DATE DUE

12/19/11			
3/12/13			

Demco, Inc. 38-293

REAL ESTATE
DEVELOPMENT

PRINCIPLES AND PROCESS

FOURTH EDITION

MIKE E. MILES

GAYLE L. BERENS

MARK J. EPPLI

MARC A. WEISS

Urban Land
Institute

1025 Thomas Jefferson Street, N.W.
Suite 500 West
Washington, D.C. 20007-5201

Library of Congress Cataloging-in-Publication Data

Real estate development : principles and process.—4th ed. / Mike E. Miles ... [et al.].

    p. cm.

  Rev. ed. of: Real estate development / Mike E. Miles, Gayle Berens, Marc A. Weiss. 3rd ed. c2000.

   1. Real estate development—United States. I. Miles, Mike E. II. Miles, Mike E. Real estate development. III. Urban Land Institute.
  HD255.R348 2007
  333.73'150973—dc22

                       2007033171

ISBN: 978-0-87420-971-6

Printed in the United States of America.

10 9 8 7 6 5 4 10 09 08 07

ABOUT ULI–THE URBAN LAND INSTITUTE

The mission of the Urban Land Institute is to provide leadership in the responsible use of land and in creating and sustaining thriving communities worldwide. ULI is committed to

- Bringing together leaders from across the fields of real estate and land use policy to exchange best practices and serve community needs;
- Fostering collaboration within and beyond ULI's membership through mentoring, dialogue, and problem solving;
- Exploring issues of urbanization, conservation, regeneration, land use, capital formation, and sustainable development;
- Advancing land use policies and design practices that respect the uniqueness of both built and natural environments;
- Sharing knowledge through education, applied research, publishing, and electronic media; and
- Sustaining a diverse global network of local practice and advisory efforts that address current and future challenges.

The Institute has long been recognized as one of the world's most respected and widely quoted sources of objective information on urban planning, growth, and development. Established in 1936, the Institute today has more than 38,000 members worldwide, representing the entire spectrum of the land use and development disciplines.

ULI PROJECT STAFF

Rachelle L. Levitt
Executive Vice President, Global Information Group
Publisher

Dean Schwanke
Senior Vice President, Publications and Awards

Nancy H. Stewart
Director, Book Production Program
Managing Editor

Lori Hatcher
Director, Publications Marketing

Barbara M. Fishel/Editech
Manuscript Editor

Duke Johns
Editorial Consultant

Michael Rohani/DesignForBooks.com
Layout and Design

Betsy Van Buskirk
Art Director
Cover Design

Craig Chapman
Director, Publishing Operations

PROJECT MANAGERS

Jason Scully
Senior Associate, Development Case Studies

Gayle L. Berens
Senior Vice President, Western Region Office

Anne Frej
Director, Office/Industrial

Adrienne Schmitz
Senior Director, Residential and Community Development

About the Authors

Mike E. Miles, PhD, is the *PLUS* Portfolio Manager for Guggenheim Real Estate, manager of $2.8 billion in assets. Before forming Guggenheim Real Estate, Miles served as portfolio manager for the Fidelity Real Estate Asset Manager, a series of institutional investment vehicles combining public securities with direct real estate ownership. Before joining Fidelity, he was executive vice president of the Prudential Realty Group and managing director of Prudential Real Estate Advisors. Miles also served as vice president of finance for Albert Investment Corporation, a real estate development firm. He was a Foundation professor of real estate and associate dean of the Business School at the University of North Carolina at Chapel Hill and is a past president of the National Council of Real Estate Investment Fiduciaries and the American Real Estate and Urban Economics Association. He has received two of the real estate investment industry's most prestigious awards: the Robert Toigo Award for leadership in real estate portfolio management from *Institutional Real Estate* and the Graaskamp Award for contributions to real estate research from the Pension Real Estate Association. He was also editor of Institutional Investor's *Real Estate Finance* for ten years. He is a graduate of Washington & Lee University and holds an MBA from Stanford University and a PhD from the University of Texas at Austin.

Gayle L. Berens is senior vice president, Western Region Office, at ULI, where she is responsible for the strategy and policies for the ULI Western Region, which makes up approximately 35 percent of ULI's membership. Previously Berens was senior vice president for education and was responsible for ULI's conferences, professional development programs, study tours, and academic projects. For most of her tenure at ULI, she served as vice president, real estate development practice, where she managed the publications and education programs related to the practice of real estate and land development—from commercial to residential to parks. In addition, she oversaw five awards programs, including the interdisciplinary ULI Gerald D. Hines Student Urban Design Competition. Berens is coauthor of *Urban Parks and Open Space,* published with the Trust for Public Land, has also served as project director for many publications, and has written many articles for *Urban Land* and case studies for ULI. She is a graduate of the University of Wisconsin Green Bay and holds an MS from Georgetown University.

Mark J. Eppli, PhD, is professor and Robert B. Bell, Sr., chair in real estate at Marquette University in Milwaukee,

Wisconsin. Before joining Marquette in 2002, he was professor of finance and real estate in the School of Business and Public Management at the George Washington University for eleven years, where he directed the MBA program in real estate and urban development. Additionally, he has been an instructor for the Urban Land Institute's Real Estate School since 1992. Eppli is widely published on a range of real estate–related research topics. His research includes shopping center economics, single-family housing valuation, commercial mortgage default, and the new urbanism. Before entering academia, Eppli pursued a career in commercial real estate. He was manager of research and investment analysis with PM Realty Advisors and was also employed in the commercial real estate department at General Electric Capital. Eppli earned his BBA in finance and his MS and PhD from the University of Wisconsin, concentrating in real estate and urban land economics.

Marc A. Weiss, PhD, is chair and CEO of Global Urban Development, an international nonprofit policy education and research organization with offices in Barcelona, Beijing, London, Prague, Singapore, Sydney, and Washington, D.C. He is executive editor of *Global Urban Development Magazine*, a member of the steering committee of the United Nations Habitat Best Practices Program, a member of the Metropolis Commission on Financing Urban Services and Infrastructure, a member of the board of directors of the International Downtown Association, and the director for research for the World Future Council. He previously served as a public policy scholar and editor of *Global Outlook* at the Woodrow Wilson International Center, as coordinator of the congressionally mandated Strategic Economic Development Plan for Washington, D.C., as special assistant to the Secretary of the U.S. Department of Housing and Urban Development in the Clinton Administration, as director of the Real Estate Development Research Center and associate professor of urban development, planning, and preservation at Columbia University, and as deputy director of the California Commission on industrial innovation. He is the author or coauthor of many books, articles, and reports, including a widely acclaimed book on urban development and planning, *The Rise of the Community Builders.* He earned a BA with honors in political science from Stanford University and an MCP and a PhD in city and regional planning from the University of California, Berkeley.

Contributors

The authors would like to thank many people for their contributions to this fourth edition of *Real Estate Development: Principles and Process*. In particular, they would like to thank Jason Scully of the ULI staff for his doggedness in bringing this project to completion.

Contributing Authors (Fourth Edition)

Deborah L. Brett
President
Deborah L. Brett & Associates
Plainsboro, New Jersey

Richard Burns
President
GNU2
San Anselmo, California

John B. Detwiler
Direct Property Investments
Guggenheim Real Estate LLC
Charlotte, North Carolina

Douglas R. Porter
President
The Growth Management Institute
Chevy Chase, Maryland

Lynne B. Sagalyn
Professor
Penn Design School and Wharton School
University of Pennsylvania
Philadelphia, Pennsylvania

Jason Scully
Senior Associate
Development Case Studies
ULI
Washington, D.C.

Ronald I. Silverman
Partner
Cox, Castle & Nicholson
Los Angeles, California

Michael A. Stegman
Director of Policy
Program on Human and Community Development
MacArthur Foundation
Chicago, Illinois

Rebecca R. Zimmermann
Principal
Design Workshop
Denver, Colorado

Additional Contributors

Anne Frej
Director, Office/Industrial
ULI
Washington, D.C.

Saman Rooentan
CoStar
Rockville, Maryland

Raymond Torto
CBRE Torto Wheaton Research
Boston, Massachusetts

Paul Wildes
Charles Schwab Investment Management
San Francisco, California

Bret Wilkerson
Property and Portfolio Research
Boston, Massachusetts

Greg Williams
Reis, Inc.
New York, New York

ULI Staff

Alex Bond
Joan Campbell
Rick Davis
Robert Goodspeed
Aaron Gottlieb
George Kelly
Cynthia Laguna
Christopher Portillo
Alisa Rosenbaum
Thomas Sprenkle
Kathryn Terzano
Karrie Underwood
Ronnie Van Alystne

Preface

The impetus for writing the fourth edition of this textbook on the real estate development process has not changed since the first edition was published in 1991: real estate development continues to have an enormous effect on our society, and no other single textbook is designed to give future decision makers a complete look at the complex decision-making process involved in real estate development.

Development affects everyone as it shapes the built environment. Development produces shelter, one of the three needs fundamental to every human being's survival. As such, it constitutes a significant portion of gross private domestic investment, which represents our nation's investment in the future. In 2007, the total value of real estate in the United States was estimated to be around $30 trillion—two-thirds single family and one-third commercial—and it continues to climb. More important, development today determines in many respects how we will live in the future. Now more than ever, development patterns and building design and materials are being scrutinized as to how they contribute to global warming and climate change.

The inherently interdisciplinary character of the real estate development process and its entrepreneurial nature give development a special status and create a decision-making environment best suited to a well-rounded, disciplined, thick-skinned person. Though many activities related to development now take place under the corporate or institutional umbrella, the activities themselves still bear a distinctive entrepreneurial stamp.

Real estate development is also unusually dynamic, with rapid changes occurring in the links among construction, technological advances, regulation, marketing, finance, property management, and so on. The dynamic nature of the process contributes a factor of extra excitement and makes development the most challenging component of the real estate industry.

This textbook captures an understanding of the development process delineated with an eight-stage model of real estate development, first elaborated by coauthor Mike Miles in his PhD dissertation. The interrelated activities that collectively constitute the process are the academic/technical portion of development. With such knowledge of the overall process firmly in hand, the reader can then proceed to perform the additional detailed studies of particular product types and local markets necessary for successful development.

The book is divided into eight parts. *Part I, Introduction,* lays out a general framework of the development process in eight interactive stages, describing the primary players in the development process and the magnitude of dollars, land, and labor involved in contemporary development. As part of that, we take a close look at demographics and the spatial setting in which real estate is located.

In *Part II, The History of Real Estate Development in the United States,* coauthor Marc Weiss provides a context for development to date—looking at the trends and activities from colonial days to the present. This historic picture is clearly one of a dynamic relationship between public and private players. The players' exact roles have changed over time, but it has always been and always will be true that the public sector is a partner in the development process.

Part III, Finance, introduces the financial tools necessary for the decision-making period of the development process. (Part III was revised almost entirely for this edition.) Nothing else we describe in the book is possible without financing. Chapter 7 explores the relationships of the various players in the tenant market and the investment capital markets. Chapter 8 examines the logic behind real estate financing decisions, focusing on financing decisions as capital structure decisions, particularly the best combination of debt and equity, to achieve the investor's goals. These lessons are then illustrated in a case study of a credit presentation. Chapter 9 goes through the discounted cash flow process and how judgments are made about whether or not to invest in a project. Appendix C briefly describes the distinction between level one and level two of real estate ventures.

In *Part IV, Ideas,* the book moves on to the process of generating ideas for specific development projects. There we discuss the sources of ideas and how those ideas are refined as the developer starts to move through the initial two stages of the development process. The part emphasizes the role of market research as a decision-making tool.

Part V, Planning and Analysis: The Public Roles, deals with the public perspective of development. Chapter 13 focuses on the public's role in zoning, land use policy, impact fees, and financing of infrastructure and how the decisions made in the public sector affect private developers. Chapter 14 discusses public/private partnerships and a more proactive role for public sector players. And Chapter 15, which has been substantially rewritten and updated, looks at affordable housing, always an important political issue as our generally affluent society continues to leave certain people behind. Beyond its direct relevance, this chapter serves as food for thought. Future developers will be faced with new and increasingly difficult social issues as they change the structure of the urban terrain. Throughout the book, we emphasize the public sector as a partner in the development process. Part V explains in greater detail the kinds of roles the public sector plays.

Part VI, Planning and Analysis: The Market Perspective, moves from a public to a private perspective. The chapters in this part deal with the feasibility studies and market analyses that facilitate decision making and with structuring the development team. The developer is responsible for seeing that all participants collectively are suited to the task and that the enterprise is worthwhile. Chapter 16 defines and outlines a holistic version of the feasibility study—the most important decision aid and management tool in the development process. The feasibility study remains a living document that is constantly revised throughout stages four through seven of the process. Chapter 17 covers the most important element of the feasibility study—market analysis. Properly collected and validated data are critical components of insightful market research and help establish a connection between supply and demand trends and forecasts for the competitive marketplace as well as property-specific cash flow and valuation assumptions. And Chapter 18 helps the analyst appreciate idiosyncratic features of the data while identifying various data sources and related forecasting models.

Part VII, Making It Happen, deals with everything from contract negotiations to construction to the formal opening. Thus, it reviews the legal aspects of putting the team together as well as the critically important management of the construction phase of development. Chapter 19 includes a considerable section on the environmental issues facing developers, particularly hazardous waste, wetlands, and air and water pollution, and how they affect financing, contracting, and managing the development process.

Part VIII, Making It Work, looks at the concerns that continue once the building is completed. Developments should never occur without planning for the project's operation. Thus, Chapter 21 explores the real estate management triad (property, asset, and portfolio managers). Chapter 22's emphasis is on marketing, sales, and leasing—work that continues once the development is completed. Finally, Chapter 23 deals with the future, reviewing what has passed and how development decision makers combine an analysis of today's market conditions with consideration of possible future market conditions to establish prospective cash flows. Developers must anticipate many different aspects of the future. By rigorously studying existing trends, developers can predict reactions and interactions with the expectation of developing what the public will perceive to be better buildings.

To integrate the many areas covered in the textbook, we include three case studies, two of which are woven throughout the text and integrated into the eight-stage model that forms the core of the text and the third of which appears as *Appendix A: Europa Center Case Study.* Europa Center was the case study that appeared in the first three editions and covers the development of two phases of the Europa Center office buildings in Chapel Hill, North Carolina. It began in the late 1980s, and we continue the story through phase two and to 2007.

The second case study appeared in the third edition. Museum Towers in Cambridge, Massachusetts, looks at the development of twin multifamily towers in a pioneering location on land that was purchased a decade before the project was actually started. This case study takes the reader through the process in a tough development environment from the perspective of an experienced, slightly maverick developer.

And with this edition, we've added a new case study—Elevation 314, the story of a small-scale developer who is committed to building a green building from the ground up. We found this case study particularly relevant to the growing trend toward seeking sustainable solutions in real estate development.

Insofar as it was possible, all the information in the textbook has been updated. The figures have been updated, and the profiles, feature boxes, and photos are new or updated. All bibliographies have been supplemented and revised.

This text is intended for university students in schools of business, planning, architecture, engineering, and law. It is also a useful beginning point for individuals shifting careers, either into development or between roles in development. While the text certainly does not guarantee success and/or financial reward, it does introduce readers to a process that is both enjoyable and rewarding. Once smitten with the development process, few people want to return to less challenging pursuits.

Note that we have chosen to use "he" throughout the text when referring to a developer, simply to enhance readability. The use of the pronoun does not reflect any bias on our or ULI's part. Although the number of men in development outweighs the number of women, the number of women involved in development is growing steadily, and women are entering the field in many capacities.

Many people over many years had a hand in producing the fourth edition of this textbook, including academics from several different fields, practitioners from across the country, and numerous members of ULI's staff. Among the ULI staff, the authors would like to thank Rachelle Levitt, Dean Schwanke, Adrienne Schmitz, Anne Frej, Karrie Underwood, Lori Hatcher, Betsy VanBuskirk, and especially Barbara Fishel and Nancy Stewart for their remarkable patience. Jason Scully deserves special kudos for his tireless efforts.

Beyond ULI, other people who deserve a special thanks for their contributions are listed elsewhere. We are particularly indebted to our coauthors from the first, second, and third editions—Richard Haney, Emil Malizia, and Ginger Travis—whose contributions were invaluable. We would also like to thank

Nancy Sedmak-Weiss, Sand Companies, Inc., Associated Bank, and Inland Companies, Inc., for their assistance.

In addition, we offer a special thanks to developers Russell Katz, Whit Morrow, and Dean Stratouly, who allowed us to look at the development process through their eyes.

Mike E. Miles, Gayle L. Berens,
Mark J. Eppli, and Marc A. Weiss

October 2007

Contents

PART II. THE HISTORY OF REAL ESTATE DEVELOPMENT IN THE UNITED STATES

PART V. PLANNING AND ANALYSIS: THE PUBLIC ROLES

PART VI. PLANNING AND ANALYSIS: THE MARKET PERSPECTIVE

PART VIII. MAKING IT WORK

PART 1

INTRODUCTION

The principles and process of real estate development should not be studied without looking at both the people who are involved in the process and the people who are the ultimate users of the product. Although this book focuses on the role of the developer or the development company, many people affect and are affected by real estate development. We all consume the end product. Individuals ultimately provide financing for a project. Individuals make up the public sector that allows a development to be built. People in many allied professions produce the buildings that are used by people of many different backgrounds and income levels.

Anyone who is thinking about going into real estate development should try to understand who helps a development come to fruition and how they do it. Most important, developers must understand the users and their needs. Without users, buildings—no matter how aesthetically pleasing or how theoretically functional—have no value.

Part I looks at the people who make a development possible—the developer as prime mover, those of our society who will be the users, and the many players who work with the developer to provide what the end user wants/needs.

CHAPTER 1

The Real Estate Development Process

Real estate development is the continual reconfiguration of the built environment to meet society's needs. Roads, sewer systems, housing, office buildings, and lifestyle centers do not just happen. Someone must initiate and manage the creation, maintenance, and eventual re-creation of the spaces in which we live, work, and play.

The need for development is constant, because population, technology, and taste never stop changing. New generations, new lifestyle choices, and revolving immigrant groups, coupled with the evolution of technology, drive economic changes in consumer tastes and individual preferences.

Whether current consumer, new citizen, or real estate professional, all of us inhabit the built environment. Further, through the legislative/political process, we collectively continue to alter the rules of the development process. Therefore, we should all understand the development process. The development process creates the houses we live in, the mixed-use development down the street, the 25-story office tower downtown, the warehouse that stored the paper this book was printed on, and the convenient (but to some tastes terribly unattractive) fast-food restaurant on the commercial strip.

Both public and private participants in real estate development share compelling reasons for understanding the development process. The goals of private sector participants are to minimize risk while maximizing personal and/or institutional objectives—usually profit (wealth maximization) but often nonmonetary objectives as well. Few business ventures are as heavily leveraged as traditional real estate development projects, magnifying the risk of ruin but also increasing the potential for high returns to equity. Large fortunes have been and continue to be made and lost in real estate development.

The public sector's goal is to promote sound and smart development, ensuring that construction is attractive and safe and that new developments are located and designed to enhance the community, provide needed space, and boost the economy. Sound development means balancing the public's need for both constructed space and economic growth against the public responsibility to provide services and improve the quality of life without harming the environment.

The public and private sectors are involved as partners in every real estate development project. A key tenet of this book is that all participants enjoy a higher probability of achieving their goals and objectives if they understand how the development process works, who the other players are, how their objectives are interwoven, and the need to achieve consensus.

This book was written for people who need to understand real estate development from the perspectives of both the public and private sectors. Its aim is to be useful to present and future developers, city planners, legislators, regulators, corporate real estate officers, land planners, lawyers specializing in real estate or municipal law, architects, engineers, building contractors, lenders, market analysts, and leasing agents/brokers. Readers are assumed to have already acquired the fundamentals of real estate and/or city planning. This book summarizes but does not repeat in great detail basic information about real estate law and finance, urban economics, and land planning and design. Although the focus of our book is the individual entrepreneurial developer, it is important to note that developers can also be financial institutions, corporations, universities, medical centers, private investors, cities, municipalities, and others. The process laid out in this book remains essentially the same—no matter who the developer is. Market decisions still have to be made, pro formas still need integrity, designers have to be consulted, and so on. The process might be layered by various institutional procedures and committees and boards of trustees, but the product is achieved by going through the same steps. In fact, many institutions and cities are hiring entrepreneurial developers on a fee basis to manage a project's development within the larger organizational framework.

Throughout, the book includes profiles of developers and the diverse set of professionals who work with developers. Their career paths are always interesting and often surprising. Their perspectives on development are especially valuable because these individuals have lived the process we are describing. Development decision making has become more difficult as the world has grown more complex, and developers' and professionals' insights help frame the development process in human terms.

In addition to the various profiles, the book focuses on three developers and three projects. One profile is of Russell Katz, a young developer who was originally trained as an architect. An ardent supporter of green buildings, one of his goals in developing Elevation 314, a four-story, 52-unit apartment complex, is to demonstrate the potential of environmentally friendly architecture.

The other project involves two residential towers developed in Cambridge, Massachusetts, by Dean Stratouly of Congress Group Ventures. Museum Towers is the story of a development in a pioneering location.

In addition to Katz's and Stratouly's experiences, Appendix A of this edition includes an account of Whit Morrow's Europa Center. Originally interspersed throughout the pages of previous editions of this book, the case study of Europa Center has changed as this book has changed. In the first edition, Morrow recounted in his own words all phases of the development process for this Class A office building: from conception through planning, permitting, financing, and construction to completion, leasing, and ongoing management. In subsequent editions, we learned how the building functioned over time and about the need for related development.

These projects tell stories of unexpected complications and their resolution through the words of the developers.

To begin the discussion of the development process, this chapter lays out the functions of the process and its many players:

▶ The definition of real estate development;
▶ The eight-stage model of real estate development;
▶ The characterization of developers and their reputations;
▶ The development team;
▶ The public/private partnership;
▶ Market and feasibility studies; and
▶ Design.

The next two chapters complete the introduction by defining the playing field—the spatial economics of the contemporary city—and then defining the roles of the various participants in the process. Chapter 2 describes the raw materials of the development process—demographics—while Chapter 3 adds detail and contemporary color to the process and the players.

Part II presents a long-term historical perspective on real estate development in the United States. Part III then covers the financial mechanics that support development decision making. Finance is not the goal, however; rather, finance constitutes the logic that allows the developer to bring together several participants (each with its own set of objectives) in a coordinated effort that will ultimately make a profit. The book then proceeds through the eight-stage model to look in detail at decision making in the real estate development process.

DEFINING REAL ESTATE DEVELOPMENT

A real estate development starts as an idea that comes to fruition when consumers—tenants or owner-occupants—occupy the bricks and mortar (space) put in place by the development team. Land, labor, capital, management, entrepreneurship, and broadly defined partnerships are needed to transform an idea into reality. Value is created by providing usable space over time with associated services. It is these three things—space, time, and services—in association that are needed so consumers can enjoy the intended benefits of the built space. Although the definition of real estate development remains simple, the activity continues to grow more and more complex. The product of the development process—a new or a redeveloped project—is a result of the coordinated efforts of many allied professionals.

Developments do not happen without financial backing and often require multiple agreements to be negotiated by multiple financial players. Only then can physical construction or reconstruction be started, involving the myriad of design professionals, construction workers, engineers, and so on. Before, after, and during the process, the developer works with public sector officials on approvals, zoning changes, exactions, building codes, infrastructure, and so on. Increasingly, community groups in many cities demand to be key players in the development

process, and the time needed to work with them has to be factored into the development equation. Finally, selling or renting the space to users at the intended (or higher) price is the act that proves the entire project was justified. This consummation requires the expertise of marketing professionals, graphic artists, salespeople, Web site developers, lawyers, and others. The developer must ensure that all these elements—and many more to be identified later in this book—are completed on schedule, are properly executed, and are reasonably within budget.

Today, development requires more knowledge than ever before about the specifics of prospective markets and marketing, patterns of urban growth, neighborhood associations, traffic, legal requirements, local regulations, public policy, conveyances and contracts, elements of building design, site development, construction techniques, environmental issues, infrastructure, financing, risk control, and time management. Ever-increasing capacities and complexities along each of these dimensions have resulted in increased specialization. As more affiliated professionals work with developers, the size of the development team has expanded and the roles of some professionals have changed. Although greater complexity has generated the need for better-educated developers (educated both in book knowledge and hard knocks), it has not changed the steps they usually follow in the development process.

THE EIGHT-STAGE MODEL OF REAL ESTATE DEVELOPMENT

Developers follow a sequence of steps from the moment they first conceive a project to the time they complete the physical construction of that project and begin ongoing asset management or sell the finished product. Although various participants of the development process may delineate the sequence of steps slightly differently, the essence of the steps does not vary significantly. At a minimum, development requires the following elements: coming up with the idea, refining the idea, testing its feasibility, negotiating necessary contracts, making formal commitments, constructing the project, completing and opening it, and, finally, managing the built project. This text seeks to capture that essence in the eight-stage model depicted in Figure 1-1. Succeeding chapters detail the activities that collectively make up the eight-stage model of the development process.

Before proceeding further with the model, a few points about development must be emphasized. First, the development process is hardly straightforward or linear. A flow chart similar to that shown in Figure 1-1 can freeze the discrete steps and guide an understanding of development, but no chart can capture the constant repositioning that occurs in the developer's mind or the nearly constant renegotiation between the developer and the other participants in the process. And don't forget that redevelopment of existing projects requires many of the same steps as development. Moreover, in very large projects, individual development components can be "nested" within a larger development plan. For example, during the development of a large-scale community like Stapleton in Denver, Colorado, individual components of the community may be in different stages while the overall development plan is in stage six—construction.

Second, development is an art. It is creative, often extremely complex, partly logical, and partly intuitive. Studying the components of real estate development can help all players make the most of their chances for success. What cannot be taught are two ingredients essential to the success of the real estate developer/entrepreneur: creativity and drive. At times, a smart developer will choose to move in a different order than the one suggested here.

Third, at every stage, developers should consider all the remaining stages of the development process. In other words, developers should make current decisions fully aware of the implications of these decisions not just for the immediate next step but for the life of the project. By doing so, they ensure that the development plan and its physical implementation come closest to the optimum for the duration of the entire development process and, equally important, for the project's long expected life.

Fourth, the development process requires interaction among the different functions (construction, finance, management, marketing, and government relations) in each of the eight stages as well as interaction of the functions over time.

It is a huge mistake to underrate the importance of asset management and property management after the project is built or to overlook provision for them during design and construction. For example, operating a building with every up-to-the minute technological bell and whistle may require technical competence beyond the general management skills typical of most property managers. In addition, asset managers need to remarket space continually and to upgrade or remodel buildings periodically to keep the space competitive in an evolving market. Institutional investors and corporate owners are also keenly aware of the periodic need for and cost of major remodeling to prolong the economic life of buildings. Careful planning during stages one through seven should enable developers to find ways to minimize the frequency and cost of retrofitting buildings. Whether or not developers manage the property for the long term, they are responsible for considerations involving asset management during the first seven stages. Given that developers' actions largely determine future operating costs and that the expected magnitude of such costs represents a significant part of the project value (i.e., what it will sell for), today's developers focus sharply on making building operations appropriately cost-efficient.

Fourth, although the model for development is based on reality, it also represents an ideal version of the process and gives an elegant means of imparting the information. The various stages of the model assume a well-informed developer, a thorough analysis of the market, accurate assessments of the cost of construction, and so on. They assume a businesslike approach to the process. They do not totally account for the lucky intuitive person who had a gut feeling about something and used all sorts of unconventional means to get the project built. Real estate development has been full of stories of those people whose gut has led them to being very successful in the business. They are becoming less common because of more and tighter regulations, declining amounts of developable land, and so on, but they still exist. You will hear from one such maverick, Pamela Bundy, who is profiled in Chapter 19.

Figure 1-1	The Eight-Stage Model of Real Estate Development

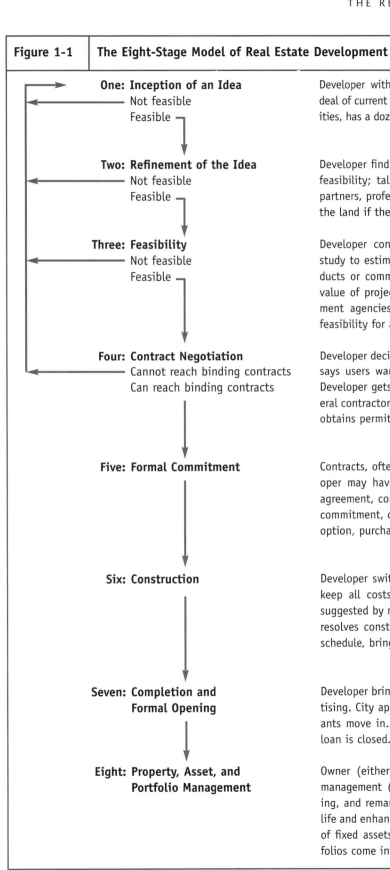

One: Inception of an Idea
— Not feasible
Feasible ⌐

Developer with extensive background knowledge and a great deal of current market data looks for needs to fill, sees possibilities, has a dozen ideas, does quick feasibility tests in his head.

Two: Refinement of the Idea
— Not feasible
Feasible ⌐

Developer finds a specific site for the idea; looks at physical feasibility; talks with prospective tenants, owners, lenders, partners, professionals; settles on a tentative design; options the land if the idea looks good.

Three: Feasibility
— Not feasible
Feasible ⌐

Developer conducts or commissions a more formal market study to estimate market absorption and capture rates, conducts or commissions feasibility study comparing estimated value of project with cost, processes plans through government agencies. Demonstrates legal, physical, and financial feasibility for all participants.

Four: Contract Negotiation
— Cannot reach binding contracts
Can reach binding contracts

Developer decides on final design based on what market study says users want and will pay for. Contracts are negotiated. Developer gets loan commitment in writing, decides on general contractor, determines general rent or sales requirements, obtains permits from local government.

Five: Formal Commitment

Contracts, often contingent on each other, are signed. Developer may have all contracts signed at once: joint venture agreement, construction loan agreement and permanent loan commitment, construction contract, exercise of land purchase option, purchase of insurance, and prelease agreements.

Six: Construction

Developer switches to formal accounting system, seeking to keep all costs within budget. Developer approves changes suggested by marketing professionals and development team, resolves construction disputes, signs checks, keeps work on schedule, brings in operating staff as needed.

Seven: Completion and Formal Opening

Developer brings in full-time operating staff, increases advertising. City approves occupancy, utilities are connected, tenants move in. Construction loan is paid off, and permanent loan is closed.

Eight: Property, Asset, and Portfolio Management

Owner (either developer or new owner) oversees property management (including re-leasing), reconfiguring, remodeling, and remarketing space as necessary to extend economic life and enhance performance of asset; corporate management of fixed assets and considerations regarding investors' portfolios come into play.

Fifth, it is imperative to remember that the development process is inherently interdisciplinary and dynamic. It is not a game won by exhibiting exceptional depth in one particular area, say, electrical design. Rather, it is a complex process that demands attention to all the different aspects of creating the built environment—political, economic, physical, legal, sociological, and so on. Good management of the interactions among various disciplines—with special attention to the areas that are most crucial to the specific project—is essential to successful development. Further, many of the components of this interdisciplinary world are experiencing an accelerating rate of change, and all the interfaces among the disciplines are constantly in flux.

Finally, U.S. real estate development is global in perspective. Financing is increasingly provided by international sources, tenants are served globally, and international building firms offer the full gamut of construction services. And although your architect may be based in San Francisco, the engineers might be working out of a less expensive part of the country and the drawings for the project might be done in India. Most important, continued immigration results in lifestyle shifts that are changing what people want in the built environment. As different ethnic groups continue to settle in metropolitan areas, the configuration of cities and the needs of citizens shift. Developers must be prepared to respond to these changes.

CHARACTERIZING DEVELOPERS

Developers are like movie producers in that they assemble the needed talents to accomplish their objectives and then assume responsibility for managing individuals to make sure that development potential is realized. They are proactive; they make things happen. As we will see in later chapters, a great deal of uncertainty is associated with the development process, just as with the introduction of any new product. Unlike most new products introduced (say, a new MP3 player), real estate development involves long-term commitments (buildings last for decades). Thus, the cost of making a mistake is extraordinarily high. Just how much of the related risk the developer

assumes personally is an important issue that commands significant attention throughout this book. Regardless of which risk control devices the developer finds appropriate for a particular project, the developer ultimately is responsible for managing all aspects of that project. Obviously, successful developers must be able to handle (and thrive under) intense pressure and considerable uncertainty.

It is an error to assume that all developers are alike. Some, for example, develop only one type of property such as single-family houses; others develop anything commercial or industrial. Some developers carve out a niche in one city and refuse opportunities outside it; others work regionally, nationally, or internationally. Some developers run extremely lean organizations, hiring outside expertise for every func-

MUSEUM TOWERS
The Development Company

NAME
Congress Group Ventures (two partners)

FOUNDED
1980

PURPOSE
Originally established to rehabilitate a historic property in downtown Boston; moved into development of commercial space, condominiums, and apartments

Sample of Projects Completed from 1980 to 1999

Russia Wharf
Boston
Historic rehabilitation

One Memorial Drive
Cambridge, Massachusetts
Office building

28 State Street
Boston
Office building redevelopment

Wayland Business Center
Wayland, Massachusetts
Office building redevelopment

continued on page 15

tion from design to leasing; others maintain needed expertise in house. Some work in publicly traded companies, often real estate investment trusts (REITs), while others prefer to stay private, forgoing certain capital market advantages to avoid the short-term press of quarterly earnings. In between are many gradations. As in most professions, developers range from those who put reputation above profit to those who fail to respect even the letter of the law. Likewise, in ego and visibility, developers vary enormously. Some name buildings for themselves; a few cherish anonymity.

One of the projects featured in our case studies, Museum Towers, was developed by a company that started with a historic property it converted from industrial to office space. Since its inception, the company has developed office, retail, multifamily, and light industrial projects.

Our other featured case study tells the development story of Elevation 314. This apartment building is only the third project and the first construction project (the other two were renovations of existing apartment buildings) to be developed by 38-year-old (as of January 2007) developer Russell Katz.

ELEVATION 314
The Development Company

NAME

Montgomery Oaks Management, Inc.

Purpose

To develop and manage real estate in the Washington, D.C., metropolitan area

Projects Completed

Elm Gardens
Washington, D.C.
Rehab of a 36-unit, 1960s-era garden-style apartment complex

The Sheldon
Washington, D.C.
Rehab of a 12-unit apartment building originally constructed in 1918

continued on page 16

Private developers/entrepreneurs must balance an extraordinary number of requirements for completing a project against the needs of diverse providers and consumers of the product. As Figure 1-2 shows, developers first need the blessing of local government and possibly neighbors around the site. Often, to obtain public approval, developers are required to redesign the project. Therefore, appropriate flexibility is one of a developer's most crucial traits. Second, developers need to be able to identify tenants or buyers (the users) who will pay for space over time with associated services. Third, developers lead an internal team of specialists who depend on a given developer for their livelihood (the staff) and recruit external players whose business is contracting with developers. Fourth, developers demonstrate the project's feasibility to the capital markets and pay interest or offer equity positions in return for funding (finance). In every one of these areas as well as in interactions between areas, developers practice some form of risk management, initiating and managing a complex web of relationships from day one through the completion of the development process.

This book refers many times to the "development team" that designs and builds the developer's idea. It is worth noting that probably only 1 percent (perhaps fewer) of the people in real estate development are developers/entrepreneurs. The other 99 percent include a wide range of professionals, support staff, and building tradespeople who are indispensable players. Clearly, challenging work abounds in real estate development for all participants, not just for the developer. Understanding the decisions facing the developer is critical to all participants, just as it is for the general public.

The developer's job description includes shifting roles as creator, promoter, negotiator, manager, leader, risk manager, and investor, adding up to a much more complex vision of an entrepreneur than a person who merely buys low to sell high. Developers are more akin to entrepreneurial innovators (like Bill Gates, Warren Buffet or Michael Dell)—people who realize an idea in the marketplace—than to pure traders skilled primarily at arbitrage.

Balancing roles is part of the developer's art, something that can be described but not taught.

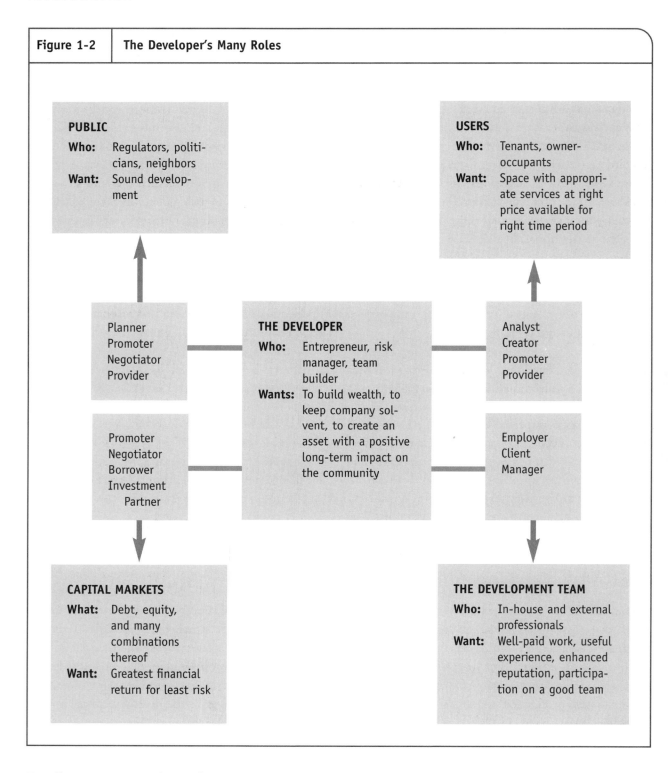

Figure 1-2   The Developer's Many Roles

PUBLIC
Who: Regulators, politicians, neighbors
Want: Sound development

USERS
Who: Tenants, owner-occupants
Want: Space with appropriate services at right price available for right time period

Planner
Promoter
Negotiator
Provider

THE DEVELOPER
Who: Entrepreneur, risk manager, team builder
Wants: To build wealth, to keep company solvent, to create an asset with a positive long-term impact on the community

Analyst
Creator
Promoter
Provider

Promoter
Negotiator
Borrower
Investment
Partner

Employer
Client
Manager

CAPITAL MARKETS
What: Debt, equity, and many combinations thereof
Want: Greatest financial return for least risk

THE DEVELOPMENT TEAM
Who: In-house and external professionals
Want: Well-paid work, useful experience, enhanced reputation, participation on a good team

Equally important and equally unteachable is the drive that makes developers persevere to the desired end despite problems and obstacles. Developers tend to be highly focused. This quality, perhaps more than the profit motive, accounts for the negative public image of some developers. Yet such focus can lead to the design and construction of innovative projects. Without drive, no development would occur. As noted in later chapters, the potential roadblocks are numerous.

Sometimes, though, the tenacity that drives developers to produce a successful project can lead to disastrous results. The savings and loan debacle of the 1980s was in part the result of developers' desire to develop because they liked to do deals and because money was available. Many buildings were erected without enough thought given to proper market studies or design considerations or even the basic need for more space, leaving an inventory of unneeded buildings around the country that should never have been erected. Presumably all facets of the industry (particularly the regulators of financial institutions) are wiser now and will not easily repeat this expensive mistake. We hope this book will contribute to a healthier, more thoughtful way of doing business.

DEVELOPERS' REPUTATIONS

Deserved or not, developers are not always held in high esteem by the general public. Without even knowing the individual or firm, people are often wary at the mention of a developer's involvement in a project in their locality. Given the impact that their work has on a community, it is not surprising that developers offend some people. Their product, which is so clearly manifested in the built environment, is there for everyone to see and criticize. And often their public persona is as much a part of a project as the product itself, making developers an easy target to blame for everything from increased traffic to a shortage of parking. Successful developers can earn a lot of money, and certain elements in the community often resent such wealth.

Developers are also subject to attack because they engineer change in communities that is sometimes hard to accept, especially for long-time residents. Yet they provide a service as community builders. They facilitate the production of shelter for living and working. They make possible new retail/entertainment areas, recreation areas, and health care facilities. Ideally, they do so within the rules established by the public sector—planners, government staff, and elected officials—and to the satisfaction of most of the community.

More and more as growth infringes on every community in the United States, the appearance of NIMBYism ("not in my backyard") is inevitable. As more communities feel saddled with projects they deem wholly unworthy of their affection, they seem less able to distinguish good development from bad development and good developers from bad developers. Neighbors await the bulldozer with trepidation. Against a backdrop of growing animosity, developers, city planners, elected officials, and others involved in community growth have learned the hard way about the necessity of involving the wider community in guiding development. The intense involvement of the neighbors has added another layer of activity to the process and has extended development time, as some projects require hundreds of meetings with neighborhood groups and other interested parties.

As in any profession, some developers are models of ethical behavior, making innovative and attractive contributions to the built environment. And some exhibit little sensitivity for community standards, at times appearing on the front page of newspapers under indictment for shoddy construction and bribery.

Communities will always grow and change, with or without developers. With a good developer, however, growth and renewal can be managed and made to have a more positive effect on a community.

THE DEVELOPMENT TEAM

If developers consistently play one role throughout the development process, it is that of a leader who can coordinate people and help realize a particular vision. Developers almost never work in isolation. To design, finance, build, lease or sell, and manage their dream, developers must engage the services of many other experts—public and private—some of them professionals and others entrepreneurs themselves.

Developers vary in the technical expertise they bring to the team. Earlier in their careers they might have been architects, lawyers, contractors, brokers, land planners, or lenders. Increasingly, more developers are actually getting advanced degrees in development or in real estate finance. They must, however, hire the expertise they lack—whether they keep their experts on the payroll or contract for outside assistance. Developers must be able to find the right

Formerly a barren rail yard along Michigan Avenue in Chicago, Illinois, Millennium Park was funded through a public/private partnership, with more than $215 million of the $475 million total cost coming from private donations. *Courtesy of U.S. Equities Realty*

people, keep them motivated and on schedule, and ensure that their collective work is appropriate—or the project may not be successfully completed.

Often developers, like any team leader, motivate players with incentives other than money—with pride in the project, with the hope of future work, and with fear of the consequences of nonperformance. Knowing when and with whom to use different incentives is part of leading the development team.

With each project, developers must shape and sell an idea to secure commitments from others. Thus, they are first and foremost promoters. Developers then spend a considerable part of their time managing other people, particularly as design and construction begin. They have both the plan and the responsibility for making it happen; they are quarterback, coach, and team owner rolled into one. (See Chapter 3 for a more detailed discussion of the roles of other players.)

THE PUBLIC SECTOR: ALWAYS A PARTNER

Private sector real estate developers have a public sector partner in every deal—no exceptions—whether or not they choose to recognize that partner. The government—federal, state, and local—controls the U.S. system of capitalism under which private developers operate. Real estate development is a highly regulated process. Property law, public infrastructure, financial market rules, zoning, building permits, and impact fees are all part of the public sector's realm. In some cases, the public sector may participate directly in the development process as a private developer's equity partner working toward the achievement of a public goal, such as downtown redevelopment. Chapter 14 provides an in-depth discussion of public/private partnerships in which the public sector is a formal, risk-bearing partner in a development project. Although more and more

Decorated with sculptures and art from world-class artists such as Frank Gehry and Anish Kapoor, the 24.5-acre (9.9-hectare) Millennium Park has generated an unrivaled economic boon to nearby developments, both residential and commercial. *Courtesy of U.S. Equities Realty*

local governments are initiating development projects, the public sector more often is engaged in a less formal partnership. Nonetheless, if developers do not work hand in hand with local governments, giving them the same amount of respect and attention they would give a private sector partner, delays and problems are likely to occur. Likewise, developers should also not overlook the people in the neighborhood who will be directly affected by the project.

Time is money in real estate development, and overlooking or antagonizing neighbors and public sector partners often costs a developer time, which translates into more interest payments and more significant costs. More important, the public sector can permanently delay a developer and can even change the rules in the middle of the game. Changing the plan and/or design midstream is usually quite expensive. In fact, changes forced by the public sector can easily make a project infeasible. When it happens at a

later stage in the development process, developers often face huge difficulties because of the costs already incurred. For these reasons, it pays for private developers to treat the public sector as a partner from the outset. The partnership is like a marriage: it can take many forms, but if it fails, it is painful.

MARKET AND FEASIBILITY STUDIES

Textbooks on marketing and market research seldom cover real estate in great detail. Likewise, when real estate textbooks discuss market research, they typically fail to draw connections to the broader principles of marketing. Still, developers, planners, public officials, lenders, and investors need to use fundamental concepts of marketing to make better-informed decisions about real property.

Developers tend to rely on market research to make decisions at several stages in the development process, but especially when it is time to convince lenders to lend them money. Some lenders remember the huge oversupply of space in many markets during the early 1990s. Developers can rarely rely on instinct or optimism to assure prospective lenders that the project will capture market share from competitors. A rigorous market study early in the process stimulates development ideas, improves initial concepts, and serves as an important risk control device.

Beyond convincing lenders and investors, market research is useful in development planning. Residential developers, for example, can use a market study of a projected design for a specific site to answer several questions. What is the anticipated employment growth rate in the market area? What is the anticipated household growth rate in the market area? What is the best configuration and size of housing units for the proposed residential subdivision? How many units will the market absorb, at what price, and over what period of time? What percent of that demand will the project capture and why? How should units be marketed to each targeted consumer group? The market study's bottom line reveals how much operating income or revenue over what period of time the developer can expect a particular project to generate, given market conditions and expected competition.

Equally important, the developer can use a market study to help determine what project types will gain the support of various neighborhood and public sector participants. In a sense, development creates "public goods" by placing long-lived products on the land, and everyone must live (at least visually) with the products for many years. The underlying research into the market area should include both regulatory requirements and the attitudes of neighbors and other "publics." Not only does market research guide the project's size and design; it also indicates ways for the developer to win public approval and/or gain various entitlements.

Furthermore, market studies should be versatile, for they can help accomplish other objectives. They can, as noted, be used to help obtain financing. After a project is financed, a market study can also be used as a marketing guide for the sales or leasing staff. To be salable, a project often needs an identity in con-

sumers' minds; the market study should provide a competitive analysis and identify a market niche that permits the proper targeting of advertising and promotion.

A feasibility study completes the analysis (see Chapter 16 for details). Simply put, the project is feasible if its estimated value exceeds estimated costs. Value is a function of projected cash flow and a market-derived capitalization or discount rate (defined in Chapter 9).

Local real estate markets respond to neighborhood, regional, national, and international trends, be they development of interstate highways, amendments to the U.S. tax code, changes in oil prices, or fluctuations in the value of the dollar in world markets. A thorough market study looks beyond the primary market area to wider trends affecting local supply and demand. Ultimately, the project's revenues will reflect these trends. Moreover, savvy developers look for fresh design and marketing ideas outside local markets. Thus, developers must understand their local markets as well as recognize and respond to broader trends (the latter task may be easier said than done, as explained in this text's concluding chapter).

Information, of course, carries a cost. The more data an analyst gathers and the more time the analyst spends manipulating the data, the higher the price tag on the study. In all risk control techniques, the developer must weigh the cost in relation to the magnitude of the risk. In market studies, cost depends on the level of detail, who performs the analysis, and how much rigor a developer wants (or is forced by lenders or regulators) to pay for.

The future is not a straight-line extrapolation of the past. Although the market analyst scrupulously examines past performance and is exacting in determining current market conditions, the future is what matters most to real estate developers. Developers look for indications of the kind of space that will satisfy society's needs over a project's long expected life. The future is not just the one year or five years that it takes to develop a project; it is the entire useful life of the project, which may be 30, 50, 100, or 200 years. No one can fully anticipate the future, yet the developer's challenge is to be at least a few steps ahead.

DESIGN: NEVER AN AFTERTHOUGHT

Good design has never been more important than it is today. Taking a cookie-cutter design off the shelf and applying it to an available site is not often the winning strategy in competitive markets where space needs are changing. Serious attention to the market—which means to the people who will use the project—can show developers and their architects and planners how to capture market share from competitors or how to build for a new niche.

Design has emerged as a versatile method of establishing contact with and discriminating between specific market segments. Buildings convey images that send direct messages, and architects who want to contribute successfully to development teams have had to become proficient in creating the appropriate design message. At the same time, it is important to remember that for some uses and certain tenants, the appropriate image is pure functionality—that is, the most functional bay sizes and core elements, covered with a skin whose operating costs are low.

Proficiency in design is hard won, for the right image is frequently elusive. Each player in the development process brings to the process some expectation of how the completed project will look and function. For example, hoping to maintain their town's character, public sector players bring images of desired interac-

---

MUSEUM TOWERS
A Summary of the Project

LOCATION

Eight and Ten Museum Way (formerly 15 Monsignor O'Brien Highway), Cambridge, Massachusetts

Museum Towers at North Point was built in what many would consider a pioneering location. Located in east Cambridge, generally east of the Charlestown Avenue Bridge, Museum Towers is in the eastern section of the North Point development district, a 70-acre (28-hectare) development zone master planned to provide a mix of commercial and residential development, upgraded infrastructure, and an extensive park network. The eastern portion was the last large parcel of undeveloped waterfront property in Cambridge.

North Point is adjacent to the highly successful Kendall Square and east Cambridge (Lechmere Canal) development areas, which have become vibrant centers of commercial development and professional job growth.

The eastern section of North Point is located across from the Museum of Science and bordered to the west by Monsignor O'Brien Highway, to the north by the Gilmore Bridge, to the east by I-93, and to the south by the Charles River, directly across from the west end area of downtown Boston. The site had been used for industrial purposes and was known as "the lost half-mile of the Charles River." For decades, it had been the wrong end of Cambridge.

LAND

Original site 4.11 acres (1.7 hectares), three parcels of land. The site is bounded to the north by a 40-foot-wide (12-meter-wide) private access way (Main Road) and beyond that by a parcel of land owned by the Massachusetts Water Resources Authority. Industrial Way, owned by the Massachusetts Bay Transportation Authority, borders the site to the east. To the east of Industrial Way is the site of North Point Park, which is owned by the Metropolitan District Commission. This parcel is clearly separated from all other nearby development by roadways, although these uses are very visible from the site and are clearly "industrial" except for the Museum of Science.

LAND COST

$13 million

BUILDINGS

Two 24-story apartment buildings joined at the base by a low-rise area of apartments, support space, a central lobby, a health club, and a 490-vehicle parking garage.

PROJECT COST

$78 million

INITIAL CHRONOLOGY

Land purchased—October 1987
Site preparation began—Fall 1995
Building construction began—Early 1997
Building certificate of occupancy issued—1998

continued on page 42

tions with surrounding areas. Different members of the development team might have visions of the project that range from minimalist to cosmetically dazzling. In the final analysis, the developer/entrepreneur charges the architect (and other design professionals) with solving the design problem and resolving the diversity of pictures into a single, coherent image. Still, the ultimate responsibility for good design rests with the developer.

The Museum Towers project was developed in Cambridge, Massachusetts, home of MIT and Harvard University and across the Charles River from Boston. In the 1980s, the area was a developers' paradise—but everything crumbled in the early 1990s.

Development of Elevation 314 started during a fortuitous time in Washington, D.C. Low but steadily rising housing prices in the early 2000s were transforming neighborhoods all across the city, and Takoma—the neighborhood where Elevation 314 is located—was no exception. Looking beyond short-term profits, developer Russell Katz wanted the ben-

efits that accrue from long-term ownership. Built with the environment in mind, Elevation 314 sports many green features, including a geothermal heating and cooling system, energy-efficient appliances, bamboo flooring, low–volatile organic compound finishes, and a stormwater management system comprising a green roof and bioretention area.

Configuring the built environment to create specific images has a long and instructive history. Early merchandisers knew that building a massive single structure sent a message of abundance that a profusion of small branch outlets could never achieve. In a similar vein, books of house plans containing Greek revival designs sold particularly well at the beginning of the 20th century. It was not only the floor plans or the efficient space that was popular but also the strong identification with the image of an earlier democracy that attracted homebuilders. Today, most travelers can readily identify the quality and cost of a motor hotel simply by the image the

ELEVATION 314
A Summary of the Project

LOCATION

314 Carroll Street, N.W., Washington, District of Columbia

Though it is officially part of Washington, D.C., the Takoma neighborhood has a close relationship with the bordering city of Takoma Park, Maryland. Elevation 314 is less than a quarter-mile (0.4 kilometer) from the D.C./Maryland border. Although both Takomas were once considered transitional and potentially dangerous, the area started to change in the late 1990s when buyers discovered the rich inventory of moderately priced, pre–World War II houses on tree-lined streets. Although many houses in the area sell for large sums of money, home values there are still slightly lower than those in many other parts of the Washington metropolitan region.

LAND

The 0.79-acre (0.32-hectare) triangular site sits directly across the street from the Takoma Metro station. It is bordered to the west by an elevated railroad right-of-way with train tracks for both freight trains and the Metro Rail trains. Originally located at the base of a small hill, the tracks were

elevated by excavating the land under them. As a result, the site includes some steep changes in grade.

LAND COST

$1,000,000

BUILDING

A 52-unit, four-story apartment building designed to be environmentally friendly, the project includes a geothermal heating and cooling system, a green roof, and bamboo floors.

PROJECT COST

$8,900,000

CHRONOLOGY

Land purchased—March 2001
Building construction began—November 2002
Sales/leasing started—July 2004
Project completed—September 2004

continued on page 43

building projects. Creating a formal image that becomes a vital, interactive component in a project's success is neither accidental nor mysterious. It results from careful consideration of design criteria during all eight stages of the real estate development process—not just exterior design but also all the functional aspects of interior design that are critical to tenants' efficient use of constructed space. (Later chapters deal with integrating both exterior and interior design criteria during the eight-stage development process.)

Finally, the implications of successful design go far beyond creating an effective structure. Architects, like the other players in the development process, are bound by ethical obligations. They understand space and urban design far better than laypeople. If architects do not see it as their responsibility to innovate and advance the state of the art, then society will not live up to its potential, at least not as related to improving the built environment. Architects must often convince developers, who must make it happen.

SUMMARY

As we move forward with the introductory framework in Chapters 2 and 3, it is important to keep the following concepts in mind:

1. Everyone is in some way connected to the development process. Consequently, the developer should see the public sector as a partner.
2. The developer ultimately is responsible for creating space over time with associated services that meet society's needs.
3. Because the development period decision-making environment is complex and interactive, a model is useful so that future ramifications of current decisions can be more easily evaluated.
4. Development is an art that requires drive and creativity coupled with "appropriate" flexibility and risk management.
5. Development of the built environment is a long-term activity that justifies considerable planning. Provision for ongoing operating management should be a critical element of such planning.

TERMS

Many of the following terms are introduced in this chapter and explained later in greater detail:

▶ Asset management
▶ Built environment
▶ Capital markets
▶ Corporate owners
▶ Development team
▶ Entrepreneur
▶ Equity
▶ Feasibility studies
▶ Infrastructure
▶ Institutional investors
▶ Interdisciplinary
▶ Leverage
▶ Market studies
▶ Niche
▶ Operating costs
▶ Private sector
▶ Public sector
▶ Real estate development
▶ Risk control
▶ Value

REVIEW QUESTIONS

1.1 What is real estate development?
1.2 Why does every real estate development project involve both the public and private sectors?
1.3 What is the role of the developer in the development process?
1.4 What are the eight stages of development as delineated in this textbook?
1.5 What are the advantages of using such a model? What are the pitfalls?
1.6 Why is real estate development inherently an interdisciplinary process?
1.7 Why and how do developers use market research and feasibility studies?
1.8 Discuss the importance of good design in development.
1.9 Discuss the many roles a developer must play.
1.10 What role does time play in the real estate development process?

CHAPTER 2

The Raw Material:
Land and Demographics
In the United States

The preceding chapter summarized the activities that constitute the development process. This chapter describes both U.S. demographic trends and the spatial setting in which real estate development takes place. This is the playing field on which a dynamic game is constantly unfolding. Chapter 3 completes the introductory framework by reviewing the functions and motivations of the primary participants in the development process. Collectively, these three chapters provide the foundation for understanding how society's needs are met by the real estate development community.

Searching for future opportunities requires ongoing examination of basic demographic and economic indicators as well as how they are expected to change. Understanding the recent past and the present tells us where we have been, while carefully prepared projections can tell us much about the future users of real estate. Demographic data trends are important in understanding national, regional, and local markets; they are used to analyze a particular site and its development potential.

This chapter looks at:

► Population growth;
► Employment growth and economic cycles;
► Land supply; and
► The interaction of real estate values, the gross domestic product, national wealth, and employment.

The chapter overall clearly shows the importance of the real estate and construction industries in the nation's overall economy. It also looks forward, suggesting how the built environment will need to change to accommodate technological change and related population shifts.

Keep in mind as you read this chapter that the data presented here represent a moment in time compared with a long history. By the time the author has collected the information, the editor has made her changes, the graphic artist has laid out the text, and the book has been printed, the data will be out of date. Or a major event such as a tsunami in Asia or a hurricane in the South can cause sudden economic

The authors are indebted to Deborah L. Brett, Deborah L. Brett and Associates, Plainsboro, New Jersey, for her extensive revisions to this chapter.

changes or unusual large-scale demographic shifts. It is important, however, to focus on demographic changes over time and their effect on real estate development. This chapter provides historical context on the basic issues that developers should think of and possible resources for finding current data and trends. The chapter in itself is not intended to be a resource for demographic trends but an introduction to some of the issues that developers need to look at. A lot more will be said on these topics as we move through the development process.

POPULATION GROWTH

Population growth, the formation of new households, and the creation of jobs are the key drivers of real estate demand. Real estate development opportunities materialize when people with purchasing power increase in number in a particular location. In the 2000 Census, the U.S. Census Bureau counted more than 282.2 million Americans, an increase of 13.5 percent compared with a decade earlier. The nation gained 13.6 million households, creating demand for new housing, retail space, and entertainment venues. Business expansion generated jobs, requiring new office buildings, factories, and warehouses. But population growth is not the only determinant of real estate demand. Opportunities also emerge in mature, stable communities as older, worn-out properties are renovated or redeveloped for new uses. In general, though, development opportunities expand with population growth.

National and regional populations grow in two ways: more people are born than die and more people migrate in than leave. Figure 2-1 shows decade-by-decade changes in the total number of Americans. In the earliest days of our country, immigration was the key source of population growth. This trend continued through the early part of the 20th century, but then immigration dropped to a trickle during the 1940s and 1950s. In a dramatic reversal, both the number of newcomers and their share of population growth rose dramatically after 1980. As shown in Figure 2-2, legal immigration during the 1990s was at an all-time high. Yet the official immigration rate

(the number of legal newcomers per 1,000 residents) was still less than half that seen at the turn of the last century. Illegal immigrants, mainly from Mexico and Central America, add to the totals. Demographers estimate that as of 2006, about 12 million undocumented immigrants live in the U.S, making up about 5 percent of the workforce.[1]

Today, 12 percent of Americans are foreign born,[2] compared with fewer than 5 percent as recently as

Figure 2-1	Population Growth in the United States: 1790 to 2006	
Census	Number of People	Increase over Previous Decade (Percent)
1790	3,929,214	–
1800	5,308,483	35.1
1810	7,239,881	36.4
1820	9,638,453	33.1
1830	12,866,020	33.5
1840	17,069,453	32.7
1850	23,191,876	35.9
1860	31,443,321	35.6
1870	39,818,449	26.6
1880	50,155,783	26.0
1890	62,947,714	25.5
1900	75,994,575	20.7
1910	91,972,266	21.0
1920	105,710,620	14.9
1930	122,775,046	16.1
1940	131,669,275	7.2
1950	151,325,798	14.9
1960	179,323,175	18.5
1970	203,302,031	13.4
1980	226,542,199	11.4
1990	248,718,302	9.8
2000	282,216,952	13.5
2004	293,628,158	–
2006	299,398,484	–

Source: U.S. Census Bureau, Population Division.

1970 (see Figure 2-3). The expanding number of foreign-born residents accounted for 35 percent of U.S. population growth during the 1990s and about half the new wage earners joining the labor force.[3] And despite stricter scrutiny of potential entrants into the United States after September 11, 2001, immigrants continue to flock to our shores.

Immigration is an important factor in the continued growth of border states such as California and Texas. Newcomers also help to maintain the population in gateway central cities such as New York, Chicago, Los Angeles, and Miami. Increasingly, however, immigrants gravitate toward nontraditional destinations: heartland agricultural states such as Iowa and Minnesota and growing metropolitan areas with available service sector jobs such as Atlanta and Raleigh-Durham. Although new Americans can strain local government resources, they are an important source of demand for housing, stores, and service businesses. Immigration presents opportunities for entrepreneurs who see new needs and ways to satisfy them. Catering to ethnic tastes and consumer preferences can enhance market penetration, a strategy adopted not only by neighborhood retailers but also by such mass market chains as JCPenney and Wal-Mart. Gradually, as immigrants move into the economic mainstream, they support the real estate market as buyers of both new and existing housing. Homeownership rates for naturalized citizens (immigrants who become U.S. citizens) are about the same as for native-born Americans.[4]

Greater longevity also contributes to population growth. Average life expectancy at birth was 68.1 years in 1950; the average American born in 2003 was expected to live almost 78 years.[5] In the United States today, the rate of population growth (net natural increase plus immigration) is lower than that of most emerging nations, as seen in Figure 2-4, but is much higher than western Europe and Japan. The population growth rate in the United States is expected to slowly decrease over the next decade. Nevertheless, the sheer number of new Americans will be significant. Census Bureau demographers project that the population of the United States will reach nearly 350 million by 2025.[6]

National Demographic Trends

As it expands, the population's characteristics are changing dramatically, and the nature and composi-

Figure 2-2	Legal Immigration to the United States				
	Legal Immigration by Decade	Population at Start of Decade	Average Annual Immigration per 1,000 Population	Population Increase in the Decade	Legal Immigration Share of Population Increase (Percent)
1901–1910	8,795,386	75,994,575	11.6	15,977,691	55.0
1911–1920	5,735,811	91,972,266	6.2	13,738,354	41.8
1921–1930	4,107,209	105,710,620	3.9	17,064,426	24.1
1931–1940	528,431	122,775,046	0.4	8,894,229	5.9
1941–1950	1,035,039	131,669,275	0.8	19,161,229	5.4
1951–1960	2,515,479	151,325,798	1.7	27,997,377	9.0
1961–1970	3,321,677	179,323,175	1.9	23,978,856	13.9
1971–1980	4,493,314	203,302,031	2.2	23,240,168	19.3
1981–1990	7,338,062	226,542,199	3.2	22,176,103	33.1
1991–2000	9,095,417	248,718,302	3.7	32,712,033	27.8
2001–2004	3,780,000	281,422,246	3.3		

Sources: U.S. Immigration and Naturalization Service and U.S. Census Bureau, *2000 Census.*

Figure 2-3	Foreign-Born Persons as a Percent of U.S. Population	
	Number	**Percent**
1910	13,516	14.7
1920	13,921	13.2
1930	14,204	11.6
1940	11,595	8.8
1950	10,347	6.9
1960	9,738	5.4
1970	9,619	4.8
1980	14,080	6.2
1990	19,767	7.9
2000	31,107	11.1
2004	34,000	12.0

Source: U.S. Census Bureau, 2000 Census.

Figure 2-4	Projected Population Growth Rates: Developing Nations versus Mature Economies	
Projected Annual Rate of Population Growth (Percent)		
	2000	**2025**
Developing Nations		
Congo (Kinshasa)	3.2	2.5
Ecuador	2.0	1.2
Egypt	2.0	1.1
Haiti	1.5	1.4
India	1.6	0.9
Malaysia	2.0	1.4
Mexico	1.8	1.0
Philippines	2.2	1.3
Turkey	1.3	0.6
United States, Europe, and Japan		
France	0.5	0.1
Italy	0.0	−0.5
Japan	0.2	−0.6
Norway	0.5	0.3
Russia	−0.4	−0.5
United Kingdom	0.4	0.2
United States	1.0	0.8

Source: U.S. Census Bureau, International Data Base, 2002.

tion of the population will be as important as its total size in determining opportunities for future real estate development. A look at demographic trends tells us not only how many more people will reside in the United States ten or 20 years from now but also their ages, household composition, educational attainment, and ethnicity. Looking beyond the totals helps predict and segment consumers' needs and desires more accurately.

Demographers used to talk about the population pyramid, with large numbers of children on the bottom and relatively few old people at the top. In 1970, the nation's median age was 28. By 2000, it was greater than 35, and by 2010, it will be greater than 37. In 2030, America's age distribution will be closer to a pillar than a pyramid (see Figure 2-5). Age cohorts younger than 75 will be increasingly equal in size. The baby boomers (born 1946 to 1963) constituted 35 percent of the population in 1970 but will account for only 20 percent of the nation's total in 2030.

The middle-aged baby boomer bulge will start to retire in large numbers after 2010. Fewer working-age adults will support nonworking seniors and children as the population ages, creating concern for employers, who will need more skilled workers to fill positions in factories, warehouses, stores, and office buildings.

As demonstrated by the 2030 demographic profile in Figure 2-5, no single generation will be large enough to dominate public policy making, and each group will be equally important in terms of numbers of real estate consumers (although their relative purchasing power will be quite different). Politicians and retailers will have to please all age groups in a way that has not been true historically. If the distribution of population by age is overlaid with variations in income, race/ethnicity, and household characteristics, the large number of discrete target markets becomes clear. This number of markets creates an opportunity for developers because the real estate industry has been slow to properly segment overall demand and thus address this growing diversity.

For retailing, an aging population means higher disposable income, better-educated and savvier consumers, and more money spent on discretionary purchases than on necessities. For housing, the large number of empty nesters suggests new demand for second homes and for primary housing in locations not affected by perceived school quality. Senior citizens will seek specialty housing catering to households segmented by lifestyle preferences, health needs, and ability to pay. In the late 1980s, developers believed that an affluent, aging population also translated into strong demand for upscale active retirement communities. In practice, however, senior citizens have not totally accepted either age-restricted

living or its high prices. The result has been slow product absorption for some developments. In this case, demographics alone was insufficient to gauge demand: increasingly, focus groups and other research are used to evaluate consumers' desires in terms of features, functions, and benefits of the built product.

Some developers focused on expanding the supply of assisted living facilities catering to an increasingly frail population. They were financed largely by real estate investment trusts specializing in assisted living facilities and nursing homes that gained the confidence of investors.[7] Many assisted living market segments were overbuilt, however, requiring state agencies to find ways to assist developers in providing affordable assisted living options as an alternative to costly (and often unnecessary) nursing home beds.

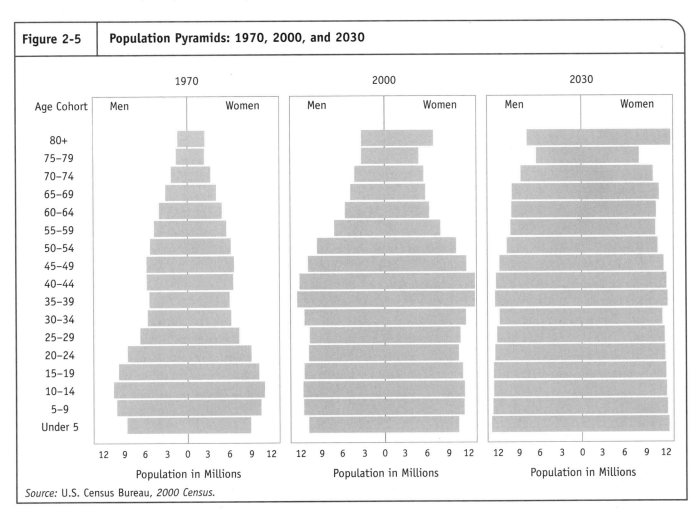

Figure 2-5 **Population Pyramids: 1970, 2000, and 2030**

Source: U.S. Census Bureau, *2000 Census.*

In the coming decades, the U.S. population will become more ethnically and racially diverse—partly because of differences in the age composition and birthrates of the existing minority population but also because of new immigrants and their offspring. Non-Hispanic whites constituted 76 percent of the population in 1990 but will represent only 65.1 percent by 2010. Hispanics (13 percent of the total in 2000) will be the fastest-growing minority in absolute numbers, reaching nearly 16 percent of all Americans by 2010.[8] It is important to recognize that immigrants are not simply Asian or Hispanic or European; they constitute different segments of the broader categories. Thais and Japanese, Puerto Ricans and Peruvians, French and Italians are all very different subgroups of Asian, Hispanic, and European. Within each cultural group many socioeconomic variations further segment the populations. Real estate entrepreneurs need to be sensitive to the different cultural and economic norms that are reflected in shopping and housing choices.

Similarly, households are not homogeneous, and neither are their housing preferences. Demand is shrinking for the mass market suburban tract house as household needs and personal preferences become more diverse. Niche marketing will be the key to successful development into the 21st century. More than one-fourth of all households consist of a single person, and their numbers are rising rapidly. Growth in single-person households is fueled by adults who never marry, high divorce rates, and an increase in the number of older widows and widowers. Homeownership is increasingly attractive to singles, and their numerical growth will help offset a decline in future demand from families with children. In 2005 single women purchased 1.5 million homes—or one-fifth of all homes sold. Compare that with 1981, when single men and single women bought about 10 percent each of all homes sold. In 2005 single men purchased only 9 percent of the homes, compared with the 20 percent purchased by women. That change in activity was the result of a series of demographic and societal shifts: women marry later, they live longer than men, the divorce rate is still high, making many women single in mid-life, and women earn more money than they used to.

The number of traditional married-couple-with-kids families has declined sharply—from 40 percent of all households in 1970 to 20 percent in 2004 (see Figure 2-6 for changes over several decades).[9] Only 33 percent of all households include any children under

Figure 2-6	Changing Composition of American Households		
	Percent of All Households		
Household Type	1970	2000	2025
Family Households	81.2	68.1	67.1
Married Couple	70.5	51.7	51.3
With Children under 18	40.3	23.5	20.4
Other Family	10.6	16.4	15.8
With Children under 18	5.0	9.3	7.6
Nonfamily Households	18.8	31.9	33.0
Living Alone	17.1	25.8	27.7
Not Living Alone	1.7	6.1	5.3

Sources: U.S. Census Bureau, *2000 Census*, 100 Percent Data, Table P18; projections from Martha Farnsworth Riche, "How Changes in the Nation's Age and Household Structure Will Reshape Housing Demand in the 21st Century," *Issue Papers on Demographic Trends Important to Housing* (Washington, D.C.: U.S. Department of Housing and Urban Development, Office of Policy Development and Research, 2002), Table 2.

18. A growing share of families with children—more than 31 percent—has only one parent (or another adult relative) at home, up from 11 percent in 1970.

To gauge demand, homebuilders focus on aggregate growth in the number of households nationwide and in their trade areas. During the 1970s and 1980s, demand for homes and apartments was fueled by household formations that exceeded the rate of population growth. Average household size continues to fall, from 3.14 persons in 1970 to 2.76 persons in 1980 to 2.57 persons in 2004. Americans are having fewer children as overall affluence rises, and more people are living alone. The number of households is still growing, but at a slower rate than in the past. Consequently, aggregate demand for shelter will not grow at the same pace as in the past. Harvard University demographers project that the United States will gain 11.7 million new households between 2000 and 2010 and another 12.1 million in the following decade, yielding growth rates of 11.1 percent and 10.3 percent, respectively.[10]

Residential and retail developers closely monitor household income characteristics and are alert to how age, race, and household composition affect both affordability and taste. As shown in Figure 2-7, income can vary dramatically by age. Earning power is greatest in the 45 to 54 age bracket, followed by 35- to 44-year-olds, and then by people 55 to 64. Over the next ten years, "middle-aged" household growth will be high, generating demand for discretionary goods and services and for move-up housing and second homes.

Household income data vary dramatically by place of residence (metropolitan versus nonmetropolitan areas, central cities versus suburbs), by household type, and by race. For example, median household income in 2004 was $47,994 in the Northeast but only $40,773 in the South. For non-Hispanic whites, it was $48,977 but for African Americans only $30,134.[11]

Census income data underestimate household purchasing power because many households fail to report all their earnings. In fact, a growing underground economy operates beyond the realm of traditional reporting practices. The magnitude of the so-called "informal economy" varies among markets, and unreported activities take many forms (second jobs paid in cash, street vending, agricultural barter,

Figure 2-7	2004 Median Household Income by Age of Householder
All Households	$44,389
15–24	$27,586
25–34	$45,485
35–44	$56,785
45–54	$61,111
55–64	$50,400
65+	$24,509

Source: U.S. Census Bureau, *Income, Poverty, and Health Insurance Coverage in the United States: 2005.* www.census.gov.

tutoring, home improvement work, domestic services)—all legal activities that produce cash that eventually makes it into the hands of retailers, landlords, and homebuilders. No definitive methods exist to estimate the extent of unreported income in an individual market, but it is an important element in consumer demand in inner cities, blue- and pink-collar suburbs, and rural areas.

In addition, market analysts who focus only on current earnings miss part of the wealth picture—household assets that will be inherited by today's younger households. In 2004, U.S. families had a median net worth of $93,100 and a mean worth of $448,200 held in investment vehicles ranging from equity in owner-occupied homes to interest-bearing accounts, stocks, bonds, and retirement plans. Net worth is highest for households aged 55 to 64, whose 2004 median net worth was $248,700 and whose mean worth was $843,800.[12] Many young households, which may not be earning much right now, will enjoy greater affluence upon inheriting family assets. Senior citizens, on average, have modest cash incomes but can tap into savings, investments, and home equity to pay for units in active retirement communities or assisted living facilities.

Finding Demographic Data

Good historical data about national demographic trends can be found in many different places. The U.S. Census Bureau's Web site (www.census.gov)

provides a wealth of data that are constantly being updated and reinterpreted. The Web site provides easy access to population and housing data in the American Community Survey. These data are collected every year instead of every ten years.

Income data are best found through the Bureau of Economic Analysis (BEA) on its Web site (www.bea.gov). Most of the data provided thus far in this chapter are national data. But developers are more likely to use data for metropolitan statistical areas (MSAs) and possibly neighborhoods after reviewing national trends. Historical income data for MSAs are available from the BEA; two major suppliers are Moody's Economy.com (formerly Regional Financial Associates) and Global Insight (formerly DRI/WEFA). In the past, BEA updates could lag up to five years, which meant that suppliers were in fact forecasting five years of the past as well as the future. Fortunately, BEA updates state statistics much more frequently—the lag at the state level is only four months—and forecasters can then adjust MSA numbers to match state numbers.

EMPLOYMENT GROWTH AND ECONOMIC CYCLES

Whereas demand for housing and retail space is primarily a function of population and of household growth and composition, demand for other commercial property development—office buildings, factories, research and development facilities, warehouses—is more closely tied to changes in the labor force and employment. The office construction boom of the 1970s and 1980s was fueled, in part, by a dramatic shift in the U.S. economy from production of goods to delivery of services and the concomitant growth of white-collar occupations. Manufacturing jobs dropped as a share of total employment, but the service sector—a diverse mix of jobs heavily concentrated in business services and health care—grew dramatically. Women entered the labor force in increasing numbers, and new technology created opportunities for both professional and clerical services and knowledge workers. Typical anchor tenants of new office buildings were expanding law, account-

ing, and investment firms, and corporations and banks seeking to enhance their images.

Aggressive expansion ended by 1989. The lending excesses of the 1980s led to failures in the savings and loan (S&L) industry and to bank mergers, and real estate lending came to a screeching halt. Growth in the labor force had been slowing for some time, but then employers cut back. Total wage and salary employment dropped by more than 1 million jobs between 1990 and 1991 and showed only a slight increase in 1992.

Economic recovery began in earnest in 1993 and soon became a long-term boom. Nonfarm jobs increased by more than 21 million between 1993 and 2000. A significant share of the new jobs was in industries that use office space—data processing, advertising and media, business services, communications, finance, and the professions. Occupancy in office buildings quickly improved, and by 1997 new construction was well underway in both central business districts and suburban office nodes. But in 2001, the bursting dot-com bubble brought economic expansion to a halt, and job losses in 2002 totaled more than 1.1 million. As the economy weakened, office vacancy rates spiked up.

Trends in employment by industry and occupation suggest that the share of total jobs found in office-prone industries will continue to grow, as seen in Figure 2-8. The Bureau of Labor Statistics (BLS) predicts that close to 19 million new jobs will be created in the rapidly growing service sector between 2004 and 2014. By 2014, the service sector's employment is expected to reach 129 million, accounting for almost four out of five jobs in the U.S. economy.[13]

Despite the strength of the service sector, future demand for new office space will not match that of the previous three decades. Much of the growth in service sector jobs will be found at health care providers (home health care agencies, assisted living facilities, or nursing homes) that do not require much multitenant office space. In banking, insurance, and government, a focus on consolidation, improvement in productivity, and cost containment resulted in job cutbacks and vacated office space in the 1990s, a trend that is likely to continue.

Figure 2-8	Employment in Office-Using Industries: Share of Total Nonfarm Jobs

Year	Share (Percent)
1985	19.1
1990	20.4
1995	20.9
2000	22.6
2005*	23.1
2010*	23.6

*Projected.
Source: Economy.com. Projections as of May 2003.

Employment growth is just one of several determinants of demand for commercial and industrial real estate. Fast-paced development of state-of-the-art warehouse space in the 1990s resulted primarily from new technology and changing methods of operation, not job growth. Retail employment has grown along with shopping center square footage, but demand for new store space is more a function of residential development patterns, store design trends, and growth in purchasing power.

Regional and Metropolitan Shifts

Population, household, and employment growth suggests opportunities for real estate development

Figure 2-9	Employment by Major Industry: 1994, 2004, and Projected to 2014 (Thousands)					
	1994	2004	2014	Percent of Total 1994	Percent of Total 2004	Percent of Total 2014
Nonfarm Wage and Salary Employment	114,984	132,192	150,877	100.0	100.0	100.0
Mining	577	523	477	0.5	0.4	0.3
Construction	5,095	6,964	7,756	4.4	5.3	5.1
Manufacturing	17,020	14,329	13,553	14.8	10.8	9.0
Utilities	689	570	563	0.6	0.4	0.4
Wholesale Trade	5,247	5,655	6,131	4.6	4.3	4.1
Retail Trade	13,491	15,034	16,683	11.7	11.4	11.1
Transportation and Warehousing	3,701	4,250	4,756	3.2	3.2	3.2
Information	2,739	3,138	3,502	2.4	2.4	2.3
Financial Activities	6,867	8,052	8,901	6.0	6.1	5.9
Professional and Business Services	12,174	16,414	20,980	10.6	12.4	13.9
Educational Services	1,895	2,766	3,665	1.6	2.1	2.4
Health Care and Social Assistance	10,912	14,187	18,482	9.5	10.7	12.2
Leisure and Hospitality	10,100	12,479	14,694	8.8	9.4	9.7
Other Services	5,202	6,210	6,943	4.5	4.7	4.6
Federal Government	3,018	2,728	2,771	2.6	2.1	1.8
State and Local Government	16,257	18,891	21,019	14.1	14.3	13.9

Source: Bureau of Labor Statistics, "Employment by Major Industry Division, 1994, 2004, and 2014," December 17, 2005 (http://stats.bls.gov/news.release/ecopro.t01.htm).

nationally, but internal mobility data help identify *where* construction should occur. Movement across regions, between states, and within metropolitan areas creates demand for new homes, shopping centers, entertainment facilities, office buildings, and hotels. At the same time, a net loss of households or jobs results in higher vacancies, lower rents, and softening home prices.

The U.S. population continues to shift from older metropolitan areas of the Northeast and Midwest toward the Sunbelt, the mountain states, and the Pacific Northwest (see Figure 2-10). More than half of all Americans lived in the Rust Belt in 1970. By 2000, the share had dwindled to 42 percent. Between 1990 and 2000, the country's population grew at a rate of 13.2 percent; at the state level, however, growth varied wildly (see Figure 2-11). Because of California's prolonged recession in the first half of the decade, its decade-over-decade population growth rate (13.8 percent) was only slightly above the national average (13.1 percent). California's net domestic migration (movement into the state from elsewhere in the United States) was strongly negative during most of the 1990s. More Americans left California than moved in, a reversal of earlier trends. International immigration and natural increase were largely responsible for the state's continued growth. In contrast, Georgia, North Carolina, and Nevada attracted Americans from other states. Nevada is the nation's fastest-growing state,

based on percentages; its population increased by 66 percent in the last decade.

Population expands fastest where jobs are created (and stagnates or declines in ailing economies). New England's economic boom of the 1980s turned into a recession in the early 1990s. States heavily dependent on income from a single industry—petroleum in the case of Texas, Oklahoma, Colorado, and Louisiana—were severely depressed during the mid-1980s. Texas and Colorado, however, aggressively courted non-energy businesses and recovered less than a decade later. Metropolitan areas such as Austin, Portland, Sacramento, San Francisco, and Seattle thrived during the technology boom of the late 1990s, only to suffer severely weakened space demand after the dot-com crash. Property markets in metropolitan areas with diverse economies are better able to withstand cyclical fluctuations than are regions dependent on one or two key industries or employers.

Population shifts have political ramifications that ultimately influence real estate interests. As people move from the Northeast and Midwest to the South and West or from central cities to suburbs, congressional districts are reapportioned accordingly. In 2000, New York and Pennsylvania each lost two seats in the U.S. House of Representatives, and eight other states lost one congressional delegate. Arizona, Florida, Georgia, and Texas each gained two seats, while California, Colorado, Nevada, and North Carolina each picked up one.

Population figures for MSAs and consolidated metropolitan statistical areas (CMSAs), as seen in Figure 2-12, underscore the Sunbelt/Frostbelt dichotomy. Lifestyle preferences—increased interest in outdoor sports and hobbies—encourage both young adults and retirees to seek milder climates. Many Sunbelt markets have lower real estate costs and lower taxes, factors that encourage both employers and workers to move to metropolitan growth magnets such as Phoenix, Atlanta, and Dallas. Note, however, that the New York and Chicago metropolitan areas did grow in the 1990s, while growth rates slowed significantly in former rapidly growing areas like metropolitan Los Angeles, San Diego, and Tampa.

Figure 2-10	Population of the United States by Region				
	Percent Share				
	1970	1980	1990	2000	2005
Northeast	24.1	21.7	20.4	19.0	18.4
Midwest	27.8	26.0	24.0	22.9	22.3
South	30.9	33.3	34.4	35.6	36.3
West	17.1	19.1	21.2	22.5	23.0

Source: U.S. Census Bureau, *2000 Census.*

Figure 2-11	Percentage Change in State Populations: 1990 to 2005 (Total U.S. Growth = 19.1%)		
Under 10 Percent	**10–30 Percent**	**30–50 Percent**	**Over 50 Percent**
Connecticut	Alabama	Colorado	Arizona
District of Columbia (–9.3 %)	Alaska	Florida	Nevada
Iowa	Arkansas	Georgia	
Louisiana	California	Idaho	
Maine	Delaware	North Carolina	
Massachusetts	Hawaii	Texas	
Michigan	Illinois	Utah	
New York	Kansas		
North Dakota (–0.3 %)	Kentucky		
Ohio	Maryland		
Pennsylvania	Minnesota		
Rhode Island	Mississippi		
West Virginia	Missouri		
	Montana		
	Nebraska		
	New Hampshire		
	New Jersey		
	New Mexico		
	Oklahoma		
	Oregon		
	South Carolina		
	South Dakota		
	Tennessee		
	Vermont		
	Virginia		
	Washington		
	Wisconsin		
	Wyoming		

Source: U.S. Census Bureau, *State and Metropolitan Area Data Book: 2006,* Administrative and Customer Services Division, Statistical Compendia Branch, http://www.census.gov/compendia/smadb/SMADBrank.html.

Central cities were more successful in retaining their population base during the 1990s than in previous decades. Some cities that lost population in the 1970s and 1980s, such as Chicago, registered net gains. Households were encouraged by new entertainment venues and recreational facilities. Redevelopment generated new office space, cultural facilities, hotels, and downtown housing. Immigrants were drawn to New York, Los Angeles, Houston, and Boston. In the aggregate, however, the shift of households from older cities

Figure 2-12	Population Change in the 20 Largest MSAs and CMSAs: 1980 to 2000			
	Population in 2000 (Thousands)	Rank in 2000	Percent Change 1980–1990	Percent Change 1990–2000
Northeast/Midwest				
New York-Northern New Jersey-Long Island, NY-NJ-CT-PA CMSA	21,200	1	3.4	8.4
Chicago-Gary-Kenosha, IL-IN-WI CMSA	9,158	3	1.5	11.1
Philadelphia-Wilmington-Atlantic City, PA-NJ-DE-MD CMSA	6,188	6	4.3	5.0
Boston-Worcester-Lawrence, MA-NH-ME-CT CMSA	5,819	7	6.5	6.7
Detroit-Ann Arbor-Flint, MI CMSA	5,456	8	−2.0	5.2
Minneapolis-St. Paul, MN-WI MSA	2,969	15	15.5	16.9
Cleveland-Akron, OH CMSA	2,946	16	−2.7	3.0
St. Louis, MO-IL MSA	2,603	18	3.2	4.5
South/West				
Los Angeles-Riverside-Orange County, CA CMSA	16,374	2	26.4	12.7
Washington-Baltimore, DC-MD-VA-WV CMSA	7,608	4	16.2	13.1
San Francisco-Oakland-San Jose, CA CMSA	7,039	5	16.4	12.6
Dallas-Ft. Worth, TX CMSA	5,222	9	32.5	29.3
Houston-Galveston-Brazoria, TX CMSA	4,670	10	19.6	25.2
Atlanta, GA MSA	4,112	11	32.5	38.9
Miami-Ft. Lauderdale, FL CMSA	3,876	12	20.8	21.4
Seattle-Tacoma-Bremerton, WA CMSA	3,555	13	23.3	19.7
Phoenix-Mesa, AZ MSA	3,252	14	39.9	45.3
San Diego, CA MSA	2,814	17	34.2	12.6
Denver-Boulder-Greeley, CO CMSA	2,582	19	13.7	30.4
Tampa-St. Petersburg-Clearwater, FL MSA	2,396	20	28.2	15.9

Source: U.S. Census Bureau, U.S. Census 2000 Redistricting Data (P.L. 94-171) Summary File and 1990 Census. Released April 2, 2001.

to suburbs continues. Many Sunbelt cities can grow because they are able to annex adjacent unincorporated land—an opportunity not available to most cities in the Northeast or Midwest ringed by incorporated suburbs. Figure 2-13 highlights population losses in Washington, D.C., Philadelphia, Detroit, Cleveland, and St. Louis, a pattern also seen in smaller cities such as Pittsburgh, Buffalo, Baltimore, Milwaukee, and New Orleans (pre-Katrina). In these places, the influx of immigrants and the attractiveness of city living for

young adults could not outweigh the desirability of suburban schools and modern homes on spacious lots.

For local public officials, growth is a source of civic pride and means an expanding tax base, but it also triggers the need for costly public services and infrastructure. Rapid growth without adequate school, road, water, or sewer capacity often engenders no-growth attitudes among longer-term residents. Numerous states and metropolitan areas are implementing smart growth strategies designed to direct

Figure 2-13	Population Change in Central Cities				
	Population in 2005 (Thousands)	2005 Rank	Percent Change 1980–1990	Percent Change 1990–2000	Percent Change 2000–2005
Northeast/Midwest					
New York City	8,143	1	3.5	9.4	1.7
Chicago	2,842	3	–7.4	4.0	–1.8
Philadelphia	1,463	5	–6.1	–4.3	–3.6
Detroit	886	11	–14.6	–7.5	–6.8
Boston	559	24	2.0	2.6	–5.1
Cleveland	452	39	–11.9	–5.4	–5.5
Minneapolis	372	48	0.8	3.9	–2.6
St. Louis	344	52	–12.4	–12.2	–1.1
South/West					
Los Angeles	3,844	2	17.4	6.0	4.1
Houston	2,016	4	2.2	19.8	3.2
Phoenix	1,461	6	24.6	34.3	10.6
San Diego	1,255	8	26.8	10.2	2.6
Dallas	1,213	9	11.3	18.0	2.1
San Francisco	739	14	6.6	7.3	–4.8
Washington, D.C.	550	27	–4.9	–5.7	–3.8
Seattle	573	23	4.5	9.1	1.9
Denver	557	25	–5.1	18.6	0.6
Atlanta	470	35	–7.3	5.7	13.0
Miami	386	45	3.4	1.1	6.6
Tampa	325	56	2.9	8.4	7.4

Source: U.S. Census Bureau, Population Finder.

development into areas with adequate utility capacity and transportation networks and to encourage walkable communities.

The real estate industry, like any other producer of goods and services, profits by satisfying buyers' needs and wants. The developers, builders, and salespeople who pioneer new products and techniques spot trends early and assume that they can profit accordingly. Looking at broad demographic data is useful not only to look at the big picture of

trends in the United States and its regions but also to stimulate obvious questions. Is the same trend affecting my local market? Will it continue in the future? What opportunities does it present?

Finding Employment Data

Employment statistics are compiled by the BLS of the U.S. Department of Labor, whose Web site (www.bls.gov) is comprehensive but a bit confusing at times. For more than 60 years, the BLS used the Standard

Industry Classification (SIC) system to collect employment data by industry. The SIC system was not flexible enough, however, to handle rapid changes in the U.S. economy such as developments in information services, new forms of health care provision, and high-tech manufacturing, and a new system, the North American Industry Classification System (NAICS), was developed jointly with Canada and Mexico. The new system uses a six-digit coding system (compared with the previous four-digit system) to classify employment into 20 industry sectors.

The BLS provides timely data for MSAs and the larger CMSAs (two or more adjacent MSAs or smaller micropolitan regions that are combined such as Washington, Baltimore, and Northern Virginia). These data are used to produce forecasts of not only employment growth but also population and income estimates for MSAs. BLS uses two surveys to provide employment data (see Chapter 18).

A reasonable number of organizations such as the well-known Economy.com and Global Insight compile, interpret, and forecast employment information, usually using BLS data. Job Watch of the Economic Policy Institute (www.jobwatch.org) provides some employment information, most of it with analysis from its experts. The Economic Research Service of the U.S. Department of Agriculture provides some employment information, primarily on rural areas.

LAND SUPPLY

The United States contains 3,718,694 square miles (9.6 million square kilometers) of land,[14] which supports an estimated population of more than 300 million people as of January 2006.[15] Physically, both Russia and Canada are slightly larger than the United States. China is slightly smaller.

Compared with a country such as the Netherlands, where overall land use is intensive, the United States boasts extensive and relatively unused deserts, mountains, dry plains, tundra, and swamps. Developed land takes up only 5.5 percent or 107 million acres (43.3 million hectares) of total land area in the United States.[16] The present land-to-people ratio in the United States is about 8.1 acres (3.3 hectares) per

person (79 persons per square mile [205 per square kilometer]), which may seem inconceivable to someone living in New York City but may sound crowded to a Montana rancher.

In addition to vast rural areas, significant quantities of undeveloped land exist even in the urbanized metropolitan areas of the United States. These reserves result from leapfrog suburban development, abandoned or dying central-city neighborhoods, and relatively low-density development patterns in new urban areas. In recent years, however, the high cost of infrastructure—roads, water, and sewerage—and decreasing federal funds for extending services have led community groups, planners, and real estate interests to seek ways to constrain suburban sprawl through farmland preservation programs, limits on utility extensions, impact fees, and/or incentives for development in designated growth areas. Consequently, demand for developable land—that is, properly zoned land with the necessary infrastructure in place—has driven up land costs sharply in some areas, thereby producing higher-density commercial and residential land uses. At the same time, metropolitan areas continue to expand outward geographically as the effect of population growth exceeds the impact of increased density. In 1960, metropolitan areas housed 63 percent of the U.S. population on 9 percent of the country's land area. By 2000, 80 percent of the nation's population lived in metropolitan areas.

Americans' love of space is exemplified by recent trends in homebuilding. Despite experiments with smaller houses in the early 1980s, U.S. citizens continue to demand more interior living space. The median new single-family house grew from 1,385 square feet (129 square meters) in 1970 to 1,595 square feet (148 square meters) in 1980 to 2,140 square feet (199 square meters) in 2004. A significant corollary to less land/more house is the steadily increasing proportion of new houses with two or more stories: 17 percent in 1970, 31 percent in 1980, and 52 percent in 2004.[17] The perception that more living space with less land (but still some land around the house) is better than no land seems to explain Americans' tenacious demand for single-family detached housing and thus for relatively low-density, owner-occupied residential development. It also suggests why small homes in desirable city neighborhoods and close-in suburbs are being torn down and replaced with larger residences.

Who Owns the Land? How Is It Used?

With 672 million acres (272 million hectares), or about 29.2 percent of the nation's 2.3 billion acres (931 million hectares), the federal government is the largest single landowner in the United States; in fact, Uncle Sam owns 60 percent or more of four states: Alaska, Nevada, Utah, and Idaho.[18] State and local governments collectively own another 12 percent of the nation's land, leaving private landowners and Native Americans on trust lands to share the remainder of the pie (nearly 60 percent). As urbanization pushes the boundaries of metropolitan areas outward, farm acreage is declining. At its peak in 1954, more than 1.2 billion acres (485.8 million hectares) was under cultivation. By 2002, only 941 million acres (381 million hectares) was still being farmed—a 5 percent drop since 1990.[19] Moreover, individually owned farms are gradually being replaced by a smaller number of larger, corporate-owned agricultural holdings. The family farm certainly has not disappeared, but globalization of food production, processing, and marketing is changing farm ownership and operations.

Although government, forest product companies, utilities, and railroads still control extremely large land holdings, real estate in the United States is widely owned by individual citizens and small partnerships. For social and political reasons (and not merely because of the huge land mass), middle-income people could acquire land inexpensively and easily during the 17th through early 20th centuries. Throughout U.S. history, governments at all levels have actively promoted private ownership of land and homes. During the 20th century in particular, a variety of programs and policies advanced homeownership: the Federal Housing Administration's mortgage insurance program and the Veterans Administration's mortgage guarantee program (which revolutionized home mortgage lending in the 1940s and 1950s); the federally facilitated secondary mortgage market for home loans (through the quasi-federal corporations known as Fannie Mae and Freddie

Mac); tax legislation benefiting both homeowners and private investors in commercial and industrial real estate; and, most important, provision of the infrastructure needed to support private property ownership. As of early 2007, nearly 70 percent of all U.S. householders own their homes. And the total value of owner-occupied housing (debt and equity) is far greater than that of commercial real estate.

Ownership of commercial and industrial properties rests in the hands of users such as corporations and retail chains, institutional investors, pension funds and large investment pools like REITs, and private individuals, often through partnerships and limited liability companies. On the debt side, commercial banks still hold the largest share of mortgages, but since the 1990s securitized debt (commercial mortgage–backed securities, or CMBSs) is capturing a growing share of the market. In contrast, savings associations are losing market share of both equity and debt; since the early 1990s, they have focused on owner-occupied homes and small rental properties.

Apartment ownership is diverse and widespread. According to the National Multi Housing Council (NMHC), the top 50 apartment owners in the United States in 2006 had an ownership interest in 2.64 million units, approximately 16 percent of rentals in buildings with five or more units. Among the top 50 owners, 13 are publicly traded REITs, which accounted for 922,741 apartments or 35 percent of the units covered in the NMHC survey.

Foreign Ownership of Real Estate In the United States

The relative ease of acquiring property that U.S. citizens take for granted strongly attracts foreign investors to U.S. real estate. In many other developed nations, real estate markets are much smaller, and laws dramatically restrict foreign investment. American property attracts offshore capital for several reasons: the country's perceived political and economic stability, the sheer size of the market, the potential for appreciation, and the U.S. trade deficit. American land and buildings also offer opportunities for asset diversification. A survey conducted for the

National Association of Realtors indicates that foreign investment in U.S properties increased to $40.6 billion in 2002, up from $38.3 billion in 2001.[20] Japan continues to be the largest offshore investor in the aggregate, followed by Canada, Germany, the Netherlands, and the United Kingdom.

Foreign landownership and investment in agricultural land were of concern to federal and state elected officials in the 1970s. In 1978, Congress directed the U.S. Department of Agriculture to conduct an annual inventory of foreign-owned farmland, and considerable public discussion of the dangers of foreign ownership ensued. At the end of 1997, offshore interests held slightly more than 1 percent of U.S. farm and forest land (14 million acres [5.7 million hectares]). Nearly half (45 percent) of the foreign holdings are forest lands, much of it controlled by Canadian paper companies.[21]

Although offshore investors continue to purchase highly visible office, hotel, and resort properties (and are increasingly attracted to rental apartments), their overall influence on U.S. property markets should not be a source of political concern. Real estate accounts for about 3 percent of foreign investment in American industry, and it attracted only 2.6 percent of offshore capital invested in this country in 2004 (see Figure 2-14).

Figure 2-14	Foreign Direct Investment in U.S. Real Estate (Billions of Dollars)			
	Capital Inflows		Direct Investment Position	
	2000	2004	2000	2004
Real Estate	$3.47	$2.54	$42.68	$47.58
All Industries	$314.01	$95.86	$1,214.25	$1,526.30
Real Estate Share	1.1%	2.6%	3.5%	3.1%

Source: Bureau of Economic Analysis, "Foreign Direct Investment in the U.S.: Country and Industry Detail for Capital Inflows" (www.bea.gov/bea/di/fdi21web.htm).

REAL ESTATE, THE GROSS DOMESTIC PRODUCT, WEALTH, AND EMPLOYMENT

It should come as no surprise that, given their central importance to the U.S. economy, real estate development, construction, and investment are highly regulated by government at all levels. Real estate is the largest component of gross private domestic investment in the U.S. gross domestic product (GDP). Forty percent of 2004's domestic private investment ($960.2 billion) was in real property assets, and 69 percent of that amount was for housing (see Figure 2-15).[22]

As just one example of the scale of housing investment, owners of existing residential property (all types) spent $233 billion in 2003 for improvements, repairs, additions, and alterations.[23] Owner-occupants accounted for $176 billion of the total invested in improvements.[24] (These figures do not include governments' investment in real property.)

For individuals, real estate is an extremely important component of wealth. Besides providing shelter and psychic benefits such as pride and security, housing equity constitutes more than one-fifth of total personal net worth.[25] The importance of the real estate industry in the United States is also reflected in national employment figures. In 2005, the U.S economy provided more than 134 million nonfarm jobs, of which 1.5 million were in real estate businesses and another 7.4 million in construction.[26] Overall, 6.6 percent of the nation's employment is attributable to real estate development, management, and sales, suggesting why the industry is important to the nation's economic health.

It would be a mistake to note the magnitude of employment in the real estate industry without also recognizing its cyclical nature. Real estate–oriented employment shrinks and swells in parallel with construction starts, which, in turn, tend to move broadly up and down with interest rates and the balance between the supply of and expected demand for real estate. The employment figures for construction workers in Figure 2-16 show how many workers enter and leave construction in response to opportunity. Between 1990 and 1992, the number of construction workers

Figure 2-15	Annual Private Fixed Investment in Land Improvements for 2004 (Billions of Dollars)
Nonresidential Structures	
Commercial and Health Care	$ 126.8
Manufacturing	16.5
Power and Communication	39.1
Mining	47.4
Other (Including Farm)	65.0
Subtotal	$ 294.8
Residential	
Single Family	$ 474.8
Multifamily	34.4
Manufactured Homes	7.5
Improvements and Other	148.7
Subtotal	$ 665.4
Total	$ 960.2

Source: Bureau of Economic Analysis, "Survey of Current Business," March 15, 2006.

Figure 2-16	Employment in Construction and Real Estate: 1990 to 2005

Year	Construction	Real Estate
1990	5.26	1.63
1991	4.78	1.62
1992	4.61	1.62
1993	4.78	1.67
1994	5.09	1.73
1995	5.27	1.75
1996	5.53	1.81
1997	5.81	1.87
1998	6.15	1.93
1999	6.54	1.98
2000	6.79	2.01
2001	6.83	2.03
2002	6.72	2.03
2003	6.73	2.05
2004	6.98	2.08
2005	7.28	2.13

Source: U.S. Department of Labor, Bureau of Labor Statistics, Current Employment Statistics survey program, http://www.bls.gov/ces/home.htm.

dropped by 650,000, only to increase by 2.7 million during the expansion during 1993 to 2005.

Workers in the real estate sector—in sales, finance, and management—have also felt the impact of cyclical fluctuations. Downsizing at real estate firms was a fact of life from 1990 through 1992, when commercial development activity shrank and residential sales slowed as a consequence of the real estate depression of the early 1990s. During 12 years of recovery and expansion (1993 to 2005), real estate businesses added 510,000 jobs. Commercial property markets weakened beginning in 2001, but as of summer 2006, the real estate industry as a whole was booming. Cycles are a way of life in this business, because long development lead times make it impossible to quickly adjust to abrupt changes in demand.

PREDICTING THE FUTURE

For real estate players in all markets, understanding the present and past is the necessary first step in pro-

jecting future opportunities. Extrapolation is not simple, however. Economic conditions have a way of confounding the forecasters who lay down a straight-edge and draw a line through two points in the past to project the future. Many changes are unforeseen. Some cities that lost population during the wave of suburbanization in the 1960s and 1970s grew again in the 1990s—thanks largely to immigration. By the early 2000s, retailers that were once found exclusively in suburban enclosed malls started seeking streetfront locations in city neighborhoods. Singles, once found only in rental apartments, are buying homes and condominiums in record numbers. "Smart growth" is a term unknown just two decades ago.

Moreover, not all property cycles operate in unison. Apartments were especially hard hit by the weak job market in 2002 and 2003, at the same time that record-low interest rates drew buyers into the for-sale market. Full-service hotels were affected by lower occupancy and room rates as travel declined after September 11, 2001. By 2005, however, hotel occupancy had reached nearly 70 percent, approaching historic record levels. The lesson for real estate practitioners is to stay well informed. Participants in the industry should assume that the unforeseen is always just around the corner—and be ready to confront it.

SUMMARY

Throughout, this book stresses that real estate practitioners who best anticipate the future will reap the greatest rewards. Prudent players do not take the built world for granted. Technology, consumer preferences, government policy, demographics, sources of capital, and economic underpinnings all evolve—at times slowly and at other times rapidly in response to crisis.

The economic setting of the real estate industry has become much more volatile than in earlier decades. In the early 1980s, real estate markets in the "oil patch" experienced the deepest recession since the Great Depression (in some places even worse than the early 1930s). In the late 1980s, huge investments of institutional capital led to dramatically overbuilt commercial real estate markets in many cities. Several successful development companies and professional real estate investors saw their fortunes reverse during the early 1990s when some property markets crashed. Not only small players—the carpenter turned contractor and the part-time real estate agent turned investor—but also large companies became casualties. Markets rebounded strongly in the late 1990s, only to fall victim to another economic downturn with the dot-coms. But then they rose again in the early 2000s.

Understanding the scope of the built environment, the institutions that support it, and their history cannot guarantee that observers will survive recessions or reap big profits in boom times. But a sense of perspective can put a developer or owner one step ahead of the competition and is a basic requirement for working with (or competing against) the best. All the participants in the development process need to understand the raw material that constitutes the playing field and how it is likely to change over time.

TERMS

- ▶ Baby boomers
- ▶ Consolidated metropolitan statistical area (CMSA)
- ▶ Demographics
- ▶ Downsizing
- ▶ Empty nesters
- ▶ Gross domestic product (GDP)
- ▶ Investment-grade properties
- ▶ Metropolitan statistical area (MSA)
- ▶ Population pyramid
- ▶ Purchasing power
- ▶ Service sector
- ▶ Single-person household
- ▶ Smart growth

REVIEW QUESTIONS

2.1 Why is ownership of real estate more attractive in the United States than in many other countries?

2.2 Why have U.S. developers looked outside the country for development opportunities?

2.3 Why is real estate so important to the U.S. economy?

2.4 Describe the anticipated changes in the composition of the U.S. population.

2.5 How does immigration affect demand for real estate?

2.6 How does employment growth influence the demand for commercial space?

2.7 Why is it important for real estate players to stay well informed about trends?

2.8 How significant is the construction industry to the nation's overall economy?

2.9 How does the aging baby boom generation affect the population pyramid?

2.10 How might the housing market be affected by a population where less than 30 percent of all households have children under the age of 18?

2.11 How will the significant growth in the "Professional and Business Services" and the "Health Care and Social Assistance" employment sectors affect the demand for real estate?

2.12 What portion of land in the United States is developed?

NOTES

1. Jeffrey Passel, *Size and Characteristics of the Unauthorized Migrant Population in the U.S.: Estimates Based on the March 2005 Current Population Survey.* Pew Hispanic Research Center, March 7, 2006.

2. U.S. Census Bureau, *Native and Foreign-Born Population by State: 2003,* Table 41. Updated July 11, 2005.

3. D'Vera Cohn, "Immigrant Workers Fed '90s Boom," *Washington Post,* December 2, 2002.

4. In 2002, more than three-fourths of foreign-born families who arrived in the United States before 1980 owned their homes.

5. National Center for Health Statistics, *National Vital Statistics Report,* February 28, 2005.

6. U.S. Census Bureau, *Resident Population Projections: 2005 to 2050,* Table 3.

7. As of May 2005, the National Association of Real Estate Investment Trusts listed 12 health care REITs with an equity market capitalization of nearly $13.4 billion, or 4.7 percent of the total equity REIT market.

8. U.S. Census Bureau, *Projected Population of the United States by Race and Hispanic Origin, 2000–2050,* Table 1-A.

9. U.S. Census Bureau, Census 2000 Summary File 1, Tables P18 and P19.

10. George Masnick and Zhu Xiao Di, "Projections of U.S. Households by Race/Hispanic Origin, Age, Family Type, and Tenure: A Sensitivity Analysis," in *Issue Papers on Demographic Trends Important to Housing* (Washington, D.C.: U.S. Department of Housing and Urban Development, Office of Policy Development and Research, 2003).

11. U.S. Census Bureau, Current Population Reports, *Income, Poverty, and Health Insurance Coverage in the United States: 2004,* P60–229 (Washington, D.C.: U.S. Government Printing Office, 2005).

12. Brian K. Bucks, Arthur B. Kennickell, and Kevin B. Moore, "Recent Changes in U.S. Family Finances: Evidence from the 2001 and 2004 Survey of Consumer Finances," *Federal Reserve Bulletin,* Vol. 92 (February 2006), pp. A1–A38.

13. Projections released by the Bureau of Labor Statistics December 3, 2001. They do not reflect Census 2000 counts or the economic effects of the events of September 11, 2001.

14. U.S. Census Bureau, *Statistical Abstract of the United States: 2002,* Table 335 (Washington, D.C.: U.S. Government Printing Office, 2002), p. 210.

15. U.S. Census Bureau estimate as of January 3, 2006.

16. U.S. Department of Agriculture, Natural Resources and Conversation Services, Natural Resources Inventory 2002, *Annual NRI Land Use,* April 2004. Excludes federal land and acreage in the District of Columbia and Alaska.

17. U.S. Census Bureau, *Characteristics of New Housing,* Series C25, available at www.census.gov/const/www/charindex.html#singlecomplete.

18. U.S. Census Bureau, *Statistical Abstract of the United States: 2003,* Table 348, p. 222. Figures as of September 30, 2003.

19. U.S. Department of Agriculture, National Agricultural Statistics Service, *Farms and Land in Farms* (Washington, D.C.: U.S. Government Printing Office, February 28, 2003).

20. National Association of Realtors, *Foreign Investment in U.S. Real Estate: Current Trends and Historical Perspective* (Chicago: Author, December 2005).

21. U.S. Department of Agriculture, Economic Research Service, *Foreign Ownership of U.S. Agricultural Land through December 31, 1997,* SB #943 (Washington, D.C.: Author, 1998). According to the USDA, foreign ownership of agricultural acreage has remained fairly steady since 1981, at slightly above or below 1 percent of all privately owned agricultural land in the United States.

22. Bureau of Economic Analysis, *Survey of Current Business* (Washington, D.C.: U.S. Government Printing Office, March 15, 2006.

23. Joint Center for Housing Studies, *The Changing Structure of the Home Remolding Industry: Improving America's Housing 2005* (Cambridge, MA: Harvard University, 2005).

24. U.S. Department of Commerce, *Expenditures for Residential Improvements and Repairs* (Washington, D.C.: U.S. Government Printing Office, 2003).

25. Federal Reserve Bank Flow of Funds Report, "Balance Sheet of Households and Non-Profit Organizations," Series Z.1, Table B.100. As of Q4 2002. Issued March 6, 2003.

26. U.S. Department of Labor, Bureau of Labor Statistics data series.

CHAPTER 3

Developers and Their Partners

To fully appreciate the role of developers in shaping the built environment, it is necessary to understand the function and motivation of the major participants in the development process. Although this chapter deals with the individual participants, the full complement of players should be seen as a team. Only then can the developer's multiple roles be completely understood.

Developers ultimately are responsible for the created space and how it will function over the life of a project, but because many different skills are needed to develop the kind of space society needs and wants, developers themselves usually do not provide all the expertise. Rather, they select, motivate, and manage the team needed to get a job done.

By assuming ultimate responsibility, developers must make sure that team members command the skills to do their part of the job and collectively meet development objectives. Development is a dynamic art that occurs over a considerable period of time—usually one to several years. During that time, the many changes likely to be made to the original development plan may require new skills and different players. The longer the development takes, the more

likely it is that the participants or individuals and companies will change along the way. Companies may lose key employees, or a merger may subsume the original lending institution.

Because pressures tend to become intense during the middle stages of the development process, initial contracts alone are often not enough to ensure that all team members will perform as agreed. There is no time to stop the development process for a year to engage in a lawsuit—at least not without incurring great financial pain. Successful developers recognize that the ultimate responsibility for a project's success in the context of an intense, dynamic process requires the ability to anticipate and respond to change.

Throughout the process, developers not only continue to verify that the overall project is feasible but also check to see that the development still makes sense for each individual participant, given changing situations. If the project becomes a loser for any individual participant, that participant may create problems for the rest of the team. As you consider the roles of the various participants, try to keep this challenging management task in mind so that you can see how exciting (and sometimes frightening) the development process can be.

This chapter looks at the roles of the major players in the development process, among them:

► Private sector developers;
► Public sector developers;
► Public/private partnerships;
► Architects;
► Urban designers;
► Engineers;
► Land planners;
► Landscape architects;
► Contractors;
► Environmental consultants;
► Transportation consultants;
► Appraisers;
► Attorneys and accountants;
► Real estate leasing agents and sales brokers;
► Financial players;
► Property managers;
► Market researchers;
► Marketing and public relations consultants;
► Regulators; and
► Final users.

After this detailed description of the various members of the development team, the chapter and the entire introduction conclude with a discussion of new trends in development. Although the eight-stage model first described in Chapter 1 is time honored, major evolutionary changes are occurring within this model. After seeing how each team member fits into the model, we conclude by looking at these evolutionary changes to the development process.

PRIVATE SECTOR DEVELOPERS

Like most businesspeople, developers seek the maximum possible return while minimizing risk and the commitment of their time and money. In development, the return consists of several components:

► The development fee, which is the stated direct compensation for developing the project;
► Profits on any sale to long-term investors (i.e., sale price less all costs needed to produce a fully functioning project);

► Possibly a long-term equity position (for which the developer may or may not contribute cash), in which case the developer's goals are similar to those of passive investors (discussed later);
► Personal and professional satisfaction in advancing a new concept or improving the urban environment; and
► Enhanced reputation, which creates future opportunities for development.

A developer's commitment of time is usually the length of the development period, which is increasing in most jurisdictions. If developers choose to retain ownership of a completed project, however, their commitment extends until the project is sold. Although the equity interests discussed later may also wish to minimize the time of their involvement, unlike developers they are not involved primarily in selling their time. Other professionals on the development team are either paid by the hour (job) or participate in only a portion of the development process; thus, they are less sensitive to the overall length of the development period.

Private developers may also profit through the ownership of entities that sell services to the development: insurance agencies, mortgage banking firms, leasing companies, management companies, or even general contracting firms. To the extent that these arrangements are made at arm's length and represent clearly understood agreements, developers are simply compensated for performing additional functions. On the other hand, if compensation for activities in which developers have an interest is above standard, any excess should be considered an addition to the development fee.

Private developers' financial exposure arises in two different ways. First, developers spend time and money before gaining assurance that a project will be built (i.e., before stage five, formal commitment), and naturally, developers seek to minimize such expenditures. Second, in addition to their own equity position (both contributed capital and debt for which developers are personally liable), developers might guarantee investors or lenders, or both, either a maximum project cost or a minimum occupancy level. As primary risk bearers, developers' financial exposure depends on

In a "merchant builder" arrangement, the University of Washington paid Lorig Associates a prenegotiated fee to develop Nordheim Court, a 2.8-acre (1.1-hectare), 146-unit dormitory complex housing 460 students. *Doug J. Scott/dougscott.com*

noting that to be fully effective developers must also possess clarity of vision. They must also be focused dreamers with the ability to convince others that they can make their dreams a reality.

To make the development happen, developers must be annoyingly persistent but not inflexible. Inflexible developers often find that their projects may never be built. The best developers encounter obstacles along the eight-stage road and must maintain some flexibility and willingness to be consensus builders. Local authorities and community groups can have a powerful impact on a project, and developers increasingly face design review boards that often require alterations in the appearance of a building. Only by adopting a flexible stance will developers secure all needed approvals. Developers who are willing to alter their original plans to accommodate at least some of the concerns voiced by those who will be directly affected by a proposed development most often find success at the end. Of course, too much compromise can result in an unfocused project and/or financial failure.

Today's developers have arrived at their life's work from fairly diverse starting points, as indicated by the profiles of different developers featured throughout this book. Some people know when they graduate from college or business school that they want to become a developer and immediately begin working for a development company in one capacity or another, learning as much as they can before striking out on their own. Some students enter graduate school seeking a degree in real estate development. For others, family landholdings prompt them to enter the development business. In other cases, developers get started simply because they have invested in real estate. As their interest in real estate development grows, they start to participate directly in the process. Often contractors, architects, and other participants described in this chapter decide to move up to the lead role of the developer in the process.

Dean Stratouly did not start out as a developer. He became an engineer because he did not know what else to do and eventually discovered that he liked to take risks and liked to make big deals. Becoming a real estate developer was a natural fit.

the amount of their direct financial commitment plus the magnitude of any guarantees they make and the likelihood of the guarantees' being called on.

Some developers work as "merchant builders." A client such as a retailer, health care provider, university, REIT, or public sector agency hires a developer to see a project through from beginning to completion. Such developers are usually hired for a fee, like a consultant, with a bonus paid at the end for successful completion and timely delivery of the product. In these cases, developers assume no personal financial risk. Although the fees are not small, they do not match what developers might earn when they operate as traditional developers and assume considerably more risk.

Developers' personal qualities are a vital element in the development process. Chapter 1 referred to the drive and creativity that characterize developers,

MUSEUM TOWERS
The Developer, Dean Stratouly, Speaks for Himself

I was a Navy brat, so while I was born in Boston, I grew up in a whole series of places ranging from Boston to San Diego, Hawaii to Connecticut. All in all, it was a fairly unstable childhood, but being able to deal with such instability is an important characteristic of a developer.

I went to a Catholic boys' school in Connecticut during the time of the Vietnam War. Coming from a family with a military service background, my father wanted me to go either to the Naval Academy—his first choice—or to West Point—which would have been marginally acceptable—or possibly the Air Force Academy. The boys' school administrators thought I should go to a Catholic college, one of the five schools that everybody went to—Notre Dame, Holy Cross, Boston College, Villanova, or Georgetown. But they were all-boys' schools and I wanted to be around blond cheerleaders. So I applied to the University of Southern California as an anthropology major.

My father went berserk. As a compromise, I ended up going to Worcester Polytechnic, which was an engineering school. There was no rhyme or reason for my going there except that I was good at math and science and reasonable at English and it seemed the path of least resistance. The idea was to get a job when I got out. No more. No less.

When I graduated, I went to work in the nuclear power plant business and ended up with the company that had developed Three Mile Island. I was with them until 1980 and made a nice salary selling nuclear power plants.

It was actually very good training for being a developer, because the power plant projects were very large with complicated engineering and construction processes, difficult union issues, and multilayered financing. Everything you did had to be reviewed by various groups, so I had to learn to make presentations. Like real estate development, it had the elements of social controversy, economic risk, and long-term design and planning processes.

After about five or six years when I traveled nonstop, Three Mile Island erupted and the company was bought by another group. There were all sorts of changes occurring and I decided to move on. I was living in Chicago at the time and wanted to move to either the East Coast or the West Coast. I called a friend in San Francisco who was leaving for Tokyo for several weeks, and he offered me his apartment. After that I went to visit a girl in Boston that I was dating, and I ended up marrying her and staying in Boston.

continued on page 226

Russell Katz started out as an idealistic architect who yearned for more control over his projects. Becoming a developer gave him this control and allowed him to put into practice the green building techniques that he learned in graduate school.

PUBLIC SECTOR DEVELOPERS

Increasingly, the public sector orchestrates large-scale property development projects, in essence functioning as a developer. But public sector developers must be distinguished from private sector developers. They are motivated by economic development goals or altruistic ends such as neighborhood revitalization or the need to create housing for certain income levels. The active pursuit and planning of development by the public sector has spawned a new breed of developer who could be referred to as a "public entrepreneur."

The term "public entrepreneur" is reserved for those public development professionals who plan, design, and financially structure the large-scale projects of such importance to the community that the government not only shares in their cost but also may assume much of the risk. Public entrepreneurs, with access to both public and private resources and using properly structured transactions, can help make projects happen at minimum cost to the city while stimulating additional private investment. Unlike private developers, public entrepreneurs are usually salaried employees. For three reasons, their compensation is generally higher than that of other planning professionals. First, they have developed a particular set of technical, analytical, and communication skills that are in scarce supply in the public sector. Second, they have the personality to make things happen in the public sector. Third, they are highly valuable to their cities.

The public sector works with developers in many ways. In Atlanta, the Metropolitan Atlanta Rapid Transit Authority (MARTA) has acted more like an entrepreneur in promoting development around rail

ELEVATION 314
The Developer, Russell Katz, Speaks for Himself

I'm 38 now [January 2007]. When I was growing up, I always liked buildings and I had a high level of sensitivity to the environment. I first wanted to be an artist. I liked to paint and draw. Then I got into architecture. I went to architecture school at the University of Virginia for my undergraduate degree. It was a nice program—quite liberal arts based, so I could take lots of different classes and not focus solely on architecture because it never fully held my attention. I didn't think it covered everything. It always seemed to stop short of the full picture of who actually uses the buildings and, beyond that, the impact that they have.

When I got out of architecture school, I went to Europe for some years. First I worked for the Guggenheim Museum because I was thinking about going back into the arts. Then I worked for Hans Hollein in Vienna, Austria, doing some pretty interesting architectural work. I worked with Coop Himmelb(l)au also. Some of it was pretty avant-garde work at the time in Vienna.

I came back to the States with a good enough résumé to get into some good schools. I ended up at Yale, which I loved—it was a great school for me. Once again I could cross-pollinate ideas with students from other departments and create independent studies to get into other disciplines. I got very involved with theater, developing plays and sets. We developed a whole play that ended up being put on at the drama school. We actually started the play with the set. We made the set first; then the writer wrote the play and we collaborated. Then we brought in directors and actors and went back and forth over the process. I met some friends there who also had the same basic interest in the environment that was not really being cultivated or satisfied at all through the curriculum.

One class we took at Yale was an eye opener. It was an elective, and there were students there from the forestry school, which was a lot more advanced in terms of thinking about environmental issues than the architectural school. This was in the early to mid-1990s. I think it was an awakening time for a lot of people. We got a lot of information about the environmental impact of buildings.

At the same time throughout architecture school, I was thinking about what I liked and what I didn't like about the practice of architecture. For me it always seemed like too much of a marginalized profession without enough power to realize a vision. I was, from early on, interested in how to get myself into a position where I could make decisions that would become based on what I thought needed to be done instead of trying to find a client or find somebody who actually had the resources to do things.

I learned that, for me, academia was an important environment to grow in. So much of the knowledge I got was from the relationships I developed with other students, in terms of learning where they came from, what they wanted to do, the things they were looking into, and the things that we shared.

That kind of held true through Yale and into my first job working with a great guy named Turner Brooks in Vermont for a few years. At the time it was interesting because a lot of the people who were into environmental studies considered him to be a green architect. He didn't really know what that meant—he'd just build really smart buildings that were well insulated and well situated and oriented and so forth. He used local material. It's funny how sometimes people, just because they are trying to do something with good quality, are actually doing good things in ways they don't even know.

I'm quite involved now with the UVA school of architecture. I'm on the board that advises the dean, with other developers and architects and landscape architects. It's a really interesting group, and one of the things we talk about is how development that is run from the MBA side is really different from the development that is run from the architecture side.

From the MBA side, you're looking more at the case studies and financials. You're relying a lot more on what's been done before in order to justify what you intend to do. If you are coming from the architecture side, I think you see potential in a broader spectrum. That's been a big value for me. I feel that the world would be a better place if there were more designers who knew that development would be a good opportunity instead of the perceived distrust and animosity between the fields.

After working as an architect on a number of projects, I decided it was time to get into development and learn how to do what I kept thinking I wanted to do. So I returned to Washington where I had grown up even though I hadn't been there for probably 15 or 16 years. I made the decision partly because it was where I had grown up, and I had some contacts in construction, real estate law, and development that I knew I could rely on. I had been living in New York and was familiar with Boston, where I had relatives who are developers. I knew what the real estate property prices were in all three cities.

I couldn't believe what could be done in Washington—this was 1998. With the same amount of money that it would take to buy a two-bedroom apartment in Brooklyn, I could get a 36-unit apartment building in Washington, next

continued on next page

ELEVATION 314

The Developer, Russell Katz, Speaks for Himself (continued)

to a Metro station. So the scales were jarringly different. I decided to move quickly and bought a 36-unit apartment building in Takoma, D.C., right next to the Metro station for 400-something-thousand dollars. My experience was in design work, but I quickly realized how complicated it was going to be to just figure out how to make a development project work.

I was pleased to get that building. It was in terrible condition, but the structure was good. The plumbing and electrical were, by and large, okay. There wasn't a lot of design to do. I could really just focus on the budget and on working in the District. I spent a lot of time focused on the tenant relationship, and tenant rights, and ownership rights. Rent control is a highly complicated field unto itself. I also concentrated on financing, managing the apartments, and renting them out.

It took about six to nine months to get it all put together. I met with the tenants a lot. It has to be a collaborative process. I applied a lot of my philosophies about environment to it. Wanting to be a good contributor to my environment for me is a great, simple philosophy that you can apply to many things. The environment means to me the local environment, the physical context, which is what we talk about a lot in architecture school, yet context has to include people, the social structure, the community, and also of course the ecology—both local and expanded. You have to look at the architectural context as an environment, the social context as an environment, and the ecological context as an environment. And you have to give all those things the same respect.

The goal was to work with the tenants to come up with a plan by which they could still have their lower rents protected by rent control, and allow me to improve the building. Like many buildings in Washington, D.C., at that time, it was derelict. But because of the low rents that were being paid, it would have taken somebody to write a check every month and essentially make a charitable contribution to make the building decent. It was an upside-down deal—not a healthy project.

I did the general contracting work myself, which was quite a burden. It was quite an interesting and difficult process, but it worked and I bought another building near Dupont Circle under the same kind of circumstances. This was a lot easier, actually, because it was a smaller building and it was pretty much vacant when I got it. In the end, I got myself a good business going.

I hired a manager to start taking over the day-to-day responsibilities. In the beginning, I handled all the renting and communication for all the maintenance and everything else. Then I started getting people in place to take care of that for me.

When I started looking for a new project, I found an empty piece of land close to the first apartment building in Takoma, D.C. There I decided to do a really significant project that would satisfy all the interests that I had. And that is the Elevation 314 project, which is a green building next to the entrance to the Metro station. It has a big impact on its physical environment and the community there, and it is a good environmental citizen.

continued on page 249

stations. In 1998, MARTA issued a request for proposals (RFP) for dense residential and office mixed-use development of a 47-acre (19-hectare) site around the Lindbergh Station in Buckhead. The agency chose a proposal from Carter Associates, an Atlanta-based full-service commercial real estate firm. The aggressive plan calls for 4.8 million square feet (446,100 square meters) of retail, office, hotel, and residential uses. Lindbergh City Center exemplifies the advantages of working with the public sector as a strong partner. The city government and the transit agency were "codevelopers" of the project in that they have financial interests in its success and its success depends in part on their zoning and permitting decisions and infrastructure investments.

PUBLIC/PRIVATE PARTNERSHIPS

A public/private partnership is one in which a private developer works with public authorities and public resources to develop a project that has both public and private components. Because of the shrinking supply of land in major metropolitan areas and the increased regulations and required public input, public/private partnerships are becoming a visible force in development. Some firms now specialize largely in public/private partnership developments.

A public/private developer is not the same as a public developer or entrepreneur. The public/private developer is a private developer working for profit but teaming up with a public partner in exchange for access to public resources and assets and providing the public partner with a new development or a component of a new development that can serve the public good.

LCOR Realty, based in Berwyn, Pennsylvania, is a private developer that specializes in public/private partnerships. LCOR developed the James F. Oyster School/Henry Adams House in Washington, D.C. In exchange for building a brand new public elementary school, LCOR was granted the right to build a private apartment building on part of the school's property. In a partnership with the District of Columbia Public Schools, LCOR employed a public/private financing structure to help make the new Oyster School possible and to realize the value of an underused asset—the school's excess land. In this arrange-

A public/private partnership among the Peterson Companies, Foulger-Pratt, Argo Investment Company, and Montgomery County, Maryland, revitalized downtown Silver Spring with the addition of new infill buildings and parking garages and the rehabilitation of existing structures. *R.C. Kreider Studios, Inc.*

ment, both public community and private market demands were satisfied by a simple public/private partnership.

ARCHITECTS

Architects are central to the development process from the perspective of aesthetics, physical safety, and community acceptance, yet the role of the architect in a project is not always fully understood or appreciated. The naive view of an architect is someone who simply draws the developer's or his own ideas and then produces a set of specifications used for obtaining construction bids and guiding the construction process. In fact, architects offer a menu of services to developers and, like other players, may work as outside professionals or as in-house, salaried members of the development team (although it is more and more unusual for developers to retain an architect on staff).

The relationship between architect and developer usually follows one of two models. The *design-award-build* contract breaks the project into two distinct phases, with the architect completing the design phase before the developer submits the project for contractors' bids. The other alternative, the *fast-track* approach, involves the contractor during the early stages of design. The contractor's early input can suggest ways to save on costs (value engineering), making the project more economical and efficient to construct. Fast-track construction is really more about reducing time to completion, however, than about saving money.

With development becoming increasingly complicated, architects are now involved in the development process much earlier than in the past. Architects acquire extensive experience with the regulatory and physical constraints placed on development and are a valuable asset in communicating with other consultants as well as coordinating designs. Architects can also help guide a developer in selecting a site for a specified use or develop alternative concepts for a site and head the land use team to bring a concept to fruition. Architects can also be instrumental in helping a developer secure planning and zoning approvals, working with community groups to understand their needs and preferences for proposed projects, and incorporating some of their suggestions without destroying the integrity of the proposed project. Renderings of projects can be instrumental in winning public approval for the high-density and mixed-use projects that are becoming increasingly common. Moreover, it may be that architects have a more favorable public image (whether or not earned) than developers and thus may be effective in dealing with the public and public sector agencies.

Beyond assistance in basic planning and community relations, an architectural firm can provide the developer with several basic services: programming (surveying users to determine their needs), predesign services (schematics) and final design, design development, preparation of construction contract documents, assistance with bidding or negotiations, administration of agreements between the developer and the builder or contractor, representing the developer on site, and overall project administration and management. The schematic design is a diagram that relates the space to the building's functions and is then transformed into at least a preliminary idea of what the building will look like. The final design is a refined rendering of the building's facade as well as a preliminary delineation of at least the major components of the interior space.

During design development, more players are brought in to refine the interior space and structural components. In addition, exact space allocations must be made for the heating, ventilation, and air-conditioning (HVAC) system, elevators, interior stairwells, plumbing, column size, and so on. As these refinements are incorporated into the architect's renderings, the building begins to assume its final design. The schematic phase and the design development phase require much iteration, with the developer heavily involved along the way.

The next phase of the architect's involvement is often assembling the construction package, including the package that is sent to contractors to solicit bids. The package includes the rules for bidding, standard forms for detailing the components of the bid, detailed specifications for identifying all components of the bid, and detailed working drawings. The architect, along with the developer, then usually reviews the bids and selects the best-qualified (or the lowest-cost qualified) contractor for the job.

The architect's contractual relationship in the development process is with the developer and not with the builder/contractor. Likewise, the contractor's relationship is with the developer. In their separate agreements with the developer, they acknowledge each other's roles and the roles of other parties and agree to allow other parties to fulfill their roles.

Once construction begins, the architect is usually responsible for monitoring—but not supervising—the work site, depending on the agreement the developer has with the architect. The architect is expected to inspect the site periodically to determine whether contract documents are being adequately followed. The developer also relies on the architect to confirm that predetermined phases during construction have been satisfactorily completed. The approval involves a certificate of completion necessary for disbursement of the contractor's fee. The architect's approval is usually required for each construction loan drawn from the construction lender.

Although architects may continue monitoring the project during construction, the degree of supervision varies as a result of time constraints (the need to be on site at particular times). Architects are also important in closing the loan as the project moves from construction to permanent financing. They must attest to compliance with plans and specifications and bear legal liability for the plans and specifications for some number of years (the term varies by state). Architects are licensed under health and safety laws and must pass an examination administered by the National Council of Architectural Registration Boards (NCARB), which has promulgated standards and criteria adopted by licensing boards as their standard for admission to licensing examinations. Registration takes about eight to ten years—five to seven years of study at a university and three years as a paid intern in an architectural or related practice.

An architect can be paid in several ways. A standard contract provided by the American Institute of Architects (AIA) provides the basis for defining the relationship between developer and architect. Many developers hire architects initially on an hourly basis until the project is better defined and the scope of services clear. When the developer and architect establish that they will continue working together, they often negotiate a contract whereby an architect's fee is a percentage of the construction cost. Typically, the fee ranges from 3 to 7 percent, although it can be as little as 2 percent and as much as 10 percent. One disadvantage of the fee approach may be that the architect has less incentive to operate cost-efficiently on behalf of the owner. More important, some projects might be complicated to design but easy to build or vice versa. Further, what constitutes construction costs must be carefully delineated.

An architect can also be compensated under the terms of a *fixed-price* or *stipulated-sum* contract, which outlines the services expected of the architect. The stipulated sum generally includes the architect's direct personnel expenses, other direct expenses (such as salaries and benefits), other direct expenses chargeable to the project (such as consultant services), indirect expenses or overhead, and profit. If, at the request of the developer, the architect performs any additional duties, he bills the developer for additional compensation. A design/build firm would typically be paid in this way. An architect is (unless otherwise specified) entitled to reimbursement for such expenses as telephone calls, travel, photocopying, and so on. An architectural firm can also be hired for a stipulated sum per unit that is based on the number of square feet or apartment units.

For certain projects, developers should not underestimate the need to make full use of an experienced architect. What works in New York may not work in Dallas, and a good architect understands that. An architect may also increase the functional efficiency of a building. For service providers such as hotels and health care facilities, efficiency is critical, and architects can enhance or undermine the work environment for employees. On the other hand, it may not be cost-efficient or necessary to use a world-class architect to design a duplex on a simple site in a town where the developer has already built 100 similar homes.

The level of community involvement typically associated with any development has increased so much that developers need to stand ready to consider altering their ideas—conceptually and visually. In the case of some design features, the developer can compromise with the review board; in the case of other items, compromise may be inappropriate. The architect can help explain and differentiate between design features. A good architect can be a great asset to a developer in the midst of a strenuous approval process. Therefore, it is essential that the developer and the architect feel comfortable working together, that they understand each other's positions and concepts, and that they communicate with each other throughout every step of the development process.

Developers should investigate candidate architects as thoroughly as possible. They should look at finished buildings (not just unbuilt plans), talk to clients of the candidate architects, ask around, and interview prospective architects thoroughly to ascertain their level of understanding of the different services they will provide.

An architect is a key player in the development process and ultimately is responsible for much of the mark a developer leaves on society. A building stands in a city or town for a long time. People walk past it, drive past it, use it, and love it or hate it for years. Many cities are known and distinguished by their architecture, which often provides the charm that draws visitors. Developers have to think about how their buildings fit with what already exists and how people will see and use their buildings ten, 20, 30, or 100 years into the future.

URBAN DESIGNERS

In addition to architects, developers of large projects often employ an urban designer. Urban designers develop design plans for development and redevelopment projects. They seek to coordinate the individual buildings with public spaces, the spaces in between the buildings, the larger neighborhood, the city, and the regional culture. Urban designers create master plans, strategic plans, detailed site plans, or visions. Often, working closely with neighborhood groups and other interested parties, urban designers produce the plan and detailed drawings of key development

Narrow streets lined with trees and sidewalks are intended to encourage the residents of Issaquah Highlands—a 2,300-acre (931-hectare) master-planned community on the outskirts of Seattle, Washington—to walk more. *Port Blakely Communities*

elements that guide future growth in a neighborhood or a special district such as a waterfront or a master-planned community.

A large-scale project such as the redevelopment of the Anacostia waterfront in Washington, D.C., often requires multiple teams of urban designers. The Anacostia Waterfront Corporation is targeting 900 acres (364 hectares)—of more than 3,800 acres (1,538 hectares)—along the eight-mile-long (12.9-kilometer) Anacostia waterfront for directed redevelopment. This underused and misused neighborhood has long been ignored and used as a dumping ground. But before any real development could begin, a long process was required to develop the Anacostia Waterfront Initiative Framework Plan, which is intended to guide development and improvements. The various multidisciplinary urban design teams provided the visions and steps for development in the redevelopment area.

In recent years especially, urban designers have become known for holding charrettes with neighborhood groups. These charrettes are usually multiple-day (four or five) workshops in which interested parties collaborate to achieve an agreed-upon scheme

for a site, a city, or another area. Through this process, a shared vision arises, usually making the approval process go more smoothly because of the intensive initial work the developer has already done.

The urban designer is often very important in presenting visual representations of the development to government authorities and community groups to win their approval. A talented designer can quickly move the developer through the approval process. Many urban designers originally trained as architects, although they can also be landscape architects or city planners who chose to specialize in visual design.

ENGINEERS

Several different kinds of engineers play important roles in the development process. Specifically, engineers are critical to physical safety, and their failure to deliver a safe product can have life-threatening consequences. Several types of engineers with specific expertise—structural, mechanical, electrical, civil—are required to ensure that the design can accommodate the required physical systems. Structural engineers usually work with the architect, particularly during the initial design phase, to ensure that plans are structurally sound and that mechanical systems will adequately serve the project. Structural engineers can assist in identifying cost-saving measures that simultaneously satisfy structural design and construction requirements. They are also responsible for producing drawings for the construction contractor that explain the structural system in detail, especially connections and the sizing of the structural elements. Mechanical engineers usually design necessary HVAC, plumbing, life safety, and other mechanical systems. Electrical engineers design electrical power and distribution systems, including lighting, circuitry, and backup power supplies.

Engineers are generally engaged by the architect and maintain close relationships with the architectural staff as the project unfolds. In more complex developments, engineers might also function as construction managers, supplementing the architect in supervising construction. Architects often hire engineers as the main design subcontractor; the success of the design phase depends on a good working relationship between the architect and engineers. Typically, as head of the design team, the architect is responsible for the work of the engineers. Often, they are included in the architect's budget.

Engineers must be licensed by the state where they operate, and plans cannot be approved unless they are signed by a professional engineer. Like architects, engineers are licensed under health and safety laws and bear legal liability for their plans and specifications for some number of years. The duration of liability corresponds to the nature of the undertaking and the time for recognizing defects. Effective project coordination is necessary to prevent problems; it relies on communication and intense planning and coordination early in the process. Experienced developers facilitate meetings with all architectural and engineering project personnel to define the scope of the project and communication channels and to discuss each discipline's goals and objectives in depth.

Many types of engineers can work on a project. Civil engineers may be contracted with for their expertise in land development, particularly for the design and construction of such infrastructure as streets, and water, sewer, gas, electricity, telephone, cable, and storm drainage systems. They must ensure that all civil systems meet the health, safety, and welfare requirements of the state where the project will be located.

Structural engineers assist the architect in designing the building's structural integrity. They work closely with soils engineers to determine the most appropriate foundation system and produce a set of drawings for the general contractor explaining that system in detail. Soils engineers or geotechnical engineers are responsible for determining the soil's bearing capacity, the required depth of footings, various types of loads, the level of the groundwater table, the presence of any toxic materials, and related items. A geotechnical investigation is especially important when development is proposed for a new site. Soils engineers can help transform a site with poor soil into a developable site by advising the construction engineer on the use of fill and soil replacement. Most geotechnical engineers perform a range of tests, including soil borings, seismic tests, percolation tests, and compaction tests. Geotechnical engineers are particularly important in assessing whether the past uses of a site have included hazardous materials.

Environmental engineers may also be needed for a proposed development, particularly if an existing structure on the site—whether scheduled for renovation or demolition—contains any asbestos or other hazardous substances. In redevelopment, environmental engineers check for various types of mold. Increasingly, all participants in the process are focused on not allowing mold to establish itself during construction.

As a subcontractor, the engineer's fee schedule is usually included in the architect's budget; it ranges from 4 to 7 percent of the overall architectural fee. Engineers should be licensed by the state and should be members of a professional engineering society such as the National Society of Professional Engineers (NSPE), the American Society of Mechanical Engineers (ASME), or the American Society of Heating, Refrigerating, and Air-conditioning Engineers (ASHRAE).

LAND PLANNERS

For the land development phase of a project and for larger building projects, a land planner is often needed to help develop the master plan, which locates site improvements according to their physical properties and maximizes the uses that will bring the highest value. A land planner builds on the works done by a surveyor, who determines a property's physical and legal characteristics—existing easements, rights-of-way, and dedications on the site—and prepares a site map plotting these characteristics. This site map reveals how much of the site is buildable and, in coordination with town zoning and building codes, establishes the maximum possible square footage for the project. Surveyors generally prepare two types of surveys: a boundary survey, which determines the boundaries of the site by examining easements and other legal rights, and a construction survey, which plots the location of relevant infrastructure—water, sewers, electricity, gas lines,

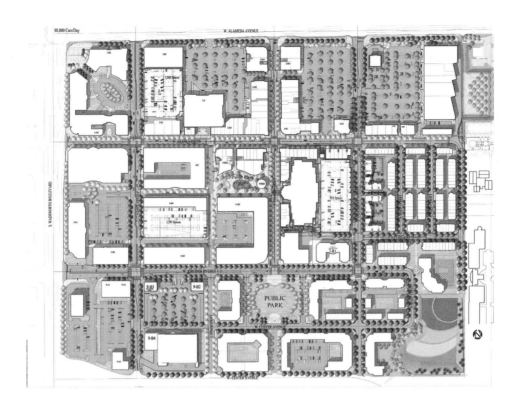

Developed by Continuum Partnership, Belmar is a 22-block, 104-acre (42-hectare) mixed-use project comprising retail and office space and housing built on the site of a failed enclosed mall in Lakewood, Colorado. *Continuum Partnership*

and roads—to assist in planning connections to utility services.

A land planner works closely with the developer to determine the suitability of the site for the proposed development and makes alternative recommendations if necessary, working with input from engineers, marketing consultants, architects, and other team members. The land planner works with the developer to emphasize the important elements of the site, from natural features to the programmed or marketing themes that the developer wishes to stress. A part of the land planning process is testing the site capacity for the amount and type of uses envisioned by the developer.

The land planner deals with the site's limitations and possibilities. On the one hand, natural, environmental, and legislative limitations define acceptable uses and densities of development on the site. On the other, developers have certain expectations for the creation of a viable development on the site. Balanc-

ing the constraints with the potential is key to the challenges the land planner faces.

The master plan prepared by the land planner takes into consideration the potential natural amenities of the site (such as trees, water features, and rolling hills) and the potential constraints (floodplains, wetlands, and steep inclines, for example). The planner is usually responsible for determining traffic patterns and overall circulation, allocating open space, locating on-site uses and amenities, and so on. In bringing together the various issues related to site development, the land planner must also consider the impacts of all land planning decisions on cost and schedule.

Often the land planner works with the developer to create "themes" for the overall site development. An emphasis on creating a special sense of place, often enhanced by the architecture and landscape design, guides the land planner in determining the highest and best use for areas within the site. This vision of the developer and land planner sets the framework for the placement of buildings, infrastructure within the site, site features (such as special entries or focal points within the site, landscape amenities, and private and shared public spaces), and other amenities.

Some of the land planner's expertise and contribution to the development can overlap with those of the urban designer, which were identified earlier, and/or the landscape architect, which are identified below. Land planners are often housed in landscape architecture offices, or landscape architects are found in land planning firms, so it is not always possible to draw a clear line between their responsibilities on the development team.

The main professional society for land planners is the American Planning Association (APA), which has no licensing requirements but offers its members certification through the American Institute of Certified Planners (AICP).

LANDSCAPE ARCHITECTS

Landscape architects bring to a development team a specialized set of skills that once were often overlooked but now play a greater role in the planning process. Landscape architecture encompasses the analysis, design, planning, management, and stewardship of the natural and built environment. Landscape architects are responsible both for site planning in the context of the existing environment and for creating a sense of place by enhancing the natural environment to complement the built environment.

In today's development market, most communities and potential buyers or tenants are concerned with the elements of the landscape that help define the character of their development. In seeking to create a distinctive image for their projects, developers often rely on the landscape design as much as they do the architecture to help define the special nature or theme of the project, especially in residential and mixed-use development projects, where the landscape design can help unite and define areas for the various uses.

Landscape architects produce the master plans for all landscaping and hard surfaces. They create the landscape environment through selection and siting of plant materials, landscape forms, and strategic use of light and shade as defined by the designed yet natural environment. They design roadways, walkways, outdoor lighting, outdoor seating, water features, railings, signs, grates, retaining walls, bus shelters, picnic shelters, outdoor waiting areas, outdoor play areas, and bicycle and walking trails. Landscape design can often be used to create a sense of place, allowing tenants and residents to feel a sense of privacy within small site areas, and landscape forms can be used to soften the overall development. Architecture can create boundaries necessary to define different use areas in a tightly packed site, and landscape design can humanize those boundaries, maintaining them but making them softer and more in scale with the people who use the site. Landscape architects work with developers to create not just specific development sites but also transitions between adjacent land uses. Moreover, the demands on a site's appearance have never been greater. Developers are spending more money than ever on the living environment surrounding their static products. In recent years, the quality of our environment has become a major concern, and, as a result, people are more aware of the quality of their "natural" surroundings.

Above all, it is important to realize that landscape architects help create places that capture the imagination of the public. Examples include New York City's Central Park, immediately recognizable by its bridges and landscape, or entire communities such as Prairie Crossing, a conservation development in Grayslake, Illinois, which is known for protecting more than two-thirds of its site from development while also protecting the most valuable native vegetation and other environmental assets.

Landscape architects develop entire greenways and park systems that help define and humanize large urban areas such as Olmsted's "Emerald Necklace" in and around Boston (see the Museum Towers case study for more discussion about the parkland that the developer donated to the city on that project).

Landscape architects can also provide consulting services for wastewater management, wetlands mitigation, the preservation of wildlife habitats, ecosystem management, xeriscaping and irrigation, sustainable site design, and land reclamation. In addition, landscape architects can contribute to a development's bottom line by extrapolating site amenities from what could be environmental problem areas.

As the general public becomes more concerned with sustainable environments, the landscape architect is called upon to implement plans that use local vegetation and require less maintenance, irrigation, and control. Some enlightened developers and their clients understand that a "wilder" landscape can also provide a haven for beneficial birds and insects, and the landscape architect is therefore challenged to develop plans that accommodate the architecture of the planned project and are sustainable and sustaining. Sustainable site design helps ensure the long-term health of a project by keeping down the cost of landscape maintenance and making it financially feasible for owners or managers to maintain landscape features in good condition. Potential users will be turned off by dead or dying plants.

Increasingly, landscape architects are drawn into the environmental debate as developers face more stringent environmental rules and stronger public opposition to development. Landscape architects, working with urban designers, are often needed to design environmentally sensitive or sustainable development schemes to be presented to regulators, zoning officials, and community groups. Accordingly, developers must rely on the expertise of land stewards to help them manage the delicate environment—both natural and political.

The American Society of Landscape Architects (ASLA) is a national professional society representing the landscape architecture profession in the United States. Forty-nine states license landscape architects.

CONTRACTORS

Contractors are builders and managers of builders who turn ideas on paper into enduring physical forms: houses, apartment buildings, warehouses, stores, offices, and public buildings. Our highly specialized society often takes for granted constructed space and its providers, yet without builders, each of us would face a simple choice: build our shelter ourselves or do without.

A general contractor (GC) typically executes a contract with the developer to build the project according to the plans and specifications developed by the architect and engineer (or sometimes according to the plans drawn up by the would-be homeowner who orders a house built) for a fixed price within a set time frame. General contractors then divide the contract among different subcontractors to perform different tasks: excavation, pouring and finishing concrete, rough carpentry, installation of mechanical, electrical, and plumbing systems, finish carpentry, and so on. General contractors schedule subcontractors' work and monitor quality to ensure that subcontractors' performance satisfies the general contractor's obligations to the developer. Typically, the GC's contract is executed with the developer, and subcontractors' contracts are executed with the general contractor, who pays the subcontractors as their work is completed. Many variations of these contractual arrangements are possible and appropriate in certain situations.

General contractors are often chosen through a selective bidding process in which the developer asks a number of contracting firms to submit proposals or general statements of qualifications that include descriptions of past projects, references from clients and lenders, résumés of key employees, and, possibly, verification that the company is bondable (that an insurance company will stand behind the contractor's contractual obligations).

In the open bidding process, a developer sends out a notice requesting bids and statements of qualifications. Because the bidding process is very time consuming for contractors, many are reluctant to participate in open bids unless they think they have a reasonable chance of being selected; thus, this process does not always attract an adequate number of responses. Consequently, it is not uncommon for a developer to negotiate a contract with a single contractor with whom the developer has had prior experience.

Besides the obvious motivation of money, both general contractors and subcontractors work for a variety of nonpecuniary reasons: to gain experience, to enhance their reputations, to be their own boss, and to perform physical work they enjoy. The contractor (or subcontractor) submitting the lowest bid is not always the best choice; the best player for the development team may have other critical attributes, such as more experience or greater reliability. The lower carrying costs implied in a shorter construction period can compensate for a higher construction bid. In some cases, developers experienced in building serve as their own general contractors and enter directly into contracts with subcontractors.

Contractors' fees are based on the size, difficulty, and risk involved in the project. A contractor may be expected to charge a fee equivalent to 5 percent of total hard costs—in addition to project overhead and on-site supervision costs. The contractor obviously calculates the time and talent required to complete the project as a basis for a fixed or percentage fee. Often the construction lender requires that the contractor guarantee a maximum cost.

General contractors may do some of the actual work in their companies but typically subcontract out the actual building. They then are responsible for quality control and timeliness of completion through their contract with the developer. Subcontractors periodically bill the general contractor for work completed to date. The general contractor withholds a portion of the billed amount to ensure final performance by the subcontractors. General contractors periodically assemble all the subcontractors' payment requests and submit them, along with a request for a portion of the general contractor's fee, to the developer.

Subcontractors vary dramatically across functions and developments. On a large project, the HVAC contractor is likely a large, well-capitalized company with several engineers on staff. On the other hand, the stonemason on a duplex development probably works out of the trunk of his car.

Associated Builders and Contractors (ABC) and Associated General Contractors (AGC) are just two of several trade associations for contractors.

ENVIRONMENTAL CONSULTANTS

Environmental consultants (closely related to environmental engineers, discussed previously) perform environmental site reviews that in some states are critical considerations in a developer's decision to build. As environmental regulations grow more complex, developers need help in navigating the regulatory maze and deciding whether a site's environmental issues are too complicated and costly to make land purchase or development worthwhile. Regardless of whether a developer chooses to engage an environmental consultant, developers must conduct two basic types of environmental reviews during the life of a project: one to analyze the project's economic, social, and cultural impacts on the surrounding built environment, and the second to determine, in conjunction with soils engineers, mitigation for any hazardous materials detected on site.

If, for example, a developer thinks a site might contain legally defined wetlands, he can engage an environmental consultant to perform an assessment, delineate any wetlands, and confirm the jurisdiction (federal or state) under which the wetlands are regulated. Similarly, an environmental site review can determine the presence of hazardous materials and indicate the cost and feasibility of removing them. An environmental review may even extend to testing for toxic wastes or as a possible first step to researching previous uses to determine the likely presence of toxic materials.

Environmental consultants can help developers identify the regulatory approvals needed for a proposed project or the types of permits required as a condition of approval. The National Environmental Policy Act of 1969 gave each municipality the right to create its own environmental laws, so regulations vary widely from place to place. Environmental consultants can also prepare environmental impact statements (EISs) or reports (EIRs) often required by zoning. They can provide advice on stormwater management, wildlife management, urban forestry, solid waste disposal—in short, all the environmental matters that communities increasingly regulate.

TRANSPORTATION CONSULTANTS

As with environmental consultants, the role of transportation consultants is expanding. Few issues generate as much controversy during the approval process as traffic and transportation. Transportation consultants can provide needed expertise and assess impor-

Featuring 347 units and 20,000 square feet (1,860 square meters) of retail space, Del Mar Station also serves as a transit stop, with the Los Angeles County Metropolitan Transit Agency's Gold Line light-rail train running through the middle of the project. *Conrado Lopez*

tant issues such as how many cars and trucks will enter and leave the site at various times of the day, what the capacity is of existing roads, highways, and intersections, and how the existing streets will accommodate new levels of traffic. The federal Clean Air Act Amendment of 1990 instituted traffic control measures as a strategy for reducing air pollution emissions from cars, trucks, and buses. Moreover, enforcement of the Clean Air Act and provisions for

reducing travel by employees have increased the need for greater compliance by employers and made additional demands on transportation consultants. Communities have adopted such traffic control measures as high-occupancy vehicle (HOV) lanes, ride-sharing programs, expanded public transportation programs, and expanded pedestrian and bicycle facilities.

The federal government withheld billions of dollars of federal transportation aid from the city of

Atlanta in 1998 because of chronic air pollution. In response, the governor of Georgia created the Georgia Regional Transportation Authority (GRTA), which has broad powers to approve or veto most road and other transportation projects and to build and operate mass-transit systems in 13 metropolitan counties that do not meet federal air pollution standards ("nonattainment" under Clean Air Act standards). In addition, developments of regional impact (DRIs), which are large-scale developments likely to have effects outside the local government jurisdiction where they are located, are required to undergo a review by GRTA. GRTA can approve or deny the use of state and federal funds to create transportation services and access that may be required as a result of the DRI. Thus, developers need to work with transportation consultants to assess potential problems and levels of traffic.

Transportation consultants may have wide experience in several specialties, including parking, traffic, and other transportation-related issues, and developers often call on them to put together plans to meet the requirements of local jurisdictions. For example, if a jurisdiction has set a cap on the number of parking spaces that can be built for a development, a transportation consultant can help the developer establish certain programs to accommodate office tenants—ride sharing, parking incentives for car pools, fare incentives for use of mass transit, and shuttle bus service between the project and transit facilities.

Most cities require traffic impact studies for developments over a minimum size. Communities now actively assess whether or not the potential increase in traffic is worth the jobs that may be created. Transportation consultants can conduct traffic impact studies to investigate such issues. In addition, they can explain the impact of proposed government exactions and possibly find better ways to satisfy public objectives.

Because parking is one of the significant factors for real estate developments and cities in general, parking consultants can provide an array of parking-related services, from planning circulation for parking garages to designing access roads to developing shared parking plans for mixed-use projects.[1] With parking often an expensive part of a development

project, parking consultants can help evaluate the cost-effectiveness of surface parking versus a parking structure. They can also assess the location of ingress and egress points and the cost of parking. For tenants, few issues are as important as how much parking is available and how close it is to the building. A parking consultant may be a transportation consultant with expertise in parking or a specialist who deals with no other transportation issues. Further, a parking consultant may be needed early in the design process so that the architect can incorporate parking recommendations in the overall design.

In choosing any kind of transportation consultant, developers must first be careful to clearly define the project and then select a consultant with knowledge of the required specialty. A transportation consultant could be paid according to several arrangements: a lump-sum fee, costs plus a fixed fee, salary costs times a multiplier, time and materials, or a percentage of construction costs for the parking structure.

APPRAISERS

Appraisers produce an estimate of a property's value based on standardized valuation methodologies. That is, they estimate the market value of property and typically prepare a formal document called an appraisal. Appraisers can be part of multiple stages of the development process—before, during, and after project completion. Appraisers are responsible primarily for valuation of a project. Thus, they may be necessary when a developer transfers ownership, seeks financing and credit, resolves tax matters, and establishes just compensation in condemnation proceedings. The appraisal report typically states the property's market value and offers supporting evidence. Three methodologies are generally used to complete an appraisal: the *income approach,* the *market approach,* and the *cost approach* (a more detailed look at these approaches can be found in the finance section).

Appraisers also complete market studies, marketability studies, and feasibility studies. For example, before a development is initiated, appraisers can analyze the market for a particular project type and help a developer assess a potential project's marketability.

Appraisers can also provide a broad range of services from investment analysis to testifying in lawsuits.

Like any professional who works with a developer, the appraiser must be selected with care. The S&L debacle of the 1980s was blamed in part on appraisers' inflated valuations of properties. Since then, federal law has mandated that appraisers working on projects for federally insured institutions be licensed or certified by the state, thereby providing tighter state control over appraisers.

The Appraisal Qualifications Board of the Appraisal Foundation has established four recommended levels of education and experience for appraisers: 1) licensed real property appraisers can value complex residential projects (of one to four units) worth less than $250,000 and noncomplex residential projects (of one to four units) with a transaction value of less than $1 million; 2) certified residential real property appraisers can value any residential project of one to four units without regard to value or complexity; 3) certified general appraisers can value any residential or commercial property of any size; and 4) appraiser trainees must work under the direct supervision of a licensed or certified appraiser. The required levels of education and experience vary accordingly.

The national Appraisal Institute also awards several designations: 1) MAI—experienced in valuation and evaluation of all types of property and permitted to advise clients on residential and commercial real estate investment decisions; 2) SRPA—experienced in the valuation of all types of property; 3) SREA—experienced in real estate valuation and analysis and permitted to advise clients on investment decisions; and 4) SRA and RM—residential appraisal.

ATTORNEYS AND ACCOUNTANTS

Because of complex legal interactions between buyers and sellers, lenders and borrowers, contractors and subcontractors, landlords, and users, lawyers and accountants are important players in the development process. Often different types of attorneys are required for different facets of real estate development. Taxes, land use, leases, and construction contracts require different legal specialties or subspecialties. Attorneys sometimes serve as the developer's chief liaison with regulators, and zoning attorneys who know a particular zoning jurisdiction very well can take the lead in obtaining approvals for the project. Above all, attorneys are essential for producing partnership agreements, contracts for acquiring property, and loan documents, all without which development cannot proceed.

The great development lawyer is usually not the great litigator. Given the intense time pressure of the development process, the great development attorney is the one who anticipates problems and then structures legal documentation to minimize the necessity of resolving differences in court. Lawyers are generally paid by the hour, although fixed prices for certain transactions are not uncommon.

The great development accountant now comes in two forms. The developer still needs to have bills paid accurately, and, as we will see in stage six, paying construction invoices is not a simple task. Further, new investment participants in the process have extensive reporting requirements. For example, real estate investment trusts must report to the Securities and Exchange Commission (SEC), and pension funds must report to the Department of Labor. The growing complexity of rules increases the need for a group of skilled accountants and lawyers.

REAL ESTATE LEASING AGENTS AND SALES BROKERS

Real estate sales brokers and leasing agents are hired to act in the name of the developer in leasing and selling space to prospective tenants or buyers. Their function, particularly in leasing large industrial and commercial spaces, is to carry out one of the most complex financial negotiations in the development process. Leasing agents secure tenants and negotiate leases while keeping in mind the developer's personal goals with respect to rates of return and tenants' creditworthiness. Brokers must balance the various users' individual needs against the developer's financial model. Clearly, leasing requires more than quoting the number of square feet at a price per square foot. Leasing involves setting the long-term price per square foot and specifying who bears the responsibility for operating costs. One of the most important aspects of real estate leasing is fitting a particular tenant into a space that fits its needs while keeping the remaining unleased space in contiguous blocks that will fit other tenants' needs.

Brokers and leasing agents are the key implementers of the marketing plan. They canvass prospects; show the product's features, functions, and benefits; negotiate the transaction; and provide critical feedback to the developer for use in modifying the project. Developers must decide early in the development process whether leasing is to be carried out by in-house staff or outside professionals. Developers must find the right agent for the job and structure the agent's compensation to align the agent's motivations with the developer's objectives.

FINANCIAL PLAYERS

Joint Venture Partners

Any individual or institution that provides the developer with equity funding during the development period in return for a share of development profits can be called a joint venture partner. (The term "joint venture partner" is not a precise legal term.) The joint venture partner's equity contribution often bridges a portion of the gap between the project's cost and the debt financing available for construction. The remainder of the gap, if any, must be filled by the developer's equity.

Joint venture partners attempt to achieve the maximum ownership interest and share of returns from the development while making the minimum possible financial exposure. The joint venture partner "helps" the developer provide the capital needed to cover the difference between the project's total cost and available debt financing. The risk to joint venture partners is a function of the size of their contribution (in the case of no personal liability) or of the size of their contribution plus the amount of debt (in the case of personal liability for debt financing).[2] In either case, partners are usually concerned with the size of their obligations (especially if the project fails) as well as the developer's talent and financial strength, which reduce project risk. Depending on the site of

the development, potential joint venture partners range from wealthy local individuals to large funds run by the major investment banks.

Construction Lenders

Construction lenders (frequently commercial banks) are responsible for debt financing during project construction and for seeing that the developer completes the project within budget and according to plans and specifications laid out by the architect. In short, construction lenders lend the money to build a development. Under the terms of the construction loan, construction lenders generally certify the degree of completion before each payment or draw, that is, amounts the developer "draws" from the loan commitment to pay periodic project expenses.

Construction lenders face the risk that construction costs will exceed the amount of the construction loan that they have agreed to provide, requiring the developer to cover the difference. If the developer is unable or unwilling to cover the difference, construction lenders usually have the option of foreclosing on the property or extending the size of the construction loan beyond the size specified in the original loan documents. Such an extension creates the possibility of a long-term loan position, something banks try to avoid, as their sources of funds are primarily short term. Construction lenders weigh the risk of these undesirable outcomes against the expected return (in interest and loan origination fees) to be earned by lending the funds. (The financing section provides considerable detail on how the development lending process works.)

Permanent Lenders

Permanent lenders finance the completed project through a long-term mortgage by taking over financing from the construction lender. Permanent financing usually has fixed interest rates, and, although the loan is typically amortized over 20 to 30 years, the term of the loan is often limited to ten years. The size of the permanent loan is determined by the value of the property and the cash flow that the property generates to pay debt service.

Like other players on the development team, lenders may also have nonpecuniary motives for par-

GERALD D. HINES
Owner, Hines Interests
Houston, Texas

Born in 1925 in Gary, Indiana, Gerald Hines learned at a young age that he did not want to follow in his father's footsteps as an employee of U.S. Steel. During the summers of World War II while still in high school, Hines got the only taste he needed of manual labor. Determined to receive a university degree, Hines's plans for matriculation were postponed by notice of his enlistment in the Army. After serving as a lieutenant in the combat engineers for the remainder of the war, Hines returned to Indiana, where he earned a Bachelor of Science degree in mechanical engineering from Purdue University in 1948. After Purdue, Hines moved to Houston, where he would go on to begin his career as one of the nation's most prominent developers.

Starting as a mechanical systems designer provided an easy transition into the development business. "I just got to know buildings very well. Then I thought I would like to build them," Hines remarks. The Houston real estate market, then ballooning with oil money, provided an ideal environment for developers. Hines erected his first building in 1952—a straightforward combination of office and warehouse space. After completing several more projects consisting of office and warehouse space, he began his career in earnest in 1957.

As the sixties came to a close, Hines's firm—Gerald D. Hines Interests—had grown to a staff of 35 employees with nearly 100 completed projects under its belt. By the end of that decade Hines began office development along a stretch of I-610 known as the West Loop with the 22-story Post Oak Tower in 1970. In the same year, the first phase of the 420,000-square-foot (39,000-square-meter) Houston Galleria shopping center opened. This project proved to be a watershed for Hines's career and became the springboard for future ambitious projects. Modeled after Milan's 19th-century Galleria Vittorio Emanuele, famous for its high-end shops and elegant design, the Houston Galleria attracted many upscale tenants and proved to be a runaway success. The popularity of the design and its many retail and dining options led Hines to develop several more parcels near the Galleria over the next 27 years.

Not wasting any time, Hines hit the mark again with the development of One Shell Plaza in 1971, his first high-rise venture in downtown Houston. For this project, he commissioned Bruce Graham of Skidmore, Owings & Merrill, the preeminent corporate architecture firm in the country, to design the building. The building has several notable attributes: an Italian travertine marble exterior, wind-bracing columns at eight points, giving it its undulating facade, and its height (at the

time it was the tallest building, at 50 stories, west of the Mississippi River). Originally intended to serve as regional offices for Shell Oil Company, it was quickly requisitioned for its world headquarters. After the successful completion of One Shell Plaza, it became apparent that Hines's intent was to target the high end of the market while incorporating innovative structural and other cost-saving methods into the designs.

Riding the tremendous wave of success of One Shell Plaza, Hines was energized to undertake another bold project. For this building, Pennzoil Place, he brought in acclaimed architect Philip Johnson of Johnson/Burgee Architects. Hines recognized the reward in thoughtfully planning a project and continued the trend of avant-garde design for the corporate headquarters of the Pennzoil Company in Houston. The building, consisting of two trapezoidal towers only ten feet (3 meters) apart, has 45-degree angled roofs and an all-glass facade. It has been described as "one of the most architecturally influential buildings constructed in the United States during the 1970s and 1980s." More than satisfying the chair of the Pennzoil Company's request for "a building with character that would stand out from the undecorated glass boxes around town," Pennzoil Place, developed originally for $50 million, eventually was sold for more than $200 million. The handsome profits reaped by this sale demonstrate the foresight and quality of product Gerald Hines chooses to offer the market compared with the commonplace, hastily built structures offered by his competitors.

To Hines, designing an architecturally distinctive building makes perfect business sense. He strongly believes that "buildings of quality . . . attract better tenants, command higher rents, and retain their value despite the ups and downs of the real estate market." Viewed as a patron of good design in architectural circles, Hines eschews simply budgetary considerations when developing a site. Obviously the object of a business is to turn a profit, but Hines's calculus for doing so may include opting for a slightly more expensive material or systems if they will enhance overall quality and the eventual resale value of the product. "A well-designed building," he says, "is the first to fill up—the main objective, after all—and the last to get vacated."

Despite the success of his signature corporate towers that grace the skylines of cities across the country, Hines prefers to erect building clusters that make a place. A project in which Hines takes special pride is the Diagonal Mar development in Barcelona, Spain. Acquired in 1996 as an undesirable

Gerald Hines Interests's development of the 64-story mixed-use Transco Tower and the 2.5 million-square-foot (232,340-square-meter) Galleria created a completely new suburban-style business district outside Houston's downtown.

project, Hines turned around the 84-acre (34-hectare) development into a thriving $600 million mixed-use community with a 35-acre (14-hectare) public park and the largest convention center in Spain adjacent to the complex. This prosperous makeover exemplifies Hines's eye for opportune acquisitions, even in the tricky international arena.

A man of detail, the engineer in Hines considers every aspect of his projects and works to produce the highest result.

According to Peter Rummell, a fellow developer, Gerald Hines knows how to put himself "in the consumer's position of how a project will be experienced." It is for this reason Hines consistently turns out popularly successful developments. He seeks to improve energy efficiency in his buildings and drives innovation in that sector of the business as well. Since 1992, his company has been a partner in the U.S. Environmental Protection Agency's ENERGY STAR program.

Emphasizing the theory that development is best performed by local firms, Hines has generated a corporate structure that places decision making in the hands of local offices. As his company has grown, it has expanded out of the Houston area into 39 metropolitan areas, 69 cities, and 12 foreign countries employing a total of 2,900 people. Trusting bottom-up management has allowed Hines to decentralize his organization, tapping the wealth of knowledge in local markets and giving him a further edge over competitors who favor a centralized style of management. He encourages a high level of communication along every step of the development process to ensure a dynamic exchange of ideas as well as provide a system of checks and balances for executing agreed-upon decisions. Currently, under this management structure, his is one of the largest real estate companies in the world, with control of an estimated $14 billion in assets.

Hines has proved that form can complement function in real estate development without fiscal abandon. His company has grown from a one-man operation to an international giant without losing sight of the mainstays of quality and innovative design. The company's 303 awards, including 103 ENERGY STAR Label awards, speak for the kind of product Hines strives for in each of his projects. In 2002, Hines was awarded the ULI J.C. Nichols Prize for Visionaries in Urban Development. He asked that the $100,000 from the award and a matched amount be put toward the funding of the ULI Gerald D. Hines Student Urban Design Competition, which challenges students across the country to engage in quality urban design and planning. He leaves a legacy of high standards for the nation's future developers.

ticipating in a project. Some lenders have an interest in serving particular social needs (for example, the development of low-income housing), while others are more attracted to innovative design and construction. Almost everyone enjoys an affiliation with a winner, and lenders are no exception. Successful developers bring to their team a lender whose nonpecuniary interests and preferences for risk and return fit the proposed development.

Both construction and permanent financing can be secured from a variety of sources, including commercial banks, S&Ls, insurance companies, pension funds, foreign investors, REITs, and private investors/joint venture partners. Different lenders have different areas of specialization, different requirements for returns, and different degrees of willingness to accept risk.

Long-Term Equity Investors

Long-term equity investors may or may not be involved during the construction period. They might either contract to purchase the completed property before construction begins (basing the price on pre-construction estimates of value) or invest after the project is completed. In the first case, the contract is usually signed before the point of commitment—the time immediately preceding the beginning of construction. Whatever the time of investment, the price is often not payable until completion; therefore, the funds are often not available to the developer. A purchase commitment before construction may, however, substitute for or supplement the permanent loan commitment as a takeout for the construction lender.

Long-term equity investors are often passive investors during the development period and do not share development risks. On completion of the project, investors want the maximum possible operating returns (sometimes guaranteed by the developer for an initial period of one or more years) for the least possible price. These returns normally are lower than those accruing to investors who participated during the development period, because the latter assume more risk; that is, they bear the uncertainties of the development process.

PROPERTY MANAGERS

Property managers are typically employed full time when the development is close to opening and then during the project's life as an active facility. Property managers provide valuable duties—direct oversight, maintenance, and control of the property and constant contact with and management of tenants—and they are responsible as intermediaries between tenants and the developer/owner. Smart developers recruit property managers for insight during the design stage, particularly if they are building a management-intensive project such as a hotel, housing project for seniors, or health care facility. The ongoing success of these projects depends largely on how well they are managed, and poor design may impede good management. A properly designed, properly run development under the management of a good property manager can save the owner a great deal of money.

One of the biggest decisions regarding property management is whether to provide in-house management services or to contract with an outside property management firm. This decision is often based on several factors: location of the project, size of the development firm, availability of trained in-house personnel, and the developer's desire to be involved in the project's day-to-day operations. Compensation is typically a percentage of gross revenue—often 2 to 5 percent—but can also be a fixed amount. Commissions for leasing are usually separate from the management agreement.

A good source for locating a property management firm is the local chapter of the Institute of Real Estate Management (IREM), which is part of the National Association of Realtors®.

MARKET RESEARCHERS

A major part of the upfront work that affects the go/no go development decision is a market study. Market researchers can tell a developer whether or not sufficient demand exists for the proposed project, who the competition is, whom the product might appeal to, how quickly it will lease or sell, and so on. In general, the developer uses the market researcher's work to determine the revenue assumptions for the economic analysis of the proposed project. (See Chapters 17 and 18 for a more extensive look at market studies.)

A market consultant's fee is usually determined by the scope of the work. The consultant who prepares an extensive market report is most often compensated on a lump-sum basis as determined by a contract. If a quick, preliminary report is required, the developer may pay the consultant on an hourly basis.

MARKETING AND PUBLIC RELATIONS CONSULTANTS

Without the right kind of project promotion, even the best project can flounder. Accordingly, the development team often needs marketing and public relations personnel to help design a marketing strategy for the product.

Marketing and public relations may begin long before ground is broken and continue through the building of the project and after project completion. Often developments cannot be started until they are 50 to 75 percent preleased or presold, so a good marketing consultant can be invaluable to a developer. The marketing strategist may work with the broker to find and sign on tenants or to presell units. Good public relations in the form of news releases, newsletters, neighborhood parties, and mailings can generate positive attitudes toward a project before it is started and can even help diffuse opposition to the development during the permitting process.

Once developers know what they want from the public relations firm, they should generate a short list of candidate firms based on referrals or colleagues' recommendations. The market consultant should be familiar with the appropriate market and the type of project the developer proposes. Prospective firms are probably listed in local business journals. In addition, the firm's principals and employees may be members of the Public Relations Society of America and the American Marketing Association.

Payment can take the form of a fixed fee or an hourly rate for a short-term project. For large projects, however, many developers find it useful to establish a long-term relationship with a firm by keeping the firm on retainer and relying on the firm to provide marketing and media relations during all phases of the project.

REGULATORS

Public regulation of the development process should produce a fair and efficient system for allocating land uses and spur high-quality development. Developers must comply with local zoning requirements and subdivision regulations and must often obtain approvals locally for site plans and special use permits—all before development can begin. Once a project is underway, a host of regulations and regulators come into play to ensure safe construction and a safe building. Additional regulators abound at the regional, state, and national levels. Their functions range from environmental and consumer protection to oversight of financial intermediaries, mortgage instruments, and lending practices.

In practice, the various rules and regulations often conflict. Rather than producing more harmonious, well-designed projects, such policies sometimes gen-

erate mundane projects that manage to meet all codes and other regulations but lack inspiration. (See Chapter 13 for more detailed information on the public sector as regulator.)

If society's needs are to be met through the private sector's development process, rule makers and regulators must learn how to protect the public interest without erecting roadblocks to well-designed, creative projects that respond to market needs. The development process has become so complex and costly that the only way to enhance the quality of the finished product is for the developer to view and treat the public sector as an active participant on the development team. Our perspective in this text is that the public sector (as represented by the various regulating bodies) is always the developer's partner. Try to avoid a bad marriage.

FINAL USERS

A description of participants in the development process would be incomplete without mentioning the

Many of the first residents of Wild Sage Cohousing in Boulder, Colorado, played an active role in the development of this 34-unit mixed-income cohousing community. *Wonderland Hills Development*

final users of the space: the direct consumers of the finished product. Developers anticipate users' needs when articulating the original project concept. The market study further elaborates on the idea and guides developers in developing products that fit their intended market(s). Ultimately, the final users determine the success of the project by accepting or rejecting the finished product as it is delivered to the marketplace.

Users often contract for space before construction begins (preleasing). By working with the developer's marketing representative, final users can make sure that the finished product meets their needs and, in doing so, become active participants in the development process.

EVOLUTIONARY CHANGES IN THE DEVELOPMENT PROCESS

Developers are ultimately the responsible parties when it comes to managing the creation of our built environment. They tend to be driven, innovative people who work with an extensive team of professionals to complete a complex and dynamic process. This process is best described by the eight-stage model laid out in Chapter 1. The model shows the time-honored relationships that continue to be fundamental in real estate decision making today. This process, along with an understanding of the history, current situation, and projected trends in demographics and land use, makes up the essential framework needed to consider 1) whether or not a development is feasible, 2) how best to create a development, and 3) how to manage the job.

Evolutionary changes require adjustments and additions to the traditional, time-honored eight-stage model.

Availability of Data

Good developers have always relied on a great deal of background information gleaned over a lifetime of conversation, observation, and reading—newsletters, newspapers, academic journals, and the like. Data are fundamental to sophisticated players in the marketplace. Turning data into useful information

can make money for a developer. At the very least, assimilation of such historical and current public information can help developers avoid large losses.

Throughout the discussion of the eight-stage model, we will refer to a host of traditional information sources. What is new is the extent and delivery capacity of the information available today. Technology now allows vast databases to be easily accessible to the development community over the Internet. As we work through the details of the eight-stage model in the remaining chapters, we will refer to companies such as Co-Star, which provides a sophisticated online commercial property equivalent of a residential multiple listing service where brokers, investors, or owners can know which buildings have a vacancy as well as the exact vacancy in every building in an area as large as New York City, with all asking rent terms and pictures of both the interior and exterior space.

We have truly seen a revolution in the availability of data. As the leader for the process, the developer needs to use these data to produce the insights needed to establish and refine the idea for development.

A Much Longer Venture Capital Period

As we move through detailed discussions of stages one, two, and three of the development process, we will review the traditional financing cycle, which moves from land acquisition financing to land development financing to construction financing to permanent financing. This sequence still holds, but the time required to move from the early stages to the closing of the construction financing has lengthened. Why? Because building sites are more complex in infill locations, negotiations are more difficult with ever more participants in the development process, and a host of other reasons. Why does it matter? Because the cost of funds is considerably higher in the early stages of the development process. A lender lending money for hard construction has relatively high-quality collateral. A lender or investor putting up the capital necessary for planning and political work over a period of many years before construction can start does not have good collateral. In fact, this kind of financing is much like the financing that a venture capital company would extend to a new small business. If the business fails, not much is there to liquidate and sell. The longer time period before construction means a longer venture capital period and thus a longer need for expensive financing. This issue significantly affects how relationships among the development team are structured throughout the first five stages of the development process.

A More Important Level Two Perspective

James Graaskamp's definition of a project's feasibility, written in the early 1970s, is still the best definition available: "A real estate project is 'feasible' when the real estate analyst determines that there is a reasonable likelihood of satisfying explicit objectives when a selected course of action is tested for fit to a context of specific constraints and limited resources."[3] It has always been important to understand the feasibility of not just the project but also of participating in the project for all members of the development team, particularly the developer.

What changes with the increasing complexity of the process and the longer venture capital period is the importance of focusing on feasibility for the individual members of the team (level two). Because timing of the project has been extended, everyone has to worry about how they personally are doing above and beyond (but connected to) the success of the overall project. As we will see throughout the text, it is the developer's responsibility to consider the viability of the venture for each member of the development team.

Wall Street (and Related Avenues)

During the 1990s, securitization became much more important in real estate investment. As will be explained in Part III, very few large publicly traded real estate companies existed before 1990. In fact, the market value of all REITs was less than $10 billion. As of 2006, more than 200 publicly traded REITs had assets totaling more than $500 billion.

This change has two obvious impacts on the development environment. First, it creates a new level of reporting and thus greater availability of information. The SEC requires public companies to report their financial status, and Wall Street analysts provide con-

siderable commentary on these public companies. More important, the investment banker mentality has hit real estate development. Morgan Stanley, Goldman Sachs, Merrill Lynch, and all the top investment bankers now are involved in real estate investment and, more particularly for our purposes, in investment in real estate during the development process. Wall Street moves to a different beat from commercial banks, insurance companies, and wealthy families that have traditionally dominated the development process. Today's developer must contend with a faster and often harder world.

Increased Pressure on the Public Sector

A primary theme of this text is that the public sector is always a partner in the development process. As covered in Part II, the evolution of community planning, environmental safeguards, hazardous waste cleanup, and so on has produced a more complex environment in which the public sector has ever greater influence.

Government at all levels is under tremendous pressure to perform better and often with fewer resources, and must deal more rapidly with a more complex environment. Your public sector partner was always unstable and is now insecure as well—not particularly good for real estate development, as will be seen in subsequent chapters.

SUMMARY

This chapter describes the players in the development process and some challenges they face. Given that each development has different characteristics, developers must choose their consultants and coworkers with full knowledge of what is required for a specific proposed development. The importance of engaging reliable people cannot be overstated. With so many varied aspects of a project, the developer alone cannot fully understand and attend to all tasks; he or she must be able to trust participants on the development team and their honesty and competence. Partners should be chosen with a clear appreciation of both the time-honored fundamentals described in Chapter 1 and the evolutionary changes described in this chapter.

TERMS

- ▶ Appraiser
- ▶ Bearing capacity
- ▶ Design-award-build
- ▶ Development fee
- ▶ Ecosystem management
- ▶ Environmental consultant
- ▶ Environmental engineer
- ▶ General contractor
- ▶ Geotechnical engineer
- ▶ HVAC system
- ▶ Liability
- ▶ Request for proposals (RFP)
- ▶ Structural engineer
- ▶ Subcontractor
- ▶ Sustainable site design
- ▶ Traffic impact study
- ▶ Transportation consultant
- ▶ Valuation

REVIEW QUESTIONS

3.1 What are the most common forms of compensation for developers?

3.2 What are some of the ways in which a public sector developer operates?

3.3 Describe the architect's role in the development process.

3.4 Why are contractors critical to the developer's work?

3.5 Describe the expanded role of a landscape architect.

3.6 Why do developers need environmental and transportation consultants more often now than 20 years ago?

3.7 Why are appraisers involved before, during, and at project completion?

3.8 Describe the various types of financial players and when they are involved in the development process.

3.9 Do you agree with the authors' list of evolutionary changes to the development process? Do you think other societal changes affect how developers get their projects completed?

NOTES

1. Shared parking is the use of parking spaces to serve two or more individual land uses, often concentrated at different times of the day, without conflict or encroachment.

2. Personal liability provides the lender with investment collateral that can include all investor assets.

3. James A. Graaskamp, "A Rational Approach to Feasibility Analysis," *Appraisal Journal,* October 1972, p. 515. The late James Graaskamp, former chair and professor, Department of Real Estate and Urban Land Economics at the University of Wisconsin–Madison, was a noted author, teacher, and mentor. See Chapter 16 and the profile of Graaskamp in Chapter 21.

PART II

The History of Real Estate Development In the United States

One of the best ways to anticipate the future is to understand the past. Thus, Part II thoroughly reviews the evolution of development in this country from colonial days to the present. This historic picture is clearly one of a dynamic relationship between public and private players. Part II sets forth a full backdrop for the eight-stage model that follows.

The role and degree of involvement of the public sector might have changed over time, but it has always been and always will be true that the public sector is an active partner in private development. Students of real estate development should not underestimate the place of the real estate market in the economic life of the nation. Ownership of land and buildings is a fundamental right that Americans cherish and is more widespread in the United States than in any other country.

As you read through this section, keep in mind the adage that "history repeats itself." This adage is especially true when you look at the boom and bust nature of the development business.

CHAPTER 4

The Colonial Period To the Late 1800s

Real estate has been a part of the American tradition for a long time. To paraphrase Calvin Coolidge, the business of the United States is real estate. The ownership of land and buildings in the United States is notably widespread; millions of people own, buy, and sell real property. Mass participation in the real estate market has been a fundamental characteristic of the economic life of this country since its origins.

The settlers and colonists who migrated here from many parts of the world came in search of greater freedom and prosperity—and owning land was essential to attaining both goals. Throughout the 18th and 19th centuries, Americans fought for greater legal rights and opportunities to become property owners. They battled for changes in the laws and administration of colonial governments, and later, after the successful war for independence, they lobbied the federal government and state and local governments for basic reforms to establish and protect private property rights, thereby making it easier and safer to obtain and develop land.

No institution or practice was left untouched by this sweeping movement: legislatures and the courts established and enforced new laws and definitions of the rights inherent in property and contracts, land was physically surveyed and real estate market mechanisms organized to facilitate sales, a vast array of subsidies was granted to prospective settlers to enable them to afford to own land, and enormous public investments in improved transportation and infrastructure helped make the land accessible and productive. All these actions were designed to increase property values for the new private owners, and in many cases they succeeded.

The story of how these changes came about and how modern attitudes toward land evolved begins in this chapter and continues through Chapters 5 and 6. Specifically, Chapter 4 covers the history of real estate development from the colonial period to the late 1800s by examining:

▶ Real estate as an American tradition;
▶ Land subdivision and residential development; and

This chapter was written and updated by Marc A. Weiss, PhD, chair and CEO, Global Urban Development, Washington, D.C.

▶ The role of railroads and railroad barons in real estate development.

REAL ESTATE AS AN AMERICAN TRADITION

The extensive privatization of U.S. land is a remarkable story, if only because the nation's settlers initially held land in a highly centralized pattern of ownership and control. During the colonial period, most land was in the hands of the various governors by authority of the English crown and other sovereign powers; beginning in the 17th century, it was purchased or violently appropriated from the Native American tribes that inhabited the continent when the European settlers first arrived.

In the early 1600s, settlers were brought to this country to farm land owned by the Virginia Company; they were paid for their labors in both money and shares of stock. The early settlers quickly rebelled against this practice, however, and insisted on ownership of the land they were farming. In 1616, the Virginia colonial governor acquiesced, granting free and clear title to a minimum of 100 acres (40 hectares) for each farmer—an action that set an important precedent for patterns of settlement in the country.

Colonial governors had many different methods of distributing the ownership of land. Outright grants were given for farming the land; settling the frontier; serving in the military, in a religious order, or as an educator; and demonstrating political connections. Large parcels of land were sold to investors, speculators, land developers, and settlement ventures. In Massachusetts and other New England colonies, governors granted and sold land to groups for establishing towns.

Once independence was achieved and the colonies formed the United States, the federal and state governments together still owned the overwhelming share of all land. Much more land was added to the public domain during the next century through the Louisiana Purchase, the annexation of Texas, the war with Mexico, the purchase of Alaska, and several treaties with Spain and Great Britain. Much time and effort were expended dispensing this land from public to private ownership. Of the total current U.S. land area of 2.3 billion acres (931.2 million hectares), only 20 percent of it was never in the public domain. The federal government disposed of more than 1 billion acres (405 million hectares) through land sales and land grants to veterans, homesteaders, railroads, and state governments. The states, in turn, sold or granted much of their public lands to private individuals and companies.

At first, public land was put into private ownership mainly through sales of large numbers of acres to individual investors. The sales occurred as a result of negotiated deals, public auctions, and fixed prices per acre set by Congress. This approach reached its peak in 1836, when the federal government sold 20 million acres (8 million hectares), most of it for $1.25 an acre ($3 per hectare). The problem with this technique was that many prospective frontier settlers could not afford to pay even the minimum government price to purchase federal land, let alone the often much higher prices asked by private speculators who bought public land wholesale and attempted to resell it retail. The huge numbers of land-hungry pioneers were also voters, however, and they rebelled in the mid-19th century as their forebears had done two centuries earlier in Virginia.

Fee Simple Real Estate Transactions

In 1862, Congress responded to this political "Free Soil Movement" by passing the Homestead Act, enabling settlers who did not already own sufficient land to be granted title to 160 acres (65 hectares) for each adult in the family simply by living on and improving the "homestead" for a period of five years. No cash payments were required, thereby opening up ownership to a wide segment of the population that had previously been excluded. Unfortunately, the system was subject to a great deal of fraud and abuse, allowing large landowners and wealthy investors to obtain substantial public acreage at bargain prices.

Despite the abuses, the Homestead Act was extremely popular and was followed in the 1870s by additional federal laws granting free 20- and 40-acre (8- and 16-hectare) parcels to settlers engaging in mining and tree cultivation. In all, the government gave away nearly 300 million acres (121.5 million hectares) of public land to private owners through the various homesteading programs—almost as much land as through cash sales.

The creation of the fee simple system of complete property rights through private ownership, including the ability of one private party to convey those rights to another through sale, lease, or trade, generated a vibrant real estate market that attracted substantial amounts of investment capital. In the early years, the money moving into and out of real property was extremely volatile and subject to wide fluctuations in amounts and prices. By the late 18th century, land speculation had already become a main preoccupation of U.S. citizens. Legendary fortunes were made and lost as the steady influx of immigrants entered the new nation. Rapidly rising prices frequently led to a mania for land gambling. Many people, including Charles Dickens's character Martin Chuzzlewit, got caught up in the excitement and the greed and were swindled in the process; countless others were eventually disappointed when the inevitable financial panic led to a drastic drop in prices. Every time new territory was opened for settlement and land was subdivided for sale, the speculative boom/bust cycles repeated themselves. Many colorful books and articles have recounted tales of glory and grief in American "land bubbles" both before and after they burst.[1]

"Land-jobbing" or "town-jobbing" by obtaining land and selling it through promotional schemes to speculators and settlers was one of the principal means of accumulating wealth in the early days of the United States, and all the major business and government leaders—from Benjamin Franklin to George Washington—engaged in it. Indeed, the father of our country was a professional land surveyor in addition to being a planter, general, and president. An energetic entrepreneur in the real estate business, Washington was heavily involved in one of the country's first big development deals—the establishment of the District of Columbia as the nation's capital.

Developing the District of Columbia

The selection of the site for and development of the District of Columbia as the Federal City was based

Advertisement for the public auction of lots in Washington, D.C., in 1792, where the lowest acceptable bid was $3.

on President Washington's plan for encouraging private land sales and trading. In fact, speculative real estate activity in the nation's capital was so overheated before it crashed that the Duke de La Rochefoucauld, a visiting French dignitary, wrote in 1797:

> In America, where more than in any other country in the world, a desire for wealth is the prevailing passion, there are few schemes [that] are not made the means of extensive speculations; and that of erecting the Federal City presented irresistible temptations, which were not in fact neglected. . . . The building of a house for the President and a place for the sittings of Congress excited, in the purchasers of lots, the hope of a new influx of speculations. The public papers were filled with exaggerated praises of the new city; in a word, with all the artifices [that] trading people in every part of the world are accustomed to employ in the disposal of their wares, and [that] are perfectly known, and amply practiced in this new world.[2]

Both the federal and state governments used land sales as a primary method of raising revenues to pay for public improvements. Washington, D.C., was to be developed on this basis, with President Washington and future Presidents Thomas Jefferson and James Madison among the private bidders for the purchase of subdivided urban lots at the initial public auction in 1791. Only 35 lots were sold at that time,

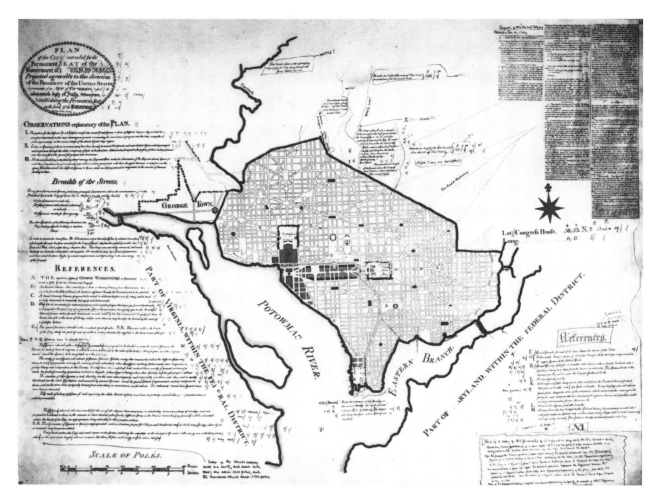

L'Enfant's 1792 plan for the Federal City. Although it was implemented slowly, more than two centuries later much of L'Enfant's original plan for a majestic city to rival any of the great European capitals is now complete.

leading to additional promotional efforts that culminated in the wholesale purchase on credit of 7,235 lots by a syndicate headed by Robert Morris, a Philadelphia merchant, well-known Revolutionary War financier, and major real estate investor in Pennsylvania and New York. Morris and his partners, James Greenleaf and John Nicholson, promised to bring needed capital for land development and building construction into the Federal City, starting with the "Morristown" project, 20 two-story brick houses near the capitol. George Washington also built several for-sale rowhouses in the same area.

In 1791, President Washington commissioned Major Pierre Charles L'Enfant to design a long-term plan for development of the entire Federal City, including the layout of the street system and the public buildings. Though little of L'Enfant's scheme was immediately adopted, much of his grand conception was eventually realized over the next two centuries. In the 1790s, the federal government tried to stimulate new investment and economic and population growth by requiring all those who purchased lots to construct permanent, good-quality, two-story brick or stone buildings, with minimum and maximum prescribed heights to ensure uniformity in the appearance of the streetscape.

Unfortunately, Robert Morris's syndicate defaulted on its payments for the Washington lots and failed to complete construction of Morristown, and all three principals were sent to debtors' prison. Land prices fell precipitously, and the federal district remained for decades what Charles Dickens called "the City of Magnificent Intentions."[3] Nevertheless, the city named for George Washington eventually proved him right—that extensive public and private investment, good planning, quality development and construction, desirable location, a sound economic and employment base, and a growing population would ultimately produce a healthy real estate market with rising long-term values.

Ground Leases

Ground leases formed the basis for the wealth of many early Americans. Under the terms of a long-term ground lease, the landlord received rental payments for the use of land. Renters could occupy the land themselves, lease it out for ground rent, sell their interest in the lease, or improve the property and then collect a building rent. Without surrendering the role of owner, landlords delegated control of the distribution, development, and use of land to the land tenants.[4]

The fact that this practice was common in 18th-century England was incentive enough for George Washington. By 1773, Washington had gained ownership of 20,000 acres (8,100 hectares) on the Ohio and Great Kanawha rivers. On July 15, 1773, he advertised for settlers in *The Maryland Journal and Baltimore Advertiser*. He indicated that he would divide the land "into any sized tenements that may be desired, and lease them upon moderate terms, allowing a reasonable number of years rent free, provided, within the space of two years from the next October, three acres for every 50 contained in each lot . . . shall be cleared, fenced and tilled."[5]

New York's most noteworthy landlord was Trinity Church. Starting with a crown grant of 32 acres (13 hectares) from Queen Anne in 1705, the vestrymen of the church accumulated approximately 1,000 city lots by the end of the 18th century. Before 1770, the church leased lots at a single rate: £2 annual ground rent for the first seven years, £3 a year for the second seven years, and £4 annually for the remainder of the 21-year term. The vestrymen calculated graduated increases to cover the doubling of land values, which they expected after 21 years.

Trinity's common leases ran for 21 years and anticipated occupancy. Such a term was long enough to allow tenants to benefit from any buildings they constructed on the lot. In contrast, longer leases, especially those running from 63 to 99 years (with rent increases at intervals of 21 or 33 years), projected a property interest that extended beyond the lifetime of the tenant. Under these longer leases, the tenant, who paid a fixed ground rent, retained any increases in the rent-generating value of property.[6]

Even today, several of New York's important buildings sit on land leased from Trinity Church and from such families as Goelet, Rhinelander, and Astor, all of which were active in the 18th-century real estate market.

The Holland Land Company

Although the story of the promotion of U.S. land and town sales is punctuated by a get-rich-quick hype and a string of broken promises and dreams, it is also the story of the fundamentals of real estate development as an entire continent's rural and urban land was brought into productive economic use. One example is the Holland Land Company, which bought 3.3 million acres (1.3 million hectares) of land in western New York State from Robert Morris in 1792. Morris had purchased the vast property on credit, hoping that rising prices would yield huge profits through quick turnover.

The Holland Land Company, a group of Dutch financiers and wealthy investors, acquired the immense territory with the intention of subdividing it into large parcels and rapidly dispensing the tracts wholesale to major investors. A serious downturn in property markets brought on by the financial panic that ensued after the collapse of Robert Morris's syndicate in Washington, D.C., however, led the Holland Land Company to reassess its strategy. Out of necessity, the principals decided to engage in long-term, value-added investment and development. Land would be sold retail to new settlers who could be induced to migrate to the region on the promise of infrastructure and services that would make both farmland and town sites physically accessible and economically viable locations for commerce, industry, and permanent residence.

In 1797, the Holland Land Company hired Joseph Ellicott, an experienced Pennsylvania land surveyor, to serve as chief land agent and to direct company operations in upstate New York. For the next two decades, Ellicott implemented a comprehensive long-term plan for the development of the territory and the retail sale of land. Included in the company's holdings was the city of Buffalo, which Ellicott laid out at the western boundary of the territory along Lake Erie.

Ellicott's long-term development strategy included the construction of hundreds of miles of roads through the wooded wilderness and the building of towns at strategic points along newly developed transportation routes. The company located land offices in the towns, and Ellicott engaged in a wide variety of promotional activities to stimulate population growth and settlement in both the towns and the hinterland. In addition to building long-distance roads, the Holland Land Company assisted in the construction of sawmills, gristmills, distilleries, and potash refineries to stimulate regional economic activity that would enhance demand for land sales and leasing. Further, when a town center was first platted and opened for development, the company frequently subsidized the pioneering private owners of general stores, inns, taverns, grain mills, ironworks, smithies, and other providers of essential goods and services. The company also donated land for schools, churches, and public squares.

Joseph Ellicott successfully sold a great deal of land and, within a decade, had brought more than 200,000 new settlers to the Holland Land Company's vast territory, prompting the president of Yale College to write in 1810, "It is questionable whether mankind had ever seen so large a tract changed so suddenly from a wilderness into a well-inhabited and well-cultivated country."[7] Unfortunately, most of the settlers who had bought land on credit with little or no downpayment found themselves unable to meet the credit terms to complete their purchases. Thus, they became essentially tenants of the Holland Land Company, and, in 1820, the company attempted to bail out of the situation by reselling all its land to the state of New York. The legislature refused to buy it, and the company was forced to squeeze more cash from the settlers or repossess their holdings.

Neither approach proved economically or politically worthwhile, and, in 1830, the company helped organize the New York Life Insurance and Trust Company, which began to refinance Holland Land's creditors by converting the unpaid sales contracts into first mortgage loans. In 1836, a powerful local businessman and politician named William H. Seward arranged for Wall Street and European investors to purchase the loans, a popular act that helped elect Seward governor of New York in 1838. As Seward put it, "In less than 18 months, 4,000 persons whom I found occupying lands, chiefly under expired and legally enforceable contracts of sale, and excited and embarrassed alike by the oppression and uncertainty of ever obtaining titles, became freeholders."[8]

In 1835, the Holland Land Company had sold its property to a New York investment syndicate for $1 million, leaving continuation of the massive enterprise for large-scale land development to a new group of real estate entrepreneurs. Fortunately for the Dutch owners of Holland Land, they managed to sell their holdings before the major economic depression of 1837. But the enduring heritage of Holland Land's nearly four decades in the land development business was not the record of financial deals; rather, it was Joseph Ellicott's national role model as an early American "community builder."

John Jacob Astor

An alternative model to either short-term speculators or long-term land developers of for-sale properties is the "Astor method," based on the real estate career of John Jacob Astor, one of the country's richest and best-known businessmen in the first half of the 19th century. Astor, who had started as a fur trader in the Pacific Northwest, owned a tremendous amount of real estate, including several land parcels and buildings in Manhattan, that he began accumulating in 1810. His philosophy of real estate was to purchase land at low prices and wait patiently for the market to change and for urban growth to drive values exponentially higher. While waiting for these long-term increases, he collected substantial rental income from his extensive commercial and residential real estate holdings.

Astor was always eager to buy properties when he could get a bargain, and he rarely sold except when he needed money to purchase more real estate or, occasionally, when values skyrocketed. Astor once sold a lot near Wall Street for $8,000 to a man who was convinced that he had outwitted Astor. The buyer said, "Why, Mr. Astor, in a few years this property will be worth $12,000." "No doubt," said Astor, "but with your $8,000 I will buy 80 lots north of Canal Street. By the time your lot is worth $12,000, my 80 lots will be worth $80,000." Needless to say, he was correct.

During the crash of 1837, Astor acquired several lots and buildings at "distress sale" prices and foreclosed on hundreds of properties on which he held or obtained the mortgages. He seldom invested in any significant improvements, preferring to lease properties and earn profits primarily from rental income. Often, Astor settled for a 5 percent return on the current value of land and left the risk of construction and property management to others. By 1840, Astor was the country's wealthiest man, with an annual income of more than $1.25 million from ground rent alone and an estate worth more than $20 million, largely attributable to the tremendous growth in the value of his urban real estate assets. Shortly before his death in 1848, he declared, "Could I begin life again, knowing what I now know, and had money to invest, I would buy every foot of land on the island of Manhattan."[9]

Capital Improvement Projects

Just as the Holland Land Company discovered it had to invest in infrastructure to enhance the value of its real estate assets, the federal, state, and local governments undertook wide-ranging development of roads, canals, ports, and a host of other facilities to enable them to turn public lands into private holdings and, most important, to promote population and employment growth. "Boosterism" and public investment went hand in hand. Often capital improvement projects were financed either by issuing bonds to be repaid from user fees such as bridge, highway, and canal tolls or by combining rail and transit fares with revenues from the sale or lease of nearby land that had increased in value because of new infrastructure. For more than 200 years, private developers have used this same model when installing major improvements. In addition, private utility, transit, railroad, and other companies have frequently relied on these methods, sometimes with public powers of land acquisition or even outright grants of public land. In other cases, taxpayers voted to sell bonds for improvements to be repaid through increased property taxes. Voters anticipated that future population growth would increase the tax base and property values so that both the public treasury and private landowners who purchased local real estate would benefit by "boosting" the area with expensive new government-financed construction.

The public sector's role was crucial in facilitating successful development and widespread ownership. Forms of intervention ranged from the ubiquitous rectangular survey that opened up the West, to regulations such as building codes, the legal protection of property transactions, and land use controls that have enhanced the physical environment, public safety, and property values. Further, the role of financing has been essential to the success of real estate ventures, as the saga of the Holland Land Company demonstrates. In addition, as will be seen later, the federal and state governments, through controls on currency, regulatory oversight of publicly chartered financial institutions, and macroeconomic policies, have played a major role in encouraging and monitoring the apparatus of money and credit that has enabled U.S. real estate development to thrive and grow.

LAND SUBDIVISION AND RESIDENTIAL DEVELOPMENT

Although the disposition of public lands involved millions of acres sold or granted by the federal and state governments and resold by private investors and developers, the nature of land subdivision fell into two different categories: larger acreage for farming or other essentially rural uses, and smaller lots for towns and urban uses. As cities grew in the 19th century, more and more land was subdivided into building lots within existing urban areas and in the open countryside to establish new cities. Many of the rural enterprises never succeeded, leaving ghost towns in their wake, but some did emerge from modest beginnings. Chicago, for example, grew in a brief seven decades from a tiny hamlet inhabited by a few hundred pioneers in the 1830s to the fifth largest city in the world by 1900. The biggest single use of land in these metropolitan communities was allocated to house the steadily growing population. Land and, in some cases, buildings were continually carved up to provide dwelling units for new residents.

Given the abundance of cheap land, inexpensive construction materials, and a constant stream of innovations in transportation technology that made residential dispersion possible, an enormous amount of urban housing in the United States consisted of single-family detached dwellings. In the older and more crowded cities of the early 19th century, attached rowhouses (typically constructed in block groups by speculative builders) and multifamily dwellings converted from spacious mansions accommodated a high-density population that walked to work in areas where available space was limited. Later in the century, a number of other dwelling types made their debut, including luxury apartment buildings, squalid tenements, and two- to four-family structures whose modest-income owners often lived in one of the units and, in some cases, constructed the building themselves.

Unlike in most other countries, the U.S. urban real estate market allowed for mass participation. Vacant building lots were frequently sold on credit with only small downpayments required, making it possible for a wide range of potential purchasers to enter the market. Millions of people bought lots, including families that wanted to build their own houses, entrepreneurial builders who wanted to construct dwellings for sale or rent, and investors who wanted to turn over land for a fast profit or hold it for long-term gain. Many subdivisions had only the most rudimentary improvements such as unpaved streets and lacked basic amenities like sanitary and storm sewers, a supply of fresh water, or curbs and sidewalks. In higher-income communities, developers sometimes installed key improvements in advance of sales and added those costs to lot prices. A more common approach was for infrastructure and ameni-

Sears, Roebuck and Co. had a booming do-it-yourself homebuilding business in the early part of the 20th century. On the cover of this catalog of houses from 1929, Sears advertises itself as "the world's largest building material dealers," a different Sears from the one we know today.

ties to be built after the initial sale of land, paid for by individual lot owners through special tax assessments. To reduce the costs of property ownership for people of limited means, subdivisions intended to house the working classes generally did without many amenities. Often these subdivisions even lacked basic features such as sewers and paved streets. As with building and housing codes, society's minimum acceptable standards for neighborhood development are much higher today than a century ago.

In the 19th century, most urban subdivisions, whether already built up and inhabited or new and vacant, lacked any significant land use controls. Mixtures of lot sizes and shapes and of building densities, heights, forms, occupancies, and uses were typical and could be limited only through actions by private owners. Deed restrictions in the form of private contracts were the one regulatory device available to developers and property owners, but they were difficult to establish and enforce and were used mostly in a small number of new, high-income residential neighborhoods. By the 1920s, the extensive use of private deed restrictions and the introduction of public controls through zoning and subdivision regulations brought new elements of stability and order to residential real estate development.

Not only was it possible for the first time for millions of people to become urban property owners, but many were also actively engaged in the real estate business. Selling one's own or someone else's property as an agent was a completely unregulated activity in the 19th century and occupied the time and energy of a substantial segment of the population, especially during boom times. Regrettably, some vendors indulged in unethical, fraudulent, fly-by-night practices that at times lent sales agents, developers, and landlords an unsavory image and later led to calls for reform by angry private citizens, concerned industry leaders, and progressive public officials.

In addition to ownership, sales, and property management, building construction was a widespread endeavor. Most contractors and subcontractors, particularly in the residential field, were small-scale operators, often shuttling back and forth between the roles of contractor and laborer. Nearly all houses were built under contract to the owner/users, many of whom constructed their dwellings with the help of family and friends. Stock architectural plans were readily available; only a small percentage of houses, mainly for the wealthy, were truly custom-designed by professional architects. By the early 20th century, the Sears catalog was selling many different models of prefabricated houses that came in pieces along with a manual explaining how to assemble them, much like today's Swedish furniture. Contract work was the principal mode, but many large and small builders also constructed houses as speculative investments, though the norm was generally just one or two and seldom more than five such houses per year. Merchant homebuilding, as this method came to be known, did not begin to dominate the housing industry until the 1950s. The standard approach for even sophisticated real estate

developers was primarily to sell finished building lots, not completed houses.

Advances in Transportation and the Rise Of Suburban Development: Llewellyn Park, New Jersey, and Riverside, Illinois

The ability to plan and develop large-scale urban, primarily residential neighborhoods and communities depended on new advances in transportation technology that enabled residents to reach their places of employment without being confined to the tight boundaries, high densities, and mixed uses of the "walking city." By the early 19th century, the population of cities began to spread out and to differentiate uses by location. Commuter ferry service by steamship across rivers and other bodies of water served as one means of circulation. Ground transportation started with both the omnibus—a horse-drawn urban stagecoach—for short in-city trips and the steam railroad for longer, inter- and intracity travel. Later, horse-drawn passenger cars running on rail rights-of-way, cable cars, electric streetcars or "trolley" cars, elevated and subway rail transit, electric rail, and, finally, the gasoline-powered automobile all helped turn the landscape into its present vast, low-density suburban world of houses, highways, industrial and office parks, shopping malls, and parking lots.

The first generation of major residential land developers was spawned by the coming of long-distance railroads in the 1840s and 1850s. Their developments were essentially elite, upper-middle-class suburbs in pastoral settings located on railroad lines connected to large central cities. Two of the earliest and best known of these suburbs are Llewellyn Park, New Jersey, and Riverside, Illinois.

Llewellyn Haskell, a successful New York merchant, together with eight partners, purchased 400 acres (162 hectares) of land near West Orange, New Jersey, in the 1850s. The location was only 13 miles (21 kilometers) from Manhattan and directly on a railroad line into the city. Haskell was attracted by the natural beauty of the site, with its hills, streams, woods, and views of a mountain to the north and New York City to the east. His goal was to create a model community for "the wants of citizens doing business in New York, and yet wishing accessible, retired, and healthful homes in the country."[10] To further this goal, Haskell hired as his chief planner Alexander Jackson Davis, a well-known architect of luxurious and romantic country estates and author of *Rural Residences,* one of the bibles of stylish residential architecture.

Haskell and Davis worked together to make the most of the site's parklike environment. Missing was the familiar gridiron pattern of straight streets meeting at right angles; instead, roads and lanes curved with the natural contours of the land. The use of curvilinear streets later became a standard feature of suburban residential land development, but, in 1856, it was a bold innovation for a new real estate venture. The developer and his architect-planner also created "the Ramble," a 50-acre (20-hectare) natural park that followed a stream at the side of the mountain. The Ramble was left in its natural state except for the addition of some curving pedestrian paths. Haskell organized a property owners' association to hold title to and maintain this common area, establishing another important precedent for new community projects—open space and recreation facilities dedicated by the developer.

Haskell also wrote restrictions into the deeds prohibiting industrial and commercial uses of the land, requiring large minimum lots (three acres [1.2 hectares]), and barring fences on people's property. These and other rules were all designed to preserve Llewellyn Park as a quiet and green paradise for wealthy residents, who entered the exclusive private community through a security gatehouse. Haskell and Davis both moved there, the lots sold at high prices, and the partners earned an excellent return on their investment. The suburb's attractiveness as an elite enclave was so well conceived and executed that, more than a century later, the community remains as Haskell originally envisioned it.

Riverside is more familiar to many urbanists because it was planned by the famous American landscape architects Frederick Law Olmsted and Calvert Vaux, the designers of New York City's Central Park. Emery Childs and a group of investors acquired 1,600 acres (648 hectares) of undeveloped land on the Des Plaines River and formed the Riverside

Downtown Philadelphia, 1897, when streets were clogged with horse-drawn carriages, trolley cars, and pedestrians.

Improvement Company in 1868 to build a new suburban community combining "the beauties and healthy properties of a park with the conveniences and improvements of the city."[11] The site was located nine miles (14.5 kilometers) west of downtown Chicago on the Burlington Railroad line, and Olmsted and Vaux were impressed by its attractive natural features, calling it "the only available ground near Chicago [that] does not present disadvantages of an almost hopeless character."[12]

Olmsted and Vaux planned a central 160-acre (65-hectare) park along the river and several smaller parks and recreation areas. The streets were laid out in a naturalistic curvilinear pattern, and several other innovations in high-quality community planning and design were included in the development of this commuter suburb. Deed restrictions provided for an impressive array of controls, requiring everything from mandatory 30-foot (9-meter) setbacks, minimum home construction costs, and design review for houses, to prescribed rules for maintaining private lawns. Olmsted and Vaux also proposed a limited-access parkway from Riverside to downtown Chicago, an unrealized idea in 1868 that was a half century ahead of its time for American suburban development.

The Riverside Improvement Company hired William LeBaron Jenney, Chicago's leading architect, to review the house plans of those who purchased lots and to design the Riverside Hotel (built in 1870) overlooking the river. Jenney also built his own house in the new community and helped set a tone for the kind of style the developers and landscape planners desired.

Unfortunately, Emery Childs's and the Riverside Improvement Company's luck was not as good as that of Llewellyn Haskell and his partners. The costly improvements installed to develop Riverside were not supported by vigorous land sales in the first few years. Many people still considered Riverside too far away from the city. Market demand, access to capital, and lot prices all fell dramatically after the 1871 Chicago fire, and the company went bankrupt during the national depression of 1873. By the 1880s, however, sales of lots and construction of houses in Riverside increased significantly. Despite the early disappointments, Riverside, which today is a historic district, was eventually built as a middle-class suburb according to Childs's vision, Olmsted and Vaux's plan, and Jenney's design. It served as an important early model for many later suburban developments from Roland Park in Baltimore to the Country Club District of Kansas City.

Although the elite suburbs located along commuter railroad lines represented the earliest examples of large-scale residential subdivisions, further advances in transportation technology later in the 19th century enabled people of more modest means to move to suburban-style neighborhoods and to travel by electric transit to their jobs. "Streetcar suburbs" began to appear on the outskirts of growing cities. Often these new subdivisions, which today are urban neighborhoods, started as unincorporated areas that were later annexed to the nearby central city.

The development of subdivisions during this period was tied to the availability of mass transit. Sometimes the private transportation company was also the land subdivider, with the enormous profits on land sales helping to pay for an initially money-losing transit operation that used cheap promotional fares to encourage people to buy lots and build houses in a sparsely settled community. Real estate entrepreneurs of this type ranged from Boston's

Henry M. Whitney, the leading subdivider of Brookline, Massachusetts, to F.M. "Borax" Smith, the largest land developer in Oakland, California. Developers who did not own transit companies usually had to pay subsidies to induce a transportation firm to extend its operations to outlying locations. The subsidies were an essential business cost for the developer, because without transit service, there would be no market for the subdivided land.

Samuel E. Gross

Most subdividers were small-scale real estate dealers, though some, especially the transit and utility companies and other large landowners, often sold a high volume of building lots. Rarely did any subdivision developer build more than a handful of houses, usually just enough to help define the character of the community and create an established, lived-in image. One exception to this general pattern was Samuel E. Gross, a flamboyant residential subdivider who built thousands of houses in the Chicago area in the 1880s and 1890s, mainly inexpensive and affordable houses for skilled blue-collar and white-collar workers earning modest incomes.

Samuel Gross had gone bankrupt in the Chicago real estate business during the 1873 panic, but, after working as a lawyer and a playwright, he reentered the real estate market in 1880. By 1892, he had sold 40,000 lots and built and sold 7,000 houses in the Chicago metropolitan area. Many of his subdivisions were in the nearly 20 new suburbs he developed. The best known is Brookfield, originally called Grossdale, located adjacent to Riverside.

This popular developer engaged in extensive and dramatic advertising campaigns, emphasizing the requirements of his easy-payment financing plan: a 10 percent downpayment, low monthly installments, and generous refinancing for delinquent borrowers. Where he built houses, he charged a single price for the house and lot. In addition, he always made sure that a major transit line ran through his subdivisions, sometimes by working in partnership with Charles T. Yerkes, Chicago's "traction king."

Gross also included major utilities and infrastructure in his developments and added special quality touches to the residential environment. Houses ranged from a modest four-room cottage that sold for $1,000 ($100 down and $10 a month) to larger and more expensive houses, such as a nine-room model that sold for $5,000. Most of the houses were built from orders and downpayments taken from customers, though Gross also maintained a small inventory available for immediate sale. He built from stock plans but provided touches to individualize the design and trumpeted this fact in his advertising.

Gross was aided in the production of inexpensive houses by the development of the balloon-frame method of construction in Chicago during the 1830s and 1840s. This technique, which used light wooden two-by-fours hammered together with machine-made nails rather than heavy timbers and elaborate joints, saved a tremendous amount of construction time, labor, and materials. By the time Gross entered the real estate business, the balloon-frame house had revolutionized homebuilding in the United States and, together with cheap land, made homeownership much more affordable in the United States than in Europe.

Samuel Gross's somewhat bigger houses and more extensive amenities were reserved for middle-income subdivisions such as Grossdale. The marketing of his explicitly working-class subdivisions, however, stressed a small house and a modest environment designed to keep down the cost of the lots. Nonetheless, even in the most moderate-cost subdivisions, Gross always planted a considerable number of trees. His basic real estate development and marketing activities, involving small, inexpensive houses and lots sold on easy credit, were so well received that the Workingman's Party nominated Gross for mayor of Chicago in 1889. He declined the honor, but two years later the city's *Real Estate and Building Journal* crowned Samuel Eberly Gross "the Napoleon of homebuilders."[13]

The Growth of Inner-City Slums

While new housing was being built for the upper class, the middle class, and the more skilled working class, unskilled, low-income workers were still crowded into inner-city neighborhoods called "slums." Close to factories and warehouses that were

This photo, taken by Jacob Riis in 1888, depicts the living conditions in some of New York City's slums.

the major sources of employment for people who still walked to work, slums claimed the worst housing, the greatest overcrowding, and the highest rates of disease. In 1890, journalist and social reformer Jacob Riis attempted to arouse the nation's conscience with his photographically documented book *How the Other Half Lives*,[14] and, four years later, Carroll Wright, the U.S. Commissioner of Labor, systematically documented the deplorable conditions in his study of the slums of Baltimore, Philadelphia, New York City, and Chicago.[15]

Even though the individuals and families living in the slums had low incomes, landlords often packed so many rent-paying customers into a building and spent so little money on maintenance that slum properties could be highly profitable. Not only were older structures constantly converted to house greater numbers of cash-poor immigrants flocking to the central cities in search of economic opportunity, but new tenements and other forms of high-density residences were also frequently built. Many of even the newest structures lacked such basic necessities as indoor plumbing and windows that brought light and air into all rooms. Lot coverage was extremely high, with little open space around buildings and no place for people to congregate and recreate other than the streets and alleys, both of which were frequently covered with mud and littered with garbage.

In cities from New York to San Francisco, housing reform movements during the late 19th and early 20th centuries began to organize for stricter laws to regulate the minimum quality and standard features of new residential construction and existing housing. Unfortunately, these movements frequently met with stiff resistance from elements of the real estate industry. Where the movements did succeed, they often encountered the fundamental problem that many of the slum tenants could not afford to pay the higher rents necessary to finance the major physical improvements needed.

One strategy to reduce rents was to encourage philanthropic capitalists to build housing for workers under limited-profit financial arrangements. These efforts were intended as both physical models of better construction and design, and economic and social

models to stimulate more extensive investment. Some real estate development firms, such as Alfred T. White's City and Suburban Homes Company of New York, became involved in these activities. Most of the leaders in this movement came from business and professional fields not directly related to the real estate industry. All together, however, these efforts did not produce enough housing to make even a dent in the immediate problem, though over the long run they had important symbolic value in helping to raise minimum standards and educating developers about better methods of planning and building low-cost housing.

Yet another approach, led by middle-class professional social workers, was to form settlement houses in slum neighborhoods. Settlement houses provided public health and education services to local residents to help them improve their living conditions and enhance their opportunities. Social workers in settlement houses also assisted members of the community in organizing labor unions and agitating for economic, political, and social reforms from business and government. Often the same people who contributed to the work of settlement houses were also involved in various attempts to regulate slum housing publicly and to promote the private, limited-dividend construction of new low-rent dwellings. The problem of housing the poor has a long history in this country and is marked by many serious initiatives that have not yet achieved long-term success (see Chapter 15).

THE ROLE OF RAILROADS AND RAILROAD BARONS IN REAL ESTATE DEVELOPMENT

The coming of the railroad in the mid-19th century profoundly affected life in the United States. Railroads quickly became the prime mover of people and goods around the nation, into and out of cities and towns. In the 18th and early 19th centuries, water-based transportation routes had made some land accessible, permitting many towns to develop mainly because of their location near navigable bodies of water. In the first half of the 19th century, canals expanded the number of accessible sites for land devel-

The growth of railroad construction brought with it a frenzy of land speculation like that along this line connecting Houston and New Orleans, circa 1880.

opment. But canals were nothing compared with the railroads. Tracks could be laid almost anywhere, and the volume of land potentially available for development thus expanded tremendously. At times, this expansion led to feverish speculation; no investor could predict with certainty which sites with access to rail transport would be in demand and at what price.

As railroads became the principal mode of long-distance passenger and freight transportation, areas depended on access to rail service for growth and, in many cases, even for survival. In the early years, some municipalities even organized their own short-haul rail corporations; later, many towns went deeply into debt paying huge subsidies to private railroad firms for providing service to their communities. Once regular rail service was established, local citizens bought land and marketed it to newcomers. Clearly, railroads and real estate development were twin forces for change in many growing areas.

The giant railroad corporations, the country's first truly big businesses, were intimately involved in real estate activity. The interstate long-distance rail carriers obtained their franchises and capitalization through the federal government's grant of not only rights-of-way but also millions of acres of land along their proposed routes. Between 1850 and 1871, the federal government granted 130 million acres (52.6 million hectares) of public land to railroad compa-

nies. The rail carriers received about half the land within six to 40 miles (10 to 65 kilometers) of the rights-of-way, with the government retaining the other half. The land was divided by sections into one-square-mile (1.6-square-kilometer) parcels, and the railroads were granted every other section. Public officials argued that once the railroad was built, the government could sell its remaining sections for at least twice as much as it could have otherwise, though it did not always work out that way in practice. After the tracks were laid, the railroads and the government went into competition with each other over subdividing and selling their alternate sections.

Railroads entered the real estate promotion business in an enormous way. In addition to selling land, many railroad companies held onto their vast acreage, mortgaging it to bankers and bond buyers to obtain capital. Indeed, when some politicians and citizens tried to force the railroads to sell their publicly granted land, the companies responded that the assets were tied up as collateral and that they could not sell the land without the permission of their lenders—an argument upheld by the U.S. Supreme Court.[16] Over the years, railroads have retained ownership of immense quantities of rural and urban land. They have sold it, leased it, and developed it. It has been used for agriculture, forestry, mining, and recreation, and for commercial, industrial, and residential developments. In many

The lobby of the luxurious 500-room Breakers hotel, built by Henry M. Flagler in 1896 in West Palm Beach, Florida.

cities today, railroads are still the biggest private landowners, and some have formed real estate development divisions to earn a greater return on their assets. Santa Fe–Southern Pacific's Mission Bay, a large mixed-use real estate development project near downtown San Francisco, is one such example.

The Effect of Railroads on Industrial Development

The railroads completely reshaped the industrial landscape of cities. Originally, in the preindustrial era of older cities, everyone was packed together within walking distance of the center, and artisan workshops were frequently inside or next to people's homes. Later, as cities expanded and manufacturing grew in importance, much manufacturing located in separate multistory "loft" buildings with high ceilings and open floor space. With the increasing demand for industrial space, supplying it became an important

branch of the real estate business. Nonetheless, small manufacturers still needed to be concentrated near the center of the city to take advantage of water port facilities—the lifeblood of the transportation system. With the advent of the railroads, however, manufacturing and warehousing could spread out to many possible sites along the rail lines, and rail spurs and feeder lines were built to connect local shippers to the main, long-haul trunk lines.

By the latter part of the 19th century, large factories and factory complexes with workers' housing were built on new sites, owing to the railroads' cooperation in bringing in raw materials and shipping out finished products. In addition to the construction of entire factory towns for large manufacturers such as the new steel mill cities of Gary, Indiana, and Birmingham, Alabama, decentralized industrial parks began to appear on the outskirts of large cities and in nearby suburban locations. Unlike the giant factories, these parks were primarily speculative real estate ventures. In some cases, the early parks were partially owned and financed by the railroad firms to promote more intensive use of their developed land and transportation services.

By the early 20th century, Chicago real estate developers had established both the Central Manufacturing District and the Clearing Industrial District. Each was located on the southwest side, far from the downtown area. Many manufacturing and warehouse firms relocated to the new districts to take advantage of cheaper rents, larger one-story floor spaces, easy access for cars and trucks to load and unload shipments, proximity to mass transit for workers, and, most important, excellent connections to railroad sidings. These industrial parks were professionally managed and offered low-rise and low-density buildings, newly developed and well-maintained grounds, clean sites, and, compared with the older loft neighborhoods and downtown railyards, more attractive landscaping. Although this type of industrial development did not become prominent in the United States until the 1950s, the earliest models were established in the 1910s and 1920s.

Railroad Barons as Real Estate Developers

Two railroad barons played a crucial role in shaping the patterns of real estate development and urbanization for entire regions: Henry M. Flagler on Florida's east coast and Henry E. Huntington in southern California.

Henry M. Flagler and the Growth of Southern Florida

Henry M. Flagler was one of John D. Rockefeller's original partners in the petroleum business; he became extremely wealthy through the growth of the Standard Oil Company. By the early 1880s, Florida was experiencing one of its periodic land booms. St. Augustine, where Flagler vacationed in 1885, was considered a favorable location because of its healthful climate. Flagler became captivated by the town and decided to develop it into a premier resort city for the upper classes, creating a southern version of Newport, Rhode Island. Flagler hired two young New York architects, John Carrère and Thomas

Hastings, to design the massive and luxurious Spanish-style Hotel Ponce de Leon, named for the man who had searched in St. Augustine for the fountain of youth. The Hotel Ponce de Leon opened in 1888 and proved so successful that, by the following year, Flagler built the Alcazar, a large entertainment center that included mid-priced hotel rooms. He also purchased a new, small luxury hotel called Casa Monica, which he renamed the Cordova. In addition, he built 14 expensive cottages for winter guests. The Alcazar contained ballrooms, theaters, swimming pools, and an array of other facilities, including Roman, Russian, and Turkish baths.

In the process of arranging for goods to be shipped to St. Augustine and marketing his hotels to the northeastern states, Flagler discovered that transportation to the site was a problem. To alleviate that problem, he began to acquire and reorganize local railroad lines. Eventually, he consolidated the lines and created the East Coast Lines, laying tracks southward along the coast toward Daytona Beach and thereby acquiring thousands of acres of public land grants from the state for his railroad-building activities. When Flagler's rail lines reached the Lake Worth area, he built the Royal Poinciana, which, with 1,500 rooms, was the world's largest hotel when it opened in 1894. Two years later, he built Breakers, a 500-room hotel. Around this time, Flagler also created the resort community of West Palm Beach, which soon after eclipsed St. Augustine. The elite from New York, Philadelphia, and Chicago traveled on Flagler's trains to this winter pleasure palace, and, by 1900, it had truly become the "Newport of the South."

During 1894 and 1895, Florida suffered from a series of winter freezes, and Flagler decided to extend his rail lines farther south, where the winter weather was even warmer. He settled on Dade County and negotiated thousands of acres in land grants from private landowners in exchange for promising to bring rail service to a little town called Fort Dallas on the Miami River and Biscayne Bay. When the railroad reached the site in 1896, the town was incorporated as Miami, and Flagler built a huge hotel there, the Royal Palm, which opened in 1897. He also built a rail terminal, an electric plant, a sewage system, waterworks, docks and wharves, and, after dredging the Miami River, a harbor for ocean vessels. In addition, he laid out miles of streets; donated land for a civic center, public buildings, schools, parks, and churches; and started a newspaper called the *Miami Metropolis* at a time when the city had only a few hundred year-round residents. By 1910, rapidly growing Miami was already the state's fifth-largest city, with a resident population of 11,000 and tourist accommodations for 100,000 visitors. Flagler took advantage of his extensive holdings to subdivide a tremendous amount of land for highly profitable sales and to develop additional hotels and other properties.

Besides the various railroad land grants, Flagler had acquired several large landowning companies in Florida—including a former canal promoter—and consolidated them all into his Florida East Coast Canal and Transportation Company, which also became the holding company for his railroad lines. Flagler made enormous profits by the timely linking of his land sales and development activities to the provision of rail service. In 1897, he added shipping to his transportation and development plans, founding the Florida East Coast Steamship Company to offer improved access from Miami to Havana, Nassau, and Key West, again building hotels and other projects and selling land in Nassau and Key West. His final project was extending the railroad to Key West, a major engineering achievement. Henry Flagler rode the inaugural train 225 miles (363 kilometers) over land and sea from his home in West Palm Beach to Key West for the grand opening in 1912. When he died a year later, the hotel, railroad, and land baron left an enduring legacy on the form and pattern of development and growth in the Sunshine State.

Henry E. Huntington and Southern California's First Boom

At the same time Henry Flagler was building the Hotel Ponce de Leon on the Atlantic Coast, southern California was in the midst of a wildly speculative land boom brought on by the arrival of transcontinental railroad service. Los Angeles was a small pueblo community of fewer than 6,000 inhabitants when it first began negotiating in the early 1870s for

the Southern Pacific to extend its railroad lines to the town. The Angelenos offered free land, an ownership share in their local railroad, $600,000 in cash borrowed through municipal bonds, and other subsidies to the Southern Pacific before its chief executive, Collis P. Huntington, finally agreed to expand to Los Angeles during the 1880s.

The Atchison, Topeka, and Santa Fe Railroad was also building a new line over the mountains to terminate in Los Angeles, and, by 1887, the Santa Fe and the Southern Pacific were fighting a rate war to establish dominance in the market for coast-to-coast travel to southern California. At one point, they cut fares so low that passengers could ride all the way from Kansas City to Los Angeles for one dollar. The rate war brought in vast numbers of tourists, and the new rail connections to the East and Midwest set off a subdivision boom that lasted for one frenzied year and then quickly crashed. In Los Angeles County, 1,350 new subdivision maps were recorded in 1887, compared with ten in 1880 and 70 in 1890. In 1887, real estate transactions in the city of Los Angeles topped $100 million; only New York City and Chicago had more that year. Prices for acreage and for subdivision lots rose ten to 20 times higher within the year, only to drop back down again by 1888.

In all, the 60 new cities and towns covering 80,000 acres (32,400 hectares) that were laid out and marketed in 1887 and 1888 contained enough land to house several million people at low densities. Yet, by 1889, fewer than 3,500 people were living in those communities. Though Los Angeles itself grew to a population of 50,000 by 1890, other boom towns quickly became ghost towns. One such town was Border City on the Mojave Desert, platted by Simon Homberg on land bought from the federal government. With great fanfare, he sold lots that cost him about ten cents each to East Coast investors for $250 each; when the buyers found out the true nature of their nearly worthless purchase, the market dried up like desert air.

The land speculation boom and bust in 1887 and 1888 left the Los Angeles real estate market in a somewhat weakened condition during the 1890s, and the national depression of 1893 added to local difficulties. Nonetheless, the long-term prospects for Los Angeles's growth turned out to be promising. Even during the 1890s, the population doubled in size, and, by 1901, the city was poised for a major revival of real estate activity. The most important figure in this revival was Henry E. Huntington, vice president of the Southern Pacific Railroad and nephew of its president, Collis Huntington.

When Collis Huntington died in 1900, Henry inherited an enormous fortune. He did not succeed in gaining control of the Southern Pacific, however, and left his position to embark on an entirely new venture in urban development based on interurban railroads. Huntington moved from San Francisco to Los Angeles and incorporated the Pacific Electric Railway in 1901. Earlier he had acquired the Los Angeles Railway, a downtown-oriented commuter service. The Pacific Electric, on the other hand, reached far out into the suburbs and to sparsely settled and mostly undeveloped areas of the vast metropolis.

Huntington laid out a transportation network over southern California that stretched from the San Fernando and San Gabriel valleys of Los Angeles County all the way to Newport Beach on the Pacific Coast in central Orange County. By 1910, his various railway companies together covered more than 1,300 miles (2,100 kilometers), making Huntington the owner of the largest private interurban transit system in the world. Many southern California communities owed their rapid growth in the first two decades of the 20th century to Huntington's rail service. By 1920, the population of Los Angeles City reached 576,000, and Los Angeles County was home to nearly 1 million people. The landscape of the metropolitan region was so strongly shaped by Huntington's rail network that many of today's freeways follow the old Pacific Electric rights-of-way.

The normal practice for streetcar extensions before Huntington's rise called for landowners to pay the transit company for capital costs in anticipation of the appreciation in property values once service was instituted. Huntington did not bother to pursue such an incremental strategy. He had his own capital and easy access to lenders and investors. Besides, he was his own biggest landowner along most of the

suburban transit routes. The Huntington Land and Improvement Company and several other of his entities bought, subdivided, and sold real estate wherever the Pacific Electric's "big red cars" rolled along their tracks. Huntington brought rail service to areas he considered ripe for land development, even when the existing ridership was minimal. In many cases, those areas did grow rapidly once they became accessible through electric rail transportation. Depending on the target market, Huntington developed a wide variety of residential subdivisions, with lots of different sizes and prices and different deed restrictions, landscaping, street plans, and utilities.

In subdividing and selling land, Henry Huntington often worked closely with William May Garland, one of Los Angeles's leading real estate brokers and developers. Huntington was also a partner in the powerful syndicate headed by the owners of the *Los Angeles Times.* The syndicate made an estimated $100 million profit on the purchase of 108,000 acres (44,000 hectares) of arid land in the San Fernando Valley and the subsequent subdivision and reselling of that same newly irrigated land after the completion of the 238-mile (384-kilometer) Owens Valley Aqueduct, which was paid for by the taxpayers of Los Angeles (and immortalized in the motion picture *Chinatown*).

Huntington's real estate developments ranged from exclusive upper-class areas in Pasadena and San Marino, where his own house was located (which is now the Huntington Museum and Library), to middle-class communities such as South Pasadena, Huntington Beach, and Redondo Beach, to working-class suburbs such as Alhambra, where Henry Huntington developed industrial land and even established his own large factory to promote industrialization and the availability of new homesites. Huntington Beach and Redondo Beach had oil wells, and, though residential development was the primary focus of Huntington's subdivisions, many of his projects also included commercial development, particularly retail stores and hotels; some even included industrial land uses such as power stations.

Another element of Huntington's ambitious metropolitan real estate development strategy was to move into the utilities business as a way of providing

Downtown Los Angeles lined with streetcars and automobiles in the midst of a southern California real estate boom fueled by extensive rail service to outlying areas.

necessary services to enhance the value of the land he was selling and to take advantage of his ownership of considerable land acreage and the transit system. Given that the Los Angeles Railway and the Pacific Electric were major users of electricity, Huntington established the Pacific Light and Power Company to provide hydroelectric and steam power both to his transit operations and to the areas that he was developing. By 1913, Pacific Light and Power was supplying 20 percent of the metropolitan region's electricity and natural gas as well as all the power for Huntington's streetcars. Having acquired so much rural land to obtain a source of water to generate power, Huntington also organized the San Gabriel Valley Water Company to supply fresh water to San Marino, Alhambra, and the greater Pasadena area.

The interrelationship of transportation, infrastructure, utilities, and real estate development that Henry Huntington exemplified on such a grand scale is aptly illustrated by a local joke from 1914. A mother was taking her daughter on a trolley ride to the beach. The daughter asked, "Whose streetcar are we riding in?" Her mother replied, "Mr. Huntington's." Passing a park, the girl asked, "What place is that?" "Huntington Park," responded her mother. "Where are we going, mother?" "To Huntington Beach" was the answer. Finally arriving at the sea, the child ventured one more query: "Mother, does Mr. Huntington own the ocean or does it still belong to God?"[17]

SUMMARY

This chapter reveals how real estate in the 1800s began to contribute significantly to the country's overall economic growth. The railroads' twofold involvement in real estate—as transporters and as land developers and owners—strongly promoted new development.

Once the federal and state governments began privatizing the public lands, real estate became the great American pastime. At the same time that large tracts of land were exchanging hands and undergoing subdivision and development, the public sector was becoming more involved in financing those activities. It was also looking to the real estate industry for new sources of public revenue. Thus, the period saw the creation of large private fortunes made hand in hand with government support.

The next chapter explores the industry's continuing evolution from the late 1800s through World War II.

TERMS

► Capital improvement project
► Deed restrictions
► Fee simple
► Ground lease
► Homesteaders
► Land development
► Slums
► Subdivision
► Syndicate

REVIEW QUESTIONS

4.1   How was public land put into private ownership?

4.2   Describe the fee simple system of private ownership.

4.3   What was the Holland Land Company noted for?

4.4   What effect did private deed restrictions and public controls have on real estate in the 19th century?

4.5   Who was Llewellyn Haskell?

4.6   What is the balloon-frame method of construc-

tion, and what effect did it have on residential development?

4.7   Describe the evolution of slums.

4.8   Discuss the role of the railroads in land development.

NOTES

1. See, for example, A.M. Sakolski, *The Great American Land Bubble: The Amazing Story of Land-Grabbing, Speculations, and Booms from Colonial Days to the Present Time* (New York: Harper, 1932); Glenn S. Dumke, *The Boom of the Eighties in Southern California* (San Marino, Calif.: Huntington Library, 1944); and Homer B. Vanderblue, "The Florida Land Boom," *Journal of Land and Public Utility Economics*, May 1927, pp. 113–131, and August 1927, pp. 252–269.

2. Sakolski, *The Great American Land Bubble*, pp. 147, 164.

3. Larry Van Dyne, "The Making of Washington," *Washingtonian*, November 1987, p. 172.

4. Elizabeth Blackmar, *Manhattan For Rent, 1785–1850* (Ithaca, N.Y.: Cornell Univ. Press, 1989), p. 36.

5. Sakolski, *The Great American Land Bubble*, p. 9.

6. Blackmar, *Manhattan For Rent*, pp. 31–32.

7. Sakolski, *The Great American Land Bubble*, p. 82.

8. Ibid., pp. 84–85.

9. Eugene Rachlis and John E. Marqusee, *The Land Lords* (New York: Random House, 1963), p. 3.

10. Kenneth T. Jackson, *Crabgrass Frontier: The Suburbanization of the United States* (New York: Oxford Univ. Press, 1985), p. 77.

11. Ann Durkin Keating, *Building Chicago: Suburban Developers and the Creation of a Divided Metropolis* (Columbus: Ohio State Univ. Press, 1988), p. 73.

12. Jackson, *Crabgrass Frontier*, p. 80.

13. Keating, *Building Chicago*, p. 76. See also Gwendolyn Wright, *Moralism and the Model Home: Domestic Architecture and Cultural Conflict in Chicago, 1873–1913* (Chicago: Univ. of Chicago Press, 1980).

14. Jacob Riis, *How the Other Half Lives: Studies among the Tenements of New York* (New York: Scribner's, 1890).

15. Carroll D. Wright, *The Slums of Baltimore, Chicago, New York, and Philadelphia. Seventh Special Report of the Commissioner of Labor* (Washington, D.C.: U.S. Government Printing Office, 1894).

16. *Platt* v. *Union Pacific R.R. Co.*, 9 U.S. 48 (October 1878).

17. William B. Friedricks, "A Metropolitan Entrepreneur Par Excellence: Henry E. Huntington and the Growth of Southern California, 1889–1927," *Business History Review*, Summer 1889, p. 354.

CHAPTER 5

The Late 1800s to World War II

I n the latter half of the 19th century, a massive wave of industrialization took place in the United States, much of it concentrated in cities. Urban areas became magnets for an immense population migration from rural areas at home and abroad, people looking to start their own businesses or to work in the factories, stores, and offices of the expanding metropolis. Adna F. Weber's landmark 1899 study, *The Growth of Cities in the Nineteenth Century,* fully documents this rapid urbanization, which he called "the most remarkable social phenomenon."[1] As cities gained population, they also spread out over a great deal of additional territory, with technological and organizational improvements by the public and private sectors in transportation, utilities, infrastructure, and urban services encouraging the mass movement of industry and residences away from the crowded city center. All but the richest and the poorest moved to outlying neighborhoods in search of newer and better housing and, in many cases, homeownership on cheaper land. Factories and warehouses moved along with the workers to industrial districts where space costs were lower, facilities were more modern, and it was easier to ship goods.

This chapter looks at the changing growth of cities and the increasing involvement of government and regulators in real estate development. It was a volatile era, encompassing two world wars and the Great Depression. The chapter covers several topics:

► Central business districts and commercial development;
► The beginning of the public sector's modern role;
► The real estate boom of the 1920s;
► Finance; and
► The Great Depression and World War II.

CENTRAL BUSINESS DISTRICTS AND COMMERCIAL DEVELOPMENT

What was left behind in the city center as people began moving farther and farther out of the city? High-volume, high-value activities that represented

This chapter was written and updated by Marc A. Weiss, PhD, chair and CEO, Global Urban Development, Washington, D.C.

Pittsburgh's downtown experienced remarkable growth in the late 1800s. Liberty Avenue, circa 1910, was one of the main streets leading to the convergence of the Allegheny and Monongahela rivers.

both the new concentration of wealth and power and the rise of the new administrative and consumer-oriented society. The central business district or "downtown" was the region's focal point for the largest banks, insurance companies, corporate headquarters, newspaper publishers, government functions, professional offices, general and specialty retailing and wholesaling, hotels, cultural activities, and much more. The main railroad and streetcar lines all terminated in and radiated out from downtown, bringing in and taking home most of the metropolitan population every day to work, shop, obtain services, and be educated and entertained.

As land values rose in the central core, many industrial and residential land uses were outbid, forced out, torn down, and replaced by an incredible commercial building boom. In downtown Pittsburgh, for example, more than 400 new buildings were completed in just a five-year period in the late 1880s and early 1890s, and nearly as many were completed over the next decade.

The Growth of the Skyscraper

No symbol of the prosperous new corporate-commercial city and its growing downtown was more potent than the tall building or "skyscraper." Most skyscrapers were office buildings that replaced church spires as the highest points of reference—though perhaps not reverence—for the entire urban community and its rural hinterland.

By the 1880s, the invention of a workable electric elevator made it possible for buildings to rise above the previous six stories that represented the limit of how many flights of stairs people were willing to walk on a daily basis. Indoor plumbing, electric lighting, and other inventions made building interiors livable and functional, while the advent of structural steel frame construction enabled builders to transcend the constraints on physical height imposed by traditional masonry construction. Instead of thick, heavy load-bearing walls that could support only so much weight and volume, the new steel skeletons with light masonry curtain walls and plate-glass windows allowed buildings to soar hundreds of feet in height in the 1880s and eventually to top 1,000 feet (305 meters) half a century later.

Life insurance companies erected many of the earliest and most prominent office buildings. The largest of these firms had substantial long-term capital to invest in real estate, needed their own headquarters, and desired to communicate visually their financial strength to millions of current and prospective policyholders. In New York City in the late 19th century, Manhattan Life, Mutual Life, Equitable, Prudential, Metropolitan, and others competed to build the tallest and most impressive structure. A similar battle took place among major metropolitan newspaper publishers, who desired the symbol of a distinctive office tower as a marketing device to boost circulation, advertising revenue, and prestige. Again in New York City, the Tribune and Evening Post Buildings took the early lead but were soon eclipsed in 1892 by publisher Joseph Pulitzer's New York World Building, which, at 309 feet (94 meters), was the first structure in the city taller than the steeple of Trinity Church. Not to be outdone, the *New York Times* fought back a decade later with the 362-foot (110-meter) Times Tower.

Two years later, the Singer Sewing Machine Company, a manufacturing corporation whose consumer products were distributed globally, stunned both the insurance and newspaper businesses by announcing plans to construct a new headquarters building more than 600 feet (183 meters) tall. The Singer Building on Broadway in lower Manhattan, designed by the distinguished architect Ernest Flagg, was, when completed in 1908, twice as high as nearly all of New York's and the world's other skyscrapers—and 40 feet

(12 meters) taller than the Washington Monument in the nation's capital. The *New York Times* called a 34-story building under construction at the same time "a comparative dwarf alongside the Singer Tower"; ten years earlier this "dwarf" would have been the world's tallest building.[2]

Singer, however, was rapidly overshadowed by the Metropolitan Life Tower, which, when completed in 1909, was nearly 100 feet (30 meters) taller. Some city residents became so alarmed by the perceived negative impact of the new towers on urban overcrowding, sunlight, and safety that they lobbied municipal authorities to impose limitations on building height. By the 1890s, Boston and Chicago passed such restrictions, to be followed by Washington, D.C., Los Angeles, and several other cities. In most cases, the maximum permitted building height ranged between 100 and 200 feet (30 and 61 meters). But by the 1920s, many of these regulations had been lifted or modified to allow continued vertical expansion.

Even though corporations put their names on skyscrapers for advertising value and usually also owned their headquarters buildings, they definitely did not occupy all the office space. A great deal of it was leased to a variety of business and professional tenants. Not surprisingly, the new downtowns spawned a specialized real estate industry in architecture, construction, brokerage, and property management. The demand for office space was sufficiently strong that real estate developers and investors also put up purely speculative buildings to compete with the large company headquarters structures. In New York City, Singer's neighbors included the Trinity Building and the United States Realty Building, both built speculatively without an anchor or "name" tenant. A more famous example is the attractive and unusual triangle-shaped Flatiron Building on Fifth Avenue and Broadway, designed by the well-known Chicago architect Daniel Burnham and completed in 1903. The Flatiron Building was occupied primarily by wholesalers and many other small firms.

The most important early commercial office building developers were the Brooks brothers from Boston. Peter and Shepherd Brooks were Boston property investors who in 1873 acquired the seven-

Once New York City's most famous skyscraper, the Flatiron Building (originally known as the Fuller Building), at the intersection of Fifth Avenue and Broadway, was designed by Daniel H. Burnham and completed in 1903. The facade is rusticated limestone, with French Renaissance details.

story Portland Block, Chicago's first office building equipped with a passenger elevator. From this initial investment, the Brooks family developed many of the key structures that pioneered the world-famous Chicago school of architecture, noted for the design and construction of large commercial buildings during the late 19th century. The Portland Block, completed in 1872, was designed by William Le Baron Jenney, who later served as architect for the Home Insurance Building, considered by many to be the first modern skyscraper because of its pioneering use of steel frame construction. The Portland, also the first building in which every office enjoyed direct sunlight, paid off handsomely for the Brooks brothers and was completely occupied from the 1870s until its demolition in 1933. Peter and Shepherd Brooks hired Owen Aldis, an attorney, to manage the Portland Block and serve as their real estate agent in

Chicago. By the turn of the century, Aldis was managing 20 percent of the office space in downtown Chicago. He and his nephew, Graham Aldis, became national leaders in commercial building investment and management.

In 1881, Peter and Shepherd Brooks decided the downtown Chicago real estate market was robust enough to support construction of the city's first ten-story building, the Montauk Block. Peter Brooks wrote Owen Aldis that "an office building erected to suit modern notions, thoroughly equipped with modern appliances, would fill up with modern tenants, leaving the old and unremodeled houses to the conservative fogy."[3] He wanted a building whose modern construction techniques, attractive and simple design, and quality materials, methods, and maintenance would project a businesslike image of efficiency and strength: "The building throughout is to be for use and not for ornament. Its beauty will be in its all-adaptation to its use."[4] The architectural partners Daniel Burnham and John Wellborn Root designed the Montauk Block plus two other Brooks-Aldis office buildings of the 1880s, the Rookery and the Monadnock Block. The Brooks brothers and Owen Aldis teamed up to develop two other major Chicago office structures in the 1890s, the Pontiac Building and the Marquette Building, both designed by another famous architectural firm, Holabird and Roche.

Peter and Shepherd Brooks's and Owen Aldis's guidelines for the design of their numerous buildings included "height sufficient to warrant the use of elevators, as much light as possible, easy maintenance, high percentage of rentable space, and ornament sufficient to avoid absolute plainness."[5] Aldis also wrote rules for building management when the Marquette was completed in 1894, with the basic thrusts of the eight points being that building first-class space and providing first-class services are the best investments. It certainly turned out that way for Peter and Shepherd Brooks, who earned a substantial return on their investment in developing and owning Chicago office buildings. Owen Aldis also did extremely well financially from his investments and fee income. The buildings developed by Brooks-Aldis were fully rented when they opened in the 1880s and 1890s, and, though the Montauk was demolished in 1902, the others maintained high occupancy rates all the way through the mid-1960s. Interestingly, Aldis's leasing strategy was to "arrange [a] typical layout for intensive use." He went on to note:

> A large number of small tenants is more desirable than large space for large tenants because: a) a higher rate per square foot can be added for small tenants; b) they do not move in a body and leave the building with a large vacant space when hard times hit; c) they do not swamp your elevators by coming and going by the clock.[6]

The Growth of Downtown Hotels, Apartment Buildings, and Department Stores

High-rise office buildings were among the most distinctive new features of the rapidly growing urban downtowns, and they were soon joined by other prominent new structures and land uses. Large hotels, many of them also rising many stories, were an increasingly vital feature of downtowns, attracting business customers and the rapidly expanding tourist trade to meetings, social functions, entertainment, and, most important, the thousands of new guest rooms. Henry Flagler's thriving Florida hotel operations, though winter resorts, also anchored the downtowns of several growing cities, particularly Miami. In New York City, the heirs and descendants of John Jacob Astor built the luxurious Waldorf-Astoria Hotel in the 1890s on the site of their parents' mansions. Elsewhere, Potter Palmer in Chicago, Henry Huntington in southern California, and other developers built similar "grand hotels."

Another emerging urban innovation of the late 19th century, related to the residential hotel, was the apartment house. As land values rose in the central area, it became increasingly uneconomical to build or maintain single-family detached houses or attached townhouses other than as mansions for the wealthiest people. Spacious apartments, complete with the latest physical amenities and a wide assortment of extra services, provided an attractive alternative for many upper- and middle-class urbanites desiring to live close

to the business and entertainment world of downtown. Some of the buildings with the most services and facilities, including dining rooms, were even called apartment hotels. This vertical lifestyle had already become popular in Paris by the mid-19th century, and, when first transplanted to the United States, the apartments were often referred to as "French flats."

The original American prototype for the French flat was the fashionable Stuyvesant Apartments in Manhattan, developed by rich socialite Rutherford Stuyvesant in 1869. Richard Morris Hunt, the first U.S. architect to be trained at the Ecole des Beaux Arts in Paris, designed the Stuyvesant. By 1900, apartment buildings accounted for an increasingly important use of land in New York City, Chicago, Boston, San Francisco, Washington, D.C., and a few other cities. Luxury apartments and working-class tenements were located in separate neighborhoods close to downtown, and middle-class multifamily dwellings were built farther out along the many avenues and boulevards traversed by streetcar lines.

The other major innovative urban land use was massive, multistory facilities for retail trade, originally called dry goods or general stores and, by the late 19th century, department stores. These massive structures, often designed as "pleasure palaces" with ornate exteriors and lavish interiors, catered especially to women shoppers. The stores employed service-oriented sales personnel and offered special events and promotions. The first major department store was Alexander T. Stewart's elaborate dry goods center, the Marble Palace, which opened in 1846 on Broadway and Chambers Street in New York City. Later in the century, larger and more spectacular department stores covering entire city blocks and serving as major downtown institutions flourished in many cities, including Filene's in Boston, Rich's in Atlanta, Marshall Field's in Chicago, The Emporium in San Francisco, Dayton's in Minneapolis, Hudson's in Detroit, Robinson's in Los Angeles, and several others. In every case, these stores acted as magnets for the real estate market. When Marshall Field's changed locations in Chicago from Lake Street to State Street in 1867, its new site became the prime "100 percent corner" almost immediately.

The Waldorf-Astoria Hotel, built in the late 1890s by the descendants of John Jacob Astor in Second Empire style.

One of the greatest of all the department store ventures was Wanamaker's in Philadelphia. John Wanamaker and his partner, Nathan Brown, opened Oak Hall, their original men's and boys' clothing store, on the ground floor of a six-story building on Sixth and Market streets in downtown Philadelphia in 1861. Their business philosophy, which Wanamaker elaborated throughout his long retailing career, called for selling decent-quality merchandise

at one everyday low price and guaranteeing money-back returns on all goods. Wanamaker emphasized a democratic, egalitarian ethic with his slogan "no favoritism."[7] Every customer was to be treated with equal respect, to be charged the same low prices, and to be served properly. In the early years, Wanamaker's made only cash sales, refunded only cash, and paid its workers daily in cash.

By the 1870s, Oak Hall proved so successful that John Wanamaker purchased an abandoned rail depot from the Pennsylvania Railroad and built the world's largest department store, a huge two-acre (0.8-hectare) dry goods emporium at Thirteenth and Market streets. Perhaps foreshadowing today's successful retail centers in former train stations, such as Union Station in Washington, D.C., Wanamaker dubbed his store "the Grand Depot." The new store opened in 1876 in the midst of the centennial celebration of the Declaration of Independence, which brought 10 million visitors to Philadelphia over a six-month period for a major exhibition in Fairmount Park. And one of the big tourist attractions was Wanamaker's Grand Depot. A year later, Wanamaker was already expanding, building an addition on Chestnut Street that connected through a stylish arcade to the main store. The Chestnut Street store, with its own separate and ornate entrance, was designed to specialize in "ladies' goods," which eventually became an even bigger business for Wanamaker's than its already brisk trade in men's and children's clothing, hats, and shoes. Linens, appliances, housewares, furniture, pianos, and everything else imaginable were eventually added to various departments in the acres of retail space. Sales reached nearly 100,000 items on a single day in December 1896, breaking all previous records.

For many years, John Wanamaker's at Thirteenth and Market, with its distinctive clock tower, was known around the world as one of Philadelphia's central landmarks. In 1908, the Chestnut Street store was demolished and replaced by a much larger, block-long structure, complete with its own subway station. In 1896, Wanamaker acquired Alexander T. Stewart's flagship store, built in 1862 at Tenth and Broadway in Manhattan as an "uptown" branch of

The grand atrium of Wanamaker's downtown Philadelphia store in 1911. This neoclassic, 13-story building was a block long.

THE BEGINNING OF THE PUBLIC SECTOR'S MODERN ROLE

As cities grew larger and more complex in the late 19th and early 20th centuries, governments became increasingly involved in providing municipal services, promoting the development of public infrastructure, and regulating private real estate development. The advent of industrialization reinforced the urban trend away from the "walking city" and toward a growing separation of work and residence so that commuting, traffic congestion, and transportation technology all became more important public concerns. As greater numbers of people migrated to cities, issues ranging from overcrowding to pollution to public health and safety to the need for light, air, and adequate recreation all became subjects of heated debate. Concern over these issues led to various proposed solutions, to new forms of public intervention in private markets, and to the rise of urban and metropolitan planning.

Industry and trade brought rising prosperity to the cities, though many citizens disliked the unpleasant side effects such as filth and noise. In response and to celebrate their new wealth and power and the success of U.S. democracy, municipalities launched "City Beautiful" campaigns to construct attractive and often monumental public buildings—city halls, libraries, museums, and schools. Another element of this movement was the establishment of public parks, both large "pleasure gardens" and smaller neighborhood parks and playgrounds. New York City established its massive Central Park during the 1850s, and the principal designer, landscape architect Frederick Law Olmsted, then spent the next four decades designing parks and parkways in many cities across the country, including San Francisco's Golden Gate Park, Brooklyn's Prospect Park, and park systems for Boston, Chicago, and Buffalo.

Along with civic centers and parks came parkways—wide streets that coursed through parks or other natural settings—and boulevards—tree-lined thoroughfares bordered by buildings and other urban scenery. Although these roads initially were intended for leisurely promenading in carriages or automobiles, many of them later turned into principal trans-

the Marble Palace, and reopened it as Wanamaker's New York City store. After a decade of growing sales, Wanamaker constructed a huge 16-story structure next to the old A.T. Stewart's Building, creating again one of the world's largest shopping complexes, with three separate stores: The Woman's Store, The Man's Store, and the Wanamaker Galleries of Furnishing and Decoration. (The last included "The House Palatial and Summer Garden," which brought in 70,000 shoppers on opening day.) By the time John Wanamaker died in 1922, Wanamaker's, like other major department stores, was beginning to build suburban stores at prime locations near commuter train stations. Despite the subsequent urban decentralization, the role of Wanamaker and other central city department store owners in creating the modern commercial downtown is an enduring legacy.

portation arteries overflowing with traffic. Given that 30 to 40 percent of the land in a typical city was used for streets and highways, the constant need to expand and upgrade the roadways preoccupied local governments. Further, local governments assumed responsibility for franchising, regulating, financing, building, maintaining, planning, and coordinating the movement of people and goods around and through urban areas. Structures such as docks, port facilities, bridges, and tunnels for cities on water; railroad lines and railway terminals for every city; and streetcars, subways, mechanized transit lines, and trucking all came under the purview of the public sector. These new areas of activity added to the already expanding demands for the public provision of infrastructure and utilities such as water and sewer systems and to the burgeoning growth of essential services, from police protection to street cleaning.

A good example of this expansion of government led by private initiative is the 1909 Plan of Chicago sponsored by the Commercial Club, a powerful downtown business group, and authored by businessmen and professionals led by architect Daniel Burnham. The purposes of the plan were to establish the central area firmly as a modern corporate and commercial downtown, to reclaim the lakefront for recreational use and the development of luxury housing, and to encourage suburban growth by constructing radial highways emanating from downtown Chicago and designating regional forest preserves to maintain suburban open space. Nearly $300 million in public funds was spent during the first two decades of the 20th century to implement the plan, supplemented by a great deal of private investment and massive promotional campaigns by the Commercial Club and the Chicago Plan Commission.[8] The plan had wide-ranging effects:

► Downtown rail lines were covered over and air rights developed for parks, office buildings, and consolidated passenger terminals.
► The wholesale produce market was relocated to accommodate construction of the bilevel boulevard-style Wacker Drive along the Chicago River.

► Building the Michigan Avenue Bridge opened up the Magnificent Mile retail and office district and the Gold Coast residential neighborhood on the near north side.
► Other new bridges built over the Chicago River improved access to downtown.
► Chicago's "frontyard" was redeveloped and filled in with attractive new lakefront parks such as Grant Park and Burnham Park, museums, cultural institutions, the Navy Pier, and expanded and improved existing lakefront parks.
► Several major streets were widened and new thoroughfares developed.
► Suburban regional parks were created.

Public works proved to be a strong stimulus for private commercial and residential development, and Chicago citizens who voted for the many bond issues were pleased with the results.

One problem of urban living was the threat of fire from so many wooden buildings so close together. Major portions of Boston, Baltimore, Chicago, and San Francisco had been destroyed by conflagrations in the late 19th and early 20th centuries, and smaller fires were a common occurrence in cities everywhere. To safeguard the dense urban environment, cities not only organized fire departments but also increasingly promulgated building codes to improve the safety of urban structures. By the late 19th century, some municipalities prescribed fire-protective limits in the center city, requiring all new buildings to be constructed of brick. In addition to focusing on fireproof materials, building codes regulated building materials and methods of construction to increase the safety and longevity of structures. Because building codes regulated only general construction, many cities also developed specialized housing codes to require minimum standards of habitability for new and existing dwelling units.

Also in the latter part of the 19th century, cities began to limit to certain areas within the city those hazardous but necessary business and industrial activities that might cause fires or expose people to disease, harm, or noxious odors. Selective prohibition of these uses by geographic location was an early form of land use zoning. The first local government to initiate a broad zoning law was Los Angeles, which in 1908 divided the entire city into residential and industrial districts. Many cities, including Los Angeles, also imposed limitations on building height, with Boston and Washington, D.C., establishing differential height districts to allow taller buildings in the downtown than in the rest of the city. By 1916, New York City combined height and use restrictions with regulations on lot coverage and building bulk to create "comprehensive zoning." A series of U.S. Supreme Court decisions between 1909 and 1926 validated this new form of public limitation on private property rights, and, by the end of the 1920s, most large cities and many smaller towns and suburban villages (more than 1,000 in all) had enacted zoning ordinances and established planning agencies to implement the new regulations (see Chapter 13 for more detailed information about zoning practices).

Why did property owners agree to abridge their rights and exchange laissez-faire laws for stricter government supervision? In some cases they did not agree, and a great deal of protest and controversy ensued. But overall, the private sector—not just community groups but also many real estate entrepreneurs—strongly favored the growing number of public laws and codes regulating urban development and land use. They supported zoning restrictions to stabilize real estate markets, increase property values, and encourage new investment because they understood that the restrictions enabled them to build or buy property with less risk of unfavorable change on the adjoining lots and the surrounding neighborhoods. They welcomed subdivision controls for introducing a level of coordination that enabled both private developers and local governments to plan, finance, and construct more efficiently the new infrastructure and amenities that were essential to the success of real estate development projects.

Even before the introduction of zoning and other types of government controls, real estate owners and developers had created their own system of private restrictions that were written into property deeds as contractual obligations. Deed restrictions—a private form of land use regulation that evolved in the 19th

Built in 1900, the 15-story Continental Building in downtown Baltimore, a classic early skyscraper in the Chicago style.

century—established the precedents and models later used in promulgating public sector development controls. Several state and local governments supported the application of these privately negotiated restrictions on property owners by publicly enforcing them in civil courts. More direct and extensive public intervention came in the 20th century after leaders of the real estate industry recognized that greater powers and flexibility for local governments were needed to regulate urban property and land uses more broadly and extensively than private efforts had been able to accomplish.

THE ROARING TWENTIES

After a relatively dry spell in the period immediately before, during, and after World War I, the construction of downtown office space burgeoned in the 1920s, in structures of all shapes, sizes, and heights.

Near the end of the decade, the Thompson-Starrett Company of New York, one of the world's largest private construction firms that specialized in skyscrapers, surveyed the country's 173 largest cities and found nearly 5,000 buildings ten stories or higher, many of them built during the 1920s. This list included hotels, department stores, manufacturing lofts, civic centers, and other private and public structures, but private office buildings predominated.[9]

Although New York City accounted for more than three-fifths of the total for the entire country, many other cities had significant and growing numbers of skyscrapers. Boston, Chicago, Detroit, Los Angeles, New York, and Philadelphia all had more than 100 buildings taller than ten stories. Baltimore, Cleveland, Dallas, Houston, Kansas City, Minneapolis, Pittsburgh, St. Louis, San Francisco, Seattle, and Tulsa each had at least 30 buildings ten stories or higher. The growth in the height and bulk of these structures was made possible by new building technology but was fueled also by the increasing economic productivity and urban wealth of the 1920s and the tremendous expansion of cities both outward and upward. By the late 1920s, financing was flowing freely from institutional lenders, equity syndicators, and mortgage bond houses, further encouraging the construction of speculative office space. New organizations and methods of equity financing through the sale of stock—under the aegis of such firms as the Fred F. French Investing Company or Harry Black's United States Realty—and debt financing—through the likes of the S.W. Straus mortgage bond company—fed the rapid private development of high-rise commercial and residential buildings.

Of the buildings listed in the 1929 census of skyscrapers, 377 were more than 20 stories high, with 188 in New York City, including what was then the world's tallest: the 55-story, 792-foot-high (241-meter) Woolworth Building constructed in 1913 by the Thompson-Starrett Company. This neogothic "cathedral of commerce" was the corporate headquarters of the F.W. Woolworth Company, and its owner, Frank Woolworth, had paid $13 million in cash to build a monument to his empire of retail stores. The building had no mortgage, and though it advertised the Woolworth name, most of the office space was leased to other firms.

By the late 1920s, office buildings were going up so fast and American business tenants, investors, and real estate developers were all in such a confident mood that several new structures, including the 77-story, 1,030-foot-high (314-meter), art deco Chrysler Building, far surpassed the Woolworth Building in height and prominence. The building that was to become the world's tallest for more than four decades, the Empire State Building, was not a corporate headquarters like some of the other giant skyscrapers but rather a purely speculative office building built quickly in what many considered a poor location (see Figure 5-1).

The Rise of Urban Apartment Buildings And Suburban Single-Family Houses

One of the most notable trends of the 1920s was the tremendous increase in the construction of apartment buildings. Outside of New York City and a handful of other major cities, earlier waves of urbanization in the United States had been based on a relatively low-density pattern of small, detached single-family houses, attached rowhouses, or duplexes. Some cities, including Boston, had triple deckers, and in many cities, large older houses were subdivided into multiple apartments.

This pattern began to change dramatically during the 1920s. Real estate investors, developers, lenders, and contractors all became active participants in the production of new apartment buildings. The apartments were built primarily as rental units, though in a few cities, some of the buildings were sold to occupants for cooperative ownership. The new structures, built mainly with brick or stucco exteriors, ranged from fashionable luxury residences with doormen and other services to more modest housing and from individual six-unit buildings to high rises and large complexes equipped with schools, parks, and community centers.

Perhaps the largest private rental housing development of the decade was the 2,125-unit, moderate-income Sunnyside apartment complex in New York City, with rents subsidized through a ten-year property tax abatement provided by the municipal government. The Metropolitan Life Insurance Company developed

| Figure 5-1 | The Story of the Empire State Building |

The site of the Empire State Building was attractive to its investors because a very large parcel of land, 197 feet by 425 feet (60 meters by 130 meters), was available. The old Waldorf-Astoria Hotel, which sat on that parcel, was slated to be demolished when the new hotel on Park Avenue was completed. After developer Floyd Brown, who had bought the site in 1928, defaulted on his mortgage payments, the property was sold to the Empire State Company, and the hotel was demolished just a few weeks before the stock market crashed in October 1929. Despite the crash, the Empire State Company, partially owned by the du Pont family and headed by former New York Governor Al Smith, decided to move forward with the project in the face of what it incorrectly perceived to be a brief economic downturn. The company invested a total of $45 million to acquire the site, demolish the hotel, and design and construct the world's tallest building, all in less than 18 months! The actual construction, managed by the general contracting firm of Starrett Brothers and Eken, took less than a year. At the peak of activity, 3,500 construction workers were adding one story a day. By the official opening on May 1, 1931, the building stood 1,250 feet (381 meters) tall, with 85 floors of offices and the equivalent of another 17 floors devoted to the magnificent mooring mast and observation decks.

When completed, the Empire State Building's skeleton consumed 57,000 tons (51,700 metric tons) of steel. The finished building contained 51 miles (82 kilometers) of pipe, 17 million feet (5.2 million meters) of telephone cables, and seven miles (11 kilometers) of elevator shaft.

One reason for the speed of construction was that in those days commercial leases in New York expired on April 30, and if the Empire State Building were not ready for occupancy on May 1, the company would have to wait an entire year to attract tenants—a costly delay. The rationale for building it so tall was that the syndicate had paid record high prices for a location at 34th Street and Fifth Avenue that was less than ideal for a quality office skyscraper: the principal office districts were at 23rd Street near Madison Square, 42nd Street near Grand Central Station, and downtown around Wall Street. The Empire State Building stood alone in the middle of a low-rise section of hotels, department stores, shops, and loft buildings, relatively far from the Grand Central and Pennsylvania Railroad Stations and several blocks from the nearest subway lines. The extreme height and distinctiveness of the building were designed to serve as an advertising beacon to attract office tenants.

Similarly, key architectural features were intended to maximize the net revenue that could be generated by the

The completed Empire State Building in 1931—the symbol of New York for more than 75 years. The facade is made out of limestone, granite, aluminum, and nickel, with a hint of art deco ornamentation.

rentable space. For example, the building is less bulky than was permitted under the zoning laws. By designing almost the entire building as a setback tower over a wide, five-story base, the developers increased the rents per square foot by offering offices that were quieter and had more natural light. By building shallow floors with window access for every office, the developers also eliminated the disadvantage of their location relative to other tall buildings, offering prospective tenants panoramic and unobstructed views. In this design, constructing less space per floor made each square foot more valuable. Similarly, rather than building a simple flat rectangular structure that would have produced four corner offices on each floor, the Empire State Building was recessed in the north and south towers so that the extra angles of the structure would yield eight to 12 corner offices per floor, adding significantly to the potential rent.

continued on next page

Figure 5-1	The Story of the Empire State Building *(continued)*

The physical achievement of the Empire State Building obscures the fact that, like today's projects, it too had to meet legal and financial requirements for feasibility. John Jacob Raskob, one of five partners in the development, asked his architect, William Lamb, "Bill, how high can you make it so it won't fall down?" The real question was, how high and still profitable? The answer depended on a stipulation in New York City's 1916 zoning ordinance that above the 30th floor, a building could occupy no more per floor than one-fourth of the total area on its lot. With two acres (0.8 hectare) of ground, the Empire State tower could cover half an acre (0.2 hectare). Lamb determined that 36 million cubic feet (1 million cubic meters) would be a profitable size; he then began playing with alternatives. The 16th iteration (Plan K) was it: an 86-story tower. His client Raskob declared, "It needs a hat" and in a creative burst suggested a mooring mast for a dirigible. The 200-foot (61-meter) mast, intended to be an international arrival point for lighter-than-air craft, extended the building's total height to 1,250 feet (381 meters). Because of high winds, the mast never worked as intended, but it was eventually used for observation. During the Great Depression, income from the observation platform offset large office vacancies and kept the Empire State Building in business.

Unfortunately, all the developer's sophisticated planning and marketing strategies designed to cope with the basic circumstances of no preleased tenants, a poor location, and a terrible office market during the Great Depression were in the short run to little avail. The building stood mostly vacant throughout the 1930s and was widely nicknamed "The Empty State Building." With the return of full employment and prosperity in the 1940s, however, the building filled up and has proved successful. Rather than being a symbol of a corporate, government, educational, medical, or cultural institution, the Empire State Building stands after more than 75 years as a symbol of commercial real estate development.

the apartments in 1922 to help ease New York's severe housing shortage. As an experiment in direct ownership and management of rental housing, Sunnyside proved economically successful and induced the insurance firm to build many larger apartment projects across the country during the 1930s and 1940s.

Living in Parisian-style apartments suddenly became more fashionable for many middle- and upper-income people. For families across the income spectrum, apartments offered a cost-effective form of housing. Rents were relatively high because of the lack of supply resulting from the low level of new residential construction during and immediately after World War I. With the growth in postwar housing demand, apartments became a good investment. The volume of apartments increased steadily throughout the decade, remaining at a high level of new construction starts through 1928. Starts of single-family housing, by contrast, peaked in 1925 and dropped sharply thereafter. Nearly 40 percent of all the dwelling units built during the 1920s were multifamily units. Further, the annual percentage of total residential construction devoted to multifamily dwellings rose from approximately 25 percent in 1921 to more than half

of all residential building permits issued in 1928. In every region of the United States and in all urban areas, the absolute number and relative percentage of apartments expanded significantly.

New single-family houses also were built in record numbers during the 1920s. The peak year, 1925, established an all-time high for starts of new housing that remained unsurpassed until 1950. The level of U.S. nonfarm homeownership escalated by more than 5 percentage points from 1920 to 1930. Urban decentralization and suburbanization spread in all directions across the metropolitan landscape, the number of private automobiles increased by the millions, disposable income and savings among the middle class rose substantially, and land subdividers carved up an astonishing amount of acreage at the periphery of cities into building lots for sale. Massive land speculation and wild price escalation ensued in many rapidly growing areas of the country, helping to induce an unfortunate degree of mismanagement and fraud. In Florida alone, enough lots were subdivided, many of them in swampland or literally under water, to house the entire population of the United States.

At the height of the boom, new suburban subdivisions came onto the market daily along the country's "crabgrass frontier." Although most of the subdivisions were only modestly improved with basic infrastructure and amenities, a small but significant group of community builders was increasingly developing large-scale, well-planned, fully improved subdivisions complete with extensive landscaping, parks and parkways, and shopping centers. This pattern of development, with roots in the 19th century, became more common and expanded in both the scale of operations and degree of capital investment during the 1920s. The most eloquent exponent of this trend was Jesse Clyde Nichols of Kansas City, Missouri, developer of the world-famous Country Club District and a founder of the Urban Land Institute (see profile).

The Spread of the Garden City

Part of what inspired J.C. Nichols to build his ideal of a stable, family-oriented, and beautifully landscaped community was his exposure to the European Garden City movement during his college years. In 1898, Sir Ebenezer Howard published the first edition of his international classic, *Garden Cities of Tomorrow,* and the following year founded the International Garden City Association in London.[10] By 1904, Letchworth, the first of the English garden cities, was under construction. The Garden City movement was a response to the rapid growth and overcrowding of the grimy, unsanitary, and crime-ridden industrial cities of the West. Howard envisioned balanced, self-contained, and modestly sized communities, each with an adequate economic base of manufacturing employment near workers' housing; democratically self-governing institutions with public ownership of land and community facilities; physically well-planned surroundings with plenty of greenery, open space, and easy transport; and linkages to a regional system of small cities separated by a permanent greenbelt of agricultural land.

The philosophy of the Garden City movement comprised four elements: environmental reform, social reform, town planning, and regional planning. Many development efforts, including J.C. Nichols's Country Club District, were motivated primarily by interests in

▶ **PROFILE**

J.C. NICHOLS AND THE DEVELOPMENT OF THE COUNTRY CLUB DISTRICT IN KANSAS CITY, MISSOURI

Jesse Clyde Nichols returned home to Kansas and entered the real estate business upon graduating from Harvard University in 1903. He started as a small, speculative homebuilder, building and selling single-family houses on vacant lots in a partially improved subdivision. Two years later, he acquired a ten-acre (4-hectare) subdivision just south of the city limits of Kansas City, Missouri, and began planning his vision: the long-term development of a large and high-quality urban community. By 1908, with capital from a group of wealthy investors, he had gained control of more than 1,000 acres (405 hectares) on Kansas City's south side, calling it the Country Club District to emphasize its proximity to the Kansas City Country Club. Eventually, those 1,000 acres would contain 6,000 houses, 160 apartment buildings, and 35,000 residents.

By the 1920s, J.C. Nichols had already established the Country Club District as one of the most attractive and expensive communities in the region. The J.C. Nichols Company employed the well-known landscape architect George Kessler, who had previously designed a "City Beautiful" plan for Kansas City that included an elaborate park and parkway system, to do the initial planning and landscaping of the Country Club District. Later, S. Herbert Hare became the Country Club District's chief landscape designer. Nichols worked with the city government to extend and build two of the new parkways, the Ward and the Mill Creek, through the Country Club District, giving the community excellent transportation connections to the downtown and a vital community amenity. Ward Parkway became among the most fashionable addresses in Kansas City.

Nichols relied extensively on long-term deed restrictions to control the design, cost, and use of all private property in the district. For years, he advertised the Country Club District as "the one thousand acres restricted." Nichols invested heavily in a wide range of community facilities from landscaped parks to public art and in an ambitious program of community activities from pageants and regattas to flower shows. In

continued on next page

J.C. Nichols's Country Club District promised "spacious grounds for permanently protected homes, surrounded with ample space for air and sunshine."

addition, he was one of the first developers to establish a mandatory homeowners' association that collected fees to help legally enforce, revise, and renew deed restrictions, finance and maintain community facilities and activities, and establish an active, participatory community identity.

J.C. Nichols engaged in practices that were unusual for real estate developers in his day, and he was generally ahead of his time. Nichols regularly installed first-rate infrastructure in advance of development, adding its costs to the prices of the lots for sale. He also engaged architects to design model homes and built many houses both on a speculative basis and under contract with lot purchasers. Finally, Nichols saw the potential for developing and owning retail centers as a profitable enterprise and as a strategy for building community atmosphere, and over the years he developed and owned many neighborhood shopping centers. His flagship was a regional retail and office complex in the heart of the district called Country Club Plaza, developed beginning in 1922. Designed with a unified Moorish-Spanish architectural theme and controlled by centralized management, the plaza provided both

on- and off-street parking, was well located for public transit, and drew a walk-in trade from residents of apartment buildings and workers in office buildings that Nichols developed nearby. Even today, both the district and the plaza are the "in" places to live and shop in Kansas City.

The restrictive covenants unfortunately discriminated against racial, ethnic, and religious minorities, as was standard on most deed restrictions before the U.S. Supreme Court ruled such provisions legally unenforceable in 1948. And the district in general catered primarily to upper-income people, though beginning in the 1930s and 1940s, Nichols shifted some of the newer subdivisions to smaller houses and lots for a middle-income clientele. Yet for creative and successful real estate entrepreneurship over half a century, Nichols's achievements stand out. He provided leadership to the real estate community as an officer of the National Association of Realtors®, to the urban planning community as a founding member of the American Planning Association, and to large-scale developers in particular as the first chair of the Urban Land Institute's Community Builders Council.

environmental reform and town planning, with far less stress placed on the other two elements.

Radburn

The most ambitious attempt to give full expression to Ebenezer Howard's ideas in the United States was with the City Housing Corporation (CHC) of New York

headed by Alexander Bing. Bing, who along with his brother Leo was a successful developer of luxury apartment buildings in Manhattan, became more public spirited during his service as a housing consultant to the federal government during World War I. After the armistice, he was determined to embark on a path of social reform. Linking up with a group of visionaries called the Regional Planning Association of America headed by critic Lewis Mumford and architects and planners such as Clarence Stein, Henry Wright, and Catherine Bauer, Alexander Bing attracted sufficient investment capital to establish the City Housing Corporation with the intention of building a garden city in the United States. After developing one successful preliminary project called Sunnyside Gardens in New York City, the CHC bought a large parcel of land in Fair Lawn, New Jersey, within commuting range of Manhattan, and, in 1928, began developing Radburn, "a town for the motor age."

Planned and designed primarily by Clarence Stein and Henry Wright, Radburn incorporated many innovative features, such as the separation of vehicular and pedestrian traffic through the use of bridges, underpasses, and footpaths. Another major innovation was the use of extra large "superblocks" with interior parks and culs-de-sac to create common open green space, keep automobile through-traffic away from houses, and economize significantly on the typical costs of land and infrastructure development. Radburn also modeled new ways of establishing an unincorporated self-governing community through strict, comprehensive deed restrictions and an active and well-funded homeowners' association. Although Radburn received global publicity and many of its planning ideas were widely imitated, it ran into the economic crisis of the 1930s, and only a small portion of the original design was actually built. The CHC encountered serious cash flow problems and was eventually forced into bankruptcy. Yet the development of Radburn remains one of this country's best-known and most-admired experiments in for-profit, speculative community building by a private real estate developer.

Shaker Heights

Shaker Heights is a model suburban community near Cleveland, Ohio, where the Van Sweringen brothers developed the financial skills that enabled them to take over a major railroad and an important section of downtown Cleveland—with almost none of their own money. Oris P. and Mantis J. Van Sweringen were minor land developers in the Cleveland area in 1900 when they first approached the Buffalo syndicate that owned the property formerly occupied by a Shaker

religious community. For more than ten years, the Buffalo group had been attempting to sell the property, which was valued at $240,000. The Vans, as they became known to Clevelanders, eventually convinced the Buffalo syndicate to give them a free 30-day option on a small section of the property. The option agreement contained a further option for an additional section twice the size of the first for a period twice as long as the first period. If they exercised that option, the Vans would receive additional options.

The Van Sweringens were consummate salesmen and convinced a number of Cleveland's leading citizens to join their development syndicate. After exercising a few of the options, they bought the entire property of 1,400 acres (567 hectares), which they later expanded to 4,000 acres (1,620 hectares).

The Van Sweringen brothers had learned during an earlier venture that transportation was critical to successful suburban development, but the president of the Cleveland Railway Company rejected as impractical their proposal that the company contribute an extension to the existing railway line to serve the new Shaker Heights community. As a result, they decided to build their own railroad.

First, they identified a ravine in which the railroad tracks could run without hindrance of any grade crossings and then began to buy the needed land. Eventually, it was necessary for them to purchase an entire railroad (called the Nickel Plate) for $8.5 million to complete the right-of-way. In addition, they acquired four acres (1.6 hectares) of land in downtown Cleveland's Public Square to construct a terminal for their new commuter railroad.

By June 1929, they had spent more than $2 million on their development of Public Square, including a new railroad station, a 36-story office tower, a department store, and a hotel. By then, more than 15,000 people lived in Shaker Heights, on land valued at more than $80 million.[11]

The Birth of Industry Trade Associations

The vigorous spirit of reform and modernization that characterized the early 20th century paralleled the tremendous growth and institutional development of the real estate industry through the movement for "professionalization." Many elements of the flourishing real estate business organized trade associations to upgrade standards of practice; to isolate, ostracize, and, where possible, eliminate unsavory activities; and to cooperate with the public sector and other segments of the business world and the general public to protect the interests of real estate and enhance its political stature and economic viability.

The National Association of Realtors® (NAR), for example, was established in 1908 to seek government licensing of the brokerage business. Operating through local boards of Realtors®, the NAR lobbied for public regulation of all participants in the larger industry combined with self-policing of smaller and more select groups of members. The NAR promoted real estate education and research and played a role in many public policy issues, from urban planning to property taxation. Its Home Builders and Subdividers Division was a national leader in the formulation of federal housing policy in the 1920s and 1930s.

Two other groups organized during this period were the Building Owners and Managers Association (BOMA International) and the Mortgage Bankers Association of America (MBA). BOMA represented the owners and property managers of the rapidly growing number of skyscrapers and other large commercial buildings in central cities and later also in the suburbs. Its focus was on professional training for management combined with a unified voice for relevant public policy issues. The MBA was originally called the Farm Mortgage Bankers Association, but it adopted an urban focus and assumed a new name during the early 1920s. At that time, mortgage bond houses and mortgage lending companies—allied with real estate brokers, developers, and life insurance companies—were rapidly evolving and expanding the variety of capital financing instruments available to acquire and develop property. The MBA later increased its national prominence with the advent of the federal government's new housing finance system in the 1930s and 1940s.

FINANCE

In real estate more so than in most other investments, capital costs are generally high relative to current incomes; therefore, the means of financing is a critical factor in the ability to engage in transactions and in the likely success or failure of projects. To compensate for the first problem, real estate is normally a valuable physical asset that makes excellent collateral for securing loans. Thus, while cash or equity investment has always been important in financing real estate, increasingly during the past two centuries, new institutions were created and methods devised to establish real estate as a highly leveraged form of enterprise operating chiefly on borrowed funds. Easily available credit has usually fueled real estate booms as well as excessive speculation and overbuilding. Conversely, when lenders turn off the spigot, tight money becomes the bane of the industry, leading at times to decreasing supply, declining sales, falling prices, rising defaults and foreclosures, and illiquid markets—as was the case in 1991 and 1992.

An important source of credit has always been sellers, including landowners and building owners, subdividers, and speculative builders. Sellers "taking back paper" in the form of land contracts, purchase-money mortgages, second mortgages, assumables, and a host of other "creative financing" instruments, all of which permit purchasers to buy now and pay later, have been significant players in the history of U.S. real estate markets. Beginning in the 1880s, subdivider William E. Harmon launched what became a successful enterprise by selling subdivision lots with as little as a 5 percent downpayment and the rest due in small monthly installments.

Before the advent of the Federal Housing Administration (FHA), mortgage insurance, and Veterans Administration (VA) home loan guarantee programs, "builders' mortgages" were an essential component in the sale of one- to four-unit housing. Developers acquiring acreage from farmers and other rural landowners often negotiated complex transfers of ownership and repayment schemes in an attempt to bridge the gaps of time and cash flow. Brokers also entered the field; many real estate sales firms maintained mortgage and loan departments as a service to their clients and helped generate a greater volume of sales (and thus sales commissions) and additional profits from the loan business itself.

Another traditional supplier of funds for real estate has been networks of local investors, including direct financing from friends, relatives, and wealthy individuals, lending through the vehicle of a trust company or mortgage company and providing equity capital by forming or joining syndicates and limited partnerships. Richard Hurd, most famous today for writing the classic *Principles of City Land Values* in 1903, for many years headed the Lawyers Mortgage Company in New York City, gathering money from prosperous investors and then making first mortgage loans on commercial and residential real estate that was strictly limited to high-quality rental buildings or "income properties" in the best locations.[12] Hurd's instincts for good value and his low-risk strategy led to a successful track record in loan safety and relatively high yields.

In contrast to Richard Hurd, mortgage bond houses such as S.W. Straus flourished during the 1920s by selling securities backed by the frequently overinflated values of new office and apartment buildings. Before the 1929 stock market crash, funds flowed into mortgage bond sales, and securities dealers arranged for highly speculative new construction simply as a minor detail associated with issuing and selling more bonds. After the crash, even the most optimistic appraiser had to admit that the buildings were grossly overvalued; not only did the borrowers default for lack of sufficient tenants to generate cash flow but the bond houses themselves also went bankrupt and left vast numbers of investors with little or nothing of what had often been promised as a guaranteed high yield and timely return of principal and interest.

Throughout the 19th century and up to the 1920s, the main source of financing for home mortgages was private individuals who operated mainly through the various methods described in the preceding paragraphs. Since that time, financial institutions have played the dominant role in all types of real estate finance; indeed, the growth of these institutions is an important part of the story of real estate development. This chapter looks at the histories of these financial intermediaries to obtain a clearer perspective on their contemporary decision making. Chapters 7, 8, and 9 examine how these financial intermediaries operate today.

Commercial banks are the oldest of the institutions that have been involved in making both construction loans and mortgage loans. These banks have participated heavily in real estate lending, often to the point of insolvency during periods of economic and financial crisis. Financial "panics" and banking problems were so common in the 19th century that when the federal government introduced national bank charters in the 1860s, the charters expressly prohibited urban real estate mortgage lending. State-chartered commercial banks were under no such constraints, however, and continued to be major real estate lenders. National banks were permitted to get back into urban mortgages beginning in 1916, and they expanded real estate lending significantly during the 1920s.

Because commercial banks relied primarily on short-term deposits to obtain funds for lending, they generally preferred and were often required to lend for short terms, either through construction loans or through mortgages on properties for as short a term as one year. Until well into the 1930s, most bankers considered a three- to five-year mortgage loan to be both long term and risky. Normally, though, short-term mortgages were renewable; in fact, borrowers simply assumed that they could keep rolling the loans over for years to come. When the market turned down and the banks got into trouble, however, lenders called the loans or refused to refinance them, often forcing borrowers into default and foreclosure. Historically, the system of real estate credit has been far more unstable than it is even in today's volatile world.

Life insurance companies have always been important players in real estate, both as owners and as lenders. Since the mid-19th century, 25 to 50 percent of life insurance companies' investment portfolios have been in real estate assets. Life insurance companies have traditionally been involved in financing and purchasing large-scale projects such as office buildings, shopping centers, and apartment complexes. Beginning in the 1920s, some life insurance companies also entered into mortgage lending on single-family houses.

Mutual savings banks have also been major real estate lenders. Located primarily in the northeastern United States, mutual savings banks were significant institutions in some cities. Nationally, however, their role and influence in residential lending was eclipsed by the advent of savings and loan associations. Also called building and loan associations, homestead associations, cooperative banks, and thrift institutions, S&Ls evolved in the mid-19th century specifically to promote homebuilding and homeownership for people of modest incomes. Savings were pooled through monthly savings plans, and money was loaned for the construction or purchase of one- to four-family dwellings. Though S&Ls charged higher interest rates than other mortgage lenders in order to pay a higher return to their depositors, their loan terms were more favorable in two ways: higher leverage—they lent up to 75 percent of the property's appraised value when most other lenders advanced only 40 percent or 50 percent on first mortgages; and longer terms—S&Ls used amortized monthly loan repayment plans for up to 12 years while most other lenders used nonamortized balloon mortgages with semiannual interest payments and the entire principal due in one to five years.

By the 1920s, S&Ls had emerged as the leading residential lender among financial intermediaries, particularly for single-family homes. Life insurance companies and commercial banks dominated commercial and industrial real estate lending. Although syndica-

tions, mortgage companies, and a variety of other noninstitutional lenders remained important, the major trend in real estate lending was the increasing role of financial institutions, especially in the field of housing. For example, the institutional share of residential mortgage debt increased from less than half during the 1890s to two-thirds by 1912. The total percentage of owned houses that were mortgaged rose from 25 percent in 1890 to nearly 40 percent in 1920 and to more than 50 percent in New England and the Mid-Atlantic states, where the larger financial institutions were concentrated. More and more, "sweat equity" was being supplanted in real estate by a debt-driven system that encompassed entrepreneurial producers and institutional financiers.

THE GREAT DEPRESSION AND WORLD WAR II

The long boom of the 1920s came to an abrupt end when the stock market crashed in October 1929. Though most people believed that the economic downturn was only a temporary setback—that prosperity was just around the corner—in fact the Great Depression was the longest and most severe economic depression in our nation's history. Starting in 1929, output and employment fell steadily for four straight years, finally hitting bottom in 1933. At the low point, one out of every four people was out of work, desperately seeking but unable to find any kind of job.

The bubble had burst on the real estate boom even before the stock market crash, though many eager speculators had not realized that they were in for such a hard landing. Most real estate markets had reached their peak in 1926, the same year that the Florida land boom collapsed. Investment in real estate, construction, property sales, and values had been slowly spiraling downward since 1926. Real estate activity, though declining in most markets, was still continuing at a high level relative to the early 1920s or the previous decade, and, in certain categories such as construction of new urban office and apartment buildings, the markets still appeared to be flourishing.

By the late 1920s, however, the speculative craze for subdivision lots was abating, and many of the

Soup lines formed in major cities across the country to feed the many unemployed workers during the Great Depression.

legions of people who had bought on credit in antici-pation of rapid and profitable resales were defaulting on their loans and property tax assessments. A major disaster loomed. Soon most of the mortgage bond issues were in default and foreclosure, with many bondholders losing their capital, leading to widely publicized investigations of fraud and corruption during the 1930s, similar to the S&L collapse in the 1980s. As banks increasingly faced a crisis of liquidity after 1929, they refused to make new real estate loans or to refinance existing ones, often calling in loans to be repaid immediately. That approach was self-defeating because it brought the further collapse of markets and the failure of thousands of banks. Millions of deposi-tors lost much or all of their savings.

Through 1931, new investment, development, sales, and leasing continued in many markets, and real estate entrepreneurs kept hopes alive; in the fol-lowing year, however, everything began grinding to a halt, and bankruptcy became the normal state of affairs. Financing was unavailable, and real estate plummeted in value. Much of the market was frozen, flooded with for-sale and rental properties that no one wanted—even at heavily discounted prices and rents. By 1933, nearly half of all home mortgages were in default and 1,000 properties were being fore-closed each day. Annual construction starts of new housing had dropped by more than 90 percent from the record-breaking peak of 937,000 units in 1925 to the dismal trough of 93,000 units in 1933.

Into this escalating crisis stepped the federal gov-ernment, at first gingerly under President Herbert C. Hoover—with considerable prodding in 1931 and 1932 from the Democratic Congress—and then forcefully under the New Deal of President Franklin D. Roosevelt. Failing banks and securities markets were reorganized and stabilized as federal deposit insurance and a new regulatory apparatus helped restore the public's and investors' confidence. Public works programs were initiated on a massive scale that dwarfed any previous peacetime federal spending, with billions of dollars to employ millions of jobless workers in building and rebuilding the nation's infra-structure—roads, bridges, tunnels, highways, dams, power plants, airports, waterways and ports, railroad

and transit lines and terminals, parks, playgrounds, schools, health clinics, community centers, civic administration buildings, public housing, and a host of other facilities.

The ever-changing and -expanding alphabet soup of federal agencies—the RFC, PWA, CWA, WPA, TVA, and many others—played key roles in financing, contracting with, and mobilizing state and local gov-ernments and the private sector. Collectively, this effort built a better economic future while putting people immediately to work and stimulating the rebirth of economic activity and growth. In many real estate mar-kets during the worst years of the 1930s, government-supported development and redevelopment projects were the only action in town. These mainly federal public works initiatives helped encourage two forms of entrepreneurship that flourished during the New Deal: the powerful public works manager, best symbolized by New York's Robert Moses (see profile), and the large-scale private contractor, exemplified by Califor-nia's Henry J. Kaiser (see profile).

Bailing Out the Financial Institutions

Public works was only one of the strategies New Dealers used to revive both the general economy and one of its most important sectors: the construction and development industry. By 1933, the field of pri-vate housing had suffered an almost complete col-lapse, and the entire system of residential financing that had grown so rapidly during the 1920s with its crazy quilt of land contracts, second and third mort-gages, high interest rates and loan fees, short terms, balloon payments, and various other high-risk and speculative practices had come crashing down like a house of cards. In the wake of this panic of defaults and foreclosures, the federal government intervened to transform the rules of the financial game and move the sale and construction of private housing out of the doldrums.

The first federal actions in housing finance focused on bailing out the savings and loan associations. S&Ls had mortgaged 4.35 million properties during the 1920s, lending out more than $15 billion to home-builders and purchasers. By the early 1930s, thousands of these institutions were insolvent as a result of bad

ROBERT MOSES

Robert Moses directed the construction of parks and parkways for the state of New York beginning in the 1920s. In 1933, Mayor Fiorello LaGuardia appointed him parks commissioner for New York City. During the New Deal, LaGuardia lobbied in Washington for billions of dollars in federal public works funds, and Moses built many of the projects, including the complex and expensive Triborough Bridge, which opened in 1936. As chair of the Triborough Bridge Authority, Moses discovered that semi-independent public authorities could amass considerable long-term power so long as the authority's management continued to control an activity that generated sufficient revenue to repay debt and accumulate a surplus. These authorities could successfully finance their operations through the sale of bonds and then retire those bonds through a dedicated revenue source, such as bridge tolls. (In the early days of the Triborough, the federal Reconstruction Finance Corporation was the only willing bond buyer, though later private investors bought the bonds.) Moses's extensive multibillion dollar development activities as head of several authorities for more than three decades helped establish public authorities as critical organizations in the real estate field. During the early 1970s, for example, under the leadership of Austin Tobin, one of Robert Moses's most powerful competitors among public authority chief executives, the Port Authority of New York and New Jersey built the massive twin office towers of the World Trade Center in lower Manhattan, at that time the world's tallest buildings.

loans, overvalued properties, and the inability to raise sufficient new capital. President Hoover and the Congress responded to the crisis by establishing the Federal Home Loan Bank System in 1932, which merged and reorganized bankrupt S&Ls, encouraged the creation of new federally chartered S&Ls that would be better capitalized and more strictly regulated, and, most important, provided vitally needed liquidity for federal- and state-chartered thrifts, helping to free them from their traditional dependence on short-term commercial bank credit. Two years later came the Federal Savings and Loan Insurance Corporation, which greatly strengthened the attractiveness of S&Ls to savers by insuring deposits and helping to standardize the management of thrift institutions. S&Ls also were granted a series of income tax and regulatory benefits in exchange for the requirement that they continue to lend money primarily for residential mortgages (a requirement that remained in force until the Reagan Administration's monetary "reforms" of 1982).

Other dramatic structural changes occurred in the 1930s. The federal government created the Home Owners' Loan Corporation (HOLC) in 1933 and the Federal Housing Administration in 1934. The HOLC refinanced more than $3 billion of shaky or defaulted mortgages and introduced long-term (15-year) self-amortizing loans to many borrowers who were not familiar with the idea.

The Rise of the Federal Housing Administration

Although the HOLC was a temporary bailout operation that stopped making loans in 1936, the FHA was a permanent program that launched a revolution in housing finance. The FHA's mutual mortgage insurance system reduced the investment risk for lenders and brought the twin S&L principles of long-term amortization of mortgage loans and high loan-to-value ratios into the world of commercial banks, life insurance companies, mutual savings banks, and mortgage companies—institutions that had not previously used such underwriting practices. The FHA's initiatives encouraged lenders to increase the first mortgage loan-to-value ratio to an unprecedented 80 to 90 percent, to extend the length of the loan repayment period to 20 and 25 years, to eliminate second mortgages, and to lower interest rates and total loan origination fees significantly.

Among its many reforms, the FHA rationalized, standardized, and improved methods and practices of appraisal, universalized the use of title insurance, required the lender's monthly collection of property

HENRY J. KAISER

Henry J. Kaiser was a general contractor who built public works. Initially a road builder for governments in the western United States and Canada, in 1930 he put together a consortium of six large construction firms and successfully obtained the federal contract to build the massive Hoover Dam on the Colorado River in southern Nevada.

Beginning in 1933, Kaiser established a close working relationship with U.S. Secretary of the Interior Harold L. Ickes, who was one of a handful of key New Deal officials controlling the federal public works purse strings and dispensing billions of dollars in government contracts. During the 1930s, Kaiser-led teams won federal contracts to build both the Bonneville and the Grand Coulee dams, in addition to doing part of the work on the San Francisco–Oakland Bay Bridge and constructing Oakland's Broadway Tunnel and several other large projects. Headquartered in Oakland, California, Kaiser achieved national recognition as a shipbuilder during World War II and as a manufacturer of cement, gypsum, aluminum, chemicals, steel, automobiles, cargo planes, and jeeps.

During the war, Henry Kaiser built a substantial amount of emergency housing for the workers who were flocking to Richmond, California, Portland, Oregon, and Vancouver, Washington, to construct Kaiser's "liberty ships" for the U.S. Navy. After the war, Kaiser became interested in mass-producing houses and formed, in 1945, a partnership with Fritz Burns, a major southern California developer. Their new company, Kaiser Community Homes, built thousands of small, inexpensive, two- and three-bedroom single-family detached houses on the West Coast until it ceased production in 1950. During the mid-1950s, Henry Kaiser retired as chief executive of Kaiser Industries, remarried, and moved to Hawaii, where he became a major developer of resort hotels, recreational subdivisions, houses, shopping malls, golf courses, and convention centers until his death in 1967 at the age of 85.

taxes and property insurance as part of the loan payments, and helped popularize other methods for stabilizing real estate transactions and financing procedures. The FHA's insured mortgages became a standardized product and a safe investment that helped establish a nationwide mortgage market in place of previously idiosyncratic and localized submarkets. The entire home mortgage lending system began to shift from lending primarily on the security of the property in the event of foreclosure to lending mainly based on the borrower's projected income and ability to repay without default—a major conceptual change.

The FHA also promoted cost-efficient production of small houses and affordable homeownership for middle-income families. The FHA's conditional commitment enabled subdivision developers and merchant homebuilders to obtain debt financing for the large-scale construction of new residential neighborhoods and communities, complete with finished houses and full installation of improvements and ready for immediate occupancy by people who were able to buy with modest savings because they qualified for FHA-insured mortgages. The FHA model of real estate development represented a dramatic advance over the previous methods of subdividing and selling unimproved lots that had been fairly common in the 1920s.

The FHA's property standards and neighborhood standards helped improve the minimum level of quality in the design, engineering, materials, equipment, and methods of land development and housing construction. The FHA's Land Planning Division encouraged private planning by developers and builders and public planning by state and local governments to ensure the coordination of accessible transportation, recreational facilities, utilities, services, and land uses through comprehensive plans, official maps, zoning laws, requirements for setbacks, and regulations for subdivisions. The Land Planning Division also played a key national role in reshaping the design of suburban housing tracts, upgrading the use of deed restrictions for private planning and development, and reorganizing and extending the role of local and metropolitan public planning.

In addition, the FHA introduced new techniques for analyzing market demand and using stricter underwriting criteria to limit overbuilding and excessive sub-dividing. This element of market control was explicitly aimed at eliminating "curbstone" subdividers and "jerry-builders" and replacing them with community builders. More sophisticated market analysis and greater market control became necessary as a result of the FHA's primary emphasis on long-term financing of large numbers of homes in newly developed neighbor-hoods. FHA underwriters needed to know before development began that the market commanded a suf-ficient number of potential buyers for the planned houses, and that purchasers' incomes, market demand, and property values would either remain stable or rise over the 25 years the mortgages would be insured. The FHA's "risk-rating system" weighed several factors affecting the supply of and demand for housing, including patterns of urban employment, distribution of income, population growth, changes in the housing stock, formation of households, the locational dynam-ics of residential neighborhoods, and future land uses and property values.[13]

Within two years of the FHA's creation, new fed-eral and state laws to stabilize and restructure the com-mercial banking system, along with the creation of the Federal Deposit Insurance Corporation in 1933, enabled commercial banks to participate in the FHA's program. Life insurance companies and mutual sav-ings banks also took advantage of FHA insurance. They acted as primary lenders and also purchased and sold standardized and relatively low-risk FHA-insured loans. FHA-insured mortgages made possible the 1938 creation of the Federal National Mortgage Association (Fannie Mae). Fannie Mae, capitalized by the federal government's Reconstruction Finance Corporation (RFC), initiated a strong secondary market for FHA-insured mortgages, purchasing loans from primary lenders to provide them with both the liquidity to make new loans and additional income gained through the retention of servicing fees. This national secondary mortgage market helped smooth out the fluctuations in real estate business cycles as well as compensate for geographic differences in the availabil-ity of mortgage funds. Fannie Mae was particularly vital to the growth of modern mortgage banking com-panies, many of which started their high-volume busi-

nesses in the 1930s and 1940s based mainly on making FHA-insured loans for resale to Fannie Mae or to a life insurance company, a savings bank, or another group of lenders and investors.

The FHA's underwriting guidelines strongly favored new housing over existing homes, suburban locations over central-city sites, entire subdivisions over scattered building lots, single-family houses over apart-ments, and Caucasians over African Americans. For older cities and racial minorities, these policies were inequitable, discriminatory, and disastrous. But for the growth of white, middle-class suburbs, they were cru-cial. Though the FHA did insure mortgages on subur-ban garden apartments, its overall policy helped reverse the late 1920s trend toward increased construction of apartment buildings and instead boosted large-scale homebuilding and suburban homeownership.

By the late 1930s, the U.S. economy and housing markets were reviving, and the FHA was insuring more than one-third of all new homes; 98 percent of the FHA's insured mortgages were on single-family detached houses in new suburban subdivisions. The FHA's highest volume was in California, where the country's suburban future was already under construc-tion in the late 1930s. Fred Marlow, who headed the FHA's southern California office from 1934 to 1938, and Fritz Burns formed a private development com-pany and, beginning in 1942, built more than 4,000 FHA-insured houses in a new southwest Los Angeles subdivision called Westchester. The purchasers of the houses were primarily workers in the nearby and rap-idly growing aircraft industry. Westchester became a model for postwar suburban tract housing, and Fred Marlow and Fritz Burns both served as presidents of the National Association of Home Builders.

Housing after the Great Depression

While construction of new homes finally began rising after the long slump, much of the older housing stock was badly deteriorated and getting worse as a result of overcrowding, lack of maintenance, and other direct effects of the Great Depression. In 1937, President Roosevelt declared in his second inaugural address that "one-third of a nation [was] ill-housed, ill-clad, and ill-nourished."

Housing in a low-income Washington, D.C., neighborhood circa 1937.

In 1919, Edith Elmer Wood, a talented housing reformer with a PhD in political economy from Columbia University, wrote *The Housing of the Unskilled Wage Earner,* an eloquent book documenting the problems of low-income shelter and arguing for government aid as part of a positive solution. In 1935, the federal Public Works Administration (PWA) under Harold Ickes published Wood's *Slums and Blighted Areas in the United States.* Wood demonstrated in considerable detail that more than 36 percent of the American people were living in very substandard housing. In her 1919 book and in her *Recent Trends in American Housing,* published in 1931, Wood described various private, philanthropic, and public sector efforts to build decent and affordable housing in many areas of the country.[14] Except for New York City and a handful of other cities, however, substan-

tial government involvement did not begin to emerge until the early 1930s. The collapse of the private housing industry opened the way for public support and programs to stimulate employment and economic activity in urban real estate development.

Starting with RFC loans for limited-dividend housing companies building apartments at moderate rentals, the federal government established the PWA Housing Division in 1934 and the U.S. Housing Authority (USHA) in 1937 to support the removal of the worst slum dwellings and their replacement with brand new publicly owned rental housing. Under USHA's formula, local governments owned the housing, which was built by private contractors. Local authorities borrowed the funds by selling 40-year tax-exempt bonds to private investors, and the federal government repaid the principal and interest on the bonds through annual contributions. Operating costs of the housing were to be paid by the local government through rents collected from the tenants. By the time that World War II interrupted and changed the nature of the public housing program to providing temporary shelter for war workers, USHA and its predecessors had already produced more than 100,000 units of decent, safe, and sanitary dwellings in low-rise buildings. These well-constructed and attractively landscaped buildings provided a welcome new environment for many low- and moderate-income families.

Nathan Straus, chief administrator of USHA from 1937 to 1941, had been an early pioneer of private, limited-dividend housing development in New York City. During 1934 and 1935, he developed Hillside Homes in the Bronx, which was the largest private housing development built with a federal loan from the PWA. Clarence Stein served as the architect for Hillside Homes, and Starrett Brothers and Eken were the general contractors. The 26-acre (10.5-hectare) project consisted of low-rise and garden apartments for 1,400 families and included landscaped interior garden courts, a public school, a large central playground, clubrooms, a nursery school, a community center, and other recreational facilities. Straus, though initially a private developer, authored *The Seven Myths of Housing* in 1941, a spirited defense of America's public housing programs.[15]

Rockefeller Center

A major private development that tore down several blocks of older tenement housing was Rockefeller Center in New York City, one of the few big projects during the 1930s that was not publicly funded or subsidized. Rockefeller Center stands as the forerunner of today's large-scale urban mixed-use developments and continues to be among the best known and most successful of such projects.

Rockefeller Center's original parcel of land between Fifth and Sixth avenues and 48th and 51st streets belonged to Columbia University, which leased it for 46 years to John D. Rockefeller, Jr., in October 1928 at an annual rent of nearly $4 million—ten times the existing rental yield from the site.

The Rockefeller family lived on 53rd Street near Fifth Avenue and already owned a great deal of property in the neighborhood. In autumn 1928, New York City was in the midst of the real estate boom that preceded the stock market crash, and Rockefeller was extremely optimistic about his prospects for redeveloping the area. He originally planned to build a new Metropolitan Opera House on the site. The directors of the opera company wanted to relocate from their 45-year-old facility at 40th Street and Broadway because of encroachment by the garment industry. Ironically, the opera company eventually turned down Rockefeller's many appeals to become the centerpiece of his ambitious real estate venture, preferring to remain in place until the mid-1960s, when it finally moved to a new opera house built as part of the massive urban renewal project called Lincoln Center for the Performing Arts.

The Sixth Avenue portion of Rockefeller's site was considered a blighted area in 1928 because of the elevated railroad tracks running along the avenue. By 1939, a new Sixth Avenue subway was constructed and the elevated tracks removed, opening up new opportunities for private redevelopment. The Rockefeller Center site was extraordinarily large, and it was highly uncertain how all the land could be redeveloped and space occupied in the marketwide context of economic depression, falling rents, and rising vacancies. Teams of architects worked for several years on many different schemes, both with and without the opera house as a focal point. The buildings were planned in a relatively unified architectural theme of style and materials, enhancing the new and unusual image of a mixed-use center in a single development project. Innovative design features included the addition of private streets to cut up the long east-west blocks and the creation of the first privately developed public plaza in the city, which today houses the world's most famous outdoor ice-skating rink.

Lacking the high culture of opera, Rockefeller turned to mass culture as his best prospect for attracting commercial tenants to this untested location. By the mid-1930s, he had filled the 70-story RCA Building (now called the GE Building)—his main high-rise office tower—with radio, motion picture, and vaudeville businesses, including RCA, RKO, and NBC, that were thriving even during the Great Depression. He also developed on Sixth Avenue his own entertainment facility for the general public, the Radio City Music Hall, as well as the Center Theatre for opera and large-scale musical shows. Magazine, news service, and book publishers also gravitated to new office buildings in Rockefeller Center. On the Fifth Avenue side, Rockefeller constructed low-rise structures for international retail and office tenants, taking advantage of proximity to prestigious retailers across the street. By the early 1940s, the development had clearly succeeded as a desirable location for corporate office space, and since the 1950s, Rockefeller Center has expanded to the west across Sixth Avenue, with tall office buildings and major tenants ranging from Time-Life to McGraw-Hill to the Rockefeller family's own Exxon. At the same time, travel agents at street level, below-ground retail shops, and a tightly controlled and well-maintained environment all helped turn what was initially a risky, speculative, expensive, money-losing venture into the premier private real estate development of the Great Depression decade.

The Professionalization of Real Estate Development

Two new private organizations, both spin-offs of the National Association of Realtors®, emerged from the crucible of economic crisis and political reform that characterized the 1930s. The Urban Land Institute started as a small, elite organization of primarily large commercial and residential developers. ULI was charged with focusing on education and research, public policy issues, and improving standards and practices of private development. Initially, ULI organized into two key subgroups. The Central Business District Council sponsored a series of studies on urban decentralization and urged federal, state, and local government officials to establish and provide funds for urban renewal, urban highways, and other programs to redevelop physically and revitalize economically the commercial core of older central cities. The Community Builders Council, which

sponsored ULI's *Community Builders Handbook,* published in 1947, concerned itself with promoting high-quality, large-scale residential and commercial development in suburban areas.[16]

The National Association of Home Builders (NAHB) was formed in 1943 to lobby the federal government during wartime to allow the continued private development of for-sale and rental housing with the aid of FHA mortgage insurance. Some government policy makers favored limiting new housing to public construction and ownership during the wartime emergency, arguing that such an approach would be more cost-efficient and easier to manage in the context of allocating scarce resources for the war effort. The Home Builders Emergency Committee, led by Hugh Potter, a former lawyer and judge who developed River Oaks in Houston, fought for publicly subsidized housing for war workers to be built and owned by the private sector. In the end, a compromise permitted the development of housing under both public and private ownership. In the process, the Home Builders and Subdividers Division of NAR split from the parent organization and merged with a completely separate group called the National Home Builders Association. Together, the two groups became NAHB, with Fritz Burns of Los Angeles as the founding president of the new organization, which grew from an initial 1,300 members to more than 25,000 in less than a decade.

During World War II, the real estate industry in certain locations received an enormous economic boost from the surge in demand for new construction, land, and space in existing buildings. Yet many ventures not directly related to the war economy were put on hold for the duration, and some entrepreneurs eagerly awaited peacetime. Many people were apprehensive, fearing a replay of the Great Depression after the soldiers and sailors returned home and the production of so many new guns, tanks, ships, and planes was no longer necessary. Others were more optimistic, seeing a wave of growth precipitated by the rising disposable incomes and pent-up consumer demand that was accumulating during the war, when most people were earning much more than during the previous decade but were unable to spend their new wealth because a great deal of U.S. production capacity was diverted to the global battlefields. By 1948, the optimists were proved correct in their predictions, and the postwar suburbs—dependent on the automobile, homeownership, and a consumer boom—were in full swing.

SUMMARY

Expansion in the real estate industry characterizes most of the period from the end of the 19th century through the first half of the 20th century. Aggressive downtown commercial development and residential movement to the suburbs changed the face of the nation's cities and metropolitan regions.

The growing involvement of the public sector reinforced the private development process, and the changes in lending policies brought about by the creation of the FHA made residential development easier and dramatically increased the number of homeowners in the United States.

Chapter 6 looks at postwar development trends and how the real estate industry evolved into its present situation.

TERMS

- ▶ Central business district (CBD)
- ▶ City Beautiful movement
- ▶ Community builders
- ▶ Comprehensive planning
- ▶ Federal Housing Administration (FHA)
- ▶ Federal National Mortgage Association (Fannie Mae)
- ▶ Garden city
- ▶ Greenbelt
- ▶ Industrialization
- ▶ Mortgage
- ▶ Public Works Administration (PWA)
- ▶ Skyscraper
- ▶ Steel frame construction
- ▶ Subdivision controls
- ▶ Trade association
- ▶ Zoning

REVIEW QUESTIONS

5.1 What happened to downtowns as transportation allowed people to move farther and farther out of the city?

5.2 Discuss the history of the skyscraper—its construction, its symbolism, and how it shaped cities.

5.3 Discuss the role of the downtown department store at the turn of the century.

5.4 What was the City Beautiful movement?

5.5 What was a garden city and how did the movement evolve?

5.6 How did real estate trade associations come about?

5.7 How did the advent of creative financing change real estate markets in the United States?

5.8 What strategies were used in the New Deal to revive the Great Depression economy?

5.9 What was the role of the Federal Housing Administration in financing housing and homeownership?

5.10 Why was Rockefeller Center such an important project?

NOTES

1. Adna Ferrin Weber, *The Growth of Cities in the Nineteenth Century: A Study in Statistics* (New York: Macmillan, 1899), p. 1.

2. Paul Goldberger, *The Skyscraper* (New York: Alfred A. Knopf, 1981), p. 7.

3. Kenneth Turney Gibbs, *Business Architectural Imagery in America, 1870–1930* (Ann Arbor, Mich.: UMI Research Press, 1984), p. 45.

4. Ibid.

5. Ibid., p. 54.

6. Earle Shultz and Walter Simmons, *Offices in the Sky* (Indianapolis: Bobbs-Merrill, 1959), pp. 33–34.

7. *Golden Book of Wanamaker Stores* (Philadelphia: John Wanamaker, 1911), p. 47.

8. Marc A. Weiss and John T. Metzger, "Planning for Chicago: The Changing Politics of Metropolitan Growth and Neighborhood Development," in *Atop the Urban Hierarchy*, ed. Robert A. Beauregard (Totowa, N.J.: Rowman & Littlefield, 1989), pp. 123–151.

9. Thompson-Starrett Company, "A Census of Skyscrapers," *The American City*, September 1929, p. 130. See also Marc A. Weiss, *The Rise of the Community Builders: The American Real*

Estate Industry and Urban Land Planning (New York: Columbia Univ. Press, 1987); and Marc A. Weiss, "Skyscraper Zoning: New York's Pioneering Role," *Journal of the American Planning Association,* Spring 1992, pp. 201–212.

10. Ebenezer Howard, *Garden Cities of Tomorrow* (London: Faber & Faber, 1945), especially the introductory essays by Lewis Mumford and Frederic Osborn; and Marc A. Weiss, "Developing and Financing the 'Garden Metropolis': Urban Planning and Housing Policy in Twentieth-Century America," *Planning Perspectives,* September 1990, pp. 307–319.

11. Eugene Rachlis and John E. Marqusee, *The Land Lords* (New York: Random House, 1963), pp. 60–86.

12. Richard M. Hurd, *Principles of City Land Values* (New York: Real Estate Record and Guide, 1903).

13. Marc A. Weiss, "Richard T. Ely and the Contribution of Economic Research to National Housing Policy, 1920–1940," *Urban Studies,* February 1989, pp. 115–126; Marc A. Weiss, "Marketing and Financing Homeownership: Mortgage Lending and Public Policy in the United States, 1918–1989," *Business and Economic History,* 1989, pp. 109–118; and Weiss, *The Rise of the Community Builders.*

14. Edith Elmer Wood, *The Housing of the Unskilled Wage Earner* (New York: Macmillan, 1919); *Recent Trends in American Housing* (New York: Macmillan, 1931); and *Slums and Blighted Areas in the United States,* Public Works Administration, Housing Division Bulletin No. 1 (Washington, D.C.: U.S. Government Printing Office, 1935).

15. Nathan Straus, *The Seven Myths of Housing* (New York: Alfred A. Knopf, 1941).

16. Community Builders Council, *The Community Builders Handbook* (Washington, D.C.: ULI–the Urban Land Institute, 1947).

Post–World War II To the Present

For the duration of World War II, most new private construction was put on hold except for industrial and residential development directly related to the war effort. On the heels of a decade-long economic depression, most U.S. real estate markets were badly underbuilt by 1945. In particular, the demand for housing was pressing. Eleven million servicemen and -women were returning home to communities where few unoccupied houses were available. By 1947, more than 5 million families had either doubled up with other families in overcrowded dwellings or were occupying temporary shelters. New housing construction quadrupled to a half million homes in 1946, but production fell far below demand, and newly deregulated housing prices were skyrocketing.

After a bumpy start, the homebuilding industry eventually rose to the challenge. With government assistance in the form of mortgage financing, new highways and infrastructure, permissive zoning and planning, and other tools, housing starts reached an all-time high of more than 1.5 million new units by 1950, mostly single-family homes to accommodate the new suburban baby boom.

Against this backdrop of postwar economic growth, this chapter explores the evolution of the real estate industry since World War II, examining:

▶ Suburbanization and the postwar boom;
▶ The office building boom;
▶ Urban renewal;
▶ The expansion of interstate highways and the growth of the suburbs;
▶ The urban crisis in race, housing, and neighborhoods; and
▶ The 1970s through the early 2000s.

SUBURBANIZATION AND THE POSTWAR BOOM

In 1944, Congress prepared for postwar growth by passing the Servicemen's Readjustment Act—the "GI Bill"—which established both the Veterans Administration (now the Department of Veterans Affairs) and

This chapter was written and updated by Marc A. Weiss, PhD, chair and CEO, Global Urban Development, Washington, D.C.

Inexpensive two-bedroom Levittown homes made it possible for families to purchase a home with little money down and low monthly payments—a real boon to World War II veterans who were starting over in the late 1940s and early 1950s.

the VA home loan guarantee program. Under this program, an eligible veteran could obtain a low-interest, highly leveraged mortgage loan to buy a home, in some cases with no downpayment. In the original legislation, homeownership loan guarantees were available only to veterans for the first two years following their return to civilian life, but by 1946 the housing shortage became so severe that Congress soon extended the program for ten years. Billions of dollars were authorized for the FHA, VA, and Fannie Mae during those postwar years, most notably in the landmark Housing Act of 1949, which declared as a national goal "a decent home and a suitable living environment for every American family."

The production of housing reached an unprecedented volume. Fifteen million homes and apartments were built in the 1950s, more than double the number in the 1940s and more than five times the 1930s total. With two-thirds of the housing constructed in the rapidly expanding suburbs, many central cities began losing population after 1950.

Formerly agricultural land was subdivided into suburban tracts on a grand scale all over the United States. The greatest growth occurred in the Sunbelt states, especially California, Texas, and Florida—new centers of what President Eisenhower called "the military-industrial complex."

The FHA's and VA's promotion of large-scale homebuilding and the availability of mass financing through life insurance companies, S&Ls, mutual savings banks, and other sources led residential developers to grow rapidly in size as the entire housing industry dramatically increased total production.

By 1949, 10 percent of the builders constructed 70 percent of the homes, 4 percent of the builders constructed 45 percent of the homes, and just 720 firms built 24 percent of the homes. These figures reflected a radical change from the prewar years, and they were to continue changing during the 1950s, with the large homebuilders further expanding in size, scale, and volume. Part of the postwar change in the real estate industry can be attributed to the experience gained during the war, when the federal government encouraged and subsidized residential developers to mass produce private housing for war workers.

The biggest of all the homebuilders immediately after the war was Levitt & Sons, developers of Levittown, New York. Levittown was the country's largest private housing project at the time. The first homes were completed in fall 1947, and, by the early 1950s, Levitt & Sons had built 17,500 homes on 4,000 acres (1,620 hectares) of potato fields in Hempstead on central Long Island, about 30 miles (48 kilometers) east of New York City. *Time* magazine devoted a cover story to Levittown in July 1950, calling the firm's president, William Levitt, "the most potent single modernizing influence in a largely antiquated industry."[1] The Levitts priced most of their newly built homes at $7,990—$1,500 less than any of their competitors—and still managed to earn a $1,000 profit on every home sold.

Abraham Levitt and his two sons, William and Alfred, started in the housing business on Long Island in the late 1920s, building individual luxury houses and, later, a small subdivision called Strathmore-at-Manhasset. During World War II, the Levitt firm entered into government contracts to construct 2,350 homes for war workers in and around Norfolk, Virginia; what the Levitts learned about high-volume methods of production became the basis for their postwar planning and development. At Levittown, William Levitt turned the entire development into a mobile assembly line, with teams of workers moving from house to house to perform 26 specific, repetitive tasks. Everything was carefully programmed and tightly controlled. The Levitts bought materials in bulk, producing them to their own specifications. Subcontractors were required to work only for them; Levitt specially trained and managed construction crews. Materials were preassembled in central facilities and delivered to each construction site just in time for that day's set of repetitive assignments. The emphasis was on speed, and, at peak production, homes in Levittown were completed at the astounding rate of 35 per day.

With an advance commitment from the FHA to insure mortgages on thousands of homes, the Levitts were able to obtain the credit they needed to construct houses and to develop roads, sewers, parks, schools, swimming pools, a shopping center, and other facilities. Levitt simplified the sales transaction to two simple half-hour steps that made purchasing easy for people who had never before owned a home. Many of the purchasers were veterans who could move in with no downpayment other than $10 in closing costs and then pay $56 a month for principal, interest, taxes, and insurance, considerably less than the monthly rent for a comparable apartment. The two-bedroom homes came equipped with modern appliances, and the quarter-acre (0.1-hectare) lots offered plenty of room for expansion. Regrettably, the Levitts restricted their American Dream to whites only. Before the civil rights movement of the 1960s, restrictive practices were common among most new housing developments. Even the FHA and VA—two federal government agencies—actively supported discriminatory policies against racial minorities.

Levitt & Sons built two other Levittowns, both in the suburbs of Philadelphia: in Bucks County, Pennsylvania, in the early 1950s, and in Willingboro, New Jersey, in the late 1950s. They built the last of their large housing projects, Belair, in Bowie, Maryland, during the early 1960s. The Levitt style of mass-produced community development had its share of critics who disdained the communities' architectural and social conformity, which were best characterized during the 1950s by John Keats's *The Crack in the Picture Window* and William H. Whyte's *The Organization Man.*[2] Although many other big devel-

opments flourished during the postwar years, the original Levittown in Hempstead, Long Island, still stands as an American cultural symbol of postwar housing construction.

NEW YORK CITY'S POSTWAR OFFICE DEVELOPERS

A surge in office building construction in Manhattan occurred a few years after the end of World War II. New demand began to fuel a long-dormant market. New York City led the nation in the production of office space by a significant margin. Harold and Percy Uris alone developed almost 9 million square feet (840,000 square meters) of office space in Manhattan from 1947 to 1962, which was twice as much as that developed in the entire city of Chicago during the same period.[3]

Most of this office construction was undertaken by family organizations led by the second or third generation in the business. Several of these families had gained significant experience before the war by developing large apartment buildings. The move to office buildings was triggered as much by the continued imposition of wartime rent controls on apartment buildings as by the demands of the commercial and financial sectors.

Family-owned office developers viewed themselves as long-term investors. They constructed buildings with the intention of holding them in the family portfolio for an indefinite period. Often, sites were assembled over extended periods of time and warehoused until the appropriate moment to build. Before demolishing the existing buildings on a site, these office developers either allowed the leases to expire or compensated tenants for surrendering the remainder of their term.

Project financing was usually simple in concept. The office developers secured a long-term mortgage commitment or "takeout," often from an insurance company. (Takeouts are so called because they signal to construction lenders that a permanent loan is in place to take out, or pay off, the construction loan once the building is leased.) This commitment served as security for a construction loan from a commercial bank. After constructing the building and satisfying any leas-

The American Dream—a typical FHA-financed residential subdivision in San Diego circa 1964.

ing requirements, the office developers transferred the short-term construction loan to the long-term mortgage lender. The developers or a few passive investors usually provided the needed equity capital.

In addition to the Uris family, major office developers included family firms such as Durst, Fisher, Rudin, Tishman, Kaufman, and Minskoff. They developed long-term trust relationships with suppliers, contractors, and professionals that were also family-operated businesses. Of that group, none were more significant than the architectural firm of Emery Roth & Sons. The Roth firm had worked for some of New York's office developers at the turn of the century, and succeeding generations of family firms turned to Roth when they moved from apartment to office development.

URBAN RENEWAL

Even though suburbanization hit the country like a tidal wave in the 1950s, the movement of population and employment away from central cities was already evident three decades earlier. While downtown development flourished in most cities during the 1920s, the neighborhoods surrounding the central business district, sometimes called "the zone of transition," had stopped growing and started to deteriorate. Once the Great Depression took root, development in most central cities ground to a halt, a condition that continued in the commercial core through World War II and into the years immediately after. By the mid-1950s, many U.S. cities had not seen a single new office building constructed in nearly 30 years. Most of these cities were also losing large numbers of manufacturing jobs after the growth spurt induced by the war. Railyards, factories, and warehouses were abandoned, with little demand for new occupancy. Many old houses and apartments in the zone of transition fell into poor physical condition and lacked tenants. Offices, retail stores, hotels, and restaurants all suffered from declining markets and vitality. Civic leaders feared that the heart of the city would die a slow economic, political, and cultural death.

The remedy proposed by many downtown business, real estate, and civic groups was first called district replanning, then urban redevelopment, and, finally, urban renewal. The idea was to rebuild centrally located slums and blighted areas—clear away old and underused commercial and industrial structures, move out poor and minority residents, and tear down their housing—and replace them with shiny new office towers, convention centers, hotels, shopping malls, and luxury housing. Local governments would use their powers of eminent domain to condemn and acquire the land, demolish the structures, replan and redevelop the area with new infrastructure and public amenities, and sell the land at a discount to private developers who, with tax subsidies and other financial inducements, would invest in and construct new privately owned developments.

Initially, state and local governments operated urban renewal programs. One of the most ambitious efforts was the Pittsburgh "Renaissance," which was spearheaded by a coalition of corporate executives headed by Richard King Mellon, scion of the family that owned Gulf Oil, Alcoa, and Mellon Bank, and by Mayor David Lawrence, an energetic New Deal Democrat. Working through the Allegheny Conference on Community Development, state and city officials and private sector leaders devised a master plan that guided the rebuilding of downtown's "Golden Triangle" as well as part of the nearby Lower Hill neighborhood, which was largely populated by African Americans. Several new high-rise office buildings, a state park, two parkways, a convention center, a sports arena and stadium, luxury apartments, and a mix of other new public and private development projects replaced the older buildings that had previously occupied one of downtown Pittsburgh's key sites.

The main obstacle to extensive state and local urban renewal was its high public cost. Local taxpayers balked at the magnitude of the funding needed for full-scale renewal, although occasionally subsidies provided sufficient economic incentive in the form of real estate tax abatements for large investors and developers to bear the direct expenses. Such was the

case with the Metropolitan Life Insurance Company's Stuyvesant Town and Peter Cooper Village, two massive private residential redevelopment projects built on Manhattan's East Side during the 1940s. Drawing on the precedent of the 1930s, when the federal government had for the first time granted billions of dollars for public works to state and local governments to rebuild the infrastructure and amenities of central cities, several key lobbying groups demanded that Washington pay for urban renewal through a federal grant program. Title I of the Housing Act of 1949 created such a program, which was strengthened and modified by the Housing Act of 1954 and by many subsequent legislative enactments. Under Title I, the federal government paid anywhere from two-thirds to three-fourths or more of the "writedown," the total direct public subsidy minus the revenue from the sale of land to private redevelopers.

By the 1960s, the impact of Title I was apparent in the form of new private and public buildings in many central cities throughout the nation. Most of these development projects brought needed new investment into the urban economy. They helped create jobs, increase the tax base, improve the physical, cultural, and recreational environment, modernize the use of urban land, and add attractive structures as well as public open spaces.

Some efforts at clearance, however, merely produced holes in the ground but no new development; projects such as St. Louis's notoriously nicknamed "Hiroshima Flats" cleared sites that failed to attract bids from private developers. These sites became a more blighting influence on the community than the buildings that had been demolished. Urban renewal projects also meant dramatic displacement of small businesses and of low- and moderate-income residents. Unless they owned property, those who were displaced received no compensation and, in most cases, little or no relocation assistance—either in the form of money or new facilities or dwellings. Even when relocation housing was available, it was seldom located in the same neighborhood. Between 1949 and 1967, for example, 400,000 residential units were demolished under Title I, but only 10,000 new public housing units were built on urban renewal sites. By the

▶ PROFILE

WILLIAM ZECKENDORF

As head of Webb & Knapp, William Zeckendorf was America's best-known national developer in the 1950s and 1960s, buying and selling land and existing buildings in and near many large cities and constructing major projects from Mile High Center and Court House Square in Denver to Roosevelt Field Mall on Long Island to Plâce Ville-Marie in Montreal to Century City in Los Angeles. He assembled the land for the site of the United Nations in New York and achieved distinction in urban design through the work of his chief architect, I.M. Pei. His most aggressive efforts were federally subsidized urban renewal projects. Beginning in the 1950s, Webb & Knapp built L'Enfant Plaza, a mixed-use office complex, the Town Center apartments, and Waterside Mall shopping center in Washington, D.C. In Philadelphia, Zeckendorf developed the Society Hill Towers and townhouses near the waterfront of the historic city and restored many of Society Hill's colonial rowhouses. Webb & Knapp, using the talents of architects I.M. Pei and Henry Cobb, won the contract to redevelop Society Hill through a design competition. Webb & Knapp also won design competitions to build the University Gardens apartment complex in the Hyde Park neighborhood of Chicago and an even larger project in Pittsburgh's Lower Hill area. In New York, where Webb & Knapp had its headquarters, Zeckendorf and Pei teamed up to develop three major Title I urban renewal residential developments in Manhattan: Park West Village, Kips Bay Plaza, and Lincoln Towers. Zeckendorf was also involved with downtown redevelopment planning in Cincinnati, St. Louis, San Francisco, Cleveland, and Hartford.

middle 1960s, such statistics led to outcries of "Negro removal" and considerable controversy. As a result, the program underwent substantial improvement during 1968 to 1970 but was abolished in 1974.[4]

With the power of suburbia's attraction and the long period of downtown stagnation uppermost in their minds, lenders, investors, and users of downtown space were very cautious during the 1950s and early 1960s. Therefore, despite all the financial incentives, most local governments found it difficult to persuade private developers to participate in downtown renewal efforts. One successful high-risk developer who bucked the conservative mood and plunged headfirst into the urban renewal program in cities all across the country was William Zeckendorf (see profile).

In the early days of urban renewal, the largest investors, lenders, and, in many cases, joint venture developers of projects were the country's leading life insurance companies. They had emerged from the war with tremendous amounts of cash to invest, and real estate assets appeared to offer a good economic return. Companies such as Equitable, which developed the Gateway Center office complex in Pittsburgh's Golden Triangle; New York Life, the developer of Chicago's Lake Meadows racially inte-

grated middle-income apartment complex; Prudential, which built and occupied the main office tower in Boston's Prudential Center; and Metropolitan Life and John Hancock were all players in the urban renewal game in various cities. They developed corporate office skyscrapers, shopping facilities, and residential towers and townhouses.

THE EXPANSION OF INTERSTATE HIGHWAYS AND THE GROWTH OF THE SUBURBS

Though urban renewal was controversial for displacing residents and businesses and received much attention for its efforts to reshape central cities, it was dwarfed by the impact of the interstate highway program on the urban landscape. Downtown corporate interests lobbied heavily for the federal government to fund the interstate highway program, which was initiated in 1956. They wanted to bring these new superhighways into the heart of the nation's cities. It was to be the last, best hope for downtown. New expressways radiating in all directions from the central core were expected to bring workers, shoppers, tourists, and middle-class residents to urban downtowns while reducing traffic congestion on city streets and improving speed and accessibility. In the process of building this grand and expensive automobile-based transportation system, displacement decimated inner-city communities and created many new land use patterns. "One Mile," Robert Caro's dramatic chapter on New York City's Cross-Bronx Expressway in *The Power Broker*, paints a vivid portrait of the human drama behind a small portion of the vast network of urban interstate highways.[5]

Ironically, the downtown expressways turned out to be two-way streets that allowed city businesses and residents to leave as well as to enter the center city, thereby disappointing the most ardent advocates of urban renewal. Together with the suburban beltways and highways that surrounded and bypassed the urban core, the interstates that radiated from the cities' centers opened up a new frontier of suburbanization, and many hallmarks of downtowns—office buildings, department stores, and hotels—moved or expanded to rapidly growing developments near the interchanges of two or more major suburban transportation arteries.

The Growth of Suburban Shopping Centers

Even before the federal interstate highway program was launched, state and local highways in the suburbs offered promising locations for a new type of large-scale development project, the shopping center. By 1954, total retail sales in suburban centers already exceeded the retail sales volume in major central cities. Though antecedents to the modern shopping center existed before the war—J.C. Nichols's Country Club Plaza in Kansas City, Hugh Prather's Highland Park Shopping Village in Dallas, and Hugh Potter's River Oaks Center in Houston—these centers were built primarily to serve existing communities. It was only after World War II that construction of the first free-standing regional shopping centers—not tied to any specific residential development—drew patrons from a wide geographic area.

By the early 1950s, shopping centers were springing up on the periphery of cities everywhere, from Cameron Village in Raleigh, North Carolina, to Poplar Plaza in Memphis, Tennessee, to Shopper's World in Framingham, Massachusetts, near Boston.

One of the most widely heralded of the new suburban malls was the Northgate Shopping Center, about 20 miles (32 kilometers) from downtown Seattle. Developed by Allied Stores and opened in 1950, Northgate featured a large Bon Marché department store as the anchor tenant. Smaller stores flanked what at that time was considered a major innovation in design: a central outdoor ground-level pedestrian mall with an underground truck tunnel that hid deliveries and removal of solid waste. Surrounding the mall was the necessary sea of parking spaces, and it was considered a bold step to turn the mall storefronts away from the automobile traffic and parking lots. In 1954, Northland Center outside Detroit, developed and anchored by J.L. Hudson's department store, opened as the largest regional shopping center at that date and the first to offer attractive amenities and open space. *Architectural Forum* even compared Northland, which was designed by Victor Gruen, to Rockefeller Center.[6]

Two years later, another department store company, Dayton's of Minneapolis, built Southdale Center, the first fully enclosed, heated, and air-conditioned suburban shopping mall. Located in Edina, Minnesota, Southdale was also designed by Gruen, America's leading shopping center architect, who had won critical acclaim for Northland and later went on to design nearly 100 other malls. To block the threatened construction of a nearby competing mall and thus reduce the risks to its expensive project, Dayton's broke with previous shopping center development practices by inducing another department store, Donaldson's, to come to Southdale as a second anchor. Southdale set new standards for the design, construction, leasing, and management of shopping malls. Other department store chains and speculative shopping center developers quickly followed the new trends.

The year after Southdale opened, James Rouse, an independent developer, built the fully enclosed Harundale Mall in the Baltimore suburbs. In 1961, Rouse and Victor Gruen teamed up to design and develop Cherry Hill, a 78-acre (31.5-hectare) shopping center in the Philadelphia suburb of Delaware Township, New Jersey. The shopping center became such a suc-

Before 1956, Southdale, Minnesota, was farmland. But in 1956, Dayton's opened Southdale Center, the first fully enclosed, heated, and air-conditioned suburban shopping mall.

cessful focal point and symbol of the suburban area's economic and cultural life that township residents later voted to change the community's name to Cherry Hill.

Many of the early shopping centers proved to be highly popular and profitable, and, over the past five decades, those with available land expanded their retail square footage as well as the number of stores and the number and size of department store anchors. The total number of shopping centers in the United States has grown exponentially, from a relative handful at the end of the war to 7,000 at the beginning of the 1960s to more than 48,000 by 2005, including several hundred large regional malls and a host of different types of smaller centers. In 1954, the International Council of Shopping Centers was formed to represent developers, owners, and managers of this innovative suburban phenomenon; by 2007, ICSC represented more than 65,000 members.

The Growth of Suburban Industrial Parks

The decentralization and suburban growth fostered by the new highway system influenced more than the location of housing and retail centers. Industry and commerce also began moving to suburbia to locate near major transportation arteries. Manufacturing plants that had previously depended mainly on rail-

road lines now relied more heavily on trucking. They found highway-accessible suburban locations, whose land costs and rents were cheaper than inner-city sites, to be increasingly available for expansion or relocation. In the 1950s, industrial parks, office parks, research and development parks—with full utilities, plenty of parking, access roads, attractive landscaping, and, occasionally, nearby services—sprouted across suburbia, particularly near the interstate highways. Cabot, Cabot & Forbes Company of Boston earned a national reputation for successfully developing many of these projects.

Cabot, Cabot & Forbes (CC&F) was an old-line real estate investment management company for Boston's Brahmin elite. In 1947, 26-year-old Gerald Blakely convinced senior partner Murray Forbes to hire him to develop suburban industrial parks. The role of MIT and Harvard in pioneering new science and technology for the war effort suggested that the Boston area could become a significant center of research and manufacturing for electronics and related industries. Blakely also assumed that engineers and scientists then moving to the expanding residential suburbs farther out from the city would appreciate shorter commuting times to nearby industrial and office parks. He focused his development strategy on Route 128, a circumferential state high-

TRAMMELL CROW

Initially a leasing agent for existing warehouse space, Trammell Crow began building new warehouses in 1948 in Dallas's 10,000-acre (4,050-hectare) Trinity Industrial District along the Trinity River. A federally funded flood control construction program in 1946 had rendered this area, formerly considered an undesirable floodplain, newly ripe for development when Crow first approached the industrial district's owners, John and Storey Stemmons, to negotiate a deal to obtain land. The Stemmons brothers decided to go into partnership with Crow. With financing from several local banks and from such life insurance companies as Pacific Mutual and Equitable, Crow and the Stemmons brothers developed more than 50 warehouses over the next two decades. Working with different partners, Crow built another 40 warehouses in the Trinity Industrial District and branched out to build warehouses in Denver, Atlanta, and many other cities. Crow has been a partner in constructing tens of millions of square feet of warehouse space—more than any other single developer—ranging from speculative multitenant facilities to custom-built single-tenant projects.

In his travels to find tenants for his inventory of warehouse space, Crow became fascinated by Chicago's massive 24-story Merchandise Mart, built by Marshall Field in 1934 as the world's largest wholesale showroom facility and featuring more than 4 million square feet (372,000 square meters) of space. By the mid-1950s, Crow launched a new plan to build trade marts in the Trinity Industrial District. Over the next three decades, the Dallas Market Center became Crow's largest and best-known development. The project became feasible in 1955 when John and Storey Stemmons donated 102 acres (41 hectares) of land to the state of Texas for a planned interstate highway with service roads for the Trinity District, making the site for Crow's trade center just two blocks from an on/off ramp and a short ten- to 15-minute commute to downtown Dallas and the airport. The highway (I-35), known in Dallas as the Stemmons Freeway, opened in 1959.

Rather than build one enormous multipurpose structure like the Merchandise Mart, Trammell Crow's strategy was to build an entire complex of attractive and modern buildings—one structure at a time—that would specialize in specific product lines. In partnership with the Stemmons brothers, Crow constructed the Dallas Decorative Center in 1955 for decorators and the design trade, then developed the Home-furnishings Mart in 1957 for the furniture and fixtures business, the Trade Mart in 1960, the Apparel Mart in 1964, the World Trade Center in 1972, and the Infomart in 1984 for the high-tech information industry. He also built Market Hall in 1963, which was the largest privately owned exhibition center in the United States, and the 1,600-room Loew's Anatole Hotel, which opened in two stages in 1979 and 1981. This hotel has so many amenities and facilities that it helped turn the Dallas Market Center into a focal point for nighttime activity and added to the center's attractiveness as a location for conducting business and holding conventions and trade shows.

Trammell Crow entered the hotel business through his association with architect-developer John Portman of Atlanta. This team built the Atlanta Decorative Arts Center in 1960 and over the next two decades developed two huge urban renewal projects, Peachtree Center in Atlanta and, together with David Rockefeller, Embarcadero Center in San Francisco. Both projects involved the construction of multiple high-rise office buildings and the development of a large Hyatt Regency Hotel. Beginning in 1960 with the opening of the Trade Mart in Dallas, Crow included large indoor atrium lobbies in his buildings. The atrium lobby has since become a standard feature of Crow's wholesale market centers, office buildings, hotels, apartment buildings, and even industrial parks. Portman, as chief architect, achieved public recognition for the large atrium lobbies in the Atlanta and San Francisco Hyatt Regency Hotels, and the ensuing publicity accorded this innovative hotel design helped set off a wave of similar developments during the boom in downtown and suburban hotel construction that ebbed and flowed during the 1970s and 1980s.

way then under construction west of Boston in a semicircle about 12 miles (19 kilometers) from the center of the city.

Blakely acquired land in Needham and Waltham—two suburban towns along Route 128. It took several years to raise the necessary private financing, win support from local governments for the required zoning changes, and convince the state government to build the appropriate highway interchanges and access roads. In the mid-1950s, Cabot, Cabot & Forbes finally opened three large facilities: the New England Industrial Park in Needham, the Waltham Industrial Center, and the Waltham Research and Development Park. All three centers were soon fully occupied, and CC&F was quickly searching for more sites to capture a major share of the rapid economic growth then taking place around Route 128.

By the mid-1960s, Cabot, Cabot & Forbes had built 13 of the 19 industrial parks along Route 128. It also developed the 800-acre (325-hectare) I-95 Industrial Center farther away from Boston near I-495, Technology Square in Cambridge near MIT, industrial parks in Pennsylvania and California, and several office buildings and shopping centers. Gerald Blakely became a millionaire, and CC&F acquired assets worth hundreds of millions of dollars, all from an initial investment of several hundred thousand dollars for land acquisition and site planning. In 1967, the National Association of Industrial and Office Properties (NAIOP) was formed to represent developers, owners, and managers of such parks.

With manufacturing comes distribution and wholesale trade; for developers, that means warehouses and showrooms. Trammell Crow, the country's largest developer of the postwar period, started out as a specialist in providing space for industry's needed storage and wholesaling facilities, building millions of square feet of warehouses and trade marts in his hometown of Dallas and across the country. As the U.S economy grew, especially in the Sunbelt, so did Crow's ambitious development, construction, and leasing activities (see profile).

Hotel and Motel Development

The growth of the interstate highway system and the wave of postwar suburbanization also dramatically affected the hotel business. Before the late 1940s, most hotels were located in the center of cities and towns. The exception was resort hotels located near lakes, rivers, oceans, mountains, and other vacation destinations. Large hotels almost always commanded a prominent site in the city or town center, from the Astor family's Waldorf-Astoria in Manhattan to Henry Flagler's Royal Poinciana in West Palm Beach. When the primary mode of transportation was by railroad, hotels served travelers through their proximity to train stations.

Beginning in the 1920s, "roadside inns" opened along major thoroughfares to accommodate automo-

bile drivers, but this type of lodging was usually small and nearly always a local mom-and-pop business. Further, roadside inns quickly acquired a seedy image, denounced by FBI Director J. Edgar Hoover in 1940 as "dens of vice" whose main clientele was the "hot pillow trade."[7]

In 1952, Kemmons Wilson and Wallace Johnson opened the nation's first Holiday Inn "hotel courts" in Memphis, with clean rooms, free parking, modest prices, and a respectable family image bolstered by the widely advertised offer of free accommodations for children under 12 when accompanied by their parents. The Holiday Inn hotel chain expanded rapidly during the 1950s and 1960s, initially building inns along highways and taking advantage of key locations on the new interstate system. Holiday Inn later moved into urban areas and resort communities and, by the 1980s, became the world's largest hotel chain.

The earliest hotel chains such as Hilton and Sheraton evolved from large downtown hotels that, in general, were independently owned and managed. But, with the 1950s explosion of motels, motor hotels, and motor inns at freeway exits and interchanges and near airports, chains such as Ramada Inn, Howard Johnson's, and TraveLodge quickly proliferated, as did cooperative referral organizations such as Best Western and Friendship Inns that represent large groups of independently owned hotels and motels. By 1954, the number of motel rooms in the United States exceeded the number of hotel rooms for the first time, and, by 1972, the nation had twice as many motel rooms as hotel rooms.

Not only did the focus of new development shift from the center of town to the outskirts; much more of the growth occurred in the Sunbelt states and the intermountain West than in the Northeast and Midwest. In 1948, more than half of all hotel rooms in the United States were located in the Northeast and Midwest. By 1981, the south Atlantic states along the coast from Virginia to Florida claimed nearly one-quarter of all U.S. hotel rooms, with another 40 percent located in the rest of the Sunbelt and the Rocky Mountain states. In addition, the size of hotels and motels grew steadily larger; between 1948 and 1981, the number of properties decreased slightly while the

A typical motel outside Washington, D.C., in the early 1950s.

number of rooms grew by 35 percent. At the same time, different product types emerged, with hoteliers offering conference centers, budget motels, residence suites, and a multitude of other new categories. Unfortunately for the industry, all this expansion and competition led to a dramatic decline in average occupancy rates, which fell from 85 percent in 1948 to just over 63 percent in 2005, according to the American Hotel and Lodging Association. In 2005, there were nearly 48,000 hotel and motel properties in the United States with more than 4.4 million guest rooms and a total sales revenue of nearly $123 billion.

Probably the most important changes in the lodging industry were the entry of investors into the business and the reemergence of many large chains, such as Hilton, Hyatt, Marriott, and Sheraton, as contract management firms. The many new and complicated methods by which hotels and motels are owned and operated have created an opening for real estate developers in speculative hotel development, both for individual projects and as components of mixed-use developments. Some developers also own and operate hotels, motels, conference centers, and resorts as a long-term investment, although many more are involved on a shorter-term basis in the construction and sale of such properties. Today, hotels and motels are considered a key sector of the real estate development industry, and most of the growth and interest in hospitality business investment has taken place in the half century since the dawn of the postwar suburban age.

THE URBAN CRISIS: RACE, HOUSING, AND NEIGHBORHOODS

In 1957, the editors of *Fortune* magazine published a book entitled *The Exploding Metropolis*. The title referred primarily to the burgeoning postwar suburbs, but the volume also included articles on downtowns, central cities, and rising racial conflict. A chapter titled "The Enduring Slums" concluded with an ominous statement: "One way or another, we will continue to pay plenty for our slums."[8] Written at the time of the bus boycott in Montgomery, Alabama, led by the Reverend Martin Luther King, Jr., and the first stirrings of the civil rights movement, the words proved a perfect introduction to the 1960s and the title of the book a prologue for the events that would unfold in our cities during the decade. Along with the migration of white middle-class homeowners to the suburbs, another massive urban migration was taking place: African Americans were moving to central cities in

Washington, D.C., after the 1968 riots. The destruction of the inner city was extensive, and it took almost 40 years for it to be revitalized.

record numbers. The African American population in northern and southern cities was growing rapidly, and, particularly in many of the older industrial cities of the North, the new immigrants from the rural South overflowed the boundaries of established and highly segregated ghetto areas. Three million African Americans migrated from the South to the North and West in the 1940s and 1950s; by 1960, two-thirds of that population was concentrated in the 12 largest cities. The percentage of African Americans in Chicago, for example, jumped from 8 percent in 1940 to nearly 25 percent in 1960 (and 37 percent in 2000).

The unfortunate legacy of racism cast a cloud over this dynamic process of urban growth and change. Newly arrived African Americans were forced in many cases to live in overcrowded, overpriced, poor-quality housing simply because they were restricted from buying or renting in many white neighborhoods. When they did attempt to break through the "color line," African Americans frequently met with verbal intimidation and physical violence. In response, many metropolitan areas launched interracial antidiscrimination movements for "open housing." At the same time, however, most cities were beginning to lose industrial jobs, either to

the suburbs or from the entire metropolitan region. As a result, new rural-to-urban migrants during the 1950s and thereafter had fewer economic opportunities than their predecessors. In fact, the competition for jobs with existing residents intensified and contributed to racial tensions. Finally, most city government agencies, bureaucracies, and politicians proved unreceptive to these African American newcomers, who were often denied access to adequate municipal services and political representation. In particular, schooling became a volatile issue, with numerous battles fought over racial desegregation.

Other groups of "new minorities" also gained a foothold in some cities during this period, most notably Puerto Ricans in New York City, Cubans in Miami, and Mexican Americans in many communities, especially in Texas, Arizona, Colorado, and California. By the 1970s and 1980s, large numbers of Hispanic Americans from Central and South American countries and a dramatic influx of Asian Americans, including Chinese, Japanese, Koreans, and Vietnamese, had become major forces in U.S. urban life. What came to be called the "urban crisis" of the 1960s, however, largely revolved around the economic and social injustice suffered by African Americans.

| Figure 6-1 | Community Development Corporations: Building Bridges to Prosperity |

The harsh economic and social changes that have ripped at the fabric of our nation's central cities and inner-ring suburbs have not caused these communities to give up hope. Many have reclaimed their neighborhoods and begun the process of renewal by building bridges to mainstream economic opportunity.

As the federal government's support for urban development and housing initiatives diminished during the 1980s, corresponding growth occurred in private nonprofit community development corporations (CDCs) and other community-based development organizations to help fill the gap. These groups built and managed affordable housing and created jobs by developing neighborhood shopping centers, incubator buildings for small businesses, industrial parks and other facilities, and recreation and services such as community medical clinics, preschools, and employment training and placement centers to serve local needs.

According to a national census of CDCs conducted by the National Congress for Community Economic Development in 1998, an estimated 3,600 CDCs were actively operating in the United States. Since the emergence of the first CDCs in the late 1960s, it is estimated that they have produced more than 247,000 private sector jobs and more than 550,000 units of affordable housing.

To support this growing movement of CDCs, state and local governments, private foundations, corporations, and banks expanded funding for community-based development. In the 1990s, the federal government redirected additional resources for neighborhood developers through programs such as low-income housing tax credits, community development block grants, HOME investment partnerships, empowerment zones, and enterprise communities (see Chapter 15 for more detail).

In addition, today such national intermediaries as NeighborWorks America (also called the Neighborhood Reinvestment Corporation), the Local Initiatives Support Corporation (LISC), Enterprise Community Partners (founded by James Rouse), and Living Cities: the National Community Development Initiative provide technical and financial assistance to community-based groups for economic development and affordable housing. Nationwide advocacy and community organizing groups such as Citizen Action, ACORN (Association of Community Organizations for Reform Now), and the Industrial Areas Foundation also work to expand grass-roots community development activities. These growing national initiatives have been supplemented by local partnerships in most cities—New York, Los Angeles, Chicago, Atlanta, Baltimore, Boston, Cleveland, Detroit, Miami, Denver, Kansas City, Houston, Washington, D.C., and many more—to mobilize funds and management expertise for community development activities. For example:

▶ In Newark, New Jersey, the New Community Corporation partly owns a profitable, high-volume supermarket in an area all but abandoned by private businesses. New Community emerged from the ashes of the 1967 riots to restore the spirit and fabric of life in the Central Ward, starting with building or renovating 3,000 affordable homes and apartments for 7,000 low- and moderate-income residents. Altogether, New Community runs a variety of businesses providing 2,300 jobs, and it operates employment training and placement services for area residents and major employers, placing 1,000 low-income people every year in full-time jobs. New Community's successful efforts at revitalization have brought private investment in homes and businesses back to central Newark, ranging from homeownership and a successful business loan fund to the first major new shopping center in decades.

▶ Headquartered in San Francisco, BRIDGE Housing Corporation is the leading builder and manager of affordable rental housing and for-sale homes in California and one of the largest in the country. Founded in 1983, this nonprofit enterprise has developed and currently manages more than 12,000 affordable homes and apartments with an estimated market value greater than $3 billion. BRIDGE has won more than 50 state, national, and international awards for developing high-quality, mixed-income residences that increase the amount of affordable housing for low- and moderate-income families and senior citizens, expand homeownership, and improve communities. BRIDGE has also launched a number of innovative financing programs, including the BUILD Initiative. Working with $100 million of California Public Employees Retirement System (CalPERS) investment capital, BUILD acquires underused properties in existing urban communities, redevelops them into residential and mixed-use infill projects, all of which have an affordable housing component, and ultimately sells them.

The battle grew increasingly heated throughout the 1950s and 1960s, with violent skirmishes in the 1950s exploding into full-scale rebellion during the 1960s. Local police, white workers, and white residents directed much early violence against their African American neighbors and coworkers. Later, African Americans fought back, battling in the streets with law enforcement officials, including the National Guard, looting stores, and burning or vandalizing buildings and cars, usually in their own neighborhoods. Long hot summers of riots descended on U.S. cities, from New York's Harlem in 1964 and Los Angeles's Watts in 1965 to Detroit and Newark in 1967 and dozens of other cities in 1968 in the wake of the assassination of Dr. Martin Luther King, Jr. In all, nearly 200 people were killed and 20,000 people arrested nationwide, with property damage estimated in the hundreds of millions of dollars.

Eventually, many concerned citizens mobilized to address the interconnected set of problems that had helped spawn dissatisfaction and disorder. The most obvious inequity was the legally and officially sanctioned segregation and discrimination that had long pervaded U.S. life. Beginning in the 1940s, the powerful political coalition and moral force of the civil rights movement finally began to sweep away many discriminatory barriers through a series of federal, state, and local laws and court decisions. In 1962, President John F. Kennedy issued an executive order banning racial discrimination in federal housing programs, and, after President Kennedy's assassination the following year, President Lyndon B. Johnson carried through on a host of successful legislative efforts, including the landmark Civil Rights Act of 1964 and the Voting Rights Act of 1965.

To solve the underlying problems, however, legal rights had to be supplemented by economic and social action. In 1960, the Ford Foundation launched its Gray Areas Program to foster the revitalization and redevelopment of urban neighborhoods with minority populations, simultaneously trying to improve housing, social services, employment training, jobs, business opportunities, crime prevention, and public education. These pilot projects paved the way for a vast array of public efforts, from the many programs and organizations grouped under the War on Poverty starting in 1964 to the comprehensive neighborhood-based Model Cities Program of 1966. One of the most innovative public/private partnerships was the creation of community development corporations (CDCs), entrepreneurial institutions that attempted to combine the best features of business investment and management with government services and citizen participation.

In 1967, the Ford Foundation worked with New York's two U.S. Senators, Robert F. Kennedy and Jacob K. Javits, to establish the Bedford-Stuyvesant Restoration Corporation in a predominantly African American neighborhood of Brooklyn. A combination of public and private nonprofit funding plus for-profit activity has helped many other CDCs grow and mature since the 1960s in a wide variety of neighborhoods that are home to diverse ethnic and religious groups. Today, thousands of CDCs and other types of neighborhood development organizations exist in U.S. cities and rural areas, building and managing affordable housing, health clinics, office and industrial parks, and shopping centers; and providing preschool education, child care, job training and placement, and a host of other family and community services. Much of today's minority and urban political, business, and philanthropic leadership has emerged from these organizations and movements. Esteban Torres, who founded The East Los Angeles Community Union (TELACU) in the 1960s to serve a rapidly growing Hispanic population, was elected to the U.S. Congress from east Los Angeles in 1982. Franklin A. Thomas, who headed the Bedford-Stuyvesant Restoration Corporation for many years, was named president and chief executive officer of the Ford Foundation in 1979.

The Federal Government's Response to the Urban Crisis

One major response to the 1960s urban crisis was the 1965 creation of the federal government's cabinet-level U.S. Department of Housing and Urban Development (HUD). Robert C. Weaver, a lifelong activist for better-quality affordable housing and a strong opponent of racial discrimination, was appointed secretary of HUD, becoming the first

African American member of a U.S. president's cabinet. In 1961, President Kennedy appointed Weaver to head the Housing and Home Finance Agency (HHFA), HUD's predecessor. Before then, Weaver had served as the New York State rent administrator. Under Weaver's direction as HHFA administrator and then as HUD secretary, federal involvement in subsidized housing changed dramatically. Since the 1930s, the federal government's housing focus was largely limited to mortgage insurance and guarantees and the secondary mortgage market, mostly for the benefit of middle-income homeowners but also to foster the development of middle-income suburban rental apartments. In encouraging private development, these activities received active support from the real estate development industry. The other emphasis at that time concentrated on public housing for low- and moderate-income families. Public housing was a small program nationwide, directed primarily to larger cities, and was extremely unpopular within the real estate community. Some of the original base of support for public housing in the 1930s and 1940s had dwindled, the result of rising affluence and increasing racial tensions. Catherine Bauer, one of public housing's most famous advocates, wrote in 1957 that "public housing, after more than two decades, still drags along in a kind of limbo, not dead but never more than half alive."[9]

By the late 1950s, the incredible postwar demand for new suburban single-family houses had largely been satisfied, and builders and developers began searching for new products and markets. One potential market yet to be tapped was individuals and families whose incomes were still too modest to afford new homes and apartments priced at the lower end of the private market. Such households could, however, be served by the private sector if public subsidies were available. Proponents of low-income housing began to view the subsidized public/private approach as a way to break what Catherine Bauer called "the dreary deadlock of public housing."[10] On the other side of the barricades, the National Association of Home Builders (NAHB), recognizing the economic potential of this new business opportunity for its members, reconsidered its position and became a key supporter of federal subsidies to produce privately owned housing for moderate-income families.

With NAHB's backing, the federal government launched new affordable housing programs in the 1960s, including the Section 221(d)(3) program (below-market mortgage interest rates), the Section 202 program (housing for the elderly), and several others. These programs generally served a target market of people with somewhat higher incomes than public housing residents. Soon these assisted housing programs were producing a large volume of new rental apartments.

In 1968, the landmark National Housing Act set forth the enormously ambitious goal of producing 600,000 subsidized homes and apartments each year for ten consecutive years. The act included both a program to assist the production of rental housing (Section 236) and a subsidy program to reduce the cost of mortgage interest to encourage homeownership for low- and moderate-income families (Section 235). Both programs expanded rapidly in the early 1970s but ran into problems, ranging from poor management and outright fraud to the economic recession and inflated oil prices of 1973. In 1974, the Section 236 program was replaced by the Section 8 New Construction and Substantial Rehabilitation programs.

Particularly during the 1960s and 1970s, these programs helped produce literally hundreds of thousands of new homes and apartments, many of good quality. Unfortunately, the federal government drastically cut back most of these programs during the 1980s, entirely eliminating some and reducing others by as much as three-fourths of their annual budget compared with the late 1970s. (The Section 8 program is discussed in Chapter 15.)

State and local governments as well as philanthropic institutions and nonprofit organizations have contributed resources to the nation's complex system of housing production. Some for-profit builders have made development of rental housing and homeownership for low- and moderate-income families a major component of their business. For example, HRH Construction Corporation, under the leadership of Richard Ravitch in the 1960s and 1970s, developed more than 25,000 affordable apartments, including

▶ PROFILE

ABRAHAM KAZAN

Perhaps the biggest of all of America's private builders of affordable housing was Abraham E. Kazan. Kazan was a Jewish immigrant from Russia who joined the Amalgamated Clothing Workers, one of the newly emerging labor unions of the early 20th century. Kazan helped organize a credit union and a union-sponsored bank to make financing more available for affordable rental housing and homeownership. In the 1920s, his union was instrumental in passing the New York State housing law that provided subsidies for moderate-income rental apartments. Kazan formed the Amalgamated Housing Corporation in 1927 and, with property tax abatements under the new state law, built the first two affordable developments: Amalgamated Houses in the Bronx and Amalgamated Dwellings on the Lower East Side of Manhattan. These historic landmark residential complexes were financed primarily by the

Metropolitan Life Insurance Company and the Amalgamated Bank. Both developments were structured as limited-dividend cooperatives to make the attractively designed new housing permanently affordable for moderate-income working families.

In 1951, Abraham Kazan formed the United Housing Foundation, a nonprofit organization that built numerous large-scale cooperative housing developments in New York City during the 1950s, 1960s, and 1970s. His final project was Co-op City, which, with more than 15,000 apartments, is still the largest private housing development in the United States. All told, Kazan constructed more than 33,000 cooperatively owned affordable apartments in over half a century of real estate development. Today, the United Housing Foundation and other institutions like the National Cooperative Bank help to carry on his legacy.

Waterside, an attractive high-rise residential complex built in Manhattan in 1974 on a platform overlooking the East River. HRH is now owned by Starrett, another large builder and owner of affordable housing developments, the most notable of which is the massive Starrett at Spring Creek in Brooklyn.

Development Movements in Inner-City Neighborhoods

As the wholesale clearance and displacement associated with urban renewal grew increasingly controversial and expensive in the 1960s and early 1970s, many community activists and urban policy makers searched for alternative methods to save and improve the existing housing stock. Their goal was to preserve and revitalize the fabric of neighborhood life for existing residents and businesses. Over time, the idea of neighborhood conservation and housing renovation gained popularity as reflected in new government programs such as Section 312 home rehabilitation loans, federally assisted code enforcement, and community development block grants (CDBGs) to assist the revitalization process.

One of the biggest stumbling blocks was "redlining"—real estate lenders' refusal to lend money on

properties in older inner-city neighborhoods inhabited by people with modest incomes—and property insurance companies' denial of homeowners' insurance in those neighborhoods. Whites were as negatively affected by redlining as nonwhites; although whites normally had an easier time obtaining a mortgage to buy a house in the suburbs, those who chose to remain in the inner cities often could not even get a home improvement loan. For many years, the federal government redlined properties through the FHA and VA, but, by the late 1960s, various legislative and policy directives led to reform of this harmful practice. After these reforms, the FHA and VA became the only available sources for home loans in many inner-city neighborhoods. Most private lenders and insurers, however, including banks, insurance companies, S&Ls, and mortgage companies, continued redlining. In the 1960s and 1970s, a movement emerged to reverse this tide.

Gale Cincotta, a housewife and PTA leader in the west side Chicago neighborhood of Austin, helped lead a crusade for community stabilization and improvement. She began her efforts with the discovery that commercial banks and thrift institutions were taking millions of dollars in deposits from local

Figure 6-2	Greenlining Neighborhoods with Community Development Financing

Over the past 35 years, many community development financial institutions (CDFIs) have emerged in cities across the country. CDFIs are specialized financial institutions that work in market niches that have not been adequately served by traditional financial institutions. They provide a wide range of financial products and services, including mortgage financing for first-time homebuyers, financing for needed community facilities, commercial loans and investments to start or expand small businesses, loans to rehabilitate rental housing, and financial services needed by low-income households and local business. CDFIs include community development banks, credit unions, loan funds, venture capital funds, and microenterprise loan funds. These diverse organizations provide vitally needed capital and credit to revitalize neighborhoods.

The ShoreBank Corporation of Chicago, owner of the ShoreBank (formerly known as South Shore National Bank), was one of the first of these organizations, offering a full range of residential, commercial, and consumer loans, deposit banking services, venture capital for small businesses and real estate development, job training, and social services to communities traditionally underserved by lending institutions. Since 1974, ShoreBank has lent nearly $3 billion for community development, including 52,000 affordable homes. ShoreBank has banks and affiliated nonprofits in Chicago; Cleveland; Detroit; Ilwaco, Washington; and Portland, Oregon, as well as business development services in Michigan's Upper Peninsula and consulting services around the world. In 2000, ShoreBank expanded its focus to include environmental issues because of the belief that true prosperity comes only with environmental well-being. Since then, ShoreBank has invested $182 million in loans that contribute to a healthier environment. President Clinton and Congress recognized the importance of greenlining neighborhoods in 1994 by creating the Community Development Financial Institutions Fund to provide financial resources and technical support for new and existing community development lenders and investors.

residents but refusing to lend even thousands of dollars to those very same customers. Cincotta's neighborhood battle against redlining and in support of "greenlining" united people across racial, ethnic, religious, and geographic boundaries—all could agree to help preserve their own communities. Starting with the Organization for a Better Austin, Cincotta later helped establish the Chicago Reinvestment Alliance and the National People's Action, which led to city, state, and federal intervention and eventually to a variety of neighborhood lending and fair insurance agreements with banks, thrifts, and insurance companies. These agreements have helped bring needed loan and grant money and homeowners' insurance back into long-ignored communities where existing property owners are eager to reinvest and upgrade their homes and where for-profit and nonprofit developers are ready and willing to rebuild homes, apartments, and stores.

From Gale Cincotta's movement came two key national laws: the Home Mortgage Disclosure Act (HMDA) of 1975 and the Community Reinvestment Act (CRA) of 1977. Both laws discourage redlining and encourage affirmative lending. A related initiative is the federal government–supported NeighborWorks America (also called the Neighborhood Reinvestment Corporation), which promotes conservation of communities through the successful Neighborhood Housing Services plan pioneered on the north side of Pittsburgh in the mid-1970s. Congress and the federal financial regulatory agencies strengthened the Community Reinvestment Act in 1989. President William J. Clinton and Comptroller of the Currency Eugene Ludwig further strengthened the CRA in 1994. Congressional amendments to the Fair Housing Act in 1992 plus subsequent civil court rulings have helped reduce property insurance redlining. The Community Reinvestment Act played an essential role in expanding available capital for neighborhood development by encouraging billions of dollars in new loans and investments during the past three decades.[11]

The Downtown Revival

While residents of inner-city neighborhoods were struggling to pump economic life into their communities and physically improve their immediate surroundings, corporate and civic leaders were engaged in an identical process focused on the areas around the central business districts of their respective cities. Most downtowns that experienced real estate booms during the 1920s languished for the next two or three decades without any significant new development. The postwar urban renewal and interstate highway programs were designed to jump-start the process of downtown development through the combination of land assembly, public improvements, and public subsidies. By the 1960s, these government programs were beginning to yield results. The growth of the service economy and the white-collar workforce stimulated the construction of new office buildings, and the rising incomes and changing lifestyles of both young and old led to new investment in retail development and, in some cities, even the construction and renovation of downtown housing.

In 1985, the Urban Land Institute published a survey conducted by the Real Estate Research Corporation that documented the long hiatus in office building development in 24 of the nation's biggest cities from the 1920s to the 1950s, followed by massive growth from the late 1960s to the mid-1980s.[12] The survey documented the completion of new, privately owned, large high-rise office buildings (100,000 square feet [9,295 square meters] or more) located in central business districts. In some cases, no office towers had ever been built in these cities before the postwar years; in most other cases, major cities lived through several decades without any development of these tall symbols of progress and prosperity. The following list documents the lean years for construction of urban office skyscrapers:

► Atlanta—before 1961;
► Baltimore—1929 to 1963;
► Boston—1930 to 1966;
► Chicago—1934 to 1957;
► Cleveland—1928 to 1964;
► Dallas—1921 to 1943;
► Denver—before 1957;
► Detroit—1929 to 1962;
► Fort Worth—1930 to 1969;

► Houston—1929 to 1960;
► Los Angeles—before 1964;
► Miami—before 1967;
► Minneapolis—1929 to 1960;
► New York City (downtown)—1933 to 1956;
► New York City (midtown, excluding Rockefeller Center)—1931 to 1950;
► Newark—1930 to 1962;
► Philadelphia—1931 to 1968;
► Pittsburgh—1933 to 1950;
► St. Louis—before 1970;
► St. Paul—1931 to 1973;
► San Diego—before 1963;
► San Francisco—before 1955;
► Seattle—1929 to 1969;
► Tampa—before 1971;
► Washington, D.C.—before 1970.

During the past five decades, these cities made up for the long drought in office tower development. From 1970 through 1983, for example, the central business districts of these cities added 627 new, privately owned high-rise office buildings of more than 100,000 square feet (9,295 square meters), for a total of more than 340 million square feet (31.6 million square meters) of new office space! The most active downtown office markets during this 14-year period were New York City, Chicago, San Francisco, Houston, Washington, D.C., Denver, Boston, Los Angeles, Dallas, Philadelphia, Atlanta, and Seattle. Many of these—and other—cities experienced an accelerated volume of office tower construction after 1983 and for much of the remainder of the 1980s, and again from the mid-1990s to the present.

Along with the growth of office space and high-rise office buildings came a gradual revival in the fortunes of retail space, with large department stores partially eclipsed by new specialty multistore shopping malls. The success of Chicago's Water Tower Place, an enclosed vertical mall with two department store anchors and 130 retail stores on seven levels, led to similar developments in other cities during the 1970s and 1980s. Boston's Copley Place, for example, was developed by the Urban Investment and Development Company, the same firm that built Water Tower Place.

A similar innovative development is the TrizecHahn Company's Horton Plaza in San Diego, an architecturally distinctive vertical downtown shopping mall that is not fully enclosed to take advantage of the city's year-round dry and temperate climate.

Even more widely publicized was the success of the tourism-, entertainment-, and food-oriented "festival marketplaces" that relied exclusively on specialty shops rather than on department store anchors. Unquestionably, the leading developer in this field is the Rouse Company, headed in the 1970s by its charismatic founder James Rouse. The first two such marketplaces, both surprisingly successful for a new concept attempted in what were considered unfavorable locations, were Boston's Faneuil Hall Marketplace, opened in 1976, and Baltimore's Harborplace, opened in 1980. *Time* magazine was so enthusiastic about the impact of these two developments on the revitalization of urban downtowns that it featured James Rouse on its cover in 1981 under the heading, "Cities Are Fun!"[13] By 1990, the Rouse Company was operating 14 such centers in cities around the country, the largest being Pioneer Place in Portland, Oregon. James Rouse's last venture, the Enterprise Development Company, which he established in 1982 as a revenue-generating venture to help finance affordable housing and community development through his Enterprise Foundation (now called Enterprise Community Partners), has also developed and operates several festival marketplaces. Interestingly, many downtown projects, including Horton Plaza and the various central-city retail and mixed-use centers developed by the Rouse Company and the Enterprise Development Company, were urban renewal projects whose initial costs were heavily subsidized by their city governments.

The fundamental idea of the festival marketplace—that the urban shopping experience is "fun"—accelerated in the 1980s and 1990s with the development of urban entertainment centers. These complexes combine retail stores with entertainment activities ranging from cinemas to skating rinks to roller coasters. In many cases, the stores themselves are designed for play, ranging from Niketown to Dave & Buster's to the Sharper Image to the Discovery Channel Store. The entertainment venues include a Ferris wheel at Navy

Faneuil Hall Marketplace consists of 160 stores and 219,000 square feet (20,346 square meters) of gross leasable retail space housed in three 536-foot-long (163-meter long) converted industrial and public market buildings, all of which were originally built before 1826.

Pier in Chicago and a variety of sports from batting cages to golf practice greens at New York's Chelsea Piers to an amusement park at the Mall of America just outside Minneapolis. Many of these urban entertainment centers highlight the joys of strolling along to view and enjoy the crowds and action, and some have made that aspect the most prominent feature of their names, such as Third Street Promenade in Santa Monica, Coco Walk in Coconut Grove near Miami, and Universal CityWalk near Universal Studios close to Los Angeles. Some of these centers have an ethnic appeal, like Harlem USA in New York City or Jump Street USA in Philadelphia. The notion of re-creating city street life as a key aspect of shopping and entertainment, first expressed by Disneyland in California and Disney World in Florida, is being imitated not just by many urban development projects but even in suburban retail malls, where the look and feel of "Main Street" is becoming increasingly popular.

The Wave of New Communities

James Rouse was also heavily identified with another key trend of the 1960s and 1970s: the attempt to create new large-scale, mixed-use communities as an alternative to both big crowded cities and suburban sprawl. Beginning in the early 1960s, a Rouse Company subsidiary called Community Research and Development secretly purchased more than 16,000 acres (6,480 hectares) of mostly contiguous farmland in Howard County, Maryland, halfway between Baltimore and Washington, D.C., and began planning and building the new community of Columbia. Rouse convinced his main lender, the Connecticut General Life Insurance Company (CIGNA), to provide financial backing for the massive community development project, beginning with the cloak-and-dagger operation of land acquisition that involved several hundred transactions.

Rouse assembled a team of distinguished city planners and social scientists to advise him on how to produce a better design for urban living. They devised such innovations as a prepaid community health insurance plan, a minibus system, shared multipurpose community facilities for worship, recreation, and other uses, and a focus on quality education and active community participation. Although Columbia endured financial hard times with the collapse of its homebuilding program during the national economic recession from 1973 to 1975, it survived to become a thriving community of almost 100,000 people.

Built around residential villages and created lakes, Columbia has a "downtown" that features a regional shopping mall (which was owned and operated by the Rouse Company until the Rouse Company was purchased by General Growth Properties in 2004), office centers, entertainment and cultural facilities, and branches of five colleges and universities. The community, intended to accommodate both residential villages and business centers, includes various industrial and office parks that employ more than 63,000 people—not all residents of Columbia. For many years there has been talk in Columbia of creating a town center to establish an urban core for the city. Thus far, it has not happened, but the new owners of the Rouse Company resurrected the idea and developed new plans in 2005.

Housing is targeted to a wide range of income groups and includes numerous subsidized, moderate-income rental apartments. Racial integration, one of Rouse's explicit goals, has been achieved through a policy of nondiscrimination: nearly one-fourth of Columbia's population is African American. The Rouse Company also helped launch a successful home-building firm, Ryland Homes, which now operates nationwide but is still headquartered in Columbia.

Columbia was just one of a wave of new communities privately developed during the 1960s and 1970s. Most of these efforts were concentrated in Sunbelt climates, especially California, Texas, and Florida, though many other states were also represented. Some of the developments were associated with resource-based corporations such as oil companies that already owned large amounts of land—for example, Reston, Virginia, previously owned by Gulf Oil and then by Mobil, and Clear Lake City, near Houston, Texas, owned by Exxon. Other new communities such as Las Colinas, Texas, evolved from large agricultural and cattle ranches. Several developments in California were the legacy of the Spanish land grants, whose massive, contiguous, undeveloped acreage survived into modern times under single ownership.

California ranches that became new urban centers in the past few decades include Thousand Oaks, Valencia, Laguna Niguel, Mission Viejo, Rancho Santa Margarita, and, the biggest of them all, the Irvine Ranch. Owned by the Irvine Company, the ranch consisted of more than 100,000 acres (40,485 hectares), nearly one-fifth of all the private and public land in Orange County. By the early 1960s, postwar suburbanization and the construction of two interstate highways brought metropolitan growth to the northern boundaries of the Irvine Ranch. The Irvine Company hired architect William Pereira to design a master plan for the new city of Irvine to be built around a new campus of the University of California. Irvine is still growing rapidly today, home to more than 200,000 people. In addition to the city of Irvine, land originally part of the Irvine Ranch was developed for urban uses in Newport Beach, Laguna Beach, Costa Mesa, Tustin, and several other communities in central Orange County.

Additional types of new communities developed since the 1960s include retiree- or adult-oriented centers such as Leisure World in Florida, California, and other states; recreation-oriented subdivisions and second-home communities in many areas of the country; and urban "new-town-in-town" mixed-use residential complexes in some big cities. Because the initial costs of land acquisition, planning, infrastructure, and development are high and take many years to pay back through sales and leasing of land and buildings, one lesson learned from these types of developments is that they require strong, long-term financial investment to succeed. Eventually, prices appreciate substantially once a critical mass of the community is developed, but time and patient investors are necessary ingredients. The federal government's New Communities Program, managed by HUD in the 1970s, sponsored developers who, for the most part, were too thinly capitalized and received woefully inadequate operating support from HUD. Consequently, most of the HUD-supported new community projects went bankrupt. One exception is the Woodlands, a HUD-supported new community near Houston owned for nearly three decades by the Mitchell Energy and Development Corporation. The Woodlands was able to draw from both the corporate resources of its parent firm during a time of high profits and from the substantial personal commitment of the company's owner and chief executive, George Mitchell, to build the town of his dreams.

Certainly the single most catalytic development was the entry of the Disney Corporation into central Florida. In 1965, Disney purchased 27,000 acres (11,000 hectares) of undeveloped swampland near Orlando and began to develop Walt Disney World, including the Magic Kingdom and EPCOT Center. Two years later, Florida's legislature created Disney's own private government, the Reedy Creek Improvement District, which enjoys full powers of taxation, borrowing, servicing, regulation, and development. Disney's intention was to control the pace and type of development surrounding its main facilities, something the company had been unable to do with its 250-acre (100-hectare) Disneyland in Anaheim, California. Despite Disney's careful plans, the overwhelming response to the East Coast theme park set off a wave of speculation, population and employ-

ment growth, and real estate development in the greater Orlando metropolitan region that has not yet subsided four decades later. On opening day in December 1971, cars were backed up for 15 miles (24 kilometers) on the new interstate highway to enter the Magic Kingdom.

Today, Disney continues to expand, building a motion picture and television theme park and studios (together with MGM), a wild animal park, many distinctively designed resort hotels by well-known architects such as Michael Graves and Robert A.M. Stern, a major shopping center called Downtown Disney, office buildings, recreation facilities, and housing, including the whole new communities of Lake Buena Vista and Celebration. For a time, Disney was heavily involved in residential development throughout Florida, acquiring the Arvida Company, a major land development and homebuilding firm now owned by the St. Joe Company. Disney is currently concentrating its development plans for Florida entirely on metropolitan Orlando. The result of Walt Disney's choice of a sleepy spot on a map is that Orlando today boasts 110,000 hotel rooms, more than any metropolitan region in the United States except Los Angeles and New York, and one of America's busiest airports. Metropolitan Orlando's population increased by 50 percent during the 1980s, and by 20 percent in the 1990s.

The heavy investment in new communities and large-scale development at the periphery of big, established central cities led to a new phenomenon in the 1970s and 1980s—the growth of "urban villages," "edge cities," "suburban megacenters," "technoburbs," and "growth corridors." These concentrations of super regional shopping malls, office and industrial parks with enormous quantities of space, major highway interchanges, and low- to medium-density housing are often located in more than one government jurisdiction and create a prime activity area away from the traditional central-city downtowns. Some of these new suburban multiuse developments have grown around a large suburban shopping center, such as Tysons Corner, Virginia, or Woodfield Mall in Schaumburg, Illinois. In other cases, a highway such as Route 1 in the vicinity of Princeton, New Jersey, or I-285 north of Atlanta has been the focal point. The image of these centers ranges from the corporate office complexes headquartered in Fairfield County, Connecticut, to the research and industrial parks of Silicon Valley in Santa Clara County, California. Nearly every major metropolitan region now has multiple suburban central business districts that compete with and often surpass the older urban downtowns.

Real estate developers have played major roles in planning and creating these large-scale mixed-use complexes away from the traditional central business districts, from J.C. Nichols's Country Club Plaza in Kansas City to William Zeckendorf's Roosevelt Field on Long Island and Century City in Los Angeles. One of the best-known projects is Gerald Hines's development of the Post Oak–Westheimer area as Houston's main high-end retail center and a thriving location for office space and hotels. In 1969, Hines opened the Galleria shopping center (now owned by Simon Property Group), a mixed-use facility that now contains 2.5 million square feet (232,340 square meters) of retail space and four department store anchors. The project also includes two large Westin Hotels and three major office buildings. The 25-story Post Oak Tower office building in the Galleria, completed in 1973, was at that time one of only two Houston office towers with more than 500,000 square feet (46,500 square meters) of space located outside downtown. In 1983, Hines built the 64-story, 1.6 million-square-foot (148,700-square-meter) Transco Tower (now called Williams Tower) in the Post Oak area. Williams Tower, designed by New York architects Philip Johnson and John Burgee, is thought by some to be the world's tallest office building located outside an urban central business district. The Galleria–Post Oak center, which continues to be Hines's flagship project, has had a major national impact on retail and mixed-use development.

Gerald Hines Interests has been among the biggest commercial developers in the United States during the past four decades, with major office buildings, shopping centers, and hotels in Houston and many other cities on its list of credits, including Atlanta, Boston, Chicago, Detroit, Minneapolis, New York, and Washington, D.C. Hines's international expansion in the 1990s has resulted in projects in Barcelona, Beijing, Buenos Aires, Moscow, Paris, and other large cities around the world.

THE 1970s THROUGH 2007

Real estate development has always been a cyclical industry. Since the 1930s, economists such as Homer Hoyt, Roy Wenzlick, Clarence Long, Leo Grebler, and Manuel Gottlieb have been collecting data and analyzing historical patterns of the ever-changing rise and fall in the volume of real estate activity and the value of property.[14] Downturns may be caused by general economic recessions or depressions, changes in money markets that restrict the supply or drive up the cost of money, and overbuilding that generates too many buildings competing for too few tenants or buyers. Upturns may be caused by a significant increase in demand as a result of population, employment, and income growth; changes in money markets that lead to a plentiful supply of relatively low-cost financing; and speculative responses to rapidly increasing rents, prices, profits, and perceived values.

The past several decades have seen a great deal of cyclical fluctuation precipitated by a wide variety of factors. A boom in the late 1960s and early 1970s fueled by strong economic growth, military spending, and modest inflation heralded a bust from 1973 to 1975 that was induced by the shock of quadrupled oil prices, double-digit inflation, and a severe economic recession. A boom in the late 1970s stimulated by the entry of a large portion of the baby boom generation into housing and job markets gave way to a crash in the early 1980s caused by extremely high interest rates and a contraction in financing, combined with high unemployment and a severe economic recession. In the mid-1980s, money flowed freely again, job growth was strong, and real estate development took off on a speculative binge that by 1990 was squeezed by extraordinarily high vacancies, low occupancies, large unsold inventories, falling prices, rents, and yields, and the most defaults, foreclosures, and bankruptcies since the Great Depression. Yet, by 1993 and 1994, relatively low mortgage interest rates and rising job growth led to a new

The Woodlands, which opened in 1974, is a HUD-supported planned new community on 25,000 acres (10,117 hectares) of heavily forested land 27 miles (43.5 kilometers) north of downtown Houston. Pictured here is the Woodlands country club, with industrial buildings in the background.

boom in home sales and residential construction. In 1994, single-family housing construction starts reached 1.2 million homes, the highest total since 1978. Through the impetus of the Clinton Administration's successful national homeownership strategy, by 1997 the national homeownership rate reached a new all-time high of 65.7 percent, surpassing the previous record set in 1980. It continued to rise each year thereafter, reaching 69.2 percent at the end of 2004.[15] But by 2007, there were troubling signs of rapidly increasing defaults and foreclosures, especially among economically challenged homeowners with adjustable-rate mortgages (ARMs) and "subprime" loans carrying significantly higher interest rates as a result of additional credit risks taken by lenders. Timely, coordinated intervention by the public and private sectors will be necessary to maintain the decade-long momentum of rising homeownership.

As always, this pattern displayed much variation. Within a metropolitan area or a multistate region, some neighborhoods and communities flourished while others languished. In the early 1980s, Dallas continued to thrive while Houston was in a decline—but, by the late 1980s, both cities' fortunes began to reverse. Throughout this period and all across the nation, new office towers and shopping centers coexisted with abandoned housing and the homeless. Cycles also varied between regions. Beginning in the mid-1970s, the Southwest boomed while the Northeast stagnated, both affected by the dramatic rise in energy prices. In the 1980s, energy prices fell substantially, and the Southwest sank while the Northeast rose again. In addition to the prime factor of geographic location, the relative fortunes of real estate differ cyclically by product type. During the late 1980s, when office buildings and hotels were generally overbuilt in most markets, developers and investors turned to residential apartment buildings and industrial warehouses. By the late 1990s, Class A downtown office buildings and luxury hotels had once again become "hot" properties.

The massive population influx of the postwar baby boomers who reached adulthood and formed separate households, the shift in population growth from the Frostbelt to the Sunbelt, the substantial increase in single and divorced households, and the rise in the numbers, income, and wealth of senior citizens all had a major impact on housing development. The housing industry responded by building and rehabilitating a record volume of homes and apartments in the 1970s and maintaining high production through much of the next three decades. Condominiums as a new form of individual apartment ownership burst onto the scene in the early 1970s, accounting for a significant portion of new and converted multifamily housing since then.

Prices, especially of single-family homes, rose rapidly in many markets as demand outran supply, with the costs of new and existing housing and developable land outpacing the previous two decades' increase in household income. The gap in wealth between homeowners and renters widened. Both longstanding tenants and newly formed families, taking advantage of the anticipated appreciation in equity and the available tax benefits, strained their resources to rush into homeownership before prices escalated higher. Mostly on the East and West Coasts at various times from the mid-1970s to today, housing sales and prices rose and fell in successive waves of speculative frenzy followed by recessionary panic. Construction of multifamily housing received a major boost in the early and mid-1980s when the Economic Recovery Tax Act of 1981 provided for syndications, accelerated depreciation, passive losses, and other income tax benefits. The reduction of these benefits under the Tax Reform Act of 1986 immediately triggered a significant reduction in investment in and development of new rental housing as well as a rapid decline of the syndication industry. The importance of congressional actions and federal administrative and judicial decisions highlighted by these tax laws encouraged major real estate firms to strengthen the National Realty Committee as a vital Washington lobby.

Contributing to the instability and wide cyclical swings characterizing the late 1960s to the early 1990s was the impact of a higher level of general price inflation than most U.S. citizens had ever experienced, in combination with revolutionary changes in capital markets and real estate finance. The easy availability of relatively low-cost, fixed-interest, long-term residential mortgages at a time of rapidly rising interest rates in the late 1970s, for example, helped finance and encourage the boom in homeownership. It also led to the near insolvency of savings and loan institutions. Under deregulation, thrifts began to compete for funds from 1980 to 1982 by paying interest on deposits that was higher than the interest they received on much of their mortgage loan portfolios. The S&Ls were borrowing short term and lending long term—a very risky proposition. This disaster of deregulation was followed by another in 1982, when S&Ls were permitted to move away from home mortgage lending and into commercial real estate markets, to engage in equity deals, to purchase "junk bonds," and to get involved in many high-risk ventures while bearing no risk of failure to depositors, because all their deposit accounts were federally

insured for up to $100,000 each. A combination of corruption in some cases, poor judgment in others, and bad luck from cyclical downturns, especially the massive real estate depression of the late 1980s in the energy-producing states, led to widespread bankruptcy among S&Ls. Consequently, in 1989, the government began taking over much of the thrift industry. The federal Resolution Trust Corporation (RTC), created to handle the S&L debacle, entered the 1990s as the owner of real property worth many billions of dollars. Indeed, the RTC became a major force in the future fortunes of the real estate industry as it sold off its vast property from failed S&L holdings during the first half of the 1990s.

The collapse of many thrifts, the difficulties experienced by a large number of commercial banks, and tighter federal regulations on real estate lending meant that, in the early 1990s, developers faced considerable challenges financing new projects. By the early 1990s, a mood of cautious, selective lending prevailed, especially for commercial development. This pattern was a complete reversal of the dominant trend in the mid-1980s, when highly leveraged nonrecourse debt from financial institutions was plentiful and many developers rushed to construct new space, often without sufficient demand for occupancy at projected rents or sale prices.

Although the decline of the thrifts left a temporary vacuum for financing new commercial development, it has had little impact on financing home purchases because of the dramatic growth in securitization and mortgage banking and the rapid expansion of the secondary mortgage market during the past few decades. Secondary mortgage market financial institutions purchase mortgages from banks, S&Ls, and others, pool the mortgages, and sell fixed-income investment securities (bonds) that pass through to the investors' portions of the monthly loan principal and interest payments. Through the medium of large government-backed agencies such as Fannie Mae (Federal National Mortgage Association), Freddie Mac (Federal Home Loan Mortgage Corporation), and Ginnie Mae (Government National Mortgage Association) and a host of private securities firms, mortgage companies have been able to draw capital from a wide range of institutional investors. Insurance companies, pension funds, depository institutions, and global investors now participate in the secondary mortgage market. These sources of capital provide ample funds for primary lenders and borrowers, though sometimes at higher real interest rates than before deregulation, when funds for housing were partially sheltered from competition on the capital markets.

Pension funds, life insurance companies, private equity funds, and other institutional investors have also begun playing a much greater role as lenders, purchasers, and joint venture partners for both new development and the acquisition, refinancing, and redevelopment of existing properties. Since the 1970s, the growth of real estate investment funds for both individuals and institutions has generated a new industry in which financial advisers play an increasingly prominent role in development and management. At the same time, real estate is becoming more professionalized. New trade associations such as the Pension Real Estate Association, the National Council of Real Estate Investment Fiduciaries, and the National Association of Real Estate Investment Trusts signal the financial and organizational changes recently experienced by the real estate industry.

In particular, real estate investment trusts have grown rapidly in recent years, drawing billions of dollars into real estate investment from the public capital markets and reflecting the burgeoning expansion of the stock market and mutual funds in the mid-1990s. Total market capitalization of 119 publicly traded REITs in 1990 was less than $9 billion; by 2006, the number of publicly traded REITs tracked by its national association had increased to 183, and their collective share value had grown to more than $438 billion. Many of these REITs provide equity financing for the acquisition and development of real estate (see Chapter 7 for more details).

An important recent source of debt capital for real estate development has come through the dramatic increase in commercial mortgage–backed securities, rising from less than $5 billion issued in 1990 to more than $202 billion issued in 2006. With total market capitalization of $700 billion in 2007, securi-

tization and the secondary mortgage market are bringing global capital to commercial real estate, just as they have been doing for financing of residential homeownership since the 1980s.

A related change is the increasing involvement of large corporations in real estate. Most industrial and commercial firms have traditionally ignored the profit potential of the land and buildings they own and use. Beginning in the 1960s, however, many resource-based companies such as the railroad, forestry, oil, mining, and agricultural giants that owned surplus land entered the real estate business to develop everything from rural recreational subdivisions to urban mixed-use complexes. The federal government also encouraged corporate entry into the high-volume production of housing through HUD's Operation Breakthrough. With the failure of many of these 1960s commercial and residential developments, however, corporations withdrew to safer and more familiar business activities. But the threat of hostile takeovers and leveraged buyouts financed by undervalued real estate, played out against the cost-conscious era of international competition in the 1980s, led to renewed interest among many major companies to use their real estate assets more intensively and productively, manage them more effectively, and sell to or enter into joint ventures with developers more frequently. This interest was reflected in the growth of a key professional organization, the National Association of Corporate Real Estate Executives. In 2002, the International Development Research Council (IDRC) merged with NACORE to form CoreNet Global, whose members manage $1.2 trillion in assets globally.

The growing presence of large institutions in real estate was matched by the growing size of many development firms. As early as the 1960s, large national developers emerged in the homebuilding field, including Kaufman & Broad, Centex, Ryan Homes, National Homes, Ryland, and U.S. Home. Similarly, shopping center developers such as Edward DeBartolo, Melvin Simon, Alfred Taubman, Ernest Hahn, and James Rouse went national. In the 1970s and 1980s, they were joined by nationwide office developers such as Trammell Crow, Gerald Hines,

Figure 6-3	Real Estate Securities

The development industry's constant need for capital and the average citizen's desire for a "piece of the action" have combined over the years to create a market for real estate securities. The health of that market has varied with conditions in both the real estate and securities markets. Today's alphabet soup of REITs and REMICs (real estate mortgage investment conduits) had its genesis in the 19th century.

One of the earliest issuers of publicly held securities in real estate was the American Real Estate Company. Organized in 1888 with capital of $100,000, the company fueled its growth by selling almost $15 million of bonds and "certificates" on an installment basis throughout the United States. Unfortunately, a downturn in the metropolitan New York market in 1914 led to its bankruptcy and eventual liquidation.

In 1925, Fred F. French financed construction of Tudor City, a 12-building project with 2,500 apartments in midtown Manhattan, by selling $50 million of preferred stock. French made a gift of one share of common stock with each share of preferred stock that was purchased. The preferred stock was to be redeemed after ten years. French retained a share of common stock for each share issued to the public. In addition, he obtained mortgage financing in an amount equal to 50 percent of the total project cost.

Harry Black, president of the George A. Fuller Company and builder of the Flatiron Building, founded the United States Realty and Construction Company in 1903 with capitalization of $66 million, $30 million in preferred stock and $33 million in common stock—the largest publicly held real estate organization of the time. In early 1929, Black extended French's financing concept by issuing stock for the total cost of the construction of each new building, altogether eliminating the use of mortgage financing.

Public participation in mortgage debt financing became big business in the first third of the 20th century. Both guaranteed and plain (nonguaranteed) mortgage bonds were issued. Typically, a bond issue covered a single development project. Commercial banks and title insurance companies guaranteed repayment of principal and interest on the bonds. By 1931, mortgage bonds accounted for more than 17 percent of total urban mortgage debt. Unfortunately, with the onset of the Great Depression, more than 60 percent of those bonds defaulted.

The Real Estate Board of New York's creation of the New York Real Estate Securities Exchange in early 1929 recognized the importance of real estate securities. Exchange members included 500 traders who generated a volume of $309 million in 1930. A victim of the chaos in the securities markets, the exchange ceased operating during the 1930s.

The stock market crash of 1929 had a devastating impact on real estate securities. More than 80 percent of the real estate corporations listed in the relevant Moody's manual in 1929 had either reorganized or disappeared completely from that publication six years later.

The 1950s dawned with a renewed vigor for real estate development as well as with a significant increase in both personal and corporate income taxes. These elements combined to propel a new breed of real estate syndicators. Louis Glickman, Harry Helmsley, Marvin Kratter, Lawrence Wien, and others were in the forefront of syndicators offering limited partnership interests to the general public. Both new construction and acquisition of such famous structures as the Chrysler Building and the Empire State Building were included in this wave of real estate equity syndication. Eventually, many of the individual syndicates were combined as investors traded their interests for shares in new publicly owned companies.

During this period, well-known real estate firms participated in the parade for stock ownership. Among them were Webb & Knapp, Arvida, the Uris brothers, and Kaufman & Broad. They joined a handful of pre-Depression survivors such as City Investing, Starrett, and Tishman.

In particular, a boom in the public offerings of single-family homebuilders occurred in the 1960s. The difficulty in raising financing for each individual development project along with a credit crunch in 1966 swelled the ranks of publicly traded homebuilding companies to 41 by 1972.

In 1960, passage of the Real Estate Investment Tax Act permitted the formation of real estate investment trusts. Each shareholder would be taxed as if investing in a partnership, yet the REIT had limited liability and other features similar to a corporation. Most of the new REITs were formed between 1968 and 1973, and many were mortgage trusts rather than equity trusts. They often borrowed heavily in the short-term money markets while lending for longer time periods. A decline in the fortunes of the real estate market and a steep increase in short-term interest rates beginning in 1973 resulted in the collapse or reorganization of many REITs during the 1970s.

The 1980s witnessed a return to public limited partnerships. This time, the underwriters and promoters were mainly large stock brokerage and investment banking firms such as Merrill Lynch. The Tax Reform Act of 1986, however, changed the rules of the game sufficiently to make these investments unattractive to typical investors because real estate losses could no longer be used to offset ordinary earned income.

Figure 6-3	Real Estate Securities *(continued)*

The 1990s saw the explosive rebirth of REITs, although the new breed consists mostly of equity ownership trusts rather than the mortgage debt trusts that were popular in the 1960s. In addition, enabling legislation made it easier for pension funds to invest in these securities, and corporate pension funds have been pouring billion of dollars into real estate. And a rapidly increasing number of individual 401(k) plans have been adding real estate as an investment option. As of 2006, approximately 180 REITs existed in the United States. Further, Wall Street reentered the mortgage market through the vehicle of mortgage-backed securities (MBSs), whereby a group of mortgage loans are packaged together and sold to institutional and individual investors looking for predictable revenue streams by receiving a share of the timely repayment of principal and interest on the packages of debt. By far the largest volume of growth in MBS investment during the 1990s was in home mortgages, primarily issued by Fannie Mae and Freddie Mac. The total outstanding market value of these securities is more than $6 trillion. More recently, the volume of capital market investment in commercial mortgage–backed securities has been steadily rising. These relatively new financial instruments, issued by Wall Street investment banking firms, are used in the long-term debt financing of commercial, industrial, and income-producing residential rental properties; they are becoming increasingly important for attracting institutional investor capital to finance commercial real estate development. The total value of CMBSs grew from less than $5 billion in 1990 to more than $700 billion by 2007.

John Galbreath, Lincoln Property, the Urban Investment and Development Company, and Tishman Speyer, along with major life insurance companies such as Prudential, Metropolitan, and Equitable and several large Canadian development firms, including Olympia & York, Cadillac Fairview, and TrizecHahn. Many of the largest developers built office, retail, hotel, industrial, apartment, and mixed-use projects. The entry of the Canadians into the U.S. development market also signaled a trend toward international development, as many major North American developers looked to Europe for new projects and prospects beginning in the 1990s—and even more aggressively in the first decade of the 21st century. The Urban Land Institute's establishment and rapid growth of ULI Europe is a good example of the rising trend toward international real estate activity by U.S. developers.

One profound change that began with the movement for neighborhood participation in the 1960s and accelerated after Earth Day in April 1970 was a growing concern for the effects of real estate development on the natural, physical, and human environments. The 1969 National Environmental Policy Act and its various state equivalents led to public regulators' and legislators' use of environmental impact reviews to decide whether proposed development projects should be approved. The 1966 National Historic Preservation Act helped focus attention on conserving existing structures rather than permitting their demolition to make way for entirely new developments. These and many other new federal, state, and local laws and practices— growth controls, sewer moratoriums, impact fees, linkage payments—all slowed the approval process and added to the costs of public and private real estate development in many communities.

In the 1970s, 1980s, and 1990s, California, which in the 1950s and 1960s was considered a developer's paradise for obtaining public infrastructure and services along with fast and favorable regulations, became an embattled and difficult state in which to build new projects, with active protests by citizens, strict and time-consuming regulatory processes, and extensive and costly taxes and fees. This change in the political scene helped reduce overbuilding, especially residential development, but it also contributed greatly to the rapid escalation of housing prices. Clearly, supply could no longer keep pace with demand.

The California syndrome was repeated in the Northeast during the housing boom of the mid-1980s. In some cases, developers joined the ranks of civil rights and affordable housing activists to

Consisting of 763 rental units and 450 for-sale units, Park DuValle is a 125-acre (51-hectare) low-income community in Louisville, Kentucky. *Urban Design Associates*

attack exclusionary zoning and other related practices. The New Jersey State Supreme Court's *Mount Laurel* decisions mandated regional fair share housing, and Massachusetts's statewide "antisnob" zoning law attempted to deal with the exclusionary practices of many suburban towns. NAHB, HUD, ULI, and other public and private organizations have searched for solutions that lower housing costs through regulatory reform.

Part of the problem is that many levels of government have trimmed their expenditures for roads, bridges, and a vast array of other needed infrastructure and services. The tax revolt of the 1970s and 1980s led to reduced maintenance and the neglect of vitally needed replacement and expansion of key facilities. In the context of overburdened infrastructure, new private development often appears to exacerbate traffic congestion, air and water pollution, crowded schools, and other undesirable environmental outcomes without generating sufficient tax revenues to improve overall conditions. Developers find themselves increasingly involved in public relations campaigns and public policy initiatives to build support for proposed projects. They work with local residents, business and civic groups, community leaders, and government officials to gain project approvals based on agreements to pay for a greater share of public facilities and amenities and to mitigate the perceived negative effects of proposed development.

During the 1990s, this form of cooperation and negotiation renewed the search for cooperative physical and financial solutions that meet society's needs for adequate and affordable housing, attractive and livable environments, and dynamic and efficient urban economic development. These solutions included "smart growth" initiatives designed to reduce suburban sprawl by reinvesting in existing developed urban and suburban areas; increasing residential and commercial densities, particularly around transit stations and other key transportation crossroads; and preserving agricultural and recreational land and open space. Many states and localities, including Maryland, Oregon, Florida, New Jersey, Vermont, Tennessee, Georgia, Utah, Maine, Washington, Colorado, and California, are now working on smart growth management.[16] Under the leadership of President William Clinton and Vice President Albert Gore during the 1990s, the President's Council on Sustainable Development served as a major forum for promoting smart growth in states, regions, and communities across the country. More recently, Smart Growth America and its sister organization, the Smart Growth Leadership Institute, headed by former Maryland Governor Parris Glendening, are providing policy education and technical assistance for smart growth initiatives. With the rapidly growing worldwide threat of global climate change caused by excessive emissions of carbon dioxide and other greenhouse gases that are increasingly becoming trapped in Earth's atmosphere, the need for concerted actions to preserve the natural environment and save the world from the destruction of human, animal, and plant life has now become a major priority that will eventually require new and much more sustainable methods of real estate development.

Another sign of the growing interest in sustainable development and smart growth was the rise of a new organization, the Congress for the New Urbanism. Architects and planners such as Peter Calthorpe and Andrés Duany, public officials such as former HUD Secretary Henry Cisneros and former Milwaukee Mayor John Norquist, civic leaders like Neal Peirce of the Citistates Group and John Parr of the Alliance for Regional Stewardship, and an increasing number of real estate developers such as Robert Davis, Henry Turley, and Christopher Leinberger have captured the public's imagination with community planning and urban design concepts and practices that bring back the best in traditional neighborhoods of the old "walking cities" in America and Europe combined with new ways of organizing daily life in a rapidly changing world. Architect-planners like Ray Gindroz have used new urbanism ideas in designing and planning developments ranging from upscale environments such as the Disney Company's new community of Celebration near Orlando, Florida, all the way to inner-city low-income neighborhoods like Park DuValle in Louisville, Kentucky.

Along with the new urbanism has come a new regionalism. As metropolitan areas grow far beyond the boundaries of their central cities, the need for increased regional cooperation and coordinated metropolitan economic development strategies has become vital and urgent. The "new economy" that has emerged is knowledge- and information-based, technology- and communications-intensive, and globally oriented, and it places a premium on the competitiveness and productivity of metropolitan regions to generate and sustain prosperity and quality of life. For communities and regions to succeed in the global marketplace, investing in the fundamental assets of people and place that encourage vibrant economic activity—including quality of the metropolitan transportation and infrastructure systems, education and workforce development, research and technology, the physical and social environment, financing and capital formation, trade promotion and business development—is vitally necessary to grow dynamic businesses and industry networks that will increase jobs, incomes, and wealth, and generate an enviromentally sustainable quality of life for every family and community.

Establishing advanced technology centers that produce a wide variety of goods and services is seen as an effective means of generating and sustaining prosperity and quality of life for many regions—from

Akron, Ohio, to Austin, Texas. Creating the necessary climate of innovation and entrepreneurship depends on public/private collaboration across governmental boundaries and jurisdictions involving cities, suburbs, counties, states, and even nations where regions cross international borders such as Buffalo and San Diego. In addition, metropolitan initiatives in cities from Portland, Oregon, to Jacksonville, Florida, focus on environmental preservation and restoration. Many of these initiatives in places like Atlanta, Baltimore, Cleveland, and Detroit also address key issues of poverty, racial and ethnic divisions and disparities, and rebuilding inner-city and inner-suburban neighborhoods with modest success and many challenges. Americans will increasingly see themselves as citizens of metropolitan economies, and the search for solutions to designing more effective governance and implementing successful regional collaboration will grow even more pressing in the 21st century.

SUMMARY

This chapter has described and analyzed the growth of a mature, modern, and professional real estate development industry with more complex sources of financing and greater sophistication in relating to government and the general public. In the time since World War II, developers have increasingly specialized in different product types—offices, shopping centers, industrial parks, hotels, and housing. They have built larger and more efficient organizations and faced tough economic challenges such as inflation and recession. Sensitivity to racial, ethnic, and environmental issues has become much more important. The new global economy will bring even more dramatic changes in real estate development.

TERMS

- ▶ Civil Rights Act of 1964
- ▶ Community development corporation (CDC)
- ▶ Community Reinvestment Act (CRA)
- ▶ Department of Veterans Affairs
- ▶ Festival marketplaces

- ▶ GI Bill
- ▶ Gray Areas Program
- ▶ Greenlining
- ▶ Industrial parks
- ▶ Junk bonds
- ▶ Limited partnership
- ▶ Military-industrial complex
- ▶ Model Cities Program of 1966
- ▶ National Housing Act of 1968
- ▶ Neighborhood development organization
- ▶ Neighborhood Reinvestment Corporation
- ▶ New communities
- ▶ New urbanism
- ▶ Power of eminent domain
- ▶ Redlining
- ▶ Syndicator
- ▶ Takeout
- ▶ Title I
- ▶ Urban entertainment center
- ▶ Urban renewal
- ▶ VA home loan guarantee program
- ▶ Veterans Administration
- ▶ Voting Rights Act of 1965
- ▶ War on Poverty

REVIEW QUESTIONS

6.1 How and why did homebuilding production methods change after World War II?

6.2 Describe the urban renewal efforts of the 1950s and 1960s.

6.3 How and why did retailing change in the 1950s and 1960s?

6.4 What spurred the urban crisis of the 1960s and what housing-related programs were initiated because of it?

6.5 What is a CDC and what is its role in community building?

6.6 What is a new community?

6.7 Real estate is always said to be a cyclical business. What are some of the financial cycles that have occurred since 1970?

6.8 Describe the growth of real estate securities from 1888 to their current form as REITs.

NOTES

1. "Housing: Up from the Potato Fields," *Time,* July 3, 1950, p. 67. See also Marc A. Weiss, *The Rise of the Community Builders: The American Real Estate Industry and Urban Land Planning* (New York: Columbia Univ. Press, 1987).

2. John Keats, *The Crack in the Picture Window* (Boston: Houghton Mifflin, 1957); and William H. Whyte, Jr., *The Organization Man* (New York: Simon & Schuster, 1956).

3. Tom Schactman, *Skyscraper Dreams: The Great Real Estate Dynasties of New York* (Boston: Little, Brown, 1991), p. 218.

4. Marc A. Weiss, "The Origins and Legacy of Urban Renewal," in *Federal Housing Policy and Programs: Past and Present,* ed. J. Paul Mitchell (New Brunswick, N.J.: Rutgers Univ. Center for Urban Policy Research, 1985), pp. 253–276; and Ann R. Markusen, Annalee Saxenian, and Marc A. Weiss, "Who Benefits from Intergovernmental Transfers?" *Publius: The Journal of Federalism,* Winter 1981, pp. 5–35.

5. Robert A. Caro, *The Power Broker: Robert Moses and the Fall of New York* (New York: Random House, 1974), pp. 850–894.

6. "Northland: A New Yardstick for Shopping Center Planning," *Architectural Forum,* June 1954, pp. 102–119. The article begins, "This is a classic in shopping center planning, in the sense that Rockefeller Center is a classic in urban skyscraper–group planning, or Radburn, N.J., in suburban residential planning." On Northland and Victor Gruen, see also Howard Gillette, Jr., "The Evolution of the Planned Shopping Center in Suburb and City," *Journal of the American Planning Association,* Autumn 1985, pp. 449–460.

7. Kenneth T. Jackson, *Crabgrass Frontier: The Suburbanization of the United States* (New York: Oxford Univ. Press, 1985), p. 254.

8. Daniel Seligman, "The Enduring Slums," in *The Exploding Metropolis* (Garden City, N.Y.: Doubleday, 1957), p. 132.

9. Catherine Bauer, "The Dreary Deadlock of Public Housing," *Architectural Forum,* May 1957, p. 140.

10. Ibid.

11. Marc A. Weiss, "Leveraging Private Financing and Investment for Economic and Community Development," *Global Urban Development Magazine,* March 2006, pp. 1–11; Marc A. Weiss, "Community Development," in *Private Finance and Economic Development: City and Regional Investment* (Paris: Organization for Economic Cooperation and Development, 2003), pp. 55–73; and Ayse Can Talen, Marc A. Weiss, and Sohini Sarkar, "The Future of Microfinance in the United States: Research, Practice, and Policy Perspectives," in *Replicating Microfinance in the United States,* ed. James H. Carr and Zhong Yi Tong (Washington, D.C.: Woodrow Wilson Center Press, 2002), pp. 331–360.

12. Real Estate Research Corporation, *Tall Office Buildings in the United States* (Washington, D.C.: ULI–the Urban Land Institute, 1985).

13. "He Digs Downtown: For Master Planner James Rouse, Urban Life Is a Festival," *Time,* August 24, 1981, pp. 42–53.

14. See, for example, Clarence D. Long, Jr., *Building Cycles and the Theory of Investment* (Princeton, N.J.: Princeton Univ. Press, 1940); Homer Hoyt, *The Urban Real Estate Cycle: Performances and Prospects,* Technical Bulletin No. 38 (Washington, D.C.: ULI–the Urban Land Institute, 1950); Roy Wenzlick, *The Coming Boom in Real Estate* (New York: Simon & Schuster, 1936); Leo Grebler, David M. Blank, and Louis Winnick, *Capital Formation in Residential Real Estate: Trends and Prospects* (Princeton, N.J.: Princeton Univ. Press, 1956); Manuel Gottlieb, *Long Swings in Urban Development* (New York: National Bureau of Economic Research, 1976); and Marc A. Weiss, "The Politics of Real Estate Cycles," *Urban Land,* March 1992, pp. 33–35.

15. Marc A. Weiss, *National Housing Policy in the U.S. for the 21st Century* (Washington, D.C.: Global Urban Development, 2002); and Henry G. Cisneros, Marc A. Weiss, and Craig S. Nickerson, *The National Homeownership Strategy: Partners in the American Dream* (Washington, D.C.: U.S. Department of Housing and Urban Development, 1995).

16. Marc A. Weiss, *The Smart Growth Experience: Lessons from the United States* (Washington, D.C.: Global Urban Development, 2002); and Marc A. Weiss, *State Policy Approaches to Promote Metropolitan Economic Strategy* (Washington, D.C.: National Governors Association, 2002).

PART III

FINANCE

Without financing (debt, equity, or some combination), no real estate development is possible, so it is critical for developers to keep up with trends in real estate finance and different sources of capital. Still, keeping up is hard without a solid foundation. Part III provides that foundation, covering both the theory and analytics of real estate finance. Building on this foundation, the rest of the book adds the complexities of development so as to allow the investment logic to lead to better development decisions.

Chapter 7 explores the relationships of the various players in the tenant market and the investment capital markets; Chapter 8 discusses the logic behind real estate financing decisions. Specifically, it looks to a proposed development's expected income stream to understand why lenders lend and investors invest. First, it explores the property income pro forma, which is the standard means of categorizing property income and expenses. Then, the property's net operating income is used to value the proposed development and find satisfactory returns for the lender and developer. The chapter closes with a case study of a credit presentation for Clackamas Ridge in Portland, Oregon, comprising information presented by the loan officer and credit officer of a bank to the loan committee when seeking approval for a loan. The Clackamas Ridge case discusses the many important details of getting a loan proposal accepted.

Expanding on the topic of mortgage loan underwriting in Chapter 8, discounted cash flow analysis of a real estate investment and why investors invest are the subjects of Chapter 9. The analysis begins with an explanation of investment rates of return, followed by a detailed presentation of the mechanics of the process. After setting up and solving numerous single-period and multiple-period discounted cash flow analyses, we apply that methodology to Gateway Business Center, a multitenant office building in Milwaukee, Wisconsin. The chapter concludes with a discussion of the different forms of equity ownership and structures for real estate ventures.

CHAPTER 7

Real Estate Finance: Background

The real estate market for income-producing properties is best described in terms of the tenant space market (the supply of and tenants' demand for space) and the real estate capital market (the supply of and demand for investment dollars used in the real estate development process). The intersection of the two markets is where the real estate market emerges.[1] Historically, real estate markets in the United States—both space and capital markets—were local. When a new tenant space was needed, local developers would gather several wealthy investors together and form a limited partnership to provide the equity (ownership capital), a local bank would fund the construction mortgage (short-term construction debt underwritten by the credibility of the developer and strength of the market), and a life insurance company would fund the permanent mortgage (long-term debt underwritten by the property's income). As we will learn in this chapter, the old model of investment capital for real estate is now only one of several models currently used.

The supply of and demand for tenant space determine a property's income stream. Stated another way, the property income stream is determined by the local space market and the quality and location of the subject property in that market—that is, the specific property's features, functions, and benefits to a tenant. The strength of the tenant market is apparent in the lease contracts—the lease term, rental rate, and tenant's creditworthiness. Property income depends on the local market demand for tenant space in a particular property type.

The real estate capital market is the market for the investment dollars used to purchase and develop real estate. Investments in commercial real estate directly compete with U.S. stocks, bonds, and other instruments. Real estate investments or developments are funded with debt and/or equity.

This chapter first covers the relationship between the space and the capital markets, focusing on recent innovations in the capital market. With that foundation, it then reviews the traditional real estate financing cycle, elaborating on the usual sequence of development financing. The second half of the chapter expands on the motivations of the major institutions involved, as developers are likely to make better decisions if they better understand the different sources of capital. In all financing decisions, it is helpful if the developer is able to stand in the lender's shoes. With that perspective, the developer is more likely to approach the right source of capital with the right loan request.

THE RELATIONSHIP BETWEEN SPACE AND CAPITAL MARKETS

Conceptual Foundations

The most common form of property valuation in the United States applies a capitalization rate (cap rate) to a property's income stream. In this approach, the property's net operating income (NOI, or the property income stream after property operating expenses have been paid) is divided by the capitalization rate (a means of valuing the property based on growth prospects and perceived risk of the property's cash flows relative to other investment opportunities) to derive value:[2]

$$Value = \frac{Net\ Operating\ Income}{Capitalization\ Rate}$$

If the perceived risk per unit of return by investing in real estate is lower than investing in other financial and nonfinancial assets (i.e., real estate investment has higher risk-adjusted return than competitive investments), then investors will acquire more real estate, driving down property capitalization rates as property prices are bid up. Property prices continue to increase to the point where the risk-adjusted return matches that of the market for other investments.

Conversely, if the risk-adjusted return for real estate investment is inadequate, capital flows away from the sector, reducing the price of real estate, until risk-adjusted rates of return increase to the point where returns are appropriate for the perceived risks. In short, capital market participants chase risk-adjusted return across investment alternatives worldwide. On the other hand, the property income stream or NOI depends solely on what is occurring in the local space market. The ability of a property to generate an income stream depends on the demand for space, competing properties, and locational factors that include everything from the quality of the local labor force to the price of

electricity to the business climate to the weather. The location's quality is priced in the tenant space market in the form of net rents. As a result, the relationship between the real estate space and capital markets can be thought of as occurring in the following way:

$$Value = \frac{Local\ Tenant\ Space\ Market}{Capital\ Market}$$

The intersection of the tenant space market and the investment capital market is where real estate value emerges. As the tenant market begins to strengthen, property income streams increase as landlords secure leases with higher rents. The strengthening of the tenant space market also reduces a property's perceived investment risk, and prospective investors are willing to pay a higher price for a less volatile income stream, thus accepting a lower capitalization rate or return on the real estate. Alternatively, as space markets weaken and the rents and viability of tenants in a building are less secure, property values decline as the risk premium embedded in the capitalization rate increases. All else being equal, the risk premiums of income-producing real estate move in the same direction as the perceived risks of the space markets. Alternatively, property values move in the opposite direction of property risk premiums and capitalization rates.

Market Overview

On the investment side of real estate, the value of institutional investment in commercial real estate in the United States for 2006 is estimated at $4.26 trillion, with approximately 75 percent ($3.2 trillion) of that amount invested in public and private real estate debt (see Figure 7-1). Private sources of debt, which include banks and life insurance companies, account for $2.4 trillion of that debt. The other $823 billion in commercial real estate debt is attributable to loans that have been securitized or sold on Wall Street in the form of commercial mortgage–backed securities (CMBSs). The remaining investment of $1.1 trillion is invested in equity or the ownership of real estate, of which $352 billion is invested in public equity (REITs) and $705 billion is invested in private real estate investment vehicles.

Figure 7-1	Real Estate Capital Sources in 2006	
	Billions of Dollars	**Percent of Total**
U.S. Real Estate Capital	**Real Estate Capital Sources**	
Private Debt	2,379.5	55.9
Public Debt	821.2	19.3
Private Equity	705.0	16.6
Public Equity	352.4	8.3
Total	4,258.1	100.0
Debt Capital	**Debt Capital Sources**	
Private Debt		
Banks, S&Ls, Mutual Savings Banks	1,792.7	56.0
Life Insurance Companies	293.5	9.2
REIT Unsecured Debt	251.2	7.8
Pension Funds	42.1	1.3
Subtotal	2,379.5	74.3
Public Debt		
Commercial Mortgage Securities	685.8	21.4
Government Credit Agencies	108.0	3.4
Mortgage REITs	27.3	0.9
Public Untraded Funds	0.2	0.0
Subtotal	821.2	25.7
Total Debt	3,200.7	100.0
Equity Capital	**Equity Capital Sources**	
Private Equity		
Private Investors (Larger Properties)	451.8	42.7
Pension Funds	162.3	15.3
Foreign Investors	55.5	5.0
Life Insurance Companies	30.4	2.9
Private Financial Institutions	5.1	0.5
Subtotal	705.0	66.7
Public Equity		
REITs (Equity and Hybrid)	315.0	29.8
Public Untraded Funds	37.4	3.5
Subtotal	352.4	33.3
Total Equity	1,057.4	100.0

Source: Compiled by Roulac Global Places from various sources, including Amercial Council of Life Insurers, CMSA/Trepp Database, Commercial Mortgage Alert, Federal Reserve, FannieMae.com, FDIC, FreddieMac.com, IREI, NAREIT, PricewaterhouseCoopers, and Reis.
Note: As of second quarter 2006. Excludes corporate, nonprofit, and government equity real estate holdings as well as single-family and owner-occupied residences.

The primary measure of return in the real estate investment market—capitalization rates—has generally maintained a tight band between 5 percent and 10 percent, according to the National Council of Real Estate Investment Fiduciaries (www.ncreif .com). Capitalization rates in 2006 were approaching or were at record lows, a record that goes back to 1980, when the data were first collected. Reasons for the low capitalization rates include 1) the perceived riskiness of owning commercial real estate, 2) good prospects for growth in current income streams, and 3) relatively low prospective returns on stocks and bonds.

The economic growth of a geographic area determines the strength of a regional tenant space market. Space markets in the United States are rarely in equilibrium for long; rather, they pass through equilibrium on their way to being overbuilt with space or undersupplied with space, often following the path of the local gross regional product (GRP). The demand for and supply of real estate in narrow space markets is not fluid. Space markets are lumpy, with large additions to the market coming in the form of periodic additions of new buildings or, alternatively, the razing of an economically obsolete building. Similarly, the demand for space is seldom fluid for individual space users. Although employers often hire additional staff one person at a time (with each additional white-collar employee occupying approximately 150 to 200 square feet [14 to 18.5 square meters] of office space), they contract for space intermittently, adding or shedding space as needed, often when the lease expires.

The broadest measure of demand for space markets is growth in the gross domestic product. As shown in Figure 7-2, annual growth in GDP in the United States has averaged 3 percent since 1980 and 2.5 percent since the beginning of 2000 through the third quarter of 2006. The 2001 recession slowed economic growth in the 2000s (recessions are the

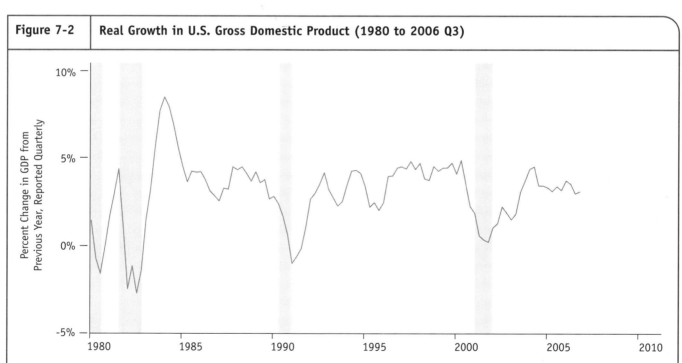

| Figure 7-2 | Real Growth in U.S. Gross Domestic Product (1980 to 2006 Q3) |

Source: U.S. Department of Commerce, Bureau of Economic Analysis.
Notes:
Data use seasonally adjusted annual rate and are reported quarterly.
Units are reported in billions of chained 2000 dollars.
See *A Guide to the National Income and Product Accounts of the United States* at http://www.bea.gov/bea/an/n.
Shaded areas indicate recessions as determined by the National Bureau of Economic Research.

shaded areas in the figure). If GDP growth rates do not exceed labor productivity growth rates, few, if any, new jobs are created. New employment fills U.S. office and industrial space, and the salaries from these new jobs fund retail purchases and fuel housing demand. Annual output per hour, or labor productivity, in the United States increased 2.1 percent since 1980 and 3 percent from the beginning of 2000 through the third quarter of 2006 (see Figure 7-3).

Employment growth in the United States depends on economic growth: if the economy is not growing and, more specifically, growing at a rate faster than labor productivity increases, few new jobs are created. For the period from the beginning of 1980 through the third quarter of 2006, employment grew at an average annual rate of 1.5 percent per year, with the annual employment growth rate forecast at 1 to 1.5 percent between 2005 and 2010 (see Figure 7-4).

In addition to being described in terms of a location (in a city or metropolitan area), tenant space

markets can also be described based on the type of space provided. Generally speaking, U.S. commercial space markets are categorized into five distinctly different property types: office, retail, multifamily, industrial, and hotel.[3] Each type has a different risk profile, even when located in the same geographical area as another type. And with the increase in mixed-use developments, the risk equation gets somewhat more complicated.

The supply of and demand for space differ across location and property type for several reasons. First, developers—especially small developers—often specialize in one type of space. For instance, office developers seldom develop multifamily housing, and multifamily developers seldom develop hotels. Thus, the suppliers of one type of space (say, office space) usually supply only that type of space and thus do not have a significant impact on the supply of other space types. (It is not the case, however, for large developers such as Forest City Enterprises or Hines, both of which

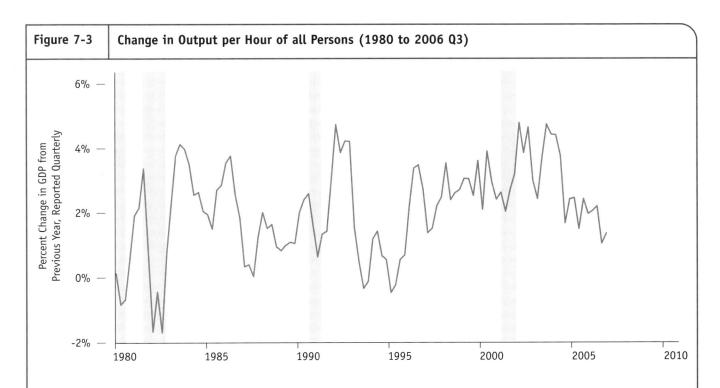

| Figure 7-3 | Change in Output per Hour of all Persons (1980 to 2006 Q3) |

Source: U.S. Department of Labor, Bureau of Labor Statistics.
Notes:
Data are seasonally adjusted and reported quarterly.
Shaded areas indicate recessions as determined by the National Bureau of Economic Research.

| Figure 7-4 | U.S. Payroll Employment (1980 to February 2007) |

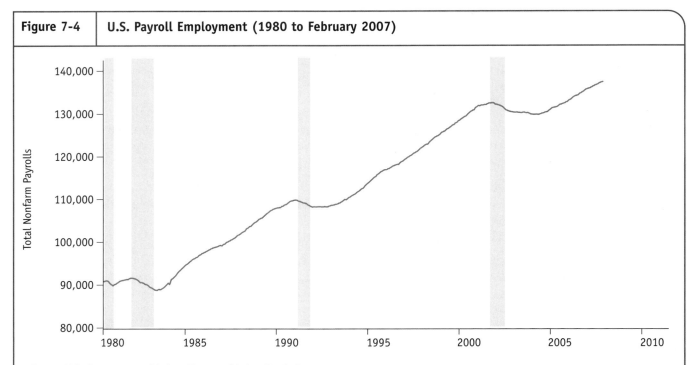

Source: U.S. Department of Labor, Bureau of Labor Statistics.
Notes:
Units in thousands.
Data are seasonally adjusted and reported monthly.
For information on survey methodology, see *BLS Handbook of Methods*, Chapter 2 (http://stats.bls.gov:80/opub/hom/homch2_itc.htm).
Shaded areas indicate recessions as determined by the National Bureau of Economic Research.

develop residential, office, retail, and hotel space. In addition, more developers are expanding their product types as the number of mixed-use developments increases.) Second, demand for space differs by market; that is, total new white-collar employment per thousand differs city by city. For instance, New York City has more white-collar employees per thousand new jobs than a manufacturing-based city such as Milwaukee, Wisconsin; thus, the absorption of office space per new employee may differ dramatically from one city to another.

Third, the amount of space for each new employee may differ based on the type of white-collar job created. For example, the many law firms and the amount and quality of space needed per attorney in Washington, D.C., is much greater than the amount of space needed for an employee at a regional call center. Fourth, not all space is created equal. Attor-

neys are often located in central business districts, where law firms often pay premium rents for premium space and quality locations; conversely, call centers are usually located in the fringe suburbs, where land and space are less expensive. Finally, the type of space and days of the week that space is needed differ across potential hotel and retail locations. For instance, a tourist destination or airport hub city would clearly demand more hotel space than other similarly sized cities; moreover, hotel clientele varies by day of the week and month of the year.

Overall, the supply of and demand for space may differ, possibly dramatically, among and even within cities. The review of the space markets in this part of the text largely ignores the differences within and among different space markets. Instead, the text briefly discusses each property type, addressing one or more broad drivers for space market demand, changes in the stock of space, property vacancy rates, and rental growth rates.[4]

Space Markets

The quality and stability of a property income stream are determined by the strength of the space market and the relative position of a property in that market. The strength of space markets is made explicit in all lease contracts through the rental rate, lease term, and rent escalations, among other lease terms. Site-specific and market attributes determine the size and volatility of a property income stream, that is, its NOI. The quality of a space market from a landlord's perspective is demonstrated by its ability to constrain new supply and generate new demand. For instance, in a market area with few municipal (legal) or physical limitations on new space, the risk of new supply is high; the Atlanta and Dallas areas are good examples.[5] Alternatively, in a market with a core of high-growth companies, desirable amenities, and constraints on the land, demand for space is likely to remain strong; New York City and San Francisco are good current examples.

For markets to grow, new employment must occur, and for new employment to occur, economic growth (GDP) must outpace the rate of productivity increase. From 1993 to the third quarter of 2006, the average increase in worker productivity was 2.6 percent, but during the 20 years before 1993, the average increase in the productivity of U.S. nonfarm workers was 1.7 percent. If GDP growth simply equals the improvement in unit productivity, little if any job growth will occur; growth in the economy comes from population growth and existing employees' greater productivity. A rough rule of thumb to estimate demand for office space in the United States is that for each additional 100 jobs, approximately 20 are in detached office space (detached from manufacturing facilities and not in build-to-suit facilities), with each office employee using 150 to 200 square feet (14 to 18.5 square meters) of space. In early 2007, the U.S. economy was growing by about 150,000 new jobs per month (see Figure 7-4).

The nationwide overbuilding of office space in the late 1980s sent vacancy rates above 15 percent for more than a decade (see Figure 7-5). As expected, these high vacancy rates left effective rent growth rates for office rent flat to negative for the duration of that period.[6] As market vacancy rates improved and fell below 10 percent, however, the effect on rents was a rise of more than 5 percent per year for several years in the late 1990s (see Figure 7-6); that is, rental rate increases outpaced inflation and the increase in the cost to develop new buildings. As space markets weakened again during the 2000–2003 cycle following the dot-com bust, effective rental growth rates dropped abruptly but picked up again a few years later. In sum, net effective rent levels are inversely affected by the supply of space.

Employment growth also fuels the demand for industrial space. It is instructive to look at industrial capacity use rates in the United States as a demand driver for industrial space (see Figure 7-7). (Capacity utilization reveals how intensely manufacturing equipment is being used: if the use rate is low, it is unlikely that companies will demand more industrial space to expand capacity. As of the middle of the first decade of the 2000s, capacity utilization grew greatly from a 20-year low; therefore, the demand and rental rates for industrial space are expected to increase in the following years (see Figures 7-8 and 7-9).

Space absorption for retail space and apartments is similar to that for office and industrial space. As might be expected, changes in personal or disposable income and consumer sentiment directly affect retail spending and thus the demand for retail space (Figure 7-10). As per capita income has continued to grow over the last 20 years, absorption of retail space has remained positive (Figure 7-11), thus keeping effective rents growing (Figure 7-12). The retail sales growth rate began weakening in 2006, indicating what is likely to be weak growth in net retail rents in the coming years.

Changes in U.S. population characteristics, specifically the creation of young adult households, have resulted in an increase in demand for housing units. Figure 7-13 reveals population changes across the baby boom, post–baby boom, and echo baby boom age cohorts and predicts the likely change in number of young adults who will form households. The young adult populations are growing, which will

| Figure 7-5 | U.S. Office Supply and Demand (1990–2008) |

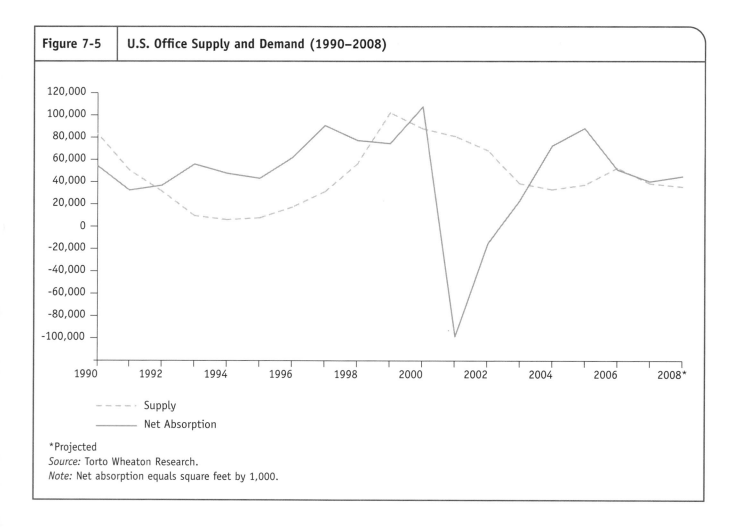

*Projected
Source: Torto Wheaton Research.
Note: Net absorption equals square feet by 1,000.

create a continued strong demand for housing in the coming decade.

A second demand driver for housing units is immigration. Population growth from immigration in the United States is focused on a limited number of markets—namely, markets in California, Florida, Texas, New York, and Illinois—but has spread recently to a large number of cities in areas of the countries not typically associated with high influxes of immigrants.

As the result of a variety of factors, homeownership rates in the United States soared from 64 percent in the mid-1990s to a record high exceeding 69 percent in 2005 (see figure 7-14),[7] reducing the demand for rental units and increasing multifamily vacancy rates (see Figures 7-15 and 7-16).[8] (Production of new rental units had lagged as developers responded to the growing interest in condominium ownership.) But just as

quickly, changes in the economy turned the tide again. In 2005 for the first time in years, the number of renter households rose in all parts of the country, and subsequently vacancy rates fell and effective rental rates bounced back.

Capital Markets

Real estate capital markets are often described as four quadrants: private debt, public debt, private equity, and public equity. Historically, capital that was used to fund real estate investments was provided by private capital sources. The most common sources of private debt are banks and life insurance companies. Although banks and life insurance companies may be publicly traded, if the mortgage debt they issue is not publicly traded, the debt is considered private debt. Since the early to mid-1990s, however, more capital

Figure 7-6	Office Vacany Rates and Changes in Effective Rent (1980 to 2011)

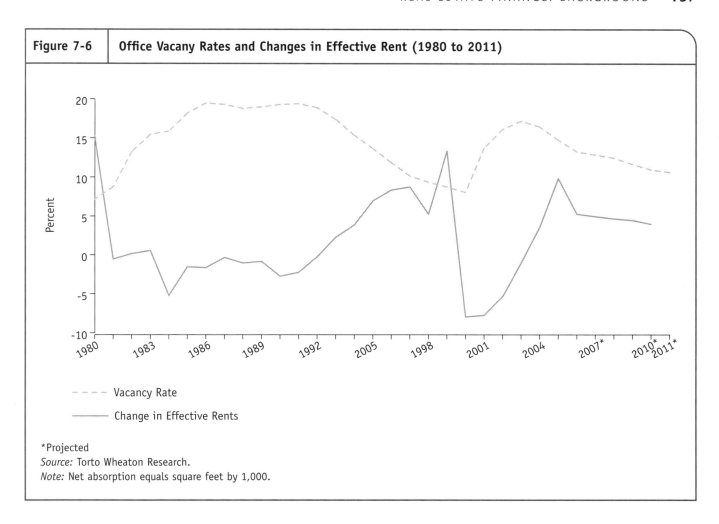

--- Vacancy Rate

—— Change in Effective Rents

*Projected
Source: Torto Wheaton Research.
Note: Net absorption equals square feet by 1,000.

for real estate has come from public sources. The distinction between private and public sources of real estate capital is whether or not the investment capital is publicly traded.

Public sources of capital came of age in the 1990s. Public capital—both debt and equity—is generally raised in public auction markets, usually organized stock and bond markets in New York, with proceeds from issuing these public securities used to fund real estate investments. Commercial mortgage–backed securities are the primary source of publicly traded debt. CMBSs are fixed-income investments similar to corporate bonds that are collateralized by pools of commercial mortgages rated and sold in the fixed-income (bond) markets.

The most common form of public equity or ownership of real estate is the real estate investment trust.

REITs usually invest in real estate on behalf of investors who purchase shares of REIT stock for return of dividends and appreciation of stock price. The following paragraphs discuss the sources of debt and equity capital that fund real estate projects.

Real Estate Debt

Private Sources of Real Estate Debt

Debt capital flows into commercial real estate have varied dramatically over the years. Before the mid-1990s, private debt was the dominant source of capital. In 1987, a cyclical high-water mark for the private debt market, more than $100 billion in capital flowed into real estate. This generous supply of capital pushed real estate development to unsustainable levels, leaving all segments of the property market

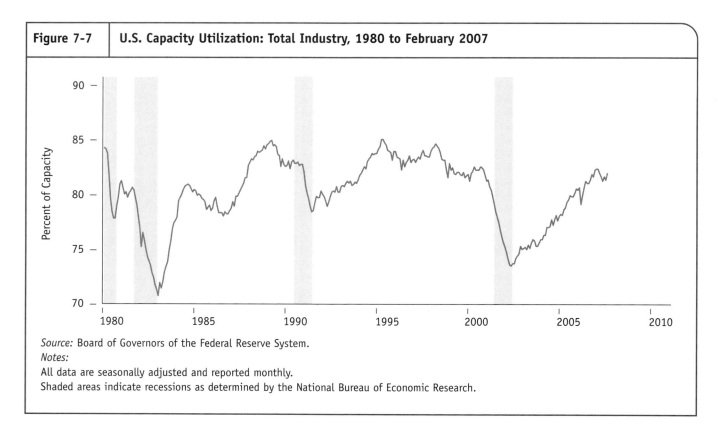

Figure 7-7 | U.S. Capacity Utilization: Total Industry, 1980 to February 2007

Source: Board of Governors of the Federal Reserve System.
Notes:
All data are seasonally adjusted and reported monthly.
Shaded areas indicate recessions as determined by the National Bureau of Economic Research.

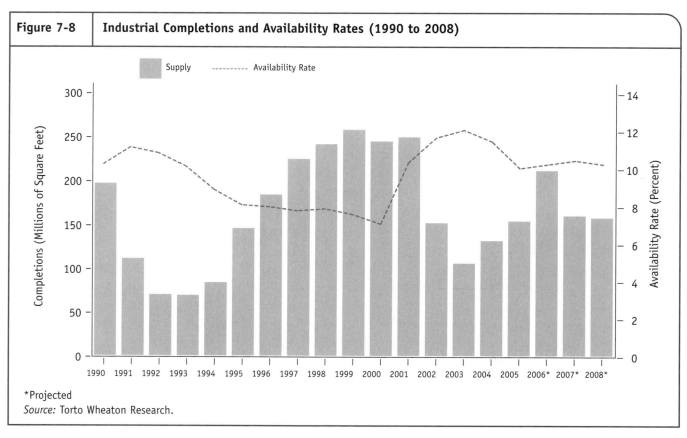

Figure 7-8 | Industrial Completions and Availability Rates (1990 to 2008)

*Projected
Source: Torto Wheaton Research.

Figure 7-9	Industrial Vacancy Rates and Changes in Effective Rent (1980 to 2011)

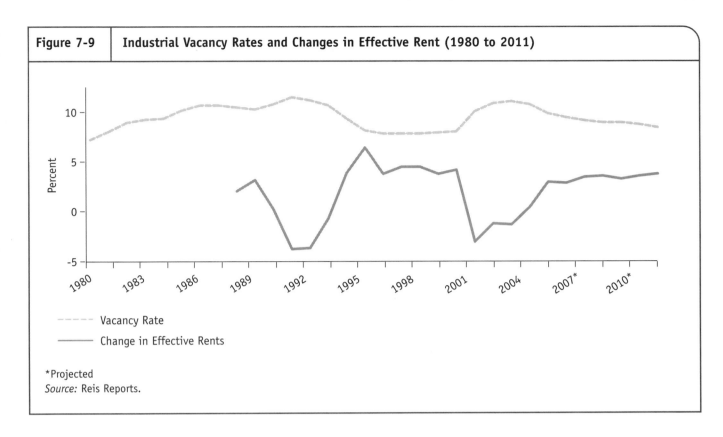

Vacancy Rate

Change in Effective Rents

*Projected
Source: Reis Reports.

other than the multifamily market significantly over-built in virtually all cities in the country. Private sources of debt, which were the dominant source of capital in the 1980s, departed from the market in the early to mid-1990s; from 1990 to 1994, $152 billion in private real estate debt flowed out of real estate, $57 billion in 1992 alone, precipitating the worst downturn in commercial real estate since the Great Depression.

Figure 7-17 reveals the aggregate sources of public and private capital in commercial real estate. Note several very important factors in the figure. First, commercial banks, S&Ls, and mutual savings banks are the dominant source of private debt, with $1.79 trillion in total loans outstanding. Banks and thrifts provide the majority of construction loan financing but more recently have been sizable players in the permanent and miniperm market as well ("mini" refers to the shorter three- to seven-year term of these permanent loans).[9] Further, banks were one of the few sources of private debt that stayed in the market during the real estate downturn in the late 1980s and early 1990s,

when they were a positive source of debt capital throughout most of the downturn in the market.

As a result of federal deregulation of financial institutions in 1979 and 1980, S&Ls became commercial real estate lenders on a large scale for the first time. This new source of debt capital for real estate developers and owners helped to fuel some of the overbuilding in the early to mid-1980s. Of the many different sources of private capital, none were more volatile than S&Ls. Freshly deregulated, these formerly staid institutions that largely supplied single-family mortgages to homeowners could now operate across state borders, became publicly traded, and provided commercial real estate developers with a new source of capital.

Somewhat paralleling the experience in the S&L industry was the life insurance industry, which lent heavily to real estate developers and owners in the early 1980s and withdrew from the market in the late 1980s. It should be noted, however, that life insurance companies are significant private market debt players, as they continue to replace maturing loans

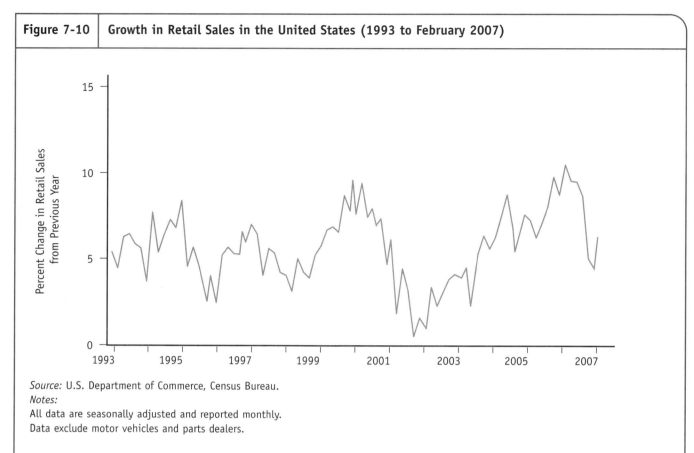

Figure 7-10 | **Growth in Retail Sales in the United States (1993 to February 2007)**

Source: U.S. Department of Commerce, Census Bureau.
Notes:
All data are seasonally adjusted and reported monthly.
Data exclude motor vehicles and parts dealers.

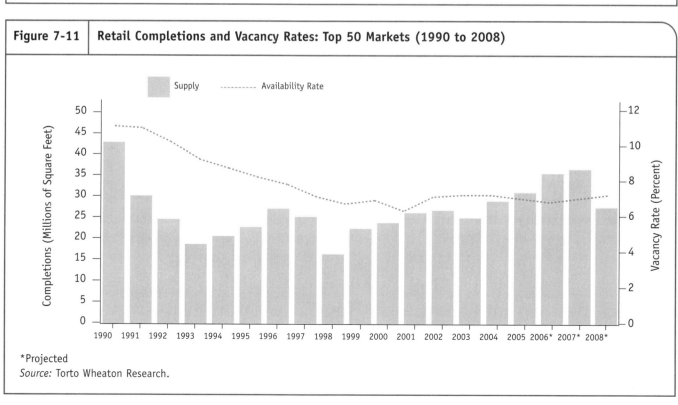

Figure 7-11 | **Retail Completions and Vacancy Rates: Top 50 Markets (1990 to 2008)**

*Projected
Source: Torto Wheaton Research.

| Figure 7-12 | Retail Vacancy Rates and Changes in Effective Rent (1980 to 2011) |

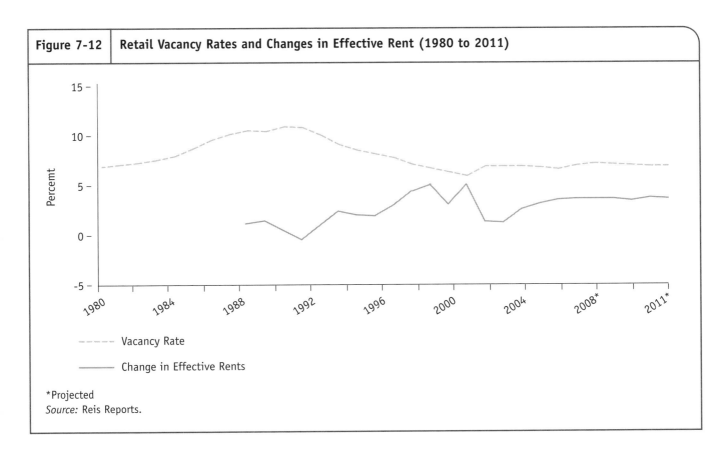

----- Vacancy Rate

——— Change in Effective Rents

*Projected
Source: Reis Reports.

that were made ten years earlier and make new permanent loans. Life insurance companies generally lend money for top-quality income-producing properties and generally are considered more conservative in their underwriting methods than CMBS pools. As such, most life insurance companies did not fail like many of the S&Ls that made construction loans. Many life insurance companies now fulfill some of their real estate investment needs by purchasing A, BBB, and BB tranches of CMBS issuances.

Finally, REIT unsecured debt and pension funds also provide debt capital to the commercial real estate market.

Public Sources of Real Estate Debt

The exodus of several of the private debt players from the debt markets in the late 1980s and early 1990s because of the market downturn left a void for new players to fill. As the federal government rationalized failed S&Ls, it quickly realized that the sheer magnitude of the loans acquired from these thrift institutions required a

new means of disposing of nonperforming and underperforming loans. Some of these loans were sold as mortgage pools to Wall Street investors and groups of investors, thus creating the public debt market.

Commercial Mortgage–Backed Securities

The big story in commercial real estate lending over the past decade has been the emergence of commercial mortgage–backed securities as a viable and ongoing source of capital for income-producing commercial real estate, which has $661 billion in U.S. commercial mortgages outstanding as of 2007 Q1 and new CMBS issuances in 2006 of $202 billion (see Figure 7-17). CMBSs are bonds collateralized by commercial property loans; most, if not all, mortgages in CMBS pools are permanent loans. Although CMBSs are a relatively new source of long-term real estate debt, all indications are that they will continue to grow in volume and in their share of the total market for permanent loan financing. They have brought a new source of capital for real estate, creating greater

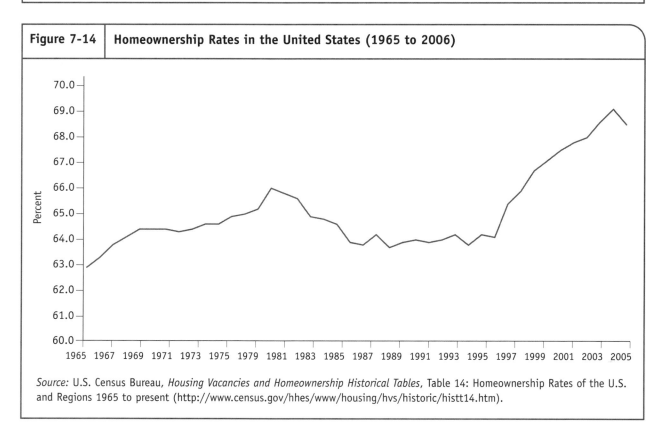

Figure 7-13	Population Characteristics of the United States			
Group Characteristic	Born	Approximate Age in 2006	Population in Age Cohort (Thousands)	Population Change from Previous Cohort
Young Generation Y	Post-1986	10–19	39,689	2.88%
Old Generation Y	1977–1985	20–29	38,587	3.76%
Generation X	1965–1976	30–39	37,189	–17.01%
Young Baby Boom	1955–1964	40–49	44,813	18.91%
Old Baby Boom	1946–1954	50–59	37,685	

Source: U.S. Census Bureau.

Figure 7-14	Homeownership Rates in the United States (1965 to 2006)

Source: U.S. Census Bureau, *Housing Vacancies and Homeownership Historical Tables*, Table 14: Homeownership Rates of the U.S. and Regions 1965 to present (http://www.census.gov/hhes/www/housing/hvs/historic/histt14.htm).

liquidity and competition for commercial real estate mortgages.

A variety of lenders and debt intermediaries originate loans that are then placed with other loans in pools. The borrowers of CMBS loans have little if any knowledge of the bondholders, the ultimate source of funding for the loans. Commercial banks, insurance companies, investment bankers, mortgage bankers, and mortgage brokers, among others, are primary originators of such loans. Banks and mortgage bankers are active participants in the securitization process. Money market funds and life insurance companies are major investors in CMBSs, which are a much more liquid form of real estate investment than whole loans (i.e., permanent loans).

In securitizing loans, banks and mortgage bankers do not actually supply the funds that flow to the projects for which the loans were originated. They are

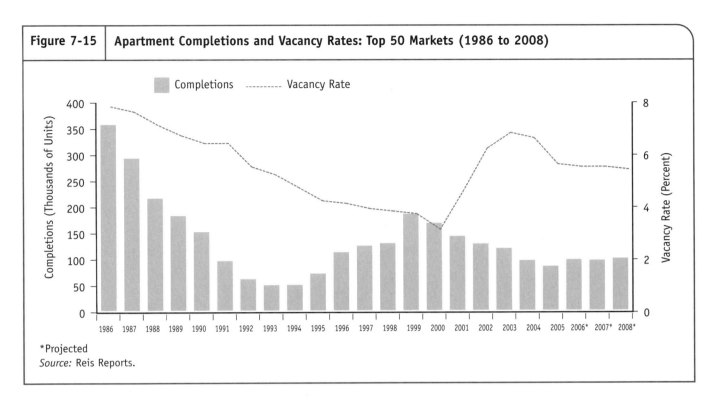

Figure 7-15 | **Apartment Completions and Vacancy Rates: Top 50 Markets (1986 to 2008)**

*Projected
Source: Reis Reports.

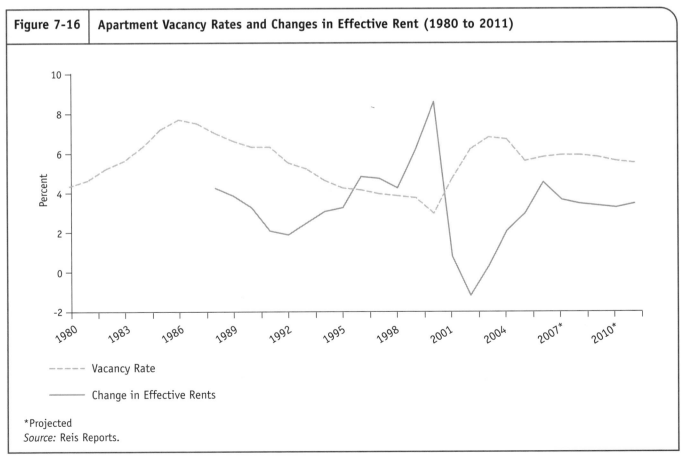

Figure 7-16 | **Apartment Vacancy Rates and Changes in Effective Rent (1980 to 2011)**

*Projected
Source: Reis Reports.

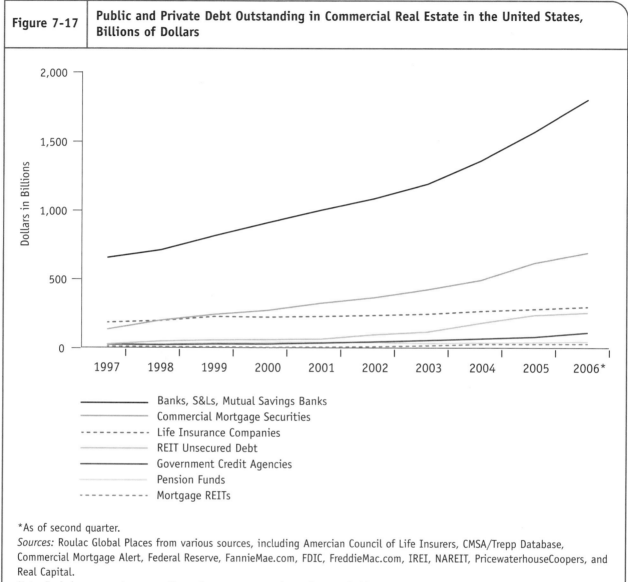

| Figure 7-17 | Public and Private Debt Outstanding in Commercial Real Estate in the United States, Billions of Dollars |

Legend:
Banks, S&Ls, Mutual Savings Banks
Commercial Mortgage Securities
Life Insurance Companies
REIT Unsecured Debt
Government Credit Agencies
Pension Funds
Mortgage REITs

*As of second quarter.
Sources: Roulac Global Places from various sources, including Amercian Council of Life Insurers, CMSA/Trepp Database, Commercial Mortgage Alert, Federal Reserve, FannieMae.com, FDIC, FreddieMac.com, IREI, NAREIT, PricewaterhouseCoopers, and Real Capital.
Note: Excludes corporate, nonprofit, and government equity real estate holdings as well as single-family and owner-occupied residences.

primarily middlemen, matching sources of long-term debt with users of long-term debt. Investments in CMBSs, including Fannie Mae and Freddie Mac investments in multifamily loans, have grown dramatically. CMBSs are second only to banks in the level of investment outstanding in commercial real estate loans.

A number of large commercial banks such as Wells Fargo, Chase, Bank One, Wachovia, and NationsBank have established their own conduit or CMBS operations in which some of the loans that they underwrite,

originate, and service are pooled and sold in the form of mortgage-backed bonds on Wall Street. Although banks do not hold these loans for investment purposes, they often underwrite them using the same ratios that they use for underwriting loans in their own portfolios.

CMBS lenders generally lend on C+- to B+-grade assets, a segment of the market that both banks and insurance companies in the past often shunned. These loans, originated by (but not held by) banks, life insurance companies, investment banks, mort-

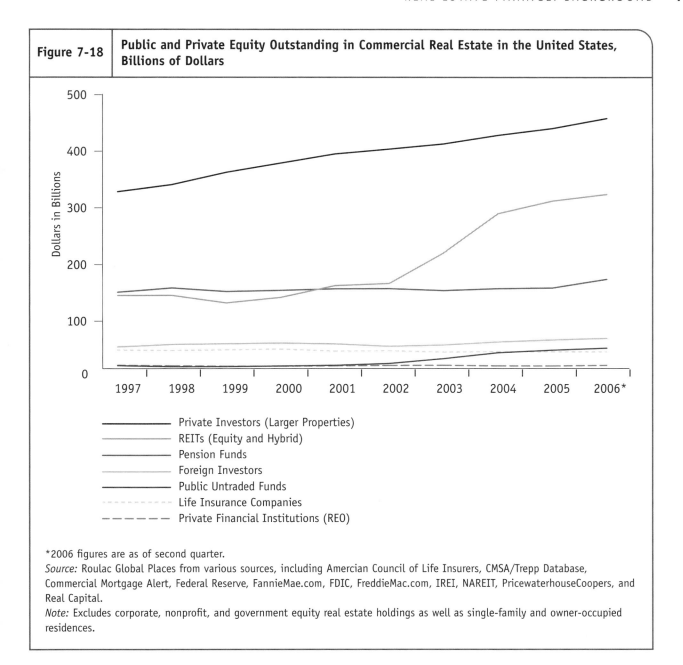

Figure 7-18 | **Public and Private Equity Outstanding in Commercial Real Estate in the United States, Billions of Dollars**

*2006 figures are as of second quarter.

Source: Roulac Global Places from various sources, including Amercian Council of Life Insurers, CMSA/Trepp Database, Commercial Mortgage Alert, Federal Reserve, FannieMae.com, FDIC, FreddieMac.com, IREI, NAREIT, PricewaterhouseCoopers, and Real Capital.

Note: Excludes corporate, nonprofit, and government equity real estate holdings as well as single-family and owner-occupied residences.

gage banks, and credit companies, are combined into pools of commercial mortgages of $1 billion to $3 billion. The pools are diverse according to property type and geographic location but have fairly homogeneous loan terms. These pools are then rated by third-party debt rating agencies that determine the size of the different credit tranches or credit ratings: AAA, AA, A, BBB, BB, B, or nonrated.

Also worth noting is the flow of capital from federally related pools, that is, Fannie Mae– and Freddie Mac–funded multifamily debt. (Fannie Mae and Freddie Mac are AAA-rated companies whose primary business is the securitization of residential mortgages.) Both Fannie Mae and Freddie Mac are publicly traded on the New York Stock Exchange, but they were both originally chartered by the federal government. As such, the debt issued by these two organizations maintains the implicit guarantee of the U.S. government. Therefore, Fannie Mae and Freddie Mac are often able to quote loan originators a lower risk spread than most CMBS pools. As they are chartered for housing debt only, Fannie Mae and Freddie Mac can pool mortgages only against commercial properties that are primarily residential. In recent years, both federally chartered organizations have stepped up lending to multifamily developments and in 2006 had $108 billion invested in multifamily mortgages.

The Equity Market for Real Estate Capital

Equity investment in commercial real estate has largely followed the path of the debt markets. After several years of large growth in capital flows into private equity investment in commercial real estate in the early 1980s, private sources of equity departed the markets in the early 1990s (see Figure 7-18). With the traditional private equity sources on the sidelines, the public market stepped in in the form of REITs. More recently, private equity sources in the form of "private equity funds" such as Blackstone have returned as active participants in the equity real estate markets.

Equity investment in commercial real estate has been the domain of private investors, with more than $450 billion invested in commercial real estate. In the past, as local private investors and investment companies were most familiar with the demand for and supply of space in their own markets, they were best prepared to capitalize on market needs. Beginning in the 1980s, however, national pension funds began to compete with local private investors. Throughout the 1980s and 1990s, pension funds continued to invest in commercial real estate; they currently invest $162 billion in U.S. commercial real estate.

Foreign direct investment in U.S. real estate has varied over the years. The Japanese were significant players in the 1980s, the Dutch and Germans poured investment capital into real estate in the 1990s, and the Australians presently are the largest source of foreign capital flowing into commercial real estate.

Real Estate Investment Trusts

The flow of public equity capital into commercial real estate is solely attributable to REITs—both publicly traded and public untraded funds. More than 90 percent of REIT investments are made in commercial

real estate equity investments rather than commercial real estate debt and hybrid investments. As the result of a dearth of private equity capital during the early to mid-1990s, REITs reentered the market and became a viable long-term investment vehicle for the first time. Although REITs have been a congressionally approved means of publicly holding real estate since the early 1960s, they were underused as an investment vehicle until 1993, when the umbrella partnership REIT (UPREIT) structure was created. The UPREIT structure allows private real estate partnerships to transfer the ownership of their partnership interests to an operating partnership controlled by the UPREIT. This arrangement was very appealing to U.S. private investors in limited partnerships, because this transfer could be completed without triggering federal income taxes. During the early to mid-1990s, UPREITs were one of the few sources of equity capital in a market undergoing extremely thin trading volumes.

As UPREITs acquired partnership interests, they bought out some limited partners and paid off some debt obligations through money raised on Wall Street in REIT offerings. The growth in REIT capital flows was tremendous in the mid- to late 1990s but slowed in 1999 and 2000 as the promise of this new source of public capital did not live up to expectations.[10] Interest in both public and private real estate investment returned with vigor in the early 2000s, with REITs among the best-performing sectors of the overall stock market. The total equity investment by REITs in commercial real estate in 2006 was more than $550 billion. REITs generally have a broader appetite for real estate than pension funds, often venturing outside traditional areas of real estate investment. In summary, Wall Street embraced public equity investment in real estate in the mid-1990s, and in the early 2000s REITs performed well, with prices soaring and dividend yields in turn falling.

THE REAL ESTATE FINANCE CYCLE

Real estate development typically involves a series of financing arrangements—predevelopment financing, short-term construction financing, interim financing, and permanent financing—depending on the project's stage in the development process. As a project progresses through the development process, its investment risk generally diminishes. Therefore, the interest rates and rates of return required by lenders and equity investors decrease as the development progresses. Predevelopment debt and equity carry the most risk and the highest expected returns. Financing the purchase of well-designed and well-located buildings with creditworthy tenants carries very low risk and correspondingly low investment returns. For the developer, it is necessary to assess risk versus return of various sources of debt and equity when deciding where to go for financing at each stage.

Much of the remainder of this chapter is concerned with the motivations and investment needs of the financial partners in commercial developments. For a project, lenders are primarily concerned about two loan risks: loss of loan principal and nonpayment of debt service (principal and interest payments). On a broader level, lenders are also concerned with matching the maturity of their loan assets with the maturity of their liabilities (such as bank deposits, life insurance claims, and retirement payments). Equity investors, on the other hand, are motivated by cash flow, value appreciation, and the benefits of tax shelters.

Debt and equity investors differ in the amount of risk they will accept. Consequently, they require different rates of return. Debt investors generally are more risk averse than equity investors. They are less willing to invest in risky projects such as land acquisition, land development, and preconstruction loans. Lenders are more willing to provide the majority of financing for completed developments that have creditworthy tenants secured on long-term leases with the rental income stream in place. Equity investors invest in riskier projects or in the risky portions of projects, but they require a higher rate of return for these investments.

Predevelopment Sources of Funds

Generally speaking, real estate projects in the predevelopment stage are the riskiest investment stage for two reasons. First, any positive cash flow from rents is one or more years in the future, and the more distant the time until the stream of income is received, the riskier the investment. Second, the probability that any project in the predevelopment stage will be completed and occupied is small compared with the probability that projects in more advanced stages will be completed and occupied. At the predevelopment stage, it is difficult to obtain equity financing and next to impossible to obtain debt financing without more collateral than that provided by the site. If a developer is willing to pledge other assets to secure a predevelopment loan, however, predevelopment debt financing is possible.

A number of predevelopment tasks require front-end capital yet pose substantial risk that they will not be completed: rezoning property to an appropriate use, securing tenants, completing conceptual designs, and conducting engineering, environmental, traffic, and other studies. Typically, developers cover predevelopment costs with their own equity capital and "sweat equity," the unpaid work or sweat in the early development stages of commercial real estate. High-risk, high-return capital may be available, however, usually from a joint venture partner. The usual joint venture agreement is a limited liability corporation or a limited partnership involving a money partner as the limited partner and the developer as the general partner. But developers can arrange joint ventures with other kinds of equity partners—for example, a landowner, a public utility seeking to sell a brownfield site, a high-profile corporation wishing to demonstrate its commitment to the community, or the owner of a hard-to-sell building.

Investors in other development projects in the neighborhood are a good potential source of equity in the early stages of a project. Whereas outside parties may view a particular neighborhood as risky, local residents or investors that have already committed development funds there may view the development site differently. Moreover, the proposed development may provide some indirect benefit for adjacent or nearby property owners. By enhancing the image of the neighborhood, the proposed development could enhance the financial position of the neighboring sites. For that reason, these local investors may be willing to invest in the proposed development.

Obtaining control of the development site is a predevelopment task that can take many forms, from purchase to option to lease agreement. The financing of these alternative approaches to site control is discussed in the following sections. Whatever the approach, finding the funds to control the site is among the developer's biggest financial hurdles during predevelopment.

Land Acquisition

A variety of sources provide land acquisition funds. Although commercial banks are a preferred source of land loans, banks often require other collateral or strong credit histories to make the loan. Some REITs and financial service companies provide financing for land acquisition. Mortgage companies and life insurance companies infrequently finance land acquisition, and, when they do, it is with the hope of becoming the construction lender and permanent lender. These capital sources sometimes charge penalties ranging from 0.5 percent to 2 percent of the land acquisition and development loan if they are not the subsequent lender.

Banks, S&Ls, and other sources of debt financing for land acquisition and development invariably offer recourse loans, that is, loans that make other assets of the borrower available as collateral for the loan. For the developer, it is risky business. A developer who personally signs a recourse loan is usually pledging all of his or her personal net worth as collateral for the loan.

Landowners can provide financing for the land. Such financing is typically in the form of a seller-financed loan (known as a "purchase money mortgage") providing 70 to 90 percent of the sale price, with the developer contributing the balance in equity capital. The deed to the land is transferred to the developer if the developer meets specific conditions and makes the required periodic payments. Such financing can be an attractive option for the seller, who can report the transaction as an installment sale and thus defer income taxes. Seller financing can also be an attractive alternative for the developer, who needs to raise only 10 to 30 percent of the land value to control the site for development.

With a purchase money mortgage, the seller/lender may agree to a subordination clause that makes the seller a second-lien holder on the property. By enabling a financial institution to take a first-lien position, the seller makes it possible for the developer to obtain construction financing. Almost without exception, construction lenders require that they have the first lien against the property, guaranteeing that they will receive all property liquidation proceeds until the construction loan is paid in full. Only after the first lien is paid in full will the second-lien holder receive any proceeds. Subordination makes seller financing much riskier, and, to compensate sellers for the additional risk, sellers usually require a higher price for the land or a premium interest rate. Construction lenders and permanent lenders include the debt service payments on seller-financed loans in their calculation of the debt service coverage ratio. Therefore, if seller financing is in place, construction lenders almost always lower the amount of the loan they will make.

Despite the problems it poses for construction lenders, seller financing can be one of the best alternatives for a cash-strapped developer because of the leverage—the use of borrowed funds to finance the development—it offers. Moreover, the confidence that land sellers have about the potential of their land is likely to translate into seller financing that provides a higher degree of leverage for the developer than any available alternative for financing land acquisition. A developer with few assets and little capital may find that seller financing is the only way to obtain control of the land. But, as the next two sections illustrate, ownership is not the only way a developer can gain control of the land. Other strategies for land control include land purchase options and ground leases.

Land Purchase Options

Under a land purchase option, the developer agrees to pay a landowner a relatively small, nonrefundable cash payment to take the land off the market during a specified option period. The cash payment, which often ranges from 1 to 10 percent of the land value, can take a variety of forms. It may be a lump sum paid at the time the agreement is signed. It may be debt service payments on the seller's land loan during the option period. Some land purchase options include bonus payments to the landowner if the property is rezoned successfully to accommodate the use or uses the developer proposes.

A land purchase option is a relatively low-risk method of controlling the site before committing significant resources to the project. While the site is under option, the developer can work on other steps in the development process—further land assembly, government approvals, rezoning, environmental assessment, due diligence, signing anchor tenants, building design, and project financing. If successful, the developer exercises the option and begins construction. If, on the other hand, conditions do not favor proceeding with the project, the developer walks away from the option, leaving his nonrefundable deposit with the landowner. Some short-term option agreements require a refund of the deposit according to provisions in the agreement.

Option contracts include a sale contract of the land, but the seller retains ownership until the option is exercised and the property is purchased. If the option is exercised, the option payment is usually applied to the sale price. The contract spells out the option price and purchase price, the terms and conditions of the option, how the option can be exercised, how it may be extended, the developer's right of access, the landowner's responsibility to cooperate, and much more. A developer might encounter a variety of land purchase options:

▶ Straight Option—An owner agrees to sell the land to the developer during a specific period for a set price.
▶ Escalating Option—Additional nonrefundable payments are required over time to keep the option open.
▶ Purchase Price Variant of an Escalating Option— The purchase price escalates if the land purchase option is extended in time or if the value of the land is increased through zoning changes or municipal variances.
▶ Rolling Option—Larger land tracts can be purchased in stages.
▶ Lease and Re-lease Option—The developer leases the land from the seller for a period of time, after which the developer can re-lease or purchase the land.
▶ Declining Balance Option—A smaller portion of the option payment is applied to the purchase price as the option period continues, creating an incentive for the developer to exercise the option early.

Ground Lease

Ground leases constitute another method of financing the land. Instead of purchasing the land, the developer rents it for a long period of time. A ground lease can protect the landowner's long-term financial interests while it enables the developer to begin the project with minimal capital.

In a typical ground lease, rental payments are based on the value of the land. Improvements usually are not included in a ground lease. (Lease agreements that cover land and improvements, such as some master leases, are not referred to as ground leases.) Lease terms are typically long (from 25 to 99 years), and the agreement usually contains a provision to extend the lease. A ground lease is usually structured as an absolute net lease, meaning that the lessee is responsible for all expenses associated with the property. Land rents usually escalate according to a predetermined schedule, an agreed-upon index such as the consumer price index (CPI), or changes in the property's rental income.

The use of a ground lease offers advantages and disadvantages for developers. Among the advantages are that no downpayment on the land is needed, the developer's leverage is increased, the developer can sublease the land, and lease payments are deductible as an expense for federal income tax purposes. Among the disadvantages are that a ground lease can be difficult to negotiate, escalations in ground rent can grow faster than the building's cash flow, the developer does not participate in future land appreciation, and when the lease term ends, improvements revert to the landowner. (If the improvements are expected to have value at reversion, the ground lease frequently includes a provision that the developer be paid for the value of the improvements.)

For the landowner, a ground lease also offers advantages and disadvantages. Among the advantages are a possibly significant improvement in the value of the land over time, a stream of income that entails few management responsibilities, and ownership of the improvements at the end of the lease. Among the disadvantages are the possibility of default by the lessee, less control over the land, and forgone development opportunities during the period of the ground lease.

Once the developer has secured control of the land, obtained any necessary zoning and planning changes, and met preleasing requirements, it is ready to commence construction—if construction financing has been arranged.

Construction Financing

Commercial banks traditionally have been the primary source of financing for construction. They still are, but alternatives to bank-financed construction loans are available. Developers can obtain construction loans from pension funds, life insurance companies, and other nonbank lenders that are more known for their role as providers of permanent financing. Larger, well-capitalized developers can issue commercial paper (short-term, unsecured promissory notes issued by a large corporation or REIT) to finance construction. A few well-capitalized developers use only equity to fund the construction of their industrial projects.

In their search for a construction loan, many industrial developers look first at local and regional banks. For large projects, national banks and consortiums of banks are likely sources. Construction lenders generally require some preconstruction leasing. The preleasing requirement often ranges from 30 to 70 percent of the building's space, depending on market conditions, the developer's experience, and the developer's collateral.

Although the real estate asset is typically what is offered as collateral for a construction loan, negotiations between the lender and the developer ultimately determine what secures the loan. A real estate development's collateral value is based on the cash flow expected at completion. The collateral value of a completed but unleased project may be only a fraction of its completed and fully leased value.

Nonrecourse construction loans put the lender in a risky position during construction and lease-up, because during foreclosure the lender has recourse only to the real estate that secures the loan and not to any other assets of the borrower. Ever since the real estate market crash of the early 1990s, however, construction lenders have routinely sought personal liability or recourse for loans. Some permanent lenders as well have sought at least partial liability for takeout or permanent loans. (Partial liability means that the borrower provides a guarantee for part of the loan.)

Funds borrowed during construction (construction loans) are largely the domain of local, regional, and national banks and S&Ls. Most construction loans are adjustable rate and usually have a two- to four-year term. The term often extends six to 18 months beyond the completion of construction, until the property income is stabilized (that is, occupancy is 90 to 95 percent and tenants are beyond the rent concession period). Construction loans rely heavily on the creditworthiness of the developer and the level of equity investment made by the developer. Construction lenders are also acutely aware of the supply of and demand for tenant space in the market, wanting to ensure that the property is fully leased at or near completion of construction. Life insurance companies and others also provide construction financing, albeit less frequently. Currently, CMBSs do not supply the market with construction loan financing; this market is serviced exclusively with private sources of capital. Most construction loans are recourse or partial recourse loans.

The following paragraphs describe the major sources of construction financing for real estate developers: commercial banks, S&Ls, finance and credit companies, corporate debt, and mortgage bankers and brokers.

Commercial Banks

The dominance of commercial banks in nonresidential real estate lending has grown since the early 1990s. According to the Federal Reserve, 44 percent of the cumulative debt investment outstanding in commercial real estate is in the hands of commercial banks as of 2006. The large size of banks' real estate loan portfolios has been a matter of concern to bank investors, debt-rating agencies, and government regulators since the late 1980s, when widespread problems in commercial real estate lending surfaced. Despite this concern, banks are likely to remain the dominant debt financier for commercial real estate construction loans in the near term. Banks are the only institutions with extensive local commercial lending experience and ties to regional and national mortgage conduits and loan participation networks.

In their efforts to match the generally short-term nature of their primary liabilities (checking accounts and savings deposits), banks traditionally have concentrated on assets with a short-term maturity such as construction loans. The interest rate on most short-term bank loans is tied to the money market and other short-term interest rates. Developers should assess the project for changes in short-term interest rates when they estimate construction interest costs. Developers of large or multiphase projects that require longer-term construction loans may obtain them from a consortium of lenders that may be formed to share the risk of a large loan or a loan with a long time horizon.

Reflecting the higher risk of construction loans, the risk premium is usually higher than on permanent loans. Construction loan rates usually range from 0.5 to 2 percentage points above the prime rate (the short-term interest rate banks charge their most creditworthy commercial customers), but they may be as high as 6 percentage points above the prime rate, depending on market conditions and the bank's assessment of the credit risk posed by the project or the developer. Stronger borrowers with larger projects often negotiate an interest rate spread over LIBOR (London Interbank Offered Rate). LIBOR is a short-term cost-of-funds index for banks. Spreads over LIBOR usually range from 2 to 4 percent, again depending on market risk and borrower's collateral provided. Upfront loan fees (expressed as points, with one point being equivalent to 1 percent of the loan amount) also vary with the market and the perceived risk of the project and/or the developer. A charge of one-half to two points is common on most construction loans. An additional point frequently is charged to extend the loan to accommodate construction delays or a difficult lease-up period.

Most construction loan agreements call for interest to accrue (or be periodically added to the principal) through the construction period rather than requiring periodic interest payments. When construction is complete and the building is leased, the developer obtains a permanent loan or sells the project and pays off the total amount of the loan, which includes the accrued interest and the principal balance. Banks change their construction lending practices dramatically depending on the capital market and space market cycles. They may increase prelease requirements and require borrowers to invest more equity in weak space and/or capital markets.

S&Ls

The reputation of S&Ls as thrift institutions—places where thrifty individuals could safeguard their savings—took a beating in the late 1980s and early 1990s, when scores of thrifts failed from the weight of poor lending decisions. Commercial real estate lending was a major culprit. As of 2006, S&Ls are the second largest issuer of multifamily debt in the United States at $102 billion (behind banks at $147 billion) and the fourth largest source of debt capital in the United States at 7 percent of the entire commercial real estate debt market.

Historically, S&Ls used depositors' passbook and other short-term accounts to fund long-term single-family home mortgages. In the late 1970s and early 1980s, however, interest rates rose to historically high levels and short-term rates exceeded long-term rates. The profitability of S&Ls began to sink, and the federal government—which insured S&L deposits through the Federal Savings and Loan Insurance Corporation (FSLIC)—responded by allowing S&Ls to broaden their lending activities and removing interest rate ceilings on their deposits.

Emboldened by rising deposits, the removal of investment restrictions, and the safety net of federal insurance, many S&Ls moved into the commercial real estate business and made risky loans on industrial and other development projects. Arguably, they did not fully understand the risks. The deterioration of the commercial real estate market in the last half of the 1980s sparked that period's thrift crisis.

Because the federal government insured the deposits, U.S. taxpayers bore the brunt of the damage. The FSLIC was dismantled and its regulatory duties handed over to the Resolution Trust Corporation, a government corporation created by the Financial Institutions Reform, Recovery, and Enforcement Act of 1989 (FIRREA). New rules were promulgated for S&Ls. These institutions still can make land, construction, and permanent loans, but the strict parameters imposed by FIRREA have reduced S&L participation in the commercial mortgage market.

Credit and Finance Companies

Some large U.S. corporations use their power in financial markets to establish entities known as credit companies that issue low-cost debt backed by the full faith and credit of the corporation and relend the money to real estate entrepreneurs. Some of these companies, such as GE Capital, provide construction and redevelopment financing. Credit and finance companies profit on the spread between the cost of their funds and the interest rate they charge on loans to developers. In the second quarter of 2006, credit and finance companies held approximately 3 percent of the entire market.

Compared with bank and S&L financing, the lending activities of credit companies are less entangled in federal regulatory oversight. The federal government regulates the investments of banks and S&Ls to protect the safety of their (federally insured) deposits. Because credit companies' source of funds is not the deposits of individuals, they are not subject to this kind of regulation. Therefore, they often are willing to lend on projects that are too complex, too risky, or otherwise outside the lending parameters of banks and thrifts. Recognizing the higher risk profile of their real estate debt investments, many credit companies require healthy risk spreads (3 to 5 percent) over their cost of funds and often participate in the appreciation of the asset when sold.

Permanent Financing

Long-term loans based on the income stream on commercial real estate are called "permanent loans." Historically, the primary sources of long-term debt financing for real estate developments have been life insurance companies, with commercial banks playing a limited role. When real estate values dropped in the early 1990s, insurance companies withdrew from the permanent loan market, leaving developers, property owners, and the Resolution Trust Corporation without a reliable source of long-term property financing. This lack of capital pushed up the financial returns on long-term permanent loans, which lured Wall Street investors into the market. Today, CMBSs are an important source of funds in the permanent financing landscape.

Permanent loans are offered to property owners when the building is fully occupied and income has stabilized. Most permanent loans are from life insurance companies and CMBS issuers and are generally nonrecourse; permanent loans issued by banks may or may not be recourse.

A property must meet six primary requirements before a permanent loan is issued to "take out" the construction lender. First, a certificate of occupancy (CO) must be obtained. A CO is a municipal approval that generally states the building is built to code. A CO must be issued before tenants can occupy a building. Second, property income must be stabilized. Income stabilization occurs when the occupancy rate reaches 90 to 95 percent of the building and the tenants are paying rent.

Third, a minimum debt service coverage ratio must be met. Most permanent loans are fixed-rate, ten-year loans with a 30-year amortization schedule. In general for the permanent lender to take out the construction loan, NOI must be 1.2 to 1.6 times higher than annual debt service. In other words, for each dollar of debt service (principal and interest payment), property net income must be $1.20 to $1.60, depending on the perceived risk of the property type and space market.

Fourth, a maximum loan-to-value (LTV) or loan-to-cost ratio is applied to the property value. Maximum ratios are generally 70 to 85 percent of the property value or property cost. As the name of the ratio suggests, this principal preservation ratio measures the amount of collateral per dollar loaned. The loan-to-cost ratio is used for construction loans, and an LTV ratio is then applied when the property is built and occupied and the income stream is in place to value the asset.

Fifth, the borrower must obtain lien waivers—statements that subcontractors have been paid in full and will not place liens or claims against the property—from construction subcontractors. And sixth, permanent lenders require that the loan be funded during a prespecified time period, or "funding window."

The permanent lender's LTV and debt coverage ratios are of critical importance to construction lenders. If, for instance, the completed project falls short of leasing projections or property value estimates, the permanent lender will be unwilling to take out the construction loan because the development does not meet required debt coverage and loan-to-value ratios.

Developers often arrange permanent financing before they seek a construction loan. When a permanent financing commitment is in place, it is much easier to obtain a construction loan. In most instances, the construction loan's principal and accrued interest both are paid from the takeout or permanent loan. Thus, a takeout commitment or commitment by a permanent lender to fund the project once certain hurdles are met improves the construction lender's risk position. As noted, takeout commitments are conditioned on a certificate of occupancy, minimum property occupancy, minimum debt service coverage ratio, maximum LTV ratio, lien waivers, and funding windows. The interest rate spreads on construction loans are typically higher than on permanent loans, giving the developer an incentive to replace the construction loan as soon as possible.[11] Moreover, most construction loans are recourse, while most permanent loans are nonrecourse, giving borrowers a second incentive to replace a construction loan as soon as possible.

By providing long-term capital, the permanent lender assumes some of the project's long-term market risks. Historically, permanent financing was expected to remain in place through more than one market cycle. The typical loan was for a 30-year, fixed-rate, fully amortized mortgage. More recently, most permanent lenders have attempted to reduce the refinancing risk or the risk that the property's value might fall over time by shortening loan terms to ten years and by using a 30-year amortization schedule on these loans.

Long-term financing is commonly provided in the form of a mortgage or a trust deed, both of which involve the commitment of property as collateral for the repayment of the loan. Mortgages come in many forms:

▶ Fixed-Rate Mortgage—The most common permanent loan, in which the interest rate is held constant during the loan term.
▶ Adjustable-Rate Mortgage—The interest rate is tied to an index. Also known as a variable-rate mortgage, this instrument protects lenders against rising interest rates and inflation and shifts interest rate risk back to the borrower.
▶ Blanket Mortgage—A single mortgage that covers multiple properties, with a release provision allowing individual properties to be released of the mortgage without retiring the whole mortgage.
▶ Package Mortgage—Personal (non-real-estate) items may be included in the loan.
▶ Open-End Mortgage—The borrower may obtain additional funds at a later date.

Two leading sources of permanent financing are commercial mortgage–backed securities and life insurance companies. Life insurance companies are able to invest a large amount of capital in long-term mortgages because their source of capital is long term, continuous, and predictable. They receive a constant flow of funds from premium payments, and they can accurately predict their future outlays from actuarial tables. To meet future death benefit outlays, life insurance companies must invest their capital to preserve the principal while maintaining an adequate investment return. Therefore, life insurance companies often lend on the best properties in a market and usually underwrite the investment conservatively (using lower LTV and higher debt service coverage ratios). Life insurance companies are a principal source of permanent financing for real estate.

Life insurance companies took an investment hit along with other lenders and investors when the bubble burst from the overbuilding of the 1980s and the value of commercial real estate declined. Since then, new government regulations, new industry standards, and pressure from investors have led life insurance companies to reduce the proportion of their assets held in mortgage loans. Life insurance companies once held one-third of their total assets in mortgages, but as of the second quarter of 2006, investment in commercial real estate mortgages by life insurance companies was $294 billion, or approximately 10 percent of all commercial mortgages. Despite their recent pullback, life insurance companies remain the third largest institutional provider of commercial mortgages (behind banks and CMBSs). Life insurance companies continue to be a significant source of permanent loans for commercial real estate, and they are also major investors in CMBSs.

Problems in the Cycle and Potential Interim Financing

Interim financing bridges the gap between construction loans and permanent loans—when such a gap exists. Many construction loans are for projects in which the developer has a permanent (takeout) loan commitment. If all construction loans included an unconditional takeout agreement, the need for interim financing would disappear. But sometimes obtaining a forward permanent loan commitment is not possible or not advisable for either the developer or the lender. Alternatively, it is possible that when the project is complete, the permanent lender will not fund the takeout loan commitment because certain conditions have not been met. Thus, some construction lenders—especially commercial banks— will commit to convert their construction loans to an interim loan and, if necessary, to a short-term permanent loan called a "miniperm," with a three- to five-year maturity.

Committing to interim financing can be a risky proposition for the lender. An interim loan is usually required if things did not go as expected during construction and lease-up (construction delays, difficulty in obtaining municipal approvals, problems in leasing, for example). To compensate for this risk, the interim lender often exacts an origination fee at the time the construction loan is closed as well as charges a high risk premium if the interim commitment needs to be funded. The interest rate is likely to be less than the rate on the construction loan and more than the rate on permanent loans. From the developer's perspective, an interim loan buys time for the project in the marketplace.

SUMMARY

Real estate development is capital intensive, meaning that a large amount of money is necessary to complete most development projects. As most developers do not have the wealth or the desire to personally fund such investments with their own money, they seek investment capital from other sources—debt, equity, or some hybrid of the two.

The supply of and demand for tenant space is a function of the economic growth in a narrow market or submarket. Alternatively, the supply of and demand for investment capital or the dollars invested in commercial real estate are international markets. The value of real estate occurs at the intersection of the local tenant space market and the international investment capital market, where the local space markets determine the expected property income stream and the investment capital determines the expected rate of return necessary to purchase that income stream. Real estate investments compete with investments in stock, bonds, and other opportunities worldwide.

The real estate finance cycle involves a series of different financing arrangements based on the types of risk presented at each stage of development. During the predevelopment stage, the real estate development carries the greatest risk. As a property is constructed and occupied, many of the development risks are dramatically reduced or eliminated. As such, different sources of capital are available at different stages of the real estate development.

TERMS

- ▶ Capital markets (and four quadrants)
- ▶ Construction financing
- ▶ GDP (growth of)
- ▶ Ground lease
- ▶ Interim financing
- ▶ Land purchase options
- ▶ Permanent financing
- ▶ Private debt
- ▶ Private equity
- ▶ Public debt

▶ Public equity
▶ REIT
▶ Space markets

REVIEW QUESTIONS

7.1 Discuss how the market for commercial real estate consists of the space market and the capital market.

7.2 Explain how the quality and stability of a property's income stream are determined by its space market.

7.3 Describe the four quadrants of the capital markets. How have the capital markets grown from two to four markets?

7.4 How did the debt capital market contribute to the overbuilding of commercial real estate in the early 1980s?

7.5 What is a CMBS?

7.6 What are the three largest sources of equity capital for commercial real estate? Which has grown fastest over the past decade?

7.7 In the early stages of the commercial real estate development process, what is the primary source of capital? Why?

7.8 What are the primary differences between a construction loan and a permanent loan?

7.9 What six primary requirements must a property meet before a permanent loan is issued to take out the construction lender?

NOTES

1. Jeffrey D. Fisher, "Integrating Research on Markets for Space and Capital," *Journal of the American Real Estate and Urban Economics Association*, Vol. 20, 1992, pp. 161–180. Another insightful conceptual discussion of the space and capital markets in the United States is provided by Denise DiPasquale and William Wheaton, "The Market for Real Estate Assets and Space: A Conceptual Framework," *Journal of the American Real Estate and Urban Economics Association*, Vol. 20, 1992, pp. 181–190.

2. Capitalization rate valuation is discussed in detail in Chapter 8.

3. Apartments are usually included in the commercial real estate markets, as they provide a stream of rental income like other property types. Condominiums and single-family residences are excluded from a discussion of the commercial real estate markets, however, as they are owner occupied and therefore not included in investment real estate.

4. The supply of and demand for space in different geographic markets is analyzed by a variety of national, regional, and local firms such as Reis Reports, Torto Wheaton Research, CoStar, Global Real Analytics, and PPR (Property and Portfolio Research). Most commercial real estate brokers and appraisers maintain space market data for their locale. See Chapter 18 for more information on specific providers.

5. Generally speaking, growth in rental income is a function of the growth in the cost of developing new space. In a market unconstrained by municipal zoning and the physical availability of land, property income streams can grow only as fast as the growth in land costs and construction costs. Limited land and strict municipal land use regulations often increase the cost and risks associated with new development, which is forced onto irregular infill sites for which municipal approvals are uncertain. Higher development costs and difficult municipal approval processes often limit the development of new space until a point where the costs and risks associated with new development are met by higher rents, increasing property rents across the entire market.

6. Effective rents are the economic rents that landlords effectively receive during the lease term and include the effect of free rent.

7. The increase in homeownership rates can largely be attributed to events in the mortgage market. First, long-term fixed-rate mortgage interest rates were at the lowest they had been in 45 years, making homeownership more affordable. Second, credit scoring became an efficient and transparent means of predicting mortgage default, which reduces the uncertainty surrounding the decision about whether or not to lend money. Third, innovations in the residential mortgage market provided a range of financing options for households with limited wealth to make a downpayment or with limited income to make monthly payments. Finally, new subprime mortgage lending instruments opened the mortgage markets to many who previously were excluded because of relatively minor credit problems.

8. There are approximately 110 million households in the United States. If homeownership rates increase by 3 points, approximately 3.3 million apartment units will become available, all else being equal.

9. Banks and life insurance companies also originate loans that are sold for the CMBS markets. These loans are not considered private debt (that is, debt that is held in whole-loan form on the balance sheets of banks and life insurance companies).

10. REITs fell on hard times for several unrelated reasons. First, in May 1998 the U.S. Treasury limited the growth of REITs by clearly delineating "rental income" and thus the types of passive investments that REITs can make in real estate. Second, the New York Federal Reserve issued a warning about the rapid expansion of this industry in fall 1998. Finally, some of the hype surrounding the income growth and expense efficiencies that REITs could obtain through the real estate platform were not realized.

11. When the Treasury yield curve has a steep upward slope (i.e., short-term interest rates are considerably lower than long-term rates), short-term construction loans may carry a lower rate of interest than long-term permanent loans.

CHAPTER 8

Real Estate Finance: The Logic behind Real Estate Financing Decisions

Chapter 7 described the financial marketplace in which the real estate developer competes for construction and permanent loans. This chapter and the next focus on the financial analysis tools available to lenders, investors, and developers.

The income productivity of a property is measured using the stream of cash flow benefits that the property is expected to generate in the future. Property cash flow benefits come in two forms: the periodic payment of net rents and the sale of the property. The primary valuation techniques used to determine the value of future benefits today use a static, or one point in time, capitalization rate valuation or apply a dynamic valuation approach using discounted cash flow analysis. Both of these methods are regularly used to generate estimates of property value. This chapter focuses solely on static cash flow analysis and "lender metrics"; Chapter 9 addresses discounted cash flow analysis.

This chapter discusses:

▶ Estimation of net operating income;
▶ The lender's perspective of the property's value;
▶ The equity perspective on debt financing; and

▶ A case study of the credit presentation for Clackamas Ridge, a commercial real estate venture.

NET OPERATING INCOME

One of the most frequently used terms in real estate financial analysis is net operating income of the property, a concept introduced in Chapter 7. NOI measures the property's productivity and is the source of the returns to lenders and equity investors. A basic statement of NOI looks like this (a detailed discussion of NOI for the Clackamas Ridge case study is presented later in this chapter):

> *Potential Gross Income*
> *−Vacancy and Concession Allowance*
> *Effective Gross Income*
>
> *Effective Gross Income*
> *−Operating Expenses*
> *Net Operating Income.*

Just as the name suggests, NOI is the income from the operation of a real estate property. It does not include the effects of property financing, nor is it affected by capital expenditures or depreciation. Property NOI is a number that is not easily controlled by the owner or manager, as rents, vacancies, and operating expenses are disciplined by the market. Most information that is included in a property's NOI should be verifiable through a comparison of comparable rents, market vacancy rates, and operating expenses with industry norms and billing statements.

Potential Gross Income

In its simplest form, potential gross income (PGI) is the rent a property could generate if it were fully occupied with no discounts. Things are seldom that simple, however. Potential gross income is likely to include numerous other income sources such as contract rent, rent escalations, expense reimbursements, and miscellaneous income. Contract rent is the stated rent per square foot times the number of square feet occupied. In the case of apartments and hotels, rent is usually stated in terms of rent per unit rather than rent per square foot. Many office, retail, and industrial leases also include a rent escalation clause in the lease agreement. Rent escalations are rent increases used to keep rents in line with market rents when multiyear leases are offered. Rents are typically escalated on the anniversary date of the lease. Rent escalations can be stated as a dollar increase per year (or dollar increase per square foot per year), a percent increase in rent per year, an increase based on an inflation index such as the consumer price index, or, in the case of retail, a function of retail sales called an overage rent escalator.

With the exception of indexed and overage rents, the calculation of rent escalations is largely self-explanatory. Indexed rents use published inflation indices to increase rent on a period-to-period basis. Indexed rents protect the landlord from unexpected increases in inflation during a multiyear lease term; they can also protect the tenant from a fixed-rent escalation that may outpace the rate of inflation. Overage rents, also referred to as "percentage rents," are used primarily in retail leases and are based on tenant sales. If tenant sales exceed a threshold, the landlord receives rent escalations based on a percent of sales over the sales threshold.[1] For instance, if tenant sales for a tenant with a 6 percent overage rate are $350 per

square foot ($3,770 per square meter) and the sales threshold or breakpoint is $300 per square foot ($3,230 per square meter), the overage rent escalation per square foot is $3 ([$350–$300] × .06) or $32.40 per square meter ([$3,770–$3,230] × .06).

Most office, industrial, and retail leases require the tenant to reimburse the landlord for certain property expenses or increases in property expenses. These expense reimbursements are considered income to the property owner. Three general types of expense reimbursement clauses are possible (note that each real estate market may have slightly different names for each type of expense reimbursement):

▶ Gross—The landlord pays all property operating expenses and expense increases. Apartment lease agreements are most often gross leases.
▶ Modified Gross or Full Service—The landlord pays all expenses up to a lease-defined expense stop, and all expenses over the expense stop are passed through to (or paid for by) the tenant. An expense stop involves per-square-foot expenses incurred in the first year of the lease term, and only increases in expenses in years two and beyond of a lease are passed through to the tenant. Modified gross expense pass-through clauses are most commonly found in office leases.
▶ Net—The tenant is responsible for all property expenses and expense increases (with the possible exception of management fees). A net lease is the same as a modified gross lease with an expense stop of zero. Most industrial and retail leases include net lease pass-through clauses. In a "net net" lease, the tenant is responsible for any necessary capital expenditures such as extensive roof repairs beyond regular operating expenses.

The expense stop ensures the landlord is estopped from having to pay expense increases. Gross leases have no expense stop, and the landlord is therefore responsible for all property expenses. No expenses are passed through to the tenant. In modified gross leases, the landlord pays expenses up to a predefined amount per square foot or expenses per square foot in a predefined lease year. The expense stop in net leases is effectively zero, with the tenant responsible for all expenses and all expense increases during the term of the lease. For example, say a property has expenses of $10 per square foot ($108 per square meter). Expense reimbursements for a gross lease, a modified gross lease with an expense stop of $8.50, and a net lease are as shown below.

Expense Reimbursement Clauses in Leases			
Lease Type	**Gross**	**Modified Gross**	**Net**
Operating Expenses	$10.00	$10.00	$10.00
Expense Stop	n/a	$8.50	$0
Expense Reimbursement	$0	$1.50	$10.00

As the example shows, none of the expenses are billed back to the tenant in a gross lease, and $1.50 and $10 per square foot ($16 and $108 per square meter) are billed to the tenant in the modified gross and net leases, respectively.

Vacancy and Rent Concessions

To obtain effective gross income (EGI), vacancies and other negative income items must be accounted for in the property pro forma. Similar to income statements for large corporations, real estate revenue contains negative income items, or items that decrease the amount of income. Such items in corporate income statements might include loss on merchandise returns and missing or stolen merchandise. For real estate, such items, often included in an allowance for vacancies and concessions, might include vacancies, collection losses, and free rent.

The appropriate vacancy rate on a property should be applied to an income stream that is potentially less than a fully occupied building; in most instances, it would include the entire potential gross income. The two exceptions are creditworthy tenants on long-term leases and income that would be maintained regardless of the occupancy rate such as rooftop and possibly parking income.

For most properties today, the line item for vacancies needs to be expanded from the narrow identification of the loss from unoccupied space to include other reductions in income. Other negative income items include collections loss (loss of income from a tenant that is occupying space but not paying the contractually agreed-upon rent), free rent, rent buy-outs, tenant moving allowances, and above-standard tenant improvements. Landlords are often required to give rent concessions to tenants in the form of free rent when the market for tenant space is overbuilt. But even when the market is not overbuilt, landlords often provide new tenants free rent during the period when the space is being fitted out with tenant improvements. Subtracting these negative income items from PGI yields EGI, effective gross income. Rent concessions other than vacancy rates and free rent may be difficult to identify, but they can dramatically affect property income.

Operating Expenses

Operating expenses are the periodic expenditures necessary to maintain income from the property—real estate taxes, common area maintenance, utilities, insurance, the management fee, and, possibly, a replacement allowance for capital expenditures. Periodic debt service payments, property depreciation, and capital expenditures are not included.

The largest operating expense in most real estate investments is real estate taxes. Real estate taxes are paid to the local municipality and usually fund municipal services such as public schools, police and fire protection, and road repairs. Because of the impact real estate taxes have on the income pro forma, it is strongly recommended that investors obtain a detailed analysis of the municipality's spending budget to estimate future increases in real estate taxes. The second-largest expense is common area maintenance, that is, the cost necessary to maintain the property in good working order. Such expenses include cleaning, maintenance of the landscaping and parking area, servicing of the heating and elevator systems, and similar day-to-day operations. Utility costs are for the gas, electricity, and water necessary to operate the building. Hazard/liability insurance is needed to insure the building physically and to protect it from tenant actions. Both utility and insurance costs have increased significantly for many property owners in recent years. Management fees are usually stated as a percent of EGI and are paid to the parties that take care of the day-to-day needs of the building and tenants. Depending on the building, management fees usually run from 2 to 5 percent of EGI. A single-tenant warehouse building may require a management fee lower than 2 percent, but a busy mall with high turnover, many inline retailers, a constant flow of customers, and large common areas may require more than 5 percent.

The replacement allowance for capital expenditures provides funds for replacing building components that wear out such as the roof, exterior painting, surface of the parking area, heating and cooling systems, and elevators. Some landlords also include the costs of tenant improvements (the costs involved in making the space habitable for a new tenant) in the replacement allowance. Although replacement costs and improvements are real cash outflows for the landlord, they are not property expenses, and because they are not expenses, they are not passed through to tenants to be reimbursed. As such, most property owners place replacement allowance for capital expenditures in below-line (that is, below the NOI line) accounts. Most lenders like to see a replacement allowance for capital expenditures included in the NOI. This conflict is common and is discussed later in this chapter and again in Chapter 9.

Most operating expenses should be verifiable with invoices and payment receipts and through the audit of the property books. Generally, operating expenses are periodic payments made to maintain a property and do not extend the economic life of the asset.

Net Operating Income

Property NOI is potential gross income minus allowances for vacancies, concessions, and operating expenses. NOI does not include mortgage debt service, capital expenditures associated with significant building improvements and the release of tenant space, and property depreciation. The costs of re-leasing space, which include tenant improvement costs and lease commission payments, occur intermittently and are not considered periodic payments of expenses. Similar to tenant improvements, building improvements occur intermittently and often extend the life of the building. Property depreciation

is used to determine taxable income and is not included in a property's operating expenses.

The development's features, functions, and benefits determine how the project's rent compares with other projects in the market, but the market is the constraining factor. PGI is constrained by the competing properties in the market, and significant increases in rents bring increased vacancies if other properties in the market are not raising rents similarly. Because calculations of NOI are based on market assumptions, NOI is a "same-for-all" number[2] that measures the amount of income expected to be available to be divided between debt and equity investors. How that income is divided depends on the financing decision, which is typically viewed as separate from decisions about the property's operations.

ESTIMATING COLLATERAL VALUE FROM THE LENDER'S PERSPECTIVE

Property NOI reflects the strength of the tenant space market through the income that is produced from the lease contracts and the related expenses incurred for the property. With a defensible NOI in hand, we must now determine how to value income from the property. Two approaches typically are used to estimate property value: capitalization (cap) rate valuation and discounted cash flow analysis valuation. The capitalization rate is referred to as a "static cash flow analysis," as one point in time, where the static cash flow estimate is capitalized to value the income stream. Conversely, the discounted cash flow analysis uses a dynamic multiperiod estimated stream of income to value a property. The cap rate approach to value is discussed in the following sections, the discounted cash flow analysis in Chapter 9.

The Appraisal Institute supplies two definitions of the direct capitalization approach to value: "A method used to convert an estimate of a single year's income expectancy into an indication of value in one direct step, either by dividing the income estimate by an appropriate rate or by multiplying the income estimate by an appropriate factor" and "a capitalization technique that employs capitalization rates and multipliers extracted from sales. Only the first year's income is considered. Yield and value change are implied but not identified."[3]

Direct cap rates are widely used in the industry to value properties with established income streams and to value proposed projects where income streams can be readily estimated. Most commonly, cap rates for the new property are derived from cap rates on comparable, recently sold properties.[4]

To estimate an appropriate cap rate, it is critical to obtain verified cap rates where the property income stream is identified and a property sale price is verified, as small changes or errors in the application of a cap rate can return a wide range of value estimates.

The formula for the direct cap rate approach to value is relatively simple: cap rate (R) is a function of the property net operating income (NOI) divided by the property value (V). That is,

$$R = \frac{NOI}{V},$$

where

V = the value of the property,

NOI = the property NOI, and

R = the capitalization rate.

Alternatively, to determine the value of a property using a cap rate,

$$V = \frac{NOI}{R}.$$

Remember that one of the limitations of the capitalization rate approach is that cap rates explicitly value only the NOI of the property's first year of operation. In the next chapter, we will relax that assumption.

The Lender's Decision

Because of the large amount of capital necessary to build or develop real estate, obtaining debt financing can be the developer's most difficult hurdle, particularly on more innovative developments. Lenders know the key role they play by providing debt financing and frequently tout what they call the golden rule of real estate lending: He who has the gold makes the rules. And because lenders have the gold, they often make the rules regarding a project's financial viability. The two primary rules lenders apply to the property

income stream are called the debt service coverage ratio (DSCR) and loan-to-value (LTV) ratio. The DSCR measures the property's cash flow adequacy, while the LTV ratio assesses the property's collateral value.

Both the developer and the lender construct a property income pro forma and value the property in a similar manner. They both start with market rents at comparable properties and estimate vacancies and operating expenses to determine a stabilized NOI. With a reasonable income estimate in place, the next step is to estimate the expected return rate that a likely purchaser would expect on his investment in the property. Comparing the location, improvements, and other attributes of similar properties with the subject, the analyst determines a cap rate that is appropriate given the riskiness and growth potential of expected NOI. Using a cap rate valuation, a reasonable estimate of value is determined using a stabilized property NOI. With good estimates of property income and value, the important lender ratios can be applied to the property.

Loan Underwriting Process

The loan underwriting process for a development proposal in this section comprises six steps; however, the number of steps, terminology used in each step, and sequence of the steps may vary from lender to lender. When a developer submits a loan application to a lender, the proposal must include information on the space market, the property's location, proposed improvements, the borrower's creditworthiness, the construction team, and financial analyses. In the process of underwriting the development, the lender must verify the developer's assumptions, adjust them as needed, and then independently assess the project's viability.

Each step in the underwriting process includes a series of additional questions that both the developer and lender must address. Note that the six steps begin with a broad or macro view of the market and the property's location in the market and narrow to a micro view of the improvements and borrower. The final step of the underwriting process combines all the collected quantitative and qualitative data into an analysis of the development's financial viability.

The lender expects certain items to be addressed in a loan proposal; they are covered in detail in the case study, Clackamas Ridge Commercial Real Estate Credit Presentation, later in this chapter. Chapters 16 to 18 (covering the feasibility study and market and data analysis) provide more detail on the first three items listed below. Consequently, more attention is paid here to the last three items.

With relatively minor variations, a loan proposal for most lenders includes:

▶ Market and submarket analysis;

▶ Location analysis of the subject site;

▶ Appropriateness of the proposed improvements for the site;

▶ Creditworthiness of the borrower;

▶ Evaluation of the developer's construction team and property management plan; and

▶ Financial viability of the proposed improvements.

Much of the loan underwriting process flows from the lender's analysis of the property's market and submarket. To determine whether the market is strong enough to generate occupancy and rental rates that will justify the proposed development, the lender must obtain satisfactory answers to questions about demand, supply, and market timing. What is the market's demand for this kind of space over time? How much competition does the development face from existing and future industrial properties? Is the project's timing good?

The answer to the question of timing depends on the answers to several other questions. How long will it take for the new space to be absorbed? Are unanticipated construction delays possible or likely? How would the developer pay for any increased costs associated with the delays? Are market conditions likely to change adversely before the project's completion and lease-up?

The second step in the typical loan underwriting process—a location analysis—involves determining the site's accessibility and suitability for its target tenants. Is the development convenient to the kinds of amenities, services, and resources that the target tenants need or prefer? The location analysis also involves issues of developability. Is the proper zoning in place? Do the community and the project's neighbors generally support the development? Are utilities available? Is the site in a growth corridor?

Step three of the process is to determine the appropriateness of the proposed improvements for the site. Does the site have physical constraints to development? Does the site contain species habitat that will need to be protected? Will the site require environmental remediation? Do subsoils support the development? Does the proposed building suit its location? For instance, a highly finished flex building might be deemed out of place in a heavy-industrial park and, for that reason, not be economically viable.

Recall the lending cycle discussed in the preceding chapter. The developer typically gets a permanent loan commitment first, then a construction loan. The permanent lender is concerned primarily with the first three items above, as they drive long-term value. The construction lender, given the takeout from the permanent lender, is most concerned with the fourth and fifth steps above, as they determine the likelihood of completing the project on time and on budget and hence being able to count on the permanent loan takeout.

Most development or construction loans are recourse; that is, in the event of default, the lender has recourse to other assets of the borrower in addition to the property pledged as collateral. Thus, the lender's analysis of collateral includes an investigation of the borrower's assets and associated liabilities. In addition, the lender must investigate how the borrower's repayment of its existing liabilities might deplete the income stream and assets available to satisfy the contemplated loan.

Evaluation of the developer's construction team and property management plan is of critical importance to the construction lender. The construction team must have a proven record of completing projects on time, on budget, and in accordance with architectural and engineering specifications (known as building to specifications or "building to spec"). Missing development and construction deadlines can cause costs to escalate, and missing completion dates can give prelease tenants the right to renegotiate or cancel their leases. If a project is not developed to project specifications, the structural and mechanical integrity of the building or development plan may be compromised, which can lower the collateral value of the property.

The building that the developer constructs will ultimately provide security for the loan. The value of the property that the borrower pledges as collateral must exceed the amount of the loan. And the building must be built to spec. Some developers are skilled at "value engineering" to reduce a project's construction costs, but often value engineering reduces a building's economic life, or, as a result of value engineering, the building is constructed with lower-cost materials that might be more costly to maintain and require replacement more often.

The lender is also concerned about what happens after construction is complete. Does the borrower have the necessary property management skills, or has the borrower hired the appropriate property management team to market and lease or sell the asset and maintain the property's collateral value and income stream? The property management team is responsible for assuring that tenants' creditworthiness is adequate. The signed leases—and tenants' willingness and ability to pay the rent—are key considerations in assessing the value of the collateral. Preconstruction lease commitments of strong (creditworthy) tenants ensure that their portion of the rental income will be generated when the building is complete, thereby reducing the risk that the property's cash flow will not be adequate to cover debt service (monthly interest and principal payments) for the permanent lender.

Although good property management cannot save a poorly conceived and executed project, poor property management can destroy a good project. Hence, the borrower's proposed property management plan is an important factor in the decision to lend money to the borrower. Good property management includes maintaining an efficient and safe development, meeting space users' needs, solving operations problems, and repairing property in a timely manner.

The cost of replacing high-quality tenants typically exceeds the cost of retaining them. Lenders therefore look for evidence of the management team's skills in tenant relations. They also examine executed leases and sales contracts to evaluate the manager's ability to structure favorable lease or sale terms. (Favorable lease terms, from the lender's point of view, are ones that best enable the borrower to service the debt.)

In the sixth step, the lender assesses the financial viability of the proposed improvements and the project's economic feasibility. This analysis uses the data, findings, and conclusions from the preceding analyses. Step six is essentially an underwriting step that covers everything from the project's concept to its cash flow and its ultimate sale to the next investor or, if the developer plans to hold the property, the management plan. The lender's primary analysis tools are the pro forma cash flow statement and possibly multiperiod discounted cash flow analysis. The lender's goal is to determine whether the development will "pencil out." A detailed discussion of the important lender ratios follows.

Underwriting the Property

The lender uses several ratios to assess the proposed development's financial viability, but before discussing those ratios, it is necessary to discuss the role of the construction and permanent lenders. As noted in the previous chapter, the permanent lender makes a commitment to loans based on the proposed development's long-term economic viability. The construction lender relies on the permanent lender's commitment.

The property receives no income during construction, as tenants do not pay rent during construction. Moreover, the value of a partially complete building is difficult to estimate. Construction loans typically begin with a zero balance, and the construction lender pays out "draws" during construction to cover a portion of the cost of the completed building to that date. Most construction loans do not receive any interest during the construction of a building; instead, interest is accrued and added back to the principal of the loan because there is no property income to cover the mortgage payments. Therefore, the construction lender often receives no debt service payments until late in the loan, if at all, making the construction lender's exit strategy very important. All principal and most, if not all, interest on construction loans are received when the loan matures.

Once construction is complete and the property income is stabilized, the construction loan is usually "taken out" by a permanent lender. At that point, the amount of the permanent loan depends on the income the property generates and on the lender ratios that the permanent lender applies to that income stream. Therefore, the amount of the takeout (or permanent) loan, which funds the construction loan, depends on the income the property generates. Because the construction lender receives most, if not all, of the principal and interest on the construction loan at maturity from a permanent lender, the construction lender is very concerned about the permanent lender's ratios, as they are critical to the borrower's exit strategy.

Primary Lender Ratios

The lending decision by the permanent lender is based in large part on two ratios: the debt service coverage ratio and the loan-to-value ratio. The lender ratios use the developer's financial pro forma income statement, current interest rates, and investor rates of return. Therefore, lenders insist that the financial statements for a proposed project be carefully constructed, complete, and accurate. To calculate the DSCR and LTV ratio, the analyst must be able to calculate the mortgage constant and be able to value the property.

Mortgage Constant

The mortgage constant (MC) is the interest and principal payment necessary to pay down a one-dollar loan over a set number of years with a level payment stream. It expresses the relationship between annual debt service requirements (principal and interest) and the amount of the loan. The mortgage constant is based on market interest rates for permanent mortgages plus the principal to pay off the loan over a set period of time. Specifically, when the annual debt service is known, the mortgage constant is:

$$MC = \frac{Annual\ Debt\ Service}{Loan\ Amount}.$$

In the past, amortization tables showing interest rates and maturities were common in real estate text-

books. Today, most analysts use the functions in a spreadsheet program such as Excel. Figure 8-1 shows the steps to calculate the mortgage constant if such a program is not available.

A higher interest rate or a shorter loan amortization period causes the annual debt service for a given loan to rise and thus increase the mortgage constant. The higher the mortgage constant, the lower the justified loan amount. Many developers pursue a strategy of bargaining for the lowest interest rate and the longest amortization term that the lender will accept, knowing that such a strategy will result in the lowest mortgage constant, the smallest debt service payment, and ultimately the largest loan amount.

Debt Service Coverage Ratio

The debt service coverage ratio is the single most important measure for determining the acceptability of a loan application. To calculate the DSCR, divide the project's net operating income by the project's annual debt service as follows:

$$DSCR = \frac{Net\ Operating\ Income}{Annual\ Debt\ Service}.$$

A property with a 1.30 debt service coverage ratio produces $1.30 of net operating income for every $1 of debt service. The DSCR determines the adequacy of the development's projected cash flow to service the debt. The DSCR is an indication of the borrower's financial risk. The lower the DSCR, the smaller the cushion of available NOI per dollar borrowed and therefore the higher the lender's financial risk.

For real estate projects, lenders generally require a DSCR between 1.20 and 1.60. Lenders on projects deemed riskier than average require a higher DSCR, and lenders on projects deemed relatively low risk accept a lower DSCR. A lower-risk property would likely have a roster of creditworthy tenants on long-term leases that occupy most, if not all, of the building.

Construction lenders use the DSCR to evaluate the riskiness of construction loans, even though no operating income is generated during the construction period. The construction lender must be satisfied that the anticipated cash flow generated by the project will be sufficient to obtain the permanent takeout mort-

Figure 8-1	Calculating the Mortgage Constant

To calculate the mortgage constant based on current interest rates and a lender-prescribed amortization period using a hand-held calculator, assume the following permanent loan terms:

Loan Amount:	$1
Loan Term:	30 years
Interest Rate:	7 percent

To calculate the annual mortgage constant, first calculate the monthly mortgage constant, because most commercial loans are paid monthly. The keystrokes necessary to calculate the monthly debt service using a Hewlett-Packard 12-C calculator are as follows:*

1. f and CLX: The combination of *f* and then **CLX** clears all registers in the calculator of previously entered data.
2. 1 and PV: Entering *1* and then **PV** places one dollar in the present value register, which is the same as saying that the loan amount is one dollar.

3. 30 g and n: Entering 30 *g* and then *n* takes the term of the loan in years (30) and makes it monthly by multiplying 30 by 12, for 360 months in a 30-year loan.
4. 7 g and i: Convert the annual interest rate to a monthly rate by dividing the 7 percent interest rate by 12, to arrive at 0.0058333.
5. PMT = Entering **PMT** asks the calculator to calculate the monthly debt service necessary to monthly amortize one dollar at 7 percent over a 30-year amortization period—0.006653 × 12 = 7.98363 percent.

Another way to look at this result is that if the borrower pays 0.6653 cents monthly for 360 months on a loan of one dollar, the debt will be extinguished at the end of 360 months. In other words, debt service payments for a $1 million loan are $6,653 monthly and $79,836 annually.

*The keystrokes necessary to calculate the monthly debt service payment are similar on most calculators. If you do not have an H.P. 12-C calculator, consult your instruction manual, go to the Web page provided by the maker of your calculator, or use one of many other online references to the calculator by typing in your calculator's brand name and model into your preferred search engine (Google or Yahoo, for example).

gage that will be used to repay the construction loan. Thus, short-term construction lenders measure the sufficiency of a project's income using the DSCR and the takeout lender's expected interest rate. The importance of the debt service coverage ratio in determining the size of a loan cannot be overstated. Whether the loan is securitized through a CMBS or held as a whole loan by a commercial bank or insurance company, the debt service coverage ratio is the critical ratio that lenders use to assess a project's viability.

Loan-to-Value Ratio

The loan-to-value ratio expresses the relationship between the amount of a mortgage loan and the value of the property securing it:

$$LTV = \frac{Loan\ Amount}{Property\ Value}.$$

The higher the LTV ratio, the larger the loan relative to the value of the property and thus the lower the equity invested in the property. With less equity invested in a project, the risk is greater to the lender because the equity cushion is smaller in the event that property values erode over time. For projects that are still in the conceptual stage, most lenders use a loan-to-cost (LTC) ratio in place of the LTV. The LTC ratio divides the loan amount by the total construction budget, as follows:

$$LTC = \frac{Loan\ Amount}{Total\ Construction\ Budget}.$$

To ensure that the developer provides an adequate equity cushion, construction lenders often apply both a loan-to-cost and a loan-to-value ratio to assess the equity investment in both circumstances.

As a matter of policy, banks and insurance companies often mandate specific loan-to-value ratios for their investments in different types of real estate. Federal and state regulators often specify maximum loan-to-value ratios for the real estate investments of regulated institutions like banks and insurance companies.

When a lender is considering a loan proposal using the LTV ratio and the DSCR, he underwrites the property to the lower of the two justified ratios. For instance, if we assume that the maximum indicated loan amount using the DSCR is $12 million and the maximum indicated loan amount using LTV is $12.5 million, the maximum loan the lender would make is the lower of the two, or $12 million. Each ratio quantifies different risks. The DSCR measures the property's ability to meet monthly debt service payments, or the adequacy of the cash flow to meet debt service; LTV is a principal preservation ratio measuring how far property value can fall as a percent of the purchase price (or construction costs) before the collateral value of the property is less than the mortgage amount. Because separate risks are measured with each ratio, the lender accepts the lower maximum loan amount.

RETURNS TO EQUITY INVESTORS AND THE EFFECTS OF LEVERAGE

As discussed in the previous chapter, investment capital for real estate comes in two forms: debt and equity. So far, we have discussed why and how lenders lend on real estate projects. Because lenders often provide 60 to 80 percent of the capital in a real estate development, it may be appropriate to discuss the needs and ratios of the debt participants first. But the riskiest capital in any investment is the equity investment. The lender has the first claim on both cash flows from a property and proceeds from the sale of an asset in the event the property runs into financial difficulties. Because of the first-loss position that an equity investor takes, raising equity capital can be the most challenging assignment. Like the debt investor, the equity investor carefully underwrites the proposed development from both a qualitative and quantitative perspective. And, similar to investment in debt, the

feasibility of a real estate investment is often narrowed to a couple of important investor ratios.

Although some equity investors (including many pension funds) purchase and develop real estate "all cash" (without the use of debt financing), most real estate investors use some debt financing to magnify equity returns. To appropriately measure the equity investor's rates of return, we first need to extend the income pro forma beyond NOI.

Property Cash Flow

To determine investors' rates of return on property cash flow, we need to account for capital expenditures. Capital expenditures are investments in a property that have a multiyear life and include tenant improvements (expenditures necessary to make the space habitable for a new tenant such as carpets, demising walls, and drop ceilings), leasing commissions (paid to secure a tenant on a multiyear lease), and capital improvements (improvements intended to extend the building's economic life).

> *Net Operating Income*
> *−Tenant Improvements*
> *−Leasing Commissions*
> *−Capital Improvements*
>   *Cash Flow from Operations*
> *−Financing Costs*
>   *Cash Flow after Financing.*

All capital expenditures have a multiyear life and are not considered annual expenses for repairs and maintenance. Subtracting capital expenditures from NOI returns cash flow from operations (CFO). Subtracting the annual debt service payments, principal, and interest from CFO returns cash flow after financing (CFAF).[5]

Return on Assets

Return on assets (ROA) measures the overall return to the property, assuming an all-equity purchase. Return on assets is the investment return before the effects of financing.

$$ROA = \frac{CFO}{Purchase\ Price}.$$

You should recognize that ROA is similar to the direct capitalization rate we used to estimate property value. The only difference between the cap rate and the ROA is that the ROA includes the costs of capital expenditures in the calculation of return. The expected ROA of an asset varies similarly to the cap rate on a property; however, the ROA is expected to be 1 to 2 percent lower than the cap rate.

Return on Equity

While the ROA measures the return of the entire property or asset, the return on equity (ROE) measures the return to the equity position.

$$ROE = \frac{CFAF}{Equity\ Investment}.$$

Because the ROE is based on cash flow after financing and the equity invested (cash), it is often referred to as the "cash-on-cash return." Expected ROE for real estate projects can vary widely; the expected ROE depends largely on the amount of borrowed funds and the interest rate/mortgage constant of those borrowed funds.

Benefits and Costs of Using Debt Financing

A basic benefit of debt is that it can be used to leverage the return on equity upward. This "positive" leverage occurs when the cost of debt financing (the mortgage constant) is lower than the overall return generated by the property (the ROA). In such situations, the percentage return to the equity investor is greater using debt than it is with no debt. Moreover, certain tax benefits may also be associated with the use of debt. Interest payments are typically tax deductible, and debt increases the tax basis beyond the equity investment, thus enhancing the tax shelter generated from depreciation. The use of debt financing also reduces the minimum investment necessary in any given project. Because investors have limited resources, a reduced minimum investment in one project allows them to spread their wealth over several investments, that is, to diversify. Diversification reduces portfolio risk, and lower risk means higher value.

Moreover, by combining various debt and equity structures, the decision maker can create risk-return opportunities to fit investors' specific needs. This flexibility to tailor the investment to suit the client (investor) is an additional benefit of debt financing.

If a property maintains positive leverage, it appears to be a free lunch for the borrower—that is, positive leverage creates a return multiplier. But that is only part of the story. The reality is that the basic relationship between risk and return is not suspended in the case of using debt. When equity investors borrow money to magnify equity returns, they assume the cost of greater variability in property cash flows or higher risk. And, at the extreme, if the project's income drops below the level of debt service, the investor may face the choice of paying the monthly debt service from other income sources or default on the loan.

In addition to creating more risk, borrowing entails various direct costs. Financial institutions charge fees for their services. Further, as the debt service coverage ratio decreases and the LTV ratio increases, the lender's risk exposure increases. In response, lenders raise the interest rate charged to the developer. Finally, the paperwork required in mortgage lending and the lender's time (as a financial intermediary) must also be considered.

THE CLACKAMAS RIDGE COMMERCIAL REAL ESTATE CREDIT PRESENTATION: A CASE STUDY

Clackamas Ridge is a proposed apartment development by Joseph Bullingo of Bullingo Properties, Inc.[6] The proposal, dated November 29, 2006, is for an $11.28 million construction loan request on 135 apartment units. The Clackamas Ridge Commercial Real Estate Credit Presentation is an example of how a construction lender looks at a construction loan and the important attributes in approving the loan. The credit presentation closely matches the loan proposal outline shown in Figure 8-2; it is a checklist of items that developers should include in all loan proposals to a lender. The credit presentation is a ten-page internal bank document that is used to decide

Figure 8-2	Outline of Loan Proposal

Cover Page
Picture of Building
Table of Contents
I. Investment Merits
   Improvements
   Location
   Site Description
   Market
   Mitigating Factors
   Investment
   Summary
II. Summary of Salient Facts
   Loan Request
      Loan Amount
      Index
      Spread
      Rate
      Term
      Amortization Period
      Annual Debt Service
      Debt Service Coverage Ratio (DSCR)
      Loan-to-Value (LTV) Ratio
      Loan per Square Foot (gross)
      Loan per Square Foot (rentable)
      Loan per Unit
      Loan per Bed
   Property Information
      Number of Buildings
      Number of Units (if residential)
      Unit Mix
      Square Footage (gross)
      Square Footage (rentable)
      Efficiency Rate
      Year Built
      Number of Elevators
         Passenger
         Service
      Parking
         Surface
         Covered

Land Area (acres)
Average Rent per Square Foot
Number of Tenants
Average Lease Terms
      Rent per Square Foot
      Utilities Paid by
      Janitorial Paid by
Pro Forma Expenses per Square Foot
Borrower
Loan Guarantor (if applicable)
Management and Leasing Firm
III. The Property
   Locational Narrative
   Locational Maps
   Subject Photographs
   Neighborhood Photographs
   Aerial Photographs (of the subject and subject
      neighborhood)/Legend
   Site Plan
   Floor Plans
   Elevations
IV. The Economics
   Pro Forma
   Rent Roll
   Operating History
V. City Economy
VI. Property Type Market Summary
VII. Rent Comparables
   Photographs and Summaries
   Locational Map
VIII. Sales Comparables
   Photographs and Summaries
   Locational Map
IX. Neighborhood Analysis
   1-, 3-, 5-Mile Demographics
X. Articles
XI. Borrower's Résumé
XII. Management/Leasing Firm's Ability to Manage and
    Lease the Building

Source: H.A. Zuckerman, *Real Estate Investment and Acquisition Workbook* (Prentice Hall,1998), p. 338.

whether or not to lend funds for the construction loan. In other words, the credit presentation is an overview of the proposed development through the eyes of the loan officer, who then presents the information to the bank's trustees to approve the loan.[7]

The Credit Request and the Property's Strengths and Weaknesses

As one might expect, the credit presentation begins with the name and address of the borrower or the borrowing entity (see Figure 8-3), followed by an executive summary providing an overview of the critical information of the deal. The request is for an $11.28 million construction loan, with a 135-unit apartment complex the primary collateral for the loan.

The pricing of the loan is critical to the lender and ultimately determines the interest rate charged to the borrower. In this case, the loan is priced 250 basis points, or 2.5 percent, over the 90-day LIBOR with an interest rate floor of 4.5 percent. In November 2006, the 90-day LIBOR rate was 5.3 percent. (LIBOR is an interest rate that banks charge each other and does not include a risk premium for lending to a developer.) Based on the risk of the market, borrower, and collateral from the analysis in the credit presentation, Affiliated Bank determined that a 2.5 percent risk premium over the bank's cost of money (that is, the 90-day LIBOR) would be appropriate. Therefore, the interest rate is the greater of 7.8 percent (5.3 percent plus 2.5 percent). Additionally, the construction lender is charging the borrower a 0.5 percent point fee, or $56,400 ($11,280,000 × 0.005).

The loan matures in three years. Although the construction period is expected to be only ten months, the lender expects that it will take an additional 16 months after construction is completed to lease the building to full occupancy. Allowing for six to nine months of stabilized operation returns approximately the three-year term of the construction loan. In the event there is no takeout lender, Affiliated Bank will automatically fund a miniperm loan for two years if the property is leased to 90 percent and has a minimum NOI of $1,125,000. The miniperm will be on a 30-year amortization schedule.

The construction loan can be prepaid at any time without penalty.

The source of funds to repay the loan is a loan refinancing; as such, the construction lender expects that Bullingo Properties is building the property to own and will refinance it with a takeout or permanent loan. Alternatively, in the event a takeout loan is not available or that long-term interest rates have increased dramatically, a two-year miniperm loan with a 30-year amortization schedule is available through the construction lender, Affiliated Bank.

Primary underwriting metrics, which include the LTV ratio, DSCR, and related measures, come next. First, the loan per unit is $83,556, which is very important to the lender to determine what he needs as a break-even sale price in the event the borrower defaults. The sale comparables later in the chapter indicate that $83,556 is comfortably less than comparable sales in the units greater than $100,000 each. The requested loan amount of $11.28 million is 78 percent of the expected appraised value when the property is completed and stabilized.

Note that the DSCR is 1.22 times pro forma NOI and 1.20 times cash flow from operations. Several critical assumptions must be considered to calculate these ratios. First, pro forma NOI is calculated based on expected rents approximately one year from the time of completion. Therefore, property income is a best estimate based on rent comparables. Second, the permanent loan mortgage constant assumes a 7.5 percent interest rate and a 30-year amortization term. Note that the interest rate of 7.5 percent is different from the construction loan interest rate. The 7.5 percent rate is the expected interest rate on permanent mortgages in three years; the construction lender uses the permanent lender's interest rate to determine the debt service coverage ratio. Recall that because there is no property income to apply a debt service coverage ratio during construction, the DSCR uses the expected interest rate on permanent loans when the property is completed and stabilized.

Finally, the lender wants to make certain that the developer has equity in the project. The developer defers his $550,000 and includes it as "soft equity" in

Figure 8-3	Affiliated Bank Commercial Real Estate Credit Presentation

BORROWER:	Bullingo Properties, Inc
ADDRESS:	366 Elligsen Road
	Wilsonville, OR 97070
CONTACT NAME/PHONE:	Joseph Bullingo
REFERRAL SOURCE:	

CREDIT REQUEST

Borrower:	Bullingo Properties, Inc., owned by Mr. Joseph Bullingo
Request:	$11,280,000 construction loan on 135-unit apartment complex
Purpose:	Construction of a 135-unit apartment complex in Wilsonville, Oregon
Pricing:	250 bps over 90-day LIBOR with a 4.5% floor
Fees:	½%
Maturity:	3 years. Additional 2-year miniperm option if $1,125,000 NOI is achieved at 90% occupancy with pro forma expenses
Amortization:	Interest only; if miniperm is taken, amortization will be 30 years
Prepayment Penalty:	Prepayable at par at any time
Repayment Source:	Refinance
Secondary Repayment Source:	Cash flow
Collateral Description:	135-unit apartment complex, assignment of leases and rents, guaranteed by Mr. Joseph Bullingo
Guarantor Name(s)/Amount:	Joseph Bullingo/unlimited
Loan per Square Foot per Unit:	$83,556 per unit
Maximum LTC:	79%
Estimated Value/LTV:	$15,400,000/73% LTV. Appraised by Wilsonville Appraisal Associates dated November 29, 2006
DCR:	Pro forma ($11,280,000 @ 7.50% for 30 years)
	1.22 before replacement reserves, 1.20 after replacement reserves
Cash/Equity in Deal:	Total project cost of $14,300,000. Equity will be contributed as $550,000 of Developer Fee, with the balance of $2,470,000 in cash from Mr. Bullingo and other equity investors.

STRENGTHS AND WEAKNESSES

Strengths

A) Moderately sized apartment complex that will take a short time to construct and should be absorbed in less than one year

B) Very experienced owner/developer with good net worth

C) Good location with great access and visibility

D) Substantial cash equity in transaction

Weaknesses

A) Overall apartment market is softer than in years past as potential renters can afford entry-level townhouses at current interest rates.

the development. In that the developer is not putting cash in the deal and is instead investing his fee, many construction lenders find this source of equity less convincing as collateral. In this case, however, Joe Bullingo and his partners also are contributing $2.47 million in cash in the deal. Most construction lenders like to see approximately 50 percent of the equity in a project contributed in cash. Figure 8-3 closes with some general comments on the strengths and weaknesses of the deal.

Ownership, Recourse, and Property Attributes

Figure 8-4 reveals several ownership, recourse, and property attributes. The 51 percent controlling interest in the asset is held by Joe Bullingo, with 49 percent of the equity provided by other partners. Joe Bullingo is pledging his entire net worth as collateral for this loan. His other assets include a 197-unit complex. Although Joe Bullingo's net worth is an impressive $3.7 million, only $260,800 of that amount is considered unencumbered and liquid, providing a meager $304,536 in personal cash flow. Another way of looking at the developer's personal situation is that his assets are providing less than 1 percent of collateral and that most of his assets are already pledged as collateral, with a relatively small $260,800 available to fund a property in case the lease-up period is extended and he has to fund some portion of the property out of pocket. Similarly, in the event foreclosure proceedings are necessary, the lender may have a difficult time obtaining additional collateral over and above the unencumbered and liquid assets of $260,800.[8]

The borrowing entity is referred to as a "single-purpose entity." A single-purpose entity is commonly used in real estate today to further protect the lender from a borrower that may go bankrupt. The primary purpose of a single-purpose entity is to make the asset being used as collateral "bankruptcy remote." A bankruptcy-remote entity is one in which the borrower can go bankrupt but the asset is not affected by the borrower's bankruptcy—that is, it is remote. Although placing the asset in an entity that is separate from the developer's other assets and liabilities pro-

tects the lender in the event of the borrower's default, it may require that the property be retitled and some other legal work.

"Sources and uses of funds" on the figure is much as the title suggests—the source of the investment capital. The collateral is a 135-unit apartment complex on a ten-acre (four-hectare) site with full amenities in the units, numerous common and other areas, and more than two parking stalls per unit.

Property Development Costs, Location, and Market

Development costs, the property's location, and the market are discussed in Figure 8-5. Most construction lenders have in-house staff for engineering and property costing services; if they do not, they use subcontractors. Such services are critical to make certain that construction costs as presented are reasonable and accurate. A cost estimate that is too high arguably reduces the amount of equity in the deal; for example, the $550,000 development fee may actually be much higher, which reduces the cash investment by the developer and his partners. Too low a cost estimate can be equally destructive, because additional equity could be required in the middle of the project and, at that time, it can be very difficult to raise.

Note that the price for the shell and core of $9,571,475 constitutes a vast majority of the cost without any real detail provided. (Chapter 19 discusses fixed-price and cost-plus construction bids.) The shell and core (that is, construction hard costs) are priced using a fixed-price estimate; if the borrower has no changes in plans, the maximum construction price of the shell and core is $9,571,475. Having no change orders is unlikely, so the amount includes a 2 percent contingency. An additional $2,569,692 is required for soft costs. Soft costs are the related expenses and services necessary to the development of a building—construction interest, architect and engineer fees, real estate taxes during construction, and developer fees, for example—but they are not part of the actual construction of the project.

In analyzing development costs, the lender considers several items. First is the price of the land. Is the land cost at market value, and is the price reasonable?

Figure 8-4	Section Two of the Credit Presentation

OWNERSHIP

Name	Ownership Percentage
Joseph Bullingo	51%
Various other equity partners	49%

GUARANTY

Guarantor's Name	Date	Liability	Net Worth	Personal Cash Flow	Unencumbered Liquid Assets
Joseph Bullingo	9/31/06	Unlimited	$3,713,510	$304,536	$260,800

OFFICER COMMENTS

Borrower is requesting $11,280,000 construction loan on a to-be-built apartment complex located in Wilsonville, Oregon. The property will be a three-story, wood-frame building with underground parking for approximately 136 vehicles. Additional outside on-site parking will be available. Loan will be full recourse to the borrowing entity as well as Mr. Bullingo personally.

BORROWER

The borrowing entity will be a to-be-formed single-asset single-purpose entity with Mr. Bullingo controlling 51% of the partnership. Mr. Bullingo will contribute developer's fee and cash to balance the loan. Mr. Bullingo is an existing customer of Affiliated Bank, N.A., with a loan outstanding on a 197-unit apartment complex in Hillsdale, Oregon. The property opened for occupancy in September 2005. Lease-up has gone slower than expected and is currently 80% occupied. The property is currently cash flowing based on current rates. Mr. Bullingo is an experienced real estate developer who has been in the construction business since 1968 and in 1991 started Bullingo Companies.

SOURCES AND USES OF FUNDS

	Sources
First Mortgage	$11,280,000
Cash Equity	$2,470,000
Developer Fee	$550,000
Total	$14,300,000
	Uses
Construction Costs	$14,300,000
Other	$0
Total	$14,300,000

SECURITY

Property Type	135-unit apartment building consisting of two wood-frame, three-story buildings over heated parking. Each unit will have a dishwasher, food disposal, refrigerator, range, and microwave, in-unit washer and dryer, walk–in closet, individual heating and cooling unit, and private balcony or patio. Each building will have one elevator. The complex will have additional storage facilities, meeting rooms, outdoor pool and spa, sun deck, fitness center, and picnic area. Parking will be provided on a 1-to-1 basis underground, and 204 additional outside on-site parking spaces will be provided at over 2 to 1.
Size	135 units. The site is approximately 10 acres.
Approximate Year Built	New construction
Occupancy	New construction
Environmental Issues	None anticipated
Lease Expiration Schedule	N/A—Apartments
Major Tenant Analysis	N/A—Apartments

Figure 8-5	Section Three of the Credit Presentation

DEVELOPMENT COSTS

LAND COSTS	BUILDING COSTS		COSTS PER UNIT
Land Acquisition	$1,257,237		
Land Development	890,396		
Total Land Acquisition and Development Costs		$2,147,633	$15,908
BUILDING HARD AND SOFT COSTS			
Shell and Core	$9,571,475		
Total Hard Costs		$9,571,475	$70,900
Contingency (4% of total soft costs)	$100,000		
Interest Reserve	987,000		
Loan Fee	75,737		
Architectural/Engineering	382,210		
Appraisal	15,000		
Environmental	2,500		
Permits/Fees	163,565		
Real Estate Taxes	35,800		
Marketing and Lease-up Costs	125,000		
Developer Fee (5.75% of total hard costs)	550,000		
Other Soft Costs	132,880		
Total Soft Costs		$2,569,692	$19,035
Total Building Costs		$14,288,800	$105,843

Notes: The land has been purchased at the indicated price. Hard costs include a 2% contingency. Interest reserve equals $987,000. Based on a 12-month construction period, half out, 23 units leased at opening and 7 per month thereafter. Total interest reserve and lease-up costs equal $1,112,000, which assumes that during construction, 50% of the loan is drawn on average (i.e., 50% of the loan is drawn at a 7.0% construction interest rate, or 50% × $11,280,000 × 7.0% = $394,800) or $394,800 of construction interest in year 1. Additionally, the rental income generated during lease-up in year 2 is assumed to fund 25% of the interest cost, requiring an additional interest reserve of $592,200 ($11,280,000 × 7.0% × 75% = $792,200), for a total interest reserve of $987,000. The market study anticipated 33 units preleased, with absorption of 12 to 15 units per month.

General Contractor	Bullingo Companies
Third-Party Property Manager	Bullingo Companies

LOCATION

The property is located in the city of Wilsonville, which is a second-ring suburb of Portland located approximately 20 miles south of downtown Portland. Wilsonville is a high-growth city with a population of approximately 16,000 people and an expected growth rate through 2015 of 2.8% (relative to a 1.1% growth rate for the U.S.). The five-mile and ten-mile "Market Areas" consist of approximately 56,000 and 297,000 people, respectively. The property has great access and visibility to Interstate 5, which is a major four-lane highway that connects Wilsonville to Portland. Interstate 5 intersects with Interstate 205 approximately five miles north of the site. The site is part of a master-planned community that includes single-family residential, multifamily residential, a municipal golf course, and the subject site. A Safeway-anchored retail center is just south of the subject site. Additionally, Wal-Mart is planning a new store, and additional retail land is currently being marketed for sale approximately one mile south of the site. Overall, the location is considered good for an apartment building.

MARKET

The overall Portland apartment market has experienced some softness over the past several years primarily because of low interest rates for home loans and because many who could afford the rents at higher-end apartment properties can afford newly constructed townhouses. According to the appraisal, the overall metropolitan area vacancy rate increased from 4.4% in 2005 to 5.7% in September 2006. The Wilsonville market contains 1,700 units and had a vacancy rate of 4.7% in September 2006. The subject market (including surrounding cities) has an overall vacancy rate of 5.8% for a universe of approximately 2,900 units. We used a 5% vacancy rate in our underwriting.

The purchase price of the land is the indicated price on the development cost summary, which is preferable. To reduce the required equity investment, developers often submit an inflated land price. Lenders must also make certain that there are no other sources of developer fees other than those explicitly stated. For instance, some developers may charge an administrative fee or other similar fees to subcontractors, again to reduce the amount of equity required in the deal. Finally, to keep costs down, some developers reduce construction costs by using low-cost construction materials. Some omit contingency reserves, which in the end is short-sighted.

The location of the collateral property is in a rapidly growing suburb of Portland, Oregon. Located in a master-planned community near I-5 and numerous retail and community amenities, the property appears well situated. But the Wilsonville market currently has a 5 to 6 percent vacancy rate, and the addition of 135 units to the market is a 5 percent increase in the stock of units. Additionally, the effects of recent low interest rates have further softened the market, as high-end renters can afford newly constructed townhouses—both significant risks to the proposed project.

Rental Rates and Rent Comparables

Estimating rent is the most critical component in constructing a property income pro forma, and the best place to begin is comparable rents. Figure 8-6 shows comparable rents for Clackamas Ridge. An analysis of comparable rents must first define the unit of comparison—rent per unit per month. Once properties comparable in location and amenities have been identified, information on the comparables should be obtained by talking to the property manager of each development through a property consulting or appraisal firm or through a commercial realtor's association. If the information is obtained from a third party, the information must be verified and, ideally, several properties visited to see unit amenities and common area amenities and to verify rental rates and rent concessions. Based on the location, unit attributes, and property amenities, the subject property is likely to be in the bottom half of the luxury apartment market in the Wilsonville, Oregon,

market. Also note that the comparable properties maintain an occupancy rate of 92 to 99 percent, and currently no concessions are given.

Figure 8-7 presents rental rates for each type of unit. Rental rates can vary significantly by unit size (primarily number of bedrooms); therefore, the figure also provides a brief discussion of the rents for each type of unit. The pro forma rents shown in the figure present the number of units, unit size, and monthly rent for each unit type. Dividing the monthly rent by unit size yields the monthly rent per square foot. Taking the number of units times the unit size times the monthly rent per square foot and dividing that quantity by 135, the total number of units, yields the weighted average rent for each unit type. Specifically, for the 12 three-bedroom/two-bathroom units of 1,295 square feet (120 square meters) at $1.04 per square foot ($11.20 per square meter), these units add $120 to the weighted average rent ([12 units × 1,295 square feet per unit × $1.04 rent per square foot per month]/135). Totaling the weighted average rents yields an average unit rent of $1,113. In other words, the average rent per unit, with the average weighted appropriately to the type of units that will be added to the market, is expected to be $1,113 in today's market. Because of the weakness of the current apartment market, however, it is expected that rents one year from now, when the units are delivered to the market, will remain at $1,113.

Pro Forma Income Statement

The pro forma income statement (Figure 8-8) is the Holy Grail for lenders underwriting a development. The estimates of property cash flow and property value depend on this statement. If the base rents in the income pro forma are incorrect, that error is compounded in future calculations; therefore, a complete and accurate underwriting of property rents depends on an accurate pro forma. Using $1,113 rent per unit for 135 units for 12 months a year yields $1,803,060, with another $25,000 expected in vending income, equaling $1,828,060 potential gross income. When a market-determined vacancy rate of 5 percent is taken into consideration, effective gross income is reduced to $1,736,657.

Property expenses begin with real estate taxes. Because of the size of this expense, real estate taxes should always be verified based on current tax rates and the expected market value of the property. Management fees are $69,466 (4 percent of effective gross income), with the remaining expenses being reasonable estimates based on similar properties in the market and industry norms. Subtracting total operating expenses from effective gross income yields a property NOI for Clackamas Ridge of $1,152,331. The capital expenditure necessary to release the units is estimated to be $150 per unit across all units; if 40 percent of the units are expected to turn over each year, the cost per turnover unit is $375. These capital expenditures reduce NOI by $20,250 to $1,132,081 for cash flow from operations. Assuming a permanent mortgage interest rate of 7.5 percent amortized over 30 years returns a mortgage constant of 8.390574 percent. Multiplying the mortgage constant by the $11.28 million mortgage loan amount returns a debt service payment of $946,457. Subtracting the debt service from the cash flow from operations yields $185,624 in cash flow after financing.

Figure 8-6	Rent Comparables for Clackamas Ridge							
					Rent			
Property	**Location**	**Size**	**Occupancy**	**One-Bedroom**	**Two-Bedroom**	**Three-Bedroom**	**Comments**	
Comp 1	Clackamas Square Advance, OR	154 unis	92%	$940–1,030	$1,170–1,030	$1,535–1,605	Built in 2000, garage included	
Comp 2	Heritage Reserve Skunk Hollow, OR	394 units	96%	$959–1,019	$1,065–1,430	$1,375–1,599	Built in 1999, attached garage	
Comp 3	Avalon at Mulloy Mulloy, OR	224 units	92%	$895	$1,075–1,280	$1,510–1,570	Built in 1998, garage included	
Comp 4	Oak Hill Wilsonville, OR	282 units	97%	$930–1,054	$1,274–1,374	$1,554–1,619	Built in 1997, attached garage	
Comp 5	Park Ridge Wilsonville, OR	112 units	94%	$925	$1,100–1,200	$1,425–1,625	Built in 2001, attached garage	
Comp 6	Oakwood Green Skunk Hollow, OR	343 units	95%	$905–940	$1,065–1,100	$1,185–1,220	Built in 2000, garage included	
Comp 7	Avalon Bay at Sherwood Sherwood, OR	348 units	99%	$825–925	$950–1,120	N/A	Built in 1987, garage included	
Comp 8	Crescent Heights Wilsonville, OR	343 units	93%	N/A	N/A	$1,205–1,265	Built in 1995, attached garage	
Comp 9	Goose Valley Mulloy, OR	282 units	96%	$889	$1,139–1,329	$1,389–1,449	Built in 1998–2000, garage included	
Subject	**Clackamas Ridge Wilsonville, OR**	**135 units**		**$764–860**	**$960–1,171**	**$1,295**	**To be built, underground parking included**	
Comp 10	North Park Sherwood, OR	415 units	93%	$840–890	$976–1,101	N/A	Built in 1987, garage included	
Comp 11	High Ridge Middleton, OR	339 units	93%	$835–880	$955–1,060	$1,225	Built in 1988, garage included	

Figure 8-7	Rental Rates for Clackamas Ridge

Studios   1 comparable available at $1.20 per square foot. Pro forma rents for studio units at Clackamas Ridge are $1.31 per square foot.

One-Bedroom   10 comparables ranging from $.90 to $1.26 per square foot, with an average of $1.09 per square foot. The best comparable is Goose Valley at $1.16 per square foot. All comparables built after 1996 are higher than $1.06 per square foot. Pro forma rents for Clackamas Ridge 1-bedroom units are between $1.10 and $1.17 per square foot.

Two-Bedroom   12 comparables ranging from $.84 to $1.35 per square foot, with an average of $.96 per square foot. The highest comparable is Avalon at Mulloy at $1.35 per square foot. All the comparables that were built after 1996 are higher than $1.03 per square foot. Pro forma rents for Clackamas Ridge 2-bedroom units are between $1.09 and $1.15 per square foot.

Three-Bedroom   8 comparables ranging from $.70 to $1.07 per square foot, with an average of $.85 per square foot. The highest comparable is $1.07 per square foot. All the comparables that were built after 1996 are higher than $.85 per square foot. Pro forma rent for Clackamas Ridge 3-bedroom units is $1.04 per square foot.

Overall, rents projected at the subject are at the low-middle end of the comparable range but in some cases exceed the comparables. This is justified in that most of the comparables are older properties. According to the market report prepared for the subject by Greenfield Research, the project rents should be achievable because of the location and the new construction.

Pro Forma Rents

Number of Units	Unit Type	Unit Size (Square Feet)	Monthly Rent Per Unit	Monthly Rent Per Square Foot	Weighted Average Rent
3	Studio	533	$700	$1.31	$15.52
6	1 Bedroom/1 Bathroom	764	$895	$1.17	$39.73
27	1 Bedroom/1 Bathroom	806	$925	$1.15	$185.38
6	1 Bedroom/1 Bathroom	860	$950	$1.10	$42.04
12	2 Bedrooms/1 Bathroom	960	$1,050	$1.09	$93.01
3	2 Bedrooms/1 Bathroom	1,011	$1,150	$1.14	$25.61
54	2 Bedrooms/2 Bathrooms	1,046	$1,200	$1.15	$481.16
6	2 Bedrooms/2 Bathrooms	1,123	$1,250	$1.11	$55.40
6	2 Bedrooms/2 Bathrooms	1,171	$1,250	$1.07	$55.69
12	3 Bedrooms/2 Bathrooms	1,295	$1,350	$1.04	$119.72
135					$1,113.26

Primary Lender Ratios

Recall earlier portions of the underwriting process that revealed an estimated cost of construction of $14,288,800, which is capitalized with $11,280,000 in debt financing and $3,008,800 in equity funding.

Based on pro forma NOI and a 7.5 percent mortgage interest rate, the debt service coverage ratio on property NOI is 1.22 and on cash flow from operations is 1.20. In other words, for each dollar of debt service, there is $1.20 of cash flow from operations and $1.22 in NOI. The primary reason for default on a loan is an inadequate cash flow to service the debt; a 1.22 DSCR on NOI is very "tight" and does not leave much room for error in the cash flows.

Using the pro forma NOI and a 7.5 percent cap rate, the value of the development is $15,364,000,

Figure 8-8	Financial/Cash Flow Analysis for Clackamas Ridge	
PRO FORMA INCOME STATEMENT		
	All Units	**Per Unit**
Revenue		
Base Rents	$1,803,060	$ 1,113/month
Other Income	25,000	
Potential Gross Income	1,828,060	
Less Vacancy Allowance	–91,403	5.00%
Effective Gross Income	$1,736,657	
Expenses		
Real Estate Taxes	$202,500	$1,500
Other (Payroll)	85,000	630
Utilities	81,000	600
Repairs/Maintenance	67,500	500
Insurance	63,860	473
Other	15,000	111
Management	69,466	4.00%
Total Operating Expenses	$584,326	$4,328
Net Operating Income	$1,152,331	$8,536
Capital Expenditures	–20,250	$150
Cash Flow from Operations	$1,132,081	
Debt Service	946,457	$7,011
Cash Flow after Financing	$185,624	
Ratios		**Calculations**
Proposed Loan Amount	$11,280,000	
Proposed Equity Investment	$3,008,800	
Estimated Cost of Construction	$14,288,800	
Debt Coverage on NOI	1.22	$1,152,331/$946,457
Debt Coverage on Cash Flow from Operations	1.20	$1,132,081/$946,457
Value at 7.5% Cap Rate	$15,364,000	$1,152,331/.075
Loan-to-Value	73%	$11,280,000/$15,364,000
Loan-to-Cost	79%	$11,280,000/$14,288,800
Value per Unit	$113,800	$15,364,000/135
Loan Exposure per Unit	$83,556	$11,280,000/135
Breakeven Occupancy	84.85%	($584,326 + $20,250 + $946,457)/$1,828,060
Breakeven Mortgage Constant	10.04%	($1,736,657 – $584,299 + $20,250)/$11,280,000
Breakeven Rent at 95% Occupancy	$1,008	($584,326 + $20,250 + $946,457)/135/12/0.95
Return on Assets (using estimated construction cost)	7.92%	$1,132,081/$14,288,800
Return on Equity (using proposed equity investment)	6.17%	$185,624/$3,008,800

which makes the value of the property higher than the $14,288,800 cost of construction. As such, the LTV and LTC ratios are 73 percent and 79 percent, respectively. To compare the price per unit and loan exposure per unit, divide the value of the property by the number of units (135); the value per unit is $113,800 and the loan exposure per unit $83,556. These unit prices compare favorably with similar units that recently sold in the market (Figure 8-9).

Based on eight comparable sales, the $113,800 value per unit is right in the range of recently sold units, and the $83,500 loan exposure per unit is 15 percent lower than any of the recent sales. Additionally and importantly, the comparables are listed from the lowest to highest capitalization rate. The 7.5 percent cap rate used to value the property was based on the eight comparable properties, with comparables 4, 5, and 7 being most similar to the subject. Although

| | | | | | Price per | |
| | | | Sale | Sale | Square Foot | Cap |
Property	Location	Size	Date	Price*	per Unit*	Rate
Comp 1	Solara Fair Oaks, OR	394 units	March 2006	$54,250,000	$137,690	6.3%
Comp 2	Overlook Apartments Fair Oaks, OR	394 units	October 2005	$45,728,000	$116,061	6.7%
Comp 3	Avalon Park Fair Oaks, OR	282 units	July 2005	$29,020,000	$102,908	6.7%
Comp 4	Westwood Village Milwaukie Heights, OR	334 units	February 2006	$36,740,000	$110,000	7.1%
Comp 5	Clackamas Trails Sherwood, OR	124 units	July 2005	$14,012,00	$113,000	7.1%
Subject	**Clackamas Ridge Wilsonville, OR**	**135 units**			**$113,800/value $83,556/loan exposure**	**7.5%**
Comp 6	Jefferson Square Apartments Mulloy, OR	110 units	April 2004	$10,935,000	$99,409	7.5%
Comp 7	Ivy Ridge Middleton, OR	282 units	December 2005	$33,200,000	$117,730	7.2%
Comp 8	Running Brook Apartments Skunk Hollow, OR	90 units	June 2005	$9,300,000	$103,333	8.0%

Figure 8-9 — Sale Comparables for Clackamas Ridge

APARTMENT SALE COMPARABLES

Sale comparables indicate comparable apartment complexes have been trading in the range of $99,000 to $137,690 per unit. Our loan per unit is $83,556. Several additional comparables have traded in the range of $75,000 to $85,000 in the past two years. Because of the new construction, quality of construction, and amenity package, it is reasonable to conclude that the stabilized value will be in excess of $100,000 per unit. Avalon Bay recently sold a portfolio of apartments in the Portland market at an average price of $98,500 per unit. All the properties were built in the late 1980s and early 1990s.

According to the market report, potentially 770 market-rate apartment units in the market area are scheduled to start construction in 2004. One such project is a 288-unit project proposed by Mr. Donald Schultz, who has confidentially said that he is not planning to move forward because of high construction costs. The other project in the immediate area that is currently under construction is a 245-unit apartment complex that is being built by Mr. Jerry Nelson of Piper Jaffray. The project will be a bond transaction that will have some "affordable" units.

The owner will develop and act as general contractor for the subject property, which will help keep construction costs down.

The underwriter has investigated all the comparable rental properties and sale comparables. Overall, the underwriter believes the property will perform at the market rents described above.

*Several more comparable sales in the $75,000–85,000 range for inferior product have occurred over the past two years.

Comments

High-end apartment complex, newer property, great location

High-end apartment/townhouse complex, great location, older property

High-end apartment complex, great location, older property, small units

Townhouse complex in an infill location similar to the subject

Most comparable in age and style. Better location.

Four-story wood-frame building, built in 1998, similar location

Townhouse complex, similar location

Older unattractive property. Good location.

comparable 6 was also similar, the sale date was approximately 2.5 years earlier and therefore less relevant.

Other Lender and Equity Ratios

In addition to the DSCR and LTV ratio, most lenders also look to other functions to assess the quality of the loan—such as value per unit and loan exposure per unit, discussed above. Both those numbers are very informative for lenders, especially when compared with recent similar sales (see the bottom portion of Figure 8-9).

Another important ratio is breakeven occupancy (the minimum occupancy rate necessary for property cash inflows to meet all cash outflows), sometimes called the default rate. The breakeven occupancy shown, 84.85 percent, takes the property's fixed outflows and divides them by PGI:

$$Breakeven\ Occupancy = \frac{Total\ Operating\ Expenses + Capital\ Expenditures + Debt\ Service}{Potential\ Gross\ Income}.$$

Conversely, the maximum vacancy rate that a property can sustain before the developer has to make debt service payments out of pocket is 15.15 percent (100 percent − 84.85 percent). A breakeven mortgage constant and a breakeven rent at 95 percent occupancy are also calculated in the income pro forma. These two numbers reveal that the mortgage constant can increase from 8.39 percent to more than 10 percent before the property cash inflows do not cover the debt service payment. The lowest average rent that the borrower can collect and still meet all fixed payments is $1,008, or approximately 90.5 percent of the anticipated $1,113 average rent.

Equity ratios are also of concern to the lender. If the borrower is not making any money on a project or, worse, losing money, the chances increase dramatically that the borrower will not act in the lender's best interests. The lender therefore wants to make certain that the development is a good one for the property owner as well. Dividing cash flow from operations by estimated construction costs yields a 7.92 percent ROA. The 6.17 percent ROE (cash flow after financing divided by the equity investment) is considerably lower than the ROA. Because the debt service constant of 8.39 percent is higher than the ROA of 7.92, leverage is negative, lowering ROE.

Although Affiliated Bank approved the Clackamas Ridge construction loan, the loan officer and several of the bank's trustees felt it was a very tight approval. If it were not for the fact that Joe Bullingo had an ongoing relationship with the bank and the loan officer, it is likely that this loan would not have been approved, as both the DSCR and LTV ratio were at the bank's minimum and maximum, respectively. Additionally, the borrower's personal cash flow position was troubling, because his 197-unit apartment complex was filling much more slowly than anticipated. In short, the existing relationship between this borrower and the bank made a difference in approval of the loan.

SUMMARY

The financing decision can have an enormous impact on investment risks and expected returns. Two criteria dominate the financing decision, especially from the lender's perspective. First, the property's value must provide adequate collateral to cover the loan, with a cushion of value shown in the loan-to-value ratio. Second, regardless of the adequacy of the collateral, the property must have an expected income stream adequate to service the loan, with the cushion of income measured by the debt service coverage ratio. Loan underwriting places tremendous weight on the credibility of comparable information in the construction of the income pro forma. The weaker the reliability of the data, the larger cushion the lender will require.

The use of debt dramatically affects both expected risk and returns for the equity position. Positive leverage occurs when the cost of debt is lower than the overall return to the property; in such cases, leverage increases expected equity returns. Negative leverage occurs when the cost of debt exceeds the overall return to the property; thus, leverage reduces expected equity returns. The use of leverage to raise expected returns carries with it financial risk. Leverage increases variability of the equity cash flow. Should NOI become insufficient to service the debt, default and possibly foreclosure may result.

TERMS

- ► Capitalization
- ► Capitalization rate (cap rate)
- ► Debt service coverage ratio (DSCR)
- ► Discounted cash flow (DCF) analysis
- ► Loan-to-value (LTV) ratio
- ► Mortgage constant
- ► Negative leverage
- ► Net operating income (NOI)
- ► Operating expenses
- ► Positive leverage
- ► Pro forma cash flow statement

REVIEW QUESTIONS

8.1 Discuss the three different ways property owners escalate tenant rents in multiyear leases.
8.2 What is an expense stop, and how is it used in gross, modified gross, and net leases?
8.3 What is a capitalization rate, and how is it used to value commercial real estate?
8.4 What are the two primary ratios commercial property lenders use? What risks does each ratio assess?
8.5 What are the six steps in underwriting a commercial loan? Why is each section important?
8.6 What are capital expenditures, and why are they usually not included as an expense in the calculation of net operating income?
8.7 What are rent comparables, and how are they used to construct an income pro forma?
8.8 What are sale comparables, and how are they used in the valuation of a proposed development?

NOTES

1. Percentage rent rates in the overage rent clauses of retail leases are 6 to 10 percent of tenant sales over a contractually defined threshold. Large anchor stores pay a rent escalator of 1 to 2 percent of sales over the sales threshold.
2. "Same-for-all" means market determined after adjustment for situs. The best corner gets more rent than the next best corner.
3. Appraisal Institute, *The Appraisal of Real Estate*, 12th ed. (Chicago: Author, 2001), p. 529.
4. Several other methods of estimating the property cap rate have also been advanced over the years, among them the band-of-investment approach and the Ellwood method. These methods,

however, are far less defensible than using actual capitalization rates from comparable sale transactions when they are available.

5. For a detailed discussion of the back-of-the-envelope analysis, see William Poorvu, "Cash Flow REITs and the Back of the Envelope," *Real Estate Finance*, Winter 2000, pp. 7–15.

6. To protect the developer and the bank that supplied the information, Clackamas Ridge is not the actual name of the development, Joseph Bullingo is not the name of the developer, and Wilsonville is not the actual location of the development. The facts provided, however, are for an actual construction loan in a town similar to Wilsonville, which is part of a U.S. city sim-ilar to Portland, Oregon. The credit presentation follows the format of a bank with $20 billion in assets and more than 200 retail banking outlets. We are thankful to the anonymous bank for supplying us with a live deal with all the details.

7. The presentation has been edited down.

8. Liquid assets are investments that can be easily converted to cash such as bank accounts, certificates of deposit, and publicly traded stocks and bonds. Illiquid assets are those that take significant time and effort to convert to cash. Real estate investments are considered illiquid because it can take three months to three years to sell an asset.

CHAPTER 9

Discounted Cash Flow: The Equity Perspective in More Detail

INVESTMENT VALUE

Real estate investment is motivated by a combination of three investment benefits: 1) periodic cash flow, 2) residual cash flow from appreciation, and 3) a potential tax shelter. During the 1970s, most of the investment interest in real estate was caused by real estate appreciation, generated in large part because real estate investment was being used as a hedge against inflation. The rise and fall of real estate syndications in the 1980s were heavily predicated on real estate tax shelter benefits (or lack thereof). In the 1990s, periodic cash flow from operations was the strongest benefit of real estate investment. Well into the new millennium, it appears that property cash flow and, to a lesser degree, property appreciation are foremost in the minds of the real estate investment community.

Valuation models used for real estate should explicitly address each of these three benefits to the investor. Only current period income/cash flow is explicitly included in the direct capitalization valuation model. The capitalization approach discussed in Chapter 8 implicitly includes real estate appreciation and tax benefits in the capitalization rate. In other words, the cap rate is adjusted down (or up) for

higher (or lower) potential property appreciation. Similarly, the cap rate is adjusted down (or up) for greater (or lower) expected tax shelter benefits.

Alternatively stated, the direct capitalization method measures the current return of a real estate investment based on the anticipated property NOI and property price—that is, Capitalization Rate = NOI/Value—without explicitly accounting for property appreciation and tax shelter benefits. Direct capitalization does not include any explicit provision for measuring capital expenditures (capital improvements, tenant improvements, and leasing commissions) in the valuation of real property, as these costs are included in the property pro forma after or below the line for NOI.

For most income-producing real estate, it may be wise for the investor to look at property income using both a cap rate method and the more detailed discounted cash flow analysis.

DISCOUNTED CASH FLOW ANALYSIS

Discounted cash flow (DCF) analysis values the expected income streams from a property as if the cash flows were all to be received today. If we assume that cash flows in the future are not as valuable as cash flows today, we need to reduce future cash flows using a process called "discounting." To keep things simple, if an investor did not care whether he received a dollar today or a dollar tomorrow on a real estate investment, we could simply add the expected cash flow streams from a property to determine the property's value. Because few, if any, investors are willing to take no investment return on a property, the real estate analyst must reduce future cash flows by the return he expects from a project.

The expected rate of return or discount rate on a project is largely affected by two things: 1) the perceived riskiness or volatility of the cash flows from the real estate investment; and 2) the investment alternatives available. The stability of property cash flows is largely a function of the tenant space market (see Chapter 8). The discussion in this chapter is on the effects of the capital markets on real estate investments and the application of the rates of return in a discounted cash flow analysis.

Expected Rate of Return

The expected rate of return (or discount rate) on real estate investments is determined in a competitive investment market. Stock, bond, and real estate investments compete with each other for investment capital. Conversely, the many different sources of investment capital—individual investors, REITs, pension funds, corporations, for example—compete with the others for different investments. As such, the expected rates of return on real estate and all other investments are determined in a highly competitive marketplace.

When considering investment alternatives, most investors look to the rate of return on U.S. Treasury obligations as the baseline investment return. The lowest rate of return any investor should be willing to accept for an investment of a given term should be that of U.S. Treasury securities of a similar term. Investment in commercial real estate is usually considered a long-term investment, as the transaction costs of purchasing and selling real estate make short-term direct investment in real estate difficult. Over the last 50 years, the average long-term U.S. Treasury rate of return was 6.5

percent.[1] The U.S. Treasury interest rate is considered "risk free," because the full faith and credit of the federal government back the debt.[2] On September 6, 2007, the ten-year U.S. Treasury bond yielded 4.51 percent.

This 4.51 percent risk-free rate of return includes an inflation premium and a real rate of return, two of the three needed components of return on all investments. The other component of an interest rate is a risk premium.

Inflation Premium

Embedded in or part of the 4.51 percent ten-year U.S. Treasury interest rate is an inflation premium. Long-term rates of return include an inflation premium, as investors must be compensated for the expectation in the marketplace that prices in the future will be higher than prices today. To keep pace with inflation, investors' returns include an inflation premium. Currently, the inflation premium component of the ten-year Treasury rate is estimated at 2.19 percent.[3] In summary, the inflation premium is the first component of an interest rate where the investor expects a return that must meet the expected increase in prices, or inflation, in the long term.

Real Rate of Return

A second component of an interest rate is the real rate of return. Investors are not interested in their investments' simply keeping up with the rate of inflation; they also require a real rate of return in excess of inflation when investing in U.S. Treasury securities. The real rate of return is another way of saying what the investor is *really* getting over the rate of inflation. The real rate of return does not compensate the investor for risk, which is embedded in the risk premium. Generally, the real rate of return is approximately 2 to 4 percent on ten-year U.S. Treasury bonds.[4] In sum, the U.S. Treasury interest rate or the risk-free interest rate includes two components, the real rate of return and the inflation premium, but does not include a risk premium.

Risk Premium

All investments other than investments in U.S. Treasury securities include a risk premium. The risk premium or spread to Treasuries (the difference in rates between similarly termed risky debt securities or a loan that is not backed by the U.S. federal government) compensates the investor for his willingness to make an investment that may default, be difficult to sell, experience price volatility over time, or incur other risks associated with the investment. An investor considers each risk and "prices" it or includes it in the risk spread or spread to Treasuries. For instance, the investment in a commercial mortgage includes the possibility of the borrower's defaulting on the loan. Even if the borrower is in good standing, the lender may have limited ability to sell or liquidate the loan (known as "liquidity risk"). Over the past several decades, the approximate risk premium on long-term permanent commercial mortgages is 1 to 3 percentage points over similarly termed U.S. Treasury securities. The spread to Treasuries is highly dependent on the perceived riskiness of a loan, which is measured using the property loan-to-value ratio and debt service coverage ratio (see Chapter 8). The spread to Treasuries has been lower than long-term averages in recent years, however. Thus, taking a risk spread of 2 percentage points for a commercial real estate mortgage over the current ten-year U.S. Treasury rate of 4.51 percent combines for a commercial mortgage interest rate of approximately 6.51 percent.

Like commercial real estate loans, equity investment in real estate is also risky. As real estate debt has the first claim on property cash flow and asset value in the event of default, equity investments in real estate have an expected return and risk premium that exceeds the expected rate of return and risk premium on long-term commercial mortgages. Over the past several decades, unleveraged (no debt is used) total returns on real estate investments by pension fund managers have averaged approximately 9.4 percent.[5] Although the average return is lower than what most pension investors expected over this period (attributed to significant overbuilding of space in the middle to late 1980s, which depressed total rates of return on all-equity purchases of high-quality investments in real estate during that period), most pension funds today are investing in high-quality income-producing real estate with the expectation of 8 to 10 percent total rates of return on all-equity investments in real estate.

Another source of equity capital for real estate is real estate investment trusts. REITs are publicly traded securities that invest in commercial real estate. Generally speaking, REITs invest in assets of good to high quality and use debt to leverage or increase the returns (and the volatility or riskiness) of property cash flows. Over the past 30 years, REITs have maintained an average rate of return of 13.5 percent. Investment returns on stocks over that same 30-year period averaged 12.4 percent. Overall, long-term investment returns on REITs are similar to stock returns, but it should be noted that year-over-year returns on REITs often differ dramatically from stock indices.[6]

DETERMINING A DISCOUNT RATE

The expected rate of return on real estate investments is a function of the risk of the investment. A completed and leased building by General Electric (a AAA-credit-rated company) for 30 years has a very low risk profile and therefore would command a very low total rate of return (discount rate) if sold in the market, say 6 to 7 percent. The low risk premium and therefore low expected rate of return increase the value of future cash flows today because the discount rate (the rate at which we discount future cash flows) is low. Alternatively, the risk of developing an office building on a brownfield site that needs to be rezoned and has no preleasing in an overbuilt office market poses many risks—environmental, municipal approval, development, lease-up, and market. All these risks suggest an expected rate of return that could be 25 to 30 percent (maybe higher) on the equity investment, and there is little chance a lender would provide debt capital on such a risky deal.

All space markets and submarkets depend on the economic and population growth of the area where they are located and the supply of competitive space. As such, the risk profile of an investment in a market or submarket changes as one moves from the central business district to the suburbs to the exurbs. The risk of a central city location could be slower economic and population growth relative to the suburbs, but it may also be difficult for new competition to build in the area. Alternatively, many suburbs may contain numerous sites available for competitive development but greater opportunity for economic and population growth.

To determine the discount rate for a property, it is best to find comparable properties that were recently sold and find out what competitive sources of capital expect for a rate of return. One source of that information is the local commercial property appraisal community, which may have both survey data on expected rates of return and information about specific, comparable properties. Some regional appraisal and consulting firms publish expected property rates of return. Direct discussions with brokers and principal investors may also be fruitful. The commercial real estate industry has become much more open in recent years, and it is more common to find willingly shared formal and informal information about property income streams and returns.

Tenant and Space Market Risks

Expected rates of return are affected by the perceived riskiness of the property, tenant, and capital markets. Refer again to the earlier example of the General Electric leased building. If the full faith and credit of G.E. are behind 30 years of lease payments, the property analyst can virtually ignore the risks of an overbuilt space market because the need to re-lease the G.E. space is unlikely to occur for another 30 years. Few are lucky to have such a tenant, however. Additionally, creditworthy tenants know the value that they bring to a real estate development and they negotiate lower rents, resulting in low returns and low investment risk for the developer and property owner.

Most real estate developments incur a range of property-specific risks. Managing these risks is critical in estimating an expected rate of return. For instance, developing a new office building in an overbuilt market sounds like a risky proposal, but if 60 percent of the building is preleased to six different tenants, much of the perceived risk is mitigated. The recognition and mitigation of risk is critical in commercial real estate development and investment. (Chapter 16 discusses several risk management techniques available to control development and investment risk.)

Another significant source of risk in commercial real estate is market risk. Most leases are relatively short term—three to seven years—and lease-up or re-leasing can pose significant risks to the developer and investors. Both debt and equity sources of capital are acutely aware of vacancies in the market and submarket where the property is located. When leases expire on a commercial building, not only might the space remain vacant for months (or years) but also leasing commissions to secure new tenants and tenant improvement costs are likely to be significant. If that expiring lease is for a sizable portion of the building, property cash flows may be very volatile during this period, making it difficult to meet mortgage debt service payments.

Capital Market Risks

Capital flows into investments that return the highest risk-adjusted return. For instance, during the high-tech stock run-up in prices in the late 1990s, investors perceived little downside risk by investing in new technology and telecommunication stocks. As a result, tremendous amounts of capital flowed into largely unproved technologies with little if any sales revenue and profits and the expectation that technology would change virtually all aspects of our lives. Many of these technologies were unable to generate profit, capital beat a hasty retreat from the technology sector, and the tech market bubble burst. Real estate investments are subject to some of the same pressures as stocks, bonds, and all other investments. In the short run, excess capital flows into a particular investment segment, reducing the cost of capital because the perceived risk of making that investment is lower than the reality of that investment. In the long run, excess capital flowing into commercial real estate is likely to increase the amount of commercial real estate, oversupplying the market with space and reducing rents and thus property returns.

Determining the expected rate of return for a property is as much an art as it is a science. Analyses of comparable sales can be one important source of expectations for returns. Numerous appraisal and real estate consulting firms collect return rates on properties that can provide some guidelines. From that point, it is imperative that the real estate analyst determine the overall risk profile of the subject development or acquisition and the anticipated growth in the supply of and demand for space to further refine the riskiness and thus expectations of returns on a real estate project. Add to the mix the perception of risk—real or not—and its contribution to estimating expected rates of return.

DISCOUNTING A SINGLE CASH FLOW

Discounted cash flow models discount the expected property income stream to estimate the value of a property today. Alternatively, the value of a property is the amount that an investor is willing to pay for a stream of future cash flows. For example, assume that you would like to purchase a zero coupon bond, which distributes no interest payments and returns only $1,000 at maturity, in exactly one year. After reviewing the expected return on similar securities or comparables, you have determined that 6.5 percent is a reasonable expected rate of return. To determine the value today of $1,000 in one year, we must discount the $1,000 for one year. The present value, or discounted cash flow, analysis for a single-period discount, is as follows:

Present Value = Future Value × Discount Factor
Present Value = Future Value × $1/(1 + i)^n$
Present Value = $1,000 × $1/(1 + .065)^1$
Present Value = $1,000 × 1/1.065
Present Value = $1,000 × 0.93897
Present Value = $938.97.

First, the present value, or value today of a future expected amount, must be discounted. The size of the discount factor depends on the discount rate (i) and the number of discount periods (n). With a discount rate of 6.5 percent and the number of years as one, we obtain 1/1.065, which returns 0.93897. Multiplying the discount factor by the future value of $1,000 returns a value today of $938.97.

Now let's use all the same information as above but assume a two-year zero coupon bond; that is, we receive no interest payments for two years and get only $1,000 at the end of Year 2. The discounting process is identical to the example above, with one exception: the number of periods now is two ($n = 2$).

Present Value = Future Value × Discount Factor
Present Value = Future Value × $1/(1 + i)^n$
Present Value = $1,000 × $1/(1 + .065)^2$
Present Value = $1,000 × 1/1.13423
Present Value = $1,000 × 0.88166
Present Value = $881.66

The 6.5 percent discount factor is compounding (i.e., the use of an exponential term of two), which returns a present value of $881.66. We could continue with a three-year holding period and beyond, but we would simply be changing the number of compound periods and completing the same calculation. The steps using a handheld calculator are shown in Figure 9-1.

Figure 9-1	**Calculator Inputs for Present Value Analysis**

Using a Hewlett-Packard 12-C calculator, we calculate the present value *(PV)*, given a future value *(FV)*, interest rate *(i)*, and term *(n)*:

PV = (FV, i, n)
PV = (1,000, 6.50, 2)

Entering these cash flows into the calculator as follows returns the present value:

f	CLX
1,000	FV
6.5	i
2	n
PV =	–$881.66

After clearing the memory registers by entering *f CLX*, we then enter 1,000 *FV*, 6.5 *i*, and 2 *n*. We are telling the calculator that we will receive $1,000 in two years and would like to have the money discounted at a 6.5 percent rate to determine the value today. Entering *PV* asks the calculator to calculate the present value of the information that was input. The *PV* is a negative $881.66. The negative result indicates that we should be willing to pay $881.66 to purchase a cash flow stream that provides $1,000 in two years; however, *the present value is not negative.* The value of a positive cash flow stream can only be positive; what the calculator provides is what the investor should be willing to pay today—a cash outflow of $881.66—for a cash inflow of $1,000 in two years. (Inputs to an Excel or similar spreadsheet are identical to what was used for the calculator using the *PV* or present value function.)

DISCOUNTING MULTIPLE CASH FLOWS

Discounted cash flow analysis using multiple cash flows is simply an expansion of discounting a single cash flow. Suppose a real estate investment is expected to produce an income stream and sale proceeds (reversion) as shown below and that a discount rate of 9 percent is considered appropriate for the perceived risk of investing in the project. That is, a rate of 9 percent is considered reasonable to compensate the investor for the risks associated with the real estate investment over the five-year investment horizon.

Year	Income	Reversion
1	$110,000	
2	111,000	
3	112,000	
4	115,000	
5	125,000	$1,470,000

The formula for present value analysis or discounted cash flow analysis of the property investment is as follows:

$$PV = \text{(Discount Factor}_1 \times \text{Cash Flow}_1) +$$
$$\text{(Discount Factor}_2 \times \text{Cash Flow}_2) +$$
$$\text{(Discount Factor}_3 \times \text{Cash Flow}_3) +$$
$$\text{(Discount Factor}_4 \times \text{Cash Flow}_4) +$$
$$\text{(Discount Factor}_5 \times \text{Cash Flow}_5)$$

Note that there are five separate cash flows to discount and five separate discount factors at which to discount them. Although the discount rate of 9 percent stays the same for each cash flow, the number of periods needed to discount the cash flows changes. The calculation below places the property cash flows into the discounted cash flow analysis model. Note that the property income is added to the reversion price to obtain $1,595,000 ($125,000 + $1,470,000) in Year 5.

$$PV = [\$110,000 \times 1/(1 + .09)^1] +$$
$$[\$111,000 \times 1/(1 + .09)^2] +$$
$$[\$112,000 \times 1/(1 + .09)^3] +$$
$$[\$115,000 \times 1/(1 + .09)^4] +$$
$$[\$1,595,000 \times 1/(1 + .09)^5]$$

Although the DCF model appears complex, we are simply replicating the discounting process five times to discount five separate cash flows. The next step is to calculate the discount factors each year; alternatively, the analyst can find present value discount factors from a table.[7]

$$PV = (\$110,000 \times 0.91743) +$$
$$(\$111,000 \times 0.84168) +$$
$$(\$112,000 \times 0.77218) +$$
$$(\$115,000 \times 0.70843) +$$
$$(\$1,595,000 \times 0.64993)$$
$$PV = \$1,398,936$$

The estimated value of $1,398,936 (actual results may be ± $10 because of rounding the discount factor) is based on the expected property income and the estimated sale price in the fifth year and on the expected return or discount rate of 9 percent. An investor who pays the estimated price and then receives the forecast stream of income plus the reversion will receive a 9 percent annual return.

At this point, it is instructive to clarify the difference between present value and net present value. *Present value* is the value today of a sequence of future cash flows, usually the series of cash flows from a property plus the reversion sale price, as we have discussed to this point. *Net present value* subtracts the purchase price, or cash outflow at time zero, from the expected property inflows—in short, the net present value "net out" the purchase price from the present value of the future income streams. In the Hewlett-Packard 12-C example in Figure 9-2, we enter zero for cash flow zero by entering no purchase price at time zero, as the NPV calculation is equivalent to the present value of the cash flows.[8]

Calculating the present value of a stream of uneven cash flows (that is, the cash flow amounts are different each year) in Excel uses a method to determine net present value similar to the handheld calculator. First, we must combine the property income and anticipated sale price in Year 5 into an annual property cash flow line as we did in cell G8 (see Figure 9-3).

Next, identify the discount rate and type it into cell C10 and find the NPV function in the Excel program. While residing in cell C13, select the f_x icon if

Figure 9-2	Tools to Calculate the Present Value of Unequal Cash Flows

Calculating the present value of a five-year income stream, while instructive, is rather cumbersome. Most financial calculators allow you to key in the cash flows and calculate the present value more simply. What follows are two examples of how to calculate the present value of a stream of income, one using the HP 12-C calculator, and the second using an Excel spreadsheet.

Calculating the present value of a stream of income using a handheld calculator is rather straightforward. First, the analyst must remember that the income stream must be entered sequentially (that is, in the order the income is received) and that for each period only one cash flow can be entered. Therefore, the property income in Year 5 must be added to the reversion or sale of the property, as both are received at the end of Year 5. Thus, property cash flows (CF) will look like the following:

Period	Cash Flow
CF_0	0
CF_1	110,000
CF_2	111,000
CF_3	112,000
CF_4	115,000
CF_5	1,595,000

The following example is for the HP 12-C, which, even though it is based on technology that is 25 years old, still reigns as one of the most popular calculators among real estate professionals.[a] More recent calculators have a menu screen that prompts the user to enter the appropriate cash flow. The keystrokes necessary to discount the cash flows listed above are as follows:

f	CLX
0	g CF_0
110,000	g CF_j
111,000	g CF_j
112,000	g CF_j
115,000	g CF_j
1,595,000	g CF_j
9	i
f	NPV = $1,398,938

The key strokes to calculate the present value are as follows. First, f CLX clears all registers, 0 g CF_0 enters a zero in time zero, and 110,000 g CF_j enters 110,000 in cash flow register CF_j (as this is the first cash flow). The key strokes 111,000 g CF_j enter 111,000 in the second cash flow register or period $j = 2$, and so on for the next three years. Then enter the discount rate of 9 in i or the interest/discount rate register. Finally, enter f NPV, which asks the calculator to determine the net present value, returning $1,398,938.

[a]We cannot present the keystrokes for each brand and model of calculator available; however, using your favorite search engine on the Internet (such as Google or Yahoo), enter the model of your calculator and "present value analysis," and a variety of Web pages will appear.

you have the function icon available on your tool bar, or click on *Insert* and then select f_x or *Function*. Under *All* or the *Financial* function categories, find *NPV* and click on it. At this point, a pop-up menu appears requesting a *Rate* and *Value1*. For the *Rate*, enter *C10* or the cell where you have placed the discount rate cell, then enter *C8:G8* or the range of the property cash flows for *Value1* through *Value5*, and then select *O.K.* Although the prompt for *Value1* suggests that you should enter only a single value, a range of values works fine; you can enter the range by typing in *C8:G8* or dragging the cursor across cells *C8* through *G8*. At this point, cell *C13* should reveal $1,398,938.

If it does not, go back and retrace your inputs because something was entered incorrectly. If what fills your cell is #######, you need to reformat your column to a greater width or format your number to fit the cell; you do both of these actions using *Format* on your tool bar. Again, because we entered only the cash flow stream CF_1 through CF_5, *NPV* returns the same as the present value of the cash flows. To restate, the inputs for the NPV function are =*NPV (discount rate, cash flows CF_1 ... CF_n)*, where we reference cell *C10* for the discount rate and cells *C8:G8* for the cash flows to be discounted, which returns the present value of the cash flows as $1,398,938.

Figure 9-3	Discounted Cash Flow Example on Microsoft Excel				
	B	**C**	**D**	**E**	**F**	**G**
4						
5		Year 1	Year 2	Year 3	Year 4	Year 5
6	Property Income	$110,000	$111,000	$112,000	$115,000	$125,000
7	Reversion Sale Price					$1,470,000
8	Property Cash Flow	$110,000	$111,000	$112,000	$115,000	$1,595,000
9						
10	Discount Rate	9.00%				
11						
12						
13	Present Value	$1,398,938				
14						

The formula for calculating net present value using Excel is NPV (rate, value 1, value 2, value 3, . . .). In this example, the rate is in cell C10, and the values range from cell C8 to G8. Simply click on an empty cell and enter = NPV (B7, B5:F5). The computed NPV is presented in cell C13.

INTERNAL RATE OF RETURN

The internal rate of return (IRR) is the property discount rate that makes property inflow equal property outflow. In other words, the IRR is an iterative process to determine the rate of return on an investment, given predetermined equity investment or cash outflow and a series of investment cash inflows. Many real estate investors like to use the IRR as a comparative measure between and among alternative property investments, as the IRR is always stated per dollar or unit of investment so that the IRR of a $50,000 investment can be directly compared with the IRR of a $50 million investment.

The primary difference between an IRR calculation and a PV calculation is that the present value determines the value of an income stream today given a specified discount rate. An IRR, on the other hand, calculates the rate of return on a property given a purchase price (cash outflow) and a stream of future cash inflows. Figure 9-4 presents a calculation of IRR. Start with a purchase price or a cash outflow at time zero. In the example, we assume that the investor is willing to pay $1.2 million for the property income stream. Based on a $1.2 million cash outflow at time zero and series of positive income streams in periods one through five, what is the total rate of return or IRR on the property?

First, it is necessary to place both the cash outflow at time zero and the series of cash inflows in the same row, as shown in row 10 in the figure. Next, find the IRR function resident in the Excel program. While residing in cell *C12*, select the f_x icon if you have the function icon on your tool bar or click on *Insert* and then select f_x or *Function*. Under the *All* or *Financial* function categories, find IRR and click on it. A pop-up menu should request that you enter a *Range;* in that range, enter *C10:H10* or the range of all of the property cash flows for *Value 0* through *Value 5.* Then select *O.K.* Note that for the calculation of the IRR, cash flow begins with cash flow zero, while for the calculation of NPV, cash flows begin with cash flow one. At this point, cell *C12* should say *12.96%.* If it does not, retrace your inputs, as you entered something incorrectly. Alternatively, you may need to format the cell for the *Percent* format. To do so, select *Format, Cells, Percentage,* and the number of decimal places you want presented.[9]

Figure 9-4	Internal Rate of Return Example on Microsoft Excel					
	B	**C**	**D**	**E**	**F**	**G**	**H**
4							
5		Year 0	Year 1	Year 2	Year 3	Year 4	Year 5
6	Property Income		$110,000	$111,000	$112,000	$115,000	$125,000
7	Reversion Sale Price						$1,470,000
8	Property Cash Flow		$110,000	$111,000	$112,000	$115,000	$1,595,000
9	Purchase Price	−$1,200,000					
10	Investment Cash Flows	−$1,200,000	$110,000	$111,000	$112,000	$115,000	$1,595,000
11							
12	Internal Rate of Return	12.96%					
13							

The formula for calculating internal rate of return using Excel is IRR (value 0, value 1, value 2, . . .). In this example, the range of values is from C10 to H10; simply click on an empty cell and enter = IRR (C10:H10). Note that Excel needs at least one positive and one negative value for the calculation. The computed IRR is presented in cell C12.

GATEWAY BUSINESS CENTER CASE STUDY

We now apply the mechanics of discounted cash flow analysis to the Gateway Business Center, an industrial property in Brookfield, Wisconsin, a suburb of Milwaukee. The Gateway Business Center Offering Memorandum (see Appendix B) provides actual property attributes, leasehold income, and capital market return parameters for modeling and analyzing the cash flows to estimate a purchase price for the asset.[10]

Applying Discounted Cash Flow Analysis To Gateway Business Center

Investment risk can be managed or accounted for in one of two ways: risk-adjusted property cash flows or a risk-adjusted discount rate. *Risk-adjusted property cash flows* can be reasonably completed using the property income streams if the impact of the risk on the investment cash flows can be roughly estimated. Alternatively, investment risk can be accounted for by *risk-adjusted property discount rates,* where a higher discount rate is used to account for riskier cash flows. When property cash flow risk cannot be reasonably

adjusted for in the cash flows, a risk-adjusted discount rate is used to account for a greater risk of investing in a property. Overall, real estate investors attempt to account for investment risk in the property cash flows when completing a discounted cash flow analysis and then use standard discount rate risk premiums to account for the possibility of incorrect cash flow assumptions.

Investment risk can be accounted for in property income streams by modeling the multiyear lease contracts that define the property income stream. Generally speaking, risk is endured when the landlord is responsible for increases in property expenses or tenant leases expire or tenants go bankrupt, and so on. The expiration of tenant leases is a particular risk that landlords and lenders alike account for when assessing the riskiness of property cash flows. During lease rollovers, the landlord is likely to endure reduced or nonexistent rental income, fewer expense pass-throughs to the tenant, and the costs of renegotiating a new lease or securing a new tenant. Additionally, leasing commissions and tenant improvements surrounding the loss of a tenant can significantly affect property cash flows below the NOI line. The increase in the volatility of property cash flows from expired leases and the management of that risk is very difficult to complete when using a cap rate valuation that analyzes a single-year cash flow; thus, a DCF analysis is very helpful in identifying and managing this risk.

Overall, DCF provides a better means of managing property investment risk by explicitly addressing risk factors in assumptions about the property's cash flow. If a DCF is thoughtfully constructed, it should assist both investor and lender in managing the risks of a real estate investment. As lease terms, tenants' creditworthiness, growth in property expenses, and rental markets change from property to property and market to

Figure 9-5	Opportunity Summary	
Total Square Footage		72,510 SF
3235 Intertech Drive (South Building)		38,180 SF
3275 Intertech Drive (North Building)		34,330 SF
Current Number of Tenants:		5
Time Warner		*33,455 SF*
Diebold		*4,725 SF*
United Leasing Associates		*6,329 SF*
Prestige Electrolysis		*5,802 SF*
EZ International		*12,653 SF*
Currently Vacant		9,546 SF
Year 1 Net Operating Income		$529,975
Asking Price	$ 6,700,000 (7.9% cap rate)	

market, being able to directly address some of these risks explicitly in property cash flows is very helpful.

The remainder of this section is dedicated to the Gateway Business Center Offering Memorandum (Appendix B). The Gateway Business Center Offering Memorandum is an excellent example of how commercial real estate is offered for sale and includes many, if not all, of the important components of a property sale document. In addition to presenting the Gateway Business Center offering, we analyze the property cash flow using a lease-by-lease analysis program called ARGUS.

The following discussion reviews the information provided in the offering memorandum and analyzes the property investment over a ten-year holding period.

Gateway Business Center

Executive Summary

The Gateway Business Center Offering Memorandum begins with an executive summary of the property. The offering is a 100 percent fee simple ownership interest in two flex industrial/office buildings located at 3235–3275 Intertech Drive, Brookfield, Wisconsin (see Figure 9-5). The executive summary includes several noteworthy items, among them a description of the property and tenancy and financial highlights.

The Property

The discussion of the property begins with a physical description of the collateral, which is two buildings totaling 72,510 square feet (6,740 square meters) of net rentable area that were built in 1997 with decorative split-face block construction on approximately 5.5 acres (2.2 hectares) of land. The property is currently divided into six tenant suites; each suite has dock-height and/or drive-in loading. The building allows the landlord to increase or decrease suite sizes easily. The property has truck parking in the rear of the building and car parking in the front of each building for office employees. The property, located approximately two miles (3.2 kilometers) from I-94, offers immediate access to Highway 190 (Capitol Drive).

Tenancy Highlights

After the physical description of the property, the next most important attribute is the quality of the property cash flows, which depends on tenants' creditworthiness. The building is 87 percent occupied and currently houses five companies. One space is vacant. The property has maintained a stable list of tenants for nine years and includes both national and local companies with triple net and modified gross leases. Time Warner Telecom (www.twtelecom.com) is the anchor tenant of the property and occupies 46 percent of the building space. Time Warner (NYSE: TWX) has been a tenant in this project since its inception in 1997. One of the primary draws of the building to Time Warner is the building's high-speed fiber-optic lines that are also available to the business park. Diebold (NYSE: DBD) is also a tenant in the 3235 Building and recently signed a lease in the Gateway Business Park for 63 months. Local companies that reside in Gateway Center include Prestige Electrolysis (www.prestigeelec .com), EZ International (www.ez-international.com), and United Leasing Associates (www.ula.net).

Financial Highlights

The executive summary includes three important financial highlights (see Figure 9-5): 1) Year 1 NOI of $529,975, 2) asking price of $6.7 million, and 3) 7.9 percent cap rate based on the asking price and first-year property NOI. The combination of the asking price, Year 1 NOI, and the cap rate summarize the financial opportunity with the expected investment, expected income stream, and expected return. An abbreviated five-year summary of property cash flows (see Figure 9-6) indicates that property income streams are expected to be stable to growing in the coming years, largely attributable to the Time Warner lease, which does not expire until Year 9 (2014).

From the information included in the executive summary, a potential investor can quickly assess the property as collateral, the income stream generated from the property, and the investment return based on a suggested asking price.

Property Overview

"Property Overview" includes a summary of the property systems and structure and a series of pictures of the collateral property and its location in the market. Property and site attributes are critical to assess the current and future viability of the collateral. In other words, if the building is functionally, physically, or locationally obsolete, a purchaser would place a higher discount rate on the property cash flows to account for the higher risk associated with leasing the building in the future. A building's functional obsolescence can be assessed using the property highlights shown in Figure 9-7. The property highlights provide potential purchasers with a quick rundown of the building systems, which should reveal the degree of functional obsolescence in the building systems and plans.

Each building and site attribute is important to a potential investor who wants to make certain that the property will meet the needs of current and future tenants and meets current environmental guidelines. For instance, because the building was erected in 1997, it should not contain any lead paint, asbestos, or other banned materials that are now considered health hazards. The 200+ stalls of parking provide approximately three stalls per 1,000 square feet (93 square meters) of net rentable area (a 3:1 parking ratio), an industry standard for this type of building. The 12 dock-high and drive-in truck doors provide an appropriate number of loading docks for the building; they are located throughout the two buildings, allowing the layout to be easily configured for multiple tenants. The lighting, concrete structure, reinforced floors, and gas-fired HVAC system are all indications of the property's collateral value.

A potential purchaser can also assess the quality of the property's physical location through a series of maps, building photographs, and aerial photographs. Some simple maps locating the subject in a neighbor-

Figure 9-6	Summary of Cash Flows				
Year Ending	2006	2007	2008	2009	2010
Potential Gross Income	$701,689	$747,306	$734,719	$765,653	$786,381
Vacancy	0	($52,311)	($39,582)	($48,027)	($50,399)
Effective Gross Income	$701,689	$694,995	$695,137	$717,626	$735,982
Operating Expenses	$171,714	$175,756	$180,199	$185,671	$191,114
Net Operating Income	$529,975	$519,239	$514,938	$531,995	$544,868

Figure 9-7	Gateway Business Center: Property Highlights
3235–3275 Intertech Drive, Brookfield, Wisconsin	
Square Footage:	72,510 SF
Site Size:	5.5 acres
Land To Building:	3.30:1
Percent Office:	±50%
Age:	1997
Parking:	200+
Construction:	Concrete block
Clear Height:	18′
Loading:	Ten (10) exterior docks, two drive-in doors
Roof Structure:	Rubber membrane
Sprinkler System:	Wet system
Lighting:	Metal halide
Floor Thickness:	Six inches reinforced
Zoning:	Office, Light Industrial
HVAC:	Gas fired in warehouse, rooftop HVAC in office
Railserved:	No
Utilities:	Gas, electric, water—provided by WE Energies

hood and its market are critical to potential buyers, and visualizing the proximity of the asset to primary surface and interstate roads further helps to understand the quality of the property's location. Interior and exterior photos reveal the quality of the asset and its state of obsolescence. Aerial photos also provide potential buyers with a better sense of land use patterns in the area and the possibility of future development.

Financial Analysis

Although bricks and mortar are necessary to house tenants, when determining a property's value the actual cost of construction is of secondary importance to the cash flow stream that the property can generate. Revenue is generated from tenant leases, which run for multiple years and usually expire during the holding period of the asset. Most institutional investors assume an investment holding period of seven to 15 years, with a ten-year cash flow analysis the most common. To financial analysts, an income-producing property is simply a portfolio of

leases or fixed-income contracts of differing maturities, which is what they look to value. Therefore, to complete a ten-year cash flow analysis, the property analyst must be able to project tenant income based on existing lease contracts and to project what market rents will be for the space when existing lease contracts expire.

"Financial Analysis" provides prospective purchasers the set of assumptions used to determine property market rental rates, lease rollover assumptions, and expense and capital improvement costs. "Tenancy" complements "Financial Analysis" in that income from the lease contracts is presented in the lease abstracts for each tenant. A commercial real estate cash flow analysis program called ARGUS combines the anticipated income from existing lease contract income with the prospective income likely to come from the space after the primary leases have ended. Although the function of the Offering Memorandum is to sell the asset, it is in the seller's best interest to be forthright about its financial information.

Discussing the property income stream needs to start with General Assumptions to Projections (shown on pages 11 and 12 of the Offering Memorandum in Appendix B). Figure 9-8 addresses the first part of the general assumptions for the Gateway Business Center's prospective cash flows, beginning with a property holding period of ten years. Current occupancy of the building is 87 percent, and the vacant space is expected to be leased on July 1, 2006, effectively returning a 93.5 percent occupancy rate for the building in Year 1. Thereafter, a 5 percent general vacancy rate is applied to account for loss of income from bad credits and other reductions of the ongoing rental income. Property expenses and capital improvements are expected to grow at the inflation rate, 3 percent.

Although in reverse order from a property pro forma, property expenses are entered into a lease-by-lease analysis program before revenue is entered. Expenses must be established before entering lease contract data so expense reimbursement data can be entered for the lease contracts and market leasing assumptions. Building expenses are obtained from past actual expenses for the building; the following projected expenses and structural reserves were used for 2006:

CAM and Utilities	$48,658
Insurance	$7,251
Real Estate Taxes	$87,737
Management Fee	4% of Effective Gross Revenue
Structural Reserves	$0.10 per square foot

CAM (common area maintenance) and utilities includes the ongoing and daily expenses to operate the building—for example, building cleaning, parking lot maintenance, landscaping expenses, and all utility expenses. Insurance costs include purchasing insurance against numerous perils for the structure; insurance for contents of the leased space and business interruption insurance are usually the responsibility of the tenant. Real estate taxes are usually the largest property expense, approximately half of all property expenses. The property management fee is 4 percent of effective gross revenue and pays for the salary of the property manager and administration of the building. A small structural reserve is set aside for future and ongoing costs associated with the replacement of significant building components such as the roof, HVAC system, and elevators.

The triple net leases in these buildings allow for pass-throughs (reimbursement by the tenant to the landlord) of CAM, utilities, insurance, real estate taxes, and management fees. The modified gross lease for the Time Warner space allows only increases in these expenses to pass through to the tenant. Structural reserves do not pass through to the tenants, as structural reserves are for the replacement of capital items and are not considered expenses; only in rare cases do tenants reimburse the landlord for structural reserves.

We now shift attention to how the space will be re-leased when leases expire. The subject property contains two types of spaces—flex space leases and office space leases. The only difference between flex and office space is that flex space leases designate approximately 30 percent of the space as office space, while office space leases designate approximately 80 percent of the space for office use. Rents, lease terms,

Figure 9-8	Gateway Business Center: General Assumptions to Projections		
Analysis Period	Ten-year analysis begins January 1, 2006		
Occupancy	The asset is currently 87% occupied by five tenants. For purposes of this analysis, the pro forma assumes that the asset will be 100% occupied by July 1, 2006.		
Growth Rates	General Inflation	3%	
	Expenses:	3%	
	Capital Improvements	3%	
General Vacancy Rate	5% year 1 excluded; natural 13% vacancy exists for first 6 months of year 1 in analysis		

Figure 9-9	Gateway Business Center: Flex Space Leases	
New Lease Assumptions	Subject Units:	Diebold, EZ International, Prestige, Vacancy
	Rate:	$5.75/SF (±30% office)
	Type:	NNN
	Term:	Five years
	Rent Growth:	2.5%
	Return Factor:	65%
	Downtime:	Six Months
	Abatements:	Two Months
	Commission	
	New:	8%, 3%, etc. . . . on the NNN Rent
	Renewal:	4%, 1.5%, etc. . . . on the NNN Rent
Tenant Improvements	New:	$5.00/SF
	Renewal:	$2.00/SF

Figure 9-10	Gateway Business Center: Office Space Leases	
New Lease Assumptions	Subject Units:	Time Warner, United Leasing
	Rate:	$8.75/SF (±80% office)
	Type:	NNN
	Term:	Seven years
	Rent Growth:	2.5%
	Return Factor:	65%
	Downtime:	Six Months
	Abatements:	Two Months
	Commission	
	New:	7%, 2%, etc. . . . on the Gross Rent
	Renewal:	3.5%, 1%, etc. . . . on the Gross Rent
Tenant Improvements	New:	$5.00/SF
	Renewal:	$2.00/SF

and lease-up costs are likely to differ between the two types of spaces for property cash flows.

Lease Assumptions for the Flex Space Market

Lease assumptions for the flex space are used to determine property cash flows after existing lease contracts expire. In other words, we use information from existing lease contracts to model property income until the lease contract expires; upon expiration, we use the market lease assumptions to model the income from the space. Three tenants in the buildings occupy space that is approximately 30 percent office and thus considered flex office/industrial space

(Diebold, EZ International, Prestige). Additionally, the current vacant space is also expected to attract a flex space user.[11] When the lease contracts for these three tenants expire in 2008, 2009, and 2010, assumptions about the flex leases are used to determine the expected property income stream after the lease expires. Current market rent for flex space is $5.75 per square foot ($61.90 per square meter) per year, triple net, with a five-year term.

It is also assumed that market rent will grow 2.5 percent per year and that 65 percent of the existing tenants will renew their lease contracts. When tenants do not renew, it is expected to take six months to find a new tenant and to generate no rent for the first two months of the new lease because the space will be reconfigured to suit the tenant or the tenant will have been offered free rent as an inducement.

Both assumptions—downtime (the period necessary to reconfigure the space for the new tenant) and rent abatements (reductions in rent to attract new tenants or keep existing tenants)—are applied to flex and office market assumptions about re-leasing the space. If a tenant does not renew its lease, the ARGUS program, based on our inputs, assumes six months of downtime and two months of rent abatement. If the tenant stays, leasing commissions are half the rate they would be if they depart, and tenant improvements are $5 per square foot ($54 per square meter) to secure a new tenant, compared with $2 per square foot ($21.50 per square meter) if the tenant stays (Figure 9-9).

Lease Assumptions for the Office Space Market

Two tenants (Time Warner and United Leasing) use about 80 percent of their space for offices. As this space is expected to be leased to office tenants in the future, a different set of assumptions are needed in the cash flow analysis. Here again, when the lease contracts for these two tenants expire in 2012 and 2014, the office lease assumptions are used to determine property income after the lease expires. Office space is assumed to be re-leased at $8.75 per square foot ($94.15 per square meter) per year, triple net, for a seven-year term. Market rent is expected to grow at 2.5 percent per year,

and 65 percent of existing tenants are expected to renew their leases. Like flex space, downtime and rent abatements are six months and two months, respectively. Leasing commissions are 7 percent in Year 1 of the lease and 2 percent each year thereafter, based on gross rent and leasing commissions half the rate of that paid if the tenant stays. Tenant improvements are $5 per square foot ($54 per square meter) to secure a new tenant, compared with $2 per square foot ($21.50 per square meter) if the tenant stays.

Tenancy

With the background data on property growth and inflation factors and with the property expenses and lease assumptions in place, we can now identify and model tenant-by-tenant income streams. Section Four of the offering, "Tenancy," provides information about existing lease contracts on the buildings. The stability and duration of the income stream generated by these existing lease contracts is critical in underwriting the property from both equity and debt investors' perspectives. Rental income and expense reimbursement from the existing leases generate a stream of income across many years and allow a lender to calculate a debt service coverage ratio and the equity investor to calculate an annual return on equity. Using the information provided in the Property Rent Roll (Figure 9-11), additional information from the lease abstracts (pages 15 to 19 of Appendix B), and the general and property-specific assumptions presented earlier, we can generate a lease-by-lease income stream using the ARGUS software.

To reveal how the information is input and used in the ARGUS lease-by-lease analysis, the income information for the EZ International space is detailed in Figure 9-12. From the rent roll in Figure 9-11 and EZ International's lease abstract on page 17 of the Offering Memorandum, we know that EZ International signed a 61-month triple net lease ("net" under "expense reimbursements" in Figure 9-11) that began September 1, 2003, and expires September 30, 2008. EZ International leases 12,653 square feet (1,175 square meters) at a rental rate of $5.53 per square foot ($59.50 per square meter) per year, which is the stated rent in both the rent roll (Figure 9-11) and on page 17 of the Offering

Figure 9-11	Gateway Business Center: Rent Roll					
Description	**Area**	**Rent**	**Rent Adjustments**			
Tenant Name **Lease Dates** **Lease Term**	**Square Feet** **Building Share**	**Current** **Base Rent**	**Date**	**Rate per** **Square Foot**	**Expense** **Reimbursements**	
Time Warner 9/99–8/14 15 years	33,455 46.14%	$11.74/SF	9/09	$12.24	Mod. Gross (Base Year 99)	
Diebold, Inc. 7/05–9/10 5 years 3 months	4,725 6.52%	$6.70/SF	10/06 10/07 10/08 10/09	$6.85 $7.00 $7.15 $7.30	Net	
EZ International 9/03–9/08 5 years 1 month	12,653 17.45%	$5.53/SF	–	–	Net	
Prestige Electrolysis 10/98–9/09 11 years	5,802 8.00%	$6.80/SF	–	–	Net	
United Leasing Associates 10/05–2/12 6 years, 5 months	6,329 8.73%	$6.31/SF	2/07 2/08 2/09 2/10 2/11	$6.56 $6.83 $7.10 $7.38 $7.68	Net	
Vacancy: Suite 300 Projected 7/06–6/11 5 years	9,546 13.16%	$5.75/SF Pro forma	2.5% Annual increase		Net	

Memorandum. Based on this lease contract information and the assumptions about flex space rollover, the cash flows for EZ International are presented in Figure 9-12.

EZ International pays $69,971 (12,653 square feet times $5.53 per square foot) in base rent annually. Additionally, its prorated share (EZ International's 12,653 square feet divided by 72,510 total square feet in the building, or 17.45 percent) of all expenses is $29,964 ($171,714 × 0.1745), which returns total potential revenue of $99,935 in Year 1 of the property cash flow analysis. Because EZ International's lease does not expire until 2008, no leasing and tenant improvement costs are incurred until

then. EZ International's rent remains the same in Year 2 of the property cash flow analysis, as the lease does not have an escalation clause. Rental revenue is $69,971 again in 2007, but expense reimbursements increase to $30,669 ($175,756 × 0.1745).

On September 30, 2008, in Year 3 of the cash flow analysis, the lease contract with EZ International expires. The ARGUS cash flow model uses the flex lease assumptions to project the rental revenue from this space beginning October 1, 2008. For EZ International's space, the base rent for the first nine months of 2008 comes from the contractual rent; base rent for the remaining three months is based on the market lease assumptions for flex space (9/12 × $69,971 +

3/12 × $76,438), yielding a base rent of $71,588. The new rent per square foot is $5.75 ($61.90 per square meter); it increases at 2.5 percent per year, returning a market rent of $6.04 per square foot ($65 per square meter).[12] If a new lease begins December 1, 2008, the landlord loses two months of rental income (2/12 year times $76,438, or $12,740), as there is a 35 percent chance EZ International will not renew the lease. Base rent abatements include free rent for a new tenant; again, there is a 35 percent chance that EZ International will not renew the lease, thus requiring rent abatements of $4,459 ($76,438 × 2/12 × 0.35), returning a scheduled base rental revenue for EZ International of $54,389. Expense reimbursements dip in 2008 because the two months of downtime assumes that the space is not leased and thus no expense reimbursements are collected.

Tenant improvements and leasing commissions must also be paid in 2008. Tenant improvement costs again depend on whether the space is leased to a new tenant or EZ International re-leases the space. Tenant improvement costs are the weighted average of $5.30 ($5 increased at 3 percent for two years) and $2.12 ($2 increased at 3 percent for two years), returning a weighted average tenant improvement cost of $3.24 per square foot [($5.30 × 0.35) + ($2.12 × 0.65)]. Tenant improvements are calculated at $40,942 ($3.24 × 12,653 square feet).[13] Leasing commissions for Years 1 to 5 are 8, 3, 3, 3, and 3 percent, respectively, of the new lease. If a new tenant lease is required and if the lease is renewed, half of that expense is anticipated. In short, there is a 20 percent leasing commission for a new tenant and a 10 percent leasing commission for a lease renewal based on the new rental rate of $76,438. Weighted average leasing commission based on expected chances of lease rollover is 13.5 percent [(.20 × .35) + (.10 × .65)] of the average year's rent, or $10,199.[14] Finally, the market lease assumption for flex space includes a rent escalation clause that is tied to the CPI. As such, on the lease anniversary date (December 2009), the rent escalates by $2,293; however, only one month of this escalation occurs in 2009 and thus the rental escalation is $191. In another five years (2013), the lease renewal/rollover for the EZ International space expires again, and the landlord again incurs a new

rent, turnover vacancy, abatements, tenant improvements, and leasing commission in 2013 and 2014.

The modeling of tenant income is rather cumbersome as described above, which is why we use a lease-by-lease analysis program such as ARGUS. It is critical when using it, however, to understand the flow of income from the property and the volatility or risk that is created by tenant rollovers. The total tenant cash flow can be thought of as a portfolio of tenant income streams, as the income from each tenant and the income from the vacant space are combined. In short, using ARGUS and postulating a series of tenant release assumptions, vacancy rates, and other factors helps to determine the "most likely case" or a risk-adjusted cash flow projection.

Gateway Business Center Property Income Analysis

Unleveraged Cash Flow Analysis

An unleveraged cash flow analysis can now be completed to determine the investment internal rate of return (IRR). Income from both the lease contracts and the income expected after each lease expires—using the market lease assumptions along with property expenses—are combined into a ten-year cash flow analysis. The base rental revenue for Gateway Business Center is expected to be $601,403 in Year 1 (see Figure 9-13). Additionally, the property is expected to produce $100,286 in total expense reimbursement revenue, which returns a total potential gross revenue of $701,689. Both base rental revenue and expense reimbursements are obtained by summing the income for these two categories across the five tenants and the vacant space. As the vacant space of 9,546 square feet (890 square meters), or 13 percent of the total square footage, produced no income for the first six months of the year, no general vacancy was taken in Year 1; thus, property effective gross revenue is also $701,689. Reducing effective gross revenue by $171,714 in total operating expenses returns a net operating income in Year 1 of $529,975. Operating expenses are an estimate of expected expenses based on the previous years' actual expenses. Tenant improvement costs from the vacant space of $95,460 ($10 ×

Figure 9-12	Cash Flow and Summary for EZ International						
For the Years Ending	**Year 1** **Dec-2006**	**Year 2** **Dec-2007**	**Year 3** **Dec-2008**	**Year 4** **Dec-2009**	**Year 5** **Dec-2010**	**Year 6** **Dec-2011**	**Year 7** **Dec-2012**
Potential Gross Revenue							
Base Rental Revenue	$69,971	$69,971	$71,588	$76,438	$76,438	$76,438	$76,438
Absorption & Turnover Vacancy			−12,740				
Base Rent Abatements			−4,459				
Scheduled Base Rental Revenue	69,971	69,971	54,389	76,438	76,438	76,438	76,438
Base Rental Step Revenue							
Porters' Wage Revenue							
Miscellaneous Rental Revenue							
CPI & Other Adjustment Revenue				191	2,490	4,858	7,297
Parking Revenue							
Retail Sales Percent Revenue							
Expense Reimbursement	29,964	30,669	26,204	32,400	33,349	34,225	35,266
Total Potential Gross Revenue	99,935	100,640	80,593	109,029	112,277	115,521	119,001
Leasing and Capital Costs							
Tenant Improvements			40,942				
Leasing Commissions			10,199				
Total Leasing and Capital Costs			51,141				
Potential Net Cash Flow	$99,935	$100,640	$29,452	$109,029	$112,277	$115,521	$119,001
For This Tenant:							
Lease Expiration Date			9/08				
Potential Market Rent per Square Foot	5.75	5.89	6.04	6.19	6.35	6.51	6.67
Scheduled Base Rent per Square Foot	5.53	5.53	4.30	6.04	6.04	6.04	6.04
Retail Sales per Square Foot							
Average Occupancy	12,653	12,653	10,544	12,653	12,653	12,653	12,653

9,546), leasing commissions of $11,539, and capital reserves of $7,251 reduce the property NOI to a $415,725 cash flow before debt service and taxes.[15] Assuming the investment is $6.6 million funded with all equity, the property returns a 6.3 percent return on equity (ROE) ($415,725/$6,600,000).

In Year 2 (see Figure 9-13) of the cash flow analysis and every year thereafter, property expenses grow at 3 percent per year and market rent (the rental rate used when a lease ends) grows at 2.5 percent, with the exception of a management fee that is 4 percent of effective gross income. Additionally in Year 2, a 7 percent general vacancy rate is applied to the total potential gross revenue.[16] None of the tenant leases expire in Year 2, so there are no leasing and tenant

improvement costs, which increases cash flow before debt service to $511,770, or a 7.75 percent ROE. Because 46 percent of the space is leased to Time Warner, whose lease expires in Year 9 (2014), expected investor ROE is narrowly banded between 6.3 and 8.6 percent in the first eight years of property operation. In Year 9, tenant rollover costs for the Time Warner space significantly affect cash flows and reduce the ROE to 4.2 percent.[17]

Although finding ROE for each year is interesting, a better measure of return is the property's total rate of return or IRR. Before determining the property's IRR, however, the analyst must also estimate the property sale price at reversion (the end of the ten-year holding period) and include the net sale

Year 8 Dec-2013	Year 9 Dec-2014	Year 10 Dec-2015	Year 11 Dec-2016
$77,275	$88,645	$88,645	$88,645
−7,207	−7,387		
	−5,171		
70,068	76,087	88,645	88,645
8,794		2,438	4,958
33,267	33,857	38,405	39,489
112,129	109,944	129,488	13,3092
	48,887		
	11,827		
	60,714		
$112,129	$49,230	$129,488	$133,092
11/13			
6.83	7.01	7.18	7.36
5.54	6.01	7.01	7.01
11,599	11,599	12,653	12,653

Leveraged Cash Flow Analysis

Figure 9-14 presents a leveraged property analysis. Note that the addition of debt in this figure does not affect the property income from operations because both the property NOI and cash flow before debt service are identical to unleveraged property analysis. Placing a $5 million ten-year interest-only mortgage at a 6.5 percent interest rate (a U.S. Treasury interest rate of approximately 4.5 percent and a commercial mortgage risk premium of 2.0 percent return a 6.5 percent mortgage interest rate) requires a $325,000 interest payment each year. A $5 million mortgage has a 75.76 percent LTV ratio, a debt service coverage ratio on NOI of 1.63, and a debt service coverage ratio on cash flow before debt service of 1.28 in Year 1 of the discounted cash flow analysis (see Figure 9-14). Additionally, the debt service coverage on NOI for all years is solid, ranging from 1.58 to 1.84. A more relevant measure of debt service coverage, however, is the coverage based on cash flow before debt service, which ranges from 0.84 to 1.74.

In Year 9 when the Time Warner lease rolls over, property cash flow is inadequate to service the debt. To manage this risk, the lender would likely require the borrower to escrow some portion of the previous years' cash flows to mitigate the risk of a delinquent payment. The inclusion of debt in the capitalization of the purchase generally increases the property ROE into double digits, but in Year 9 the investor is expected to have a negative ROE. In short, the use of leverage generates much greater volatility in investors' ROE but also generates a higher average ROE. As the interest payments are a required fixed amount against a varying property cash flow stream, the more volatile ROE to the investor creates a range of −3.17 percent to 15.06 percent. In short, the annual (or monthly) presentation of property cash flow streams allows the lender to manage property cash flow volatility.

To calculate the IRR of the property to the equity investor, several adjustments need to be made relative to the unleveraged case presented in Figure 9-13. First, in Figure 9-14, the use of debt reduces the equity investment to $1.6 million (the $6.6 million purchase price minus the debt capitalization of $5

price in the Year 10 cash flow analysis. Assuming an 8 percent cap rate on Year 11 NOI, the sale price at the end of Year 10 and 2 percent in sale transaction costs return net sale proceeds of $7,411,177.[18] Adding net sale proceeds to Year 10 cash flow before debt service of $558,337 returns a Year 10 property cash flow of $7,969,514. The IRR is 8.12 percent when assuming a $6.6 million purchase price at time zero and ten years of positive property cash flows. Although an IRR around 8 percent is rather low by historic standards, current market expectations for unleveraged property IRRs are 8 to 10 percent. Given the strong creditworthiness of the rent roll, an 8.12 percent unleveraged IRR may be appropriate, given how we adjusted property cash flows for risk.

Figure 9-13	Gateway Business Center: Unleveraged Property Analysis

For the Years Ending	Year 0 Dec-2006	Year 1 Dec-2007	Year 2 Dec-2008	Year 3 Dec-2009	Year 4 Dec-2010	Year 5 Dec-2011	Year 6
Potential Gross Revenue							
Base Rental Revenue		$601,403	$631,674	$637,083	$650,476	$661,633	$661,651
Absorption & Turnover Vacancy				(12,740)	(5,988)	(4,998)	(10,350)
Base Rent Abatements				(4,459)	(2,096)	(1,749)	(3,623)
Scheduled Base Rental Revenue		601,403	631,674	619,884	642,392	654,886	647,678
CPI Escalation					191	2,580	6,103
Expense Reimbursement Revenue							
CAM & Utilities		32,055	36,719	36,721	39,061	40,770	41,771
Insurance		5,193	5,888	5,889	6,237	6,491	6,642
Real Estate Taxes		45,712	54,120	54,123	58,345	61,427	63,232
Management Fee		17,326	18,905	18,102	19,427	20,227	20,062
Total Reimbursement Revenue		100,286	115,632	114,835	123,070	128,915	131,707
Total Potential Gross Revenue		701,689	747,306	734,719	765,653	786,381	785,488
General Vacancy			(52,311)	(39,582)	(48,027)	(50,399)	(45,359)
Effective Gross Revenue		701,689	694,995	695,137	717,626	735,982	740,129
Operating Expenses							
CAM & Utilities		48,658	50,118	51,621	53,170	54,765	56,408
Insurance		7,251	7,469	7,693	7,923	8,161	8,406
Real Estate Taxes		87,737	90,369	93,080	95,873	98,749	101,711
Management Fee		28,068	27,800	27,805	28,705	29,439	29,605
Total Operating Expenses		171,714	175,756	180,199	185,671	191,114	196,130
Net Operating Income		529,975	519,239	514,938	531,955	544,868	543,999
Leasing and Capital Costs							
Tenant Improvements		95,460		40,942	19,337	16,220	33,753
Leasing Commissions		11,539		10,199	4,794	4,001	8,286
Capital Reserves		7,251	7,469	7,693	7,923	8,161	8,406
Total Leasing and Capital Costs		114,250	7,469	58,834	32,054	28,382	50,445
Cash Flow before Debt Service and Taxes		$415,725	$511,770	$456,104	$499,901	$516,486	$493,554
Return on Equity		6.30%	7.75%	6.91%	7.57%	7.83%	7.48%
Equity Investment	$6,600,000						
Property Sale							
Sale Transaction Costs							
Net Sale Proceeds							
Property Cash Flows	($6,600,000)	$415,725	$511,770	$456,104	$499,901	$516,486	$493,554
Internal Rate of Return	8.12%						

million). The use of debt and the need to make debt service payments also reduce annual cash flows. Upon sale of the asset, repaying the principal to the lender reduces net sale proceeds. As property unleveraged IRR is higher than the mortgage interest rate (that is, leverage is positive), the use of debt magnifies investment returns to the equity investor, or the investment IRR for the $1.6 million of equity

Year 7 Dec-2012	Year 8 Dec-2013	Year 9 Dec-2014	Year 10 Dec-2015	Year 11 Dec-2016
$675,565	$679,004	$673,158	$643,616	$650,797
(10,704)	(7,207)	(70,218)	(6,300)	(14,609)
(3,746)		(25,976)	(2,430)	(6,128)
661,115	671,797	576,964	634,886	630,060
11,178	17,917	14,687	19,382	29,091
43,855	45,572	46,659	62,719	63,602
6,952	7,207	7,231	9,347	9,478
66,990	70,086	76,072	113,092	114,684
21,241	21,963	20,855	32,266	32,340
139,038	144,828	150,817	217,424	220,104
811,331	834,542	742,468	871,692	879,255
(46,838)	(51,715)		(55,159)	(47,961)
764,493	782,827	742,468	816,533	831,294
58,100	59,843	61,638	63,488	65,392
8,658	8,918	9,185	9,461	9,745
104,763	107,905	111,143	114,477	117,911
30,580	31,313	29,699	32,661	33,252
202,101	207,979	211,665	220,087	226,300
562,392	574,848	530,803	596,446	604,994
23,049		178,145	23,089	
10,316		69,116	5,559	
8,658	8,918	9,185	9,461	
42,023	8,918	256,446	38,109	
$520,369	$565,930	$274,357	$558,337	
7.88%	8.57%	4.16%	8.46%	
			$7,562,425	
			$151,249	
			$7,411,177	
$520,369	$565,930	$274,357	$7,969,514	

rises. That said, the use of $5 million in debt (a 76 percent LTV ratio) reduces the equity investment to $1.6 million, producing a leveraged IRR of 12.45 percent. If the equity investor is looking to obtain a leveraged IRR of 12 percent, this property exceeds the investor's return requirements.

Investment Analysis with Equity Return Splits

Few real estate investors or developers have the equity necessary to undertake a new investment or development and thus usually need to solicit equity investors for their deals. Often developers provide only a deferred fee in a deal and the only "hard equity dollars" come from limited partner investors.[19] To entice limited partners to fund the needed equity investment, developers who take on the role of general partner in a limited partnership are often required to subordinate their investment returns to the limited partner investors. As developers are often thought to be more optimistic than their limited partner investors, limited partners often require that they obtain a preferred return on their investment. In return, limited partners often are willing to forgo a larger portion of the property cash flow upside and property sale upside for more stable or assured income stream.

Figure 9-15 presents a series of investment analyses using different investment splits. The property cash flows come from the Gateway Business Center cash flow analyses presented in Figures 9-13 and 9-14. Summary cash flows from Figure 9-13 are presented under "IRR—Unleveraged Investment," returning the same 8.12 percent IRR. Under "IRR Leveraged Investment," cash flows from Figure 9-14 show a return of 12.45 percent IRR. In both these cases, we assume that a developer was able to fund the entire purchase price of $6.6 million or to provide the entire equity investment of $1.6 million.

"Leveraged Investment and Equity Investor" in Figure 9-15 presents debt funding of $5 million, a limited partner's equity investment of $1.2 million, and a general partner's investment (possibly through deferred developer fees) of $400,000. In this structure, the limited partner receives an 8 percent preferred ROE on his investment before the general partner/developer receives any property cash flow. Additionally, if the limited partner does not receive an 8 percent return in a previous period, that short-

Figure 9-14	Gateway Business Center: Leveraged Property Analysis						

For the Years Ending	Year 0 Dec-2006	Year 1 Dec-2007	Year 2 Dec-2008	Year 3 Dec-2009	Year 4 Dec-2010	Year 5 Dec-2011	Year 6
Potential Gross Revenue							
Base Rental Revenue		601,403	631,674	637,083	650,476	661,633	661,651
Absorption & Turnover Vacancy				(12,740)	(5,988)	(4,998)	(10,350)
Base Rent Abatements				(4,459)	(2,096)	(1,749)	(3,623)
Scheduled Base Rental Revenue		601,403	631,674	619,884	642,392	654,886	647,678
CPI Escalation					191	2,580	6,103
Expense Reimbursement Revenue							
CAM & Utilities		32,055	36,719	36,721	39,061	40,770	41,771
Insurance		5,193	5,888	5,889	6,237	6,491	6,642
Real Estate Taxes		45,712	54,120	54,123	58,345	61,427	63,232
Management Fee		17,326	18,905	18,102	19,427	20,227	20,062
Total Reimbursement Revenue		100,286	115,632	114,835	123,070	128,915	131,707
Total Potential Gross Revenue		701,689	747,306	734,719	765,653	786,381	785,488
General Vacancy			(52,311)	(39,582)	(48,027)	(50,399)	(45,359)
Effective Gross Revenue		701,689	694,995	695,137	717,626	735,982	740,129
Operating Expenses							
CAM & Utilities		48,658	50,118	51,621	53,170	54,765	56,408
Insurance		7,251	7,469	7,693	7,923	8,161	8,406
Real Estate Taxes		87,737	90,369	93,080	95,873	98,749	101,711
Management Fee		28,068	27,800	27,805	28,705	29,439	29,605
Total Operating Expenses		171,714	175,756	180,199	185,671	191,114	196,130
Net Operating Income		529,975	519,239	514,938	531,955	544,868	543,999

fall flows into the subsequent period, and the limited partner receives that return as well before the developer receives any property cash flow. In Year 1 of Section III cash flows, the equity investor receives the entire $90,725 cash flow after debt service, as $90,725 is less than the $96,000 necessary to obtain an 8 percent preferred rate of return ($96,000 = 8 percent of $1,200,000). The developer does not participate in the property's cash flow in Year 1 and therefore has zero ROE.

In Year 2 of "Leveraged Investment and Equity Investor," the $186,770 cash flow after debt service trickles down a long waterfall. First, the equity investor receives his $96,000 preferred return. Second, the equity investor receives his shortfall payment from Year 1 of $5,275. Third, the developer receives his 8 percent return of $32,000 ($400,000 × .08), as $53,495 cash flow after debt service remains. This cash flow is split 60 percent to the equity investor and 40 percent to the developer (as stated in the assumptions), providing an additional $32,097 to the equity investor and $21,398 to the developer. It is worth noting that although the developer funded 25 percent of the needed equity, he receives 40 percent of the cash flow after the equity investor's preferred return is met. This additional portion of the cash flow is a reward for taking a subordinate position to the equity position's preferred ROE. This process continues for the remainder of the holding period, with the developer required to fund the cash flow shortfall in Year 9. Note that the shortfall funded by the developer—$50,643—was added to the developer's investment in Year 9.

Year 7 Dec-2012	Year 8 Dec-2013	Year 9 Dec-2014	Year 10 Dec-2015	Year 11 Dec-2016
675,565	679,004	673,158	643,616	$650,797
(10,704)	(7,207)	(70,218)	(6,300)	(14,609)
(3,746)		(25,976)	(2,430)	(6,128)
661,115	671,797	576,964	634,886	630,060
11,178	17,917	14,687	19,382	29,091
43,855	45,572	46,659	62,719	63,602
6,952	7,207	7,231	9,347	9,478
66,990	70,086	76,072	113,092	114,684
21,241	21,963	20,855	32,266	32,340
139,038	144,828	150,817	217,424	220,104
811,331	834,542	742,468	871,692	879,255
(46,838)	(51,715)		(55,159)	(47,961)
764,493	782,827	742,468	816,533	831,294
58,100	59,843	61,638	63,488	65,392
8,658	8,918	9,185	9,461	9,745
104,763	107,905	111,143	114,477	117,911
30,580	31,313	29,699	32,661	33,252
202,101	207,979	211,665	220,087	226,300
562,392	574,848	530,803	596,446	604,994

continued on next page

With the property cash flows appropriately split between the equity investor and developer, we now look to the allocation of the property net sale price of $7,411,177. Net sale proceeds are first allocated to the lender's $5 million loan. Then the investor's initial investment of $1.2 million is returned, then the developer's investment of $450,643. Note that the developer's investment increased from $400,000 at time zero to $450,643 at property sale. The increase of $50,643 comes from the additional equity required of the developer in Year 9, which was necessary to fund negative cash flow. Thereafter, the remaining net sale proceeds of $811,178 are equally distributed to the limited partner investor and the developer, based on the contractual agreement. Here again, as the developer is subordinating the return of his equity investment to the limited partner's investment, the developer captures fully 50 percent of net sale proceeds after repaying debt and equity investments (having funded 25 percent of the equity). Because the developer is taking a greater risk, he receives a higher IRR based on cash flow projections. As shown under "Leveraged Investment and Equity Investor" in Figure 9-15, investor IRR is 11.36 percent, while the developer receives a 14.55 percent IRR.

Section IV in Figure 9-15 is the same as Section III above, except that the IRR lookback provides the equity investor with a preferred total rate of return and a preferred ROE before the developer receives a split of the net sale proceeds after the loan and equity investment are repaid. With the IRR lookback, the net sale proceeds first pay back the outstanding loan balance; then equity is returned to both the investor and developer. Next the equity investor receives his $465,000 reversion split, which is based on an IRR lookback of 12 percent. Then the developer receives his reversion split of $148,000 to obtain his IRR lookback of 12 percent. Finally, the remaining net sale proceeds of $188,872 are split equally between the equity investor and the developer. The IRR lookback is a calculation in which the investors' investment cash outflow and all subsequent annual inflows are lined up sequentially. If the investor has not received a 12 percent IRR after the return of his investment, a portion of the net sale proceeds is added to his cash flow until a total rate of return or IRR of 12 percent is received. For the equity investor to receive a 12 percent IRR, he needs $465,000 of net sale proceeds over and above the return of his investment; similarly, the developer needs $148,000 of additional sale proceeds to obtain a 12 percent IRR. Only after each investor has received a 12 percent IRR are the sale proceeds then split 50/50 based on the investment agreement, which in the end returns 12.30 percent to the equity investor and 12.88 percent to the developer. The use of an IRR lookback is a means of allocating net sale proceeds to create a preferred total rate of return to the equity investor.

Figure 9-14	Gateway Business Center: Leveraged Property Analysis (*continued*)

For the Years Ending	Year 0	Year 1 Dec-2006	Year 2 Dec-2007	Year 3 Dec-2008	Year 4 Dec-2009	Year 5 Dec-2010	Year 6 Dec-2011
Net Operating Income		529,975	519,239	514,938	531,955	544,868	543,999
Leasing and Capital Costs							
Tenant Improvements		95,460		40,942	19,337	16,220	33,753
Leasing Commissions		11,539		10,199	4,794	4,001	8,286
Capital Reserves		7,251	7,469	7,693	7,923	8,161	8,406
Total Leasing and Capital Costs		114,250	7,469	58,834	32,054	28,382	50,445
Cash Flow before Debt Service and Taxes		415,725	511,770	456,104	499,901	516,486	493,554
Debt Service							
Interest Payments		325,000	325,000	325,000	325,000	325,000	325,000
Principal Payments		0	0	0	0	0	0
Total Debt Service		325,000	325,000	325,000	325,000	325,000	325,000
Cash Flow after Debt Service		90,725	186,770	131,104	174,901	191,486	168,554
Debt Coverage Ratio on NOI		1.63	1.60	1.58	1.64	1.68	1.67
Debt Coverage Ratio on Cash Flow before Debt Service		1.28	1.57	1.40	1.54	1.59	1.52
Return on Equity		5.67%	11.67%	8.19%	10.93%	11.97%	10.53%
Equity Investment	1,600,000						
Loan Amount	5,000,000						
Property Sale							
Sale Transaction Costs							
Outstanding Loan Balance							
Net Sale Proceeds							
Property Cash Flows	(1,600,000)	90,725	186,770	131,104	174,901	191,486	168,554
Internal Rate of Return	12.45%						

MUSEUM TOWERS

How Recent Innovations Can Affect the Financing of a Development

Museum Towers was built in what many would consider a pioneering location. Located on the river in east Cambridge, on a formerly industrial site, the area was known as "the lost half-mile of the Charles River." This apparently marginal piece of land was purchased for $13 million in 1987. The original site included three parcels on 4.11 acres (1.66 hectares). In 1996, the developer/owner, Congress Group Ventures, sold 50,000 square feet (4,645 square meters), and, as part of its development deal, gave away an acre to the state for a park and several thousand square feet to the city for roads, ending up with a 2.07-acre (0.84-hectare) site.

The Museum Towers project consists of two 24-story towers with 435 rental apartment units and a gross building area of 619,500 square feet (57,553 square meters). The towers are joined by a central lobby and a 490-space parking garage. In total, the project contains four studio apartments, 181 one-bedroom units (40 in the low-rise portion of the towers), and 250 two-bedroom units. Most of the one-bedroom units have only one bathroom; the two-bedroom units have two full bathrooms. The base building is mostly cast-in-place concrete with precast concrete exterior panels. The floors are poured concrete. The windows are aluminum frame with a combination of awning windows, fixed windows, and sliding doors. The exterior doors are a combination of metal and glass in metal frames. The towers, part of the 40-acre (16.2-hectare) North Point Park, feature great views of downtown Boston.

	Year 7 Dec-2012	Year 8 Dec-2013	Year 9 Dec-2014	Year 10 Dec-2015	Year 11 Dec-2016
	562,392	574,848	530,803	596,446	604,994
	23,049		178,145	23,089	
	10,316		69,116	5,559	
	8,658	8,918	9,185	9,461	
	42,023	8,918	256,446	38,109	
	520,369	565,930	274,357	558,337	
	325,000	325,000	325,000	325,000	
	0	0	0	0	
	325,000	325,000	325,000	325,000	
	195,369	240,930	(50,643)	233,337	
	1.73	1.77	1.63	1.84	
	1.60	1.74	0.84	1.72	
	12.21%	15.06%	–3.17%	14.58%	
				7,562,425	
				151,249	
				5,000,000	
				2,411,177	
	195,369	240,930	(50,643)	2,644,514	

MUSEUM TOWERS *(continued)*

The Congress Group's pro forma showed that, when the project stabilizes, it is expected to generate annual net operating income of $8,874,391, a very attractive 11.6 percent return on investment. Like all developments, however, this return is only expected. Despite the attractiveness of the concept and the site and the very tight residential market in Cambridge, potential long-term lenders were understandably not willing to equate this expected NOI with an existing reality, i.e., "in-place NOI." On the plus side, the quality of the location, the idea, and the development group convinced a lender—Fleet Bank—to provide a first lien miniperm, a construction loan that extends beyond completion of the construction for a year or two so that the developer can demonstrate stabilized operations. After stabilization, a larger first lien can typically be obtained based on calculation of a maximum loan. The developer's problem is how to get to "stabilized" NOI and thus in a position to maximize the permanent loan. Although the financing process involves a series of negotiations that vary from development to development, some common strategies are involved. Three that were important in the process followed by Congress Group Ventures in financing Museum Towers are often critical for development financing: 1) leverage as inexpensively as possible; 2) get the cheap money and always have an exit strategy; and 3) consider alternative sources for high-risk dollars.

Strategy One: Leverage as Inexpensively as Possible

Congress Group Ventures wanted to maximize the eventual permanent loan because doing so would provide the cheapest overall financing (debt equity). Use of the miniperm provided by Fleet Bank allowed a slightly longer period in which to stabilize NOI before negotiating for permanent financing.

Nevertheless, the decision to go with the miniperm was not an easy one for the Congress Group. Long-term interest rates were relatively low in 1996, as pressure from the CMBS conduits had forced the traditional long-term lenders to reduce their spreads. Further, interest rates on short-term construction loans were lower than they had been for many years. Thus, a potentially attractive alternative to the miniperm was to negotiate for a longer-term loan immediately. But because the pro forma was, in fact, only a pro forma and not current operating income, it was not possible to obtain a first lien commitment of the size the Congress Group felt the project warranted. Consequently, the Congress Group went for the miniperm.

Because Museum Towers was a large, high-quality, highly visible project, the Congress Group approached a prominent local lender that could benefit from the association. Fleet Bank agreed to make a first lien miniperm of $55 million. The initial term was for three years with an upfront fee of 0.75 percent and a variable interest rate. To fix the rate, the Congress Group then conducted an interest rate swap, with the result a variable rate to Fleet Bank and a fixed rate (8 percent) to the Congress Group. The miniperm included a two-year extension option for an additional payment of 0.375 percent and an interest rate for the extension period of LIBOR plus 175 basis points. Thus, the miniperm provided the Congress Group with three years to build the project and the option for another two years to stabilize NOI to maximize the permanent loan.

In negotiating the terms, the Congress Group had to consider not just the cheapest rate for the money but also

continued on next page

Figure 9-15	Gateway Business Center: Investment Analysis Using Different Investment Cash Flow and Sale Return Splits					

	Year 0	Year 1	Year 2	Year 3	Year 4	Year 5
I. IRR—Unleveraged Investment						
Property Purchase	$6,600,000					
Cash Flow		415,725	511,770	456,104	499,901	516,486
Property Sale						
Property Cash Flows	(6,600,000)	415,725	511,770	456,104	499,901	516,486
Return on Equity		6.30%	7.75%	6.91%	7.57%	7.83%
Internal Rate of Return	8.12%					
II. IRR—Leveraged Investment						
Loan to Value Ratio	75.76%					
Loan Amount (calculated)	5,000,000					
Interest Rate	6.50%					
Loan Amount	5,000,000					
Property Cash Flows	(6,600,000)	415,725	511,770	456,104	499,901	516,486
Debt Service	(325,000)	(325,000)	(325,000	(325,000)	(325,000)	(325,000)
Mortgage Balance						
Property Cash Flows	(1,600,000)	90,725	186,770	131,104	174,901	191,486
Return on Equity		5.67%	11.67%	8.19%	10.93%	11.97%
Internal Rate of Return	12.45%					
III. IRR—Leveraged Investment and Equity Investor				Required Investment		
Equity Investor Preferred Return on Cash flow				8.00%	Mortgage Amount	
Equity Investor Percent of Cash Flow after Preferred Return				60.00%	Equity Investor Amount	
Equity Investor Percent of Sale Proceeds				50.00%	Developer	
Cash Flows		415,725	511,770	456,104	499,901	516,486
Debt Service		(325,000)	(325,000)	(325,000)	(325,000)	(325,000)
Cash Flow after Debt Service		90,725	186,770	131,104	174,901	191,486
Equity Investor Position						
Cash Flow Preferred Return		90,725	96,000	96,000	96,000	96,000
Arrears Cash Flow Preferred Return			5,275	0	0	0
Cash Flow Split		0	32,097	1,862	28,141	38,092
Return of Investment						
Reversion Split						
Equity Investor Proceeds	(1,200,000)	90,725	133,372	97,862	124,141	134,092
Return on Equity		7.56%	11.11%	8.16%	10.35%	11.17%
IRR for Equity Investor	11.63%					

MUSEUM TOWERS *(continued)*

How Recent Innovations Can Affect the Financing of a Development (continued)

how all the "loan terms" affected other important parts of its strategy.

Strategy Two: Have an Exit Strategy

Although this project is the kind a developer might want to own over the long term, the Congress Group was smart enough to know that no individual developer is bigger than the cycle. It is always possible that the economy will hit another period like the middle 1980s, when so many new projects were developed that even the best products began to suffer. Today's informed developers have learned the hard lesson: they must always consider the eventual sale.

It looked as though a REIT would be a logical long-term holder of this property. Because REITs like to show growth in earnings, they typically do not develop the majority of their properties. Rather, they often prefer to

Year 6	Year 7	Year 8	Year 9	Year 10
493,554	520,369	565,930	274,357	558,337
				7,411,177
493,554	520,369	565,930	274,357	7,969,514
7.48%	7.88%	8.57%	4.16%	
493,554	520,369	565,930	274,357	7,969,514
(325,000)	(325,000)	(325,000)	(325,000)	
				(5,000,000)
168,554	195,369	240,930	(50,643)	2,644,514
10.53%	12.21%	15.06%	–3.17%	
		(6,600,000)		
		5,000,000		
		1,200,000		
		400,000		
493,554	520,369	565,930	274,357	558,337
(325,000)	(325,000)	(325,000)	(325,000)	(325,000)
168,554	195,369	240,930	(50,643)	233,337
96,000	96,000	96,000	0	96,000
0	0	0	0	96,000
24,332	40,421	67,758	0	3,171
				1,200,000
				380,267
120,332	136,421	163,758	0	1,775,438
10.03%	11.37%	13.65%	0.00%	

continued on next page

MUSEUM TOWERS *(continued)*

buy properties after they have been developed and stabilized by entrepreneurial developers. If, at the end of the three-year miniperm, a REIT were a viable option, the Congress Group would sell; if not, it would pay the additional 0.375 percent fee, extend the loan for two years, and wait.

Another option with the miniperm is to sell to another investor. Here, the CMBS market is important. With the con-

duit loans pressuring traditional lenders, the Congress Group anticipated that attractive financing would be available should an entrepreneurial, possibly European, investor be the eventual buyer (as opposed to a REIT). The Congress Group was actively involved with a few larger European institutions (Boston being a favored American city in Europe) as well as a number of apartment REITs. One particular apartment REIT, Smith Residential, specialized in high-rise inner-city projects in the Northeast. The Congress Group cultivated a particularly close relationship with it.

Strategy Three: Consider Alternative Sources for High-Risk Dollars

No discussion of financing would be complete without considering the high-risk capital. If the developer cannot or does not want to put up all the required equity, then a partner may be needed. This approach can involve very complex relationships, and this topic will be revisited many times throughout this text. In the case of Museum Towers, the overall project cost of $78 million would be initially financed with the $55 million miniperm from Fleet Bank. The Congress Group did not want to put all the remaining $23 million into the project, however. In fact, it preferred to pull out some of the $13 million it had already invested. A logical place to look was the opportunity funds.

Although earlier in this chapter we concluded the discussion of opportunity funds by noting that any good idea is financeable, it may cost a great deal to attain such financing. The group of opportunity funds, however, includes some segmentation. Museum Towers was not a highly speculative project, given the housing market in Cambridge. Consequently, the Congress Group looked for a lower-risk opportunity fund (sometimes called "value-added funds"). The Congress Group found such an opportunity fund, also located in Boston, that it hoped would appreciate the tightness of the Cambridge market. Working with the Fidelity Real Estate Group, the Congress Group arranged a participating secured second mortgage. The site and improvements were the basic collateral along with certain pledges of equity interest in the project from the developer. These notes were subject to Fleet's first lien and had a similar term.

Face Amount—$16,500,000
Term—Five years
Base Interest Rate—15%
Additional Interest—50% of net operating cash flow and net capital appreciation during the term of the notes until Fidelity has earned a 20% internal rate of return; thereafter, Fidelity's participation drops from 50% to 30%

continued on next page

Figure 9-15	Gateway Business Center: Investment Analysis Using Different Investment Cash Flow and Sale Return Splits (*continued*)

	Year 0	Year 1	Year 2	Year 3	Year 4	Year 5
III. IRR—Leveraged Investment and Equity Investor (*continued*)						
Developer Position						
Cash Flow Return			0	32,000	32,000	32,000	32,000
Cash Flow Split			0	21,398	1,242	18,760	25,394
Return of Investment						
Reversion Split						
Developer Proceeds	(400,000)		0	53,398	33,242	50,760	57,394
Return on Equity		0.00%	13.35%	8.31%	12.69%	14.35%
IRR	14.55%					
IV. IRR—Leveraged Investment and Equity Investor with an IRR Lookback Rate of 12%						
Equity Investor Position						
Cash Flow Preferred Return		90,725	101,275	96,000	96,000	96,000
Cash Flow Split		0	32,097	1,862	28,141	38,092
Return of Investment		0	0	0	0	0
Reversion Split		0	0	0	0	0
Equity Investor Proceeds—with Lookback	(1,200,000)	90,725	133,372	97,862	124,141	134,092
Equity Investor IRR Look back to:	12.00%					
Reversion Split after 12% IRR lookback						
Equity Investor Proceeds	(1,200,000)	90,725	133,372	97,862	124,141	134,092
Equity Investor IRR	12.30%					
Developer Position						
Cash Flow Return		0	32,000	32,000	32,000	32,000
Cash Flow Split		0	21,398	1,242	18,760	25,394
Return of Investment		0	0	0	0	0
Reversion Split		0	0	0	0	0
Developer Proceeds	(400,000)	0	53,398	33,242	50,760	57,394
Developer IRR	12.00%					
Reversion Split after 12% IRR lookback						
Developer Proceeds	(400,000)	0	53,398	33,242	50,760	57,394
Developer IRR	12.88%					

MUSEUM TOWERS (*continued*)

How Recent Innovations Can Affect the Financing of a Development (continued)

This debt structure allowed the Congress Group to pull $6,500,000 out of the project ($78,000,000 total cost – $55,000,000 first lien – $16,500,000 second lien = $6,500,000) while retaining control and the majority of the upside. The leverage from Fleet's financing produced expected equity returns of just over 25 percent. By bringing in Fidelity and further positive leverage, the expected equity return to the Congress Group was raised to over 40 percent. The expected return to the slightly lower-risk Fidelity portion was 21.5 percent and to the much lower-risk Fleet portion about 9 percent. These differences in expected returns reflect each entity's different risk position.

continued on page 248

	Year 6	Year 7	Year 8	Year 9	Year 10
	32,000	32,000	32,000	(50,643)	36,051
	16,222	26,948	45,172	0	2,114
					450,643
					380,267
	48,222	58,948	77,172	(50,643)	869,076
	12.06%	14.74%	19.29%	−12.66%	
	96,000	96,000	96,000	0	192,000
	24,332	40,421	67,758	0	3,171
	0	0	0	0	1,200,000
	0	0	0	0	465,000
	120,332	136,421	163,758	0	1,860,171
					73,767
	120,332	136,421	163,758	0	1,933,938
	32,000	32,000	32,000	(50,643)	36,051
	16,222	26,948	45,172	0	2,114
	0	0	0	0	450,643
	0	0	0	0	148,000
	48,222	58,948	77,172	(50,643)	636,809
					73,767
	48,222	58,948	77,172	(50,643)	710,576

prescribed based on the perceived riskiness of the space markets and cash flows of proposed investment.

To better understand the space market and how real estate analysts look at the space markets, we completed a lease-by-lease analysis of the Gateway Business Center, where we accounted for many of the risks of investing in commercial real estate in the cash flows. We began the cash flow analysis by estimating the expected revenue from the tenant. At the end of the lease, we used market lease assumptions to estimate what cash flows might be received at the expiration of the original lease agreement. Then including property expenses, mortgage payments, and a reversion sale, we used the property cash flows to complete a series of property return analyses. We learned that the inclusion of debt makes property cash flows more volatile on an annual basis but that debt can also magnify property return rates—both good and bad. We also considered the possibility of limited partners' receiving a preferred or preferential return before the developer, who receives returns only if the equity investor has met or exceeded his return thresholds. We use this tool (DCF) later in the chapter on feasibility when we discuss development decision making.

TERMS

▶ Capital market risk
▶ Expected rate of return
▶ Inflation premium
▶ Internal rate of return
▶ IRR lookback
▶ Preferred return
▶ Present value
▶ Real rate of return
▶ Return on equity
▶ Risk-free rate of return
▶ Risk premium
▶ Space market risk

REVIEW QUESTIONS

9.1 What combination of investment benefits does real estate provide, and how have investments changed over time?

SUMMARY

This chapter has explored discounted cash flow analysis. By projecting property cash flows over the entire investment holding period, we are better able to delineate the risks inherent in real estate investments.

In Chapter 7, we discovered that discounted cash flow analysis ties space markets and capital markets together. The strength of space markets is revealed through lease contracts and market lease assumptions. The discount rate or required rate of return is similarly

9.2   What is discounted cash flow analysis?

9.3   What are the three primary components of a discount rate?

9.4   What are the benefits of using a lease-by-lease cash flow analysis program like ARGUS to analyze commercial real estate acquisitions?

9.5   Why is a property internal rate of return different in unleveraged and leveraged cash flow analyses?

9.6   How does leverage affect the volatility of the return on equity?

9.7   In an investment with equity provided by both investors and the developer, why are the equity investors often provided a preferred return?

9.8   Which investor does an IRR lookback protect and how?

NOTES

1.   Based on data provided by the St. Louis Federal Reserve at http://research.stlouisfed.org/fred2/series/GS10/downloaddata, the ten-year U.S. Treasury interest rate from 1953 to July 2007 was 6.48 percent.

2.   Financial theory suggests that short-term U.S. Treasury obligations (three-month Treasury bills) are the only risk-free asset, as longer-term U.S. Treasury obligations incur interest rate risk, which is the possibility that rates change over time. Because real estate investments are generally long-term investments, we will refer to the long-term U.S. Treasury interest rate as the risk-free rate.

3.   Inflation-indexed Treasury securities that mature in 2017 currently yield 2.32 percent, indicating that ten-year Treasuries have a real rate of return of 2.32 percent, or a 2.32 percent return over inflation. Next subtract the 2.5 percent real rate of return from the ten-year Treasury interest rate of 4.51 percent to obtain the implied 2.19 percent inflation premium on ten-year Treasury obligations. For time-series data on ten-year and inflation-indexed Treasury securities, see the St. Louis Federal Reserve Web page at http://research.stlouisfed.org/fred2/categories/22.

4.   Using ten-year inflation-indexed Treasury bonds, the real rate of return on a recently issued inflation-indexed Treasury bond that matures in 2017 (in ten years) averaged 2.32 percent, with the most recent week's market (September 6, 2007) requiring a 2.32 percent inflation-indexed or real rate of return.

5.   The National Council of Real Estate Investment Fiduciaries' quarterly average rate of return annualized for the period 1978 to 2003.

6.   The National Association of Real Estate Investment Trusts provides average returns on REITs in *NAREIT Real Estate Chart Book*. The numbers provided above were obtained from the April 2006 edition.

7.   Most introductory finance textbooks provide present value discount factors; alternatively, using an Internet search engine and typing in "present value discount factor tables" returns several discount factor tables.

8.   For a more detailed discussion on present value and net present value analysis, you may want to search the Internet or find a basic financial management textbook.

9.   Although a particular cell format presents data based on the requested format, the Excel program maintains seven or more significant digits in the electronic memory.

10.   Parts of the Offering Memorandum (see Appendix B) are reproduced as figures in this chapter to further illustrate important components of the offering. Some numbers presented in the offering memorandum differ slightly from those presented in the figures, which is attributable to differences in assumptions for the cash flow analysis. We are grateful to the Inland Companies of Milwaukee, Wisconsin, for the use of this case.

11.   See the building plans on page 10 of the Offering Memorandum to see the space layout for each tenant.

12.   Note that $6.04 × 12,653 square feet returns a base rental revenue of $76,424 but that increasing the $5.75 market rent in 2006 at 2.5 percent returns a rental rate of $6.04109 without rounding, and thus $76,438 in base rental revenue.

13.   Results may differ slightly because of rounding.

14.   The average year's rent must be adjusted down from $76,438 because the first year has a rent abatement of $4,459.

15.   The vacant space needed significant tenant improvements and thus $10 per square foot was used. In addition, a full leasing commission was used to estimate leasing commissions for the vacant space.

16.   Note that general vacancy is reduced by the absorption and turnover vacancy reported in the second row of the cash flow analysis. In years when absorption and turnover vacancy is larger than the assumed 7 percent general vacancy, as is the case in Year 9, the general vacancy is zero.

17.   For a full discussion of the investor's ROE, see Chapter 8.

18.   Year 11 NOI is used to estimate the sale price at the end of Year 10, as the next investor will value the income stream that he expects to obtain based on when he purchases the building (Value$_{10}$ = NOI$_{11}$/cap rate = $604,994/.08 = $7,562,425). An 8 percent cap rate is a slight increase in the cap rate over the purchase cap rate of 7.9 percent to account for the property's physical and functional obsolescence.

19.   The ownership structure for a real estate investment can come in many forms, including a general partnership, a limited partnership, a limited liability corporation, and a Subchapter S corporation. We assumed a limited partnership for the equity splits discussed here.

PART IV

IDEAS

Some of the best ideas seem so simple that people assume they appear like the proverbial lightbulb over cartoon characters' heads. Unfortunately, that "ah, ha!" experience is rare. Instead, most ideas are a combination of intuition, interest, creativity, and deliberate, rigorous market research. Developers need new ideas so their firms can stay in business. Sometimes opportunities result from the developer's deliberate efforts. At other times, an almost unconscious processing of information leads to ideas for the next development. At still other times, opportunities seem to present themselves from nowhere.

No matter how the ideas for the development come about, developers have to know when to go ahead with those ideas or when to abandon them before too much time and money are invested in a losing proposition. The next three chapters look at the formation of ideas in general and in the context of development in particular (stage one) and how and when the decisions are made to refine the idea and move forward (stage two). Market research is a critical element in the decision-making process, just as it is throughout the entire development process.

Stage One: Inception Of an Idea

Knowing the roles of the various participants in the development process, having the ability to apply financial logic to the process, and keeping the historical evolution of the public/private partnership clearly in mind, we are ready to move forward with stage one of the development process—inception of an idea. Of all the activities that constitute real estate development, generating plans for prospective projects should be the least mechanical and most creative. The excitement of identifying an unfilled human need and creating a product (and a marketing campaign) to fill it at a profit is the stimulus that drives development—even if the product is as technically uncomplicated as self-storage units or pads for mobile homes. The best ideas result in products that serve the user well and add value to the community and do so at a profit. It is often difficult if not impossible to manage your way out of a bad development idea, so everything that follows is predicated on getting stage one right.

Where do developers get their ideas? How do they know which ideas deserve further analysis and which do not? No magic formula exists for generating good development ideas, because everyone receives different data and processes it into information differently. The spark comes from the way different pieces of information are put together to solve a problem—as well as from the quality and uniqueness of multiple insights. One thing that is certain is that developers generally need background information to make the most of good ideas. Such information, along with experience, results in what is often called "a feel for the market." This feel does not earn the developer any money, but, without it, a developer is likely to lose money and do a disservice to the community.

Although generating development ideas might often be thought of as unpredictable and intuitive, in truth, a portion of generating ideas is methodical and calculated. Developers need future projects if they hope to keep their firms active in the business. Thorough market research has become as important as a developer's drive to complete a project. Successful developers are rigorous in their planning but not so regimented as to lose the creative spark.

Human experience and observation go a long way when developers try to understand real estate markets. Developers, members of the development team, investors, regulators, and policy makers can be more effective and successful if they look at all knowledge (history, current conditions, and forecasts) as potentially useful when envisioning new projects. In a sense, the development players unconsciously perform market research during almost all their waking moments when they read, drive, eat, play, meditate, or interact with other people. They also perform more structured market research when they rigorously analyze the regional economy and local population growth, employment figures, zoning provisions, traffic counts, occupancy rates, and consumer surveys. Curiosity, interest, and observation enhance the formal approaches to generating ideas.

Although marketing and market research underlie every stage of the development process, the basics of marketing and market research are highlighted at four points in the development process (see Figure 10-1).

As a starting point to the eight stages of the development process, this chapter covers the following topics:

- ▶ Different motivations behind ideas;
- ▶ The back-of-the-envelope pro forma;
- ▶ Generating ideas through strategic decision making and market research;
- ▶ Techniques for generating ideas;
- ▶ Words of warning and signposts; and
- ▶ Risk control during stage one of the real estate development process.

The Museum Towers and Elevation 314 case studies introduced in Chapter 1 are continued, illustrating stage one of the development process.

DIFFERENT MOTIVATIONS BEHIND IDEAS

Although idea inception may seem the fuzziest stage in the real estate development process, it can also be the most enjoyable stage—even for individuals who are compulsive about order. Simply put, it is exciting to think about creating a new built environment. In fact, a developer frequently devotes 20 to 30 percent

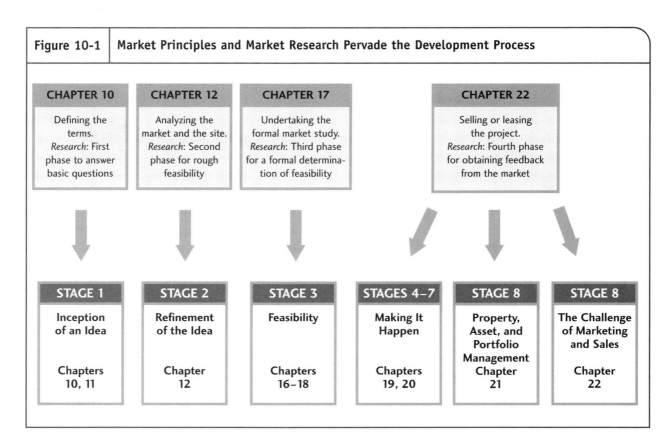

| **Figure 10-1** | **Market Principles and Market Research Pervade the Development Process** |

CHAPTER 10	**CHAPTER 12**	**CHAPTER 17**	**CHAPTER 22**
Defining the terms. *Research:* First phase to answer basic questions	Analyzing the market and the site. *Research:* Second phase for rough feasibility	Undertaking the formal market study. *Research:* Third phase for a formal determination of feasibility	Selling or leasing the project. *Research:* Fourth phase for obtaining feedback from the market

STAGE 1	**STAGE 2**	**STAGE 3**	**STAGES 4–7**	**STAGE 8**	**STAGE 8**
Inception of an Idea Chapters 10, 11	Refinement of the Idea Chapter 12	Feasibility Chapters 16–18	Making It Happen Chapters 19, 20	Property, Asset, and Portfolio Management Chapter 21	The Challenge of Marketing and Sales Chapter 22

or more of the time required for a project to idea inception. Every new insight serves as a catalyst, which, when melded with the developer's background and experience, generates still more ideas. In this way, the developer moves repeatedly through stage one of the development process many times a day.

This chapter characterizes developers as professionals constantly involved in informal brainstorming; they search their background and current experience for an idea that offers potential. In the development process, however, ideas may emerge in many different ways. For example, developers often discover a site looking for a use. For one reason or another, the owners of a particular parcel, whether public or private, want the site to be developed, thereby creating possibilities for the developer. Sometimes the site is already developed and the existing structure needs to be redeveloped. Perhaps a building stands on the site and must remain, but the owner is seeking a new use for the building. Or perhaps the existing building will be expanded or additional buildings built on the site. Alternatively, developers might encounter a use looking for a site, which is frequently the case when corporations want to expand, introduce a new product, or restructure their operations, thereby creating a need for constructed space (a fast-food restaurant, for example, looking for a high-traffic corner or a bank seeking a location for a new branch). Finally, powerful forces of the capital market might be at work, setting capital to look for a development opportunity.

In all these cases, the developer must have the background—relevant experience in development and familiarity with the latest changes in the industry—to be able to respond to the stimulus. Successful developers also have extensive contacts who can function as a sounding board for new ideas and suggest potential members of the development team.

Jim Chaffin, Jr., a resort and recreational developer responsible for Snowmass Village, Colorado, Spring Island, South Carolina, and Semiahmoo in Blaine, Washington, among others, believes that the best development ideas come from creative dreaming balanced by knowledge of the industry and trends—economic, sociographic, psychographic, and demographic (see the profile on the next page).

Even though the developer is typically the driving force, landowners, space users, or sources of capital are periodically the catalysts for development ideas. For example, organizations such as railroads and paper companies that own vast tracts of land have created development subsidiaries to plan and develop land already owned by the company. Many large corporations have established real estate units or subsidiaries to develop space as well as to manage their leased space. Some have gone so far as to spin off a separate company to develop and manage their extensive real estate holdings. Although the initial push comes from many sources, eventually someone (inside or outside the corporation) must take charge and become the developer.

It is, of course, possible for an idea—a purely entrepreneurial idea—to spring from the developer's own imagination. Often, however, a combination of motivations triggers a development idea. When developer Joseph Alfandre acquired 352 acres (143 hectares) outside Washington, D.C., he knew he wanted something different from the typical suburban communities that were being re-created across the United States. No land planning firms he went to could satisfy his desire to do something unusual on the site he called Kentlands. Then he met architect and planner Andrés Duany, with whom he conducted a seven-day charrette to develop design and planning principles for the site. With participation from citizens and political bodies, the developer and architect came up with a surprisingly dense neotraditional site plan on a modified grid system with no culs-de-sac or on-street parking, and shared open space that defines the character of the community. Since that time, hundreds of such neotraditional communities have been built in the United States and Canada. What seemed radical and was subjected to much early criticism is now commonplace. Likewise, in the early 1980s, entrepreneur Ian Schrager, creator of New York's legendary Studio 54, developed his first boutique hotel in New York and started a phenomenon that has changed the hotel business. Using big-name designers, he made each hotel a lifestyle statement designed to attract clientele who think of themselves as chic and added a restaurant

JAMES J. CHAFFIN, JR.
President, Chaffin/Light Associates
Snowmass Village, Colorado
Spring Island, South Carolina

Jim Chaffin is a cofounder (with James W. Light) and president of Chaffin/Light Associates, a firm that specializes in developing resort and recreational communities. Since 1978, the company has developed internationally recognized communities with superb recreational facilities, conservation-based development principles, and distinctive community operating programs. Chaffin has been involved in the development of communities across the country, beginning with the Sea Pines Company at Hilton Head Island, South Carolina (Sea Pines Plantation, Hilton Head Plantation, Amelia Island in Florida, Kiawah Island in South Carolina, Palmas del Mar in Puerto Rico, Brandermill in Richmond, Virginia, and many more). With his partner Jim Light, he has gone on to develop Snowmass Village in Colorado, the Semiahmoo resort in Washington, Spring Island, Callawassie Island in South Carolina, and the Roaring Fork Club near Aspen, Colorado. Chaffin is active in several professional and community organizations, including ULI, the National Real Estate Advisory Council of the Trust for Public Land, the Board of Managers of the University of Virginia, and local arts and education groups.

GENERATING IDEAS FOR NEW PROJECTS

Chaffin believes that the process for generating new ideas should be both systematic and creative. "To have one without

Chaffin/Light's Roaring Fork Club, near Aspen, Colorado, is a golf and hunting club designed with sustainability in mind. A very limited number of homes are planned, and an environmental trust has been established to ensure the continuation of environmentally sensitive practices in the area. Robert Shafer

the other is a big mistake. Developers should know the fundamentals of market analysis and be able to dream." Even though some poor ideas are successful because of circumstances or market aberrations, Chaffin believes that developers who are aware of the economic, social, political, and environmental conditions of the global community will come up with the best product ideas or "create the most stimulating places for people to live and work."

Now that Chaffin has a solid track record as a developer, he finds that many deals come to him. Well over half his opportunities involve a site that somebody wants developed, about 20 percent come about because he or his partner has an idea that demands a site, and another 10 percent represent capital coming to the firm in search of an investment.

Chaffin's starting point in the process of generating ideas is to think about his previous experience. "Who have been my customers in the past? What did they expect? Was I able to deliver? What have I learned from those experiences?" The next step is to examine the economic, sociographic, and demographic trends of the area and analyze demand. "Start with the fundamental questions. Who are my potential customers? How many? How fast will they respond? Who else is competing for the same customers and how are they doing? And so on."

FROM SEA PINES TO SPRING ISLAND

Like many major recreational community developers of his generation, Chaffin got his start working with Charles Fraser (the same Fraser of Fraser Morrow Daniels referred to in the Europa Center Case study in Appendix A) at Sea Pines Plantation on Hilton Head Island, South Carolina. That project set new standards for recreational communities by putting aside 1,200 (485 hectares) of the development's total 5,200 acres (2,105 hectares) for open space, establishing architectural controls on building design, protecting environmentally sensitive areas, and developing extensive outdoor amenities such as golf courses, tennis courts, marinas, and walking/cycling trails.

Chaffin then went on with his partner Jim Light (also a former employee of Sea Pines) to develop resort and private club communities in the Colorado Rockies, the Pacific Northwest, southern California, and the South Carolina coast. Their interest in conservation led to Spring Island, a 3,000-acre (1,215-hectare) high-end golf/residential island community near the coast of South Carolina. The Spring Island Company has preserved one-third of the island and with it a plethora of wildlife, including bald eagles, wood storks, deer, quail, fox squirrels, and a 600-acre (243-hectare) live oak forest. "When I visited the island for the first time Thanksgiving weekend 1988, I was awed by its natural beauty and so frustrated to know that the original developer had approvals to build 5,500 homes on the island that when the developer couldn't fulfill his options, we decided to grab it." Chaffin and Light's efforts to preserve the project's most important amenity—nature— have included the creation of the nonprofit Spring Island Trust to maintain a 1,000-acre (405-hectare) nature preserve and manage a staff of working naturalists and their nature laboratory, supported by a 1.5 percent transfer fee on the sale of all lots to perpetuity.

Although Chaffin's associates thought he was a little idealistic to undertake Spring Island and cautioned him to wait until he was approaching retirement before indulging himself in such a project, he went ahead based on his knowledge of the market and his gut feeling. "I really had a feeling that people were moving back to basic values. Families wanted to be outdoors in a real place, sharing real experiences and safe adventures." His goal was to complete a high-quality project that is sustainable and ecologically sound and to set an example for other developers. The community has received many national awards for its environmental stewardship, and it has been financially successful ("striking a balance between environmental sensitivity and economic sensibility"). Several developers have used Spring Island as a model for developments in other locations.

In 1996, planning began for the Roaring Fork Club near Aspen, Colorado. A 300-acre (120-hectare) family fly fishing and golf club, the project has limited residential development to 48 hand-hewn log cabins, sensitively located around the golf course and along one mile (1.6 kilometers) of "gold medal" fishing waters. Similar to Spring Island, Roaring Fork Club has established a 501(c)(3) environmental trust for environmental programs in the Roaring Fork Valley.

Subsequent projects in Colorado, South Carolina, and North Carolina continued the Spring Island focus of ultra low-density development and preservation of the environment.

ADVICE FOR WOULD-BE DEVELOPERS

"I think a liberal arts education with a graduate degree in business or law or real estate is most beneficial to a developer for several reasons. Developers have to be able to communicate well. They have to be interested in the entire planet and must be aware of what's going on in the world, to be good observers and listeners so they can see and hear what the market is telling them. They need discipline and passion, persistence and courage, all with a healthy dose of humility. We're all deal junkies. We look at a deal and think that we can make it work. But no matter how great the opportunity, you have to be able to admit not having the capital, personnel, experience, or energy to take on a project that's not right for you. And for that you need discipline and rigor."

Chaffin's strongest advice to students: "Don't ever think you are as smart as everybody thinks you are during the good times because you're not going to want to believe you're as dumb as they think you are during the bad times." (See www.chaffinlight.com.)

and bar that in themselves usually became destinations. Many other hoteliers have imitated his approach; in some cases, they have taken the next step of attracting more business clientele while maintaining the trendy look and reputation.[1]

Although an initial idea may be rough, James Graaskamp's "situs"—all the ways a project affects its surrounding environment as well as all the effects of that environment on the project—is the key concern. The type of project must generally fit the location, which, in turn, must fit the tenant and fit the financing. Ultimately, this fit usually reshapes the original idea, as demonstrated in the next several chapters. And when "fit" and "reshaping" are being considered, it is important not to lose sight of ethical obligations. As the pressures of the development process intensify, the developer must remain alert to any moral hazards lurking in the substructure.

THE BACK-OF-THE-ENVELOPE PRO FORMA

Stage one of the development process ends when the developer tests the new idea with a "back-of-the-envelope" pro forma—a simple comparison of value and cost. At this stage, ideas are not sufficiently refined to be subjected to the type of detailed analysis that incorporates the computerized discounted cash flow models described in Part III. And because most ideas generated at this stage are never carried out, the developer cannot justify the expenditure of a great deal of money or time to analyze fully every aspect of each idea.

To prepare a quick pro forma, the developer typically uses his concept of the target user to estimate how much rent the user might be willing to pay for a particular type of space with appropriate services in a particular location. For an income-producing property, the projection consists of a rough estimate of income per square foot and operating expenses per square foot without detailed attention to the configuration, length of lease, number of elevators, and the many other factors that will be determined during the later stages of development decision making. The next step is to multiply the project's leasable square feet by the estimated revenue per square foot. The developer then subtracts the projected operating expenses and multiplies the result by ten to twelve (the inverse of an 8 to 10 percent cap rate). This back-of-the-envelope pro forma follows the same format as the one introduced in Part III. It differs only in the level of detail. The rough estimate of value thus inelegantly generated is then compared with a rough estimate of cost, which at this point typically is projected from estimates of what the land might sell for plus site development costs and construction costs per square foot of the proposed structure. If value exceeds cost, at least based on the rough numbers, the idea remains viable. If cost exceeds value, it is back to the drawing board.

For example, consider a project with 200,000 leasable square feet (18,600 square meters). If expected annual market rental rates were $18.25 per square foot ($196 per square meter) for the proposed tenant and a 93 percent occupancy rate were appropriate, then the owner would collect $16.97 per square foot ($18.25 × 0.93) ($182.60 per square meter, or $196 × 0.93). If expected operating expenses total $7.30 per square foot ($78.55 per square meter) annually for this type of project, then $9.67 ($16.97 − $7.30) represents the project's anticipated net income per square foot ($104.05 per square meter, or $182.60 − $78.55). Multiplying $9.67 by 200,000 square feet of leasable space yields $1,934,000 of net income per year ($104.05 × 18,600 square meters yields $1,935,000). Capitalizing it at 10 percent ($1,934,000 ÷ 0.10) results in a value of $19,340,000. If the land for this project costs $4,000,000, expected site development costs are $500,000, and construction per square foot costs about $95 (a total of $19,000,000 [$95 × 200,000 square feet]), then developing the project would total about $23,500,000. The projected cost thus exceeds the value, and the developer would need to search for another site,

a higher-paying tenant, or, most likely, a better idea. Note that when capital is readily available or tenants are in place, cap rates are lower. If the market cap rate for this project were 8 percent, then the estimated value would be $24,175,000 ($1,934,000 ÷ .08) and this hypothetical example would be a go from the back-of-the-envelope perspective.

Like most research-driven activities, the vast majority of ideas are not financially viable. Thus, most of the time, stage one ends with the best possible device to control risk: the decision to stop. The prospect of a "no-go" decision is a fact of life and a natural part of the development process. But the compensation for nine (or 999) ideas that die on the back of the envelope is one good idea worth refining in stage two.

It is important to note, too, that when developers calculate a back-of-the-envelope pro forma and it looks like a go, it is not a guarantee that the idea will live beyond the next stage. Developers are part dreamers, and everything to this point is a rough estimate. Once other players become more involved—which occurs upon getting a positive value from the back-of-the-envelope pro forma—they may temper the dream with realities and improved information that make it impossible to go ahead with the project.

GENERATING IDEAS THROUGH STRATEGIC DECISION MAKING AND MARKET RESEARCH

The rise of large development companies, corporate real estate departments, and large numbers of professionals with extensive university training has accelerated the application of strategic planning to the creative side of real property development. This trend is noteworthy given that the public often views developers as freewheelers unfettered by bureaucracy. In fact, as shown in Figure 10-2, market research is a strategic tool applied throughout the development process. Although the specifics of strategic planning are beyond the scope of this book, all members of the development team should appreciate strategic planning's overall framework and aim.

Strategic planning consists of formulating goals (ends) and determining courses of action (using the

With buildout expected by 2015, the plans for the 4,000-acre (1,619-hectare) master-planned community of Daniel Island, in Charleston, South Carolina, call for 6,000 homes, two golf courses, 2 million square feet (185,800 square meters) of office space, 1.2 million square feet (111,480 square meters) of retail space, and three schools. *©Steve Uzzell*

Figure 10-2	Market Research in the Real Estate Development Process
Stage	**Market Research Provides**
1 Inception of an Idea	Background for brainstorming, initial information for a back-of-the-envelope pro forma
2 Refinement of the Idea	Specific input for refining the rough idea
3 Feasibility	Input for rigorous market analysis to convince all participants in the process that the development is a feasible project and feasible for them personally
4 Contract Negotiation	Supporting information needed for hard negotiations between the different participants in the process
5 Formal Commitment	Support material for legal documentation
6 Construction	The basis for planning marketing tactics and adapting to changing market conditions during construction. Marketing feedback loop is critical.
7 Completion and Formal Opening	Current market data for implementing the operating plan and ongoing marketing effort
8 Property, Asset, and Portfolio Management	Input for all capital expenditure decisions, leasing and re-leasing, and eventually repositioning the project

associated means available) to achieve those goals. The choice of a project affects the development company's organization, and, before deciding on projects, developers should think about how large an organization they want to control, the extent of desired vertical or horizontal integration (the amount of structure they are willing to accept), and the talent, ambition, and money available to the organization. Any idea selected for implementation becomes de facto part of an organizational strategy; in fact, developers can identify specific projects and locations and consider those choices part of the organizational strategy they want to pursue. Ideally, developers should think beforehand about how a particular project might fit into a strategy for their organization. In other words, to use marketing research effectively for a project, developers should have a clear idea of why they want to undertake the project and how much of their money, personnel, and reputation they are willing and able to commit to it. (Note how Graaskamp's definition of feasibility fits easily into a strategic planning framework: "A real estate project is 'feasible' when the real estate analyst determines that there is a reasonable likelihood of satisfying explicit objectives when a selected course of action is tested for fit to a context of specific constraints and limited resources.")[2]

Organizational strategies differ in detail and formality, depending on the size and focus of the development company. Small developers may have a strategy that exists only in their heads. In contrast, the development arm of a large corporation must usually prepare an organizational strategy for its real estate business that fits into the larger corporate strategy. In such an environment, fairly rigid procedures for making a go/no-go decision must be followed. In development, it is hard to separate the strategic idea from the team that will try to implement it. Consequently, it is usually good practice to move quickly from the *what* of the idea to the *how.* To keep the text as readable as possible, however, this chapter focuses on the *what* of strategic planning, with the how to follow in subsequent chapters.

TECHNIQUES FOR GENERATING IDEAS

Ideas often appear to arise intuitively; however, certain formal techniques can be used to stimulate creativity.

Of the various formal techniques, brainstorming, the nominal group process, the Delphi method, environmental scanning, focus groups, and surveys (or a combination of the types) are those most frequently used to generate and test development ideas. These techniques are sufficiently systematic and precise to help generate ideas without making exorbitant demands on limited time and money.[3]

Brainstorming is a group (or individual) exercise devoted to producing the largest possible number of creative ideas during a given period of time. To encourage an atmosphere of creativity, the group or individual initially accepts every idea, no matter how unusual. Whether pursued in a group or individually, brainstorming should follow several rules: write down every idea, defer judgment on the value of ideas, list as many ideas as possible, try not to let participants get too far afield while still pursuing radical thoughts, and, most important, look for combinations of listed ideas. After a brainstorming session is completed, the development team can study the lists more closely and select the most promising combination of ideas for potential projects.

The *nominal group process* is a technique for establishing priority among ideas identified by a group. It can be used to analyze in more detail ideas generated through brainstorming and is particularly useful when a development team is responsible for achieving consensus about goals and courses of action to achieve those goals. Participants are first asked to write down their ideas in silence after a facilitator has clearly explained the problem or issue. A facilitator then lists the ideas that people have developed on their own, helps clarify them, and screens opinions based on the group's preferences. Members then submit a written, confidential vote on the various alternatives. Preferred projects emerge from the process. The usefulness of the nominal group process depends on the developer's willingness to work with a group—usually the development organization or a larger development team that includes outside consultants—to establish priorities among project ideas. The nominal group process is often used in public sector development when consensus is critical.

The *Delphi method,* first used to analyze military strategies and the impacts and implications of new technologies, offers a formal approach for bringing expert opinion to bear on a research question. Developers can use the technique to gather the informed opinions of market experts about a complex question without having to actually bring them together at one time. One obvious real estate application is in forecasting the supply of and demand for different kinds of space. Aiming for a consistent set of answers, the developer prepares a set of questions for a diverse group of experts, perhaps a politician, a market researcher, and a broker. After examining the experts' independent forecasts, the developer can prepare more structured and close-ended questions and then ask the experts to compare their views with others and to consider revising their opinions. The process may require several rounds of review. If the process is successful, the developer can elicit a single, coherent picture of the environment under study. Developers find the Delphi method attractive when the questions are complex, the experts are dispersed and few in number, or antipathy exists in the proposed development team.

Environmental scanning is a systematic way for developers or a development team to monitor the local, regional, national, and global environments and to predict the possible implications of environmental events. For example, a developer engaged in a large-scale project with a lengthy completion period might consider the implications of a recession on the project's feasibility. Scanning can be simplified by identifying a few readily available, easily interpreted indicators for monitoring environmental events. Examples include the prime interest rate or quarterly changes in the GDP. The developer or team specifies the events and the actions they would trigger and often writes scenarios used for playing out various implications and the results of alternative courses of action. Although environmental scanning is widely used and highly recommended for strategic organizational planning, it is a time-consuming way to generate project ideas. Although it is included here for reference, it is more commonly used in stage three with computerized sensitivity analysis.

Focus groups are most often used for modifying a proposed project to meet the desires of a potential consumer group, although they are sometimes used to

Located on the site of the first amusement park in Denver, Colorado, Highlands' Garden Village consists of 306 residential units, 75,000 square feet (6,970 square meters) of commercial space, and 65,000 square feet (6,040 square meters) of civic space. *Perry Rose, LLC*

generate ideas for future developments. Focus groups have one primary advantage over other processes: they allow the free flow of thoughts that can sometimes generate a wide range of interesting ideas.

Focus groups typically comprise eight to 12 people who meet for about two hours. A moderator leads a discussion according to a set of carefully prepared questions or objectives, but he must be flexible enough and sufficiently knowledgeable about the topic to know when to delve deeper. The moderator must also be trained to avoid steering the group to affirm preconceived notions. Critics of focus groups say that the technique is not rigorous and that its results can be misleading if the wrong participants are chosen. When focus groups are used to search for ideas that will subsequently be tested, however, these weaknesses are not critical.

Surveys are another tool used by developers to generate ideas for new products and projects and to modify projects that are underway. Many times surveys are given to residents or tenants in the developer's existing

projects to assess customer satisfaction. Or they are given to prospective customers who visit or call the sales office for information. Developers can put together a profile of probable customers and the kind of product they want, their willingness to pay for it, and so on. The advantage of this method is that the profile is generated by sales center traffic—people who have already shown a certain amount of interest by making the effort to gather information about the development.

All these generic techniques can be modified to fit the particular situation. Although these formal methods can be quite useful, entrepreneurs should not rule out some less formal techniques used by creative people, such as daydreaming, simply carrying a notepad at all times and writing down anything that is remotely related to the problem at hand, or changing some routines to leave oneself open to fresh experiences. So long as the developer enters these activities—formal and informal—with an open mind and is not merely looking for confirmation of an initial idea, new ideas and reshaped ideas will emerge.

WORDS OF WARNING AND SIGNPOSTS

Although many basic principles of market research can be applied to real estate development, a few caveats apply.

Test Marketing a New Idea

One traditional form of market research—test marketing a new product—generally does not work in real estate development, for real estate products are expensive, large, physically fixed to a location, and long-lasting. Thus, developers cannot simply test a new concept in hotel design by building a hotel and inviting a sample group of guests to try it. Once a large project is built, the developer is committed—at least to the part already built.

Not surprisingly, developers kick a lot of tires, show friends a lot of sketches and photographs, and visit other cities and countries to get ideas. Increasingly, they build projects in what appear to be uneconomically small phases, allowing market response to shape the later phases. But because products are so expensive, good market research is particularly important. Trial and error is seldom a viable method of proving the market.

Using Research to Make Decisions

Successful developers have been able to cope with too little relevant information, too much data, inaccurate data, and rapidly changing conditions—somehow managing to synthesize successful new ideas from insights gained from imperfect sources. Sometimes the idea is a small change in familiar elements—perhaps developing a fairly standard 300-unit apartment complex but with slightly larger master baths in a new city. Sometimes the idea is a startling new combination of elements such as Chelsea Piers Sports and Entertainment, a 30-acre (12-hectare) sports and film center located on New York City's Hudson River on four giant finger piers. The sports center was started because the developer, Roland Betts, had a daughter who was a figure skater and he himself was a hockey player; he knew too well from firsthand experience that the few rinks available in the city were not high

quality and were booked almost 24 hours a day. His frustration with that situation led him to develop the piers, which now house a sports center, ice-skating rinks, bowling, a fitness center, a rock-climbing wall, and golf (30 separate sports are accommodated in the facilities) as well as a park and restaurants and various amenities to complement the recreational activities. It was later, after Chelsea Piers was well established as a destination recreational center, that the owners took the step of building a large event space with water views—something almost unheard of in Manhattan. The developer of Chelsea Piers is particularly successful at identifying a need and responding to it.[4] Behind almost all these ideas lies some form of market research.

Given the difficulties of obtaining just the right data at just the right moment, the market research initiated in stage one must be even more organized and coordinated in subsequent stages of the development process.

RISK CONTROL DURING STAGE ONE OF THE REAL ESTATE DEVELOPMENT PROCESS

Pragmatic developers can take several steps to reduce risk in stage one of the development process. Knowing when to hedge your bets is a big part of a developer's longevity.

▶ *Know yourself.* Developers who honestly evaluate their own capabilities (financial, intellectual, and emotional) will be better situated to deal with the pressures of development. It is helpful to have well-positioned contacts in financial institutions, in groups of prospective tenants, and in construction companies. A large liquid net worth is also usually helpful. Ideas that can be successfully executed by one developer may be less viable for another. If your net worth is in the six figures and you have no construction experience beyond garden apartments, you would be stretching to attempt a $50 million high-rise residential tower without strong development partners to fill the gaps.

Figure 10-3 | Big Ideas: Taipei 101

The age of the skyscraper was born in the United States in the late 19th century, made possible by the advent of structural steel construction and workable electric elevators. Until recently, the United States held the distinction of being home to most of the world's tallest buildings. Today, however, most of the existing, planned, and under-construction tallest buildings are in Asia and the Pacific Rim.

At 1,667 feet (510 meters), Taipei 101 dominates the largely low-rise skyline of Taipei and was, for a short time, the tallest building in the world. That the 101-story structure was finished at all, at a cost of $1.7 billion, is a testament to the determination of its various backers, who forced their vision to completion in the face of a string of potentially project-ending obstacles.

Conceived by noted local architect C.Y. Lee, Taipei 101 faced its first major roadblock in the form of the Taiwan Aviation Safety Council, which halted construction on the not-unreasonable grounds that it was being built in the flight path of aircraft landing at nearby Sungshan Airport. But by pulling a few political strings, this flight path was changed so that the building's height could be maintained.

The next holdup came in March 2002, when a 6.8-magnitude earthquake struck Taipei as construction on the building reached the 56th floor. Although the unfinished structure held firm, the quake toppled two cranes on its summit, killing five workers and delaying work for seven months. In addition to that incident, a series of fires and other accidents, $60 million in cost overruns, and a forced redesign to improve the tower's aerodynamic efficiency ensured a start-stop building schedule that ultimately saw completion delayed by nearly two years.

Although some question the wisdom of building such a huge structure in one of the world's most seismically active zones, the hazards of the local environment and the many vicissitudes suffered during construction have guaranteed that the tower has been built to the most exacting engineering standards of any major building in the world. Structurally, the building is anchored by eight megacolumns extending the full height of the tower and tied to a braced core of 16 steel box columns. Reduced beam sections known as "dog-bone cuts" permit beams to rotate slightly to prevent buckling during earthquakes, providing a design with an extremely durable structure. To counter the super typhoons that hit Taiwan, special pendulums at the top of the tower are designed to absorb the impact of wind gusts as high as 150 miles per hour. These three huge metal balls act as an inertia sink, swaying in the wind so the building itself does not.

Located in the fashionable Xinyi District of Taipei, Taiwan, Taipei 101 stands tall at 1,667 feet (510 meters) and 101 floors. Colin Galloway

The building's elevators also illustrate the latest technology necessary for ultratall buildings. Sixty-one elevators, including 34 double-decker compartments, serve 78 floors of office space. Two of these elevators now rank as the fastest in the world. The two $2 million Toshiba-built cars take passengers from the ground to the 89th-floor observation deck in a smooth, 37-second ride at speeds reaching 38 miles per hour. Descent speeds are lower to keep pressure increases from rupturing passengers' eardrums.

Taipei 101's reign as the world's tallest building did not last long. Despite recent research questioning the sustainability and cost-effectiveness of such megabuildings, the prestige that accompanies their construction and use continues to be a powerful force, especially in developing countries, encouraging governments and big business to build ever higher. With advances in modern construction techniques and materials continuing apace, it seems that—literally—the sky is the only limit remaining.

Source: Condensed from Colin Galloway, "Towering Taiwan," *Urban Land*, February 2006, pp. 64–67.

World's Tallest Buildings: Completed, Under Construction, and Proposed

Building	Year of Completion	Stories	Height (Feet/Meters)	Location
*Burj Dubai	2009	160	2,313/705	Dubai, United Arab Emirates
†Center of India Tower	2008	224	2,221/677	Katangi, India
†Tower of Russia	2010	125	2,129/649	Moscow, Russia
†Three Empires Tower	N.D.	150	1,969/591	Istanbul, Turkey
†International Business Center	2008	130	1,903/580	Seoul, South Korea
Lotte World Tower	2006	N.A.	1,821/555	Seoul, South Korea
*Freedom Tower	2009	82	1,776/541	New York, New York
Taipei 101	2004	101	1,667/508	Taipei, Taiwan
*Shanghai World Financial Center	2007	101	1,614/492	Shanghai, China
*Union Square Phase VII	2007	102	1,555/474	Hong Kong
†Busan Lotte Tower	2010	102	1,516/462	Busan, South Korea
†Suyong Bay Tower	2010	102	1,516/462	Busan, South Korea
†Xujiahui Tower	N.D.	92	1,509/460	Shanghai, China
Petronas Towers	1998	88	1,483/452	Kuala Lumpur, Malaysia
†The Gateway III	N.D.	N.A.	1,476/450	Hong Kong
Sears Tower	1974	110	1,450/442	Chicago, Illinois
†Asia Tower	2008	103	1,414/431	Kaosiung, Taiwan
Jin Mao Building	1999	88	1,376/419	Shanghai, China
†Dalian International Trade Center	2007	78	1,376/419	Dalian, China

Notes: *Under construction. Year of expected completion.
†Proposed. Original expected completion date.
Source: Emporis (www.emporis.com).

MUSEUM TOWERS

Museum Towers is a fairly standard product. It did not stretch the boundaries of creativity; it did not require years of research to come up with the idea. It was a straightforward look at the market and the location. But what was ultimately built was not what Dean Stratouly intended to build.

DEAN STRATOULY EXPLAINS THE GENESIS OF AN IDEA: ANALYZING MARKET OPPORTUNITIES

The original site was 4.11 acres (1.7 hectares) and was actually three lots. We had intended to subdivide the property and develop it as a hotel and apartment building. The proposed development would have consisted of a 420-unit apartment building complex, a 207-suite hotel building, and a total of 696 parking spaces. The city's preferred use was housing, including affordable housing.

When the market went to hell in the early nineties and we were basically sitting on the property, we changed our plans when we got the opportunity to sell the hotel parcel. So, in 1996 we sold 50,000 square feet (4,650 square meters) to E.F. Institute for Cultural Exchange for $5.25 million for its

North American headquarters (the company is based in Sweden). The institute built a ten-story office project containing 250,000 gross square feet (23,200 square meters)—159,000 square feet (14,800 square meters) of office space, a restaurant on the first floor, and 132 parking spaces.

After we gave away an acre to the state for the park and a small strip to the city for roads, we ended up with a site of 2.07 acres (0.8 hectare).

The housing vacancy rate in Boston has been low for a long time, so the market was ripe for a new product. At the same time, at least three other major projects were on about the same schedule as we were—Cronin's Landing, the Village at Bear Hill in Waltham, and University Park at MIT. Some others were permitted and being constructed, and several others were still waiting for approvals. When a major real estate research firm identified Boston as the third best market in the country for apartment investment and development, people started taking notice. Only San Francisco and Orange County, California, were rated better markets.

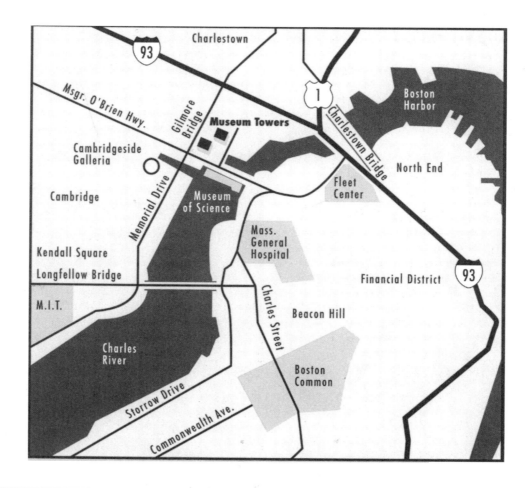

MUSEUM TOWERS *(continued)*

But other things contributed to the interest in multifamily housing here. For one thing, the state eliminated rent control in 1996—which affected about 17,000 units in Boston alone. The unemployment rate in Cambridge was very low throughout the 1990s and was about 2 percent in 1999. The state also made some big tax cuts in favor of business and investment. In addition, the high-tech economy was great and the overall job market (education, medicine, and financial services in addition to technology) strong. Cambridge has always attracted entrepreneurs and innovators because of its highly educated workforce. Moody's rates the Cambridge government "Aa1." The vacancy rate was less than 2 percent, and interest rates were at historic lows. We had a site that had waited nearly ten years. What more do you need?

So for this project, the idea wasn't a big lightbulb going off in my head. It was market driven, because my original idea was different from what we ended up with. Developers gotta be flexible.

continued on page 265

ELEVATION 314

Unlike Museum Towers, Elevation 314 was intended to be a nontraditional product from the start. The building was the result of environmental and architectural theories that Russell Katz had been thinking about since college. Elevation 314 gave him a chance to put these theories to the test.

RUSSELL KATZ EXPLAINS THE GENESIS OF AN IDEA

For me Elevation 314—which we named both for its location at 314 feet (95.7 meters) above sea level and for its street address at 314 Carroll Avenue—was a combination of having to do something and wanting to do something special. On the one hand, I have a family and I have to provide for them. I have to be able to put food on the table and take care of my kids and wife. It's a financial imperative for me to work and make some money. I couldn't rest on my laurels with what I had already done. But more than that, I was compelled by an idea that my environmental philosophy should be combined with good business practices.

Probably 99 percent of buildings get built for financial reasons—for an investment or building to sell for a profit. Green buildings, at that time [the early 2000s], were way too often an institutional gesture or a personal gesture. They were cabins in the woods, university buildings, or nonprofit buildings. Or more likely they were the result of a rich individual who has a concern for the environment and therefore builds himself a very nice house.

Green buildings and builders were fringe elements, but interest was increasing. The market had evolved so much since I first started learning about it in the 1980s. At the time I started Elevation 314, if you wanted a green building material it had been in use for years. And you probably had a number of options to choose from. Often there were two or three different sources or contractors supplying it. It seemed that since the 1980s, a sort of fringe green movement had developed, and by the early 2000s it was ready to become part of the mainstream.

I wanted to make a difference and make something that would prove a point and bring a product to a market that is completely underserved. I envisioned a nice building that could do good for the community but would also serve a market niche that nobody was serving then. To do all of this as a good investment in a money-making venture would break down some of the barriers that you run up against all the time when you are talking about green buildings.

At the time, when I was talking about green buildings to people in the industry—whether it was investors, contractors, or subcontractors—all I heard was, "How much more does it cost?" "Why do you think people want to spend more for that?" But that wasn't the point. We were trying to figure out how to make a building green. We were asking questions like, "If we had a budget of $105 to $110 a square foot [$1,130 to $1,185 a square meter], can we do geothermal heating and cooling? Can we do bamboo floors?"

I made some early decisions that I held to. One was that I wanted to invest for the long term in the building but also in my ability to develop green buildings. The building renovations I did before Elevation 314 were basically green renovations. I didn't use the LEED [Leadership in Energy and Environmental Design] checklist or try to get them certified in any way; I used what I knew was within the budget to make them green, including buying them because they were close to Metro stations and also in walkable areas. They are environmental also in that they were derelict buildings where we kept as much as we could and tried not to create a lot more waste.

As I conceived the project, I saw something that I thought was being missed by the marketplace. Developers

ELEVATION 314 *(continued)*

were just generally doing the same things over and over, building strip malls, office buildings, and apartment buildings. Not much different from what I saw growing up, except that now the urban core was becoming valued more highly than it had been before. Real estate in D.C. and in most cities across the country was becoming more valuable, while the suburbs, especially new suburbs built farther and farther out, were becoming untenable. But you didn't see a hardcore green movement in the marketplace, even though there was a lot of interest.

I'd say there's a thirst and a vibe about this thing, especially now, but back then 90-something percent of the buildings that were getting built had no green elements. I felt strongly that I was either going to do this thing and do it well and make it green or it wasn't going to work. In that case, I was going to change my course, maybe change my city. It was an all-or-nothing move to say that I have this idea, and now I'm looking for its location. I was looking for empty land in a place that would work for me. Which would mean in the city, near the Metro, and walking distance to things that you need to do during the day and in a neighborhood that had some upside to it that I could feel.

I started out with three criteria, or pillars, of development that had to stand at the end of the day. One of them related to design, architecture, sensitivity, and beauty—the pillar of beauty. This project had to be a beautiful thing to see and to occupy. For me that beauty meant that it would not be a trophy building but a building that plays a role in a context. Still, it had to be sublime; the proportions had to be just right, the lighting had to be just right, and there had to be places that would be comfortable and compelling to be occupied.

The second pillar was that it had to be a green building. It had to be a good environmental citizen. And the third one was that it had to be a smart business proposal. It had to make money, and at the end of the day it had to support itself and reward the risk that I'd taken in doing it.

Based on these criteria and the site, the idea of the project began to form itself. I ended up deciding that Takoma is really a bedroom community and that it needed some more retail. When you are located on a main street, you've got to reinforce the street with the retail. That was a decision that took some weeks.

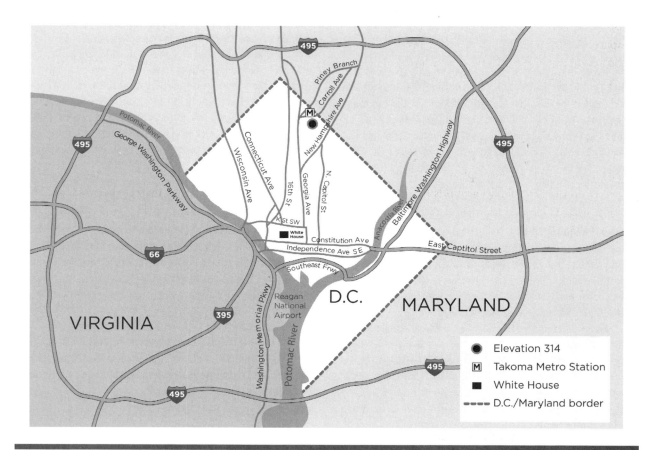

ELEVATION 314 *(continued)*

The acoustic consultant played a key role because the site is hard up against the train tracks and across the street from the subway and bus station. The design had to start developing itself from that point of view: "How do we create something that will be usable?"

Mitigation of the noise caused by the site's location next to the train tracks was a major consideration in guiding the design. Special types of insulation and vibration-softening construction materials were used, but one of the most important design aspects was the use of space in the building. None of the units abut the railroad tracks. Between the units on this side of the building and the railroad tracks are the hallway and some service spaces. Inside these units, the

bathrooms and living rooms are further buffered by the placement of bathrooms, kitchens, and closets.

To capture quiet space, we developed a courtyard concept for the building. That was an architectural idea informed by the site, the context, the sounds, and so on. We started thinking about the facades and the form and how it would relate to the context. This is not a trophy building. Not every building is a Frank Gehry museum. A lot of buildings make up the fabric. This was to me a fabric building, but I wanted it to be subtle and beautifully proportioned and finely detailed. I wanted a kind of a quiet building. If you look at it you'll see a lot more but it's not yelling at anybody.

continued on page 289

▶ *Know your image.* Often the public perception of a developer is that of gunslinger (without the white hat). Successful developers often see themselves as risk averse and functioning more like movie producers. By drawing on several individuals' talents, they package ideas and create a product intended to satisfy society's needs for space. Aspiring developers should understand both what a developer does and how the public views the development profession. If you keep the public perception firmly in mind from the beginning, you will be more likely to dot all the i's and cross the t's so that your idea is appropriately documented to win the support of others.

▶ *Know your team.* Self-perception and public perception are useful backgrounds for self-preservation. Developers must determine the quality of all participants in the development process at an early juncture. During stage one, as developers decide on a general type of project, a general location, and a general type of tenant, they must also think about players they might recruit for the development team to make the development possible. People who demonstrate both excellent track records and financial strength and are easy to work with will reduce long-term risk. Naturally, such people often cost more. Risk reduction is seldom free. The developer must decide what costs are justified from the perspective of reducing risk.

▶ *Coordinate.* From the beginning, developers must coordinate the activities and functions of the individuals involved in the process. This task becomes even more critical in later stages, when the developer adopts a more managerial role. Even at the beginning, however, developers must talk to—not just read about—contractors, subcontractors, potential tenants, city managers, and community groups. The team coordinated by the developer should function more smoothly than a collection of talented free agents.

▶ *Keep current.* To the extent that developers stay current in their reading and networking, they are more likely not to move beyond stage one when available information suggests an idea is not feasible, economically or otherwise. Trends in the national economy, supply conditions, the political climate, and tax laws can shift quickly and interact in unexpected ways. Reading newsletters and attending local and national meetings cannot guarantee profits, but keeping abreast of major events can help minimize financial losses.

▶ *Behave ethically.* Personal relationships and ethics are critically important in the development process because it is often difficult to rely on the courts for a speedy resolution when problems arise. In development, time is money—a lot of money—and developers lack the luxury of time to stop and sue. The stronger the personal relationships and business ethics of all those involved, the safer the development for all concerned, including the general public.

SUMMARY

Inception of an idea is the first stage in the development process. Several techniques are available for generating ideas: brainstorming, the nominal group process, the Delphi method, environmental scanning, focus groups, and surveys. Ideas come from several different motivations and inspirations, but, regardless of the source, ideas must be tested quickly with a back-of-the-envelope pro forma. Ideally, idea generation is integrated into the development company's strategic planning using market research to add rigor to the process. Regardless of the level of rigor or the techniques employed, several potential pitfalls can derail even the most promising proposed project. Accordingly, formal consideration of risk control is necessary even during the first stage of the development process.

From the beginning (stage one), the developer is the ultimate responsible party. He does not have to do every job (not even generating ideas), but he is responsible for each job's getting done well. A developer must maintain the mind-set of a "do-er" rather than a consultant. Strategic planning is useful, but the developer has to make it happen.

Stage one is clearly the most important stage of the development process. Although weak leadership and poor management can ruin a good development idea, the converse is not true. Strong leadership and great management cannot save a bad idea. Remember, Napoleon lost at Waterloo because fighting everyone at once was a bad idea.

The best risk control technique is "don't." Moreover, everyone will tell you to "stay within the boundaries of the market." On average, this advice is good, but the boundary should not be the market just as consultants see it today. Rather, the boundary should be set where the market will be upon completion of the development. The developer can use examples from other times and other places (along with current local market rents) to estimate future demand.

TERMS

- ▶ Back-of-the-envelope pro forma
- ▶ Brainstorming
- ▶ Delphi method
- ▶ Design charrette
- ▶ Environmental scanning
- ▶ Focus groups
- ▶ Nominal group process
- ▶ Situs
- ▶ Strategic planning

REVIEW QUESTIONS

10.1   What are the three most common motivations from which ideas for new developments emerge?

10.2   Describe a back-of-the-envelope pro forma and what it is used for.

10.3   What are some of the formal techniques that developers can use to generate ideas?

10.4   Describe the techniques of risk control that developers can use at this stage. How do they help developers hedge their bets?

10.5   Summarize the advice developer James J. Chaffin, Jr., gives to would-be developers. Do you agree or disagree with his advice?

NOTES

1. See www.kentlands.org and www.ianschragercompany.com.

2. James A. Graaskamp, "A Guide to Feasibility Analysis" (Chicago: Society of Real Estate Appraisers, 1970).

3. The references at the end of the book provide excellent descriptions of basic techniques for generating ideas (although not in the context of real estate development).

4. For a more complete description of Chelsea Piers, see Alexander Garvin and Gayle Berens, *Urban Parks and Open Space* (Washington, D.C.: ULI–the Urban Land Institute, 1997), pp. 126–133; Michael D. Beyard et al., *Developing Urban Entertainment Centers* (Washington, D.C.: ULI–the Urban Land Institute, 1998); and www.chelseapiers.com.

Market Research:
A Tool for
Generating Ideas

The previous chapter makes it clear that before starting any project, developers should understand the market. This chapter provides more context and detail around that basic concept. Subsequent chapters use the insights from Chapter 11 in specific situations.

The market comprises types of property (such as light industrial), owners (players in the capital market), and tenants (players in the space market) located in a particular geographic area. A strong overall market does not necessarily equate with a good development opportunity. Neither does a weak market mean that a good idea cannot be implemented successfully. Further, a good market from the perspective of demand may be oversupplied; at the same time, a good idea may prove successful in a low-growth market. Although poor implementation can undermine the most promising opportunities in any market, understanding the market is a necessary prerequisite to generating ideas. Flawless implementation (stages four through eight) cannot redeem a bad idea.

The word *market* is used in many different ways. It can be a public gathering held for buying and selling merchandise. It can be a store that sells a particular type of merchandise. In real estate development, a market can be defined as a subgroup of a general population that is considered to contain potential buyers or users of a specific property type. This definition of market usually includes a demographic makeup (age, income, household size, education, and so on) and motivations of its constituents. A market can be described in broad terms such as the U.S. homebuying market or in very detailed, specific terms such as retired second homebuyers with a net worth greater than $1 million interested in large family homes with golf course footage within 60 minutes of a particular metropolitan area.

Market research is the tool for discovering who buyers and end users are and what motivates them to buy. This information provides the groundwork for estimating product demand.

This chapter discusses the elements involved in understanding a market by focusing on:

▶ The basics of marketing and market research;
▶ Ten critical questions that market research must answer;

The authors are indebted to Rebecca Zimmermann, Design Workshop, Inc., for rewriting this chapter.

▶ The use of data analysis to draw conclusions; and

▶ The connection between market research and the development of ideas in stage one of the development process.

THE BASICS OF MARKETING AND MARKET RESEARCH

Real estate developers, like all businesspeople, need to pay close attention to their customers. And "market research" is a means of discovering specific intelligence about a particular market, that is, the customers. It is done by collecting, organizing, and interpreting data from local, regional, and national sources to determine potential sales of a product, service, or facility. The best market researchers combine skills in detective work, statistics, interviewing, and data organization to create an end product that is timely, informative, and concise.

Common areas of research can take the form of demographic summaries, analysis of the current state of the geographic area and comparable projects, and use of statistical data to make projections about the future.

Developers who pay careful attention to markets fare far better than those who do not. It is important to note, however, that market research should not be viewed narrowly. Market research needs to be an integral part of every aspect of the development continuum:

▶ Due diligence—research conducted before buying a real estate property;

▶ Entitlements—research completed to understand the most desirable zoning and development conditions to seek;

▶ Programming—research conducted to determine what should be built and when, that is, to define the sequence, product mix, and amenities;

▶ Project positioning—research that informs the market niche for the project; and

▶ Sales—research to determine the most effective marketing and sales programs.

Those who market a product must first analyze market opportunities by paying careful attention to the macro- and microlevels of the market. The macrolevel includes the major forces that influence society: technology, tastes, demographics, sociocultural developments, political attitudes, legal structures, and economic trends. The micro (or industry) level includes both current and potential suppliers, customers, and competitors as well as the public that regulates or influences the market. With an understanding of macro- and microlevel markets, marketers then research and select target markets with, at a minimum, good information on customers who have purchased or leased a similar real estate product in the past. Developers also collect market intelligence on potential consumers and competitors.

Although it is obvious that deals driven by the market tend to be the most successful, examples abound of deals executed for reasons other than simply satisfying current market demand. Until 1986, when tax reform eliminated several provisions favorable to real estate, incentives in the federal tax code prompted a number of otherwise uneconomic developments. When financing was readily available, many dubious projects were developed because some participant in the process benefited even if the project did not succeed. Further, some unsuccessful projects were developed to realize the dream of a particular developer, who paid insufficient attention to the market.

If any such non-market-driven projects were successful in the past, it is best to consider them lucky rather than useful models for future practice. When developers can persuasively demonstrate that they have identified customers with unfilled wants and needs, they can use the collected market information to garner public support and financial backing for a project. When the project is not justified by the market but is considered socially necessary, as in the case of housing for the very poor (see Chapter 15), developers should understand the extent of the subsidy required.

The following review briefly summarizes the basic marketing concepts relevant to the development process. Marketing is the intermediary function between product development and sales. It is the marketer's job to ensure that consumers look beyond price and functionality when they are weighing their buying options. Marketing specialist Philip Kotler argues that marketing should not be narrowly construed as the process of selling products but more broadly understood as satisfying human wants and needs. The following overview draws heavily from Kotler's well-known marketing textbook:[1]

▸ Marketing is a social and managerial process by which individuals and groups obtain what they need and want through creating, offering, and exchanging products of value with each other.

▸ Marketing occurs because humans have needs, wants, and demands, some of which can be satisfied by products (goods, services, and ideas).

▸ If people have a choice among products, their choice is usually guided by their notion of value and their expectation of satisfaction.

▸ Although products can be obtained in several ways—producing them ourselves, coercion, begging, or exchange, for example—most of us acquire goods by exchange. Therefore, most of us become specialists in producing particular products, which we trade for other things we need.

▸ A market consists of all the potential customers sharing a particular need or want who might be willing and able to engage in exchange to satisfy that need or want. The size of that market depends on how many people share the need or want, have resources that interest others, and are willing and able to offer those resources in exchange for what they want.

▸ A marketer is someone seeking one or more prospects who might engage in an exchange of values.

▸ Marketing management is the process of planning and executing the conception, pricing, promotion, and distribution of goods, services, and ideas to create exchanges with target groups that satisfy customers' and organizations' goals.

Industry and market, sellers and buyers are linked in four ways. Sellers send 1) goods or services produced by industry and 2) communicate to the market; in return, they receive from the buyers 3)

Radio City in Toronto, Ontario, consists of two high-rise condominium towers containing studio and one- and two-bedroom units. Because the project is located in the Church Street neighborhood—commonly referred to as Toronto's "Gay Village"—developer Context Development's marketing campaign included a focus on gay men that was so successful that informal surveys suggest that the ownership base is 90 percent gay men. *Ben Rahn, A-Frame Inc.*

money and 4) information. In essence, marketing is the activity that turns the crank: potential transactions become real transactions when people are stimulated to exchange money (or something else of value) for something they want or need.

People—employees—create and manage marketing campaigns to achieve a company's objectives—no less in real estate development companies than at Apple or General Mills. In theory, marketing objectives ought to be part of most management functions, including, for example, the construction process. In practice, however, the task of finding and keeping customers is at times left solely to the marketing staff—which, in real estate development, means leasing agents or salespeople. As in any company, projects are more successful when the people marketing the product understand how the product is produced and financed and can communicate what they learn from dealing directly with the customers to those producing and managing the project. It is the developer's job to ensure that such feedback occurs regularly throughout the development process.

Developers can be susceptible to the field-of-dreams syndrome, too often assuming that "if you build it, they will come." Even experienced developers, because of their past successes, might assume that their next project will be successful just because they are building it; that is, "their" supply will create its own demand. Such assumptions are very dangerous.

Market research has multiple purposes and many uses, including the ability to find and analyze data that will lead to a strategic conclusion on how the project should address:

▶ *Product positioning.* Product positioning refers to where the product fits in the buyer's, tenant's, or investor's mind. To correctly position the product, the researcher must know who the market is and what motivates the people in it. For example, a residential product positioned as value-priced homes near transportation centers would be well suited to lower-income families who need public transportation to get to work. Market research is also important in repositioning existing real estate projects—determining how to change a project to be more competitive and successful in the changing marketplace.

▶ *Product type and characteristics.* Market research helps to inform decisions about the size, layout, features, and style of the real estate product. Characteristics include a broad spectrum of items such as architectural style and quality of finishes. Buyers' preferences come into play at this point.

▶ *Amenities.* Amenities are the set of goods and services available to buyers or users. They are often included in the lease or purchase price as part of the primary real estate offering. For corporate real estate tenants, it could mean spacious entryways, a health club, or VIP parking.

▶ *Product mix.* Product mix refers to the amount and placement of different sizes and types of the product, for example, the percentage distribution of one-, two-, or three-bedroom units in an apartment or condominium project. This exercise can be especially complex with mixed-use projects, where retail, commercial, and residential often coexist.

▶ *Price points.* Most developments do not have a structure of one price for all users. A pricing model allows for strategically targeting the product to different buyer groups. It also provides for pricing to be based on the distinct characteristics of each unit, such as corner units or those with the best views. Determining how to best capture value and meet demand calls for some creativity.

▶ *Absorption rates.* The absorption rate is defined as the pace of sales or leasing divided by the total number of units or amount of space in the development. It is important to be able to accurately project how fast demand will absorb the product. This estimate is critical to the accurate measurement of the financial return of a property.

Market research helps determine what the product should look and feel like, whether it will be absorbed, and, if so, how quickly and at what price points. But market research is also used for more strategic answers to the development process. Thus, market research often involves many end users or audiences. The primary purposes of a market study include:

▶ *Determining the size of the market.* The size of the potential buyer pool must first be calculated to effectively estimate how many sales can be anticipated. From this calculation, the project's estimated share of the market can be determined.

▶ *Supporting feasibility analysis.* Market research is often used to help determine whether an idea can actually succeed within a certain time period (see the discussion of stage three of the development process). Market research is necessary to determine the demand and come up with conclusions on financial inputs such as projected absorption rates, product mix, and price points. These inputs are then used to create the development pro forma.

▶ *Determining the marketing strategy.* Another use of market research is to discover what the target market will respond to positively. The marketing strategy is then crafted to convey this message. The research provides direction in forming this strategy.

▶ *Communicating findings to a variety of stakeholders.* Research reports are not just for developers. They can be used to fortify arguments or justify a change in direction. They can be used as public relations tools and to satisfy regulatory requirements. And they can be used as sales tools and resources for educating investors about the project and its potential.

▶ *Gaining entitlements.* Market research is often required to substantiate the idea of the project to the approving government authorities. How well does the proposed project support the intent of the community's general plan or of regional comprehensive plans? The market researcher's task is to help various participants recognize the relative merits of the project.

▶ *Providing background information for the loan process.* As explained in Part III, investors and lending institutions may require market research to be completed before an investment or loan is made for the project. Credible research is critical for decision making.

Real estate differs substantially from standard mass-produced and nationally advertised products. Market research is often more complex. For example, real estate products are highly differentiated. They serve several functions for different space users and are produced in more styles than most common household products. Above all, real estate is distinguished by the importance of location. Unlike all other products, people cannot take real estate home. Instead, the customer must move to the product.

Constraints on supply are far more variable for real estate. Unlike for mass manufacturing, local conditions of site availability and political entitlements often control the volume of competing supply and direct the developer's opportunities.

In addition, market data are much less certain in the case of real estate. The distinctiveness of different locations and market niches combined with the volatility of local economies and construction cycles require that developers must work hard to know their markets.

TEN CRITICAL QUESTIONS THAT MARKET RESEARCH MUST ANSWER

Whether for a new residential project, a retail center, or an office park, several fundamental questions should be part of every market research effort. The researcher must understand the importance of these questions as well as methodology and sources for addressing the questions.

1. What are the trends in this type of development?

Trends are the guideposts that arise through the collective experience of many professionals in multiple industries. Numerous trends combine to create common themes—experiences and expectations that will influence the future of real estate development.

New projects and ideas are created that look at an old problem from a different angle. Just like styles of blue jeans, real estate users' needs and preferences change constantly. What we see as important tomorrow is sure to be different from what was important yesterday. It is easy to tell, for example, the differences between a house built in the 1960s, 1980s, or today. But what about the house built in 2015? Without looking at trends, we are simply throwing darts, hoping to hit what buyers' preferences will be then. This question becomes particularly important in real estate development, because initial market research is often done years before the actual product is sold. We need to be able to look into the future and make decisions based on what we think buyers and users will demand at the delivery date. Then we can make estimates based on where we want to be positioned in the market.

Every use in Victoria Gardens—a mixed-use development that includes three department stores, 120 upscale shops, restaurants, cafés, movie theaters, and a range of civic uses—was chosen to meet the demand of the rapidly growing Inland Empire region of southern California. *Brent Moore—RMA Photography*

The best way to determine trends is to look at how products and people's preferences have changed over time. The places to find relevant data are published articles and interviews with buyers that provide insight into their motivations. A researcher should bring together many different sources to come up with an opinion about where the market is heading. The key is to determine not only what they want today but also how preferences might change in the future. For example, the number of retirees and empty nesters returning to lively urban locations is increasing. A generation ago, the idea was practically unheard of; now this group is a critical component of the rebirth of intown housing. Keep in mind that trends are predictions about the future based on momentum from the past. They are not always right, but the better and more complete the data, the better our guesses will be.

One technique in turning volumes of market data into a succinct set of trends involves interviewing stakeholders or leaders in the industry, researching current periodicals, and observing the performance of projects. Write down the key messages from each source on index cards or type them in a spreadsheet and group them based on common themes. These themes can then be grouped into trends.

2. What is the current market?

The current market is a concrete view of what buyers want today. Research reveals who potential customers might be so the developer can decide on product strategy. One way to determine potential customers is to profile current buyers and tenants. Doing so provides tools to make informed decisions about the characteristics of the product to be developed. It is important to know who these people are and something about their lives. From this information, one can make inferences about amenities, price points, absorption rates, and product types and mix.

Demographic statistics are the first place to look for information on the current market. They can be found in U.S. Census numbers and state and regional demographic agencies such as the Web site of the Colorado demographer (http://dola.colorado.gov/demog/populationtotals.cfm). (See Chapter 2 for a larger discussion on demographics.) Other sources of current market data are industry numbers from real estate brokers and analysts who publish up-to-date reports on the makeup of their customers. Interviewing recent buyers to learn what motivated them to purchase a property provides more specific information. Finally, newspaper and other print and electronic media publish articles on the state of a current market that are useful sources.

3. What is the depth of this market?

The main reason for researching the depth of the market is to find out what the size of a potential market is and what percentage of that market must be captured to reach target revenues. Developers need to figure out whether they are taking a piece of the pie or making the overall pie larger. For example, will a new Class A office building in downtown Los Angeles take market share from existing buildings nearby or will it attract new tenants who would not otherwise have rented space in that market? In many slow-growth cities, the residents who are moving into downtown housing are not new residents but residents coming from other neighborhoods in search of a different lifestyle.

It can be quite a challenge to quantify market depth. Industry experts who focus on the particular market and comparable projects and their market shares are great sources of information. When specific market numbers are available from these sources, statistical analysis is possible.

4. What are the market's perceived values?

Demographics and the rest of the statistical data tell only part of the story of the market. Asking questions about what is important to buyers, users, or tenants yields more information. What motivates them? What, for example, motivates real estate buyers at high-end resorts? Are they looking for the best prices, or are they looking for something to satisfy their egos? Are they more interested in a solid real estate investment, or do they simply want a retreat to relax and get away from their busy lives? Once these values are determined, the product should be designed to reflect these values and satisfy buyers' wants.

Psychographics is the study of psychological profiles of potential buyers of a product. Some common sources for this information are Claritas (www.claritas.com) and VALS (www.sric-bi.com/VALS), which provide data on the relationships between demographics, personality types, and consumer behavior. These models place buyers into psychographic groups, each with particular characteristics and motivations. Another way to find information about values is through targeted focus groups where subjects are asked to make decisions that provide insights into their values and priorities.

5. What opportunities and challenges does the current market profile present?

Aside from the challenge of matching the product to the market, each market profile has its distinct opportunities and challenges. For example, most real estate developments entail specialized political and public perception issues. Most people want the convenience and low prices of a big-box store like Wal-Mart, but they do not want it next to their home. One of the most common methods of evaluation is through a SWOT (strengths, weaknesses, opportunities, and threats) analysis. Strengths and weaknesses explore internal aspects of the project or elements that can be controlled or changed by the developer. Opportunities and threats evaluate how external influences can affect the project—and most of them (such as interest rates and natural disasters) are beyond the direct control or influence of the developer. Many of these issues are key in determining a project's feasibility.

To answer this question, the researcher should strive to study all the people affected by a project, including buyers, investors, government and other regulatory agencies, and community groups. Perhaps most important, the answer to this question includes public perception. The landscape is littered with projects that have failed or gone over time and cost budgets because the developer underestimated negative public perception. Interviews with all the affected parties is the best way to get this information. Local media such as newspapers and Internet blogs are other sources of local opinions.

6. How do you determine and gain an understanding of your target market?

Once the larger market has been determined, the researcher must narrow it down to determine product mix and desired amenities. An example is moving from the broad apartment rental market to the narrow market of young active professional city-dwelling singles with incomes higher than $100,000 per year. In general, the more precise the target market determination is, the easier it is to position the product in it. Narrowing the target market is also critical in designing an efficient marketing strategy: to reach young active professional city-dwelling singles with incomes higher than $100,000 per year, for example, ads in *The Wall Street Journal* are less effective than direct mail to members of the area's high-end athletic club.

Numerous resources are available to gain understanding of the target market, from focus groups to surveys to interviewing others who sell to the market. Because it is a subset of the overall market, the study group is smaller and more specialized. If a researcher

were to study young active professional city-dwelling singles with incomes higher than $100,000 per year, for example, perhaps the best approach would be to hand out surveys at a downtown bar at happy hour or on the club level of a stadium during a professional football game.

7. What are market positions, development programs, price points, absorption, and lessons learned for competitive projects? Who are their buyers?

It is essential to research the competition, not only to know what other choices potential buyers will have but also to get ideas about how to make your product better. An objective evaluation of the competition's strengths and weaknesses can be used to better position your product. This research should lead to conclusions regarding which elements you want to mimic and which ones should be differentiated. It also assists in understanding buyers' expectations.

The best place to look for information about competing projects is their marketing materials and their sales centers. Web sites, brochures, and sales kits provide detailed information about their offerings. Some information such as absorption rates is harder to find because of the proprietary nature of numbers. Multiple listing services available in some markets also list sale prices and days on the market for homes. Assessment offices in many cities and counties have addresses of buyers. Sales representatives from competing projects share information about how the product is selling or leasing. A visit to the sales center with well-thought-out questions will reveal who buyers are and their likes and dislikes about the project. The researcher should also look at third-party reviews (often conducted by industry experts) of the competitive landscape.

8. What are market positions, development programs, price points, absorption, and lessons learned for comparable projects? Who are their buyers?

Comparable projects (projects that have similar traits to your proposed project but are not necessarily in competitive markets) are just as critical to look at, as they may provide important lessons to be learned. Assessing the product mix, amenities, price points, and product position of comparable developments in other markets can be very instructive. For example, looking at the best beach resorts may provide useful ideas that can be applied to a mountain resort development.

Marketing materials from comparable projects are the most readily available information sources. Interviews with the project's developer or sales team may help justify why the project qualifies as comparable and what attributes are best to analyze.

9. What are the opportunities and challenges presented by the competitive and comparable projects?

If people have a choice among products, their choice is usually guided by their notion of value and their expectation of satisfaction. Along with discovering what the competitive landscape is and gathering ideas from other projects, lessons can be learned about the successes and failures of other developments. This task is critical in market research, as it can save time and money to avoid making the same mistakes the competitors made. Moreover, looking at other projects may show an opening in the market; for example, if all the competitive projects are modern high rises, perhaps more traditional, low-rise buildings would be desirable. And seeing how the projects sold can help determine whether unmet demand still exists. The researcher must accurately describe these opportunities and challenges to best meet the needs of the market.

To translate lessons learned into conclusions, the researcher must be specific about his or her findings. The most common areas to look at are competitive and comparable projects (questions 7 and 8 above). One possible source is the *ULI Development Case Studies* series (www.uli.org/casestudies), which often detail the opportunities and challenges faced and how they were addressed.

10. What conclusions can be drawn about all aspects of the projects?

Drawing conclusions is often the most challenging task, as it requires the synthesis of a large amount of data. Collecting data is relatively easy, but determining what it means and its relevance to a specific proj-

Planned to have 1,350 single- and multifamily homes at buildout, expected in 2012, Northwest Crossing is a master-planned community in the small town of Bend, Oregon, that was designed to appeal to empty nesters, retirees, and families with children. *West Bend Property Company*

ect are more difficult. In an ideal world, the data themselves lead to obvious logical conclusions, but this situation rarely happens. Thus, drawing on past experience helps one interpolate incomplete information or predict future behavior. Conclusions from the research should answer questions about:

► The market—Who are the buyers? What are their characteristics? What do they want?
► Positioning—Where should the product fit in potential buyers' minds relative to other choices?
► The development program—What is the best way to provide a product that will be in demand yet financially feasible?

- ▶ Marketing—What is the best way to get our message to buyers? How do we convey our value proposition?
- ▶ Opportunities for differentiation—Where can we stand out compared with other possible choices? What makes us special?
- ▶ Price points—How can we best capture the value we created? How should pricing be structured?
- ▶ Absorption rates—How quickly can the product be sold or leased? How should we match development time frames to this information?

ANALYZING THE DATA AND DRAWING CONCLUSIONS

Despite the fact that many real estate companies struggle because they failed to conduct the proper research to assess market opportunities, buyers' needs, competitive challenges, and internal weaknesses in their product, far too many companies still believe that organized market research is unnecessary. Simply collecting a wealth of data will not aid a developer's decision-making process, however. Data must be carefully selected and placed in a meaningful framework that links the proposed project with the market and connects the present with the future.

As this text demonstrates, project planning and decision making never stop; they are continuous processes because products, markets, the development organization, the competition, and the environment change continuously. Market research should accumulate knowledge through a sequence of analyzing market conditions, market positioning, product design, sales strategy, and market response.

Deciding whether to conduct market research internally or hire a consultant is one of the early development decisions to be made. Both approaches have advantages and disadvantages. If an internal team completes market research, existing staff can be used for no additional fees. Further, the inside team member learns the market more completely. Internal staff, however, may not have adequate research skills, may lack experience, may not have the benefit of working on similar projects over a long period of time, and may not be able to provide candid conclu-

sions. It is often difficult for someone in a company to go against assumptions or conclusions that a more senior member of the same firm has already made. An outside consultant can bring a fresh perspective and extensive experience. The right decision depends on the particular development.

However produced, market research informs the marketing strategy for the product. The marketing strategy is a detailed plan for meeting marketing objectives and should include a clear statement of the target market, measurable objectives for serving the market, a marketing budget (a critical part of the project's overall feasibility), and the marketing mix. Projects tend to be more successful when marketing people understand how the product is produced and financed and can communicate what they learn from customers to those producing and managing the project. It is the developer's job to ensure that such feedback occurs regularly throughout the development process—regardless of whether internal staff or outside consultants provide marketing.

Conclusions drawn from the market research should help identify market segments—geographically, financially, or behaviorally. Since the 1950s, developers' geographic scope and product mix have increased with the size of their companies. Now, in addition to serving a variety of geographically and functionally segmented markets, developers search for important socioeconomic and behavioral distinctions among potential customers. Research on these different factors identifies target market segments that usually consist of a distinctive combination of people, lifestyles, purchasing power, and place. Identifying new markets or niches in established markets is a crucial application of marketing research to real estate development. The underpinnings of the research into market segments include sociology and urban history—again demonstrating the interdisciplinary nature of real estate development.

Information is everywhere and fairly easy to access. The challenge is filtering it to get something useful. Kalle Lasn, founder of Adbusters, reports that more information is available in today's Sunday *New York Times* than the average person born in the Renaissance would see in an entire lifetime. The

Figure 11-1	Sources of Research Data

COMMERCIAL REAL ESTATE INFORMATION

Free market reports (international to local) from large brokerage firms:

CB Richard Ellis	www.cbre.com/
Colliers International	www.colliers.com/
Cushman & Wakefield	www.cushmanwakefield.com/
Oncor International	www.oncorintl.com/
CRESA (tenant perspective)	www.cresapartners.com/
Grubb & Ellis	www.grubb-ellis.com/

Free market reports from other sources:

Studley Report	www.studleyreport.com/
Globe Street	www.globest.com/
Society of Industrial and Office Realtors®	www.sior.com/
NAIOP	www.naiop.org

Market reports for a fee:

Torto Wheaton	www.twr.com/
REIS	www.reis.com/
PPR	www.ppr-research.com

Comparable property reports for a fee:

CoStar Group	www.costar.com/

National and regional building size/use information:

Energy Information Administration	www.eia.doe.gov

Construction costs:

RS Means	www.rsmeans.com/

RESIDENTIAL REAL ESTATE INFORMATION

National home sales data:

National Association of Realtors®	www.realtor.org/

Local home sales data (similar for other cities):

Denver Board of Realtors	www.dbrealtors.org/

New home sales:

National Association of Home Builders	www.nahb.org/
American Housing Survey	www.census.gov

RETAIL REAL ESTATE INFORMATION

International Council of Shopping Centers	www.icsc.org/
Retail Tenants (most for a fee)	www.retailtenants.com/

GENERAL INFORMATION

Globe Street	www.globest.com/
ULI	www.uli.org/
REBUZ	www.rebuz.com/
Mapquest	www.mapquest.com/
MIT Libraries	www.libraries.mit.edu

DEMOGRAPHIC INFORMATION

All demographics:

ESRI	www.esribis.com/
U.S. Census	www.census.gov/
Colorado Demography (similar for other states)	www.dlg.oem2.state.co.us/demog/demog.htm/

Employment statistics:

U.S. Bureau of Labor Statistics	www.bls.gov/

Colorado retail sales (similar for other states):

Department of Revenue	www.revenue.state.co.us/stats_dir/taxstats.html/

prospect of gathering marketing data can be daunting, but tools are available to help get to the right information quickly.

The Internet has had a significant impact on market research. What used to take weeks to find can now be done in hours, as information is available quickly and extensively. Market conditions can be found by studying updates and reports from real estate brokers. Comparable projects can be studied through their marketing materials and third-party reviews. Local, regional, national, and industry-specific news articles provide up-to-the-minute status on legal and regulatory initiatives and information about public opinion. Sites such as the U.S. Census Factfinder allow researchers to view public data from many different angles. Web sites for local municipalities provide detailed information on the local business climate and area amenities. All this information can be overwhelming, and it is important to know how to use search engines and key Web sites to find the specific information needed without having to spend too much time digging.

For example, the CoStar Group provides information on more than 1.2 million commercial properties, enhanced by photographs, floor plans, and 3-D images. It includes details such as comparable sales, buildings for sale, cap rates, income and expense data, lease expirations, and loan terms. It claims to cover "virtually every building in every major city" as well as millions of tenants, owners, and brokers using a 700-person research team. The U.S. Census Web site provides access to the American Housing Survey, which includes data by housing types that reflect year-to-year changes in homes and households.

Figure 11-1 provides a list of some of the sources for research data. It is not exhaustive, however, and these resources are always changing—companies merge, new ones form, Web sites change.

THE CONNECTION BETWEEN MARKET RESEARCH AND DEVELOPMENT IDEAS

With this general review of marketing fundamentals and the role of market research as it applies to the development process in place, we can now return to stage one. Good ideas flow from specific sources with specific knowledge of the industry and its markets. Developers need to understand themselves, their company, the competition, the other players who help build and finance projects, the regulatory and socioeconomic environment, and, most important, potential clients. Where does this knowledge come from? Practical experience, reading, and formal inquiries into specific topics are all important sources of knowledge.

When entering a new market where they have little or no experience, developers obviously assume added risk. To limit risk, developers must pay special attention to assessing their position in the marketplace as well as to the realism of their goals and objectives.

When making decisions about his Museum Towers project, Dean Stratouly had to take a look at his firm and its capacity and develop a strategy for going forward.

Watching experienced developers at work leaves the impression that real estate development is much more an art than a science. But formal research requires patient and systematic investigation to discover the facts and principles pertinent to the subject of inquiry. How does such a time-consuming process relate to generating good development ideas?

Consider the creativity of jazz musicians whose improvisations prompt critical acclaim. Their music appears spontaneous; they create it as they go. In fact, the apparent freedom and ease of play stem from years of study and practice. Through practice, they have mastered the techniques of their instrument and of jazz forms. Through study, they have come to understand the relevant principles. By reading about the principles or listening to the interpretations of great jazz players, they refine their knowledge of the medium. Thus, freedom and discipline and improvisation and technique interact. In fact, creativity and logic generally work together.

Structured research provides the discipline, fuels the logic, helps set the criteria, and to some extent even prompts the intuition by which people respond creatively to events occurring around them. Most successful real estate developers have at one time or another engaged in careful, systematic study of

MUSEUM TOWERS
Getting Started

Once I settled in Boston, I got a job with an architecture/engineering firm that had in its client pool something called a "real estate developer." Don't forget that I was coming from the nuclear power plant business, where projects cost billions of dollars and take ten to 12 years to complete and a very sophisticated group of people are involved in economics, design, and construction. So when I started dealing with our client who was the real estate developer, I was surprised at how little he knew about the design and construction process and how unsophisticated his approach was to market and location decisions.

It was all fairly ad hoc—you know, the market seems good, that's a good location, let's see if we can put something up. Very much back of the envelope. This particular developer and I struck up a relationship that grew from our firm's providing him services to my doing some consulting for him to our actually becoming partners. In 1980, we started working on a project together that went extremely well, and I decided to leave the architecture/engineering firm and go do this development stuff.

I joined with Ed Berry in 1980. Ed had two partners locally and a relationship with several guys in New York, one of whom is my current partner. I actually started in this business with a company that we called the Russia Wharf Company, because we were redeveloping a historic project that had been the site where the trade came in from Russia to Boston. We started the project the year that Russia invaded Afghanistan and Russia wasn't very popular in the U.S. I was standing on the corner of Congress Street and Atlantic Avenue in downtown Boston, ready to sprint across that street. It was a hot August day, and a big crowd of people were getting ready to make the dash. A couple of tourists noticed the Russia Wharf sign, and one said, "Look at this! The Russians are everywhere—even in Boston."

I walked into the office and said to my partner, "We've got to change the name of this Russia thing." Since we were on Congress Street, we decided to call it the Congress Group. We needed to make the decision fairly quickly, because we had just acquired our next project and we needed names for the partnerships.

In 1982, Ed and I bought out the other partners. Everything we did from 1980 to 1986 included equity participation from a group in New York. We had an agreement that all our projects would be financed with this group of individuals of high net worth, who had access to other individuals with high net worth. Then in late 1986, Ed and I split up Congress Group, and a partner in New York and I re-formed Congress Group Ventures.

continued on page 280

specific markets and property types. In addition, they have tested ideas for projects by planning, building, and leasing space. Thus, even in cases where the inception of an idea appears to be a flash of brilliance—something truly original—the idea can often be traced to the interplay of past study and analysis of widely known facts and basic principles. The new idea is usually a reworked combination of known elements. More typically, good development ideas replicate to a great extent previously tried ideas that are tailored to a particular niche.

ASKING THE GREAT "HOW COME?"

Successful development responds to the needs of space users and, to a lesser extent, to the requirements of government and citizens/neighbors. The successful projects highlighted in the profile of Shaheen Sadeghi, shows how developers effectively use information about the market and good ideas to satisfy diverse interests. Products, places, people, and capital add up to many useful areas of inquiry.

Once the developer and the marketing staff believe that they have arrived at a good choice for a proposed development, they must still ask one nagging question: How come no other developer has stumbled across this fine opportunity? Is something wrong with the idea? Why do we see the opportunity more clearly than others? Asking such skeptical questions brings added discipline to the marketing process. The question is especially important for out-of-town developers who may be less knowledgeable about local politics and market trends but more sophisticated about development in general.

As part of their research, developers must identify and recognize the competition so they can position their own product competitively to reach the target market. Better price, quality, and location are obvious attributes of competing real estate products. Only slightly less important are reputation, expertise, and financial depth.

Simply discovering a development opportunity is not enough. For the development firm to prevail, it may also need to secure the best site or come up with the best design or arrange the earliest loan commitment or obtain needed entitlements or secure the key anchor tenant or develop the best marketing plan before other developers come up with the same idea. When a developer follows a systematic marketing approach, an objective evaluation will likely reveal when the developer does have a competitive edge and is thus well advised to proceed.

▶ PROFILE

SHAHEEN SADEGHI
President, LAB Holdings Corp.
Costa Mesa, California

Shaheen Sadeghi is the founder and president of Little American Businesses, Inc., a specialized retail shopping center developer founded in 1991 in California's Orange County. Sadeghi has dubbed his two signature developments the Lab and the Camp, two "anti-malls" with unconventional design, clientele, and tenant base. Traditional malls have attempted to be all things to all people; in the process they can lose any sense of place or belonging to shoppers. Sadeghi's current two anti-malls break the mold for retail centers. Located across the street from each other, both are outdoor destinations with modern styling and central areas for gathering. They house a range of tenants: national brands like Patagonia and Urban Outfitters stand next to local yoga and health food shops. The eclectic mix attracts members of sophisticated and individualistic shoppers, regardless of age, who dislike repetitive product offerings, aesthetics, and dysfunctional traditional shopping malls.

"Cities are burned out on strip and megamalls. They want culture," says Sadeghi, "and successful retail developers have a responsibility to build the culture, not just the buildings."

FROM FASHION TO NICHE RETAIL

Sadeghi never set out to be a real estate developer. A 1977 graduate of New York's Pratt Institute, Sadeghi began his professional career as a fashion designer. After working among internationally acclaimed couturiers, he relocated to California to design for the more youth-oriented sportswear industry. After a stint with Catalina Sportswear, Sadeghi served for eight years as a designer and product manager for Jantzen, a men's watersport brand owned by VF Corporation. He later served as executive vice president of Gotcha Sportswear, supervising domestic and international product development and procurement. During his time at Jantzen and Gotcha, he traveled extensively to research and develop the sportswear companies' product lines. Sadeghi ended the fashion segment of his professional life as the president of Quiksilver, a leading manufacturer of surf- and sportswear.

It was Sadeghi's experience at Quiksilver that set the stage for the anti-mall. The company wanted to grow, but its reputation and integrity prohibited it from locating next to mainstream retailers in traditional shopping centers. The company's clientele was younger and often hostile to the corporate establishment. Generations X and Y's (born after 1964 and 1979, respectively) had greatly different taste in retail from their parents. Quiksilver risked alienating its core customers if it located in malls or sold to mass market department stores. Sadeghi supported a direct sale approach, keeping the integrity of the brand, by helping open Quiksilver shops, now known as Boardrider's Club shops, exclusively featuring the multiple Quiksilver product lines. Retail development designed to provide space for niche and lifestyle retailers was simply not being built, despite the demand.

Sadeghi seized the opportunity and left his position as president of Quiksilver in 1991. Together with his wife, Linda, also a sportswear apparel executive, they stepped into the world of commercial real estate development. The Lab, which opened in December 1992, comprises three renovated buildings on the former three-acre (1.2-hectare) site of a military equipment manufacturer. Its now more than 50,000 square feet (4,645 square meters) of retail space houses 14 tenants, two or three of which are recognizable brands that serve as anchors. The rest of the spaces were intentionally designed much smaller to accommodate local merchants. This project is the first and only known recycled retail center, reusing much of the material from the previous night goggle factory demising walls.

The second anti-mall in his portfolio is the Camp, completed in 2002. This environmentally friendly center contains such features as a percolation system that contains rain

continued on next page

runoff so no water is washed to the oceans, a grass roof, and indigenous plantings throughout. Its tenants occupy five newly constructed buildings with simple and clean designs. The 3.6-acre (1.5-hectare) site was designed with a campus-like feel along a central gathering plaza. Whereas the Lab has always targeted sophisticated urban youth, the Camp targets outdoor enthusiasts, no matter the age.

The anti-mall has garnered international press and acclaim. The Orange County *Register* has honored Sadeghi as one of the area's "Top 100 Most Influential" and as one of the California *Apparel News*'s "25 Most Influential People in Fashion." His upcoming projects will branch into mixed-use lofts and LEED-certified apartments, but his distinct style of retailing will remain the central component of his business model in the long term.

RETHINKING RETAIL

Sadeghi's early career focus on international business models and shopping preferences played an influential role in his future real estate endeavors. Through his trips abroad, Sadeghi discovered that retail shopping should be influenced by regional and local demands instead of offering a standardized national product. Culture matters in retailing, a concept that has led other developers to build lifestyle centers or outdoor, faux-mainstreet shopping districts. Although lifestyle centers attempt to inject a measure of culture into retailing, they do not always adapt to the tastes and preferences of the local clientele. Sadeghi tailors the retail district—or a segment of it—to the culture of the surrounding area.

The trendy, hip lifestyle of California's Orange County was the right location for the anti-mall concept. The county is extremely wealthy, is close to outdoor activities, and is largely suburban—and thus needs a gathering place. The anti-malls have thrived despite being located less than two miles (3.2 kilometers) from the enormous South Coast Plaza Mall, underscoring how different the shopping experience is. They have proved particularly popular with consumers who identify with subculture activities like surfing or extreme sports. Himself an extreme sports participant, Sadeghi knew that small, focused retail centers would be a strong draw for like-minded consumers.

The Lab and the Camp have found a lucrative niche in retailing. The very nature of the niche mandates constant reevaluation and change, however. As consumer tastes change, niche retail must change with it. Recruiting new tenants is endless, as the anti-mall has to swap outdated tenants for new trendy ones. It requires constant monitoring of youth culture and broader retail trends, a process the company refers to as the "anthropology of retailing." Sadeghi plans to stay ahead of the curve: "We are constantly searching for the next wave of consumers in America."

Sadeghi strongly believes the anti-mall concept can be applied outside Orange County. Retail across the United States is changing in major ways as retailers and developers try to court the dollars of the maturing Generation X and Y—and younger. Regardless of the direction retail takes, Sadeghi has the background and experience to meet the demands of any future trend.

SUMMARY

The importance of marketing principles and market research to real estate developers cannot be overemphasized. Marketing begins long before the leasing of space—and even before design of the product; it begins with the notion that any development must start with the needs and wants of customers and satisfy those needs and wants competitively.

Market research is the investigation into needs and wants (demand) and into products and competitors that might satisfy those needs and wants (supply). Although usually thought of as formal, focused, and systematic, market research for generating development ideas involves a large informal component made up of experience, observation, reading,

conversation, and interdisciplinary analysis. Prudent developers equip themselves to undertake both types of inquiry. The generation of ideas, marketing, and market research embrace both intuitive and rational elements. Successful developers are able to integrate the intuitive with the rational. Formal knowledge of marketing principles and market research enhances the use of both faculties.

This chapter has taken a broad view of marketing and market research as befits the earliest of the eight stages of the development process. Chapter 12 covers refining the project idea and sharpens the focus of the market research. Chapters 17 and 18 show how focused market research results in a formal market study, which constitutes one component of the feasibility analysis. If a developer formally commits to the project idea in stage five, then the market study (which has evolved in stages one through four) becomes a building block in the marketing plan that drives sales or leasing in stages six through eight (Chapters 20 through 23).

TERMS

▶ Absorption rate
▶ Due diligence
▶ Macrotrends
▶ Market segmentation
▶ Marketing strategy
▶ Microtrends
▶ Product positioning
▶ Psychographics
▶ SWOT analysis

REVIEW QUESTIONS

11.1 Describe Philip Kotler's attitude toward the customer and how it affects marketing principles.

11.2 What are four major differences between marketing real estate and marketing traditional products?

11.3 Identify and discuss the many users of market research in the development process.

11.4 What is societal marketing, and why are real estate developers forced to engage in it?

11.5 Discuss how a developer can determine whether a development is taking a share of the pie or making an existing pie larger.

NOTE

1. Philip Kotler, *Marketing Management,* 12th ed. (Englewood Cliffs, N.J.: Prentice-Hall, 2005).

CHAPTER 12

Stage Two: Refinement Of the Idea

Most ideas do not survive beyond stage one; they succumb to qualitative limitations such as image or they die in red ink on the back-of-the-envelope pro forma. But, occasionally, the developer's back-of-the-envelope figures show promise, and the development idea continues to generate interest. When that happens, the process moves to stage two: refinement of the idea.

This chapter elaborates on the objectives of stage two:

▶ A more detailed scanning of the environment relevant to the particular development idea;

▶ Choosing the appropriate site;

▶ Deciding what can be built on the site: initial design feasibility;

▶ Negotiating for the site;

▶ Discussing the project with other players;

▶ Segmenting the market and differentiating the product;

▶ Financial feasibility; and

▶ Risk control during stage two.

The chapter concludes with a discussion of the factors involved in deciding to move ahead with

Museum Towers and the community's involvement in the development of Elevation 314.

OBJECTIVES OF STAGE TWO

Considering the complexity of what happens in stage two, "refining the idea" is a deceptively simple phrase. The intent is clear: the developer's idea must either evolve into a particular project design associated with a specific piece of land or be abandoned before extensive resources are committed to the concept. Finding and acquiring a site and making an initial determination of legal and physical feasibility are the primary tasks in stage two. Now we move from the idea of building office space to a preliminary design for a 100,000 square-foot (9,300-square-meter), four-story office building with more specific features, functions, and benefits.

Associated with these primary physical tasks are marketing, financial, and management functions, which combine with the physical tasks to allow the developer to feel reasonably confident of the project's feasibility at the end of stage two. This comfort level permits a significant increase in "resource commitment" during stage three. During stage three, the developer must demonstrate feasibility to all participants in the development process. In stage two, however, it is the developer who must become convinced of the project's feasibility, because it is largely his funds that will be expended (that is, put at risk) during stage three to convince the other participants of the project's viability.

Several key concepts underlie site selection, the first of stage two's physical tasks.

First, finding the right site is crucial. In the United States, land typically represents anywhere from 10 to 30 percent of a project's total cost. In some markets, the cost of residential lots represents more than 50 percent of the median price for new and existing houses. Although many legally and physically feasible sites where a structure could be constructed might be available, one site will often be preferable in the eyes of prospective tenants. Location is the key to realizable rent: a better site might generate 10 percent, 20 percent, or even 50 percent more rent, depending on its particular components. Because it costs roughly the same amount to construct a given building on any of the physically possible sites (barring any unusual natural features that must be accommodated), the increase in rent is said to be attributed to the land.

The developer must exercise great care during site selection. In many urban areas, a distance of only a few blocks might separate vastly different neighborhoods. Thus, selection of the optimal site provides the greatest positive divergence between cost and value.

Further, at this point, the developer's profit motive often conflicts with the desire to control the level of financial commitment early in the development process. This dilemma leads to a Catch-22: the developer must tie up a site early, before fully demonstrating its feasibility, to capture the maximum profit on the land. Unfortunately, to do so he must spend money, increasing his financial exposure. Clearly, minimizing outlays of cash in the early stages is a prime method of controlling risk, but the developer who waits to tie up land until he can demonstrate its physical, legal, political, and economic feasibility may have to pay a premium (and others may be willing to pay more). If the developer purchases the land outright only to discover that the idea proves infeasible, he may have to resell the land at a considerably lower price. Consequently, developers typically use some type of an "option to buy" to tie up a site during stage two.

In any development undertaking, the public sector is the developer's partner in site selection. Public sector officials enforce the rules, while the body politic determines how the rules will change in the future. (The developer can try to influence change, for example, by lobbying for a rezoning.) Zoning regulations reflect the public partner's general position regarding development. Today, zoning in most jurisdictions grants a developer the right to present a proposed site plan, though it does not necessarily allow the developer to develop retail or office space. Zoning practices vary across jurisdictions. In Florida, for example, statutes require a municipality to prove the existence of adequate infrastructure before a plan for development is approved. In general, the time required today for project approval often extends the development period to the point that developers must either risk more of their own money (if it is available) or seek the equivalent of venture capital to fund the project during planning and approval.

In many areas of the United States, the influence of well-organized neighborhood groups intent on having a direct say in development in their community has grown significantly. Incurring the opposition of such groups almost certainly affects planning and approval. At a minimum, developers facing community opposition will likely experience substantial delays and significant expenses for engaging the services of additional professionals (primarily attorneys and planners) to help them work with the community.

In the process of finding a site and specifying a proposed project, developers must undertake many, if not all, of the following tasks simultaneously:

▶ Scanning the environment for significant forces—possible competitors, government jurisdictions, political power bases as described in the preceding chapter;

▶ Analyzing the market, that is, the areas or neighborhoods in the market that might offer an appropriate site;

▶ Analyzing the competition—competing development companies and competing projects—and refining the subject development to maximize its competitive position;

▶ Continuing to refine financial feasibility—periodically retesting the back-of-the-envelope numbers for financial feasibility and undertaking preliminary projections of the timing of cash flows over the development period, remembering the importance of level two feasibility;

▶ Setting market, physical, legal, and political criteria for the proposed project;

▶ Discussing the project with elected and appointed officials and city planners to ascertain their interests and any possible constraints on the project;

▶ Determining initial design requirements for the site;

▶ Analyzing possible sites to identify the site that best satisfies the criteria;

▶ Choosing the site;

▶ Negotiating for the selected site and structuring a contract (usually one that constitutes an option) to secure the site; and

▶ Controlling risk during idea refinement—testing the design's preliminary feasibility by discussing with engineers, architects, land planners, contractors, and/or financial sources a project design that fits the prospective tenant market.

Completion of these tasks culminates in a decision to move the idea to stage three (formal feasibility), rework the idea, or abandon the idea.

The process of refining the idea is complex not only because so many activities are involved in identifying the right use for the right site but also because many of the activities must be carried out simultaneously and interactively. (Figure 12-1 captures this complexity in two dimensions.) The answer to the overarching question—is this idea feasible on this site?—is conditioned on the answers to many other questions posed at about the same time but not always answerable quickly, completely, or at all. Therefore, refining the idea is typically not a straightforward process. Developers must tolerate some disorder, uncertainty, and risk as they try to bring an

idea to physical reality. Each development requires a slightly different approach. Sometimes developers press hard and commit more resources early in stage two. In other situations, developers let certain political pressures "work themselves out" before proceeding. Still, at some point, the developer must acquire control of the land, make contact with other potential members of the development team, and undertake initial project design; typically, these activities occur during stage two of the development process. Although there are often good reasons to deviate from the sequence outlined in the eight-stage model—for example, one site might be far superior to all others and the owner will sell only for cash—it is important to remember that developers frequently incur penalties through increased risk or decreased reward when tasks are completed too far out of the logical sequence of the development process.

A MORE DETAILED SCANNING OF THE ENVIRONMENT: COMPETITORS AND GOVERNMENTS

Home-grown developers know the projects, financial depth, and political clout of their competitors in the local market, but newcomers must identify the competition as well as determine what the market will want. Further, all developers—whether home-grown or newly arrived—need to understand the ways in which trends in local politics and regulations are likely to affect the viability of their projects. They need to forge relationships with city officials, politicians, and the general public. Indeed, understanding the human and organizational sides of a market may be as important to formulating successful development ideas as understanding the physical patterns of infrastructure, interactive land uses, and urban growth patterns.

Learning about competitors, governments, regulatory frameworks, and politics is an ongoing process for developers. In a dynamic real estate market, competition, regulation, and politics are all subject to continuous change. One developer might perceive an opportunity to develop apartments in one submarket only to find that an established apartment developer

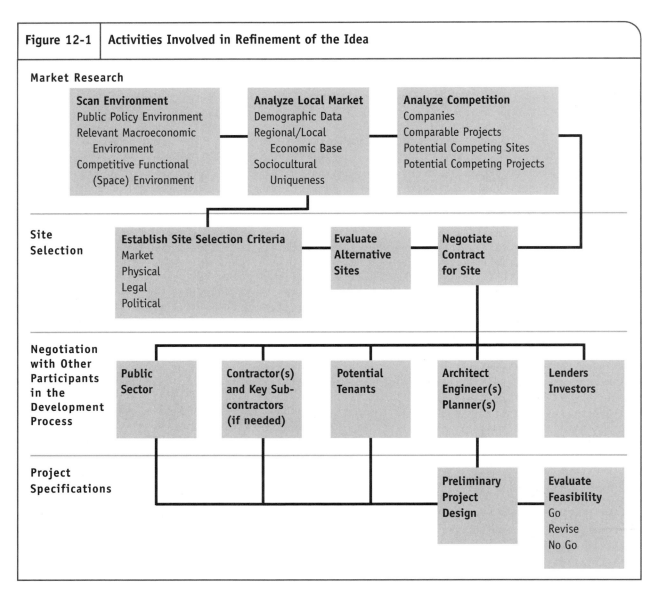

Figure 12-1 | Activities Involved in Refinement of the Idea

Market Research

Scan Environment
Public Policy Environment
Relevant Macroeconomic
   Environment
Competitive Functional
   (Space) Environment

Analyze Local Market
Demographic Data
Regional/Local
   Economic Base
Sociocultural
Uniqueness

Analyze Competition
Companies
Comparable Projects
Potential Competing Sites
Potential Competing Projects

Site Selection

Establish Site Selection Criteria
Market
Physical
Legal
Political

Evaluate Alternative Sites

Negotiate Contract for Site

Negotiation with Other Participants in the Development Process

Public Sector

Contractor(s) and Key Sub-contractors (if needed)

Potential Tenants

Architect Engineer(s) Planner(s)

Lenders Investors

Project Specifications

Preliminary Project Design

Evaluate Feasibility
Go
Revise
No Go

with solid political connections and a favorable public image is already planning such a project. Unless the new entrant can clearly distinguish its project from those of established developers, the newcomer might be well advised to find another submarket, as he is at a possible regulatory competitive disadvantage relative to the locally established developer.

A developer might find an opportunity only to confront rigid opposition from the public sector. The market for apartments might exist simply because residents successfully opposed previous project proposals. Or the local council or planning board might decide to limit apartment construction as a strategy for avoiding adverse fiscal impacts. In other instances,

constraints through building codes could represent more subtle impediments to development. Overlong project review might prevent a developer from retaining site control at an affordable price. Infrastructure might appear to be adequate, but other planned projects scheduled for completion before the developer's proposed project could consume available service capacity and lead to moratoriums on new development. And impact fees and exactions (see Chapter 13) can reduce the project's profitability.

The Culture of Urban Growth Patterns

Even harder to explain than the role of transportation, technology, immigration, and economic oppor-

A cornerstone of downtown Los Angeles's revival, the Frank Gehry–designed Walt Disney Concert Hall seats 2,265 people and is home to the Los Angeles Philharmonic. *Federico Zignani*

tunity in shaping U.S. cities is the culture or personality of a city and how that personality influences what gets built. In many cases, a city's ability to foster a climate of sensitive entrepreneurship is central to its growth.

The success story of the last century is Los Angeles. Other than its benign climate, Los Angeles can boast few natural advantages. In 1880, the city was on its way to nowhere, its ports were inferior to those of San Francisco and other western cities, and, most important, it had no water. Urban historians such as Roger Lotchin, who have studied the evolution of Los Angeles, often attribute the city's remarkable growth

to an entrepreneurial spirit among its leaders—the people who organized the California Institute of Technology, the people who brought water to Los Angeles in 1900 via the first 250-mile (403-kilometer) aqueduct, and the people responsible for the Colorado River Compact in 1928 and eventually the Hoover (now Boulder) Dam.[1] Los Angeles exists because people made it happen. And it continues to evolve because of people. Today, Los Angeles is undergoing a renaissance that few would have expected. The light-rail system has the highest number of passenger miles annually in the country and is expanding. Grand Avenue is being remade into a vibrant downtown regional center with housing, performance centers, shopping, restaurants, and more. From 1999 to 2006, nearly 6,500 housing units and 32 commercial properties were built or rehabilitated in downtown Los Angeles. And as of mid-2006, 6,600 additional housing units were under construction. In today's urban environment, cities can still make it happen, and a sense of history can enhance any developer's appreciation of the entrepreneurial opportunities awaiting discovery (see Chapters 4 through 6).

Models of urban growth provide developers with a useful framework for understanding a city's current patterns of land use and indicate to some extent the future direction of change. These theoretical urban models focus on where growth takes place and how different land uses interrelate. For several reasons, people and firms cluster in concentrations rather than spreading uniformly over the territory. One major reason is to minimize the "friction of distance." Because resources are needed to move people, goods, and information, agglomerations can reduce the costs of moving and handling goods, thereby fostering economies of scale. Because cities are agglomerations of people and activities, all cities reduce some of these transfer costs. Most large cities evolved around nodes where transportation lines met (often a break or transfer between modes of transportation such as water to rail).

People congregate to pursue economic opportunities that are less available at lower social and physical densities. The modern city has taken on economic functions that overshadow the historically important reasons of defense, religion, government, and local trade. The new telecommunications infrastructure often locates at existing transportation hubs (large cities or their newly developing suburban areas near regional airports) to profit from existing large markets, thereby strengthening existing urban centers. The Internet backbone generally has been built to connect existing population concentrations, although there are important differences in access that materially affect cities' competitiveness.

Urban Economic Theories

When searching for a site, developers can organize the sea of existing data by using three simple theories of urban economics: concentric zone theory, axial theory, and sector theory. *Concentric zone theory* holds that, assuming no variations in topography or transport corridors or limits on land supply, cities grow in concentric rings, with the most intensive uses located at the center. Over time, more competitive land uses replace less competitive uses, which move outward from the center. Generally, land values decline the farther land is located from the central, most intensive uses. The concentric zone theory held up fairly well until the early 1900s and the advent of new transit options. Consequently, it explains best the original shape of our older cities. Today it is useful as a starting point. The logic is still sound, but there are many reasons for deviation.

Axial theory came next and accounts for development along transportation corridors, which typically radiate outward in several directions from the city center. Over time, advances in transportation systems and improvements in transport technology have changed the patterns of access in many cities and, consequently, land values. Transportation routes usually form paths along which development locates as new areas become accessible. Activity still locates efficiently, but it is commuting time rather than physical distance that drives location.

Sector theory holds that because geographic features and differential access exist in the real world, waves of development tend to move outward from the center, forming wedge-shaped sectors (like a pie cut into wedge-shaped pieces) that follow the path of least resistance and lower costs. In addition, agglomeration of supporting activities influences business location.

Careful analysis of the development of particular cities over many years often reveals a sectoral pattern of growth, possibly overlain by the more recent network of circumferential highways that have created new suburban nodes. In fact, during the late 19th and early 20th centuries, Homer Hoyt (the originator of the sector theory) based his general model of urban sectors on such an evolution of U.S. cities.[2]

Atlanta is a good example of a city with no major geographic restrictions preventing concentric spread. In fact, the railroad line and its terminus established the original city center, which still serves as the

BARRY MANDEL
President, The Mandel Group
Milwaukee, Wisconsin

Milwaukee, like many other cities in the United States, is experiencing a wave of urban housing development. Much of this development is occurring along the Milwaukee River—once a center for the industrial economy. Known as the Beer Line "B" site because of its prior use as a rail yard that served the flourishing breweries, this land sat vacant for 20 years, consisting primarily of abandoned buildings, coal piles, and empty, blighted parcels. In 1999, the city concluded the planning study that presented a blueprint for the area's redevelopment. A catalyst for that revitalization was hometown developer Barry Mandel's East Pointe development. One of Milwaukee's leading developers and a pioneer in the development of Milwaukee's downtown housing market, Mandel is known for his creative uses of former industrial sites and making a real commitment to high-quality successful housing developments in downtown Milwaukee. Thanks to efforts by the city and developers like Mandel, downtown Milwaukee has experienced a revitalization, a 25 percent increase in population since 1997, and a 35 percent increase in riverfront property values.

Mandel's initial developments have spurred the downtown housing market and have led the way for other developers. By 2006, the Mandel Group had developed and constructed more than $100 million in residential and retail developments and had financed, purchased, or sold roughly $200 million of developments. With more than 1,000 units and commercial developments representing $375 million in the pipeline for downtown Milwaukee, the Mandel Group will continue to maintain its status as one of Milwaukee's premier real estate developers.

STARTING YOUR OWN BUSINESS

Mandel was raised in a family that was familiar with the real estate business, specifically, single and multifamily developments. Growing up in the business, Mandel realized his calling at an early age. He remembers as a child sitting around the table talking about real estate deals and taking drives to look at new subdivisions. Both his education and work experiences have helped him to refine his skills to become a developer. An economics major at the University of Wisconsin–Madison, Mandel diversified his educational experience by also taking business courses. Mentored by his adviser, James Graaskamp, Mandel wrote his senior thesis on housing rehabilitation in the Madison student housing market. After he earned his law degree from Georgetown University, Mandel practiced real estate, securities, and tax law in Kansas City, Missouri. He

believes that he was very fortunate because he started his business as a transition from being a partner with Trammell Crow Residential. As part of his separation from Trammell Crow Residential, he explains, he had all the key aspects that were necessary to start his own company: income, land, a handful of associates, and a financial partner to provide equity. As part of the transition, he was left with a management company that started an operating business, nine square blocks of downtown Milwaukee, and a financial partner that had participated with him when he was a partner at Trammell Crow Residential.

Starting out as a company with six employees, the Mandel Group now has more than 100 employees and has diversified its product type by adding condominiums and retail space to its original portfolio of apartment developments. With a larger company, Mandel believes, it is harder to make a significant impact with respect to one particular deal or person. He has also assumed a much more difficult management role. He believes the key traits of a good president are being a great manager and being able to understand and motivate people and think strategically. He strives to concentrate on the person and not specifically the task and to mentor each person to reach his or her highest potential. He believes it is crucial to allow flexibility to complete tasks as long as it is consistent with the core values, mission, and purpose of the company. Mandel has overcome the obstacles of Milwaukee's small market—little population growth, household growth, or job growth—to build a successful company.

KEYS TO SUCCESSFUL DEVELOPMENT

When looking for property to purchase, Mandel looks for the very best locations, which typically are infill locations that will have an advantage now and into the future. Mandel gets ideas for new developments by traveling all over the world. He does not copy ideas, but travel enables him to see what others have done in different cities and then consider how it might be done in another community.

A successful development is not just construction of a building; it is building a relationship with the neighborhood and the community. It needs to relate to the community with respect to its architecture and use and to become part of the neighborhood, not just a building with a fence around it. Mandel believes the success of a development is measured by its profitability, by whether it works in the context of its location, and by whether it gives back to the community where it

continued on next page

Barry Mandel considers East Pointe—a 1999 ULI Award for Excellence winner—one of his most successful projects. An infill development in downtown Milwaukee, the project mixes housing with stores and open space. The Mandel Group

was built. These goals can be difficult to achieve, however, because infill locations, especially in urban areas, have become technically difficult. If the site is riverfront, it probably was previously an industrial site, so it may have environmental, geotechnical, and structural issues and, in addition, with changing building codes, require much more sophisticated construction techniques.

Mandel refers to East Pointe as his most successful development. It is a 19-acre (7.7-hectare) mixed-use development in downtown Milwaukee started at a time when financial institutions and developers shied away from urban housing. It was vacant land that was cleared for a freeway, leaving a scar on the neighborhood. East Pointe mended that scar with a mix of uses: apartments, condominiums, retail space, and parks. The project's success was recognized by receipt of the 1999 ULI

Award for Excellence. Mandel believes his properties are successful because they maintain a certain quality standard throughout and because they are well planned and integrated into the neighborhood.

CHANGING DOWNTOWN MILWAUKEE

Barry Mandel's passion is building urban developments in his hometown. "We have significantly contributed to the critical mass of housing in downtown Milwaukee. We have made downtown a much better place to live," Mandel says. His developments have changed from neotraditional to modern to object architecture, which is a building that stands out from the surrounding buildings and is in itself an architectural statement. For a successful downtown resurgence, according to Mandel, a critical mass of housing, jobs, recreation, entertainment, restaurants, and public venues must all be present. Because of an increase in the number of baby boomers and their children wanting to live in the city (in separate units), the demand for housing has increased in downtown Milwaukee. Mandel suspects the reason is that boomers no longer need their large homes in the suburbs after their children leave, and they are changing their lifestyle. The age that most children marry is progressively getting older, so more young people are also looking to live in the city. With the change in architectural needs, Mandel is attempting to change the product mix to fit the demands of Generation Y. The Mandel Group's work has been consistent with the efforts of the mayor and the Department of City Development. "We have dovetailed with their vision in taking a new urbanist approach to urban development," explains Mandel.

Downtown redevelopment involves many obstacles and challenges. Mandel believes that Milwaukee faces three main challenges. First, the economy and slow job and population growth are all obstacles to development. Second, the difficult technical aspects of developing urban areas such as environmental and geotechnical issues impede development. Third, it is difficult to provide some affordable housing in urban areas, because the very nature of urban development makes it more expensive. Mandel has been able to overcome these obstacles, however, and become a successful pioneer in downtown Milwaukee's housing market. Believing that Milwaukee's downtown redevelopment is a trend that will escalate for at least the next ten to 15 years, Mandel sees a positive future for downtown Milwaukee. He sees Milwaukee expanding desir-

able areas and, over time, creating niche neighborhoods like other major U.S. cities. Areas with distinctive features such as lakefront or riverfront development will be premium locations, but Mandel believes the tide will rise for all locations.

ADVICE FOR WOULD-BE DEVELOPERS

When hiring new associates, Mandel usually looks for applicants who have a background in law, business, architecture, urban planning, or engineering. He considers being a self-starter and having an entrepreneurial spirit imperative. One important trait, he believes, is to be able to learn continuously and thus be able to see outside the box. One way to do so is to attend meetings of professional organizations such as ULI, learn from your competition, and recognize that competition comes in all shapes and sizes (especially when you deviate from the product type you are most familiar with). He believes his membership in ULI gives him perspective, knowledge, and camaraderie.

Mandel believes that major issues in the world economy and economic growth are the future obstacles to real estate development. The most important skill for a successful developer to possess is to stick with it through all business cycles. Mandel's strongest advice to students: "Don't be confused by a good market. Fundamentals are always important and no developer is infallible. Measure the risk and keep in mind risk management. Don't bargain or compromise your reputation or brand. Location is important, but good timing can be even more important."

central business district. As strong north/south corridors developed in response to the influence of the rail lines, the first upper-income residential area expanded to the north of downtown on physically attractive land. Over many years, the higher-income residential areas continued to be developed northward, forming a wedge-shaped sector moving outward to the northeast and northwest. The major industrial zone moved outward south of downtown and today extends to Hartsfield-Jackson Atlanta International Airport and the Atlanta–Fulton County stadium. The lower, flatter industrial zone also happens to be downwind of the northern residential areas. In fact, many cities with prevailing winds from northwest to southeast have evolved with higher-income residences located in the northwest and industrial uses situated in the southeast.

As the perimeter highway around Atlanta developed, new nodes of office and retail development

sprang up. Primarily north of downtown, these nodes formed the base point of new sectors that pushed Atlanta's urban fringe farther out and created a multi-centered pattern and many more new low-density "edge cities."[3]

These types of edge cities are often worthwhile investment locations because of the availability of land there, but they each have their own issues, depending on when they were developed. For example, inflexible street systems do not easily accommodate additional development.

In recent years, recognition has been growing of "edgeless cities," sprawling suburban office developments located even farther from the city center that never reach the scale, density, or cohesiveness of edge cities. This type of development grew steadily in the 1980s and 1990s, and the amount of office space in edgeless cities is now estimated to be double that of edge cities.[4]

Clearly, no simple theory can fully explain the richness of our urban environments. Still, the developer who is well grounded in models of urban growth can have a competitive advantage in finding appropriate sites for new ideas. These straightforward models make it easier to assimilate new data and forecast future land uses.

The models are also helpful for understanding transitions that result in the replacement of one land use with another. In Atlanta, for example, developers have purchased entire residential subdivisions with the express purpose of redeveloping the land more intensively for nonresidential and/or more intensive residential uses. Redevelopment of parts of existing sectors is another useful insight enjoyed by those who can organize facts by combining these and other urban economic theories. By using the theories of urban growth, developers should have a better grasp of the long-term development potential of any site they are considering.

CHOOSING THE SITE

Developers find sites in various ways. One obvious way is by keeping abreast of real estate listed for sale. More commonly, developers (or other members of the in-house development team) often study zoning and tax maps for prospective parcels, examine deed records, and then approach owners of property not listed for sale. The grapevine is yet another source: an attorney might happen to mention over lunch that a competitor is strapped for cash or that a family seeks liquidity on the passing of a generation.

Developers love real estate, are fascinated by it, and think about it most of the time. They go to professional meetings to get new ideas and more background. They regularly take time wherever they are visiting to "kick the tires." They get out, talk to people, and see sites, creating a specific database in their heads.

But besides using the intuitive, gut-level database, developers also use computerized spatial databases. Many cities and government agencies have spent the past decade developing powerful data-rich geographic information systems (GISs) that com-

bine spatial data such as road maps, parcels, and satellite imagery with real estate databases such as Assessor Parcel Information. Once delegated to GIS professionals, new tools are being developed that allow individuals with no GIS training to access the information through easy-to-use software and Web sites. Today, in fact, many people use the expression *geographic information sciences* instead of the original *systems,* as several statistical techniques have been more effectively combined with spatial mapping. These systems allow individuals to search detailed property information, retrieve a map of properties with a high-resolution satellite photo, and pull up demographic information such as income and education level for the surrounding area. Much of these data can be found quickly and easily, and much of it is available for free online. As usual, the best information may require both cash and a person trained in GIS.

Many local and regional government agencies are using GIS technology to support economic development. GIS is used to assist in identifying ideal locations for transit-oriented, mixed-use, and high-density residential developments. A properly developed GIS can assist an agency in identifying the best locations for developing these types of land use. For example, a city or developer may want to identify infill opportunities by identifying areas that meet multiple criteria—underperforming land of minimum area with the fewest built structures and within walking distance to transit, for example.

Local governments are also using these systems to determine which areas should be subject to increased densities, financial incentives, and infrastructure enhancements that will attract developers to the area. For example, New Mexico Biz Sites (www.nmbizsites.com) offers access to information that can assist developers looking for land or businesses looking to relocate or expand. The Web site application allows users to view, create, and print maps; perform site selection searches; review potential incentives; and customize and analyze demographic and business data. Some other local agencies are developing similar systems that allow posting of available land and buildings for sale or lease, creating

Figure 12-2	Major Factors in Site Selection

ZONING	ENVIRONMENTAL IMPACT
▶ Legal use of the site	▶ Adverse impacts on air, water, and noise levels
▶ Restrictions on density and layout	▶ Amount and type of waste project will generate
▶ Allowable contiguous land uses	▶ Other areas of concern, including historic districts, parks, open space, trees, wildlife habitats
▶ Likelihood of obtaining variances	
PHYSICAL FEATURES	**GOVERNMENT SERVICES**
▶ Size	▶ Police and fire service
▶ Soils	▶ Garbage collection
▶ Topography	▶ Schools, health facilities, and other government services
▶ Hydrology (floodplains, subsurface water)	▶ Impact fees, property taxes, and permit fees
UTILITIES	**LOCAL ATTITUDES**
▶ Sewage (often most constraining factor)	▶ Defensive: How powerful are antidevelopment forces?
▶ Water (important constraint in certain parts of the United States, particularly the Southeast and Southwest)	▶ Neutral: What social costs does the project impose? What are the benefits to the locality? Is the project in the public interest?
▶ Computer lines, fiber optics, cable television, telephone, gas, oil, electricity; usually readily available except in large-scale projects	▶ Offensive: What are local attitudes toward growth and how can they be used to help shape, refine, and specify the project to be built?
TRANSPORTATION (ALL MODES)	**PRICE OF THE LAND**
▶ Transportation linkages	▶ Cost of land, including site development
▶ Traffic	**DEMAND AND SUPPLY**
▶ Availability of public transportation	▶ Population growth, trends, and projection
▶ Especially important in determining access and in evaluating ingress, egress, and visibility of alternative sites	▶ Employment growth, trends, and projection
	▶ Income distribution and probable change
PARKING	▶ Existing and planned supply
▶ Usually needed on site; therefore, interacts with zoning and physical features	▶ Competitive environment, including comparison of relevant features, functions, and benefits
▶ Is structured parking warranted?	

Source: Modified from material in G. Vincent Barrett and John P. Blair, *How to Conduct and Analyze Real Estate Market and Feasibility Studies* (New York: Van Nostrand Reinhold, 1988). Used with permission.

an online marketplace for real estate combined with the local economic development department.

Two main GIS models used to forecast where development will occur and what the impacts will be are spatial interaction models and spatial diffusion models. Currently, through spatial interaction models (also known as gravity models), users have the capability of, for example, forecasting traffic flows, store patronage, and shopping center revenue as one means of assessing the desirability of a retail site. Spatial diffusion models can help predict population movements, growth or decay of neighborhoods, and development of new neighborhoods. Such models allow developers to visualize complex spatial information and anticipate future opportunities. Government agencies are using these models to develop policies and programs to support future growth.

Despite the evolution of advanced computer models, technology will not replace old-fashioned tire kicking. Developers work in an uncertain world, and to anticipate emerging trends, they will continue to rely on personal contacts—with people and sites. Further, developers recognize the advantages of imperfect information and will not readily give up any comparative advantage by freely transferring their personal insights or proprietary information to publicly available databases.

Dean Stratouly spent a lot of time thinking about the political situation in his city. For many developers, a city's political climate is as important as the

MUSEUM TOWERS
The Site

We bought the site, which was 4.11 acres (1.7 hectares), in October 1987 with the belief that Cambridge would become hot. The site was on the river but in an unattractive industrial area. You have to understand what was happening in the market at that time. This marginal piece of land was put on the market for $10.5 million. Three companies were chasing it, and the day I bought it, one of the other bidders ran into the president's office with a check for $1 million and said, "Whatever Stratouly's giving you, put this million on top of it." It was a lot of money, reflective of the market at the time, and way overpriced. Just after we bought it, the stock market took the largest percentage drop in history. Timing is everything.

This site was at the corners of Somerville, Charlestown, and Cambridge, an area known as North Point. A high-end residential product wasn't conceivable there ten years earlier. When we purchased it, the site contained a bottling company with more than 400 people working in it. The company wanted to move to a new location and so decided to maximize the investment it had made in real estate.

The city of Cambridge had put a moratorium in place that was to expire in December 1987. We agreed to voluntarily extend the moratorium while they rezoned the area, provided that we controlled the rezoning process so the city wouldn't try to kill us. The moratorium was put in place because of a neighborhood reaction against the amount of development going on in East Cambridge.

The zoning that had been there was good old-fashioned zoning designed to allow you to do what you want—big FAR (floor/area ratio), no height restrictions—it was great.

But the city began to panic after I bought the land. They figured out that we were here, other developers were over there, and then another developer tied up another piece of land and the next thing they knew, the city was confronted with the fruits of its own success, which would result in more development on the riverfront. The North Point district is made up of about 70 acres (28.5 hectares) of land with 13 different landowners, ranging from a husband/wife team to Boston & Maine Railroad. Their knowledge and understanding of real estate matters was all over the map, so we

organized all the landowners and spent one year and 17 days rezoning the full 70 acres. And it was torture. That was the balance of 1987, all of 1988, and into 1989.

The amount of fighting was unbelievable because we had to divide the land and put roads in certain areas—through buildings and properties—so we had to do land swaps. Then some people complained that their land would be less valuable, and so on. It was unbelievable. We needed a vote from the city council, but before we could get to the council, we had to get the landowners and two neighborhood groups to agree on a master plan. Then we had to get the planning board to agree on the master plan before it could be presented to the city council. Eventually we succeeded.

And then the world stopped moving. Boston's economy went into a high-speed nosedive, and everything ground to a halt.

At the same time I was working on this site, we had several other projects underway: 42 acres (17 hectares) on the Southeast Expressway in the middle of permitting a 4 million-square-foot (372,000-square-meter) biomedical research center, the American Express Building in Providence, Rhode Island, a condominium project in New York City, a ten-acre (4-hectare) parcel in Cambridge off the Massachusetts Turnpike, and a project in Connecticut.

We bought our development site. I didn't take an option because I don't believe in options when the entitlement lead time is hard to measure and potentially very long. It took us until 1991 to get our permits. Between then and 1998, when the project was completed, we hung on. We wrote a lot of checks—thousands of dollars—begged for equity, and tried to get someone to believe in our project and not take us for a ride. The area was nothing but warehouses and railroad cars. The river was basically inaccessible from the site. And we had promises from the state that it would build a park along the river. But we didn't know if those promises were real.

At the time, no one was buying land, so we couldn't have really sold it for a reasonable price. Land was like leprosy then—untouchable.

continued on page 293

appropriateness of the site and the vibrancy of the market.

The Site's Physical Characteristics

An appropriate site is not simply the gross number of square feet but, more important, the number of *buildable* square feet with the appropriate configuration. Ten acres (4 hectares) may be more usable than 40 acres (16 hectares), for example, if part of the 40 acres is located in a floodplain or if the 40 acres is configured as one long, narrow strip along the side of a mountain. Ingress and egress, infrastructure easements, and publicly mandated vision corridors can further complicate site selection.

Soils further help determine a site's potential for development; soils must exhibit adequate load-bearing capacity for the structures the developer plans to construct. In many areas, soils are not a problem, but would-be developers should not take soil conditions for granted. Even where soils are generally suitable for construction, special conditions such as abandoned landfills may create problems that even long-time residents have forgotten. Newcomers in town should talk to more than one knowledgeable local broker, builder, banker, geologist, or soils engineer about soil conditions. The developer does not want to learn after the deal is closed that poor bearing qualities (or the soil's expansion and contraction properties or the amount of rock or the underground water patterns) well known to local builders will add extra costs in excavation and foundation work. Even the oldest members of a community may be unaware of long-abandoned cemeteries that are legally protected.

Other considerations include hazardous wastes and possibly even the requirements for an archaeological survey. Unless specified otherwise in the land sale contract, it is the developer's job to see that hazardous wastes are removed (see Chapter 19), and the expense can be ruinous. No developer would assume this responsibility knowingly unless the cost of remediation could be built into the economics of the deal. In any event, many cases warrant elaborate and costly hazardous waste studies that must be conducted by environmental professionals. In stage two, however, the developer wants to hold down major cash outlays and make careful tradeoffs between expenditures and the assumption of risk. Ideally, the developer structures contracts that allow him to back out of a purchase if significant environmental contamination is discovered. Even with such contracts, however, the developer is still out of pocket the cost of the environmental study.

Some government agencies require an archaeological survey. If a survey turns up artifacts, archaeologists may then have to excavate the area by hand, possibly delaying development for months. This possibility is not as great in urban and suburban areas as the likelihood of discovering hazardous wastes, but developers should nonetheless be aware of it. Even in New York City, when an African American cemetery was discovered on a site in lower Manhattan, construction of a federal courthouse was delayed until a decision could be reached about the proper means of dealing with the remains.

Developers should also consider a site's ties to the surrounding infrastructure. How far is the site from water and sewer service? Where is major road access possible? Increasingly, developers need more than access to water and roads; they need to ascertain whether the local municipality can and will provide sufficient water and sewer infrastructure and surrounding road capacity. Where water or sewer systems are at capacity, new development may be prohibited until additional public facilities can be planned, financed, and constructed. Likewise, in more intensively used areas, a city may properly deny access from certain directions to any given site. And such denial can turn an otherwise attractive site into an infeasible one—despite high demand, ideal topography, parcel configuration, and soils.

Twenty-five years ago, developers who had access to needed municipal services could expect the city to deliver them with no upfront charge. No longer. More and more, developers absorb some or all of the costs of constructing adequate infrastructure such as roads (see Chapter 13).[5] Dean Stratouly of Museum Towers had to provide all utilities, rebuild an intersection, build roads in the development, and then give it all to the city. Today, developers must be concerned with a municipality's ability to provide essential services and their own ability to afford the related fees.

The Site's Legal Characteristics

Other considerations are permitted uses and the intensity of use. A site may be zoned for multifamily housing but at such a low number of dwelling units per acre that, given development costs, the idea is infeasible. Assuming variations in allowable densities, the price may be quoted per multifamily dwelling unit rather than price per square foot of land. Figure 12-3 provides an example of these two

Figure 12-3	Analysis of Alternative Sites Based on Permissible Density				
Alternative Site Number	Size (Acres)	Allowable Number of Dwelling Units per Acre	Price	Price per Square Foot	Price per Dwelling Unit
1	3.0	25	$561,900	$4.30	$7,492
2	2.5	18	$350,650	$3.22	$7,792
3	3.2	21	$510,175	$3.66	$7,592

methods of comparison. Prices per dwelling unit are much more tightly clustered than prices per square foot of site area.

Developers must look at current zoning for both the tract under consideration and the surrounding parcels as well as at the flexibility of current zoning and the possibility of future changes. The way developers work with the city within the existing rules or to change those rules and the way developers of competing sites influence the legal and political process are important considerations. The town or neighborhood is usually a potent force. Finding a way to get what you need, given the particular political climate, is a major way developers "add value."

Beyond zoning, subdivision regulations are usually in place not only in metropolitan areas but also in "extraterritorial jurisdictions," that is, in areas that a city may eventually annex. Subdivision regulations typically specify the quality of the needed infrastructure. Developers must meet those requirements if they plan to dedicate that infrastructure to the city, which, in turn, is expected to provide ongoing maintenance. In most cases, developers prefer to dedicate infrastructure to avoid the costs of lifetime maintenance and eventual reconstruction.

Besides subdivision regulations, building codes can present problems, particularly if building inspectors are unfamiliar with innovative designs and technologies planned for the given development. The ideal building code specifies a particular standard, not a particular material. In some cities, materials suppliers have managed to write their particular products into the building code, a practice that can be an especially difficult issue for manufactured housing whose construction takes place far from the installation site.

Highly rigid building codes restrict a developer's creativity in fitting a product that satisfies consumers' evolving needs to a particular location.

INITIAL DESIGN FEASIBILITY

In larger developments or in smaller developments on difficult sites, developers customarily have professional help in determining the feasibility of design (project layout) before committing large sums of money to site acquisition. Determining the feasibility of design requires engineering and architectural information that may include the results of soils tests, exact grade measurements, ingress and egress to the site, other site specifications, and various projected land and building configurations.

In working through design services, developers often engage outside consultants—possibly a land design professional, an architect, and an engineer—to survey the site to determine how well it satisfies development objectives. The associated financial outlays increase the developer's exposure if the project should ultimately prove infeasible. Managing this tradeoff is another big part of the developer's job.

Think of the investigation as beginning with the ground. In many areas, a soils engineer must determine the soil's load-bearing capacity and address problems related to groundwater and stormwater runoff. Changing the direction of water can be extremely expensive, but ignoring drainage can be disastrous. Soils and mechanical engineers, working as part of the development team (for a fee), often go beyond a simple determination of physical viability to suggest better ways to handle problems. The soils engineer, the architect, and sometimes the grading subcontractor work-

---

Figure 12-4 | **A Site Looking for a Use**

San Francisco's Mission Bay development covers 303 acres (123 hectares) of land in the South of Market neighborhood just outside downtown San Francisco. For more than 20 years, this well-located former rail yard has been a site searching for its highest and best use. Today a major transformation is underway to create a major mixed-use neighborhood there. Development will take place over 20 to 30 years; the total cost is expected to exceed $4 billion.

As early as 1981, community opposition and market forces dashed plans for 40-story high rises to be constructed on the site. Two votes in the late 1980s rejected proposals to bring baseball South of Market along the waterfront. Then in 1991, the owner of most of the site, Catellus Development Corporation (a spin-off of the Santa Fe Pacific Corporation), obtained approvals to go ahead with the high rises, but a weak economy stopped those plans. In 1995, Catellus sought a new scaled-down plan and began once again to seek approvals from the city. The time seemed right to try again as the South of Market neighborhood boomed with the new Museum of Modern Art, the Yerba Buena projects, the expanded convention center, the growth of restaurants and nightlife, and the opening of the Embarcadero Promenade, a 2.5-mile-long (4-kilometer), 25-foot-wide (7.6-meter) pedestrian zone built along the river after the elevated Embarcadero freeway was damaged in the Loma Prieta earthquake and ultimately torn down.

Planning of Mission Bay has been handled by a series of mayors, planning directors, redevelopment authority staff, and corporate incarnations. When the Mission Bay plan was adopted in 1998, Catellus owned nearly all the land in the area. Since then, much of the property has been sold to other developers and investors. In September 2005, Catellus was acquired by ProLogis, a publicly traded real estate investment trust, which has assumed development management responsibilities.

Plans call for the construction of $200 million in public infrastructure in Mission Bay, to be financed through special assessments and increased property taxes generated by the development. Upon completion, the right-of-way and utility improvements will be accepted for operation and maintenance by the city. The Redevelopment Agency will operate the park system, funded by annual assessments against private property in the development area.

The development program for Mission Bay includes:

► 6,000 housing units, with nearly 1,700 (28 percent) affordable for moderate-, low-, and very-low-income households. Redevelopment Agency–sponsored non-profit developers will build 1,445 of the affordable units on 16 acres (6.5 hectares) of land contributed to the agency; the remaining 225 affordable units will be included in privately developed projects.
► 6 million square feet (557,600 square meters) of office/life science/technology commercial space.
► A new University of California–San Francisco research campus containing 2.65 million square feet (246,300 square meters) of building space on 43 acres (17.4 hectares) of land donated by the developer and the city.
► 800,000 square feet (74,350 square meters) of city- and neighborhood-serving retail space.
► A 500-room hotel with up to 50,000 square feet (4,650 square meters) of retail entertainment uses.
► 49 acres (20 hectares) of public open space plus eight acres (3.2 hectares) of open space on the UCSF campus.
► A new 500-student public school.
► A new fire and police station.

The San Francisco Giants stadium, AT&T Park, is a centerpiece of the development. Built on city-leased land with $300 million in private funds (the first privately financed ballpark since the early 1960s), the park is easily accessible by foot (it is located a very short distance from the financial district) and is served by more public transportation than any other ballpark in the country. In addition, some 6,500 dedicated parking spaces as well as scattered sites throughout the neighborhood within a five- to ten-minute walk of the ballpark are available to fans.

---

ing in concert may be able to advise the developer on a better way to work with the grade of a site—from designs that use the existing grade to create a specific image to engineering solutions that permit development on difficult grades to finding more cost-efficient ways to cut, adjust, and bank the land.

Starting from the developer's initial idea of building configuration, the architect lays out an initial building footprint on the site and, given intended access points, determines whether or not the building and its associated parking can be placed on the site. The layout must honor environmental features as well as setbacks and guidelines specified in the local subdivision regulations without compromising the image the developer hopes to create. Most important, it must do it all with an eye toward how tenants will perceive the final product. Sensitivity to the natural environment and the situs at this stage can pay off with easier permitting later.

In some cases, assistance from architects, engineers, land planners, and/or subcontractors can be obtained without paying for it upfront. Large developers who generate a great deal of business can call on professionals they have previously engaged and expect some services at deferred costs. Although astute developers minimize costs and capitalize on past relationships appropriately, successful developers also know when to spend additional dollars. The developer's role is to decide which items require additional investment as a means of controlling risk and to enhance future returns.

The primary design contract is usually executed with the architect. The contract signed in stage two establishes a relationship that usually continues for the duration of the project. Figure 12-5 provides suggestions about what to expect from an architect, what not to expect, and how to select an architect.

During the process of selecting the site and designing the physical product that fits the anticipated client to the site,[6] it is wise to remember that urban land value relies more on the land's visibility and proximity to customers and services than on its inherent productivity (the soil's fertility, coal reserves, or timber stands, for example). Thus, when developers evaluate alternative sites, they focus on situs, including access to appropriate residences and related businesses, pedestrian and vehicular traffic flow, and proximity to any off-site amenities that make the site more or less attractive to prospective customers.

NEGOTIATING FOR THE SITE

At this point, the developer faces a Catch-22. Work in stage two has shown that the site is probably feasible physically, legally, and politically. Still, it has yet to be subjected to a complete feasibility study. In an effort to keep down money at risk during this venture capital–like period, the developer does not want to purchase the land. At the same time, however, the more the idea for development becomes public knowledge, the more money the current landowner is likely to ask for the land. Thus, assuming the refined idea and subsequent feasibility study may prove positive, the developer's objective is to obtain the right to buy the land at the current price without committing a great deal of money.

The most obvious solution is an option. Ideally, the developer would like to pay $1 for the right to buy the land at today's stated price at any time over the next five years. Regrettably, owners are not enthusiastic about tying up their land for a long time without significant remuneration. Thus, depending on the landowner's objectives and the current attractiveness of the site, negotiations lead to a tradeoff between the developer's desire to pay as little as possible for the option with as long a lead time as possible and the owner's desire to receive a large payment for a short option period.

An option agreement is a more complex document than first meets the eye. Even in the most straightforward transaction, the option, if exercised, becomes a contract of sale and legally drives the entire process of land purchase. Accordingly, the option must specify all necessary requirements for the transfer of title from the seller to the buyer, including any details about financing by the seller such as release clauses and subordination agreements that facilitate subsequent financing (see Chapter 7 for a discussion of different option types and structures).[7] The option almost always grants the buyer the opportunity to examine the quality of the seller's title as well as time to arrange financing, permits, and, possibly, even a zoning change. The agreement must not only specify the price and any warranties in the deed (and any possible deed restrictions) but also include escape clauses based on the results of environmental or engineering tests.

The option is a forward-looking agreement that should be as complete as possible and anticipate future actions as well as reactions to those actions. If the developer, for example, needs a rezoning to permit construction of the proposed project on the chosen site, the option agreement might contain a clause specifying that the developer has 120 days to propose the change to the town council and that the option will run until 90 days after the council's decision or one year, whichever comes first.

Figure 12-5	Working with an Architect

WHAT TO EXPECT FROM AN ARCHITECT

1. High-quality design that satisfies the owner's program.
2. Timely answers to the owner's requests and suggestions.
3. Alternative suggestions and schemes during the early phases of the project; an architectural problem never has only one solution. An open mind to requests for modifications of the project when necessary.
4. Sensitivity to and understanding of zoning and building codes, environmental issues, and other government restrictions.
5. An understanding of construction costs relating to particular types and uses of buildings.
6. Ability to interact constructively with government agencies and to understand the positions of groups opposing the project.
7. Ability to be a team player, joining and frequently meeting with owners, consultants, and others who contribute to the project.
8. Suitable graphic presentations that portray the project in its best light to government agencies and local interest groups.
9. Good (not perfect) construction documents that are well coordinated with documentation from other consultants.
10. Architectural supervision throughout the construction of the project, with field reports on each site visit; it is easier to respond to a contractor's questions on the job than to make serious corrections later.
11. Timely and accurate processing of all paperwork—change orders, bulletins, pay requests, and final certifications as required by lenders (with the wording not in conflict with what an architect is allowed to sign under professional liability insurance).

WHAT NOT TO EXPECT

1. Cut-rate fees, free services, or work on "spec"; high-quality service with the proper amount of time spent by experienced professional personnel requires proper remuneration; if a large, upfront payment is a problem for the developer, deferred payments should be an option.
2. The ability to design anything; special consultants with proper training and experience should be used for traffic, parking, interiors, graphics, landscaping, and so on.
3. A guarantee of the contractor's work; architects cannot guarantee work over which they have no control or have not put in place.
4. Work on a fixed fee before the program and final scope of the project are determined.
5. Changes by the owner without affecting the architect's fee, construction costs, and schedule.
6. Detailed, highly accurate cost estimates unless a professional cost estimator is on staff or has been retained to perform such work.

HOW TO SELECT AN ARCHITECT

1. An architect should not be hired on the basis of aesthetic competence alone. The most attractive project can be totally unsuccessful in terms of financial performance, profitability, and quality of construction.
2. An architect or the key person on staff who will manage the project should be highly experienced in the specific project type.
3. An architect should not be hired based on an extensive portfolio of renderings of unbuilt projects.
4. You should talk to the owners and/or users of other projects the architect has designed to determine the project's success and the architect's responsiveness throughout the project.
5. It is essential that the owner can relate to and respect the individual assigned to the project.
6. The owner should make sure the architect's current workload allows for the required attention to the project and its on-schedule completion.

Source: Adapted from Charles Kober, the Kober Group, Santa Ana, California.

As with all real estate contracts, the economic content of the option agreement is in theory very flexible; the developer is limited only by the extent of his imagination. In fact, the agreement might not, strictly speaking, be an option. For example, in a low-downpayment, nonrecourse purchase, the developer actually buys the property but with 95+ percent financing provided by the seller, with the seller's only recourse to the property. In economic terms, this particular arrangement differs little from paying 5 percent of the asking price for an option.

At times, it can be useful to include landowners in the development process. Sometimes landowners want to take a long-term equity position in a developed structure. At other times, when the seller owns surrounding parcels, that can be the incentive needed to encourage participation of the landowner as a financer of the development.

DISCUSSING THE PROJECT WITH OTHER PLAYERS

As we have stressed throughout this text, developers do not work in isolation. They talk to other industry professionals and community members who might be affected by the proposed development, thereby both refining the idea and initially planning its tactical implementation.

Contractors

During the project's early stages, developers need to determine how many people in the area have the expertise needed to construct the project. Some general contractors take on all types of projects; others specialize in one type of project or another. In a dynamic market, developers must also determine how many of the general contractors have the time to construct another project.

Interestingly, the business cycle affects the quality of available building tradespeople. Construction workers tend to move up the line during a boom period when ample work is available. In other words, the rough carpenter becomes a finish carpenter, the finish carpenter becomes a superintendent, and the superintendent becomes an independent general contractor. As the business cycle peaks, construction costs may escalate and quality suffer, as less-experienced people are the only ones available to do the labor.

From the perspective of marketing, contractors can outline for developers the typical functions and features as well as the quality of materials and finishes in comparable buildings in the market area. Typically, contractors also estimate the cost of construction; their input is one of the critical elements in both the informal feasibility in stage two and the formal feasibility in stage three.

Tenants

During this stage, developers begin discussions with a range of possible tenants to determine users' specific requirements and to refine the general idea of market demand established during stage one. As the idea becomes better defined and tied to a particular site, developers must begin serious discussions with likely tenants. Despite appropriate use of the market research techniques covered in the preceding chapter, they may find that the initially targeted users do not want precisely what has been proposed. Designing a project with the desired features, functions, and benefits is much more cost-effective than adding such items to a completed structure. Conversely, developers can eliminate items tenants do not want enough to justify the cost.

The focus on marketing at this stage is to tailor the product to make sure it serves customers' needs. Refining an idea (stage two) and then formally determining its feasibility are the critical links between a good idea and fully occupied space (stage eight). During stage two, the developer moves from general use to a specific project design and evolves a marketing strategy for eventual execution by the sales and leasing staff.

Property Managers

Early in the process, the developer usually begins working with a property manager knowledgeable in the particular field. This input is even more critical when a proposed project will involve extensive, ongoing services. Keeping tenants satisfied requires good management, and good management requires a building realistically designed to accommodate the targeted tenants and their day-to-day needs. Property managers can be very valuable in helping to avoid a costly design mistake and planning design features that will make the building easier to manage and/or reduce operating costs. Knowledgeable managers can advise the developer about everything from appropriate floor plans to the right tradeoff between elevator cost and speed.

Lenders

Because most developments require some type of outside financing, developers should usually contact potential lenders and investors at an early stage. A typical sequence begins with discussions with permanent lenders—institutions that might want to finance the project for the long term and are willing to take the long-term market risk or at least some portion of

In response to feedback from the community of Port Credit, just south of Toronto, Ontario, developers FRAM Building Group and Slokker Canada Corporation reduced the density of Port Credit Village—a mixed-use project consisting of a range of housing types and office and retail space—and thereby fast-tracked the project through the approvals process. *Philip Lengden*

it (see Chapters 7, 8, and 9 for a more detailed review of the process).[8] Lenders have preferences; some finance only certain types of projects, and others finance projects only in certain ways. To obtain the most advantageous and compatible source of financing, developers may rely on their knowledge of financial markets, or they may obtain assistance from a mortgage broker. Hiring a mortgage broker represents an additional expense and does not relieve the developer of the responsibility of making financial decisions. Developers must still choose the appropriate source of financing and the appropriate structure for the particular transaction.

Developers also need a lender to finance construction. The construction lender assumes the risk that the project will not be completed on time and within budget; it does not typically assume the long-term market risk (which is assumed by the permanent lender and the equity investor or investors). So long as the project is built according to plans and specifications, the construction lender generally has a "takeout" in the form of a permanent loan commitment.

At this early stage, developers seek merely an understanding of lenders' interests in the geographic area and type of project and, most important, of any specific guidelines lenders have, such as parking requirements that exceed city minimums or sprinkler systems that go beyond code requirements. By determining their interests at this stage, developers can often refine a project to increase the number of potential lenders, heighten lenders' interest, and, it is hoped, lower financing costs.

Investors

Developers might also want to discuss the project with long-term equity investors, those who take the higher-risk position over the project's expected life. In recent years, the most common long-term equity investors in real estate capital markets are "opportunity funds" (pools of capital from sophisticated investors), real estate investment trusts, pension funds, wealthy individuals, and even syndicates of less wealthy individuals. Many other long-term investors, however, such as insurance companies, major corporations, and even municipal governments, have become involved in the real estate development process at different times in the capital market cycle. By anticipating some of the equity investors' needs at an early stage, developers can refine their ideas more effectively—again with an eye to minimizing overall financing costs.

An important issue is whether to bring in equity investors at the beginning or end of the development process. Early equity investors typically want a greater portion of the project's cash flow because they assume some of the development risk, but the early involvement of equity investors reduces the risk to permanent and construction lenders, thereby lowering the cost of debt financing. Depending on a developer's financial position, the nature of the project, and lenders' demands, a developer must, at least by stage three, decide when to involve outside equity investors. Typically, the longer a developer can wait, the higher his potential profits. Just as developers can use a mortgage broker to help them determine the shape of debt financing, they can also seek outside counsel on equity investments. For larger projects, the counselor might be a national or international investment banker, for medium projects a mortgage brokerage firm, and for smaller or tax-oriented projects a local syndicator. Although specialized assistance

may increase the developer's awareness of options, it does not replace the developer's responsibility for making the final decisions.

Higher-Risk Investors

Because the development process now takes longer than ever before, many projects today involve a period that requires something resembling "venture capital" and, consequently, a class of investors distinct from traditional real estate equity investors. Developers must often command substantial upfront capital or otherwise demonstrate the ability to secure it. Money for expenditures before construction is the hardest kind of money to raise and also the most expensive. Traditionally, venture capitalists have not financed real estate development. Those who do, however, are a relatively few wealthy individuals. The other source is "opportunity funds" managed by Wall Street firms and independent investment boutiques. Note that some firms—opportunity funds and mortgage brokers, for example—are involved in multiple roles in development finance.

The Public

Possibly the most important player developers must talk to at this stage is the general public, as represented by government, neighborhood associations, and other advocacy groups. The public sector is always the developer's partner in a long-lived investment that requires substantial infrastructure. The developer must "sell" the project and its benefits to both elected and appointed public officials and to relevant citizen groups with the hope that, by the end of stage three, the public will have a favorable impression of the project.

Public officials can offer suggestions that enhance the value of the finished project and, more important, speed approval time. Just as lenders and investors exhibit different preferences and concerns, so do government officials and agencies. Developers should investigate regulators' desires and how the project might satisfy public needs in various jurisdictions. Sources of information on local policy and politics include newspapers, the municipality's master plan, elected and appointed officials, other developers working in the local market, political consultants who specialize in the local market, and public meetings where multiple groups express their opinions.

Whether as regulators or codevelopers (see Chapter 14), public officials seek to protect the public interest. Understanding the public (the development site's neighbors and the public at large) is an important aspect of market research. Although tenants rent space or buy units, the public is exposed to the physical asset created by the developer as part of the long-lived built environment. Savvy developers want to satisfy the public—or local citizens might not let developers serve their intended customers. The public is primarily concerned about the project's appearance, its fit to the land, its compatibility with surrounding land uses, its impact on the community in terms of on- and off-site costs, and its benefits, such as taxes generated, jobs created, and new amenities and services offered.

Federal Realty Investment Trust, for example, found strong proponents in city government when it went through the approvals process for its Santana Row project in San Jose, California. Working in collaboration with the planning department, it was able to find solutions to suburban zoning ordinances that did not apply to a cutting-edge project governed by new urbanist design principles. Among other things, Federal Realty obtained approvals for shared parking between uses, redefined the parameters for parks and open space to fit the project's context, and rewrote the local ordinance covering lighting, signage, and graphics. The project had a rough start—but not for the developer's lack of innovation and creativity in working with the public sector. This early collaboration, it is hoped, made working through a difficult period a bit easier (see Chapter 13).

Developing in a neighborhood with many active citizens' groups meant Russell Katz had to involve the community and local government in the development process. As a result, the plans for Elevation 314 were refined through civic involvement.

SEGMENTING THE MARKET AND DIFFERENTIATING THE PRODUCT

After introducing the project to others involved in the development process and evaluating their responses, developers must decide whether the project is worth taking to stage three, the formal determination of

---

ELEVATION 314
Involving the Community

In every project, the government is a partner, and you can never get away from the government. There were times when the government intervened and became a mediation ground. There were also times when the government was trying to do things that were unfair, and there were times when everything lined up perfectly. I was always clear with everybody about what I intended, and if I changed my mind I explained it. It's an incredible process—it can be draining but also invigorating.

The community is also a partner. You can't really get away from the community and why would you want to? The community was heavily involved in this project. The District is a city in which local communities have power and a voice—an organized voice. There are ANCs [advisory neighborhood commissions] to start with but also community groups that are self-organized and –operated, and Takoma as a neighborhood is even more organized than most.

I dealt with two community groups in Takoma that were highly organized. Then there were the neighbors.

Truly the first thing I did after having the property under contract was to make a dozen phone calls to the chairs of the local groups, to the local ANC rep, to all of the neighbors who are adjacent to the property and along the street, and to the local council member, who at that time was Adrian Fenty (he was elected mayor of Washington, D.C., in fall 2006). I would call them up and say, "I'm Russell Katz. I just bought that property that you can't miss because it's right there at the Metro. I'm not sure what I'm going to do with it, but I'll let you know how I progress. And if you hear anything good or bad, just give me a call. Here's my cell phone number." I would do this just to open a line of communication.

Farther on in the process when I would get to a point where I thought the project was starting to look like something that could be presented, I'd call up the community people who registered interest and say, "I got something I can show you."

continued on next page

ELEVATION 314 *(continued)*
Involving the Community

I'd go to meetings with Plan Takoma or Historic Takoma, and they were always very gracious. I would present a project and take questions—and they were not always gracious—but I got feedback. Some people would tell me that they wished I didn't exist, and some people would say, "I like what you are doing, but I don't know if you thought about the following alternatives. . . . " Some people would say, "I like that, but I don't like this."

I got a lot of information, and, being young and impatient, sometimes found it frustrating. But I'd always make myself shut up and take notes and never react in anger, even though sometimes people really wanted me to—because some people out there are just angry. If somebody called and said, "I want to know more. Can you come by my house on a Sunday?" I probably would have done it. I didn't have kids so it was easier.

I spent a lot of time listening to everybody. And I made it clear that I was doing this myself, that I was not some nameless, faceless corporation and that I'd listen. So the building was incredibly informed. I think four or five times we produced progress sets for the schematic design and design development, and I left copies at the library. The library is two blocks away from the project, and people

Directly across the street from the Takoma Metro station, Elevation 314 is also adjacent to the elevated railroad tracks for both CSX freight trains and the Washington Metro Red Line trains. Russell Katz

were able to go there and check the plans. Beyond going to meetings, I would just send a mass E-mail saying, "Hey, it's at the library."

Even some of the people who were the nastiest and the meanest and who didn't want me to be there at all informed the project in really beneficial ways. Site constraints and being right next to the Metro and freight train tracks created some major challenges. We had a tough time getting both fire stairs in. In an early design, one of them ended up on the front corner of the building where the clock is now. It made sense in terms of buffering sound and egress and using as little square footage as possible. I quite frankly couldn't figure out where else to put it. A particular person in the neighborhood whom I did not get along with and I still think was a lot nastier than she had to be raised hell about it. She said, "You can do better than that. When I'm walking over there from my house across the tracks I don't want to see a big empty blank thing there. I want to be welcomed as I walk under the bridge."

We ended up moving the stair tower into the building, and at the bottom floor we tucked away a little tunnel out to the street. We were able to make that whole sidewalk corner glass and retail. It's a really nice corner and that's just because somebody challenged us on it. That's just one example, and there were a lot of examples. In the end, I was really lucky, and I was brave enough to take shots because the building went through a trial by fire before it was fully designed.

I recommend this approach to any developer, although I think it's definitely got its risks. In general, the open-book policy has been, in my life, the way to go. If you're not strong enough and proud enough of what you're doing to put it out there for critical comment, then there might be a reason why. That was a profoundly informative part of the whole process, and that's government and community.

Early on we had some scares that had the potential to drastically alter our plans. As we were excavating the area for construction, we found fuel tanks on two separate occasions. There was some speculation that one of the fuel tanks serviced the CSX trains. Rather than being welded, this 20,000-gallon (75,700-liter) tank was riveted together. Although the tank did leak, the hard-packed clay in which it was buried kept the fuel from contaminating the surrounding soil. Later, we uncovered another tank that was probably used to store motor oil. Most likely this tank was part of a gas station that used to be on the site but had long since been demolished. And once again we

ELEVATION 314 *(continued)*

Involving the Community

lucked out, because that tank did not leak. Although the discoveries of these tanks slowed down the construction schedule, soil tests showed that there was no unsafe contamination and that remediation was not needed.

On another occasion, we had to reevaluate our design in relation the site's boundaries. The original plans called for the building to be built from property line to property line. When we were getting ready to prepare the construction documents, we laid out the site with pins. It was then that I realized the sidewalk was half on government property and half on my property. I just kind of assumed that the sidewalk was on the government's property. I never pulled out a tape measure to see. The way we had designed the building left the sidewalk too small. And that really stinks when you are already that far into the project. When we put the pins in, I wasn't there, but I got phone calls right away. At that point, we were already getting into construction documents. But we

had to move it back three feet (1 meter) or so, because the sidewalk wouldn't function if it weren't wide enough.

The street and the sidewalk and the way people walk along the buildings are very important. We had to revise the project to create a good streetscape. The facade reflects that, too. Typical concrete-frame construction tends to have 20 to 30 feet (6.1 to 9.1 meters) of space between columns. But I think that proportion is much better suited to car travel than foot travel. So we spent a lot of time looking at buildings in terms of walking, walking speeds, and the rhythm that you get into as you walk. Blocks can feel long or short depending on how they are broken up. In the end, we took the 25-foot (7.5-meter) space between columns and broke it in half. On Elevation 314's facade, we built columns every 12.5 feet (3.8 meters). I find that it makes it really comfortable to walk along the front of the building.

continued on page 400

feasibility. In stage three, the emotional and financial stakes go up. Before then, the developer initiates some more detailed market research. (Figure 12-6 builds on material from Chapter 11, distinguishing between market research during stages two and three.) The more thorough the research, the more precisely developers can define their market niche, reduce risk, and maximize returns. Unfortunately, high-quality research is not usually free, so developers must decide how much research is appropriate for the particular project at each stage in the development process.

While talking with other players, developers continually think about who will use the proposed space and how the general public will react to the project. They need to move from the broader idea of building apartments in Madison, Wisconsin, for example, to the narrower plan of building 225 one- and two-bedroom units in a colonial-style three-story garden apartment complex located on the northwest corner of Midvale Boulevard and Mineral Point Road targeted to single persons and couples without children earning more than $60,000 per year. How do developers accomplish this task?

They consider the features, functions, and benefits offered by the competition. In searching for the winning strategy that will capture sufficient market share at the highest price, developers move back and forth between considerations of cost and market appeal. As explained in Chapter 11, they segment demand and differentiate their own product from the competing supply. In fact, when considered in terms of market research, refining an idea can be viewed as the interactive process of segmenting the market and differentiating the product at a particular location.

In an effort to keep costs down, developers often perform much of the market research during stage two. The discussions with other professionals are only one component; other parts of the research effort include making telephone calls to see who has vacant space, driving around to inspect competing projects, delving through public records, and checking the newspaper for announcements of new projects. All this information goes into the developer's database and provides insight into the existing supply, the characteristics of space users, and unmet needs (demand).

Figure 12-6	Office Market Segmentation

STAGE TWO: REFINEMENT OF THE IDEA

▶ Analyze competing projects and developers to determine what is selling or leasing.

▶ Consider trends creating demand for more specialized uses.

▶ Consider trends changing locational requirements for key tenant groups.

▶ Define segments based on users' needs, for example, large floor plates, low rent, central city versus suburban location.

▶ Compare potential supply and development controls across spatial submarkets.

▶ Remember the goal: to capture a share of the market by differentiating the product from competitors' products and to satisfy the demand for space of a particular group of users (a market segment).

▶ Understand potential space users to target marketing and promotion.

▶ Keep an open mind: remember that a differentiated product could lead to the discovery of a new product to serve a changing market.

STAGE THREE: FEASIBILITY

▶ Forecast demand and supply to gauge overall market conditions in the metropolitan area and quantify sub-market conditions.

▶ Specifically designate the key characteristics for describing products: location, size, physical features, price, quality, age, and amenities.

▶ Relate characteristics to differences among space users to define relatively homogeneous segments of space users.

▶ Use careful assessment of supply and demand in each market segment to forecast rents, inventory, absorption, and vacancies for each segment over the next three to five years.

Adapted from: David E. Dowall, "Office Market Research: The Case for Segmentation," *Journal of Real Estate Development,* Summer 1988, pp. 34–43.

Developer Shaheen Saghedi took the concept of segmentation to a new area when he developed a special and different kind of opportunity—the "anti-mall," a seemingly radical idea based on sound market principles (see the profile in Chapter 11).

Dean Stratouly took a chance on a site in a developing but promising area. But the developer looked at many factors and potential risks and rewards before proceeding.

FINANCIAL FEASIBILITY

An ongoing function during idea refinement is translating all the collected information (completed analyses) into a framework that relates potential risks and rewards to the developer's objectives. As noted in Chapter 1, developers rarely build projects for money alone. At this point, they need to address each goal explicitly and determine how the project may need to be modified to meet that goal. Still, the big item is financial feasibility.

Developers continually revise the initial back-of-the-envelope analysis as they refine the idea. Refinement means better estimates of hard and soft costs and better projections of revenues and expenses. The pro forma does not have to be complex, but the more sophisticated and insightful it is, the better. During idea refinement, the developer should listen and talk to knowledgeable people and potential tenants, not beat a spreadsheet to death.

During stage two, financial feasibility goes a critical step beyond stage one: developers must begin estimating cash flows during the development period. Can the developer finance the project through startup? It hardly matters that the project's completed value exceeds cost if the developer cannot survive to completion. A key part of the analysis at this stage is figuring out how much startup capital is needed and where it will come from. And do not forget the concept of level two feasibility elaborated in the first section. As quarterback of the entire process, the developer is concerned not only with

MUSEUM TOWERS
Researching and Selecting Target Markets

The site is located in a "North Point Residential, Office, and Business Zoning District" or NP/PUD-6 District, also known as a planned unit development (PUD) district. This district was established to provide a transition from the industrial sector to a mixed-use area. Residential uses—as well as hotel/motel, retail, entertainment, recreational, office, industrial, transportation, and utility uses—are permitted. The property meets the requirements of the PUD except for the maximum height, which is 50 feet [15 meters]. Museum Towers obtained a special permit from the city of Cambridge in June 1989 to go up to 24 stories.

The location is somewhat isolated, but the improvements have made a big difference. If everything else—the park and infrastructure improvements—goes according to plan, the location should become more popular. This kind of revitalization is not unprecedented in the Boston area. A project at the Charlestown Navy Yard, for example, Constitution Quarters, is a luxury rental apartment constructed in a neighborhood that wasn't known as a luxury market. But that project's done well because of the quality of the building. Cambridge has two new rental developments—Church Corner and Kennedy Lofts—in the Central Square area, which isn't exactly a desirable neighborhood. But both those projects have done very well, beyond expectations.

We figured that with the apartment rent, storage unit rent, parking fees, and retail rent, the project had a potential annual income of over $12 million.

continued on page 398

whether the overall project is viable but also whether participation in the process is a financial winner for each prospective member of the development team.

RISK CONTROL DURING STAGE TWO

The method of land acquisition can itself be a means of controlling risk during stage two. Because a developer seeks to limit financial exposure before formally committing resources to a project, controlling the site through an option or a low-downpayment, nonrecourse, seller-financed purchase is one way to minimize exposure during stage two.

Any option and/or purchase agreement should ideally (from the developer's perspective) contain contingency clauses and specify that protective warranties will be included in the deed. Developers should ensure that the seller has provided all possible guarantees to the title's quality. Beyond that, the other terms of the sale (which should be included in any option) can help limit the developer's risk. One common provision, for example, stipulates that the developer will receive the downpayment and/or option amount back with no further responsibility if desired entitlements cannot be obtained.

In most real estate transactions, constructive notice to the general public takes place by recording the instrument. The first instrument executed typically is the option agreement to acquire the land. So long as it is in proper form and, in most states, notarized, it can be recorded. Recording this agreement places it in the chain of title and thus gives notice to all others of the developer's right to the land. At times, this step can be particularly helpful in reducing the possibility that a landowner will execute subsequent contracts that use the land for purposes other than the developer's intent.

Release clauses and/or subordination clauses in the option or purchase agreement are also useful techniques for controlling risk. A release clause is possible in a seller-financed mortgage. Essentially, it allows a borrower or developer to obtain a first lien on a portion of the land by paying a portion of the seller's financing note. For example, if a developer purchases 100 acres for $10,000 an acre (40.5 hectares for $24,700 per hectare), a release clause might provide that any one of ten ten-acre (4-hectare) parcels included in the overall tract could be released from the lien if the developer makes a $150,000 payment. Thus, if the developer wants to begin the development with a ten-acre (4-hectare) site and needs a first lien for the construction lender, the original purchase money mortgage (seller financing) could be removed from that ten-acre site with a payment of $150,000 as opposed to payment of the entire note for $1 million. Note that if the developer does not obtain such a clause at note origination, the seller/lender will be in position to "extract more" when the developer subsequently tries to obtain a partial release.

Subordination clauses accomplish a similar objective while providing developers with something extra. They too must be written into any option agreement so that they are subsequently included in the seller's financing. An agreement to subordinate by the seller (lender) is a promise to move from a first lien position to a second lien position under specified circumstances. For example, a seller who owns thousands of acres in a particular area and wants to encourage a particular developer to develop one site within that area might agree to subordinate its claim of financing on that one site to the bank's construction financing. Thus, when the purchase closes, the seller (lender) will have a first lien. When the developer begins construction and needs to give the construction lender a first lien, the seller then agrees to move to a second lien position. Subordination is superior from the developer's perspective because it enhances his ability to borrow money. From the construction lender's perspective, the landowner's subordinated interest looks almost like equity in that it is an investment that is paid after the bank's loan. In effect, if the landowner subordinates its claim, the land serves as collateral for the development, even though the developer has not yet paid for it. If the seller financing requires a monthly debt service payment, however, the bank will include both the debt payment it receives and the one the seller receives when determining a justified loan amount.

In addition to eliminating the uncertainties associated with a site's availability, developers can control risk by helping to ensure that a project is acceptable to the community. If developers can show from the beginning that the development plan fits or coordinates well with the city's master plan, fewer time-consuming delays are likely.

Informally presenting the project to city officials and building inspectors to elicit their responses can eliminate potential opposition later in the process. Not only do such officials become more committed to the project but, like other participants, they too make suggestions that the developer can choose to incorporate into the proposed idea. It is important to note, however, that elected officials sometimes leave office during the time required for the approval of large projects to become final. Therefore, it behooves developers to seek approvals and opinions in writing. Although documentation does not always secure a developer's position against changes in policy and rules during the process, it does help.

More and better market research is another technique for controlling risk, but, as noted earlier, it can be expensive. The best risk control technique in stage two is to keep down the invested time and dollars so that the option of stopping remains viable.

SUMMARY

Stage two in the development process involves what many people see as the real heart of real estate development, further refining the idea generated during stage one. Toward the end of stage two, the rough idea is linked to a specific site that is legally, politically, and physically capable of supporting that idea. Moreover, the developer, through a series of conversations, believes that one or more general contractors will be available to construct the project, that tenants will be interested, that lenders will want to lend money, and that appropriate equity interests can be attracted to the project.

By this time, the developer has probably decided whether the development idea is feasible. Nonetheless, a formal feasibility study is often necessary to convince other participants such as investors, lenders, tenants, and the public sector. Although 99 out of 100 ideas generated in stage one fail the back-of-the-envelope pro forma test, the pass rate is much higher in stage two. Perhaps one in ten ideas passes this stage. If the refined idea still seems feasible, the developer takes it to stage three, at which point financial and emotional commitments become much greater.

TERMS

► Axial theory
► Concentric zone theory
► Extraterritorial jurisdiction
► Floor/area ratio
► Geographic information system (GIS)
► Lien
► Market segmentation
► Option agreement
► Sector theory
► Subordination clause
► Urban economics
► Venture capital

REVIEW QUESTIONS

12.1 Describe some of the key concepts involved in site selection and how developers go about assessing potential sites.

12.2 What is the Catch-22 developers face when they find a site that meets their initial criteria but that has not yet been subjected to a thorough feasibility analysis?

12.3 What services can architects provide to developers at this stage of the development process?

12.4 What are "market segmentation" and "product differentiation"? Why are they important in the real estate development planning process?

12.5 How can developers control risk during stage two?

12.6 In Dean Stratouly's description of rezoning, the situation sounds extremely stressful and aggravating. But this is one of his first steps in a long development process. What is the impetus for him to continue the project?

12.7 Russell Katz has demonstrated that community involvement in a project can be highly beneficial. What are some ways to engage the community constructively in the development process?

NOTES

1. Roger W. Lotchin, *The Martial Metropolis: U.S. Cities in War and Peace, 1900–1970* (New York: Praeger, 1984). See also Marc A. Weiss, *The Rise of the Community Builders* (New York: Columbia Univ. Press, 1987), Chap. 4.

2. For a fuller discussion of these and other urban economic concepts, see John F. McDonald and Daniel P. McMillen, *Urban Economics and Real Estate: Theory and Policy* (Oxford, U.K.: Blackwell, 2006); Alan Rabinowitz, *Urban Economics and Land Use in America: The Transformation of Cities in the Twentieth Century* (Oxford, U.K.: Blackwell, 2004); Arthur O'Sullivan, *Urban Economics,* 5th ed. (New York: McGraw-Hill, 2002).

3. For more information about the definition and growth of edge cities, see Joel Garreau, *Edge City: Life on the New Frontier* (New York: Anchor, 1992).

4. For more information on edgeless cities, see Robert Lang, *Edgeless Cities: Exploring the Elusive Metropolis* (Washington, D.C.: Brookings Institution Press, 2003.)

5. For a good look at traffic in America, see Anthony Downs, *Still Stuck in Traffic: Coping with Peak-Hour Traffic Congestion* (Washington, D.C.: Brookings Institution, 2004); Robert T. Dunphy, *Moving beyond Gridlock* (Washington, D.C.: ULI–the Urban Land Institute, 1997); Susan Hanson and Genevieve Guiliano, eds., *The Geography of Urban Transportation,* 3rd ed. (New York: Guilford Press, 2004); and Bruce Katz and Robert Puentes, *Taking the High Road: A Metropolitan Agenda for Transportation Reform* (Washington, D.C.: Brookings Institution Press, 2005). Developers should never underestimate the potential for protest against proposed developments simply because of the traffic the developments will generate or the traffic residents think will be generated. Traffic has become a headache for most residents of urban areas.

6. See Adrienne Schmitz and Deborah L. Brett, *Real Estate Market Analysis* (Washington, D.C.: ULI–the Urban Land Institute, 2001) for a useful way of relating site selection to the process of refining the project design to fit the local market.

7. The many items likely to be specified are covered in most elementary textbooks and more completely in James Karp and Elliott Clayman, *Real Estate Law,* 6th ed. (Chicago: Dearborn, 2005); George Seidel, Robert Aalberts, and Janis Cheezem, *Real Estate Law* (Belmont, Calif.: South-Western, 2002); and Daniel Hinkel, *Practical Real Estate Law* (Clifton Park, N.Y.: Thomson Delmar Learning, 2003).

8. See William Brueggeman and Jeffrey Fisher, *Real Estate Finance and Investment* (Boston: McGraw-Hill/Irwin, 2002); Terrence M. Clauretie and G. Stacy Sirmans, *Real Estate Finance Theory and Practice* (Belmont, Calif.: South-Western, 2005); and other similar real estate finance textbooks. In addition, publications by Goldman Sachs real estate research, Lehman Brothers real estate research, Morgan Stanley, and Prudential, among others, can provide current discussions of financing terms and financial innovations.

PART V

Planning and Analysis: The Public Roles

The government is always a partner in any real estate development. Development professionals should never underestimate the importance of this relationship—whether a formal public/private partnership or simply zoning and land use policies that affect what and how development can be implemented.

Because of the importance of this issue, all of Part V is devoted to it. Chapter 13 explores the role of the public sector as it relates to zoning, land use policy, impact fees, financing infrastructure, and the like. Chapter 14 examines many varieties of partnerships that cities have formed with private entities to accomplish development and revitalization goals. Chapter 15 looks at affordable housing—what it is, why we need it, and some of the financing issues involved in its production. Even though we could have focused in depth on many different types of development, we chose affordable housing as the illustration, because the number of homeless and the number of persons living in substandard and unaffordable housing continue to increase in virtually every area of the country.

CHAPTER 13

The Roles of the Public Sector

Historically, the United States has relied on spontaneous economic forces (the "free market system" or "free enterprise") to carry out urban development. The right of private individuals to own and determine how they will use real estate has been a cherished and constitutionally protected tradition. But even in this context of private initiatives in the marketplace, the public sector has always been a strong force in establishing the rules of the development game. Government statutes and court decisions provide the legal framework for landownership and contractual understandings. Government policies and programs promote development by planning and securing the funding for supportive infrastructure. Government regulations prescribe standards to guide the character and location of private development.

Moreover, the roles of the public sector as regulator of private development and provider of needed facilities and services have been constantly evolving. In recent years, many local governments, constrained by limitations on their powers of taxation and by voters' changing attitudes toward development, have shifted much of the burden of financing infrastructure to the private sector. Some communities have imposed limits on development in response to voters' wishes to slow or even stop growth. Environmentalists and other interest groups have persuaded governments to adopt more rigorous standards and complex requirements to protect specific areas, natural features, and historic buildings. The real estate industry functions within a climate of changing public/private responsibilities and goals. Remember Jim Graaskamp's classic definition of feasibility. Both formal rules and moral responsibilities must be considered.

For that reason, developers increasingly find themselves working closely with government officials to ensure that their projects meet public objectives. In almost every local jurisdiction, developers must respond to official public plans, zoning and subdivision requirements, and other policies and regulations that affect their development plans. Increasingly, too, regional public agencies and state governments are stepping into the land development process to make additional demands on both local governments and developers. If

This chapter was written by Douglas R. Porter, president, The Growth Management Institute, Chevy Chase, Maryland.

developers are to succeed in their endeavors, they must anticipate public needs and desires for private development and seek to mesh the interests of private development with public goals and requirements.

This chapter examines the following important roles of governments as they affect the development process and the development industry:

- ▶ Regulator of private development; and
- ▶ Provider of needed public infrastructure and facilities.

These roles frequently go hand in hand, one dependent on the other. The chapter's central theme is that real estate development is a shared process in which the public and private sectors continually interact—it is hoped for their mutual benefit.

THE PUBLIC SECTOR AS REGULATOR

Developers usually first come in contact with local government regulations early in stage two of the development process, even before they acquire a site. Public/private interactions increase in frequency and intensity as proposed projects are subjected to intensive scrutiny during the approval process's leading to final permits for construction and occupancy (stages four and five). Along the way, developers must deal with public expectations for development that are framed in comprehensive plans and zoning ordinances as well as satisfy public standards and requirements for development expressed in subdivision regulations and building codes. In addition, developers may find their projects affected by growth management ordinances and provisions that can postpone or restrict development. The extent to which developers understand the regulatory process and its components can spell success or failure for their proposals.

In many communities and in many ways, public officials and agencies are intensifying their involvement in the development process. Many developers expected the real estate recession of the late 1980s and early 1990s and the property rights movement to induce local governments to ease restraints on development. Indeed, property rights groups have been partially successful in enacting state legislation

and winning some favorable court decisions. But although these events resulted in some communities' pulling back from regulatory constraints—especially rural areas eager for development—most growing communities in recent decades have strengthened rather than weakened public guidance of the development process. Many have adopted growth boundaries or policies to slow development in their jurisdiction. In local elections, voters continue to approve expenditures for purchasing and preserving open space while opposing those for improving infrastructure systems required for development. An expanding constituency of interests in many regions seems to be pressing for greater restrictions on growth and higher standards of development. Environmentalists, quality-of-life advocates, and NIMBYists of every kind have influenced public attitudes toward community development. Virtually across the nation, development is blamed for congested highways, overcrowded schools, loss of valued natural qualities, and other impacts on quality of life and fiscal stability.

These attitudes are reflected in a crop of new concepts (or restatements of past concepts) that are enlivening community discussions about appropriate forms of development. Phrases such as *smart growth, new urbanism, traditional neighborhood designs, transit-oriented development,* and *green development* are being bandied about as effective prescriptions for improving community development. Their contributions toward enlightening or confusing the issues are discussed in a later section.

The Legal Foundation for Public Regulations

State and local governments' regulation of land development is based on the police power—the requirement of government to protect the health, safety, and general welfare of citizens. The police power is not a constitutional power of the federal government except in cases of interstate commerce, land held in federal ownership, and private land subject to major federal public works such as dams and irrigation systems. Rather, the police power is reserved for the states. Most states enacted enabling legislation in the 1920s and 1930s to give local governments the police power (authority) to regulate real estate development for purposes of health, safety, and general welfare. Since then, local officials have grown accustomed to thinking of these regulatory powers as theirs by right. They believe that regulations affecting the growth and character of their communities should be determined and administered by local governments. Developers also have tended to support local control of development in the belief that state governments are too removed from the realities of development in local areas. Increasingly, however, states are moving to reassert a role in managing the development process.[1]

Courts recognize the legal rights of local governments to exercise the police power, but they are also concerned with safeguarding private property rights. The history of land use law in the United States describes the working out of an uneasy—and continuously evolving—balance between the rights of local governments to protect the public health, safety, and general welfare and the rights of individuals to unfettered enjoyment of private property. That balance has shifted over the years as courts have expanded their interpretation of "health," "safety," and "general welfare" to include aesthetic and other concerns. The courts also have tended to grant local governments wide latitude in adopting legislation under the police power. Under the doctrine of "legislative presumption of validity," the courts give great deference to regulations that are properly enacted by local governments, generally holding the regulations valid unless clearly proven otherwise. Local governments' use of the police power to regulate land development therefore has grown considerably in scope and application.

Two early U.S. Supreme Court cases, *Welch v. Swasey* in 1909 and *Hadacheck v. Sebastian* in 1915, established the right of local governments to regulate development. (All references to court cases in this chapter can be found in Figure 13-1.) A major judicial step supporting regulation of the police power occurred in 1926, when the U.S. Supreme Court, in *Euclid v. Ambler Realty,* upheld zoning as a valid form of regulation. Through countless court decisions since then, the courts have consistently upheld the right of local governments to regulate land use and development so long as they establish a legitimate

public interest and follow due process in adopting and administering regulations. Indeed, under the police power, governments may severely limit private property owners' rights to use their property. In appropriate circumstances, governments may legally curtail or prohibit development to preserve floodplains, wetlands, sand dunes, and habitats of endangered species, and they may restrict the amount or height of development to protect erodible hillsides, mountain views, access to beaches, solar access, and other public interests.

Rights to use the police power are, however, constrained by court decisions and limits self-imposed by local governments. The question of just how restrictive regulations can be continues to vex developers and public officials. If regulations are too restrictive, they may be viewed as a "taking" of private property without compensation, which is prohibited by the Constitution. Two famous U.S. Supreme Court decisions in 1987 and in 1992 sounded warnings to local governments about overly expansive use of the police power. In *Nollan v. California Coastal Commission,* the Court ruled that the commission had not established an appropriate connection between a regulation and the public interest when it required property owner Patrick Nollan to allow public access along his beach frontage to provide public views of the ocean. The Court indicated that, in future cases of this type, it would more closely scrutinize government actions to ensure that regulations were properly related to public purposes. Then, in *First English Evangelical Lutheran Church of Glendale v. County of Los Angeles,* the Court ruled that if regulations are found to be so restrictive as to constitute an effective taking of property, then the public authority may be required to compensate the owner as if it had actually taken title. (In this case, however, a state court later determined that the regulations, which prevented the rebuilding of structures destroyed by a flood in a floodplain, were not a taking.)

Two other cases further bind public restrictions on landowners' rights. In 1992, in *Lucas v. South Carolina Coastal Council,* the U.S. Supreme Court held that a taking had occurred and that damages were due because the council's regulations against

Figure 13-1	Some Important Land Use Cases

Welch v. Swasey, 214 U.S. 91 (1909). The U.S. Supreme Court upheld Boston's height restrictions within districts.

Hadacheck v. Sebastian, 239 U.S. 394 (1915). The U.S. Supreme Court upheld as a proper exercise of the police power a city ordinance that prohibited the continuation of brick manufacturing within designated areas as a nuisance to nearby residents.

Village of Euclid, Ohio v. Ambler Realty Co., 272 U.S. 365 (1926). Euclid was the first U.S. Supreme Court case to uphold zoning as a valid form of regulation of the police power.

Golden v. Planning Board of Town of Ramapo, 285 N.W.2d 291 (N.Y. 1972). This case is one of the first and most important cases upholding regulations for timing, phasing, and quotas in development generally and in Ramapo specifically, making development permits contingent on the availability of adequate public facilities.

Southern Burlington County NAACP v. Mt. Laurel Township, 336 A.2d 713 (N.J. 1975) and 456 A.2d 390 (N.J. 1983). In these two cases, the state court ruled that Mt. Laurel Township and other New Jersey municipalities must provide for development of a fair share of lower-cost housing and imposed court oversight of the process. The state court affirmed the rulings in subsequent cases, including most recently *Toll Brothers, Inc. v. West Windsor Township*, 803 A.2d 53 (N.J. 2002).

Avco Community Builders, Inc. v. South Coastal Regional Commission, 132 Cal. Rptr. 386, 553 P.2d 546 (1976). The California Supreme Court held that Avco did not have vested rights to develop a property despite having secured local approvals and expending more than $2 million. The decision led directly to the state Development Agreements Act.

Penn Central Transportation Co. v. New York City, 438 U.S. 104 (1978). The U.S. Supreme Court upheld New York City's imposition of landmark status on Grand Central Station as a justifiable regulation that required no compensation, thus preventing construction of an office building over the station.

Kaiser Aetna v. United States, 444 U.S. 164 (1979). The U.S. Supreme Court upheld the owners of a private lagoon in their claim that a taking had occurred when they were forced to allow public use of the lagoon.

Agins v. City of Tiburon, 447 U.S. 255 (1980). This case was one of a series in which the U.S. Supreme Court held that the cases were not "ripe" for a decision, usually meaning that the plaintiffs had not exhausted the administrative procedures that might have resolved their complaint before going to court.

First English Evangelical Lutheran Church of Glendale v. the County of Los Angeles, 482 U.S. 304 (1987). This decision was the first by the U.S. Supreme Court claiming that a regulatory taking of property can require compensation to the owner, even if the regulation has only a temporary effect.

Nollan v. California Coastal Commission, 483 U.S. 825 (1987). The U.S. Supreme Court ruled that the California Coastal Commission had not established an appropriate connection between a requirement for an exaction and the cited public objective for the exaction.

Lucas v. South Carolina Coastal Council, 112 S. Ct. 2886 (1992). The U.S. Supreme Court ruled that damages are due in the relatively rare situations in which a government entity deprives a landowner of "all economically beneficial uses" of the land.

Dolan v. City of Tigard, 114 S. Ct. 2309 (1994). The U.S. Supreme Court ruled that the government has the burden of justifying permit conditions requiring dedication for which the property owner is not compensated.

Tahoe-Sierra Preservation Council, Inc. v. Tahoe Regional Planning Agency, 535 U.S. 302 (2002). The U.S. Supreme Court decided that moratoriums that prohibit or otherwise reduce issuance of development permits during some period of time are well-established planning tools that do not automatically create a taking of property requiring compensation.

Kelo v. City of New London, 125 S. Ct. 2655 (2005). The U.S. Supreme Court ruled that the city of New London's use of eminent domain to take private property for the purpose of economic development satisfies the "public use" requirement of the Fifth Amendment. The Court's decision deferred to the time-honored preference given to legislative powers.

beachfront development deprived Lucas of all use of his two lots on the ocean. And in 1994, *Dolan v. City of Tigard* found that city requirements for significant setasides of property for public purposes before allowing rebuilding of a downtown store constituted a taking. The court said that such dedications should impose no more than a proportionate degree of burden on the landowner. These decisions demonstrate the necessity of governments' regulation of development following strict rules, with due caution for the rights of private property owners. Local governments can still exercise the police power to restrict development, however, as indicated by a 2002 case, *Tahoe-Sierra Preservation Council v. Tahoe Regional Planning Agency.* The *Tahoe* decision by the U.S. Supreme Court affirmed that the agency's adoption of a temporary moratorium did not effect a taking. The Court explained that takings issues depend on the particular set of factors involved in the case and should not be subject to a precise formula.[2]

A 2005 Supreme Court case, *Kelo v. City of New London,* set a new standard for the use of eminent domain and transfer of land from one private owner to another to further economic development. The city of New London, Connecticut, condemned privately owned property so that it could be used as part of a comprehensive economic redevelopment plan. The benefits that a community enjoys from economic development qualified as a permissible public use under the Fifth Amendment. Property rights activists and others have criticized the decision as a gross violation of individual rights in favor of broader community economic development goals.

The other, perhaps more widely significant, brake on governments' use of the police power is public opinion as expressed in the political arena. Many U.S. citizens own property and place great store in their rights to use it. It is not surprising, therefore, that public officials, when deciding to regulate land use and development, usually attempt to allow property owners a reasonable economic use of their property. Public officials' attitudes toward this issue, however, vary considerably from state to state. What might be considered reasonable regulation in California or Colorado might be anathema in Virginia or Texas.

Thus, local governments have a great deal of latitude in determining how to regulate development. State enabling legislation provides a starting point and court decisions erect a legal framework, but final decisions often depend on the attitudes and perspectives of the public officials making them.

The Local Regulatory Process

Cities, counties, and other local governments undertake to regulate development according to state enabling statutes and, in some cases, in conformance with home rule charters granted by the state. The mainstays of local governments' regulatory programs are comprehensive plans, zoning ordinances, subdivision regulations, and capital improvement programs. Many communities adopt additional measures to manage growth and development.

A *comprehensive plan* describes the desirable ways in which a community should develop over a ten- to 20-year time frame. A plan usually consists of written development goals and policies, supplemented by maps, that provide guidelines for local officials as they make decisions about the quality, location, and amount of development. Depending on state enabling statutes, comprehensive plans may be either merely advisory in nature or legally binding on public decisions. Comprehensive plans may also include or be supplemented by more detailed plans for specific development elements such as housing and infrastructure systems or for particular areas of importance such as central business districts and historic neighborhoods.

Zoning ordinances are the most widely used form of land use regulation. They establish a variety of districts, depicted on maps, and spell out requirements and standards for permitted uses of land and buildings, the height and size of buildings, the size of lots and yards around buildings, the supply of parking spaces, the size and type of signs and fences, and other matters in each district. When a local government adopts a zoning ordinance, every property within the government's jurisdiction is designated for a specific district, and the property's use is regulated by the ordinance provisions for that district. The ordinance also establishes procedures for changing zoning. (Figure 13-2 describes a number of special

Figure 13-2	Selected Zoning Innovations

Planned unit development. An optional procedure for project design, usually applied to a fairly large site. It allows more flexible site design than ordinary zoning by permitting options or relaxing some requirements. A PUD frequently permits a variety of housing types and sometimes other uses as well. Usually a PUD includes a plan that is implemented in phases through specific subdivision plans.

Cluster zoning. Zoning provisions that allow groups of dwellings on small lots to be located on one part of a site, thereby preserving open space and/or natural features on the remainder of the site. Minimum lot and yard sizes for the clustered development are reduced. Like PUDs, cluster site designs are subject to more detailed reviews.

Overlay zoning. A zoning district, applied over one or more other districts, that contains additional provisions for special features or conditions such as historic buildings, wetlands, steep slopes, and downtown residential uses.

Floating zones. Zoning districts and provisions for which locations are not identified until enacted for a specific project. Such zones are used to anticipate certain uses such as regional shopping centers for which locations will not be designated on the zoning map until developers apply for zoning. Floating zones usually require special review procedures.

Incentive zoning. Zoning provisions that encourage but do not require developers to provide certain amenities or qualities in their projects in return for identified benefits such as increased density or rapid processing of applications. Incentives are often used in downtown areas to gain

open space, special building features, or public art in connection with approved developments.

Flexible zoning. Zoning regulations that establish performance standards and other criteria for determining appropriate uses and site design requirements rather than prescribing specific uses and building standards. Performance provisions are rarely applied to all zoning districts but are often used for selected locations or types of uses (e.g., PUDs).

Inclusionary zoning. Zoning that requires or encourages construction of lower-income housing as a condition of a project's approval. Provisions may include density or other bonuses in return for housing commitments and may require housing on site or allow construction at another site.

Transferable (or transfer of) development rights (TDRs). A procedure that permits owners of property restricted from development to recoup some lost value by selling development rights to developers for transfer to another location where increased densities are allowed. TDRs are often used to preserve buildings of historic or architectural importance and sometimes to preserve open space or farmland.

Form-based codes. Codes written in plain English that use matrices, diagrams, and other illustrations to communicate the preferred physical character of an area. Unlike traditional zoning, which regulates land uses on a site, form-based codes regulate the building forms—the scale, mass, and relationships between buildings—on the site. They also differ from design guidelines, which are usually not enforced by municipal law.

zoning approaches that may be incorporated into local ordinances, and Figure 13-3 describes some new concepts in community planning and design that affect zoning practices.) In stage two, developers check the current zoning for properties they wish to develop as well as procedures for rezoning.

Subdivision regulations provide public control over subdivision of land into lots for sale and development. They contain requirements and standards regarding the size and shape of lots; the design and construction of streets, water and sewer lines, and other public facilities; and other concerns such as

protecting environmental features. The regulations require all subdivision developers to obtain approval of detailed plans before they can record and sell lots. (Figure 13-4 presents a typical set of requirements and procedures for subdivision plan approval.)

Capital improvement programs are adopted by local governments to provide a construction schedule for planned infrastructure improvements; they also identify the expected sources of funds to pay for the improvements. Usually updated each year for a multi-year period, the capital improvement program is a guide to when and where improvements will be made.

Figure 13-3	New Concepts in Community Planning and Design

Smart growth. General principles describing desirable qualities of new development that have been broadly accepted and supported by many public, private, and nonprofit organizations across the nation. Although lists vary, they usually include the following principles: compact multiuse development, open space conservation, expanded mobility through multiple transportation modes, enhanced livability, efficient management of infrastructure systems, and infill, redevelopment, and adaptive use in built-up areas. Some additional principles often espoused are affordable housing, regional collaboration, and streamlined regulations.

Green or sustainable development. A more comprehensive worldview of development principles, formally defined as development that meets the needs of the present without compromising the ability of future generations to meet their own needs. Development contributes to a sustainable future when it uses renewable resources such as solar energy and preserves nonrenewable resources such as environmentally sensitive landscapes, while also promoting a sound economy and social advancement.

Site designs that sustain important natural landscape and hydrologic features bordering and within developed areas and building designs that capture the benefits of renewable resources such as solar and geothermal energy, reused or manufactured materials, natural lighting, and on-site stormwater infiltration.

New urbanist or *traditional neighborhood development*. Traditional grid-style designs for neighborhoods, communities, and areas that feature relatively dense compact development and multiple uses oriented toward pedestrian-friendly streets and civic spaces, all within walking distance of each other.

Transit-oriented development (TOD). Development oriented around a transit system that is intended to encourage greater use of that system. TOD is encouraged as a means of revitalizing neighborhoods through the development of housing and commercial uses that promise to reduce transportation expenses and allow increased walking and transit trips while generating revenues for transit agencies, developers, and cities.

Figure 13-4	The Minor Subdivision Approval Process City of Walnut Creek, California

The following guidelines cover procedures for subdivisions of four or fewer lots. A subdivision is defined as the division of any improved or unimproved land for the purpose of sale, lease, or financing. A subdivision also includes the conversion of a structure to condominiums. The state Subdivision Map Act provides general regulations and procedures that local governments must follow in the regulation of subdivisions. The city also has a subdivision ordinance that provides specific city guidelines and standards for the regulation of subdivisions.

The tentative map review procedure is designed to ensure that specific features such as grades, drainage and sanitary facilities, trees, and street alignments of a subdivision conform to city regulations and policies and are arranged in the best possible manner to serve the public. The tentative map is prepared by the applicant's civil engineer.

The tentative map is evaluated for its consistency with the General Plan and zoning and the compatibility of site and public improvements with surrounding development.

Special attention is focused on the preservation of valuable natural topographic features, preservation of existing trees, and the integration of the development to existing terrain as well as the pattern of existing development.

A parcel map must be submitted to the Engineering Division after the tentative map has been approved. The parcel map is a map based on a survey showing the location of the parcels approved on the tentative map. It must be prepared by a civil engineer or licensed land surveyor in accordance with the requirements of the state Subdivision Map Act and the city subdivision ordinance. It is a legal description of the parcels created by the subdivision and is filed with the County Recorder.

How Do I Apply for a Minor Subdivision?

1. Project Consideration

Early in the consideration of a potential minor subdivision, you should carefully review the city's General Plan and

continued on next page

Figure 13-4	**The Minor Subdivision Approval Process** **City of Walnut Creek, California** *(continued)*

zoning designations for the location of the proposed sub-division. It is important that the proposed minor subdivision be consistent with the city's subdivision ordinance, zoning regulations, and the General Plan. For your convenience, these documents may be found on the city's Internet site. In addition, local utilities and other special agencies should be contacted regarding requirements for future development in the area. The process and submittal information for vesting tentative maps are very different from those for standard tentative maps.

2. Review by Staff Preliminary Review Team

You may submit a preliminary proposal to the city's preliminary review team (PRT) before the formal application. Doing so allows planning, engineering, and transportation staff to review the request and provide useful information that may save you time and expensive revisions later in the process. The city's PRT meets weekly and is intended to provide feedback on preliminary requests. PRT is a cursory review, not a comprehensive analysis of the project. It allows the staff to review the request and make comments on possible environmental concerns, General Plan and engineering requirements, traffic, layout, and design criteria. This early review and input by staff could save you possible delay and expensive plan revisions later in the process. Staff can also review the history of other development proposals on the site and review the required data and procedures to be followed throughout the process.

3. Filing the Application

You should submit the completed application to the Community Development Department. You will also be required to make an initial deposit at the time of submittal for processing the application. The final charge will be based on the actual cost of staff time required to process the application to final action and for processing the parcel map and improvement plans. A staff planner will review the materials to make sure all the required information is provided. After the project is submitted, the planning manager briefly reviews the application and assigns the project to a staff planner. The staff planner assigned to the project will be your primary contact and staff liaison throughout the process. Your application is then routed to outside agencies and city divisions that will provide input to the project. Within 30 calendar days after the applica-

tion is submitted, the staff planner assigned to the project will provide you with a Notice of Application Status indicating whether the application is complete for processing or additional information is required.

4. Environmental Review

Minor subdivisions are categorically exempt from environmental review if the following criteria are met: 1) the subdivision is in conformance with the General Plan and zoning; 2) no variances or exceptions are required; 3) all services and access to the proposed parcels are available; 4) the parcel was not involved in a division of a larger parcel in the previous two years; and 5) the parcel does not have an average slope greater than 20 percent. In the event an environmental assessment is necessary, information on timing and sequence of this process is contained in Environmental Review Procedures, which will be provided you upon request.

5. Community Development Department Review (Tentative Map)

After your application has been certified as complete, the Planning Division will analyze the tentative map for site planning, subdivision design, conformance to zoning regulations, design standards, and applicable codes. Staff will consider comments from other city divisions or departments, public agencies, and interested persons. After the Planning Division has reviewed the tentative parcel map, the application is referred to the zoning administrator, who then schedules a public hearing. Owners of land within 300 feet (91 meters) of the property that is the subject of the proposed application will be notified by mail at least ten days before the hearing. The zoning administrator may require that the public hearing be held by the Planning Commission when there is extraordinary public concern about the minor subdivision. Having considered all documents and input, the zoning administrator will either approve, conditionally approve, or deny the tentative map in accordance with the provisions of the subdivision ordinance (Section 10-1.403, Walnut Creek Municipal Code).

6. Appeals of Zoning Administrator's Action

The zoning administrator's decision is final unless an appeal is filed by any interested person. The appeal must be made within ten days after notice of the zoning admin-

Figure 13-4	**The Minor Subdivision Approval Process** **City of Walnut Creek, California** *(continued)*

istrator's decision is mailed to the applicant. A public hearing will be held before the Planning Commission, and a decision will be made either affirming, modifying, or reversing the decision of the zoning administrator. The city council hears appeals of the Planning Commission's action.

Other Required Actions

A parcel map must be submitted to the Engineering Division after the tentative map has been approved. The specific requirements for the parcel map, including those for the Subdivision Improvement Plan, are available from the city's Engineering Division and should be carefully followed to prevent delay of the project. The city engineer will approve or disapprove the parcel map along the improvement plan. If approved, the subdivider must enter into a subdivision improvement agreement and provide security to ensure completion of the improvements. The parcel map must be filed with the county recorder's office.

Following approval of the tentative map, the design review commission must review and approve final plans for the dwelling units and other structures. Information on the timing and sequence of this process is contained in Design Review Procedures.

Source: City of Walnut Creek, California, Planning Division, www.ci.walnut-creek.ca.us/planning.

From the developer's perspective, the capital improvement program provides a useful indication of longer-term plans but is typically conclusive only about infrastructure improvements that are to be funded over the next year. Developers are forced, however, to evaluate the likelihood of funding for future infrastructure beyond the "conclusive" first year.

In addition to these basic forms of regulation, various growth management techniques have gained favor with many local governments. These techniques tend to provide more direct public control over the amount, type, timing, location, and quality of development than traditional planning and zoning. Many types of growth management techniques are in use today. They range from the adoption of exacting standards for development to broad restrictions on the location or amount of allowable development. For example, suburban jurisdictions may increase minimum lot sizes, cities may adopt growth boundaries and prohibit development in environmentally sensitive areas, and some locales may limit the number of building permits they issue. The Portland, Oregon, metropolitan growth boundary has been established for decades with only minor expansions in response to growth. Howard County, Maryland, under growth pressures from the Washington, D.C., area, requires lots of three acres (1.2 hectares) or more in much of its rural area. All the municipalities in San Diego County, California, impose some type of limit on the amount of development permitted each year.

A popular regulatory technique that goes beyond traditional planning and zoning is the use of requirements for "adequate public facilities." Such regulations make development contingent on the existence of adequate capacity in the local infrastructure systems that will serve new development. Developers covered by such requirements could find their proposals grinding to a halt. In some places, developers can provide such infrastructure to move forward with development—though at a higher cost. When the service capacity problem is a congested major highway, however, developers may be forced to defer development until the government constructs more capacity. (Figure 13-5 describes some of the more common types of growth management techniques.)

Regulations adopted by local governments establish procedures that require property owners and developers to obtain zoning, building, and eventually occupancy permits. Applications must be submitted for these permits, usually with supporting documentation. If the type of development is allowed "by right," according to the permitted zoning for the property, an

Figure 13-5	Major Techniques for Managing Growth

Urban growth boundary/urban service limit. Boundaries established around a community within which the local government plans to provide public services and facilities and beyond which urban development is discouraged or prohibited. Boundaries are usually set to accommodate growth over ten to 20 years and are intended to provide more efficient services and to protect rural land and natural resources. Communities in Oregon, Florida, Colorado, Maryland, Washington, and California use urban growth boundaries extensively.

Designated development area. Similar to an urban growth boundary in that certain areas in a community are designated as urbanized, urbanizing, future urban, and/or rural, within which different policies for future development apply. Used to encourage development in an urbanizing area or redevelopment in an urbanized area.

Adequate facilities ordinance. A requirement that approvals for projects are contingent on evidence that public facilities have adequate capacity for the proposed development. When facilities are found inadequate, development is postponed, or developers may contribute funds to improve facilities.

Extraterritorial jurisdiction. Power of local governments in some states to plan and control urban development outside their boundaries until such areas can be annexed. Such controls may also be effected through intergovernmental agreements, such as between a city and a county.

Affordable housing allocation. A requirement in some states that local governments must plan to accommodate a fair share of all housing types geared to regional housing needs. Targets can then be met through various programs to encourage or mandate lower-income housing (see "inclusionary zoning" in Figure 13-2).

Growth limit. Establishment of an annual limit on the amount of permitted development, usually affecting the number of building permits issued and most often applied to residential development. Such limits require a method for allocating permits, such as a point system (see below). Limits may be adopted as either an interim or a permanent measure.

Growth moratorium. Temporary prohibition of development based on an immediate need to forestall a public health, safety, or welfare problem such as lack of sewage treatment capacity or major traffic congestion. A morato-rium may apply to one or more types of development communitywide or in a specific area. Moratoriums typically remain in effect for one to three years to allow time for the problem to be solved, but they may last for many years.

Point system. A technique for rating the quality of proposed developments by awarding points according to the degree to which projects meet stated standards and criteria. Typically, the various factors are weighted to reflect public policies. Point systems are frequently used in flexible zoning and with techniques to limit growth.

administrative official can approve the zoning permit without further action. If the proposed development is allowed only under certain conditions or requires a change in zoning, special hearings and other procedures are necessary, some of which can take months or even years. Zoning changes may also require revisions in comprehensive plans, thus extending the process even further. (Figure 13-6 illustrates typical procedures that many communities follow.)

As development regulations become more complicated, developers face many decisions about making their way through the permitting process. Frequently, to develop a marketable product or to maximize their investments, developers request changes in the adopted plans or zoning or turn to special procedures that allow alternative uses or more flexible design treatment. A request for changes or special procedures usually exposes a project to closer scrutiny by public officials and the general public and often creates opportunities for public officials to require additional contributions of amenities or infrastructure.

The use of these special "discretionary" procedures has grown in recent years. In part, this growth has occurred because public officials have discovered that they can control the size and quality of development more directly through case-by-case reviews than through written regulations. In part, developers have found regulations too restrictive and thus request

---

Figure 13-6 | **Typical Procedures for Development Approval**

This figure outlines a "generic" process used by many communities for subdivision plan review, rezoning, or comprehensive plan amendments.

Concept Phase

Developer	▶ Identifies site, defines preliminary development concept
	▶ Evaluates feasibility of concept with consultants
	▶ May test ideas with citizen groups

Preapplication Phase

Developer	▶ Prepares basic descriptions of proposed project, including location, types of uses, general densities, public facilities
	▶ Meets with public staff to discuss concept, define initial issues, determine appropriate approval procedure
Public Staff	▶ Checks conformance of proposal with official plans and regulations
	▶ May test preliminary concept with other agency staff

Application Phase

Developer	▶ Prepares reports, drawings, plans for application
Public Staff	▶ Routes application to other agencies
	▶ Meets with developer to resolve questions, problems
	▶ Initiates official notice of upcoming public hearing(s) to public, adjacent owners
Developer	▶ Prepares final plans
Public Staff	▶ Prepares final report and recommendations to public officials

Public Decision Phase

Public Officials	▶ Conduct one or more public hearings at which developer presents plans (perhaps before multiple agencies)
Public Officials, Staff, and Developer	▶ Propose modifications or conditions necessary for approval
Public Officials	▶ Approve, approve with conditions, or deny application

---

special procedures that permit greater flexibility. But special interest groups and citizens' groups have also discovered that such procedures open opportunities for participating in decisions (see Figure 13-7 for an example). Developers increasingly find that they must spend almost as much time coming to terms with neighborhood or special interest groups as with the public officials charged with project approval. In many instances, developers must employ consultants and prepare special studies to respond to questions and demands from such groups. Developers in many communities have had to become (or hire) public relations experts to have their projects approved.[3]

Depending on the circumstances, however, developers may find the results worth the effort, especially if their projects draw favorable public attention in the process. In fact, more than one developer has been able to use "required" amenities as major marketing tools. When one project in Florida was required to retain an eagle habitat, the developer's marketing materials featured the habitat as the project's centerpiece. Many developers have learned to use required stormwater retention ponds and stream buffers as natural features that add value to adjoining development. Developers who must safeguard stands of trees usually find that lots near wooded acres command higher prices.

A time may come, however, when the local regulatory process needs to be rethought and reorganized. Communities have frequently formed task groups, comprising both public and private interests, to

Figure 13-7	**The Project Approval Process:** **Santana Row** **San Jose, California**

Covering an 18-block area and including 680,000 square feet (63,200 square meters) of retail and restaurant space, 1,201 housing units, two hotels, and seven parks, Federal Realty Investment Trust's Santana Row is one of the nation's largest mixed-use projects constructed by a single developer. Modeled after another of Federal Realty's earlier developments, Bethesda Row, Santana Row is credited with bringing new life to San Jose through its tailored design. The project transformed a suburban development pattern into a high-density urban area while creating a pedestrian-friendly environment. The focus of the design was on creating a memorable main street experience. Achieving this goal, Santana Row has become widely popular. The path to success, however, was not without setbacks for the developer. The dot-com boom that was intended to fuel the high-end retail and residential leasing threatened to sink the venture after the tech market went bust. Although weathering this recessional storm, the development faced catastrophic losses resulting from a fire just one month before the scheduled grand opening in late 2002. Destroying the largest building of the development, the fire threatened to permanently cripple the project. The highly antici-pated residential units would not open their doors for another two and one-half years following the fire, but Federal Realty recovered its construction losses, lost income, and operating expenses through a $129 million insurance settlement.

Approval Process

By early 1998, the concept was submitted to the city of San Jose as a general development plan, in recognition that current zoning ordinances would have to be rewritten to accommodate a fully integrated, mixed-use urban design in a suburban setting. The specific plan was entitled in June 1998. From 1999 through 2003, numerous other major entitlements were received that supported this planned unit development.

Featuring a development type that was innovative in the San Jose market, Santana Row faced many challenges obtaining permits and approvals. Developer Federal Realty Investment Trust had to work closely with the local government to build the 18-block mixed-use retail and residential district. Federal Realty Investment Trust

Figure 13-7	**The Project Approval Process:** **Santana Row** *(continued)* **San Jose, California**

The approvals process was not without controversy. Seeing the project as a threat to their livelihood and the value of retail land, many downtown San Jose merchants and real estate interests fought against it. Balancing this negative feedback were strong proponents in city government.

The public interaction process was elaborate. Federal Realty managed the community and political efforts through the offices of two former councilmen and the mayor. Most of the attendants at public hearings were neighborhood residents, who kept up with the project through a dedicated Web site and newsletter and collaborated with Federal Realty on finding solutions to their concerns.

Several issues were tackled during the approvals process:

▶ Getting permits issued in a timely manner. Federal Realty collaborated with San Jose's planning staff to develop procedures specific to Santana Row that would facilitate decisions based on preapproved design and building standards. To expedite approvals, planning staff also assisted other city agencies involved in the permitting process.

▶ Satisfying various environmental requirements, among them relocating an endangered species of burrowing owl, moving and replanting 17 50-year-old oak trees at a cost of $30,000 per tree, and controlling outdoor lighting to prevent interference with the operations of Lick Observatory.

▶ Finding solutions to suburban zoning ordinances for a project governed by urban design principles. Among other things, Federal Realty obtained approvals for shared parking between uses, redefined the parameters for parks and open space to fit the project's context, and rewrote the local lighting, signage, and graphics ordinance.

Setbacks

Between 2001 and opening day in November 2002, Federal Realty experienced three major blows in developing Santana Row. First, the bottom dropped out of the high-tech industry around the time that construction of Phase I began. Silicon Valley's economy was hit hard: companies closed, jobs were lost, and people left the region.

Next, the terrorist attacks of September 11, 2001, cast further doubt on the country's economic vitality, crippling the travel and tourism industry, impeding retail sales, and slowing speculative business ventures.

Finally, just 30 days before the originally scheduled grand opening, a devastating $100 million, eight-alarm fire destroyed the Santana Heights building, the largest of nine on the site at that time. The nearly completed structure had covered six acres (2.4 hectares) and consisted of four floors of stores and luxury apartments above an underground garage. Thirty-six shops in various stages of construction and 242 townhouses and flats were destroyed.

Solutions were timely and pragmatic. Federal Realty faced the economic decline head on by reducing the average rent on residential units from an anticipated $3.07 per square foot to $2.05 per square foot ($33 to $22 per square meter) and by negotiating creative lease terms with retail tenants to obviate risk, such as shorter terms and kick-out plans based on sales volume. In an even more unusual move, the REIT became an investor in six restaurants to help them achieve successful, on-time openings. All remain profitable, with sales ranging between $700 and $1,000 per square foot ($7,500 and $10,760 per square meter). Insurance covered the $129 million in damages, and rebuilding began almost immediately.

update comprehensive plans and regulations and/or to review and recommend ways to "streamline" the regulations and regulatory process. Most public officials believe that involving their constituencies in these procedures will lead to wider consensus on new plans and regulations and therefore less opposition to implementing them. Thus, communities often engage

in intensive "visioning" or goal-setting exercises to describe future directions and qualities of growth based on projected trends and new understandings of desired community qualities. The results become the foundation for revising comprehensive plans and amending development regulations. In addition, task groups can review and simplify complex or overlapping requirements and lengthy, bureaucratic procedures to reduce wear and tear on both the public and private sectors in the permitting process. Design and construction standards can be brought in line with community objectives, particularly if reducing housing costs is a concern.

Chances are that reconsiderations of community goals, plans, and regulations will be partly set in motion by, and include intensive discussions of, new concepts of community planning and design that have risen to general public knowledge over the past decade. The most prominent concepts, as summarized in Figure 13-3, include smart growth, sustainable development, new urbanism, traditional neighborhood design, transit-oriented development, and green development. Because these terms have become popular as ways to describe the shape and quality of future community development, developers and builders should become familiar with them. One caution: All the terms require further definition in applying them to the particular circumstances and goals of specific communities and neighborhoods. Developers and builders should seek to be involved in such a process, which often affects the character of local comprehensive plans, zoning, and other development regulations.

Regional Regulatory Actions

Regional agencies in many metropolitan areas provide planning or other services for local governments. Although they are generally viewed as relatively unimportant players in the development process, they have often been given responsibilities for coordinating plans and financing for transportation improvements, and many administer major regional infrastructure systems for such services as water supply, wastewater treatment, regional parks, transit, and air quality monitoring. In some cases, they also may issue permits for expanding these services to serve new development. In addition, some regional agencies have worked out agreements with local governments to establish growth boundaries or otherwise affect patterns of regional development. The Denver Regional Council of Governments and the San Diego Association of Governments, for example, work with local governments to define growth objectives and

areas. Other nongovernmental regional organizations may represent important interest groups that can support or block proposed developments. Thus, developers should recognize the potential effects of regional actions on the development process in their communities.

State Regulatory Actions

Although state governments delegate most regulation of land use and development to local governments, states have always exercised some control over development. For example, states typically build most of the major highways and roads on which so much development depends. State agencies also preserve large amounts of open space in parks and conservation areas. In addition, to preserve water quality, most states regulate municipal and individual water supply and sewage treatment systems and have enacted various environmental laws that affect where and how urban development will take place. A number of states, for example, have adopted environmental protection acts similar to the federal act that requires many major projects to undergo environmental evaluations. State powers of taxation and infrastructure spending also play a significant role in community development.

In general, state agencies pursue these programs with little attention to coordination among agencies or with local governments. In the past 15 to 20 years, however, a number of states have enacted more specific statutes—in the form of growth management laws—to control urban development. The first wave of such laws appeared in the early 1970s, primarily as an outgrowth of the environmental movement. Legislatures in Vermont, Oregon, California, Florida, Colorado, Rhode Island, North Carolina, and Hawaii enacted laws that were intended to curb excesses of urban growth and to protect natural resources.

Ten years later, most of those laws were found wanting because they had either failed to achieve their objectives or had stirred up unproductive controversies. A second wave of state growth management acts began with Florida's 1985 enactment of a sweeping new law aimed at strengthening previous requirements for local planning and requiring state-

Figure 13-8	Summary of Requirements in Florida's Local Government Comprehensive Planning and Land Development Regulation Act (Adopted in 1985, Amending the 1975 Act)

All of Florida's 67 counties and 410 municipalities are required to adopt local government comprehensive plans that guide future growth and development. All comprehensive plans must conform to state goals and the requirements of the act within a specified time period, or the plan will be prepared by the regional planning body. All plans must include a capital improvement element, and no development permits shall be issued unless public facilities are adequate to serve the proposed development (a "concurrency" provision).

The coastal zone element of each plan must meet new and tougher requirements.

The state Department of Community Affairs must review and approve local plans according to rules drafted by the department and approved by the legislature.

All plans must address future land use, housing, transportation, infrastructure, coastal management, conservation, recreation and open space, intergovernmental coordination, and capital improvements.

All plans must be reviewed every five years.

Land development regulations must be adopted to implement the plan within a specified time period after the plan is approved. Citizens are afforded several opportunities to challenge decisions that may be inconsistent with the Growth Management Act.

---

level planning. Florida's law was quickly followed by actions in Vermont, Maine, Rhode Island, New Jersey, Georgia, Washington, and Maryland. All the acts set state goals for development and require local plans, state agency plans, and, in some cases, regional plans to be consistent with these goals. Requirements for consistency mean, in essence, that public plans for future development must meet the spirit and intent of state goals. In addition, most state acts require local governments to formulate follow-up programs to implement the plans. The states expect that the laws will improve the quality of development regulations and the predictability of the development approval process because all local governments are required to plan according to specified standards and procedures and are required to back up plans with solid implementation programs. (Tennessee and some other states have since adopted laws reflecting some of these features but in no sense as strong as Oregon's and Florida's laws. Figure 13-8 summarizes the requirements of Florida's growth management law.)

In the growth management states, once a local plan has been reviewed or approved by a state agency and the community has adjusted its zoning and other regulations to the new plan, development approvals

and permits proceed in a traditional manner. In Oregon, which has the most extensive experience with state growth management, builders have generally supported the law because it provides a predictable approval process for proposed developments. On the negative side, the multiple layers of plans and bureaucracies in some states may breed a sluggish and somewhat inflexible approval process that is slow to adjust to rapidly changing market conditions and/or emerging technologies.

Beginning in the mid-1990s, some states tried new strategies. Maryland, followed by a few other states, passed a law limiting state expenditures for infrastructure improvements to growth areas defined by local governments. Other states, including Pennsylvania, have encouraged local governments to follow smart growth principles in preparing comprehensive plans.

State and local regulation of development promises to become more, not less, complex and generally more restrictive. Developers, in addition to their knowledge of the physical, financial, and economic factors of development, will have to become more skillful at working with public officials and the general public to complete their projects successfully. As detailed in Chapter 16, the increased complexity and restrictiveness lengthen the early stages of the development process and often increase the amount of capital needed before traditional construction financing is available.

PUBLIC/PRIVATE ROLES IN PLANNING AND FINANCING INFRASTRUCTURE

Governments generally play a major role in planning, financing, and constructing the capital facilities that provide essential services for the general public. For several reasons, providing infrastructure for community development is viewed as a primary government function. First, many facility systems, such as roads and water and sewer lines that serve large areas and benefit many people, must be closely interrelated. Second, some public facilities and services such as schools should be made available even to people who cannot afford to pay their direct costs. Third, governments frequently expand infrastructure systems to support economic development in the community and region.

The private sector is also heavily involved in providing capital facilities. Sometimes, public facilities and services such as water supply and distribution are owned and/or operated by private companies or semipublic authorities. In addition, developers of real estate projects are usually required to plan, finance, and build roads and other infrastructure necessary to support proposed development within—and frequently outside—project sites.

Therefore, planning and financing infrastructure have traditionally been joint responsibilities shared by the public and private sectors. The particular ways those responsibilities are shared have changed over time. In recent years, for example, a greater share of the burden of designing and constructing capital facilities has been shifted to the private sector, as overall public expenditures for capital facilities have failed to keep pace with increases in either economic activity or population. Local governments, in turn, are beset with rising costs for social services and taxpayer revolts against increased taxes to pay for expanding infrastructure systems. Consequently, public officials are turning to the private sector to "make development pay for itself"—a favorite phrase in rapidly growing communities.

Public/private participation in planning and financing facilities also depends on the type of infrastructure system involved. Funds for major highways, for example, come chiefly from federal and state gasoline and other vehicle-related user taxes, whereas minor highways are usually funded from state and local tax sources, with some contributions from developers of projects adjoining the roads. Local streets are usually financed and built by developers, although local governments generally assume responsibility for maintaining them so long as they are built to the standards specified in the subdivision ordinance. In these times of fiscal restraint, public officials and developers are experimenting with many forms of public/private planning and financing of infrastructure.

It is a given that infrastructure paid for by the developer increases overall project costs. All things being equal, it reduces the likelihood that any development idea will be feasible. Things are seldom equal, however. New infrastructure may provide your development a comparative advantage. On the other hand, if you must pay for infrastructure that a competitive property in a nearby jurisdiction obtains free of charge, then your development is at a comparative disadvantage.

Sources of Public Capital Funds

Local governments obtain capital for infrastructure improvements from their annual budgets, from the issuance of municipal bonds, and from state and federal funding programs. Often several sources are combined to fund improvements. Local officials may tap annual budgets to finance construction or reconstruction of major streets, for example, but revenues earmarked for street projects also flow from fuel, motor vehicle, and other taxes and from state and federal funding programs that collect revenues from some of the same sources. Improvements in municipal water supply systems are often financed from revenue bonds repaid through user fees, although general revenues and general obligation bonds may be used instead. Local water and sewer systems within development projects

As with the development of most master-planned communities, the plans for Plum Creek in Kyle, Texas, called for infrastructure improvements to support the new community. For Plum Creek, these improvements included new roads and sidewalks, parks, jogging trails, and an elementary school. A second phase calls for the construction of a commuter rail station, scheduled to open by 2012, that will take Kyle citizens to nearby Austin. *Sam Newberg*

are generally financed and installed by developers who must sometimes pay a hookup or tap-in fee as well to help fund major improvements such as trunk lines.

For long-term investments in capital improvements, local governments often depend on funds derived from the issuance of general obligation bonds or revenue bonds. General obligation bonds are backed by the full faith and credit of the municipality and thus carry a fairly low interest rate. Revenue bonds are repaid from specified sources of revenue,

usually fees and charges for services, and carry a somewhat higher interest rate. Interest rates for both types of public bond issues are usually lower than rates for privately issued bonds, as bondholders find municipal bonds attractive because the interest income earned on the bonds is generally exempt from federal taxation. In addition, investment bankers have invented a large variety of general obligation and revenue bonds to suit various local government needs and/or the conditions of today's bond market.

Bonds are repaid from several revenue sources. For many years, the basic source was property taxes, but by the mid-1980s, property taxes had dropped to less than half (47 percent) of all revenues collected from local sources, and their decline as a share of all local revenues continues today. In place of property taxes, sales and income taxes and various types of excise taxes, fees, and charges have become more significant. Excise taxes or taxes on specific types of uses or activities, such as those on aircraft landings and hotel rooms, help fund airport improvements and convention centers. User fees and charges are much favored sources of revenue for many capital facilities because consumers pay them for services rendered. Many communities now rely on a variety of fees and charges, including landfill charges, fees for use of recreation areas, automobile license fees, and public parking charges. In addition, especially for large-scale systems such as transit and regional parks, communities often earmark increases in sales taxes to pay for improvements.

Impact Fees and Exactions

One type of fee that has become familiar to developers in many communities is the impact fee. (Sometimes other terms are used such as "systems development charges" and "development impact fees.") Impact fees are one form of a broad spectrum of developer contributions called *exactions* that require developers to contribute to the provision of public facilities related to their developments. Contributions may include dedication of land to the public sector, construction of facilities, or payment of fees to be used for the construction of public facilities. The importance of this financing approach has increased over the past few decades as more local governments turn to the private sector to fund infrastructure improvements.

Often, subdivision regulations require developers to fund, build, and dedicate for public use the basic facilities required for residents and tenants of a new development, such as local streets, sewer and water lines, drainage facilities, and parks and recreational facilities. Many jurisdictions also require developers to fund selected improvements to major streets within or at the borders of their projects or at nearby intersections. In addition, it is not unusual for subdivision ordinances to require developers to provide drainage improvements in the general area of the proposed project and to reserve sites for schools. Such requirements usually include standards for determining the appropriate size and character of the facilities.

More and more communities are imposing impact fees because they help pay for project-related facilities located beyond the bounds of development projects. For example, developers often must pay hookup or tap-in fees to connect their projects to water and sewer systems; such fees are used to improve trunk lines, pumping stations, treatment plants, and the like outside the project site. Impact fees also pay for large parks and recreational areas that serve residents of many developments, or they may be levied to help fund major highway sections and interchanges, drainage systems, schools, and many other types of facilities. The ordinances that impose such fees normally spell out methods for calculating them, thereby permitting developers to determine their expected payments in advance. Most communities allow developers to build facilities directly to offset required fees.

Impact fees can range from a few hundred dollars to many thousands of dollars. Clancy Mullen, of Duncan Associates, conducts an annual survey of impact fees across the nation (see www.impactfees.com). For example, for the 206 local jurisdictions outside California, fees in 2000 averaged $5,361 for single-family homes and $3,204 for multifamily units, including all types of facilities for which fees were demanded. Average fees for other types of development ranged from $1,445 per 1,000 square feet (93 square meters) of industrial space to $3,159 per 1,000 square feet of retail space. Most localities charged fees for roads and schools; half charged fees for water and sewer facilities; less than 40 percent charged fees for drainage, parks, libraries, fire and police, general government, and other facilities. Averages in rapidly growing states such as Florida, Arizona, and Maryland tended to be higher.

Average fees charged by California jurisdictions are about 40 percent higher than the national averages, in part the result of higher development costs and in part the result of state restrictions on local sources of infrastructure funding such as those imposed by Proposition 13. Mullen's survey shows that total fees for single-family homes average $8,479 in California compared with $6,106 in states outside California. Total fees of $20,000 and more are not uncommon in California communities, and some combined fees in that state's jurisdictions reach more than $60,000 per home.

Although exactions and fees may be specified in regulations, many jurisdictions also negotiate with developers to exact other contributions. Such exactions become possible when developers request a rezoning or the use of special procedures such as planned unit developments that require approval by a board or legislative body. Public officials (and neighborhood groups) often find that negotiations present an excellent opportunity for requesting additional contributions from developers. Legally, developers are obligated to offer only facilities and improvements that primarily benefit their developments, but developers pressed to move forward with a project often agree to other contributions as well, including such offerings as scholarships for neighborhood youths and relandscaping of neighborhood parks.

Fees and exactions raise three major issues that deserve consideration: legal constraints, equity, and administrative concerns.

Legal Constraints

The extent to which local governments can demand contributions from developers, and for what purposes, have generated a considerable amount of litigation in state and federal courts (some of the major cases are summarized in Figure 13-1). Three constitutional guarantees—just compensation for taking property, equal protection under the law, and due process—limit local governments' powers to require exactions. Exactions must be clearly related to a public purpose, they must be applied equally to all types of development and not have an exclusionary effect, and they must not be imposed in arbitrary and capricious ways. Under the police power that allows local governments to regulate land development, exactions must be necessary for protecting health, safety, and public welfare.

The general test, applicable in virtually all states, is that exactions should bear a "rational nexus" to a development's impacts on local public facilities. A local gov-

ernment may, for example, require a developer to improve a certain road intersection if the developer's project will generate enough traffic to warrant the improvement. The local government cannot, however, legitimately require developers to pay for improvements to distant intersections that will seldom serve traffic generated by the developer's project.

The legal foundation for impact fees is more complicated than for other forms of exactions. Fees must be allowable under the police powers granted by the state to the local government rather than defined as a form of tax for which specific state authorization is usually required. Calculation and administration of impact fees must meet stiffer criteria than for typical tax revenues. To avoid double taxation, fee amounts should take into account regular taxes that property owners will pay for public improvements and must not include funds needed to correct existing deficiencies (for which existing residents are responsible). Local governments must expend collected fees within a reasonable time for facilities that will benefit the developments that paid the fees.

Equity Considerations

Exactions raise some issues about who should pay for infrastructure improvements. At one time, it was assumed that the general community should be responsible for funding major infrastructure systems, while developers should be primarily responsible for facilities needed on their development sites. Developers point out that past generations of residents benefited from wide public sharing of infrastructure costs and that many citizens besides those in their projects, including future generations of users, benefit from improvements. But urged by taxpayers, public officials are increasingly concerned with ensuring that developers contribute to overcoming any adverse impacts of new development on the capacity of the community's public facilities.

Another issue concerns government services financed on the basis of ability to pay: that is, people who earn more should pay more. Elementary and secondary education, for example, is normally considered important enough to society as a whole that it is financed largely by property tax revenues that on average reflect levels of personal wealth. Which capital facilities should be financed in this way and which should be targeted for payment by specific fees is a continuing issue. Moreover, much infrastructure confers value on property it does not directly serve: a good park system, for example, improves everyone's property values in addition to offering direct benefits to park users.

Administrative Concerns

Exactions and fees pose two administrative concerns: the general lack of administrative guidelines or rules for determining exactions and the difficulties inherent in the use of impact fees. Many exactions of land or improvements, especially those located off the development site, are negotiated during project approval procedures. Seldom do guidelines exist to determine the appropriate types or amounts of exactions, to suggest how financial responsibilities should be shared among public and private interests, or to guide negotiations. As a result, developers often complain of extortionary exactions unrelated to the impacts of their projects; at the same time, public officials frequently believe that developers escape contributing enough.

These problems are supposedly solved in large part by relying on impact fees whose requirements call for predictable measures of impact and specified payment amounts. It takes expert knowledge, time, and effort to create legally sound and politically stable fee programs. Once enacted, impact fee programs require correctly calculated fees to be collected for each project and timely expenditures to be made for the construction of facilities that benefit fee payers. For these reasons, cities such as San Diego that use impact fees as a major financing mechanism employ a full-time staff to administer fee programs.

Fees and exactions should not be viewed as a panacea; such contributions rarely cover all the costs of required infrastructure. Instead, fees and exactions should be employed as one of several sources of revenue within an overall public program of financing capital facilities. In this context, they may generate essential funds that permit development to proceed. In effect, developers "pay to play."

Indeed, infrastructure improvements funded by fees and exactions often add market value to the proj-ects they serve. Public requirements for open space or drainage, for example, usually enhance the value of many building sites. Environmental features preserved from development often become valuable amenities for residents and tenants in the surrounding area. Other benefits relate to management of the development process. Developers who have paid impact fees enjoy greater assurance that needed public facilities will be built. Further, developers who construct facilities have a significant amount of control over the timing and quality of those facilities and can make certain that facilities are in place when they need them.

Special Taxing Districts

Special taxing districts are another means of planning and financing infrastructure. Districts are especially useful in providing specific services to targeted users. They may encompass one or more development projects in a single neighborhood or local jurisdiction, or extend across several jurisdictions. Types of districts include those organized for single purposes such as constructing roads, building junior colleges, and promoting soil conservation or for multiple purposes such as almost all the facilities and services required to serve new development.

State legislation spells out requirements for initiating, financing, and operating specific types of districts. For this reason, types of districts vary considerably from state to state and even within states. Special taxing districts are allowed in all states but are particularly numerous in some states, including Illinois, Texas, California, Florida, and Pennsylvania.

States may allow local governments to establish assessment districts or public improvement districts to levy a special tax on property owners who will benefit from improved facilities. The districts may be governed by special boards or commissions or by the city or county governing board sitting as the district board. Budgets and actions are usually subject to the local government's review and approval. Alternatively, property owners, including developers, who wish to establish a financing mechanism for capital facilities, may petition either a local government or a state agency to establish a district, which may function as an independent authority.

A 1.1-acre (0.4-hectare) mixed-use project combining housing and retail in the Longfellow neighborhood of Minneapolis, Minnesota, West River Commons was financed in part through TIF funds. *Sam Newberg*

Special taxing districts are especially useful to developers because creation of a district circumvents the need to tax existing residents for facilities required for new development and spreads the costs of improvements over a targeted group of owners for a repayment period of 15 to 20 years. Districts are also invaluable in developing areas where local governments have little incentive, administrative capacity, or financial resources to fund infrastructure.

One type of special district popular in several states is a tax increment financing (TIF) district. TIF districts obtain revenues from earmarked property taxes raised only from new development to finance capital improvements. Assessments are based on net increases over the existing property tax base. For this reason, TIF districts are often used in redevelopment areas to provide funds for improvements.

Establishing special districts requires a considerable amount of time and talent. They can be initiated only according to specific state provisions relating to the voting powers of the property owners involved, organization of the managing board, types of facilities to be constructed, and financing plans and revenue sources. Securing financing involves the services of bond counsels, underwriters, rating agencies, and insurers. Planning and undertaking infrastructure construction and managing the district demand still other specialties. In any case, special taxing districts offer a useful alternative to local government financing of infrastructure (see Figure 13-9).

Privatization

In recent years, many local governments have experimented with the use of private companies to build and operate public facilities. It is not a new idea: private water companies, private solid waste disposal facilities, and private transit companies are not uncommon. Semiprivate authorities manage many toll roads and bridges. Special taxing districts that provide basic services are often managed by private companies under contract to the districts. In many small- and large-scale developments, community associations own and manage recreational and other facilities.

Proponents of privatization claim that private companies provide superior service at lower cost (partly the result of more efficient management but also because of lower wage scales). Public officials, however, often worry that private companies may make unreasonable profits or fail to provide equal, adequate service to all residents. Perhaps for these reasons—despite a great deal of interest in privatization and some highly publicized examples—the nation has not seen a rush to convert public facilities and services to private operation. On the other hand, an increasing percentage of new intercity highways are privately owned toll roads.

Planning, Design, and Construction

Planning and design of infrastructure improvements may be carried out by public agency staffs or by contractors employed by public agencies. Developers usually employ consultants to design the improvements required in their projects, with the engineering drawings subject to public approval. Design and construction standards for facilities are specified by public agencies for individual public works projects or, in the case of development projects, spelled out in subdivision regulations. In the latter case, the subdivision drawings indicate the standards of construc-

Figure 13-9	**TIF Districts in Arlington Heights and Palatine, Illinois**

Tax increment financing districts are becoming quite popular in many metropolitan areas such as Chicago. Not only does the city of Chicago designate many such districts to aid redevelopment but suburban jurisdictions also find TIF funding an appropriate financing vehicle for supporting development of public/private projects.

The village of Arlington Heights, about 24 miles (39 kilometers) northwest of downtown Chicago, established several TIFs to raise funds to rebuild its downtown. The TIF districts have succeeded in providing the financial edge needed to stimulate private investments in downtown, including a centrally located mixed-use "town square," another mixed-used development, and a performing arts center, all near a rebuilt commuter rail station. New public parking garages and streetscape improvements have provided the most visible sign of TIF investments, but the TIFs also have allowed the village to provide gap financing for several projects, grants and loans for facade improvements and interior renovations of about 35 buildings, and relocation assistance for business residents displaced by new development. As of 2002, $27 million in TIF dollars had leveraged $133 million in private investment, and projected revenues are expected to fully pay off TIF-backed bond issues well ahead of the target date.

The village of Palatine, just up the Metra rail line from Arlington Heights, also has used TIF financing to revitalize its declining town center. The village designated most of the downtown area as a TIF district and has been attracting development by carefully targeting TIF-generated funds, which are expected to total about $40 million. The first project developed corporate offices and retail space in Gateway Center, next to the train station, including a TIF-supported large public parking structure. Other projects assisted by TIF funding include six residential projects and a mixed-use development that have added more than 400 residential units to downtown. The TIF district has invested in the parking garage, streetscape improvements, environmental cleanup, and acquisition of properties to create future sites for redevelopment.

Sources: Case studies prepared by Douglas Porter for *Developing around Transit: Strategies and Solutions that Work* (Washington, D.C.: ULI–the Urban Land Institute, 2004).

tion for each type of facility. Before proceeding with construction, developers are usually required to post a bond to ensure the satisfactory completion of the facilities. During construction, public inspections determine that facilities adhere to standards. Frequently, the completed facilities are then dedicated to the local government for public use, although they may become the responsibility of a community or homeowners' association organized to manage the common facilities.

SUMMARY

All real estate development is a public/private joint venture in some form. Developers should expect to interact closely with public officials and administrators in the course of achieving their objectives. Developers must understand and adhere to regulations, rules, and established public procedures in selecting sites, designing projects, and carrying out construction. In addition, they can take advantage of optional regulatory approaches that offer special project or design opportunities. Thus, both personally and through trusted consultants, developers should acquire a keen knowledge of local regulations affecting development.

This principle also holds for the provision of needed infrastructure to support proposed developments. Especially as more communities attempt to shift the costs of infrastructure to the private sector, developers are well advised to keep abreast of facility and financing requirements and options that can have an important effect on a project's financial viability.

In both cases, developers find it good business practice to know local public officials and administrators and to participate in community decision making regarding future development. Developers can lend their special understanding of the practical aspects of development to discussions about new comprehensive plans, rezoning, annual capital improvement programs, and other public actions that directly affect the climate for development in their communities. At the end of the day, successful development requires the meshing of public and private objectives.

TERMS

▶ Capital improvement program
▶ Comprehensive plan
▶ Exactions
▶ General obligation bond
▶ Growth management techniques
▶ Impact fees
▶ Linkage fees
▶ New urbanism
▶ Planned unit development (PUD)
▶ Police power
▶ Revenue bond
▶ Smart growth
▶ Special taxing district
▶ Subdivision regulations
▶ Taking
▶ Tax increment financing (TIF)
▶ Zoning ordinances

REVIEW QUESTIONS

13.1 What is the police power and how is it enforced? Who has a stronger obligation in the exercise of the police power—the federal government or the states? Why?

13.2 What are the mainstays of local governments' regulatory programs and how do they affect development?

13.3 What are the roles of state and regional agencies in regulating development?

13.4 What does the popular phrase "make development pay for itself" mean? How does that attitude manifest itself?

13.5 What are the main sources of capital for infrastructure improvements?

13.6 Discuss how legal constraints, equity, and administrative concerns affect fees and exactions.

13.7 What are special taxing districts?

NOTES

1. See Douglas R. Porter, "The States: Growing Smarter?" in *Smart Growth: Economy, Community, Environment* (Washington, D.C.: ULI–the Urban Land Institute, 1998), pp. 28–35; and David O'Neill, *Smart Growth Toolkit* (Washington, D.C.: ULI–the Urban Land Institute, 2000).

2. For a complete explanation of the takings issue, see Robert Meltz, Dwight H. Merriam, and Richard M. Frank, *The Takings Issue: Constitutional Limits on Land Use Control and Environmental Regulation* (Washington, D.C.: Island Press, 1999); and Douglas T. Kendall, *Takings Litigations Handbook: Defending Takings Challenges to Land Use Litigations* (Cincinnati, Ohio: American Legal Publishing Corporation, 2000).

3. See Deborah Myerson, *Involving the Community in Neighborhood Planning: A ULI Community Catalyst Report* (Washington, D.C.: ULI–the Urban Land Institute, September 2004); and Douglas R. Porter and Suzanne Cartwright, *Breaking the Development Log Jam: New Strategies for Building Community Support* (Washington, D.C.: ULI–the Urban Land Institute, 2006).

CHAPTER 14

Meshing Public and Private Roles In the Development Process

Development in the United States has traditionally occurred through a conventional process in which the public and private sectors perform independent functions and therefore tend to remain at arm's length from one another. As a general rule, simple projects in strong markets have historically followed conventional modes of development, and any mix of function between the public and private sectors has been seen as a conflict of interest on the part of local government. As detailed in preceding chapters, the public sector was expected to perform the functions of regulation and broad planning, providing the needed services—schools, roads, water, sanitation, fire and police protection—to support new development. The private developer originated projects based on information about the market and formulated a specific plan for a project with public policy in mind—all without the public's direct involvement in stages one and two of the process. Consequently, the public sector did not assume any

of the entrepreneurial risks or absorb any project-specific costs typically borne by the private sector.

This development scenario changed dramatically in the late 1970s with a proliferation of new-style real estate projects defined by their special public/private status. Variously referred to as partnerships, joint developments, codevelopments, or just public/private deals, these projects have reshaped the conventional development process by expanding the public sector's traditional sphere of activity. In a number of ways—as developers, lenders, equity investors, land lessors, and, in selected cases, operators—public agencies have become more active in the development arena and, in so doing, have assumed new risks. With each succeeding decade, the number of public/private projects has continued to grow, and the concept has been applied to a more diverse array of projects. Increasingly, these public/private partnerships are structured as creative alliances that may result in net benefits for all parties. Public sector entities can leverage and maximize public

The authors are indebted to Lynne B. Sagalyn, PhD, professor of city and regional planning, School of Design, and professor of real estate development and planning, Wharton School, University of Pennsylvania, for her extensive revisions to this chapter.

Figure 14-1	Downtown Silver Spring, Silver Spring, Maryland

Downtown Silver Spring is an urban mixed-use infill and historic rehabilitation project anchored by restaurants, retail space, offices, and cinemas in Silver Spring, Maryland. An inner-ring suburb of Washington, D.C., the area had experienced decades of flight and changing demographics.

Montgomery County designated the four-block site as the Silver Triangle urban renewal area in the 1980s and condemned and assembled the land, but several attempts to redevelop the site failed. The area was littered with several underused structures that had fallen into disrepair, including the historic 1938 art deco Silver Theatre and Silver Spring Shopping Center complex, a landmark of early 20th-century commercial architecture and one of the nation's first automobile-oriented shopping centers.

After two unsuccessful attempts to redevelop the area, a public/private development partnership was assembled to create a gathering place for this urban community that integrates existing structures with new construction and features a traditional street format punctuated by two plazas. Future phases will include a town square, a civic building, and a residential component.

The project, which has been a catalyst for further redevelopment in the area, features approximately 440,000 square feet (40,900 square meters) of retail space, 185,000 square feet (17,200 square meters) of offices, a 179-room hotel, more than 3,800 parking spaces, public plazas and other open space, and 23 movie screens in two facilities. Today, the area draws visitors from a wide area who come to shop, dine, see a movie or play, relax with friends, and attend community events.

Downtown Silver Spring was developed by a public/private partnership governed by a development agreement between Montgomery County, Maryland, and the private sector developer, PFA Silver Spring, LC—a partnership among the Peterson Companies, Foulger-Pratt, and Argo Investment Company, all Washington, D.C., metropolitan area firms with broad experience in developing office, retail, residential, and mixed-use projects. The firms' combined body of experience appealed to Montgomery County Executive Douglas Duncan. In May 1997, Duncan entered into an exclusive agreement with PFA Silver Spring to negotiate a joint development plan for a mixed-use project on the urban renewal area site. The agreement, which did not specify a time frame or an end date for the conception of a plan or development of the site,

required the development team to remain intact throughout the process.

The following month, the development team began meeting with the 31-member Silver Spring Redevelopment Steering Committee—a group of stakeholders representing civic, business, and community groups whom Duncan appointed to address issues related to the redevelopment and revitalization of downtown Silver Spring—to discuss concept plans, a massing scheme, and tenant mix. The steering committee's limited assignment was to determine whether the ultimate plan for the site would revitalize downtown Silver Spring. Its mission did not include reviewing potential tenants, leases, architecture, or other project elements.

In April 1998, Duncan and PFA signed a general development agreement that specified the conditions under which the county and PFA would work together to develop a mixed-use urban entertainment and retail center incorporating existing historic structures and featuring a traditional street format punctuated by urban plazas. The agreement mandated the restoration of the Silver Theatre and the Silver Spring Shopping Center facade and parking lot and outlined the responsibilities of the development team and the county.

Shortly thereafter, the county and the American Film Institute (AFI) signed a formal agreement to move the national arts organization's East Coast exhibition program from the Kennedy Center for the Performing Arts to Downtown Silver Spring, where it would occupy and operate the historic Silver Theatre. The county agreed to spend up to $7.8 million to restore the 400-seat theater and develop an adjacent facility that would include a 200-seat theater and a 75-seat theater as well as state-of-the-art audiovisual equipment, offices, a conference room/library, and concession and retail space.

The developers initially faced a hostile community environment. Citizens were concerned about the demolition of existing properties, including the Maryland National Guard Armory, and community leaders and preservationists had fought for years to save the Silver Theatre and Silver Spring Shopping Center. The public/private development team used a proactive approach, working with the community before fully developing a plan that put local residents' fears to rest.

Figure 14-1	Downtown Silver Spring, Silver Spring, Maryland *(continued)*

PFA representatives attended an extended series of meetings with members of the community. A variety of county advisory boards and committees also provided input throughout the planning and development process, including the Silver Spring Redevelopment Steering Committee; the Silver Spring Citizens Advisory Board, which represents citizens and businesspeople and advises elected officials and the Silver Spring Regional Services Center on matters of community and regional importance; and the Silver Spring Urban District Advisory Committee, which provides information and advice to the Silver Spring Regional Services Center regarding promotions, maintenance, service levels, and budgetary guidance for the urban district. The Silver Spring Regional Services Center proved to be an effective liaison for the project's public and private sector partners. The partnership also established regular communications with local nongovernmental organizations, including the Silver Spring Historical Society, the Art Deco Society of Washington, and civic associations, which helped generate support for the project from existing neighborhoods and local businesses.

Financing for Downtown Silver Spring came from both the private and public sectors. The public sector's participation was governed by a complex development agreement between PFA and the county. PFA furnished more than $189 million in private investment through a combination of the partners' equity, tenants' equity, and construction debt provided by two national banks and guaranteed by the PFA partners. Montgomery County contributed

continued on next page

A mix of new and rehabilitated buildings oriented along the existing street grid of Silver Spring, Maryland, Downtown Silver Spring includes about 440,000 square feet (40,900 square meters) of retail space, 185,000 square feet (17,200 square meters) of offices, a hotel, movie theaters, structured parking, and multiple open spaces. R.C. Kreider Studios, Inc.

Figure 14-1 | **Downtown Silver Spring, Silver Spring, Maryland** *(continued)*

$96 million, and the state of Maryland provided $35.4 million. Historic preservation tax credits were used to restore and redevelop the AFI Silver Theatre and the Silver Spring Shopping Center.

Montgomery County conveyed the land to PFA through a series of $1 per year, 99-year ground leases. The property is divided into four blocks, which roughly correspond to seven land parcels or sections. Each parcel has its own ground lease and ownership entity. The county required each section to be 60 percent preleased before PFA could execute the lease for that section. PFA paid the county the appraised value for the office and hotel sections; the retail portions of these parcels were conveyed with a deed restriction similar to the ground leases in the rest of the project. (The developer also will pay the appraised value for the residential section.) This structure allowed PFA to survive an economic downturn in the cinema business, enabling it to build the right things at the right times rather than simply what would make financial sense in the short term.

The development agreement also contains incentives to keep PFA involved in Downtown Silver Spring. Lease and deed restrictions in effect for the project's first ten years allow PFA to finance 100 percent of the cost of the project or sell it at cost, but if the developer finances or sells any project for more than cost, the county will reap 50 percent of the profit. After ten years, the properties will be deeded over to the respective ownership entities.

The project is located in the state-designated Silver Spring Enterprise Zone, allowing the state to issue prop-erty tax credits on any new expansions, renovations, or capital improvements to properties. Downtown Silver Spring also lies inside a county-designated "green tape zone," which gives projects in the zone special priority in reviews and inspections, and in the county's Arts and Entertainment District, which reduces the taxes paid by the theaters.

Both the public and private partners say that they are pleased with the development and their economic returns. As of late November 2005, the retail space was 92 percent leased, and the office space was fully leased. Both rents and the developer's return on cost are well above pro forma estimates. The leasing success enabled PFA to close on permanent financing on the retail and office components in December 2004, even before construction was complete.

Successful urban redevelopment generally depends on both the public and private sectors' having a financial stake in the deal. Both must buy into a common vision for the project, and both must take risks as well as benefit from subsequent rewards. When another county government in the region asked the Peterson Companies whether they could duplicate Downtown Silver Spring in its county, the developer responded, "Yes, but only if you can participate as Montgomery County did—by assembling the land, putting together a ground lease structure, building and operating public parking garages, and so forth."

Source: Condensed from "Downtown Silver Spring," ULI Development Case Study, Vol. 35, No. 21, October–December 2005 (www.uli.org/casestudies).

---

assets, increase their control over the development process, and create a vibrant built environment. Private sector entities can achieve greater access to land and infill sites and receive greater public support throughout the development process.

Several forces contributed to the public sector's heightened engagement in the development process. In particular, cutbacks of federal urban aid in the 1980s pushed local governments to innovate and improvise to meet their city planning and economic development objectives.[1] At the same time, local pressures compelled local governments to search for new

sources of funds after a rash of tax-cutting referenda (beginning in 1978 with California's Proposition 13) made raising taxes or going to the voters for approval of new bond issues a political risk. In an environment of fiscal restraint and rising land values during the 1980s, local governments came to view development as a strategic resource that could be harnessed to revitalize downtowns, capture hidden land values, finance needed infrastructure, stimulate economic growth, and generate jobs. Even during the first half of the 1990s, when property markets were experiencing severe distress, public/private development lost none of its

appeal as an economic development strategy, although the deals were certainly fewer in number and harder to put together. With the pickup in development activity in the second half of the 1990s, the public/private approach was evident in suburban infill projects, historic landmark redevelopments, military-base conversions, brownfield developments, affordable housing development, transit-oriented development, and waterfront parks. In recent years, the use of public/private partnerships to encourage the development of entertainment complexes, recreational facilities, and cultural facilities has increased.

This chapter looks at the nature of interactions between government and private developers and the character of their joint projects. In particular, it examines:

▶ The objectives of public/private development;
▶ The process involved in forming public/private partnerships; and
▶ The practical problems and policy issues associated with public/private development.

THE OBJECTIVES OF PUBLIC/ PRIVATE DEVELOPMENT

Each decade since the 1940s has seen the promulgation of federal, state, and local public policies aimed at stimulating the development of projects that would otherwise not occur. The ways in which government has sought to influence private investment decisions span a wide spectrum of policy approaches. At one end of the continuum are "carrot-oriented" regulatory actions (incentive zoning and transfer of development rights) and programmatic assistance (tax abatements) through which local government provides subsidies to attract desired types of private investment. With these policy approaches, the benefits of public assistance are available to all who meet the qualifying conditions of entitlement.

At the other end of the continuum are more active public intervention strategies that rely on bargaining and custom-tailored negotiations with private firms over the terms and conditions of individual projects. In this instance, selective processes of competition rather than prescribed incentives determine private firms' access to development opportunities.

Intervention in the market has successfully stimulated revitalization in center-city commercial cores and suburban downtowns, inner-city neighborhoods, and waterfront districts through the development of mixed-use projects, retail centers, commercial buildings, stadiums and convention centers, and residential clusters. Several cities have earned acclaim for their joint public/private efforts—Baltimore, Boston, Cleveland, New York, Indianapolis, Long Beach, Milwaukee, Minneapolis, Philadelphia, Portland, Oakland, and San Diego, among others. Each city has developed its own method of leveraging private investment to stimulate revitalization of that city's economy. Some more "entrepreneurial" local governments have, through their own initiative and their willingness to take risks, become joint venture partners with private developers on projects.

Baltimore, for instance, entered into several joint venture agreements, both for the revitalization of its well-known Inner Harbor and for other large and small development projects. An early example was the development of Coldspring, an in-town planned community instigated by Baltimore's Department of Housing and Community Development (HCD). In addition to complete master planning and overall coordination, HCD provided land, infrastructure, parks, public facilities, and financing in an agreement with the F.D. Rich Housing Corporation in 1978. In meeting its goals for the site, which was the last large undeveloped tract in the city, HCD specified the exact form of development that was to occur and limited the developer's profit to 10 percent. Assuming a role as senior partner in Coldspring, HCD succeeded in meeting its goals for affordable housing and other aims for the site. Both risk and reward for the developer were considerably lower than in conventional private developments. Following its early successes, the city has developed a significant track record in public/private development. More recently, it participated in an adaptive use of the former American Can Company factory, with the goal of stimulating redevelopment in a relatively untested neighborhood. This mixed-use development in the Canton neigh-

Mixing commercial and retail space in what was once a can factory, the Can Company in Baltimore, Maryland, was redeveloped through a public/private partnership. *Struever Bros. Eccles & Rouse*

borhood includes more than 60,000 square feet (5,575 square meters) of retail and 140,000 square feet (13,000 square meters) of commercial space and serves as the centerpiece of southeast Baltimore's renaissance.[2]

In another early initiative, the Philadelphia Redevelopment Authority entered into a joint venture in 1974 with the Rouse Company to develop the Gallery, a downtown retail/office project incorporating many of the attractive features of suburban shopping malls. Private developers were not interested in the site because of the perceived risk in revitalizing the Market Street area and the large number of funding sources involved. Acting as both joint developer

and general contractor, the redevelopment authority provided $18 million toward two-thirds of the costs of the shell. The Rouse Company provided $20 million in equity for the project, covering one-third of the costs of the shell in a 99-year ground lease arrangement under which Rouse also finished the space and sublet it. Within a few years of the Gallery's opening in 1977, city officials initiated an expansion of the project, which included a second retail phase (Gallery II), an office tower (One Reading Center), and a parking garage linked to transit improvements.

Public/private efforts in Chicago led to the successful adaptive use of the Reliance Building, the city's first modern skyscraper, as the Burnham Hotel, a 122-room boutique hotel in the Loop—the heart of the city's central business district. The Reliance Building, reflecting downtown Chicago's office market in the 1980s, had slipped into disrepair. To protect a treasured landmark, the city purchased the building and quickly stabilized it by restoring the exterior. The city then issued a request for proposals (RFP) and awarded a contract to the winning development team, headed by the locally based McCaffery Interests, on the basis of the team's proposal to convert the office building into a hotel that would suit its status as architecturally significant. With the award of the development contract, the city established a TIF program that added $2.5 million to available development funds. The city had already spent almost $8.6 million in TIF-generated funds in two phases to restore the exterior. Private financing exceeding $19 million succeeded in producing a project notable for its contribution to and catalyst for the rejuvenation of a declining downtown district.[3]

The success of early efforts spawned subsequent waves of public/private projects, many of which have been even more ambitious in scope. MetroTech Center (see Figure 14-2), for example, has helped reshape the core of downtown Brooklyn. Another example is CityPlace in West Palm Beach, Florida, one of the largest and most ambitious town center projects built to date in the United States, with more than $550 million in total investment.

Other projects have extended the public/private model beyond downtown to meet neighborhood needs for long-undersupplied services, particularly retail space. Vermont-Slauson shopping center in south central Los Angeles, for example, is a 154,000-square-foot (14,300-square-meter) community center developed in the late 1970s in a high-crime, high-density, low-income neighborhood. This public/private effort has served as a prototype for developing inner-city neighborhood retail services. Similarly, a nonprofit community development corporation in partnership with a for-profit partner completed the $9.8 million supermarket-anchored Lake Park Pointe Shopping Center in 1999 in the North Kenwood area of Chicago's South Side, a revitalizing mixed-income community.

The development of supermarkets and supermarket-anchored shopping centers has been especially important to community developments in cities all across the nation, and many successful efforts to date owe their origins to the public/private approach. Under the leadership of The Retail Initiative, a nonprofit organization created in the early 1990s to finance equity gap–investments in supermarket-anchored centers, cities and institutional investors joined forces with the initiative and community development organizations to develop centers in Chicago, Dallas, New Haven, New York, Philadelphia, and San Diego. The Boston-based Initiative for a Competitive Inner City has been another important force of information and promotion stimulating corporate investment in urban retail.

Based on a strong understanding of the public/private partnership model, development firms such as Magic Johnson's Canyon-Johnson Urban Development Fund and Los Angeles–based CIM Group, Inc., have acquired, developed, and redeveloped real estate in urban neighborhoods throughout the country. These firms and others, encouraged by growing sources of private equity capital, are undertaking transformative neighborhood projects such as CityVista, a $200 million mixed-use project on the 3.2-acre (1.3-hectare) site of the former Wax Museum in Washington, D.C. Selected as developer by the National Capital Revitalization Corporation through an RFP, Lowe Enterprises is creating a mixed-income community of both affordable and market-rate apartments and condominiums as well as retail, including a 52,900-square-foot (4,920-square-meter) supermarket.

Museum Place in Portland, Oregon, is another instance of urban neighborhood development based on a public/private partnership. This one-block project located close to light-rail, streetcar, and bus lines is the cornerstone of a new pedestrian-oriented community being developed by the Portland Development Commission (the city's development agency) and local developer Sockeye Development LLC. Part of a three-block redevelopment project in the West End area of downtown Portland, the city's goal is to infuse the low-income neighborhood with new retail and expand the housing opportunities in the district on the fringe of downtown.[4]

| Figure 14-2 | MetroTech Center: Economic Development in Brooklyn |

MetroTech Center is a 16-acre (6.5-hectare), seven-building corporate campus in downtown Brooklyn. Developed through a partnership of the city of New York, Polytechnic University, and Forest City Ratner Companies, the $1 billion-plus project represents the fused interests of public and private capital investment.

Formally initiated in 1982 after several years of preliminary feasibility study by the city's public development agency (in response to Polytechnic's pressing concerns about the deteriorating environment around the school and its negative impact on recruiting faculty and enrolling students), the development of the MetroTech project was conceived as a way to revitalize downtown Brooklyn by developing facilities that would attract high-tech businesses and back-office operations.

The city's investment took shape in two distinct forms. The first consisted of traditional redevelopment assistance for land acquisition, relocation, demolition, and infrastructure

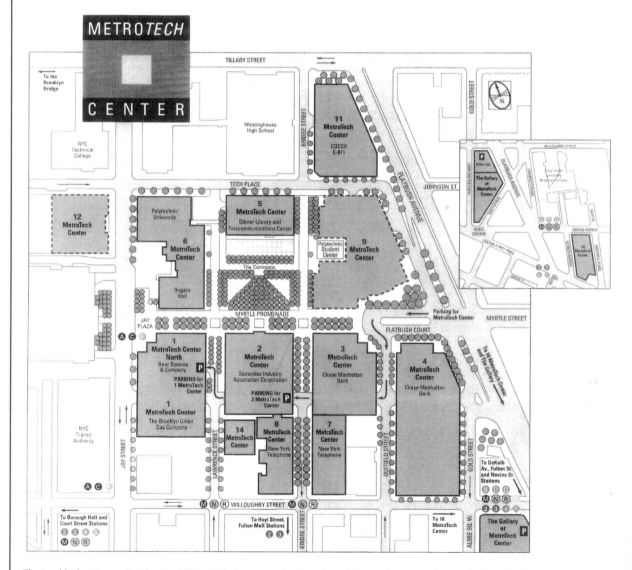

The ten-block, 16-acre (6.5-hectare) MetroTech Center required a variety of innovative approaches to develop this dense, intensely urban mixed-use project.

Figure 14-2	MetroTech Center: Economic Development in Brooklyn *(continued)*

needed to ready the site for private development. The second consisted of an aggressive economic development package of tax incentives, discretionary benefits, and energy cost savings designed to lower occupancy costs for corporate tenants. According to the developer's projection, the package would result in rents $5 to $15 per square foot ($54 to $161 per square meter) less than in Manhattan for new construction.

In combination with strong private investment, the development succeeded in attracting a critical mass of corporate tenants. Office towers totaling 5 million square feet (464,700 square meters) surround a two-acre (0.8-hectare) park-like open space that provides a campus feel for the project. Ground floor space in each building provides retail services for the center's tenants.

Such blue chip tenants as Chase Manhattan Bank, Brooklyn Union Gas, Bear Sterns & Company, Goldman Sachs, Morgan Stanley & Company, and the Securities Industries Automation Corporation occupy the MetroTech office buildings. In addition, as part of its obligations to the public development partnership, Polytechnic University built a new library and the Center for Advanced Telecommunications Technology (under the sponsorship of New York State) and renovated existing academic space. It continues its development as a major technology center.

Sources: Forest City Ratner Companies Web site (www.fcrc.com) and MetroTech BID Web site (www.metrotechbid.org).

Over time as public/private projects develop strong performance records, public agencies, universities, school districts, and port authorities will continue to expand their development activities, embarking on high-visibility public/private development ventures to renovate landmark structures such as San Francisco's Ferry Building 5 and to build sports arenas, cultural facilities, and entertainment complexes. Entertainment-based projects such as the Sony Metreon—the centerpiece of San Francisco's Yerba Buena Center, an 87-acre (35-hectare) mixed-use project in South of Market—and Block E, a large-scale entertainment, retail, and hospitality project in downtown Minneapolis, can be said to constitute a third wave of public/private projects.

The public/private approach has proved to be critical to large-scale projects with complex site conditions, infrastructure demands, or environmental contamination. The open-ended and unpredictable nature of environmental cleanup, for example, requires high rates of return to attract private capital. The major impediment to redevelopment of brownfield sites is often risk, not cost.

Public/private projects are diverse in scope. For any city, individual characteristics and history determine the types of projects and forms of assistance that best meet local public goals. Generally speaking, public entrepreneurship is most beneficial in the case of complex projects proposed for weak markets if a city can capitalize on its resources and use incentives to make a real estate project feasible for both public and private participants. In contrast, in strong markets, the public sector may be presented with select opportunities to capture benefits from the rising values of publicly owned land.

Although the majority of public/private projects have involved revitalization directed toward urban cores and distressed neighborhoods of the nation's cities, in the 1980s the strength of local real estate markets prompted some suburban governments to enter into public/private development. A case in point is Fairfax County, Virginia. In 1987, the county board of supervisors entered into a development partnership with the Charles E. Smith Company and the Artery Organization to build a new $83.4 million government center on 100 acres (40 hectares) of existing county land at no cash outlay to taxpayers. Instead of floating bonds for the project, the county swapped 116 acres (47 hectares) of its adjoining land (which would be zoned for commercial and residential development) for tenancy (and ultimately building ownership after 75 years), $24.6 million in cash, and $16.6 million in other forms of compensation. The county had bought 183 of those acres (74 hectares) for $4.1

Figure 14-3 | **Block E, Minneapolis, Minnesota**

Block E is a large-scale mixed-use urban project in downtown Minneapolis that combines retail, entertainment, hospitality, and parking uses. Deriving its name from the city block where it sits, Block E is the result of a public/private partnership between the city of Minneapolis and McCaffery Interests, an experienced urban infill developer based in Chicago. The city contributed the land and issued bonds in support of the funding for public improvements necessary for the project. Bond payments are being fully paid through tax increment financing and by an allocation of a portion of the entertainment tax levied by the city. The city invested about $39 million in clearing the block, locating utilities, and building an adjacent parking ramp.

McCaffery Interests understood that downtown Minneapolis desperately needed a mixed-use complex containing a bookstore, movie theaters, other entertainment venues, and restaurants. The impetus for Block E stemmed from the city's desire to reduce nuisance crime and clean up a portion of Hennepin Avenue between Sixth and Seventh streets. The site had been vacant (except for the Shubert Theater) since 1988. Although it was occasionally used for outdoor entertainment events, the site had been largely underused for some time. The city considered various uses for the site, including a park, but eventually decided on and approved a program that called for the development of a retail/entertainment complex.

After a false start with another developer, the city allowed McCaffery Interests an extension on the RFP and to take over the Block E development program in 1999. The site was essentially level (except for the historic but vacant Shubert Theater, which was moved nearby in 1999), but the developer faced some uniquely Minneapolis problems. Famous for its downtown skyway system that evolved in response to the harsh climate, the city of Minneapolis requires all buildings in its grid to have a second elevated entrance, in this case to two skyways. The developer and the architect sought to strike a balance between the necessity for the skyways and the desired appeal of the street. Designers had little choice but to celebrate the skyway bridges by making them icons of the project itself. The skyway that crosses First Avenue, connecting Block E to the Target Center, is the most dramatic in the city, with bold red coloring and soaring cables that resemble those of a suspension bridge. The skyway across Hennepin is only slightly less dramatic; it is brightly colored and lit to create a theatrical effect in the heart of the theater district.

Construction of Block E began in September 2001. Subsequent events and the decline in the retail economy proved to be a challenge for the leasing team. Letters of intent that had been relied upon, some leases, and many negotiations were either canceled or delayed. Nonetheless, demand for space picked up as the economy slowly recovered, and the project was 98 percent leased by February 2004.

The fractious political climate during the Minneapolis mayoral election of 2001 posed another challenge to the project. Block E had been approved, though not unanimously, by the outgoing mayor and city council and was under construction at the time of the election. Yet it became a lightning rod for the debate over public financing of downtown improvements and, as a result, suffered negative press even before it opened. More than anything else, the passing of time, combined with the project's lease-up, has helped Block E weather this temporary public relations setback.

The developer was also publicly criticized for his intention to include national chains such as Hard Rock Cafe, GameWorks, and Borders Books at the expense of local merchants and entrepreneurs.

---

million in 1979; the 116 acres (47 hectares) involved in the land exchange was valued at $42 million.[5]

Capturing the value of municipal land and other assets as a fiscal objective distinguishes another set of public/private projects, typically those initiated by public transit agencies, which, as a residual of their primary function, often control desirable development parcels. The Washington Metropolitan Area Transit Authority (WMATA), for example, manages transit-related site development through its joint development program, which was a pilot started in 1969 and then expanded in 1981. The early efforts at the Rosslyn, Virginia, Metro stop proved to be a financial success. Some 2.7 million square feet (251,000 square meters) of office space, almost 600 residential units, and more than 600 hotel rooms were built near the stop. By 2003, the amount of office space and number of hotel rooms had quadrupled, and an additional 4,000 residential units had been added. But the planners learned that their successes came at a price. They did not anticipate the kind of "place" they were making and for the past 15 years have been trying to repair some of the place-making damage the development caused. They applied the lessons learned to later developments throughout the corridor, however, and now WMATA can boast of many transit-oriented mixed-use development successes—many of which are destinations—throughout the metropolitan area. Ridership on the system continues to grow, making it the second most used transit system in the country, after New York.

From the perspective of city planning or real estate, joint development of transit-related sites often seeks close coordination of residential and commercial development at transit stations.[6] From the perspective of transit, joint development aims to meet many goals—generation of additional sources of revenue, increased rail ridership, enhanced convenience for riders, a public amenity, and architectural distinction through direct physical connections between private building entrances and rail stations.

Whether for urban revitalization, economic development, or to capture value, the growth of public/private development initiatives has been fostered by a shift in public values favoring entrepreneurial behavior. Further, the broad definition typically accorded "public purpose" provides a rationale that allows every type of public agency to become involved in real estate development: local governments, redevelopment authorities, transit agencies, port authorities, school districts, quasi-public development corporations—even the U.S. General Services Administration, the U.S. Navy, and the U.S. Postal Service.

THE PROCESS OF FORMING PUBLIC/PRIVATE PARTNERSHIPS

Public/private partnerships dramatically redefine the traditional roles of the public and private sectors in the development process. In such ventures, joint par-

ticipation by the public and private sectors is a prerequisite to developing a project in which each partner shares risks and benefits. Even though joint efforts involve many steps similar to conventional development, they differ in several ways:

▶ Business agreements between private firms and government detail the terms and conditions of development and involve the private sector in the public planning process much earlier than is traditionally the case, even under conventional urban renewal.

▶ Relatively limited public resources are used (leveraged) to attract larger amounts of private investment for community and economic development.

▶ Public commitments of financial resources to a project engender concerns about public accountability and create expectations for financial returns in exchange for the risks taken.

▶ The active involvement of the public, private, and community sectors creates more complex sets of public/private interactions.

▶ Public objectives (including community goals, design criteria, affirmative action, and hiring of residents) must be considered in addition to private objectives.

Public/private partnerships offer many advantages. Developers anticipate a more cooperative regulatory environment when a government agency is their partner.[7] Developers perceive government entities as more apt to approve and often to accelerate the approval process for those projects in which public agencies have an investment. For the public sector, public/private partnerships afford more control over projects throughout the development process and enable cities to achieve a variety of social objectives, for example, affirmative action, use of minority contractors, and the creation of jobs for low-income residents. Public/private projects, however, typically involve increased public review and comment, specific contracting requirements, and attention to political concerns, as was the case when the city of St. Louis Park, Minnesota, set out to create a new town center (see Figure 14-4). Under most conditions, the receipt of public monies and the participation of a

| Figure 14-4 | **Excelsior and Grand: Creating a New Town Center** |

Seeking to create a pedestrian-friendly town center, the city of St. Louis Park, Minnesota, entered into a public/private partnership with TOLD Development Company to develop Excelsior and Grand, a $150 million mixed-use project on 16 acres (6.5 hectares) that contains apartments, condominiums, retail space, and a town green linked to an existing city park. The project is the result of nearly ten years of community input and visioning and the city's close work with planners, market consultants, the developer, the architect, lenders, contractors, and landscape architects to create a civic amenity as well as additional future tax revenue for the city.

Planning for the development, which is located in the eastern portion of St. Louis Park, a first-ring suburb one mile (1.6 kilometers) west of the Minneapolis city limits, began in the mid-1990s with a vision. One of the city's desires was for community and connectivity, and the creation of a mixed-use town center fit that vision. At the time, the portion of the site along Excelsior Boulevard was lined with blighted single-use properties housing a variety of businesses, including bars, pawnshops, and sexually oriented businesses. These uses were generally unpopular in the community, and thus the area was targeted for redevelopment.

In 1996, the city initiated a series of charrettes funded by the Metropolitan Council's Livable Communities grant program, which helps local communities leverage their development plans. The charrettes brought prominent Twin Cities urban designers together to sketch plans for the Excelsior and Grand area, then called Park Commons East. The charrette process was combined with market studies of the retail and residential components as well as pro formas to assess what uses and densities were required to make the project financially feasible. This process informed the planners that densities would have to be increased from earlier designs. As a result, a town green area was narrowed from 300 to 180 feet (91.5 to 55 meters), and the density was increased to contain four-story buildings.

To ensure timely approvals for development at Excelsior and Grand, the city of St. Louis Park drafted an entirely new mixed-use zoning code (MX). Based on mixed-use and new urbanist projects around the United States, the zoning code allowed for vertical mixed-use development and diagonal on-street parking.

Using a request for qualifications (RFQ), the city chose a developer in 1999. This relationship ended in 2000, however, because of external pressures requiring the developer to focus on its east and west coast projects. The developer also had difficulty achieving a balanced pro forma for the project. During a second, accelerated process, this time an RFP, TOLD Development Company was selected in 45 days, mainly because of its experience with commercial development. TOLD retained ESG Architects, which has substantial experience in designing residential properties, as project architect.

TOLD inherited a set of design standards, a mixed-use zoning code, most approvals already in place, and traffic studies and environmental work already completed, making the project very attractive to the developer and enabling it, together with the city, to focus on the difficult task of developing and financing the mixed-use project. The public involvement in the planning process continued after TOLD was selected as the developer, with the company participating in more than 40 public meetings as well as weekly meetings with city staff. The current master plan for Excelsior and Grand evolved from this planning.

Financing for the project came from a variety of public and private sources. Approximately 20 percent of the financing, or $30 million of the $150 million project cost, was derived from public sources. The Metropolitan Council's Livable Communities grant program funded the charrettes and the initial market studies, and the Minnesota Department of Trade and Economic Development funded the demolition of existing structures. Very little site cleanup or soil contamination was associated with the project. A TIF district, created for the area in 1978, assisted the city with the cost of land assembly.

The U.S. Department of Housing and Urban Development provided financing for Phase I of the project at a loan-to-value ratio of approximately 80 percent, with equity furnished by TOLD. The interest rate for Phase I was 6.95 percent. Phases II and III were financed through a construction loan provided by US Bank. Similar bank debt will be provided for the development of Phase IV.

This four-phase project is planned to include 86,000 square feet (8,000 square meters) of retail space and 416,000 square feet (38,700 square meters) of residential space, including rental apartments and for-sale condominium units. Ground was broken for Phase I in summer

| Figure 14-4 | Excelsior and Grand: Creating a New Town Center *(continued)* |

2001. By early 2005, the first two phases, comprising 337 apartments, 124 condominiums, and more than 65,000 square feet (6,040 square meters) of retail space, were completed and ready for occupancy. Construction of Phase III started in February 2005. It will feature 86 loft-style condominiums and 14,000 square feet (1,300 square meters) of retail space on the first floor. Phase IV will comprise approximately 113 additional condominiums and 5,000 square feet (465 square meters) of retail space on the first floor, similar to Phase II. Of the 337 rental units, 18 are designated affordable under the Section 8 Housing Program. TOLD has assumed management of the project.

The willingness of the entire development team, including the city, to create a vision and implement it through an open, transparent process has been at the heart of Excelsior and Grand's success. Municipal officials say the stars aligned for the project, with the public will and vision to see blighted properties redeveloped, the availability of public money for planning and project financing, and a development team that was willing to try something riskier than a more traditional project. Representatives from TOLD note, however, that recent changes to TIF laws in Minnesota will restrict the potential for future projects like Excelsior and Grand and that other sources of necessary public money will need to be found.

A public partnership between the city of St. Louis Park, Minnesota, and TOLD Development Company, Excelsior and Grand provides a new town center for this inner-ring suburb of Minneapolis with its mix of apartments, condominiums, and retail and open space on 16 acres (6.5 hectares). Bob Perzel

Source: Condensed from "Excelsior and Grand," ULI Development Case Study, Vol. 35, No. 2, January–March 2005.

public partner also mean greater disclosure than in a private project. At the same time, politically active pressure groups are more likely to be a problem for private developers as a result of the publicity that usually accompanies public/private ventures.

Figure 14-5 describes how two levels of government worked together to execute the cleanup and

redevelopment of New York's 42nd Street, long known for its reputation as a center for vice, crime, pornography, and sleaze. In reviewing Figure 14-5, consider the private developer's perspective in terms of how different types of active public support may be enlisted, how many different constituencies may become involved in a project, and how a model of the development process takes on great importance in the complex world of public/private development.

Strategic Decisions in the Implementation Of Public/Private Projects

In implementing a public/private project, the public sector faces five fundamental tasks:

▶ Selecting a developer;
▶ Determining the terms and conditions of the opportunity for development, including forms of public assistance;
▶ Negotiating disposition and development agreements;
▶ Resolving problems and conflicts that arise throughout the development process; and
▶ Monitoring performance responsibilities and payments of project revenues due over the life of the agreement.

From a strategic perspective, some of the decisions a city must make in the early stages of planning a public/private venture (often when city decision makers are least informed about a project's development potential or are still evaluating possibilities) ultimately come to shape both the agenda for negotiations and the tools available for managing the initiative. One such decision concerns the process of selecting a developer. The choice is typically between an auction-bid competition or a development-prospectus competition through which a parcel is offered for disposition and a developer selected on the basis of comprehensive responses to a request for qualifications or a request for proposals. For nearly all public/private ventures, the RFQ/RFP has been the preferred option; the auction-bid approach generally offers government less flexibility in controlling the development process and less control over the composition of the benefits package.[8]

In attracting private developers' interest and specifying the ground rules for participation in the project, the RFP sets the stage for future implementation of the project. The RFP can be short and open ended or long and detailed with respect to a project's land uses, design guidelines, and business terms; regardless of the RFP's length, however, it requires the public

entity to assess its specific objectives for the project with an eye to broadly defining the character of the private development, identifying public roles and available types of assistance, structuring a set of project-specific planning conditions and business points to which developers must respond, and providing for an orderly and clearly understood procedure for evaluating proposals. These tasks are roughly analogous in timing to the activities in stages one through three of the conventional development model. (Most of the detail covered in Chapters 10, 11, 12, 16, 17, and 18 is relevant background for preparing the RFP.)

The level of specificity for each of these elements is often a matter of market conditions. For example, when the market is weak and the site untested, attracting the attention of qualified developers may require a detailed prospectus and thorough feasibility study. Conversely, when the market is strong, less documentation may be needed, but correspondingly more attention must be devoted to other matters, particularly the detailed terms and conditions for the contemplated business deal. Differences in market dynamics, site characteristics, a given project's public objectives, and the legal alternatives available for designating developers are all important considerations when selecting a developer and thus make generalizations about the "best" approach inappropriate.

When land for public/private development is publicly owned, a second strategic decision is whether to sell or lease the parcel. A sale can generate substantial upfront revenues for use in other public projects, eliminate the risk of future nonpayment, and, under certain conditions, promise higher dollars for the public treasury than lease arrangements.[9] In terms of controlling land use, restrictive covenants can be attached to property deeds as a condition of sale, as was the case with urban renewal dispositions. As a means for managing the development of large-scale public/private projects, however, many big cities have found that leasing affords more strategic advantages.[10]

Los Angeles's disposition of the land underlying California Center is illustrative. The last remaining parcel in the city's long-running Bunker Hill urban renewal project, the 8.75-acre (3.5-hectare) site was also the only large parcel of land left in downtown

| Figure 14-5 | 42nd Street at Times Square: Marshaling Public and Private Resources for a Transformation |

One of the most visible examples of redevelopment that took advantage of public and private resources is New York's 42nd Street at Times Square—or the new 42nd Street as bespeaks its radical transformation in perception and reality. The emergence of the new 42nd Street has become a worldwide symbol of renewed optimism about the dynamics of city life in general and public/private projects focused on entertainment in particular. Long associated with a lengthy list of urban ills, conditions of social depravity, vice and high crime rates, and the easy availability of every form of sexual pleasure, West 42nd Street has reemerged as New York's prime entertainment mecca, a drawing card for families, out-of-towners, and native New Yorkers alike.

This historic one-block stretch of midtown Manhattan—also the nexus of the city's transportation system since 1904 when the first of several subway lines to converge on Times Square was completed—is now the new home for corporate tenants. Condé Nast Publications, Skadden Arps, Reuters, Ernst & Young, and others occupy four new office towers with more than 4.1 million square feet (381,040 square meters) of space on corner sites at 42nd Street on Seventh Avenue and Broadway. An additional 1.6 million square feet (148,700 square meters) of office space was added in the new 52-story headquarters for the New York Times Company; it was designed by architect Renzo Piano in connection with Fox & Fowle Architects and jointly developed by the New York Times Company and Forest City Ratner Companies. The block is once again home to newly renovated live theaters: New York's art nouveau masterpiece, the 1,800-seat New Amsterdam now operated by Disney; the city's first theater dedicated to children's programming, the 500-seat New Victory Theater; and the 1,821-seat Ford Center for the Performing Arts (refashioned from the combined Lyric and Apollo theaters), designed for musical productions. On the north side of 42nd Street are the new home for the Roundabout Theater Company (in the old Selwyn Theater); The Duke on 42nd Street, a 199-seat theater for national and international performing artists; a new ten-story building festooned with dozens of glass louvers and a computer-controlled network of multicolored lights home to rehearsal studios and workshop offices for nonprofit arts groups; and E-Walk, a 193,000-square-foot (18,000-square-meter) entertainment/retail center that includes a 13-screen, 100,000-square-foot (9,300-square-

The new 42nd Street at Times Square has become a worldwide symbol of renewed optimism about the dynamics of city life in general and public/private projects focused on entertainment in particular.

meter) Sony/Loews theater complex and a 45-story hotel. On the south side of 42nd Street in the space of three other theaters (the Empire, Harris, and Liberty) is a 335,000-square-foot (31,100-square-meter) retail project that includes a 25-screen AMC multiplex cinema, the 60,000-square-foot (5,575-square-meter) Madame Tussaud's wax museum, and other retail attractions. Built in 1905 by the *New York Times* and the source of the district's name, the old Times Towers (now called One Times Square) is completely vacant yet generates substantial revenues from its 26 billboards and electronic signs. The iconic building—where thousands gather to watch the ball drop on New Year's Eve—and its signs serve as a visual entry point for the eight-block stretch of Broadway from 42nd Street to 50th Street and its new generation of flashing neon, kinetic lights, and supersigns.

This vast transformation and cleanup of 42nd Street—a saga of stops and starts, 47 lawsuits, continual controversy, and market reversals over the course of nearly 25 years since the public/private project was initiated by the public sector—has been a joint undertaking by an unusually powerful coalition between the city and state. Under a memorandum of understanding signed in 1980, the city of New York and the state of New York through the entrepreneurial public development entity, Urban Development Corporation (UDC, now called the Empire State Development Corporation), agreed to cooperate in the redevelopment of the 42nd Street block between Broadway and Eighth Avenue.

continued on next page

Figure 14-5	**42nd Street at Times Square: Marshaling Public and Private Resources for a Transformation (continued)**

The compelling force of this institutional coalition came from the singular combination of three powers only UDC could bring to the deal-making process: the police power of eminent domain to condemn land (the city's public development arm did not have clear statutory authority to undertake the power, and, though the city did, its process was viewed as terribly cumbersome and relatively slow), the legal status (as would-be landowner) to negotiate customized tax agreements for commercial projects, and a distinctive statutory power to override local land use regulations.

As part of the agreement, UDC accepted the lead role of implementing agency for the project. The city retained the rights of approval on financial terms and changes to UDC's General Project Plan, which governed the redevelopment land use program. Most significant, the public approvals that are the legal ballast to the project were undertaken pursuant to state regulations and therefore did not go through the city's traditional lengthy approval process.

In city-state agreements executed in 1988, 1991, and 1994, UDC agreed to transfer its interest and obligations to a wholly owned subsidiary whose sole activity would be development of the 42nd Street Development Project (42DP). Thus, although UDC was the original condemning authority, title to the properties lies with 42nd Street Development Project, Inc. In addition, the city in 1988 created an independent nonprofit organization, New 42nd Street, Inc., and charged it with long-term oversight of the renovation and ongoing operations of 42nd Street's historic theaters.

As the implementing agency, 42DP has been responsible for day-to-day management of the project (including property management, condemnation, relocation, and fee and fixture trials) as well as development of the plan, marketing, attracting tenants, and negotiations with developers. The city retained consent rights on all "material" actions by 42DP and UDC. 42DP's core activities have been funded through UDC and were repaid directly by developers or will be reimbursed through developers' revenues related to site development.

From the perspective of implementation, at least two structural characteristics distinguish this project from other large-scale public/private efforts in the nation. The first was the city's policy mandate that it take no direct financial risk for the costs of acquiring, through condemnation, the 13-acre (5.3-hectare) project area. It managed to do so through an innovative public/private deal structure designed to shift that risk to private developers (principally Prudential Insurance Company as the money partner behind Times Square Center Associates, the joint venture that held the development rights for the four office tower sites). The second was the public coalition between the city and state that was instrumental in carrying out the city's financial mandate and acting as a political bulwark against constant opposition that continuously delayed condemnation and troubled implementation of the project. In turn, when the real estate market collapsed in the early 1990s and effectively killed the initial concept of office/mart/hotel for the project, the leadership and resources of 42DP, in concert with the staying power of the public/private coalition, provided the basis for rescripting the project. It was a rare second chance for any large-scale redevelopment project. This new plan, with its clear and timely focus on entertainment-based activity, reinforced the historic and enduring thematic attraction of 42nd Street at Times Square.

Source: Lynne B. Sagalyn, *Times Square Roulette: Remaking the City Icon* (Cambridge, Mass.: MIT Press, 2001).

when the Community Redevelopment Agency solicited development proposals in 1979. After two moribund decades, the market in downtown Los Angeles heated up, and to capture the benefits of its position as landowner, the agency decided to offer the parcel on a long-term lease basis. The RFP called for a mixed-use project of 3.5 million to 4.4 million square feet (325,300 to 409,000 square meters) with a substantial allocation of housing uses; a major public benefits package, including a new, freestanding structure for the Los Angeles Museum of Modern Art, which was to form the focus of the entire development; and an adjacent 1.5-acre (0.6-hectare) central park as well as other pedestrian open spaces to be provided, owned, and maintained by the developer. These public amenities would not substitute for direct financial returns—which, according to the RFP, should reflect prevailing market practices and include provisions for inflation-protected rents, escalations pegged to rising property values, and profit-sharing participations.[11]

Forms of Assistance

The nature of public investment in projects has taken the form of subsidies for land redevelopment and such capital improvements as infrastructure, parking garages, transit systems and stations, public amenities (e.g., outdoor plazas, pedestrian malls, other open space), and complementary facilities such as convention centers and stadiums. Such improvements ready a site for private development, provide needed amenities, and/or create an improved programmatic environment in which a project is more likely to succeed. Indirect—or softer—forms of assistance designed to improve project feasibility can be passed on to developers in several ways: through density bonuses, government agencies' commitments or guarantees to lease space in a new development, transfers of development rights, land and/or building exchanges, air rights transfers, regulatory relief from zoning and building codes, reduced processing time for project approvals, coordinated design of projects in an area, arbitration of any disputes that might arise, and work with or organization of neighborhood and business groups. These public actions typically do not require an outlay of public money but provide the developer with savings in time and money, reduced risk, or increased opportunities for development.

For example, the San Francisco Giants' stadium, SBC Park, was built on land acquired under a ground lease from the Port Authority of San Francisco. The Giants privately financed the construction of the ballpark, using revenues derived from the facility. The public contribution toward construction was an allocation by the city and its redevelopment agency of a portion of the property tax increment generated by the new ballpark to pay for certain public infrastructure elements, including a waterfront promenade and public plazas.[12]

After the cutbacks in federal aid in the late 1970s, cities received fewer categorical aid dollars from Washington with which to fund their projects, yet they continued to support projects through the issuance of tax-exempt bonds—at least until the 1986 Tax Reform Act curtailed the use of such bonds for private-purpose projects. Continually pushed to rely more and more on local resources, cities established a broad inventory of incentive tools and financing techniques from which to fashion their assistance packages: tax increment financing, special assessment districts, tax abatements, dedication of sales or special-purpose taxes, urban development action grant paybacks, eminent domain, land write-downs, land swaps, ground leases, lease/purchase arrangements, second mortgage financing, loan guarantees and credit enhancements, loan subsidies, capital improvements, leases for office space, and value-creating tradeoffs based on zoning bonuses.

In return for the increased risk associated with providing substantial assistance, the public sector can take a direct financial stake in projects to secure a specified percent of a project's cash flow (a pseudo-equity interest) through such mechanisms as participatory leases and profit-sharing agreements.

Although used with some frequency in the past, profit-sharing agreements have not always produced substantial revenues for many cities. The economic logic of the subsidy in many downtown or inner-city neighborhood projects works against a big return. To kick off a project, the city invests funds early in the development process. Then, so as not to burden the project before it reaches an economically viable operating position, profit-sharing revenues typically are structured as triple-net revenues, with the city last in line to receive any cash flow. In other words, the cost-revenue account is likely to be negative for many years. Such was the case in Boston, where officials waited 17 years before realizing any profit from Faneuil Hall Marketplace. In that project, the city acts as a limited development partner, sharing a percentage of the development's net cash flow in lieu of collecting property taxes and relying on conventional lease terms.[13]

Notwithstanding the evidence to date, sharing profits affords cities other nonfinancial benefits. Although large public subsidies are always potentially controversial, profit-sharing arrangements in effect provide a political solution to the buy-high/sell-low problem of writing down the cost of redevelopment. They offer political protection to city officials vulnerable to charges of giving away too much. Even if the anticipated revenues are small or expected far in the future, a financial agreement to share returns is perceived as a sign that the city is acting responsibly and effectively.[14]

Cities aim to be pragmatic in packaging assistance. Their objective is to create combinations of incentives that make a real estate investment feasible for both the public and private participants. In this case, feasibility means overcoming serious obstacles and problems—land assembly, negative impacts of the surrounding area, excessive or premium costs, heavy upfront capital investments—that inhibit private development or renovation. Through diverse and numerous means, the public assistance package reconfigures the risk/return relationship of private investment through one or more financial tactics: reducing capital costs, absorbing the demands for new infrastructure, lowering operating costs, or reducing debt service burdens.

In determining whether significant levels of public assistance for development and financing will be required, public officials typically proceed through several steps:

1. Determine total development costs by project component.
2. Determine the level of private financing available (see Part II) by:

   ▶ Estimating the income-producing capacity of the project;
   ▶ Capitalizing net operating income;
   ▶ Determining loan value;
   ▶ Determining available equity financing; and
   ▶ Calculating total private funding capacity.

3. Identify the gap between project costs and available private resources.
4. Structure assistance to close financing gaps and to gain reasonable project returns.

Although the terms and conditions of public aid are tailored to the needs of individual projects, local governments structure assistance within the framework of three widely held (if informal) general policy principles:

1. Public aid should be delivered through cost-sharing mechanisms.
2. Investment of public dollars requires a return for risk taking apart from increased collections of property taxes, based on some form of loan recapture or profit participation in future project revenues.
3. The timing and conditions of public commitments should be linked to specific private obligations and responsibilities that must be performed.

In each instance, the public sector seeks to create binding ties in the form of mutually dependent commitments and business interests that establish incentives for the completion of an economically viable project. Generous upfront subsidies can carry risky projects through the first uncertain years, but experience has shown that they cannot turn weak projects into successful ventures. Beyond the task of making development feasible, the hard part of crafting public/private deals is finding ways to ensure the efficacy of public investment in joint development ventures. When deciding on the measures to apply in helping developers close financing gaps, public entities must define and measure the public risk of and reward for their actions (see Figure 14-6).

Cities and states today have become more sophisticated about claims of benefits from private projects and are acting accordingly by critically scrutinizing the cost/benefit ratio attached to projects with large subsidies. One area where this scrutiny is most visible is the provision of publicly subsidized financing for stadiums and arenas, especially when voters are being asked directly—through the ballot box—to pay the price. If voters want stadiums, they often do not want to shoulder the costs or to subsidize a team's owner, so voters' rejections of referenda on stadium-financing questions are not unusual. A "no" vote on stadium financing is not always the final word, however, and therein lies a big part of what is a nationwide fierce, tough, and controversial debate over municipal assistance to sports stadiums.

| Figure 14-6 | **Analyzing Financial Returns to the City: Portland's South Waterfront** |

A primary purpose of public investment is to obtain a public benefit or return on investment exceeding what could be expected without a major public commitment to development.

To accomplish revitalization goals, cities are implementing increasingly creative terms to inflate their ability to provide low-cost financing and subsidization. The city of Portland, Oregon, for example, adopted the North Macadam Urban Renewal Plan in 1999 to establish a 409-acre (165.5-hectare) urban renewal area within which the Portland Development Commission will focus efforts to encourage private development, cure blight, and enhance economic development.

The first phase of redevelopment took place in 2003, when a private development team acquired several blocks in the Central District of the South Waterfront, a 130-acre (52.6-hectare) plan area just south of downtown Portland. It is a largely vacant former industrial area, with few businesses remaining. The Central District comprises 31 acres (12.5 hectares) in the heart of South Waterfront.

The city is assisting the development team by providing critical infrastructure and public amenities as a form of project financing in return for revitalization of blocks in a TIF zone and a local improvement district (LID).

Development Manager:
Williams & Dame Development, Inc.

Initial Development, Phase I (2003–2008)

To begin implementation of the South Waterfront plan, the Portland Development Commission, Oregon Health & Science University (OHSU), and private development partners North Macadam Investors (NMI), River Campus Investors (jointly owned by NMI and OHSU), and Block 39 executed a development agreement that establishes roles and responsibilities of public and private partners for delivering the following program in the 31-acre (12.5-hectare) Central District:

At Buildout

▶ 250 student units
▶ 400+ affordable units
▶ 2,050 market-rate condominiums and apartments
▶ 150- to 200-room hotel/conference facility
▶ OHSU research/clinical buildings (approximately 1.5 million square feet [139,000 square meters])
▶ OHSU parking garages (3,500 spaces)

▶ A four-acre (1.6-hectare) greenway for pedestrians, habitat, open space, and transportation
▶ A new two-acre (0.8-hectare) neighborhood park
▶ New transportation options, including streetcar, tram, bus, new streets, and hiking, biking, and running trails

Financing

The Central District will be financed by a mix of public and private investment totaling $1.9 billion at buildout. Phase I investment, through 2008, includes $440 million private investment in direct new building development and $122 million in public projects financed by public and private resources ($70 million from public sources, including $30.8 million in TIF), and $52 million from private sources, including potential district-wide LID funds. (These terms are as described in the development agreement between the Portland Development Commission and the development partners dated August 22, 2003, and might not reflect the terms of all successive development agreement amendments.)

Terms of the Agreement

The city sought to engage the development team by providing funding for public projects in their entirety or on a percentage basis. A financing plan outlines funding priorities, emphasizing projects essential for the development team's economic success. Successful completion of these projects was essential to achieving the public goals for each project, which would lead to creation of taxable value and economic development stimulus. The city received both monetary and nonmonetary returns for its contributions.

Total investment by the city in the form of TIF; system development charges for all publicly owned projects, facilities, and land; land sales/loans; and non-TIF and LID contributions totals more than $65 million (excluding an additional $23.5 million obtained by the city from the state and federal governments).

The city's contributions and expected returns are as follows:

1. Transportation

▶ City's contribution. Streetcar extension/service into the Central District. Buildout of tram and funding of approximately 15 percent of operations and maintenance (O&M) costs.

continued on next page

Figure 14-6	**Analyzing Financial Returns to the City: Portland's South Waterfront** *(continued)*

► City's return. Return on funds from infrastructure necessary for establishment of the TIF and LIDs. OHSU to fund approximately 85 percent of O&M costs (percentage of riders estimated to be OHSU-related).

2. Streets

► City's contribution. Street improvements, including demolition of existing improvements in existing rights-of-way, remediation of any subsurface environmental contamination, and construction of north/south streets and walkways. Street and road O&M.

► City's return. Development team constructs east/west streets and walkways and dedicates all rights-of-way to city. Increased TIF and LID funds resulting from buildout of condominiums, apartments, office space, and hotel according to schedule and provisions set forth in development agreement. The city essentially mandates a development schedule that will ensure cash flow to TIF and LID.

3. Subsidization of Potentially Commercial OHSU Research Space

► City's contribution. $5 million in TIF funds for construction of OHSU building.

► City's return. Establishment of a bioresearch facility as the cornerstone of a bioresearch center and catalyst of future bioresearch facility development. OHSU must design, construct, complete, and occupy the structure in accord with the schedule set by the city.

4. Greenway and Parks

► City's contribution. Park and greenway construction. Shared responsibility for funding O&M costs.

► City's return. Development team clears greenway, constructs access for the handicapped, and regrades greenway parcels, paying for initial improvements. Development team conveys greenway parcels to city upon substantial completion of the riverfront blocks. City receives additional revenue for maintenance in the form of system development charges for the greenways as well as assessments on property owners living adjacent to the greenway.

5. Affordable Housing Subsidies

► City's contribution. Affordable housing subsidized in

the form of $3 million in TIF funding and up to $10 million in federal low-income housing tax credits.

► City's return. Mixed-income neighborhood resulting from the generation of more than 400 units of affordable housing (250 required).

6. Low-Cost Financing

► City's contribution. Interim financing of TIF and LID assessments as necessary for the public projects.

► City's return. Expedited return on funds from TIF and LID assessments.

In addition, the development team designs, obtains all permits for, and constructs the stormwater and sanitary infrastructure and dedicates easements for necessary infrastructure to the city.

These terms parallel a trend by cities whereby the risk of acquiring land in designated redevelopment areas is put firmly on the shoulders of the developer. The city reimburses the developer for infrastructure expenses or completes infrastructure and improvements on its own through traditional methods such as financing or economic development zones. The complexity of these deals is in the execution. The development agreement merely outlines responsibilities, and the relationship between the city and development team is paramount to the plan's success.

Analyzing Potential Returns

A city should consider several questions when analyzing the potential returns for a deal such as this one:

► What are the opportunity costs associated with the temporary tax abatement on property of potentially rising value? Can increases in property values for areas surrounding the subject property be projected?

► How does the city account for its costs related to the project, including soft administrative costs?

► How critical to the city is the developer's purchase of the property? (It is the purchase that triggers an increase in the percentage of participation in the cash flow.)

► Not counting the value of social goals, such as minority employment, what is the net present value of the city's investment in the project? Have long-term financial pro formas been developed so that such value can be calculated? What discount rate should be used in calculat-

Figure 14-6	Analyzing Financial Returns to the City: Portland's South Waterfront *(continued)*

ing the net present value of the city's investment?

▶ What value should be placed on the projected new jobs to be generated by the project?

▶ What is the procedure, if any, for renegotiating any portions of the deal in the event of unforeseen circumstances?

Cities like Portland—and many others—are fine-tuning their skills in analysis and negotiation to leverage public dollars for revitalization. As the competition for public money increases and deals become more complex, cities will need to hone these skills even more to use resources as wisely as possible.

Source: Portland Development Commission, "South Waterfront District FAQs"; "South Waterfront District Fact Sheet"; and "South Waterfront Central District Project Return on Investment Analysis Update." For more information, see www.wddcorp.com and www.thesouthwaterfront.com.

Figure 14-7	The Pros and Cons of Publicly Subsidized Financing for Sports Stadiums and Arenas

Pros for New Stadiums

▶ Foster local economic growth;

▶ Generate new jobs and new taxes;

▶ Stimulate spending in neighborhood restaurants, bars, and hotels;

▶ Create spillover opportunities for real estate development;

▶ Meet local citizens' desires for entertainment and pride of place for local sports team.

Cons for New Stadiums

Stadiums are poor sources for economic development, as most empirical studies have shown, because:

▶ The projected economic impacts rarely materialize.

▶ Stadium-related jobs are often seasonal and pay low wages.

▶ They only change the way people spend money on entertainment rather than generate new revenue.

▶ The value of publicly subsidized financing is often distorted in economic studies.

▶ Costs typically exceed benefits.

▶ Cities have more pressing needs—schools, transit, infrastructure—for scarce public funds.

Economic studies need to answer three questions:

▶ How do the costs of a proposed stadium compare with its benefits? Who benefits and who pays?

▶ What is the impact of a new stadium on local per capita income?

▶ What is the likely impact of a new stadium on the rate of growth of the local economy?

Common Criticisms of Economic Studies

▶ Impact or cost/benefit studies are rarely commissioned by "independent" players, and the results typically are consistent with the positions (pro or con) of their sponsors.

▶ Estimates of benefits (direct revenues and spillovers) are imprecise because data are limited and assumptions suspect or optimistic.

▶ Multipliers—one of the key variables of any economic impact analysis—used by most studies are based on decades-old data.

▶ Econometric studies of economic impacts are also suspect, because economists disagree on methodological approach and conceptual models for measuring impacts are weak.

For more information, see David C. Petersen, *Developing Sports, Convention, and Performing Arts Centers*, 3d ed. (Washington, D.C.: ULI–the Urban Land Institute, 2001).

The 685,000-square-foot (63,639-square-meter), 20,000-seat Nationwide Arena in downtown Columbus, Ohio, was developed through a public/private partnership in which construction and site costs for the arena were paid for by a subsidiary of Nationwide Insurance, the Dispatch Printing Company, and multiple private investors. The city supported the development through tax increment financing for the necessary infrastructure improvements. *Greg Bartram/Nationwide Arena*

With increasing regularity, sports franchises have used their monopoly-type power to pressure governments for a new or substantially refurbished stadium; the present stadium may be too old or too small or without the amenities, luxury boxes, and suites that raise the revenue to develop a top team. Alternatively, city officials may actively seek a franchise when the city has no sports team or may view an additional franchise as an element of its economic development strategy for downtown or a significant enhancement to the community's quality of life. Somerset Ballpark, for example, was built as a public/private venture between New Jersey's Somerset County and the Somerset Patriots, an unaffiliated minor league team in the Atlantic League.[15]

In either case, cities have to figure out how much and in what form they should contribute to the build-ing of a new stadium for a privately owned team or risk losing that team to another city that seems (at least during the heat of negotiations) only too willing to promise team owners a new stadium. Despite the trend toward public financing, the San Francisco Giants' stadium, SBC Park, and the Verizon Center, a professional sports arena in downtown Washington, D.C., were built entirely with private funds.

The political stakes of such debates are high, with pros and cons targeting both economic and strategic issues (see Figure 14-7). Economists continue to cast doubt on the monetary benefits cities reap from subsidizing new stadiums. Heavy public financial assistance is highly controversial, so how the public assistance package is put together is key to the political acceptance of a city's decision making. Sports sta-

Figure 14-8	James F. Oyster Bilingual Elementary School

In 1995, the James F. Oyster Bilingual Elementary School building in Washington, D.C., was overcrowded and deteriorated, and it poorly supported the school's nationally acclaimed English/Spanish dual-language immersion program. Built in 1926, the school's space was constrained and failed to comply with the Americans with Disabilities Act. The challenge was what to do and how to finance improvements at a time when the city government, in fiscal crisis, had no capital funds.

Led by concerned parents, the local school community began a crusade to secure alternative sources of financing for improving the school facility. The result of that effort was an innovative public/private partnership among the school system, the city, and LCOR Incorporated, a national real estate company that specializes in public/private development.

The partnership proposed a new educational and residential complex (not just a rehab of the old facility) that would combine an inviting, modern school and an elegant rental apartment building on existing school property. To finance the school—the first new one to be constructed in the District of Columbia in 20 years—the District would issue a 35-year, tax-exempt bond package to be repaid entirely with revenue generated by the Henry Adams House, a private apartment building. The result was an $11 million new school constructed at no cost to D.C. taxpayers.

The new school, completed in May 2001 and officially opened in June, is a state-of-the-art facility featuring a computer lab, library, gym, and classrooms designed to accommodate the school's bilingual education program, where every class is taught by English- and Spanish-speaking teachers. The facility also includes a 33-car garage as well as office space for after-school programs that previously had been housed in a converted closet. Many spaces in the school are available for community use.

Although the project is unusual, the development and financing approach applied in this context are highly replicable. Government entities, including school districts across the country, own trillions of dollars of land, a significant share of which is excess or otherwise underused. Projects such as this one (in which school land was in effect traded for capital) offer a way for governments to maximize the value of noncapital assets such as land to finance needed school construction.

Source: Reprinted with permission from the National Council for Public/Private Partnerships, www.ncppp.org.

diums may rely on specialized types of "export" taxes such as hotel and motel taxes, car rental taxes, or a tax on visiting athletes; cities also have created sports lotteries and put in place a "temporary" sales tax or surcharge on an existing sales tax to partially finance stadium construction. The private side of the equation offers a number of special sources of funds: corporate sponsorships, stadium-naming rights, luxury boxes and charter seats, concession rights, advertising revenues, and parking fees.[16]

The terms of assistance and conditions of development contained in public/private agreements are complex. This complexity reflects the many tradeoffs made during the course of negotiations in which the public's set of objectives is reconciled with both its limited resources and the demands of private investment. Similarly, the roles adopted by the public sector—broker, facilitator, lessor, builder, lender, investor—reflect both the range of multifaceted issues (bureaucratic, financial, political) to be addressed and the conditions in local real estate markets at the time those roles are defined.

Organizations and the Public/Private Process

As public/private ventures have evolved, the involvement of state and local organizations has expanded in innovative ways. Various types of government structures, including an array of quasi-public government bodies, development corporations, and city departments with expanded functions, have been organized to handle public/private development. Other actors have joined as well—nongovernmental institutions such as health care providers and educational institutions, nonprofit organizations, and intermediary groups such as business improvement districts. In one particularly notable example, a group of concerned parents in Washington, D.C., became the moving force behind an innovative partnership among the school system, the city, and LCOR Incorporated that developed a new educational and residential complex, the James F. Oyster Bilingual Elementary School and Henry Adams House (see Figure 14-8).

Public/private development is frequently organized under a quasi-public institutional structure that permits an organization to operate with greater flexibility and fewer restrictions than a city agency involved in development. Though partially publicly funded, a quasi-public development organization can conduct negotiations in private—a particularly useful feature as developers are reluctant to negotiate when the details of their financial dealings are made public. Examples of quasi-public organizations are the Centre City Development Corporation in San Diego and the Milwaukee Redevelopment Corporation (see Figure 14-9).

The Centre City Development Corporation (CCDC) is a public nonprofit corporation created in the early 1970s to facilitate public/private partnerships to revitalize downtown San Diego. CCDC's partnership with developer Ernest W. Hahn created the highly successful Horton Plaza retail/entertainment complex and led to large-scale development of offices, hotels, and residential units. Adoption in 1992 of the Centre City redevelopment project expanded CCDC's area of responsibility to include almost all of downtown's 1,500 acres (607 hectares). Commercial and residential development is envisioned to accommodate more than 50,000 residents by 2025.[17]

A dedicated and specialized public development partner is crucial. The many responsibilities carried out by the public partner—brokering regulatory approvals, negotiating with other public agencies, shepherding the development proposal through the environmental impact and community review processes, and providing financial assistance—can expedite progress through the inevitable hurdles encountered by these projects. And more so than with other types of development, the risks of public/private development are political. Gauging both the level of political commitment to carry through with a project and the government's ability (in financial matters and personnel) to deliver on agreements is central to a developer's qualitative assessment of project feasibility.

PRACTICAL PROBLEMS AND POLICY ISSUES

Shared Decision Making

The public interests at stake in joint venture projects draw governments into the management of development and the details of decision making associated with stages four through seven of the conventional development process—decisions typically left to the private sector. As cities share more of a project's financial risk, they ask for more control. When, for example, public interests take charge of developing parts of a project, as was the case in the $95 million mixed-use Town Square project in which the city of St. Paul, Minnesota, built a park on the third level of a retail mall, it is clear that shared control is the most practical way to proceed. In that instance, although it was possible to settle some of the major issues early in the development process, St. Paul could not anticipate all the details well in advance of actual construction. Further, the demands of mutually dependent construction schedules that overlapped in time and space ruled out the hands-off control style of urban renewal. For St. Paul to cut a straightforward deal, prepare and transfer the property, and then merely monitor the developer's performance until the project was completed according to plan would have been practically impossible. The deal in St. Paul was an implied agreement to share both design and management decisions throughout the development period and to cope with problems by renegotiating any earlier understandings. Frequent trips back to the bargaining table helped move the project beyond unexpected obstacles.[18]

The ground lease form of land disposition similarly creates an ongoing business relationship. For the developer, leasing minimizes the upfront capital investments and makes more efficient use of taxable deductions; for the government agency, retaining ownership of the land allows the public to benefit

Figure 14-9	Milwaukee Development Corporation

The Milwaukee Development Corporation (MDC) is a not-for-profit corporation and the successor organization to the Milwaukee Redevelopment Corporation (MRC), which was originally created in 1973 to provide private sector leadership and financial support to revitalize downtown Milwaukee, Wisconsin. Established as a private organization with a board of directors comprising chief executive officers of major area corporations, the MRC raised $3 million in seed money in its first years of operation by selling stock to more than 40 Milwaukee-based firms. In 1983, MRC reorganized as a nonprofit corporation with operating funds coming from membership dues rather than from the sale of stock. Any return from the MRC's development partnerships has been reinvested in civic projects.

The MRC worked closely with city and county governments in its early days to promote economic development through catalytic real estate developments. It met with business and government leaders to identify priorities and to establish an agenda for downtown revitalization. Among the first targeted priority districts was the central retail area west of the Milwaukee River. The focus of development was a $150 million venture that included the construction of a Hyatt Regency Hotel, Henry Reuss Federal Plaza, and the Grand Avenue, a retail development stretching over four square blocks of downtown Milwaukee.

To develop the hotel, the MRC made a cash equity investment in the project, while the city participated in landscaping and the construction of a skywalk. For the office building, the MRC optioned much of the land, and the city assembled a portion of the land. For the retail center, the MRC forged a coalition with the city and the Rouse Company—developer of the retail center—and developed the entire $70 million project. It provided more than $16 million of the equity, purchased two of the buildings used in the redevelopment, acquired other land in the project area, and executed a lease of the retail space with the Rouse Company.

The organization also became a joint venture partner in the development of the 354-unit Yankee Hill, the first major housing development in downtown Milwaukee in 20 years. Completed in 1988, the $30 million market-rate rental project has been a resounding leasing success. MRC also worked with the Mandel Group and WISPARK, the Wisconsin state electric utility's real estate subsidiary, to develop East Point Commons, a 20-acre (8-hectare), nine-block project on the edge of downtown with 188 rental units, a 40,000-square-foot (3,700-square-meter) supermarket, and 18,000 square feet (1,700 square meters) of neighborhood retail services.

In 1998, MRC and the Mandel Group, Inc., created Library Hill, an attractive residential development in a formerly blighted area of the city through a distinctive financial partnership. The city wished to develop 139 units of market-rate rental housing and street-edge retail on a strategically located site, but a gap existed between the construction cost and the projected value of the development. To fill this gap, MDC and 18 of its member companies guaranteed the letter of credit that in turn guaranteed $17.8 million of tax-exempt bonds issued by the city of Milwaukee. These bonds brought the interest rate down low enough to bridge the difference between the project's construction cost and its rental income. In fact, lower interest rates combined with the project's outstanding rental success resulted in the probability of the bonds' early retirement.

In 2005, the MDC was reorganized as an affiliate of the Milwaukee Metropolitan Association of Commerce (MMAC) with the express purpose of broadening its mission to include regional economic development. The formula for development requires MDC's involvement in sponsoring planning studies; local government's assistance with property acquisition and relocation, public improvements, and financing when required; and a private sector entity's undertaking the development alone or as a joint venture with MDC. As the business community's not-for-profit civic developer, the Milwaukee Development Corporation continues to initiate and promote projects that support the community. Currently, MDC is taking the lead in a new five-year economic development campaign known locally as "Milwaukee 7."

Also in 2005, MDC became involved in the Kenilworth project, a mixed-use development on a 2.5-acre (1-hectare) site owned by the board of regents of the University of Wisconsin–Milwaukee. Plans call for the site to be subdivided into two parcels and developed with both university-related and commercial uses. One parcel will be leased to the Redevelopment Authority of the City of Milwaukee (RACM), which will, in turn, contract with a joint venture of the MDC and a private developer (Weas Development Company) to create student apartments, retail space, and facilities for the Peck School of the Arts. After development is completed, RACM will lease the property back to the university for a term of 30 years, with an option to purchase at

continued on next page

Figure 14-9	Milwaukee Development Corporation *(continued)*

fair market value. MDC and Weas will lease all the 26,500 square feet (2,500 square meters) of retail space for 30 years. The university will lease the second parcel to MDC and Weas under a 99-year ground lease with renewal options.

Source: Milwaukee Development Corporation, www. mmac.org.

Plans call for a condominium development on the site. The redevelopment authority will finance the project with a bond issue supported by a bank guarantee and the university's rent commitment in the operating lease.

from rising land values through lease payments and percentage rents, thereby capturing the residual value of the built improvements. Alongside these benefits, however, lies the potential for conflict and tough lease negotiations, especially if the RFP does not include a sample lease document that sets out terms and conditions affecting the developer's bid.

Structuring a ground lease that is acceptable to a long-term lender is the developer's major concern. In strong markets, government often does not subordinate the land lease to the development financing; for reasons of both business and policy, public officials generally want participation in project revenues above a base fixed rent. To control its exposure to the political as well as business risks of assuming a proprietary interest in a private investment, the public sector seeks tight lease conditions and, through participation formulas, protection against charges that the developer is earning a "windfall." Both positions present problems to institutional lenders seeking protection from the potential loss of control through foreclosure by the government fee owner.[19]

The practical problems of implementing public/private development rule out anything but an active role in project decision making for the public sector. Attempting to anticipate upfront all conditions that might arise in the course of development would not only extend the process indefinitely but also be unrealistic. Reconciling initial differences, finding efficient cost-sharing arrangements, coordinating public and private construction schedules, recasting the deal when crisis threatens the project, and managing the process in light of public review all call for flexibility in responding to the economic and political events that often challenge public/private projects.

For private developers, participation in a public/private development means changing normal business practices to accommodate the demands of a politically accountable partner. As we will see in future chapters, time pressure increases dramatically in stage six of the development process, making the public sector's active role quite stressful for the private developer and putting heavy pressure on public sector participants in the decision process as well. Consequently, the terms of agreement between the parties negotiated in stage four and signed in stage five must be even tighter and more goal aligning in public/private ventures.

Conflicts and Accountability

As the public sector has become more involved in making deals, concerns have surfaced about its objectivity in regulating development and about whether public/private development leads to a conflict of interest for the public sector. The dual role of the public sector creates a two-part dilemma: the potential conflict of interest inherent in the public sector's role as land seller and as land regulator. At its simplest, the conflict arises because a city's goals in selling versus regulating land are potentially at odds, with the city's role as seller perhaps improperly influencing its regulatory role.

The following questions should be considered in examining whether such a conflict exists:

▶ Is the city overlooking longer-range public interest goals?
▶ Can cities make good deals, especially when bargaining with sophisticated private parties?
▶ Are regulatory concessions given away too cheaply?

JOSEPH P. RILEY
Mayor, City of Charleston

Charleston, South Carolina

With no formal education in either architecture or urban design, Mayor Joseph P. Riley has demonstrated an uncanny knack for creating a powerful sense of place for citizens and tourists alike while revitalizing the centuries-old city of Charleston, South Carolina. With a developer's vision and an architect's attention to detail, his best teaching was not found in the classroom but in walking the streets, examining urban design blemishes and triumphs, and being receptive to the town's voice. Riley's tenure as mayor of Charleston began following a six-year term in the South Carolina House of Representatives. In his early years as a representative, membership in the progressive wing of the Democratic party signaled his reformist position on civil rights and social equality deeply dividing the state.

Indeed, once elected mayor of Charleston in 1975, Riley increased the number of African Americans on the city council by 50 percent and appointed the city's first black police chief. In 2000, his "Get in Step" campaign to march four days to the state capital to remove the Confederate flag from atop the South Carolina State House was met with national media coverage and credited with the flag's ultimate removal. Racial harmony and equitable consideration of the needs of all citizens, regardless of social class, are pillars of Riley's mayoral canon. In fact, to confront the port town's slavery-dominated past, Mayor Riley has proposed the construction of a $60 million international African American history museum, set to be the first of its kind in the world.

His resolve to cure the social issues of his early political years is matched by his unrelenting attention to the structural importance of the public domain. Mayor Riley spends much of his time considering development issues. He often works directly with developers to bring to fruition buildings and spaces that will prove most appealing and beneficial to the community. While touring in Europe on a Marshall Fellowship, Riley noticed the costly materials that were used in public areas. He learned from his travels that it is the city's duty to provide beauty at its own expense for communal enjoyment and should view such costs as an investment. In the long run, Riley posits, thoughtful improvements pay dividends by making the city more desirous to vacationers, businesses, and investors. He likens cities to family heirlooms in that "we are to pass them on to future generations in just as beautiful condition—if not more beautiful—as the way we found them."

Illustrative of the mayor's insistence on the public's benefiting from development, the accomplishment of Waterfront Park has become iconic of Charleston's celebrated revival. The

Located on the shore where the Cooper River flows into the Charleston Harbor, the 13-acre (5.3-hectare) Waterfront Park is one of Riley's successes. Bill Murton, City of Charleston

land used for the development of the park was originally sought after by a developer who planned to turn an overlooked stretch along the Cooper River into a mixed-use complex. Riley had another idea: one prohibiting private development of this property. Instead of opting for the private development, Riley recognized the chance for economic and social revival through public works and consequently envisioned the potential for Waterfront Park. He described the 13-acre (5.3-hectare) park abutting the river as "a gift to the future," saying the alternative project will add tax revenues to local coffers and raise the price of real estate in the vicinity. After his time and efforts in the design and construction of the park, Riley's foresight paid off by significantly raising nearby land prices and creating a meaningful public space that could be enjoyed by all.

Likewise, the preservation of Charleston's historic features is something Riley adamantly pursues. Although when he first took office in 1975, 27 percent of its citizens lived below the poverty line, its convention facilities were vastly underused, and commercial space vacancies exceeded 1 million square feet (93,000 square meters), the developments he inspired coupled with stringent regulatory guidelines breathed new life into Charleston. The guidelines include "burying" parking facilities out of sight behind shops and restaurants whenever possible

continued on next page

and setting noise ordinances in popular residential neighborhoods to preserve quality of life. Immediately following Hurricane Hugo, which stripped many structures' rooftops in Charleston in 1989, Riley was quick to allow property owners to repair damages, but he set the conditions of the repairs to abide by the city's high design standards: if the original material were not available at the time to fix a roof, it would later be replaced with a more historically appropriate material.

So effective was Riley's city management that in 1986 he helped found the Mayor's Institute on City Design. This program, which convenes twice a year nationally and four times a year regionally, invites six to eight mayors from cities around the country to introduce a critical urban design problem found in their city. An interdisciplinary team helps to correct the setback. In 2006, the program celebrated its 20-year history and the more than 700 mayors who have participated

in the institute. Reflecting Riley's stance on the value of diversity and identifying many similarities between challenges in small and large cities, much of the success of the program has been in its inclusion of mayors from all sizes of cities and every major region of the United States.

For his tireless efforts as a statesman at the local, regional, and national levels, Mayor Riley has won much praise. In 1985, he was presented a Presidential Award for Design Excellence by Ronald Reagan for public housing in Charleston, and in 2000, he became the first recipient of the ULI J.C. Nichols Prize for Visionaries in Urban Development. Riley believes that the true job of a leader is to understand the "best aspirations of citizens." His attitude toward his position as a civil servant is best summarized by his insistence that public administrators have a "moral imperative" to create beautiful, meaningful places.

▶ Are planners as deal makers focusing on short-term real estate activity rather than on long-range comprehensive planning?

▶ Can traditional notions of due process be fulfilled when deals are hammered out behind closed doors?

The potential for conflict of interest is great, especially when real estate markets are strong. So far, however, conflicts have surfaced only infrequently, particularly given the large number of public/private projects. One such conflict arose with a government center project in Fairfax County, Virginia. In this case, the county was accused of selling the land at too low a price to develop its new building. Critics said the county should have held onto the land (which rose substantially in value after the trade) and sold bonds to finance the government center. The issue to consider is a question of public stewardship. Does gaining income for the city through the disposition of city-owned land further the public interest?[20]

Public/private deal making also poses difficult issues of political and financial accountability. With development agreements too complex to work out in public forums, meetings must be held behind closed doors. But for a local government to grant formal

approval, the city council needs to understand the agreements; nonetheless, council members are not always fully briefed on the choices and tradeoffs that are factored into the decision-making process. The complexity of public/private deals also underscores the importance of balancing the need to provide timely information to both council members and the public against the need to protect the city's effectiveness in ongoing negotiations with private developers. In practice, the city council typically faces the choice of accepting a deal as it is or running the risk that a rejection would mark the council as the spoiler of a project that has been years in the making.

Ideally, a full accounting of costs and benefits should accompany the evaluation of a deal; with several different agencies involved in negotiations and cost sharing, however, it is often hard to track all the direct costs and indirect subsidies. Certain aspects of a deal are simply too difficult to value. Although design amenities, subway improvements, and below-market loans can be valued by referencing market equivalents, other benefits such as employment preferences and environmental mitigation commitments have no obvious market prices. These differences make it hard to standardize evaluation techniques and to define the value of tradeoffs in a public/

private deal. As a result, public officials must devote substantial time and resources to effectively communicating the objectives of public/private development and to disclosing public commitments, risks, and expected returns. Mayor Joseph P. Riley of Charleston, South Carolina, advocated for public/private joint ventures and built the community support necessary to make them successful.

SUMMARY

The shift to public/private development evolved from the efforts of local government to manage the redevelopment process with greater control than that afforded by regulatory strategies and arm's-length relationships with private developers. The success of public/private development has made it an important strategy for stimulating local economic development and financing selected items of capital infrastructure. It is also a means of implementing complex redevelopment projects. The highly visible record of public/private projects from the 1980s until today has reshaped the landscape of downtowns across the country. The tangible results of this type of development approach contrast sharply with the legacy of political controversy, acres of cleared but eerily vacant land, and years of frustration that had resulted from failed urban renewal projects developed under a strategy of command and control on the part of the public sector in the 1960s and 1970s. The strong record offers tangible evidence that the public/private approach is a pragmatic solution to the earlier bureaucratic problems that beset the federal urban renewal program, proving that it is a strategy extremely well suited for coping with the complexity and risks of attracting the types of projects officials have wanted to revitalize their cities. Consequently, city governments, public authorities, and other special-purpose agencies have strong incentives to build a foundation for public/private partnerships by establishing planning and consensus-building processes, resource mobilization efforts, and institutional mechanisms the set the groundwork for successful joint ventures.

The scope and focus of urban public/private development activity continues to evolve. Building on past experience, much of which was concentrated on large-scale building of downtowns, cities today tend to focus more on smaller-scale projects targeted at rebuilding neighborhoods, creating transit hubs, revitalizing waterfronts, and creating town centers with a mix of uses. And there is little reason to expect that the drive for off-budget financing of public infrastructure and civic amenities among suburban governments will abate. Land-owning public authorities as well are likely to continue to pursue efforts to capture value through joint development. No matter the market conditions, the motives for pursuing public/private development remain strong. That fewer opportunities may exist will only make that handful of opportunities the intense focus of limited resources for both public and private sector players.

Given that the management of development from the public perspective is so difficult, public bodies should do everything within their power to facilitate strong and consistent management. Particularly important is coordinating all public agencies to avoid undue time delays.

TERMS

- ▶ Financing gap
- ▶ Investment tax credits
- ▶ Joint development
- ▶ Land leasing
- ▶ Municipal bonds
- ▶ Public/private joint venture
- ▶ Quasi-public organization
- ▶ RFP
- ▶ RFQ
- ▶ TIF
- ▶ UDAG
- ▶ Urban renewal
- ▶ Value capture

REVIEW QUESTIONS

14.1   Why has the number and size of public/private joint ventures grown over time?

14.2   What are the opportunities for working in a public/private partnership for a city? For a developer? What are some of the practical problems or points of tension in such a business relationship?

14.3 Describe the five key decisions the public sector faces in implementing a public/private project.

14.4 Why is city assistance, both financial and organizational, needed to facilitate public/private development projects?

14.5 What are the special issues that a proposed shopping center in an inner-city location faces?

14.6 What are some of the financial techniques that cities can use and have used to accomplish their goals for revitalization and for reducing their risk?

NOTES

1. See Lynne B. Sagalyn, "Explaining the Improbable: Local Redevelopment in the Wake of Federal Cutbacks," *Journal of the American Planning Association*, 1990, pp. 429–441.

2. See "The Can Company," *Development Case Study CO30005* (Washington, D.C.: ULI–the Urban Land Institute, 2000).

3. See "The Burnham Hotel at the Reliance Building," *Development Case Study CO31016* (Washington, D.C.: ULI–the Urban Land Institute, 2001).

4. See "Museum Place," *Development Case Study C034008* (Washington, D.C.: ULI–the Urban Land Institute, 2004).

5. Richard F. Babcock, "The City as Entrepreneur: Fiscal Wisdom or Regulatory Folly?" in *City Deal Making*, ed. Terry Jill Lassar (Washington, D.C.: ULI–the Urban Land Institute, 1990), pp. 9–43.

6. See Robert T. Dunphy et al., *Developing around Transit: Strategies and Solutions That Work* (Washington, D.C.: ULI–the Urban Land Institute, 2004).

7. Babcock, "The City as Entrepreneur," p. 14.

8. Empirical studies of auction dispositions for housing in both Boston and New York, for instance, revealed critical limitations—low levels of rehabilitation investment and immediate property tax recidivism. See Christine A. Flynn and Lawrence P.

Goldman, *New York's Largest Landowner: The City as Owner, Planner, and Marketer of Real Estate*, Report for the Fund for the City of New York, 1980; and H. James Brown and Christopher E. Herbert, "Local Government Real Estate Asset Management," unpublished report for the Lincoln Institute for Land Policy Seminar, September 1989.

9. The infusion of cash can be duplicated with prepayment of rent, and the risk of nonpayment can be nearly eliminated with the purchase of a riskless government security, as was the case for Copley Place, a large-scale mixed-use project in Boston.

10. See Lynne B. Sagalyn, "Leasing: The Strategic Option for Public Development," Working Paper (Cambridge, Mass.: Lincoln Institute of Land Policy, 1993); Robert Wetmore and Chris Klinger, "Land Leases: More Than Rent Schedules," *Urban Land*, June 1990, pp. 6–9; and Lynne B. Sagalyn, "Negotiating Public Benefits: The Bargaining Calculus of Public/Private Development," *Urban Studies*, December 1997, pp. 1955–1970.

11. Community Redevelopment Agency of the City of Los Angeles, "Development Offering: Remaining 8.75 Acres of Bunker Hill, Downtown Los Angeles," September 1979.

12. Jesse C. Smith, "Vitalizing Urban Property," *Urban Land*, July 2005, pp. 50–54.

13. Lynne B. Sagalyn, "Measuring Financial Returns When the City Acts as an Investor: Boston and Faneuil Hall Marketplace," *Real Estate Issues*, Fall/Winter 1989, pp. 7–14.

14. Lynne B. Sagalyn, "Public Profit Sharing: Symbol or Substance?" in *City Deal Making*, ed. Lassar, pp. 139–153.

15. See "Somerset Park," *Development Case Study CO30013* (Washington, D.C.: ULI–the Urban Land Institute, 2000).

16. David C. Petersen, *Developing Sports, Convention, and Performing Arts Facilities*, 3d ed. (Washington, D.C.: ULI–the Urban Land Institute, 2001).

17. Retrieved December 10, 2005, from www.ccdc.com.

18. For a more complete description of Town Square, see Frieden and Sagalyn, *Downtown, Inc.*, pp. 140–142.

19. In the case of percentage rent, lenders hesitate because they fear a reduction in the amount of income to be capitalized when a large percentage of the income stream is committed to a ground lessor. In the event of foreclosure, the valuation impact would be substantial unless the lessor had agreed to subordinate the percentage provision in the lease.

20. Lassar, *City Deal Making*, p. 3.

CHAPTER 15

Affordable Housing

For many American homeowners, the early 2000s were the best of times. By 2004, homeownership reached almost 70 percent, and homeowners' combined home equity was more than $10 trillion. Household wealth fueled consumer spending, as more people than ever drew on their equity to finance education, retirement, vacation homes, and various luxury items. But as housing prices continue to rise in most major markets in the United States and mortgage rates creep up, the dream of homeownership moves farther and farther out of reach for many working families. It is no longer just very-low-income families who suffer from lack of affordable housing. Today, many young married couples who in the past could plan on buying a small starter home must now defer that dream because of skyrocketing housing costs, and many workers with steady jobs cannot afford to live close to their jobs. Problems of affordability are worsening—and are moving up the income level. In just three years, from 2001 to 2004, the number of households paying more than half their incomes for housing increased by almost 2 mil-

lion, to a record 15.8 million households. Although affordability pressures are highest among renters, they also affect a large proportion of homeowners as well.[1]

This chapter introduces the concept of affordable housing and examines it through the lenses of both the public and private sectors. This type of development, formerly infeasible for private developers without massive direct government subsidies, can potentially be quite attractive to private developers as the result of a combination of tax and risk-sharing incentives. The chapter also discusses the nature and extent of the problem of affordability, outlines past and current activities and policy considerations, and discusses ongoing public and/or private efforts to increase the supply of affordable housing (see Figure 15-1). It looks in depth at the following topics:

▶ Definitions of affordable housing and low income;

▶ The evolving roles of federal, state, and local governments and the private sector;

▶ Low-income rental housing; and

▶ Affordable ownership housing.

Diane R. Suchman, consultant, wrote an earlier version of this chapter. Michael A. Stegman updated the text for this edition.

Figure 15-1	Public Policy Issues

Several key policy issues must be addressed in formulating a response to the extensive, complex, and difficult problems associated with affordable housing.

Achieving a Consensus for Action

The problem must be recognized and its key components and priority needs agreed to, including what, if any, responsibility the public must assume.

Allocating Scarce Resources

How should scarce funds be allocated to provide assistance? Who should receive assistance, how much, and in what form? What are reasonable goals? Should few households be provided with sufficient resources, or should the same dollar amount be stretched or leveraged to reach a greater number of households with smaller subsidies?

Roles and Responsibilities

What are the appropriate roles for the federal, state, and local governments and for the private sector, including nonprofits? What impact will devolution—the passing down of responsibility from the federal to state governments—have on the production of affordable housing and vouchers for families who need to obtain market-rate housing? How and to what extent should the poor be empowered to decide for themselves how their needs can best be met? How can the participation of the parties be encouraged, sustained, and coordinated?

Related Issues

Maximization of financial resources. We must identify, generate, and/or tap additional sources of funding and find ways to leverage available funds. We must find the means to streamline and simplify the financing of low-income housing so that an efficient and replicable delivery system can be established.

Supporting physical and social services. Without supportive services and programs for revitalization, physical shelter deteriorates rapidly and does little to improve the lives of the poor. Related issues such as inadequate income, education, job training, drug counseling, security, and medical and social services must be addressed if goals for housing are to succeed.

Populations with special needs. Certain population groups—the elderly, the disabled, single-parent households,

rural households, immigrants, the homeless—have special needs that cannot be adequately met by policies and programs designed for more typical populations.

Preservation of low-income housing. The preservation of low-income housing is particularly critical, given the tens of thousands of contracts that have expired between owners and HUD for federally subsidized housing units. In a five-year period, owners of more than 160,000 formerly HUD-assisted multifamily units opted not to renew their subsidy contracts and raised their rents to market rates.[a] What incentives can Congress extend to owners to ensure that the units are not converted to market-rate housing and rents pushed beyond the reach of the nation's low- and moderate-income households? How can the debt on these properties be restructured to make it financially feasible for owners to maintain them in the low-cost housing stock while at the same time minimizing the claims to the FHA fund? Once constructed and operating, how can low-income housing be preserved to ensure its long-term affordability and to avoid rapid deterioration and decay? Where will funds for operation and maintenance come from? Where will funds for capital expenditures come from? How can commitments to long-term affordability best be ensured?

Responsiveness versus efficiency. How can the tension between the need for local solutions and responsiveness to social goals and the need for systemization and efficient production be resolved?

Subsidies for middle- and upper-income owners. As many advocates of low-income housing point out, the groups receiving the largest federal subsidy are middle- and upper-income homeowners through the income tax deduction for interest paid on home mortgages. The U.S. Office of Management and Budget estimates that the revenue forgone to the U.S. Treasury as a result of the deductibility of mortgage interest on up to $1 million in principal on home mortgage debt will exceed $365 billion between 2002 and 2006.[b] The elimination of this deduction has been a major part of the housing policy debate for decades, leading to the capping of the mortgage interest deduction in the late 1980s. Although its complete annihilation is extremely unlikely, the subsidy will likely be the subject of lively debate well into the future. Other substantial subsidies to middle- and upper-income owners include the deductibility from federal income taxes of state and local property taxes on owner-occupied homes, estimated to be $99.2

Figure 15-1 | **Public Policy Issues** *(continued)*

billion between 2002 and 2006, and the exclusion of capital gains on home sales, estimated to be almost $70 billion between 2002 and 2006.[c] This latter subsidy will be even

deeper in future years as legislation that passed in 1997 virtually eliminated the payment on any capital gains on home sales for most taxpayers.

[a]Michael Bodaken, "Taking the Right Steps to Preserve Affordable Housing: The Correct Path Lies Just ahead," Guest Commentary, *Affordable Housing Finance*, July 2003, p. 6.
[b]Data are for fiscal years. U.S. Government Printing Office, Joint Committee on Taxation, Estimates of Federal Tax Expenditures for Fiscal Years 2002–2006, January 17, 2002, Table 1, p. 22.
[c]Ibid.

A DEFINITION OF AFFORDABLE HOUSING

Because it is so broad, the term "affordable housing" means different things to different people, and it has different implications in different places. Some define affordable housing as housing that has not risen rapidly in price over the last several years. Others think of affordability in terms of houses that young people entering the market for the first time can buy. Some might equate affordability with rental rather than with for-sale housing, and still others consider affordable housing synonymous with government-subsidized housing or even with public housing. In fact, the term encompasses a wide spectrum of housing types, housing prices, and housing occupants.

As a general rule, housing can be considered affordable for a low- or moderate-income household if that household can own or rent the housing for an amount up to 30 percent of its household income[2]—a standard that federal, state, and local government agencies generally use. Mortgage lenders also use it as one important criterion in qualifying buyers of market-rate housing for mortgage loans. Home sellers and their real estate agents generally do not seriously consider potential homebuyers if the price of a home is more than two and one-half to three times a prospective borrower's income, with this standard derived from the 30 percent ratio.

According to the 30 percent standard, the term "affordable housing" can apply to any income group. As a practical matter, however, discussions of public policy usually speak of affordability as:

▶ Low-income rental housing—housing that requires subsidies for production or for occupants or both to make it affordable to low- and very-low-income households; or
▶ Affordable ownership housing—market-rate, unsubsidized housing for moderate-income households, particularly first-time buyers, and subsidized ownership housing for low- and moderate-income homebuyers.

The 30 percent definition for affordable housing suffers from serious limitations when applied to low-income households because it ignores variations in the size of families. Obviously, the larger the family, the harder it is to find adequate housing at the 30 percent of income level. It is also problematic in determining whether a given geographic area contains an adequate supply of affordable housing, as it compares only numbers of households at various levels of income with numbers of housing units at the prices or rents these households can afford. This standard fails to consider that access to housing also implies a certain amount of choice in housing types and locations so that various needs, particularly the commute to work, can be accommodated. Studies have shown that minority households of the same income level as nonminority households often pay higher prices for housing because of limited access and choice. Thus, a simple comparison of the number of households at a given income level with the number of housing units that households at these income levels can afford is inadequate in capturing the problem of affordability faced by many minority households as a result of discrimination in housing markets.[3]

Nonminority low- and moderate-income households are also susceptible to limited housing choices and limited access. Discrimination or "steering" by sellers, real estate agents, brokers, leasing agents, lenders, mortgage insurers, or the secondary market can limit the effective supply of housing available to certain households. More subtly, affluent communities might rely on socially and legally acceptable arguments to fight the development of lower-cost housing, even though the underlying force behind their arguments could in fact be veiled racial discrimination.

THE WORKING DEFINITION OF LOW INCOME

The criteria used to determine whether a household is eligible for government housing assistance are generally used to define the phrase "low income." In most cases, according to the U.S. Department of Housing and Urban Development (HUD), the following criteria apply:

▶ Very low income—A four-person household with an income less than 50 percent of the local area median family income. In this category, a four-person household with an income less than 30 percent of the local area median family income is considered "extremely low income";

▶ Other low income—A four-person household with an income from 50 to 80 percent of the local area median income.

▶ Moderate income—A four-person household with an income from 80 to 95 percent of the local area median income.[4]

Given that median income differs by locality, a household with a fixed income could fall in different defined categories of income in different areas of the country. The percentages vary somewhat along with variations in family size. Using a standard of "relative deprivation" ensures that a certain proportion of households will, by definition, always fall into each of the designated categories. Generally speaking, however, extremely low-income and very-low-income households cannot compete effectively for market-

rate housing in many locations in the Northeast, on the West Coast, in Hawaii, parts of Florida, and urban pockets in other parts of the country. Moderate-income households face the same plight.

These measures do not, however, take into consideration other aspects of a household's financial situation: ownership of assets and equity in a home (which may be significant in some groups such as the elderly); government assistance such as food stamps, Medicare, and housing assistance (although Temporary Assistance to Needy Families [TANF], the successor to Aid to Families with Dependent Children [AFDC], is taken into account when calculating income); and employer-provided benefits such as payments for health insurance premiums, which can add significantly to an employee's total compensation package.

PUBLIC AND PRIVATE SECTOR ROLES IN DEVELOPING AFFORDABLE HOUSING

Since the 1980s, changes in the political landscape have seen the federal government's reducing the role it plays in the provision of affordable housing. As a result, state and local agencies have become much more actively involved. Likewise, private developers, community development corporations (CDCs), and other nonprofit organizations are also becoming major players. With more actors from many different arenas becoming involved in affordable housing, the number of projects developed through public/private partnerships has risen dramatically. Increasingly, public/private partnerships are becoming the norm in developing residences that are affordable.

The Federal Government's Role

In the early part of the 20th century, production of housing at all levels was considered an activity of the private sector. The federal government's role was limited to expediting mortgage lending associated with homeownership. From the Great Depression through 1980, however, the history of the federal government's involvement in housing—through financial assistance to producers and occupants, direct production, tax incentives, insurance and credit programs, specialized thrift institutions, the creation of a secondary market, and neighborhood revitalization programs—was one of expanding responsibility. Especially during the 1970s, federal housing programs supported massive production of low-income housing.

Housing policy shifted dramatically beginning in the late 1970s. Between 1978 and 1990, the federal government systematically dismantled its programs for the production of assisted housing and withdrew funding support for affordable housing. Federal authorizations for housing dropped by 70 percent between 1978 and 1989. The government's retreat from affordable housing is more clearly revealed in HUD's budget when the effect of inflation is removed. In 1978, at the peak of federal spending for housing, the budget authority reached $73.8 billion. By 1980, direct spending for housing was only $54.1 billion, and, by 1990, spending dropped to only $13.7 billion—less than one-fifth its 1978 level.

The National Affordable Housing Act (NAHA) of 1990 renewed the federal government's commitment to housing, and between 1989 and 1993, federal authorizations for housing (current dollars) rose from $9.6 billion to $21.2 billion—an increase of 120 percent.

In 1992, the HOPE VI program was launched with the goal of replacing severely distressed public housing projects with mixed-income housing. It combined grants for physical revitalization with funding for management improvements, supportive services for residents, and housing vouchers to enable some public housing residents to rent apartments in the private market. The goals of this ambitious redevelopment and community building program were to:

Figure 15-2	Sources of Housing Funds 2002

☐ No Funds
░ State Funds Only
▓ County/Municipal Funds Only
■ State and County/Municipal Funds

Sources: The State of the Nation's Housing, 2005 (Cambridge, Mass.: Joint Center for Housing Studies, Harvard University, 2005); and *Housing Trust Fund Progress Report,* 2002, Center for Community Change.

▶ Improve the living environment of severely distressed public housing through demolition, rehabilitation, reconfiguration, and replacement;

▶ Revitalize public housing project sites;

▶ Provide housing that would decrease the concentration of very-low-income families; and

▶ Build sustainable communities.

HOPE VI has received mixed reviews from city officials, neighborhood leaders, and public housing residents. There is no question that it removed some of the most distressed housing environments from communities and, in many cases, replaced them with improved mixed-income developments that have contributed to the revitalization of surrounding areas. At the same time, though, it eliminated a substantial number of public housing units that have not been replaced by permanent affordable housing. And it is charged that the original residents of HOPE VI projects have not always benefited from the program.[5]

As of July 2007, the fate of HOPE VI was undetermined. Since fiscal year 2004, the second Bush Administration has advocated for the elimination of the program's funding. Bipartisan support for HOPE VI, however, has kept the program alive, even in the face of large budget cuts: the program's budget dropped from more than $570 million before fiscal year 2004 to $100 million in fiscal year 2006. In 2005 and again in 2006, both the House and the Senate introduced bills to reauthorize HOPE VI. Although these bills failed to pass, the 110th Congress in March 2007 introduced another bill (S. 829), which, as of July 2007, was in the early stages of the legislative process.

HUD's budget flattened during the mid-1990s as HUD restructured many of its multifamily programs to restore the financial standing—and reduce the risk—of its loan portfolio. Some of the losses in federal spending for housing were restored in the new millennium. In 2005, HUD's budget authority reached just over $31 billion—a level not achieved since 1978.[6]

In recent years, however, the majority of these resources have gone toward renewing subsidy contracts for existing assisted housing projects rather than for new production that would expand the supply of affordable housing.[7] These increases notwithstanding, funding levels for housing remain uncertain and subject to the vagaries of congressional appropriations. What is fairly certain is that the funding levels for housing production programs of the late 1970s will not be reached again as the federal government struggles with a budget deficit and turns more toward tax expenditure programs, state and local government programs, and the private sector for the provision of affordable housing.

State and Local Governments' Expanding Roles

In the mid-1980s, after decades of leadership in public sector assistance for affordable housing, the federal government began looking increasingly to state and local governments to provide decent and affordable housing for the populace. Since that time, many state and local governments have picked up the slack and now administer programs, some of which are modeled after defunct federal programs.

Although not all states and localities have risen to the challenge of devising or identifying resources for housing, the range of responses to date demonstrates determination, creativity, and considerable success in tapping into existing resources or creating new ones. Indeed, data from the American Housing Survey for the United States for the years between 1987 and 1997 suggest that state and local governments gradually assumed larger roles in the provision of rental housing for their poorest households. The number of poverty-level renters assisted through rent reductions attributable to state and local subsidies rose from 314,000 in 1987 to 380,000 in 1995.[8]

The history of state and local governments' assistance to *poverty-level* citizens who wish to become homeowners has been less straightforward. In 1987, state and local housing programs provided assistance to 220,000 poverty-level homeowners, and, by 1991, the number of assisted poverty-level homeowners had risen to 314,000. But by 1997, only 263,000 poverty-level homeowners used lower-cost mortgages available from state and local housing programs. Whether this reduction represents a retreat by state and local governments as they increasingly target limited resources to the neediest renting households or the decrease is attributable to waning demand cannot be discerned from the data.

The Private Sector's Roles

In an environment of decreasing federal involvement and scarce state and local resources, the private sector is increasingly being called on to pinch-hit, and many participants have stepped up to the plate. Private sector participants include for-profit developers who have received incentives in the form of low-income housing tax credits (LIHTCs) and tax-exempt rental housing bonds, banks and other financial institutions such as insurance companies and pension funds, trade unions, foundations, philanthropic groups, and nonprofit housing developers. The anticipated users of low-income housing are also sometimes participants in the process, though the extent of their participation varies from place to place and often from project to project.

Today, nonprofit housing developers such as CDCs are significant nongovernmental players who produce record numbers of affordable homes, often in conjunction with for-profit developers. They also play an important role in keeping the need for affordable housing in front of decision makers. Many charities and foundations, including the Freddie Mac Foundation, the Ford Foundation, and Habitat for Humanity, have made affordable housing a primary cause. The challenges are great, however: getting an affordable housing project to fly can test even the savviest financier.

TYPES OF AFFORDABLE HOUSING

The provision of all types of affordable housing requires a creative search for reduced costs at every step of the process. Increasing the supply of low-income *rental* housing demands that governments and developers generally seek below-market financing and direct subsidies and take advantage of available tax expenditure programs such as LIHTCs and municipal tax-exempt bonds. To produce affordable

ownership housing, on the other hand, the general approach is to minimize the direct costs of development: land, land development, and construction. The differences between affordable rental and ownership housing are explored throughout the remainder of this chapter.

Low-Income Rental Housing

The nation's affordable rental stock has been shrinking for more than three decades as a result of demolition, abandonment, and the conversion of units from affordable to market-rate housing. From 1993 to 2003, the inventory of affordable units dropped by 1.2 million.[9] The effective shortage is even greater than the numbers imply, partly because higher-income households are able to outbid lower-income households for the least expensive units. For example, in 2001, higher-income households occupied 2.7 million of the 7.9 million lowest-cost units.[10]

Difficulty in finding affordable housing is an issue that spans income groups, but the problem is most serious for renters at the low end of the income spectrum. The number of very-low-income renters grew by 13.5 percent between 1985 and 1995, driven largely by the growth in poor single-parent families. In comparison, the number of renters with very high incomes fell by 5 percent. Low-income renters are concentrated in center cities, many in inner cities. Thus, they are disproportionately affected by high crime rates, low educational attainment, and other ills of urban life.[11]

Low-income households rely heavily on government programs to secure housing that is both affordable and adequate. Although more than 4 million renter households with incomes less than half the area median receive housing assistance, HUD estimates that this number represents only about a quarter of the renters with incomes that low.[12]

Shrinking Supply

A shift in the focus of federal government policy in the 1980s away from the production of low-income rental housing units toward the provision of housing certificates and vouchers that enable eligible households to obtain private sector housing led to a reduction in the production of new subsidized rental homes. The discontinuation of the federal government's newer production programs, particularly Section 8 (new construction, substantial rehabilitation, and moderate rehabilitation) during that time has further contributed to the decline in housing production. As a result, new affordable rental supply in many places across the country lags far behind population growth.

The losses resulting from cuts in new production programs have been exacerbated by the loss of existing housing units built under the early federal production programs (Section 221(d)(3) and Section 236 programs). Contracts between private owners of housing built under those programs during the 1960s and 1970s are expiring. If contract rents fall below the basic costs of maintenance and operation, private owners of assisted units built under these programs will disinvest in their property, thereby accelerating the removal of units from the inventory of affordable housing. Owners of assisted units also upgrade and convert units, raise rents, and, in effect, remove additional units from the affordable stock. Compounding these losses, many more of the most obsolete and deteriorated public housing units have been torn down as part of the Hope VI public housing transformation initiative, further shrinking the affordable rental inventory.[13]

Budget cuts and HUD's restructuring of the multifamily housing program will likely continue to take their toll on the supply of subsidized units. Legislation designed to preserve project-based Section 8 housing at rents consistent with local markets may cause additional hemorrhaging. Section 8 contract rents in many areas are currently above market rents. As contracts expire and HUD aims to get contract rents more in line with market rents before renewal, some property owners may not renew at the lower rent levels, opting instead to remove their units from the stock of low-cost assisted units.

The availability of public rental housing is also problematic. According to a report by HUD's Office of Policy Development and Research, tenants in public housing in 1997 waited, on average, nearly one year for a public housing unit to become available. A more recent study of hunger and homelessness in 23 cities conducted for the U.S. Conference of Mayors suggests that the situation has not gotten any better. For public housing, the average wait in 2003 was 36 months in Denver, 24 in Kansas City and Philadelphia, 60 in Trenton, and 36 in Washington, D.C. The shortest waits were in Nashville (two months), Louisville (eight), Boston (11), and Burlington, Vermont (nine).[14] Nonetheless, in the early 1990s, 10 percent of public housing units stood vacant as public housing authorities waited for funding from HUD to undertake needed maintenance.[15] Indeed, many of the units in public housing projects desperately need repair and modernization. HUD's analysis of the 1993 American Housing Survey revealed that nearly 12 percent of the public housing stock in which very-low-income renters reside was structurally inadequate because of low initial construction standards or poor maintenance. Rather than attempt to redevelop all these units, HUD and Congress decided to demolish them and replace them through a combination of housing vouchers and a modest amount of mixed-use, mixed-income new housing financed largely through the HOPE VI program.

Increasing Need

At the same time the inventory of affordable rental housing has declined, the demand from poor and moderate households needing such housing has remained strong. For the lowest-income renters, less affordable housing means that they must spend a higher proportion of income on housing costs. Because housing is generally the first claim on income, households with limited incomes often cannot afford other necessities like food, medication, insurance, and savings. The problem of crowding is also more pronounced when focusing on extremely low-income households. It is estimated that 2.5 million households live in crowded or structurally inadequate units.

Working families with children are another group that faces strong pressures to find affordable housing. It is estimated that among the nation's working families with children, 10 million are poor or near poor. The median income of working poor families with children is just $12,000 and, of near-poor families with children,

The affordable apartments of Chatham Square—a HUD HOPE VI mixed-income project located north of downtown Alexandria, Virginia— are designed to look like the expensive, high-end townhouses of the market-rate component. *Cameron Davidson*

only $27,000. These households often spend more than half of their incomes on housing, they often live in crowded and substandard conditions, and they are increasingly forced to live farther from their workplaces in areas where housing is less expensive.

In the future, pressures for affordable housing will grow, largely because of increasing numbers of immigrant families. Immigration is expected to account for about one-third of household growth in the decade ahead, and children of immigrants will be a major contributor to the demand for housing.[16]

Homeless Populations

One manifestation of the increasing need for low-cost rental housing is the large number of homeless individuals and families on the streets of many U.S. cities. In 1990 for the first time, the U.S. Census Bureau sent enumerators to locations typically associated with the homeless population to try to develop a sense of the magnitude of the problem. The bureau attempted to count persons who do not live in typical households but instead reside in homes for unwed mothers, drug and alcohol treatment centers, agricultural workers' dormitories on farms, group homes for the mentally ill, and other nonhousehold living arrangements. According to the 1990 Census of Population and Housing, nearly 460,000 persons were found at these locations. And although the Census Bureau cautions that the data undeniably underestimate the number of homeless, it is difficult to know the magnitude of the undercount.[17] Although not based on the Census Bureau's enumeration, more recent survey data suggest that "between 700,000 and 800,000 people are homeless on any given night, and that over the course of a year, between 2.5 and 3.5 million people will experience homelessness in this country."[18]

Because of the controversies that technically flawed enumerations of the homeless raise, policy makers have turned their attention away from counting to improving the provision of comprehensive services to homeless families and individuals. With annual federal funding levels of more than $1.2 billion a year, the federal government has adopted a goal of ending chronic homeless in ten years.[19]

Proponents of a decennial sampling rather than a head count of the population and housing units say that sampling guarantees a more accurate count of the homeless, immigrants, minorities, and other populations difficult to enumerate. Better representation of these groups will give them better representation in Congress as district lines are redrawn and thus better access to federal program funding. But the U.S. Supreme Court struck down the use of sampling for enumeration for Census 2000.

Federal Government Activities

Federal government subsidies for rental housing fall into two broad categories—supply side and demand side. Supply-side subsidies are given to developers and owners to produce housing that is affordable to low- and moderate-income households. Demand-side subsidies are provided to eligible households to seek housing in the private market. During the early 1980s, the federal government began shifting toward demand-side subsidies.

The Housing Choice voucher program, also known as Section 8, has been one of the major demand-side programs since it was established in 1974. The program provides vouchers to eligible households to help them pay the rent on privately owned units of their own choice. Under the program, households may select any accommodations that rent for no more than the fair market rents established by HUD. Fair market rents vary by metropolitan area (or county for nonmetropolitan areas) and by number of bedrooms and, in theory, reflect typical asking rents for apartments in the area. Since 1998, 75 percent of all new voucher holders must have extremely low incomes, at or below 30 percent of the area median income. Today, about 1.8 million households use rental assistance vouchers.[20]

Detractors of demand-side subsidies believe that housing markets are inefficient and that income-related housing allowances rather than subsidies for new production may be insufficient to spur developers to supply housing that is affordable for the nation's low- and moderate-income families. In any event, most production (supply-side) programs provide few units that are affordable for low-income households without additional demand-side rental subsidies. Nevertheless, the two types of subsidies can be used together quite effectively.

As is the case with public housing, the waiting lists for housing vouchers are quite long in many cities. The Conference of Mayors' study cited above found that the average wait ranged from 12 months in Boston and Burlington to 48 months in Providence.[21]

Federal supply-side activities help augment demand-side programs. HUD has contributed significantly to the provision of affordable housing over the years through direct spending programs, but the U.S. Department of the Treasury arguably has become even more instrumental in this effort through its tax expenditure programs: tax-exempt bonds and LIHTCs (see Figures 15-3 and 15-4). LIHTCs are one of the largest federal subsidy programs that support the development of various types of rental housing for lower-income residents. Essentially, the LIHTC is a credit against regular federal income tax liability for investments in the acquisition and rehabilitation or construction of qualified low-income rental housing. Since its inception in 1987 until 2006, the LIHTC program assisted in the production of approximately 1.8 million affordable units.[22]

Other significant federal programs support the supply of affordable housing:

▶ The Home Investment Partnership Act program (HOME), which includes grants from the fed-

Figure 15-3	Tax-Exempt Bond Financing

Tax-exempt bonds issued by state or local governments have helped finance the development of low-income multifamily housing. Issuers sell bonds to investors whose income from such investments is exempt from federal—and, in most cases, state—income taxes. Consequently, issuers can market bonds at lower-than-conventional interest rates. Issuers usually seek a bond rating from one of the rating agencies (Standard & Poor's or Moody's, for example) whose credit rating further reduces the interest rate payable on the debt. Issuers might also use some form of credit enhancement to obtain a higher rating based on the credit enhancer's credit from the rating agencies. Such credit enhancement is also needed to provide liquidity if the debt is variable rate. For example, the bond issue could be secured by either a letter of credit or bond insurance. A letter of credit gives the bonds the same rating as the bank issuing the letter.

The Tax Reform Act of 1986 restricted the range of private uses eligible for tax-exempt funding and reduced the annual volume of bonds that may be issued for the remaining permitted uses. Most private-purpose bonds, including bonds for ownership and rental housing, are subject to unified state-by-state volume ceilings equal to the greater of $75 per resident or $228.6 million, with the annual volume cap adjusted for inflation since 2000.[a] That is, they are subject to the unified private activity bond volume cap. Therefore, housing must compete with alternative private uses, like economic development projects and student loans, for this limited resource. Before passage of the Tax Reform Act of 1986, multifamily housing bonds were not limited, while the separate cap for mortgage revenue bonds was higher in many states than is the unified volume cap on bonds for all permitted private activities combined. Projects financed with tax-exempt bonds that use low-income housing tax credits are subject to this unified private activity bond volume cap rather than to the volume cap for tax credits (discussed in Figure 15-4). As a result of increasingly fierce competition for tax credit allocations, project owners have opted for tax-exempt financing to avoid the "beauty contest." Now, even tax-exempt bond allocation has become more competitive.

Under the Tax Reform Act of 1986, public agencies may issue a tax-exempt bond if a Section 501(c)(3) tax-exempt entity uses the proceeds for its exempt purposes and complies with other restrictions. Such an organization can use the bond proceeds to develop or acquire housing that it will own. The bonds are not subject to the volume cap applicable to most multifamily bonds. Each Section 501(c)(3) organization can use up to $150 million of bonds issued for housing on its behalf. The bonds tend to sell at an interest rate that is about 25 basis points lower than other tax-exempt bonds, as interest on the bonds is not a tax preference subject to the alternative minimum tax. One potential disadvantage of these bonds, however, is that these projects do not qualify for low-income housing tax credits.

[a]National Low Income Housing Coalition, "2003 Advocates' Guide to Housing and Community Development Policy: Housing Bonds," at www.nlihc.org/advocates/housingbonds.htm.

Source: Updated from Diane R. Suchman et al., *Public/Private Housing Partnerships* (Washington, D.C.: ULI–the Urban Land Institute, 1990), p. 15.

eral government to states, localities, and Native American tribes based on relative housing need as demonstrated in the participating jurisdiction's Comprehensive Housing Affordability Strategy (CHAS). Private developers or agencies in these participating jurisdictions can then apply for and receive funds in the form of equity investments and interest-bearing or non-interest-bearing loans for the provision of affordable housing, primarily through rehabilitation of existing structures but also through new construction in some cases. All housing developed with HOME funds must serve low- and very-low-income families. (HOME funds have been used extensively to provide housing for low-income elderly renters, as discussed in the following section. HOME funds can also be used to provide assistance to first-time homebuyers to purchase homes at below-market interest rates.) This program has helped to produce or rehabilitate hundreds of thousands of rental units since the early 1990s.

Figure 15-4	Low-Income Housing Tax Credits: Changing the Project Economics

To encourage production of low-income housing, the Tax Reform Act of 1986 authorized a ten-year federal income tax credit for investments in mixed- or low-income rental housing to replace the abolished incentives of the Economic Recovery Tax Act (ERTA) of 1981. Incentives for the real estate sector under ERTA included accelerated depreciation rates for real property, shorter useful lives, five-year amortization of expenses for rehabilitation, and a full write-off of interest and taxes during the construction period. By 1986, the economy had recovered and ERTA was no longer needed to stimulate the economy. Not wishing to eliminate the positive side effect ERTA had on the production of affordable housing, lawmakers introduced the low-income housing tax credit in the 1986 tax legislation.

The tax credit offers investors one of two levels of benefit. Over a ten-year period, it returns either 70 percent or 30 percent of the costs (present value of total eligible development costs) of the investments in qualifying units, depending on the size of the credit. For properties placed in service in 1987, the credit percentages were fixed at 9 percent (credit against federal income tax liability) for eligible expenditures in new buildings and at 4 percent for eligible expenditures in existing buildings or buildings constructed using 50 percent or more of tax-exempt bond financing (see Figure 15-3). Investors receive the credit annually for ten years. The size of the credit can be fixed or can float until the time the property is placed in service and is based on an average of federal interest rates. Therefore, actual rates may vary; that is, the 9 percent credit may actually be 7.82 percent, and the 4 percent credit may actually be 3.35 percent, for example.

The pool of credits is limited. Each state receives an annual allocation of tax credits that, effective in 2002, was raised from the greater of $1.75 per capita, or $2 million. Starting in 2003, tax credit allocations are also adjusted annually for inflation.[a] States can also receive additional credits through a reallocation of a national pool of unused credits at the end of each year. Unused credits, however, are becoming very scarce. Developers/investors must apply to state housing finance agencies or other designated allocators of the credits in a competitive process, demonstrating that their proposed properties meet an array of federal requirements for setasides and rent restrictions. Tax credit properties that are more than 50 percent financed with federally tax-exempt housing bonds do not need to apply for tax credit allocation but do need to receive volume cap bond allocations for the issuance of the bonds.

An important caveat pertains to investors who do not intend to maintain the property in the low-income stock over the long haul. If the elected percentage of units for low- and very-low-income tenants is not maintained for 15 years, the tax credit investor must pay interest and a penalty and repay part of the tax savings of the credits (which is also considered preference income for the alternative minimum tax).

[a]Changes in tax credit limits were proposed in H.R. 4577, Departments of Labor, Health and Human Services, and Education, and Related Agencies Appropriations Act of 2001.

▶ Section 221 and Section 236, two federal programs that provide below-market-rate mortgages to private and nonprofit developers of rental housing for low- and moderate-income families;

▶ Locally allocated community development block grants (CDBGs)[23];

▶ Supportive housing finance programs, including the mortgage loan purchase programs of the federally chartered secondary mortgage market players—Fannie Mae, the Federal Home Loan Mortgage Corporation (Freddie Mac), and the Government National Mortgage Association (Ginnie Mae)—FHA and VA traditional mortgage insurance and guarantee programs, FHA's risk-sharing programs,[24] and Rural Housing Services/Rural Development (formerly Farmers' Home Administration [FmHA]) subsidies for rural housing programs;

▶ Historic Preservation Tax Incentives program, which may be used in producing low-income housing;

The result of a partnership between the Multnomah County library system and Shiels Obletz Johnson, The Bookmark Apartments at the Hollywood Library in Portland, Oregon, consists of 47 apartments on top of a neighborhood library and 815 square feet (75 square meters) of retail space. *Lara Swimmer/ESTO*

▶ Fair market incentives to encourage private owners to keep affordable that housing built with federal assistance and originally designated as affordable; and

▶ Public housing.

Shifting Federal Focus to the Elderly and Populations with Special Needs

The federal government shifted its focus during the 1990s from affordable housing for the low-income population in general to housing for the growing number of low-income elderly and special-needs populations. In 1999, at least 1.4 million very-low-income elderly individuals nationwide had what HUD calls "worst case needs," paying more than 50 percent of income on shelter or living in substandard housing but receiving no housing assistance.[25] Elderly renters are of particular concern because they typically do not have any home equity to tap into to meet basic needs and they are the most likely group to have disabilities. The two main programs designed to alleviate the housing problems faced by the nation's elderly include Section 202 supportive housing for the elderly and HOME investment partnerships.

Under the Section 202 program, capital advances are made to eligible, private, nonprofit sponsors to finance the development of rental housing with supportive services for the elderly. The advance to the sponsor, who may work with a private, for-profit developer, is interest free and does not have to be repaid so long as the housing remains available for very-low-income elderly persons for at least 40 years.

HUD compensates the developer/owner for the difference between the operating costs of the units built under the program and the amount the resident can afford to pay, which, according to program rules, is about 30 percent of income.[26]

The HOME program began several years after Section 202. Unlike the Section 202 program, housing built with HOME funds is not limited to elderly residents. Another major difference between the two programs is the sources of financing for the projects built under the programs. Financing for housing built under the HOME program typically comes from many sources, including grants from state or local housing programs, conventional bank mortgages, and proceeds from syndication of LIHTCs. Financing for projects built under Section 202 is much simpler, with HUD's capital advance being the only significant source of funds for most projects.[27]

The 1990s also ushered in increased funding for programs geared toward populations with special needs. Similar to the Section 202 program, Section 811, Supportive Housing for Persons with Disabilities, was established to provide interest-free capital advances to nonprofit private organizations that do not have to be repaid so long as the housing built with program funds remains available for the intended program beneficiaries for 40 years. Like the Section 202 program, the nonprofit sponsor may work with a for-profit developer with certain restrictions. Recent funding for Section 811 housing has been between $240 million and $250 million a year, which has been enough to fund fewer than 2,000 incremental units a year while renewing expiring subsidy contracts. As a result of cutbacks in the program (the only one that produces affordable and accessible housing specifically for the nonelderly disabled), only 41 percent of eligible very-low-income renter households with a disabled member under age 65 receive direct housing assistance.[28]

State Activities

Most state housing—and economic development—related activities are administered by state housing finance agencies (HFAs), which oversee both multifamily rental and single-family ownership programs. HFAs generally receive and administer the federal allocation of LIHTCs and tax-exempt bond authority, which are in great demand by private developers of affordable multifamily housing (see Figures 15-3 and 15-4). HFAs also oversee allocations from federal HOME funds.[29]

Each state has specific programs, but many are derived from HUD demonstration programs; thus, they have some common elements:

▶ Below-market interest rate financing for new construction, acquisition, and/or rehabilitation of affordable housing;
▶ Below-market interest rate financing for construction or rehabilitation of housing for populations with special needs;
▶ Loan guarantees to qualified lenders for affordable and special needs housing.

Many HFAs such as the one in California participate in a risk-sharing pilot program with the FHA. Under risk-sharing programs, FHA assumes up to 50 percent of the default risk on affordable multifamily rental housing. The creditworthiness of the HFA is consequently "enhanced" so that investors will accept lower interest rates on the HFA's bonds. The lower interest rates may be passed on to the developers in the form of low-cost financing. This system is similar to passing on to developers the cost savings from the sale of tax-exempt bonds over taxable bonds in the form of below-market-rate financing.

In response to restrictions imposed by the Tax Reform Act of 1986 on the type of private activities eligible and the volume of tax-exempt bond financing (which is the thrust behind the below-market-rate financing programs), states began experimenting with a variety of programs and funding techniques, including:

▶ Off-budget funding vehicles such as housing trust funds to produce housing and assist occupants—in New Jersey, for example, proceeds from a statewide realty transfer tax are put into a housing trust fund to which developers of affordable housing can apply for funds;
▶ State tax credit programs such as California's and Connecticut's efforts to piggyback state credits on federal LIHTCs;

▶ Revised building codes and housing standards to reduce costs and to facilitate production; and

▶ Simplified procedures, requirements, and delivery systems for the production of subsidized housing.

Local Activities

Most states delegate the authority to regulate the private housing market to local governments, which then establish and enforce zoning policies, land use restrictions, development fees, subdivision and design requirements, building codes, rent controls, and other regulations that reflect local priorities and objectives. These regulations affect where and what different types of housing can be developed, how much it costs, and how it is maintained.[30]

Unfortunately, some state and local government activities and legislation can actually impede rather than promote the provision of affordable housing if left unchecked. Overregulation can drive up land and production costs, pushing home prices and rents out of reach of low-, moderate-, and, in some cases, middle-income households. Zoning and regulations such as those limiting high-density development or specifying minimum lot size can make the production of affordable housing difficult and effectively exclude low- and moderate-income families. Where low-density development is widespread, dwelling costs tend to be higher and individuals' dependence on automobiles for transportation greater. The results are high infrastructure costs, increased traffic congestion, high levels of energy use, increased air pollution, and shortages of certain categories of (lower-wage) labor.

In addition, certain regulatory measures discourage developers from building or preserving lower-cost, market-rate rental housing. Rent controls in particular can be a major disincentive to the production of affordable rental housing. Exclusionary zoning also limits the production of affordable housing by allowing only the production of low-density single-family housing in areas zoned for it. Historically, the frustrating length and difficulty of the permitting process for higher-density housing added substantially to the cost of producing housing and deterred many otherwise willing developers of multifamily housing from entering the market.

On the positive side are many examples of creative approaches taken by local governments, often through local HFAs, to create the environment for the production of low-income housing.

Inclusionary zoning (sometimes termed "inclusionary housing") helps increase the supply of affordable housing for moderate-income renters or buyers by encouraging or requiring developers to set aside affordably priced units. This process uses incentives to offset the added cost of affordable units for developers while allowing them to still make a reasonable profit. Incentives can include increased density, reduced impact fees, tax abatements for affordable units, and accelerated processing. Inclusionary zoning programs frequently are used in combination with other programs such as housing trust funds, community land trusts, and other local housing finance resources.

Housing trust funds provide public funds for the production and support of affordable housing. Operating through loans and grants, they can be used to support developers, nonprofit groups, government entities, and homebuyers or renters. Activities range from new construction or rehabilitation of affordable housing to assistance with rents and downpayments.

Through a community land trust, a nonprofit trust retains ownership of the land associated with affordable housing but sells the house itself—typically to a moderate-income first-time buyer. The land is leased to the homeowner, which means that only the house can be sold. Typically, it is sold back to the trust or to another low-income household for an affordable price.

Other techniques are available:

▶ Using real estate taxes and new sources of revenue (such as fees on new developments and community loan funds) as well as tax-exempt or taxable bond financing to support low-income housing;

▶ Donating or otherwise making available surplus publicly owned land at low cost or through land lease arrangements;

▶ Using linkage programs or regulations that require contributions to the development of low-income housing as a condition for obtaining

| Figure 15-5 | The Fairfax County Affordable Dwelling Unit Ordinance |

In Fairfax County, Virginia—a suburb of Washington, D.C., and one of the most affluent counties in the United States—the 2003 median family income was $93,000, and the median cost of a single-family home was approximately $380,000. To afford such a house, a family of four would have had to earn about $109,000 a year, but 53 percent of the county's families earn less than that amount. Fairfax County, long aware of this discrepancy, has worked to find a suitable solution through its Affordable Dwelling Unit (ADU) Ordinance.

In 1971, Fairfax County passed a mandatory zoning ordinance that required developers of projects with more than 50 dwelling units to ensure that 15 percent of the units would be affordable to households earning between 60 and 80 percent of the area median income. The Virginia Supreme Court overturned this ordinance in 1973 on the grounds that it constituted a "taking" of private property without just compensation.[a] Fifteen years later, a local affordable housing advocacy group, AHOME (Affordable Housing Opportunity Means Everyone), began lobbying at the state and local governments for a new affordable housing ordinance. Because Virginia is a Dillon's Rule state, Fairfax County could not devise the ordinance on its own: the state legislature had to grant local planning and zoning authority to the county.[b] Thus, AHOME not only had to persuade local politicians of the value of an affordable-housing ordinance but also had to work with state lawmakers to obtain enabling legislation that would give jurisdictions the right to pass inclusionary zoning ordinances. In 1989, Virginia amended its state code to allow localities to adopt such ordinances; the Fairfax County ADU Ordinance was enacted the following year. To ensure that the enforcement of the ordinance could not be regarded as a taking, developers are granted a density bonus in return for providing affordable dwelling units.

The ordinance applies to developments of 50 units or more for which the developer has proposed densities exceeding those allowed under the R-1 designation. (Developments with fewer than 50 units or for which additional density has not been proposed or both are not required to include affordable units; however, the developers of such projects are required to donate 0.5 percent of each unit's estimated sale price to the county's affordable-housing trust fund.) Developments of single-family homes receive a 20 percent density bonus, but 12.5 percent of the units must be affordable (the percentage of affordable dwelling units may be lower, depending on proffers or mitigating circumstances). A 10 percent density bonus is allowed for multifamily buildings without elevators or multifamily buildings of three or fewer stories with elevators, and up to 6.25 percent of all units must be affordable. Originally, the ordinance had excluded multifamily buildings of four stories or more that included at least one elevator, but in 2003, the county board of supervisors voted to include mid-rise developments in the ordinance. Developers of mid-rise projects may obtain density bonuses of up to 17 percent in exchange for up to 6.25 percent ADUs. Developments in which 50 percent of the parking is structured are required to provide no more than 5 percent ADUs.

Fairfax County affordable-housing activists continue to lobby for increases in the percentage of affordable housing units in each development. As of 2003, Fairfax County had 1,436 affordable units, despite the fact that the ordinance had been in place for close to 15 years. The program was not immediately popular with developers, who claimed that they were losing profits and that projects were being slowed down by the NIMBY syndrome. Developers can appeal the ADU requirement, but the county rarely makes exceptions. Circumstances such as infeasibility or proffers may decrease the ADU requirement, but not eliminate it.

Over the past decade, the ordinance has been amended to ease the burden on developers and builders. Developers are now allowed slight increases in sale prices in exchange for using a sympathetic design or to cover the cost of enhancing the appearance of the units. In 1998, the ordinance was amended to allow developers to complete up to 90 percent of the market-rate units upon completion of 90 percent of the required ADUs. (Previously, developers could not complete more than 75 percent of the market-rate units before completing 100 percent of the ADUs.) To ensure appropriate square footage and amenities, the county provides developers with guidelines for the construction of the units.

For a household to qualify for a unit, its income must be at or below 70 percent of the median income for the Wash-

[a]*Board of Supervisors of Fairfax County v. Degroff Enterprises, Inc.,* 198 S.E.2d 600 (VA 1973).
[b]Dillon's Rule is named after Judge John F. Dillon, a 19th-century authority on municipal law. Dillon's Rule of strict construction says that any powers not explicitly granted to local governments are implicitly denied to local governments.
Source: ULI–the Urban Land Institute, *Developing Housing for the Workforce: A Toolkit* (Washington, D.C.: Author, 2007).

| **Figure 15-5** | **The Fairfax County Affordable Dwelling Unit Ordinance** *(continued)* |

ington, D.C., standard metropolitan statistical area. Prospective buyers are not permitted to have owned a home in the past three years and must attend a course on homeownership. The names of buyers who are approved are placed in a lottery. Priority is given to those who live or work in Fairfax County or have children under 18 at home. There are hundreds of names on the waiting list, and, because not many units are produced in a given year, those who do not meet the priority requirements are unlikely to receive a unit.

The units are sold under a restrictive covenant that maintains their affordability for 15 years (a number that was recently lowered from the original 50 years). In exchange for the opportunity to purchase a below-market-rate unit and to ensure that the unit remains affordable, annual appreciation is linked to the consumer price index. Owners are also given appreciation credit for improvements to the unit. The county oversees appraisal, pricing, and sale of the units. The county is also responsible for ensuring that the owner does not rent out the unit and for discouraging owners from taking refinancing offers from predatory lenders. If a unit goes into foreclosure, the affordability covenant is null and void, and the unit must be sold to the highest bidder. Owners may sell at any time, and one-half of the net gain goes into the county's affordable-housing trust fund.

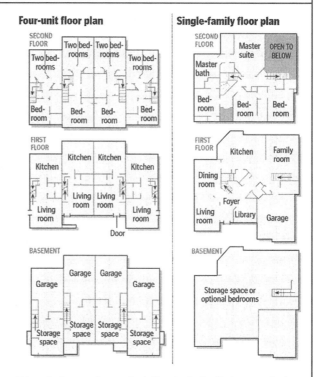

Although the townhouses look like single-family houses, the layouts are quite different. Edgemoore Homes

Designed to blend in with luxury single-family homes that range from 4,000 to 5,000 square feet (370 to 465 square meters), the affordable housing component (mandated by Fairfax County's inclusionary zoning ordinance) of the 105-unit Edgemoore at Carrington development consists of two buildings, each containing four affordable for-sale townhouses. Edgemoore Homes approvals for commercial, office, and other types of development;

► Providing credit enhancements such as mortgage insurance, letters of credit, or funding reserves that reduce risks and make investment in low-income housing more secure for private developers or investors and often make lower interest rates possible;

► Using local housing vouchers, as in Pennsylvania and Maryland;

► Employing land use concessions and flexible zoning provisions, subdivision ordinances, density allowances, building code requirements, and waivers or reductions of fees to add value to a project;

► Fast-tracking the approval process to save developers time and money;

► Using funds creatively, as in San Francisco's use of linkage payments to fund loan origination fees;

► Forgiving or abating real property taxes; and

► Allocating funds repaid for urban development action grants to low-income housing.

Private Sector Participants

Private development entities typically produce and often manage low-income housing. In some cases, for-profit private developers construct low-income housing exclusively or in conjunction with other market-rate developments through linkage programs or in fulfillment of inclusionary zoning requirements.[31] Because of their entrepreneurial approach, for-profit developers can be more efficient producers of housing, but they require sufficient incentives to enable them to make a profit and monitoring to ensure that they fulfill the public purpose.

Nonprofit community-based developers typically know and understand firsthand their communities' needs and resources and generally enjoy a strong local political base and community support. They tend to be accountable to the community and demonstrate a long-term commitment to low-income housing. Further, they are less likely to displace current residents and more likely to involve neighborhood people in their work. For these reasons, they have an advantage when seeking certain charitable and public funds.

Such groups, however, are often hampered in their effectiveness by several factors. Most CDCs have small, often overworked, staffs with limited experience or technical capability, especially in the areas of financial feasibility analysis and financial packaging. In addition, CDCs are frequently undercapitalized, waiving development fees even when they are allowed. As a result, CDCs suffer chronic shortfalls in operating revenues needed for predevelopment and ongoing operating costs.

Although production has declined in recent years as a result of reduced federal funding, CDC-based housing development has not dried up, and indications are that many CDCs have gained added skills and sophistication to enhance their production capabilities. For example, in the 23 cities that constitute the National Community Development Initiative (NCDI), "The number of CDCs capable of producing more than ten housing units per year grew from 104 groups in 1991 to 184 groups in 1997."[32]

One such nonprofit corporation, Enterprise Community Partners, works with community-based organizations to acquire sites and buildings for development. For more than two decades, it, along with its equity partners, has joined with various financial institutions, governments, and community organizations. For example, in 2006 alone, Enterprise estimates that, along with its community-based partners, it built or preserved 23,142 affordable housing units and invested $1.2 billion in affordable housing and community development.[33]

Limitations on Financing

Financing affordable rental housing can be quite complex. The essence of the problem of financing low-income housing is the need to fill the "affordability gap"—the difference between shelter costs and what a family can afford to pay. The size of the gap and thus the magnitude of the problem vary with locality.

Financing low-income housing is complicated by the fact that no single source of subsidies is available that can on its own make a project financially feasible. Resources available for financing low-income projects are fragmented and vary according to different types of projects and locations. Projects typically require funds

---

Figure 15-6	Highland Park: A Small City Takes Big Steps to Meet Affordable Housing Needs

As one of Chicago's older suburbs, Highland Park has always taken pride in the diversity of its housing. Small bungalows and multifamily residences mix with traditional Georgian and Tudor homes as well as distinctive lakefront and "ravine" mansions. To maintain this distinctive character, the city established a housing commission in 1973. During the 1970s and 1980s, community leaders succeeded in developing three projects that provide 153 apartments and townhouses for low- and moderate-income families and seniors using federal Section 8 grants.

Since the early 1990s, however, demolitions and conversions of affordable units to more expensive homes has added to rising home prices and pushed out many lower-income families and long-term residents on fixed incomes. Recognizing that action needed to be taken and that federal funding was growing scarce, the city has created a housing trust fund and a community land trust and adopted a housing tear-down fee and an inclusionary zoning program. For a city of 31,000 residents, it is a remarkable achievement that is already paying dividends in preserving housing affordability in an increasingly upscale community.

The process has been guided by the "Affordable Housing Needs and Implementation Plan" adopted by the City Council in 2001 as an element of the city's Master Plan. It recommends the adoption of inclusionary zoning that requires developers of market-rate residential projects to include a proportion of affordable units in the development. It also recommends a series of action steps toward the establishment of a housing trust fund and a community land trust.

The housing trust fund, the city's primary financing mechanism for developing and preserving affordable housing, is managed by the Housing Commission. It has a dedicated source of revenue from the tear-down tax, demolition permit fees, and fees in lieu of constructed inclusionary units. The trust fund provides a major source of funding for the community land trust, a nonprofit organization that acquires land or buildings to be used for affordable housing. This organization operates independently of the city. Its board of directors comprises city, community, institutional, and community land trust homeowner representatives. In addition to funds from the housing trust fund, it receives funds for its operation and development activities from a variety of public and private sources, including foundation and government grants and federal and state housing agencies.

The inclusionary zoning ordinance, the first in Illinois, applies to residential developments of five or more units, including new construction, renovation of multifamily buildings to increase the number of units, a change in use from nonresidential to residential, and conversions of rental properties to condominiums. Twenty percent of the units must be affordable to individuals or families earning up to 120 percent of the area's median income of about $75,000 for a family of four. Half the units must be affordable to households earning no more than 80 percent of the area median income. Current residents of Highland Park and public and business employees are given priority for occupying units.

A density bonus of one additional market-rate unit is allowed for each affordable unit. In planned unit developments, an additional half-unit of market-rate housing may be allowed for each required affordable unit. All development-related fees applying to the affordable units are waived. Under certain circumstances, developers can contribute cash to the trust fund, dedicate land, or provide units at another site in lieu of including affordable units on the site. Rental units must be kept affordable for 25 years, for-sale units in perpetuity. Affordable units must be dispersed throughout the project, visually compatible with market-rate units, and built concurrently with market-rate units.

Source: Douglas R. Porter, president, Growth Management Institute, Chevy Chase, Maryland.

---

from many sources, and it is not unusual for five or six sources of funds to support a single project such that funds from one source become the basis for securing commitments for funds from other sources.

In addition, because each provider of funding has its own social agenda and underwriting criteria, financing arrangements must be flexible enough to respond to the various requirements. The resulting financing packages are time-consuming and expensive to structure and require sophisticated financial expertise. Because they are tailored to a particular project, time, and place and involve local resources,

THOMAS L. SAFRAN

Affordable Housing Developer

Award-winning Los Angeles affordable housing developer Tom Safran is a product of the late 1960s, when his native Chicago was a hotbed of political activity and an urban crisis was percolating all across America. Safran knew when he was in college that he wanted to do something to help failing cities. After completing his undergraduate degree at Trinity College in Hartford, Connecticut, he went back to Chicago to enroll at the University of Chicago in political science and urban studies. In the summer before his second year, Safran took a year's internship at HUD in Chicago and Washington, D.C., that extended into almost five years. He eventually ended up in southern California, where he worked as a consultant to several housing authorities and, at the same time, began work on his MBA at the University of California at Los Angeles.

At UCLA, while delivering a presentation on developing a hypothetical project using the newly created Section 8 program funds, Safran was struck with the notion that perhaps he could undertake such a project. But never having worked in the private sector, he knew he was not a savvy deal maker. In fact, he had no idea how to structure a deal or how to tie up a piece of property, which was his first goal. Somehow, though, with only $1,000, Safran managed to tie up a piece of property that no one else had been able to claim simply because he persuaded the owner to consider his offer. Safran worked with the property owner to bring him into the deal and relocate him. With the final piece of the puzzle in place, Safran built his first project.

That was the beginning of Safran's 30-plus years in the development of affordable housing. Since that time, Thomas Safran & Associates has developed more than 2,800 units of affordable rental housing for seniors and families—projects that are known for their attention to design. Although Safran maintains sole proprietorship, he depends heavily on his nine-person management staff and three-person development team to maintain the quality that he seeks in everything he does. Safran has a keen interest in design and believes that low-income housing does not have to be unattractive. His awards attest to Safran's point—the 1978 Exceptional Design Award from the Inglewood Planning Commission for his first project, the 1980 Honor Award for Project Design from HUD for Ponderosa Village, the 1983 Hollywood Beautification Award for Multifamily Residential and Residential Landscaping for Hollywood Fountain North and South, the 1993 National Award of Merit in Project Design for the Strathern Park Apartments, the 1995 ULI Award for Excellence in the small-scale residential category, the Downtowners of Distinction Award from the Los Angeles Downtown News. And the list goes on.

Underscoring the challenge to financing affordable housing, Safran's Skyline Village was funded with tax-exempt bonds, 4 percent LIHTCs, five permanent loans, and $9 million in bond funds provided by the California Housing Finance Agency. Thomas Safran & Associates

Safran's commitment to superior design helps him attract high-quality low-income residents as well as "sell" affordable housing, especially family developments, to communities that would not otherwise accept it.

Good Management Is Key

Safran's group puts great stock in good management. Resident managers are hired during project construction so that they will develop a commitment to a given project. As a result, they go the extra step in selecting good residents. And good residents are critical to a project's success.

Selecting tenants begins with a careful screening, including thorough background checks of job history and rent history that cover at a minimum the past two residences. Managers also visit every potential resident's current home with all family members present to develop a sense of the household's attitude toward home and family. In addition, residents must sign lease agreements that some might consider particularly strict. The agreements clearly limit the number of occupants in a unit and precisely define "occupant" and "visitor." The agreements also forbid any kind of illegal drug use. Ground rules are very stringent. Family units are subject to inspections twice a year, senior units once a year. Income is recertified annually. Without question, resident managers' concern has paid off. Thomas Safran & Associates exhibits a remarkably low delinquency collection rate—less than half of 1 percent. Safran refers to this stringent screening process when neighborhood groups protest his developments. He explains that often, affordable housing residents are better neighbors than market-rate housing residents because of a stricter screening process and lower turnover rates.

Day-to-day issues and decisions rest with the resident managers and the vice president of property management, who oversees the resident managers. In response to some difficult lessons learned over the years, Safran himself approves all new resident managers as well as all evictions for reasons other than nonpayment of rent. When hiring staff, Safran says, "I look for people who have a passion for what they're doing. I also require a certain sensitivity in my employees toward the people they're serving. My employees can't be in this business just for making money. They must be interested in what we do and how we do it. We're providing housing for the same people as public housing authorities are, but we're committed to doing it better."

The Deal Maker

Despite his apparent success, the next project is not always clearly waiting for Safran. His main role in the organization is that of deal maker; he creates and initiates new projects. But the deal-making function depends on so many other factors that, at any one time, Safran might have three or four potential deals in the works. Indeed, some of them might fall through because of a lack of appropriate funding, a jurisdiction's reluctance to give approvals for the type of project proposed, or a variety of other reasons.

Developing affordable housing requires the careful selection of neighborhoods. Safran tends to stay out of neighborhoods plagued with problems block after block; however, he likes to go into areas where a cluster of problem properties is surrounded by decent buildings. On occasion, Safran or his staff has had to deal with gangs or displacement problems, but such matters are all part of the social environment that is unavoidable for developers of affordable housing.

Safran prefers to develop the types of property with which he feels most competent, namely, affordable housing for families and the elderly. But he has also undertaken some mixed-use development (housing with retail) and in 2006 had in the works a small market-rate rental project and a large mixed-use project (consisting of retail space, workforce for-sale housing [housing for people who do not qualify for government housing subsidies but cannot afford market-rate units in their communities], and low-income senior rental units). He also purchased a single-room occupancy building with Section 8 housing certificates. But affordable housing is his specialty and passion. "The competition is much tougher than it used

to be. A lot of private developers are looking for opportunities, particularly in southern California, where the office market dried up, and they saw affordable housing as a wide-open market." And since the tax credit program has been made permanent, there is much more competition for funds and less available land, so more developers have shifted to redevelopment rather than new projects. Though relocation costs are high, Safran cites higher demand and an already established neighborhood as benefits of this current trend.

Safran calls himself a limited-profit developer. He neither earns as much money as the typical private developer nor assumes as much personal risk, but he also does not have nonprofit status and the advantages that can come with it. His company's goal is "to enhance the world in which we live and enrich the lives of the people who reside in our buildings." He explains, "I live by it and my staff has to live by it. To me, integrity in this business is essential. My word is everything. Public agencies have to trust me and want to do business with me. I think that should be true for every developer, but it might be more important in this type of development because so many people's well-being is affected." Nonetheless, he is convinced that a frequently mistaken assumption holds that nonprofit sponsors are inherently better suited to developing affordable housing than "greedy" private developers. The perception is that nonprofits and community-based groups will stay around and take care of their buildings, while private developers will either abandon them or turn them into market-rate housing after 20 years.

"The best part of what I do is create a nice environment—a home. I like to help upgrade neighborhoods and provide a nice home for people, which I believe can turn around lives in some cases." Safran believes that his success is partly the result of an ability to blend a strong business sense with a social conscience.

Tenacity is another requisite for Safran's work. "I spend a lot of time figuring out ways to get around obstacles. You also need creativity and vision to see the possibilities where others might not. One of my staff once said that the best lesson he learned working in this office is that 'no' means 'maybe' and 'maybe' means 'yes.' That pretty well describes what it takes." When hiring new young associates, Safran looks for someone with a "tenacious charming personality who won't take 'no' for an answer and recognizes that you must stay in the game to accomplish your goals."

Financing Affordable Housing

"Probably the hardest thing about this type of development is coordinating the endless varieties of approvals and financing. It can be numbing to put a deal together because of the

continued on next page

inconsistencies from one group to the other," says Safran. Because financing is generally layered, the developer has to meet standards (legal, occupancy, design, and more) for each source of funding.

Safran likes to use his favorite project, Strathern Park in the Sun Valley section of Los Angeles, as an example of the complexity of financing. This $25.5 million project, which provides 241 apartment units to low- and very-low-income residents, was completed by layering seven different sources of funding. First, the Los Angeles CRA funded a land acquisition loan for $4.3 million. This loan, in addition to more than $2 million in seed money that Safran advanced to the project, financed the acquisition of the project as well as many predevelopment costs.

Upon funding of the $7.8 million construction loan from Wells Fargo Bank, the CRA's land loan was taken out by $5.2 million in loan funds from HUD's housing development action grant program (HoDAG), which was administered jointly by the CRA and the Los Angeles Housing Preservation and Production Department. At the same time, the CRA funded a long-term gap loan for $6.3 million, to be disbursed along with the conventional construction loan.

Financing Sources	*Amount*
Preconstruction Sources	
Seed Capital from the Developer	$2,000,000
Land Acquisition Loan from the CRA	4,300,000
Total	$6,300,000
Construction Sources	
Partial Equity from Tax Credit Investor	$3,900,000
Permanent Gap Loan from the CRA	6,300,000
HUD HoDAG	5,200,000
Wells Fargo Construction Loan	7,800,000
Total	$23,200,000
Permanent Sources	
Full Equity from Tax Credit Investor	$7,800,000
Permanent Gap Loan from the CRA	6,300,000
HUD HoDAG	5,200,000
California Community Reinvestment Corporation	6,200,000
Total	$25,500,000

During the predevelopment phase of the project, the developer received an allocation of 9 percent federal low-income housing tax credits from the state, which were syndicated through the Boston Financial Group, bringing a total of

$7.8 million in equity investment to the project. A portion of this capital was made available to the project at the start of construction. The remaining amounts were contributed to the project on completion of construction, on permanent loan funding, and after a period of stabilized occupancy.

After completion of the project, the construction loan was taken out by a combination of investors' equity and a long-term $6.2 million first trust deed loan from the California Community Reinvestment Corporation. The $5.2 million HoDAG loan (second trust deed) and the CRA's $6.3 million gap loan (third trust deed) remained in place, payable out of surplus cash flow.

Skyline Village, a 73-unit affordable housing complex set against the backdrop of downtown Los Angeles, was another challenging project for Safran. Thomas Safran & Associates first introduced the Skyline Village project to the city of Los Angeles in 2000. Over the next few years, the company was successful in securing the participation of more than seven different agencies and six deeds of trust to make the apartment complex a reality. Although the development team originally sought to finance the project with 9 percent LIHTCs, the competition for those credits in California was too strong and the deal had to be restructured to use tax-exempt bonds and 4 percent tax credits, which generated about $5.4 million in tax credit equity. Alliant Capital was the syndicator (Limited Partner Equity), and Bank of America was the investor.

The rest of the project was financed by obtaining five permanent loans, each secured by deeds of trust. The California Housing Finance Agency also provided about $9 million in bond funds for a loan-to-lender deal with Bank of America. The bank then used the funds to provide the project with a construction loan.

Construction Sources and Uses	*Amount*
Construction Loan	$10,966,000
Los Angeles Housing Department	2,872,000
Limited Partner Equity	1,923,000
Deferred Developer Fee	1,200,000
Century Housing (bridge loan)	550,000
Affordable Housing Program Broadway	292,000
Deferred Costs/Fees	177,000
Total	$17,980,000

Skyline Village has amenities not usually offered in affordable housing complexes, including a community room, a computer lab with broadband Internet access, an exercise room, two playgrounds, a basketball court, and a gas barbecue grill. "We build places where we would want to live," says Safran. Rents vary depending on income levels but are offered for

▶ **PROFILE** *(continued)*

Permanent Sources of Funds	Amount	Rate & Terms
LP Equity	$5,411,000	
California Department of Housing and Community Development	4,056,000	55-year/3%
California Housing Finance Agency	3,750,000	40-year/5.35%
Los Angeles Housing Department	3,265,000	45-year/5%
MHP Deferred Developer Fee	635,000	
City of Industry Funds	566,000	
Affordable Housing Program Broadway	292,000	
GP Equity	5,000	
Total	$17,980,000	

those who make 60, 50, and 35 percent of the area median income and stipulate that no more than 30 percent of income should be allotted for rent. When the project was available for leasing, approximately 2,600 people applied for the 73 units.

The Future of Affordable Housing

Safran believes that developing affordable housing today is both easier and harder than when he started. Because of increased competition for both funds and land, it is more difficult to complete projects. But with more established programs

such as the California state law requiring 20 percent of redevelopment funds be spent on affordable housing, specific funds are available. Protesting has diminished from neighborhood groups because of a larger sample of successful affordable housing projects and a greater recognition of the need, causing communities to earmark more money for low-income housing.

Safran stresses the importance of being able to quickly respond to changes caused by the economy. One example is the California multifamily insurance crisis. Thomas Safran & Associates was less affected by the crisis than other multifamily development companies because of good management and maintenance. The number of companies willing to insure affordable housing projects greatly declined, but because of their expertise in the field, Safran's premium was increased at a much lower rate than other affordable housing developers.

"There's always going to be a need for housing, especially affordable housing. I encourage people to explore this type of development because it involves a lot of reward and opportunity. You have to limit your financial expectations, but the internal reward can be tremendous."

Thomas Safran & Associates is developing a new project that combines an affordable rental senior project with retail and a for-sale affordable workforce housing product. In California in particular—but in almost all areas of the United States—housing for the workforce is becoming less and less affordable. Thomas Safran & Associates is seeking to provide for-sale housing to working families at reasonable prices.

the packages are typically unique to the projects they support and therefore not replicable from place to place or even from project to project in the same city.

Spurred in part by the requirements of the Community Reinvestment Act of 1977 (CRA), a variety of banks, insurance companies, and pension funds provide financing for the development of low-income housing. In addition, some private organizations have created special programs that set aside funds for low-income housing projects, while several insurance companies have initiated social investment programs that provide limited amounts of specially targeted funds for low-income housing.[34]

Some banks such as the South Shore Bank of Chicago aggregate and hold in low- and non-interest-bearing accounts funds deposited by individuals, gov-

ernment agencies, and foundations. These so-called "linked deposits" are earmarked for investment in community development projects. Because these banks are insured by the Federal Deposit Insurance Corporation, depositors assume no real risk on linked funds used for community projects.

In some cases, financial institutions have pooled resources through various consortia for the purpose of making community development and mortgage loans in distressed communities. Players in the secondary mortgage market, through their purchases of loans secured by homes in inner cities, minority neighborhoods, and affordable housing, have been instrumental in expanding the supply of mortgage credit. New products being developed by the secondary market and the adaptation of underwriting guidelines to meet the needs of nontraditional buyers have gone a long way toward expanding opportunities for homeownership.

Many private sector organizations serve as intermediaries that raise and distribute funds as well as provide various kinds of technical support for developers (usually nonprofit developers) of low-income housing. Intermediaries can include public/private housing partnerships such as the Boston Housing Partnership or the Cleveland Housing Network, both of which operate locally to support nonprofit community-based developers. They might also include private national organizations such as the Local Initiatives Support Corporation (LISC), a nonprofit corporation created in 1979 by the Ford Foundation; the Enterprise Foundation, established by developer James Rouse in 1982; and the Housing Assistance Council.

An example of these national intermediaries is NeighborWorks America, which was chartered by Congress in 1987 as the Neighborhood Reinvestment Corporation (NRC) to revitalize deteriorating urban neighborhoods and to promote affordable housing. The organization, which changed its name in 2005, provides financial support, technical assistance, and training for communities across the nations, including the NeighborWorks network—a nationwide network of more than 240 community development organizations working in more than 4,500 communities across the country. From 2001 to 2006, the network has helped minority families achieve homeownership at four times the rate of conventional lenders. One of the organization's more important contributions to spurring the production of low-income housing was the creation of its local government secondary market, which enables the delivery of loans to low-income borrowers who cannot satisfy standard underwriting criteria.[35]

| Figure 15-7 | Ten Principles for Developing Affordable Housing |

In response to the growing demand for affordable housing, the Urban Land Institute's Affordable Housing Council convened a one-day workshop in March 2006. Professionals with diverse and deep experience in the field identified the following ten principles for developing affordable housing with the goal of aiding those who wish to develop housing for low- and moderate-income households.

1. Inspire Leadership

Although leadership is essential for many endeavors, it is particularly important for developing affordable housing because of the length and complexity of the development process. Leaders need to address two great challenges: defining the problem and creating solutions. Affordable housing leaders must make the case for the importance of affordable housing to a community and create and articulate a compelling vision for solutions to the lack of affordable housing.

Efforts to provide affordable housing may get lost among competing needs in a community, particularly when public resources are limited. Leaders can ensure that their cause receives the attention and funding it deserves by documenting the need for affordable housing and its community benefits, especially the key role it plays in maintaining a healthy, vibrant regional economy. In addition, strong leadership can counter the negative stereotypes and misperceptions that many people have about affordable projects.

2. Build Community Support and Trust

Building community support and trust begins with clear and open communication with everyone, from the highest elected officials to the neighbors of the proposed development. Full, direct, and proactive communication in partnership with local government must be part of the process from the beginning. One of the first steps is to explain the benefits of—or establish the need for—affordable housing. Residents of a community may have a general sense that the lack of affordable housing is a problem, but they often do not fully grasp the connection between a community's affordable housing and its economic health.

The planning and marketing tools used for describing a proposed affordable housing development must be visual and must accurately simulate its real-life neighborhood effects. Visual, virtual-reality tools can be a powerful antidote to preconceived notions about affordable housing, many of which were formed by the failed high-rise public housing projects developed after World War II.

Figure 15-7	Ten Principles for Developing Affordable Housing *(continued)*

3. Learn the Alphabet—and Do the Math

Financing options for affordable housing are an alphabet soup of loans, grants, and various other programs containing numerous qualifications and restrictions. This soup includes but is not limited to some of the programs mentioned throughout this chapter—LIHTCs, HOPE VI, CDBG, HOME funds. In addition, states, counties, cities, and other jurisdictions often offer numerous financing and incentive programs. Developing affordable housing requires in-depth knowledge of these options as well as the ability to stitch a number of them together seamlessly to create a development proposal that pencils out financially.

Developers of affordable housing are often constrained on several levels by both lending and program requirements. Lenders require covenants that ensure timely payments, establish reserves, and maintain various metrics (such as the loan-to-value ratio and the debt service coverage ratio). Further, sale and rental rates as well as a host of maintenance and public service issues are restricted or mandated by program requirements. Knowing the programs and their parameters is the first step in establishing long-term financial success for an affordable project.

4. Know Your Market and Your Customers

Developers of affordable housing must have a thorough knowledge of the market where they work. This knowledge should encompass the political, social, and cultural facets of the community as well as the underlying market fundamentals. Developers must know most elected officials and community leaders as well as developers of competing market-rate and affordable projects. Establishing and maintaining good relationships and trust go a long way toward avoiding misunderstandings and surprises down the road.

In-depth knowledge of the community allows developers to anticipate community concerns and proactively address them. Knowing the political situation can tell developers whom they can (and cannot) count on for support. Moreover, finding a champion in city hall can make the entitlement process significantly easier.

Despite the facts that, in most areas of the nation, the demand for low-income housing far exceeds the supply and most new affordable housing communities lease up quickly and maintain waiting lists, projects that include market-rate housing require a more thorough market analysis.

Market studies can help verify and quantify demand and allow for greater leverage in underwriting the development and gaining public support. In addition, market studies can become selling points in convincing public officials and the community of the need for a proposed project.

Developers should seek to understand the concerns of nearby businesses and homeowners in relation to the proposed project. Ascertaining a project's potential residents is an important part of gathering information, and knowing the characteristics of prospective residents can help developers sell their project to community stakeholders.

5. Nurture Partnerships

An ideal partnership provides benefits to both partners, with the pairing creating an entity that is stronger than its individual parts. Affordable housing partnerships must be carefully crafted to benefit each partner—just as business partnerships would be. A successful partnership relies on the strengths of each partner.

For-profit developers contribute real estate savvy, contacts with end users, and an understanding of financial resources; nonprofit developers may be able to access LIHTCs; and public sector entities can help resolve land assembly problems, ensure that the site is ready for development, ease the entitlement process, and invest in land or infrastructure costs. A public sector partner's smoothing of the entitlement process keeps the private sector developer confident, on track, and on schedule—and helps make it possible for the developer to assume the risks and produce an outcome that reflects both the community vision and the market reality.

6. Select Sites for Opportunity and Choice

Low- and moderate-income families do not differ from other families in their desire for housing with access to basic amenities and advantages. Accordingly, developers should site affordable housing to maximize economic and social opportunities for its residents as well as to allow for quality-of-life amenities such as access to good schools, safe streets and parks, and public transportation.

In the past, affordable housing projects typically were relegated to the most disadvantaged neighborhoods in their municipalities. The large-scale public affordable housing developments of the mid-20th century characteristically

continued on next page

Figure 15-7	Ten Principles for Developing Affordable Housing *(continued)*

fostered concentrations of poor families, which had devastating effects for both the public housing residents and adjacent neighborhoods. Isolating affordable housing in distressed neighborhoods with poor schools and substandard social services severely limits opportunities for upward mobility among residents and breeds a culture of endemic poverty, hopelessness, and despair.

Affordable housing must be made available in a variety of markets and types of neighborhoods, not just in central-city neighborhoods. Rapid job growth in suburban locations has intensified the need for nearby affordable housing. In cities, inner suburbs, and other built-up areas, the production of affordable housing should be an important component of infill and revitalization strategies. Demand for affordable housing also exists in rural areas, where wages may be significantly lower than in cities.

The reality, of course, is that developers of affordable housing often cannot compete without funding assistance for land in many areas where affordable housing is needed. Further, proposals to develop affordable housing in good neighborhoods are almost bound to engender community opposition, which results in a lengthier entitlement process and legal entanglements that add expenses to pro formas that have very little room for such additional costs. Inclusionary zoning ordinances that call for the voluntary or mandatory inclusion of "affordable" units in new housing developments offer one entry for affordable housing in a number of communities where it is scarce.

7. Strive for Healthy, Balanced Communities

A healthy community provides a variety of housing types appropriate for residents in all stages of the life cycle, safe and affordable housing for people in all income groups, and housing opportunities close to jobs. The majority of U.S. communities have always lacked racial diversity, but many were much more economically diverse 75 years ago than they are today. In the early 20th century, a typical community blended an assortment of housing types and residents of disparate incomes and backgrounds. Today's typical community is more economically segregated, a result chiefly of the migration of many upper- and middle-income households to homogenous housing developments in the suburbs—made possible by the expanding interstate highway system—and the segregation and isolation of poorer families in high-density public hous-

ing concentrated, as a matter of government policy, in the poorest urban neighborhoods.

In neighborhoods with little affordable housing, the introduction of mixed-income communities can jump-start the process for bringing about diversity, affordability, and balance. Much of the affordable housing being constructed today aims to create balanced communities by providing a variety of housing at a variety of prices. People with rising incomes or growing families can move up without having to move out of the community. Seniors can downsize without leaving their family and friends. Adult children can stay in the neighborhood where they grew up. Households can move from subsidized housing to a home of their own without having to relocate. The presence of long-term residents who stay active and vested in their community helps maintain both stability and a sense of community.

From the developer's perspective, a mixed-income, mixed-product development mitigates the development risk by appealing to a variety of potential customers. Market-rate units can help cross-subsidize the income-restricted units, making the development more financially feasible. The proper ratio of market-rate, workforce, and low-income housing units in any one community is a matter of some debate, and the answer may vary based on the situation in the surrounding community. Many developers think that at least 50 percent of the units in larger mixed-income communities should be market-rate housing to ensure community stability and provide options for families to move up from subsidized or small units.

8. Use Design to Foster Community, Safety, and Pride

The lessons from the failures of public housing projects built in the mid-20th century have not been lost on today's designers of affordable housing, many of whom are creating award-winning communities. Good design can foster a sense of community, provide for the safety of residents, and ultimately create community pride. In fact, one of the greatest lessons from public housing's failed approach is to focus on building communities and neighborhoods, not projects and developments.

Resources for the development of affordable housing are typically limited, which demands creativity from developers and design professionals. They put significant effort into value engineering interior and exterior spaces to create the

Figure 15-7	Ten Principles for Developing Affordable Housing *(continued)*

most value for the least cost. This process may involve reassessing how spaces are used and challenging traditional thinking about design and density. The following design guidelines can help designers and developers think about what is needed to create high-quality affordable housing and great communities:

▶ *Create curb appeal.* Attractive housing fosters residents' pride.

▶ *Scale projects to respect the neighborhood.* A proper scale helps to promote a healthy connection between the development and its surrounding neighborhood.

▶ *Foster a sense of ownership.* Involve your target market in the design of the building(s).

▶ *Orient windows to put "eyes" on the street.* Street watching can instill a sense of ownership in residents and serves as a de facto neighborhood watch program.

▶ *Provide adequate light and air circulation in the homes.*

▶ *Know where to cut costs and think long term.* Drastically reducing room sizes or installing cheap equipment or finishes will not save money in the long term because of increased maintenance costs.

9. Empower Residents

Well-planned affordable housing is a long-term investment and a key component of a healthy community. Although a current project is temporarily the developer's undertaking, the developer is building permanent homes, relationships, connections, lifestyles, and community.

Community participation is key. Community members must be involved in initial project meetings and residents consulted on unit design, programs, and planning. Participation keeps the energy high and provides residents with a meaningful role in project development. An inclusive, people-driven process will gain acceptance from the businesses, neighborhoods, and politicians affected by the project. Broad community support is essential to ensure the project's success.

By listening to the community and responding to its vision, the developer can create a development plan focused on common goals related to a healthy environment, a strong economy, and a high quality of life. Collective decision making increases pride and investment in the community, which in turn encourage high-quality maintenance and adherence to community rules and policies on the part of residents.

Developers of affordable housing should incorporate programs that encourage ownership by facilitating transitions from rental to ownership housing and building wealth. Various federal, state, local government, and private initiatives provide financing, technical assistance, and education resources to encourage affordable homeownership. Developers should consider partnering with lenders, local governments, and neighborhood residents to educate potential homebuyers on realistic homebuying goals.

10. Orchestrate Sustainability

Developers of affordable housing build for the long term. Market-rate for-sale housing developments sell out in a matter of years, and market-rate rental properties are often sold after a specified holding period. Affordable housing developments, on the other hand, often are required to remain affordable over the long term. Developers of affordable housing must develop, finance, and manage the property for longevity, which means integrating sustainability into all aspects of the project.

The period for which affordability requirements are in place is commonly known as the compliance period. Although it is difficult to predict how the area around the project will develop over the compliance period, it is a good idea to try to establish a terminal value that reflects the likely status of the property given its geography, assumed capital improvements, and likely demographics while also taking into account inflation. Building for sustainability offers the best chance of maintaining long-term value.

Sustainable development is high-quality development, but it does not need to be high-cost development. Through creative design and value engineering, developers can create sustainable communities while maintaining affordability. Key qualities of sustainable affordable housing are that it promotes economic vitality, fosters environmental integrity, and encourages a sense of community today and for future generations. More specifically, such housing should promote health, conserve energy and natural resources, and provide easy access to jobs, schools, and services. It is best to take a holistic approach to sustainable affordable housing that focuses on people instead of buildings.

Source: ULI–the Urban Land Institute, *Ten Principles for Developing Affordable Housing* (Washington, D.C.: Author, 2007).

Corporations sometimes make direct contributions to developers or housing partnerships that specialize in low-income housing, indirect contributions to intermediary organizations, and in-kind donations of goods, property, and expert time. Corporations and other large employers such as Fannie Mae and Freddie Mac often initiate special programs designed to assist their employees in obtaining housing in expensive localities. "Employer-assisted housing programs," designed to enable employees to live near their jobs, can take the form of assistance with downpayments, low-interest mortgages, equity sharing, rent subsidies, or contributions to local communities' efforts to develop affordable housing.

Finally, foundations invest in low-income housing developments through such vehicles as program-related investments (PRIs).[36] They have also been the chief supporters of intermediary organizations, including many local housing partnerships. Moreover, foundations provide grant money directly to nonprofit community-based housing developers and to housing partnerships.

In the 26-block Fall Creek Place neighborhood of Indianapolis, Indiana, 58 historic houses were restored and 369 new houses built on vacant lots, with 51 percent of the units reserved for households earning 80 percent or less of the area median income. *Chris Palladino*

Affordable Ownership Housing

Another aspect of what is commonly termed "the affordability problem" is the increasing inability of households of moderate means—especially young households—to purchase a home. The problem has crept steadily up the income ladder. During the 1980s, household incomes began to polarize: the proportion of households with higher incomes and the proportion of households with lower incomes increased, while the proportion in the middle declined.

The Definition of Affordable Ownership Housing

The definition of "affordable" as it relates to ownership, as opposed to rental, housing has long divided analysts in the housing, real estate, academic, and government communities. Several mathematical expressions and affordability indices for homeownership have emerged in an attempt to summarize the relationship among home prices, household incomes, and the structure of mortgage financing costs.

Affordability indices generally fall into two broad categories. The first category embraces household affordability indices, which measure whether a specific type of buyer can afford a specific home. The second broad category of indices encompasses market measures of housing affordability that can be divided into two subcategories: the share of homes within a specific market that a typical household can afford and the share of households that can afford a typical home in a particular market—the housing opportunity index (HOI).

The Nature of the Problem

After 40 years of steadily increasing rates of homeownership, the proportion of households that own their own homes dropped steadily from a peak of 65.6 percent in 1980 to a stabilized rate of around 64 percent in 1994. But the positive effects of the strong economy and falling interest rates could be felt in the early 2000s. In 2002 homeownership increased to a record 67.9 percent, in 2003 it reached 68.3 percent, and in 2004 it reached 69 percent before dropping slightly in 2005. Despite a homeownership boom that has been remarkably broad-based, a wide gap exists between white and minority homeownership rates that has improved little since 1994.[37]

The overall figures mask glaring differences among household types. Young households—those aged 25 to 34, historically the age of first-time homebuyers—have been most affected by the affordability problem, with their rate of homeownership well below 1980 peaks. Older households have fared better, as evidenced by the substantial increase in their homeownership rates between 1980 and 1997. The increase in homeownership rates among the elderly is primarily the result of a shift in national wealth toward the elderly and of a healthier elderly population. Also important is market acceptance of different variants of reverse mortgages, which allow elderly households to tap into the equity in their homes. They can use the proceeds for the costs of operating and maintaining their homes, in-home care, and other services that help them remain in their homes longer.

The incidence of the problem of affordable homeownership is uneven, varying considerably among housing markets. The first reason relates to demand. During the 1980s, the maturing of baby boomers created a surge in demand for entry-level houses. At the same time, the decentralization of employment to suburban locations translated into increased demand for workers' housing in suburban areas. In addition, the number of households as a proportion of the population increased dramatically during the 1970s and 1980s as more people remained single well into their adult lives. Some observers believe that as baby boomers age and create continuing strong demand for move-up housing, the entry-level housing they can be expected to vacate will create affordable housing for the next generation of first-time buyers, namely, households lower on the income ladder. To be sure, this moving up of boomers has already begun.

The second major contributor to the problem of affordability is financing. Except for those with the deepest pockets, housing producers need financing to undertake a real estate project. They need pre-development financing to pay for land acquisition, feasibility studies, site planning, and so on, and construction financing to pay for all the hard and soft

costs of actually preparing the site and building the houses. Mortgage financing must also be available to homebuyers to purchase the homes, as more than 90 percent of homes are sold with mortgages. High interest rates, limited sources of funding, or other unfavorable terms thwart the production of affordable housing. Indeed, unfavorable financing terms and high interest rates of the late 1980s and early 1990s played a great part in the decline in affordability, particularly for young first-time buyers. With enactment of the Financial Institutions Reform, Recovery, and Enforcement Act (FIRREA) in 1989, residential developers faced additional concerns for a period, specifically with regard to restrictions on the amount of loans that could be obtained for land acquisition and, more generally, on sources of capital for development. That period of high interest rates and stringent underwriting criteria has passed, but financial cycles will continue to create difficulties.

The Community Reinvestment Act strongly encourages loans for the construction, rehabilitation, and purchase of homes in low- and moderate-income areas, and banks that do not meet their obligations to these underserved communities face stiff penalties under the law. In 1999, a Federal Reserve Board study of 500 large financial institutions—that together accounted for 70 percent of all lending under CRA—found that these institutions made $58 billion in home loans, $59 billion in small business loans, and $13 billion in community development loans to lower-income borrowers in their CRA assessment areas.[38]

As noted, another factor limiting housing production is overregulation, which often serves to limit the amount of new affordable housing that can be built in a community. Housing and land development regulations are enacted to serve legitimate public purposes such as protecting a community's health and safety. Yet it is ironic that "excessive" regulations or overregulation may adversely affect the communities they are supposed to protect through:

▶ Restrictions on building or sewer, water, and utility connection permits;
▶ Limitations on the amount or location of developable land through the establishment of urban

limit lines and zoning of insufficient amounts of vacant land for residential use;

► Exclusionary zoning that limits the types and densities of residential development allowed in a community;

► Excessive subdivision regulations such as unnecessarily high standards for grading and drainage, street spacing or width, pavement thickness, curb and sidewalk design, lighting, utility mains, or other physical improvements to the site;

► Requirements that developers construct, or pay fees for the construction of, infrastructure beyond that required to serve the expected residents or occupants of the specific project;

► Complex and time-consuming permitting procedures that increase developers' holding costs and risk exposure; and

► Environmental regulations that, for example, control air pollution, protect water supplies, limit the demand for water, preserve wetlands and endangered species, and manage and require the removal of toxic wastes. Such regulations serve the public good but can add time and expense to a project.

Because increased construction expenses are also a factor in the rising cost of homeownership, unnecessarily costly specifications or standards for construction materials and standards can also hinder the development of new affordable housing.

HUD has created a national Web-based forum, the Regulatory Barriers Clearinghouse, where local jurisdictions and others can report and share with others their most successful regulatory reforms. To further encourage local actions, the agency has also decided to award extra points to program funds for applicants that are able to demonstrate success in removing regulatory barriers to affordable housing.[39]

Two of the most pervasive and difficult issues confronted by communities seeking to encourage the

Located in affluent Irvine, California, Montecito Vista is a 162-unit garden-style apartment complex comprising two- and three-bedroom units reserved for those making between 30 and 50 percent of the area median income. *www.blakephotography.net*

production and purchase of affordable houses are the lack of political will among leaders to support production of affordable housing and resistance to including lower-cost housing in their communities, even though the location of moderately priced dwellings in expensive neighborhoods has not been shown to affect property values. Housing is usually the largest single expenditure for any household; thus, homeowners are highly motivated to protect and enhance their investment. People apparently prefer to live among others of similar or higher incomes. Yet mixed-income housing developments have successfully attracted residents in many communities.

Encouraging the Production of Affordable Ownership Housing

Potential homeowners face two primary difficulties: making the downpayment and meeting the monthly payments. Federal housing programs as well as innovations by private mortgage lenders are geared toward helping households overcome either or both of these two barriers. Traditional FHA mortgage insurance, by insuring mortgage lenders against loss from defaults, has expanded the pool of mortgage money available to households that would not qualify under conventional underwriting standards. Because HUD insures up to 97 percent of the first $25,000 of home value, 95 percent of the value between $25,000 and $125,000, and 90 percent of the value above $125,000, private financial institutions are willing to make mortgages that require low downpayments. FHA-insured loans then significantly lower the downpayment barrier. Interest rates on FHA loans are also lower, thereby reducing monthly payments below those required with conventional financing. The Department of Veterans Affairs has a similar loan guarantee program. Private mortgage insurance companies perform a function similar to the FHA and VA in lowering the downpayment required by lenders, although downpayments are still higher than those required under the FHA insurance and VA guarantee programs.

Unparalleled economic growth and low interest rates combined with an aggressively supportive public policy environment propelled homeownership rates to record levels during the 1990s and into the new millennium. Despite a declining economy that dipped into recession in 2000 and 2001, historically low interest rates sustained these gains, including impressive growth in homeownership rates among low- and moderate-income families, minorities, and nontraditional households.

Much of the growth among these latter groups was made possible by the widespread introduction of "affordable" mortgage products featuring flexible underwriting—including low downpayments, higher debt ratios, and reduced cash reserves—combined with the use of nontraditional means of verifying creditworthiness.[40] For example, home purchase loans requiring downpayments of 5 percent or less were nearly four times (15 percent) more common in 2001 than in 1990 (4 percent).[41] Freddie Mac's Alt 97 mortgage, which is targeted to buyers with little savings but good credit, features 3 percent down and only part of the upfront cash having to come from the borrower's own resources. Underscoring the potentially huge impact of these new mortgage products, it is estimated that the Alt 97 mortgage has increased "the relative probability of homeownership for young households by 27.1 percent, for black households by 21 percent, and for center-city households by 15 percent."[42]

Combined with the strong economy, these mortgage innovations helped proportionately more low- and moderate-income families buy homes. Between 1993 and 1997, for example, the number of home loans to families with incomes at or below 80 percent of the median increased by 38 percent, compared with 27 percent growth for loans to higher-income families.[43] For a roughly similar period (1994 to 2001), minorities accounted for 40 percent of the national net gain in homeowners, even though they account for just 25 percent of all households.[44]

During the second Bush Administration, HUD announced two efforts to expand homeownership opportunities for lower-income and minority families. The American Dream Downpayment Initiative, begun in fiscal year 2004, provides grants to help homebuyers with downpayments and closing costs.[45] The Zero Downpayment Mortgage was part of the administration's fiscal year 2005 budget. Through the FHA, it provides additional help to families who are closed out of the homebuying market because they lack the ready cash for a downpayment.[46]

Tax savings, by reducing the real cost, also encourage homeownership. Homeowners of all income levels are allowed to exclude from income for federal income tax purposes interest paid on mortgages for primary and secondary residences as well as real estate property taxes paid to state and local governments. To the extent that they hold greater amounts of mortgage debt, upper- and middle-income homeowners receive a disproportionate share of the subsidy from the mortgage interest and property tax deductions. But low-income homeowners benefit as well.

Various groups have demonstrated that reductions in the cost of housing production can be achieved through regulatory reform. Through the Joint Venture for Affordable Housing, HUD and the National Association of Home Builders (NAHB) demonstrated the cost savings that could be realized by updating or eliminating certain regulations governing residential land development and construction. Working with builders constructing houses ranging from $30,000 to $60,000 in 18 communities nationwide, HUD and NAHB documented cost savings of $855 to $15,647 per unit as a consequence of regulatory reform. Among the 18 communities, cost savings averaged about 15 percent.

Regulatory reforms have taken several forms, including:

▶ Zoning for higher densities;
▶ Encouraging planned unit development zoning and clustering housing units to reduce development costs and raise housing densities;
▶ Allowing zero-lot-line zoning;
▶ Streamlining entitlements and permitting;
▶ Modifying building codes to allow the use of less expensive building materials and more flexible construction standards; and
▶ Waiving or streamlining fees.

Communities can also enable the production of lower-cost housing by promoting manufactured housing and other alternative building types. Modular housing units, which are generally 90 to 95 percent complete when delivered to the site, have been used successfully, especially on infill sites, to construct inexpensive housing quickly and efficiently. Much of the cost savings come from standardization, efficient land use and construction, and reduced construction time, which translates into savings in carrying costs. Not surprisingly, the building trades have opposed modular housing, perhaps because it requires less on-site labor; in addition, building inspectors may find that modular housing is complicated to inspect. Even the building trades, however, are now realizing that the highly skilled labor force required in certain cost-cutting production techniques will be a boon to training and wages in the industry.

Favorable court rulings in litigation involving exclusionary zoning and antidiscrimination have gone a long way to ensure that manufactured or modular housing is not arbitrarily excluded from planned residential developments. Moreover, the secondary market supports this type of housing through various new products. The next step is for such housing to be included as a viable alternative to site-built housing in any jurisdiction's CHAS. Many states have already adopted sophisticated planning legislation that recognizes affordable housing as an element of the comprehensive plan.[47]

SUMMARY

The issue of housing affordability for moderate- and low-income households is great and will continue to expand. Aging baby boomers are swelling the ranks of retirees, many of whom are living on fixed incomes and unable to keep pace with spiraling housing costs. The polarization of incomes will continue to widen the gap between the housing haves and have-nots, with more middle-income households pushed toward the have-nots. Production of affordable housing, albeit increasing, is still unable to keep up with the growing demand. Existing affordable housing is being lost as homes filter up and landlords command higher rents, or deteriorating as landlords do not undertake necessary maintenance because rents are unable to cover even operating expenses.

Housing is a continuum, and when lower-income households are unable to secure decent housing at affordable rents, reverberations are felt throughout the market. The pool of prospective first-time home-buyers diminishes as renting households are squeezed by high rents and unable to save for downpayments. Thus, the young renting households who in a previous time would have moved up to homeownership continue to rent. Current homeowners with considerable equity in their homes move up to large, well-appointed homes, thereby widening the gap between the housing haves and the have-nots.

Federal, state, and local initiatives for affordable rental and ownership housing have met with mixed success. For example, the 1990 NAHA incentives offered to private owners of federally subsidized housing to maintain their affordable rental properties when contracts expired were very expensive. Thus, the preservation incentive program was stopped, and no new funds were appropriated before the losses stopped. In contrast, the low-income housing tax credit (a federal tax expenditure program administered by the states) has proved to be a tremendous incentive for private developers, with roughly 60,000 units of affordable housing being built annually in recent years using the credits. State programs that provide below-market-rate financing to developers to build affordable housing and purchasers to buy affordable housing have also been successful, with more than 650,000 units of affordable housing produced and 2 million mortgage loans made since the beginning of the program in the 1970s.

Private sector participation has been significant. For-profit and nonprofit developers such as CDCs are increasing their production of affordable rental and ownership housing, spurred on by tax incentives. Individual financial institutions are forming affiliates that specialize in community development lending, including mortgage loans for affordable housing. Financial institutions are pooling resources in loan consortiums to make mortgage loans for affordable housing. Life insurance companies and pension funds are putting money in economically targeted investments. Affordable housing is climbing to the top of many foundations' and charities' social agendas.

To achieve the goal of the Housing Act of 1949 of "a decent home and suitable living environment for every American," all participants in the development process will have to be ever more creative.

TERMS

- ▶ Community development block grant (CDBG)
- ▶ Community Reinvestment Act of 1977
- ▶ Demonstration programs
- ▶ Exclusionary zoning
- ▶ Fannie Mae
- ▶ FHA
- ▶ FIRREA
- ▶ Freddie Mac
- ▶ Ginnie Mae
- ▶ Housing vouchers
- ▶ HUD
- ▶ Linked deposits
- ▶ Market-rate housing
- ▶ National Affordable Housing Act of 1990 (NAHA)
- ▶ Rent control
- ▶ Risk sharing
- ▶ Special-needs program
- ▶ Tax Reform Act of 1986
- ▶ Urban development action grant (UDAG)

REVIEW QUESTIONS

15.1 Define "affordable housing." Why is there confusion when it comes to identifying what affordable housing is?

15.2 Which groups are finding it difficult to afford adequate housing?

15.3 Discuss the role of state and local governments in providing housing and the type of programs and techniques they use.

15.4 Define "low income."

15.5 Discuss various programs for low-income housing.

15.6 How does the private sector participate in providing low-income housing?

15.7 What are some of the factors affecting the cost of housing?

15.8 What are some of the regulatory reforms that have encouraged the production of affordable housing?

NOTES

1. Joint Center for Housing Studies, *The State of the Nation's Housing, 2006* (Cambridge, Mass.: Joint Center for Housing Studies, Harvard University, 2006).

2. Thirty percent was selected because the U.S. Department of Housing and Urban Development uses this standard in its determinations of affordability for most of its housing programs. (Until 1981, HUD's standard of affordability was 25 percent of income.)

3. Although the affordability standard does not consider family or household size, the income limits for household eligibility for HUD programs are adjusted from a four-person base according to household size. Additional adjustments to income limits for program eligibility reflect unusually high- or low-income areas or high or low housing costs. Other sliding scale standards of affordability for low- and moderate-income households base the share of income that a household can comfortably spend on housing on both the size and income of the household. HUD programs, however, do not use the sliding scale standards—perhaps because of the difficulty in administering programs tied to so many definitions of affordability.

4. HUD's definition of low income is not generally as low as another common measure of economic deprivation—the "poverty line," which is defined by the U.S. Census Bureau in terms of a household's ability to purchase a hypothetical "market basket" of goods and services. (The poverty line is used to determine eligibility for certain kinds of government assistance other than housing.) From a national perspective, the income ceiling for HUD is about 50 percent higher than that of the Census Bureau. Thus, many more households are classified as poor under HUD's definition.

5. Susan J. Popkin, Bruce Katz, et al., "A Decade of HOPE VI, Research Findings and Policy Changes," posted May 18, 2004, by the Urban Institute (www.urban.org).

6. *State of the Nation's Housing, 2005.*

7. Michael A. Stegman, "The Fall and Rise of Public Housing," *Regulation*, Summer 2002, pp. 3–4.

8. Since 1995, no source of national data has been available on the number of households receiving state and local housing subsidies.

9. Namely, housing stock that is affordable at 30 percent of income to the third of renter households with an income of $16,000 or less, according to *State of the Nation's Housing, 2006.*

10. *State of the Nation's Housing, 2003*, p. 28.

11. *State of the Nation's Housing, 2006.*

12. Ibid.

13. Stegman, "The Fall and Rise of Public Housing," p. 4.

14. U.S. Conference of Mayors and Sodexho, "Hunger and Homelessness Survey. A Status Report on Hunger and Homelessness in America's Cities," December 2003, p. 84.

15. U.S. Department of Housing and Urban Development, "A Picture of Subsidized Households, 1997." Accessed July 11, 2007, from www.huduser.org.

16. *State of the Nation's Housing, 2005.*

17. U.S. Census Bureau, "Fact Sheet for 1990 Decennial Census: Counts of Persons in Selected Locations Where Homeless Persons Are Found," CPH-L-87 (Washington, D.C.: U.S. Government Printing Office, 1992).

18. National Alliance to End Homelessness, "A Plan, Not a Dream: How to End Homelessness in Ten Years." Accessed January 11, 2004, from www.endhomelessness.org/pub/tenyear/demograp.htm.

19. Department of Housing and Urban Development, "Martinez Ends Tenure as Chairman of Interagency Council on Homelessness with Recommitment to End Chronic Homelessness in Ten Years," News Release No. 03-032, March 28, 2003. Accessed July 11, 2007, from www.hud.gov/news/release.cfm.

20. National Low Income Housing Coalition. Accessed March 10, 2006, from www.nlihc.org.

21. U.S. Conference of Mayors and Sodexho, *Hunger and Homelessness Survey*, p. 84.

22. *State of the Nation's Housing, 2006.*

23. Since their authorization in 1974, CDBGs have provided a flexible source of funding for community and economic development. HUD gives CDBGs to qualified cities and counties on the basis of entitlement; smaller cities and towns compete for project-specific funds through state governments. Money may be used for projects in which 70 percent of the beneficiaries are low- and moderate-income households and for programs that eliminate slums and blight and serve "urgent community needs."

24. The FHA has introduced several risk-sharing demonstration programs, which are similar to traditional mortgage insurance except that FHA shares the risk with state and local housing finance agencies (in the case of the credit enhancement program) and with qualified lenders (in the case of the reinsurance program) rather than assumes the entire risk of loss from mortgage defaults.

25. U.S. Department of Housing and Urban Development, *A Report on Worst Case Housing Needs in 1999: New Opportunity amid Continuing Challenges.* Executive Summary. January 2001, p. 2.

26. U.S. General Accounting Office, *Housing for the Elderly: Information on HUD's Section 202 and HOME Investment Partnerships Programs.* Report No. GAO/RCED-98-11. (Washington, D.C.: U.S. General Accounting Office, November 1997).

27. Ibid.

28. *State of the Nation's Housing, 2006.*

29. Michael A. Stegman and J. David Holden, *Nonfederal Housing Programs: How States and Localities Are Responding to Federal Cutbacks in Low-Income Housing* (Washington, D.C.: ULI–the Urban Land Institute, 1987), p. 75.

30. Bruce Katz and Margery Austin Turner. "Rethinking Shelter," *Urban Land*, March 2004, p. 56.

31. Housing linkage programs, in which approvals for non-residential construction are conditioned on the applicant's direct provision of market-rate and/or affordable housing or payment of fees for housing in lieu of such provision, flourish during periods of strong commercial construction activity. As a result, housing linkage programs virtually came to a halt with the lull in office

construction in the late 1980s and early 1990s. Despite the resumption of office construction during the mid-1990s, mandatory linkage programs have not reached the importance they had during the 1980s.

32. Begun in 1991 in 23 cities, the National Community Development Initiative is an "effort to increase the capital available to community development corporations by pooling more funding than any one philanthropic or private sector source could be expected to provide." In its three funding rounds, NCDI resources have come from a total of 11 foundations, six corporations, and the federal government, through HUD. See Christopher Walker and Mark Weinheimer, *Community Development in the 1990s*. Accessed July 11, 2007, from www.urban .org/pubs/comdev90/summary.html.

33. *Thinking Differently: Acting Boldly*. Annual Report 2006. Accessed July 11, 2007, from www.enterprisecommunity.org/ about/annual_report/2006/annualreport_2006.pdf.

34. Congress passed the Community Reinvestment Act in 1977 to encourage banks to meet the credit needs of low- and moderate-income neighborhoods in their local communities. The CRA requires banks and other financial institutions to prepare a statement of their investment in the community every one to five years, depending on size. The statement must outline the types of credit offered by the institution to the community. The appropriate supervisory agency (the Board of Governors of the Federal Reserve System, the Federal Deposit Insurance Corporation, the Office of Thrift Supervision, or the Office of the Comptroller of the Currency) rates each covered institution under its purview according to specific guidelines regarding reinvestment in the communities that the institutions are supposed to be serving.

FIRREA amended the CRA to give the public access to regulators' examination assessments and CRA ratings. Over the years, the focus of the CRA has shifted from the identification of community needs, which are now assumed, to financial institutions' actual performance. Enforcement is a large element of the legislation as it currently stands.

35. Accessed March 15, 2006, from www.nw.org.

36. The Ford Foundation instituted PRIs in 1968. PRIs are not grants but investments made by a foundation from its endowment or annual earnings. Investments can take the form of loans, loan guarantees, or equity.

37. *State of the Nation's Housing, 2005*.

38. Enterprise Foundation, *Comment to the Millennial Housing Commission*, June 28, 2001, p. 18.

39. *HUD Proposes New Initiatives to Reduce Barriers*. Accessed July 11, 2007, from www.huduser.org/rbc/rbcNews/ Nov-25-03.html.

40. R.G. Quercia, M.A. Stegman, W.R. Davis, and E. Stein, with the Joint Center for Housing Studies, Harvard University. "Performance of Community Reinvestment Loans: Implications for Secondary Market Purchases," in *Low Income Homeownership: Examining the Unexamined Goal*, ed. N.P. Retsinas and E.S. Belsky (Washington, D.C.: Brookings Institution Press, 2002), p. 51.

41. *State of the Nation's Housing, 2002*, p. 18.

42. Quercia et al., 2002, p. 352.

43. R.G. Quercia, G.W. McCarthy, and S.M. Wachter, "The Impacts of Affordable Lending on Homeownership Rates," *Journal of Housing Economics*, Vol. 12, no. 1, p. 31.

44. *State of the Nation's Housing, 2002*, p. 14.

45. *American Dream Downpayment Initiative*. Accessed July 11, 2007, from www.HUD.gov.

46. "Bush Administration Announces New HUD 'Zero Down Payment' Mortgage," News Release No. 04-006. Accessed July 11, 2007, from www.hud.gov.

47. S. Mark White, "State and Federal Planning Legislation and Manufactured Housing: New Opportunities for Affordable, Single-Family Shelter," *The Urban Lawyer*, Spring 1996, pp. 263–291.

PART VI

PLANNING AND ANALYSIS: THE MARKET PERSPECTIVE

Development involves the cooperation of many different entities, and each must be informed with sufficient data about the level of risk involved in the project, whether for the project itself or for the firm. Part VI examines issues related to market information—finding it, using it, and understanding its relationship to the development project.

Chapter 16 defines and outlines a holistic version of the feasibility study—the most important decision aid and management tool in the development process. The developer uses it to evaluate the idea across all dimensions of the project—physical, legal, market, and financial—and to assemble the development team. The feasibility study remains a living document that is constantly revised throughout stages four through seven of the process.

Chapter 17 covers the most important element of the feasibility study—market analysis. Properly collected and validated data are critical components of insightful market research and help establish a connection between supply and demand trends and forecasts for the competitive marketplace as well as property-specific cash flow and valuation assumptions. Chapter 18 describes idiosyncrasies of the data while identifying various data sources and related forecasting models.

CHAPTER **16**

Stage Three: The Feasibility Study

Although developers probably have a strong intuitive feel for a project's ultimate viability based on the results of activities that occur during stage two, typically they must still formally demonstrate the project's viability to other participants. The formal demonstration of viability is the goal of stage three—the feasibility study. If the project survives refinement of the idea (stage two), then it is more likely to be a viable project than the rough idea that survived stage one. During stage three, developers commit additional dollars to the project to perform more detailed analyses along several dimensions. Consequently, a strong intuitive positive feeling for the project is necessary coming out of stage two to induce the developer to make the additional financial commitment. At the end of stage three, developers can still decide not to undertake a project, but at a significantly higher cost than at the end of stage two. The cost goes beyond dollars—it includes relationships, time, reputation, and credibility.

Development is more than a series of numbers gleaned from the marketplace; it involves entrepreneurial energy and creativity as well. Still, even the most creative, intuitive developers who bring to the marketplace new concepts of space (over time with

associated services) benefit from running all the numbers and systematically addressing all the issues. In addition to serving as a marketing tool to bring all the members of the proposed development team together, the feasibility study is an important management tool providing multiple forms of risk control over several subsequent stages of the development process.

This chapter begins with a comprehensive definition of feasibility and then moves to the initiation of the feasibility study and an overview of the market study. The market study is so critical that Chapters 17 and 18 are devoted exclusively to its preparation. The present chapter discusses other traditional elements of the feasibility study, newer topics under the broad headings "the enterprise concept" and "the notion of venture capital," and techniques to control risk during stage three. It covers the following major topics:

▶ The definition of feasibility;
▶ Initiating the feasibility study;
▶ An overview of the market study;
▶ Preliminary drawings;
▶ Initial construction and total cost estimates;
▶ Lenders and investors;

- Building permits and other government considerations;
- The value statement and formal estimate of feasibility;
- The enterprise concept;
- The notion of venture capital;
- Level two feasibility; and
- Techniques of risk control during stage three.

In thinking about the feasibility study, certain broad principles should be kept in mind.

1. Among its other uses, the feasibility study is an excellent organizational tool. It brings together everything about the development in a consistent format, usually by using a computer program to facilitate sensitivity analysis. As the development moves through the eight stages, the feasibility study is continually refined and modified, with estimates becoming increasingly concrete with the passage of time.

2. The developer should produce one feasibility study, with relevant sections for each participant in the development process. He probably does not want to share the details of the equity financing with the contractor or the lead tenant, but he does want to be certain that all the assumptions in the equity section are internally consistent with the assumptions in the building cost and leasing sections. The developer should not prepare an independent feasibility study for each participant, even though each must be induced to make an individual commitment. A single feasibility study for the entire project allows the developer to see how the individual participants will achieve the development goal collectively.

3. A complete feasibility study is an extensive undertaking. To ensure its full benefit, the study should not end with a mere finding of "sufficiency," i.e., a determination that the project's value exceeds the cost of making the development "feasible." Rather, the feasibility study should be considered an optimization tool. By using computer-aided sensitivity analysis, the developer should examine every major decision and every significant feature, function, and benefit of the proposed project to see whether it is the best plan, not simply an acceptable plan.

4. The eight stages of the development process provide a convenient and logical framework within which to explore the many interactive aspects of real estate development. In fact, the feasibility study might not always be clearly delineated at the third stage of the development process. It might start during refinement of the idea, and final design might spill over into the fourth stage—contract negotiation. Like the entire development process, the feasibility study should be seen as inherently interdisciplinary.

THE DEFINITION OF FEASIBILITY

The best definition of feasibility remains the one that renowned real estate educator James A. Graaskamp advanced in his classic 1972 article, "A Rational Approach to Feasibility Analysis": "A real estate project is 'feasible' when the real estate analyst determines that there is a reasonable likelihood of satisfying explicit objectives when a selected course of action is tested for fit to a context of specific constraints and limited resources."[1]

Each phrase of Graaskamp's long definition is important. First, feasibility never demonstrates certainty. A project is feasible when it is reasonably likely to meet its goals; even favorable results from a feasibility study cannot guarantee a project's success.

Second, feasibility is determined by satisfying explicit objectives that must be defined before initiating the feasibility study. It is not just a matter of satisfying the developer's explicit objectives, though such objectives may be the initial driving force. The other players have objectives that must be met, the most important of which are the objectives of the public sector partner and the final user.

Third, the definition talks about a selected course of action and testing it for fit. In other words, logistics, particularly timing, matter. It is not simply a question of whether or not an idea might work; rather, it is a question of whether a particular plan for turning an idea into bricks and mortar is likely to work within a specific time frame.

Fourth, the selected course of action is tested for fit in a context of specific constraints, which include all the legal and physical limitations enumerated in stage two of the development process. In addition to the obvious constraints associated with both the public sector's involvement and the land itself, people and capital are limited. For a project to be feasible, it must be feasible given the amount of capital and number of people to be dedicated to the project, according to a specific course of action at a particular time.

This broad definition of feasibility goes far beyond the simple idea of value exceeding cost. When the word "constraints" is pushed into the ethical dimension (as suggested by Graaskamp), then both personal and social ethics as well as formal legal and physical constraints must also be satisfied.

INITIATING THE FEASIBILITY STUDY

The feasibility study is the formal demonstration that a proposed project is or is not viable. In addition to maps, pictures, and résumés, a typical feasibility study includes an executive summary, a market study, preliminary drawings, cost estimates, information about terms and sources of financing, government considerations, and the estimate of value.

Depending on the size and complexity of the development, the feasibility study can vary dramatically in length, scope, and cost. At one extreme, if the project is a duplex in an area already developed with other duplexes and is to use architectural drawings from a previously built project and the same contractor and lender, then the feasibility analysis is a simple activity that involves the new market information described in Chapters 10 through 12 applied to a proven course of action. In other words, new market data are used to project rent and absorption, with most other factors refined modestly from preceding developments. In such a simple case, developers would probably choose to perform the feasibility study with in-house staff at limited cost.

This simple case contrasts sharply with a 5,000-acre (2,025-hectare) master-planned community and business park. Such a community includes several types of developed real estate and requires extensive infrastructure as well as above-ground construction. Because the project is likely to take many years to complete, the recognition of long-term trends is

A complex project like the 35-story Agbar Tower (Torre Agbar) in Barcelona, Spain—the building has a three-layer facade consisting of concrete, corrugated aluminum, and 59,600 reflective, tinted glass louvers—will require a much lengthier and more extensive feasibility analysis than a smaller or less complex project. *Rafael Vargas*

One of the first new projects to be built in the U Street district in Washington, D.C., in decades, the Ellington is an eight-story, 192-unit apartment building with 17,000 square feet (1,580 square meters) of retail space. *Steve Hall*

more important—even for designing the first stage of the project. An idea for a complex, expensive, long-term project often results in a complex, expensive feasibility study that involves at least one and possibly more outside professionals such as architects, land planners, soils engineers, hazardous waste experts, and even public relations consultants. More than one architect might be used to specify designs for key facilities as well as any architectural constraints for projects slated to be constructed by outside builders.

Because the relationship between developers and local governments is more dynamic and complex than in the past, interaction with and involvement of various government bodies will probably be substantial from the outset. In some jurisdictions, developers use political consultants who function like pollsters to test the local political waters and then help prepare and deliver the developer's message.

Likewise, market analysis and tenant relations are more complex because of the possibility that people will move to the location not simply from within the city but also from around the country and possibly from around the world. The developer must coordinate all the professionals and ensure that they are all talking about precisely the same project so that they can collectively determine its feasibility.

For the developer who chooses to use an outside analyst to produce the feasibility study, numerous specialized companies and professional organizations are available to perform the work. Real estate advisory firms, appraisal companies, business consultants, and the real estate divisions of most large accounting firms can be commissioned to perform a feasibility study.

Because various state and federal regulatory agencies oversee the lenders who bear a portion of the risk in major developments, affected financial institutions are usually required to include some feasibility work as one of the items they examine in underwriting the loan. An outside feasibility study prepared by a well-respected firm meets this requirement. By the latter part of the 1980s, for example, Rule R-41c (Appraisal Policies and Practices of Insured Institutions and Service Corporations) required lenders to mandate that appraisals of development projects constitute more than simply a collection of a few comparable facts illustrating current conditions. Instead, lenders are required to formally estimate a project's "highest and best use" based on a schedule of space absorption over time. Further, as a measure of risk control, appraisers must estimate the "as is" value of partially completed projects as well as their projected values upon completion. (See Part III for more detail.)

Although the government hoped to end the unsubstantiated assertions of financial feasibility and property values that led to many financial disasters during the 1980s, more recent regulatory attitudes have placed a greater burden on lenders. Regulators no longer spell out what lenders must demand of appraisers and other market analysts. Rather, lenders are required to demand whatever analyses are necessary and appropriate in the particular situation—a Catch-22 for most lenders. If they do not require substantial analysis by an independent party and a loan subsequently goes into default, then the regulators will fault them for not performing sufficiently detailed due diligence. Lenders, on the other hand, do not know ahead of time what level of analysis is adequate to avoid loan losses. They do not want to put too much cost burden on their customers (developers/borrowers), but they want to leave a paper trail in case problems develop later. Most important, lenders want to make money. Avoiding loans on losing developments is a big step in that direction.

Before examining each individual component of the feasibility study, it is instructive to consider all the components as a single unit. An analysis of the collective items listed below yields an answer to whether or not an idea is feasible, using Graaskamp's broad definition of feasibility.

The Essentials:

▶ Executive summary
▶ Maps
▶ Photographs of the site
▶ Renderings
▶ Market study
▶ Electronic valuation model derived from market study
▶ Documented cost projections
▶ Development schedule
▶ Background on key players, including project consultants

Critical Analytic Elements:

▶ Idea and target market for the project, from the big picture down to an absorption schedule for today in the particular market niche—progressing from world to nation to region to city to neighborhood to site;
▶ A careful enumeration of target market demand—number of people, their requirements, their income—tied to the specific project concept;
▶ Identification of competitive properties along with the major features, functions, and advantages of each;
▶ The foregoing information tied into a discounted cash flow model;
▶ A sensitivity analysis to move from feasible to optimal, with an individual evaluation of each variation of the plan;
▶ A review of risks in the optimal configuration, with appropriate risk management techniques;
▶ Confirmation that the project is feasible for each participant (see "Level Two Feasibility" below).

AN OVERVIEW OF THE MARKET STUDY

The market study is usually the most crucial item in a feasibility analysis. It analyzes all the long-term global, national, regional, and local trends that were initially identified during idea refinement in stage two. These trends are now formally brought to bear on the existing local situation as the analyst projects an absorption schedule for the project. This task is so important that real estate market studies for various property types are the entire focus of Chapters 17 and 18.

The first step in a market study is an examination of national economic conditions (including international influences) and projected long-term trends as well as careful consideration of the characteristics of the region, locality, neighborhood, and site. Long-term national trends are often extremely important to the site. It has been well documented, for example, that, nationally, the types of jobs available and types of job seekers in central cities are mismatched. The United States has moved increasingly away from the strong back (manufacturing) and toward the strong mind (information processing) in numbers of available jobs. Entry-level jobs for high school dropouts that used to be available in manufacturing have declined drastically in central cities; jobs involving information processing have increased in number but are out of reach for most dropouts.

This national trend is particularly apparent in certain regions and is directly relevant to development in many central cities. Developers of office space in central cities may find that prospective tenants worry about their ability to attract needed high-level administrative staff at a given location. At the same time, suburban retail developments might have difficulty finding individuals willing to take lower-paying service positions at fast-food restaurants and retail shops. In both cases, the lack of available workers near the location may decrease the value that prospective tenants place on a proposed project. Market analysts should not lose sight of such important national trends as they project operating numbers for a specific site, and they must remember that even modestly sized projects have two- to five-year time horizons for planning, construction, sales, and leasing, thus increasing the importance of sound forecasting.[2]

As a second step, market analysts investigate comparable properties to determine the features, functions, and benefits of those properties that are important to the market. Because market analysis is expensive, the analysis should focus on projects that are directly competitive with the proposed development or useful in providing insights into market pref-erences. Understanding and even quantifying the value of particular features can help developers specify the key features of the proposed development. If the best leasing in the area has been achieved by an office building that has no fitness center but more parking than the competition, then extra parking is more important than a fitness center; thus, the subject property should be designed accordingly.

Third, the market study concludes with projected absorption schedules for the market segment and for the specific property. How many units at what price over what time period will the target market be likely to absorb? It is necessary to segment the market carefully by defining all the features, functions, and benefits of comparable projects to be able to predict the overall absorption rate for the market segment. The developer can then attach value to the distinctive features of the subject property and compare it with the market to estimate the proposed development's capture rate and expected rents.

PRELIMINARY DRAWINGS

If an idea's viability is established (at least in the developer's mind) in stage two, more money must usually be committed to drawings in stage three. Preliminary drawings show exterior elevations and specify floor layouts with rentable square feet or salable units, parking, type of HVAC systems, and the like. Part of this work was done in stage two, but the formal feasibility study requires drawings much closer to final design plans than those needed for stage two.

Although different architects and engineers can be used for the initial architectural layout and the final construction drawings, it is usually more efficient to use the same architect and engineer throughout the entire process. Such consistency reduces the learning curve involved in bringing in new players and prompts their commitment to and understanding of the development team's objectives. Developers must decide the level of talent/sophistication (read "cost") needed of the architect and engineer as well as the amount of their time to use at each stage. The more complex and innovative the job, the more important it is to hire competent professionals and bring them into the process earlier. On the other hand, for simpler projects that are much like other projects and on sites much like other sites, it is probably not cost-efficient to bring in "starchitects" with a full team of supporting engineers. The developer must decide on the quality, quantity, and timing of design talent.

High-quality design is becoming much more important as more communities implement design standards and as clients become more discriminating. High-quality, high-performance design can go a long way toward the successful leasing and management of the finished project. Landscaping is also increasing in importance as part of the overall design package. A creative landscape architect can enhance and beautify an already striking project and contribute to the overall image of a development.

Bilbao, Spain, for example, has centered economic development plans around striking architecture. The unusual architecture and high style of the Bilbao Guggenheim, designed by Frank Gehry, was expected to bring perhaps 500,000 visitors to Bilbao the first year. Instead, it brought 1.36 million visitors and $160 million in revenue to the former shipbuilding town that few ever visited. The city's solution to its economic decline was culture and design, and, in addition to the museum, a new exhibition center was constructed and a new sports arena will break ground in 2008. Both projects were designed by internationally renowned architects. Many cities have followed Bilbao's lead and commissioned a high-profile architect to design a public building. For example, the Milwaukee Art Museum commissioned Santiago Calatrava, and the city of Chicago commissioned Frank Gehry for a band shell in Millennium Park.

Outside professionals can bring valuable experience to the development team and reduce risk when a development company lacks experience in a certain type of project or has not yet established a good track record with local government bodies. As specialists, architects play a crucial role in the development process, but they cannot design the project unless they are aware of other players' activities and objectives. To be successful, the final product must be marketable, manageable, and cost-effective. Communication and feedback among the members of the development

Drawings of Broadway and Pine—a green mixed-use building with 44 units of affordable housing over a Walgreens drugstore—were useful for the design team and for communicating the plans to community members and neighbors. *GGLO*

team are essential from the beginning, because preliminary drawings must compare and trade off three basic items: marketing appeal (the project's eye appeal to prospective tenants), the project's physical cost, and the ease of ongoing management. A beautiful building that costs too much to construct and is difficult to manage is not a successful development. On the other hand, a low-budget project could be both visually unappealing and difficult to manage and therefore even less successful. Optimal results occur when property management (described in Chapter 21) is combined with the factors discussed in this chapter and with the concepts of marketing discussed throughout the text. The development team's clear communication of marketing information to the architect stimulates the design of manageable space that is attractive to prospective tenants.

A balance among marketing appeal, cost, and ease of management cannot be achieved without fitting the project to a specific site; after all, the primary distinguishing characteristic of real estate is its specific, unchangeable location. A project that fits one site well is often far less successful when replicated on a second site. Fitting the project to the site requires

MUSEUM TOWERS
Working with the Architect

Museum Towers is not a "high-design" project. When all the adjoining public work is complete, it will have tremendous views and a very convenient location. With those attributes, we didn't think we needed to overpay on design. We did spend a considerable amount of time with interior design people, making sure that the kitchens and baths were superior to the older competition, but the project won't win any design competitions.

BUILDING SPECIFICATIONS

Location
Eight and Ten Museum Way (formerly 15 Monsignor O'Brien Highway), Cambridge, Massachusetts, in the North Point neighborhood, directly across the Charles River from the west end area of downtown Boston.

Lot Size
Total parcel area—90,169 square feet (2.07 acres)—8,380 square meters, or 0.83 hectare

Building Size
Total gross square feet—618,710 (57,500 square meters)
Total rentable square feet—410,444 (38,145 square meters)

Units
Total number of units—435
Average area per unit—944 square feet (88 square meters)
Mix of units—four studios, 180 one-bedroom units, 251 two-bedroom units

Parking
490 spaces in a 103,200-square-foot (9,590-square-meter) underground garage

Common Area/Mechanical
88,566 square feet (8,230 square meters)

Retail Space
2,500 square feet (235 square meters)

Health Club
14,000 square feet (1,300 square meters)

Tenant Storage Space
200 units

Elevators
Six high-speed elevators, three in each tower, that travel at the rate of 700 feet per minute (213 meters per minute)

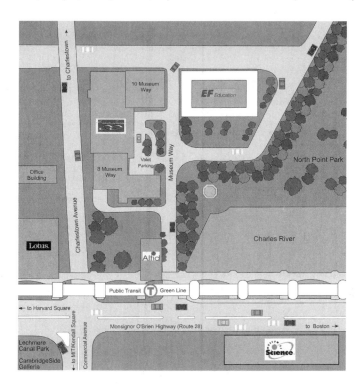

Museum Towers is located close to several main arteries and two subway lines.

MUSEUM TOWERS

Working with the Architect (continued)

Windows
Combination of awning windows, fixed windows, and sliding doors with insulated glass in aluminum frames

STANDARDS

Partitioning—Wall Finishes
Gypsum wallboard with plaster

Ceilings
Gypsum wallboard with skim coat of plaster and sprayed, textured finish; suspended acoustical tile in commercial areas

Floors
Poured concrete

Electrical Lights
Incandescent and fluorescent

Floor Coverings
Carpeting in unit living and common areas; resilient tile in storage, janitor, and utilities areas; ceramic tile in bathrooms; sheet vinyl in kitchens

Exterior Doors
Combination of metal and glass in metal frames

Exterior Unit Doors
Solid wood

Interior Unit Doors
Hollow-core wood, bifold, six panel

HVAC
Individually controlled water source heat pumps with circulated warm and cool water from a central system

Hot Water
Individual electric units in each unit

Utilities
Sewer and water—city of Cambridge
Electricity and natural gas—Commonwealth Energy

Trash Removal/Disposal
Trash chutes on each floor

Life-Safety Systems
High-rise fire alarms and smoke detectors, emergency lighting, sprinkler system, stair pressurization, and smoke exhaust systems

Security
Twenty-four-hour concierge service; card-access security systems; closed-circuit television with videotape surveillance in each building

continued on page 405

creativity and is frequently a time-consuming process, but it is an invaluable device for controlling risk. Early refinements in the design can prevent the development of structures that are hard to build, manage, or lease. Good planning can also reduce or eliminate opposition from the public sector.

Space is created for people, not vice versa. Moreover, space that appeals to people can generate a new market in the future beyond the demand indicated in the market study. Today, heightened interest in the functionality and aesthetics of constructed space leads to research into the value created by outstanding architecture and specifically addresses the question of whether or not buildings that clearly are design landmarks (or are particularly attractive) bring a higher return to the developer and investor.[3] Whether or not such research eventually proves that

greater returns accrue to "great" architecture, developers find some lenders and investors want to be associated with "big names."

Besides being concerned about how a building fits its site and serves its intended tenants, developers also need to think about how a building blends into the urban setting. For example, Pittsburgh—with its many corporate headquarters buildings, three rivers, and mountains—has been said to have one of the most stunning skylines of any major U.S. city. In contrast, other writers have characterized Dallas as "a bunch of spectacular buildings screaming at each other." Dallas's cityscape seems less to bring together a harmonious group of different buildings than to show different buildings that compete with each other. The lesson is that an individual building may appear attractive in isolation but, once built, must

ELEVATION 314

Constructing a Green Building

From the beginning, Elevation 314 was designed to be environmentally friendly. It is not just the big things—like a green roof or geothermal heating and cooling—that make a building green, but also the small things.

BUILDING SPECIFICATIONS

Location
314 Carroll Street, NW, Washington, D.C. in the Takoma neighborhood and across the street from the Takoma Metro station.

Lot Size
Total parcel area—34,531 square feet (3,210 square meters)

Building Size
Total gross square feet—67,348 (6,260 square meters)
Total residential gross square feet—54,058 (5,025 square meters)

Floor/Area Ratio (FAR)
Actual FAR—1.5

Units
Total number of apartment units—52
Number of retail spaces—2
Mix of units—26 two-bedroom units, 6 one-bedroom-with-study units, 20 one-bedroom units

Car Parking
38 spaces total: 19 in a 7,143-square-foot (665-square-meter) underground garage, and 19 on grade

Retail Space
2,988 square feet (280 square meters)

Storage/Laundry/Bicycle Parking
3,838 square feet (355 square meters)
47 bicycle parking spaces in basement

Mechanical
Approximately 1,600 square feet (150 square meters)

Tenant Storage Space
40 units

Elevators
One elevator using KONE's EcoDisc system, chosen for its energy efficiency and because it does not use oil or hydraulic fluids.

Windows
Insulated glass in window frames using recycled aluminum from Thermal Windows, Inc.

Partitioning—Wall Finishes
Gypsum wallboard and plaster finished with paints using low levels of volatile organic compounds

Ceilings
Gypsum wallboard and plaster

Floors and Floor Coverings
Bamboo and tile on concrete or just painted concrete on the first and second floors. On the third and fourth floors, the flooring is bamboo on wood framing with extra layers of sound insulation.

Electrical lights
Compact fluorescent

Floor Coverings
Bamboo, ceramic tile

Exterior Doors
Aluminum framed with double-pane insulated glass

Exterior Unit Doors
Balcony doors are made with fiberglass and double-pane insulated glass.

Interior Unit Doors
Hollow core masonite

Geothermal Heating and Cooling System
Closed-circuit system pumps water through pipes reaching a depth of 520 feet (160 meters) underground. The water returns to the surface at a temperature range of 55 to 65 degrees Fahrenheit (13 to 18 degrees Celsius). The chilled water is then pumped through the building. Individual heat pumps in each unit allow residents to adjust the temperature. Savings come from the benefit of borrowing the temperature of the earth; the system is most efficient when cooling the building.

Hot Water
Electric hot water heaters accompany each heat pump for each apartment. During the winter, energy from the water heaters supplements the work of the heat pumps, and in the summer, extra heat from the heat pumps is used to condition the hot water. Thus, in the summer, the hot water heaters use very little, if any, energy.

Utilities
Gas ranges, all others electric

Trash Removal/Disposal
Full recycling, including glass, plastic, metal, paper, and corrugated cardboard, is included in the rent. A dumpster is

ELEVATION 314

Constructing a Green Building (continued)

available for all other trash. Residents have also installed a compost system with the help of management.

Life-Safety Systems
Sprinklers throughout the building use the Antronnix monitoring system.

Security
All entries are controlled by a DoorKing access control system. Tenants use magnetic cards for entry. Building entrances and other locations on site are under surveillance of video cameras. Tenants can view entry camera to see who is requesting entry.

Bioretention Area
Courtyard stormwater management system comprising a green roof and bioretention area retains stormwater runoff

and uses native plants to filter water and to break down toxins.

Additional Green Features
20 percent of concrete is fly ash additive. More than 90 percent of steel used in the project comes from recycled sources.

All wood and bamboo in building come from sources certified for sustainability.

Only ENERGY STAR–rated appliances are used.

All electrical fixtures use low-energy compact fluorescent bulbs.

All paints, sealants, caulks, and adhesives were chosen for their low levels of volatile organic compounds.

continued on page 476

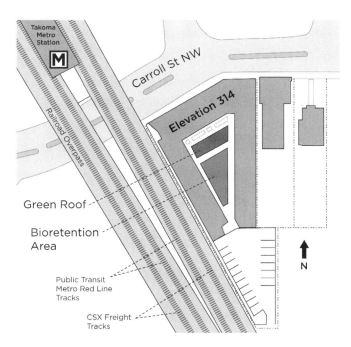

Elevation 314 site plan. Russell Katz

interact with its surroundings. Context is an important element of design.

Truly great architecture synthesizes the elements of context and design. Size and scale, massing and setbacks, landscaping, circulation in the parking area, lighting, stylistic details, relationships, image, range of difference—not to mention form and materials—

are all important in what is usually referred to as "the context of the building." Likewise, foreshadowing and the entry, contrast and consistency, form and space relationships, volume, ordering systems, edges in transition, activity areas, levels, circulation in movement, the building's footprint, human scale, surfaces and materials, varied elements, ornamenta-

Figure 16-1	Going Green

In the last two decades, the green building movement has made an enormous leap forward. Environmentally sustainable projects representing every sector of the real estate industry have been constructed around the world. Green is now gold, and architects and developers are more aware of the performance value and the marketing value of a green building. What green issues do developers need to know?

WHAT IS GREEN BUILDING?

The prevailing tenet of green building is to produce a harmonious interaction between the built and natural environments. Proponents of green buildings believe that dwellings, industrial and health facilities, and offices do not have to be in contention with the natural environment in and around which they are constructed and that fresh air, vegetation, and natural lighting should be part of the built environment, not just available in the natural environment. Employees who work in green buildings are said to be more productive, patients recover faster, and people lead healthier lives.

Energy efficiency is paramount to the green building doctrine—not just through the construction and maintenance of the building but also in the embodied energy of the materials. For example, if bamboo has to be shipped from halfway around the world to make the final product slightly "greener," the embodied energy, or the energy that it takes to process and ship the material to the construction site, obviates any energy efficiency gained by using the product. Extensive consideration to minimize such counterproductive practice goes into each green project to ensure that it has been constructed with the least detriment to the natural environment. Smarter, cleaner, healthier buildings are the objective of green builders.

ORIGINS

Since the 1970s energy crisis when America's addiction to oil and other nonrenewable fossil fuels became painfully apparent, a small group of architects, real estate developers, and engineers from around the world have been working to develop buildings that have a minimal impact on the environment. Initial commitments to this ideal were spotty at best. Pockets of devotees could be found, but the majority of private real estate developers dismissed

green buildings as not being profitable (the materials were too expensive) and being too difficult to get constructed because of the need for educating workers.

In the past, environmental benefits alone were not enough to persuade most mainstream consumers to dole out the higher upfront costs associated with building green. As demand for sustainable buildings grows, however, green building practices and technology are gaining momentum and shedding the higher costs once associated with the previously untested development style. Green branding along with capital cost neutrality and operational cost effectiveness are driving up profits, and conventional development methods are consequently being succeeded by more energy-efficient and environmentally friendly ones.

CERTIFICATION SYSTEMS

To determine whether or not a project can be considered "green," various organizations assess building planning and construction and offer certification based on certain criteria. The following green classifications are awarded by different oversight groups:

▶ Leadership in Energy and Environmental Design (LEED)—U.S. Green Building Council

▶ Building Research Establishment Environmental Assessment Method (BREEAM)—codeveloped in the United Kingdom by Energy and Environment Canada (ECD) and the Building Research Establishment (BRE)

▶ ENERGY STAR (Environmental Protection Agency).

Because the process of certification can be cumbersome and expensive, many public building programs are developing their own criteria for green.

Certification such as LEED is awarded based on many factors, but a handful of green principles constitute the foundational tenets of green development:

▶ Being made from salvaged, recycled, or agricultural waste content;

▶ Conserving natural resources;

▶ Reducing environmental impacts during construction, demolition, or renovation;

▶ Saving energy or water;

| Figure 16-1 | Going Green *(continued)* |

▶ Contributing to a safe, healthy indoor environment; and

▶ Avoiding toxic or other emissions.

METHODS OF BUILDING GREEN

To achieve the green criteria, large strides have been made in planning, design, and construction innovation. Common green building practices include:

▶ Site oriented toward mass transit or within walking distance of retail/grocery/workplace;

▶ Roofs covered with soil, drainage systems, and landscaping to help decrease the "heat island" effect and slow water runoff;

▶ Minimization of paints and adhesives that contain volatile organic compounds (VOCs), which produce noxious fumes and decrease ambient air quality;

▶ HVAC and cabling under the floor to reduce costs when relocating employees within an office;

▶ Use of rapidly renewable resources such as bamboo (applied in anything from furniture to flooring), soybeans (used to bind plywood instead of formaldehyde), and wheat (byproducts used to make wheatboard, which can substitute for particleboard);

▶ Natural light available to wider reaches of the office by orienting workspaces toward windows;

▶ Low-emissivity glass to reduce the effect of the exterior temperature on the office environment;

▶ Implementation of systems that monitor and manage energy use, including motion-sensor lighting;

▶ Low-flush toilet fixtures and waterless urinals.

BENEFITS OF ENVIRONMENTAL DESIGN

▶ Insurance companies may start linking lower premiums to high-performance buildings because of reduced risk of mold and other environmental hazards.

▶ Flexible design can help cut the cost of relocating employees within a building.

▶ Interactive, well-planned design minimizes surprises that can lead to costly errors and delayed completion.

▶ Green building often enhances the preexisting built environment, commanding higher lease premiums for landlords by differentiating the product from others in the market.

▶ Green building enhances labor productivity and decreases absenteeism through more desirable, healthier office conditions.

▶ Green features increase asset value and command higher sale prices.

SUMMARY

Unpredictable energy prices, increased greenhouse gas emissions, and the fear of irrevocable global warming have all begun to weigh more heavily on consumer decision making. With public attention fixed on such issues, it is logical to assume that the current practice of construction and maintenance of buildings, which is estimated to account for 30 percent of the aggregate energy consumption in the United States, will change substantially. With low to no increased upfront costs and sometimes even lower capital costs resulting from thorough planning and resource allocation, the dollars and cents of green building is starting to appeal to more and more developers. Developers often find that the approval process for obtaining building permits is met with less resistance when the intended project meets green criteria. The triple bottom line (economic profits, social benefit, and decreased environmental impact) is becoming the standard for conscientious and profit-seeking firms alike. Energy cost savings of up to 50 percent are common in many green buildings, and HVAC systems can frequently be downsized, saving both upfront and long-term capital. In a 2000 evaluation, for example, Hines, an international development firm, reported that it was generating $13 million in savings from its ENERGY STAR–rated buildings. Moreover, green buildings often produce something better than just the sum of their parts. They have the power to reshape communities and become a symbiotic addition to the living environment where they are built. Green building is fast becoming the rule rather than the exception.

—Chris Portillo

tion and color, and landscaping are important design considerations.

For a nonarchitect, this list may sound like an expensive set of intangible combinations. The ideal way for most individuals to learn about architecture is to visit great buildings and to study how their architecture fits with the city and how the space functions for those who inhabit it. It is probably one of the most enjoyable parts of kicking tires in the real estate business.

INITIAL CONSTRUCTION AND TOTAL COST ESTIMATES

The cost estimate for project construction should include the land, usually optioned or contracted for in stage two, the needed infrastructure, and the planned site improvements. In large, complex developments, both the latter requirements can be extremely expensive. Off-site infrastructure costs, whether assumed voluntarily or imposed on the developer by regulation, must be combined with on-site costs of water, sewers, streets, and the like to obtain an estimate of the total cost of infrastructure. Beyond needed infrastructure, the basic development costs are the land and the physical improvements to it that are necessary to bring the site to a condition that is ready for above-ground construction. In Tokyo, where a hectare of land (about 2.5 acres) can sell for more than a small ranch in South Dakota, land is usually the costliest item; in the United States, the greatest cost is usually attributable to the construction of the building—the bricks, mortar, and labor necessary to build the space.

Although it is easy to list cost categories, it is difficult to estimate the dollars associated with those costs. The cost of the land will probably be known after stage two, though with some variability for more complex options, lease fees, subordination agreements, and the like. In most cases, the most difficult cost to estimate accurately is infrastructure. Without extensive soil borings, it is difficult to know where rock is located and hence how expensive it will be to remove it or route pipe around it. And even with the advice of the best soils engineer, sometimes the handling of water is more expensive than expected. Every

experienced developer can relate war stories about problems encountered during construction—and underestimating the cost of infrastructure often heads the list.

Above ground, readily accessible guides are available for estimating construction costs. The guides break down cost elements and include monthly updates for cost inflation as well as adjustments for the geographic location of the proposed development.[4] The breakdown between materials and labor or at least their components is usually based on cubic, square, or linear footage. Other above-ground improvements—for example, parking lots, trees, lights, and signs—are often categorized under landscape architecture.

Developers should use standard industry cost guides to compile in-house cost projections to compare with local general contractors' estimates. In-house cost projections should yield an estimate that is close to general contractors' own cost estimates. When a significant difference occurs, the developer needs to recheck the figures and discuss them in more detail with the general contractors. If discrepancies remain, they must at least be explainable.

At times, the estimating process requires the developer to meet with individual subcontractors. For example, if an unusual amount and type of glass is to be used in a particular project, the developer might find it advisable to discuss with the glass subcontractor the specifics underlying the cost estimates used in the feasibility study. Information gleaned from talking to contractors and subcontractors helps redefine and improve parts of the project so that the proposal becomes more attractive to tenants, less expensive to construct, more cost-effective to operate, or some combination of the three.

Beyond the costs of land with improvements and above-ground construction, an estimate of total costs involves a substantial amount for marketing, financing, preparing taxes, insurance, consultants, and other administrative costs. Depending on the type of project, marketing could start months or even years before completion. Market research should start even earlier. Postconstruction costs for operations during initial periods of moderate occupancy are part of the

MUSEUM TOWERS
Choosing Players

I can't tell you how important it is to work with people you trust. If you're trying to make a decision about buying a building or a permitting issue or cooling towers, you have to be able to look at people and understand something about their personality, how credible they are. You have to get a sense of who they are and what their agenda is and where they're trying to go compared with where you're trying to go.

I'm fortunate because I've had the same project team for 20 years. The same mechanical engineer, electrical engineer, plumbing engineer, structural engineer. I've got one lead law firm. Even in the office, I need to be sure that everybody who works for me is working toward the same goal. I tell them that everybody has to do what's necessary to make sure we meet our pro formas. If you expect to come to work at nine o'clock and go home at five o'clock Monday through Friday, it's the wrong place to be.

Loyalty is a big piece of it. Trust is a big piece of it. And the loyalty and trust start off with capability. My construction guy, for example, is one of the best in the business. In the early eighties, I fired a construction company and hired another one that had a young assistant project manager.

The project manager and the assistant manager both came to the meeting. The project manager was so full of himself, but the assistant project manager was a straightforward guy. So I hired them on the condition that the assistant would be the project manager. We've been together ever since. There was something about the way he answered questions that made me trust him. I hired him after he finished that project, and he's been with us ever since.

He's stuck with me, too. In 1989, we had 55 people in the company; by 1992, we were down to seven people, and then I had to cut everybody's salary by 20 percent. I know that my construction guy was offered several jobs, one of which would have doubled his salary, but he said he helped me get into this mess and he'd help me get out. That kind of loyalty you can't buy.

I make mistakes every day—some really big ones sometimes. It doesn't do me any good to have well-paid people on staff telling me what I want to hear. People need to know that they're going to get treated fairly and not see their heads roll when they deliver unpleasant news to me. My construction guy and I fight. You should see the fights sometimes. But I trust him.

continued on page 457

total marketing cost. Advertising, commissions, and special concessions to tenants during the initial leasing period usually represent the major portion of the costs of marketing the development.

Lenders charge fees. Long-term lenders charge a commitment fee for the promise to take out or replace the construction lender. Construction lenders typically charge origination fees (points) and certainly charge interest. Additional points may be charged at the permanent loan at closing.

Local governments expect to collect property taxes throughout the development process, making such taxes another very real cost of development. Insurance should include fire and extended coverage in addition to various forms of liability coverage. Accounting costs and a variety of overhead costs should also be included in the overall cost estimate. The inclusion of both overhead and a development fee over and above overhead costs indicates that the developer is planning to draw some profit during the

construction period. (See "Level Two Feasibility" later in this chapter.)

Most estimates of marketing, borrowing, property taxes, insurance, and administrative costs can be based on experience and a projection of future trends. It is possible, for example, to know what market brokerage fees are, to estimate the amount of media time needed for advertising and the cost of that time, and, based on trends in the marketplace, to project the lease-up period, an essential part of accurately estimating the cost of initial periods of low occupancy. Likewise, estimates of financing costs can be based on a combination of projected construction time and projected interest rates.

Overall, past experience can be helpful in estimating costs for a standard product in a familiar location. Looking at the history of recent comparable developments can provide updated information, allowing a developer to adjust for recent changes. Clearly, it is important to plan for the impact of any changes in tax law, any changes in public policy, and evolving market conditions.

Finally, costs for contingencies should be included for every project. In an uncertain world, where feasibility is only "reasonably likely" and not guaranteed, it is important to set aside funds for unexpected costs and cost overruns. Because the total cost estimate is based on several other estimates, it is important to provide contingency funds commensurate with project risk. In a standard development, 5 percent might be adequate; in complex mixed-use redevelopments, 10 percent may not be sufficient.

Although each development will have features specific to it, a typical cost estimate might include the following elements:

- ▶ Land cost
- ▶ Site and infrastructure development costs
- ▶ Design fees
  - Architecture
  - Engineering
- ▶ Hard costs
  - By category
  - Labor and materials
- ▶ Permitting costs
- ▶ Financing costs
  - Permanent loan commitment fees
  - Construction interest
  - Construction loan fees
- ▶ Marketing costs
  - Promotion
  - Advertising
  - Leasing commissions
  - Brokers' fees
- ▶ Preopening operating costs
- ▶ Legal fees
- ▶ Accounting costs
- ▶ Field supervision (inspection) costs
- ▶ Overhead
- ▶ Contingencies
- ▶ Development fees.

Ideally, each estimate is confirmed by market data. Some items, such as land costs, may be based on contracts or options. The largest item, hard costs, should be confirmed by comparison with 1) the cost of similar projects; 2) cost estimation services; and 3) the prospective general contractor.

LENDERS AND INVESTORS

The preliminary discussions with lenders and investors that began in stage two now progress to a much more formal level. Based on initial reactions, the developer is close to finding the most appropriate permanent lender, construction lender, and, possibly, development-period equity investor and/or joint venture partner. In stage three, the developer presents lenders and investors with more specific information about the target market, design and costs of the project, and financial structure of the proposed transaction. At this point, the developer uses the project's estimated value to encourage participation. Permanent lenders look at their prospective return and the associated risk. This exercise usually involves a projected debt service coverage ratio, a loan-to-value ratio, and an estimation of the project's ability to maintain value through long-term appeal in a particular market.

Construction lenders usually prefer a simple project designed and built by highly skilled individuals with whom they have experience. If developers always followed lenders' guidelines, however, their profit (value minus cost) would likely be slim indeed. Lenders want both low risk (often interpreted as "it's been done before") and high interest rates with many loan fees. Lenders have been known to deviate from their general preferences—but only for logical reasons and usually only if those reasons are supported by a high-quality feasibility study.

To find the appropriate financiers for a proposed development, developers must know lenders' and investors' particular needs, their histories, their self-images, and the current preferred mix for their portfolios. Accordingly, developers work to minimize the costs of financing (see Chapters 7 through 9) and maximize their flexibility by minimizing the number of rules and other constraints imposed by lenders in the loan documents.

Why does a particular investment fit one lender better than another? On the surface, the answer is fairly straightforward. Larger life insurance companies typically finance larger projects developed by national firms. Regional life insurance companies and some commercial banks are more likely to finance smaller, more local projects. Many commercial banks, because of their predominantly short-term sources of funding, are more typically construction lenders on safer projects.

Recall the typical sequence presented in Chapters 7 through 9. Usually, the developer first lines up the largest, lowest-cost permanent loan possible. This permanent loan is the "takeout" for the construction lender. The difference between the total project cost and the available financing is the required equity. If the developer does not have (or does not want to risk) much money, he needs an equity investor for the development period.

The critical concept is matching the right lender or investor to the particular development. With consolidation in the financial markets, financial supermarkets such as Bank of America or GE Capital now typically engage in a variety of real estate loans through subsidiaries and affiliates, if not directly. Again, a mortgage broker might be hired to help developers deal with the financial community. As with the selection of an architect and an engineer, the more complex and crucial the financing arrangement, the more skilled developers or their agent must be in dealing with the financial community. Developers do not have to arrange financing; instead, they could hire Goldman Sachs and get first-rate assistance. Even with a top national investment banker on the team, however, it remains the developer's job to make the project happen, and financing is critical to that outcome.[5]

BUILDING PERMITS AND OTHER GOVERNMENT CONSIDERATIONS

During stage three, it is important not to forget the most important partner in the development process—the government. Government agencies are responsible for issuing the necessary building permits for the project. In some areas, obtaining permits is a highly political process. Developers who misjudge the local political environment or suggest a project that does not fit the community's long-term interests can have difficulty even if they technically meet the letter of the law (see Chapters 13 and 14 for more detail).

Clearly, some representatives of local government need to be involved in the determination of feasibility. If the regulators understand all the pressures on the development and how the development meets both public and private objectives, they will more than likely support the project and be less likely to delay the development approval process. Often, municipal staff are technically well trained and will accept the development concept so long as it fits with the city's master plan. If the public sector is recruited early in the development process and is fully committed to the concept, it is less likely to throw up time-consuming roadblocks as the process unfolds.

Successful developers must not ignore the political side of government. Elected officials representing the public at large and individuals representing particular interest groups may mount a challenge even if a project benefits the overall jurisdiction. In many areas, the political environment has become a nightmare for developers who fail to anticipate the power of opinions strongly held by small groups. Projects endorsed earlier by elected officials may suddenly lose support when officials respond to an unexpected public outcry. Successful developers have learned to work with citizens and local governments to address

Originally the site of an underperforming enclosed mall, the site on which Winter Park Village—a 40-acre (16-hectare) mixed-use development consisting of apartments, office buildings, and retail spaces in Winter Park, Florida—now stands was eligible for municipal funding. Although the developer, Casto Lifestyle Properties, declined to use public funds, city staff worked closely with the firm to ensure that no minor zoning issues became barriers to development. *Casto Lifestyle Properties*

citizens' concerns such as unwanted traffic and possibly to make some concessions. Through the feasibility study, developers can see at an early stage of the development process the full impact of requested concessions.

Turnover in public offices can pose other problems for developers when projects conflict with the platforms of newly elected officials. When administrations change, earlier approval of a project does not necessarily guarantee that the newly elected officials will be good partners.

Some developers have taken the route of working with governments through public/private development. This partnership can be particularly complicated but ultimately rewarding (see Chapter 14).

THE VALUE STATEMENT AND FORMAL ESTIMATE OF FEASIBILITY

The result of the market study is an estimated schedule of leasing or sales for the proposed development that projects rent, occupancy, and expenses over the leasing period and number of units over the sellout period. During the feasibility study, developers must ensure that the marketing staff is planning to sell the same product that the builders are planning to construct, which in turn is the same project that the public sector is expecting to review and that lenders or investors are planning to finance.

It is also critical that projected rents or sales be based on truly comparable projects. A well-prepared feasibility analysis always includes a comparison grid in the section discussing the market study. Whether the project is for sale or for lease, the attributes of value of the comparable projects must be explicitly laid out on the grid, which shows the specific adjustments for differences between the comparable projects and the subject project, i.e., the proposed development. The comparison must be sufficiently rigorous to give readers confidence in the estimate of the project's "capture rate" of total market demand. The larger the adjustments the analyst must make to the comparables, the more likely that some error has been or will be made and the greater the need for a larger budget for contingencies and/or a higher risk premium in the discount rate. In other

words, truly unique development ideas for which no real comparable projects exist are considered risky, and the developer thus should have more reserves.

The grid that shows comparable factors should be used interactively with the grid for the proposed project to modify the project according to which features, functions, and benefits are justified by costs in relation to supply and demand in the particular market. Once the project's final amenities have been chosen, the analyst derives the expected prices (or rents) from the grid and generates the projected cash flows.

The process is straightforward: potential revenues minus vacant space equals effective gross revenue minus operating expenses equals net operating income. The difficulty comes in making reasonable assumptions for each element. (See Chapters 7 to 9 for information on the mechanics of these statements.)

Since the change in the tax laws in 1986, it has become more common to base the value side of the feasibility analysis on pretax cash flows. Under such a scenario, the net operating income plus an estimate of residual value is discounted to a present value. As explained in Chapters 7 through 9, the discount rate is taken from the marketplace. In the case of a major national project, the rate may be derived from published property indices.[6] For smaller projects, local appraisers and financial institutions maintain records of returns from comparable projects. Feasibility is a forward-looking concept, and historic returns are merely a guide to what investors require for a current project. Hence, in preparing the feasibility study, the analyst looks at historical numbers and then adjusts them for the expected inflation rate as well as for any other projected changes in market conditions that may affect the relative risk of the subject property. Once a discount rate has been determined in this manner, the analyst should confirm it by questioning investors who are actively seeking the type of project proposed for development.

By using the estimated discount rate, the analyst reduces projected operating flows to a current value that incorporates everything that can be known about the project. In other words, all the information about the market, the quality of the space relative to the competition, future trends, and the risks associated with all the projections are brought back to one value at one point in time. The analyst then compares this value with the total cost estimated earlier.

A project satisfies Graaskamp's definition of feasibility if the value (adjusted for risk) exceeds the total cost, where the total cost includes all the logistics as well as all the items necessary to satisfy the legal, physical, and ethical rules and where the developer commands the financial and human resources necessary to bring the project to fruition. Thus, the developer uses both appropriately defined value and completely specified costs to determine formal feasibility.

After estimating the value based on net operating income, the analyst should construct an after-financing and after-tax scenario to show how all the participants fit into the project. Ideally, the sum of the parts should be greater than the whole. In other words, if tax benefits occur, they should accrue to the appropriate investor.

Once the entire cost and all the value statements have been determined, the developer should run a sensitivity analysis to see whether some feature of the project can be improved. For example, a slight increase in operating costs may be justified if it substantially lowers the project's total cost. If the cost and income statements are set up on a simple computer spreadsheet, it is easy to check the tradeoff between operating costs and visual appeal, between construction costs and management costs, and so on. By using sensitivity analyses, a feasibility study moves beyond a static financial analysis and becomes a dynamic planning tool.

One important caveat is in order. Electronic spreadsheet models are often used to force feasibility: it is easy to change a number here or there to produce a value that exceeds costs by an appropriate amount. But forcing the numbers will surely come back to haunt a developer during the highly stressful stage six of the process and/or during the very long life of stage eight.

THE ENTERPRISE CONCEPT

More and more frequently, development involves the combination of an operating business and the con-struction of physical space. In today's customer-focused markets, it is increasingly important that the space specifically fit the user's needs—and continue to do so over its life. In other words, some of the considerations that were always important in running a hotel are becoming more important in running a warehouse. Is a merchandise mart, for example, a real estate project or an operating business? Because such projects involve constructed space that can satisfy a range of users, all the standard questions about real estate development apply. The constructed space is, however, specially oriented toward the functioning of a particular business, and if that business fails, the next best use will often generate a far lower rent from the next user. Consequently, traditional real estate feasibility analysis is interwoven with modern business planning. Conversely, well-designed space for a highly specialized user can generate operational efficiencies and permit higher rental rates from the end users.

Operations management is assuming a more important role in all phases of real estate—and is critical as the developer considers the complex combination of real estate development and the ongoing needs of a business and the customers of that business. The enterprise concept is a view of the development process as a living, breathing organism with ongoing problems of cash management, just like an operating business. For a proper feasibility study, it is necessary to decide how much of the ongoing business risk is "developmental" and how much will be passed on to tenants or to long-term investors. The part passed on generally reduces the developer's risk so long as the lease agreements and tenants' credit are both strong and/or the role of the permanent investor is unconditional. The more a building is combined with significant management operations such as a hotel, where food, beverage, and other services are critical to realizing income, the more complex the feasibility study. Two kinds of questions are involved: 1) How crucial is the operating management to the project's long-term success? And how good is the management (on a relative basis) selected for this development? and 2) Is the developer or the tenant responsible? Or has the developer passed this risk on

Located in 250,000 square feet (23,200 square meters) of renovated industrial buildings on 11 acres (4.5 hectares) of a decommissioned navy yard in Philadelphia, the corporate office campus of Urban Outfitters is designed to be complementary to the brand's urban style and fashion sensibilities.

through an unconditional presale to a long-term investor? A hotel exemplifies the enterprise concept, but if a net lease with Hyatt is in effect for 20 years, the developer is creating an investment that will receive bondlike returns. Alternatively, if the developer plans to own and operate the hotel, the development investment is considerably riskier.

The more small, short-term tenants involved, the more the development must be seen as an operating business. The active marketing required in such circumstances must focus on the ongoing "business aspects" of the project. As players involved in the development process have come to realize the importance of seeing the whole enterprise, feasibility studies have changed significantly. Some feasibility studies

look more like formal business plans than traditional descriptions of the value and cost of constructed space.

THE NOTION OF VENTURE CAPITAL

Another aspect growing in complexity is the increasing likelihood of the need for the real estate equivalent of "venture capital." For a large-scale mixed-use project, two to six years might elapse between the time the developer moves from stage two to the beginning of construction in stage six. During that time, the formal feasibility study is undertaken, much of the design work is done, extensive government relations are worked out, and long-term tenant relations are negotiated. All these phases require out-of-pocket cash the developer must pay out during this period. Consequently, the source of operating money becomes an extremely important consideration. Because the amount of money may be large and because developers usually take great pains to minimize the amount of their own money involved before commitment, substantial front-end dollars from other sources may be needed.

In such a situation, it is probably appropriate to judge this interim period—the period between the end of stage two and the beginning of stage six (construction)—as more of a "venture capital period" than a traditional real estate financing period. The dollars invested may be substantial. Further, a great deal of risk is associated with the investment because of uncertainties as to whether the project, whose exact size and value are unknown, will ever be undertaken. Consequently, investors during this period look for extraordinarily high returns, not unlike traditional venture capitalists. An extended venture capital period changes the investor's, the lender's, and even the developer's traditional roles. (We are not suggesting that such financing comes from venture capitalists but that this financing comes from higher-risk investors—like venture capitalists—and is usually noticeably expensive.) All the traditional players are still important, but the need for venture capital financing introduces an additional level of complexity. If the project does not proceed to stage six, the investors do not receive a low return. In fact, they lose all their money. After all, plans for an infeasible development have little or no resale value.

The astute developer uses as much of the less expensive financing (e.g., commercial banks) as possible and as little of the expensive financing (e.g., venture capital) as possible.

The development company is a business, and its collection of development projects must be structured so that the development company remains viable. Thus, to keep the development company solvent, the developer may at times need to trade longer-term profits (the percentage of the difference between value and cost) for higher immediate development fees and for a way to mitigate the need for large amounts of venture capital.

LEVEL TWO FEASIBILITY

A project may eventually be feasible, but the developer needs to eat every day; therefore, it is instructive to think of the project's feasibility as level one and the developer's position as a participant in the process as level two (see Appendix C, "The Real Estate Game"). The developer must be concerned with the level two perspective of every participant in the development process.

Although a given project might appear feasible, that is, value substantially exceeds cost, the level one relationship is a necessary but not sufficient condition. All participants in the process must see a similar relationship between the value to them of participating in the process and the cost of their participation. If, at any point in the process, any participant suddenly finds that its level two participation ceases to be "feasible," the whole project may be endangered. Despite legal obligations to perform, most people become less enthusiastic about even the most exciting project when their participation starts to cost money rather than generate the expected profit. As an ongoing risk control technique, the developer uses the feasibility study not just at level one but also to think about each participant's level two perspective. The electronic spreadsheet should first show overall project feasibility calculations (level one feasibility) and then the cash flow position of each primary participant, particularly the developer himself (level two feasibility). The developer tries to anticipate problems so as to have sufficient flexibility in keeping the development team together.

TECHNIQUES OF RISK CONTROL DURING STAGE THREE

Several techniques are available to control risk during stage three. The most common ones follow:

1. Information and data analysis in the feasibility analysis is clearly a major risk control technique, which will be used throughout the remainder of the development process. The more time, high-quality information, and effort that go into esti-

mating all revenues and costs, the more likely it is that the development decision will be sound. In almost all cases, the better the forecast, the less risk involved in the development. On the other hand, the feasibility study for a large project is expensive and time-consuming. Overdoing the feasibility analysis is a waste of time and money that can seriously extend the length of the development process—much to the detriment of the developer. How much is enough but not too much? That is where the developer's judgment comes into play.

2. The financing arranged during stage three critically affects the sharing of project risks. Different lenders and equity investors have different preferences. The construction lender wants early equity contributions, a floating-rate loan with strict procedures for dispensing funds, and both the developer's and any equity investors' guarantee of personal liability. The developer, however, prefers an interest rate cap, easy procedures for requesting payments, no personal liability, and the right to contribute his own cash after the bank puts up its cash. How these desires are traded off depends on the quality of the project, the relative strength of the lender and the developer, and current conditions in the capital markets. In a lender's market, the developer may have to take on greater risk. When financing is readily available from many sources, lenders are more likely to accommodate developers' desires and take a greater share of the risk.

Permanent lenders likewise must consider certain interests in the tradeoff between risks and returns. The higher the debt service coverage ratio and the lower the loan-to-value ratio, the more likely it is that the lender will be paid on schedule and, in the event of default, collect the total loan balance. Investors also bring their own perspectives to the financing arrangement. They want to make their cash contributions late and receive assurance that, in the event of the need for additional cash, the shortfall would be made up by the developer or the lenders. Certainly, investors do not want to be personally liable, but they do want to maximize their after-tax returns.

3. A formal review of the architect's design plan by operating, marketing, and construction professionals as well as by public officials is critical in controlling risk. A formal review by all players in stage three will make stage four's negotiations much easier.

4. The developer must check to ensure that utilities and other infrastructure are available. Even though a project is legally feasible and publicly desirable, the city might be unable to provide sewer, water, or other infrastructure services. The developer must begin discussions early, document meetings, and, whenever possible, obtain formal commitments for public facilities and services.

5. When considering all the costs of infrastructure for a project, developers try to go beyond negotiations for "permissions" and ask the city for concessions in return for providing it with something of value. A joint venture with other private sector users or with the general public, which is a beneficiary of the development, might be both possible and appropriate. Sometimes when sharing costs is not possible, the developer finds it feasible to acquire some of the surrounding land and capture some of the increased value that results from the development (unfortunately, doing so increases risk, but the return may justify the incremental cost).

The idea is not to forget the concept of situs—the interactions of a project with surrounding sites and the impact of those surrounding uses on the subject property. This principle is basic to real estate. No site operates in isolation. In a competitive world, it is useful to share costs and, at times, to capture some of the benefits of the development and property uses on surrounding land. It is not always possible, but it is useful to consider the possibility.

A graphic example of the impact of situs is the difference between the development of Disneyland in Anaheim, California, and Disney World in Orlando, Florida. At Anaheim, all the peripheral "action" accrued to the benefit of others. Recognizing this loss of profitable opportunities, the huge site acquired for Disney World has allowed Disney to reap much of the benefit of additional development such as resort hotels and shopping districts that feeds on the central theme park's facilities.

6. The developer must check to make sure that a building permit has been issued to the chosen contractor; in addition, in some cities, it is important to make sure that subcontractors have obtained the appropriate permits. In their haste to get a job, contractors sometimes overlook certain rules or promise something that the company cannot legally deliver. Further, it is wise to ensure that both contractors and subcontractors are properly licensed to do the work. Checking details is a good way to control risk.

7. It is often useful to provide structural warranties in the architect's contract. (Some people even consider insuring the contract when the architectural firm is small.) After the windows fell out of the John Hancock building in Boston, it became obvious to many developers that they personally were not adequately prepared to undertake a final review of all the technical aspects of construction. Warranties from the architect, suppliers, and builders and a guarantee that all participants have sufficient financial worth to make a lawsuit worthwhile mean that the developer has a remedy in the event of disaster. Although it is seldom a good idea to stop development for a lawsuit, the potential for a successful lawsuit often encourages players to perform up to their commitment. The more concrete the legal documentation of responsibilities, the easier it is to convince individual players that serious problems will result if they fail to perform. Thus, structural warranties and, more important, clearly drawn contracts can be tools for negotiating from strength. These possibilities must be anticipated during stage three's economic discussions; if they are not, stage four's legal negotiations will be far more difficult.

SUMMARY

The definition of feasibility presented in this chapter is noticeably broad. It begins with a formal definition of the development's objectives, which may involve money, ego, civic enhancement, and other related

WaterColor, a 499-acre (202-hectare) mixed-use, master-planned community adjacent to the premier new urbanist community of Seaside, Flordia, was able to generate synergy between the two projects through its careful design and site plan. *Prema Katari Gupta*

items. The defined objectives are then tested for fit in the context of specific market, legal, physical, and ethical constraints as well as limited financial and human resources. A project is feasible when it is reasonably likely (almost never certain) that its objectives can be achieved in a particular situation.

The primary task in the feasibility analysis is to produce a sound market analysis, one that culminates in a projection of net operating income for the subject property over the relevant time frame. Based on these projections, the developer estimates value for the project by using discounted cash flow analysis. A project is said to be feasible when that value exceeds all the projected costs of development.

The feasibility analysis is more than a technique for controlling risk during stage three of the development process. Once completed, the formal feasibility study is the sales tool used to bring together all the different players needed to fulfill the objectives of development. During stages four through seven, the feasibility study is constantly refined; it remains probably the single most important management tool in the development process.

TERMS

- ▶ Enterprise concept
- ▶ Feasibility analysis
- ▶ Formal feasibility
- ▶ Market study
- ▶ Operating efficiency
- ▶ Optimization tool
- ▶ Preliminary drawings
- ▶ Sensitivity analysis
- ▶ Takeout loan
- ▶ Venture capital

REVIEW QUESTIONS

16.1 Define feasibility.

16.2 What is a feasibility study, and why is it necessary for a development?

16.3 What are the essential elements of a feasibility study?

16.4 What is the role of the architect at this stage of the development process?

16.5 How do developers know whether general contractors' estimates of construction costs are appropriate?

16.6 How and why do construction contingencies change?

16.7 Describe some of the techniques that can be used to control risk during stage three.

16.8 Discuss the enterprise concept and the impact it can have on the type of space that is developed.

NOTES

1. James A. Graaskamp, "A Rational Approach to Feasibility Analysis," *Appraisal Journal,* October 1972, p. 515.

2. *Emerging Trends in Real Estate*®, produced annually by the Urban Land Institute and PricewaterhouseCoopers, is one of the industry's longest-running and most-respected annual investment studies. Based on surveys and interviews with more than 400 of the industry's leading authorities, it examines the outlook for real estate capital markets and contains a comprehensive annual forecast for all categories of the commercial real estate industry, including apartments, regional malls, downtown offices, warehouses, community shopping centers, suburban offices, research and development space, power centers, full-service hotels, and limited-service hotels. Since 2005, the report also has started tracking trends in the housing industry. Starting in 2006, three separate reports were published: United States, Europe, and Asia Pacific.

3. See, e.g., M. Atef Sharkawy and Joseph Rabianski, "How Design Elements Create and Enhance Real Estate Value," *Real Estate Review,* Summer 1995, pp. 83–86; Kerry Vandell, "Will Good Design Pay? The Economics of Architecture and Urban Design," in *Real Estate Investment Strategy: A Year 2000 Perspective* (New York: Prudential Realty Group and Univ. of North Carolina, 1989); and "The Design Dividend," a research project on the investment return accruing to owners of well-designed projects by the Property Council of Australia, published in 1999 and updated in 2006, www.propertyoz.com.au.

4. Information is available from, for example, Marshall & Swift (www.marshallswift.com) and McGraw-Hill Construction (a network including *Architectural Record, Design-Build, Engineering News-Record,* Dodge, and Sweet's Group) at www.construction.com.

5. Lehman Brothers, Morgan Stanley, Goldman Sachs, Citigroup, and others describe the risk profile and property cash flows that attract certain larger lenders to particular transactions in publications and on their Web sites.

6. For example, the NCREIF Property Index, published quarterly by the National Council of Real Estate Investment Fiduciaries, Chicago (www.ncreif.com).

CHAPTER 17

Market Analysis: Collecting, Validating, and Understanding Market Data

If you can't "buy" the assumptions as presented, you cannot afford the real estate product about which those assumptions were made, no matter how "good" the site and "attractive" the building.

—JAMES A. GRAASKAMP

Real estate market analysis forms the basis for the assumptions that are made about the future value of a real estate development. If a developer cannot defend the cash flow projections with analysis and reasonable data inputs, the feasibility of the entire development is unsubstantiated, and simply hoping that the type of space proposed is what the market desires and that rental rates will return a sufficient cash flow to service the debt and provide a reasonable return to the equity investor is not enough.

Real estate market analysis is a critical risk management technique in that it provides the backup for the set of assumptions used in the cash flow analyses and therefore reduces or at least delineates the riskiness of projected cash flows. Thus, the market study functions as the backbone of the real estate development process by providing the critical inputs to the feasibility analysis

discussed in Chapter 16. Before proceeding to the increasingly sophisticated econometrics applied to metropolitan-level forecasting (Chapter 18), this chapter looks at the nuts and bolts of data collection, verification, and analysis. Specifically, the chapter covers:

▶ Market analysis as a process—market studies, marketability studies, and market analysis as part of the feasibility study;
▶ Data collection and validation—validating supply data, and understanding and validating demand data;
▶ Defining the relevant market area and the competitive submarket, and market disaggregation; and
▶ Presenting the research and conclusions.

MARKET ANALYSIS AS A PROCESS

Market analysis is the identification and study of the market for a particular economic good or service.[1] Markets are created at the intersection of market participants' needs and desires (demand for space) and

Richard Schwien, EDAW Inc., provided updated information on geographic information systems.

characteristics and amenities of the built environment (supply of space).

Real estate markets can be subdivided into different property types: office, retail, residential, hotel, and industrial, among others. Each property type can be further segmented into smaller markets by price, location, and functionality. Market segmentation is the process of identifying and analyzing submarkets of a larger group of property markets. As a first step, office markets can be segmented into central business district and suburban, retail markets can be segmented into regional malls and strip retail, and residential can be segmented into single-family housing and multifamily housing. This segmentation continues down to the site level, where competition for a specific activity on the specific site is determined in stage two of the development process.

Most real estate market analyses include both a broad *market study* and a narrow *marketability study*.

Market Studies

Market studies report and analyze aggregate supply and demand data. Aggregate data assist the developer in understanding the effective supply of and demand for space of a broadly defined user group.

Supply analysis is carried out using data from local, regional, and national providers. Analysis of the supply of competing projects takes into consideration the following factors:

► Inventory and quality of existing space;
► New construction of space (under construction and proposed);
► Features, functions, and benefits of existing and proposed space;
► Overall vacancy rate and characteristics of vacant stock;
► Recent absorption of space (including types of tenants);
► Market rents (and the reasons rents differ across locations and by quality of space); and
► Lease terms and concessions (i.e., free rent, tenant improvement allowances, and so on).

Whereas supply analysis looks at the projects that could be construed as competition, demand analysis investigates the potential users of the space. Potential space users are usually identified by analyzing the expected needs and preferences of users as well as the expected changes in their needs and preferences over time. An analysis of regional demographic, employment, or income data is often the first step in a demand analysis, because changes in population, workforce, or income levels drive demand for most new space. It is somewhat difficult to provide a "generic" list of the critical factors to be included in a demand analysis, because users' needs can differ greatly. Still, most demand analyses include some important inputs:

► Population and population changes;
► Employment and employment changes;
► Income and income changes;
► Other macroeconomic and local factors; and
► Psychological, image, and other perceptions that often include factors that are difficult to quantify.

When assessing the anticipated demand for different types of space, it is clearly important to assess existing population, employment, income, and other macroeconomic and local factors. What is frequently more important to real estate developers is how these numbers change over time. Existing demand generally fills existing space, but changes in the factors listed above often create demand for new space. It is also important to look beyond the economic numbers at how the target market views its lifestyle and how this self-image may change over time. Emerging software developers for computer games want very different office space from new hedge funds serving the investment needs of high-net-worth families.

Marketability Studies

Most market analyses also include a marketability study. The marketability study addresses a narrow market or market niche. Thus, the developer can adapt the real estate product, price, and merchandising appeal to better fit the market and attract a group of users with particular behaviors or preferences. Marketability studies generally include four steps:

1. Profile the space user to be served by the development.

2. Identify the revenue unit and the associated service necessary to capture that revenue unit.
3. Fully define the product in terms of features, functions, and benefits.
4. Delineate pricing strategy, including sales logistics.

The marketability study refines the aggregate findings of the market study for the subject project. In the marketability study, the set of income assumptions (rental rates, rental growth rates, and space absorption rates) is generated for the specific development.

The market analyst should be able to establish a connection between trends in supply and demand in the competitive marketplace and cash flow assumptions for the specific property. The analysis can be enhanced by postponing early judgment on conclusions about demand for the specific property and instead focusing initially on 1) collecting market data at the most highly disaggregated levels available; 2) validating the integrity of the data; 3) constructing multiple data series[2] that pertain to a variety of assumptions influencing performance of the property (supporting the sensitivity analysis described in Chapter 16); and 4) rigorously defining the submarket where the subject property will compete after the data have been analyzed.

Market Analysis as Part of Feasibility

Recall at this point where the market analysis fits into the eight-stage model of real estate development described throughout this book: after the developer initially tests and refines the project idea, a market analyst undertakes systematic research both to make sure the developer's assumptions are realistic and to create tools for marketing to be done later in the development process. Market studies bracket the questions to be answered, and marketability studies focus the analysis. These studies provide the "topline" revenue estimates used in financial feasibility analysis that substantiate estimates of NOI. Better studies also indicate the degree of confidence that the estimates deserve and therefore help developers set an appropriate premium for risk in the discount rate.[3]

Market research is conducted for the benefit of different players at different stages of the development process. It is helpful to know who performs the analysis at each stage of development as well as each player's objectives. In stages one and two, for example, developers take the lead in analyzing the market, albeit informally. In stage three, developers continue to use national forecasting services (Chapter 18) and now may ask a market analyst to formally evaluate the subject property's income potential and provide inputs to the financial feasibility analysis to make the final decision on the project's viability. The developer might also commission and present the results of an economic impact analysis to garner public support for the project.

In stage four, developers negotiate the contracts needed to build a project that appears feasible. At this point, other participants must reach their final decisions about whether or not the market will support the project as proposed and, consequently, how likely they are to achieve their individual objectives (level two feasibility). Lenders are required to underwrite loans to determine the project's expected market value in accordance with accepted professional standards. Investors study all the issues—financial, environmental, and other related attributes—of a project or property ("due diligence"). Like other participants in the process, they must decide whether the proposed project's estimated value justifies their participation. Major tenants often employ in-house market analysts or outsource firms to assess competing sites. Even local governments may want assessments of the project from their particular perspectives before committing their support.

In many areas, the public sector is being called on to sponsor market studies and help rationalize proposed development or redevelopment projects. Although the public sector's in-house capability or resources to hire market analysts are often limited, the public sector has a legitimate role in providing reliable information about expected demand. Sound market analysis can improve planning and zoning practices, guide the provision of development incentives, and reduce the social costs of overbuilding by accommodating growth while protecting a community's environment and quality of life.

DATA COLLECTION AND VALIDATION

Until recently, inadequate and inconsistent market data were significant issues for real estate market analysts. Today, the sources of data are much more reliable; nevertheless, all data must still be verified, additional proprietary information must often be collected to supplement publicly available data, and analysis must be undertaken to ensure that the data directly address the critical decisions regarding feasibility (see the bibliography at the end of the book).

Market analysts should be willing to expend the effort to ask appropriate questions and to review and adjust the publicly available data as required to ensure that professionally compiled market data offer the insights needed to make conclusions about the market prospects. Although the data may not be individually compelling, the fully analyzed composite should provide the foundation for successful decision making. This section discusses what needs to be done to get the best possible information. It is even more valuable in a price-inefficient market like real estate.

Properly collected and validated data are critical when making assumptions that bridge the past with the future, which involves:

- ▶ Collecting data;
- ▶ Validating real estate market supply data; and
- ▶ Understanding and validating real estate market demand data.

This work will allow the market analyst to define the relevant submarket and present persuasive conclusions about that submarket.

Collecting Data

Data collection typically starts with the national services described in Chapter 18. This chapter assumes that "baseline" information is known and therefore focuses on moving from what is publicly available (often at a substantial price) to analysis of the narrow submarket. Real estate traditionally has been a private industry, and, despite its more public incarnations in the form of REITs and commercial mortgage–backed securities (CMBSs), it continues to be intensely private. Some people believe that the most relevant information is almost impossible to obtain and/or that sources willing to volunteer information fabricate their responses. The truth is that obtaining information from private sector real estate sources, typically brokers, developers, appraisers, and consultants, requires more finesse than working with public sector data sources or the forecasting and national data collecting firms described in the next chapter. Persistence is often the most important factor in success.

One key to effective private or public sector research is to know as much as possible before making contact with a prospective source. For example, before calling a local brokerage firm to request a market report, the analyst should try to obtain any press reports that summarize some of the report's findings. Even better, the analyst should be armed with findings from competitive firms. If it is not clear that a particular report is generally available, the analyst should avoid beginning the conversation by asking for the material and should instead inquire about the contents of press accounts by focusing on methodology and terminology. After establishing a dialogue with an information source and demonstrating respect for that source, the market analyst may find the contact more willing to share information as well as some underlying raw data or insights.

Another way to pry data from reluctant sources is to offer to exchange data. Assuming that the analyst is gathering data from multiple sources and plans to clean and organize the data, the contact may be interested in receiving an excerpt from the analyst's report in exchange for available data. Or, in some cases, earlier reports prepared by the analyst may be of interest to the contact. It is important to try to obtain a level of detail from each contact beyond what is generally available. If a contact's report addresses the market or submarket, the analyst should ask for the supporting detail about buildings. When an analyst demonstrates professional behavior and offers to share data, the information flow will usually improve. The worst that can happen is that the contact will say "no."

It is critical to remember that a successful real estate researcher must possess the skills of an investigative reporter. Interpersonal skills and persistence often represent the critical distinction between turning out stale, repackaged market analyses and producing reports that literally crackle with proprietary information and insight.

Validating Real Estate Market Supply Data

Not until the data have been validated can the market analyst have a defensible set of assumptions for the cash flow analyses. As an analyst's research becomes more focused on a specific project, some unique property characteristics may force the market analyst to narrow the focus of research. Nevertheless, an analyst can usually compile a strong profile of metropolitan or submarket supply by attending to the seven market factors noted earlier:

▶ Inventory and quality of existing space;
▶ New construction of space (under construction and proposed);
▶ Features, functions, and benefits of existing and proposed space;
▶ Overall vacancy rate and characteristics of vacant stock;
▶ Recent absorption of space (including types of tenants);
▶ Market rents (and the reasons rents differ across locations and by quality of space); and
▶ Lease terms and concessions (i.e., free rent, tenant improvement allowances, and so on).

All these indicators carry import as snapshots of current market conditions. When viewed over time, these same indicators reveal the trends that will have a significant impact on cash flows for the development and should drive investment decisions.

Multiple analyses by time period are also vital in assessing the credibility of real estate market data or, in other words, in performing an audit. An audit is a formal examination and verification process whose objective is to confirm that a data set has been compiled with accuracy, logic, and internal consistency. In accounting, audited financial statements are typically considered more credible when they reflect multiple years of a company's financial results. Reconciliations can be performed and changes in financial conditions traced back to the source.

Similarly, the real estate market analyst must obtain multiple years of market data and array the information so as to ensure internal consistency. For example, the annual change in total inventory should equal that year's new completions minus deletions. Likewise, absorption should equal the net change in occupied space. Unfortunately, in much market research, many of these key indicators appear to "float" from year to year, thereby obscuring actual trends. The reason for the frustrating shifts in data can most often be traced to inconsistencies in the survey sample. For example, the precise definition of geography and/or quality for the particular market may fluctuate, thus changing the mix of buildings included in the sample. The analyst must recognize variability in the sample and take steps to adjust the data accordingly.

Two of the most important market fundamentals in terms of their influence on future cash flows are absorption of space and rent. Hence, they deserve considerable effort to ensure the integrity of the data. Absorption is particularly vulnerable to misstatement based on changes in the survey sample. By implication, any data about absorption not supported by corresponding data on inventory and occupied space should be subjected to more intense scrutiny. Data about changes in rental rates are also highly sensitive to variations in the survey sample. In quantifying percentage changes in rent levels, the analyst must hold the building sample as constant as possible between each survey point, even if it means sacrificing a large number of observations. Three questions are critical in auditing real estate supply data:

1. What are the limits of the sample survey (i.e., geographic size of the market, minimum building size, and so on)?
2. How has the sample changed over time (understanding sample changes is critical when creating historical trend analyses)?
3. What are the quality of and amenities in the surveyed buildings?

The analyst's ability to answer these questions depends heavily on his skill as an investigative reporter.

Recognizing that net absorption is one of the most incorrectly defined and poorly understood

Residential developers are building more housing designed to appeal to empty nesters, single parents, and childless couples. Harbor Town, a 400-acre (162-hectare) master-planned, traditional neighborhood development in Memphis, Tennessee, offers a broad mix of housing types, sizes, and price ranges. *Henry Turley Company*

market concepts, the market analyst must make a special effort to distinguish the varying measures of market demand typically lumped under the heading "absorption." Net absorption is defined as total space leased minus space vacated. Frequently, statements of gross leasing activity, which usually represent a brokerage firm's estimate of all leases signed in the market during a given time period, are mistakenly labeled "net absorption." Similarly, the leasing of space in new developments is often included in net absorption, while newly constructed space is not. Although both total leasing and leasing in new buildings are insightful market measures and necessary in certain types of property-specific analyses, they should not be confused with net absorption.

Given the importance of precisely measuring a market's or submarket's net absorption, the market analyst must avoid the perils typically associated with building-level data and aggregate market statistics. Optimally, analysts should look behind the absorption estimates quoted in reports and attempt to create their own estimates based on building-by-building data. This procedure calls for determining the most accurate and comprehensive inventory (often

through combining multiple surveys and sources) and making appropriate adjustments for building size, double-counted buildings, and excluded buildings that should be included in the sample.

Understanding and Validating Real Estate Market Demand Data

The demand for real estate space is generally a function of job creation, household formation, and/or income generation. For instance, the primary source of demand for office/industrial space is white- and blue-collar employment, demand for residential housing depends more on household formation, and demand for retail space depends more on income generation. All types of space demand also depend on local economic growth, wage rates, and other economic and noneconomic forces that make a location competitive or desirable.

As detailed in the next chapter, the competitive role of an MSA or regional economy in the national or global economy must be examined. In a town or city, nodes of employment, commercial centers, or residential areas must be accessible to garner a sufficient share of the metropolitan market. The ebb and flow of metropolitan economies and areas within them is continuous; such flows show the combination of interdependence and competition that generates change and affects long-term profitability for a real estate development. Thus, both competition and cooperation among people and firms affect a locale's economic viability. Naturally, the spatial arrangements within an area (situs) are important in influencing firms' profitability and local residents' well-being. Demand for space is also influenced by varying property, wage, and income tax structures, as these factors affect space users' overall occupancy and employee costs.

Employment and Demographic Forecasts

It is important to thoroughly understand the underlying methods of collecting the many types of available economic and demographic data for analysis of the real estate market. For example, depending on the application, employment data gathered at "place of work" or "place of residence" may be significantly different. A common mistake is the inadvertent integration of the two, often made by relying on occupational employment data from the Census Bureau (gathered at place of residence) and industry-group data from the Bureau of Labor Statistics (gathered at place of work).

Economic and demographic forecasts also vary in quality and frequency. Nonetheless, even the most prestigious sources, such as Global Insight or Moody's Economy.com, should be examined for their underlying assumptions. In addition, the analyst should compare data from these sources with current actual data (for example, the Bureau of Labor Statistics for employment data) to determine whether a forecast is consistent with current conditions in an MSA and then validate data against alternative forecasts.[4]

To make informed judgments about the future, market analysts must examine trends. Forecasts of population, households, income, or employment form the basis for forecasts of a market area's space absorption. The key is to recognize patterns and how these factors change over time. For example, the surge in immigrants in recent years has boosted the U.S. housing market, and cities with strong housing markets are often in regions with significant immigrant populations. Studying historical trends to understand how absorption has changed relative to indicators of demand for space leads to better-informed forecasts of demand for a given market and eventually for a specific development. This analysis must be extended from the MSA to the relevant submarket. The same MSA-level factor may affect submarkets differently. For example, immigration may provide the new labor force that expands an industrial area, while the children of these same immigrants may overwhelm a particular school district and thus hurt a set of residential submarkets.

Economic Forecasts

Forecasts of key economic and demographic indicators are critical components of any market analysis.[5] Forecasts of absorption and growth in rents must be linked with forecasts of the growth rate from the demographic, employment, or other demand drivers for the proposed development. Viewed in this light, all demographic and economic forecasts should receive a level of scrutiny equal to that often reserved for capitalization and discount rates.

Market analysts typically are not in a position to build sophisticated models of regional or MSA economies. They can, however, obtain substantial analytic leverage by studying the models and assumptions of others. Good market analysts try to determine whether projections make sense. For example, are income forecasts supported by emerging changes in the local economy? Or are forecasted rates of in-migration sustainable, given the availability of properly zoned and serviced land? As we will see in Chapter 18, there are major national forecasters that evaluate MSAs from a real estate perspective. The analyst must decide which to use in each situation.

Market analysts make their own projections of population, jobs, and income based on analyses prepared by government agencies, universities, and other private institutions. Rather than making original forecasts for cities or metropolitan areas, analysts are usually advised to check and refine existing forecasts, some of which are frequently available at no cost from local, regional, state, and federal agencies or for a modest fee from for-profit sources. Part of being a good market analyst is developing familiarity with the appropriate sources of information. Savvy analysts collect and compare estimates from several sources, but the analyst's central job is to make reasonable estimates for subareas or market segments for which no projections exist.

As a general rule, analysts should compare all local estimates with regional or national averages. For example, analysts frequently use location quotients, which take the percentages of the workforce employed in each major industry sector in the locality and divide them by the percentage of the workforce employed in the industry sector nationally. Thus, a location quotient equal to 1.0 shows that a local industry's percentage share of total employment in the MSA is the same as that industry's national share. Industries with location quotients of less than 1.0 are underrepresented in a particular market relative to the nation. Those with location quotients greater than 1.0 show an overrepresentation or account for the locality's economic specialization. In local economic analysis, learning how a market differs from the region or nation is as important as knowing the absolute values. Comparisons with reference areas in either the same locale or other parts of the country can help the analyst understand the macroforces that are at work behind observed local outcomes.

In the comparison of forecasts, an outlier forecast is often as interesting as a consensus forecast, because it challenges the analyst to identify the reasons accounting for the deviation.[6] Variability among forecasts may indicate greater market volatility and warrant an increase in the risk premium in the discount rate or can be modeled in wider-ranging sensitivity analyses.

Population Forecasts

In forecasting population, births and deaths are relatively easy to estimate. Estimates of migration, however, can be difficult to predict. It is also difficult to aggregate population properly into consumption units as required in residential or retail studies. Regional planning agencies often provide demographic and economic information, which is also available from the Census Bureau. Subscription services collect, analyze, and sell census information. (Much of this information is available online and in multiple formats.)

Good analysts check the details. They might, for example, look at recent utility hookups and tele-

According to National Gay and Lesbian Task Force estimates, there were 3 million gay, lesbian, bisexual, or transgender Americans over the age of 65 in 2000; by 2030, the number is expected to increase to 4 million. RainbowVision, a 12.7-acre (5.1-hectare) resort retirement community in Santa Fe, New Mexico, is one of the first developments anticipating a growing demand for this demographic group. *Elena Gomez*

phone installations to estimate whether household migration is slowing or accelerating. Usually such data are highly reliable. In some areas where cable television is heavily subscribed, cable installations can also be used to gauge recent migration. National moving companies are a useful source of current information on interstate moves.

The most easily available and comprehensive information on population is usually the decennial census (www.census.gov) of the United States, which is mandated by law to take place every ten years. As the sole source of actual socioeconomic data on individuals and households by small geographic areas (census tracts and census blocks in metropolitan areas or minor civil divisions elsewhere), census figures provide excellent benchmarks. Census information is available on line, on CD-ROM, in major libraries, and in most city or county planning departments. The government regularly updates population estimates based on the most recent census (which is far less detailed and comprehensive than the decennial census), indicating the increment of population or employment that has either moved into or out of a community. The Census Bureau Web site also allows easy access to the American Community Survey, which provides population and housing data collected every year instead of every ten years. Estimates of migration are the primary source of information about population and labor force changes. (Chapter 2 has more information about collecting demographic data.)

Income and Employment

The same sources that provide information about population and income also provide information about employment. Most of the published figures ultimately depend on estimates developed by the U.S. Departments of Commerce and Labor. For example, the Bureau of Labor Statistics publishes employment statistics for metropolitan areas monthly in *Employment and Earnings.* For nonmetropolitan areas, the Economic Research Service (ERS) of the U.S. Department of Agriculture makes available numerous county-level studies free or at nominal cost. The local office of the state employment security commission tracks current employment for workers covered by unemployment insurance (see www.bls.gov/ces and www.ers.usda.gov).

The BLS uses a disaggregated input-output model to forecast national employment. Based on estimates of final demand for goods and services and estimates of productivity, the BLS generates industry-specific estimates. Using BLS estimates as control totals, the Bureau of Economic Analysis (BEA) of the U.S. Department of Commerce disaggregates the estimates to state and metropolitan areas with a combination of location quotient, shift-share, and economic base analyses plus some well-informed judgments. The BEA performs more comprehensive analyses but publishes forecasts only every five years.

One method of checking for consistency between population and employment estimates is to compute and examine the employment-to-population ratio over time. A second way to audit the data is to compare the employment-to-population ratios with national averages. By using decennial or annual estimates, analysts can determine whether the ratio is constant, trending up, or trending down. With the ratio and the trend, analysts can then compare projections of population with projections of employment. Although the two factors are interdependent, job growth tends to lead population growth. If the ratio for future projections is out of line with the past, it is worth taking the time to figure out how to adjust one or both projections.

For example, it might be reasonable to find that labor force participation rates for a locality are gradually decreasing and that the average age of the city's population is gradually increasing. If so, the employment-to-population ratio will decline over time. If independent projections of employment and population yield ratios that change erratically over time, the projections may need to be revised; at the least, the assumptions need careful checking.

Although it is difficult to come up with reliable forecasts of metropolitan-level employment, public sources such as city or regional planning agencies and state government are often as good as any source for employment forecasts. Local economic development authorities may offer useful insights, although they tend to be a bit optimistic on their area. Local com-

munity leaders can add information about an area's economic opportunities and problems that the top-down models (models that begin with aggregate data and then disaggregate the data down) do not capture.[7] It is therefore wise to complement top-down employment projections with bottom-up models (models that begin with disaggregate data and aggregate the data up). Additionally, market analysts may want to interview major employers, local bank executives, university researchers, economic development officials, and others to sample expert opinion.

Another use of the bottom-up approach is to examine the details of the employment base: the age of facilities in the area, the credit ratings of major employers, and the product mix generated by employers in the community. Some communities manufacture products on the leading edge in a particular industry. Some products face stiff local or foreign competition, while others sell in less competitive markets. For office or industrial market analyses that emphasize employment forecasts, analysts should look in an area's major industries to understand the mix of goods or services produced in the market and local firms' relative competitiveness.

Market analysts use local and regional forecasts to establish the baseline figures for the demand for space. Thus, they must comprehend the regional economy's future direction. Because the demand for space is derived from market demographics, employment, and income, concise and validated estimates of these factors are critical inputs to the market analysis.

DEFINING THE RELEVANT MARKET

Unlike the market for most consumer goods, real estate competes principally in its own locationally constrained and functionally defined submarket. Hence, proper definition of the submarket and then accurate disaggregation to that submarket are essential for accurate projections.

Defining the Competitive Submarket

With audited supply data (preferably built up from building-level information) and objective demand forecasts of population, households, income, and employment in hand, the market analyst can focus on data in the subject property's neighborhood for the marketability study. Most competitive submarkets have a narrowly defined area from which demand is drawn and competition (supply) is located. Depending on the type of property, market analysts must generate specific forecasts of employment, population, households, or income for this narrowly defined market area.

Although analysts have traditionally been forced to approximate market areas by using reports that list census tracts, ZIP codes, or county boundaries because of data limitations, GIS technology, or electronic mapping, is liberating real estate decision makers from relying on arbitrary boundaries and dense reports. GIS is a combination of data, software, and spatial analysis that allows the creation of maps and sophisticated models that can be used as a valuable tool for real estate and market analysis. Examples of GIS data include county property assessment files, geodemographic information, and traffic volume counts. Property assessment files include all a property's characteristics used by property tax assessors to arrive at assessed values as well as spatial representation of the parcel boundary in latitude and longitude coordinates of the property. Geodemographic information includes hundreds of census year demographic measurements such as income, education, race, and family composition as well as projections to present and future years. Traffic volume is key information for making decisions about commercial real estate. The most important data available are U.S. road networks in digital format, first digitized in 1990 and available from the U.S. Census Bureau as TIGER/Line data. Several commercial GIS data vendors have enhanced these data by increasing the spatial accuracy and adding additional data such as traffic volumes and enhanced geocoding, which allows users to match addresses. With these enhanced street networks, market analysts are able to perform sophisticated analysis such as service area definition, routing, driving directions, and identification of the nearest facility.

GIS software has often been referred to as a "spatial spreadsheet." Early in the 1990s and before, GIS software was very expensive and difficult to use. Today, however, commercial desktop software is based on a graphic user interface, is more user friendly, and is available from a variety of sources; it ranges in price from $100 to several thousand dollars.

GIS is not limited to desktop computers. The Internet has made geographic technology quite commonplace. The most popular use of GIS data on the Internet is by sites such as www.zillow.com, which allows anyone in the world to search for parcels by address, property type, assessed value, number of bedrooms, and so forth. These sites display a map of search results, allowing the user to pull up detailed information on each property found. Users are able to choose from a variety of maps, including high-resolution satellite images available from multiple angles, census data, crime statistics, school district boundaries, and special assessment areas.

Whether analysts are armed with elementary analysis tools or sophisticated electronic mapping technologies, their knowledge of the market's vehicular and mass-transit patterns, natural barriers, competitive projects, and economic and demographic profiles is of critical importance in defining property submarkets.

The definition of a competitive market area for a marketability study is best discussed in terms of property type. A marketability study usually begins by identifying and profiling the space user who will demand the benefits offered by the project. Some GIS data providers have developed market segments, which consist of predefined user groups classified with similar characteristics—income, education, and spending habits, for example. These segments are becoming increasingly sophisticated and can include characteristics such as political affiliation, spending habits, lifestyle choices, and health habits. Real estate developers are thus able to target specific segments when exploring opportunities for development.

The next step is to locate where those potential consumers live and work as well as whether reasonable access exists to the subject site and how the potential space users will overcome any "friction of distance." GIS data and tools can be very valuable, as this type of analysis is very difficult and time-consuming. Competitive space suppliers in the market area must also be profiled, including amenities offered.

South Campus Gateway is a four-block mixed-use entertainment, retail, office, and residential complex on the southern edge of the Ohio State University campus in Columbus. The developers used abundant low-cost parking to attract noncampus users—as well as the 50,000 nearby OSU students—to this regional destination by building 300 parking spaces more than demand studies suggested were needed. *Elkus Manfredi Architects*

For instance, residential development establishes locations from which the local population has access to jobs and local goods and services. The metropolitan area or labor market area therefore represents the overall housing market area. Market analysts, however, devote most attention to submarkets that are distinguished by the specific nature of demand or the differences among housing units, such as age, structure, or neighborhood characteristics (supply). On the demand side, tenure, location, and amenities distinguish major market segments. Preferences for tenure allocate demand to owners or renters. Adding preferences for locations and amenities leads to more refined market segments for which data might not be easily available but are of critical importance. For the marketability study, the market area where the subject project is located receives the most attention, but competitive supply almost always exists in other locations. As a result, residential market areas are often noncontiguous areas in the same labor market or metropolitan area. Residential developments in different sections of the metropolitan area often compete to attract the same in-migrants or local homebuyers and renters who are moving up.[8]

In retail analysis, submarkets are created of consumers living or working near the retail site. Retail trade areas are typically segmented into primary, sec-ondary, and tertiary areas and are defined in most instances in terms of drive time and the category of goods offered. For example, the primary trade area for neighborhood shopping centers may be limited to a five- to ten-minute drive, and the secondary and tertiary trade areas for neighborhood shopping centers will not extend much farther than the primary trade area. Super regional shopping centers, however, may have primary trade areas extending up to 20 minutes from the site and secondary trade areas of up to 40 minutes, while the tertiary trade area could extend up to and beyond an hour in some areas.

Office market areas often assume one of two forms: local services or export services. Local services such as routine medical or dental care characterize market areas similar to retail trade areas because of their orientation to local residents; local consumers visit service providers to receive services. In contrast, export services are characterized by large, noncontiguous service areas. Customers do not visit export service sites. Rather, information flows to and from the sites, and service providers (for example, accountants, architects, engineers) usually travel to deliver services to customers at their locations. Therefore, a complete office development marketability study must clearly define space users as local service providers or export service providers. Whether office space users are local or export service providers, access to a qualified labor pool, related business services, and transportation is essential.

Industrial trade areas are also noncontiguous, as most manufacturers export products to regional, national, or international markets. Unlike retailing operations, which compete for the same customers from their overlapping trade areas, industrial tenants generally sell to different customers in dispersed locations. Nonetheless, they might compete for local infrastructure, labor, intermediate goods or services, and properly zoned industrial land.

Hotel guests reside somewhere outside the locality rather than near the accommodations. The large majority of guests therefore pass through a locality rather than permanently reside there. Like retail centers and offices, hotels compete for sites at highly accessible transportation nodes or key destinations.

Although it is difficult to define a hotel's market area by a market's characteristics, hotel demand can be disaggregated by weekday versus weekend guests, business guests versus vacationers, and conference travelers, airline employees, and so on to better estimate new demand.

One goal of the new urbanism is to mix property types and income levels in the same development—a very tricky feat. (The intrepid reader is encouraged to research the development history of new urbanist communities and the personalities who designed them.) Elizabeth Plater-Zyberk has been at the forefront of this movement.

Market Disaggregation into Competitive Submarkets

The research and valuation committees of the National Council of Real Estate Investment Fiduciaries

---

▶ **PROFILE**

ELIZABETH PLATER-ZYBERK
Cofounder, Duany Plater-Zyberk & Company
Dean, University of Miami School of Architecture
Miami, Florida

Admired for her role in the promulgation of the new urbanism and her leadership at the University of Miami School of Architecture, Elizabeth Plater-Zyberk has greatly contributed to the architecture and design of today's cities and suburbs. She is revered for her role in the creation of the Congress for the New Urbanism, which has helped pioneer the movement.

Born to an aristocratic Polish family that migrated to the United States after they lost their wealth during the Soviet expansion after World War II, Plater-Zyberk was exposed to architecture at an early age. Her father was an architect, and she remembers her father taking her along to construction sites and being shown drawings of buildings, specifically old Pennsylvania farmhouses being redeveloped into modern houses. Plater-Zyberk earned her Bachelor of Arts degree in architecture and urban planning from Princeton University and a Master's degree in architecture from the Yale School of Architecture. While at Princeton, she met Andrés Duany and the two of them, later married, continue to be one of the most influential husband-and-wife teams in the field.

After receiving their degrees, Plater-Zyberk and Duany joined another couple in Miami to form Arquitectonica, a firm that reflected the young, hip Miami culture through their bold Modernist designs. They were able to overcome the obstacles of starting a small business because of the surge in Latin American investment. Their most recognized work was the design of the Atlantis building, with the square hole in it, which was made nationally famous as the backdrop for the television series *Miami Vice*.

Coming of age in the politically sensitive environment of the 1960s, Plater-Zyberk was uncomfortable with her success as a designer of picturesque buildings that lacked social responsibility. She feared that she was creating buildings that demanded attention to themselves without recognizing, and contributing to, the surrounding public space. Watching Florida's numerous large residential developments be designed as undifferentiated suburbs rather than new towns, Plater-Zyberk and Duany regarded the situation as a crisis. With the philosophy that new developments were receiving inadequate design attention and that proper architecture required much research, the couple left Arquitectonica and that style of architecture to pursue their dream and incorporate their philosophy into their work. Wanting to create a research-oriented firm, the pair formed Duany Plater-Zyberk & Company, DPZ for short.

Plater-Zyberk's first project using the principles of traditional neighborhood development, Charleston Place in Boca Raton, used a townhouse model inspired by traditional Charleston houses, which included side courtyards and porches, small gridded streets, and a compact design. This project was an urban pod in the middle of suburbia, and it turned out to be extremely popular. Trying to do something unconventional, Plater-Zyberk learned a lot about the conventions and what needed to be changed.

To promulgate their planning principles, DPZ has circulated a guide to traditional neighborhood developments. Elements of such design include neighborhoods of limited size with clear edges and a focused center; shops, workplaces, schools, and residences for all income groups close to each other; streets sized and detailed to serve the needs of both automobiles and pedestrians; buildings that define streets and squares; and well-placed civic buildings used as symbols of the community's identity that provide a place for public assembly.

SEASIDE, FLORIDA

One of Plater-Zyberk's most recognized projects is Seaside, Florida. When Robert Davis approached DPZ with a commission to plan a modern artist resort in the manner of some of the older places in Key West on an 80-acre (32-hectare)

▶ **PROFILE** *(continued)*

Through the development of Seaside, Elizabeth Plater-Zyberk and Andrés Duany were able to test many concepts, and Seaside thus became the prototype for the new urbanism. Steven Brooke

oceanfront parcel in an unincorporated part of Florida's panhandle, very few zoning codes were in place to restrain their ideas. They did, however, buck many regional architectural conventions. For example, Seaside has no culs-de-sac and no single-entry lots, and it embraces a traditional style of architecture rather than the California style that was popular at the time. The development team worked hard with the construction team to ensure the quality of the work because the construction team was unfamiliar with this style of work. To raise interest in the property, the team built a few houses initially to show what the project was like, intending to get people to buy into it.

With the philosophy that architects and planners should base their politics on behalf of public space, DPZ wrote a two-sheet zoning and design code that specified the range of dimensions, styles, colors, and forms for every detail of the home construction, from lot sizes and setbacks to window and porch trim. The uniformity cultivated a communal feeling, and economic differences were not apparent between residents and their neighbors, in turn encouraging residents to take responsibility for all public spaces.

Support and opposition were mixed throughout the development of Seaside. Initially, the atmosphere was extremely supportive because many of the young architects working on

the project were featured in various publications, keeping the buzz about Seaside strong. Some architects were also working at universities. One of these institutions, the University of Miami, was always a strong supporter of the project. Leaders in the field such as Robert Stern and Vincent Scully recognized that Seaside could have a tremendous effect on the real estate world. In addition to supporters, however, a fair share of skeptics was vocal.

The original idea was for Seaside to be a small, quiet beach town, but critics often complain that instead, it is a tourist site that has lost its original purpose. Plater-Zyberk, while agreeing that Seaside is not as quiet as they had planned, believes this sort of popularity is inevitable. Because Seaside was one of a kind and had such an appeal, it attracted more than its share of people, especially tourists who visit for only a day. And because tourism is such a large industry, it is hard for beautiful places not to be overrun. In most new urbanist communities, compromises are inevitable. A community of lesser quality will attract fewer visitors, and residents will be able to live a more peaceful life.

THE FUTURE OF NEW URBANISM

Though obstacles such as zoning codes and working with state and local officials still exist in developing new urbanist

continued on next page

communities, Plater-Zyberk believes it is much easier today to build a new urbanist project than it was in the past. The environment today is more favorable, with changed zoning codes and comprehensive city plans that now incorporate some principles of the new urbanism. Moreover, the Congress for the New Urbanism helps back changes for setting standards that are appropriate for urban areas. When she first began, Plater-Zyberk did not realize that it was somewhat difficult being a woman in her line of work. Few women and few female role models were in the field, and developers were used to talking only to men. She says, however, that she kept taking little steps forward and that they eventually added up.

Plater-Zyberk believes that in the future, the new urbanism will be the norm because of concern about sprawl and the cost of infrastructure. "Social and environmental issues will make it more logical in the long run to promote the new urbanism rather than conventional suburban development. Looking at questions such as the social cost of keeping people segregated by income, the answers will make it more convincing for more efficient urbanism."

ACADEMIC PRACTICE

Plater-Zyberk has been involved with the University of Miami School of Architecture since 1979, first as a professor, then as director of the Master of Architecture Program, then as director of the Center for Urban and Community Design, and currently as dean. Her position as dean gives her a chance to help the program grow. Though she continues to manage several projects a year at DPZ, her deanship remains her priority. As a teacher, she has learned how to clarify and conceptualize issues and to articulate her ideas and thoughts. These skills have been invaluable in her professional practice. With

the belief that research elevates the practice of architecture, Plater-Zyberk thinks highly of the research opportunities available at the university.

With numerous publications to her credit, including *Suburban Nation* with Andrés Duany and Jeff Speck, Plater-Zyberk is one of the most recognized figures in architecture and planning. Her various honors and awards, including honorary doctorates in architecture from several universities, the Vincent J. Scully Award from the National Building Museum, and the Educational Leadership Award from the AIA Miami Chapter, are a testament to her influence on the shape of America's cities and towns.

Plater-Zyberk considers the people she meets in her everyday life—family, teachers, architects, university administrators, developers, elected officials—her most important influences. Working with her husband is a rewarding experience because she believes she is always learning from him. Her advice to someone interested in architecture or planning: pursue a design that embellishes the environment and everyday life. "You can make beautiful places by building one building at a time while understanding the regional context." Stressing the importance of understanding how people would move through the streets of a new development, Plater-Zyberk explains that an architect should understand that he or she is putting together the framework for a physical environment that promotes communication.

When looking to hire new young associates, Plater-Zyberk looks for someone who sees his or her efforts as part of a larger team effort. She wants someone smart and hardworking who wants to succeed and understands that he or she must learn and will look forward to that learning. She adds, "Even if you are not good at your work at the beginning, love it to excellence."

(NCREIF) have established an articulate and well-reasoned general premise and goal for real estate market analyses:

> The Market Analysis content of an appraisal report should provide data concerning both the historical and prospective relationships between supply and demand information. In addition, this information should form the basis for assumptions set forth in the Income Approach. These issues are all interrelated, and the appraisal report should demonstrate a consistency of rationale between the issues. . . . The

appraisal report must maintain a flow of logic addressing the interplay of these factors when developing investment assumptions.[9]

To develop "a consistency of rationale" and "a flow of logic," it is critical for the analyst to select the appropriate level of data disaggregation for the type and use of the proposed development. In fact, different levels of market data or selected qualitative or quantitative classifications may reveal information on distinct aspects of the subject's historical, current, and prospective performance. Three of the most powerful levels of data disaggregation are for the metropolitan area, the competitive submarket, and the peer group. Each level of disaggregation has a specific analytical purpose and/or relationship to the performance of the proposed development.

The Metropolitan Area Market

Most market analyses rely heavily or even exclusively on data for the MSA in formulating property-specific assumptions, but relying solely on data for the MSA does not sufficiently pinpoint the competitive forces that most directly influence the proposed development's pace of absorption and rental rates. Nonetheless, analysis of the MSA is an essential first step in developing sound market-driven assumptions. To the extent that an MSA represents a well-defined economic unit, virtually any analysis of the area's economic and demographic base (the primary drivers of demand) will benefit from the use of comprehensive historical, current, and forecast data for the metropolitan area.

Likewise, an attempt to focus exclusively on the economic activity of a submarket is likely to ignore many of the factors for the metropolitan area that either promote or discourage growth throughout the metropolitan area and overlook the richest sources of demand side data. Moreover, MSA demand forecasts represent the baseline data to compare and contrast market share benchmarks and capture rates for individual submarkets.

The value of developing trends and forecasts for the MSA also extends to supply-side indicators, particularly new construction and change in rents. Because information on new construction projects is often limited to the near term, a well-developed annual time series that presents a submarket's historical share of metropolitan construction can be extremely useful in developing longer-term forecasts of construction in the submarket. With respect to assumptions for rental growth rates, metropolitan trends and forecasts are a necessary check on any forecasts developed for a submarket and a peer group market. It is likely that any one submarket's significant deviation from the average metropolitan rental growth rate will be corrected in the intermediate term or that the submarket's share of absorption and construction will adjust appropriately.

The Competitive Submarket

The definition of a competitive submarket or trade area, "a geographical area surrounding the subject site that will provide a substantial portion of the customers for the real estate project," has received considerable attention in the literature.[10] Hence, a submarket's trends in supply and demand should have a more direct impact than metropolitan trends on the performance of the subject property. As a result, a strong case can be made for relying heavily on submarket trends and forecasts in the development of property-specific cash flow assumptions. Although the characteristics of the subject property and/or peer group may justify a modification in the submarket research, trends in supply and demand in a well-defined submarket determine more precisely the parameters in which individual buildings can shift rental rate pricing and lease terms.

The Peer Group Market

Before discussing the value of peer group analysis, it is important to address the limitations that can often accompany market statistics by property class. For instance, property-type quality measures such as Class A or Class B office space market segments are often arbitrarily defined. Sometimes market classification measures are used to justify not using a part of the space inventory that is difficult to measure. Although some properties are competitive within a given classification, the most rigorous method for establishing specific parameters of a competitive position is from the bottom up, or by taking the inventory of the individual buildings that constitute the primary and secondary levels of competition.

A determination of the physical, locational, or economic factors that distinguish the subject's proper classification can be made after completing the peer group analysis. Thereafter, individual peer buildings can be ranked according to comparability with the subject development. At the same time, distinctions among properties can be evaluated and priced. These often subtle distinctions are critical factors in refining net effective rents, rental growth rates, and leasing concession assumptions used in the discounted cash flow analysis.[11]

In other words, peer group analysis is central to defining the subject property's market niche from which submarket trend analysis can be used to project future change in the niche's performance. Moreover, if the analyst can obtain historical trend data on the performance of the peer group, he can conduct a comparative analysis to ascertain market share and to quantify differentials in growth rates. If the peer group history is sufficiently extensive, the analyst may be justified in adjusting the absorption and rent growth assumptions based on the historical premium or discount recorded by the peer group.

PRESENTING THE RESEARCH AND CONCLUSIONS

The material in this chapter has thus far portrayed the tasks of gathering and validating market data that are essential components of a process that yields greater insight into a project's marketability. Once the data have been obtained, cleaned, and reconciled, no one way is available to present findings and conclusions that speak equally well to all audiences. Despite that admission, information should usually be arrayed in a way that conveys the process of discovery to the reader of a market analysis (see Figure 17-1 for a generic outline of items to be covered in a market analysis report).

This chapter places considerable emphasis on developing time-series analyses at multiple levels of market disaggregation in the belief that historical trends communicate a sense of variability, and thus risk, that analyses relying on a single point in time cannot. Therefore, the construction of trend analysis is viewed as perhaps the most important means of communicating the market study's results. Specifically, the analyst should pay attention to peaks and troughs of market performance and other measures of market cyclicity such as the levels of construction, absorption, vacancy, and rent growth that were recorded during the most dynamic periods of market and economic expansion and severe economic contraction. The same analysis should be performed for all demand indicators. Given that annual data can fluctuate significantly and distort apparently meaningful trend analysis,

the construction of time slices in two-, three-, and/or five-year increments may be helpful. To the extent that sensitivity analyses are employed, these historical

Figure 17-1 A Generic Outline of Market Analysis to Be Adapted for Specific Situations

I. EXECUTIVE SUMMARY
A. Goals and objectives
B. Methods of analysis, key assumptions, risk factors
C. Recommendations—go/no go/postpone/improve project
D. Disclaimers

II. OVERVIEW
A. National (or global) economy and key growth areas
B. Regional economic outlook
C. Local economy
D. Market delineation and site analysis
E. Proposed project description

III. DEMAND ANALYSIS
A. Projected overall demand
B. Analysis of absorption

IV. SUPPLY ANALYSIS
A. Survey of existing stock, past trends, and future supply
B. Analysis of existing zoning and possible changes
C. Consideration of business cycle and building cycle to compare projections of supply and demand

V. COMPETITIVE ANALYSIS
A. Features, functions, and benefits of the project in relation to the competition
B. Analysis of market segmentation

VI. CAPTURE RATE ANALYSIS
A. Based on analysis of the competition, estimated total absorption and absorption schedule by market segment and projected market share to account for the distinct features and competitive advantages that should attract customers and tenants
B. Final estimate of market capture rate, projected leases or sales per period, specification of price and total time to complete leases or sales

benchmarks represent a far more intuitive and factual approach to alternative future scenarios than simply varying assumptions by specified percentages.

Another important technique for conveying the quality of market research results is not to hide all the warts and contradictions in the data. Although market analysts are hired in part to resolve many of the thorniest research problems and to present lucid findings and conclusions, exposing the reader to "contradictions" in the data and explaining their resolution can add dynamism and integrity to the report.

SUMMARY

This chapter has emphasized the market researcher's responsibility to engage in data collection and validation in the context of market and marketability analyses. Data on the real estate space markets (supply) and on employment, population, and income (demand drivers) are critical to the process. Understanding collection methodologies, reconciling contradictions of multiple data sources, and aggregating/disaggregating data are critical.

Ultimately, the process of data collection and validation yields a data set that supports the two critical analytic links without which the market analysis enterprise is doomed to the irrelevancy of "background" information: the connections between the macromarket and the subject property, and the connections between historical trends and future performance. Armed with the requisite data and capable of forging vital analytic connections, the market analyst can determine what the data are saying and how to present findings in a compelling manner to support critical assumptions underlying cash flow analysis. The data as formed in market and marketability studies are the heart and soul of the feasibility analysis.

TERMS

▶ Absorption
▶ Aggregate data
▶ Bottom-up approach
▶ Consensus forecast
▶ Data series

▶ Decennial census
▶ Demographic indicators
▶ Disaggregated data
▶ Due diligence
▶ Location quotient
▶ Net absorption
▶ Outlier forecast
▶ Primary source
▶ Secondary source
▶ Top-down approach

REVIEW QUESTIONS

17.1 What is the difference between a market study and a marketability study?

17.2 What are the primary factors that influence market demand? How are they used to forecast demand for the primary property types (i.e., office, retail, multifamily, and industrial)?

17.3 What are the seven basic factors the market analyst should consider when auditing real estate supply or demand data?

17.4 Why are space absorption and rent changes two critical elements of data when analyzing a market? What kind of judgments does the market analyst make based on that information?

17.5 Why is it crucial for market analysts to gather data for several time periods?

17.6 Why must an analyst devote attention to ensuring the accuracy of absorption rates and the growth and decline of rental rates?

17.7 What are some of the resources analysts can use for forecasting population, income, and employment growth or decline?

NOTES

1. Appraisal Institute, *The Appraisal of Real Estate,* 11th ed. (Chicago: Author, 2001), p. 58; also see Appraisal Institute, *The Student's Handbook to the Appraisal of Real Estate* (Chicago: Author, 2004).

2. A data series is a grouping of aggregated information in an order or arrangement that typically shows a progression or relationship.

3. Stage three (the feasibility study) considers the full range of legal, physical, market, and financial dimensions. The market study and marketability study evaluate the subject project in

relation to the market. The financial feasibility analysis estimates risks and rewards for developers, investors, and lenders.

4. A metropolitan statistical area consists of a central city with a population exceeding 50,000, the county(ies) in which it is located, and other contiguous counties that are metropolitan in character and socially and economically integrated with the central city.

5. Demographic indicators are vital statistics on human populations that typically refer to size, density, distribution, and other significant characteristics. For real estate markets, vital statistics include population, households, and income, among others. Refer to Chapter 2 for more information on demographics.

6. An outlier forecast is one of a group of projections that differs substantially from all others in the group as well as from the group average.

7. A top-down approach to analysis first focuses on aggregated results. A bottom-up approach typically refers to developing an analysis based on the most disaggregated data available.

8. More detailed discussions are found in Adrienne Schmitz et al., *Real Estate Market Analysis* (Washington, D.C.: ULI–the Urban Land Institute, 2001); and Neil Carn, Joseph Rabianski, Ronald Racster, and Maury Seldin, *Real Estate Market Analysis: Techniques and Applications* (Englewood Cliffs, N.J.: Prentice-Hall, 1988).

9. D. Richard Wincott and Glenn Mueller, "Market Analysis in the Valuation Process." A position paper adopted by the Joint Valuation/Research Subcommittees of the National Council of Real Estate Investment Fiduciaries, published in *The Appraisal Journal,* January 1995.

10. John Clapp, *Handbook for Real Estate Market Analysis* (Englewood Cliffs, N.J.: Prentice-Hall, 1987).

11. Although gathering the information is difficult, analysts need to measure effective rent, which is contract rent minus concessions such as rent-free periods, above-average tenant improvements, moving allowances, among others.

CHAPTER 18

Data Sources Supporting Market Studies

Chapters 16 and 17 demonstrated the role of the market study as part of the feasibility analysis and the role of the entire feasibility study as a primary management tool during the development process.

Chapter 17 looked at the logic of the market study, focusing on the work done by or directly for the developer, while this chapter focuses on the secondary sources available to help analysts prepare market studies. Beyond in-house resources and the primary research done by the development team, the developer has a plethora of information sources available, most of them online. Generally speaking, these secondary sources provide background material for the study. They set the particular submarket in a regional, national, and global context. The primary research described in Chapter 17 is then used to supplement and tailor secondary sources to fit the market study for the proposed development.

Although the most critical work in the market study is auditing and fitting the data to the specific development idea (the material covered in the previous chapter), it is also important to be sure that this work starts with the best possible national and regional economic projections. The developer has available (for a nontrivial fee) several national service firms. The first three discussed in this chapter forecast future rents and returns by property type for the nation's larger MSAs. The last two provide much current leasing and pricing information. The first three help market analysts establish baselines for the local market relative to the nation, while the fourth and fifth are tools to verify current rents and cap rates in the discounted cash flow model.

Depending on the specific situation, analysts may rely more on one or another of these forecasts. To help you make that judgment, this chapter begins with an economic description of real estate forecasting. These straightforward equations explain how economists organize the data to make projections. It then covers each of the three forecasting firms in detail, including how their technology and/or data are different or superior and how the developer should use the information. The chapter concludes with a detailed description of the nation's largest real estate data providers.

FORECASTING MODELS AND METHODS

Real estate investors use forecasts to estimate value, as explained in Chapter 9. Such forecasts may be informal or formal. To the extent that the forecasts rely on outsourced work and forecasts, developers should understand how the forecasts are constructed.

In most economic models, supply and demand jointly determine price. In real estate, supply forecasts adjust with an extensive lag so that the market is seldom in equilibrium.

This chapter begins with a brief review of a generic supply and demand model and then extends it for use in determining prices for commercial real estate. By understanding how this process works, the developer can better question the firms producing MSA-level forecasts to determine which would be appropriate for use in the market study portion of the feasibility study.

Suppose we are interested in the price of an agricultural commodity, corn, for example. The basic model may take the following form:

$$Q_D = a + bP + cY$$
$$Q_S = d + eP + fW$$
$$Q_D = Q_S$$

where Q represents quantity and D and S indicate demand and supply, respectively. The model states that quantity demanded (Q_D) is a function of price P and income Y. The quantity supplied (Q_S) is a function of price P and weather W. The third equation indicates that we assume the market for corn "clears" and what is observed is a market-clearing price and a single market-clearing quantity. Thus the two *endogenous* variables, i.e., variables determined by the model, are price and quantity. The two *exogenous* variables, i.e., variables determined outside the model, are income and weather. This model is in *structural form;* that is, we have written down the model in the basic form in which we think the variables of the model interact when endogenous variables are allowed to be determined by other endogenous variables. We can always solve the equations for the two

endogenous variables (because the market is assumed to clear):

$$P = g + hY + iW$$
$$Q = j + kY + mW$$

where price and quantity are now simply functions of the two exogenous variables. This is the "reduced" form of the model.

Remember that exogenous variables are determined outside the system, but as is clear from the reduced form, they are the true determining factors for the variables of interest: price and quantity. Thus, the assumptions users make about these variables or the forecast supplier makes about these variables are absolutely crucial to the accuracy of the forecast. We return to this point in the next section when we examine the key assumptions that major forecasting services make about important exogenous variables in macromodels of the U.S. economy, such as interest rates and oil prices.

We now extend this simple model to one in which MSA-level returns or prices can be determined. First, define the following set of variables:

Q^*_{Sti} The desired supply or inventory of properties at time t in MSA i.

Q_{Sti} The actual inventory at time t in MSA i.

Q_{Dti} The demand for space at time t in MSA i.

P_{ti} The generic price for a property at time t in MSA i.

X_{ti} Demand-side variables measured for the MSA or county such as employment and per capita income.

N_t National variables such as interest rates and inflation rates.

ε_{ti} Disturbance or error terms used to indicate that even a very-well-specified model cannot capture all the relevant factors.

Supply Side

The supply side of the model recognizes that desired supply and actual supply are often different. The following equations model this fact.

$$Q^*_{Sti} = \alpha + \beta P_{ti} + \gamma N_t + \varepsilon_{ti} \qquad (1)$$

This equation states that the desired supply at time t is a function of the price that can be obtained for properties and national-level variables that may influence the ability to provide the space. In this simple model, we assume that current desired supply is a function of current price; the modeling is straightforward to incorporate lags on price in the equation (more on this subject later).

Real estate is different from many commodities, because a long lag exists before properties can be produced to take advantage of price increases. The following "partial adjustment" equation recognizes this lag:

$$Q_{Sti} = \lambda Q^*_{Sti} + (1 - \lambda)Q_{S,t-1,i} \qquad (2)$$

This equation states that the actual quantity of space supplied at time t in MSA i is a function of the desired supply at time t and *actual* supply at time t–1. The λ is a positive constant between zero and one that captures the speed with which suppliers can supply new properties. If properties could be built within a single time period (say a year or a quarter), the λ would be equal to one and we would have actual supply equal to desired supply. At the other extreme, $\lambda = 0$ means that no adjustment can take place at all. A λ between zero and one recognizes that the lag resulting from the need to acquire the land, obtain the necessary permits, prepare plans, and physically construct the building may require several time periods. The size of λ is undoubtedly different for different property types. For example, one would expect that the λ for office buildings in the CBD is probably closer to zero than the λ for suburban apartments, as urban office buildings are often larger than their suburban counterparts and thus take longer to be absorbed.

Equation 1 contains the empirically unobservable variable Q^*_{Sti}. Therefore, we substitute Equation 1 into Equation 2 to obtain:

$$Q_{Sti} = \lambda\alpha + \lambda\beta P_t + (1 - \lambda)Q_{S,t-1,i} + \lambda\gamma N_t + \lambda\varepsilon_{ti} \qquad (3)$$

Demand Side

The demand side of the market is represented by Equation 4:

$$Q_{Dti} = \delta + \kappa P_{ti} + \theta X_{ti} + \tau N_t + \varepsilon_{ti} \qquad (4)$$

where we hypothesize that in addition to price, demand is determined by national variables such as interest rates and the consumer price index (CPI), as well as economic conditions in the MSA such as unemployment rates.

So far, we have specified two equations with three unknowns: quantity of space demanded, quantity supplied, and price. If we impose the condition of equilibrium that the market must clear in every period (quantity demanded is equal to quantity supplied), we can solve Equations 3 and 4 for price and quantity (as $Q_{Sti} = Q_{Dti}$). For example, the price equation takes on the following form:

$$P_{ti} = \pi_1 + \pi_2 Q^*_{S,t-1,i} + \pi_3 X_{ti} + \pi_4 N_t + v_{ti} \qquad (5)$$

The new coefficients are linear combinations of the coefficients in the separate demand and supply equations, and the disturbance term incorporates the disturbance terms in both equations. Equation 5 states that the price of a property is determined by national, MSA, and county economic conditions and lagged supply. A straightforward extension of the model allows either desired supply or quantity demanded to be a function of lagged price. It is easy to justify lagged price in either equation because of the time involved in property development on the supply side and relocation time on the demand side. Regardless of where lagged price is introduced, the reduced form of the equation is modified as follows:

$$P_{ti} = \pi_1 + \pi_2 Q_{S,t-1,i} + \pi_3 X_{ti} + \pi_4 N_t + \pi_5 P_{t-1,i} + v_{ti} \qquad (6)$$

where price in the current period is now a function of price in the preceding period. Note that this equation requires us to have complete data, because for each MSA in the data set at each point in time, we must observe both a current and a lagged price. Depending on the data source, this requirement could be problematic, because it may not be possible to construct an accurate price for each MSA for each point in time as a result of the relatively slow turnover of commercial real estate properties. If complete data are not available, we can substitute for lagged price in Equation 6 as follows:

$$P_{ti} = \overset{*}{\pi}1 + \sum_{k=1}^{K}\overset{*}{\pi}2kQS, t{-}k, i + \sum_{k=0}^{K}\overset{*}{\pi}3k X_{t{-}k,i} + \sum_{k=0}^{K}\overset{*}{\pi}4k N_{t{-}k} + \overset{*}{v}ti \quad (7)$$

where * indicates that the coefficient or disturbance term in Equation 7 is a linear combination of coefficients and disturbances in Equation 6. Equation 7 states that current price is a function of a weighted average of past supply, demand, and national-level variables.

In the literature, both structural equation models (CB Richard Ellis/Torto Wheaton Research, Property & Portfolio Research, and Reis Reports) and reduced form models (Case and Shiller) have been used. The different forecasting services use different demand and supply data to prepare their forecasts. Even more than differences in econometric methodology, differences in data sources distinguish the various forecasts.

PRIMARY SOURCES OF DEMAND DATA

This section provides an overview of demand-side forecasts at the MSA level. Although several smaller competitors provide information, the major producers of demand-side forecasts are Moody's Economy.com and Global Insight. Differences can be found in their methodology, but both start with a standard set of macroeconomic statistics such as GDP and interest rates, which are used to create a macromodel for the U.S. economy, which is then used to prepare state, regional, county, and metropolitan area forecasts.[1]

Three variables used extensively in the models are employment, population (total and population by age group), and income. A key ingredient in forecasting any of these variables is good up-to-date historical data. Employment statistics are the work of the

Figure 18-1	Tradeoffs in Reduced Form and Structural Form Equations	
	Reduced Form (Equations 5, 6, or 7)	**Structural Form (Equations 3 and 4)**
Pros	▶ No endogenous explanatory variables; simpler methods can be used in estimation.	▶ No endogenous explanatory variables; simpler methods can be used in estimation.
	▶ Forecasting future returns requires only values for variables that are exogenous to the model.	▶ Forecasting future returns requires only values for variables that are exogenous to the model.
		▶ Model is more intuitive; we can understand the pathways through which variables influence price.
		▶ Estimated coefficients represent combinations of coefficients from the structural equations model, which may make interpretation more difficult.
Cons	▶ Estimated coefficients represent combinations of coefficients from the structural equations model, which may make interpretation more difficult.	▶ It is more difficult to estimate the dependent variables, although some forecasting services ignore the simultaneity of the model and use simple methods such as ordinary least squares to estimate structural coefficients.
		▶ The model produces forecasting equations for both price and quantity; however, reduced form equations for quantity can be obtained simply by replacing price on the left side of the reduced form.

Preliminary MSA-level data are readily available through the Internet and can be easily found through search engines such as Google or Yahoo. According to the BLS, for example, the Pittsburgh, Pennsylvania, MSA had an unemployment rate of 4 percent in February 2007; a U.S. Census population estimate for 2002 states that it is the 21st largest MSA in the nation. *www.visitpittsburgh.com*

Bureau of Labor Statistics, while income data are the work of the Bureau of Economic Analysis.

Demand-side data providers evaluate critical issues such as quality of life and relative costs to obtain their forecasts of MSA employment, population, and income growth. Such "soft" items are critical to estimates of migration across MSAs. Further, the nation's perception of what constitutes a high quality of life and any relative cost advantage changes over time.

Building Starts

Dodge maintains the most comprehensive database for the supply side of the model. It includes quarterly information about stock and construction starts per square foot from 1970 to the present for 31 building types in 3,105 counties. Dodge tracks starts through a network of more than 1,300 reporters, who obtain information from building permits and other sources. Projects are

tracked through a "project life cycle," which includes preplanning, final planning, negotiations, bids, bid results, starts, and construction. Dodge also provides data about starts of single-family houses back to 1970; unfortunately, it does not have estimates on the total inventory of single-family houses by MSA.

Because the data are for counties, analysts can "build" information to either MSAs or divisions of MSAs. For example, rather than using the new Miami MSAs (Miami, Fort Lauderdale, and West Palm Beach), supply-side information can be constructed for each division of the three, which can then be matched to comparable demand-side data from Global Insight and Economy.com.

In addition to historical information on building stock and starts, Dodge provides a five-year forecast for both variables. A one-year forecast is largely based on information from Dodge Pipeline. Beyond one year, the forecast is mainly econometrically generated using demand-side data from Economy.com. (Reis also provides supply-side information.)

Population Density

Analysts expect change in the available square footage of space to be the dominant supply-side effect on appreciation returns. Another factor to consider, however, is constraints on potential increases in supply in the most desirable areas of MSAs. For example, San Francisco has very little room for expansion because of square-foot development restrictions plus the physical boundaries of the Bay and ocean to its west and the presence of San Jose and Oakland to its east and south. San Antonio, on the other hand, has both looser zoning and almost limitless land surrounding the MSA for future development. Therefore, MSA population density is included as an additional explanatory factor.

Some analysts construct the density measure as a time-dependent variable. They start with the number of square miles in each county and then construct the number of square miles in each MSA. They then construct a log of population density using the populations in the MSAs at each point in time. Some MSAs—Las Vegas, for example—have increased density tremendously over a 30-plus-year period. Nevertheless, Las Vegas is still a low-density MSA compared with most other MSAs.

Employment Data

Employment growth (measured at the appropriate level of aggregation, either region or MSA) is one of the most important variables in forecasts. The government is the ultimate source of almost all employment data. All major forecasting services rely on data from the Bureau of Labor Statistics to produce their forecasts of employment growth by MSA. The BLS conducts two primary surveys—Current Employment Statistics, and Employment and Wages Covered by Unemployment Insurance—and all major services use both surveys in their forecasts.[2]

Current Employment Statistics

The survey of current employment statistics is a payroll survey frequently referred to as the "790 survey,"

because the reporting form used is BLS form 790. The survey is administered monthly to a sample of approximately 350,000 business establishments nationwide. The primary statistics derived are estimates of employment, hours, and earnings down to the level of MSA. This huge sample asks all establishments with more than 250 employees to participate; a representative sample of smaller firms also participates. Nearly 40 percent of the total nonfarm population is represented in the survey. Respondents extract the needed information from payroll records they are required to keep for a variety of reasons.

Bias adjustment factors (a mathematical correction that compensates for any biases that might occur in survey work) are used primarily to adjust for the inability of the survey to capture the entry of new firms. The bias adjustment uses the universal coverage provided by the ES-202 data (described next) to provide an adjustment factor. These bias adjustment factors vary by state and hence the accuracy also varies by state.

Employment and Wages Covered by Unemployment Insurance

Commonly called the "ES-202 program," the survey of employment and wages covered by unemployment insurance is a cooperative effort of the BLS and the employment security agencies of the 50 states, the District of Columbia, Puerto Rico, and the Virgin Islands. The ES-202 program is a comprehensive and accurate source of employment and wage data by industry for the nation, states, and counties. Providing a virtual census of nonagricultural employees and their wages, it also covers about 47 percent of all workers in agricultural industries.[3]

Benchmarking Employment Data

Not surprisingly, a tradeoff exists between the two sources of employment data. The 790 data are timely, as the lag between the time the data are collected and when they are released is only one month. It is a survey, however, and is subject to sampling error and possibly bias in coverage. The ES-202 data provide a virtual census, but because of the complexity of the data, the lag between collection and release is 15 months.

The BLS therefore benchmarks (corrects preceding forecasts using new, more detailed information) the 790 figures to the ES-202 figures in March each year. For example, in March 2005, the BLS benchmarked employment statistics for April 2003 through February 2004.

PRIMARY SOURCES OF SUPPLY DATA

This section provides information about what major forecasters offer, how they are different from other forecasters, and how developers can use their insights. The material presented here comes directly from the forecasting companies.

Property & Portfolio Research, Inc.

PPR (www.ppr.info/) is a leading provider of independent real estate research and strategic advisory services to the institutional real estate community in the United States. The firm provides clients with expertise in real estate market analysis, real estate portfolio analysis, mortgage risk analysis, and design of productive real estate investment strategies. Clients include commercial banks, insurance companies, Wall Street firms, rating agencies, pension funds, investment advisers, REITs, and private investors. PPR is wholly owned by DMG Information, Inc., the business information division of Daily Mail and General Trust, plc (DMGT).

PPR offers several reports for clients:

▶ *Fundamentals Reports* provide quarterly forecasts of fundamental information, including vacancy rates, demand, supply, and rent changes for 54 urban areas and five property types (apartment, office, warehouse, retail, hotel). Each report also includes an extensive market narrative, a summary of employment and demographic trends, a snapshot of the current construction in progress and planned, a list of up to 25 major projects in the development pipeline for each metropolitan area, and information about sales transactions and cap rates. Each report also includes a full 20-year historical time series.

▶ *Submarket Reports* provide quarterly forecasts of real estate fundamentals, including vacancy rates, demand, supply, and rent changes for more than 800 separate submarkets in 54 urban areas. Each report also contains a written summary of submarket conditions as well as more detailed analyses of supply, demand, vacancy rates, and rents for the major property types, including apartments, offices, and warehouse space, with five-year forecasts.

▶ *Construction Trak* is a searchable database of current and proposed commercial real estate construction projects throughout the United States for six property types (office, apartment, warehouse, retail, hotel, and seniors' housing) in 318 urban areas; it is updated weekly. Information on new supply comes from a national reporter network provided by Reed Construction Data, a business unit of Reed Business Information.

Project reports contain a detailed listing of every vital aspect of a project, including property type, location, project specifications, construction stage, and contact person. *Construction Trak* is a tool for identifying financing opportunities, acquisition deals, market research, and competitive development. Its search capabilities allow users to extract custom construction information.

▶ *Performance Service* provides forecasts of fundamentals and performance (NOI and capital value) for 54 urban areas and four property types; it also provides strategic advice and may include client-specific project work. Typical clients use this service to:

- Provide a risk-free environment to collaborate on strategic ideas;
- Run real-time analysis on multiple real estate investment strategies;
- Identify and validate investment platforms for opportunity and growth;
- Provide direct access to market economists to discuss tactical issues;
- Provide support for investing and recycling capital;
- Provide access to extensive data, research, and market analysis;

- Support marketing efforts to communicate investment strategy strengths;
- Provide an independent third-party source of qualitative and quantitative analysis;
- Provide an independent view about the concerns of institutional investors.

▶ *European Service* provides:

- Quarterly forecasts of real estate supply, net absorption, vacancies, rents, NOI, capital value, yield, and total returns for 21 European office markets, prepared semiannually;
- Quarterly forecasts of rents, NOI, capital value, yield, and total returns for ten European warehouse markets, prepared semiannually;
- Forecasts incorporating performance data;
- Quarterly historical data back to 1990, with five-year forecasts;
- Objective analysis with data consistent over time and from market to market;
- Narrative analysis of economic, demographic, and capital market trends.

▶ *Portfolio Analysis Service* applies modern portfolio theory to clients' portfolios across debt, equity, public, and private global and/or domestic markets. Clients use the service to better understand the relationship between risk and return as it applies to their existing portfolios and objectives. Once they understand their customized goals, strategies are developed that will bring them closer to those goals.

The service is used to objectively allocate funds, review and proactively adjust allocations as market cycles reduce unrewarded risk, identify acquisition/ disposition candidates based on impact on portfolio risk and return, and convey strategy to investors and management using third-party analysis.

▶ *Mortgage Risk Service* encompasses at its core PPR and Algo COMPASS^CRE, a desktop tool that calculates default metrics calibrated to historic defaults on commercial real estate mortgages. COMPASS^CRE takes into account loan structure, seasoning, growth in NOI and capital value, and market volatility. The analysis differentiates systematic risk across loan structure, metropolitan area, property type, time, seasoning period, and macroeconomic expectations (stress testing). The application directly provides complete time series measures of probability of default, loss given default, expected loss, and unexpected loss for a loan, portfolio, or securitized pool.

The service is used to quantify, compare, and manage the risk of loans, portfolios of loans, and tranches of CMBSs. The probability of default or loss given a default model creates a metric that allows the user to directly compare risk across loan structures, markets, and property types. The service is also used to decompose the sources of performance of debt instruments; price loans, portfolios, and securities more precisely; find mispriced items; and "test drive" new ideas for mortgage structures.

Reis, Inc.

A leading provider of commercial real estate market information to the investment community for more than 25 years, Reis, Inc. (www.reis.com), offers coverage of 80 U.S. metropolitan areas and more than 2,300 submarkets for the four principal property types. The company's flagship product, Reis Subscriber Edition, has been widely adopted by major institutional clients. For each metropolitan area and property type, Reis Subscriber Edition contains a full array of reports and tools, including:

▶ Market and submarket rents, vacancies, and inventory history and forecasts;

▶ *Asset Advisor*, an address-based report that provides the full Reis perspective on a given property and its surrounding area;

▶ Sales comparables, including trends in pricing and cap rates;

▶ Rent comparables;

▶ Narrative reports;

▶ Construction surveillance;

▶ Breakouts of market and submarket classes;

▶ Analysis of CMBS deals;

Before the development of Chesterfield Square in Los Angeles's South Central neighborhood in 2004, residents spent $900 million a year outside their neighborhood. An infill community shopping center, Chesterfield Square has some of the strongest sales in the region; its tenants are among the top performers for their respective chains, and they pay rents nearly as high as those on the west side of Los Angeles. *Cameron Carothers*

▶ Estimates of valuation and credit risk;

▶ Aggregation and analysis of portfolios.

All of Reis's information and analysis products are grounded in years of primary research on more than 200,000 apartment, office, retail, and industrial properties throughout the United States. Therefore, Reis is able to present market and submarket findings that are grounded in time series observations for properties rather than working backward to infer property performance from broad market assumptions.

Reis's output is weighted heavily in favor of the survey and quality assurance departments. Surveyors

are responsible for contacting owners, managers, and leasing agents to obtain information about the availability, rent, and lease terms for individual office and industrial buildings, shopping centers, and apartment complexes. Reis subjects all survey responses to a set of quality assurance and validation processes. For example, to ensure the integrity of data, data are checked and validated for both individual buildings and the aggregate market level (i.e., peer group, submarket, and metropolitan area). At the front end of the process, surveyors compare real-time data reported by building contacts with the previous record for the property and ask follow-up questions to verify any unusual changes in rents or vacancies.

On the back end, automated exception reports identify properties that deviate materially from their peer group or submarket averages. Follow-up telephone calls are used to verify or clarify information.

Aggregate market data for both the metropolitan area and the submarket are also subject to intensive quality controls. Reis's analysts are responsible for approving the results of the firm's market statistics; as part of the approval process, analysts compare Reis results with multiple local sources and reconcile discrepancies. Typically, differences among sources may result from the date of data collection, the methods employed, or the geography covered. If a discrepancy cannot be explained, analysts oversee any additional research required to ensure the integrity of Reis's market and submarket statistics.

Reis's clients use the company's findings in support of activities such as loan origination, acquisitions and underwriting due diligence, asset management and credit administration, strategic planning, market monitoring, and sale or securitization.

Torto Wheaton Research

Torto Wheaton Research (www.twr.com), an independent research firm owned by CB Richard Ellis, the world's largest real estate services company, provides research, data, analytical tools, and advisory services to its clients. TWR's research services are developed on a rigorous academic foundation using sophisticated data processing and modeling and leveraging progressive technologies to exploit the data and vast local knowledge of the parent firm.

TWR's services range from conducting customized research and analysis to interpreting data from off-the-shelf reports. TWR experts help clients analyze individual assets or a cross section of property types across the United States and Canada. It provides two main products for developers: TWR Outlook and TWR/Dodge Pipeline.

TWR Outlook provides quarterly forecasts on real estate fundamentals and capital markets across five property types (office, industrial, retail, multifamily housing, and hotel) by submarket. It provides forecasts of supply and demand, rents, and vacancy rates, and demographic and economic information

for 80 metropolitan markets and more than 700 submarkets throughout the United States and Canada. TWR Outlook can help developers:

▶ *Make accurate forecasts.* TWR uses well-tested market forecasts to design investment strategies and execute tactical decisions to buy, sell, and hold properties.
▶ *Develop leasing strategies.* Outlook provides information about future changes in rents, vacancy rates, and supply/demand drivers and about their timing, down to the level of submarkets.
▶ *Maximize returns and manage risk.* Outlook helps to anticipate changes in market fundamentals that will affect investment performance and the levels of tolerable risk.
▶ *Monitor market trends.* The service provides consistent, objective historical data to follow market and submarket fundamentals and identify trends.

The Torto Wheaton Research/Dodge Pipeline is a Web-enabled database and analysis tool for clients seeking detailed information about future commercial real estate supply in the United States and Canada. Developed in conjunction with McGraw-Hill Construction, Pipeline provides a single, comprehensive source of construction supply data, including property profiles (construction costs, start and completion dates, for example) and owner contact information, for more than 600,000 projects and six property types in various stages of development.

Pipeline tracks the complete development cycle of projects under construction from preplanning through completion as well as projects that have been deferred or abandoned. This information allows users to monitor changes in supply and to build an accurate picture of future revenue at each stage of the development cycle.

Pipeline provides unlimited search capabilities on project profiles for six property types (multifamily housing, office, retail, warehouse, housing for seniors, and hotels) and 55 subtypes. Clients can develop customized reports to track competitive developments, anticipate changes in supply, and manage exposure to risk. Its supply database provides detailed information about new construction in the preplanning stages, allowing users to identify new opportunities and contact prospects, owners, developers, and investors before projects break ground.

CoStar

CoStar Group, a publicly traded global company headquartered in Bethesda, Maryland, provides comprehensive property information for the commercial real estate industry. CoStar's suite of subscription-based online services includes several options:

▶ CoStar Property Professionals®, CoStar's flagship service, provides a comprehensive inventory of building information across all commercial property types and classes, including office, retail, and industrial. The service's retail component provides retail property search technology, demographics, mapping, photographs, and analysis tools. Subscribers also have access to powerful analytics that help track asset performance and project future trends in vacancies, rental rates, absorption, and more.
▶ CoStar COMPS Professional® provides the country's most comprehensive database of comparable sales transactions. These independently verified sales reports give users appraisal-grade access to the true story behind the sales, the principals behind corporate veils like LLCs and partnerships, and a perspective on market trends.
▶ CoStar Tenant® provides some of this country's most comprehensive information about commercial tenants—tenant profiles, lease expirations, occupancy levels, growth rates, square footage occupied, monitoring of competitive properties, and related activities.

CoStar's database numbers more than 1.2 million commercial properties with more than 5.1 billion square feet (474 million square meters) of available space as of mid-2006. The result of more than 20 years of rigorous research, the database is kept current by approximately 1,000 highly trained research professionals who canvass 66 major U.S. markets. Field researchers drive the streets in distinctive low-emission, high-tech

research vehicles photographing properties, interviewing principals, identifying space and for-sale listings, and monitoring new construction, among other tasks. Research analysts personally interview brokers, owners, property managers, and others; verify transactions; and research property details such as vacancies, subleases, lease expirations, building age, size, transaction history, true owners, cap rates, absorption, and more.

Flexibility in CoStar's online services accommodates a variety of search scenarios for commercial real estate developers, brokers, lenders, investors, owners, appraisers, and others.

The "search" and "results" features that work with CoStar's extensive database include:

▶ *Mapping functions:* Layered traffic counts, competitors for retail space, parcel boundaries, and major roads over map and aerial images;
▶ *Aerial images:* Pan and zoom features from regional to building level;
▶ *Analytics:* Forecasts of trends or tracking historical data for a particular building or market;
▶ *Demographics:* Use of census-derived demographics to find sites in particular income, population, and consumer-spending averages;
▶ *Reports:* Customizable, professional reports to support research findings.

CoStar provides a complement of more than 100 professionally designed reports that can be customized through a variety of print options.

Global Real Analytics, LLC

Global Real Analytics (GRA, www.graglobal.com) is a leader in creative applied real estate analytics, investment management, and commercial real estate index products, applying research, technology, and investment thought to global real estate investing. On January 1, 2007, Charles Schwab Investment Management (CSIM), the asset management arm of the Charles Schwab Corporation, announced its acquisition of GRA.

Maintained and published under agreements between Standard & Poor's (S&P) and GRA/CSIM, S&P/GRA commercial real estate indices are designed to be reliable and consistent benchmarks for

In 2002, Las Vegas, Nevada, had 38 million visitors, and Atlantic City, New Jersey, had 33 million; both cities had gaming revenues of around $4.3 billion. Yet Las Vegas's visitors spent an additional $4.5 billion in nongaming expenditures, while Atlantic City's visitors spent a paltry $300 million. Developed to improve the situation, the 56 restaurants and outlet stores of Atlantic City Outlets have increased the amount visitors spend when not gambling and is responsible for increasing hotel bookings by 58 percent and the number of conventioneers by 312 percent. *Dixon Photography*

commercial real estate prices by property sector and geographic region. The indices monitor closed commercial real estate sales transactions, weighing price values by asset quality, market, and sector inventory.

The initial index series comprised ten commercial real estate indices: a national composite, five geographic regions, and four national property sectors. The indices are published monthly and are available for trading futures and options on futures on the Chicago Mercantile Exchange and for over-the-counter trading through Standard & Poor's.

SUMMARY

A major question we set out to answer is how accurate forecasts are. Given the divergence in information, forecasts clearly are not all the same. So how should the analyst choose which supplier to use? Following are some general guidelines:

1. Buying real estate is expensive relative to buying forecasts, so you should buy more than one forecast. In making your decision, you should certainly diversify across demand suppliers.
2. Remember that the whole forecasting process starts at the macrolevel with someone's subjective judgment on a few key exogenous variables. All services provide you with their list of variables and assumptions, leaving you to judge for yourself whether the assumptions are reasonable.
3. You should probably choose suppliers that have an explicit dependent variable that is of interest

to you over suppliers that create indices. Using regression methods to weight the relative importance of the demand- and supply-side factors reduces the amount of subjectivity in the forecast.

4. If your potential supplier has been producing forecasts for a number of years, it should be able to provide you with measures of forecast accuracy. It is important to note that some suppliers that use regression methods estimate MSA-specific regression models with the dependent variable a function of its own lagged value plus demand and supply variables. These models are simply time series models—and relatively short time series models at that. Therefore, you should not be impressed by r-squareds of 90 percent or higher. This information is relatively easy to obtain. You should be more interested in the cross sectional performance of MSAs (at any particular time, do you want to buy a building in Dallas or San Francisco?). This calculation is a lot harder to do well, resulting in relatively low r-squareds.

5. Employment data for MSA-level forecasts, which undergo wholesale revision in March every year, are critically important. It is important to understand how fast these data are incorporated into your supplier's forecast. Experience shows that there is a three- to four-month difference in the speed with which BLS data are incorporated into the various demand-side forecasts.

It is important to remember that, whether you are buying a final forecast based on regression methods or an index, either implicit or explicit weights are used to combine the supply and demand variables. These weights—whether objectively obtained by regression methods or set subjectively—are based on historical information ("forecasting the past with ever greater precision"). If the future relationship between demand and supply variables changes in some fundamental way, then regardless of how well a model fits the past, the forecast for the future will be imprecise. If we believe, for example, that technology will fundamentally alter the amount of warehouse space needed by drastically reducing inventories, then we may need to adjust forecasts accordingly.

TERMS

▶ Benchmark
▶ Bias adjustment factors
▶ Endogenous variables
▶ Equilibrium
▶ Exogenous variables
▶ Lag
▶ Linear combinations
▶ Regression analysis weights
▶ Supply and demand

REVIEW QUESTIONS

18.1 How does real estate differ from most other commodities, and how do supply and demand models accommodate that difference?

18.2 Explain the difference between structural equation models and reduced form models.

18.3 How do users deal with the assumptions that different data providers use when making their forecasts?

18.4 The text states that the government is the ultimate source of employment data and that most of the data are estimates rather than actual numbers. What implication does this observation have for a forecaster?

18.5 Forecasts offered by the data services presented in this chapter will differ from each other. How does a user make sense of those differences and decide which one is "correct"?

NOTES

1. See www.economy.com and www.globalinsight.com for more information.

2. Very complete information about the surveys can be obtained from the BLS Web site, www.bls.gov/bls/proghome.htm.

3. Bureau of Labor Statistics, *Handbook of Methods* (Washington, D.C.: U.S. Government Printing Office, 1997), Chap. 5.

PART VII

MAKING IT HAPPEN

The diverse, creative work that goes into starting a development comes together in stages four, five, six, and seven.

During stages four and five, the nitty-gritty negotiations and detailed agreements are completed, allowing the project to begin construction. During this time, many decisions are made that will affect how well and how quickly the development is completed. Now the developer moves from the role of creator/promoter to that of manager, ensuring that time, budget, and all the participants' responsibilities are as tightly controlled as possible.

By the time a developer initiates stage six—construction—his commitment to a project is nearly irreversible, because the decision to back out from that point on would result in a tremendous financial and professional loss. Stage seven—completion and formal opening—is the initial test of how well everything was done. In this stage, users begin their assessment of the development, from the building itself to the services and amenities.

CHAPTER 19

Stages Four and Five: Contract Negotiation and Formal Commitment

Stage three of the development process—the formal feasibility study—brings together all previously completed research and projections into summary statements of value and costs. If the project is feasible, its estimated value is expected to exceed costs (broadly defined). With data, knowledge, analysis, and experience indicating that the project is feasible, the developer has the necessary information to complete the assembly of the development team. Thus, the feasibility analysis serves as a sales and negotiating tool and as a coordinating device in stage four, contract negotiation. During stage four, contracts are arranged to implement the decision to proceed with the project; during stage five, these contracts are executed.

A detailed agreement should be negotiated with and documented for each member of the development team. The developer must ensure that all the different aspects of the project are covered by the collection of individual contracts and that the various relationships among players are clearly defined. Because many of the contracts are contingent on one

another, stage five represents the joint execution of the contracts negotiated in stage four.

Contracts are another method of controlling risk. They set forth the rules for the physical, financial, marketing, and operating activities that will occur during construction, formal opening, and operation (stages six, seven, and eight, respectively). If all contracts are properly drawn and are consistent with each other, then the collective risk of all members of the development team is reduced. With proper structuring of the contracts, the developer will be able to spread the risks appropriately among the participants.

A major transition occurs in a development as it moves from stage three to stage six; stages four and five are the last opportunity to back out before major construction costs are incurred. During stage four, negotiations ensure that the project idea is still feasible as all feasibility details are confirmed in a set of formal contracts that make the costs explicit and as free of ambiguities as possible. Once the documents are executed in stage five, most of the players no longer retain the option to get out of the deal. In reality, of

The authors are indebted to the law firm of Cox, Castle & Nicholson LLP, Los Angeles, for its contributions to this chapter.

course, it is still possible to quit, but the pain (for breach of contract) can be intense and costly after contracts have been executed. During the earlier stages, developers are primarily idea generators and promoters. As the process moves toward construction, however, the developer's role becomes that of primary negotiator who brings together all the members of the team. And in stage six, the developer's role shifts to manager of the development team.

This chapter covers the following issues involved in contract negotiation (stage four) and formal commitment (stage five):

▶ Arranging financing;
▶ Environmental issues;
▶ Decisions about design and contractors;
▶ Decisions about major tenants;
▶ Decisions about equity;
▶ The government as a partner; and
▶ Commitment, signing contracts, and initiating construction.

STAGE FOUR: CONTRACT NEGOTIATION

Like the other stages of the development process, everything interacts in stage four. For example, the players do not negotiate financing without first considering the impact of the timing of financing on construction. Because so many different elements must be clarified and potential problems identified at this stage, the discussion that follows covers a variety of issues. It begins with construction and permanent financing and other sources of investment capital. It then moves to the handling of hazardous materials and other environmental concerns; consideration of contracts with architects, engineers, and contractors; leases with tenants; and contracts with financial partners during the development period and long-term equity investors.

Keep in mind as you read about stage four that, because of their many interactions, the topics are covered in a somewhat arbitrary fashion. Nowhere are these interactions more evident than in the financing arena. For example, environmental concerns must be satisfactorily addressed; acceptable architects,

engineers, and contractors must be located; preleasing or presales of a significant amount of space may be required; and the identity and contributions of any financial partners during development and long-term equity investors should be firm before the commitment for permanent financing is signed. The fewer uncertainties that exist, the less risk to the lender and the better the financing rates and terms to the developer/borrower.

The market study (Chapters 17 and 18) and the investment analysis contained in the feasibility study (Chapter 16) are part of the raw material for the loan application. Historically, developers began arranging financing by seeking a permanent lender and obtaining a permanent loan commitment and then finding a construction lender and negotiating a construction loan. Recently, it has become more common for developers to seek a construction loan without prearranging the takeout of the construction loan by a permanent loan. Given both the historical context and current customs and practices, this analysis of financing issues begins with a discussion of construction lending and then focuses on permanent financing. The discussion of construction lending includes a discussion of dynamics between construction lenders and permanent lenders, the "administrative" side of the financing challenge. And while you are reading this chapter, recall the "economic" logic for each lender or investor covered in Chapters 7 through 9.

Arranging Financing: The Construction Lender

As noted, construction lenders historically made development loans conditioned on the developer's obtaining a commitment from a so-called permanent lender; the permanent lender would provide assurance to the construction lender that, if the project is built on time, on budget, and consistent with approved construction drawings, the construction lender's loan will be paid off ("taken out") at a certain time.[1] With a permanent loan commitment in hand, the construction lender does not have to assume market or other long-term risk.

The degree to which the construction lender relies on the permanent lender's commitment is a

▶ **PROFILE**

PAMELA D. BUNDY

Washington, D.C.

In the predominantly male-dominated real estate development industry, it is no surprise that an African American female would spark curiosity for achieving flying success. So has been the case for Pamela Bundy. Bundy was born and raised in a rural Virginia town; neither of her parents earned a high school diploma. Her first job was in the family business: farming. During the summers, she and the rest of her family traveled to her uncle's tomato fields to pick tomatoes for 20 to 25 cents per basket. Although she lived very modestly in her younger years, she developed some crucial skills that would prove beneficial in her future career in real estate—a hard work ethic and the financial savvy acquired through her weekly trips to the bank to review the family's financial statement on behalf of her parents. "I knew from an early age that to control my own destiny, I had to control my money," Bundy remembers. The Friday trips to the bank bred an invaluable fiscal understanding.

Farm life was not for Bundy, and after graduating from high school, she set out for Lincoln University in Pennsylvania. It was there that she gained a broader cultural understanding and experienced many firsts. She admits to never having eaten Chinese food or having gone to a Broadway show before she went to college. After receiving a degree in psychology, Bundy considered graduate school but ultimately headed to the West Coast to enter the corporate world.

Southland Corporation's 7-Eleven is where she ended up. As a middle manager, the position brought her back to the East Coast, where she eventually settled in Washington, D.C. A blessing in disguise, being laid off from her position ignited an entrepreneurial fire that led Bundy into the real estate field. Having only a basic interest in real estate before the loss of her job, Bundy knew she wanted to be self-employed, so she took real estate appraisal courses and became a certified appraiser. Initially, to cut costs, she moved out of her apartment and into her grandmother's house and worked from there. She became committed to entering the real estate market on her own.

Her first investment was the renovation of a 5,000-square-foot (465-square-meter), four-story house in a low-income neighborhood. After turning over the house for a profit, she sought out similar residential projects she could "flip" as well. After a decade, she had accumulated enough capital to make the leap into the realm of upscale residential and commercial development.

Persistence led to one of her first major commercial deals. After deciding to try her hand at high-end residential development, Bundy pored over the market in search of the ideal location. Settling on a parcel at Logan Square, Bundy found herself

Completed in 2004 by the Bundy Development Corporation, the Icon is a 26,000-square-foot (2,415.5-square-meter) infill condominium project in the revitalized Logan Circle neighborhood of Washington, D.C. Bundy Development Corporation

in line to speak to the owner behind several larger established developers. Undaunted, she stopped by to try to meet with the owner on her way to the gym each morning. This diligence paid off when she was granted the right to develop the property, much to the chagrin of the other developers.

Larger projects thrill Bundy because she works with a different team for each one. She has no in-house employees save for an accountant/assistant and commits only to projects that she selects. She stresses that no cookie-cutter formula can be applied to new developments. "Each deal is like a piece of artwork with its own different needs," Bundy asserts.

To stay competitive in Washington's evolving market, Bundy has begun attending Harvard Business School. "I recognize that I am a female pioneer," she says, "but the market

continued on next page

has changed." She plans to branch out from the D.C. market to explore other regional options such as a 100-acre (40-hectare) farm plot in Greenville, North Carolina, where she could develop single-family detached houses—a first for her.

To date she has developed primarily residential projects in and around the District of Columbia, but Bundy has landed spots on teams to develop two major sites downtown. The first is redevelopment of the Washington Convention Center site, the second a large mixed-use project on the site of the former Wax Museum. Combined costs of the two projects are expected to exceed $1 billion, and she will work with the likes of Hines, the real estate development giant, and renowned British architect Sir Norman Foster.

Civic engagement is a priority for Bundy, and she generously gives her time to local causes. For her pioneering accomplishments in real estate, she has received several awards, including the 2004 Women Who Mean Business Award from the *Washington Business Journal* and the 2004 Entrepreneur of the Year Award from the Parren J. Mitchell Foundation. Bundy attributes her success to being a good student. She has found role models in the industry who became mentors and followed their counsel.

Her advice to aspiring developers: "Be willing to walk away from a deal. If you are bringing substantial equity for a project, and they are not offering you a fair share of the profits, walk away."

factor of both the construction lender's internal practices and the willingness of permanent lenders to issue commitments for takeout financing. Some construction lenders rely on the permanent loan commitment for repayment. Depending on the construction lender's internal practices, it will either not lend more than the permanent loan's initial funding amount unless and until the economic conditions for subsequent permanent fundings are satisfied or, more problematic for the developer, until each condition of the permanent loan commitment, short of completion of the improvements, is satisfied. Other construction lenders may agree (with the permanent lender) that the portion of the construction loan not covered by the initial permanent loan funding will be placed into a subordinate position on the project, subject to repayment upon satisfaction of the conditions for the subsequent funding.

Given the relationship between the construction loan and the permanent loan, anticipating what the permanent lender will require for loan approval can represent a threshold for obtaining the construction loan. The most crucial part of the feasibility study (completed in stage three) for long-term lenders is the market analysis. Most long-term lenders look at the feasibility study submitted by the developer and then adjust it according to their own perceptions of the market. Sophisticated permanent lenders maintain a substantial database on the markets where they lend

money. They underwrite the loan—that is, they analyze the market, the cost of the proposed project, and the demand for the project—based on their perception of community needs. The feasibility study is the developer's sales tool to "help" the lender's underwriting.

Depending on the state of the market, some construction lenders may not require permanent commitments as a condition of loan approval. Even without the express requirement, however, construction lenders typically expect that they will be paid off in a short time and therefore usually view their risk as short term.

As described in the finance section (Part III), short-term loans tend to come from institutions with shorter-term liabilities in their portfolios. Balancing asset and liability maturities reduces the institution's risk. For that reason, commercial banks are the leading construction lenders. With thousands of commercial banks across the country, the institutions (or their branch operations) are more likely to be located close to a given project; accordingly, they are able to supervise construction and reduce risk. Construction lenders that are not located near a project often engage local construction disbursement agents to supervise the project in their absence.

Given the lender's time horizon, a construction lender focuses on the developer's experience and reputation, the professionalism of the architect, the reputation of the general contractor, the complexity of the project, and other risks specific to the project. The more complex the project and the more inexperienced the developer and other participants in the process, the greater the risks to the construction lender.

For major projects, it is not unusual for a number of lenders to collectively provide construction financing. A single lender may not want to assume the multimillion-dollar risk inherent in a large project. The structures for such an arrangement are varied, ranging from a traditional loan participation arrangement in which a lead lender commits to making the loan and seeks out loan participants who have no direct relationship with the developer, to an agency lending arrangement in which each lender executes its own commitment with the developer and one of the lenders is appointed as the agent to act on behalf of all lenders in dealing with the developer. The latter option is riskier for the developer, as no lender agrees to fund any shortfall that may arise as a result of another lender's failure to fund its share of the loan.

The interest rate on a construction loan typically varies and is most often tied to some index, generally the lender's prime rate or LIBOR (London interbank offered rate). Depending on the index, the lender typically charges a spread over the index from one to two points (for a prime-based lender) to as much as four points (for a LIBOR-based lender). Because these indices can be volatile in a rapidly changing global financial market, a risk exists that the interest reserve in the construction loan may not be large enough to accommodate unanticipated increases in the interest rate. During periods of low interest rates, lenders often require a minimum (or "floor") interest rate, ranging from 4 percent to 6 percent. Borrowers, mindful of the interest escalation of the 1980s, often bargain for a maximum (or "ceiling") rate as well.

The conditions under which the developer is permitted to draw down the construction loan can be the source of a great deal of negotiation. Typically, the developer and construction lender agree on a line-item budget for the project (usually based on the feasibility study), with draws advanced against that budget. Many lenders do not permit draws against a particular line item if, in the opinion of the lender's consultants, the draws will leave insufficient funds in

the line item to complete that portion of the project. Most lenders, however, permit the developer to use a portion of the "contingency" line item in the budget to cover a shortfall or to move any savings in other line items into a deficient line. If neither of these devices is available, the loan may become "out of balance"; that is, sufficient funds will not be available to complete the project. The lender may then require the developer to deposit sufficient funds with the lender to bring the loan into balance; the lender will disburse the developer's funds first. Developers can generally persuade a lender to agree, however, that demonstrable cost savings relative to a particular line item can be added to the "contingency" line item.

Alternatives available to developers who do not care to place their cash with the lender include providing the lender with additional security, such as a letter of credit, to ensure that sufficient funds will always be available to complete the project. Reluctantly, a developer (or the development period venture partner) may put up additional cash or provide the additional security if 1) the developer believes he will ultimately achieve substantial cost savings when bringing the loan into balance, or 2) the anticipated value of the project justifies a potential infusion of cash. Clearly, construction lenders need to keep a close watch on the entire construction and funding process to avoid any loss in the event of foreclosure.

Arranging Financing: The Permanent Lender

As noted, construction lenders sometimes require a permanent lender to "preapprove" certain of the closing conditions in the permanent loan commitment as part of the takeout commitment. Regardless of the specific terms of the financing, the permanent lender provides longer-term capital than the construction lender and thus assumes some of the project's longer-term market risks.

Historically, the developer and lender expected financing to remain in place through one or more market cycles. Under those conditions, permanent loans ran for 30-year terms on a fixed-rate, fully amortized basis. In recent years, the permanent lending community has attempted to limit the market risk it is willing to accept. The result has been shorter loan terms' "ballooning" (coming due) in five to ten years but still with 30-year loan amortization schedules or interest-only or partial interest-only loans. (Recall from the financing section that longer amortization schedules are helpful in terms of the debt service coverage ratio.) Further, interest rates on some loans now are adjusted periodically so that the lender is somewhat insulated from (and the long-term owner exposed to) major shifts in interest rates.

Competition is a key consideration for permanent lenders. The astute permanent lender analyzes the postdevelopment market needs of the community, comparable projects under construction, and sites that, while not under construction, offer the potential for long-term competition. Permanent lenders are concerned with the project's ability to sustain cash flows sufficient to pay operating expenses and debt service over the term of the loan. At the same time, they need to anticipate potential demand for the project at the date of any balloon payment, thereby minimizing the risk that no replacement financing will be available.

The development and project management team play a major role in the lender's decision making. The permanent lender looks to the leasing and property management capabilities of the developer or, if these services are not to be provided by the developer, to the brokers and the management company to be engaged by the developer. Specifically, the permanent lender is interested in any management contract that the developer proposes to execute and the capability and experience of the management company. Understandably, the long-term management track record of the developer and/or management company is a prime consideration for the permanent lender, as poor management can adversely affect the property income stream and thus the ability to make debt service payments and reduce the collateral value of the property.

As the lender analyzes the proposal in light of its understanding of the market, it might also determine whether the loan fits into its portfolio. Most lenders have crafted diversification strategies that require diversification by region, product type, developer, and tenant. Further, many lenders attempt to match

permanent loan receipts (assets) on the one hand with payment obligations (liabilities) on the other. For example, if an insurance company has guaranteed a certain yield to a pension fund as part of an investment contract for a defined period of time (referred to as a GIC or guaranteed investment contract), the lender will attempt to match the term of the pension investment contract (liability) with the term of the permanent loan (asset).

Once the lender decides to make a loan on the project, it either issues a commitment letter or accepts the developer's application for financing. Both the letter and the application typically include loan amount, interest rate, term of the loan, and a period of time within which the loan must be closed, i.e., funded by the lender. In short, in the context of the so-called takeout loan, both documents provide that the lender will make the described loan within a certain time, say, 24 to 36 months in the future, upon the satisfaction of certain terms and conditions. Such conditions usually include completion of the project in accordance with approved plans and specifications, satisfaction of any leasing requirements, and proof of acceptable title insurance and an ALTA (American Land Title Association) survey.

Today, a new issue confronts developers, largely as the result of three concurrent influences: permanent lenders' portfolio management, the go-forward funding nature of the commitment, and historically low interest rates. Because of the confluence of these issues, permanent lenders are more frequently entering into interest rate "swaps" and "hedges" to protect them if the interest rate for the committed permanent loan is lower than the prevailing interest rates at the date of funding. In some way, the lenders attempt to pass the cost of an interest rate "hedge" to the developer.

The precise economic terms of a loan depend on the availability and cost of financing in the capital markets generally and other market conditions that bear on the relative bargaining strength of the parties. Often, the amount of the permanent loan is funded in stages according to the ability of the project to achieve certain leasing levels. In such cases, the major portion of the loan is funded upon satisfaction of physical construction. Additional amounts are funded as leases are signed for more than preestablished rates and with tenants of acceptable quality.

Arranging Financing: The Mezzanine Lender

Conventional financing, i.e., construction financing and/or permanent financing, does not always fund all development costs. Typically, construction loans fund only 60 to 75 percent of development costs, and permanent loans are usually for an amount equal to, and in some instances slightly more than, the construction loan. Only with a truly great development idea is the permanent loan sufficient to permit the developer to recoup all the equity investment.

In the past, developers used a variety of equity structures (partnerships, syndications, private placements, and others) to raise the shortfall to complete the development. (A discussion of equity structures follows.) In recent years, however, a new source of funding has become more available: mezzanine financing.

Originally, mezzanine financing typically was used for speculative developments where the goal was to sell the project in three to five years. Now, mezzanine financing is used in a variety of circumstances where a developer wants to get his equity investment out earlier or wishes to obtain financing in lieu of equity, thereby minimizing his risk.

Basically, the mezzanine lender makes a loan to the developer or the equity holders in the development (i.e., the partners, members, or shareholders) in an amount ranging from 50 percent to as much as 100 percent of the shortfall between the construction lender's (or permanent lender's) loan and the equity investment. For example, assume that the total costs for a particular development are $10 million and that the developer can obtain $7.5 million in construction financing. As an alternative to raising the $2.5 million in equity, a developer might consider obtaining mezzanine financing for a substantial portion, say $1.5 million, of the required "equity" investment. In this situation, the developer limits his investment to $1 million and, through the leverage, improves the residual equity's tax position. The project must generate sufficient cash flow to cover the higher debt service of the permanent and mezzanine debt.

Mezzanine lending is inherently riskier than conventional lending. The mezzanine lender usually requires the loan to be secured by a subordinate deed of trust. More often than not, however, the "senior lender" (i.e., the construction lender or the permanent lender) will not permit a junior encumbrance, and the mezzanine lender is forced to secure the loan with a pledge of the equity in the developer. In either event, the mezzanine lender's security is less secure than the first priority lien granted to the conventional lender.

The inherent risk underlying mezzanine financing translates into higher borrowing costs, which come in the form of more loan fees and higher interest rates than conventional development loans (first liens). Moreover, in addition to higher standard loan costs, mezzanine lenders may require a share of the profits. So-called "participation interests" usually amount to both a share of the project's cash flow after financing (if any) until the project is sold or the mezzanine loan is otherwise repaid, and a percentage of the profits from the sale (i.e., the net proceeds after payment of the development loan, repayment of the principal amount of the mezzanine loan, and a return of any cash equity contributed by the developer). As an incentive to developers to finish projects on time and to lessen the risk to mezzanine lenders, mezzanine lenders may require that their percentage of participation interest increase over the term of the loan.[2]

Sources of Development Financing

The evolution of global financial markets continues apace. From the perspective of real estate development, several things have happened over the last ten or 15 years that have created new opportunities. Specifically, we have seen further consolidation in banking, volatile behavior from the large life insurance companies, and a significant increase in the lending presence of Wall Street.

During the 1990s, considerable consolidation, particularly among the large banks, reduced the number of depository institutions in this country. In the 1980s, no one would have thought that North Carolina National Bank would become NationsBank and eventually acquire Bank of America. It was a period of rapid evolution at the top of the American commercial banking business. The new financial giants are clearly aggressive and determined to serve a bigger part of the overall financial community than commercial banks have traditionally served.

From the perspective of real estate, this change has meant that the larger financial institutions are now financial supermarkets. They make construction loans, they originate permanent loans and sell them to others, and, in general, they continue to look for new ways to generate fees through service to their customers. Clearly, developers can explore multiple options with large commercial banks. As always, the overall cost of financing, the size of the loan, and the "flexibility" of the loan terms are the developer's concerns.

Life insurance companies have traditionally been a major source of financing for commercial real estate. As noted earlier, life insurance companies have invested in multifamily lending and commercial lending and have held extensive portfolios of commercial real estate equity. The introduction of risk-based capital rules in the early 1990s gave big insurance companies the incentive to move away from equity ownership. They have done so but have maintained a significant position in commercial real estate lending. Unlike banks, life insurance companies have focused primarily on longer-term commercial lending.

The big change for large life insurance companies has been the reintroduction of correspondent programs, i.e., subcontracting some of the loan origination work to outside firms to be able to maintain a national presence without the full cost of staff in multiple markets. The new correspondent firms are very cost efficient, which allows the life insurance companies (through their correspondents) to make not just very large loans but also smaller loans. Thus, small developers as well as large developers now have access to the pools of savings managed by large life insurance companies.

Wall Street now provides a variety of funding sources. As explained earlier, many commercial loans now are packaged and securitized, allowing real estate borrowers to reach a much larger audience of savers and investors. The S&L crisis in the late 1980s brought about the packaging of existing loans and loan portfolios held by defunct S&Ls, and thus began the securitization trend. Today the vast majority of new commercial mortgage–backed securities (CMBSs) come from "conduit programs."

Conduit loans are originated specifically to be securitized. Some conduit loans are originated by Wall Street lenders. In addition, to increase loan pools, Wall Street firms also have correspondent relationships with mortgage bankers located around the country. The local mortgage bankers originate loans under terms specified by the investment banks, with the loans then pooled by the investment banks (possibly with the investment banks' own loan portfolios) and securitized.

This conduit structure allows developers to tap a vast new array of investors for financing through the Wall Street–operated conduit. The permanent loans usually are nonrecourse to the developer (that is, the lender may look only to the collateral for recovery) and are very competitively priced. Further, conduit lenders generally hold themselves out as able to close quickly.

Although attractive, conduit loans also come with exacting rules for "documenting" loans, as loan originators do not intend to be the ultimate investor/lender. In particular, conduit lenders require complex lock-box agreements and have stringent insurance requirements. Further, in an effort to protect the real property security from the developer's creditors, conduit lenders insist that the developer's company be structured in a certain way (so-called bankruptcy-remote, single-purpose entities), which may result in higher transaction costs for the developer.

Conduit lenders also need to answer to investors' need for long-term stability with regard to the income stream of the loan pool. As a consequence, conduit lenders also use a variety of provisions to protect the income stream by restricting prepayment of the loans. The first such method is a prohibition against prepayment of the loan for some but not all of the term. Depending on the term of the loan, the so-called "lockout" period ranges from one year from the date of funding (for short-term loans) to as much as seven to ten years from the date of funding (for longer-term loans). Although not a problem for every developer, developers need to consider whether or not these restrictions materially affect their exit strategy. The second such method is the requirement that a premium accompany any prepayment. For example, the lender may require a "yield maintenance" premium penalty, which maintains the yield or interest rate to the lender during the remaining term of the loan if the loan is prepaid. Thus, the prepayment penalty is the interest shortfall that the developer must actually make up to maintain the lender's yield or interest rate (which, depending on the term of and interest rate on the loan, can be significant).

In a twist on the basic story, conduit lenders may prohibit any prepayment but nevertheless permit the developer to obtain a release of the real property collateral if the developer purchases replacement collateral that will provide the same income stream as the loan over the term of the loan. When the real property collateral is replaced with so-called "defeasance collateral," typically U.S. Treasuries, the loan remains outstanding, but the borrower has obtained a release of the property from the conduit lender's lien. To obtain a similar income stream, however, the developer must purchase U.S. Treasuries that replicate the loan payments and loan balance at maturity. This requirement, for obvious reasons, severely limits the developer's ability to release the underlying real property collateral.[3]

The biggest current problem with CMBS financing involves ongoing loan administration. Selling a property encumbered with securitized debt takes longer than selling the same property with traditional nonsecuritized debt. Further, with traditional debt, the long-term investor can much more easily change loan terms if the change benefits the lender. With a securitized loan, changing terms is much more difficult.

The Common Thread in All Forms of Financing

A developer should ensure that all financing options are explored, by himself or a member of the development team or a third party retained to obtain the financing. Whoever is seeking the financing should try to stand in the lender's shoes. Only when the developer is able to anticipate all the ways the lender may be compensated (interest rates, points, participation, and so on) and appreciate any nonmonetary objectives the lender may have (compliance with new regulations, civic duties, among others) is the developer able to obtain the lowest overall cost of financing with the fewest restrictions. Finally, it remains important to fit the financing not just to the lending institution's financial and nonmonetary objectives

MUSEUM TOWERS
Financing

The way our company is set up, I'm the person who takes the lead in fighting with public officials and neighborhood groups. My partner lives in New York, and he's involved in every project but in a very different way from my involvement. He talks to the players on the phone, he reads everything, and he provides good counsel and financial support. He's excellent at dealing with the facts. He doesn't deal with tenants or permitting agents. He deals with the banks, the lawyers, the lawyers in the banks, and that's it. He's the first one to admit that if he were running the company on a day-to-day basis, we would never get anything permitted. Nothing would get built. And we'd have no tenants. His temperament and ego wouldn't allow him to sit through the public hearings. Being called an asshole and a liar in public on a nightly basis just doesn't sit well—nor should it—but it is what it is.

When we first financed the project, we got low-risk money—prime plus one. Not bad. But then, in 1994, we were forced to restructure the debt. I don't know if I can tell the story without crying. From 1990 to 1994 were the worst four years of my life. Everything had changed in real estate. You couldn't borrow money. The money you did borrow was outrageously expensive: you could borrow it from loan sharks on the North End of Boston for less. We found out we were close to getting construction of this project financed; in fact, Chase Manhattan Bank held the existing land mortgage that had financed cost overages (beyond our initial equity) up to this date (when you carry a project for years, the preconstruction costs are huge). We struck a deal on a repayment plan. But unbeknownst to us, while we were spending another $1 million to redesign and repermit the project, they sold the mortgage. The group they sold it to was a collection of bright, talented lawyers and finance people. You know how the guys on the North End that lend you money might come at you with baseball bats? Finance guys come at you with legal fees. It's the same thing. It's just slower and more painful the way they do it on Wall Street.

continued on next page

MUSEUM TOWERS *(continued)*

We spent eight months negotiating with our new lender, and it was a bare-knuckles fight. It's situations like this when you learn how good your partner really is and what you're made of. It was war.

The day before Thanksgiving, my wife called me in tears. She said the sheriff had just showed up at the house and left a bunch of boxes. I went home to my pregnant wife and two giant boxes. It's one thing to fight with me—it's another thing to get my wife and kids into it. So we got the largest law firm in Boston, which has some equally nasty litigators to represent them. We had nasty people on both sides. And the battle began. It was awful, but some of my greatest moments were in this fight. At one point, we met with their attorney, a good ol' boy, very calm and tranquil but a shark. He is like getting cut with a razor blade—deep, fast, seemingly not painful, but you bleed to death anyway. So he approached the problem by acknowledging that he realized that I didn't have any money, that it was really my partner who did, and that it wasn't worth suing me. So he suggested that they take me out of the deal but that I continue working for them. I told him that I wasn't interested in that kind of deal. He said, "Dean, we can make your life really miserable." I said, "I can make your life equally miserable. That land in Boston, without the permits, is worth nothing. And you know who controls those permits? Me. And you'll never see those permits." They hired local counsel and discovered that in fact I did control some of the permits and that the others would be difficult for them to get. In the end we got our money, but it was $3 million more than we were settling on with Chase. It was a horrible experience.

Once everybody had established his position and they understood what we had, they were reasonably pragmatic. To them it was just another transaction, just another restructuring: it was nothing personal like it was for my partner and me. We got the deal to work, and they made a ton of money on it. In the end they were decent guys. In fact, when we did a press announcement about Museum Towers, I got a handwritten note from the guy who runs the firm. Decent.

There are a couple of banks that to this day I hold some personal malice toward. That experience has given me a whole new view of working with lenders. Just like lenders want to know who their borrowers are, well, guess what: I want to know who the lender is. I won't allow the wholesale sale of our notes. We've walked away from three deals because they wouldn't give us the right of approval. That's a big difference in how we do business.

Of course, paying the original lender was just part of the story. We needed a construction loan. The Boston market had improved dramatically, and our now fully entitled land was very valuable. Still, we weren't able to get a construction loan to cover all the remaining costs. (Fleet Bank agreed to a floating rate, roughly 8 percent, on a $55 million first lien.) We found a higher-risk mezzanine lender to provide a participating second lien. For an expected total return of 21 percent, the Fidelity Real Estate Group closed the gap between the value of what we had created (our real cash invested was much larger) and what the lower-cost first lien holder would provide. The gap financing was expensive, but we felt that keeping most of the upside was the smart thing to do.

continued on page 466

---

but also to its self-image. Most institutions, for example, picture themselves as experts in certain areas or dedicated to leadership in certain fields. When a project "fits" the lender's self-image, the lender tends to stretch a little to get the business. Likewise, individual loan officers have self-images, and the smart borrower fits the financing to the individual loan officer as well as to the institution.

ENVIRONMENTAL ISSUES

Awareness of the environment increased dramatically in the 1970s as the courts took an active role in protecting the nation's natural resources. This awareness has picked up momentum in recent years, and today developers realize they must do more than simply ensure that their property does not violate any environmental protection laws. Such laws apply to the contamination of the environment by hazardous or toxic materials, wetlands protection, endangered species, and more. The federal, state, and local laws pertaining to these aspects of the environment are a starting point, but sensitive site planning, design, and construction in the development process can help turn restrictions into opportunities for healthier, more attractive, and more energy-efficient developments. Being environmentally friendly can be a sales tool.

Several federal and state laws profoundly affect real estate development. Two federal laws stand out: the Comprehensive Environmental Response,

Before Southside Works—a 34-acre (13.8-hectare) mixed-use project comprising apartments, offices, and retail spaces—could be developed, environmental remediation was needed because the land was once the site of a steel mill and designated a brownfield.
Walter Larrimore

Compensation, and Liability Act (CERCLA, more commonly known as the Superfund law) and the Clean Water Act. Lenders, developers, buyers, and sellers have all been touched by these far-reaching laws.

Hazardous Wastes: Everyone's Concern

In response to environmental contamination problems that were perceived to be no less than a crisis, Congress enacted CERCLA in 1980. The Superfund law was adopted not only to provide funding for at least a portion of the cleanup of the nation's worst toxic waste sites but also to establish powerful legal tools to allow both regulatory agencies and in some cases private parties adversely affected by contamination to force the responsible party to undertake a cleanup program or to

recover costs if the cleanup is undertaken by the claimant. Under Superfund and its subsequent amendments, present owners and certain past owners of land contaminated with hazardous substances can be liable for the entire cost of cleanup, even if the disposal of the material was legal at the time, even if the owner had nothing to do with the disposal, and even if the disposal occurred years before passage of the Superfund law. Often referred to as "potentially responsible parties" (PRPs), the categories of parties that can find themselves liable for the cost of remediating the contamination include 1) current owners and operators of the property; 2) former owners and operators of the property; 3) persons who arranged for the disposal or treatment of the hazardous materials at the property;

and 4) persons who accepted hazardous materials for transport to disposal or treatment facilities. Liability under CERCLA can be joint and several, meaning that an owner of the property found to be contaminated can be held responsible for the entire cost of the remediation and left to try to recover contribution from the culpable parties.

Superfund's all-inclusive liability scheme caught many developers and lenders off guard. In 1985, for instance, Shore Realty Corporation and its principal stockholder were each held responsible for cleaning up hazardous wastes on land only recently purchased, even though the corporation had neither owned the property at the time the wastes were dumped nor caused the release of toxins.[4] The court did not need to rely on the traditional (and often difficult) process of "piercing the corporate veil" to find the stockholder liable. Instead, it relied on a principle included in the Superfund legislation to determine that the stockholder had enough of a role in managing the hazardous materials after the corporate acquisition to qualify as an "operator." According to the background summary included in the court's opinion, the cleanup was estimated to cost more than Shore Realty paid for the property.

U.S. v. Fleet Factors has become probably the leading case involving a lender's liability adjudicated under Superfund with a lender deemed responsible for cleanup costs after foreclosing on contaminated property. The court held that the lender retained the "capacity to manage" the hazardous materials.[5] As a result of that case, lenders over the next several years commonly would not originate a loan for commercial or industrial property unless the property received a clean bill of environmental health. In an attempt to ameliorate the harsh results of the *Fleet Factors* decision, the U.S. Environmental Protection Agency (EPA) adopted regulations to clarify the secured-lender exemption language included in Superfund, but, in early 1994, the federal Circuit Court of Appeals for the First District invalidated the regulations. The EPA shortly thereafter announced it was considering an appeal of the ruling, and the Clinton Administration's proposed reauthorization bill for Superfund in 1994, which would have resolved the issue, was not passed by Congress. Finally, legislation in 1996 eliminated the "capacity to manage" test of *Fleet Factors,* and, as a result, lenders have now returned to the marketplace although still typically demanding a thorough environmental investigation as a condition of loan approval.

In response to the excessively onerous provisions of the Superfund law, the Superfund Amendments and Reauthorization Act of 1986 (SARA) created a defense for so-called "innocent landowners," that is, landowners who did not know and had no reason to know that the property they purchased was contaminated. This defense was expanded in 2002 with passage of the Small Business Liability Relief and Brownfields Revitalization Act (the "Brownfields Amendments"), which was designed to facilitate the acquisition and development of properties believed to be contaminated. The Brownfields Amendments expanded the defense to include three classes of protected land buyers: 1) the innocent purchaser who buys the property without knowledge of the on-site contamination; 2) the contiguous landowner who buys the neighboring property without knowledge that the property has been contaminated by a nearby property; and 3) the bona fide purchaser who buys the land knowing that it is contaminated. A discussion of the technical differences in these three defenses is beyond the scope of this text, but to qualify for any one of these defenses, the landowner must prove that he made all appropriate inquiries into previous uses of the property to uncover any possible evidence of contamination. The amendment states that until the EPA provides further guidance, to meet the standard of "all appropriate inquiries" for property purchased after May 31, 1997, a party seeking to acquire property should conduct a Phase I Site Assessment according to the standard set forth by the American Society for Testing and Materials, ASTM E-1527, which has established the current custom and practice for such investigations. Moreover, if contamination is subsequently found after acquisition, the landowner is required to take all reasonable steps to stop any continuing releases and prevent any threat of future releases.

Even if a landowner qualifies for one of the defenses under the Brownfields Amendments, the problem of contaminated property may only have begun. Contaminated property probably cannot be sold except at a discount related to the cost of cleanup. Further, if a public health threat is associated with the contamination (such as contamination that releases poisonous vapors into the structures above and below ground), the exculpation against cleanup costs provided by the defenses to CERCLA liability may very possibly prove ineffective as a shield from tort liability if the facts indicate a breach of duty to the public by the owner of the property where the problem originated.

Most real estate lenders have developed their own standards that generally require purchasers to conduct what has come to be known as a Phase I Environmental Site Assessment (also known as Phase I or an ESA), which sometimes goes well beyond the requirements of the ASTM procedure. The ASTM procedure is typically implemented by conducting, for example, a background check on previous users and owners of the property; a visual inspection of the site; a review of historical records, including aerial photographs, title reports, telephone listings, and insurance maps of the property (depending on which records are available); and a careful review of regulatory agency records. In the event that any steps in the initial review indicate the possibility of contamination, the borrower will likely be required to physically sample the soils and possibly the groundwater to fully investigate the site's environmental condition. Such sampling is often referred to as a Phase II Site Inspection or simply a Phase II.

Many states have enacted laws intended to require investigation and cleanup of hazardous waste sites within their borders. Among others, California has adopted its own version of legislation modeled after CERCLA. New Jersey has enacted legislation that has earned a reputation as perhaps the toughest body of hazardous waste laws in the country. Some state laws impose penalties if the landowner does not address the requirement for cleanup; for example, if the state of California cleans up a site after failure of a responsible party to comply with a cleanup order, then, under state law, the responsible party or parties may be assessed treble damages and the state may place a

lien on the property to recover its costs. Many state enactments provide for the imposition of a lien to allow the jurisdiction that conducted the remediation to recapture the public monies spent for the cleanup, thereby avoiding a windfall to the owner (that is, the restoration of market value to the previously contaminated site). A handful of those states have adopted so-called "superlien" laws that give the state claim priority over all other liens. Lenders obviously do not want their collateral to be subject to such risks. Consequently, properties with such problems are very difficult to finance. As might be expected in an entrepreneurial society, certain companies specialize in buying and cleaning such sites. One such firm is Cherokee Investments, which has been actively involved in many large-scale properties such as Xanadu at the Meadowlands in New Jersey.

Asbestos

Asbestos was used extensively for decades to insulate, fireproof, and soundproof all kinds of buildings, particularly commercial and industrial buildings. In the mid-1970s, however, following mounting evidence that asbestos posed significant health risks (particularly lung cancer), the EPA adopted regulations that for all practical purposes ended the use of asbestos materials in newly constructed buildings. Nevertheless, the EPA has estimated that more than 500,000 office buildings and more than 200,000 apartment buildings still contain asbestos. Depending on the condition of the asbestos in those buildings, owners may be sitting on a time bomb of future asbestos remediation.

Asbestos is a natural, fibrous material mined from the earth and found in numerous locations around the world. Its mere presence in buildings does not necessarily pose a hazard; only when it exists in a "friable" condition—that is, when it can be crumbled by hand pressure, thereby causing its fibers to become airborne—does it pose a danger. When they are inhaled, the tiny asbestos fibers may lodge in the lungs, which, research indicates, can lead to lung disease such as asbestosis and cancer. Fear of asbestos-induced illness and the potential resulting claims has made bankers and investors cautious of buildings

1n 1999, asbestos in the air circulation system led to abandonment of the Leverett Saltonstall Building, a 22-story government office tower in downtown Boston. As part of the building's renovation, a structure consisting of condominiums above street-level shops was built to wrap around the original building's facade. The office spaces in the original building were modernized and remediated, and the tower was rechristened 100 Cambridge, while the condominium complex was given the name Bowdoin Place. *Woodruff Brown Photography*

containing asbestos. Many lenders and investors can be expected to buy buildings containing asbestos only if the properties are offered at prices low enough to make asbestos remediation procedures (such as encapsulation or removal) economically feasible or if the asbestos is in such a condition that it does not pose a threat to human health.

In the mid-1980s, Congress enacted the Asbestos Hazard Emergency Response Act (AHERA) to address the concern related to risks created by asbestos used in

the construction of public schools. The program required all schools to be inspected by certified inspectors trained under guidelines established by the EPA. It further mandated preparation of a "management plan" if asbestos were identified. Commercial building owners have not yet been brought within a regulatory net similar to AHERA, but under the Clean Air Act, asbestos must be handled in a health-protective manner before a building is demolished. Building owners and managers may, additionally, face common law liability as a result of claims by persons exposed to asbestos. Relatively recent regulations promulgated by the Occupational Safety and Health Administration (OSHA) now impose duties on commercial building owners to safeguard employees against the risk associated with on-site asbestos.

A few states have adopted regulations governing buildings containing asbestos. In California, for instance, owners and lessees of buildings containing asbestos must inform their employees and certain other persons of the location and condition of asbestos in the building, the results of any studies to monitor the air, and any potential health risk stemming from exposure to asbestos.

In response to investors' jitters, many owners of buildings containing asbestos have spent considerable sums of money removing asbestos. Widespread removal of asbestos from buildings, however, may not only be exceedingly expensive but also exacerbate the problem by increasing the level of airborne fibers and the associated health risks. In the 1980s, the mere presence of asbestos panicked many people, but by the mid-1990s, science and the law came closer together so that asbestos became an understandable and manageable problem in redevelopment.

Wetlands

Until 1985, the federal government subsidized farmers for draining, plowing, and planting wetlands, and bogs, swamps, and marshes—commonly known as "wetlands"—were considered nuisances. Developers and farmers alike were encouraged to convert these "worthless" areas into productive uses. Since 1985, however, the situation has changed. After centuries of mistreatment, wetlands are now valued for their enormous environmental and economic importance.

Wetlands are one of the earth's most productive natural ecosystems. They have an extraordinary ability to shelter fish and wildlife, cleanse polluted and silt-laden water, and protect against floods. Over half of North American ducks nest in wetlands in the north central United States and southern Canada. And about two-thirds of U.S. shellfish and commercial sport fisheries rely on coastal marshes for spawning and nursery grounds.

As our understanding and appreciation of wetlands expand, so do the number and scope of federal and state laws to protect them. Under Section 404 of the Clean Water Act, for instance, developers must first secure a permit from the U.S. Army Corps of Engineers (the Corps) before building in certain wetlands and other "waters of the United States." This permitting process has become controversial for a number of reasons.

▶ First is the problem of what constitutes wetlands. Using the complex federal definition, land that would appear to be dry to a layperson may constitute wetlands subject to the permitting process. A related problem is federal jurisdiction over dry washes in the Southwest: Is a two-foot-wide (0.6-meter) wash that carries water only after a rare rainfall a water of the United States? Development in wetlands (or nonwetland waters) without a permit can lead to substantial fines and, in some cases, jail time.

▶ Second, there is no way to obtain judicial review of the Corps's determination that wetlands or other waters are present except by first seeking a permit or else by defending against an enforcement action that seeks to punish a landowner for developing in wetlands without a permit.

▶ Third is the considerable disagreement about the type of activity that is subject to regulation under Section 404 of the Clean Water Act. For instance, building in wetlands clearly qualifies as "fill" under the Act. Under current court decisions in some areas of the country, however, certain dredging, agriculture, and irrigation projects may not require a Section 404 permit. Most observers expect the United States Supreme Court to resolve the scope of Section 404.

▶ Fourth, the Corps has drastically limited the type and size of projects eligible for preapproved permits under the so-called Nationwide Permit Program. Projects that are not eligible for preapproved permits must obtain an individual permit through a complicated process subject to environmental review under the National Environmental Policy Act (NEPA). The Corps permitting program is time-consuming (a recent study indicated that the average time to obtain an individual permit was 373 days) and often involves review by several federal agencies, including the Corps, the EPA, and the Fish and Wildlife Service, and state agencies, including water quality and coastal zone management boards. As a result of the increasing complexity, cost, and duration of the permitting system, most developers seek to minimize permitting time by designing their projects with reduced impacts so as to qualify for Nationwide Permits.

▶ Finally, the Corps usually issues a permit on the condition that the developer mitigate any adverse impacts on wetlands stemming from the development. In addition, a growing number of states have adopted wetlands protection laws that are more stringent than the federal laws.

Ten years ago, only a few states had enacted laws protecting wetlands; now, over half the states have wetlands laws on the books, and the list is growing.

Before receiving an individual permit to develop on wetlands, developers must first demonstrate that, for so-called non-water-dependent uses such as a mall or a housing development, no practicable, nonwetland sites exist. (Water-dependent uses include, for example, marinas and ports.) Furthermore, both the Corps of Engineers and state regulators generally require developers to minimize adverse effects on wetlands and to compensate for any wetlands lost by restoring or creating wetlands nearby. This process is generally referred to as "wetlands mitigation."

Wetlands mitigation, particularly creating wetlands, has been controversial. Wetlands are complex, dynamic ecosystems, and early attempts to create them yielded mixed results. Environmentalists argued that artificially created wetlands could scarcely be considered adequate substitutes for natural wetlands. More recently, a number of successes have occurred as biologists improved their wetland creation and maintenance techniques. During the 1990s, the regulatory, development, and environmental communities cooperated in creating a number of "mitigation banks," which permanently preserved large areas of biologically sensitive habitat with funding collected as mitigation for wetland impacts.

Oleson Woods is a 32-unit, sustainably developed affordable housing complex in Tigard, Oregon. Developer and property manager Community Partners for Affordable Housing has turned an on-site wetland into an amenity and wrapped the project's townhouses around it. Since opening, more than 55 species of plants and animals—some of which are threatened—have been spotted there. *Carleton Hart Architecture*

The Corps has also gained substantial experience in how to write and enforce permit conditions that will ensure successful mitigation and provide fallback systems and other provisions to protect the environment in case the mitigation is not as successful as hoped. Even with these improvements in mitigation, however, federal permitting for projects involving wetlands or other waters of the United States remains very problematic.

Like asbestos, wetlands create risks for lenders and investors. The development feasibility should deal with such issues, as their mitigation is essential to obtaining financing. In stage four, expect the lawyers to be very careful to "cover" their clients for such risks.

Sustainable Development

Real estate development no longer occurs in a vacuum away from environmental realities. Savvy developers understand that citizens are more and more interested in environmental issues and that it often makes sense to involve them early in the development process. Developers also understand environmentally sustainable practices help establish a strong image for a project and, in some cases, even save money. Today sustainable, "green" development is moving into the mainstream as a building practice that can minimize environmental impact and land consumption.

In the last few years, many more tools and much more information on green and sustainable development have become available. One of the most valuable is the voluntary Leadership in Energy and Environmental Design (LEED) rating system developed by the U.S. Green Building Council, which has provided guidelines and a recognition system to promote green building practices. The LEED system began as a green building evaluation and has now expanded into other areas, including neighborhoods. The LEED Neighborhood Development (LEED ND) program measures developments by location efficiency, resource efficiency, environmental preservation, and compact, complete, and connected neighborhoods, with ratings based on such factors as density, transit access, balance between housing and jobs, mixed-income housing, and energy-saving features.

Successful green projects come in all sizes and shapes—from single-family houses to larger multifamily projects like Elevation 314 to large office buildings and skyscrapers. One of the earliest green buildings, the JohnsonDiversey global headquarters in Sturtevant, Wisconsin, was built in the late 1990s before many technologies and products became available. With a tight building envelope, a heat-recovery system, efficient mechanical systems, and energy management systems, it is estimated to use 60 percent less energy than the average for a comparable office building.

The Condé Nast building, completed in 1999 at Four Times Square in New York City, was among the first environmentally friendly skyscrapers in the United States. Among other things, it features photovoltaics and fuel cells for harnessing solar energy and systems for improved air quality. The building has received numerous awards, and it has consistently outperformed the market in terms of vacancy rate and absorption.

For many development projects, environmental issues are a routine but often complex part of the project. Museum Towers was built on an old industrial site located on the "tidelands" of a river, and the environmental issues took many years to work through.

DECISIONS ABOUT DESIGN AND CONTRACTORS

By the time they enter stage four, developers usually have at least preliminary drawings of the project, and it will be necessary to make final arrangements with the architect and other design professionals, including engineers, and begin to move toward final construction drawings. At some point, and certainly before the architect draws final plans, a contract must be drafted to establish the formal relationship between the developer and the architect.

It is often useful and necessary to designate the architect as the responsible party for all design matters, as developers have difficulty closing the permanent loan unless someone is professionally responsible for the quality of all work. Thus, the contract with the architect drives related contracts with other design professionals.

Although there are no wetlands on the site and it's not within a designated 100-year floodplain, the environmental issues were murder.

We tried in the late 1980s and early 1990s to win approval for our apartment complex. But much to my dismay, MEPA (Massachusetts Environmental Policy Act) exercised jurisdiction over the project, which meant we had to do a full environmental statement. Basically, it forces you to go to a multitude of different state agencies, commissions, and authorities. It opens up Pandora's box. On top of that, the Chapter 91 Division of Waterways exercised jurisdiction, claiming that the site was filled land and that the project was located in "historical tidelands" of the Charles River, so they had jurisdiction that could not be usurped by MEPA. It was like going to a football game and watching all the guys pile on the little running back. The process dragged on so long that, by the time we got the approvals, the market had changed and our project was no longer commercially viable.

About 65 percent of Boston is landfill. It used to be a series of islands interconnected by strips of land. Boston's Back Bay used to be a bay where ships anchored. The North End, where Boston started, was about half its current size. The filling of titled land, marshes, and wetlands was granted by the King of England in the 1600s and 1700s. These licenses were granted for the creation of facilities to support commerce. The theory was that the reduction of access to the water and marshes was justifiable because the creation of commerce created a benefit that inured to the body politic on a greater basis.

Fast-forward to the late 1970s and early 1980s, and all the lawyers in the commonwealth of Massachusetts are challenging developers because they don't have fee simple title—they have licenses. So it was decided that our buildings were a change of use of the "historical tidelands," because that's not what they were originally designated as; therefore, we had to go through a new permitting process to establish that what we wanted to do with this real estate addressed the spirit of the original license to create commerce or to create a benefit for the public good. They declared that the project proposal constituted a "non-water-dependent use of tidelands," and we had to prove that our project serves a proper public purpose and provides a net public benefit to the rights of the public in the tidelands. I submit that this process is absolutely irrational, irresponsible, and exploitative.

In the middle of all this, the planning board in the city of Cambridge exerted autonomy that it may or may not have had, and the city council tried to get its name on whatever projects it could to keep politically active. And two state entities were at war with each other: MEPA tried to demonstrate that it was the ultimate permitting agency of the state government, and the Chapter 91 Division of Waterways said that, when it came to waterfronts, it had all the authority. Then a new complication arose when the executive secretary of transportation and construction for the state said that the land was previously owned by the railroad and the railroad never got a signoff from the state transportation group. Under Massachusetts General Law 4054A, you have to get a release from the state transportation secretary to change property that was originally designated as transportation dependent to use it for non-transportation-related property. So then the circle widened to include the city of Cambridge, the planning board, MEPA, Chapter 91, and the executive office of transportation and construction.

They all wanted a piece of us. Not a small piece, but a big piece, and they all wanted the other guy to go first so they could come in and really chew us up. We spent an inordinate amount of time juggling and dancing among all these groups. And MEPA forces you to go to every involved agency, each with its own agenda. For example, Health and Human Services wanted a big low-income housing component. The Massachusetts Business Commission (MBC) wanted parks. Transportation wanted roads. It just kept going and going. So we took on all four groups in parallel and just tried knocking them off one at a time. Then we had to do an Environmental Notification (ENF), a special permit application.

Let me tell you, that was 1988 and a lot of other stuff was going on in the city of Cambridge. The secretary of transportation wanted to put in a river crossing from Federal Island to Cambridge. He was having a hard time getting it through, so he suggested that if I help him get the river crossing, he'd help me.

It gets more complicated. A lot of our troubles went back to the time when railroads were big. Railroads were given the power of eminent domain all over the country, so they could come in and, with compensation for you, take your home, your farm, and your business because they were building a railroad system. The concept was the loss to an individual was secondary to the gain of the entire body politic. So the railroads amassed huge landholdings, and when the railroads started cutting back, they went into the real estate development business. But the commonwealth of Massachusetts intervened and forced the railroads to go through the commonwealth with all their deals. As the regulator of transportation systems, the commonwealth had the right to decide whether the land should remain a transportation-related use or whether the short-term gain the railroads got on the real

MUSEUM TOWERS *(continued)*

North Point Park conveys a positive environmental message and is an outstanding amenity for Museum Towers and the city of Cambridge.

estate would hurt the long-term public transportation network. The secretary of transportation is given three bites at the apple. First, the railroad had to notify Transportation when they put the land on the market. The state can take it then. Second, before the title is transferred, the railroad had to go back to the commonwealth, when it can take the land at the same price. Third, and most difficult, is that when the local building department is going to issue a building permit, the new owner has to go back to the secretary of transportation and he has to approve the building permit. In our situation, that's the point where he wouldn't give us the approval—unless we could work with him on getting the river crossing. Of course, the city of Cambridge wanted us to do the opposite. They wanted us to work against him.

MEPA was unbelievable. We did an ENF, a draft environmental impact statement, a final environmental impact statement, a supplemental final environmental impact statement, and a supplemental supplemental environmental impact statement.

But in 1998, by the time our project was built, the state began easing some of the environmental burdens on developers. The idea is that the reform efforts will ensure a faster review process among state agencies, eliminate filing of the same forms with different agencies, and stuff like that. In theory, things that took months or years to get approved will now take only a few weeks.

If I were buying this site today, without permits, I'd pay only $1 million. But it took $3.5 million just in permit costs.

continued on page 478

Most architects prefer to use the American Institute of Architects (AIA) standard contract (B-141), which was revised in 1997 (see Figure 19-1). It is usually rewritten every ten years, with occasional supplements added as needed. Of course, developers must be careful not to execute the AIA contract blindly. Like all contracts in stage four, it must be negotiated and executed so that all parties agree to produce the appropriate product, with risks and responsibilities clearly defined. The AIA standard contract is frequently modified to add items not covered, such as responsibility for professional errors and omissions insurance, indemnification, and any expanded scope of services. In fact, lenders might require several changes to the contract. What is omitted from the standard AIA contract is as important as what is included.

Because the contract was drafted by AIA, it clearly protects the architect in various ways. Therefore, developers have a strong incentive to negotiate and change the standard AIA contract. Only some preliminary budgeting (estimating costs) is included in the basic services portion of the standard AIA contract; any other budgeting must be paid for in addition to the basic price of architectural design. Indeed, the current version of the AIA contract specifies that public hearings and interior layouts are excluded from the basic contract price. If developers want any of these services, they need to be clear about whether or not they will pay extra for them. Under the AIA contract, architects also have the right to notify developers of their need for certain additional services. If the developer does not respond promptly, the architect has the right to do the work and bill the developer for those services.

Insurance of any kind (such as professional errors and omissions insurance, commercial general liability

Figure 19-1	AIA Document B-141-1997

Standard Form of Agreement between Owner and Architect with Standard Form of Architect's Services

where the basis for payment is the COST OF THE WORK PLUS A FEE with a negotiated guaranteed maximum price

1997 EDITION

THIS DOCUMENT HAS IMPORTANT LEGAL CONSEQUENCES; CONSULTATION WITH AN ATTORNEY IS ENCOURAGED WITH RESPECT TO ITS COMPLETION OR MODIFICATION.

AIA Document A201-1997, General Conditions of the Contract for Construction, is adopted in this document by reference. This document has been approved and endorsed by the Associated General Contractors of America.

ARTICLE 1.1

Initial Information

This is a new Article in which the parties describe or identify, if known at the time of contract execution, certain information and assumptions about the Project, such as the physical, legal, financial, and time parameters and key persons or entities with the Project. It includes project parameters and project team (including designated representatives of the architect and the owner).

ARTICLE 1.2

Responsibilities of the Parties

The Owner's and the Architect's responsibilities now have been combined and placed in one Article.

ARTICLE 1.3

Terms and Conditions

This new Article encompasses the former Articles Five through Nine in the 1987 Edition and includes Cost of the Work, Instruments of Service, Change in Services, Mediation, Arbitration, Claims for Consequential Damages, Miscellaneous Provisions, Termination or Suspension, and Payments to the Architect.

ARTICLE 1.4

Scope of Services and Other Special Terms and Conditions

This new Article enumerates all documents that make up the agreement between the Owner and the Architect, including the Standard Form of Architect's Services, unless another scope of services is indicated, and provides a blank space to describe any other terms and conditions that modify the agreement.

ARTICLE 1.5

Compensation

Compensation includes basis of compensation computation, services to be included, how to calculate payments for change in services, and reimbursable expenses.

ARTICLE 2.1

Project Administration Services

This new Article describes administrative services that the Architect performs at various intervals throughout the life of the Project, including submittal of design documents, project presentation requirements, project schedule updates, attendance at project meetings, filing documents, and other such tasks.

ARTICLE 2.2

Supporting Services

Formerly contained in Article Four, Owner's Responsibilities, of the 1987 Edition of B-141, this Article includes the responsibilities to furnish services or information relating to the program, land surveys, and geotechnical engineering.

ARTICLE 2.3

Evaluation and Planning Services

This new Article lists certain predesign services to be performed by the Architect, such as evaluation of the Owner's budget, schedule, and site for the Project.

ARTICLE 2.4

Design Services

This Article describes the normal design disciplines (normal structural, mechanical, and electrical engineering services) included in the agreement and contains provisions defining and describing Schematic Design Documents, Design Development Documents, and Construction Documents.

ARTICLE 2.5

Construction Procurement Services

Article 2.5 of B-141-1997 delineates in greater depth than in the previous edition of B-141 the Architect's services

Figure 19-1	AIA Document B-141-1997 *(continued)*

relating to the Owner's procurement of the contract for construction and covers the competitive bidding process and negotiated proposals.

ARTICLE 2.6

Contract Administration Services

The Architect's Contract Administration Services now are further divided into six subcategories: General Administration; Evaluations of the Work; Certification of Payments to Contractor; Submittals; Changes in the Work; and Project Completion.

ARTICLE 2.7

Facility Operation Services

This new Article provides for two meetings between the Architect and the Owner (or the Owner's Designated Representative): one promptly after substantial completion to review the need for Facility Operation Services, and the second before the expiration of one year from the date of Substantial Completion to review the building's performance.

ARTICLE 2.8

Schedule of Services

A new feature of B-141-1997, this Article enables the parties to fill in a specific number of submittal reviews, site visits, and inspections to determine Substantial Completion and final completion that will be performed before the Architect incurs a Change in Services and to specifically designate any other services that form part of the agreement between the Owner and the Architect.

ARTICLE 2.9

Modifications

Similar to Article 12 of the 1987 Edition of B-141, this Article provides a blank space for modifications the parties wish to make to the provisions of the Standard Form of Architect's Services.

Source: The American Institute of Architects, 1735 New York Avenue, N.W., Washington, D.C. 20006. Used with permission.

insurance, or worker's compensation insurance) is not included in the AIA standard contract. Of course, the cost of insurance varies with the coverage required. Developers should note these facts and determine the proper amount of insurance and the appropriate carrier.

In the current version of the AIA contract, the architect can make decisions binding on the developer and the contractor regarding disputes between the parties. Unless the developer or the general contractor takes specific actions to challenge the architect's decision, such decisions will be binding.

The contract does not specify the exact form of certification that will be required to be executed by the architect regarding the quality of the work (certification will be needed when the permanent loan is closed). Thus, the developer must specify the form in the contract so that problems will not arise at the loan closing.

The standard contract specifies that the plans drawn belong to the architect, not to the developer, even though the developer has paid for them. This provision should be changed to give the developer ownership rights to the plans, provided the developer

makes payment to the architect in accordance with the contract.

A provision in the AIA contract prohibits assignment of the contract to any other developer without obtaining the architect's consent. This provision should be deleted, for if the original developer cannot perform, the lender might want another developer to step in and finish the project to salvage the lender's position. This provision, if not eliminated, could seriously affect project financing.

The construction contract (the contract with the general contractor) usually follows the architect's contract fairly directly. Thus, it is important to determine at this stage whether disputes are to be handled by mediation, arbitration, or litigation. Architects often prefer arbitration, although some developers often fare better using at least the threat of litigation as a negotiating point. It is beneficial to the developer to have the same procedures for resolving disputes in all the developer's contracts.

A provision in the construction contract makes it possible to retain a portion of the money due the contractor based on work completed but withheld to ensure final completion. That provision must be coordinated with the loan agreement. The developer must be able to draw down the amount of money owed on the construction contract.

Although everything should be tailored to fit the specific development, developers are generally well advised to guard against the designation of allowances, as opposed to fixed prices, for certain budgeted items in the construction contract. Allowances such as $20,000 for carpeting rather than a fixed price can lead to serious problems in stage six. With allowances, a set amount can be drawn from the construction lender. If costs exceed this amount, serious financial pressures can result, as the developer, rather than the lender, is responsible for costs in excess of the allowance. (See Figure 19-2 for items that must be considered in a construction contract.) Allowances are a temptation, particularly for items that are not yet finalized. Still, without clear specification and associated clear pricing, the developer is taking a risk.

Drafting the design contract typically transitions into drafting the construction contract. For example, developers can designate their in-house staff as the primary builder of the project; those who come from a general contracting background often take this approach. Most developers, however, rely on outside construction contractors for much of their work. Like all aspects of the development process, many variations are possible, depending on the developer's in-house skills. Regardless, these are several important demands to be made as the construction contract is negotiated.

As both the developer and one of the architects designing Elevation 314, Russell Katz was very careful in choosing his development team and determining what role every participant would play. Like the conductor in an orchestra, Katz had to choose the right people and make sure that they worked harmoniously with each other.

Bidding versus Negotiations: Fixed Price versus Cost Plus

The developer and general contractor can reach agreement on a construction contract in several ways. The two ends of the spectrum are bidding and nego-tiation. In the case of bidding, the developer puts out plans and specifications to general contractors in the local area who are considered technically and financially qualified and asks them to supply one set price or a base price with additions per unit for certain items that cannot be fully planned in advance. For example, an office building might require a price for the building plus a certain amount per linear foot for interior walls. Not until leasing is completed will the developer know how many linear feet of walls are needed. In the bid itself, the contractor promises to perform the job according to plans and specifications for one cost plus a certain amount per foot for the amount of interior walls subsequently requested by the developer.

At the other end of the spectrum is the arrangement in which the developer negotiates with one general contractor, agreeing that the general contractor will perform the work and bill the developer for either a fixed price or a cost plus a certain profit margin.

Clearly, developers prefer a fixed-price contract while contractors prefer a cost-plus agreement without a guaranteed maximum price. Consequently, many jobs fall somewhere between the two extremes. It is common for a developer to negotiate with only one contractor and to obtain a "not-to-exceed price" based on the contractor's estimate of cost plus a reasonable profit margin. If the cost of the work plus the reasonable profit margin come in below the not-to-exceed price, then the developer and contractor can share any such savings.

In reality, most developments involve a great deal of the unknown, even after completion of the formal feasibility study and complete construction drawings. Often, marketing feedback during construction requires change orders. Thus, the developer is to some extent exposed to renegotiation, no matter how tightly the original construction contract is drawn. On jobs that tend to require few change orders and where public scrutiny is more intense, bidding is most common. Projects involving the federal, state, or local government, where the plans are set firmly in advance and no formal marketing occurs, are usually "bid." The bid process satisfies the public's need to know that the price is fair. Formulating a bid requires the contractor to spend considerable time motivating subcontractors to submit their bids, consolidating the bids, and submitting the complete bid package to the developer. When contractors have some clout, i.e., when they have plenty of other work, they might even refuse to bid on smaller jobs. At other times, they might bid high on the theory that they do not need the work but will obviously benefit if they are awarded the contract at the high price. In such situations, developers who have established long-term relationships with quality contractors might find it preferable to negotiate directly with one contractor.

Typically, the developer and the general contractor sign one contract, and the general contractor and various subcontractors sign another set of contracts. The developer negotiating a contract with the general contractor might, however, also demonstrate concern about the quality of the subcontractors. Depending on the job's complexity, certain subcontractors might play key roles in construction. In such situations, developers might specify in the bid package or during negotiations for a cost-plus contract that particular subcontractors be used and/or specific trade contractors be bonded.

Developers can negotiate directly with key subcontractors with whom they have a good relationship. In such situations, the developer might negotiate a price with subcontractors and then ask the various possible general contractors for a bid, requiring a particular subcontracted job to be performed by a specified subcontractor. The general contractor is then relieved of the difficulty of, first, finding a subcontractor to perform the job and, second, motivating the subcontractor to take the bidding seriously. Consequently, general contractors might be more willing to submit a bid, assuming that they respect the particular subcontractor's work. As with many aspects of the process, no hard and fast rules exist. In the absence of rules, therefore, developers must devise the process that best serves their needs.

Fast-Track Construction

During periods when interest rates are inordinately high or when the project must be completed rapidly to satisfy a tenant who is willing to pay for speed, the developer may find it beneficial to engage in fast-track construction. The idea is to have as many steps underway at the same time as feasible. One possibility is to start excavation as soon as the architect has completed the general layout and to start building the structure before the interior design has been completed. Fast-track construction always involves the developer in negotiating a cost-plus contract. When it works, fast-track construction can help the developer beat competitors to the marketplace and reduce interest costs. When coordination of activities is weak, however, the results can be disastrous. Another problem with fast-track projects is adjusting the contract price to reflect the final "for-construction" plans and specifications. The contractor's leverage increases greatly if work begins before reaching an agreement on the final price.

A classic illustration of fast-track construction out of control concerns a retail development south of Mexico City. Given Mexico's periodic high interest rates, fast-track construction has not been uncommon. Mexico's volcanic subsurface soils, however, can pose serious problems for construction. In this case, with the project half finished, the architect realized that it would be difficult to complete the project according to the original plans and within the original budget. The foundation work specified by the architect had been constructed before all the building plans were completed, yet the foundation would not support the optimal structure and the architect was not sure how best to remedy the problem. Though the developer could have brought a lawsuit against the architect, lawsuits are usually poor recourse for problems encountered under the pressure of constructing a building on time. With the high interest costs in Mexico, accelerating the opening was critical. Thus, the developer had to knock out that portion of the foundation that did not fit the new plan (which he decided to complete with a second architect). The additional cost placed considerable stress on construction financing.

Bonding

Bonding is a guarantee of completion and/or payment. The city might require developers to provide a bond to prove that they have the capacity to complete the infra-

Figure 19-2	Checklist for Construction Contracts			
		OWNER	**ARCHITECT**	**CONTRACTOR**
1.0	**Program Development**			
	1.1 Project requirements, including design objectives, constraints and criteria, space requirements and relationships, flexibility and expandability, special equipment, and systems and site requirements			
	1.2 Legal description and a certified survey; complete, as required			
	1.3 Soils engineering; complete, as required			
	1.4 Materials testing, inspections, and reports; complete, as required			
	1.5 Legal, accounting (including auditing), and insurance counseling, as required			
	1.6 Program review			
	1.7 Financial feasibility			
	1.8 Planning surveys, site evaluations, environmental studies, or comparative studies of prospective sites			
	1.9 Verification of existing conditions or facilities			
2.0	**Construction Cost**			
	2.1 Budget and funds			
	2.2 Estimate of probable costs			
	2.3 Detailed estimates of construction cost			
	2.4 Control of design to meet fixed limit of construction cost			
3.0	**Design**			
	3.1 Schematic			
	3.2 Design development			
	3.3 Consultants: structural, mechanical, electrical, special			
4.0	**Construction Documents**			
	4.1 Final drawings and specifications			
	4.2 Bidding information, bid forms, conditions of contract, and form of agreement between owner and contractor			
	4.3 Filing for government approvals			
	4.4 For use in construction			
	4.5 On-site maintenance of drawings, specifications, addenda, change orders, shop drawings, product data, and samples			
5.0	**Bidding**			
	5.1 Obtaining bids or negotiated proposals			
	5.2 Awarding and preparing contracts			

Figure 19-2	Checklist for Construction Contracts *(continued)*			
		OWNER	**ARCHITECT**	**CONTRACTOR**
5.0	**Bidding** *(continued)*			
5.3	Documents for alternate, separate, or sequential bids; extra services in connection with bidding, negotiation, or construction before completion of construction documents			
6.0	**Administration of Construction Contract**			
6.1	General			
	6.1.1 Owner's representative			
	6.1.2 Periodic visits to the site			
	6.1.3 Construction methods, techniques, sequences, procedures, safety precautions, and programs			
	6.1.4 Contractor's applications for payments			
	6.1.5 Certificates for payment			
	6.1.6 Document interpretation/artistic effect			
	6.1.7 Rejection of work; special inspections or testing			
	6.1.8 Shop drawings, product data, and samples			
	6.1.8.1 Submittals			
	6.1.8.2 Review and action			
	6.1.9 Change orders			
	6.1.9.1 Preparation			
	6.1.9.2 Approval			
	6.1.10 Closeout			
	6.1.10.1 Date of substantial completion			
	6.1.10.2 Date of final completion			
	6.1.10.3 Written warranties			
	6.1.10.4 Certificate for final payment			
	6.1.11 Coordination of work of separate contractors or by owner's forces			
	6.1.12 Services of construction manager			
	6.1.13 As-built drawings			
7.0	**Schedule**			
7.1	Design schedule			
	7.1.1 Development			
	7.1.2 Maintenance			
7.2	Construction schedule			
	7.2.1 Development			
	7.2.2 Maintenance			

continued on next page

Figure 19-2	Checklist for Construction Contracts *(continued)*			
		OWNER	**ARCHITECT**	**CONTRACTOR**
8.0	**Payment**			
	8.1 Basic design services			
	8.1.1 Accounting records			
	8.2 Construction (the work)			
	8.2.1 Progress payments			
	8.2.2 Final payment			
	8.3 Evidence of ability to pay			
	8.4 Secure and pay for necessary approvals, easements, assessments, and changes for construction, use, or occupancy			
9.0	**Construction**			
	9.1 General			
	9.2 Labor, materials, and equipment			
	9.3 Correlation of local conditions with requirements of the contract documents			
	9.4 Division of work among subcontractors			
	9.5 Right to stop work			
	9.6 Owner's right to carry out work			
	9.7 Review of contract documents for errors, inconsistencies, or omissions			
	9.8 Supervision and direction of the work			
	9.9 Responsibility to owner for errors and omissions in the work			
	9.10 Obligation to perform the work in accordance with contract documents			
	9.11 Provide and pay for all labor, materials, equipment, tools, machinery, utilities, transportation, and other facilities and services for the proper execution and completion of the work			
	9.12 Enforce discipline and good order among those employed on the job			
	9.13 Warranty for all materials and equipment			
	9.14 Sales, consumer, and use taxes			
	9.15 Secure and pay for all permits, fees, licenses, and inspections			
	9.16 Compliance with all laws, ordinances, regulations, and lawful orders			
	9.17 Employment of superintendent			
	9.18 Cutting and patching			
	9.19 Cleaning up			
	9.20 Communications			

Figure 19-2	Checklist for Construction Contracts *(continued)*			
		OWNER	**ARCHITECT**	**CONTRACTOR**
9.0	**Construction** *(continued)*			
9.21	Payments of all royalties and license fees; defense against suits and claims			
9.22	Indemnification; hold harmless			
9.23	Award of subcontracts			
9.24	Owner's right to perform work and award separate contracts			
	9.24.1 Award			
	9.24.2 Mutual responsibility			
	9.24.3 Cleanup dispute			
10.0	**Miscellaneous**			
10.1	Performance bond, labor, and material payment bond			
10.2	Tests			
10.3	Protection of persons and property			
11.0	**Insurance**			
11.1	Contractor's liability insurance			
11.2	Owner's liability insurance			
11.3	Property insurance			
12.0	**Changes in the Work**			
13.0	**Uncovering and Correction of Work**			
Source: G. Niles Bolton, architect, Atlanta, Georgia.				

structure. The developer might ask the contracting firm to provide a bond to prove that the general contractor has the wherewithal to complete the job. When issuing a bond, a surety company examines the credibility of the individuals or institutions to be bonded. The assessment covers both their capacity to do the work and their financial substance. Bonds are the most common form of guarantee, although alternatives such as a letter of credit or depositing assets in escrow can be used. Bonds enable the developer or general contractor to ask a surety company to stand behind the nonperforming firm in a lawsuit.

During stage four, a developer might want the general contractor to be bonded if the developer fears that the contractor might not be able to perform or cannot muster the financial resources to pay a judgment in the event of a lawsuit. Federal, state, and local government contracts often require the general contractor to be bonded. Often government agencies do not have the personnel to monitor construction yet want to ensure that taxpayers' dollars will not be lost.

Bonding has several different connotations. Completion bonds and payment bonds, for example, differ markedly. In the case of a completion bond, the surety guarantees that the project will be completed according to the contract, including the plans and the cost. A payment bond ensures that the surety will pay all valid claims for work performed and materials supplied arising from the project. Thus, a payment bond covers any successful mechanic's lien claims.[6]

A completion bond is very different. It provides that the project will be completed, notwithstanding the default or bankruptcy of the contractor. In this case, the surety (insuring company) will cover whatever it takes to finish the job, regardless of a contractor's claims against the developer with only a performance bond; in the event of a lawsuit in which the developer successfully secures a judgment against the general contractor, the surety on the payment bond is liable for that judgment. In this situation, the surety can use all the defenses available to the general contractor. If the developer has caused part of the problem, it might not be able to collect on the bond.

ELEVATION 314

Choosing Players and Negotiating Contracts

Many contract negotiations are involved in real estate development. There's finding the property and negotiating with your seller and even your broker. Brokers know what they'd like to get from a project, whether they are listing or selling. I have had a relationship with a broker for a long time, which is a little unusual. I get a pretty good deal with him because I'm the one with my feet on the pavement all the time.

For Elevation 314, there was no negotiation for the land because I bought it for the asking price. I like negotiations, but the best way to negotiate is if you don't need anything or if you don't really care and if the other side needs to do something. Sometimes the roles are reversed, but in the end everything is up for negotiation. In the case of 314, I felt the price was fair and I just wanted the property. The only condition I put on it was that there be a Phase II environmental study before closing. There was already a Phase I study, but I wanted more specific information: borings, sampling, and that type of research. We closed really quickly. There was no financing; it was an all-cash offer. In other cases, I've driven really hard deals, most of which haven't worked out. You have to know what you want and know what your position is, but still the negotiations go on and on. They never end.

I've gone into projects knowing I wouldn't get hurt. I didn't know how I'd do it or how it would work out. I think for me the commitment—or rather buying the property—comes quickly. I've never been big on trying to work with options and long drawn-out complicated partnerships. Where I really mix things up, especially with projects that are new like 314, is that I want to be the developer and the designer but I don't want to be the architect of record.

Most architecture firms are used to providing a full range of services. They usually start with their design concepts, then elaborate on them in the design development phase. From there they produce the necessary construction documents. But I want to do the design myself. I had to meet with a dozen architects and talk about my vision for the site and how I saw everyone's roles working together. Through this process, I found a great architectural consultant and that led to a really good civil engineer, who is also a green roof consultant. I also hired a woman whom I'd known from graduate school to work as a design consultant.

What I wanted to do, realizing that I was wearing three or four hats, was to bring in people who could embody each distinct role and defend their turf—who could serve as the conscience for each component so that when I was under a lot of pressure to save money I wouldn't destroy the project.

I ended up with many contracts to get the project done. At the beginning, it was important to get the right people and for them to know what they were supposed to do. So I made things really clear to all of them. I wanted the project to satisfy three very important criteria: the building had to be beautiful, green, and a good business decision.

I would maintain strict control over the financial part, because I was the one with everything in. I was doing the whole thing with only my own collateral and investment, and nobody can look out for that like me.

For the environmental criterion, I brought in two fantastic consultants. One of them, Michelle Scurfield, is an architect who is one of the early LEED-qualified consultants. I brought in Katrin Scholz-Barth, one of the most respected authorities in the country on green roofs, to oversee the green roof on 314. I hired Suzanne Pullman, who went to grad school with me, to work on design.

Throughout the project, I had my fingers everywhere, but I relied on these people to a tremendous extent. When we studied the heating and cooling system, we knew what we wanted but didn't know whether we could afford it. So we priced geothermal, but we also wanted solar panels. The first pricing exercises came back way too high, so I said to Michelle, "We can't even build the building if we go with geothermal. If we go a high-efficiency gas furnace with a split system, is that still green?" And she told me, "On the LEED scale of being green, we'd lose a couple of points but we're still okay." Then she said, "I might know somebody who can do it at a better price."

ELEVATION 314 *(continued)*

A green roof and bioretention area in the courtyard at Elevation 314 use carefully selected native plants to filter and break down pollutants in stormwater. Russell Katz

I'd say all these consultants paid for their services by enabling me to save costs. Michelle found a great source for bamboo floors that was cheaper than other sources. The consultants were professionals who were invested in the project and working hard. They could all be relied on, and they were all under hourly contracts. I tend not to negotiate hourly contracts. If somebody says, "This is what I do and this is how I do it," it's either a price I can afford or one I can't.

And then there are negotiations with the contractors and builders. It's a process that includes lots of interviews, references, pricing studies, and nuts and bolts. At the end of the day, there are really a lot of contracts. And different levels of negotiation that go along with them all.

I didn't have to worry about major tenants because it was an apartment building with few retail spaces. My situation was different from many condo projects that were going on at the time, where you have to presell a certain number of units. With Elevation 314, it was just me using my other buildings as collateral and all my savings—but not my house. That was the only thing I won't sign up for. It was my equity, and I didn't want partners. I thought it was going to be a tough project, and if it was going to work, it would require fast decision making. I always felt that was one of the real benefits that I got out of being a design architect and developer. We cut a lot of fat out by being able to make decisions quickly. I didn't want to muddy that by having a partner who might not agree with things I was doing.

continued on page 491

Lenders and investors clearly have less risk with a completion bond. Unfortunately, completion bonds are considerably more expensive. But regardless of the type of bond, most developers believe that when they are forced to call on a bonding agent, they will, in the best case, lose some money for time lost and higher interest rates. Thus, bonding provides some, albeit not complete, protection.

Another major decision in design and construction is whether to go with architectural supervision of the construction, hire an outside engineering firm to supervise, or have a member of the development team supervise construction. Whatever the choice, someone representing the developer must regularly inspect construction and certify compliance with design specifications and the construction contracts. Construction lenders are vitally concerned about the quality of this work, as they will substantiate the draws made under the construction loan agreement as construction progresses. Most lenders will hire their own inspector to verify the percentage of completion of the project. Likewise, architects want to be sure their ideas are properly translated into constructed space, and the general contractor wants to get paid. Consequently, provision for construction supervision is part of several of the contracts negotiated in stage four and signed in stage five.

DECISIONS ABOUT MAJOR TENANTS

Since stage one of the process, the developer has had an idea of the primary tenant and/or tenant mix anticipated for the project. In the case of a for-sale project, the developer has had some idea of the end customer. That idea is refined in stage two and further documented in stage three. In stage four, the developer must make the final decision. Possibly by applying sensitivity analysis to the pro forma numbers from the feasibility study, the developer decides how much space to allocate to major tenants and when to sign them on.

The first question pertains to major tenants. Large tenants—ranging from regional mall anchors such as major department stores, big-box power center tenants, or grocery store neighborhood anchors to tenants occupying several full floors in an office building to industrial tenants occupying a significant amount of space—know their power and drive a hard bargain. This power is greater the earlier in the development process they sign. Thus, the greater the number of major space users (particularly those with prominent names or well-recognized creditworthiness) the developer signs early, the less the net rent (rent after consideration of concessions for tenants, impact of unusual expense stops, and the like). On the other hand, large tenants draw other tenants. A regional mall is not usually possible without several anchor stores and cinemas. Signing the anchors is usually the key to drawing smaller tenants and convincing lenders of the project's long-term viability. From the developer's standpoint, however, the more space the major tenants prelease, the lower the expected average rent per square foot upon completion.

In regional malls, developers might actually give away space to the top anchor tenants and earn all their return from smaller tenants. This practice is not uncommon, as it is the advertising and name recognition of the major tenants that draw customers to the mall and thus provide the smaller tenants' livelihood. The critical decision is what percentage of the space should be allocated to major tenants. On the one hand, it is usually safer to reserve more space for major tenants. On the other hand, it is more lucrative to recruit a large share of smaller tenants if they "stay and pay." The "right anchor" changes rather quickly in retailing. In the 1980s, Sears was a strong draw; today, it might be Whole Foods that is the tenant who, if signed early, can make an idea a reality.

As noted, in addition to deciding what percentage of space to allocate to major tenants (and all gradations between major and minor tenants), developers must decide when to sign tenants. (Lenders' preleasing requirements often reduce the developer's flexibil-

---

MUSEUM TOWERS
Construction Costs

The construction company we chose to build Museum Towers was Suffolk Construction Company, a Boston-based group.

The total estimated cost to complete the project was, by category:

Land	$8,100,000
Hard Costs	53,600,000
Soft Costs	9,500,000
Project Administration	1,500,000
Loan Fees	1,800,000
Contingencies	2,900,000
Construction Interest	7,600,000
Interim Rents	(7,000,000)
Total	$78,000,000

Financing

Construction Loan	$55,000,000
Mezzanine Loan	16,500,000
Borrowers' Equity*	6,500,000
Total	$78,000,000

*Credited—actual amount invested was higher.

continued on page 494

---

ity in this regard.) Tenants signed early in the process commit to something they cannot see as well as to a possibly uncertain future opening date. To induce tenants to make an early commitment, developers must offer one or more concessions, perhaps a rent concession or a choice location.

From the developer's perspective, signing a tenant early has certain advantages. The more tenants that sign early, the lower the vacancy rate and risk to the developer if the market becomes less robust or the project less inviting after construction. Although early leasing is a way to reduce risk, many times it also requires greater concessions to tenants.

After making decisions about the advance signing of tenants and the number of name tenants, developers

In leasing the retail component of the Market Common–Clarendon—a mixed-use development in Virginia comprising for-sale townhouses, apartments, and high-end shopping—developer McCaffery Interests mixed national credit tenants such as Pottery Barn, Crate & Barrel, and the Apple Store with smaller, locally owned businesses. *McCaffery Interests*

must specify the general conditions desired in other leases. What is involved is not just rent per square foot, which varies with location, the amount of space required, and other considerations. Developers must also decide who pays what portion of which operating costs, the amount of tenant improvement allowances, and who provides what services. For example, who pays for carpeting and other interior features? If the developer pays, the rent is typically higher to reimburse the developer for the additional costs incurred. Often developers give the tenant a certain improvement allowance; the tenant then pays whatever additional amount is necessary for upgraded fixtures beyond the amount specified in the lease. From a lender's perspective, tenant allowances are reasonable because money spent on permanent interior improvements creates additional value and collateral for the first lien on the project. Given that the developer typically negotiates the first loan, it is often easier to include in those negotiations a certain tenant allowance and pass it along to tenants. The alternative is for tenants to borrow the necessary funds. Smaller tenants frequently find it difficult to finance improvements because their lenders cannot consider the affixed improvements as collateral.

Ongoing operating guidelines are also important. What services will the landlord provide? How often will the bathrooms be cleaned? How fast will the elevators travel? What kind of security will be provided? In many projects, particularly shopping centers, tenants also have obligations. What are the minimum hours of operation? How much cooperation is necessary for joint promotions? All these items must be negotiated before the execution of leases to ensure that the total marketing effort for the project matches the expectations specified in the feasibility study. Although the landlord would like higher rents with more expenses passed on to tenants and fewer allowances, the market may not tolerate such terms. Further, although the landlord may hope to pass escalations in operating expenses through to tenants, tenants hope for just the opposite. Tenants may be willing to sign before seeing more of the project, particularly if the market is overbuilt, the developer inexperienced, the project unusual, or the location unproved.

At this point, developers must also decide whether leasing is to be handled by in-house staff or outside brokers. For some types of projects and some locations, it is preferable to use outside leasing agents, at least in part. In other cases, such as leasing (or sale) of retirement housing, the product is maybe so unusual and operations so complex that developers often do well to have the needed talent on staff, where they can monitor it more closely.

The developer is accountable for all these decisions and for seeing that the corresponding documents are properly drafted. If the developer concludes that the numbers in the feasibility study cannot be met, stage four is a good time to get off the wagon.

DECISIONS ABOUT EQUITY

The difference between project costs and what can be financed is the required development equity. The ideal project is one whose value is so far above cost that the developer can obtain a low loan-to-value ratio loan and still secure a sufficiently large loan to cover all costs, including a development fee, major reserves to cover any operating deficits before lease-up, and a large reserve for contingencies. When a lender finances a real estate development project, however, it usually relies on such conservative underwriting criteria that it nearly always requires an equity

investment by the developer. Only a truly great idea gets 100 percent debt financing.

When developers cannot finance the entire project through senior debt, they must find additional sources of capital. Four basic alternatives are possible: developers provide the necessary equity from their own funds or their firm's funds, they bring in an outside equity investor or investors for the development period, they obtain a second loan, subordinate to the first, in which the lender may get part of the equity in return for lending an amount beyond that provided by first lender, or they use some combination of the first three options. These approaches have numerous variations, all of them compensating investors according to the risk associated with their contribution to equity.

In structuring an outside equity deal, developers typically extend the cash flow forecast from the feasibility study to include debt service and income taxes for each participant in each financing alternative. Potential tradeoffs can be exceedingly complex. Often, the amount of the developer's profits and exposure to risk changes materially, depending on the source of permanent debt and equity financing. It takes experience, and the discounted cash flow analysis introduced in Part III, for the developer to decide on the optimal structure for any required equity. Taking advantage of the feasibility study's electronic spreadsheet as an optimization tool, the developer performs sensitivity analyses on revised cash flows, using alternative forecasts of future events to determine the impact of each scenario on the various cash flows. Experience comes into play in specifying likely scenarios. For example, just how likely is the combination of interest rates 10 percent lower, an increase in local demand with the relocation of a major employer to the area, and a steady competitive supply as a competing property owner chooses not to expand? It takes experience and "feel" to estimate the likelihood of alternative scenarios.

If the market is hot and the developer is financially able, it is usually most rewarding to build the project with the developer's own funds and then sell interests in it upon completion. At that time, the final investor, attracted by lower risk because the development process is over, should be willing to pay a higher price. When additional capital is required for the development process itself, however, the developer must induce money before the project is built, thereby reducing the amount of cash the developer must invest. Sophisticated investors know the value of such a commitment and are likely to negotiate a more advantageous split of the rewards in exchange for assuming the additional risk. The more developers can guarantee in terms of construction costs, completion dates, and leasing, the higher the percentage of rewards they will be able to retain. The developer may also seek to develop the project using funds from one investor and then, following completion and stabilization of the project, to buy out that investor, using funds obtained from another investor who wants a long-term, lower-risk investment.

When developers lack the resources to provide all the requisite equity for a project or choose to allocate their funds differently, they usually consider the participation of outside equity investors. These outside equity investors generally invest in projects by forming a limited liability company (LLC) with the developer. The newly formed limited liability company then acquires the project being developed. High-net-worth individuals, pension funds, and other institutional investors are the primary sources of this equity capital.

The development period equity joint venture requires the developer to give away a share of the development period profits to the investor partner, along with some control over decisions about the development, ownership, and ultimate disposition of the project. Developers are frequently required to provide the investor with what is often referred to as a "preferred return" on the investor's money before the developer receives a return on his interests. This priority is often expressed as both a return on equity and an internal rate of return. Eventually, after the outside investor has received its preferred return, the developer gets a return on its capital, return of its capital, and then a split of the cash flow. The split of cash flow is often disproportionate to the relative percentage of capital invested by the developer and investor; that is, the developer's percentage share of back-end cash flow is greater than the relative percentage of capital invested by the developer—often referred to

as the developer's "promote." The number of possible deal structures is almost limitless. This area is one where the developer can demonstrate creativity. Whatever the deal, however, it needs to be formally documented in stage four.

THE GOVERNMENT AS PARTNER

Developers are usually well advised to collaborate with their public partner—the local municipality—throughout the early stages of development. In stage four, as the developer is negotiating and finalizing contracts with all the key players on the development team, it would be extremely advantageous if the developer were able to "contract" with the municipality where the project is located.

The contract with the municipality would, among other things, confirm the parties' understanding regarding the project's entitlements, fees, exactions, and dedications for which the project will be responsible and the right of the developer to develop the project in accordance with the municipality's rules, regulations, and official policies such as local zoning ordinances, as those rules existed on the date of the "contract."

Unfortunately, not all states permit municipalities to enter into these types of contracts. In some municipalities, however, state law permits a developer to enter into a "development agreement" with the local municipality. Under such an agreement, a developer is assured of the right to proceed with the development of the project during the term of the development agreement and is assured that the development may be developed in accordance with the rules, regulations, and official policies of the municipality that were in effect on the date the development agreement was entered into. For a large project that will be developed in phases, this type of assurance is essential and is frequently required by the developer's lender(s). A number of states, including Arizona, California, Colorado, Florida, Hawaii, Maryland, Minnesota, and Nevada, permit development agreements in one form or another.

A developer's right to proceed with development of the project without being concerned about having

At 4,700 acres (1,900 hectares), Stapleton is the largest infill development in the United States. The project is the result of a public/private partnership among the city and county of Denver, the Stapleton Redevelopment Foundation, and Forest City Enterprises, Inc., to transform the site of Stapleton International Airport into a community that mixes many different housing types with office and retail space. *Steve Larson*

the rules change is known as a "vested right." Until a developer has obtained a vested right, the possibility exists that the local rules could change and preclude the developer from proceeding as planned. When a developer achieves a vested right to develop varies from state to state. In some states, merely pulling a

building permit vests the developer's right to proceed with the development for a period of time equal to at least the life of the building permit.

In Massachusetts, for example, the developer's interests are vested if a building permit has been issued and construction starts within six months.

Also in Massachusetts, so long as a plat map for a new subdivision is filed before a rezoning hearing, zoning is frozen for a period of eight years. Downzoning is therefore not an immediate risk once the plat map is filed. In other jurisdictions—California, for example—no vested right is obtained to complete construction of a project until a building permit is obtained and substantial work has been undertaken and liabilities incurred in good faith reliance on that building permit. A grading permit therefore would not satisfy the California standard for vested rights.

In formalizing the relationships among parties, particularly the local municipality, developers should not lose sight of the changing face of the urban landscape. Projects that began as industrial distribution centers have become high-tech office parks and in the process made their owners extremely wealthy.

Evolving land uses are usually stimulated by growth in surrounding areas, public restrictions on the development of other land, and other forces prompting change. Although the stimulus might come from the outside, developers can create the possibility of change. Developers who realize the inevitability of change and provide as much flexibility as possible in design, tenant selection, financing, and entitlements are most likely to enjoy the benefits of "second-order effects."

The fine print in the contracts and entitlements negotiated during stage four greatly affects the flexibility to change. Developers should not ignore the details in their contracts or in the conditions to their entitlements, because those "details" can end up either restricting or maximizing the developer's flexibility. Developers should make every effort to ensure future flexibility when drawing up agreements and when reviewing conditions to their entitlements.

STAGE FIVE: COMMITMENT— SIGNING CONTRACTS AND INITIATING CONSTRUCTION

Several of the contracts negotiated during stage four can be contingent on other contracts. It is common for the permanent lender to be unwilling to make a commitment until certain major tenants have signed

a commitment. The construction lender's agreement is often contingent on a permanent loan takeout. Developers do not want to make a commitment to a contractor until they have the funds available to pay for construction, and major tenants do not want to sign a contract until they are sure the developer has sufficient money and staff to complete the project.

Hence, many of the parties examine contracts in which they are not direct participants but that are necessary for them to realize their own objectives. It is often necessary to have different contracts executed simultaneously. Regardless of whether the contracts are executed sequentially or simultaneously, most must be fairly firmly negotiated before any are signed. And a series of events must happen as the contracts are signed.

In stage five of the process, the contracts negotiated in stage four are executed. If outside investors are involved, agreements documenting the formation of entities such as partnerships or other relationships typically must be signed and filed with governmental jurisdictions. In larger projects, a public offering registered with the federal Securities and Exchange Commission might be involved. To complete the financial arrangements, the permanent loan commitment must be signed and the fee paid; similarly, the construction loan agreement must be signed and that origination fee paid. The contract with the general contractor is signed, while the general contractor signs a series of contracts with the subcontractors.

The local jurisdiction is also involved. If possible, permits are obtained in stage three or at least early in stage four, but negotiations in stage four often cause changes that require renegotiation with the city. In larger projects (and increasingly in smaller projects), local governments require impact fees and/or major off-site improvements before approving a development. These agreements must also be finalized in stage five.

As for marketing, the preleased space requires a formally executed lease, with memoranda of some (usually major) leases recorded. If an outside leasing agent or sales agent is used, a listing agreement or at least a memorandum of understanding may be necessary. A memorandum describes the type of space to be leased or sold and the conditions under which the transaction is to occur.

To close the construction loan, the developer probably will have to close on the option to buy the land and/or pay off any land loan in the event the land has already been purchased. This step is necessary to ensure that the construction lender's loan will be a first lien on the property.

On the administrative side, insurance for the construction period must be put in force—liability, fire, and extended coverage; an update on title insurance; and the like. At the same time, the developer switches to a more formal accounting system. Up to this point, the developer has probably simply aggregated all the costs associated with the project, but now a formal budget and cash controls are necessary. The budget comes from the feasibility analysis (as amended by negotiations in stage four), receives the construction lender's blessing, and becomes part of the procedure to draw down funds as construction proceeds. It is also the basis of the contract with the general contractor.

Cash controls require a look at the budget to compare funds expended and funds committed in the original plans while keeping a careful eye on remaining funds. The construction lender uses a similar procedure to keep track of the draws by the developer to fund construction.

Most important, the developer must institute some type of control mechanism for the development itself, either by directing the architect to perform a certain amount of supervision or employing an on-site construction manager. The general contractor must also use some type of formalized process for control. The most common methods are the program evaluation and review technique (PERT) and the critical path method (CPM), both of which are available for use on personal computers.

SUMMARY

Once the project is officially deemed feasible in stage three, the development team can move toward and formalize all the relationships necessary to implement the plan. During stage four, detailed relationships are negotiated, possibly leading to some changes in the plan as a result of the negotiations. And in stage five, the contracts negotiated in stage four are executed.

During stages four and five, although it is still possible for the developer to determine that the project is not feasible, it is far more expensive than it was earlier to pull out of the project. Developers who frequently arrive at stage four and decide to stop find that they have accumulated a tremendous amount of uncovered overhead. Nonetheless, failure to stop when the signals indicate a stop in stages four and five can cause disaster in stages six, seven, and eight. Developers use the feasibility study done in stage three as a management tool during stages four and five. They should be particularly careful to ensure that 1) the overall project remains feasible after all the contracts are negotiated, and 2) none of the participants in the process have lost level two feasibility through contract negotiation.

TERMS

- ▶ AHERA
- ▶ Asbestos
- ▶ Bonding
- ▶ CERCLA
- ▶ Clean Air Act
- ▶ Clean Water Act
- ▶ Commitment letter
- ▶ Construction loan
- ▶ CPM
- ▶ Ecosystems
- ▶ EPA
- ▶ Fast-track construction
- ▶ Friable
- ▶ Guaranteed investment contract (GIC)
- ▶ Hazardous waste
- ▶ Mezzanine financing
- ▶ Participating loan
- ▶ Permanent loan
- ▶ PERT
- ▶ Preferred return

▶ Prime rate

▶ SARA

▶ Superfund

▶ Surety company

▶ Takeout

▶ Vested right

▶ Wetlands mitigation

REVIEW QUESTIONS

19.1 Broadly describe how contracts help control risk.

19.2 What are the options for developers who do not have permanent financing committed before construction begins?

19.3 What is the difference between the risks taken by a construction lender and those taken by a permanent lender?

19.4 What is mezzanine financing, and why is it usually considered expensive money?

19.5 What are some different types of equity investment vehicles?

19.6 Describe the municipal approval challenges that the Museum Towers development incurred.

19.7 Describe the contract a developer must sign with an architect and some of the issues that should be negotiated.

19.8 What are two primary ways in which a developer hires a general contractor?

19.9 How do allowance items in a construction contract allocate risk?

19.10 What occurs in stage five? Why is stage five so heavily dependent on what decisions are made in stage four?

NOTES

1. Additional detail about permanent and construction loans and lenders is provided in Chapters 7 to 9.

2. Readers should use the material in this chapter and the financial logic developed in Chapters 7 through 9 as bases for exploring professional real estate journals (e.g., *Real Estate Review, Real Estate Finance, Real Estate Finance Journal,* and *National Real Estate Investor*) for new ideas that can be modified to fit a proposed development.

3. The CMBS market originally was a vehicle for placement of permanent loans with fairly safe loan-to-value ratios and high-quality real estate products as collateral. As the market has changed, new programs (most notably, short-term "interim" loans) entered the scene, thereby allowing for conduit loans for riskier ventures, such as lesser-quality real estate or loans to borrowers who intend to make significant improvements.

The one drawback with the CMBS market is that CMBS lenders need to undertake secondary market offerings to move their loans off their books. Until recently, these securitizations were "fixed" at the closing of the offering; that is, CMBS lenders could not move new loans into a previously securitized pool of loans. The fixed nature of the securitized loan pools limits the ability of CMBS lenders to make construction loans. In particular, loans that have as collateral undeveloped or partially developed land are too risky for the public markets.

In 1998, the CMBS market introduced the FASIT (financial asset securitization investment trust) structure, which allows for "postclosing" placement of loans into securitized loan pools. Thus, CMBS lenders now have an exit strategy for construction loans, and conduit lenders can make the construction loan and hold it until the property is sufficiently developed to permit placement into an existing FASIT.

4. See *New York v. Shore Realty Corporation,* 759 F.2d 1032.

5. See *U.S. v. Fleet Factors,* 901 F.2d 1550 (1990).

6. A mechanic's lien is a lien on property that comes about when a subcontractor claims to have been unpaid. Lenders find liens troublesome because they often take effect as of the first day the subcontractors furnished labor, but they appear in the title (the legal recorded history of ownership) only when filed at some subsequent date. To avoid such potential clouds on a title, some lenders use title companies as disbursing agents, particularly in states with especially strong statutes covering mechanic's liens.

CHAPTER 20

Stages Six and Seven: Construction, Completion, And Formal Opening

Stage six—construction—differs in one key way from all other stages covered so far: time becomes even more crucial. At stage six, the developer is more exposed to multiple uncertainties, most of them negative and potentially expensive. Unlike earlier stages of development, when a well-structured option may keep the developer's financial exposure to a minimum, the developer is now fully committed—with cash, guarantees, and human resources—to the development project. Once the general contract has been executed and construction commences, it is not easy to stop or make major modifications without incurring significant financial consequences. Even in the best, safest situations, when developers have arranged nonrecourse financing and are receiving substantial early development fees, their reputations—and usually a lot more—are on the line.

During the earlier stages, particularly during stages four and five—contract negotiation and formal commitment—the specific rules governing the relationships among the parties were formalized and their obligations defined. Once the agreements are signed and construction begins, the developer's focus shifts toward project management. The crucial items to be controlled are time, quality, and budget. The developer must ensure that all players perform their jobs on time, that they deliver the quality of work specified in the contracts, and that all soft costs such as ongoing marketing are carefully and continuously monitored. Although the feasibility study remains an important management tool allowing the developer to quickly evaluate potential reactions to changing market conditions, the contracts negotiated in stage four and signed in stage five have created binding obligations, so changes now are almost certainly more cumbersome and expensive to implement.

This chapter covers two stages in real estate development: project construction (stage six) and the project's completion with formal opening (stage seven). Specifically, it considers:

▶ The continuing and potentially much more intense interaction among major players;
▶ Building the structure;
▶ Drawing down the construction loan;
▶ Leasing space and "building out" the tenant space;
▶ Landscaping and exterior construction;

▶ Potential problems that might arise during stage six;

▶ Completion and formal opening; and

▶ Risk control techniques during stages six and seven.

STAGE SIX: CONSTRUCTION

In stage six, the developer (along with the other players now formally committed to the project) takes a major financial leap and begins construction. Making life exciting is the high degree of uncertainty that necessarily remains part of the process in even the most exhaustively planned and fully contracted developments. Unknowns—from unexpected subsoil conditions to labor unrest—abound. Customers can change perspective rapidly, as high-tech firms in San Jose did at the start of this century. Even the most trusted partner can fail to perform as the result of an accident, major health issues, or divorce. Remember, you, the developer, are ultimately responsible for overcoming whatever problems arise.

The Continuing Interaction among Major Players during the Construction Process

A developer's role as manager does not end and may well intensify with the hiring of a general contractor to build the project and an architect to oversee construction. The developer must still manage the general contractor and the other members of the development team. By carefully selecting a team of appropriately experienced professionals and by establishing formal and formally coordinated relationships during stages four and five, the developer is better able to manage the working relationship among the design, construction, marketing, financial, operations, and public sector players during stage six. Coordinating the players through the construction process is especially important in complex multiphase or mixed-use developments, which often involve multiple designers and builders, many different users, and several chances for the general public to express its opinion and have an impact on the process. The developer—subject to approval rights of lenders, investors, and tenants—is the final arbiter among all

the players and is responsible for making the final decision when a tough judgment is needed.

During the construction phase, so many players are involved that much of the process focuses on coordination and collaboration. For example, the architect will most likely work with his own team of design professionals, which could include a lighting designer, an acoustical consultant, a structural engineer, a mechanical engineer, and an interior design professional. The general contractor will coordinate a team of building professionals (which could include negotiations with labor unions), materials suppliers, equipment rental companies, various insurers, and lenders. Each team must work with public sector professionals—municipal inspectors, health inspectors, life safety inspectors—who will also have an interest in the development.

Developers can provide on-site management in several ways. In some instances, the architect who designed the project examines the work at various stages and certifies that it has been performed according to plans and specifications. Another approach is to hire an in-house project manager, typically an architect or engineer with a construction background who remains on site and, among other things, monitors the general contractor's performance throughout the process.

In the 1980s, substantial reliance on architectural supervision was common. With today's more complex jobs and a more sensitive physical environment, however, periodic supervision by the architect is often insufficient. On larger jobs, most developers hire someone who is on site all the time and is responsible for dealing with the general contractor's team, the design team, and the array of involved public sector officials. The more complex the job, the more frequent and unusual the problems that are likely to arise. As problems occur, somebody must be available to make decisions quickly. Either the developer himself or some member of the staff must be there to work with the general contractor.

Construction lenders are naturally interested in the arrangements for supervision and oversight of project construction. Periodic sign-offs, usually once a month, by the architect or the developer's project manager are required when the contractor asks for money and the developer requisitions a draw on the construction loan. Construction lenders (and occasionally institutional partners and permanent lenders) also inspect the construction work, but their presence reinforces rather than replaces technical reviews.

Project Manager

The project manager—whether an architect, in-house construction professional, or in-house engineer—should be experienced in the type of project under construction. Without such experience, the project manager could miss opportunities to intercept and reduce the inevitable conflicts that arise as the general contractor attempts to minimize costs, the operating and marketing people clamor for changes to make the structure more functional, the marketing people seek to please potential tenants, and the architect tries to retain a certain aesthetic concept. In an ideal situation, most conflicts would have been resolved in stages three, four, or five, but changes are often necessitated by market shifts or unanticipated construction problems encountered during stage six. An experienced and effective project manager will be better able to maintain a sense of cooperation and mutual achievement among the development team as the various inevitable conflicts are resolved.

Marketing Manager

Even when all the tenant space is preleased or the building has a single tenant (in the case of a public hospital, for example), marketing is an ongoing activity, as tenant buildout must meet the client's contractual expectations. When there is a significant amount of unleased space, ongoing marketing may be the major issue for the development team. Simultaneously with initiation of construction, the marketing strategy is implemented in full force. As detailed in subsequent chapters, this strategy usually involves advertising (which involves photography and graphic design), coordination of the sales force (which is responsible for meeting with prospects and selling or leasing space), and site visits by prospects.

Among the sales and leasing manager's responsibilities is providing feedback gathered by interacting

The marketing campaign for Museum Towers emphasized location and views.

with potential tenants to the rest of the development team. As space is leased or sold, it often becomes clear that certain aspects of design fare better in the marketplace than others. Ideally, the original overall design offers enough built-in flexibility that, during the development process, interior configurations, color schemes, and other features can be changed to suit the market as tenants' preferences are expressed and become clear (and change over time).

Financial Officer

The development team's financial officer manages the project's budget, ensures the timely payment of bills, and, beyond hard construction, ensures optimal use of available funds to achieve the plan's overall economics. Financial officers must also be sure that insurance coverage is exactly what is required and that the marketing manager is staying within budget. They also manage the relationship with the construction lender, the permanent lender, and any outside investors. Whenever feedback from the marketing staff or the architect suggests changes and the project manager is asked to estimate the cost of the suggested alternative, financial officers at the same time must determine whether the increment in value justifies the additional cost and whether the lender or the equity investor can be convinced to increase its financial commitment to the project to cover the additional costs.

Property Manager

The property manager, who ideally participated during the design stages, should also be involved during construction. As the marketing representative suggests changes and the construction manager responds with alternatives, the property manager should ensure that the proposed changes do not compromise the building's long-term manageability. Particularly when financing becomes tight, short-term decisions to solve financing problems—often referred to as "value engineering"—can cause long-term trouble. The property manager is responsible for ensuring that short-term solutions to problems during construction do not unduly complicate any important aspect of property and asset management (see Chapter 21). The future property manager, or some other member of the development team, should maintain positive relations with the various city regulatory bodies during construction. The orchestration of physical inspections by regulatory agencies as work proceeds (usually coordinated by the general contractor and the project manager) is only one aspect of managing government partners. Most development projects have several more points of contact—from shared policing of the construction site to new municipal bus stops.

Building the Structure

As noted earlier, the general contractor typically contracts with a variety of subcontractors to accomplish the physical work, buy the needed materials, and provide the needed equipment. These efforts usually involve installing the building's major systems, including the electrical, plumbing, and HVAC systems. Subcontractors are also typically engaged for excavation, foundation and concrete work, framing, drywall, roofing, trim, painting, and other specialty trades. (The developer can choose to do some or all of these functions with in-house staff.) In high-rise construction, the structural components are more difficult and the systems more complex, but the same principles apply. Although the general contractor manages the subcontractors, the project manager represents the developer's interests with the general contractor. At the same time, the developer makes sure that construction is coordinated with the ongoing marketing effort and that construction and marketing are covered by the available financing without sacrificing long-term management efficiencies.

Subcontractors vary dramatically in the size and organizational sophistication of their companies. Some subcontractors for mechanical systems are large regional or even national firms with sophisticated management procedures and accounting controls. By contrast, the masonry subcontractor or the painter could be one woman and her nephew with a few tools in the back of a pickup truck. The general contractor must choose the appropriate subcontractor for the job at hand, remembering that it is expensive to hire someone more skilled than necessary and imprudent and dangerous to hire someone less skilled than necessary. The appropriate subcontractor must have the time and resources to do the job when needed, remain financially solvent, and have appropriate insurance. Ideally, the subcontractors have earned the general contractor's trust based on reputation, past relations, and the possibility of future business. Depending on the relationship between the developer and the general contractor, the developer's in-house construction expertise, and the needs of the project, the developer sometimes hires individual subcontractors directly, often to lock in a price or a slot in the subcontractor's schedule. Regardless, developers are ultimately responsible, so it behooves them to know how the general contractor is handling the tradeoff between quality and experience versus availability and low cost in selecting subcontractors.

The general contractor's most important task is properly scheduling the different subcontractors' work and then making every effort to maintain that schedule. Although everyone appreciates the difficulty involved in putting on a roof before the walls are up, it is also difficult to know exactly how long it will take to put the walls up when the weather turns inclement. Because most construction is performed outdoors in uncertain weather conditions, even the most reliable subcontractors can fall behind schedule. If one task falls behind, the next subcontractor may be committed to another job when the previous subcontractor has

ELEVATION 314

Choosing the Right General Contractor for the Project

Construction Costs

Land	$1,000,000
Hard Costs/Site Improvement Costs	6,750,000
Soft Costs	1,150,000
Total	$8,900,000

Construction is where I had the most problems. In short, I picked the wrong builder. If there was one mistake that I made that carried throughout the project it was not putting enough value on experience. I wasn't that experienced and I never thought it would be a problem. For me, not being experienced meant that you'd come up with a fresh attitude and a lot more energy. Perhaps you'd do it better than anybody else could. Most of the consultants I used had varying degrees of experience and some had less experience than I did, but we were all the kind of people who would not stop until we had the right answer. I was accustomed to that level of honesty, candor, and hard work. I hired an architect who had not done a multifamily project. The firm had worked on a lot of big projects in the city but not multifamily.

I also hired a builder who had done renovations but had not been a base builder for a multifamily project. The builder was the weak link. There are so many different entities and companies and people that you have to rely on for a successful project. If one of the key players can't perform as they're supposed to, it puts a profound burden on the others.

The builder was inexperienced and turned out to be less than forthcoming about the problems he was having. We had a guaranteed maximum price contract with the builder. It's a very seriously negotiated contract. A guaranteed maximum price means that the builder has so much confidence in his ability to build that he will get it done for your specifications at a predetermined price—basically he's completely bid out the project and knows the costs. Up to a point, the builder was very open; I saw all the bids that fed into it and his fees and overhead expenses.

The builder's guaranteed maximum price fit the budget just fine. I came to learn much later, however, that there were significant gaps in the subcontracts that left the builder in a very bad position. Instead of coming to me and being honest, the builder tried to use change orders to deceptively reset the balance. We ended up in court over that because I wouldn't accept that the builder was not at fault for his subcontracting mistakes.

Construction was difficult as a result. I wouldn't wish that process on anybody. I have been involved in construction and architecture for a long time, and I have seriously involved myself in all my projects. Because I had the experience and I was fully invested, I was determined to figure it out. So I put more money into it, and I hired a construction manager. I also kept people on past the time that they were supposed to be working so they could continue to positively affect things. I got involved directly with some subcontractors and replaced people who weren't doing their work. It was very hard and it took a lot of very tough personal negotiations over the existing contracts. But the building got completed and to me that was the most important thing.

It took another year afterward to settle all the contract stuff; all the subcontractors settled out, and, through mediation and arbitration, the general settled in the end. The real lesson from that is that I will be more careful about selecting builders in the future, but I'll also be more careful to address every problem as it comes up. And I'll to try to negotiate settlements while everyone is still at the table.

It's kind of a shame that it was not a happy experience all the way through. But the building did get finished. And the only bad relationship I ended up with from the four- or five-year process was with the general contractor. I'm even still on very good terms with a lot of the subcontractors who worked there. I'm on good terms with the architects, the consultants, with the community, and with the local government. Construction for me was by far the hardest part of the process, and it shouldn't have been.

It's important to note that the construction problems had nothing to do with environmental elements; the problems had to do with ordering materials on time and scheduling contractors in the proper sequence and leaving gaps in contracts—really basic stuff. It had nothing to do with using bamboo instead of maple or a geothermal system instead of a split system. It was all doable but it was just poorly organized. I was not going to let the project fail, and I especially didn't want to hear people say, "See, green buildings are harder to build."

We wanted to prove that green buildings are not harder to build. We chose products and systems that had been tested over time and could be easily obtained. The concrete, for example, has a 20 percent fly ash additive, which is a standard option that happens to reduce landfill waste. Similarly, we used recycled or recyclable building materials whenever possible. All the wood used in the building came from Certified Managed Forests and is certified as sustainably harvested. The bamboo flooring was also sustainably harvested. Strategic siting and placement of windows further created savings in heating and cooling. We used

continued on next page

ELEVATION 314 *(continued)*

Elevation 314's geothermal heating and cooling system works by pumping water—using a mechanism located in the building's basement—through a series of pipes placed in 520-foot-deep (158.5-meter-deep) wells. The water returns to the building at 55 to 65 degrees Fahrenheit (12.8 to 18.3 degrees Celsius) and is then pumped throughout the building, thus saving energy because the water heaters always start heating from a consistent temperature.

low-volatile organic compound finishes. All the appliances are Energy Star rated. I consider making choices like these to be like picking low-hanging fruit.

By starting with a well-thought-out green design, we were able to achieve huge cost savings and avoid almost all construction challenges that could have been caused by building green.

With a construction cost of $115 per square foot ($1,240 per square meter), Elevation 314 was comparable with normal construction costs for the Washington, D.C., area. In most cases, we found that using green building techniques offered cost savings in addition to environmental and aesthetic benefits. For example, at $2 per square foot ($21.50 per square meter), the bamboo floors offered good looks and cost savings. The bioretention area and green roof systems are another example. The alternative to this stormwater management system was to use underground sand-filter chambers, which cost tens of thousands of dollars and require regular and difficult maintenance. Instead, the natural biofiltration system of the courtyard is a lower-cost, lower-maintenance, and more visually pleasing option.

Of all the green features in the project, only the geothermal heating and cooling system had a higher upfront cost than its conventional counterparts. The installation of the wells was in large part responsible for the higher costs. But the system will pay for itself through energy savings within seven years. Further, the equipment life span is estimated to be at least two times that of the next best system (a gas furnace and split air conditioning). Because I'm investing in Elevation 314 for the long term, equipment life is a major consideration.

continued on page 500

---

finally completed its task. Thus, four days of heavy rain can throw a schedule far more than four days behind. The general contractor must be flexible enough and forceful enough to make certain that subcontractors adjust their other schedules as necessary.

According to Russell Katz, the hardest part of developing Elevation 314 was working with the general contractor. These difficulties turned into construction delays, numerous headaches, and quite a bit of overtime for Katz's development team.

Drawing Down the Construction Loan

Lenders, not surprisingly, are reluctant to pay their entire share of the cost of a development before the collateral has been created. In fact, they normally provide funds only as construction progress is

demonstrated. Similarly, the developer is not required to pay the general contractor before the work is performed, although general contractors and subcontractors are reluctant and often unable to wait until the completion of all construction and final inspections before receiving any payments. In most construction contracts, the parties agree that the developer will pay for the work program as it progresses while retaining a set amount—often 10 percent of the cost of construction—until the end of the job. Thus, for a $100,000 construction job (with a provision for 10 percent retainage) that is 20 percent complete, the general contractor has earned a $20,000 payment but would receive only $18,000, with the developer (and in turn the lender) retaining $2,000 until completion. Only upon "satisfactory" completion does the general contractor (and through him the subcontractors) receive the amounts retained. "Satisfactory" means that all provisions of the agreement between owner and general contractor have been met and accepted by the architect, the building officials, and the developer. Thus, retainage is a major device that ensures completion in accordance with plans and specifications. It is also partial protection for the developer against default by the general contractor.

The paperwork involved in drawing down funds from the construction lender typically follows a clearly delineated path. Periodically, often every month, the subcontractor submits an invoice for work completed. The general contractor then compiles invoices from all the subcontractors and, often with input from the architect and the project manager, examines the subcontracted work to ensure that the percentage of work claimed has been completed according to the plans and specifications. If discrepancies arise, the general contractor works them out with the subcontractor(s) and eventually sends an invoice to the developer for the combined total of all subcontractors' draw requests plus the general contractor's fee and other markups and eligible costs. In this way, individual subcontractors can be paid by the end of the month for the work completed minus the amount for retainage.

The project manager (or the architect) verifies to the developer and the lenders that the total invoice submitted by the general contractor agrees with the contract between the general contractor and the developer, that the work has been completed, and that it meets plans and specifications. At this point, the approved invoices are sent to the developer's financial officer. The financial officer combines the invoice for construction costs (the hard costs) with various other "soft costs" associated with the development—insurance, property taxes, interest on the construction loan, marketing costs, and general administrative overhead, for example—and then submits a total figure to the construction lender as a draw request.

The loan agreement with the construction lender typically stipulates that the lender will provide fund-ing as needed to cover the costs so long as the costs are within budget. Thus, the financial officer uses the budget originally defined in the feasibility study and refined during stage four to produce a monthly draw request that ties to the original budget, summarizing costs to date, the amount for the relevant period, and the remaining balance available for completion, typically for each item in the cost budget. (During stage four, the developer argued for as few categories as possible to achieve more flexibility in moving funds around while the lender favored more categories to increase control.)

The construction lender verifies that the request from the developer is in accordance with the loan agreement and that all participants (the architect or project manager, the general contractor, and the financial officer) have initialed the request. The lender might decide to personally inspect the construction to ensure that the project is proceeding as the draw request indicates. Finally, the construction lender verifies that the development appears to be on time and within budget for both hard and soft costs.

Assuming that all requirements are satisfied, the construction lender deposits funds in the developer's account for the total amount of the draw. The financial officer then writes a check to the general contractor, who in turn pays the various subcontractors. Disbursements for soft costs are also made directly to the appropriate vendors and service providers by the financial officer.

One risk control device that lenders may use is to disburse funds only through title companies. In such cases, subcontractors exchange lien waivers for their appropriate draw checks. The title company can thus ensure that all subcontractors have acknowledged payment before funds are disbursed, thereby protecting the lender from mechanic's liens filed by unpaid subcontractors.

Mechanic's liens are liens on the property that arise when a contractor goes to court to seek help in collecting payment for construction work. To protect workers (considered being at risk relative to big institutions), the law provides that mechanic's liens take effect when the work is done, not when the lien is filed. Thus, the lender could lose the coveted first lien position to a previously unrecorded claim. Laws that apply to mechanic's liens vary significantly by state, and the developer is well advised to engage legal counsel familiar with applicable local laws.

The length of time from the billing cutoff date (usually the last day of each month) until funds are disbursed to the subcontractors can be critical. If the elapsed time between performance of the work and payment for the work becomes too long, a significant burden is imposed on the subcontractors.

For example, suppose a subcontractor submits a bill at the end of each month, that each month's average billing is $50,000, and that payment is received on the 15th of the following month. Under this scenario, the subcontractor must finance its work for one and one-half months or, in this example, in the amount of $75,000. This burden can be minimized by making payments more often, perhaps twice a month, or by speeding the approval and payment process so the waiting time is reduced to perhaps one week rather than 15 days. But the principle is the same: every contractor and subcontractor must be financially able to carry a portion of the work until the disbursement of funds.

Leasing Space and "Building Out" The Tenant Space

Even with extensive preleasing before construction commences, some space usually remains unleased at the initiation of construction and therefore must be marketed during construction. Ideally, tenants will pay rent on every square foot of the building on the day the project opens. One cost item in the pro forma, however, is usually an operating deficit for the period immediately after construction until the building is sufficiently leased and occupied to cover debt service and all operating expenses. A major goal of most developers is to capture this leasing reserve. If total costs include the cost of funding a deficit and the deficit does not materialize because the building is fully leased and occupied when it opens, then the budget item moves from the cost column and eventually adds to profit on the development.

Museum Towers had the advantage of an extremely favorable market and skilled professional marketers. Yet it did not achieve 100 percent occupancy, and leasing for the most expensive units was much slower than expected.

In addition to an operating budget shortfall or lease-up reserve, the lender's agreement might provide for floor and ceiling loan amounts. For example, the total amount of the loan will be only x dollars until y percent of the building is leased, at which time the remaining amount will be funded. If such a provision is found in the permanent loan, the construction lender typically lends only the floor amount, which is the permanent or takeout lender's minimum commitment. Usually this scenario requires the developer to

---

MUSEUM TOWERS
Leasing during Construction

The rental housing market in the Boston area had been extremely strong for quite some time. With a vacancy rate of less than 2 percent in 1998, rents increased across the board at a rate of 5 to 10 percent annually in the late 1990s. Renters in this market were waiting for something new for a long time, at least ten years.

Developers have to have a bit of what we call "snake oil salesmanship." Real estate development projects require a lot of selling, at every step. You gotta sell to your banks, to your partners, to the tenants, to the public, to the leasing guys so they can sell it to others. And a lot of this selling goes on while the building is being constructed, so you have to convince everyone that they're going to like what they see before they see it. It's not always easy, so as a developer, you really have to believe in your product.

On the other hand, selling real estate is like selling anything. You need a complete marketing plan and the right people to execute it. As of June 1999, we had made only one major error. We were 70 percent leased but had planned to be 90 percent leased by that time. Essentially all of the lower-priced units were leased, but we probably held out for too high a rate in the best units. Overall, the market's strength allowed us to be above pro forma revenue, which is clearly good. But if we hadn't been quite so aggressive on rates for the best units, we would have had more income during construction.

continued on page 496

put up whatever funds beyond the floor loan are needed before starting construction. This type of loan provision places pressure on the developer's financing. Usually the developer must cover the required equity before the lender begins advancing funds. Even if the construction lender will fund the loan without the "potential additional equity," there is pressure. If marketing does not proceed according to schedule, the developer will, at some point, have drawn down the full amount of the loan, which can cause problems. The developer may have to provide funds "out of pocket," or out of his own equity, for the balance of the project. As construction progresses, it is difficult to tell participants to stop and wait a month until more space is leased. Construction must continue as scheduled, or costs will surely escalate. Office space leases in major downtown buildings cover such physical details as the location of interior walls, the number of electrical outlets and plumbing fixtures, and the type of carpeting. Thus, the leasing agent's negotiations directly influence the construction crew's work and what must be financed. Meanwhile, money might not be available to pay the general contractors and subcontractors, who will not be sympathetic with the marketing staff's failure to meet the leasing expectations. The lender will not fund an amount above the floor until the additional leasing occurs—and the pressure mounts.

Developers can cover such funding shortfalls themselves or induce outside investors to cover them. But once a project is in trouble, it is much harder and more expensive to secure additional funding.

Landscaping and Exterior Construction

The initial feasibility study likely included at least one line item in the budget for landscape architecture and design—an important component in marketing a project. Many developers of large commercial projects are now nearly as careful about selecting a landscape architect as they are about selecting a building architect. Landscape elements help set the image for a project and create an environment that will appeal to future tenants. Creative landscaping distinguishes a project from the competition and therefore can accelerate leasing. Coordinated in the landscaping, visible environmental features can go a long way toward attracting clients and making a project acceptable to neighbors.

Landscape covers a wide range of additions to the built environment. In a development of less expensive single-family houses, it might involve only spreading topsoil, seeding it, and planting a few shrubs. A major downtown mixed-use project might involve porches, decks, walkways, street furniture (such as benches, lighting, and signs), intensively planted areas, and even some works of art.

Landscape planning should begin early during site design, particularly if the site has existing features that must be preserved or protected during construction. For a variety of reasons, the installation of landscape elements typically is completed late in the construction process. From the perspective of design, landscape treatments can respond to a different mix of tenants from that originally envisioned, adding an element of flexibility for the developer. Operationally, once in place landscaping must be maintained. If installed too early during the construction process, landscape materials will likely be vulnerable to destruction by construction vehicles still on site. Further, the appropriate maintenance personnel will not yet be on staff.

Potential Problems

The circumstances described in the following illustration all occurred on the same project. Such linked problems are likely to plague most developers at some point during their career.

Imagine the development of a tennis village designed to be one of the premier tennis facilities in the world. Located on a 200-acre (81-hectare) site in an established resort, this "project within a project" was planned in multiple phases. The first phase contained the main clubhouse, the central tennis courts, a small hotel, and 50 townhouses. In subsequent phases, another 300 townhouses and more tennis courts will be added.

The financing negotiated for the project allows the developer, who is putting up $500,000, to borrow up to $24.5 million as needed. The developer's joint venture partner is a "deep pocket" or well-capitalized equity investor and is personally

MUSEUM TOWERS
Initiating Construction

Construction of Museum Towers used the PERI forming system, the same system used to erect the Petronas Towers in Kuala Lumpur, Malaysia, two of the world's tallest buildings. The PERI system, developed in Weissenhorn, Germany, is a formwork and scaffolding system. Basically, a shore or support beam is put up, another beam is put on top, and a modular panel follows. When the panel is stripped out, the system comes out in pieces and is reassembled on another floor. The walls of the towers were constructed using the TRIO system, which is a modular system that uses clamping mechanisms rather than nut-and-bolt attachments. The SKYDECK system was used for the building's slabs.

The PERI system allows construction to go at a rate three or four times faster than a conventional construction system. It's also lightweight and safer than most other systems.

It isn't cheap, but building in Boston never is and we needed to minimize the time we had to pay the 20+ percent interest on the mezzanine debt.

continued on page 547

Museum Towers was constructed using the PERI forming system, the same system that was used to construct two of the world's tallest buildings, the Petronas Towers in Kuala Lumpur, Malaysia. J. Apicella—Cesar Pelli & Associates, Inc.

guaranteeing the loan for 50 percent of the development profits. The $25 million thus available will cover the initial cost of the central courts, the 70-room hotel, the clubhouse, and the first 50 townhouses and then become a revolving loan.

Under the arrangement, the developer will pay back the $24.5 million as he sells the first 50 townhouses. Assuming the units sell for $250,000 each, as projected in the feasibility study, 50 units will generate $12.5 million. This money will then be available for the developer to draw down again to continue building townhouses in subsequent phases. Accordingly, the project involves a certain amount of financing for the courts, hotel, and clubhouse, which will eventually be repaid from a permanent loan closed with the transfer of the amenities to the property owners. The revolving portion of the construction financing allows the developer to continue

building townhouses so long as the first units sell. The logistics incorporated in the feasibility study show the developer realizing no profit from the first group of townhouses. They are priced to induce the first residents to buy into a novel concept. He does, however, receive a development fee on the first phase and expects to profit handsomely on subsequent phases as he increases the price but not the cost of the remaining 250 townhouse units. If the developer stays within the forecasted time and costs, which were incorporated in the loan document, the financing package will remain intact through multiple phases of development and produce substantial profits down the road. If marketing slips or construction is delayed, problems will arise.

As the developer of this project, you are six months from completion of the clubhouse, the hotel, the stadium tennis courts, and the first 50 townhouses. Life is good; your joint venture partner is happy and the return on your investment (plus the $500,000) looks huge. At the weekly project coordination meeting, the marketing staff tells you that the two-bedroom units are sold out but that the one-bedroom units, which are essentially the same size but feature a balcony, are not selling at all. The first 50 units were planned to include 25 two-bedroom units and 25 one-bedroom units, but now the marketing staff suggests changing most of the 25 one-bedroom units to two-bedroom units. The construction manager tells you that the additional walls and minimal additional electrical service needed for the change will require $450,000 total, or $18,000 per unit. You agree to the change, remembering $625,000 allocated in the budget for contingencies.

Then it rains—every day for two weeks—in what should have been the dry season. Because the subcontractors' other commitments are also backing up, rescheduling proves to be difficult and the project slips four weeks behind schedule. Time is critical: early buyers are looking forward to the tennis tournament scheduled for September, which will be carried on national TV and has been a major selling point. Moreover, the rescheduling will cost some money. The subcontractors want incentive compensation to return promptly to the project, and their prompt return is essential to making the grand opening coincide with the tennis tournament. The interest meter will now run for a full additional month. The total added expense will likely total $325,000. What to do?

The solution to the second problem is to approach the construction lender and claim, in an appropriately humble manner, that an act of God has wiped out the amount set aside for contingencies (the original $625,000 minus $450,000 for 25 conversions to two-bedroom units leaves only $175,000). The construction lender, who initially claimed to be your partner in the development process, should understand that events beyond your control sometimes require a little more cash.

If the lender goes along with your request, however, he also puts himself in a difficult position. The original financing provides a permanent takeout loan on the clubhouse, stadium tennis courts, and hotel

for $12 million (predicated on completion of construction according to plans and specifications). If the cost overrun is allocated to these facilities, then the lender has loaned more than the agreed-upon $12 million, which is tied to his estimate of value for the improvements. What is the source of payment for the additional funding? If the lender allocates the excess amount to the townhouses, he must believe that the sale price will be sufficiently higher to cover the loan. In other words, he must assume a little more risk or believe that the price can be higher than projected in the original feasibility study. He decides, based in part on your charm, to allocate the excess to the townhouse units, believing that they can be sold at a somewhat higher price than specified in the feasibility study. These first two problems and their solution are rather common. What follows is less common.

Two weeks later, the marketing staff returns, highly upset. Architectural costs for this particular job were kept to a minimum by using the architect only through rough construction drawings. Your in-house project manager (an engineer) finalized the site plans and has managed the process to date. As the job began, the general contractor noted a large quantity of rock at the end of the site where the first phase of townhouses was to be located. Working with your project manager, he determined that if the units were relocated slightly closer to the outlying tennis courts, which were in the center of each cluster of units, far less rock would have to be moved and costs could be kept to a minimum. The project manager approved the new location of the units, and the development team was pleased because a potential problem had been solved expeditiously with only a slight shift in design and no increase in site costs.

Regrettably, when the units were moved closer, the end units with the attractive bay windows ceased to look out toward the mountains and looked instead into another bedroom window 12 feet (3.6 meters) away. According to the marketing staff, these units could not be sold for any amount close to the projected price and would have to be rented instead. Normally, you cannot expect a limited price cut on a luxury item to clear the market when the item has a flaw that is

Thirty days before its scheduled grand opening, a fire destroyed many of Santana Row's retail and restaurant spaces as well as 250 luxury apartments. Fortunately, insurance covered the fire damage, and developer Federal Realty Investment Trust was able to rebuild almost immediately. *Federal Realty Investment Trust*

obvious to even the most unsophisticated consumer. If the end units, eight of them in this first phase, are kept as rental rather than for-sale units and the $12.5 million townhouse construction loan for the townhouses is thus not fully paid back as planned, you will be short of cash as development continues. You might have to develop in smaller phases (fewer townhouses in each), which would be inefficient and raise your construction costs. This is not a story you want to tell your lender or your partner, who has guaranteed the loan.

But your troubles do not stop here. Three weeks before the scheduled grand opening, another deluge of rain falls, and a second flaw in the redesign is discovered. With the units now located closer to the tennis courts, the stormwater runoff cannot be fully absorbed by the original drainage system, and the units on the lower side of the courts flood. The flood ruins the drywall and carpeting in ten units that had been scheduled to close in two weeks.

In addition to the costs of replacing the drywall and carpeting, you must find a solution to the drainage problem. Working with your in-house engineer and the general contractor, you identify a solution that will cost $160,000 ($70,000 for new materials and other miscellaneous repairs and $90,000 to install a new "Mediterranean" drainage system on the lower side of the tennis courts). Unlike the money involved in the no-view/no-sale units, the $160,000 is needed now. The end of the construction period is near, and not much leeway is left to shift expenditures between budget categories, even if the lender would permit it. You have already asked nicely at the bank and received more money for a problem that was an act of God and not your fault. What do you do now? If you show weakness, the lender may "deem itself insecure" (a provision in most new construction loans that allows foreclosure before default if the lender decides that there is no way for you to finish successfully). If you ask your joint venture partner for help (that firm is also at risk, given these problems), it will clearly want to renegotiate the 50/50 split of the expected profits from subsequent phases of the development.

Assuming you solve that problem, the project advances to the week before the scheduled grand opening. It is August in the Southwest, and the beautiful landscaping is brown. Apparently, the flood was followed by two weeks of hot sun and the lack of water was fatal. The landscape contractor assumed that the property manager would take responsibility for landscape maintenance. Somehow the property manager did not get the signal, and $100,000 worth of plants are dead. Your high-end buyers may not go to closing with dead shrubs, and if you back off the grand opening, you could lose existing presales; that is, people who previously agreed to buy might decide they do not want to buy a unit in your development. How do you solve the problem? Remember that, as the developer, everything is ultimately your responsibility. In each stage of the development process, we have discussed risk control techniques. Which would have been appropriate for this development situation?

STAGE SEVEN: COMPLETION AND FORMAL OPENING

Training the operations staff, connecting utilities, beginning on-site operations, final marketing of the development, the grand opening, tenants' moving in, and a transition in financing from the construction loan to the permanent loan collectively constitute stage seven—completion and formal opening.

Operations personnel are brought to the site before the grand opening. Their job is to make sure that tenants get the space with associated services specified in the lease agreements. The amount of time the operations people spend on site before opening depends on their functions and on the project's size and type. In a convention hotel, for example, some marketing people may join the operations staff two years early.

The marketing people, working with the operations personnel, handle activities before the opening—advertising, promotion, VIP parties, and the like. It is often good business to throw a party to thank the people who have helped you. In the process, you generate some long-term good will in the community and the market, and you can use the opportunity to invite potential customers to visit the development. Before the party, however, the utilities must be connected, which means all obligations to the city must have been met. Building inspectors must ensure that final items were installed according to code. Mistakenly assuming that city inspections are only an annoying technicality can result in cancellation of the party. The government is always your partner.

Suppose that, during the final stages of construction, a pipe on the 25th floor bursts and water seeps in and damages key components of the fire alarm system. A fire inspection is scheduled in two days and tenants are moving in two days after that, but now the alarm system must be rewired—a process that will take longer than two days. Rescheduling the inspection will force a delay of at least two weeks even if the city inspector, whom you've been cultivating since stage three, bends over backward to be helpful. What do you tell tenants who plan to move in next week?

During the construction phase, all the interior finish work specified by tenants expected in the initial move should be completed. The marketing staff must coordinate work with the tenants so that the new occupants can move in and be ready to operate in their new space. With the tenants in place and paying rent, the permanent loan can be serviced. Typically, it is closed and the construction lender repaid during stage eight.

In addition, a shift might occur from the developer as the controlling equity interest to a new long-term equity investor. The new investor might have in-house management personnel, rely on outside property management companies, or hire the developer as manager. In fact, the developer in many cases stays on as a partner with the new investor. Even with this arrangement, a significant part of the risk shifts from the developer, who has now completed the development, to the long-term investor.

ELEVATION 314
Elevation 314 Nears Completion

One of the hardest things in the development business is just getting the project done. It's very tough to get things done when you are involved in a project that ends with gaps in the contract, and that's exactly the position the contractors left me in. Motivation is extremely difficult, but you have to find a way. There are lots of different ways of motivating people. And that goes back to the negotiation.

One of the things that frustrated me with the builder was the grand opening celebration. I'm a planner and I love organizing months and years in advance with spreadsheets and calendars and tables. I had been planning a very nice grand opening party to say "thank you" to community and government officials who'd been involved.

The schedule had me starting to ramp up to it for six months. I was doing some press releases and getting the invitations out. I was relying on the builder's word that the building would be done on the date. They kept telling me four weeks before, and then three weeks before, "We'll get it done. We'll get it done."

Mayor Anthony Williams (the mayor of D.C. at the time) among others was supposed to be there, and I had to cancel the party. It was really a disappointment for me. We ended up finishing about two and a half months later. We did end up doing a really nice grand opening, but it was after the building was pretty much occupied because I was just too busy to get back and reorganize it. It was sort of a grand opening and a party for the new tenants. It ended up being really fun because many of the people who came had been involved in the project at different times. They were able to see it occupied and talk to the tenants.

Leasing went really well. Many of the units were rented even before the building was completed. We even got partial certificates of occupancy for some units. I think we rented quickly because of the location, the unique qualities of the building, and the low rents we were able to offer, and because we kept the costs where they needed to be. I was really surprised because I thought the place really didn't look fully inhabitable when we started leasing units, but I suppose people were already able to see what they liked.

We had tenants in place even during pretty heavy construction. When we were putting in the whole bioretention system, the green roof, and the back parking lot, we had a dozen people in the building and that number was increasing every week or so. Now we maintain close to 100 percent occupancy. Renting now happens mainly by word of mouth. We don't even advertise, although we do post on the Internet when we have vacancies.

The completion in terms of the design, the management rollout, and the renting was great. It was easy because the building was so environmentally compelling. Going back to the three original pillars (a beautiful building, a green building, a financially successful building), we hit our goals. We offered units at the right price. In terms of design, it is a comfortable, serene place to be—a place that you could see yourself going back to at the end of the day. And it is environmentally advanced.

We found that as we rented up in the beginning, the percentage of people who came because it is a green building was usually about half. I thought it would be at least 90 percent, especially during the first renting phase. The few marketing materials that we created referred to it as "urban eco-living," but probably a little fewer than half the people moved in just because they liked the place, mentioning things like the high ceilings and being next to Metro. A lot of them just thought it was pretty and a beautiful place to be.

I taught my managers how to give the spiel about the environmental stuff when they were showing Elevation 314 to potential renters. As my managers explained it, they'd start the spiel but if someone's eyes started glazing over, they'd switch to talking about the high ceilings and hardwood floors. But now I'd say that most of the tenants—we've been renting for almost two and a half years now—value the environmental qualities. Those are the type of people who are ready to jump in when we have a vacancy.

continued on page 516

RISK CONTROL DURING STAGES SIX AND SEVEN

Under pressure to keep construction and marketing on schedule while keeping costs within budget, developers use appropriate risk controls. Some possible risk control techniques follow:

1. Retainage, discussed earlier, and performance bonds are useful methods of controlling construction risk. Retainage allows the developer to hold back cash to ensure the contractor's satisfactory completion of work. A surety company's guarantee of completion or performance of a general contractor's contract reduces the devel-

oper's risk by providing a "deep pocket" equity investor. (Unfortunately, even such guarantees do not eliminate the time risk.) Likewise, a bonded general contractor reduces the city's risk when infrastructure is involved.

2. Union relations are an important consideration in many areas of the country. Sensitivity to the unions and to construction workers in general can only benefit the developer. On a high-rise project in Manhattan, for example, the entire construction process can be stopped by one person—the worker who runs the construction elevator. If that person belongs to a union different from the other workers and decides to strike, the other workers cannot get to their jobs, even if they are willing to cross the one-person picket line.

3. Architectural supervision and construction project management are obviously important risk control techniques. In addition to supervising the general contractor, developers can require contractors to include warranties in their contracts. Beyond promises of structural integrity, which can be the basis of subsequent lawsuits, developers should also check that subcontractors have the necessary licenses to perform the specified work and that they are paid a reasonable amount for what is expected of them. Unless the developer is one step ahead of a potential issue, the subcontractor with a problem could eventually become the developer's problem.

4. Liability, fire, and extended insurance coverage are basic to controlling risks. For insurance to work, developers must be covered for what might happen, and the insurance must be in force at the right time.

5. By focusing on critical events, PERT and CPM and similar program management systems are useful techniques for managing time and thus controlling risk. There are many software packages available to perform critical path analysis for construction. (See the bibliography for descriptions of these operations research techniques.) Many of these packages now connect to the Internet so that project managers in the field can easily communicate with the architect in his office and the marketing staff in a prospective office.

6. Preleasing and presales reduce the risk of initial high vacancies. Careful attention to the tenant mix also helps reduce risk. If tenants "fit" together or if one tenant draws others, fewer problems with long-term vacancies are likely.

7. For small tenants, insurance covering lease guarantees or some type of letter of credit is another possible risk control technique. Depending on the strength of the market, it might be possible to obtain high rent from a small tenant. Without some type of outside guarantee that the tenant will be able to pay the rent, however, there may be no increase in value to the development from these higher rents. Although formal insurance is relatively uncommon, some form of guarantee for a smaller and newer tenant's performance is common. The guarantee can range from the tenant's designation of a cosigner to the occupant's completing a portion of the finish work, thereby enhancing its commitment to the space.

8. Net leases, expense stops, and escalations are all important devices to control risk for long-term investors, and developers should structure leases with these possibilities in mind. When market conditions permit, developers should make sure that they are not the first to absorb all the pain in the event of rapid inflation in expenses. Lessening such exposure makes long-term investors happy to raise the sale price and hence increase profits during the development period.

9. The operating agreement negotiated with tenants during the leasing process is another risk control technique. By controlling how tenants relate to one another and to the building, developers can help ensure long-term operating viability and a minimum of maintenance problems.

10. Good internal controls, particularly the accounting system, are critical during development. The closer the developer's financial officer or accountant is to the entire billing process, the less the risk of error, theft, and fraud.

11. It is essential to involve the operations professionals in project planning and to involve them

in the project early. Otherwise, both initial and long-term operation of the facility could be less efficient—and more expensive—than it should be. Poor service can establish an image that will be expensive to change later.

When evaluating whether these techniques are appropriate for any particular development, it is helpful to keep in mind the fundamental things that can be done to reduce risk. As noted in most insurance textbooks, there are six conceptual ways to reduce risk:

1. Avoid risk by stopping in stage one, two, or three before much money is committed.
2. Invest in additional research; it is possible to know more about potential market reactions by completing a more substantial feasibility study in stage three.
3. Engage in some form of "loss prevention." In development, the most obvious is a more competent development team assembled in stages four and five.
4. Transfer a potential loss to other players through the contracts negotiated in stage four.
5. Combine and diversify to reduce the pain of large losses. Buy insurance for stages six through eight, for example.

6. Assume risks. After adopting some of these concepts, the developer must assume the residual risk. Developers are the type of people who can live and work in risky environments. Successful developers price all risks and accept them (i.e., allow a residual risk) only when costs justify it.

SUMMARY

The physical structure is built during stage six of the development process, requiring constant interplay among the construction, marketing, financial, government, and operating personnel. The developer's role shifts with the move to stage six: he becomes less a promoter and more a manager. Time becomes the critical risk element. It takes an extremely competent manager to successfully coordinate all the activities that unfold simultaneously during stage six.

Stage seven encompasses the activities associated with completion and the formal opening. It requires considerations involving the public sector, tenants, the interior layout, operations personnel, and a shift in financing to long-term investors. Stage seven is the end of the active phase of real estate development and sets the stage for asset and property management—stage eight.

TERMS

▶ Construction manager
▶ Draw request
▶ Escalation
▶ General contractor
▶ Lien waiver
▶ Marketing manager
▶ Mechanic's lien
▶ Phased development
▶ Project manager
▶ Retainage

REVIEW QUESTIONS

20.1 How does stage six differ from the first five stages?

Grand opening ceremonies can play an important role in both marketing and community relations. Sereno Transit Village is a 125-unit transit-oriented rental housing complex in the Bay Area city of Vallejo, California. All units are reserved for those receiving less than 50 percent of the area median income. *Courtesy of the city of Vallejo, California*

20.2 What is the role of the developer in managing the construction process? How does it differ from the role of the project manager?

20.3 Why is appropriate scheduling particularly important for the project manager?

20.4 How can a new developer avoid some of the problems that Russell Katz experienced with Elevation 314?

20.5 Describe the process of drawing down the construction loan.

20.6 How does good landscaping add to the value of a project?

20.7 What are the elements of stage seven? Who assumes the risk at this point in the process?

20.8 Describe some of the risks inherent in stages six and seven and some ways to avoid them.

20.9 Summarize the various risk reduction strategies available to the developer.

PART VIII

MAKING IT WORK

Value is derived from a project's long-term viability, which depends heavily on the quality of ongoing management, marketing, and sales. Initially, the developer seeks to add value by matching an idea to a site and guiding the process of constructing an attractive, efficient building. At the end of the development process, the asset and property management functions work to increase value through leasing and managing the project.

At completion of construction, the development team and the development—the product—are tested. Until now, it was not possible to test the product the way other consumer goods are tested. That is why every step in the development process to this point must be conducted carefully and thoroughly, with an awareness of the project's operating future. In other words, it is important to anticipate stage eight of the real estate development process throughout stages one through seven.

CHAPTER 21

Stage Eight: Property, Asset, and Portfolio Management

Real estate development is a process that transforms an idea into bricks and mortar. Once the development is complete, it is the responsibility of the management triad—the property managers, asset managers, and portfolio managers—to deliver the cash flows envisioned in the feasibility study and to maintain the physical structure and site so as to protect the project's long-term profitability. To accomplish this task, the real property management triad must focus on one key reality: bricks and mortar are only tools to satisfy the customers, who ultimately create value through income in the form of rental payments or purchase prices.

The functions of the management triad are interrelated and overlapping, and they collectively are essential to maximizing the value of the real estate. Sometimes a single individual may perform two (or even all three) of the management functions, although the three functions are distinct.

The property management team focuses on the day-to-day operation of the physical site; their primary task is to ensure a high-quality environment for tenants and thus a continuous cash flow for owners. By constantly monitoring the submarket where the asset competes (its situs), a property manager can effectively implement the strategic directives developed by the asset manager to satisfy the portfolio manager's objectives.

Asset management broadens the focus of property management and marketing beyond one physical facility and its users to several different properties that may employ a variety of property management and marketing teams. Asset management monitors the performance of property management and provides clear guidance to allow the teams to develop strategic plans that will maximize the assets' values in the context of portfolio management's objectives and capital resources and in the constraints presented by market conditions.

After development, ongoing real estate profits are created in three basic ways: buying at the right time or at a favorable price (either from the developer or the owner of an existing property), operating a property to maximize the present value of cash flows over

John B. Detwiler, Guggenheim Real Estate, Charlotte, North Carolina, updated this chapter.

the holding period, and selling at the right time or at a favorable price. It is the responsibility of asset management to oversee all three activities on behalf of individual or institutional investors and, in effect, serve as the de facto property owner.[1]

Real estate portfolio management is even broader than asset management. This discipline necessitates a deep understanding of the owner's investment objectives to evaluate asset management performance, analyze the costs and benefits of capital improvements recommended by asset management, and orchestrate acquisitions and dispositions of assets to maximize risk-adjusted portfolio returns.

This chapter discusses the following topics in detail:

▶ The enterprise concept espoused by James A. Graaskamp, which explores the concept of a building as a dynamic business—not just bricks and mortar—competing in an ever-changing market;

▶ A definition of the real estate management triad and its increasing importance in real estate development;

▶ The fundamentals of real estate management from the perspective of development;

▶ The transition from property development to asset management and the development of a strategic plan for the asset;

▶ Management's role in implementing the strategic plan—the heart of this chapter;

▶ The influence of the public sector in the management of real estate projects;

▶ Training for property, asset, and portfolio managers to ensure that the individuals responsible for the assets are properly prepared and capable; and

▶ The corporate real estate director.

THE ENTERPRISE CONCEPT AND CONTINUING MANAGEMENT OF THE DEVELOPED ASSET

The enterprise concept, as originally espoused by James A. Graaskamp, portrays real estate as an enter-prise and thus sets the stage for business-like, aggressive management. Considered one of the most innovative thinkers among real estate academicians, Graaskamp campaigned for years for a change from the concept of real estate as bricks and mortar to the concept of a building as an operating entity, that is, a living, breathing business with a cash flow cycle similar to any other operating business. He suggested that developers should recognize that buildings are like businesses that continually need to redefine their market positions and seek new niches in the marketplace. From the standpoint of development, the enterprise concept means not only that marketing must be ongoing but also, in all probability, that the structure itself will have to adjust over time to meet new needs of the marketplace.

The notion of treating real estate assets as a business is important, because operating businesses must continually reinvent themselves to remain viable. IBM, for example, is a different company today from what it was fifteen years ago, let alone in 1911 when it was first incorporated. Google opened its door—a garage door—in 1998. By 2006 it was a multibillion dollar company and "google" had become a much-used verb worldwide. Although it is true that real estate assets have a long life and a fixed location, it is also important to note that the demands of building users are constantly evolving. If real estate developers appreciate that they are creating an ongoing business, not simply bricks and mortar, they will be more likely to incorporate into their projects the design flexibility needed for long-term operating success in a dynamic environment.

The enterprise concept is not new; it is just more important now than ever before. That is why the framework established earlier in this text focused on the extended venture capital period, level two feasibility, and a tighter connection to the business operations of prospective tenants. These aspects are all contemporary components of Graaskamp's enterprise concept.

An example of the enterprise concept in action is the Showplace Square development in San Francisco's South of Market (SoMa) district. The development originated in a cluster of underused industrial build-

▶ PROFILE

JAMES A. GRAASKAMP

Former Chair and Professor, Department of Real Estate and Urban Land Economics

University of Wisconsin at Madison

The late Jim Graaskamp was a hero and mentor to his students and others who knew him. At the time of his death in 1988, the wheelchair-bound quadriplegic professor was the driving force behind the real estate program at the University of Wisconsin at Madison. Crippled by polio since his teens, Graaskamp, who turned lecture notes with a stick held in place with his teeth, viewed his handicap as a "materials-handling problem."

His disability, however, did not prevent him from earning a PhD in 1964, teaching real estate, encouraging new theories of real estate, and consulting through his Landmark Research company. Well known for his articulate and spellbinding speeches, he was also often an outspoken critic—with many critics of his own—on national and local land use policies, often taking very unpopular positions.

Graaskamp understood that, in a world of change and uncertainty, determining a course of action is more important than merely pricing assets. Graaskamp was a visionary in the field of real estate with a strong system of ethics. He believed that the developer's profit should be the secondary motivation for a development project. For if a project fails, the negative consequences do not stop with the investor. In fact, Graaskamp wrote that a project should not be viewed as solvent if society has been shortchanged in its development. He conceptualized a real estate development process that would maximize the benefits not for just a few individuals, but for the greater society.

Feasibility analysis—the determination of what makes sense and why—was Graaskamp's major contribution to the real estate field. He developed methods for solving problems based on the tenet that, because the key characteristic of real estate is its location, most real estate problems are unique to the particular site. In response, he developed the microanalytical approach to real estate problem solving, in which the issues are defined in terms of the specific location, the individual developer, the micromarket, and other characteristics of the project.

According to Graaskamp, the real estate feasibility process should attempt to answer the following four questions:

1. *What is it that we are doing?* The three possibilities are a site in search of a user, a user in search of a site, or an investor seeking a development opportunity. If beginning with the site, the site's attributes should determine the project. Beginning with a user requires identifying a site that matches the user's requirements. When starting with an investor, the investor's objectives are the crucial element.
2. *For whom are we doing it?* Realizing that development occurs for many reasons beyond simply maximizing the investor's income, Graaskamp believed that it is important to understand the individual developer's goals.
3. *To whom are we doing it?* This question addresses understanding the market to adapt the product to its needs.
4. *Will it fly?* More than just the narrow concern of "will it sell?" this question seeks to explore broader issues regarding the project's physical, legal, and financial viability.

Graaskamp expanded on the traditional concept of highest and best use with the more idealistic "most fitting use," in which the land use is measured by its optimization of consumer satisfaction, cost of production, impact on third parties, and, finally, profit to the investor. He also defined the more pragmatic "most probable use," described as less than the most fitting use but constrained by political factors, short-term solvency, and the state of real estate technology.

Although better known for the spoken word than for his writings, Graaskamp authored *The Fundamentals of Real Estate Development*, published by ULI in 1981. In addition, his life and work were the inspiration for ULI's 1991 book, *Graaskamp on Real Estate*, and James R. DeLisle and J. Sa-Aadu's 1994 book, *Appraisal, Market Analysis, and Public Policy in Real Estate: Essays in Honor of James A. Graaskamp*. Clearly, James A. Graaskamp was, and continues to be, an influential force in real estate thinking.

Sources: James A. Graaskamp, *Fundamentals of Real Estate Development* (Washington, D.C.: ULI–the Urban Land Institute, 1981); Stephen D. Jarchow, ed., *Graaskamp on Real Estate* (Washington, D.C.: ULI–the Urban Land Institute, 1991); and Mike Miles and Mark Eppli, "The Graaskamp Legacy," *Real Estate Finance*, Spring 1998, pp. 84–91.

ings when the initial developer, Henry Adams, saw the opportunity to use the space in buildings there to satisfy a new need in the market. In the early 1980s, the SoMa neighborhood was a pioneering location; now it is a trendy area offering hundreds of thousands of square feet of design showrooms and shops selling home furnishings, from pillows to furniture. For Showplace Square to survive the twists and turns of local market trends and the neighborhood's evolution has required considerable operations savvy. Bill Poland, the long-term developer, has shown that a critical element for success for Showplace Square has been to treat it as an operating business. Recognizing that satisfied tenants need customers and products, Poland promoted trade shows and rented the vast facilities for weddings and other social functions in the evenings and on weekends to add life to the area and help create a sense of place in what was then a pioneering location. Quality basic services and creative management have made Showplace Square a successful business enterprise and hence a successful development. Poland continues to adapt to market trends and changes in the character of the area—in mid-2006 he sold a majority interest in Showplace Square to obtain the funds needed to develop condominiums and apartments in this now fashionable and well-located area. RREEF (the U.S. real estate subsidiary of Deutsche Bank) now owns this high-quality institutional asset in a fund managed for pension investors. The buildings in this location were far from "institution" quality when Henry Adams had his original vision.

An asset management focus on evolving customer or tenant demands and the recognition that the product must respond to these demands increases the likelihood of a profitable operation. Even a developer who does not plan to retain long-term ownership of a project must be conscious of long-term profitability, because the next owner will evaluate the potential return on investment, including the asset's future residual value. Residual value is maximized when the property functions well after opening (stage seven) and is expected to continue to perform well over its extended economic life (stage eight).

THE REAL ESTATE MANAGEMENT TRIAD

Against the backdrop of Graaskamp's enterprise concept, this section explores the roles of the real estate management triad in greater depth. Although property management and marketing are at the heart of the traditional management function, asset and portfolio management have expanded the management function to include a much greater range of challenges in response to both changes in the economy and society's demands for constructed space. As noted, the roles of property management, asset management, and portfolio management are separate but interrelated. In a small "portfolio," the distinctions among these three roles may be blurred and even handled by the same person or group of people, while in larger portfolios, separate teams with task-specific staff members are likely.

Figure 21-1 shows the relationships between and among property management, asset management, and portfolio management for a large real estate portfolio. Every portfolio is different, and the relative roles of the people functioning in those roles may expand or contract depending on their experience and capabilities and on composition of the portfolio.

In this example, property management is located on site and is the primary link with the rent-paying customer. (On-site property management also may be known as site management.) The main role is to provide immediate service to the tenants and to protect the property's ongoing revenue and cash flow streams. To do so, the property manager establishes a management plan, helps create a budget tied to that plan, assists in marketing and leasing space, collects rents, maintains accounting and operating records, directs and performs preventive and remedial building maintenance, supervises staff and contract personnel, addresses risk management–related issues, coordinates insurance, manages real and personal property tax valuations, and generally preserve the project's value.

In contrast, asset management is typically located off site and usually is responsible for several different properties. Asset managers may specialize in property type, geographic location, or both (such as office buildings in New York City or apartments in the Midwest). Even with such specialization, asset management assumes a broader perspective than on-site property management. Asset management "manages" the property on behalf of the owner or investor. The asset management staff often participates directly in critical property management activities such as significant lease negotiations, major capital projects, and annual budgeting.

| Figure 21-1 | The Relationship among Property Managers, Asset Managers, and Portfolio Managers |

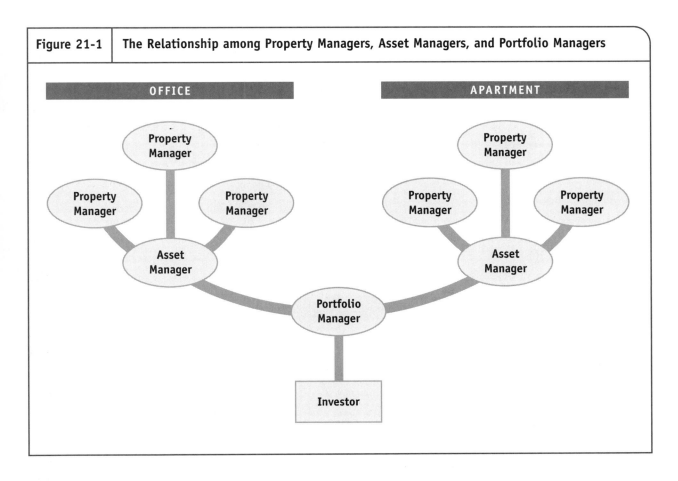

Portfolio management defines and implements a portfolio investment strategy based on the goals and parameters for risk and return of the investors in the portfolio of properties. Portfolio management oversees asset management, acquisitions, dispositions, and reinvestment decisions as well as supervises cash management and financial performance reporting to ownership. It is common for larger portfolios to invest in a manner such that exposure to product types, geography, industries, tenants, and capital events is diversified to preclude undue risk presented by a downturn in any one category. Figure 21-2 highlights the major responsibilities of the property manager, the asset manager, and the portfolio manager.

Just as asset management ensures that the capital expenditures recommended by property management generate an acceptable return on investment, portfolio management coordinates with asset management for multiple properties to balance cash needs across the entire portfolio. Portfolio management must determine the appropriate timing of a property sale because ownership interests may diverge from that of asset and property management, which may be unduly influenced by an overriding interest in preserving jobs.

By structuring all operations to maximize the value of the owners' real estate portfolios, effective managers of real estate assets (property, asset, and portfolio) are able to respond proactively to changing markets (both local rental markets and broader capital markets). In recent years, the more active investment management of pension funds and the growth of REITs have heightened awareness of the need to manage clients' portfolios with a broad perspective as well as particular real property assets.

The composition of the *property management and marketing team* varies depending on the property and the size and complexity of the project. Some functions may not be on staff but be contracted with third parties. The team could include:

Figure 21-2	Major Responsibilities of the Management Triad

Property Manager

▶ Tenant relations and retention

▶ Rent collection

▶ Control of operating expenses

▶ Financial reporting and record keeping

▶ Maintenance of property

▶ Planning capital expenditures

▶ Crisis management

▶ Security issues

▶ Public relations

Asset Manager

▶ Developing property strategic plan

▶ Analyzing whether to hold or sell the property

▶ Reviewing opportunities to reposition properties and to justify major expenditures

▶ Monitoring property performance

▶ Managing and evaluating the property manager by comparing property performance with peer properties in the particular submarket

▶ Assisting in tenant relations

Portfolio Manager

▶ Communicating with investors and setting portfolio goals and investment criteria

▶ Defining and implementing portfolio investment strategy

▶ Overseeing acquisitions, dispositions, asset management, and reinvestment decisions

▶ Accountable for portfolio performance

▶ Client reporting and cash management

▶ The senior property manager (also known as a general manager on projects with especially large staffs), who bears ultimate responsibility for operations, reporting, and team performance, with the exception of leasing.

▶ The assistant property manager, who functions as an adjunct for the senior property manager and is delegated duties in a large project that otherwise would be handled by the senior property manager in a small project.

▶ The lease administrator, who maintains records of tenants' lease compliance.

▶ The chief engineer (also known as the director of operations for larger projects), who ensures that the physical plant runs reliably and efficiently; he is responsible for preventive maintenance programs and refurbishment or replacement of equipment as needed.

▶ The construction manager, who prepares design specifications and bids, recommends contractors for construction projects larger than those able to be handled by the engineering staff on a day-to-day basis, and administers those projects

(draws, lien waivers, compliance with drawings and specifications, and so on). Qualifying projects typically include both base building improvements and tenant improvements.

▶ The director of security, who hires and trains the security staff and bears responsibility for the personal security of building occupants and for protection of the real and personal property.

▶ The project accountant, who processes accounts payable and accounts receivable and prepares balance sheets and income statements for asset management.

▶ A concierge, whose role, depending on the product type, could range from an information desk for a retail project to a person who arranges for movie or theater tickets, makes dinner reservations, and handles dry cleaning and laundry for a hotel or office. In smaller projects, the concierge may also be responsible for building security.

▶ The leasing team, which comprises one or more licensed real estate sales agents who might be dedicated to a project or handle multiple noncompetitive projects. The team's task is to identify

The duties of the marketing and property management teams can often intersect and create beneficial outcomes. A resident dog in the leasing office and a tolerant pet policy attracted many residents to Alcyone—a LEED-certified, 161-unit apartment complex located just north of downtown Seattle, Washington. *Steve Keating*

prospective tenants and negotiate the terms and conditions of a lease for when they occupy the project. Negotiations typically are closely coordinated with asset management; in some cases, asset management participates directly in negotiations.

► The marketing director or manager, who supports the leasing team by helping to establish the project's competitive position or brand and promoting that position through media such as print advertising, direct mail, Web sites, and on-site branding. The role expands in large retail centers to include programs that target tenants so as to increase the store's sales and thus benefit all tenants (and increase their rent).

The *asset management staff* includes:

► The asset manager, who is the primary conduit between the property management and marketing team and the portfolio management team, with full responsibility for all aspects of asset performance.

► The controller, who, usually supported by a staff of portfolio accountants, consolidates reports of multiple projects for a single owner, investor, or fund and conducts performance analysis pursuant to a range of standards.

► The risk manager, who underwrites and administers general liability, property, umbrella, and other forms of insurance coverage to preserve the investment against physical damage and claims arising from operations.

► The financial analyst, who models prospective cash flows and analyzes the impact of asset management decisions and changes in market conditions on rates of return.

The *portfolio management staff* includes:

► The portfolio manager, who is the proxy for the owner (and in certain instances is the owner either on an equity basis or an incentive basis). This person defines the character of the portfolio and implements the acquisitions, sales, and interim decisions that determine the correlation between the defined character and actual portfolio performance.

► Economists and research professionals, who identify macrotrends, markets, product types, and other investment opportunities or risks to facilitate the composition and maintenance of a portfolio that is consistent with the owner's objectives.

► Acquisition professionals, who are investment specialists charged with the task of acquiring property that is consistent with the risk-adjusted return and product requirements specified by the portfolio manager.

► Disposition professionals, who are responsible for the sale of property, either through direct marketing or a brokerage group. Disposition is sometimes handled by asset managers.

THE FUNDAMENTALS OF REAL ESTATE MANAGEMENT FROM THE PERSPECTIVE OF DEVELOPMENT

Input from property management should begin in stages four and five, well before the project is completed. In these stages, the various participants' roles in the development process are formalized in contract documents. Lease agreements for lead tenants specify the features, functions, and benefits expected from the building and from property management. The developer bears responsibility for a building design that will allow these lease obligations to be satisfied at a cost (capital and operating) consistent with the pro forma; it is best accomplished by engaging property management expertise earlier, rather than later, in the development process. Property managers must determine that they will be able to provide the level of service tenants expect at the costs specified in the operating pro forma based on the structure designed by the architect and built by the contractor. Certainly the financial arrangements (debt and equity) must be capable of funding the structural features necessary for adequate property management.

Engaging property management in the design process can generate design improvements that will allow the property to operate at a lower cost and compete more effectively for cost-conscious tenants—for example, adjustments to lighting designs that are more energy efficient or accessible to the maintenance staff or selection of a higher-quality carpet that, although more expensive initially, is more easily cleaned and able to maintain its good appearance for a longer period. Design that includes the proper utility cutoffs in a residential apartment community allows a single unit to be isolated, thereby allowing maintenance or emergency repairs without affecting other units and without the attendant cost and inconvenience that it would otherwise entail.

Site maintenance can also be significantly affected by decisions made during design and development. It not only involves daily maintenance of a project but also considers ongoing preventive and nonroutine maintenance necessary to ensure preservation of the value of the real estate asset throughout its useful life.

Design and development decisions that do not consider both daily and long-term site maintenance are likely to generate additional operating expenses that will reduce the asset's net operating income. It is therefore critical that all aspects of project maintenance be considered and that property management personnel be involved to ensure that daily operating issues are properly evaluated.

During construction, the remaining space is leased, the loan drawn down, the structure built, and, in the case of commercial buildings, design modifications made and interior finishes installed to accommodate the requirements of future tenants. Property management should be involved when any changes are contemplated. Although tenants may want certain features, the developer must estimate the initial cost and any incremental increase in operating expenses to determine whether changes are cost-effective in the context of the needs of prospective tenants and long-term investors.

Consider, for example, a pending lease between a cinema operator and a shopping mall owner for interior space in a project under development. Normally, such an operation would be freestanding or be accessed by a dedicated entrance. In this instance, however, a cinema was not part of the original mall design, and no separate entrance or remaining outparcel is available. The leasing agent, however, has considerable retail space that must be leased and is motivated to promote the lease. The construction manager favors the change because construction for one large tenant is simpler and less expensive than for multiple tenants in the same space. The architect revises pedestrian flow through the mall to determine whether other stores would benefit from the presence of theater patrons. Should the developer approve the arrangement?

Not necessarily. Property management's review of the revised leasing plan identifies shortcomings related to higher janitorial and security costs because the cinema will be open well beyond the normal operating hours of other mall tenants. The additional costs exceed the difference between the rent the theaters would pay and lower rent expected from the next-highest-paying prospective tenant. Quickly con-

sidering the discounted cash flow model introduced in the finance section of this book and detailed in the feasibility study, the developer understands that the operating ramifications associated with the cinema will impair, rather than create, value. In this and similar situations, the feasibility study serves as a tool for sensitivity analysis, with additional costs among the critical variables.

The property management team shifts from an advisory role to an operating role during stage seven of the development process. At that time, the management plan must be formalized so that when the management team assumes day-to-day operating responsibility at the close of stage seven, a plan is available that matches the asset's position in the marketplace as it has evolved during the construction period to the investor's needs (which also may have evolved during the construction period). The developer is responsible for ensuring that the necessary management plans are established and implemented.

The management plan determines the ease with which many of the property management functions can be performed. It should be based on a realistic assessment of the property's competitive position in the market and the owner's investment objectives and resources. The details of the management plan must be consistent with the property's ability to provide the space over time and associated services necessary to compete effectively in the market. If the services are inconsistent with the market's desires, the project is not likely to generate maximum net operating income over time. For example, providing services of no value to tenants increases expenses without a commensurate increase in lease rates, and, as a result, the property's value is not maximized.

The feasibility study prepared earlier provides the basic analyses needed in the management plan to assess the property's strengths and weaknesses as it serves its target market. The feasibility study also provides a detailed analysis of existing and potential competitive properties. Developers should use this baseline comparison throughout development to identify changes to the initial development plan that would generate higher rents and/or lower operating costs by an amount that more than offsets incremental development costs. Maintaining good tenant relations, collecting rent, paying the bills, re-leasing space, handling maintenance schedules, conserving energy, providing security, supervising personnel, and coordinating insurance all are critically important property management functions; anticipation of these tasks can create a better development project. Security, for example, is a critical concern of many tenants, and the initial design dramatically affects security. Installing adequate exterior lighting and placing entranceways so they are clearly visible from the street are important. Electronic card access systems provide tenants and visitors a greater sense of security and may reduce the need for guard service and/or electronic surveillance. Decisions made during the development process can seriously affect the cost of insurance coverage. For instance, buildings that lack complete sprinkler systems and other modern life safety systems typically incur higher insurance premiums.

Developers must consider the image conveyed by the physical structure initially and over time in establishing the initial management plan. A project's architecture clearly makes a statement about the property, a statement that is difficult to recant by the end of stage

seven. Accordingly, the management plan must be crafted to maximize the leverage afforded by the project's architecture and operational possibilities (or limitations, as the case may be). As the owner and manager of two other apartment projects, Russell Katz was able to approach the design of Elevation 314 from the perspective of both an architect and a property manager. Many of his development decisions were based on his plan to own the building for the long term.

THE TRANSITION FROM PROPERTY DEVELOPMENT TO PROPERTY MANAGEMENT

The graph in Figure 21-3 depicts the stages in the life of a real estate project. The first stage—the subject of most of this text—is the development period. As the shortest period in the life of a real estate project, the development period for some small industrial or residential projects may last less than a few years from project conception to completion and opening. On the other hand, the development period for large offices or mixed-use projects may span several years.

ELEVATION 314
Development Choices Can Affect Property Management

Property management to me is not very much fun or exciting, but it certainly is interesting. With my first two buildings, after I tired of doing all the daily management by myself, I hired professional property management companies to take care of the property management. But I was disappointed with their performance because they didn't treat the buildings like the most important things in the world. Perhaps they couldn't because they weren't their buildings: they were mine.

Neither of the companies worked the way I like to work. At the end of the day, the tenants are the most important part of a project. They are the backbone and keep everything going, and they've got to be happy. You've got to be responsive, to fix things. Strategies like deferred maintenance are crazy. I like to fix things and fix them right while investing along the way. I make capital improvements constantly. That's not the way most people work, and it wasn't the way either management company

worked. Eventually I gave up on them. I hired people who could work under me, and I trained them.

I decided to do things my own way. I set certain rules, like if a tenant calls with a repair—I don't care what the repair is—it has to be responded to within 24 hours and fixed within 48 hours. If we have a leak and there's a cheap way to fix it that'll last for a year or an expensive way to fix it that's going to last for five years, we do the expensive way every single time. As another example, when we have to put a new roof on, we go for the best that will last 30+ years, and we pay for it. When you are dealing with capital improvements for things like a new roof or new HVAC for a unit, the question you always get from the contractor, subcontractor, or vendor is "Are you planning to keep this building?"

It's such a telling question because, in our society, we move around so much that people are always fixing up and flipping. There's very little buy and hold. So there are two prices and two ways of doing things; there's the way to do things so you can sell it in a year or so you can own it for 30 years. I'm always thinking 30 years down the road. When I first got into this, going all the way back to feasibility studies and business plans, I decided that I would hold whatever I bought, renovated, or built. One of the main reasons is that all the spreadsheets I did—if I looked out more than eight to ten years—showed I'd be making more money in the long term.

And I really like the idea of getting the residual benefits of ownership. Instead of doing what I've always done as an architect—that is, get paid for my work by the hour or by the effort—I wanted to earn residual benefits from the project. The only residual benefit you might obtain in architecture is repeat business based on your reputation, and that's much less reliable. But if you build something that's going to be of value, it's going to generate monthly cash flow forever as long as you live. That's a residual benefit.

I decided that if I were going to work so hard on these things, they were going to stick with me—especially when it comes to a building like 314 where I was taking so many chances and sticking my neck out to do something special. I wanted to be the one who would get the generated benefit—the residual benefit.

Managing my two other properties revealed a real benefit—being involved in the development process from inception of idea through extended use. Through property management, I learned how my decisions as an architect and a designer affect the way the building lives. Architects have such a weird view of buildings. Nine times out of ten, they take it to the point where they hand the key over to the owner and then they never go there again. There's generally no feedback loop. I've been involved in many buildings that I've never seen again after construction was done. How does

that inform you as an architect? The architects I know tend to be involved with their buildings only if there is some litigation or if something went horribly wrong like mold or leaks. I've learned a lot from being a property manager, and it informed a lot of my decisions about the design of 314.

For example, we wanted to put in fancy dual flush toilets at 314. With these toilets, there is a half flush for urine and a full flush for solid waste. I bought a few of them and installed them in my house and in another building. We had a problem and took them apart to fix them, but we couldn't figure out the mechanism. It was too complicated—and they didn't work that well a lot of the time. Then the flapper went bad. Unfortunately, it turned out that the flapper was integral to the whole guts of the thing. It had a complicated shifting-bucket mechanism inside. Anybody who has run a building knows that flappers wear out every six months, and anybody who cares about the environment as well as water bills ends up changing flappers all the time.

There was no way I was putting in a dual flush toilet like the ones I'd tried. Each time you replace the flapper, you have to replace the whole guts of the toilet—at a cost of probably $150 a shot. I started researching toilets, and I found one called the "flapperless toilet." It is just a bucket on a pivot inside the tank, so there's no flapper at all. I can get really excited about that kind of thing because it really works: it's low tech, it's cheap to operate, and it's the most affordable toilet I saw. On top of that, it was the most environmentally beneficial one of the bunch. You don't necessarily learn things like that unless you've been a property manager.

Now we strictly manage our own properties, and I've got two fabulous managers who handle all the day-to-day stuff. Whenever a weird thing comes up, I get directly involved—and that happens weekly.

continued on page 522

A project is considered "stabilized" when it is physically complete and its occupancy rate represents a fair share of the market. The length of the period to stabilize varies by property type, market conditions, the quality of the asset, and its management. (Some poorly conceived and constructed projects go into decline the moment they are completed; that is, they are never stabilized.) When a project reaches stabilization, it typically becomes the full responsibility of property and asset managers. Until that time, the developer remains very actively involved and works

closely with the management group as part of the development team.

The developer's profit is calculated at the end of the development period as the difference between the developer's total cost and the project's market value. A long period to stabilization caused by a slow lease-up of the project often reduces the developer's profit because of operating losses resulting from expenses that exceed income during the early years. A slow lease-up may indicate weaker market conditions than projected, and the developer may be com-

| Figure 21-3 | Real Estate Project Life Cycle |

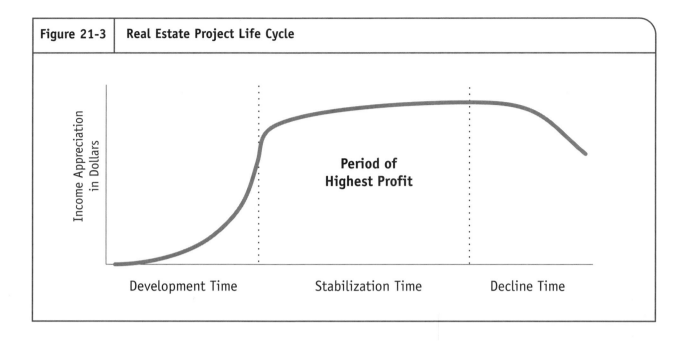

The end of the development period is the day of reckoning for the developer. Did the developer create value or not? If so, how much? If not, why not?

pelled to agree to lower lease rates, lower-quality or lower-credit tenants, and greater concessions, any one of which could reduce value and profit at stabilization.

The end of the development period is the day of reckoning for the developer. Did the developer create value or not? If so, how much? If not, why not?

Development companies are often constrained by the capital they have (or do not have) and so want to recover their capital and profit from a project as early as possible. From the developer's perspective, maximizing profits during the development period means keeping construction costs as low as possible and then completing the project as quickly as possible to minimize capital costs.

The asset manager is as interested in the value of the completed project as the developer. Although the value at completion of construction determines the profit for the developer, it also provides the baseline for measuring the performance of the property and asset managers in the future. After all, it is the charge of asset management to "add" value to the real estate. Even if the property is simply transferred from one group within a real estate company to another (from development to asset management), it is still incumbent on asset management to affirm the value of the property as if it were a new acquisition.

Transferring the Project To Asset Management

At the time the project is sold or transferred to asset management, the transition is accompanied by a "transfer package" that clearly establishes the benchmark for measuring management's future performance. The documents in the transfer package vary with the size and complexity of the project but generally include:

▶ A brief narrative describing the status of the project at transfer and any major outstanding issues. All significant construction-related documents should be incorporated into the report (including "as-built" drawings and certificates of occupancy).

▶ A comparison of actual results with pro forma results. All significant variances, both positive and negative, should be explained. Categories would include the construction budget by line item, the length of the development period, the status of leasing and rental rates, and net operating income and cash flow generated during the development period.

▶ The value of the project and assumptions used to arrive at that value (discount rate, capitalization rate, rental growth rate, vacancy rate, and so on).

▶ The total cost of development and any outstanding items that remain to be completed.

▶ The calculation of the profit created by the developer.

In an ideal world, the handoff from the developer to the management team is simple. Asset and property management would have tracked the project during its development period and would have had the opportunity to provide input into project design and the marketing strategy; as a result, there would be no surprises at project completion. In reality, however, a project rarely follows its pro forma exactly during the development period. The reasons are many and may range from increases in project scope to changing market conditions. The transfer package is thus a mechanism that enables all parties involved in the throes of a development project to take a step back and objectively measure where the project stands in the marketplace. As such, the transfer package is the first step in developing the initial strategic management plan for the property.

Developing a Strategic Plan for the Property

Let us revisit the graph of a real estate project's life cycle (Figure 21-3) and consider two projects during the development period: one that performed significantly worse than its pro forma and one that performed significantly better than its pro forma. If, in a project's initial stage of life, the project were stunted or experienced unusually prolific growth, what does the experience of the development period portend for the future? Where will the project stabilize? What can asset management do to create a better outcome?

Consider the case in which a project performed significantly worse than its pro forma during the development period (see Figure 21-4). Unfortunately, many projects in the mid- to late 1980s fit into this category, as a burst of new construction activity rapidly increased the supply of space in many markets and simultaneously caused a fall in effective rents, substantially lowering the expected net income of new projects. The Europa Center exemplifies a property that fell short of its pro forma, owing to dramatic changes in market conditions (see Appendix A). But a changing market is only one reason a project may fall short in the development period. Poor project design, a misunderstanding of users' requirements, an inaccessible location, or poor construction management also can cause a project to miss the mark. At this stage, the challenge for asset management is to determine whether a project can be reestablished on the original growth curve or to revise expectations

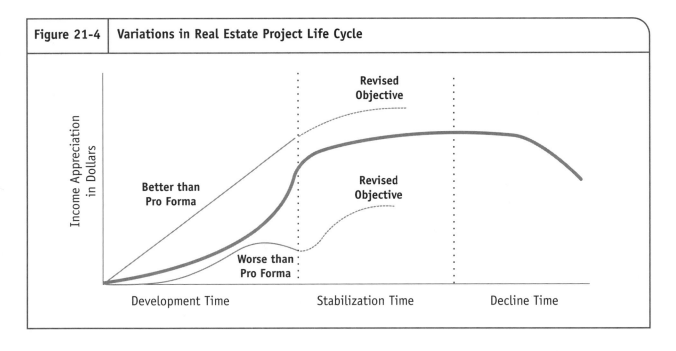

Figure 21-4 | **Variations in Real Estate Project Life Cycle**

downward in light of current market realities. Ironically, a project that performs better than its pro forma during the development period also can present problems for asset management. Consider the apartment development program created by the Prudential Insurance Company's PRISA II commingled pension fund real estate account in conjunction with several leading high-quality apartment developers such as Trammell Crow Residential in the 1990s. As background, it is important to recall that the 1986 Tax Reform Act eliminated the tax benefits of syndication and abruptly ended the extreme overbuilding of apartments. Nationwide, construction of multifamily units dropped by 75 percent from 1985 to 1992. At the same time, the real estate credit crunch that accompanied the restructuring of the banking and S&L industries translated into very limited availability of financing for new apartment construction, even in those markets where demand for high-quality apartments outstripped supply.

PRISA II responded to this inefficiency in the capital markets by developing a program to purchase to-be-built apartment communities in exchange for a financial return higher than what would be available from acquiring a top-quality existing apartment community at market prices. PRISA II's projects would be constructed in such locations as Princeton, New Jersey, Phoenix and Tucson, Arizona, Salt Lake City, Utah, and Albuquerque, New Mexico. As the demand for high-quality apartments in those markets outpaced supply, the projects benefited from an abbreviated lease-up period and rental rates that exceeded the pro forma. Astute asset managers should question whether these market growth rates and rent levels can be sustained over the long run. Are regulatory controls in the local markets sufficient to prevent a repeat of the apartment overbuilding of the early 1980s? Or is it more probable that once the capital markets achieve equilibrium, apartment construction will relapse to the boom-and-bust cycle historically typical of real estate?

Figure 21-5 summarizes the major elements of the real estate strategic planning process, with the concept of property life cycle as background. Using such tools as the transfer package, asset management must define the opportunities and challenges facing a property. This analysis is not performed in a vacuum. In fact, effective property and asset management should seek a wide variety of local experts and written reports in the course of formulating a plan. The next step is to evaluate the existing objectives (stated or implied) for the property and to revise them based on current information. In short, is the developer's concept for the property still valid or does it need to be recast? Variables that precipitate a revision of the original objectives might include changes in local market competition, tenant requirements, or portfolio considerations based on investors' needs.

Once the property's position in the market has been analyzed and defined in conjunction with the revised objectives, asset and portfolio managers are in a position to examine the various possible alternatives for the property's future. The real estate management team must agree on the preferred direction for the property as reflected in a new pro forma. The revised pro forma provides a picture of the property that, in effect, is painted with numbers integrating all the major factors that shape a property's performance. Even though the numbers in the pro forma are only estimates predicated on multiple assumptions, these numbers play a central role in providing a road map for asset management's future direction for the project. In the absence of a clear, well-documented strategic plan, the project will be subject to the arbitrary whims of the marketplace and is unlikely to achieve its full potential.

In the case of newly constructed apartments in Phoenix that were leasing at a rate higher than the pro forma, for example, the best choice for maximizing the owner's return over the short run might be to sell the property while investors' interest in apartments in the Southwest remains high. On the other hand, for a slow-to-lease office building designed for large corporate tenants, asset and portfolio management may decide to redirect the leasing strategy by pursuing smaller local firms that represent a higher credit risk but offer better long-term opportunities for rent growth. Each case demands a pro forma that logically and consistently supports the property's strategic direction.

Figure 21-5	**Property Strategic Planning Process**

Define and Analyze Property Problems and Opportunities

▶ Physical description of property

▶ Operating history

▶ Market conditions

▶ Property strengths and weaknesses compared with competition

Evaluate and Revise Objectives Based on Current Information

▶ Local market/competition

▶ Investor needs

▶ Tenant requirements

▶ Portfolio and other considerations

Consider Alternatives and Generate a Plan to Meet Objectives

▶ Review major decision points

   ▶ Hold or sell?

   ▶ Rehabilitate?

   ▶ Change the use of the building?

   ▶ Change the tenant mix?

   ▶ Change the manager/leasing agent?

▶ Create a new pro forma for the property based on the plan

Implement the Plan

▶ Staffing

▶ Marketing program

▶ Operating budget

▶ Capital program

MANAGEMENT'S ROLE IN IMPLEMENTING THE STRATEGIC PLAN

Once the strategic plan has been agreed upon, the next step is implementation. For the plan to be credible, the resources devoted to implementation must be commensurate with the objectives. For example, a plan whose established objective is to increase occupancy in an office building from only 15 percent to 80 percent in a year must have a fully staffed and aggressive leasing team armed with a full complement of marketing tools. The four main elements in the implementation of a strategic plan are 1) staffing, 2) the marketing program, 3) the operating budget, and 4) the capital program.

Staffing

As discussed in the section on the enterprise concept, commercial real estate is at its core a service business. Unless the staff at a property is properly trained and fully understands the objectives for the property, it is unlikely to manage the property satisfactorily. The appropriate quantity and quality of staff at a property

must be continually evaluated. The marketing, operating, and capital budget components of strategic plan implementation are then reviewed again with the staff that will operate the property.

Marketing Program

The marketing program—designed both to attract new customers and to retain existing ones—is critical in implementing a property's strategy. It involves not only personnel but also advertising, promotional events, commission schedules, and other factors explored further in Chapter 22.

Ongoing marketing and leasing beyond initial occupancy are typically the responsibility of property management for multifamily residential developments, while dedicated leasing professionals are generally responsible for major offices and shopping centers. For a small multifamily project, ongoing marketing might involve little more than showing available apartments to prospective tenants. For larger multifamily assets, marketing might include the creation of collateral materials, the development of effective property signs, the negotiation of contracts with prospect referral firms, the development

ELEVATION 314

Leasing

Initial Rental Rates (July 2004)

Unit Type	Total	Unit Size (Square Feet/Square Meters)	Initial Rental Rates
Efficiency with Den	1	564/52.4	$1,000
One-Bedroom	19	607–780/56.4–72.5	$1,010–1,290
One-Bedroom with Den	6	700–838/65.1–77.9	$1,375–1,640
Two-Bedroom	26	775–975/72.0–90.6	$1,625–1,875

The building is doing really well financially and otherwise except for one of the retail spaces. We have two retail spaces; both are about 1,500 square feet [140 square meters], and both are in Elevation 314. The first one rented very quickly to a local guy who wanted to open a second café (he owns a successful, larger café about two miles [3.2 kilometers] down the street). I knew him and we worked it out really well.

I found out after the fact that my broker hadn't actually found him. He went and found the broker. I wasn't getting any good leads from the broker on the second space. Unfortunately, when you own only two retail spaces, you are not the most important customer. Even though I like to think that I'm the most important customer for everybody I work with, I realized I wasn't. I wasn't getting the attention that I wanted, so I switched brokers after that space was vacant for a few months. I had very strict requirements. I didn't want to put in something that would be degrading to the environment. That cut out most people who came along.

One guy wanted to open a fast-food Asian carryout. It would have a little eat-in area and a carryout. He wouldn't agree to use dishes; he wanted to do everything with Styrofoam and plastic. That was a deal breaker for me.

The café has china and glasses, and they wash everything. When we were negotiating the lease, the owner said, "I have a lot of cardboard, but there's not enough room for cardboard recycling in the trash area and I want to recycle." I found that I could add it to my trash service for not that much money. So I supplied cardboard recycling for him on the provision that my other tenants could use it too.

That's the kind of guy I wanted to work with. His coffee is all free trade, and there's a conscience to his business that suits the building. I rejected so many potential tenants. I think that was very frustrating for the broker too. To her credit she stuck with me.

Then she brought two women who wanted to start a store selling office products for home offices. They'd have

When Elevation 314 first opened, units were available at, or slightly below, market rate. Russell Katz

recycled paper and offer recycling for toner cartridges—which could be a larger contract business than the retail side. A lot of people in the area work from home. I thought it was a great idea. But even though they were very motivated and were putting up their own money, they were inexperienced and they'd never run a business before. They were both professional women who worked in the government and had good salaries and were educated, interesting people. I really liked them a lot, but they failed at their business plan.

The space was about 70 percent built out. They hadn't opened on time (retail leases usually require you to open or else be in violation of the lease). They were on notice for being in violation, and I was trying to work with them. They put their money into a lot of the wrong things, and they took too long and ran out of money. In the end, they gave up the space, and we made a sort of walk-away deal. So then I still have an empty retail space a couple of years after the building opened and was fully occupied otherwise.

Right now I have a prospective tenant who I think is going to come through. I've met with her and we've gone

ELEVATION 314 *(continued)*

through some of the initial stuff. Her business is something that will suit the building perfectly. It's another small business owner. If all goes well, we'll have a lease signed and she'll have built-out space soon.

Fifty percent of our retail space has been a problem in terms of renting. If that was all there was, then the building would have been an abject failure. But it's not; the apartments are the driver of the building. Retail is an important part of it conceptually, but it's a small part in terms of its overall area and financial impact.

The other interesting thing about the retail space and the apartments is that we've exceeded the pro forma projections of return. As we were renting space, we raised rents from what we projected based on the rapid rent-up. The apartments ended up renting for 5 to 10 percent higher than projected, and the retail space went for 35 to 40 percent more than we originally projected in 2001. And—this is huge—the building's energy efficiency is much better than the pro forma, largely because there were no good comparables on which to base appraisal numbers so we had to use market-rate numbers. In the end, the efficiency of the building makes it much less expensive to operate, which greatly benefits the return. If you do something well and get lucky—and luck is no small part of it—there's a lot of ways to be rewarded.

As for the retail and the problems with the one space, I'm still glad we included it. I don't know that there's anything we could have done differently. When I get frustrated, my broker tells me that I have to realize that almost every person who opens a shop does it because he wants to, not

The ground floor of Elevation 314 consists of two 1,500-square-foot (140-square-meter) retail spaces that face the Takoma Metro station on the opposite side of the street. Russell Katz

because he has to. You have to be at the right place at the right time with the right person. If potential retail renters really need to make enough money to live through the next year, they'll probably just go get a job working for somebody and not open their own shops.

The building's bottom line has certainly suffered a little bit from the vacancy, but it hasn't really made much difference in the end. Retail is tough to do, and it's tough to win at. Those women spent a lot of money and paid a lot of rent without ever selling anything. That's the way the deal goes, and it's a tough one.

continued on page 562

and placement of advertisements, the coordination of cooperative advertising with local businesses to attract customers similar to those residing at the community, and the creation of corporate outreach programs targeted to areas that have traditionally provided residents for the community. In these instances, it is critical that the property management firm demonstrate its ability to track both the source and quality of the prospects generated from its marketing efforts.

For example, if during the course of a year the $15,000 spent on advertising in the *Washington Post* generates 23 leases, the advertising cost per lease is approximately $652. Likewise, if the $6,800 spent annually on advertising in the *Apartment Shopper's*

Guide generates an average of 32 leases, the cost per lease for this method of advertising is approximately $213. Such information is critical in attempting to ensure that marketing dollars are spent as effectively as possible. The developer must carefully consider advertising strategies when identifying the property management firm best able to maximize the project's value.

A significant component of value in many retail developments is derived from percentage rent, which is rent payments based on a tenant's sales volume. In this case, it is even more important for the owner to develop a marketing program that will help attract shoppers from the trade area and increase their frequency of visits so that tenant sales are driven higher for the benefit of both the tenant and landlord.

For larger commercial projects, ongoing marketing can be more complex, and the in-house marketing team and property manager typically cooperate with outside brokerage firms to achieve leasing objectives. In a major office building, for example, the listing agents or landlord's representatives are responsible for advertising and promotional activities for the project. Such activities target both the tenant or user community and that segment of the brokerage community known as "tenant representatives," which in some metropolitan markets represent 90 percent or more of prospective tenants. The landlord's representative is responsible for regular communication with these brokers, facilitates tours of the space, generates proposals for leases (or responds to formal and sometimes extensive requests for proposals), and, with legal counsel, negotiates the actual lease documents. Asset management participates actively or more passively in the process, depending on the relationships and structure of the organization, but typically has a say about final approval of leases.

Regardless of the size of the property and who handles ongoing marketing, the integrity of the revised pro forma is critical because it is used to estimate future rental rates and to include all ongoing costs of marketing the space, including brokerage commissions, rental concessions, tenant allowances, space planning/design costs, moving allowances, and legal fees. In other words, from the feasibility study to the operating budget, the bottom line should be effective rents, which are the net of all revenue and expenses associated with a lease and not simply the absolute asking rents.

Although Russell Katz experienced difficulties leasing one of the two retail spaces in Elevation 314, meeting and surpassing the pro forma projections for the residential component still allowed the project to be financially successful.

Operating Budget

Once the property's place in the market is matched to the owner's needs, the management team develops a detailed, month-by-month operating budget. The operating budget typically is based on the first year of the new pro forma. From the developer's perspective, the budget is identical to the top portion of the pro forma income statement used in the feasibility study. From property management's standpoint, the property is expected to provide the cash flow projected by the pro forma (assuming the budget is met). Thus, projections of net operating income are derived from projected gross revenues as adjusted for projected vacancies and reduced by projected expenditures for real estate taxes and operating expenses, including casualty and general liability insurance, payroll, marketing, utilities, repair and maintenance, management, and replacements. Adjustments for debt service, expenses of ownership such as asset management fees and tax preparation costs, and income taxes after net operating income are not traditional components of the property-level operating budget and are not necessarily included.

The process of creating a budget for the property is time-consuming and tedious but extremely important. Each revenue and expense line item from the property's chart of accounts must be carefully considered and detailed to ensure that all potential revenues and expenses are accurately recognized. Overstating revenues and/or understating expenses can result in overly optimistic financial projections; understating revenues and/or overstating expenses can result in overly pessimistic financial projections. In either case, the developer will be misinformed and more likely to make inappropriate investment decisions.

Optimistic projections of net operating income may result in the development of projects that cannot succeed financially. Many failed real estate assets were accompanied by financial pro formas that contained overly optimistic and unrealistic assumptions. Revenues were shown to increase at rates that, while possibly achieved in the past, could not be sustained in an environment of eroding market fundamentals. Similarly, estimated expenses were likely not properly recognized. The result was the development of assets that could not produce the income required to satisfy financial obligations.

The importance of creating a realistic and accurate operating budget cannot be overemphasized. The potential ramifications of overstating or understating net operating income for the project are severe. The most effective method for ensuring that errors are not incorporated into the development's operating budget is to require:

▶ Asset and property management to be involved as early as possible in the development process. Asset and property management personnel are the individuals who are most knowledgeable of the costs and complications of managing a stabilized project. They also are the individuals most capable of generating realistic operating pro formas.

▶ The development of detailed assumptions that describe each line item in the operating budget. By generating detailed assumptions, all individuals who assess the financial feasibility of the development will be able to comment on the logic of the financial projections and to ensure that the assumptions are internally consistent (e.g., if 50 percent of the apartments in a residential apartment community are expected to turn over annually and be leased to new residents at higher rental rates, then the associated apartment turnover costs must be included in the operating expenses).

▶ The actual operating results of similar development projects in similar locations, to be used as background in the creation of the pro forma financials. Many line items in the operating budget cannot be accurately projected without operating experience. New developments obviously lack a history on which to base projections. Therefore, compelling evidence and logic are prerequisites to any deviation from actual historical operating results associated with similar projects.

An examination of the details of the operating budget early in the development process can allow the developer to adjust the project as necessary to avoid serious errors. Although industry averages are a reasonable starting point, it is the cost of operating a particular property relative to what the market will pay for the features, functions, and benefits provided by that property that matters in the final analysis. An accurate budget is critical to providing the developer with the information necessary to make informed decisions.

Capital Program

The initial capital program often receives little attention, especially in the case of a new project, which ideally requires few additional capital expenditures in its early years. In practice, however, most projects—even well-conceived new projects—require some additional capital input either to remedy construction or design deficiencies not covered by warranties (such as inadequate drainage in a parking lot) or to meet expanded tenant requirements (such as demand for additional covered parking in an apartment project).

From the perspective of the property's life cycle, it is important to note that the upkeep of a commercial real estate building and its basic components is predictable (in the same way that a maintenance program for a new car is predictable). Accordingly, a ten-year schedule of capital expenditures should be created at the time a property is acquired. Figure 21-6 is a graph of the repair and replacement schedule for three major components of an office property—the roof, the cooling tower, and the elevators. These capital projects would be considered base building maintenance. Other projects involve tenant improvements related to releasing space as the initial terms of tenants' leases expire. Additional capital expenditures may arise as a result of changes in government regulations or market requirements. Life safety improvements, new security systems, asbestos removal, energy management programs, and retrofits to provide improved access for disabled persons are all examples of programs that have emerged in recent years but may not have been incorporated into developers' original pro formas. Although property and asset managers must be careful not to improve a facility too much and drain a property's cash flow through excessive capital expenditures, a property must be maintained at the market standard if it is to have an extended useful life and compete effectively for tenants. Further, scheduled preventive maintenance projects are usually less costly and less disruptive to tenants over the long run than crisis-driven emergency repairs.

Ongoing Planning

Strategic plans for a property should be reviewed at least annually and more frequently if circumstances

Figure 21-6	Long-Term Capital Budget Program

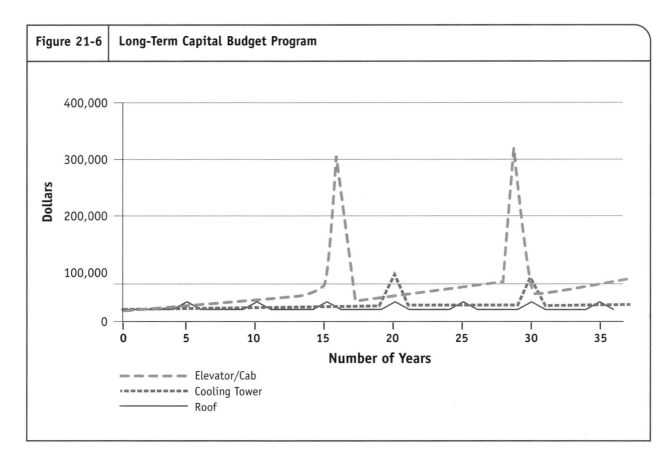

dictate. In many cases, as a result of changes in market conditions and tenants' requirements, a property strategic plan may become obsolete a short time after it is prepared. Ideally, asset and portfolio managers should look at the property with fresh eyes each year and ask themselves, "If we didn't already own this asset, would we acquire it again today? If not, why not?" By forcing the property to be "reacquired" each year, asset management invigorates the planning process and sloughs off the inertia so often endemic to the property management business.

Property Management Contracts

A property management contract provides a framework for the relationship between the property management firm and the owner. It specifies which management services the owner will pay for and which the property management firm will pay for. It determines who pays employees, who can authorize certain expenditures, who is responsible for keeping certain records, who is responsible for maintaining

insurance coverage, who handles advertising and promotion, and who takes care of compensation for the property management firm. The budget quantifies the management plan and ensures that the interests of owners and tenants are expressed consistently. Just as they must be alert to general contractors' bids that do not include all essential cost items, developers must also scrutinize management plans and budgets to ensure they are comprehensive and that the fee is sufficient to properly motivate the property management firm to devote the resources necessary to accomplish the owner's objectives. Only when the capabilities of the property management firms are thoroughly scrutinized and the management contract negotiated and committed to paper can developers be certain that a qualified organization is ready to perform all specified services at the quoted price.

Developers typically are responsible for hiring the first property management firm, unless a building is designed for a single tenant who will own, occupy, and operate the facility. Many developers have subsidiary companies that perform property management services, while others hire independent property managers. The length of the management contract varies, but the progressively more common industry standard is to provide the owner with a right to terminate the contract without cause after 30 or 60 days notice. The benefit to the owner is the ability to effect change quickly if performance is substandard, but it also ensures the property management firm's constant attention. Figure 21-7 depicts the elements of a standard management agreement.

THE INFLUENCE OF THE PUBLIC SECTOR IN THE MANAGEMENT OF REAL ESTATE PROJECTS

As discussed throughout this book, the public sector plays an integral role in real estate development because of the people-intensive nature of the product. Stage eight is no exception, as the enactment of new legislation and promulgation of new regulations require compliance. Properties and buildings not only provide space for tenants but also offer employment for a significant number of people. In its efforts to ensure that all individuals are treated fairly, that the workplace is safe, and that the environment is preserved for the long term, the public sector establishes rules in the form of legislation and building codes that apply to real estate assets. These rules often affect the project's ongoing operating expenses, requiring modifications to existing structures and/or generating liabilities that the owner, property management, asset management, and portfolio management must be prepared to address.

The real estate industry actively attempts to ensure that new legislation and regulations achieve the desired public purpose without creating undue hardships for the owners of real estate assets. Industry groups such as the National Multi Housing Council, the National Apartment Association, the National Association of Industrial and Office Properties, the Real Estate Roundtable, and the Urban Land Institute seek to ensure that all interested parties understand the ramifications of the various rules adopted by local, state, and federal governments. Legislation that appears to

Figure 21-7	A Standard Management Agreement
Article 1	Properties
Article 2	Commencement Date
Article 3	Manager's Responsibilities
Article 4	Insurance
Article 5	Financial Reporting and Record Keeping
Article 6	Owner's Right to Audit
Article 7	Bank Account
Article 8	Payment of Expenses
Article 9	Insufficient Gross Income
Article 10	Sale of a Property
Article 11	Cooperation
Article 12	Compensation
Article 13	Termination
Article 14	Subsidiaries and Affiliates
Article 15	Notices
Article 16	Nonassignables, etc.
Schedules	
A	Property Identification, Compensation Schedule, and Leasing Commission
B	Leasing Guidelines
C	Monthly Report Forms
C-1	Chart of Accounts
D	Reimbursable Employees
E	Subsidiaries and Affiliates
F	Insurance Certificate

target a specific public purpose may have the effect of creating unintended burdens that are less than desirable for real estate owners.

Two pieces of federal legislation—the Americans with Disabilities Act (ADA) and Title IV of the Clean Air Act of 1990—had an immediate and ongoing effect on both the methods and costs associated with managing real estate projects. In its most general sense, the ADA prohibits discrimination against disabled persons with respect to employment, public services, and public accommodations operated by private businesses. Its intent is to provide persons with disabilities with accommodations and access equal to, or similar to, those available to the general public (see Figure 21-8). Title IV of the Clean Air Act

---

Figure 21-8 | **The Americans with Disabilities Act**

The Americans with Disabilities Act was signed by President George H. W. Bush in July 1990. Its objective is to provide persons with disabilities access equal to, or similar to, that available to the general public. Title III affects places of public accommodation, including commercial real estate. The law also affects alterations to existing properties subsequent to January 26, 1992. Residential real estate is excluded from the ADA as it is already covered by the Fair Housing Act of 1988. Significantly, the ADA is civil rights legislation—not a building code.

The law is administered and enforced by the U.S. Department of Justice. Congress incorporated a provision into the ADA stating that "good faith efforts" and "attempts to comply" should be considered in enforcing this law. The Department of Justice has identified a compliance plan as a "good faith effort" when accompanied by constructive actions. Priorities in a compliance plan include entryways, routes from entryways to public places, restrooms, and public facilities such as telephones and drinking fountains. The cost of complying varies significantly from property to property, depending on specific building conditions and original project design. For additional insights into ADA compliance, see *ADA Compliance Guidebook*, published by the Building Owners and Managers Association International.

Located in St. Louis, Missouri, 6 North is one of the first multi-family buildings in the nation that is designed to be completely accessible and fully usable by both disabled and nondisabled people. For example, the kitchens in each of the project's 80 units (44 percent of these units are reserved for affordable housing) come equipped with adjustable-height countertops and appliances that are mounted at a height that is convenient for those with movement restrictions or in wheelchairs. Alyse O'Brien

---

of 1990 addresses protection of atmospheric ozone and mandates the recycling, production phaseout, and elimination of ozone-depleting compounds. In addition, the act prohibits the release of chlorofluorocarbons (CFCs) into the atmosphere during the maintenance, servicing, and disposal of refrigeration equipment.

Although both these acts address critical societal issues, they also potentially create costs for the development process and the subsequent ongoing operation of real estate projects. New developments are required to include certain types of equipment, while existing projects may have to undertake retrofit and maintenance to ensure compliance with the guidelines. Expanded training is necessary for both management and maintenance personnel, as even unintentional noncompliance may result in costly fines.

More recently, awareness has increased of the health implications of microbial growth, or mold, especially for persons with special sensitivity to certain types of mold. Restoration of damage caused by a leaky roof or failed waterline or drain now entails both a construction solution and a remediation solution requiring that materials presenting a risk of hosting mold be encapsulated and removed. It is also much more urgent to attend to these problems immediately before mold can develop and affect air quality, typically within 48 hours of an event.

The impact of the public sector on the planning, design, feasibility analysis, and operation of real estate projects reinforces the importance of the involvement of both the asset manager and the property manager throughout the development process. The asset and property managers, like other members of the development team, should interact regularly with the public sector during development, setting up the vital working relationship that will of necessity exist during stage eight.

TRAINING PROPERTY, ASSET, AND PORTFOLIO MANAGERS

The capabilities of the management triad are of primary concern to the developer. During implementation of the strategic management plan, capable management is critical to achieving the results specified in the operating budget. Well-trained management personnel with appropriate specialized skills are more likely to succeed in the competitive and complex marketplace.

Property Managers

Property managers and on-site property personnel are integral to the successful performance of the development project. As the role these people play in generating revenues, containing costs, and maintaining or enhancing value is progressively more appreciated, developers place greater emphasis on identifying individuals capable of performing the necessary management tasks. At the same time, more training and certification programs have become available through professional associations. The best-known is the Institute of Real Estate Management (IREM), an affiliate of the National Association of Realtors®, which offers a designation as certified property manager (CPM®) and accredited residential manager (ARM®).[2] In addition, the Building Owners and Managers Association International (BOMA) offers four professional management accreditations, the International Facilities Management Association one.[3] BOMA also publishes an array of statistics on office building operations similar to the analyses of apartment income and expenses produced by the Institute of Real Estate Management. The International Council of Shopping Centers (ICSC) generates its own statistics and jointly with ULI–the Urban Land Institute publishes income and expense data for shopping centers. All these organizations seek to enhance professionalism in the field and to provide

data that can be used in feasibility studies and long-term operating budgets.

The various professional programs aim to familiarize managers with the use of a systematic approach to record keeping, the best ways to anticipate and respond to tenants' needs, strategies for negotiating leases, legal responsibilities to tenants, and sales and marketing techniques. Techniques for tracking the many functions of building management are often best learned in professional training courses, because real estate management involves meticulous attention to detail.

Asset and Portfolio Managers

A variety of companies offer real estate investment management or advisory services. A few are subsidiaries of development companies; others are independent investment managers or subsidiaries of major financial institutions. The largest group of portfolio managers is probably pension and private investment managers who are members of the National Council of Real Estate Investment Fiduciaries (NCREIF), the Pension Real Estate Association (PREA), or the National Association of Real Estate Investment Managers (NAREIM).[4] In addition to providing advice on managing a portfolio and acquiring and disposing of properties, these companies also bear responsibility for asset and property management, whether these services are provided by affiliates or by third parties. Typically, the individuals who handle asset and portfolio management in investment management companies are university trained in management, finance, or law. Such professionals continue to enhance and develop their skills through seminars and professional literature made available by these associations. The CCIM Institute focuses on asset management; it designates those who have successfully completed training "certified commercial investment members."[5]

THE CORPORATE REAL ESTATE DIRECTOR

Real estate assets constitute a major portion of most company's balance sheets and typically represent the greatest operating costs after payroll. Not only is real estate important from the perspective of cost: access to the right space in the right location also is critical to a firm's competitiveness and its employees' quality of life. In fact, an attractive work environment is critical to attracting and retaining employees, especially in tight labor markets. For these reasons, the role of the corporate real estate director is critical.

Despite its importance, real estate is rarely a major driver of a company's business decisions, and many building owners have witnessed users abandon perfectly good real estate in the interests of a corporation's strategic change in direction. This ever-present risk underscores the importance of understanding the requirements of the marketplace and focusing on the development of well-conceived and -located projects that can appeal to a wide market. These attributes also coincide with the objectives of investors and lenders, who are averse to special-purpose or marginally located projects whose reuse may be unclear.

A detailed understanding of the value of a corporation's real estate is extremely important as the corporation attempts to minimize its cost for space while meeting all its space needs. In the early 1990s, businesses devoted considerable effort to reducing operating costs, and the corporate real estate director was a big part of the process. An accurate assessment of the value of the corporation's real estate assets can help ensure that the assets are properly reflected on the balance sheet. Effective asset management may increase the value per share and/or minimize the potential for corporate takeovers aimed at acquiring businesses for their real estate holdings.

The corporate real estate director is involved in decisions on building capacity and layout from the building user's perspective. Corporate real estate directors implement decisions to lease or buy space. They work with the firm's operating management team to create the best organization for the continuing management and monitoring of real estate assets. They also lead in creating a management information system for this purpose. They work to identify surplus or underused real property and seek ways to reuse those assets. They negotiate on the company's behalf in the lease or purchase of space. They initiate

suggestions for alternative ways of owning or leasing real estate such as the opportunity to create a joint venture if the company does not want to create its own development business but still wants to take advantage of its financial strength to reap the rewards of equity participation.

Many corporate real estate professionals are affiliated with organizations such as CoreNet Global and the National Association of Industrial and Office Properties (NAIOP).[6] Both these professional organizations offer networking opportunities and educational programs.

The rate of change in business has increased because of advances in technology, evolving business practices like integrated just-in-time production and delivery systems, and globalization. Consequently, planning effectively is more difficult than ever, which has led to high demand for flexibility—a principal that can be at odds with the fixed nature of real estate assets. What corporations now need most is flexibility, because they cannot forecast future events with great certainty. The feverish growth of the technology sector in the late 1990s led many companies to vastly overestimate product demand and lease space in anticipation of it. The pain from such overcommitment increased the corporate interest in flexibility, which can be achieved by policies requiring shorter-term leases or at least termination rights on longer-term commitments. Although this solution is beneficial to corporate users, it presents difficulties for developers and owners seeking to create predictable cash flow and for lenders seeking certainty.

Many companies have turned to external professional real estate companies to improve efficiency in managing their real estate exposure. Real estate outsourcing enables corporations to avail themselves of expertise in a variety of areas that may not be available in house and allows the corporate real estate office to maintain a lean staff. For example, Trammell Crow Company and LaSalle Investment Management, a division of Jones Lang LaSalle, have been leaders in forging alliances with major corporations such as United Parcel Service, Bank of America, and ExxonMobil to assist in the efficient management of corporate real estate holdings.

SUMMARY

▶ The triad of real estate management—property, asset, and portfolio management—provides critical functions for ensuring that real estate projects maximize their value. The importance of each of these disciplines throughout the life cycle of the asset is hard to overestimate.

▶ As espoused by James A. Graaskamp, the real estate asset should be viewed as more than just bricks and mortar. The project must be recognized as a dynamic business enterprise operating in an always-changing marketplace.

▶ The role of asset and portfolio management in real estate continues to expand and evolve. Although asset management's fundamental involvement and interaction with property management remains a priority, portfolio management is assuming a much more active role in the development and/or acquisition of assets, the positioning of the project throughout its life cycle, and the timely disposition of the asset. These responsibilities serve to preserve and enhance the value of individual assets to long-term investors.

▶ Effective property management, marketing, and leasing continue to be fundamental for both maintaining and enhancing the value of real estate projects. The detailed nature of property management requires a thoughtful and structured approach that includes early involvement in the development process, detailed management plans and budgets, consistent attention to day-to-day operations, and the flexibility to adjust to changing market conditions.

▶ Because of the people-intensive nature of real estate projects, the public sector influences responsibilities of asset and property management. New legislation and regulations are promulgated almost daily, and their effects on property can be costly from the perspective of both initial development costs and ongoing operating expenses. Proactive involvement in understanding rules and regulations by both the development and management teams is essential.

▶ Ongoing training is critical to ensure that the property management team and its on-site personnel perform well in an increasingly competitive and demanding marketplace.

▶ Real estate and/or office space is an important component of the business management side of most corporations. The value and importance of effective management of corporate real estate is gaining progressively more recognition and has heightened the importance and involvement of the corporate real estate director in the day-to-day operation of the business. This additional scrutiny has created opportunities for capable developers who are able to provide flexible solutions to satisfy the corporation's requirements.

TERMS

▶ Asset management
▶ Corporate real estate director
▶ Effective rent
▶ Enterprise concept
▶ Management plan
▶ Marketing and leasing program
▶ Portfolio management
▶ Property life cycle
▶ Property management
▶ Property management contract
▶ Property strategic plan

REVIEW QUESTIONS

21.1 Describe the differences in property, asset, and portfolio management functions and how they are interrelated.

21.2 How does property management use a management plan?

21.3 Why is the involvement of property management early in the development process important?

21.4 What are some potential problems facing asset managers, even in good markets?

21.5 What are the four main elements of a strategic plan? Discuss each one.

21.6 Why is it so important to create a realistic and accurate operating budget?

21.7 What issues does the property management contract spell out?

21.8 Why is real estate such an important asset to corporations?

NOTES

1. Richard Kateley and M. Leanne Lachman, *Asset Management: The Key to Profitable Real Estate Investment* (Chicago: Real Estate Research Corporation, 1985), p. 2.

2. See www.irem.org for more information.

3. See www.boma.org and www.ifma.org for more information.

4. See www.ncreif.org, www.prea.org, and www.nareim.org.

5. See www.ccim.com.

6. See www.corenetglobal.org and www.naiop.org.

CHAPTER 22

The Challenge of Marketing and Sales

*S*imply put, *good real estate marketing is the comprehensive process of planning, creating, and communicating activities that results in selling or leasing the most space or product for the greatest return in the shortest amount of time.* Although most marketing activities take place toward the end of the development process, it is important to consider marketing throughout the development process and treat it as a strategic element of the entire process.

This chapter uses marketing terminology that applies specifically to real estate, yet the basic concepts can be found in every good marketing textbook. The development team must have the skill to apply those concepts. The umbrella shown in Figure 22-1 is a simple model for depicting the major components of real estate marketing. *Research* is learning about the market's audiences and competition for the project. *Strategy and planning* is developing the strategic course of action based on the development plan and market dynamics. *Promotions* involves communicating to the target audiences with the appropriate messages and media to generate awareness, interest,

and traffic. *Sales* is the transaction of the lease or sale. This chapter focuses on strategy and planning, promotions, and sales.

THE MARKETING UMBRELLA

This chapter focuses on the challenge of selling real estate. For the most part, the word "sales" is used broadly to include both leasing and selling. Ideally, if members of the development team do a good job at designing the right product for the target market, sales and leasing can be a relatively straightforward exercise. But even if research and product design were nearly perfect, the team must still identify and convince prospects of the project's merits. Getting a long-term lease signed requires an effort similar to that required for getting a sales contract signed. The overriding purpose in both cases is finding and convincing prospects that a particular development better meets their space needs than any other available product. For shopping centers, marketing also includes convincing the prospective tenant's customers to shop at a particular center.

The authors wish to thank Richard Burns, GNU2, San Anselmo, California, for his contributions to this chapter.

| Figure 22-1 | The Marketing Umbrella |

Source: Richard Burns.

The marketing process should be treated as an investment in time and money that adds value to a real estate project rather than an expense item in the development budget. Time to market is one of the most important determinants of profitability, as the sooner a property can be leased or sold, the sooner the carrying cost of a non-income-producing asset can be eliminated. Marketing has the power to reduce this time frame. For example, a commercial office building with a carrying cost of $500,000 a month in financing and preopening operational costs that can be fully leased two months sooner through a dynamic marketing program will potentially add $1 million to the bottom line.

Although every sales or leasing challenge is distinctive (because every real estate project is distinctive), some commonalities exist among all of them. Just as we covered the basics of market analysis, design, financing, management, and public policy in earlier chapters, here we review the basics of sales (and sales management) from the perspective of development. This chapter moves from the initial stages of marketing through to actually selling the product, examining:

► The marketing plan and budget;
► The strategic marketing process;
► The promotions program; and
► Sales, including relations with real estate agents.

THE MARKETING PLAN AND STRATEGIC MARKETING PROCESS

The strategic marketing process is a linear series of steps whose goal is to arrive at the marketing plan of action. It begins with a well-conceived project that responds to market demand (a market looking for a project) rather than the other way around (a project looking for a market). Although it is not impossible for a dynamic marketing program to facilitate the success of a property in a poor market, it is unwise for a developer to proceed with this assumption. Marketing is a single component in the overall success

| Figure 22-2 | The Strategic Marketing Process |

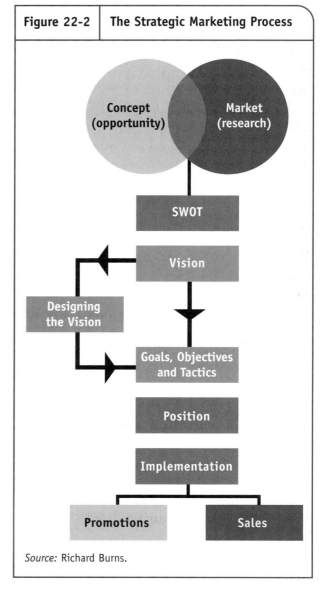

Source: Richard Burns.

of a project; it is not a panacea for poorly conceived or ill-timed projects.

No project should proceed without a thorough knowledge of the marketplace—current trends, competitive supply, and potential demand—making market research an important aspect of strategic marketing. In addition to helping the developer decide whether or not to proceed with a project, the information gathered through market research can help define the project concept and provide background information on target markets.

Once it has been determined that a development will proceed, the next step includes an analysis of its **s**trengths, **w**eaknesses, **o**pportunities, and **t**hreats (SWOT). The SWOT analysis leads to the formation of the vision, which leads to the positioning of the property. Once the vision is established, a finite set of marketing goals and objectives are identified and the tactics for achieving them defined.

The marketing plan includes a summation of the project and its target markets, results of the SWOT analysis, vision statement, goals, objectives, tactics, and positioning. It concludes with the concepts for the promotions program, the sales program, the budget, and the assignment of responsibilities.

SWOT Analysis

The SWOT analysis is a benchmarking process used to inventory all internal and external aspects of a project, both positive and negative. It delineates the internal strengths that can have a favorable influence and potentially be incorporated into a positive presentation of the development as well as weaknesses that must be overcome. The analysis identifies external opportunities and threats that are beyond the developer's control but can potentially affect the development's success.

The SWOT analysis is conducted to identify the values and virtues of the development that can be the focus of the marketing program as well as to understand the deterrents and obstacles to the project's success. It should result in a complete inventory of all factors, internal and external, that influence the marketing of the project. They will form the basis of the vision for the property and become an important resource in telling its story.

Strengths

Strengths are internal attributes of the project that differentiate it from the competition. They can include location, quality of the design and environment, entitlements, cost, amenities, management characteristics, or anything else that enables the project to be better than the competition. Knowing the project's strengths can provide guidance on the attributes and capabilities upon which to build a marketing program.

Weaknesses

Weaknesses are self-imposed limitations and problems that have a negative impact on the project's or property's attractiveness. They too can include location, quality of design and environment, entitlements, cost, amenities, management characteristics, or anything else that makes the project worse than the competition. Once weaknesses are identified, the challenge is to mitigate them. Determining which of the weaknesses can be overcome through marketing and which require programmatic or product changes is a fundamental part of the process.

Opportunities

Opportunities are situations or conditions that exist outside the property or project. They can be global and omnipresent, or they can exist at a point in time. Opportunities include, among other things, economic and market conditions (which are always subject to change), the demeanor of local jurisdictions, neighbors, the labor pool, demographic trends, and financial climate. Opportunities must be aligned with strengths to determine how best to capitalize on them. The marketing plan must leave flexibility to accommodate fluctuating economics.

Threats

Threats come from outside and require the greatest vigilance. Threats, like opportunities, vary in their magnitude and longevity. Some can be mitigated through the development or marketing program. Others may be permanent. A major threat, like a downturn in the economy, requires an adjustment to strategy. Smaller threats such as the departure of a key tenant are marketing problems and must be addressed through the marketing program.

The Vision

The vision for a real estate development can best be described as the dream for what the place is to become. This dream is measured not only in physical dimensions but also in the character and dynamics of the place that endure long after development is complete. The elements of that vision include physical qualities, environmental conditions, sociological dynamics, character, values, commitment to execution, and, ultimately, the quality of life and experience that will make the project truly different and special.

Once the attributes are identified, they should be compiled into a vision statement for the development that will provide a road map around which planning, design, construction, communications, and marketing will be based. The vision statement must be actionable. By providing the platform for telling the development story accurately and consistently, it becomes a benchmark for all marketing decisions.

Marketing Goals, Objectives, and Tactics

The marketing plan requires clear goals and objectives. A goal identifies an overarching end result for the development. For example, 50 percent of space preleased might be a goal for a new office building. Objectives quantify the goals by assigning specific quantities and matching numbers to time frames and target dates. Some objectives for the goal stated above might include establishing a relationship with a brokerage firm within four weeks or signing a major tenant for at least 15,000 square feet (1,395 square meters) within the first three months after initiation of construction.

Tactics are the distinct actions that must be taken to realize goals and objectives. In addition to the quantification of numbers and time frames, they require designation of responsibility for achieving results.

Positioning

Whereas vision is the expression of the broad development concept, positioning is the identification of the selling propositions that will establish the proj-

ect's place in the market. Positioning is the means by which to create a competitive edge for the project.

Four fundamental strategies can be used to position any real estate project: differentiating, repositioning, finding a niche, and branding. Although these strategies are not mutually exclusive, one of them should usually dominate in determining the manner in which the project is packaged and presented. The dominant and secondary positioning platforms are derived directly from the attributes of vision.

Differentiation is the most common positioning strategy. Items that differentiate a property can be all manner of things, but they must directly benefit target audiences. Larger floor plates, better amenities such as concierge service or fitness facilities in a commercial project, or recreational amenities and open space in a residential project may be the strengths on which a development can be distinguished from the competition. For example, if environmentally sensitive and sustainable design is identified as a key attribute in the visioning process, then promoting a building's "green" features would be a good way to position the project.

Sometimes difficulties or constraints on development can be turned into tools to differentiate a project. High Desert, a 1,000-acre (405-hectare) planned development in Albuquerque, New Mexico, was planned and developed under the auspices of rigidly prescribed design guidelines packaged as "Guidelines for Sustainability." The marketing presentation for High Desert was predicated on positioning the community as, first and foremost, about environmental quality. Sensitive home sites with prescribed building envelopes to protect views and vegetation, water harvesting and light pollution standards, and strict architectural and landscape provisions were all part of the commitment to the environment. What on one hand could be considered extremely restrictive or punitive development policies, albeit absolutely reflective of the community's vision, became the foundation for positioning the development in all its marketing, promotions, and communications. The community attracted buyers who embraced these values, and it quickly distinguished itself in the market and achieved extraordinary initial sales volume.

Repositioning is the process of taking an existing product and turning it into something new or different. Given the accelerating rate of change in our society, repositioning becomes an important development and marketing strategy. Repositioning can also result from rethinking how an existing property can maintain the same use yet appeal to different markets. For example, an office building that has typically relied on large-scale users that finds itself in a market where only smaller tenants are leasing could adopt a repositioning strategy based on servicing the needs of the smaller tenants by, for example, concentrating on building services that would appeal to smaller tenants such as administrative support and concierge services. Repositioning could take the form of suggesting that the development is actually a business partner in the degree to which it can support smaller firms' efficiency and productivity.

Finding an unserved or underserved niche in the market and filling it is another method of positioning. Niches can include very specific types of property to serve the special needs of distinct buyers and users. Virtually every class of real estate can be positioned according to the niche it occupies. In recent years, a wide variety of niche retail formats such as family entertainment centers and high-end specialty outlets have offered strong competition to standard regional, neighborhood, and convenience shopping centers. Many niche hospitality markets have been identified, including luxury, resort, urban, boutique, economy, destination, and ecological.

Branding is the process of endowing qualities in the project that create value and expectation for the prospect. Branding builds on visual identification. It is about name and product recognition, predictability, and creating and meeting expectations. The most often cited definition of branding is "a promise." To that end, branding adds consistent and controlled behavior to visual identity. Great brands must deliver products and services with a degree of consistency that allows customers to have their expectations met. Because of the diverse and varied nature of real estate, establishing a brand is especially challenging. Recent consolidation in the real estate industry has seen a trend toward branding the new, larger companies formed rather than trying to establish a brand through the project.

Trammell Crow was one of the first real estate companies to institute a branding strategy in the early 1980s. The approach was to brand the company through a strong corporate identity by creating a visual design standard that was applied to all properties, primarily through marketing signage at every building. It may sound simplistic, but few other real estate companies were using the approach at the time. During the same period, Lincoln Properties sought to achieve recognition and connection between its industrial and warehouses properties with a big blue strip that encircled every building. It was also a simplistic approach to consistent recognition, but this distinctive design element served as an effective branding tool.

How can the property or project be replicated elsewhere so that the brand equity accrues to the new location? Achieving branding for property requires common elements in development programs. One of the strongest examples of branded properties is Del Webb's Sun Cities. These properties are large-scale communities built for the active adult market. The first Sun City was developed in Arizona in the early 1960s. Since then the company has developed Sun Cities throughout the country. Each community is adapted to the locale where it is developed, but each has a consistency and continuity that is absolutely recognizable from one to another. Del Webb has a precise formula for every aspect of product, process, people, and performance that can be moved to any location. The brand is vested with the real estate product, and a prospective customer can expect the same level of performance, quality, and service at every property.

When corporate behavior is added to the branding equation, the challenge of brand management increases exponentially. When it comes to real estate, the most difficult aspect of brand management is controlling the people component. How do you get the organization to behave in a consistent and market-responsive manner? How can a buyer or owner expect to be treated by project personnel? Will customer service be consistent? How does management respond to exceptional situations? How consistent and predictable is the customer experience?

If branding is the choice for positioning, the decision must be made as to whether the brand represents the company or the project. Hines was another early leader in real estate branding. Beginning as a local industrial property developer, Gerald Hines believed that he could distinguish his company and products through exceptional design. In the 1980s, he established a new standard for urban and suburban office buildings by hiring well-known architects to create signature buildings. To be in a Hines building was a statement about the tenant's own brand. Everything about the Hines product was tied to this proprietary positioning, from the excellent quality of design to creativity in the marketing presentation. The brand was established around this platform, and any prospect considering a Hines building knew exactly what he could expect. Interestingly, in recent years Hines has greatly diversified the types of property it develops, making it increasingly difficult to maintain brand awareness through the building quality and design. It can be argued that the brand now accrues to the company rather than the properties.

Few progressive real estate executives do not recognize the importance of branding. In the final analysis, successful branding means standing for something, treating customers well, behaving with consistency, and delivering on promises.

The Marketing Budget

Developers like to estimate in advance the total dollar amount for marketing, leasing, and sales that will allow them to complete project leasing or sales. As most facets of development lend themselves to fairly accurate estimates, a developer's desire to estimate the precise costs of marketing, leasing, and sales is understandable. Developing a hard-and-fast number for marketing and sales expenses, however, is much more difficult than deriving estimates for most construction cost items, partly because marketing is a relatively small percentage of overall development costs. Exclusive of leasing or sales commissions, marketing expenditures typically run from 1 to 3 percent; therefore, the margin for discrepancy as a percentage of the marketing budget alone can be great.

The developer has a marketing budget by stage three, which evolves over the final five stages of development. Ongoing budget planning requires a period of time against which the investment required for marketing can be forecast. It is important to make realistic estimates; real estate developers tend to be relatively optimistic and usually designate a time frame that is too short to complete all the sales objectives. The budget should be prepared for a period that relates to other aspects of the business structure such as a fiscal or tax year or for the entire selling period. If you choose a shorter time frame, make sure everyone involved knows that the budget is not the total to be allocated and that additional funding will be required.

Three approaches to budgeting for marketing are common:

► Zero-based budgeting;
► Percentage of revenue budgeting; and
► Fixed allocation budgeting.

Zero-Based Budgeting

Zero-based budgeting assigns a cost to each line item or activity. It is the most reliable approach to preparing an accurate budget, as it anticipates everything that needs to happen through the entire course of the marketing program. This budgeting process begins with a marketing plan developed to the point of identifying all activities necessary to achieve marketing goals. As the development progresses, the description of each activity should be expanded to include a list of specific, productive actions. To ensure that no promising prospects go overlooked, a comprehensive checklist of activities appropriate to a wide range of products and markets is an appropriate starting point.

The next step is to start paring down the total by scrutinizing every item. Each activity should be justified, and those that are not should be deleted. Presumably only the strongest ideas survive, which is the purpose of this method of budgeting—casting the net as wide as possible and keeping only the best of what it catches.

To estimate the grand total, it is necessary to predict how long it will take to lease the project. Market research can provide an estimated absorption rate, but how much to spend per month to achieve that rate is a judgment call. The total of all projected expenditures should be evaluated to determine whether the total budget is in line with the development pro forma. If not, the final budget may then be adjusted to reflect the project's overall financial requirements.

Percentage of Revenue Budgeting

In the real estate industry, certain property types have established financial benchmarks for marketing budgets. The percentage of revenue budgeting approach assumes that these industry averages are reasonable gauges of what it will cost to get the marketing done. It might be useful to start with industry averages to prepare a ballpark marketing budget, assuming that if marketing costs exceed the averages, the pricing for the development might be at a competitive disadvantage. But it is important to keep in mind that, although averages are useful references, they can be misleading and may not be an accurate or appropriate gauge of the project's needs.

Averages provide only macrobudgets. They indicate what others are allocating to marketing in the aggregate, but they do not disclose what areas of the promotions menu are most effective. Moreover, the size, markets, history, economic conditions, and a host of other factors will skew the percentages. To gloat because marketing expenditures have been kept below industry averages or to be distressed because they have exceeded averages may do the project a great disservice. Most critical is committing the resources to meet marketing goals.

Fixed Allocation Budgeting

"Fixed allocation" means simply assigning an amount for marketing based on company or project financial modeling. Whether based on experience from past projects, formulas developed for the particular property type being developed, or a discretionary decision, plugged-in numbers for marketing are dangerous. This approach is not recommended and is identified here as a budgeting alternative only because many development companies use it. Relying on numbers based on past allocations is irresponsible and reflects an organization that approaches marketing as an expense. Most budgets developed as fixed allocations generally result in numerous amendments to ensure that the budgets are sufficient to allow the marketing program to succeed. Most important, such budgets must be constantly monitored. It is difficult to forecast accurately how long marketing and sales will last. Because of the idiosyncrasies of the market, fluctuating economic cycles, and a host of other conditions beyond the developer's control, marketing programs and their budgets require a measure of flexibility. Budgets should include a contingency fund that can become a reserve if market conditions dictate the need for additional time or money to complete the program.

Whichever budgeting system is used, it is critically important that the productivity of marketing and sales activities be continuously measured against leases produced or sales closed. Incorporating the list of budget line items directly into the accounting system is crucial. In that way, total return on marketing dollars expended can be tracked with some precision. It is also important to use continuing market research to measure effectiveness and to pick up on changes in the project's trade area that affect marketing. And it is essential to request feedback from the sales team and prospects. As the team develops a track record, its experience can replace the original projections for the remainder of the sales or leasing effort.

Just gathering information is not enough. In this information age, data are readily available. Knowing how to handle the data and use information to benefit the developer is a special skill that cannot be underestimated. Coordinated marketing and sales is an exercise in value creation that occurs continually throughout the development process.

THE PROMOTIONS PROGRAM

The promotions program is the mix of materials, activities, and tools used to reach the development's various audiences. Every development will have a distinct and proprietary mix of promotions. Each project's promotion program is driven by the strategy, market, market conditions, and a host of other factors.

Image, Identity, and Naming

Real estate projects benefit from well-conceived identity and image programs as a foundation for communicating the development story. A development identity and image program typically includes a logo (a symbolic representation of the project) and/or logotype (the project name in a special typographic presentation) consistent with the impression the developer is trying to convey to the target audiences.

Every development—even those that simply rely on an address for identification—requires a label. The name is the first introduction to the project and conjures up certain impressions in potential customers' minds. To that end, naming is an important component of real estate marketing. No magic formula exists for naming a real estate project, but the following criteria should be considered when selecting a name:

► The name should reflect the scale of the development. Remember that the longer the name, the smaller the place. A name like *Falling Leaf at Chortling Creek* is inevitably a townhouse cluster of a few units, while names like *Celebration* and *Anthem* represent huge communities with thousands of acres.

► The name should be meaningful and evocative, capturing the nature and character of the environment.

► The name should engender an emotional reaction and be an element of the development story.

► The name, when necessary, should be capable of being extended into a comprehensive naming system for related amenities, neighborhoods, streets, facilities, and features of the project.

► The name should be distinctive, easy to recall, and not used elsewhere.

► The name should reflect the vision for the development, implying its sociology and a lifestyle.

► The name should be a source for a compelling story in and of itself. Even if it is fabricated, the name needs a marketing-based answer when someone asks "where did the name come from?"

Marketing Environments

For many types of developments, a marketing or information center is a significant part of the promotional program. Such facilities can range from simple displays in a designated space in a building or model home to extravagant freestanding buildings dedicated to totally controlling visitors' experience.

Between the cost to create them and the ongoing expense of operations, marketing environments take considerable resources and require competent, trained staff—usually dedicated to project sales—who use the environment as their office space.

Every marketing facility, regardless of size or complexity, should be a calculated orchestration of the development story. The information should be a quality presentation, prepared with imagination. The story should unfold in a logical sequence, building on its strengths and demonstrating its benefits to the audience. For the prospect, it must be an inviting experience.

Depending on the specific characteristics of the development, certain displays and graphic sales aids are appropriate to underscore the points stressed in the sales presentation. The design of each exhibit, model, and display, the message they convey, and their placement in the facility should unfold the story with logical impact. The entire presentation must empower the sales representative in telling the story.

The centers Hines created in its signature office towers were legendary. During the construction period, Hines would lease space in an adjacent competitor's building on a high floor overlooking the Hines site. The prospect would be taken on a tour through a series of rooms displaying the development story and touting the features and benefits. Model offices complete with wall-size murals replicating the views and large-scale models of the buildings were part of the tour. The final stage of the presentation was a media show. At the conclusion of the show, the narrator would invite the audience to view the progress of the building; a full wall would rise, revealing a commanding view over the Hines site. The choreography of the presentation was flawless and added

A project's name should be meaningful and evoke an emotional response. For example, Santaluz, a 3,800-acre (1,540-hectare) gated community 30 miles (48 kilometers) north of downtown San Diego, takes its name from the Spanish for "sacred light." *DMB Associates, Inc.*

to the image and reputation that Hines was building for the company and its developments. It also was the catalyst for leasing a tremendous amount of space.

Targeted Advertising

Market research provides ideas for the creative content of the advertising message. Often an outside advertising agency is responsible for writing advertising copy and producing a logo and accompanying graphics for the property. The agency also purchases media space or time for advertising. It is not usually advisable, however, to allow the advertising agency alone to determine the target market or establish an appropriate marketing budget. These factors are the responsibility of the marketing specialist (and ultimately the developer). Larger developers typically employ their own in-house marketing staffs, research staffs, and advertising professionals. In this case, it is

entirely appropriate to use in-house resources simultaneously with outside professionals.

Deciding on the best mix of media is an important component of targeted advertising. The target market itself should suggest which media would be most productive. Even with the availability of the Internet for advertising, newspaper advertising is still the traditional medium of choice across the nation for real estate, regardless of product type. If newspaper advertising is judged appropriate for both the product and the target market, the next task is to select the newspapers in which to advertise. That decision is based on what the target market is likely to read.

Deciding where in each newspaper to place the advertisement is also critical. A basic principle to follow is to place advertising where interested customers will look for it. Communicating with an interested audience actively seeking information about a

Figure 22-3 | Celebration

Celebration's 18-acre (7.3-hectare) downtown district features apartments, shops, offices, restaurants, a movie theater, small parks, public plazas, and a lakefront promenade. Designed on the assumption that streets belong to people, not cars, most parking is placed in lots behind buildings. Adrienne Schmitz

Developed by the Celebration Company, a subsidiary of the Walt Disney Company, Celebration is a 4,900-acre (1,985-hectare) new town near Orlando, Florida, and the Walt Disney World Resort. Celebration promotes a strong sense of community through its traditional neighborhood design. Ground was broken in March 1994. The residential sales and rental program began in November 1995, and the first residents moved in by June 1996, followed by the opening of the downtown district in November that year. Since that time, homes sales have remained strong. When complete, Celebration is anticipated to have approximately 12,000 residents.

Marketing and Sales Strategy

Robert Charles Lesser & Co., based in Los Angeles, undertook initial market studies for the community in the late 1980s. RCLCO's research indicated a strong market for primary housing for young families and empty nesters, second homes, and retirement homes. Rather than deal with all these markets in Phase I, Disney decided to focus on the primary-home market, as it provided the greatest support for the school and health campus. During Phase I, covenants prohibited use of the houses for second homes. The first phase where houses can be used seasonally is Phase IV—North Village—which includes housing products targeted for second-home and retirement markets and allows houses to be rented out.

Although the company placed no national advertising, the national press was keenly interested in the project, generating a high level of interest among consumers. Because demand was so strong, the company held a drawing to establish priority for purchasing the 351 lots and leasing the 123 apartments. Five thousand people attended the Founders Day drawing in 1995, and 1,200 prospective residents put down deposits.

The Celebration Preview Center functions as an information center and headquarters for Celebration Realty, which handles all home sales. The center's ground floor houses exhibits, a video presentation, a model of the community, and an interactive computer display. Visitors with strong interest are escorted to the realty and design center on the second floor, where sample home designs and floor plans are displayed. From there, they tour model homes. Showcase Village, a collection of three models, highlights innovative building technologies and displays the latest products from suppliers and participants. Each house employs a different energy-efficient method of construction.

To build the houses for Phase I, Disney selected eight premier local homebuilders and two high-quality national homebuilding companies. Builders are free to set their own prices and margins. Disney undertook extensive research to determine the mix of product types. The company analyzed market growth, absorption by price point, and house and lot size. The research resulted in a master plan for a community that would appeal to a variety of buyers and create a vibrant town. Selling prices in all categories appear to carry a premium of at least 10 to 15 percent above comparable homes in other local master-planned communities. The estate homes are lowest in demand, perhaps because some builders set sale prices well above the recommended $500,000.

General Business Strategy

Over the years, Disney's goal has been to maintain the special values and high quality that have been Disney hallmarks while always embracing new ideas. The company tries to look at the familiar in new ways, seeing change as the essence of creativity. The company is structured like most development firms, with a general manager, a marketing division, a sales division, a residential development division that works with builders, and a financial and operations division responsible for financial planning, asset management, apartment leasing, and

Figure 22-3	Celebration (*continued*)

building maintenance. What distinguishes the company's structure from most is its new business development division, whose role is to establish strategic alliances and to work with strategic alliance partners.

The Celebration Company believes that other developers can replicate almost everything about the community, including the town center and the creation of public/ private partnerships for information technology, education, and health. At the same time, however, the company acknowledges that it would be considerably more difficult for most developers than it was for Disney to undertake so much advance research and development. The special circumstances that made it possible were that Disney owned the land, had access to substantial financial resources, and was also able to tap into strong market demand. Nevertheless, the company points out that it has a pro forma for each element of the project and that every element is programmed to generate an appropriate return over time. Further, building the infrastructure through community development districts helped the economic equation greatly.

The strategic alliances with corporate partners proved beneficial to all involved. Celebration's alliances bring industry leaders together to help create the special components that form the town's cornerstones. Since the alliance process was initiated in 1992, alliances have typically evolved through several steps: research and identification of potential partners, information sharing, letters of understanding, an operations plan, formal agreements, operations, vision, and alliance expansion. The last step often results in the identification of new products and opportunities for Disney, creating value that the company did not have in the past. The alliances often create synergistic relationships. As the partners were brought together with the common purpose of creating community, they were asked to focus not only on their own areas but also on the entire town.

In 2004, the Walt Disney Company sold Celebration's town center to Lexin Capital, a real estate investment company. The purchase encompassed 18 acres (7.3 hectares) containing 16 retail shops, six restaurants, and 105 apartments. Lexin agreed to retain the architectural design standards established by Disney.

---

product is much more useful than attempting to capture the attention of someone with no initial interest in the product. The goal is to design and place an advertisement powerful enough to induce response.

Magazines and trade publications are also often used to advertise real estate. In many communities, some magazines survive almost exclusively on real estate–oriented advertising, particularly for residential developments in rapidly growing communities. Local and statewide business magazines are natural choices for almost all types of income-producing properties. Both residential and commercial developers may find opportunities in magazines targeted to area newcomers. Product-specific trade publications are another medium for advertising property developments, particularly in the retail sector, where players are fewer and their interrelationships well established.

Compared with newspapers, magazines have longer life cycles and may deliver more highly targeted readers. The print quality of magazines is also much higher, especially if the magazines include full-

color photographs. For upscale, particularly attractive developments, these factors can be compelling inducements. Public service publications such as the local guide to radio and television symphony broadcasts can sometimes make sense when trying to establish a certain tone for a development.

Radio and television offer tremendous impact, though generally at commensurate cost, particularly in major metropolitan markets. They are especially useful for the short-term support of a special event such as a grand opening. Many metropolitan areas have radio stations targeted to just about any imaginable profile of residential buyers. The growing popularity of cable television offers creative possibilities for business-oriented developments.

Direct mail is the most highly targeted advertising medium and one of the most precise ways to communicate with target audiences. The careful selection and review of recipients on the list help to minimize wasted exposure. Numerous sources can provide demographically segmented mailing lists that make it possible to target audiences with highly customized messages. Most successful direct-mail campaigns feature repetitive mailings.

Newsletters in either hard copy or electronic form should be considered if the development requires extensive dissemination of information for promotion. They can be very effective in ongoing communications and in maintaining connections with tenants and buyers. By focusing on issues of concern to the customers, they help fill the role of a customer relations tool. They also allow developers to tell their own story in their own way while subtly implying a third-party endorsement.

Web sites have become obligatory tools for marketing real estate developments. They provide a medium for prospective customers to obtain detailed price information, view floor plans, take virtual tours of available space, and find contact information. It is important to remember that Web sites are first and foremost for information, not entertainment. Overly complex, tricky, or information-excessive pages will make legibility more difficult and fail to hold the viewer. When designed correctly for maximum marketing effectiveness, a Web site is an ideal medium to offer substantive information for prospective customers. If the site contains time-sensitive content, make sure it is updated regularly.

Many Web sites such as LoopNet provide online real estate listings that allow users to search by type of property desired and location, making follow-up easy. These Web sites provide a free or relatively low-cost means of marketing properties and providing up-to-date information for potential users.

Finally, signage is an important part of any real estate promotions program. Real estate is all about location, and the market for most projects exists within a relatively close radius of the property. Most of a project's prospects will pass by the property at some point. Creating awareness with on-site signage is highly effective and relatively inexpensive. Referencing the Web site address on the signs provides viewers easy access to the total development story.

Whatever the medium of choice, the marketing team should take care to fully estimate the costs and benefits of using that medium in a marketing campaign. In the case of Museum Towers, Dean Stratouly knew his limitations in marketing and leasing and hired professionals to help develop a strategy for leasing space in a pioneering location.

Public Relations

Targeted advertising must be reinforced by a coordinated public relations effort. It is useful to think of public relations as untargeted promotion aimed at the public at large, with the best generator of positive public relations the quality of the development itself.

Using the media means first and foremost having a compelling and newsworthy story. The technology that now drives media means everything is done at lightning speed using E-mail and the Internet. Editors receive hundreds of messages per day, and even modestly sized publications get thousands of press releases and story ideas a week. The challenge is to stand out in the crowd.

Press releases can be issued to any media outlet and on virtually any topic. Learn the form in which each publication of interest to the development's target audiences prefers to receive information. Give them what they want.

Community Relations

Almost all real estate development today generates some concern—if not outright opposition—among people who live near the project or will be affected by it. The special-interest groups that are in a position to influence the development must be considered paramount among target audiences. Although community relations programs may seem an incongruous part of a marketing program, the positive effect of a well-conceived and -executed program can reap significant benefits in facilitating the development's progress and as such can contribute immeasurably to the bottom line. Engaging special-interest groups early often results in the fine-tuning of a project to make it more attractive to consumers. And it is not uncommon for participants in these forums to become buyers or renters.

Thoughtfully receiving feedback from government and the community shows respect for the public interest. In reality, developers have some

Figure 22-4	Content, Organization, and Design of the Sales Brochure

Content

Every piece of communication must capture the message and the compelling reasons that a prospect should choose the development. Infuse passion and energy into the story. Make sure the points of distinction are evident and understandable. Always consider the story from prospects' point of view. Make it speak to their needs and push their hot buttons. Make sure the written content is not dry or founded on real estate clichés. Tell prospects how the development will benefit them and add value to their lives or businesses. Defining the development through strategic messages and connecting your message to each target audience is paramount.

The following components can be used in the presentation of any real estate development to visually demonstrate a project's story:

▶ Site and land use plans;

▶ Floor plans;

▶ Regional, local, and access maps;

▶ Aerial photos;

▶ Building elevations;

▶ Photos—of the environmental ambience, the entrance, interiors and the exterior; the surrounding area, amenities, and the lifestyle in action.

Layering

Layering information is crucial to legibility. Organizing information with a hierarchy of headlines, captions, pull quotes, column widths, and type sizes adds to the ease of reading. Identify the levels of information and select a type font, size, and weight for each. Then use them consistently throughout the document.

Typography

Type is the primary means of transmitting information. Keep it legible. Follow basic typographic rules:

Source: Richard Burns.

▶ Never set text in all caps.

▶ Set body text flush left and rag right. Try to avoid justified text (flush left and right). It is more difficult to read.

▶ Keep the text to fewer than 55 to 65 characters per line in sizes up to 14 points. Use fewer characters per line in larger sizes.

▶ When in doubt about legibility, increase the type size.

▶ Avoid mixing multiple serif and sans serif fonts in the same document. Rely instead on sizes, weights, italics, and line spacing to create different effects.

▶ Remember that blank space makes the information easier to assimilate.

▶ Keep it simple. Clutter impedes legibility.

Audit of the Printed Program

When producing printed materials, attempt to view how your materials will be seen through the eyes of your audience. Honestly assess how well you tell your story:

▶ How easy is it for a reader to understand your project?

▶ How easy is it for a reader to appreciate the things that make your project a compelling choice?

▶ Is it easy to access the information?

▶ Does the quality of the presentation and reproduction reflect the stature and scale of the project?

▶ Does the visual vocabulary reflect the project's image?

▶ Does the communications system have the flexibility and thoroughness to respond to all inquiries?

▶ Is there a call to action? Will the audience know what to do after reading the materials? Will potential customers know whom to call or how to reach the right contact?

latitude in initiating changes as a result of that feedback. Few actions of a developer can be more effective in generating favorable public relations than demonstrating responsible concern for the community and corresponding with flexibility during the development process.

A well-conceived community relations program provides relevant agencies and officials with the comprehensive information they need to discharge their responsibilities efficiently. Taking the initiative to raise and resolve potentially difficult issues can sometimes avert distressingly contentious public confrontations.

The local government was heavily involved in the development of Museum Towers, which required the developer to include some non-market-rate units.

Events

On-site events provide an excellent opportunity to promote a project and tell its development story. Ground breaking ceremonies, topping out parties, grand openings, tours for brokers, and open houses are the types of events that can help potential clients get acquainted with the development. Invitation lists should include those audiences who are prospective buyers or renters or who are in a position to influence others in favor of the development.

Events should be entertaining, but the overall focus should be on education and exposure of the development story. The development environment can be enhanced with exhibits, displays, tours, and presentations to maximize the exposure that can come from a well-executed event.

Perhaps the most obvious on-site promotion of a new development is the grand opening (stage seven in the real estate development process). Developers should invite to the opening citizens and government officials they met as part of the public relations program as well as representatives of the extended development team. Developers should also invite principal or potential prospects. In many areas, a chamber of commerce function is a worthwhile on-site promotion. The primary and secondary trade areas' customers should be included, along with area retailers and anchor tenants, corporate real estate managers, and merchants.

Not only should the physical features of a building be used as a sales tool, but the quality and depth of the property's tenancies should also be distinctly attractive to the target market. Allowing the market to experience firsthand a project's features, functions, and benefits can be a great sales tool.

A city agency asked Museum Towers to donate land to a park that will abut the property. What was originally seen as a concession to the city in the negotiations is being marketed as an amenity.

SALES

Real estate marketing makes a distinction between promotions and sales. Sales represent the step in the marketing process where an interested prospect has been identified and needs to be converted to a buyer or tenant. A broker or sales agent typically executes this step. The role of the broker or sales agent varies from project to project and depends on the developer's desires. The relationship can range from an outside brokerage company to the developer's in-house staff. The approach depends on the developer's capabilities, the property type, and market conditions. Regardless, the brokerage community inevitably becomes part of the sales process for any project. Therefore, developing relationships with local real estate agents who specialize in a specific property type is critical, regardless of whether the developer employs an in-house sales staff or an outside agency. Successful brokers know about local market conditions and often have proprietary access to prospects.

When sales and leasing are handled in house, the developer has far more control. But even with in-house sales teams, the developer must maintain a cooperative and productive relationship with outside brokers, including the commission-sharing structure to provide appropriate incentives. Brokers are not easily excited by new products unless they are convinced they can sell the property quickly and easily. Brokers want assurance that developers will pay full commissions quickly. Timely financial remuneration of cooperating brokers is the primary reason that agents bring prospects to a developer's property. To the extent that the developer can help agents build a stronger relationship with their clients, local agents become more enthusiastic about introducing their clients to the developer.

The Marketing and Sales Staff

The principles that guide the formulation and implementation of the marketing strategy, including market research and techniques for determining

MUSEUM TOWERS
Developing a Marketing Strategy

Web sites can assist owners and consumers in marketing. Owners can save money on printed material, and consumers can educate themselves about the project and its competition before touring it.

We hired Doerr Associates of Winchester to do our marketing. I'm a developer, not a marketing person, so I think it's really important to use the professionals that know what they're doing. Doerr has been around for more than 25 years, and we hired them to develop advertising strategies, direct-mail campaigns, and printed brochures and other material. We put ads in the *Boston Globe* that were designed to appeal to the "hip" professional crowd. We also developed our own Web site and advertised on Rent.Net. From the beginning, the *Boston Globe*, a very traditional apartment leasing tool, brought the greatest number of prospective tenants.

We developed a marketing slogan—Rent the Apartment; Own the City—that we put on billboards, online, on our collateral marketing materials. We paid a lot of attention to the amenities and special features, and marketed them heavily. We made some decisions about which amenities to include based on a focus group of renters who lived within two miles (3.2 kilometers) of Museum Towers. The washer and dryer in each unit, which were recommended by the focus group, have been a real boon to our marketing. High-speed elevators and security were also important. So we got elevators that travel 700 feet (215 meters) per minute, a 24-hour concierge staff, and valet parking. Every apartment has four high-speed telecommunications lines and a broadband cable-ready outlet from *MediaOne*. We run a shuttle in the morning and evening to the three closest subway stops—Lechmere, Kendall Square, and North Station.

But we also have a 15,000-square-foot (1,395-square-meter) health club with an indoor two-lane lap pool, which cost over $2 million to build. It's two floors with treadmills, cross-trainers, stair steppers, lifecycles, weights, aerobics, spin classes—you name it.

Plus we offer 200 units for tenants' storage and parking—both of which are hard to find in this market. We've even got a housekeeping service and furniture rentals. There's also a nice courtyard for our renters to use.

At the time we initiated the marketing campaign, Cambridge was a great market for high-end renters. The average household income was about $57,000, compared with the national average of about $46,000.

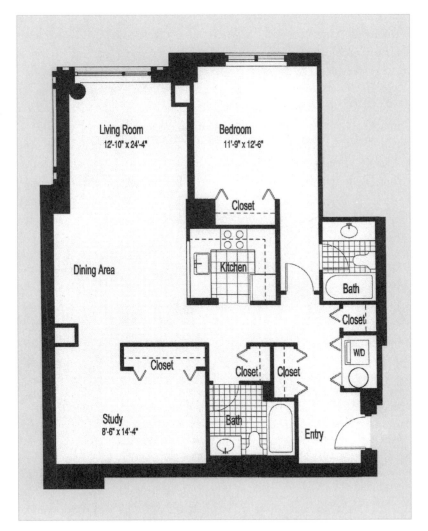

A floor plan of a typical Museum Towers apartment unit.

continued on next page

space use, must be second nature to anyone contemplating a successful career in marketing and sales. After all, sales or leasing is the final step in the overall marketing process, which began during stage one. Understanding the specific product type as well as its design and production (the construction process) is a prerequisite to selling the product knowledgeably and successfully. In development, leasing or sales almost always starts before the project is complete and often before construction begins. As a result, the marketing representative is often involved in changing plans during construction to meet tenants' needs. Marketing professionals and salespeople should be firmly grounded in the principles of real estate finance so that they can competently advise prospects of alternative financial structures for proposed lease transactions. Both marketing professionals and brokers also need to understand the financial aspects of feasibility analysis to know which tenant proposals may be acceptable to the developer or investor. And the ability to empathize with and lead people, a general management skill, is crucial to the sales process.

Keeping salespeople content and motivated is an ongoing challenge. By its very nature, the real estate sales process is characterized by rejection and failure: attempted sales far surpass completed sales, and the number of prospects far surpasses the number of buyers. Many more selling days end in defeat than in victory. Virtually all sales agents are compensated through commissions, and, although this type of incentive compensation is an inducement for agents, any effective and sustainable sales program must include continuing education. Training and education will enhance professional skills and increase confidence and motivation and lead to more sales or leases for the developer. Continuing education also creates esprit within the organization; the result is fewer turnovers in sales agents, which adds to the organization's effectiveness. Whether relying on in-house staff or an outside agency, a wise developer takes advantage of these benefits by making sure that continuing sales education is an integral part of the marketing and sales system.

To sell a product well, an agent must fully understand the product. Recognizing this fact, most developers provide some type of orientation program for new agents. It would be difficult to go too far in this endeavor, for every detail about the project's design and excellence that can be communicated to salespeople becomes ammunition for use with prospects. Most developers also acknowledge that any real estate sale or leasing transaction could take the prospect or the developer into unfamiliar financial territory. For this reason, the agent must be able to act as a financial guide, leading the prospect to a rational and com-

MUSEUM TOWERS
Setting Rental Rates

A total of 33 units, or 7.5 percent of the units, are for low- or moderate-income renters. The subsidized units include 15 one-bedrooms and 18 two-bedrooms. Although the tenants have to be qualified by the Cambridge Housing Authority, we're working very closely with CHA to screen the tenants, most of whom will be Section 8 certificate holders.

The law allows these units to be 110 percent of allowed Section 8 rents adjusted for utilities or, in this case, $772 for one-bedrooms and $920 for two-bedrooms. The remaining subsidized units will be available to tenants earning 80 percent of the median income. These tenants will pay 30 percent of their gross income, with an estimated rent of $722 for the one-bedroom units.

A model apartment with a view of the Charles River was an effective leasing tool for Museum Towers.

MUSEUM TOWERS *(continued)*

Estimated Annual Gross Income from Apartment Rentals

	Per Square Foot	Per Unit	Total
Market Units	$2.55	$2,433	$977,918
Affordable Units	$1.06	$838	$27,640
Total			$1,005,558
Annualized (x 12)			$12,066,696

Rent Schedules

Market Units	Total	Unit Size (Square Feet)	In-Place Rent/ Per Square Foot	Current Market Rent Range/ Per Square Foot
Studio	3	720	$1,225–1,400/$1.70–1.94	$1,390–1,490/$1.93–2.07
1 Bedroom/1 Bath				
Floors 2–9	61	646–864	$1,200–1,585/$1.59–2.17	$1,300–1,775/$1.63–2.43
Floors 10–19	37	701–864	$1,485–2,000/$2.12–2.85	$1,650–2,050/$2.16–2.92
Floors 20–24	25	701–864	$1,975–2,075/$2.82–2.96	$1,975–2,600/$2.66–3.38
Subtotal	**126**	**646–864**	**$1,200–2,075/$1.59–2.96**	**$1,300–2,600/$1.63–3.38**
1 Bedroom & Study/1 Bath				
Floors 2–9	9	864–889	$1,300–1,635/$1.47–1.89	$1,425–1,675/$1.60–1.94
Floors 10–19	16	864	$1,545–2,055/$1.79–2.38	$1,725–2,200/$2.00–2.55
Floors 20–24	9	862–864	$2,150–2,410/$2.49–2.79	$2,050–2,650/$2.37–3.07
Subtotal	**34**	**862–889**	**$1,300–2,410/$1.47–2.79**	**$1,425–2,650/$1.60–3.07**
2 Bedrooms/2 Baths				
Floors 2–9	30	1,044–1,337	$1,800–2,300/$1.65–2.10	$1,925–2,360/$1.72–2.20
Floors 10–19	110	1,044–1,095	$2,045–2,760/$1.91–2.54	$2,120–2,905/$1.95–2.70
Floors 20–24	52	1,072–1,210	$2,700–4,000/$2.47–3.35	$2,615–4,150/$2.39–3.47
Subtotal	**192**	**1,050–1,210**	**$1,800–4,000/$1.65–3.35**	**$1,925–4,150/$1.72–3.47**
Total Market Units	**352**	**936**	**$2,023/$2.16**	**$2,198/$2.35**
Total Market Units by Floor				
Floors 2–9	103	646–1,337	$1,200–2,300/$1.47–2.07	$1,300–2,360/$1.60–2.43
Floors 10–19	163	701–1,095	$1,485–2,760/$1.79–2.85	$1,650–2,950/$1.95–2.92
Floors 20–24	86	701–1,210	$1,975–4,000/$2.47–3.35	$1,975–4,150/$2.37–3.47
Affordable Units				
Studio	0	–	–	–
1 Bedroom/1 Bath	14	636–714	$587–801/$0.86–1.15	$700–729/$1.01–1.15
1 Bedroom & Study/1 Bath	1	1,083	N/A	$900/$0.83
2 Bedrooms/2 Baths	18	1,050–1,092	$721–908/$0.66–0.85	$736–908/$0.68–0.84
Total Affordable Units	**33**	**906**	**$763/$0.84**	**$812/$0.90**
Corporate Units				
Studio	1	720	$1,500/$2.08	$1,540/$2.14
1 Bedroom/1 Bath	7	636–714	$1,500–2,000/$2.14–2.85	$1,500–2,050/$2.14–2.92
1 Bedroom & Study/1 Bath	1	1,076	$1,975/$1.84	$2,000/$1.86
2 Bedrooms/2 Baths	41	1,072–1,095	$1,950–2,450/$1.80–2.26	$1,955–2,425/$1.80–2.24
Total Corporate Units	**50**	**1,023**	**$1,964/$1.92**	**$2,043/$2.00**
Total Units	**435**	**944**	**$1,920/$2.04**	**$2,075/$2.20**

continued on next page

MUSEUM TOWERS
The Park as a Marketing Tool

North Point Park is a 40-acre (16-hectare) park that, under the direction of the Metropolitan District Commission, was scheduled to be completed in 2000. The idea of the park was first presented to the public in 1986. It's all part of the Metropolitan Park System's plan to connect the edges of the city. The Boston and Cambridge Esplanades will be connected along the river to HarborPark and the Freedom Trail. Along the way are large-scale engineering works such as bridges, dams, pumping stations, locks, and viaducts that will all be set off and beautified with parkland and water elements. Seven miles (11.3 kilometers) of new pathways will be available along the Charles River.

The Metropolitan District Commission held public hearings and various meetings and worked closely with the New Charles River Basin Citizens Advisory Committee to solicit ideas, attitudes, and expectations about the North Point Park.

The land that the park is on was part of the site that we owned and donated to the state. Somewhere during this development process, I got religion and said, yes, I want to give up an acre (0.4 hectare) of my land to parks, yes, I want to have my site cut in half by a road, yes, I want to set aside 7.5 percent of my project for low-income housing, yes, I want to build my own utilities, yes, I want to rebuild an intersection, yes, I want to build two separate towers instead of one, yes, I want to build towers that are not as tall as I'd like, yes, I want to build a restaurant that has to be open to the public certain hours. I love being a developer.

But the park will come up around one building and wrap around the other building, right up to the health club. We have to give the roads to the city. In the end, the park will be a huge asset to the project. It will be for passive use, with trails. It'll link with other bike trails. There will be a canoe house and some kiosks. I expect the restaurant I was forced to build will also benefit from the park.

continued on page 560

---

fortable decision among possibly confusing and conflicting financing alternatives.

The need to provide education for salespeople about the specific skills of selling is less well understood. The profession of selling is built on the ability of salespeople to establish clear and compelling communication with prospects. Most often, sound communication is based on establishing as much personal rapport as possible with the prospect as soon as possible. Prospects who feel comfortable with their sales agent and are convinced that the agent is sincerely interested in their point of view are much more likely to buy or lease the product.

Building rapport with prospective buyers generally requires breaking down the prospect's emotional defenses against the sale of an item. Prospects usually perceive themselves at risk, believing that a negotiation could be critically important to them. They want to get as much information as possible from the sales agent without revealing too much about themselves, their needs, and their motives. The sales agent's challenge is almost the opposite. Building rapport with the prospect requires the agent to learn as much as possible about the prospect as an individual.

Many training courses devote time to classifying personalities that enable salespeople to identify a prospect's comfortable style of behavior. Reading the prospect's verbal and nonverbal cues in the first few moments allows the agent to place that individual into one of a number of behavioral categories and to adapt his own normal style of behavior to the prospect's behavior to lower defensive barriers. The assumption is that different behavioral types are interested in and motivated by distinctly different elements of the product.

Another body of useful knowledge is negotiation techniques. If the prospect perceives the two parties to be involved in negotiation from the outset, then they are. Many of the lessons that have been learned during negotiations, either between nations or between management and labor, are directly applicable to negotiations in real estate sales and leasing. Understanding where power comes from and how to use it can give salespeople a tremendous advantage. Likewise, understanding classic maneuvers and how best to counter them can make some of the toughest situations appear elementary.

All these techniques apply to the general objective of fostering improved communication between the participants involved on either side of a real estate sales presentation. They are adaptations of techniques that are one foundation of an education in business management. Including them in the education of sales agents can expand team members' professional capabilities.

Perhaps these obligations are the reason so many developers find it advantageous to contract with an outside brokerage agency for sales and leasing. A relatively simple negotiation between a developer and a broker sets in motion a continuing effort in which the developer may be somewhat less involved. The agency is presumed to command special expertise in handling a particular type of product in a particular market and to employ a competent and motivated staff. (The developer's administrative burden is reduced dramatically, especially in subdivision sales, where the agency is paid from the proceeds of actual sales. In the case of leasing, commissions are paid from property operations or construction and development financing.)

In sales operations, one of the principal differences between commercial and residential sales is the extent to which active prospecting takes place. In commercial developments, the developer's representatives normally identify potential individual members of the target market and contact them directly to initiate the sale. Alternatively, the developer's representatives may contact members of the brokerage community who enjoy exclusive leasing arrangements with prospective tenants.

An enterprising salesperson should spend some time calling on a developer's current clients to see whether they are content or might be thinking of expanding or relocating their facilities. Lack of attention could send current clients to a competing project. Existing relationships with current tenants offer a great advantage to the developer who is not concerned about eroding occupancy in one building to increase it in another. When the same developer controls both existing and prospective leases, timing the move is not overly worrisome. In fact, it is not uncommon for an asset manager to manage investments for multiple clients. Although in such cases moving tenants between buildings can create serious

conflicts of interest, keeping up with existing tenants' needs is still a good idea. Care should be taken, therefore, to investigate any conflicts of interest adequately before engaging an asset manager or a brokerage firm.

Defining the target market and creating a product specifically suited to it are fundamental to successful real estate sales. Although market research defines the target market in economic and demographic terms, understanding the psychographic profile of target markets is a well-established principle in marketing consumer products that is directly applicable to marketing real estate. Just as traditional demographic analysis allows salespeople to group customers on the basis of age, sex, income, and family size, psychographic analysis allows the sales force to segment the overall population into groups that share the same general outlook on life. (This approach helps in retail leasing, because it becomes possible to lease to the appropriate tenants whose merchandise or line of business fits the needs of the trade area's particular psychographic groups.)

Knowing what customers want as individuals allows sales agents to present the product so that it meets needs customers may not even perceive they have. This principle is the basis of psychographic marketing: creating products (or leasing to tenants who sell products) that meet the strongly felt needs of an identified target market segment and then presenting those products to that target so that their unrealized needs are satisfied just as their explicit needs are met. The psychographic profile represents an extremely powerful component of marketing knowledge that salespeople can use to great effect.

Building the Sale

Once the salesperson has identified an interested prospect, the challenge shifts to making a successful sales presentation. Whether the objective is generating a signed lease or an authorized purchase agreement, a planned rather than improvised presentation is always preferable, regardless of property type. The agent must identify the prospect's needs and convince him that the proffered product will meet those needs, ensuring that the value delivered is at least equal to the price.

A model custom home in the Pinehills allows potential buyers to imagine what it would be like to live in this 3,000-acre (1,215-hectare) master-planned conservation community located seven miles (11 kilometers) south of Plymouth Rock and 45 miles (72.5 kilometers) south of Boston. *Eric Roth*

Finally, the salesperson must ask for the order. It is this final part of the process that many salespeople find so difficult; it always seems to be too soon to ask. The best salespeople eliminate this stress from the decision-making process by following a planned sequence for the presentation that guarantees delivery of all needed information in a logical order as well as opportunities for ample feedback from the prospect. If the salesperson has followed the sequence and delivered all the necessary information, the prospect will want the agent to ask for an order. If the prospect were not ready to proceed, he already would have found a way to terminate the process.

Follow-Up

Effective follow-up is essential for any sales transaction. Few sales are closed in the first meeting, and good salespeople work patiently with identified prospects.

In residential sales, following up on presales is intended to encourage return visits to the sales center. The agent should follow a prearranged schedule of written and telephone contacts based on the number of days that pass since the prospect's first visit to the sales center. Generally speaking, these contacts should be friendly and not oriented toward sales. For commercial properties, the same general idea holds, though with one major exception: the intensity of follow-up should increase as the expiration date of the prospect's present lease approaches.

Reaching an agreement does not mean that follow-up should cease. One of the most important functions a sales or leasing professional can perform is to hold the deal together between signing and moving in. In Florida, for example, the signing of a purchase agreement for a new condominium merely signals the beginning of a 15-day period during which the purchaser can cancel the deal at any time for any reason. This law, reflecting government's continuing role as the developer's partner, merely acknowledges that once people make a decision, they often have second thoughts. It is up to the sales agent to anticipate this event and to take steps to prevent its occurrence.

After the tenant moves in, follow-up shifts to ascertaining that the space has been delivered in acceptable condition. Given the effort and expense of creating a synergistic marketing and sales system, it makes sense to try for more than a one-time contact with a prospect who is never seen or heard from again. It makes no sense to shepherd a prospect to an agreement only to have the deal fall apart. Likewise, it is of limited benefit to put a prospect into space the team has worked so hard to create only to have him become unhappy. The most efficient way to avoid these unfortunate circumstances is systematic and sensitive follow-up by salespeople.

SUMMARY

In successful development operations, people come to work early, work hard, move fast, and stay late. Salespeople who are not immediately productive are quickly gone. If salespeople want to avoid failure, they might consider the following suggestions:

1. Learn the property type, tenant market, customer, and trade area. Thoroughly understand the market research. Read the feasibility study very carefully. Look at comparable facilities; shop the competitors. Understand access, visibility, and road patterns. Review the plans and specifications for each building under construction. Walk around the property, preferably with someone who can explain its features, functions, and benefits.

2. Know the development company's history and its current financial condition. Look for statements of its operating philosophy and plans for the future. In retail development, visit tenants' existing units. Understand their business.

3. Read recent leases and/or purchase agreements, which demonstrate how business is conducted and with whom. Differences among recent agreements indicate areas of frequent negotiation.

4. Get to know the company's principal suppliers.

5. Estimate where the financial pressures will be felt in the organization. Compare the current status of the project with the projections included in original plans. Pressure will most assuredly be directed toward operations that are behind schedule, including marketing and sales.

6. Get to know the players on the team. Who controls what in the company? Who is reliable? Where are the territorial lines that should not be crossed?

7. Find out the current status of the relevant local market and any apparent market trends. Know how the market is doing and how it is important to potential customers. The local press is a great place to start on both counts.

8. Most important, be professional from the beginning. Work hard. Tell the truth. Never stop learning.

9. And never sell all the lakefront property first.

Few people are born salespeople, but many people can learn marketing, and everyone—whether a consumer or supplier of space—should understand what makes space appealing, marketable, and valuable to its users.

TERMS

▶ Absorption
▶ Broker

▶ Marketing
▶ Positioning
▶ Promotions
▶ Sales
▶ SWOT
▶ Target market
▶ Vision

REVIEW QUESTIONS

22.1 Describe the difference between sales and marketing.

22.2 How does market research help the marketing process?

22.3 What are the elements of SWOT analysis? How do they interrelate with each other?

22.4 What are the elements of vision?

22.5 What are the four positioning strategies?

22.6 Describe the three principal methods of developing a marketing budget.

22.7 What is included in a marketing plan?

22.8 Museum Towers has a Web site advertising the property to potential tenants. How does that kind of advertising differ from a print ad or a direct-mail campaign? What are some of the advantages and disadvantages?

CHAPTER 23

Some Closing Thoughts and A Note about the Future

There can be no fully appropriate summary or conclusion to a book about real estate development, because society's needs for built space are continually evolving. We offer instead some closing thoughts and a note about the future.

We hopefully have made the case in this book that decisions about the development of real property are critical to our society's future functioning. Indeed, a very large share of the nation's wealth is invested in real property, both residential and commercial. Further, the built environment has a major impact on almost everyone's life. The better the development decisions made today, the better tomorrow's built environment will be.

The eight-stage model of the real estate development process discussed throughout this text is a flexible strategic tool that allows developers to make better decisions today—to see the whole while focusing on a particular decision. The logic behind the eight-stage model is clearly financial, but the motivation comes from the market. Development involves complex marketing, financial, political, and production tasks as well as many different kinds of interpersonal relationships. Still, all the activity is in response to particular market segments and the consumers in those segments, whose preferences are constantly changing.

A complete understanding of the development process is impossible without a historical perspective, for history allows us to understand where we have been and how we have arrived at the present. As such, history is a useful tool for predicting the future. Development is a forward-looking activity based on knowledge and experience drawn from the past. Because constructed space can be expected to last for several decades, a long-term historical perspective is important in anticipating what society will demand over the next several decades.

This chapter about the future discusses several topics:

▶ A contemporary perspective on the past, and how best to think about what will be in the future;
▶ A few important trends and critical issues to consider; and
▶ A return to Graaskamp's complete definition of feasibility and concern for "what ought to be."

Along the way, we pay a final visit to Museum Towers and Elevation 314.

A CONTEMPORARY PERSPECTIVE ON THE PAST AND HOW BEST TO THINK ABOUT THE FUTURE

The long view—from the past and into the future—yields a portrait of recurring patterns as well as entirely new circumstances. For example, the fact that real estate development slowed after its dizzying pace in the mid-1980s and again at the end of the dot-com boom is certainly not surprising. Real estate is traditionally a cyclical business, and it has always experienced the inevitable busts that follow the booms. What was different about the 1980s was the extent of overbuilding. Typically, during the downturns of the past four or five decades, the development pendulum would swing back again within a few years. In the 1980s, however, the supply of available office space, hotel rooms, strip shopping centers, and residential condominiums compared with projected demand was so excessive that it took more than half a decade to restore balance in some markets. Nevertheless, although overbuilding was far more extensive in the 1980s than in the 1950s, 1960s, 1970s, or late 1990s, the situation was still far better than at the beginning of the 1930s. With the economic impact of the Great Depression, supply was so much greater than demand that virtually no new private office buildings were constructed in many urban areas for more than 20 years.

Until summer 2007, investers believed there was an important difference between earlier cycles—all the way back to the 18th century—and contemporary circumstances in that the more severe real estate crashes from the 1790s to the 1930s were generally accompanied by a major panic in the financial system. The S&L crisis of the 1980s is now history, and, with new regulatory safeguards in place, America's financial system is much more stable. Indeed, pension funds and other forms of institutional ownership have introduced an added element of stability that was missing during the 1930s, when the widespread default of privately insured mortgage bonds led to a long-term withdrawal of private capital from real estate. Professionally managed REITs also added to stability and allowed smaller investors to invest indirectly in real estate. Increasingly, real estate is viewed as an institutional asset, and new financial institutions and global investors will continue to bring many structural changes to real estate development in the 21st century.

Sometimes history repeats itself. The financial instruments that emerged in the 1980s and 1990s such as REITs and mortgage-backed securities resemble in many ways some of the innovations of the 1920s. Likewise, development ideas and practices of the 1990s included a return to traditional street grids in suburban subdivisions and nostalgic Main Street storefront designs for new shopping centers. Yet at the same time, recent and projected new demographic patterns of a rapidly aging population, the continuing increase in the formation of nontraditional households, and an influx of immigrant households suggest that we will continue to witness the creation of new forms of development to meet the changing and often untapped needs of different segments of the market.

In most markets, existing conditions are "fairly" priced as soon as they become widely known. Therefore, what matters in investment performance is forecasting change. Whether concerned with minute-to-minute pricing (lease decisions) or three-year forecasts (when to start Phase II of a project), the astute developer focuses on change.

This focus involves two kinds of judgment:

► Learning from the past (while monitoring the contemporary situation). This kind of judgment is econometric and data intensive. Most of the market material covered in this text deals with judgments based on documentable current conditions and historic relationships.

► Estimating what may be different in the future.

Although learning from the past is something every professional tries to do, estimating what may be different in the future is more subjective and often difficult for decision makers. Everyone will admit it is critically important not to "straight line" a forecast, but that does not mean everyone will agree on how to draw the curves. Different curves are what create the development horse race. It is not a matter of guessing the date of "the big one" in California. Rather, it is a matter of looking at the reactions to and interactions among existing trends—which can be done without a crystal ball. All investors do it implicitly, but the best ones do it explicitly as well.

A FEW IMPORTANT TRENDS AND CRITICAL ISSUES TO CONSIDER

Known Demographic Changes With Known Consequences

Beginning early in the text, we argued that much about what will be true about population cohorts is knowable. Demographics is a science that can predict with a fair degree of accuracy. The skill is in adjusting the "knowable" cohorts into demand for space, considering income changes. Both income and wealth in our society continue to become more stratified. There will eventually be a reaction to this long-running trend, and this critical trend will intersect with other important trends. Seeing these reactions and interactions from a space perspective will constitute development genius.

Employment Outsourcing and World Markets

Major corporations have become increasingly willing to outsource to smaller local firms across the United States and throughout the world. At the same time, sensing the potential advantages of globalization, many nations have reduced trade barriers. Linking the first two is ever-increasing technological capability, which enables everything from working from home to just-in-time global sourcing and assembly. Drive 30 miles (48 kilometers) east from the ports of Los Angeles and Long Beach and note the scale of the warehousing.

As outsourcing plays out across U.S. markets, space needs will change dramatically. This is another opportunity for development genius.

Green Building and Sustainable Development

Green building and sustainable development have become more than fringe movements and are set to gain even greater acceptance in the years ahead.

Since the late 1990s, the green building movement has grown into an accepted way of approaching the design, construction, and management of buildings of all types. The U.S. Green Building Council (USGBC), a leader in the field, has seen its membership swell as developers, designers, and manufacturers jump on the green bandwagon along with a rapid increase in the number of buildings certified as "green" under its LEED (Leadership in Energy and Environmental Design) rating system.

Proponents of green building argue that it costs little or no more to go green—and even when initial costs of new buildings are higher, ample opportunities are available to achieve savings down the road. With more experienced green architects and contractors and a wider range of truly sustainable products, the potential added costs of building to green standards have steadily gone down.

In the future as the market becomes more aware of the benefits of high-performance buildings with healthier indoor environments, lower energy costs, and benefits to the larger community, it may be a liability not to go green. And owners of existing nongreen buildings may find it necessary to undergo expensive environmental retrofitting to stay competitive.

The practice of sustainable development is also more widely accepted, and demanded, by communities. Concerns about sprawl, traffic congestion, pollution, and energy prices touch everyone's lives from Boston to Beijing, and pressures are strong to find solutions to these issues. With rapid urbanization affecting cities around the world, the challenge will be to act more resourcefully and sensitively toward land, an increasingly scarce commodity worldwide.

In the United States, the Smart Growth movement that began in the late 1990s started a dialogue on how to handle these development pressures in a way that is environmentally sensitive, economically viable, community oriented, and sustainable. A growing convergence between green building and smart growth is taking place today; this trend will potentially lead to a more holistic approach that integrates building design and site planning with larger-scale neighborhood design and infrastructure.

The 204 solar panels on 44-unit Colorado Court allow this affordable housing project—units are available to those who earn between 35 and 40 percent of the median income in the Santa Monica, California, area—to generate as much energy as it consumes. *Sam Newberg*

Place Making

Overlapping the move toward more sustainable development is the increasing focus on creating places that have a strong sense of identity and community or "place." Savvy developers and local governments recognize increasingly that places offering a sustainable high quality of life—in the form of efficient transportation, pedestrian orientation, recreational and cultural amenities, high-performance offices and homes, diverse neighborhoods—are most likely to come out ahead in the long run.

One byproduct of place making and sustainable development is a greater focus on mixed-use infill projects and new town center developments that offer choices for living, working, shopping, and recreation close to one another and public transit. Convenience and savings in energy costs will continue to add to the appeal of these types of development.

THE FINANCIAL MARKETS AREN'T LIKELY TO GET SIMPLER

The summer of 2007 brought a fairly major financial scare related to sub prime mortgage defaults and the resulting tightening of mortgage standards. Are we in the midst of a "subprime meltdown" or just barely in the start of an ugly recession? Despite new financial market discipline, increasing globalization in concert with financial innovation has reduced transparency in financial markets. Apparently, the rating agencies have not quite been able to keep up.

We now know that big European banks were speculating through off balance sheet special investment vehicles (SIVs) in the U.S. residential mortgage market. In several cases, they were leveraging this speculation with commercial paper. This was based on ratings from the rating agencies and the rating agencies were not adjusting fast enough to abuses in sub prime lending.

We also know that the U.S. housing market is currently overbuilt partially because of the number of buyers who couldn't afford the houses they bought. Possibly they were induced with misleading marketing about variable rate mortgages. In any case, there is a real world physical implication of the financial market problem—we have too many houses in several markets.

The retirement/resort housing market is also oversupplied as buyers bought in anticipation of future needs. Both housing markets are further overbuilt because of several years of heavy investment by "flippers," the day traders of the early 21st century.

We also now know that there is the real possibility of "contagion" across the financial markets as perceived risk to one investor/lender has caused other lenders to withhold credit. The lack of transparency in hedge funds and private equity funds compounds this problem.

At the same time, fundamentals for commercial real estate, the basic supply/demand balance, looks favorable. Still, not long after the residential lending market slowed, the commercial lending markets followed suit. Why? Because the buyers of the lower tranche (higher risk) CMBS issues were the same people buying those tranches of the residential mortgage backed securities. When those investors (many were leveraged hedge funds) got into trouble on the residential side, the investment banks became unable to unload their inventory of commercial loans into the new CMBS because there were no buyers for the high risk tranches. Consequently, they stopped lending. This led their competitors, the life insurance companies, to raise rates.

It is indeed an exciting financial world and real estate is definitely a big part of that world. Just as it is important to anticipate market trends, an eye to the ever-changing financial markets is also a good idea.

WHAT OUGHT TO BE

If you believe that everything you hear about the future is important and just about to happen, then you may qualify as the world's most gullible person. Even the authors of this text do not agree with all the suggestions made in this one chapter. We do agree, however, that one of our most important jobs is to think about dealing with the brave new world we will all inhabit. What follows is a demonstration of how to combine rigorous thought about the future with personal inspiration to produce rules for living. Clearly, you must adopt them (or not) for yourself based on updated facts, reinterpreted trends, anticipated reactions to those trends, and your own personal ethics.

▶ **Rule 1.** Do business only with people who are pleasant. In fact, as you get older, add to that only people who are fun. After all, people will be the critical resource, and you don't want any unnecessary negatives.

▶ **Rule 2.** Do not get locked into a narrow educational path unless you want to be a research scientist. If you want to be something else, breadth is important. Your best work may well occur when you are over 35, unless you're a pure math nerd, in which case you're over the hill at 28. Continued learning is facilitated by a broad educational background.

▶ **Rule 3.** You should measure personal success by a self-defined quality of life. Otherwise, you will be the victim of the "reaction syndrome" and end up in the wrong club. More important, you will end up a wimp, which leads to Rule 4.

▶ **Rule 4.** Your self-worth should be measured by what you can give away. It is incumbent on anyone who wants to have a meaningful life to contribute something to the neighborhood where he lives, if not to other regions of the world.

▶ **Rule 5.** Education must get better. Yours is a generation of high school graduates who have a poorer education (at the median) than their parents. Continuing education is a must. With a graduate degree, you are only an average player in the big leagues of this entrepreneurial world. Moreover, the half-life of information is short and getting shorter.

▶ **Rule 6.** Try not to segment things into little boxes. Breakthroughs come at the interfaces. Your continuing education shouldn't be all in the same field. Real estate is an interdisciplinary field, and the successful player needs an understanding of many different aspects of life—

sociological, psychological, architectural, and historical—as well as of business and politics.

▶ **Rule 7.** Be wary of economists. In an information society, you can give it away and still have it. This fact does not fit well in traditional economic models.

▶ **Rule 8.** Think globally, act locally. Watch Washington for destabilizing activities, but make it happen in your own world, which is probably your neighborhood or your city.

▶ **Rule 9.** Seek knowledge and eventually wisdom, not just information. There are already more newsletters in the real estate area than anyone could read on a regular basis. Beyond that, an

MUSEUM TOWERS

A Final Word from Dean Stratouly

Somebody asked me if I expect to make money from this project. Well, if I look at all the money spent over the duration of this project, back to 1987, we will make a little, maybe break even to slightly positive. If we look at the project from the time I restructured the debt in 1994 to the time when we dispose of the project, we'll do well.

With everything that was going on, it wasn't really until 1996 that I could start looking again at acquiring other land. In 1997, I actually began putting some deals together. In the early nineties, like a lot of developers, we were doing management work for banks just to eke out enough money to meet payroll. So many guys during that time continued to talk about putting together deals. And either they were being taken advantage of by the guys on Wall Street or they were overdosing on Prozac, because there was nothing going on.

The thing that scares me about development now is that there's a whole new generation of developers who don't know what "down" means. I was pretty naive when I started in 1980, but I had been around a little bit. I watched the nuclear power plant industry collapse around me. When I left, we were turning into spare parts salesmen; there hadn't been a new plant sold in years.

Now, when things are good, nobody thinks the real estate business can collapse again. Well, it can. It's a very fragile business. If you're in this for the money, you're not going to be successful at it. I love this business. I really do. I even loved it when I was failing. It's like racing a sail boat and colliding. It's an adrenaline rush. Keeps you on edge. It's hell for spouses though. One minute you have money and the next you don't.

No two days are the same. I love the construction, the machines, the mud. I even enjoy the negotiations with the banks. When I started out, I had this vision of building a national real estate company that would do design, development, marketing, property management, finance—the whole nine yards. The next thing I knew, I was sitting in an office with 50 employees and I was two or three people removed from the actual piece of real estate. I wasn't particularly happy. I'd have staff meetings once a week, project update meetings once a week, but I was running people, not building buildings. Now I'm back to being a real estate developer.

AN UPDATE BY ULI STAFF

What's happened to Museum Towers since then? In late spring 1999, the Congress Group hired Fallon Hines & O'Connor, a Trammell Crow company, to market the project for sale. The firm had worked with Stratouly and the Congress Group in the past, serving as an equity partner on the renovation of an old Raytheon plant in Wayland, Massachusetts, and was therefore familiar with his work.

After the first round of bids, the two firms expected to sell the towers for about $112 million, at a profit slightly larger than the anticipated 20 percent. The project was sold on August 19, 1999, for slightly less—a purchase price of $108 million, or $248,000 per unit. At the time of the sale, Museum Towers had a 15 percent vacancy rate, which was a little more than double the hoped-for 7 percent. As a result, the projected NOI was not achieved and Stratouly was not able to attain the expected cap rate of 7.25.

MUSEUM TOWERS *(continued)*

A Final Word from Dean Stratouly (continued)

Museum Towers is not a high-design project, but its location and amenity package have made it a very competitive property.

Although Stratouly expected to sell the project to a REIT, the final buyer was ING Clarion, the U.S. investment management arm of ING Real Estate, one of the world's largest real estate investment managers, with a portfolio of $102 billion as of February 2007. According to Mark Weld, ING Clarion's managing director for the New England region, Museum Towers was an excellent product in the right location. It was the first new mid- to high-rise development in the Boston area for at least 20 years. When the project went for sale, Boston's residential market was less sophisticated, with a less differentiated mix of products than many other cities its size. ING Clarion also saw a great potential for development in the neighborhood and believed that land values in the surrounding area would increase substantially.

ING Clarion's goal was a long-term investment in Museum Towers, but the historically low interest rates of the post–September 11, 2001, economy dramatically transformed both the national and local housing markets. Demand for condominiums surged, and it became a very hot market for conversions. Capitalizing on this demand, ING Clarion sold the property to Crescent Heights on September

20, 2004, for $145.7 million, or $335,000 per unit. Weld estimates that the cap rate was about 4 percent.

Crescent Heights saw great potential in the towers. Its strategy is to convert the units to condominiums aimed at first-time buyers, young professionals, and empty nesters. Part of this strategy involved rebranding the project with a new name: Regatta Riverview Residences.

Numerous options for customizing units allow for many different levels of buyers. Buyers can purchase units as is, they can opt for a standard package that includes new appliances, countertops, cabinets, and carpets, or they can select more high-end luxury features.

Crescent Heights also spent more than $10 million in capital improvements. It renovated all the common areas, added some new amenities, gutted and rebuilt the lobby, and created a private theater with an 80-inch (205-centimeter) television screen. Next to the theater, the party room has new carpeting, new wallpaper and paint, and a pool table.

Crescent Heights uses the party room and theater to sell to empty nesters, pointing out that although they are

continued on next page

MUSEUM TOWERS *(continued)*
A Final Word from Dean Stratouly (continued)

moving to smaller spaces, they will still be able to host parties and events. A new business center has computers, a fax machine, and a copier. The gym, which was originally leased to the Boston Athletic Club, has all-new gym equipment and is now an amenity for residents.

The conversion strategy for Museum Towers planned a three-year sellout, with the north tower converted first, then the south tower. All lease agreements were honored, and Crescent Heights maintained a steady flow of income through the conversion period, using leases that are very flexible for renters and landlord alike. In addition, according to state law, each tenant was given right of refusal with up to 90 days to purchase the unit.

Andrew Romanosky, the Midwest/Central region operations manager for Crescent Heights, states that Museum Towers was much less affected by the bursting of the condominium market bubble then many other projects in the Boston area. He points out that there will always be a demand among first-time homebuyers and young professionals and that Museum Towers is well poised to take advantage of this demand—even in a market downturn.

The combination of excellent views and a location close to downtown but without downtown's high land values has also played a role in keeping sales brisk. And

The desirable location of Museum Towers was a big factor in the ease with which it was sold.

Crescent Heights has had timing on its side. Because it started selling units close to the height of the bubble, it was able to sell them much faster and at much higher prices than originally projected.

As of February 2007, Congress Heights was very close to sellout and was expecting to finish on budget and months earlier than planned.

ELEVATION 314
A Final Word from Russell Katz

Patience is a large part of business, which is not something I'm naturally inclined to but which I've definitely learned. Time, just the ticking of the clock, can be a really powerful tool to work with. Everything takes its time. You can compress things and fight harder and force them. Or you can be lazy and nothing ever happens. But if you are attentive and lead a process through, it'll go through. I think that's like this retail thing, it's just a process.

For me, being fully invested and invested for the long term are really important, and it has worked out even better than I expected it would. It's been a great way to do things. I'm not sure what I'm doing next, but I'm certainly managing these buildings. All the hard work and investment have created a residual benefit that's supporting me and my family right now.

For Russell Katz, the benefits of retaining ownership of Elevation 314 have been both financial and experiential. Managing the property over time has allowed him to determine what to repeat and what to do differently in future projects. Jason Scully

incredible array of facts and information is at your disposal through the Internet. The challenge is to develop the conceptual framework that allows you to process this sea of information into knowledge, especially the knowledge needed to act and the wisdom to know when to run.

▶ **Rule 10.** Always fully segment your markets. Do not get trapped into measuring the MSA exclusively when you are marketing to a world of overlapping neighborhoods. Remember that we all live not in one neighborhood but rather in a series of neighborhoods. One is for our work environment, another for our social environment, and possibly many more for the different facets of our lives. When you are building space, you are satisfying the needs of people who themselves probably function in a series of overlapping neighborhoods. Consideration of the census tract is an easy first pass but not the whole story.

▶ **Rule 11.** Overall, expect continued growth in the United States. It is one of the few countries both developed enough to be comfortable and open enough economically to provide opportunity. Therefore, the best and brightest (and their money) will continue to come. Entrepreneurial immigrants still create a brain drain toward America that will make tomorrow's United States an exciting place.

▶ **Rule 12.** Remember that only change is constant in this life. This recognition will continue to force a search for spiritual certainty that will, in turn, have an impact on other aspects of our lives. Given that people, not capital, are the critical resource, the search for meaning will become increasingly important to development trends.

▶ **Rule 13.** Do not fool yourself into believing that MBA thinking (adjusting available data) is real thinking. Even the latest accounting rules drive through the rear view mirror, and appraisal practices still ignore most of the big issues that we have discussed in this chapter. If you are a little right on the future, it can make up for a lot of

smaller mistakes. No amount of getting it right in the present can make up for a major miss on future trends.

▶ **Rule 14.** In the future, you need partners—not suppliers, not customers, not acquisition targets, but partners. And partnerships should not be based solely on long legal agreements but rather on reciprocally fair deals oriented toward mutual interests and maintained in an atmosphere of good will (bad news for lawyers).

SUMMARY

This chapter only touches on what future developers need to consider as they think about upcoming development opportunities. We hope readers will be motivated to read as widely as possible and to talk to as many different kinds of people as possible. Keeping attuned to cycles and always looking for a new way to fill customers' needs can give developers an edge that spells the difference between a successful and a marginal development.

Although developers cannot continuously focus on broad societal trends given the demands of their daily operations, over the long run such trends and changes account for the biggest differences between successful and less successful developments. As providers of space over time with associated services, developers should continuously respond to the needs and wants of consumers. Sensitivity to underlying shifts in preferred locations, commuting habits, customs and cultural orientation, and household characteristics is critical to effective decision making. The developer's first job is to anticipate what society will want from the built environment—one of the most exciting, challenging, and rewarding tasks in our society.

REVIEW QUESTIONS

23.1 How can looking at the past help us in thinking about the future? Was the overbuilding of the 1980s an anomaly?

23.2 How has the trend toward "development's paying its own way" affected developers?

23.3 Do you agree with the rules for living in this chapter? How realistic are they?

23.4 What is the advantage to the developer of selling Museum Towers so soon after the development was complete? What is the advantage to holding on to the project? What goes into making the decision to hold or not hold?

23.5 Do you believe it is dangerous for new developers who haven't ever experienced the down cycle in real estate?

23.6 The authors offer one piece of advice to readers—read as widely as possible and talk to as many different kinds of people as possible. Why would it be beneficial for a developer to follow that advice? Are there any possible pitfalls?

Europa Center Case Study

Featured in the three earlier editions of this book is the case study of Europa Center. This office project was developed by Fraser Morrow Daniels, a company founded to develop real estate in the Carolinas with a geographic focus and specializing in office, residential, and hotel space.

The Research Triangle of North Carolina includes the cities of Raleigh (the state capital), Durham, Chapel Hill (the location of Europa Center), and Cary. Research Triangle Park, the University of North Carolina at Chapel Hill, North Carolina State University (in Raleigh), and Duke University (in Durham) are all located in this metropolitan area.

THE DEVELOPMENT COMPANY

Name

Fraser Morrow Daniels & Company (four partners)

Founded

1985 in affiliation with other ventures by Charles E. Fraser

Purpose

To develop real estate in the Carolinas, initially in the Research Triangle (Raleigh, Durham, Chapel Hill) of North Carolina

Projects Completed from 1985 to 1994

Park Forty Plaza—Class A office building, 125,000 square feet (11,620 square meters), Research Triangle Park, approximate cost $12 million. Savings and loan association attempted to sell to private investor, but the Resolution Trust Corporation stepped in and negated the sale. Ultimately sold to another investor. *Spring Hill*—Residential community on 65 acres (26 hectares) in Research Triangle Park, 25 single-family houses and 100 condominiums completed out of 600 housing units projected. Ultimately taken over by lender after falling victim to oversupplied apartment market.

Rosemary Square—In-town hotel in Chapel Hill projected for 188 suites/rooms, 22,000 square feet (2,045 square meters) of commercial space, and 516 parking spaces. Estimated cost: $30 million. Designed but marketing delayed by litigation until September 1987 in North Carolina Supreme Court. Project absorbed more than $2 million, and in 1989 company decided not to build project. Site subsequently developed as public parking facility, with public open space on the top level.

Europa Center—Class A office building, 95,000 square feet (8,830 square meters) in Phase I, 100,000 square feet (9,295 square meters) in Phase II, Chapel Hill. The design of Europa Center was intended to bring big-city, Class A office space to a small but sophisticated town that offered nothing precisely comparable. Not by coincidence was the project located next door to the town's first luxury hotel.

A SUMMARY OF EUROPA CENTER

Location

Chapel Hill, North Carolina (population 35,000 in 1987, 38,700 in 1994, 49,360 in 2004), home of the University of North Car-

Opened in 1987, Europa Center is a 195,000-square-foot (18,000-square-meter) Class A office complex in Chapel Hill, North Carolina.

olina; 12 miles (19 kilometers) from Durham (population 100,000 in 1987, 136,611 in 1994, 201,700 in 2004), home of Duke University; ten miles (16 kilometers) from Research Triangle Park; 28 miles (45 kilometers) from Raleigh, the state capital and home of North Carolina State University; 18 miles (29 kilometers) from Raleigh-Durham Airport.

Land

7.3 acres (3 hectares), zoned for office and industrial use, fronting U.S. 15-501 (four lanes, the main route to Durham, and, two miles (3.2 kilometers) farther east, a heavily developed commercial strip), Europa Drive (site of Hotel Europa), and Legion Road.

Land Cost

$2.1 million, $1 million allocated to Phase I, remainder to Phase II.

Buildings

Phase I—Five-story, 95,000-square-foot (8,830-square-meter) Class A office, poured-in-place reinforced concrete structure with glass curtain wall. Atrium lobby, marble, granite, and fabric panel finishes. Adjoining three-level parking deck.

Phase II—Adjoining five-story, 100,000-square-foot (9,295-square-meter) Class A office, poured-in-place reinforced concrete structure with glass curtain wall. Extended parking deck to increase spaces from 278 to 650.

Project Cost

Phase I—As of January 1987, projected at $9.3 million. Revised June 1987 to $10.5 million (construction close to budget, about $250,000 in construction changes, the remainder to fund slow leasing).

Phase II—Total construction cost about $11.3 million, including doubling of parking and three-story atrium connecting two phases. Completed 1991.

Initial Chronology

Land purchased—November 1985
Site preparation began—April 1986
Phase I building construction began—Summer 1986
Building certificate of occupancy issued—November 1987

Joint Venture Shares—Phase I

50 percent—Centennial Group buys land for $2.1 million.

35 percent—Fraser Morrow Daniels contributes up to $100,000 worth of research, planning, negotiating, and staffing, which is only partially reimbursed by joint venture.

15 percent—Centennial Group (a joint venture partner during construction) guarantees $1 million if needed to fund protracted leasing. This amount becomes additional equity in 1987 when Centennial is acquired by the construction lender and the entire financing is renegotiated to handle the slow leasing period.

THE STORY

The Europa Center project was developed in a relatively small city, at the time not known as a hot spot for development, and its developers entered the market rather naively. The following segment describes Whit Morrow's decision in his own words to pursue a career in real estate development and his surprise at the complexity of the process.

I want you to hear about real estate development from someone who is up to his eyeballs in alligators right now in the marketplace. You should know how we started, how we got to where we are now, and how we're going to get out of it and make a profit at some point.

I grew up in Albemarle, North Carolina, a small town with about 10,000 people at that time. My grandfather owned one-third of the office buildings in town, so I was vaguely aware of real estate at a young age. When I was older, I had a job making change in the old hardware store building. They had pneumatic tubes that went from the cash registers back to the central office where they kept all the money, and that was where I sat making change. That was the extent of my exposure to business before college, when I was trying to decide what I was going to do. When I headed off to college (Davidson College, 40 miles (65 kilometers) away, near Charlotte), I didn't even know what an architect was.

At Davidson College, the subject that fascinated me most was the readings we had on utopias—ideal communities. Davidson College had about 1,000 students and sat in the middle of the countryside, the most pristine Walden II *setting you've ever seen. One of the books I read was* Walden II, *of course, about how B.F. Skinner made the ideal community, designing everything the way it ought to be, with all the people fitting into his community. So I decided during my college days that I wanted to go out there like Alexander the Great and build cities. Or be an industrialist and build Hershey, Pennsylvania. I thought that was the greatest thing you could possibly do.*

Coming out of college with my BA degree, I was a little naive, and my advisers said I should go to business school. For me, going to Harvard Business School was like being drafted into the Marines. The first day or two of class when I talked about why I was there and what I wanted to do, they burst my bubble. So you want to go out and build cities, huh? Do you know what a REIT is? Do you know what a second mortgage is? I wasn't exposed to any of those things, even in college. I was totally shocked by all the intricate details that go into building a house or an office building or a street. But I survived Harvard Business School, and after learning the details, I thought I knew a lot more and got a job with the Sea Pines Company, the development company that was responsible for Hilton Head Island.

STAGE ONE: INCEPTION OF AN IDEA

As a new entrant in the Research Triangle market, Fraser Morrow Daniels relied heavily on formal inquiry, as Whit Morrow describes. The company's market research and definition of a target market reflect the steps outlined in this text, but the steps are not clearly defined. As Fraser Morrow Daniels learned more about emerging trends in the market, the firm synthesized the information and moved back and forth between market research and planning tactics to revise the initial concept.

Analyzing Market Opportunities

Why did we form a new company to undertake new ventures in a new area, and what made us choose the Research Triangle area? What did we consider in picking our products, and how did we structure our company in that environment?

The area as a whole was attractive to us; it was an area where we would personally want to live and work. We looked at several factors: growth and diversity in employment, demographics, infrastructure, government regulations, prices, product supply, availability of financing, politics (different from the regulatory environment, it is the attitude in the area, what people are thinking, what will happen when the bulldozer starts), labor supply, and quality of the natural environment.

With all those factors in mind, we started looking at the whole Research Triangle area. It was a new business environment, unlike Atlanta, for example, which is a big city with a beltway and all the traditional factors that go along with working in a fairly steady, predictable business environment. In the Research Triangle, four small cities—Raleigh, Durham, Chapel Hill, and Cary—make up the metropolitan area.

We tried to develop an overall business strategy for the 1980s and the 1990s. We looked not just at population growth but also at changing segments. Census data showed that the area was growing at a higher rate than the national average. We took what was happening in the national economy and national population statistics and compared it with local data.

Researching and Selecting Target Markets

Then we looked at Raleigh/Durham to see how the trend was playing out there. Who was moving there? Which market segments, defined by age group, were being built for shopping opportunities, for housing? What effect did those trends have on the homebuilding market and other segments?

We found that local job growth and diversification were probably the best mix of any area we looked at in the country. The factors driving the local economy were universities, state government, and growth in Research Triangle Park, where high-tech businesses were growing rather than being overbuilt or dying out. What those factors told us was that that marketplace was the place to be if we wanted to be in the development business for the next 15 to 20 years.

Developing a Marketing Strategy

Next question: What do we do and where do we do it? The first factor we started looking at was who else was doing what in the marketplace. Who were the major players? Who had been around for a long time building office buildings and shopping centers? Where were they located? We wanted to put things on a map and decide where the opportunities were. We wanted to combine that information with our analysis of infrastructure.

I went to the local map store and asked for a map of the Research Triangle area and was shocked to find that none were available anywhere. I went to the Council of Governments for the six-county area. All it had were county road maps pieced together—without even the cities on it—a map of the water supply, and a map that had schools on it but basically nothing else. No one had put together all the nitty-gritty details that are necessary for the area as a whole, making it such a peculiar opportunity for real estate development.

The Research Triangle area was also different because it had 750,000 people spread over three or four cities, which together have all the activity equivalent to one major city that attracts businesses. Individually, however, the cities are small towns. The competitors we found in this marketplace were people like the Yorks, who had started the Cameron Village shopping center 40 years earlier in Raleigh. The Davidson and Jones construction company had been building buildings for the universities and the state government. And some big companies, like IBM, had built their own campuses or leased space in other buildings.

This was a key finding. No active, competitive, national speculative office building developer was operating in the area. Nobody had gone out on a limb and built a building and hoped to fill it because of growth in the office population. There had been only companies doing it for themselves and local builders building for existing committed demand. As of 1983, the supply was 100,000 square feet (9,295 square meters) and absorption was 100,000 square feet (9,295 square meters)—totally unlike any other place in the country with a population of 750,000. Our next stop was the local chambers of commerce to talk to the people who were promoting business activity and pushing development. Raleigh's chamber had all the statistics on Raleigh and knew all about Raleigh's beltway, how long it would take to get the outer beltway built, and some other statistics as well. Durham's chamber had all its statistics, although it still had somewhat of an inferiority complex because Durham had been

just a tobacco town and isn't beautiful. In Chapel Hill, the chamber of commerce represented about 2 percent of the community's population. The university represented one part, retirees another part, and residents who commuted to jobs in other parts of the Triangle the rest of the community. So Chapel Hill's chamber was basically of no help. And people there didn't even want to talk about development.

So we were, in a sense, real pioneers (along with many other people, as it turned out) in a new business environment ripe for plucking. The people there had all their assumptions about the way it was: "Nobody's going to live in Durham. Nobody's going to move to Durham." They told us about the last developer that tried to build houses on the south side of Durham in 1972, on Highway 54 near Research Triangle Park. That developer went bankrupt. Total failure.

Well, some other newcomers realized that it was not possible to buy a nice house next to a swimming pool and tennis court, despite the high rate of growth. They took a chance and bought 750 acres (304 hectares) at dirt-cheap prices south of Durham in the same location that had failed ten years earlier near Research Triangle Park. Boom! Woodcroft was born, selling 2,000 housing units over a two-year period. That's how rapidly this business environment was changing.

It's hard to imagine, but at that time the individual chambers of commerce had no concept of a unified MSA. They were individual communities, fighting among themselves for recognition. So we took the U.S. Geological Survey maps and pieced them together to make a big map. It was the only detailed topographic map available of the whole area, and it was ten feet (3 meters) long. Standing back from it, anyone could see that a very strong link would develop between the east and west sides of the community (Raleigh to Chapel Hill) with the completion of I-40 as well as a great deal of opportunity in the middle that did not exist before because of cars backed up on two-lane Highway 54. Simple things became apparent: Research Triangle Park had no restaurants, it shuts down at 5:00 at night, there's only one hotel, and nightlife is as boring as it can be.

These ideas are very simple. The infrastructure changed: the airport built a real runway and the number of flights quadrupled. American Airlines put a hub there. Research Triangle Park accelerated from a very steady 4 to 5 percent increase over the 20 years from 1960 to 1980 to 20 percent increases every year for the next five or six years. And in the middle of this abundant land, the federal government and the state were spending oodles of money on the highway systems, and the airport was reaching huge capacity.

At the Raleigh chamber of commerce, the chief concern was developing Raleigh's outer fringe—trying to force development to the east side of Raleigh, exactly the opposite direction from Research Triangle Park. In Durham, most of the power brokers live north of town, also opposite from the Park, and the north side of Durham was being developed. Even some bright, forward-thinking people said that the solution was a replication of Research Triangle Park in that area and proposed Treyburn, a mixed-use project on 5,500 acres (2,227 hectares) northeast of Durham. But the natives still thought of Durham and Raleigh and Chapel Hill as separate cities—even though a multimillion dollar interstate highway runs right through the area between Durham and Chapel Hill within eight minutes of the heart of the Park.

Thus, we had an obvious strategy: buy 100 to 200 acres (40 to 80 hectares) to build office buildings. With the growth we saw and the communities' coming together, we foresaw the need for a large amount of office space. The old absorption rate of 100,000 square feet (9,295 square meters) per year would change. In fact, we noticed that in 1983, 500,000 square feet (46,470 square meters) of office space had been used (with some businesses building their own space on top of that). Population growth, demographics, and infrastructure combined to tell us that someone could take advantage of a big opportunity. We did just that, buying 100 acres (40 hectares) of land to develop office space. As it turned out, we were not alone in our astute observations.

As the case study of Europa Center continues, Whit Morrow talks about competition and risk and describes Fraser Morrow Daniels's search for a site and the impact of detailed market research on the company's initial strategy.

People who were buying land in the Research Triangle area started doing so based more on politics than on the economics of the area. And they started speculating on land prices a little bit, so that the situation got to be very competitive. The obvious strategy was to buy 100 to 200 acres (40 to 80 hectares) in and around Research Triangle Park and to build ten or 12 buildings over 15 years. We were just hell-bent-for-leather to develop there. We had bids in on four or five pieces of land, but the politics of the area made us uncomfortable, so we got setbacks and height amendments.

Within a year, while we were trying to buy land, at least 15 or 20 other people—with more money, more staff, more power, and more connections than we had—dived right into the marketplace. Every time we identified 100 acres (40 hectares) to buy, three other people were bidding on it, trying to buy it.

So we stopped, looked at our company, and looked at our capacity. We didn't have 500 banks trying to give us money or 2,000 employees. We were a tiny company—five or six people. So what could we do in that highly competitive business environment?

We totally shifted our strategy from becoming a big organization and doing 15 office buildings and a big office park and making our first profits on the fifth building to being a little organization. We acknowledged who we were and what the real competitive market was. We decided instead to buy ten acres (4 hectares) and build one or two buildings. We based our profit

projections on a modest goal and not on what we were going to do over a ten-year period.

We focused on the I-40 extension corridor from Research Triangle Park to the U.S. 15-501/I-40 intersection just east of Chapel Hill and looked at the major intersections closest to the population centers. There were really just two centers: Durham and Chapel Hill. And we weren't alone. We identified 23 different projects that came on line or were about to come on line during the three-year period that it takes to get something started.

In 1984 when we moved our company to the area, we wanted to be associated with the Research Triangle area. Therefore, we did not want our office in Raleigh, Durham, or Chapel Hill. We wanted to be in Research Triangle Park or on the edge of the park. We tried to lease office space, but no suitable space was available. We got into about 4,000 square feet (370 square meters) of crummy space at $14.50 a square foot ($155 per square meter). In 1989, if I had wanted to rent office space around the park, at least 500,000 square feet (46,470 square meters) was available at a net effective rent of about $12 per square foot ($130 per square meter) for Class A space.

In 1986, a lot of money was available to build office buildings in Research Triangle Park. Many banks would put up exactly what you needed, build the building, and finance all the tenant improvements on the day the building opened. And there was no shortage of potential tenants. Looking ahead, we saw that the competitive environment would be different in three years. We asked five or six banks for an extra million dollars or more to carry the finished building through the leasing period. We held out for the extra financing for a long lease-up period that lasted two years.

My partner, Charles Fraser, was unwilling to sign a guarantee that he was the sole source of that extra million dollars, and we knew the banks would not lend it to us. So Charles decided to give up half his projected profit in exchange for a financial partner who would share the risk with us. It is important for a company entering this kind of environment to ask what its staying power is, what its risk profile is, and how much of a chance it is willing to take. How much do you really believe your projections? We decided to involve a financial partner in this office venture to put up money to buy the land and to guarantee an extra million dollars if we needed it.

Any time you have a great idea that takes several years to implement, you won't be the only one there, even if you're first. Furthermore, other companies have different risk profiles. Our risk profile was such that we could not stand the heat if it came to a competitive environment with 17 projects all targeted to the same market. It was a matter of survival for us.

In a three-year cycle, your potential tenants have to recognize you. The site with only one building must be attractive. You can't sell somebody a 100-acre (40-hectare) parcel with the promise of a lake and trails; the site has to be right today. So the difference between us and some of the other players was *that when we switched from 100-acre purchases at $50,000 an acre to ten-acre (4-hectare) tracts at five times that amount per acre, the economics changed a little bit, too. You do not have to carry all that land, but you do have to pay more for the one piece that's currently available. So our strategy changed from finding a good site that we could market over ten years to one of finding a site that people stumble over every hour today—and we were willing to pay a lot for that.*

Whit Morrow explained how others had overlooked the Research Triangle, which was viewed as separate small towns rather than a single region. Growth had been sluggish in the past, but more recent indicators suggested that the area was poised for development. As Morrow's comments attest, the opportunity quickly had become too obvious, and eventually a number of other developers discovered it as well.

STAGE TWO: REFINEMENT OF THE IDEA

The Fraser Morrow Daniels development company, because it was interested in entering a new geographic area and developing products outside its previous expertise, undertook an extraordinary amount of market research when it moved into North Carolina's Research Triangle area. The firm set out to answer the basic questions raised in Chapter 10: Where do we work and what do we develop? For Fraser Morrow Daniels, stage one of the development process concluded with the decision to work in the Research Triangle and to develop several property types, including an office park.

It is important to recall that Fraser Morrow Daniels perceived an excellent opportunity to build speculative office space in the Research Triangle in the early 1980s when almost all space in the area was built to suit by local developers. This same opportunity, however, also attracted to the market a flock of much larger out-of-town developers. Thus, as the competitive situation changed rapidly in the mid-1980s, Fraser Morrow Daniels had to reassess its ability to compete with other newcomers. After evaluating the competition, Fraser Morrow Daniels realized that its own capacities were not the same as those of the other, larger players. Therefore, the firm abandoned its plans to build an office park and instead looked for a niche to fill with one or two office buildings on a smaller site.

Similarly, Fraser Morrow Daniels recognized the various climates for development in the different political jurisdictions in the Research Triangle market. The city where the firm ultimately chose a site posed the greatest political and legal difficulties of the four major Triangle cities for developers wanting to work quickly. Nonetheless, Fraser Morrow Daniels's accurate perception of the city's regulatory climate guided the company's site selection: any site would need to have the appropriate zoning already in place to avoid substantial delays.

For example, when Fraser Morrow Daniels began looking at possible office sites in Chapel Hill, it identified zoning as one binding constraint. Any site for consideration needed to have the appropriate zoning already in place; a rezoning in Chapel Hill would have been too difficult, costly, and time-consuming. Even though the site for Europa Center met the zoning requirement, Fraser Morrow Daniels found the land only after stepping back, rescanning the environment, and revising its criteria for site selection. Other binding constraints face developers: traffic (too much or too little), access, infrastructure, and adequate space for parking, for example.

In the continuation of the case study, Fraser Morrow Daniels narrows its search for a site and focuses on the Europa Center site because it eliminated uncertainties about zoning and hastened the development process. In making its decision, the company weighed the competitive edge of controlling the right site against the risk of the large financial commitment required by the outright purchase of an expensive parcel.

Back to the Drawing Board

We wanted to build west of Research Triangle Park and somewhere strategically close to the I-40 extension. We studied every single intersection in the area of I-40 and all the land around it. We collected tax maps and called landowners to ask if they wanted to sell their land. We talked to all the brokers and went after pieces of land that weren't for sale, because everything that was for sale was priced too high or was poorly located.

As part of that process, we discovered the Europa Center site, which was owned by the developers of the Hotel Europa. At first when the owners offered us the land for $250,000 an acre ($617,500 per hectare), we said it was three times more than we wanted to pay and what anybody else was paying. But the owners assured us it was a site with great potential and that they wanted to sell it to someone who would develop an attractive building. They had already turned down Kmart, which was willing to pay the price, but the city did not want a discount store on the site. In fact, the site had been for sale several times for different purposes. The owners tried to convince us that with I-40 going through, the site was worth $250,000 an acre ($617,500 per hectare), but we still said no.

Instead, we went back to our site selection criteria and looked at the overall market and what was already built on Durham–Chapel Hill Boulevard toward Chapel Hill. In addition, we looked at other factors, such as the demographics and the office/business neighborhood. No other office buildings existed there except for Eastowne (11 two-story office buildings), but Blue Cross/Blue Shield was just up the street from the Hotel Europa. We conceded that the project might fit as an office/business complex. We talked to some potential tenants who were interested in moving into an attractive building near their present location (Eastowne Park). Some potential tenants said they would like a place that was between Durham and Chapel Hill so they could combine offices. That kind of feedback pointed us toward the intersection of I-40 and Durham–Chapel Hill Boulevard (U.S. 15-501).

We were committed to developing an office building somewhere between Durham and Chapel Hill close to that intersection, and things kept coming back to the Europa site. We justified the high price by saying it would mean only $0.80 a square foot ($8.60 a square meter) more in rent.

But what about the politics in Chapel Hill? We had heard dozens of horror stories.

We decided we would go ahead with the project only if we didn't have to ask for any approvals. The site was already zoned for office buildings, and the planning board had already approved some proposed office buildings for construction. We thought the Europa site would be easy because the planning board had already blessed it, the city council had already blessed it, and we didn't have to do anything to get a site plan approved. We decided to pursue the site.

Then we started looking at the competition and the marketing significance of that competition. North Raleigh had a lot of activity and a lot of land. Downtown Raleigh had a lot of space. Downtown Durham was trying to give away land for office buildings. But in Chapel Hill, a fight broke out at every turn with anybody who wanted to develop commercial or office buildings. Every other piece of land that had been zoned for offices was already built on. Eastowne, across from Blue Cross/Blue Shield on Durham–Chapel Hill Boulevard, had two small tracts of land left, about an acre and a half (0.6 hectare) each, for office buildings. So we figured we would be the only game in town for the foreseeable future. The possibility that competitors could enter the market and attract the same tenants was relatively small.

At that time, a McDonald's restaurant was proposed in front of the site on U.S. 15-501 as an upscale building with an inconspicuous sign. And the Hotel Europa was one of the more attractive buildings in town. The project we had in mind would also be an attractive building to fit our image of the company. The Europa site became, in all our analyses, the best site available: it satisfied all our criteria for our company profile, the market profile, and the competitive environment.

The only real unknown was the political environment. We could not purchase the land contingent on certain conditions. The seller would not allow it. We had to buy the land with the existing zoning.

The planning board and city council said informally that our idea looked good and advised us to proceed with project design; they would then decide. Accordingly, we purchased the land for $5 per square foot ($53.80 per square meter) in late 1985. Several people around town chuckled. The Hotel Europa was in deep financial trouble at that time, badly needed the money, and, we discovered later, probably would have sold the land to us for $3.50 a square foot ($37.65 per square meter). But we had justified the price in our minds and paid the asking price.

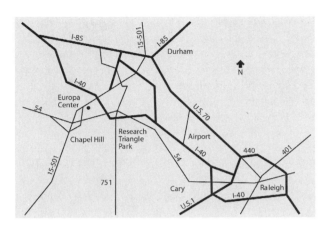

Europa Center is located on the U.S. 15-501 corridor, 1.5 miles (2.4 kilometers) west of I-40.

In the case of Europa Center, the planning board and the town staff identified traffic and traffic control as major concerns. Fraser Morrow Daniels strove to allay the city's fears and solve the traffic problem by volunteering to realign the affected intersection.

Anticipating Exactions

During our negotiations with the town of Chapel Hill, many questions arose about traffic and traffic control, a major concern of the planning board and the town staff. We knew some improvements were needed in the intersection of U.S. 15-501 and Europa Drive, primarily because of all the recent residential development nearby on Erwin Road and increased traffic between Durham and Chapel Hill. For our project to work well, we needed some traffic control signals and some adjustments in turning lanes, and we volunteered to perform the entire amount of work for $50,000. That's not a normal anticipated cost of development.

Most cities in the past have done that work themselves because they wanted economic growth. In Chapel Hill, the situation was different. We volunteered to do the work, knowing that it would otherwise not get done. We needed to allay the town's fears, and we needed to solve an anticipated traffic problem.

The North Carolina Department of Transportation completed the work, and we paid for it. It realigned the whole intersection, not just a turning lane into our project. And we managed to find a way to do it that didn't cost as much as some of the other alternatives.

For Fraser Morrow Daniels, researching the converging segments of the Research Triangle Park market required two years of analysis to break out segments of the market and to fully define supply and demand. Location emerged as a key feature in developing Europa Center in the Research Triangle office market.

Segmenting the Market

In selecting a site, we had to seek first-class, gold-plated sites that would win out at even rental rates in a competitive market.

Developers who succeed are those whose sites are good right now, today. Tenants don't want to move to the middle of the wilderness where customers don't come. Renting office space in an office environment is only 2 to 5 percent of your business budget. People will pay $0.75 per square foot ($8.05 per square meter) more to get an office space if it's the right space for their business. Being a pioneer is not necessarily good.

In deciding which land to buy, we had a choice between land selling at $1 a square foot ($45,000 to $50,000 an acre or $10.80 per square meter—$111,150 to $123,500 per hectare) and $5 a square foot ($250,000 an acre [$53.80 per square meter—$617,500 per hectare]), the Europa site next to the Hotel Europa. The less successful and less visible land was cheaper, but is the Europa land five times more valuable than the other land? Who knows? What is the bottom line?

The land component per square foot of building area turned out (at $5 per square foot ($53.80 per square meter)) to be $0.80 per square foot ($8.60 per square meter) in the building rental rate—$16.80 instead of $16 per square foot ($180 instead of $172 per square meter) to put somebody on a site next to the Hotel Europa rather than three blocks away behind a sewer plant. For $0.80 a square foot ($8.60 per square meter) in the rental rate, can you add that much more value from the tenant's point of view? If you're building only one building, absolutely.

To help us make our decision, we looked at the office buildings in the area to assess how much space was available, what quality it was, how much space was being built, what kind of tenants leased space there, who was likely to move, who was not. We listed every building in every segment of the market on a computer printout. Our list had 500 buildings. A Chapel Hill under-

Retaining the pond required many financial compromises, but leaving it in place enhanced the appeal of Europa Center and helped soothe public concerns about the project. Jim Sink, Artech, Inc.

graduate worked for me for four hours a day after school for two years calling owners, agents, and tenants and asking how many square feet of office space they had. It's this kind of nitty-gritty detective work you have to do for the project coming up three months from now.

Weighing the Pros and Cons

The site of Europa Center appeared to fit the bill: location on the major transportation artery connecting the two cities and adjacent to the highest-quality hotel at that time in Chapel Hill or Durham (see map on previous page). The land was well configured and nearly rectangular, with a pond that represented an amenity, not a problem. Access was not perfect but was possible.

The fact that the site was nearly ready for development fit with our evaluation of the overall Research Triangle Park market; although long-term prospects were good, substantial new construction was coming on line soon, and it was thus important to bring the project to fruition as soon as possible. We had already invested heavily in both research and creating an image and wanted to recapture some of those costs through a series of developments, one of which was Europa Center.

We had done an excellent job of overall background research on the Research Triangle market and had worked hard at producing a positive image in the community, but we were still taking a chance with the Europa site. Although ideally situated in the middle of growth, close to major transportation arteries, physically attractive without major constraints on construction, and appropriately configured, the location had not traditionally projected an image of quality in the community. Though located next to the most expensive hotel in the area, the hotel was only four years old and had already been through one foreclosure caused by lower-than-expected average rates and surprisingly low summer occupancy. Near the site on the east side was a subsidized housing project and, farther to the northeast, low-income retirement housing. With McDonald's and new car dealers on the south and west, the site offered excellent potential but would require substantial marketing and operating expertise to ensure a successful project. We chose particularly high-quality architecture and construction to try to influence the market's perception of the project.

Whit Morrow, unlike many competitors, viewed the cities that make up the Research Triangle as a converging market area and assumed that office growth would spread beyond Research Triangle Park (the center of the triangle formed originally by three cities) along the transportation corridors, especially I-40. Because he had compiled a list of planned office buildings for the entire Research Triangle market rather than for any one of the individual cities (Raleigh, Durham, Chapel Hill, and Cary), whose spatial distinctions were weakening, Morrow also projected the coming oversupply of office space earlier than most competitors.

STAGE THREE: THE FEASIBILITY STUDY

A Key Hiring Decision

The next step after justifying the cost of the land was to decide which architects and construction companies to use—major decisions for our company. People in the business of building offices usually have long working relationships with architects and ask for five or six bids. Our company had no history of building major office buildings, but all our lenders told us that putting up office buildings was quite simple compared with the complicated resort development we had done earlier and that it ought to be relatively easy for us.

What I wanted to do, even if it cost more money, was to hire the best, most experienced architect that I knew we could trust and the best construction company with a record of getting the job done—even if its prices weren't the best going. Our choice was the architectural firm Cooper Carry & Associates from Atlanta, which has built many office buildings.

During the development of preliminary drawings for Europa Center, the building's design underwent many changes to satisfy the requirements of the developers and Chapel Hill's city council.

Working with the Architect

Designing the project was another delicate process, because we did not have a lot of money. The architects designed the whole building for $250,000 for a chance to participate in the project, even though they would not be paid until after we got a loan funded. They had to prepare fairly complete working drawings of the whole building so that we could put it out for bids to contractors and get a firm, guaranteed maximum price. The architects did all that work before we got our construction loan.

We gave the architects general parameters: design something distinctive and relatively conservative that reflects the architecture and style of the Hotel Europa. It should be heavy on landscaping, should not remove any of the existing trees (we knew in Chapel Hill that saving the seven or eight remaining trees on the site was critical), and should not fill in the small pond (a landmark that people valued). We wanted to concentrate the building on the back of the site.

We asked the architects, based on the 50 buildings they had designed before, what the best, most compatible design for this site would be. The architects came back with about five plans and told us the only way we could get a cost-effective amount of square footage for the $5 per square foot ($53.80 per square meter) we had paid for land would be to fill in the pond, cover

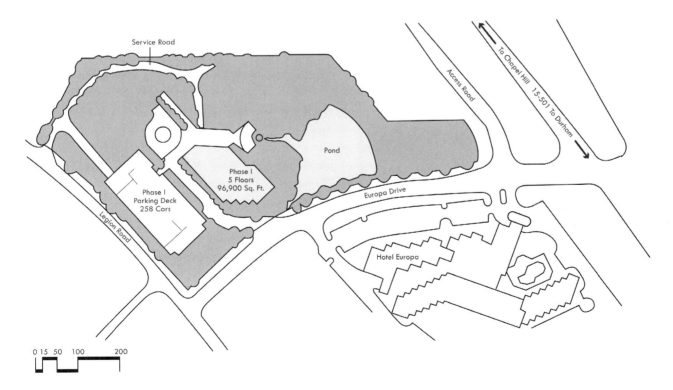

Phase I of Europa Center contains 96,900 square feet (9,005 square meters) of space (approximately 92,700 square feet (8,600 square meters) of rentable space) and 258 parking spaces in a parking deck with covered access. Landscape amenities include an abundance of trees and a pond.

it over with asphalt, and build a building there. They recommended a seven-story building.

We went back to the planning board and the town council informally and asked whether the architects' proposed plan could work. They said it wouldn't and told us to have the architects redesign the building to take into consideration the trees, the pond, and the site's general aesthetics.

Again we had to justify cost. Either we had to build a smaller building, build surface parking, and keep the pond, or we had to build the amount of square footage that it took to justify $5 per square foot ($53.80 per square meter) for the land and build structured parking. Economically, structured parking is borderline unless you've paid about $6 or $7 per square foot ($64.50 or $75.30 per square meter) for land. Based on just one building analysis, we would have been better off to build one building on this site, make less money, and buy another piece of land somewhere else for a second building; the cost of the land for the second building would be cheaper than the incremental cost of building the parking deck. But we could not identify another site that was as good as this one for a second building. The logical solution would be to put the parking somewhere else, not underground. We decided, however, that we would be better off paying the extra price, building a five-story building, adding another $0.70 a square foot ($7.50 a square meter) to the rental rate, building structured parking, and getting 200,000 square feet (18,600 square meters) of building on the site.

So we gave the architects some very tight boundaries to work within, all based on economics. They came up with a building that fit the shape of the site, reflected the architecture of the Hotel Europa, and preserved the pond and landscaping nearest the major frontage road. It took about an extra three months in the process.

The relationship with the city was complex, simply because the town council and planning board staunchly supported Chapel Hill's no-growth climate. The planning board, concerned about the building's height, wanted to see what the site would look like after construction and asked us to put up balloons that would delineate the building's top floor. The day the board was to visit the project, the wind was blowing at 20 miles an hour. We brought four high-rise cranes to the site, one for each corner, and had ribbons stretched across the tops of the cranes to outline the top of the proposed five-story building. It worked, although balloons clearly would have been cheaper. The cost of delay and rescheduling the council's site visit, however, would have been greater than the cranes.

Building Specifications

Location
U.S. 15-501 and Europa Drive

Building Size
Total gross square feet, Phase I—96,900 (9,005 square meters)
Total rentable square feet, Phase I—92,700 (8,615 square meters)

Suite Sizes
Approximately 1,000 square feet (93 square meters) to full floor (approximately 18,860 square feet [1,755 square meters]); capability of expansion in Phase II to a contiguous floor area of approximately 40,000 square feet (3,720 square meters).

Parking
258 spaces in an open-air parking structure consisting of one on-grade parking level and two elevated levels.

Elevator
Two custom hydraulic elevators in the entrance lobby; interiors of cabs finished with raised-fabric wall panels with polished stainless steel accents, carpeted floors, and polished stainless steel 9.5-foot (3-meter) ceiling with recessed downlighting.

Standards

Partitioning
All partitions to be drywall construction using ½-inch (1.3-centimeter) gypsum wallboard over two ½-inch (1.3-centimeter) metal studs; tenant allowance to be one linear foot (0.3 meter) of partitioning per 10 square feet (1 square meter) of usable area; of this linear footage, 20 percent will be soundproofed.

Wall Finishes
Interior walls will be finished with standard vinyl covering, with tenants' choice of colors; upgraded finishes available.

Ceiling
Suspended ⅝-inch (1.6-centimeter) acoustical fireguard tile with recessed edge in exposed two-foot by two-foot (0.6- by 0.6-meter) grid.

Electrical Lights
Two-foot by four-foot (0.6- by 1.2-meter), three-lamp, lay-in fluorescent energy-saving lamp and ballast fixture with parabolic louver diffuser; one per 83 square feet (7.7 square meters) of usable area.

Power Outlets
One duplex wall outlet per 100 square feet (10 square meters) of usable area.

Light Switches
One double-pole switch per 300 square feet (28 square meters) of usable area.

Telephone Outlets
One outlet per 150 square feet (14 square meters) of usable area, wall mounted in interior partitions.

Floor Covering
Standard carpet is 30-ounce tufted cut-pile nylon commercial carpet installed by direct gluedown, with colors to be selected by tenant and upgraded carpet available; vinyl asbestos tile is

12 inches by 12 inches by 1/8 inch (0.3 meter by 0.3 meter by 0.3 centimeter), available for kitchen and storage areas; four-inch (0.1-meter) vinyl cove base standard.

Entry Door
One single, full-height, three-foot-wide (0.9-meter), solid-core door in an aluminum frame, with hardware to include lockset, wall stop, and automatic closer; one set of double-entry doors provided for leased premises larger than 3,000 usable square feet (280 square meters).

Interior Doors
One single, full-height, three-foot-wide (0.9-meter), solid-core door in an aluminum frame with passage set hardware; one per 225 square feet (21 square meters) of usable area (including entrance door).

Window Covering
One-inch (2.5-centimeter) blinds with Top-Lok feature or equal provided at all fixed exterior windows.

Heating and Air Conditioning
Multiple-zone, variable-air-volume system using heat reclaim with thermostatically controlled zones; distribution for each zone uses ceiling diffusers; one supply per 150 usable square feet (15 square meters) and one return per 200 usable square feet (18.5 square meters).

Space Planning
Layout and design services that provide blueprints for construction will be furnished at no cost by the landlord.

Graphics
One tenant identification and suite number sign to be provided by landlord at entry door; one listing on building directory to be provided by landlord on interior building directory; all graphics standard throughout building.

Floor Loading
70 pounds per square foot (0.03 kilogram per square centimeter), including wall partitions.

During the initial solicitation for construction bids, Fraser Morrow Daniels used the suggestions of three contractors to revise the architects' preliminary drawings. The accompanying section of the case study reveals the motivation for selecting the contractor for Europa Center. Although selection of the architect was based on reputation, cost entered more heavily into the selection of the contractor.

The Tradeoffs in Choosing Players
We put the design out to bid to three different contractors. We reviewed the project in detail with each one, incorporating some of their suggestions for saving money, got a final price, and then chose the construction company based on price as well as on the firm's reputation for finishing jobs. In this case, we violated one of our own rules. To save $200,000 on the cost of construction, we picked the company that had a less solid reputation than the others (although all three companies were good ones). In this way, we reached the base construction price; later, we had to negotiate the parking deck, which wasn't yet designed.

For Europa Center, the changes prompted by the contractor's suggestions rippled through to the cost estimates, thus demonstrating that the feasibility study should not be considered a static document. Rather, the study should be continually refined to reflect changes in both the physical project and market conditions.

An election in Chapel Hill had considerable impact on Fraser Morrow Daniels's project. At that point in the process (well into stage three), the company was in a vulnerable position. It had committed a great deal of time and money to specify a project and obtain approval, but construction had not yet started.

Politics and Changing the Rules in Midstream
After we chose a contractor and spent a great deal of money to design the building, one political uncertainty in the process jumped up and bit us. An election in Chapel Hill in November 1985 brought new players to the game. The people who were elected vowed that no more tall buildings would be built in town and that they would lower the density of everything. We thought that wouldn't matter because our project had already been approved and we had bought the land. But we found out otherwise. If the new officials' proposals went through, the amount of time that it would take to put the new limits and restrictions in place would have been about three months. So we had three months to begin construction, for we found out that if the project was not under construction, all of the approvals were dead. There we were with a set of financial calculations based on 200,000 square feet (18,600 square meters) of building and a parking deck, already having been through planning review and site planning and in the final stages of bidding with the contrac-

The parking deck for Phase I of Europa Center just after construction. Designed to accommodate close to 300 cars, the parking deck was eventually cloaked by landscaping.

tors, with only three months to begin building without any financing. We really had to scramble. About the middle of February, the town fathers decreed that any project not under construction on April 15 probably would fall under the new rules instead of the old ones.

The Europa Center Feasibility Study

In the development of Europa Center, stage two gradually slid (rather than suddenly lurched) into stage three. The architect, from an independent firm, was involved in both stages, because architecture was not one of Fraser Morrow Daniels's in-house capabilities. Moreover, with Fraser Morrow Daniels being new to office development, the firm chose the best architect to minimize risk and establish credibility. The developer focused on fitting the building to its site and surroundings (a political as well as design decision). By acquiring a highly buildable piece of land and using the highest-quality architect, the developer hoped to realize savings by avoiding construction cost overruns and permitting delays.

The case study focuses on the tradeoff among costs, rents, and operating efficiency. Fraser Morrow Daniels intended to capitalize on the existing market for office space without creating something particularly special—a high-quality development but not a unique development. The developer worked closely with the city because the city fathers were known to be difficult. As a result, the relationship was a dynamic one. In this case, the developer came close to fast-tracking construction simply to avoid losing building permits.

During Europa Center's development, Fraser Morrow Daniels was also attempting to secure approval for a condominium hotel, also in the Research Triangle area. Located close to a state university, the hotel was projected to attract persons attending events associated with the school, so an operating tie-in was needed. In addition, the project was to be located in a historic section of town, further complicating political issues, traffic congestion, and even physical construction. Fraser Morrow Daniels, a relatively small developer working in a relatively small town, had more than $2 million invested in the project before the city finally approved it. (Much more money would be involved in a complex project in a large city.) Think about how the providers of the capital reacted when the project proved infeasible despite the eventual political approvals. The developer chose not to move to stage four, leaving the investor with $2 million worth of plans for a project that would never be built.

STAGES FOUR AND FIVE: CONTRACT NEGOTIATION AND FORMAL COMMITMENT

Fraser Morrow Daniels had no financing for Europa Center and was under pressure to begin construction before Chapel Hill's new rules restricting a building's height and density took effect.

Financing and a Quick Move to Contract Negotiation

We beat the April 15 deadline by starting construction before the completion of financial negotiations. But we traded one kind of risk for another.

It takes a long time to execute documents and to get the contractor and the architect to agree on all the final details—how they will proceed, order materials, get the grading subcontractor to come out and start bulldozing. The financial negotiations were not quite finished on April 15, but we had our site plan approved and we started clearing ground on April 14.

We called the town fathers and told them they wouldn't see a lot of building soon but that we were starting. We just didn't want to get caught on a technicality because of the political environment. If we had missed the deadline, our building would have become a three-story building instead of a five-story building and 120,000 square feet (11,150 square meters) in two phases instead of 200,000 square feet (18,600 square meters). Under those circumstances, we would have lost money on the day we started.

To get funding for Europa Center, we needed a financial partner—on this project the Centennial Group, a group partially composed of former Sea Pines people who managed a fund that they created. It was a publicly held stock company that has invested in various projects around the country. They put $2 million into the Europa project. For that, they got 50 percent of the deal. Financing was arranged through Investor S&L out of Richmond, which had a working relationship with the Centennial Group from previous development deals. Centennial as a financial partner brought more to the table than just money; it also brought a reputation and a working relationship with a lender. We funded the research, planning, purchase negotiations, staff, and so on before the joint venture and were partially reimbursed in the joint venture agreement. So we had a small initial dollar risk: $50,000 to $100,000 partially reimbursed.

We invest time and money on many ideas that never come to fruition. For every project we end up working on, we may have spent time and money on ten other ones that didn't happen. We usually wouldn't get to the stage of having invested $50,000 or $100,000 on a project that wasn't going to go anywhere. But we may spend $10,000 to $15,000 or $20,000 many times before we ever get to a project that works.

The financial models we used included a little section called "capitalized expenses"—the capital cost of building a project. It's a list covering the relative cost of doing things in a project like this. The land purchase is half of the $2 million land price, because this model is for one building (the first phase of two). Centennial holds land for the second phase for the Park Forty project and for Europa, accruing interest on it. When we use it, it will be a separate calculation. But as far as the bank is concerned, it's $1 million for land, and Centennial and our group together have another million dollars invested in another piece of land.

Our financial partners ended up bearing the risk of that million in addition to the other million for the second phase. The lender agreed to fund everything else on the list, so instead of $9,339,000, the lender loaned us $8,339,000. We negotiated the construction price of $4,985,000 with the construction company building the building. It included an allocation for the parking deck. The parking deck was not yet fully designed, so we estimated the cost and had some money allocated for it.

To attract a lender, we had to pay fees up front—in this case, 1.5 percent in the beginning and another 0.5 percent for an extension of the amount they were lending, which is about $200,000. We budgeted for interest on the construction loan at 11.5 percent during construction; fortunately, during the process, the interest rate went down.

The next item was a deficit in leasing over the 36 months of funding for the project. That amounted to $457,000 that we had to fund for operating the building while no rent was being paid and for paying the interest on the empty space. The budget also included normal design and engineering costs, the cost of finishing space for tenants at $12 a square foot ($130 per square meter), leasing commissions for the leasing agent, salaries for the developer's staff, and some other soft costs, for a total capitalization of about $9,339,000.

The management fee in the budget is the 4 percent development fee. The construction company handles construction management. We got $250,000 in fees during the construction period and the leasing period—$15,000 a month over about 17 months. After it ran out, that was all we got until we made some profit on the building.

The S&L made us an open-ended construction loan with an extension period. There was no takeout on the deal. The S&L also agreed to fund the deficit during leasing, which doesn't normally happen. The agreement stated that we would lease the office building in Chapel Hill gradually over two years after the building was finished; that's 100,000 square feet (9,300 square meters) over two years, with the first tenant moving in the first day the building is completed and then not filling the building for two years afterward.

We projected that we would lease 25 percent of the building to rent-paying tenants during the first quarter after construction, then 5 percent a month, then about 3 percent a month. That meant getting four or five tenants to move in when the building was completed and then one or two small tenants requiring 3,000 to 5,000 square feet (280 to 465 square meters) a month for the remaining year and a half.

Thirty-six months of the leasing period includes the 12 months of construction, so the deficit item in the loan is funding for the 24 months after the completion of construction. That seemed reasonable to us, and we didn't see any major competition for our project. The extension of I-40 from Research Triangle Park to U.S. 15-501 was scheduled to open about the same time our building was scheduled to be completed.

The vision of Europa Center the developers and architects sold to the financiers so they could begin construction.

But what happens if that amount is not enough? What happens if we have to come up with another million dollars? We decided that it was a good insurance policy for us to have an extra million dollars lined up before we executed the agreement on the loan. We said the two 50/50 partners jointly should be willing to give up 30 percent of the project, leaving each with 35 percent. All the third party had to do was guarantee with a letter of credit or something else that it would have the money available to lend if we didn't meet the schedule for leasing and construction costs and other things.

Instead of having to get a third party to come in as an investor, Centennial decided it would do it. The agreement was as follows: the million dollars that Centennial had put up to purchase the land was not funded by the bank. So instead of $9,339,000, the bank funded $8,339,000, and the million dollars was left in the deal, essentially as a line of credit to be used if leasing did not go according to plan. We ended up with a 65/35 deal, with Fraser Morrow Daniels receiving 35 percent and Centennial 65 percent of the project's profits.

When you calculate how much it costs to operate the building versus how much rent you're collecting, the occupancy figure drives the cost of operating the building. And the number of rent-paying tenants drives the revenue side. Our revised model gave us the $9,339,000 capital cost over three years from when we started—a building 95 percent occupied at $17 per square foot ($185 per square meter) two years out. If you rent the office space today and get six months of free rent, then start paying at $16 per square foot ($170 per square meter), your rent escalates after a year by 5 percent and after another year by another 5 percent and you're paying about $17.50 ($190) by the time we would sell or refinance the building.

What it cost to get from a raw piece of land to a fully occupied, income-producing building two years after construction, including all the interest carrying costs, was $9,339,000 total. The construction cost was $5 million, the land was $1 million, and tenant finishes, interest, marketing, and commissions were

$3.3 million. With conventional financing, owning an office building that leases at these rates provides a relatively marginal return to the building owner.

The capital cost is what we have to pay back when we sell the building. The selling price is a function of net rental income after operating costs and before debt service. When you build an office building, basically it's always for sale. Our expected profit was $2.2 million, and we expected to get 35 percent of that $2.2 million at the end.

Fraser Morrow Daniels negotiated an agreement with the contractor for Europa Center. For the developer, a cost-plus-fee contract with a guaranteed maximum price is preferable to a fixed-price contract (where the fixed price equals the guaranteed maximum price). With a cost-plus-fee contract, the developer receives the benefit of any savings (unless the contract provides otherwise); with a fixed-price contract, the contractor reaps any savings only if the actual cost of construction is less than the amount of the fixed price.

Construction Costs

The contractor gave us a guaranteed maximum price, and the agreement stated that if actual costs came in under that price, the contractor could keep half of what it saved us. The negotiations were so tight that I was certain savings would not occur.

During construction, the contractor builds the project exactly as it is drawn. If you change anything, a step or a rail or a nail, it's extra and, in some cases, a lot extra. We have learned over the years that even though a project can be improved by changing it during the process, it costs about four times as much as improving it before building starts. So you live with it the way it is bid except for critical omissions or safety features. We added a $200,000 contingency to cover just such possibilities.

In its deal for Europa Center, Fraser Morrow Daniels ended up with a 65/35 split with Centennial. A small development company, Fraser Morrow Daniels traded off a share of ownership and potential monetary rewards to share the risk inherent in leasing a new product—Class A office space in a new location—and to obtain the additional equity necessary to attract construction and permanent financing for the project (i.e., the equity that Fraser Morrow Daniels was either unable or unwilling to invest).

Initiating Construction

We formalized the relationship that had been negotiated with the S&L. Final negotiations were tough because both the S&L and Centennial were initially unwilling to expand the loan to cover the extensive leasing period we sought. When things started to get tight, it became obvious that different members of the devel-

Interior construction at Europa Center. Jim Sink, Artech, Inc.

opment team had different goals. The firm's senior partner did not want to lose his established net worth, while the younger members did not want to lose an opportunity. All members of the team realized their respective positions, however, and held firm in their negotiations with the lender/financier, eventually obtaining the desired $1 million reserve for the leasing period.

We negotiated the price of construction, dealing seriously with three potential general contractors and finally obtaining a contract that did not need to be bonded because of the general contractor's quality. The architect's judgment played a central role throughout, but we did not turn over final decisions involving rent, costs, and operating efficiency to the architect. And because quality construction was very important to us and local builders did not have much experience with Class A office buildings, we added a partner to the team to supervise construction for a salary plus a small percentage of the profits.

STAGE SIX: CONSTRUCTION

During the early stages of construction, Fraser Morrow Daniels encountered problems arising from poor on-site supervision. To correct the problem, the firm hired a professional experienced in construction management in the Research Triangle market. As both construction manager and partner in the project, he certainly cost more than his predecessor, but the predecessor was not getting the job done.

The design for Europa Center stressed both current appeal to tenants and future flexibility. With each decision it faced, Fraser Morrow Daniels considered the tradeoff between immediate cost benefits and longer-term impacts.

The Building Itself

Europa Center has a high ratio of usable space compared with the core utility and common areas (85 percent), and we maximized the amount of window space for tenants. Everyone likes windows and extra corner offices. It costs a little bit more for construction, but I don't think it affects utility costs very much.

Almost all of the mechanical systems in a well-designed multitenant building offer a lot of flexibility for different heating and cooling requirements in different zones throughout the day. We used high-efficiency glass for comfort and energy cost control. We used the best elevators so that we could move people more efficiently; in a five-story building with 20,000-square-foot (1,860-square-meter) floors, a lot of people need to move up and down. The building also has two separate sets of stairs; a freight elevator is planned in the second building.

We had to decide how much telecommunications and electronics capability to put in the building. Initially in looking at office building development, we thought we should build a state-of-the-art building with built-in computer systems (a so-called "smart" building), but we learned in talking with others that 80 or 90 percent of tenants won't pay for that extra cost: they don't yet know how to use the systems and don't want them. The best

thing to do is to build flexible conduit space and wiring into the building so those systems can be added as they become economically feasible for tenants. We got clearance for a satellite dish on the roof. Such decisions gave us flexibility about how to use the building in the future.

We also did some special on-site landscaping, changing the land plan to increase some landscaped areas. We sank the parking deck into the ground at significant cost so that it would have a low profile and be hidden by earth berms and trees. That probably cost us an extra $50,000 to $100,000. We'll landscape it so that some marginal leasing benefit might be possible. We liked that from the standpoint of design, but it was more expensive. We would have to increase rent to pay for the added costs, but which pocket could we take it out of? In a very competitive market, we probably would not recover the extra rent.

Later, the building will be more valuable because of that decision. The building is more valuable because of the parking deck. Period. The alternative to a parking deck to serve a fairly large building like Europa Center would have been to cover the entire site with asphalt.

Fraser Morrow Daniels planned to give up 15 percent of its share in Europa Center's profits to obtain a leasing reserve of $1 million, and Whit Morrow hoped the company would never need that reserve. As it happened, the firm could not lease the building during construction because prospective tenants were unfamiliar with the benefits of the proposed Class A office space. Compounding this problem was the disappearance of the planned leasing reserve.

Leasing during Construction

We anticipated signing some leases immediately after the building was completed—mostly small professional firms and service firms—but expected that it would take two full years to fill the building. And because of rent concessions that had emerged as standard in the marketplace, we were not sure when those tenants would begin paying rent. Whether we use free rent or extra tenant improvements is always a consideration. The cost of tenant improvements may add to the building's value; free rent doesn't do anything except induce tenants to move in.

And we ended with no convenient million dollars to draw on if necessary. Investors S&L bought Centennial and required that million dollar cushion in equity. Despite a valid loan contract, the bank negotiated a more secure position as part of the acquisition and absorbed the real million. We then expected to require some additional prorated contribution of capital from the partners, with a possible renegotiation of partnership shares—an eventuality that was not anticipated going into the project. But if you examine almost any real estate development deal today, the amount of profits that actually ends up with the person who generated the original idea for the project is usually a lot less than anticipated at the outset. [Authors' note: In this case, failure to anticipate all the project-level implications of the acquisition put the project in jeopardy.]

What would I do differently if I had it to do over again? Bargain for another million. Be more explicit about the long-term contingencies for which money would be used. And continue to reexamine them during negotiations for financing. The feeling that we would be more cooperative, I think, put less pressure on us to spell out every contingency and every detail in a 200-page agreement.

STAGE SEVEN: COMPLETION AND FORMAL OPENING

Because of unforeseen problems, Fraser Morrow Daniels lost about three months at the beginning of Europa Center's development and a few more months at the end. The construction company was partially responsible for several of the early delays. For instance, when the lobby was under construction, some of the granite pieces and some of the special marble from Italy arrived in the wrong size. On-site cutting and fitting of those pieces required additional time. Fabric panels for the lobby walls were missing, and some of the exterior signs arrived late. Although developers cannot foresee all the impediments to construction, they should assume that some will occur and know how to manage them. A careful developer preserves some portion of "float" in the project schedule as a hedge against unforeseen delays.

Leasing and Opening the Project

By December 1987, things were going much more smoothly for us. Europa Center was complete and had opened in November with a well-attended party. One-third of the building was committed, and we expected the building to be 50 percent leased by the end of January 1988.

The market was better. We had been pushing sales hard and pricing space competitively. Our base rate was $15 to $15.50 per square foot ($160 to $165 per square meter) instead of the projected $17 ($180)—about 12 percent under original projections. We used a combination of free rent and tenant improvements, so it will take us a little longer—two years—to reach the amount on the pro forma. We expected to be fully leased by summer 1988 and for everyone to be paying rent by 1989.

We committed 13,000 square feet (1,210 square meters) to an executive business center for small but high-profile tenants. Basically, it offers space plus services for a one-person office: a 200- to 300-square-foot (18.5- to 28-square-meter) office, a common reception area, and secretarial, telephone answering, and copy services. Tenants can even rent office furniture. It's ideal for companies with just one person in the region. Costs to tenants are about twice the base rate for space alone, and the arrangement has been very profitable for us.

One thing we found in this extremely competitive market is that almost nobody would lease space before the building was complete. Another thing we learned is that a lot of prospective tenants didn't know what Class A meant. We had to attract them to the VIP party to make them aware of our project. Our opening party in November was attended by 450 people. We started planning two months ahead in conjunction with the chamber of commerce's Business After Hours program. With all that lead time, we were able to convince the chamber to hold graduation for its leadership training class there. It makes sense to hold this type of function in an office building expected to be a major part of the business community.

We wanted to get two points across about the building: it's exciting and it's elegant. So we hired party consultants instead of planning it ourselves. They put a baby grand piano and a pianist in the lobby and a huge stream of silver balloons from the first to the third level of the atrium. We served shrimp and beverages and had a steady stream of people from 4:30 p.m. to 9:00 p.m. All kinds of people came—including some town planners and some local political figures.

After Construction

The physical construction of Europa Center went reasonably smoothly—which was to be anticipated because we hired a very talented and experienced architect, hired and paid well a construction supervisor, fully explored in advance all regulations with the relevant public officials, and bought a site that presented few physical problems.

Although the construction was smooth, marketing was anything but. In 1987 and 1988, the Research Triangle area contin-

Europa Center has the advantage of many corner offices, providing much light for occupants. Jim Sink, Artech, Inc.

ued to be highly overbuilt, like many other sections of the country. More important, approximately eight months earlier, an office tower with more than 200,000 square feet (18,600 square meters)—huge by the area's standards—was completed only four miles (6.5 kilometers) away on the southeastern side of Durham at the other end of U.S. 15-501. The earlier completion of another Class A office building that was also pursuing tenants with business in both Durham and Chapel Hill was a serious problem for us. Although we tried to woo tenants already committed to the other building, our late arrival in the market allowed the other developer to presign larger tenants. Even highly attractive rental concessions could not cause them to change their minds. And inducing them to jump after signing would involve buying out existing leases for a substantial period of remaining time.

Europa Center officially opened with 15 percent occupancy, and the leasing reserve was therefore critical. To spur activity in the building, we entered into a joint venture with another promoter for an executive office suite. That joint venture took another 20 percent of the building but certainly did not reduce our risk because we were equity partners in the venture. Despite the fact that risks were not reduced, the need for activity in the building made the joint venture a logical decision. [Authors' note: Even though plans for an executive office suite were prepared, they were never executed and the idea did not take hold until much later.]

The city fathers loved Europa Center when it opened. It was attractive to anyone thinking of moving to town because the prices looked very reasonable for the space available. The public sector partner was happy; the neighbors around it were happy. The question was how much longer the lender would be tolerant.

STAGE EIGHT: PROPERTY, ASSET, AND PORTFOLIO MANAGEMENT

Whit Morrow, Dean Stratouly, and Russell Katz, the developers profiled throughout this text, shared their real life with readers, reminding them, first, that real estate development is an art and, second, that it requires some luck. In working out the interactive design and construction of Europa Center, Morrow was slowed down, allowing his competitor (University Tower, which was eventually foreclosed on by its lender) to fill the same market niche first with two substantial projects. In a modest market niche, Fraser Morrow Daniels's Class A building had no fallback position; thus, the firm was both unlucky and a step behind in reaching the market.

When Whit Morrow left development, he became a senior executive with a medical laboratory partly to be in an environment in which professionalism counts more than art or luck.

Leasing Space

There's a major question about who will lease your building for you, especially in the Research Triangle area, where the market was just forming. We chose a national organization, Cushman & Wakefield, which leases only office space, because we anticipated

that the competition for tenants would be cutthroat. In a highly competitive environment, the tenants run the show anyway. If the company listing your space leases it, it will cost 4 percent of the value of the lease. If it is cobrokered with another company, you pay 6 percent of the value of the lease, including the cobrokerage fee. We budgeted 5 percent, because we figured that we or the leasing company could generate tenants for half the space and that the other half would be cobrokered.

The leasing process works mostly like this. The leasing company identifies tenants—trying to find businesses that are expanding or moving to the area or that could be talked out of a current lease that still has a year to run. Once the leasing agents have a prospect, they come to us and say, "This is how your building stacks up against other buildings. You're this much nicer, your location is this much better, and your rent is $1 higher. The tenant needs a loading dock; here's what it values. What will it take to get that tenant here rather than to one of the other three buildings it could move into?" Then we try to guess what the other buildings have to offer and decide how low we can go to beat them out.

Then the leasing agent says, "To get that tenant, I think we'll have to give them a lower rate and six months of free rent. They can't afford to pay for any extra finishes, but they need an extra $3 a square foot ($32 a square meter) for nice surroundings. We should offer an extra $3 per square foot ($32 per square meter) that we pay for, and I think we can get them. Or we should offer free electricity on weekends rather than charging extra." Then we say, "We're not comfortable with six months of free rent; give them four." Or we might say, "That's a great tenant. We really want them because we think they'll attract more tenants. Let's give them 18 months of free rent. They're really beneficial to the building. Let's pay something to get them in there."

After the building was 30 percent leased, more people came to us and asked to be in the building, instead of the other way around. Getting started is very tough, but the subsequent leasing is usually easier.

By April 1989, Europa Center was more than 80 percent leased. Most of the tenants were local professional companies that have been in Chapel Hill and Durham for some time. Virtually all the tenants moved up from substandard space to our space. A few companies had expanded and just needed more space. A couple were startup companies, and some were controlled and located in other parts of the country but used Europa Center as their Chapel Hill office.

Asset management and ongoing leasing are strong considerations for building owners. All the existing tenants had different lease contracts with different terms, different rates, and different escalation clauses. When overbuilding and high vacancy rates are common, tenants can pretty much get what they want by shopping around. Building owners become more and more willing to conform to a tenant's needs, first with lower prices or lower escalations and later with higher tenant allowances and a lot of special things you probably wouldn't want to fool with in a better market.

Once a building is finished and occupied, the building owner or building manager worries about the electricity, the water bill, parking, elevator maintenance, and indoor and outdoor landscaping—all the things that are essential to keeping the tenants happy and the building looking good. Because a lot of different tenants have leases with varying lengths, some leases are always coming up for renewal or people are moving out. Leasing in a building like Europa Center is a continuous process.

A Final Word from Whit Morrow

Europa Center was sold in early 1989 to a Chapel Hill family that has been a great benefactor of the community. The price was market at this stage of development, allowing the existing owner/financial institution to come close to breaking even and giving the new investor significant long-term benefits.

No profits were available for distribution to partners. It was disappointing for us, but when I look at the building, I think I would have done the project anyway because it was interesting and exciting. Our final product is gorgeous. It's the best office building in town. Everything about Europa Center is right.

It is very difficult to have a short-term perspective about real estate and still make money. After we build a project and it's occupied, there is no reason for people to continue to pay us to be involved in it, so we have to move on to different projects. As a small company, we didn't have the equity position for long-term projects. Profits from building management are not significant for a company like ours. It would have been nice to have developed ten buildings and to have ended with a continuing source of income from managing all ten, but that's not the situation we were in.

The building's capital structure, financing, and ownership evolved in a way that was not conducive to long-term ownership. We made the decision to sell the building to an investor whose objective was to manage the building over the long term, which was different from our objectives. A company with a different financial structure might value long-term growth more than immediate cash. Banks and small development companies like ours are not in a position to take advantage of the long-term benefits of owning a building, even though a project might be worth considerably more ten years from now than it is today.

The lender decided that it wanted to sell the building to recover its money. A lending institution that owns a property values it differently because of the accounting rules associated with lending. It has to depreciate and write things off and maintain reserves against potential losses, so that owning a building is not as valuable to that institution as it might be to some other type of institution. In fact, owning the building negatively affected the lender's ability to lend money. The lender knew it could make a greater profit over the short term by lending money rather than by managing a building.

I have very mixed emotions about the sale of Europa Center. Although the long-term prospects for ownership are excellent, we had evolved to a point where the lending institution had full control. It was more advantageous to the lender to sell than to hold the property for future marginal gain. Instead of selling the building, we might have restructured the financing such that we would have maintained ownership by merely replacing the lender. But a separate question arises about whether or not our small company could have properly structured itself to stay involved. In my judgment, it worked out better to sell the building outright and not to enter the building management business.

The new investor occupied the remaining 20 percent of the first building and immediately began construction of the approved second phase, a 107,000-square-foot (9,900-square-meter) building. The town managers or citizens had no objections; they now regard Europa Center as attractive and beneficial to the community. The local leasing market is better, and today Europa Center has no competition from new buildings. With other highly respected occupants in place (particularly the new investor and related subsidiaries), prospective tenants now feel secure that Europa Center is a fine building in a superior location. The completed site is truly spectacular.

As Morrow mentioned, the new owner built a second phase after buying the property in 1989. The new owner describes his perspective in the following discussion.

The New Owner's Perspective

Although Europa Center was initially well conceived, the project was generally perceived by the market as an unsuccessful venture by the time it was offered for sale. This image posed a dilemma for prospective tenants. The original developers were offering attractive lease terms to fill the building, but the uncertainty of the future ownership of the building added some risk to the agreements. When Investors S&L decided to sell the project "as is," the new owner purchased the building with the intention of holding it as a long-term investment, recognizing numerous benefits in the building. For one, it was the first and only true Class A space in Chapel Hill. It was well built and offered attractive amenities to a small market with no previous Class A space. Moreover, it was approved for more than 100,000 square feet (9,300 square meters) of additional space. The new owner felt comfortable that the market could bear a second phase of this type of attractive project.

Europa Center was purchased for $11 million, which included the land and building from Phase I and the additional land originally intended for Phase II. As a result of the long-standing relationship between the new owner and his capital sources, an unsecured line of credit was available for both the purchase and the subsequent development of Phase II.

The new owner brought in a team of on-site managers from Allen & O'Hara of Memphis. The team leader then served as the

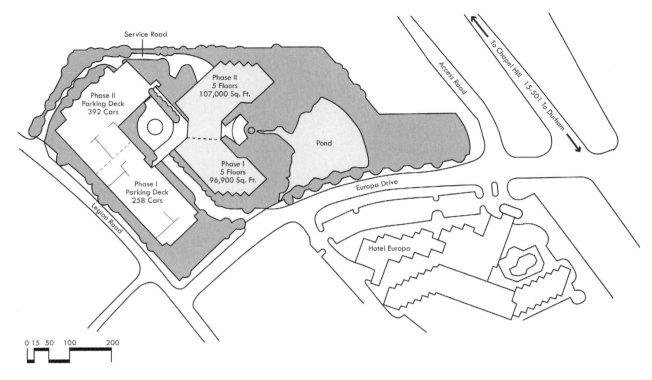

Site plan showing Phase II of Europa Center, built by new owners based on original plans developed by Fraser Morrow Daniels. Phase II contains an additional 107,000 square feet (9,950 square meters) of office space and accommodates 392 more cars.

owner's representative during the development of Phase II. The presence of the new on-site management to deal with the day-to-day issues and the sale of Europa Center to a respected and well-known member of the community changed the business community's perceptions such that the building leased up rather quickly, going from about 65 percent occupancy at the time of purchase to almost 100 percent within six to eight months.

Construction of Phase II

Soon after the purchase, plans were made to start Phase II. An Atlanta architectural firm, Cooper Carry & Associates, was retained to design Phase II; it had been the original architectural firm for Europa Center and had created the footprint for Phase II. As approvals from the city had been negotiated during Phase I, the second building could get started quickly. The architects prepared drawings for a building of 107,863 gross square feet (10,025 square meters), 99,751 square feet (9,270 square meters) of it rentable space, a three-story atrium connecting the two phases, and an expansion of the parking deck from 258 to 650 spaces.

The owner offered the construction contract to Allen & O'Hara, with which he had worked on previous projects. Based on past experience, he was confident that the firm could complete the project on time and within budget. The total cost of

construction of Phase II was estimated at slightly more than $11 million. That amount covered the hard costs of the building and parking deck, architectural and engineering fees, development fees, hard- and soft-cost contingencies, leasing commissions, and interest; it also included approximately $2 million for tenant improvements. These costs were significantly higher than for Phase I, but nearly four years had elapsed since Phase I had been planned. The cost also included the addition of a three-story atrium and the substantial expansion of the parking deck to more than double its original size. Construction financing was based on an unsecured line of credit at the prime interest rate minus 1 percent. The interim financing remained in place through lease-up and was subsequently rolled into long-term fixed-rate financing in early 1994 at a time when commercial mortgage rates were the lowest in more than 30 years.

Construction took approximately one year. Having the construction information available from Phase I simplified the job somewhat; overall, the job progressed smoothly. Excavation revealed several soil types, necessitating an increase in the size of a few footings, some to more than 20 feet (6 meters) wide. A fair number of unexpected boulders were also encountered. Neither problem required significant expense to rectify.

Expansion of the parking deck proceeded without problems, using the same contractor from Phase I. Precast concrete was used in both phases.

During initial management of the project, the owner noticed what appeared to be a limitation in the capacity of the electrical heating system. If the system went down for any lengthy period, it would take as long as four or five days to get back up to normal ranges. The system was designed to incorporate heat gain from all sources, including solar gain, gain from the presence of people, and gain from lights. After long discussions with the architect and engineers, the owner decided to use the same type of electrical heating system in Phase II as in Phase I, even though managers would be required to monitor the system closely and to use setbacks to make sure the temperature does not fall below predetermined levels.

Although no major problems were encountered in construction, several incidents related to birds caused headaches for a while. For example, construction of the three-story atrium connecting the two buildings necessitated removal of the temporary end wall of Phase I. During construction, that wall was covered with a Visqueen barrier, but, unbeknown to the contractor, pigeons gained entry through the barrier and nested in the space above the ceiling tiles on nearly every floor. The pigeon noises that could be heard throughout the project gave away the birds' presence. The problem was easily solved when the atrium was closed and the birds could no longer gain entry.

After Phase II was completed and being leased, the managers noticed that flocks of large crows were perching on the window ledges and pecking at the window caulking until an edible chunk could be torn loose. The caulking manufacturer, initially refusing to admit that birds liked the compound, eventually acknowledged it and agreed to change the formula. The windows were recaulked and that problem disappeared.

The only major delay during construction was on the interior finish work. The atrium was to be finished with a combination of Canadian and Italian granite. Although the granite was preselected from both countries, the Italian quarry experienced a labor strike just before shipping. When the strike was settled, the granite was shipped, but for some reason, the marble had to go through quarantine and could not be delivered. The result was a two-month delay. And because the Canadian and Italian granites were to be mixed in the atrium, the finish work had to be deferred until all the granite arrived on site.

Given the quality of the building and the image projected by Europa Center, the new owner decided during completion of the project to provide excess landscaping. The original landscape subcontractor went bankrupt during Phase II construction, leaving plants that had been paid for but not delivered and an irrigation system that had not been completely installed. In addition, the subcontractor had not provided adequate drainage for the trees that were to be placed in circular planters near the building entry. The general contractor took responsibility for the problem and brought in another subcontractor, thereby minimizing the financial impact. Unfortunately, the lack of proper drainage for the trees in the circular planters required

replacement of four of the trees within the first two years of operation. But the attention to landscaping detail has made Europa Center a particularly attractive project. Overall, the construction process for Phase II lasted about 13 months, and the contractor was able to bring the project in on time and on budget.

Marketing and Leasing

When the property was purchased in 1989, Phase I was about 65 percent leased at an average lease rate of about $13.50 to $14 per square foot ($145 to $150 per square meter). The market for office space during that time was slow, primarily as a result of overbuilding in the area during the late 1980s. The recently completed University Towers, a 200,000-square-foot (18,600-square-meter) office building in south Durham, had an occupancy rate of about 30 percent then, and the owners were extending attractive lease terms to fill the building. It was not uncommon to receive one year's free rent on a five-year lease in addition to a generous amount for tenant improvements. Another new project, the Quadrangle, a campus-style office

The three-story atrium connecting Phases I and II of Europa Center is finished with Canadian and Italian marble.

facility also located in Durham, was about 25 percent occupied. The Chapel Hill market is very small, so the addition of new space has a tendency to oversupply the market quickly. Further, in that small market, tenants generally prefer to see the space they are going to lease; accordingly, preleasing is somewhat more difficult than in larger cities such as Raleigh.

By the time construction began on Phase II, the market was beginning to improve slightly, and it continued to improve slowly from that point. The improvement in the market during this time was largely a result of the lack of capital for new construction during the early 1990s. Most banks and S&Ls had withdrawn from the construction lending business and were not interested in making speculative development loans. In addition, because the market was already overbuilt, few developers were interested in starting a new project in a down market. But that very lack of new office construction meant that Europa Center was well positioned to take advantage of the market as it improved.

Securing tenants for Europa Center in such a soft market was not easy. The fact that Phase I was complete provided a slight advantage during the construction of Phase II, because prospective tenants had a sense of what the new space would look like. The new owner and his long-term commitment were also major selling points. Nonetheless, the marketing team followed several leads and knocked on a lot of doors while Phase II of Europa Center was under construction.

By the time construction of Phase II was nearly complete, almost all the remaining space in Phase I had been leased and about 10 to 15 percent of Phase II preleased, but there were no anchor tenants for Phase II. Instead, the tenants were mostly local companies that wanted to locate in Class A space or small offices with regional or national affiliations. Tenants occupied from 600 square feet (55 square meters) to more than 10,000 square feet (930 square meters), but most located in 4,000- to 5,000-square-foot (372- to 465-square-meter) spaces.

With the market far from robust during that period, space was preleased at rates of about $14 per square foot ($150 per square meter), with tenant improvement allowances of approximately $12 to $14 per square foot ($130 to $150 per square meter). The real improvement in the market during that period materialized in the area of free rent; instead of providing one year's free rent on a five-year lease, the marketing team was able to secure three- and five-year leases with only three to five months of free rent. Even with the slightly improved market, lease rates of $14 per square foot ($150 per square meter) would not support the capital budget imposed by the acquisition of the project, at least over the short run.

As the project was nearing completion in early 1991, the new owner expressed concern about the pace of leasing for Phase II. He felt that a brokerage firm with national exposure would be needed to attract major tenants. As a result, he signed a one-year contract with a large national brokerage firm that specializes in the leasing of office space and kept on Allen & O'Hara as property managers that assisted in leasing the building. Over the next year, occupancy in Phase II increased from about 15 percent to approximately 30 percent. Allen & O'Hara was instrumental in securing a few small tenants over the course of the year; the new leasing company was not successful in leasing any new space in the building. In fact, a couple of potential tenants were lost to other space represented by the same brokerage company.

At the expiration of the listing contract at the beginning of 1992, Allen & O'Hara reassumed its position as primary leasing agents for the project. By then, the market had improved considerably, and the leasing momentum had picked up. New leases were signed at $15 to $16 per square foot ($160 to $172 per square meter), and free rent was no longer necessary to attract tenants. By the end of 1992, Phase II was about 70 percent occupied, and it took only an additional six months or so to bring the building to 90 percent occupancy.

Even though leasing was progressing well, a few locations in the building proved difficult to lease. One such space, at the back of the terrace-level atrium, encompassed approximately 1,500 square feet (140 square meters). The space had limited visibility and was ill suited for configuration as offices. Alternative uses were explored at length until the need emerged for on-site food facilities. At the owner's suggestion, the firm negotiated a deal with a local restaurant operator for approximately 1,200 square feet (110 square meters) of space, thus providing a viable solution to otherwise difficult-to-lease space.

Another difficult area to lease was a wedge-shaped space comprising about 3,000 square feet (280 square meters) on the fifth floor over the atrium. This space had a limited number of windows and was therefore unacceptable to the vast majority of tenants looking for quality space in a building such as Europa Center. Given the difficulty in leasing this space, the owner made the space available as executive suites. The idea was an instant success. Many regional or national companies wanted a presence in the area but could not justify the expense associated with staffing an office. The executive suite satisfied the need for small amounts of high-quality space in a Class A building. The suites leased instantly, and a waiting list developed for those offices. Interestingly, a previous Phase I tenant had leased a large amount of space from the original developer for use as executive offices, but for some reason, the space was never developed into suites.

Final Thoughts

By the end of 1994, the entire building was approximately 95 percent leased. Leases at that time were being signed at rates of about $18 per square foot ($195 per square meter), with a $5 per square foot ($55 per square meter) tenant improvement allowance. Free rent was no longer incorporated into any of the leases. It took several years for the project to lease at rates projected by the original developer. Europa Center illustrates one of the key issues associated with the development of real estate—the cyclical nature of the product. Even though few developers consider a recession or slowdown in the market when conducting their initial financial analysis of a project, real estate has been shown to suffer large swings in performance, just like any other asset class.

Since 1995, the market in Chapel Hill has tightened considerably. Occupancy at Europa Center now hovers near 100 percent and rents average $21 to $22 per square foot ($225 to $235 per square meter). Most of the older, below-market leases have been turned over. New leases offer no rental concessions or tenant improvement allowance, save some minor painting. Tenants pay for their own interior buildouts. Extensive marketing has not been necessary, as turnover has been quite low and additional space is in demand from existing tenants. In fact, one of the biggest challenges currently facing management is finding room for expansion of tenants.

With the emergence of a strong market and increased demand for space, management has discontinued the executive suite program in favor of a single tenant. As the market has tightened, the less optimal space offered as executive suites has become more desirable. Because of the additional management and furniture leasing costs associated with offering several executive suites, the owner achieves a higher return by leasing to a single tenant. The program was, however, an excellent short-term strategy for leasing unused space.

The managers have made an effort to keep the tenant mix diverse. Beyond protecting the owner against the impact of the sudden departure of a large tenant, a diversity of tenants also avoids the perception that the building is controlled by any single tenant. The largest tenant at Europa Center controls less than 14 percent of the space.

The owner and managers are pleased with the results achieved at Europa Center. This Class A project was well conceived by the original developers; it is very attractive and offers all the amenities necessary for today's office market. The extensive landscaping and attention to quality throughout the building have served the project well. The value of one amenity in particular, the parking deck, is becoming increasingly apparent over time. As the office market in Chapel Hill continues to mature, parking has become a valuable commodity, one not enjoyed by many other new office developments in the area. Indeed, the owner considers the development of the parking deck to be as much of a coup as the development of the office building itself. Although parking on the deck is currently unrestricted, management feels that it may eventually be necessary to reserve parking on the deck for tenants and visitors to Europa Center.

Large-scale upgrades of the property have not been necessary. An electronic security system has been installed, eliminating the need for a graveyard shift of security personnel. Guards

The completed Phase I of Europa Center. Jim Sink, Artech, Inc.

are still on the premises weekdays from 7 A.M. to 11 P.M. and on Saturday from 9 A.M. to 2 P.M. At all other times, the building is accessible with electronic key cards. The investment in the system was recouped in only one year. Utility upgrades have been provided to individual tenants as needed by the utilities, and management has brought in an Internet service provider, giving tenants the option to connect to the Internet.

The owner continues to view Europa Center as a long-term asset. Several other properties in the area have been flipped into REIT portfolios, a prospect the owner does not currently entertain. Europa Center continues to stand as the premier Class A office in the Chapel Hill market. Although other new office buildings have been developed, none boast the scale and amenities of Europa Center. Its position at the top of the market is fairly secure, as Europa Center now enjoys a certain amount of insulation from competition. Because of the high regulatory barriers to entering the market, it is unlikely that comparable space will be developed in the near term.

A FINAL WORD FROM AUTHOR MIKE MILES

Our 20-year look at this development affords a classic picture of the evolution of situs—all the impacts of the subject property on surrounding properties and all impacts of surrounding properties on the subject property. When Whit Morrow conceived the development, this site was the emerging new hot location. The new hotel next door was a high-end boutique on the European model. The site was (and still is) on the major connector between the two major employers in the area—the University of North Carolina and Duke University. Further, this location was in the middle of the two most upscale residential neighborhoods.

Recall that Whit Morrow was subsequently caught in a general market downturn. It affected even the better-done developments, and he faced a liquidity squeeze. The second owner, and still the current owner, is the prominent Kenan family, with several chaired professors named Kenan Professors and the football stadium named Kenan Stadium. They were appropriately capitalized to buy this well-located and very-well-built project at a fortuitous time. They have engaged solid property management and reaped the benefits of the attractive purchase price over the last several years.

Like many areas of the country that are blessed with the economic and climatic drivers that fit in today's outsource-oriented, technology-enhanced global economy, the Chapel Hill area has seen a big jump in office rents over the last year. So it should be happy days again at the Europa Center. Right? Not exactly. Another real estate truism is relevant to this story. The three most important things in real estate investing are traditionally location, location, and timing. Through 2006, with the property being in a good location, the Kenan family has also benefited from great timing on the purchase.

Today, time has moved on. The Chapel Hill area has grown, and it now includes several new high-end housing areas. Consequently, the competitive advantage of the Europa site is lessened. The road to Durham from Chapel Hill has many new stoplights, and it is now very crowded. Several people now prefer to travel on the interstate to make the journey. The boutique hotel is now a mid-priced Sheraton. Close by, on the road to Raleigh, is Meadowmont—a new small city with everything from high-priced housing to retail to office space to apartments to housing for the elderly to a very upscale fitness center. The rents in that submarket are up more than 25 percent in the last two years.

In Durham (where Duke University is located), a major new downtown renovation initiative is underway. The old tobacco warehouses have been converted to upscale retail space, restaurants, and lofts. The Duke medical campus has expanded dramatically, increasing the attractiveness of the Durham area in general. The Europa site is in between and not as appealing as either of these newer locations.

Late in 2006 armed with numerous incentives, the Durham downtown commission captured the area's oldest and largest locally grown investment firm—Smith Breeden. This firm emerged years ago as a manager of bonds for institutional investors and has grown to be a major local firm. Breeden, who lives in Chapel Hill, went on to be dean of the Duke Business School. His firm has a significant cultural and economic impact on the community. It was originally located at the best site in town—the Europa Center—but it is now moving to downtown Durham next to the renovated ballpark (from the movie *Bull Durham*). Smith Breeden's sign will be visible over the outfield fence.

So who will Europa Center get to fill space in 2007 and beyond? Its rents are still well below $25 per square foot ($270 per square meter), gross, while the best Meadowmont office space is $30 per square foot ($325 per square meter). The other tenants in the building are increasingly university related. And although there is nothing wrong with university tenants, they are not the highest rent payers. But even after all these years and strong asset management, the property looks good. It was well built and has great parking. Still, rents today are lagging the newer locations by more than $5 per square foot ($55 per square meter).

Situs evolves. As the old guys say, it really is about location, location, and timing. It's just that timing is not all about purchase price. Basis may be forever, but situs evolves.

Gateway Business Center Offering Memorandum

The Gateway Business Center Offering Memorandum is included here as a supplement to the cash flow analysis featured in Chapter 9. The memorandum is also an example of how commercial real estate is offered for sale; it includes many of the important components of a property sale document such as property attributes, leasehold income, and current return parameters of capital markers for modeling and analyzing the cash flows to estimate a purchase price for the asset. It is important to note that some of the numbers presented in the figures in Chapter 9 are slightly different from those in the offering memorandum, which is attributable to differences in assumptions for the cash flow analysis. The authors are extremely grateful to the Inland Companies of Milwaukee, Wisconsin, for the use of this case study.

Confidential Offering Memorandum

**Investment Opportunity
3235-3275 Intertech Drive
Brookfield, Wisconsin**

inland
COMPANIES

Confidential Offering Memorandum
Investment Opportunity

Gateway Business Center

3235 - 3275 Intertech Drive
Brookfield, Wisconsin

72,510 Square Feet

Confidential Offering Memorandum

3235 - 3275 Intertech Drive, Brookfield, Wisconsin

Inland Companies ("Agents") have been engaged as the exclusive agents for the sale of this 72,510 square foot investment offering located in Brookfield, Wisconsin (the "Property").

The Property is being offered for sale in as "as-is, where-is" condition, and the Seller and the Agents make no representations or warranties as to the accuracy of the information contained in this Offering Memorandum. The enclosed materials include highly confidential information and are being furnished solely for the purpose of review by prospective purchasers of the interest described herein. Neither the enclosed materials, nor any information contained herein, are to be used for any other purpose, or made available to any other person without the express written consent of the seller. Each recipient, as a prerequisite to receiving the enclosed information should be registered with Inland Companies, Inc. as a "Registered Potential Investor". The use of this Offering Memorandum, and the information provided herein, is subject to the terms, provisions, and limitations of the confidentiality agreement furnished by Agents prior to delivery of this Offering Memorandum.

The enclosed materials are being provided solely to facilitate the prospective investor's own due diligence for which it shall be fully and solely responsible. The material contained herein is based on information and sources deemed to be reliable, but no representation or warranty, express or implied, is being made by the Agents or the seller or any of their respective representatives, affiliates, officers, employees, shareholders, partners, and directors, as to the accuracy or completeness of the information contained herein. Summaries contained herein of any legal or other documents are not intended to be comprehensive statements of the terms of such documents, but rather only outlines of some of the principal provisions contained therein. Neither the Agents nor the seller shall have any liability whatsoever of the accuracy or completeness of the information contained herein, or decision made by the recipient with respect to the Property. Interested parties are to make their own investigations, projections, and conclusions without reliance upon the material contained herein. The seller reserves the right, at its sole and absolute discretion, to withdraw the Property from being marketed for sale at any time and for any reason.

The seller and the Agents each expressly reserve the right, at their sole and absolute discretion, to reject any and all expressions of interest or offers regarding the Property, and/or to terminate discussions with any entity at any time, with or without notice. This Offering Memorandum is made subject to omissions, correction of errors, change of price or other terms, prior sale or withdrawal from the market without notice. The Agents is not authorized to make any representations or agreements on behalf of the seller.

Confidential Offering Memorandum

3235 - 3275 Intertech Drive, Brookfield, Wisconsin

The seller shall have no legal commitment or obligation to any interested party reviewing the enclosed materials, performing additional investigation, and/or making an offer to purchase the Property unless and until a binding written agreement for the purchase of the Property has been fully executed, delivered, and approved by seller and any conditions to seller's obligations thereunder have been satisfied or waived.

By taking possession of, and reviewing the information contained herein, the recipient agrees that (a) the enclosed materials and their contents are of a highly confidential nature and will be held and treated in the strictest confidence and shall be returned to the Agents or the seller promptly upon request; and (b) the recipient shall not contact employees or tenants of the Property directly or indirectly regarding any aspect of the enclosed materials of the Property without the prior written approval of the seller or the Agents; and (c) no portion of the enclosed materials may be copied or otherwise reproduced without the prior written authorization of the seller of the Agents or as otherwise provided in the Confidentiality and/or Registration Agreement executed and delivered by the recipient(s) to Inland Companies, Inc.

Seller will be responsible for any commission due to Agents in connection with a sale of the Property. Each prospective purchaser will be responsible for any claims for commissions by any other broker or agents in connection with a sale of the Property if such claims arise from acts of such prospective purchaser or its broker/agents. Any buyer's agent must provide a registration signed by the buyer acknowledging said agents' authority to act on its behalf.

If you have no interest in the Property at this time,
please return this Offering Memorandum immediately to:

Thomas Shepherd
Inland Companies, Inc.
839 N. Jefferson Street, #400
Milwaukee, WI 53202

Confidential Offering Memorandum

3235 – 3275 Intertech Drive, Brookfield, Wisconsin

Gateway Business Center
Table of Contents

Executive Summary

3235 - 3275 Intertech Drive, Brookfield, Wisconsin

Gateway Business Center
Opportunity Summary

Inland Companies has been retained by the ownership as Seller's ex-clusive agent to represent them in the sale of the 100% fee simple ownership interest in two (2) quality flex buildings located at 3235-3275 Intertech Drive, in Brookfield, Wisconsin.

OPPORTUNITY SUMMARY	
Total Square Footage:	72,510 SF
3235 Intertech Drive (South Bldg)	38,180 SF
3275 Intertech Drive (North Bldg)	34,330 SF
Current Number of Tenants:	Five (5)
Time Warner	*33,455 SF*
Diebold	*4,725 SF*
United Leasing Associates	*6,329 SF*
Prestige Electrolysis	*5,802 SF*
EZ International	*12,653 SF*
Current Vacancy	9,546 SF
Year 1 Net Operating Income	$529,026
Asking Price	$6,700,000 a 7.9% cap

THE OPPORTUNITY:

This 87% occupied, multi-tenant triple net (NNN) leased property is a quality industrial/office asset. Located in the affluent Waukesha suburb of Brookfield, Wisconsin this stable property has enjoyed a quality Tenants for over nine (9) years.

THE PROPERTY:

The property was built in 1997 of decorative split-face block construction. The 72,510 SF build-ings sit on approximately 5.5 acres or approximately 239,580 SF. The property is currently di-vided into six (6) tenant suites and each suite has dock height and/or drive-in loading. This property is very flexible in that it allows the landlord to increase and decrease the tenant size eas-ily. The property has ample truck parking in the rear of the property ample car parking in the front of each building for office employees. The property offers immediate access to Highway 190 (Capitol Drive) and it is located approximately 1 mile from Highway F (Former 164 North). Interstate 94 is approximately 2 miles due south of the Center via Springdale Road.

1

3235 - 3275 Intertech Drive, Brookfield, Wisconsin

Gateway Business Center
Tenancy and Investment Highlights

TENANCY HIGHLIGHTS:

The Gateway Business Park enjoys a stable mix of both national and local companies. Time Warner Telecom (www.twtelecom.com) is the anchor tenant of the property. Time Warner has been a tenant in this project since its inception in 1997. They came to this building because of its high quality image and the high speed fiber optics that are available to the building and the Gateway Business Park. Diebold, Inc. (NYSE: DBD) is also a tenant in the 3235 Building with Time Warner. This publicly traded company just recently signed a lease in the Gateway Business Park for 63 months. Successful local companies in the Center include Prestige Electrolysis (http://www.prestigeelec.com), EZ International (http://www.ez-international.com), and United Leasing Associates (http://www.ula.net).

FINANCIAL HIGHLIGHTS:

A ten-year projection cash flow is included in the Financial Analysis Section of this offering memorandum.

Below is an abbreviated schedule of Pro Forma cash flows from years one through five of our analysis.

Year	1	2	3	4	5
Year Ending	2006	2007	2008	2009	2010
PGI	$701,200	$752,930	$742,170	$781,609	$805,332
Gen Vac (5%)	-----	($37,647)	($24,144)	($32,957)	($35,130)
EGI	$701,200	$715,283	$718,026	$748,652	$770,202
Op. Expenses	$171,694	$177,235	$181,499	$187,477	$193,093
NOI	$529,506	$538,048	$536,527	$561,175	$577,109

Executive Summary

3235 - 3275 Intertech Drive, Brookfield, Wisconsin

Gateway Business Center
Summary of Offer Terms

Before touring the Property, all prospective purchasers must submit an offer, with the bid finalists receiving a tour of the assets. A representative of the Seller is required to accompany investors during any inspections.

PROPERTY INFORMATION SUMMARY	
Number of Assets:	Two (2)
Total Square Footage:	72,510
Property Type:	Industrial/Office ("Flex")
Current Occupancy:	87%*

*For the purposes of this analysis we are assuming the building will be 100% leased 7/1/2006.

THE LETTER OF INTENT (LOI) OR OFFER SHOULD ATTEMPT TO COVER THE FOLLOWING THINGS:

- *Purchaser* – Description of purchaser, entity, and constituent partners, detailed approval process, source(s) of funding, and whether funds are discretionary or non-discretionary.

- *Purchase Price* – Total price with any financing contingencies.

- *Earnest Money* – Minimum deposit of $50,000 cash

- *Inspection Period* – We encourage the Buyer to take no longer than thirty (30) days. The thirty (30) day period shall commence on the day the Letter of Intent is fully executed.

- *Closing* – Closing shall occur no later than fifteen (15) days after due diligence period.

3

Property Overview
3235 - 3275 Intertech Drive, Brookfield, Wisconsin

Gateway Business Center
Property Highlights

3235-3275 N Intertech Drive Brookfield, Wisconsin	
Square Footage:	72,510 SF
Site Size:	5.5 Acres
Land To Building:	3.30:1
Percent Office:	+/- 50%
Age:	1997
Parking:	200+
Construction:	Concrete Block
Clear Height:	18'
Loading:	Ten (10) exterior docks, Two (2) drive-in doors
Roof Structure:	Rubber Membrane
Sprinkler System:	Wet System
Lighting:	Metal Halide
Floor Thickness	Six inches (6") reinforced
Zoning:	Office, Light industrial
HVAC:	Gas Fired in WH, Rooftop HVAC in Office.
Rail Served:	No
Utilities:	Gas, Electric, and Water WE Energies

4

Property Overview

3235 – 3275 Intertech Drive, Brookfield, Wisconsin

Gateway Business Center
Maps

This investment consists of two (2) industrial buildings totaling 72,510 square feet. Building one equals 38,180 SF and Building two equals 34,330 SF and they are located at 3235-3275 Intertech Drive in

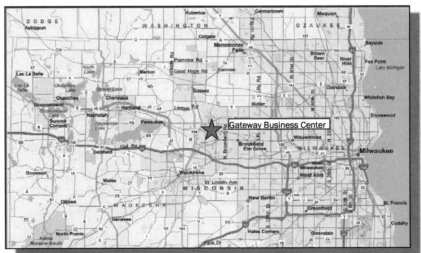

5

Property Photos

3235 - 3275 Intertech Drive, Brookfield, Wisconsin

Gateway Business Center
Exterior Photos

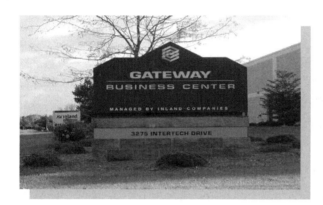

inland
COMPANIES

Property Photos

3235 - 3275 Intertech Drive, Brookfield, Wisconsin

Gateway Business Center
Interior Photos

Property Photos

3235 – 3275 Intertech Drive, Brookfield, Wisconsin

Gateway Business Center
Aerial Photo

Property Photos

3235 – 3275 Intertech Drive, Brookfield, Wisconsin

Gateway Business Center
Aerial Photo

Property Overview

3235 - 3275 Intertech Drive, Brookfield, Wisconsin

Gateway Business Center
Building Plans

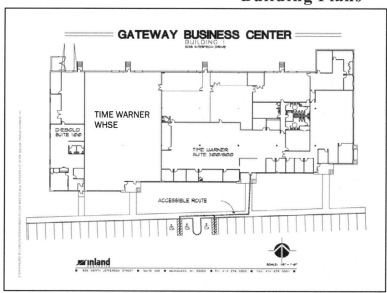

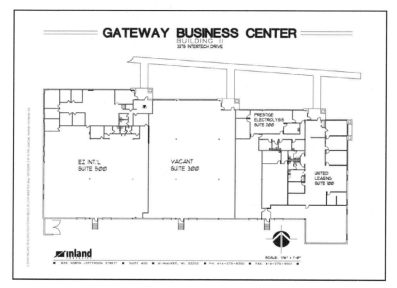

10

Financial Analysis

3235 – 3275 Intertech Drive, Brookfield, Wisconsin

Gateway Business Center
General Assumptions to Projections

Analysis Period

Ten-year analysis begins January 1, 2006

Occupancy

The asset is currently 87% occupied by five (5) tenants. For the purposes of this analysis, we are pro forma that the asset will be 100% occupied by 7/1/06.

Growth Rates

General Inflation:	3%
Expenses:	3%
Capital Exp:	3%

General Vacancy Rate

5%, Y1 excluded - natural 13% vacancy exists for first 6 months of Y1 in analysis.

New Flex Lease Assumptions

Subj. Units:	Diebold, EZ Int., Prestige, Vacancy
Rate:	$6.10/SF (+/- 30% Office)
Type:	NNN
Term:	Five (5) Years
Rent Growth:	2.5%
Ret. Factor:	75%
Downtime:	Six (6) Months
Abatements:	Two (2) Months
Commission	
New:	8%, 3%, etc...on the NNN Rent
Renewal:	4%, 1.5%, etc...on the NNN Rent

Tenant Improvements

New:	$5.00/SF
Renewal:	$2.00/SF

11

Financial Analysis

3235 - 3275 Intertech Drive, Brookfield, Wisconsin

Gateway Business Center
General Assumptions to Projections (continued)

New Office Lease Assumptions	Subj. Units:	Time Warner, United Leasing
	Rate:	$9.00/SF (+/- 80% Office)
	Type:	NNN
	Term:	Seven (7) Years
	Rent Growth:	2.5%
	Ret. Factor:	75%
	Downtime:	Six (6) Months
	Abatements:	Two (2) Months
	Commission	
	New:	7%, 2%, etc…on the Gross Rent
	Renewal:	3.5%, 1%, etc…on the Gross Rent
Tenant Improvements:		
	New:	$5.00/SF
	Renewal:	$2.00/SF
Assumable Debt	The property is being offered free and clear of any debt obligations.	

12

Financial Analysis

3235 – 3275 Intertech Drive, Brookfield, Wisconsin

Gateway Business Center
10 Year Pro Forma Cash Flow Analysis

Schedule Of Prospective Cash Flow
In Inflated Dollars for the Fiscal Year Beginning 1/1/2006

For the Years Ending	Year 1 Dec-2006	Year 2 Dec-2007	Year 3 Dec-2008	Year 4 Dec-2009	Year 5 Dec-2010	Year 6 Dec-2011	Year 7 Dec-2012	Year 8 Dec-2013	Year 9 Dec-2014	Year 10 Dec-2015
Potential Gross Revenue										
Base Rental Revenue	$629,433	$635,811	$642,974	$664,684	$681,068	$685,279	$699,763	$705,942	$680,407	$597,545
Absorption & Turnover Vacancy	(29,115)		(13,647)	(6,446)	(5,407)		(11,336)	(7,910)	(75,454)	(6,982)
Base Rent Abatements			(3,559)	(1,632)	(1,329)		(2,373)		(16,105)	(1,632)
Scheduled Base Rental Revenue	600,318	635,811	625,768	656,606	674,332	685,279	686,054	698,032	588,848	588,931
Expense Reimbursement Revenue										
CAM & UTILITIES	32,670	37,394	37,398	39,769	41,502	43,768	44,626	46,367	47,405	63,556
INSURANCE	5,193	5,888	5,889	6,237	6,491	6,827	6,952	7,207	7,231	9,347
REAL ESTATE TAXES	45,712	54,120	54,123	58,345	61,427	65,463	66,990	70,086	76,072	113,092
MANAGEMENT FEE	17,307	19,717	18,992	20,652	21,580	22,409	22,503	23,033	20,779	30,496
Total Reimbursement Revenue	100,882	117,119	116,402	125,003	131,000	138,467	141,071	146,693	151,487	216,491
Total Potential Gross Revenue	701,200	752,930	742,170	781,609	805,332	823,746	827,125	844,725	740,335	805,422
General Vacancy		(37,647)	(24,144)	(32,957)	(35,130)	(41,187)	(30,587)	(34,722)		(33,638)
Effective Gross Revenue	701,200	715,283	718,026	748,652	770,202	782,559	796,538	810,003	740,335	771,784
Operating Expenses										
CAM & UTILITIES	48,658	50,786	52,005	53,735	55,375	57,160	58,704	60,465	61,235	64,179
INSURANCE	7,251	7,469	7,693	7,923	8,161	8,406	8,658	8,918	9,185	9,461
REAL ESTATE TAXES	87,737	90,369	93,080	95,873	98,749	101,711	104,763	107,906	111,143	114,477
MANAGEMENT FEE	28,048	28,611	28,721	29,946	30,808	31,302	31,862	32,400	29,613	30,871
Total Operating Expenses	171,694	177,235	181,499	187,477	193,093	198,579	203,987	209,689	211,176	218,988
Net Operating Income	529,506	538,048	536,527	561,175	577,109	583,980	592,551	600,314	529,159	552,796
Leasing & Capital Costs										
Tenant Improvements	95,460		36,915	17,435	14,625		20,381		154,475	19,827
Leasing Commissions	12,094		10,909	5,002	4,074		7,050		48,176	5,002
Structural Reserve	7,251	7,469	7,693	7,923	8,161	8,406	8,658	8,918	9,185	9,461
Total Leasing & Capital Costs	114,805	7,469	55,517	30,360	26,860	8,406	36,089	8,918	211,836	34,290
Cash Flow Before Debt Service & INCOME TAX	$414,701	$530,579	$481,010	$530,815	$550,249	$575,574	$556,462	$591,396	$317,323	$518,506

13

Financial Analysis

3235 - 3275 Intertech Drive, Brookfield, Wisconsin

Gateway Business Center
Rent Roll

DESCRIPTION	AREA	RENT	RENT ADJUSTMENTS		
Tenant Name Lease Dates Lease Term	Sq. Ft. Bldg Share	Current Base Rent	Date	Rate/SF	Reimburse.
Time Warner 9/99 – 8/14 15 Years	33,455 46.14%	$11.74/SF	9/09	$12.24	Mod. Gross (Base Year 99)
Diebold, Inc. 7/05 – 9/10 5 yrs 3 mos.	4,725 6.52%	$6.70/SF	10/06 10/07 10/08 10/09	$6.85 $7.00 $7.15 $7.30	Net
EZ International 9/03 – 9/08 5 yrs 1 mo.	12,653 17.45%	$5.53/SF	-	-	Net
Prestige Electrolysis 10/98 - 9/09 11 years	5,802 8.00%	$6.80/SF	-	-	Net
United Leasing Associates 10/05 - 2/12 6 years, 5 months	6,329 8.73%	$6.31/SF	2/07 2/08 2/09 2/10 2/11	$6.56 $6.83 $7.10 $7.38 $7.68	Net
Vacancy Suite 300 Projected - 7/06 - 6/11 5 years	9,546 13.16%	$5.75/SF Pro Forma		2.5% Annual Increase	Net

14

Tenancy

3235 – 3275 Intertech Drive, Brookfield, Wisconsin

Gateway Business Center
Lease Abstracts

Tenant:	Time Warner Telecom
Original Commencement Date:	9/1/1999
Rentable Area:	33,455 SF
Pro Rata Share:	46.14%
Original Lease Term:	15 years
Termination Date:	8/31/2014
Current Rent:	$11.74/SF
Lease Type:	Base Year 1999, Modified Gross
Expenses:	Base year amounts – Operating Expenses = $29,042.66
	Taxes = $78,565.12, Insurance = $3,425.34,
	Management Fees = $19,275.17
Right to Sublease:	Shall not be unreasonably withheld by landlord.
	60 day written notice required.
Insurance & Damage:	Tenant must maintain in full force and effect. Limit of not less than $3,000,000 for each occurrence and annual aggregate.
Option to Renew: rent	Two (2) Five (5) year renewals at the Landlord's fair cur- market rent.
Holdover:	Subject to State of Wisconsin Law

15

Tenancy

3235 - 3275 Intertech Drive, Brookfield, Wisconsin

Gateway Business Center
Lease Abstracts

Tenant:	**Diebold, Inc.**
Original Commencement Date:	7/1/2005
Rentable Area:	4,725 SF
Pro Rata Share:	6.52%
Original Lease Term:	5 years 3 months
Termination Date:	10/1/2009
Current Rent:	$6.70/SF
Lease Type:	NNN
Expenses:	Tenant pays pro rata share of all RE taxes, CAM, and Insurance
Right to Sublease:	Shall not be unreasonably withheld by landlord. 14 day written notice required.
Insurance & Damage:	Tenant must maintain in full force and effect. Limit of not less than $2,000,000 for each occurrence and $4,000,000 for annual aggregate.
Option to Renew:	None
Holdover:	125%
Security Deposit:	None

Tenancy

3235 – 3275 Intertech Drive, Brookfield, Wisconsin

Gateway Business Center
Lease Abstracts

Tenant:	**EZ International, Inc.**
Original Commencement Date:	9/1/2003
Rentable Area:	12,653 SF
Pro Rata Share:	17.45%
Original Lease Term:	5 years 1 month
Termination Date:	9/30/2008
Current Rent:	$5.53/SF
Lease Type:	NNN
Expenses:	Tenant pays pro rata share of all RE taxes, CAM, and Insurance
Right to Sublease:	Shall not be unreasonably withheld by landlord. 60 day written notice required.
Insurance & Damage:	Tenant must maintain in full force and effect. Limit of not less than $3,000,000 for each occurrence and anual aggregate.
Option to Renew:	None
Holdover:	200%
Security Deposit:	$6,595.00

Tenancy

3235 – 3275 Intertech Drive, Brookfield, Wisconsin

Gateway Business Center
Lease Abstracts

Tenant:	**Prestige Electrolysis Supply, Inc.**
Original Commencement Date:	10/1/1998
Rentable Area:	5,802 SF
Pro Rata Share:	8.00%
Original Lease Term:	5 Years
Renewal Term:	3 Years
Termination Date:	9/30/2009
Current Rent:	$5.68/SF
Lease Type:	NNN
Expenses:	Tenant pays pro rata share of all RE taxes, CAM, and Insurance
Right to Sublease:	Shall not be unreasonably withheld by landlord. 60 day written notice required.
Insurance & Damage:	Tenant must maintain in full force and effect. Limit of not less than $2,000,000 for each occurrence and annual aggregate.
Option to Renew:	None
Holdover:	Subject to State of Wisconsin Law
Security Deposit:	$3,117.10

Tenancy

3235 – 3275 Intertech Drive, Brookfield, Wisconsin

Gateway Business Center
Lease Abstracts

Tenant:	**United Leasing Associates, Inc.**
Original Commencement Date:	10/1/2005
Rentable Area:	6,329 SF
Pro Rata Share:	8.73%
Original Lease Term:	6 Years 5 months
Termination Date:	2/29/2012
Current Rent:	$6.31/SF (2/1/2006)
Lease Type:	NNN
Expenses:	Tenant pays pro rata share of all RE taxes, CAM, and Insurance
Right to Sublease:	Shall not be unreasonably withheld by landlord. 60 day written notice required.
Insurance & Damage:	Tenant must maintain in full force and effect. Limit of not less than $2,000,000 for each occurrence and annual aggregate.
Option to Renew:	None
Holdover:	Subject to State of Wisconsin Law
Security Deposit:	$3,117.10

19

Tenant Information

3235 – 3275 Intertech Drive, Brookfield, Wisconsin

Gateway Business Center
Description of Tenants

- **Time Warner Telecom:** www.twteleccom.com

Time Warner Telecom, headquartered in Littleton, CO, is a leading provider of managed networking solutions to a wide array of businesses and organizations in 22 states and 44 U.S. metropolitan areas. As one of the country's premier competitive service providers, Time Warner Telecom integrates data, dedicated Internet access, and local and long distance voice services for long distance carriers, wireless communications companies, incumbent local exchange carriers, and enterprise organizations in healthcare, finance, higher education, manufacturing, and hospitality industries, as well as for military, state and local government. Time Warner began their business in 1993 as a joint venture with Time Warner Cable (now a unit of Time Warner Inc.). Since 1997, they have focused on delivering services to business customers, including carriers and governmental entities, and on expanding from dedicated services into switched services, Internet and data. In July 1998, they became a separate entity apart from Time Warner Cable and were reorganized into Time Warner Telecom LLC. In May 1999, they issued an IPO and became Time Warner Telecom Inc. According to North American IT Managers polled by Network Magazine, September 2003, Time Warner Telecom leads as the best ISP in the United States.

- Diebold, Inc.: www.diebold.com (NYSE: DBD)

Diebold provides a full range of self-service, software, security/facility, and card-based products, as well as consulting and support services. Founded by Charles Diebold in 1859, for over the last 140 years Diebold has been synonymous with security. Diebold is a global leader in providing physical and electronic security systems as well as facility transaction products that integrate security, software and assisted-service transactions, providing total systems solutions to financial, retail, commercial and government markets.

- EZ International: www.ez-international.com

EZ-International is a leading supplier of small electric vehicles for commercial applications. EZ's product lines include electric shopping scooters used in grocery stores and other retail environments, motorized utility carts used for a wide variety of commercial and industrial functions, and electric transport chairs employed in health care institutions, airports and similar applications.

20

Tenant Information

3235 - 3275 Intertech Drive, Brookfield, Wisconsin

Gateway Business Center
Description of Tenants

- **Prestige Electrolysis**: www.prestigelec.com

Founded in 1985, Prestige has been successful in the electrolysis supply business for over 20 years. Prestige has licensed electrologists, laser technicians, and a dermatologist consultant on staff. Their products include ultrasonic cleaners, sterilizers, probes, needles, lotions, aromatherapy products, and more.

- **United Leasing Associates:** www.ula.net

Founded in 1987, the principals of United Leasing have over 30 years of combined equipment leasing experience. They are proud members of the Equipment Leasing Association (ELA), the United Association of Equipment Leasing (UAEL), and the Wisconsin Association of Equipment Lessors. ULA leases a variety of office products including copiers, office furniture, vehicles, computers, and fax machines.

Market Analysis

3235 - 3275 Intertech Drive, Brookfield, Wisconsin

Gateway Business Center
Milwaukee Industrial Market Overview

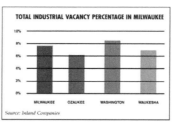

MILWAUKEE INDUSTRIAL MARKET

The metropolitan Milwaukee industrial market is slowly seeing a transformation into institutional quality industrial space, similar to other major Midwest markets such as Chicago, Minneapolis and Indianapolis. In a market that is historically 75 percent owner-occupied, the shift from heavy industrial to traditional distribution and office/service space is evident throughout. Developers building distribution space on speculation or build-to-suit within the metropolitan area are focusing on floor plates from 50,000 to 150,000 square feet with a typical clear height of 24 feet. Office/service space (flex or office/showroom) developments are offering 30,000 to 70,000-square-foot buildings with clear heights of 18 feet.

A majority of the successful post 9/11 recession industrial developments have been infill locations such as the Stadium Business Center development in West Milwaukee, near Miller Park. Brownfield redevelopment opportunities around the Interstate 94 stadium interchange and the highly anticipated 120-acre Menomonee Valley Industrial Park are revitalizing outdated industrial zones due to ease of access to interstate transportation routes and renewed interest in urban living. Major freeway infrastructure construction between the Menomonee River Valley and downtown in the next 12 to 18 months will create synergies between the new industrial developments and Milwaukee's central business district (CBD). Significant infill developments are underway and are in some cases progressing to second and third phases through the work of developers such as Real Estate Recycling and Inland Companies.

Additionally, development in the western suburbs is highlighted best by the Pabst Farms' 1,600-acre mixed-use project in Oconomowoc. Roundy's, Inc. has completed a 1.1 million-square-foot distribution facility within the industrial portion of Pabst Farms. Westerly expansion continues to narrow the gap between Milwaukee and Madison along the I-94 corridor. Briohn Development just added 4 new buildings to the Pewaukee submarket as an expansion of the Pewaukee Woods Industrial Park.

Once the economy shows tangible indicators of a recovery, expect suburban industrial parks such as Franklin Business Park, New Berlin Business Parks and Waukesha County's industrial parks to rekindle the activity levels of the late 1990s and early 2000s. A significant amount of relatively new, high-quality space within these adolescent industrial parks will provide excellent space opportunities for new emerging companies and those retooling and growing.

After a lackluster few years, industrial development momentum is surging near Milwaukee's General Mitchell International Airport. Multiple industrial land parcels south of the airport market in Oak Creek are creating speculative and build-to-suit opportunities for a number of developers controlling land, including Opus, MIE Investments and Capstone Quadrangle. Opus has kicked off its 92-acre Oakwood Crossings Development in Oak Creek. The first building under construction in this development is a 140,000-square-foot, 26-foot clear distribution building and is just one of several projects that have reinforced developer confidence in the airport market. MIE Investments (48,180 square feet) and Capstone Quadrangle (102,000 square feet) each have completed speculative buildings

located immediately off of I-94 and Ryan Road (Highway 100) in the new Creekside Corporate Park. The Dickman Company just completed a 50,000-square-foot building in the new Oak Commerce and Business Center for Bax Global, a logistics company. Although ample vacancy remains in the airport and south industrial markets, these developers are hoping to be the early birds by having new product ready to supply when the volume of activity builds on the growing momentum during the next 12 months.

Given the significant manufacturing base within Milwaukee, the industrial market has been impacted by high vacancy rates. However, vacancy rates stabilized in the last 6 months of 2004. The 2004 year-end Milwaukee industrial market vacancy rate of 7.1 percent is below the national average of 9.5 percent.

In review of first quarter of 2005 to date, and making projections for the next 6 to 8 months, many opportunities will be available within the industrial market benefiting building owners and developers. One factor is certain, current development in the suburban and infill markets and stable vacancy rates are signs that the health of Milwaukee's industrial market is returning.

— The Inland Industrial Team is a part of Milwaukee-basaed Inland Companies.

Market Analysis

3235 - 3275 Intertech Drive, Brookfield, Wisconsin

Gateway Business Center
Waukesha Submarket Size and Vacancy

	Waukesha Submarket Vacancy and Rates											

Summary/Submarket	# Bldgs	Total Bldg SF	Direct Avl SF	Sublease Avl SF	Total Avl SF	Total Avl %	Direct Vac SF	Direct Vac %	Sublease Vac SF	Total Vac SF	Total Vac %	Direct Asking Rate
SE-Wksha	11	338,079	120,388		120,388	35.6%	120,388	35.6%		120,388	35.6%	$4.31
SE-Wksha /Brookfield	172	5,185,387	546,408		546,408	10.5%	500,655	9.7%		500,655	9.7%	$4.93
SE-Wksha /New Berlin/Muskego	384	13,567,708	1,326,522	24,536	1,351,058	10.0%	1,271,404	9.4%	16,536	1,287,940	9.5%	$4.06
SE-Wksha /North	663	22,939,058	1,540,893		1,540,893	6.7%	1,190,904	5.2%		1,190,904	5.2%	$4.51
SE-Wksha /South	100	2,516,852	13,808		13,808	0.5%	7,800	0.3%		7,800	0.3%	$4.70
SE-Wksha /Waukesha/Pewaukee	624	22,751,507	1,931,606	130,646	2,062,252	9.1%	1,584,743	7.0%	0	1,584,743	7.0%	$3.85
SE-Wksha /West	81	3,184,059	102,401		102,401	3.2%	44,977	1.4%		44,977	1.4%	$3.95
Ind TOTAL:	**2035**	**70,482,650**	**5,582,026**	**155,182**	**5,737,208**	**8.1%**	**4,720,871**	**6.7%**	**16,536**	**4,737,407**	**6.7%**	**$4.14**

Property Availability Summary   Page   1   Of   1   October 13, 2005

Market Analysis

3235 – 3275 Intertech Drive, Brookfield, Wisconsin

Gateway Business Center
Demographic (3 Mile Radius)

Trade Area: 3235 INTERTECH DR, BROOKFIELD, WI 53045-5140

DESCRIPTION	Radius – 3 miles
2005 Est. Average Household Income	$111,094
2005 Est. Median Household Income	$81,404
2005 Est. Per Capita Income	$43,454
POPULATION	Radius – 3 miles
2010 Projection	29,049
2005 Estimate	27,700
2000 Census	26,558
1990 Census	21,337
Growth 2005 - 2010	4.87%
Growth 2000 - 2005	4.30%
Growth 1990 - 2000	24.47%

25

Market Analysis

3235 - 3275 Intertech Drive, Brookfield, Wisconsin

Gateway Business Center
Demographic (3 Mile Radius)
Executive Summary Report

The population in this area is estimated to change from 26,558 to 27,700, resulting in a growth of 4.3% between 2000 and the current year. Over the next five years, the population is projected to grow by 4.9%. The population in the United States is estimated to change from 281,421,906 to 295,140,073, resulting in a growth of 4.9% between 2000 and the current year. Over the next five years, the population is projected to grow by 4.9%.

The current year median age for this population is 40.4, while the average age is 39.4. Five years from now, the median age is projected to be 42.4. The current year median age for the United States is 36.2, while the average age is 37.0. Five years from now, the median age is projected to be 37.4.

The number of households in this area is estimated to change from 10,068 to 10,776, resulting in an increase of 7.0% between 2000 and the current year. Over the next five years, the number of households is projected to increase by 6.9%. The number of households in the United States is estimated to change from 105,480,101 to 111,006,738, resulting in an increase of 5.2% between 2000 and the current year. Over the next five years, the number is projected to increase by 5.1%.

The average household income is estimated to be $111,094 for the current year, while the average household income for the United States is estimated to be $64,816 for the same time frame. The average household income in this area is projected to increase 9.5% over the next five years, from $111,094 to $121,634. The United States is projected to have a 13.0% increase in average household income.

Market Analysis

3235 - 3275 Intertech Drive, Brookfield, Wisconsin

Gateway Business Center
Demographic (3 Mile Radius)
Executive Summary Report (Continued)

The current year estimated per capita income for this area is $43,454, compared to an estimate of $24,704 for the United States as a whole.

For this area, 53.6% of the population is estimated to be employed and age 16 and over for the current year. The employment status of this labor force is as follows:

- 13.4% have occupation type blue collar, 78.0% are white collar, and 8.6% are Service & farm workers.

For the United States, 46.8% of the population is estimated to be employed and age 16 and over for the current year. The employment status of this labor force is as follows:

- 23.9% have occupation type blue collar, 60.0% are white collar, and 16.0% are Service & farm workers.

For the civilian employed population age 16 and over in this area, it is estimated that they are employed in the following occupational categories:

- 24.2% are in "Management, Business, and Financial Operations", 25.5% are in "Professional and Related Occupations", 8.5% are in "Service", and 28.4% are in "Sales and Office". 0.0% are in "Farming, Fishing, and Forestry", 4.6% are in "Construction, Extraction, and Maintenance", and 8.8% are in "Production, Transportation, and Material Moving".

27

Market Analysis

3235 – 3275 Intertech Drive, Brookfield, Wisconsin

Gateway Business Center
Demographic (3 Mile Radius)
Executive Summary Report (Continued)

For the civilian employed population age 16 and over in the United States, it is estimated that they are employed in the following occupational categories:

- 13.6% are in "Management, Business, and Financial Operations", 20.3% are in "Professional and Related Occupations", 14.7% are in "Service", and 26.7% are in "Sales and Office". 0.7% are in "Farming, Fishing, and Forestry", 9.5% are in "Construction, Extraction, and Maintenance", and 14.5% are in "Production, Transportation, and Material Moving".

Currently, it is estimated that 15.5% of the population age 25 and over in this area had earned a Master's, Professional, or Doctorate Degree and 32.4% had earned a Bachelor's Degree. In comparison, for the United States, it is estimated that for the population over age 25, 8.9% had earned a Master's, Professional, or Doctorate Degree, while 15.7% had earned a Bachelor's Degree.

Most of the dwellings in this area (74.6%) are estimated to be Owner-Occupied for the current year. For the entire country the majority of the housing units are Owner-Occupied (66.7%). The majority of dwellings in this area are estimated to be structures of 1 Unit Detached (64.1%) for the current year. In the United States, the majority of dwellings are estimated to be structures of 1 Unit Detached (60.6%) for the same year.

The majority of housing units in this area (18.9%) are estimated to have been Housing Unit Built 1970 to 1979 for the current year. Most of the housing units in the United States (17.1%) are estimated to have been Housing Unit Built 1970 to 1979 for the current year.

28

The Real Estate Game:
Level One and Level Two

The real estate game is played on two levels. Level one of the game is about valuing the productive capacity of the property itself. At level one, we try to determine how well the space over time with associated services (the package being sold to the user of the real estate) serves the particular marketplace. How well it serves is determined by the rent it generates, and we have the tools (discussed in Chapter 8) to convert that expected rent to an estimate of value. This is valuation at level one of the game, and most of this textbook is written about level one.

At level two, we look at the many individual players of the game and evaluate the revenue—not only to the project but also to the individual players. Why is this distinction between level one and level two important? Simply put, when conflicting goals drive different players, the system can go haywire. For example, the United States is thought to have the most efficient capital markets in the world. How then could we have produced the multihundred billion dollar S&L crisis? At level one of the game, a vast number of projects were built that made no economic sense; that is, no rational person would have expected the marketplace to pay enough rent for the space over time with associated services to justify the cost of some of these projects. How could these projects have been built when at level one many made no economic sense? If careful analysis had indicated that these properties would cost more than they were worth, then why did the S&Ls finance them?

The answer lies in the distinction between level one and level two. As noted, public policy with regard to the S&L indus-

try changed dramatically in the 1980s. The S&Ls were in trouble at that time because they were lending long and borrowing short. They were borrowing from savers and lending on fixed-rate mortgages. When interest rates went up, their costs adjusted upward (they were flexible in the short term), but their revenues did not because they lent long term with no short-term flexibility. The political fix to this problem was to allow S&Ls to enjoy the benefits of diversification across more types of investments and across more geographic regions. The logic behind this "solution" was that diversification reduced risk and would improve the S&Ls' position. This logic was fallacious, and the real reason behind the new initiative was Congress's refusal to spend the money to fix the S&L program that existed at the beginning of the 1980s. Rather than appropriate the needed funds, Congress gave S&L entrepreneurs something like a blank check. Owners of S&Ls could speculate with taxpayers' money, generating funds with high-yielding certificates of deposit, which were federally insured, and then making aggressive investments. This action was justified by citing benefits from new opportunities for diversification, but the resulting lending policy actually increased risk.

Look at level two of the game and think about the S&L entrepreneurs' position. Would they make low-risk investments or high-risk investments? Because many S&Ls were already slightly under water at the time, a low-risk investment would have been sure death. With a high-risk investment, they had at least a possibility that things would go well. So at level two, it became quite clear what the entrepreneurs would want to do with the S&Ls—buy junk bonds and invest in speculative real estate. In essence, go for it. They had very little to lose because the taxpayers were footing the bill. This is an over-simplified explanation, but it makes the point. If you want to understand the S&L crisis, you can't do it exclusively at level one (the real estate) but must also look at level two (the players and the rules).

The structure of the game looks very similar for both level one and level two. We begin by estimating revenues that can be generated from the marketplace, and we subtract the operating expenses necessary to provide the services that were promised to the marketplace. The result is a projection of net operating income, which can be translated into cash flow and valued using the discounted cash flow method. The difference is that, at level one, we value the rents to the building, and, at level two, we value the salaries, fees, bonuses, stock options, and other compensations that the individual players receive. For the S&Ls, the associations' position looked very risky as they moved into more speculative investments. The decision makers and owners had less to lose (taxpayers had provided deposit insurance) and a lot to gain (bonuses, stock options, dividends, and more), however, if the speculations worked out well. In fact, many of the more speculative real estate loans involved large "origination" fees that translated into immediate dividends for the S&L owners. Thus, many of these people won even if the investment did not work out. Hence, the decisions that lost so much money for the associations (level one) were really very rational for the owners (level two).

Glossary

Absorption schedule. The estimated schedule or rate at which properties for sale or lease can be marketed in a given locality; usually used when preparing a forecast of the sales or leasing rate to substantiate a development plan and to obtain financing.

Affordable housing. According to the U.S. Department of Housing and Urban Development, housing that does not exceed 30 percent of a household's gross income. Sometimes used synonymously with subsidized housing, for which local, state, and federal programs exist to serve low- to moderate-income families by offering lower cash downpayments, eased loan-qualifying rules, below-market interest rates, or rent assistance. Subsidies depend on a variety of factors, including household size and disability status.

Agglomeration. Concentration of commercial activity within a given area, tending to have a synergistic effect by increasing diversity, specialization, and overall business activity. In the context of urban sprawl, an overlapping of population and government jurisdictions.

AHERA (Asbestos Hazard Emergency Response Act). Legislation passed in 1986 that requires all public schools to be inspected for asbestos by certified inspectors and mandates the preparation of a management plan if asbestos is identified.

Amenity. Nonmonetary tangible or intangible benefit derived from real property (often offered to a lessee), typically, swimming pools, parks, valets, and the like.

Americans with Disabilities Act of 1990 (ADA). A federal law that prohibits discrimination against people with disabilities in employment, public services and transportation, public accommodations and commercial facilities, and telecommunications.

Amortization. The periodic writing off of an asset over a specified term. Also the periodic repayment of debt over a specified time.

Anchor tenant. The major chain(s) or department store(s) in a shopping center, positioned to produce traffic for the smaller stores in the facility.

Appraisal. An opinion or estimate of value substantiated by various analyses.

Architect. Primarily a designer of buildings and supervisor of construction. All states require architects to be licensed under laws governing health, safety, and welfare.

Asset manager. A person who balances risk and reward in managing investment portfolios, including, but not limited to, real property and improvements. Asset managers either oversee property management or are responsible for it themselves.

Attached housing. Two or more dwelling units constructed with party walls (for example, townhouses, cluster houses, stacked flats).

Audit. In real estate development, the assessment of the credibility and reliability of real estate market data.

Axial theory. A theory of land use development that suggests that land uses tend to develop in relation to time-cost functions of transportation axes that radiate from the central business district.

Binding constraint. Legally enforceable limit on the allowable development on a given site.

Bonding. A guarantee of completion or performance, typically issued by an insurance company that will back up the bonded party in any lawsuit. In real estate, contractors, for example, are often bonded as assurance that they will complete the work.

Bottom-up approach. An approach to developing an analysis based on the most disaggregated data available.

Break-even ratio. In finance, the point at which total income is equal to total expenses.

Broker. A person who, for a commission, acts as the agent of another in the process of buying, selling, leasing, or managing property rights.

Brokerage. The business of a broker that includes all the functions necessary to market a seller's property and represent the seller's (principal's) best interests.

Brownfield. A site previously used for industrial or certain commercial uses and possibly contaminated from those uses, but developable upon cleanup.

Building efficiency ratio. The ratio of net leasable area to gross leasable area.

Build to suit. Construction of land improvements according to a tenant's or purchaser's specifications.

Building Owners and Managers Association International (BOMA). A trade association of owners and managers of apartment and office buildings.

Buildout. Construction of specific interior finishes to a tenant's specifications.

Business improvement district (BID). A public/private partnership where the business owners of a district, through legislative approval, contribute funds through a special tax to the maintenance, development, and marketing of their commercial area.

Capital. Money or property invested in an asset for the creation of wealth; alternatively, the surplus of production over consumption.

Capital improvement projects. Investments in infrastructure such as roads, bridges, and ports.

Capital market. Financial marketplace in which savings (from individuals, companies, or pension funds) are aggregated by financial intermediaries and allocated to real investors.

Capitalization. The process of estimating value by discounting stabilized net operating income at an appropriate rate.

Capitalization rate (cap rate). The rate, expressed as a percentage, at which a future flow of income is converted into a present value figure.

Capture rate. Forecasted rate of absorption in a targeted market segment for a proposed project, based on an analysis of supply and demand.

Central business district (CBD). The center of commercial activity in a town or city; usually the largest and oldest concentration of such activity.

CERCLA (Comprehensive Environmental Response, Compensation, and Liability Act of 1980). Legislation adopted to provide partial funding for the cleanup of environmentally contaminated sites by requiring the party responsible for the contamination to undertake cleanup efforts or provide compensation for cleanup costs; also known as the Superfund Law.

Codevelopment. Term that refers to the combined development of real estate by the private sector and government, where the public sector assumes risks or costs normally borne by private developers.

Commercial paper. Short-term negotiable financial instruments, usually unsecured, such as promissory notes, bank checks, bills, and acceptances.

Commercial real estate. Improved real estate held for the production of income through leases for commercial or business use (for example, office buildings, retail shops, and shopping centers).

Commitment letter. A written agreement by a lender to loan a specific amount of money at a specified interest rate within a particular period of time.

Community builder. One who engages in the platting and improvement of subdivisions.

Community Development Block Grants (CDBGs). Federal grants received by cities based on a formula that considers population, extent of poverty, and housing overpopulation and that may be used for a variety of community development activities.

Community development corporations (CDCs). Entrepreneurial institutions combining public and private resources to aid in the development of socioeconomically disadvantaged areas.

Community Reinvestment Act (CRA). Legislation enacted in 1978 that directs federal agencies with supervisory authority over depository lenders to consider a lender's record in serving local credit needs when making decisions about the expansion plans of depository institutions.

Comparable property. Another property to which a subject property can be compared to reach an estimate of market value.

Compound interest. Interest that is earned and immediately added to principal, thereafter itself earning interest.

Comprehensive planning. Long-range planning by a local or regional government encompassing the entire area of a community and integrating all elements related to its physical development, such as housing, recreation, open space, and economic development.

Concentric zone theory. Urban development theory that holds that because mobility is paramount to community growth, land uses tend to be arranged in a series of concentric, circular zones around a city's central business district.

Concession. Discount given to prospective tenants to induce them to sign a lease, typically in the form of some free rent, cash for improvements furnished by the tenant, and so on.

Condominium. A form of joint ownership and control of property in which specified volumes of air space (for example, apartments) are owned individually while the common elements of the building (for example, outside walls) are jointly owned.

Consensus forecasts. Forecasts in reference areas either in the same locale or in other parts of the country that support the findings of a particular forecast.

Construction lender. Entity or individual providing interim financing during the construction phase(s) of the real estate development process.

Construction loan. A loan made usually by a commercial bank to a builder to be used for the construction of improvements on real estate and usually running six months to two years.

Contingent interest. A form of equity participation by lenders enabling them to receive an additional return if the income property securing the loan exceeds its projected profit or cash flow goals.

Convenience goods. Items typically purchased at the most convenient locations. They are usually not very expensive or long-lasting, and their purchase involves little deliberation. Convenience goods are distinguished from shoppers goods when performing retail market studies.

Convertible loan. A loan in which the lender, in addition to receiving a stated interest rate, reserves the right to convert its debt on a project to equity and thereby participate in the profits.

Covenant. A restriction on real property that is binding, regardless of changes in ownership, because it is attached to the title. Used generally in covenants, conditions, and restrictions.

Covenants, conditions, and restrictions (CC&Rs). The limitations or restrictions placed on real estate (such as size of a building, character of landscaping, or color of house paint), usually decided by a homeowners' association.

Critical path method (CPM). A network analysis method that graphically displays the activities involved in completing a project and shows the relationship between the activities. This display can graphically show how a delay in one activity will affect other activities.

Debt service. Periodic payments on a loan, with a portion of the payment for interest and the balance for repayment (amortization) of principal.

Debt (service) coverage ratio. The ratio of the annual net operating income of a property to the annual debt service of the mortgage on the property.

Deed restrictions. Private form of land use regulation using covenants or conditions placed on the title to a property, e.g., minimum lot sizes.

Delphi method. A project analysis tool in which a group of diverse experts is presented with a set of questions on a particular topic. The responses are then compared among the group and more refined questions developed, the ultimate goal of which is the development of a single, coherent response.

Demand deposits. Shorter-term deposits, such as checking accounts, that banks typically put into relatively short-term investments.

Demographics. Information on population characteristics by location, including such aspects as age, employment, earnings, and expenditures.

Density. The level of concentration (high or low) of buildings, including their total volume, in a given area. Often expressed as a ratio, for example, dwelling units per acre or floor/area ratio.

Department of Housing and Urban Development (HUD). A cabinet-level federal department responsible for carrying out national housing programs, including Federal Housing Administration subsidy programs, home mortgage insurance, urban renewal, and urban planning assistance.

Detached housing. A freestanding dwelling unit, normally single-family, situated on its own lot.

Developer. One who prepares raw land for improvement by installing roads, utilities, and so on; also a builder (one who actually constructs improvements on real estate).

Development fee. Compensation paid to a developer in return for managing a development project on behalf of a client such as a corporation or public sector agency.

Development process. The process of preparing raw land so that it becomes suitable for the erection of buildings; generally involves clearing and grading land and installing roads and utility services.

Development team. The range of participants engaged by a developer, both public and private, to assist in the planning, design, construction, marketing, and management of a development project.

Discounted cash flow. Present value of monies to be received in the future; determined by multiplying projected cash flows by the discount factor.

Downzoning. A change in the zoning classification of property from a higher use to a lower use (e.g., from commercial to residential).

Draw. The lender's release of construction loan funds in accordance with set procedures for providing portions of the total amount as each stage of construction is satisfactorily completed.

Due diligence. A forthright effort to investigate all reasonable considerations in a timely manner, as in the case of earlier waste disposal on a parcel of land.

Econometrics. The application of statistical methods to the study of economic data and problems.

Ecosystem management. Management of the interrelationships among the biological members of a community and their nonliving environment.

Effective rent. Rental income after deductions for financial concessions such as no-rent periods during a lease term.

Eminent domain. The power of a public authority to condemn and take property for public use on payment of just compensation.

Enabling legislation. Legislation typically delegated to local government that specifies the police power the state is giving to the local government. Cities, counties, and other local governments undertake planning, zoning, and additional forms of development regulation according to state enabling statutes.

Enterprise concept. The idea that encouraging private enterprise will facilitate economic revitalization or other socioeconomic goals. Encourages owners to look at real estate as another type of private enterprise.

Entrepreneur. A venture capitalist; one who accepts personal financial risk in business ventures.

Environmental scanning. The surveying of a variety of indicators in order to gauge the overall business, economic, social, political, or financial conditions that could affect a project's development.

Equity. That portion of an ownership interest in real property or other securities that is owned outright, that is, above amounts financed.

Equity kicker. A provision in the loan terms that guarantees the lender a percentage of the property's appreciation over some specified time or a percentage of income from the property or both.

Escalation clause. A provision in a lease that permits a landlord to pass through increases in real estate taxes and operating expenses to tenants, with each tenant paying its prorated share. Also a mortgage clause that allows the lender to increase the interest rate based on the terms of the note.

Estoppel letter. A written statement made by a tenant, lender, or other party establishing certain facts and conditions with regard to a piece of real estate.

Eurodollars. U.S. dollars deposited in European foreign banks and used as a medium of international credit.

Exactions. Fee or payment-in-kind required of a developer by a local jurisdiction for approval of development plans, in accordance with state and local legislation regarding the provision of public facilities and amenities.

Exclusionary zoning. Zoning practices such as large lot requirements and minimum housing sizes that serve to exclude from a community, intentionally or not, racial minorities and low-income persons.

Exurbs (exurban area). Communities located beyond older suburbs that serve as commuter towns to urban areas as a result of the availability of highways and the need or desire for housing at a greater distance from the urban area.

Fast-tracking. A method of project management in which construction of a project actually begins before all details are finalized.

Feasibility study. A combination of a market study and an economic study that provides the investor with knowledge of both the environment where the project exists and the expected returns from investment in it.

Federal Home Loan Mortgage Corporation (Freddie Mac). Subsidiary of the Federal Home Loan Bank System (FHLBS) established in 1970 to act as a secondary mortgage market for savings and loan associations that are members of the FHLBS.

Federal Housing Administration (FHA). Federal agency created by the 1934 National Housing Act that insures residential mortgages originated by private lenders on properties and borrowers meeting certain minimum standards and requirements.

Federal National Mortgage Association (Fannie Mae). A quasi-private corporation chartered by the federal government to function as a secondary market for residential mortgages.

Fee simple absolute. The most extensive interest in land recognized by law. Absolute ownership but subject to the limitations of police power, taxation, eminent domain, escheat, and private restrictions of record.

Fee simple determinable. Fee simple ownership that terminates on the happening (or failure to happen) of a stated condition. Also referred to as a "defeasible fee."

Festival marketplace. A specialty retail center incorporating aspects of old marketplaces, including significant public spaces and a variety of activities.

Financial Institutions Reform, Recovery, and Enforcement Act of 1989 (FIRREA). A comprehensive legislative act designed to overhaul the regulatory structure of the thrift industry.

FIRE (fire/insurance/real estate). An employment classification used by the Department of Labor when analyzing the service industry.

Floodplain. Land adjacent to rivers and streams subject to overflow and flooding.

Floor amount. Initial portion of a floor-to-ceiling mortgage loan, advanced when certain conditions—for example, construction of core and shell—are met.

Floor/area ratio. The ratio of floor area to land area, expressed as a percent or decimal, that is determined by dividing the total floor area of the building by the area of the lot; typically used as a formula to regulate building volume.

Floor load. The weight that the floor of a building is able to support if such weight is evenly distributed, measured in pounds per square foot.

Focus group. Market analysis tool in which a moderator presents a set of carefully prepared questions to a group, usually eight to 12 people, in order to collect detailed and specific information on consumer attitudes and preferences.

Foreclosure. The legal process by which a mortgagee, in case of a mortgagor's default, forces sale of the mortgaged property to provide funds to pay off the loan.

Formal feasibility. Formal demonstration through the use of quantitative, objective data that a proposed project is or is not viable.

Friable. Material able to be crushed or pulverized by hand pressure such that the particles become airborne; used to describe different types of asbestos.

Garden apartments. Two- or three-story multifamily housing featuring low density, ample open space around buildings, and convenient on-site parking.

Garden city. Movement begun in late 19th century Europe that sought to counter the rapid, unplanned growth of industrial cities by constructing self-contained planned communities emphasizing environmental reform, social reform, town planning, and regional planning.

General contractor. Person or firm that supervises a construction project under contract to the owner; also known as the "prime contractor."

General obligation bond. Municipal bond backed by the full faith and credit of the issuer as opposed to being backed by a particular project.

Geographic information system (GIS). An information system that allows users to work with data that are geographically referenced to the Earth, allowing them to add, store, edit, analyze, map, and present the data. GIS, also known as geographic information science, is frequently used to assist decision making for planning and real estate development.

Government National Mortgage Association (Ginnie Mae). Agency of the U.S. Department of Housing and Urban Development that operates as a participant in the secondary mortgage market, guaranteeing privately issued securities backed by pools of FHA or VA mortgages.

Gray Areas Program. Program launched by the Ford Foundation in 1960 to foster the revitalization and redevelopment of communities in minority areas.

Green building. The practice of designing and engineering more efficient buildings to conserve materials and resources such as water and energy and to reduce other negative environmental impacts and health consequences.

Greenbelt. Area of undeveloped, open space that serves as a buffer between developed areas.

Gross income multiplier. Rule-of-thumb calculation to estimate the value of residential property, derived by dividing the sale price of comparable properties by their gross annual or monthly rent.

Gross leasing activity. The sum of all leases signed during a given time period, including renewals and leases signed in new buildings.

Ground lease. A long-term lease on a parcel of land, separate from and exclusive of the improvements on the land.

Growth management. The public sector's control over the timing and location of real estate development by various means, including legislative and administrative.

Growth path. The area of a city where development, price appreciation, and user or tenant demand are the greatest.

Guaranteed investment contract (GIC). A written guarantee to an investor of a certain yield for a defined period of time.

Hard costs. In new construction, includes payments for land, labor, materials, improvements, and the contractor's fee.

High rise. Tall building or skyscraper, usually more than ten stories.

Highest and best use. The property use that, at a given time, is deemed likely to produce the greatest net return in the foreseeable future, whether or not such use is the current use of the property.

Homesteader. A person residing on public land and establishing a homestead for the purpose of acquiring legal title to the land.

HVAC system. A building system supplying heating, ventilation, and air conditioning.

Impact fee. Charge levied (on developers) by local governments to pay for the cost of providing public facilities necessitated by a given development.

Income kicker. A provision in loan terms that guarantees the lender's receiving a portion of gross income over an established minimum, for example, 10 percent of the first year's gross rent receipts.

Industrial park. A large tract of improved land used for a variety of light industrial and manufacturing uses. Users either purchase or lease individual sites.

Infill. The development of unused or abandoned land in a built-up area, especially as part of smart growth. Often, adequate infrastructure is already present, reducing potential costs.

Inflation risk. The risk that inflation will reduce the purchasing power of monies lent.

Infrastructure. Services and facilities provided by a municipality, including roads, highways, water, sewerage, emergency services, parks and recreation, and so on. Can also be privately provided.

In-sample out-sample analysis. Market analysis technique in which the analyst strives to hold samples constant between surveys conducted at different points in time.

Institute of Real Estate Management (IREM). An affiliate of the National Association of Realtors® whose purpose is to promote professionalism in the field of property management.

Intelligent building. A building that incorporates technologically advanced features to facilitate communications, information processing, energy conservation, and tenant services.

Internal rate of return (IRR). The discount rate at which investment has zero net present value (that is, the yield to the investor).

International Council of Shopping Centers (ICSC). An international trade association for owners, developers, and managers of shopping centers.

IPO (initial public offering). The first offering of stock on a previously privately held company.

Joint venture. An association of two or more firms or individuals to carry on a single business enterprise for profit.

Junk bond. Any bond (a long-term debt obligation of a corporation or a government) with a relatively low rating. The lower the rating, the more speculative or risky the investment. Returns can be much higher than for a less speculative investment, however. Bonds are rated by credit-rating companies, the best known being Standard & Poor's.

Land development. The process of preparing raw land through clearing, grading, installing utilities, etc., for the construction of improvements.

Land planner. Individual who specializes in the allocation of desired land uses in a particular site to maximize the site's value and utility, striving for efficient internal traffic circulation, well-placed uses and amenities, and adequate open space.

Leadership in Energy and Environmental Design (LEED). A system developed by the U.S. Green Building Council to provide standards for environmentally sustainable design. LEED certification comprises four levels (certified, silver, gold, and platinum) for buildings; a number of versions of the LEED system exist for different, specialized project types, including office buildings, retail spaces, and neighborhoods.

Lease. A contract that gives the lessor (the tenant) the right of possession for a period of time in return for paying rent to the lessee (the landlord).

Lease concession. A benefit to a tenant to induce him to enter into a lease; usually takes the form of one month or more of free rent.

Lease-up. Period during which a real estate rental property is marketed, leasing agreements are signed, and tenants begin to move in.

Leverage. The use of borrowed funds to finance a project.

LIBOR (London interbank offered rate). An interest rate frequently used as an index in adjustable mortgage loans; most often the interest rate on three- or six-month Eurodeposits.

Lien. The right to hold property as security until the debt that it secures is paid. A mortgage is one type of lien.

Limited partnership. A partnership that restricts the personal liability of the partners to the amount of their investment.

Linkage. Typically, a payment to a municipality for some needed development that is not necessarily profitable for a developer (say, low-income housing) in exchange for the right to develop more profitable, high-density buildings (say, commercial development).

Loan placement analysis. The decision by a lender to hold a loan or to sell the loan in the secondary market, or the decision not to make a loan if the lender is unwilling to hold it and no secondary market exists.

Loan-to-value (LTV) ratio. The relationship between the amount of a mortgage loan and the value of the real estate securing it; the loan amount divided by market value.

Location quotient. Market analysis tool used to compare local workforce estimates with national averages, derived by taking the percentages of the workforce employed in each major industry group locally and dividing them by the percentages of the workforce employed in the industry groups nationally.

Low rise. A multistory building, usually in outlying areas, with fewer than ten stories.

Maquiladora. In Mexico, a manufacturing plant that temporarily imports capital goods duty free and then ships finished goods out of the country as exports. Most are located near the U.S. border.

Market niche. A particular subgroup of a market segment distinguishable from the rest of the segment by certain characteristics.

Market research. A study of the needs of groups of people to develop a product appropriate for an identifiable market niche.

Market study. An analysis of the general demand for a single real estate product for a particular project.

Marketability risk. The risk that a lender will be unable to sell a loan in a secondary market.

Marketing research. The study of factors that will satisfy the needs of target customers and convince them to buy or rent.

Marketing study/marketability study. A study that determines the price or rent appropriate to market a project successfully.

Mechanic's lien. A claim that attaches to real estate to protect the right to compensation of one who performs labor or provides materials in connection with construction.

Mechanistic model. A forecast method that is based on research indicating generalized algorithms that can be applied to a given property type across all markets.

Metropolitan statistical area (MSA). An urban area containing multiple political jurisdictions grouped together for purposes of counting individuals by the Census Bureau.

Miniperm loan. A short-term loan (usually five years) meant to be an interim loan between a construction loan and a permanent loan. A miniperm loan is usually securitized like any other loan; the interest rate could be less onerous than a construction loan but not as favorable as a permanent loan.

Miniwarehouse. A building, usually one story, subdivided into numerous small cubicles intended to be used as storage by families or small businesses.

Mixed-use development. A development, in one building or several buildings, that combines at least three significant revenue-producing uses that are physically and functionally integrated and developed in conformance with a coherent plan. A mixed-use development might include, for example, retail space on the ground floor, offices on the middle floors, and condominiums on the top floors, with a garage on the lower levels.

Monetary policy. The actions and procedures of the Federal Reserve System meant to control the availability of loanable funds.

Money market instruments. Investment tools such as U.S. Treasury bills and commercial paper employed by money markets.

Money markets. Name given to financial markets employing short-term investment instruments that mature in one year or less.

Mortgage. An instrument used in some states (rather than a deed of trust) to make real estate security for a debt. A two-party instrument between a mortgagor (a borrower) and a mortgagee (a lender).

Mortgage-backed security. A type of bond or note that is based on pools of mortgage loans or collateralized by the cash flows from the principal and interest payments of a set of mortgage loans.

Mortgage banking. The process of originating real estate loans and then selling them to institutional lenders and other investors.

Mortgage loan constant. Percentage of the original loan balance represented by the constant periodic mortgage payment.

Move-up housing. Typically, larger, more expensive houses that homeowners buy as their incomes increase. First homes, or "starter homes," are generally modestly sized and priced. As purchasers' incomes increase, they "move up" to larger, more expensive housing.

Multifamily housing. Structures that house more than one family in separate units (apartments). Can be high rises, low rises, garden apartments, or townhouses.

National Association of Housing Redevelopment Officials (NAHRO). Professional association of agencies and private officials involved in publicly assisted housing and community development activities.

National Association of Industrial and Office Properties (NAIOP). Trade association representing the interests of commercial real estate developers, owners, and managers.

National Association of Realtors® (NAR). The largest real estate organization in the country and probably in the world. Members are entitled to use the designation "Realtor."

National Housing Act of 1968. Legislation that created several programs designed to encourage the production and rehabilitation of low-income housing.

Neighborhood. A segment of a city or town with common features that distinguish it from adjoining areas.

Neighborhood Reinvestment Corporation. A public, nonprofit corporation created by law in 1978 that uses congressional appropriations to encourage public/private partnerships in the interest of revitalizing older urban neighborhoods.

Net absorption. The change in square feet of occupied inventory over a specified period of time, including the addition or deletion of building stock during that period of time.

Net operating income (NOI). Cash flow from rental income on a property after operating expenses are deducted from gross income.

Net present income. The value of an income-producing property at a given discount rate, minus the original investment cost.

New urbanism. An urban design movement whose goal is to create and restore compact, diverse, and walkable mixed-use towns and cities. Emphasizes a discernible town center, public spaces, the placement of buildings close to the street, and the proximity of essential community features (housing, places of employment, schools, and services) to the town center. New urbanism tries to eliminate sprawl, reduce automobile traffic, and reinforce a sense of community.

Nominal group process. A decision-making technique used to set priorities for ideas generated by a group.

Nonrecourse loan. A loan that, in the event of default by the borrower, limits the lender to foreclosure of the mortgage and acquisition of the real estate, i.e., the lender waives any personal liability by the borrower.

Not in my backyard (NIMBY). The tendency of some residents to oppose nearby development or land uses that they see as undesirable such as homeless shelters, wastewater treatment plants, and airports.

Office building. A building or area of a building leased to tenants for the conduct of business or practice of a profession, as distinguished from residential, commercial, or retail uses.

Open market operations. The buying and selling of government securities by the Federal Reserve System; a tool for controlling the availability of loanable funds.

Operating budget. A budget, usually prepared a year in advance, listing projected costs of maintenance and repair for a building.

Operating expense ratio. The ratio of operating expenses to either potential gross income or effective gross income.

Operating expenses. Expenses directly related to the operation and maintenance of a property, including real estate taxes, maintenance and repair, insurance, payroll and management fees, supplies, and utilities. Debt service on mortgages or depreciation is not included.

Opportunity cost. The return on capital invested in a particular asset compared with the return available from alternative uses of that capital.

Option. The right given by the owner of property (the optionor) to another (the optionee) to purchase or lease the property at a specific price within a set time.

Origination fee. A charge made by the lender at the inception of the loan to cover administrative costs.

Outlier forecast. A forecast in a group of projections that differs substantially from all others in the group as well as from the group average.

Participation loan. A mortgage wherein one or more lenders have a share in a mortgage with the lead or originating lender.

Passive investor. An investor who seeks no active role in construction or operation of a building but merely seeks to invest funds to earn a return. Institutional investors such as pension funds are typically passive investors.

Pass-through. Lease provision whereby certain costs flow through directly to the tenant rather than to the owner (for example, property tax increases on a long-term lease).

Pass-through certificate. An investment instrument in which the periodic debt service payments on a package of mortgage loans are paid out (passed through) to the investors owning the instrument.

Peer group. Those properties most directly comparable and competitive with a subject property.

Pension fund. An institution that holds assets to be used for the payment of pensions to corporate or government employees, union members, and other groups.

Permanent lender. A financial institution undertaking a long-term loan on real estate subject to specified conditions (for example, the construction of improvements).

PERT (program evaluation and review technique). A technique that provides project managers with a flowchart representing construction schedule times. Includes a critical path that indicates the activities that must be completed on time so as not to delay completion.

Planned unit development (PUD). Zoning classification created to accommodate master-planned developments that include mixed uses, varied housing types, and/or unconventional subdivision designs.

Points. An amount charged by the lender at the inception of a loan to increase the lender's effective yield. Each point equals 1 percent of the loan.

Police power. The right of government to regulate property to protect the health, safety, and general welfare of citizens.

Portfolio. A collection of varied investments held by an individual or firm. Real estate is often among those investments.

Preliminary drawings. Architectural renderings of a project showing definite project dimensions and volumes and including such items as exterior elevations, rentable square feet or salable units, parking, and the type of HVAC system.

Prepayment or callability risk. The risk that a borrower will pay off a loan before it has matured, thus depriving the lender of additional interest payments.

Present value. The current value of an income-producing asset, estimated by discounting all expected future cash flows over the holding period.

Prime rate. The lowest interest rate charged to the largest and strongest customers of a commercial bank for a short-term loan.

Profitability ratios. A set of single-period ratios that indicate the capacity of a project to produce income relative to the capital investment required to obtain that income.

Pro forma. A financial statement that projects gross income, operating expenses, and net operating income for a future period based on a set of specific assumptions.

Property life cycle. The three periods in the life of a building—the development period, the stabilization period, and the decline period.

Property manager. An individual or firm responsible for the operation of improved real estate. Management functions include leasing and maintenance supervision.

Psychographic profile. A detailed description of a group that goes beyond personal data, such as place of residence, and includes more psychological aspects, such as interests and levels of aspiration.

Purchasing power. The financial means (including credit) that people possess to purchase durable and nondurable goods.

Rational nexus. A reasonable connection between impact fees and improvements that will be made with those fees. Jurisdictions must be able to justify the fees they charge developers by showing that the fees will be spent on improvements related to the development. For example, a fee of $25 per square foot charged for a shopping center might not be justifiable if it is to be used for building an addition to the local elementary school. It might be justified, however, if it will be used to improve roads near the shopping center because of the additional traffic that the shopping center is likely to generate.

Real estate development. The process of converting undeveloped tracts of land into construction-ready parcels and/or components of the built environment.

Real estate investment trust (REIT). An ownership entity that provides limited liability, no tax on the entity, and liquidity. Ownership is evidenced by shares of beneficial interest similar to shares of common stock.

Real estate mortgage investment conduit (REMIC). An issue of publicly traded debt securities backed by a fixed pool of mortgages that can be used as a pass-through entity for federal income tax purposes.

Realtor®. A member of the National Association of Realtors®. "Realtor" is also a generic term used to describe professionals involved in selling property.

Recourse loan. A loan offering no protection to the borrower against personal liability for the debt, thus putting the borrower's personal assets at risk in addition to any collateral securing the loan.

Redevelopment. The redesign or rehabilitation of existing properties.

Redlining. The practice of denying loans or insurance coverage to residents in a specific geographic area, usually low-income inner-city neighborhoods.

Reliability. The ability to remain consistent under repeated tests.

Rent control. Limitations imposed by state or local authorities on the amount of rent a landlord can charge in certain jurisdictions.

Repos. Short-term repurchase agreements between financial institutions.

Resolution Trust Corporation (RTC). A mixed-ownership government corporation created by Congress to manage failed thrift institutions and their holdings.

Retainage. A portion of the amount due under a construction contract that the owner withholds until the job is completed in accordance with plans and specifications; usually a percentage of the total contract price.

Revenue bonds. Bonds issued by municipalities and backed by specific fees or service charges.

Risk. The possibility that returns on an investment or loan will not be as high as expected.

Risk control techniques. Stages in the development or construction process at which the developer can discontinue or modify operations in light of new circumstances.

Risk-free interest rate. A short-term, base interest rate calculated before various risk premiums are added; approximated by the rate on U.S. Treasury bills.

Rural Housing Services/Rural Development. Agency (formerly Farmers' Home Administration) of the Department of Agriculture that provides credit to farmers and non-farm businesses in rural areas as well as guarantees and insures certain loans.

Savings and loan (S&L) association. A type of savings institution that is the primary source of financing for one- to four-family homes. Most S&Ls are mutual (non-stock) institutions.

Secondary mortgage market. The market in which existing mortgages are bought and sold: conventional loans by Freddie Mac and Fannie Mae, FHA and VA loans by Fannie Mae, and special-assistance (HUD-regulated) loans by Ginnie Mae.

Sector theory. Land use development theory postulating that land uses tend to develop along transportation corridors outward from the city center, forming wedge-shaped sectors that follow the path of least resistance and lowest costs.

Securitization. The pooling of mortgages for securities offerings.

Security. Evidence of ownership, such as stocks or bonds.

Segmentation. The classification of a population group into segments for the purpose of identifying marketing subgroups.

Sensitivity analysis. A cost/benefit examination of the various features and aspects of a real estate development project such as operating costs, amenities, management costs, and visual appeal, and the impact of adjustments to them on the value of the project.

Setback. The part of zoning regulations that restricts a building to within a specified distance from the property frontline or edge of the public street; thus, the structure must be set back a given number of feet from the frontline.

Shoppers goods. Items purchased after some degree of deliberation or shopping around. Generally, they are differentiated through brand identification, the retailer's image, or the ambience of the shopping area. Such purchases are made less often, and the product is typically more durable and expensive.

Shopping center. Integrated and self-contained shopping area, usually in the suburbs. Classified as neighborhood (30,000 to 100,000 square feet [2,790 to 9,295 square meters] and providing convenience goods and personal services), community (100,000 to 500,000 square feet [9,295 to 46,500 square meters] and providing a wider range of goods), regional (about 500,000 square feet [46,500 square meters] with one or two department store anchors), and super regional (1 million plus square feet [93,000 plus square meters] with three or more department store anchors).

Single-family housing. A dwelling unit, either attached or detached, designed for use by one family and with direct access to a street; does not share heating facilities or other essential building facilities with any other dwelling.

Single-point-in-time analyses. Analyses of market performance and various demand indicators such as construction levels, absorption, vacancy, and rent growth recorded at only one point in time.

Situs. The total urban environment in which a specific urban land use on a specific land parcel functions and with which it interacts at a specific time. More simply, location.

Smart growth. A movement that supports concentrating growth in urban centers to avoid urban sprawl and create sustainable design and advocates compact, transit-oriented, walkable, bicycle-friendly land use, including mixed-use development with a range of affordable housing choices.

Societal marketing concept. The idea that a real estate project has an effect on more than just the users of the product and therefore must be marketed to the collective satisfaction of neighbors and regulators.

Soft costs. Outlays for interest, origination fees, appraisals, and other third-party charges associated with real estate development.

Special taxing districts. Districts established by local governments, in the form of assessment districts or public improvement districts, in which a special tax is levied on property owners to fund public improvements that will directly benefit those owners.

Stabilization. In appraisal, the use of one year's typical property income and expenses and annualized capital reserve expenditures to represent each year's income stream.

Steering. The illegal practice of directing prospective home-buyers or renters away from neighborhoods of different racial or ethnic composition.

Strip mall. A shopping center with a linear configuration and located on a highway or major street along which development has sprawled outward from a town or city center.

Subcontractor. An individual or company that performs a specific job for a construction project pursuant to an agreement with the general contractor.

Subdivision. Division of a parcel of land into building lots. Can also include streets, parks, schools, utilities, and other public facilities.

Subdivision controls. Development restrictions placed on parcels in a recorded subdivision.

Submarket. A geographic area surrounding a site that will provide a substantial portion of the customers for a real estate project.

Subordination clause. Clause in which one party agrees, under certain conditions, to yield its priority to another mortgagee.

Subprime rate. A rate that is at least three points above the current prime rate for a bond of comparable maturity. Loans at subprime rates are costlier and higher risk, and are generally given by commercial banks to customers with poor or insufficient credit.

Suburbanization. The movement of development to the suburbs created by the overflow effect of cities and by the automobile, which improved access to the inner city.

Surety company. A company that guarantees the performance or debt of another in case of default.

Sustainable development. In its most comprehensive form, a three-pronged approach to development that considers social needs, economic needs, and environmental protection; also real estate development that meets the needs of the present without compromising the ability of future generations to meet their own needs.

Syndication. The process of acquiring and combining equity investments from multiple sources (for example, syndicating units in a limited partnership).

Takeout commitment. The permanent loan commitment for a project to be constructed.

Taking. The acquisition or seizure of land without just compensation or the application of police power constraints so restrictive as to prevent any viable use of the land.

Tax increment financing (TIF). A type of special district financing in which tax revenues raised only from new development, as assessed by the net increase over the existing property tax base, are earmarked to fund capital improvements.

Taxation risk. The risk that changes in tax laws will adversely affect taxes on the interest of a loan or will undermine the value of the underlying loan collateral.

Temporary financing. Short-term financing, usually for land acquisition, preconstruction infrastructure, and construction of improvements.

Tenant. One who rents from another.

Tenant allowance. A cash payment made by the developer to a tenant (usually in an income property) to enable the tenant, rather than the developer, to complete the interior work for the leased premises.

Tenant mix. The combination of various types of tenants in a leased building.

Term or maturity risk premium. Risk premium charged by lenders to compensate for the opportunity costs of long-term loans.

Time-series analyses. Analyses of market performance and other measures of market cyclicity such as construction levels, absorption, vacancy, and rental growth recorded during periods of market expansion and contraction.

Time-value-of-money concept. The idea that because money is assumed to earn interest, a dollar today is worth more than a dollar at some future date.

Title. Evidence of ownership of real property, often used synonymously with the term "ownership" to indicate a person's right to possess, use, and dispose of property.

Title company. A company that examines titles to real estate, determines whether they are valid and any limitations on the title exist, and, for a premium, insures the validity of the title to the owner or lender.

Title I. FHA-insured property improvement or rehabilitation mortgage.

Top-down approach. An approach to developing analysis based on the use of aggregated data first.

Total marketing concept. The process of determining consumer desires, producing a product to match those desires, and persuading the consumer to purchase or rent that product.

Townhouse. Single-family attached residence separated from another by party walls, usually on a narrow lot offering small front- and backyards.

Trade area. Geographic area from which a retail facility consistently draws most of its customers.

Traditional neighborhood design. An urban design approach stemming from the new urbanism and based on a compact grid that promotes higher-density and walkable development and intensified, compatible mixed uses.

Tranche. Multiple classes of tiered bond or security ownership, interests issued by real estate mortgage investment conduits (REMICs).

Transfer package. Documentation compiled at the time a project is sold or transferred to an asset manager that attempts to measure objectively the project's standing in the marketplace in order to provide a benchmark for the asset manager's future performance.

Transferable development rights. A method of allowing landowners to sever development rights for a tract of land and sell those rights to develop, which then can be assigned to another tract of land to enable higher-density development. For example, the "sending area" may be farmland, ensuring that it will never be developed, and the "receiving area" may be an urban area with a strong demand for development, which can then benefit from the allowance of greater density.

Transit-oriented development. A mixed-use area designed to maximize access to public transportation, generally seeking to create high-density developments within a quarter mile (402 meters) of a mass transit stop.

Underwriters. Persons employed by mortgage lenders and charged with making recommendations on loan approvals or disapprovals based on their knowledge of the applicant's creditworthiness and the quality or value of any collateral to secure the loan.

Urban development action grants (UDAGs). Program of grants begun in 1977 and administered through the Department of Housing and Urban Development for the revitalization of distressed urban areas; program has been unfunded since the mid-1980s.

Urban economics. Economic concepts applied in the context of a particular urban area.

Urban renewal. Process of the physical improvement and redevelopment of an area through government action or assistance.

Validity. Execution with proper legal authority.

Value. With ratio at which commodities or services exchange, the power of one commodity or service to command other commodities or services in exchange.

Value capture. With regard to the joint development of transportation facilities, it is the government purchase, management, or control of land adjacent to these developments that allows the public to share in the potential financial and community development benefits that would not otherwise be possible.

Variance. In general, the difference between expected results and actual results. Statistically, "variance" refers to the square of the standard deviation. Can be used as a measure of risk.

Venture capital. Funds available for investment at risk *i* to a profit-seeking enterprise.

Veterans Affairs (VA). A department of the federal government, formerly the Veterans Administration, that administers the veteran benefit programs intended to help returning veterans adjust to civilian life.

Warehouse. A building that is used for the storage of goods or merchandise and that can be occupied by the owner or leased to one or more tenants.

Workforce housing. Housing for working individuals or families making between 60 and 120 percent of the area median income (AMI) for their MSA—individuals or families who generally do not qualify for housing subsidies yet cannot afford market-rate housing.

Workout. Negotiated arrangements between a lending institution and a developer unable to fulfill a loan agreement.

Writedown. A deliberate reduction in the book value of an asset, typically made because of changes in market conditions, deterioration of properties, loss of tenants, and the like.

Xeriscaping. Landscaping that thrives with little or no water.

Yield curve. The relationship between the yield on an instrument and the number of years until it matures or comes due.

Zone of transition. Neighborhoods surrounding the central business district of a city.

Zoning. Classification and regulation of land by local governments according to use categories (zones); often includes density designations as well.

Bibliography

PART I. INTRODUCTION

Basic Real Estate and Planning Books

Allmendinger, Philip, Alan Prior, and Jeremy Raemaekers. *Introduction to Planning Practice*. Chichester: Wiley, 2000.

American Planning Association. *Planning and Urban Design Standards*. Wiley Graphic Standards. Hoboken, N.J.: Wiley, 2006.

Anderson, Larz. *Planning the Built Environment*. Chicago: APA Planners Press, 2000.

Barras, Richard. *Building Cycles and Urban Develop-ment*. Real Estate Issues. Oxford: Blackwell, 2007.

Berke, Philip, and Edward John Kaiser. *Urban Land Use Planning*. Urbana: University of Illinois Press, 2006.

Brooks, Michael P. *Planning Theory for Practitioners*. Chicago: APA Planners Press, 2002.

Building Owners and Managers Institute International. *The BOMI Dictionary for the Built Environment: Terminology for Today's Property Professional*. Arnold, Md.: BOMI Institute, 2005.

Calthorpe, Peter. *The Regional City*. Washington, D.C.: Island Press, 2001.

Chavan, Abhijeet, Christian Peralta, and Christopher Steins. *Planetizen Contemporary Debates in Urban Planning*. Washington, D.C.: Island Press, 2007.

Colley, B. C. *Practical Manual of Land Development*. New York: McGraw-Hill, 2005.

Davis, Tanya. *The Real Estate Developer's Handbook: How to Set Up, Operate, and Manage a Financially Successful Real Estate Development*. Ocala, Fla.: Atlantic Publishing Group, 2007.

DeLisle, James R., and Elaine M. Worzala, eds. *Essays in Honor of James A. Graaskamp: Ten Years After*. Boston: Kluwer Academic Publishers, 2000.

Dewberry Companies. *Land Development Handbook*. 2nd ed. New York: McGraw-Hill, 2002.

Duany, Andrés, Jeff Speck, and Elizabeth Plater-Zyberk. *Smart Growth Manual*. New York: McGraw-Hill, 2003.

Evans, Alan W. *Economics and Land Use Planning*. Malden, Mass.: Blackwell Publishing, 2004.

Flint, Anthony. *This Land: The Battle over Sprawl and the Future of America*. Baltimore: Johns Hopkins University Press, 2006.

Galaty, Fillmore W., Wellington J. Allaway, and Robert C. Kyle. *Modern Real Estate Practice*. Chicago: Dearborn Real Estate Education, 2003.

Garvin, Alexander. *The American City: What Works and What Doesn't*. 2nd ed. New York: McGraw-Hill, 2002.

Graaskamp, James A. *Fundamentals of Real Estate Development*. Washington, D.C.: ULI–the Urban Land Institute, 1981.

Hall, A. C. *Turning a Town Around: A Pro-Active Approach to Urban Design*. Oxford, UK: Blackwell, 2007.

Heikkila, Eric John. *The Economics of Planning*. New Brunswick, N.J.: Center for Urban Policy Research, 2000.

Hewlet, Charlie, and Gadi Kaufmann. *Strategies for Real Estate Companies*. Washington, D.C.: ULI–the Urban Land Institute, 2007.

Hudnut, William H., III. *Cities on the Rebound: A Vision for Urban America*. Washington, D.C.: ULI–the Urban Land Institute, 1998.

Jacobus, Charles J. *Real Estate: An Introduction to the Profession*. Mason, Ohio: Thomson/South-Western, 2003.

Jacobus, Charles J., *Real Estate Principles*. 10th ed. Mason, Ohio: Thomson/South-Western, 2005.

Jarchow, Stephen P, ed. *Graaskamp on Real Estate*. Washington, D.C.: ULI–the Urban Land Institute, 1991.

Johnson, David E. *Fundamentals of Land Development: A Real World Guide to Profitable Large-Scale Development*. Hoboken, N.J.: Wiley, 2008.

Katz, Peter. *The New Urbanism: Towards an Architecture of Community*. New York: McGraw-Hill, 1994.

Keeney, John. *To Build a Nation: Infrastructure, Cities, Planning, Design*. Artarmon, N.S.W., Australia: Design Masters Press, 2007.

Kone, D. Linda. *Land Development*. Washington, D.C.: BuilderBooks, 2006.

Kotkin, Joel. *The City: A Global History*. New York: Random House, 2005.

Leinberger, Christopher B. *The Option of Urbanism: Investing in a New American Dream*. Washington, D.C.: Island Press, 2008.

Levy, John M. *Contemporary Urban Planning*. 7th ed. Upper Saddle River, N.J.: Prentice Hall, 2005.

Ling, David C., and Wayne R. Archer. *Real Estate Principles: A Value Approach*. Boston: McGraw-Hill/Irwin, 2005.

Long, Deborah H. *Ethics for the Real Estate Professional*. 6th ed. Mason, Ohio: Thomson/South-Western, 2007.

Mandelker, Daniel R. *Planning and Control of Land Development: Cases and Materials*. Newark, N.J.: LexisNexis, 2005.

Marshall, Stephen. *Cities, Design and Evolution*. New York: Routledge, 2007.

McCarthy, John. *Partnership, Collaborative Planning and Urban Regeneration*. Aldershot, Eng.: Ashgate, 2007.

McClure, Wendy R., and Tom J. Bartuska. *The Built Environment: A Collaborative Inquiry into Design and Planning*. Hoboken, N. J.: Wiley, 2007.

McMahan, John. *Professional Property Development*. New York: McGraw-Hill, 2007.

Moskowitz, Harvey S., and Carl G. Lindbloom. *The Latest Illustrated Book of Development Definitions*. Piscataway, N.J.: Center for Urban Policy Research, Rutgers University, 2004.

Mumford, Lewis. *The City in History: Its Origins, Its Transformation, and Its Prospects*. New York: MFJ Books, 1961.

Newman, Peter, and Andy Thornley. *Planning World Cities: Globalization and Urban Politics*. Baingstoke, Hampshire, Eng.: Palgrave Macmillan, 2005.

Paumier, Cyril B. *Creating a Vibrant City Center: Urban Design and Regeneration Principles*. Washington, D.C.: ULI–the Urban Land Institute, 2004.

Peiser, Richard, and Anne Frej. *Professional Real Estate Development: The ULI Guide to the Business*. 2nd ed. Washington, D.C.: ULI–the Urban Land Institute, 2003.

Ratcliffe, John, and Michael Stubbs. *Urban Planning and Real Estate Development*. New York: Spon Press, 2004.

Stein, Jay M. *Classic Readings in Urban Planning*. Chicago: APA Planners Press, 2004.

Steiner, Frederick R., and Kent S. Butler. *Planning and Urban Design Standards*. Hoboken, N.J.: Wiley, 2007.

Steuben, Norton L. *Real Estate Planning: Cases, Materials, Problems, Questions, and Commentary*. University Casebook Series. New York: Foundation Press, 2006.

Stiftel, Bruce, Vanessa Watson, and Henri Acselrad. *Dialogues in Urban and Regional Planning,* vol. 2. London: Routledge, 2007.

Wang, Xinhao. *Research Methods in Urban and Regional Planning*. Tsinghua University Texts. Berlin: Springer, 2007.

Weiss, Marc A. *The Rise of the Community Builders: The American Real Estate Industry and Urban Land Planning*. New York: Columbia University Press, 1987.

Woodson, R. Dodge. *How to Be a Successful Land Developer*. New York: McGraw-Hill Professional, 2000.

Zuckerman, Howard A. *Real Estate Development* Workbook. Gaithersburg, Md.: Aspen Publishers, 2004.

Sustainable Planning and Development

Balmori, Diana, and Gaboury Benoit. *Land and Natural Development (LAND) Code: Guidelines for Sustainable Land Development*. Hoboken, N.J.: Wiley, 2007.

Calthorpe, Peter. *The Next American Metropolis: Ecology, Community, and the American Dream*. New York: Princeton Architectural Press, 1995.

Friedman, Avi. *Sustainable Residential Development: Planning and Design for Green Neighborhoods*. New York: McGraw-Hill, 2007.

Gause, Jo Allen, Richard Franko, et al. *Developing Sustainable Planned Communities*. Washington, D.C.: ULI–the Urban Land Institute, 2007.

Halliday, Sandy. *Sustainable Construction*. Princeton, N.J.: Architectural Press, 2007.

Kahn, Matthew E. *Green Cities: Urban Growth and the Environment*. Washington, D.C.: Brookings Institution Press, 2006.

Keeping, Miles, and David Shiers. *Sustainable Property Development*. Oxford: Blackwell Science, 2002.

Pawlukiewicz, Michael, et al. *Ten Principles for Coastal Development*. Washington, D.C.: Urban Land Institute, 2007.

Porta, Sergio. *Urban Sustainability through Environmental Design: Approaches to Time-People-Place Responsive Urban Spaces*. New York: Routledge, 2007.

Porter, Douglas R., and Rutherford H. Platt. *The Practice of Sustainable Development*. Washington, D.C.: ULI–the Urban Land Institute, 2000.

Swaback, Vernon D. *Creating Value: Smart Development and Green Design*. Washington, D.C.: ULI–the Urban Land Institute, 2007.

ULI–the Urban Land Institute. *Conservation Development*. Selected References. Washington, D.C.: ULI–the Urban Land Institute, 2007 (updated annually).

ULI–the Urban Land Institute. *Green Commercial Buildings*. Selected References. Washington, D.C.: ULI–the Urban Land Institute, 2007 (updated annually).

ULI–the Urban Land Institute. *Green Housing*. Selected References. Washington, D.C.: ULI–the Urban Land Institute, 2007 (updated annually).

ULI–the Urban Land Institute. *Green Retail*. Selected References. Washington, D.C.: ULI–the Urban Land Institute, 2007 (updated annually).

ULI–the Urban Land Institute. *Sustainable Development*. Selected References. Washington, D.C.: ULI–the Urban Land Institute, 2007 (updated annually).

Wells, Walker, and Ted Bardacke. *Blueprint for Greening Affordable Housing*. Washington, D.C.: Island Press, 2007.

Williams, Daniel Edward. *Sustainable Design: Ecology, Architecture, and Planning*. Hoboken, N.J.: Wiley, 2007.

Yudelson, Jerry. *The Green Building Revolution*. Washington, D.C.: Island Press, 2008.

Specialized Publications

Beyard, Michael D., et al. *Ten Principles for Developing Successful Town Centers*. Washington, D.C.: ULI–the Urban Land Institute, 2007.

Beyard, Michael D., et al. *Ten Principles for Rebuilding Neighborhood Retail*. Washington, D.C.: ULI–the Urban Land Institute, 2003.

Beyard, Michael D., and Michael Pawlukiewicz. *Ten Principles for Reinventing America's Suburban Strips*. Washington, D.C.: ULI–the Urban Land Institute, 2001.

Bohl, Charles. *Place Making and Town Center Development*. Washington, D.C.: ULI–the Urban Land Institute, 2003.

Booth, Geoffrey, et al. *Ten Principles for Reinventing Suburban Business Districts*. Washington, D.C.: ULI–the Urban Land Institute, 2002.

Booth, A. Geoffrey. *Transforming Suburban Business Districts*. Washington, D.C.: ULI–the Urban Land Institute, 2001.

Dunphy, Robert T. *Developing around Transit: Strategies and Solutions That Work*. Washington, D.C.: ULI–the Urban Land Institute, 2004.

Fader, Steven D. *Density by Design: New Directions in Residential Development*. 2nd ed. Washington D.C.: ULI–the Urban Land Institute, 2000.

Frej, Anne, et al. *Business Park and Industrial Property Development Handbook*. 2nd ed. Washington, D.C.: ULI–the Urban Land Institute, 2001.

Frej, Anne, et al. *Green Office Buildings: A Practical Guide to Development*. Washington, D.C.: ULI–the Urban Land Institute, 2005.

Gause, Jo Allen, ed., *Great Planned Communities*. Washington D.C.: ULI–the Urban Land Institute, 2002.

Gause, Jo Allen. *Office Development Handbook*. 2nd ed. Washington, D.C.: ULI–the Urban Land Institute, 1998.

Haughey, Richard. *Getting Density Right*: *Tools for Creating Vibrant Compact Development*. Washington, D.C.: ULI–the Urban Land Institute, forthcoming.

Haughey, Richard M. *Higher-Density Development: Myth and Fact*. Washington, D.C.: ULI–the Urban Land Institute, 2005.

Haughey, Richard. *Urban Infill Housing: Myth and Fact*. Washington, D.C.: ULI–the Urban Land Institute, 2001.

Heid, James M. *Greenfield Development without Sprawl: The Role of Planned Communities*. Washington, D.C.: ULI–the Urban Land Institute, 2004.

Kramer, Anita. *Retail Development Handbook*. 2nd ed. Washington, D.C.: ULI–the Urban Land Institute, 2007.

Pawlukiewicz, Michael. *Ten Principles for Smart Growth on the Suburban Fringe*. Washington, D.C.: ULI–the Urban Land Institute, 2003.

Peiser, Richard B., and Adrienne Schmitz. *Regenerating Older Suburbs*. Washington, D.C.: ULI–the Urban Land Institute, 2007.

Petersen, David C. *Developing Sports, Convention, and Performing Arts Facilities*. 3rd ed. Washington, D.C.: ULI–the Urban Land Institute, 2001.

Porter, Douglas R. *Making Smart Growth Work*. Washington, D.C.: ULI–the Urban Land Institute, 2003.

Porter, Douglas R. *Smart Growth Transportation for Suburban Greenfields*. Washington, D.C.: ULI–the Urban Land Institute, 2003.

Schmitz, Adrienne, et al. *Multifamily Housing Development Handbook*. Washington, D.C.: ULI–the Urban Land Institute, 2000.

Schmitz, Adrienne. *The New Shape of Suburbia: Trends in Residential Development*. Washington, D.C.: ULI–the Urban Land Institute, 2003.

Schmitz, Adrienne, et al. *Residential Development Handbook*. 2nd ed. Washington, D.C.: ULI–the Urban Land Institute, 2004.

Schmitz, Adrienne, et al. *Resort Development Handbook*. Washington, D.C.: ULI–the Urban Land Institute, forthcoming.

Schmitz, Adrienne, and Jason Scully. *Creating Walkable Places: Compact Mixed-Use Solutions*. Washington, D.C.: ULI–the Urban Land Institute, 2006.

Schwanke, Dean, et al. *Mixed-Use Development Handbook.* 2nd ed. Washington, D.C.: ULI–the Urban Land Institute, 2003.

Suchman, Diane. *Developing Successful Infill Housing.* Washington, D.C.: ULI–the Urban Land Institute, 2002.

Demographic Information

Demographic Data/Statistical Sources—Government

American Fact Finder, http://factfinder.census.gov/. Provides access to data from the decennial census, the American Community Survey, the Economic Census, and annual economic surveys. Washington, D.C.: U.S. Dept. of Commerce, Economics and Statistics Administration, U.S. Census Bureau.

American Housing Survey. Washington, D.C.: U.S. Dept. of Commerce, Bureau of the Census, Data User Services Division, 2005.

Statistical Abstract of the United States. Washington, D.C.: U.S. Dept. of Commerce, Economics and Statistics Administration, Bureau of the Census, Data User Services Division, Annual.

U.S. Bureau of Labor Statistics. Monthly Labor Review. Washington, D.C.: U.S. Government Printing Office. Published monthly.

Demographic Data/Statistical Sources—Other

America's Top-Rated Cities: A Statistical Handbook. Millerton, N.Y.: Grey House Publishing, 2007.

America's Top-Rated Smaller Cities: A Statistical Handbook. Millerton, N.Y.: Grey House Publishing, 2006–2007.

Comparative Guide to American Suburbs. Millerton, N.Y.: Grey House Publishing, 2006–2007.

Demographic Data/Statistical Sources with Projections

CEDDS: The Complete Economic and Demographic Data Source. Washington, D.C.: Woods & Poole Economics, 2007.

Community Sourcebook of County Demographics. 19th ed. Redlands, Calif.: ESRI, 2007.

Community Sourcebook of ZIP Code Demographics. 21st ed. Redlands, Calif.: ESRI, 2007.

Demographics USA, 2007. Wilton, Conn.: TradeDimensions International, 2007.

Stdbonline.com. Certified Commercial Investment Member (CCIM).

Demographics—General

Anderson, Margo J., ed. *Encyclopedia on the U.S. Census.* Washington, D.C.: CQ Press, 2000.

Barrell, Doris, and Mark Nash. *Reaching Out: The Financial Power of Niche Marketing.* Chicago: Dearborn Real Estate Education, 2003.

Gause, Jo Allen, ed. *Housing for Niche Markets: Capitalizing on Changing Demographics.* Washington, D.C.: ULI–the Urban Land Institute, 2005.

Hobbs, Frank, and Nicole Stoops. *Demographic Trends in the 20th Century.* Washington, D.C.: U.S. Census Bureau, 2002.

Kemp, Thomas Jay. *The American Census Handbook.* Wilmington, Del.: Scholarly Resources, 2001.

New Strategist Publications, Inc. *The American Marketplace: Demographics and Spending Patterns.* Ithaca, N.Y.: New Strategist Publications, 2005.

Riche, Martha Farnsworth. *The Implications of Changing U.S. Demographics for Housing Choice and Location in U.S. Cities.* Discussion paper series. Washington, D.C.: Center on Urban and Metropolitan Policy, Brookings Institution, 2001.

Russell, Cheryl. *Americans and Their Homes: Demographics of Homeownership.* 2nd ed. Ithaca, N.Y.: New Strategist Publications, 2005.

ULI–the Urban Land Institute. *Demographics and Real Estate.* Selected References. Washington, D.C.: ULI–the Urban Land Institute, 2007 (updated annually).

PART II. HISTORY

The Colonial Period to the Late 1800s

Abrams, Charles. *Revolution in Land.* New York: Harper, 1939.

Akin, Edward N. *Flagler: Rockefeller Partner and Florida Baron.* Kent, Ohio: Kent State University Press, 1986.

Blackmar, Elizabeth. *Manhattan for Rent, 1785–1850.* Ithaca, N.Y.: Cornell University Press, 1989.

Dumke, Glenn S. *The Boom of the Eighties in Southern California.* San Marino, Calif.: Huntington Library, 1944.

Ely, Richard T., and George S. Wehrwein. *Land Economics.* New York: Macmillan, 1940.

Fogelson, Robert M. *The Fragmented Metropolis: Los Angeles, 1880–1930.* Cambridge, Mass.: Harvard University Press, 1967.

Friedricks, William B. *Henry E. Huntington and the Creation of Southern California.* Columbus, Ohio: Ohio State University Press, 1992.

Gates, Paul W. *History of Public Land Law Development.* Washington D.C.: U.S. Government Printing Office, 1968.

Hartog, Hendrik. *Public Property and Private Law: The Corporation of the City of New York in American Law, 1730–1870.* Chapel Hill: University of North Carolina Press, 1983.

Hoyt, Homer. *One Hundred Years of Land Values in Chicago: The Relationship of the Growth of Chicago to the Rise in Its Land Values, 1830–1933.* Chicago: University of Chicago Press, 1933.

Hurd, Richard M. *Principles of City Land Values.* New York: Real Estate Record and Guide, 1903.

Jackson, Kenneth T. *Crabgrass Frontier: The Suburbanization of the United States*. New York: Oxford University Press, 1985.

Jackson, Kenneth T. *The Encyclopedia of New York City*. New Haven, Conn.: Yale University Press, 1995.

Keating, Ann Durkin. *Building Chicago: Suburban Developers and the Creating of a Divided Metropolis*. Columbus: Ohio State University Press, 1988.

Lubove, Roy. *The Progressives and the Slums: Tenement House Reform in New York City, 1890–1917*. Pittsburgh: University of Pittsburgh Press, 1962.

Moehring, Eugene P. *Public Works and the Patterns of Urban Real Estate Growth in Manhattan, 1835–1894*. New York: Arno Press, 1981.

Platt, Harold L. *City Building in the New South: The Growth of Public Services in Houston, Texas, 1830–1910*. Philadelphia: Temple University Press, 1983.

Rachlis, Eugene, and John E. Marqusee. *The Land Lords*. New York: Random House, 1963.

Real Estate Record Association. *A History of Real Estate, Building and Architecture in New York City*. New York: Real Estate Record and Guide, 1898.

Reps, John W. *The Making of Urban America: A History of City Planning in the United States*. Princeton, N.J.: Princeton University Press, 1965.

Riis, Jacob. *How the Other Half Lives: Studies among the Tenements of New York*. New York: Scribner's, 1890.

Robbins, Roy M. *Our Landed Heritage: The Public Domain, 1776–1936*. 2nd ed. Lincoln, Neb.: University of Nebraska Press, 1976.

Robinson, W. W. *Land in California: The Story of Mission Lands, Ranchos, Squatters, Mining Claims, Railroad Grants, Land Scrip, Homesteads*. Berkeley: University of California Press, 1948.

Rosen, Christine Meisner. *The Limits of Power: Great Fires and the Process of City Growth in America*. New York: Cambridge University Press, 1986.

Sakolski, A. M. *The Great American Land Bubble: The Amazing Story of Land-Grabbing, Speculations, and Booms from Colonial Days to the Present Time*. New York: Harper, 1932.

Smith, Arthur D. Howden. *John Jacob Astor: Landlord of New York*. Philadelphia: Lippincott, 1929.

Taylor, George R. *The Transportation Revolution, 1815–1860*. New York: Harper, 1968.

Thomas, Dana L. *Lords of the Land: The Triumphs and Scandals of American Real Estate Barons from Early Times to the Present*. New York: Putnam's, 1977.

Vanderblue, Homer B. "The Florida Land Boom." *Journal of Land and Public Utility Economics* 3:2 (May 1927): 113–131.

Vanderblue, Homer B. "The Florida Land Boom." *Journal of Land and Public Utility Economics* 3:3 (August 1927): 252–269.

Warner, Sam Bass, Jr. *Streetcar Suburbs: The Process of Growth in Boston, 1870–1900*. Cambridge, Mass.: Harvard University Press, 1962.

Weiss, Marc A. "Real Estate History: An Overview and Research Agenda." *Business History Review* 63:2 (Summer 1989): 241–282.

Weiss, Marc A. *The Rise of the Community Builders: The American Real Estate Industry and Urban Land Planning*. New York: Columbia University Press, 1987.

Wolf, Peter. *Land in America: Its Value, Use, and Control*. New York: Pantheon, 1981.

Wright, Carroll D. *The Slums of Baltimore, Chicago, New York and Philadelphia. Seventh Special Report of the Commissioner of Labor*. Washington, D.C.: U.S. Government Printing Office, 1894.

Wyckoff, William. *The Developer's Frontier: The Making of the Western New York Landscape*. New Haven, Conn.: Yale University Press, 1988.

The Late 1800s to World War II

Beito, David T. *Taxpayers in Revolt: Tax Resistance during the Great Depression*. Chapel Hill, N.C.: University of North Carolina Press, 1989.

Bishir, Catherine W., Charlotte V. Brown, Carl R. Lounsbury, and Ernest H. Wood III. *Architects and Builders in North Carolina: A History of the Practice of Building*. Chapel Hill, N.C.: University of North Carolina Press, 1990.

Blackford, Mausel G. *The Lost Dream: Businessmen and City Planning on the Pacific Coast, 1890–1920*. Columbus: Ohio State University Press, 1993.

Burgess, Patricia. *Planning for the Private Interest: Land Use Controls and Residential Patterns in Columbus, Ohio, 1900–1970*. Columbus: Ohio State University Press, 1994.

Caro, Robert A. *The Power Broker: Robert Moses and the Fall of New York*. New York: Random House, 1974.

Colean, Miles L. *American Housing: Problems and Prospects*. New York: Twentieth Century Fund, 1944.

Community Builders Council. *Community Builders Handbook*. Washington, D.C.: ULI–the Urban Land Institute, 1947.

Cranz, Galen. *The Politics of Park Design: A History of Urban Parks in America*. Cambridge, Mass.: MIT Press, 1982.

Cromley, Elizabeth Collins. *Alone Together: A History of New York's Early Apartments*. Ithaca, N.Y.: Cornell University Press, 1990.

Davies, Pearl Janet. *Real Estate in American History*. Washington, D.C.: Public Affairs Press, 1958.

Eskew, Garnett Laidlaw. *Of Land and Men: The Birth and Growth of an Idea*. Washington, D.C.: ULI–the Urban Land Institute, 1959.

Ewalt, Josephine Hedges. *A Business Reborn: The Savings and Loan Story, 1930–1960*. Chicago: American Savings and Loan Institute, 1962.

Fisher, Ernest M. *Urban Real Estate Markets: Characteristics and Financing*. New York: National Bureau of Economic Research, 1951.

Foster, Mark S. *Henry J. Kaiser: Builder in the Modern American West*. Austin: University of Texas Press, 1989.

Gibbs, Kenneth Turney. *Business Architectural Imagery in America, 1870–1930*. Ann Arbor, Mich.: UMI Research Press, 1984.

Goldberger, Paul. *The Skyscraper*. New York: Knopf, 1981.

Golden Book of Wanamaker Stores. Philadelphia: John Wanamaker, 1911.

Grebler, Leo, David M. Blank, and Louis Winnick. *Capital Formation in Residential Real Estate: Trends and Prospects*. Princeton, N.J.: Princeton University Press, 1956.

Howard, Ebenezer. *Garden Cities of Tomorrow*. London: Faber & Faber, 1945.

Hoyt, Homer. *The Structure and Growth of Residential Neighborhoods in American Cities*. Washington, D.C.: Federal Housing Administration, 1939.

Hubbard, Theodora Kimball, and Henry Vincent Hubbard. *Our Cities Today and Tomorrow*. Cambridge, Mass.: Harvard University Press, 1929.

Hurd, Richard M. *Principles of City Land Values*. New York: Real Estate Record and Guide, 1903.

Jackson, Kenneth T. *Crabgrass Frontier: The Suburbanization of the United States*. New York: Oxford University Press, 1985.

Jackson, Kenneth T. *The Encyclopedia of New York City*. New Haven, Conn.: Yale University Press, 1995.

James, Marquis. *The Metropolitan Life: A Study in Business Growth*. New York: Viking, 1947.

Kahn, Judd. Imperial *San Francisco: Politics and Planning in an American City, 1897–1906*. Lincoln: University of Nebraska Press, 1979.

Klaman, Saul B. *The Postwar Rise of Mortgage Companies*. New York: National Bureau of Economic Research, 1959.

Krinsky, Carol Herselle. *Rockefeller Center*. New York: Oxford University Press, 1978.

Lotchin, Roger W. *Fortress California, 1910–1961: From Warfare to Welfare*. New York: Oxford University Press, 1992.

Mayer, Harold M., and Richard C. Wade. *Chicago: Growth of a Metropolis*. Chicago: University of Chicago Press, 1969.

Morton, J.E. *Urban Mortgage Lending: Comparative Markets and Experience*. Princeton, N.J.: Princeton University Press, 1956.

Rabinowitz, Alan. *The Real Estate Gamble: Lessons from 50 Years of Boom and Bust*. New York: AMA-COM, 1980.

Schactman, Tom. *Skyscraper Dreams: The Great Real Estate Dynasties of New York*. Boston: Little, Brown, 1991.

Schaffer, Daniel. *Garden Cities for America: The Radburn Experience*. Philadelphia: Temple University Press, 1982.

Scott, Mel. *American City Planning since 1890*. Berkeley: University of California Press, 1969.

Shultz, Earle, and Walter Simmons. *Offices in the Sky*. Indianapolis, Ind.: Bobbs-Merrill, 1959.

Starrett, William A. *Skyscrapers and the Men Who Build Them*. New York: Scribner's, 1928.

Stein, Clarence S. *Toward New Towns for America*. New York: Reinhold, 1957.

Stern, Robert A. M., Gregory Gilmartin, and Thomas Mellins. *New York, 1930: Architecture and Urbanism between the Two World Wars*. New York: Rizzoli, 1987.

Straus, Nathan. *The Seven Myths of Housing*. New York: Knopf, 1944.

Taylor, Waverly, Hugh Potter, and W. P. Atkinson. *History of the National Association of Home Builders of the United States*. Washington, D.C.: National Association of Home Builders, 1958.

Teaford, Jon C. *The Unheralded Triumph: City Government in America, 1870–1900*. Baltimore: Johns Hopkins University Press, 1984.

Thompson-Starrett Company. "A Census of Skyscrapers." *America City* 41 (September 1929): 130.

Walker, Robert A. *The Planning Function in Urban Government*. Chicago: University of Chicago Press, 1950.

Ward, David, and Olivier Zunz. *The Landscape of Modernity*. New York: Russell Sage, 1992.

Weber, Adna Ferrin. *The Growth of Cities in the Nineteenth Century: A Study in Statistics*. New York: Macmillan, 1899.

Weiss, Marc A. "Density and Intervention: New York's Planning Traditions." *The Landscape of Modernity: Essays on New York City, 1900–1940*. Eds. David Ward and Oliver Zunz. New York: Russell Sage Foundation, 1992.

Weiss, Marc A. "Richard T. Ely and the Contribution of Economic Research to National Housing Policy, 1920–1940." *Urban Studies* (February 1989): 115:26.

Weiss, Marc A. *The Rise of the Community Builders: The American Real Estate Industry and Urban Land Planning*. New York: Columbia University Press, 1987.

Willis, Carol. *Form Follows Finance: Skyscrapers and Skylines in New York and Chicago*. Princeton, N.J.: Princeton Architectural Press, 1995.

Wood, Edith Elmer. *The Housing of the Unskilled Wage Earner*. New York: Macmillan, 1919.

Wood, Edith Elmer. *Recent Trends in American Housing*. New York: Macmillan, 1931.

Wood, Edith Elmer. *Slums and Blighted Areas in the United States*. PWA, Housing Division Bulletin No. 1. Washington, D.C.: U.S. Government Printing Office, 1935.

Woodbury, Coleman. The *Trend of Multifamily Housing in Cities in the United States*. Chicago: Institute for Economic Research, 1931.

Worley, William S. *J. C. Nichols and the Shaping of Kansas City: Innovation in Planned Residential Communities*. Columbia: University of Missouri Press, 1990.

Wright, Gwendolyn. *Moralism and the Model Home: Domestic Architecture and Cultural Conflict in Chicago, 1873–1913*. Chicago: University of Chicago Press, 1980.

Post–World War II to the Present

Abrams, Charles. *The City Is the Frontier*. New York: Harper & Row, 1965.

Alterman, Rachelle, ed. Private *Supply of Public Services: Evaluation of Real Estate Exactions, Linkage, and Alternative Land Policies*. New York: New York University Press, 1988.

Barrett, Wayne. *Trump: The Deals and the Downfall*. New York: Harper Collins, 1992.

Bauer, Catherine. "The Dreary Deadlock of Public Housing." *Architectural Forum* (May 1957): 140.

Beauregard, Robert A., ed. *Atop the Urban Hierarchy*. Totowa, N.J.: Rowman & Littlefield, 1989.

Bloom, Nicholas D. *Merchant of Illusion: James Rouse, America's Salesman of the Businessman's Utopia*. Columbus: Ohio State University Press, 2004.

Boyte, Harry C. *The Backyard Revolution: Understanding the New Citizen Movement*. Philadelphia: Temple University Press, 1980.

Bratt, Rachel. *Rebuilding a Low-Income Housing Policy*. Philadelphia: Temple University Press, 1989.

Breckenfeld, Gurney. *Columbia and the New Cities*. New York: Ives Washburn, 1971.

Caro, Robert A. *The Power Broker: Robert Moses and the Fall of New York*. New York: Random House, 1974.

Carr, C.M.H. and J.W.R. Whitehand. *Twentieth-Century Suburbs: A Morphological Approach*. New York: Routledge, 2001.

Checkoway, Barry. *The Politics of Postwar Suburban Development*. Berkeley: University of California, Childhood and Government Project, 1977.

Cisneros, Henry G., ed. *Interwoven Destinies: Cities and the Nation*. New York: Norton, 1993.

Cisneros, Henry G., and Marc A. Weiss. "The Wealth of Regions and the Challenge of Cities." *The Regionalist* (Winter 1997): 42–45.

Congress for the New Urbanism. *Charter of the New Urbanism*. New York: McGraw-Hill, 1999.

Dean, Andrea Oppenheimer. "New Hope for Failed Housing." *Preservation Magazine* (March/April 1998): 52–59.

Downs, Anthony. *The Revolution in Real Estate Finance*. Washington, D.C.: Brookings Institution, 1985.

Edel, Matthew, Elliott D. Sclar, and Daniel Luria. *Shaky Palaces: Homeownership and Social Mobility in Boston's Suburbanization*. New York: Columbia University Press, 1984.

Eichler, Ned. *The Merchant Builders*. Cambridge, Mass.: MIT Press, 1982.

Eichler, Ned. *The Thrift Debacle*. Berkeley: University of California Press, 1989.

Feagin, Joe K., and Robert Parker. *Building American Cities: The Urban Real Estate Game*. Englewood Cliffs, N.J.: Prentice Hall, 1990.

Fisher, Ernest M. *Urban Real Estate Markers: Characteristics and Financing*. New York: National Bureau of Economic Research, 1951.

Frantz, Douglas. *From the Ground Up: The Business of Building in an Age of Money*. Berkeley: University of California Press, 1993.

Frieden, Bernard J., and Lynne B. Sagalyn. *Downtown, Inc.: How America Rebuilds Citie*s. Cambridge, Mass.: MIT press, 1989.

Friedman, Lawrence M. *Government and Slum Housing: A Century of Frustration*. Chicago: Rand McNally, 1968.

Galatas, Roger, and Jim Barlow. *The Woodlands: The Inside Story of Creating a Better Hometown*. Washington, D.C.: ULI–the Urban Land Institute, 2004.

Garreau, Joel. *Edge City: Life on the New Frontier*. New York: Doubleday, 1992.

Gelfand, Mark I. *A Nation of Cities: The Federal Government and Urban America, 1933–1965*. New York: Oxford University Press, 1975.

Girardet, Herbert. *Cities People Planet: Liveable Cities for a Sustainable World*. London: Wiley, 2004.

Girardet, Herbert, ed. *Surviving the Century: Facing Climate Chaos and Other Global Challenges*. London: Earthscan, 2007.

Goldberger, Paul. *The Skyscraper*. New York: Knopf, 1981.

Goldenberg, Susan. *Men of Property: The Canadian Developers Who Are Buying America*. Toronto: Personal Library, 1981.

Goodkin, Lewis M. *When Real Estate and Homebuilding Become Big Business: Mergers, Acquisitions, and Joint Ventures*. Boston: Cahners Books, 1974.

Gottlieb, Manuel. *Long Swings in Urban Development*. New York: National Bureau of Economic Research, 1976.

Grebler, Leo. *Large-Scale Housing Real Estate Firms: Analysts of a New Business Enterprise*. New York: Praeger, 1973.

Grebler, Leo, David M. Blank, and Louis Winnick. *Capital Formation in Residential Real Estate: Trends and Prospects*. Princeton, N.J.: Princeton University Press, 1956.

Griffin, Nathaniel M. *Irvine: Genesis of a New Community*. Washington, D.C.: ULI–the Urban Land Institute, 1974.

Haar, Charles M., and Jerold S. Kayden. *Zoning and the American Dream: Promises Still to Keep*. Chicago: Planners Press, 1989.

Hayden, Dolores. *Building Suburbia: Green Fields and Urban Growth, 1820–2000*. New York: Pantheon Books, 2003.

Hayden, Dolores. *Redesigning the American Dream: The Future of Housing, Work, and Family Life*. New York: Norton, 1984.

Hays, R. Allen. *The Federal Government and Urban Housing: Ideology and Change in Public Policy*. Albany: State University of New York Press, 1985.

Hays, Samuel P. *Beauty, Health, and Permanence: Environmental Politics in the United States, 1955–1985*. New York: Cambridge University Press, 1987.

Helper, Rose. *Racial Policies and Practices of Real Estate Brokers*. Minneapolis: University of Minnesota Press, 1969.

Hoyt, Homer. *The Urban Real Estate Cycle: Performances and Prospects*. Technical Bulletin No. 38. Washington, D.C.: ULI–the Urban Land Institute, 1950.

Jackson, Kenneth T. *Crabgrass Frontier: The Suburbanization of the United States*. New York: Oxford University Press, 1985.

Jackson, Kenneth T. *The Encyclopedia of New York City*. New Haven, Conn.: Yale University Press, 1995.

Jacobs, Jane. *The Death and Life of Great American Cities*. New York: Random House, 1961.

Kanter, Rosabeth Moss. *World Class: Thriving Locally in a Global Economy*. New York: Simon & Schuster, 1995.

Katz, Peter. *The New Urbanism: Toward an Architecture of Community*. New York: McGraw-Hill, 1994.

Keats, John. *The Crack in the Picture Window*. Boston: Houghton Mifflin, 1957.

Kotkin, Joel. *The City: A Global History*. New York: Modern Library, 2006.

Lachman, M. Leanne. *Decade to Decade: U.S. Real Estate Adapts to Revolution in Finance and Demographic Evolution*. New York: Schroder Real Estate Associates 1988.

Laventhol & Horwath. *Hotel/Motel Development*. Washington, D.C.: ULI–the Urban Land Institute, 1984.

Lo, Clarence Y. H. *Small Property versus Big Government: Social Origins of the Property Tax Revolt*. Berkeley: University of California Press, 1990.

Long, Clarence D., Jr. *Building Cycles and the Theory of Investment*. Princeton, N.J.: Princeton University Press, 1940.

Mayer, Martin. *The Builders: Houses, People, Neighborhoods, Governments, Money*. New York: Norton, 1978.

McMahan, John. *Property Development*. 2nd ed. New York: McGraw-Hill, 1989.

Moehring, Eugene P. *Resort City in the Sunbelt: Las Vegas, 1930–1970*. Las Vegas: University of Nevada Press, 1989.

Mollenkopf, John H. *The Contested City*. Princeton, N.J.: Princeton University Press, 1983.

Morgan, George T., Jr., and John O. King. *The Woodlands: New Community Development, 1964–1983*. College Station: Texas A&M University Press, 1987.

Olsen, Joshua. *Better Places, Better Lives: A Biography of James Rouse*. Washington, D.C.: ULI–the Urban Land Institute, 2004.

Plunz, Richard. *A History of Housing in New York City: Dwelling Type and Social Change in the American Metropolis*. New York: Columbia University Press, 1990.

Portman, John C., and Jonathan Barnett. *The Architect as Developer*. New York: McGraw-Hill, 1976.

Rae, Douglas W. *City: Urbanism and Its End*. New Haven, Conn.: Yale University Press, 2003.

Real Estate Research Corporation. *Tall Office Buildings in the United States*. Washington, D.C.: ULI–the Urban Land Institute, 1985.

Robin, Peggy. *Saving the Neighborhood: You Can Fight Developers and Win*. Washington, D.C.: Preservation Press, 1993.

Rusk, David. *Inside Game/Outside Game: Winning Strategies for Saving Urban America*. Washington, D.C.: Brookings Institution Press, 1999.

Rybczynski, Witold. *Last Harvest: How a Cornfield Became New Daleville: Real Estate Development in America from George Washington to the Builders of the Twenty-first Century, and Why We Live in Houses Anyway*. New York: Scribner, 2007.

Sabbagh, Karl. *Skyscraper: The Making of a Building*. New York: Viking Penguin, 1990.

Scott, Allen J., ed. *Global City-Regions: Trends, Theory, Policy*. New York: Oxford University Press, 2001.

Seligman, Daniel. "The Enduring Slums." In *Exploding Metropolis*, by the editors of *Fortune*. Garden City, N.Y.: Doubleday, 1957.

Sigafoos, Robert A. *Corporate Real Estate Development*. Lexington, Mass.: Lexington Books, 1976.

Sobel, Robert. *Trammell Crow, Master Builder: The Story of America's Largest Real Estate Empire*. New York: Wiley, 1989.

Teaford, Jon C. *The Rough Road to Renaissance: Urban Revitalization in America, 1940–1985*. Baltimore: Johns Hopkins University Press, 1990.

Trump, Donald J., with Tony Schwartz. *Trump: The Art of the Deal*. New York: Random House, 1987.

Walsh, Annmarie Hauck. *The Public's Business: The Politics and Practices of Government Corporations*. Cambridge, Mass.: MIT Press, 1978.

Weaver, Robert C. *The Urban Complex: Human Values in Urban Life*. Garden City, N.Y.: Doubleday, 1964.

Weiss, Marc A. "Leveraging Private Financing and Investment for Economic and Community Development." *Global Urban Development Magazine* (March 2006): 1–11.

Weiss, Marc A. "Marketing and Financing Homeownership: Mortgage Lending and Public Policy in the United States, 1918–1989." *Business and Economic History* (1989): 109–118.

Weiss, Marc A. "Metropolitan Economic Strategy: How Urban Regions Innovate and Prosper in the Global Marketplace." *Global Outlook* (January 2001): 8–12.

Weiss, Marc A. "The Origins and Legacy of Urban Renewal." *Federal Housing Policy and Programs: Past and Present*. Ed. J. Paul Mitchell. New Brunswick, N.J.: Rutgers University Center for Urban Policy Research, 1985: 253–276.

Weiss, Marc A. *The Rise of the Community Builders: The American Real Estate Industry and Urban Land Planning*. New York: Columbia University Press, 1987.

Weiss, Marc A. "Skyscraper Zoning: New York's Pioneering Role." *Journal of the American Planning Association* (Spring 1992): 201–212.

Weiss, Marc A., and John T. Metzger. *Neighborhood Lending Agreements: Negotiating and Financing Community Development*. Cambridge, Mass.: Lincoln Institute of Land Policy, 1988.

Wenzlick, Roy. *The Coming Boom in Real Estate*. New York: Simon & Schuster, 1936.

Whyte, William H., Jr. *The Organizational Man*. New York: Simon & Schuster, 1956.

Zeckendorf, William, with Edward McCreary. *The Autobiography of William Zeckendorf*. New York: Holt, Rinehart & Winston, 1970.

PART III. FINANCE

Abdelal, Rawi. *Capital Rules: The Construction of Global Finance*. Cambridge, Mass.: Harvard University Press, 2007.

Beim, David O., and Charles W. Calomiris. *Emerging Financial Markets*. Boston: McGraw-Hill/Irwin, 2001.

Berges, Steve. *The Complete Guide to Real Estate Finance for Investment Properties: How to Analyze Any Single-Family, Multifamily, or Commercial Property*. Hoboken, N.J.: Wiley, 2004.

Bergsman, Steve. *Maverick Real Estate Financing: The Art of Raising Capital and Owning Properties like Ross, Sanders, and Carey*. Hoboken, N.J.: Wiley, 2006.

Brueggeman, William B., and Jeffrey D. Fisher. *Real Estate Finance and Investments*. 13th ed. Boston: McGraw-Hill/Irwin, 2008.

Bruner, Robert F. *Case Studies in Finance: Managing for Corporate Value Creation*. London: McGraw-Hill, 2007.

Clauretie, Terrence M., and G. Stacy Sirmans. *Real Estate Finance: Theory and Practice*. 5th ed. Mason, Ohio: Thomson/South-Western, 2005.

Collier, Nathan S., Courtland A. Collier, and Don A. Halperin. *Construction Funding: The Process of Real Estate Development, Appraisal, and Finance*. Hoboken, N.J.: Wiley, 2007.

Downs, Anthony. *Niagara of Capital: How Global Capital Has Transformed Housing and Real Estate Markets*. Washington, D.C.: ULI–the Urban Land Institute, 2007.

Einhorn, David M., Adam O. Emmerich, and Robin Pankova. *REITs: Mergers and Acquisitions*. New York: Law Journal Press, 2006.

El-Gamal, Mahmoud A. *Islamic Finance: Law, Economics, and Practice*. New York: Cambridge University Press, 2006.

Emerging Trends in Real Estate. Washington, D.C.: ULI–the Urban Land Institute and PricewaterhouseCoopers. Updated annually.

Emerging Trends in Real Estate: Asia Pacific, Washington, D.C.: ULI–the Urban Land Institute and PricewaterhouseCoopers. Updated annually.

Emerging Trends in Real Estate: Europe. Washington, D.C.: ULI–the Urban Land Institute and PricewaterhouseCoopers. Updated annually.

Fabozzi, Frank J., Anand K. Bhattacharya, and William S. Berliner. *Mortgage-Backed Securities: Products, Structuring, and Analytical Techniques*. Hoboken, N.J.: Wiley, 2007.

Fabozzi, Frank J., Glenn M. Schultz, and Brian P. Lancaster. *Structured Products and Related Credit Derivatives: A Comprehensive Guide for Investors*. Hoboken, N.J.: Wiley, forthcoming.

Geltner, David M., Norman G. Miller, Jim Clayton, and Piet Eichholtz. *Commercial Real Estate Analysis and Investments*. 2nd ed. Mason, Ohio: Thompson South-Western, 2006.

Gibson, Roger C. *Asset Allocation*. 4th ed. Boston: McGraw-Hill/Irwin, 2008.

Greer, Gaylon E., and Philip T. Kolbe. *Investment Analysis for Real Estate Decisions*. New York: Kaplan, 2006.

Greer, Gaylon E., Philip T. Kolbe, and Henry G. Rudner. *Real Estate Finance*. New York: Kaplan, 2003.

Haight, G. Timothy, and Daniel Singer. *The Real Estate Investment Handbook*. Hoboken, N.J.: Wiley, 2005.

Ling, David C., and Wayne R. Archer. *Real Estate Principles: A Value Approach*. 2nd ed. Boston: McGraw-Hill/Irwin, forthcoming.

McCoy, Bowen H. *The Dynamics of Real Estate Capital Markets: A Practitioner's Perspective*. Washington, D.C.: ULI–the Urban Land Institute, 2006.

McMahan, John. *The Handbook of Commercial Real Estate Investing*: *State of the Art Standards for Investment Transactions, Asset Management, and Financial Reporting*. Boston: McGraw-Hill/Irwin, 2006.

Moyer, R. Charles, James R. McGuigan, and Ramesh P. Rao. *Fundamentals of Contemporary Financial Management*. Eagan, Minn.: Thomson/South-Western, 2007.

Nachem, Ira W. *The Complete Guide to Financing Real Estate Developments*. New York: McGraw-Hill, 2007.

Nelson, Grant S., and Dale A. Whitman. *Cases and Materials on Real Estate Transfer, Finance, and Development*. St. Paul, Minn.: West Group, 2003.

Newell, Graeme, and Karen Sieracki. *Property Investment and Finance: The Global Perspective*. Oxford: Blackwell, 2007.

Precept Corporation. *The Handbook of First Mortgage Under-writing: A Standardized Method for the Commercial Real Estate Industry*. New York: McGraw-Hill, 2002.

Sagalyn, Lynne B. *Cases in Real Estate Finance and Investment Strategy*. Washington, D.C.: ULI–the Urban Land Institute, 1999.

Sirota, David. *Essentials of Real Estate Finance*. 11th ed. Chicago: Dearborn Real Estate Education, 2006.

Stallings, Barbara. *Finance for Development: Latin America in Comparative Perspective*. Washington, D.C.: Brookings Institution Press, 2006.

ULI–the Urban Land Institute. *Financing Real Estate Today*. Selected References. Washington, D.C.: ULI–the Urban Land Institute, 2007 (updated annually).

PART IV. IDEAS

Inception and Refinement of an Idea

Christofferson-Cunningham, Ashley, and David Cathey. *Marketing and Selling to Generation X*. Washington, D.C.: National Association of Home Builders, 2002.

Domack, Dennis R. *Creating a Vision for Your Community: More on the Art of Community Development*. Madison: University of Wisconsin–Extension, Cooperative Extension Services, 1995.

Garreau, Joel. *Edge City: Life on the New Frontier*. New York: Anchor, 1992.

Hanna, Robin, and Steven Kline. *Mapping the Future of Your Community: Strategic Visioning for Community and Economic Development*. Macomb: Illinois Institute for Rural Affairs, 1997.

Jackson, Philip L., and Robert Kuhlken. *A Rediscovered Frontier: Land Use and Resource Issues in the New West*. Lanham, Md.: Rowman & Littlefield Publishers, 2006.

Krueger, Richard A., and Mary Anne Casey. *Focus Groups: A Practical Guide for Applied Research*. 3rd ed. Thousand Oaks, Calif.: Sage, 2000.

Lennertz, Bill, and Aarin Lutzenhiser, *The Charrette Handbook*. Chicago: APA Planners Press, 2006.

Okubo, Derek. *The Community Visioning and Strategic Planning Handbook*. Denver: National Civic League, 2000.

Shipley, Robert. "The Origin and Development of Vision and Visioning in Planning." *International Planning Studies* 5:2 (June 1, 2000): 225–236.

Market Research

Aaker, David A., V. Kumar, and George S. Day. *Marketing Research*. Hoboken, N.J.: Wiley, 2007.

Birn, Robin. *The Effective Use of Market Research: How to Drive and Focus Better Business Decisions*. London: Kogan Page, 2004.

Birn, Robin, and Patrick Forsyth. *Market Research*. Oxford: Capstone Publishing, 2002.

Callingham, Martin. *Market Intelligence: How and Why Organizations Use Market Research*. Sterling, Va.: Kogan Page, 2004.

Churchill, Gilbert A., and Tom J. Brown. *Basic Marketing Research*. Mason, Ohio: South-Western, 2004.

Churchill, Gilbert A., and Dawn Iacobucci. *Marketing Research: Methodological Foundations*. Mason, Ohio: Thomson/South-Western, 2005.

Fanning, Stephen F. *Market Analysis for Real Estate: Concepts and Applications in Valuation and Highest and Best Use*. Chicago: Appraisal Institute, 2005.

Franses, Philip Hans, and Richard Paap. *Quantitative Models in Marketing Research*. New York: Cambridge University Press, 2001.

Graaskamp, James A. "Identification and Delineation of Real Estate Market Research." *Real Estate Issues* 10:1 (Spring/Summer 1985): 6–12.

Kaden, Robert J. *Guerrilla Marketing Research: Marketing Research Techniques That Can Help Any Business Make More Money*. Philadelphia: Kogan Page, 2006.

Mariampolski, Hy. *Qualitative Market Research: A Comprehensive Guide*. Thousand Oaks, Calif.: Sage, 2001.

McGough, Tony, and Sotiris Tsolacos. *Real Estate Market Analysis and Forecasting*. Oxford: Blackwell, 2005.

McQuarrie, Edward F. *The Market Research Toolbox: A Concise Guide for Beginners*. Thousand Oaks, Calif.: Sage, 2006.

Peter, J. Paul, and Jerry C. Olson. *Consumer Behavior and Marketing Strategy*. 7th ed. New York: McGraw-Hill, 2004.

Peterson, Keith, ed. *The Power of Place: Advanced Customer and Location Analytics for Market Planning*. San Diego, Calif.: Integras, 2004.

Richard K. Miller & Associates. *Retail Real Estate and Site Selection*. Loganville, Ga.: Richard K. Miller & Associates, 2006.

Schmitz, Adrienne, and Deborah L. Brett. *Real Estate Market Analysis*. Washington, D.C.: ULI–the Urban Land Institute, 2001.

Wang, Peijie. *Econometric Analysis of the Real Estate Market and Investment*. London: Routledge, 2001.

PART V. THE PUBLIC ROLES

The Public Roles

Adams, David, Craig Watkins, and Michael White, eds. *Planning, Public Policy and Property Markets*. Malden, Mass.: Blackwell, 2005.

Burke, D. Barlow. *Understanding the Law of Zoning and Land Use Controls*. Newark, N.J.: LexisNexis, 2002.

Callies, David L., Daniel Curtin, and Julie Tappendorf. *Bargaining for Development: A Handbook on Development Agreements, Annexation Agreements, Land Development Conditions, Vested Rights, and the Provision of Public Facilities*. Washington, D.C.: Environmental Law Institute, 2003.

Egleston, Russell L. *Adopting and Amending Zoning by Local Law*. Watertown, N.Y.: Tug Hill Commission, 2000.

Francis, John G., and Leslie Pickering Francis. *Land Wars: The Politics of Property and Community*. Boulder, Colo.: Lynne Rienner Publishers, 2003.

Hoch, Charles, Linda C. Dalton, and Frank S. So, eds. *Practice of Local Government Planning*. Washington, D.C.: International City/County Management Association, 2000.

Kmiec, Douglas W. *Zoning and Planning Deskbook*. St. Paul, Minn.: West Group, 2001.

Loughlin, Peter J. *Land Use, Planning, and Zoning*. New York: Lexis Publishing, 2000.

Mandelker, Daniel R. *Planning and Control of Land Development: Cases and Materials*. Newark, N.J.: LexisNexis, 2008.

Marshall, Alex. *How Cities Work: Suburbs, Sprawl, and the Roads Not Taken*. Austin: University of Texas Press, 2001.

Merriam, Dwight. *The Complete Guide to Zoning*. New York: McGraw-Hill, 2004.

Owens, David W. *Introduction to Zoning*. Chapel Hill: Institute of Government, University of North Carolina, 2001.

Porter, Douglas R. *Eminent Domain: An Important Tool for Community Revitalization*. Washington, D.C.: ULI–the Urban Land Institute, 2007.

Porter, Douglas R., and Suzanne Cartwright. *Breaking the Development Logjam*. Washington, D.C.: ULI–the Urban Land Institute, 2006.

Public/Private Development. Selected References. Washington, D.C.: ULI–the Urban Land Institute, 2007 (updated annually).

Salkin, Patricia E. *Zoning and Planning Law Handbook 2006*. St. Paul, Minn.: West Group, 2006.

Salsich, Peter, and Timothy Tryniechi. *Land Use Regulation: A Legal Analysis and Practical Application of Land Use Law*. 2nd ed. Chicago: American Bar Association, 2003.

Stainback, John. *Public/Private Finance and Development*. Hoboken, N.J.: Wiley, 2000.

Stephani, Carl J. *Zoning 101*. Washington, D.C.: National League of Cities, 2001.

Warner, Kee, and Harvey Luskin Molotch. *Building Rules: How Local Controls Shape Community Environments and Economies*. Boulder, Colo.: Westview Press, 2000.

Williams, Norman, Jr., and John M. Taylor. *American Land Planning Law*. Deerfield, Ill.: Clark Boardman Callaghan, 1974. Periodic revisions and updates—last updated 2006.

Affordable Housing

Bach, Alexa, et al. *Ten Principles for Developing Affordable Housing*. Washington, D.C.: ULI–the Urban Land Institute, 2007.

Brown, David J., ed. *The HOME House Project: The Future of Affordable Housing*. Cambridge, Mass.: MIT Press, 2004.

Downs, Anthony, ed. *Growth Management and Affordable Housing: Do They Conflict?* Washington, D.C.: Brookings Institution Press, 2004.

Friedman, Avi. *Homes within Reach: A Guide to the Planning, Design, and Construction of Affordable Homes and Communities*. Hoboken, N.J.: Wiley, 2005.

Harvard University Joint Center for Housing Studies. *The State of the Nation's Housing* (published annually and available for download at www.jchs.harvard.edu).

Haughey, Richard M. *Best Practices in the Production of Affordable Housing*. Washington, D.C.: ULI–the Urban Land Institute, 2005.

Haughey, Richard M. *The Business of Affordable Housing*. Washington, D.C.: ULI–the Urban Land Institute, 2006.

Haughey, Richard M. *Developing Housing for the Workforce: A Toolkit*. Washington, D.C.: ULI–Urban Land Institute, 2007.

Haughey, Richard M. *Workforce Housing: Innovative Strategies and Best Practices*. Washington, D.C.: ULI–the Urban Land Institute, 2006.

Iglesias, Tim, and Rochelle E. Lento, eds. *The Legal Guide to Affordable Housing Development*. Chicago: American Bar Association, 2005.

Lipman, Barbara J. "Something's Gotta Give: Working Families and the Cost of Housing." *New Century Housing* 5:2. Washington, D.C.: Center for Housing Policy, 2005.

Listokin, David, and Kristen Crossney. *Best Practices for Effecting the Rehabilitation of Affordable Housing*. Washington, D.C.: U.S. Dept. of Housing and Urban Development, Office of Policy Development and Research, 2006.

Meck, Stuart, Rebecca Retzlaff, and James Schwab. *Regional Approaches to Affordable Housing*. Chicago: American Planning Association, Planning Advisory Service, 2003.

Morris, Marya. *Incentive Zoning: Meeting Urban Design and Affordable Housing Objectives*. Chicago: APA Planners Press, 2000.

National Low Income Housing Coalition. *America's Neighbors: The Affordable Housing Crisis and the People It Affects*. Washington, D.C.: National Low Income Housing Coalition, 2004.

Porter, Douglas R. *Inclusionary Zoning for Affordable Housing*. Washington, D.C.: ULI–the Urban Land Institute, 2004.

Schmitz, Adrienne, et al. *Affordable Housing: Designing an American Asset*. Washington, D.C.: ULI–the Urban Land Institute, 2005.

ULI–the Urban Land Institute. *Affordable/Workforce Housing*. Selected references. Washington, D.C.: ULI–the Urban Land Institute, 2007 (updated annually).

Wells, Walker, and Ted Bardacke. *Blueprint for Greening Affordable Housing*. Washington, D.C.: Island Press, 2007.

PART VI. THE MARKETING PERSPECTIVE

Real Estate Market and Feasibility Studies

Barrett, G. Vincent, and John P. Blair. *How to Conduct and Analyze Real Estate Market and Feasibility Studies*. 2nd ed. New York: Van Nostrand Reinhold, 1988.

Brecht, Susan B. *Analyzing Seniors' Housing Market*. Washington, D.C.: ULI–the Urban Land Institute, 2002.

Carn, Neil, Joseph Rabianski, Ronald Racster, and Maury Seldin. Real *Estate Market Analysis: Techniques and Applications*. Englewood Cliffs, N.J.: Prentice Hall, 1988.

DeLisle, James, ed. *Appraisal, Market Analysis, and Public Policy in Real Estate: Essays in Honor of James A. Graaskamp*. Boston: Kluwer Academic Publishers, 1994.

Fanning, Stephen F. *Market Analysis for Real Estate: Concepts and Applications in Valuation and Highest and Best Use*. Chicago: Appraisal Institute, 2005.

Geltner, David M., and Norman G. Miller. *Commercial Real Estate Analysis and Investments*. Mason, Ohio: South-Western Educational Publishing, 2000.

Graaskamp, James. *A Guide to Feasibility Analysis*. Chicago: Appraisal Institute, 1970.

Greer, Gaylon E., and Phillip T. Kolbe. *Investment Analysis for Real Estate Decisions*. 6th ed. Chicago: Dearborn Real Estate Education, 2006.

Kahr, Joshua, and Michael C. Thomsett. Real *Estate Market Valuation and Analysis*. New York: Wiley, 2005.

Noe, Mark W. *Go/No Go: A Hands-On Guide to Successful Real Estate Development, Building Construction, and Renovation from Concept through Desig*n. 2nd ed. London: Remark Publishing, 2001.

Peiser, Richard B., and Anne Frej. *Professional Real Estate Development: The ULI Guide to the Business*. 2nd ed. Washington, D.C.: ULI–the Urban Land Institute, 2003.

Polton, Richard E. *Valuation and Market Studies for Affordable Housing*. Chicago: Appraisal Institute, 2005.

Rushmore, Stephen, and Erich Baum. *Hotels and Motels: Valuations and Market Studies*. Chicago: Appraisal Institute, 2001.

Thrall, Grant Ian. *Business Geography and New Real Estate Market Analysis*. New York: Oxford University Press USA, 2002.

ULI–the Urban Land Institute. *Feasibility Analysis for Real Estate*. Selected references. Washington, D.C.: ULI–the Urban Land Institute (updated annually).

PART VII. MAKING IT HAPPEN

Contract Negotiation and Formal Commitment

AIA Contract Documents. Washington, D.C.: American Institute of Architects. Updated regularly.

Angley, Steven, Edward Horsey, and David Roberts. *Landscape Estimating and Contract Administration*. Albany, N.Y.: Delmar, 2002.

Blum, Brian A. *Contracts: Examples and Explanations*. Boston: Aspen Publishers, 2007.

Brennan, Daniel S., and the American Bar Association. *The Construction Contracts Book: How to Find Common Ground in Negotiating Design and Construction Contract Clauses*. Chicago: American Bar Association, 2004.

Collier, Keith. *Construction Contracts*. 3rd ed. Englewood Cliffs, N.J.: Prentice Hall, 2001.

Cushman, Robert F. *Construction Law Handbook*, New York: Aspen, 2004.

Cushman, Robert F., and Peter J. King. *Construction Owners Handbook of Property Development*. New York: Wiley, 1992.

Friedman, Milton R. *Friedman on Contracts and Conveyances*. 6th ed. New York: Practising Law Institute, 2004.

Frier, Bruce W., and James J. White. *The Modern Law of Contracts*. St. Paul, Minn.: Thomson/West, 2005.

Hafer, Randall F., ed. *Construction Subcontracting: A Legal Guide for Industry Professionals*. New York: Wiley, 1991.

Hess, Stephen A. *Design Professional and Construction Manager Law*. Chicago: American Bar Association, 2007.

Hinkle, Buckner, Jr., W. Alexander Mosley, and Richard F. Smith. *Discovery Deskbook for Construction Disputes*. Chicago: American Bar Association, 2006.

Hinze, Jimmie. *Construction Contracts*. 2nd ed. New York: McGraw-Hill, 2000.

Sabo, Werner. *Legal Guide to AIA Documents*. 4th ed. New York: Aspen, 2001.

Stein, Gregory M., Morton P. Fisher, and Gail M. Stern. *A Practical Guide to Commercial Real Estate Transactions: From Contract to Closing*. Chicago: American Bar Association, 2001.

Stokes, McNeill. *Construction Law in Contractor's Language*. 2nd ed. New York: McGraw-Hill, 1990.

Sweeney, Neal J., and Overton A. Currie. *Construction Law Update*. New York: Wiley, 2006.

Sweet, Justin. *Sweet on Construction Industry Contracts: Major AIA Documents*. New York: Wiley Law Publications, 1987.

Werner, Raymond J. *Real Estate Law*. 11th ed. Englewood Cliffs, N.J.: Prentice Hall, 2001.

Werremeyer, Kit. *Understanding and Negotiating Construction Contracts*. Kingston, Mass.: R. S. Means, 2006.

Construction, Completion, and Formal Opening

Allen, Edward, and Joseph Iano. *Fundamentals of Building Construction: Materials and Methods*. 4th ed. New York: Wiley, 2003.

Ching, Francis D. K., and Cassandra Adams. *Building Construction Illustrated*. 3rd ed. New York: Wiley, 2000.

Cushman, Robert Frank, and Michael C. Loulakis. *Construction Business Formbook*. New York: Aspen Publishers, 2004.

Fisk, Edward R., and Wayne R. Reynolds. *Construction Project Administration*. 8th ed. Englewood Cliffs, N.J.: Prentice Hall, 2006.

Gambatese, John Anthony, James B. Potock, and Phillip S. Dunston. *Constructability Concepts and Practice*. Reston, Va.: American Society of Civil Engineers, 2007.

Green, Stuart. *Construction Management: A Critical Review*. Oxford: Blackwell, 2007.

Halpin, Daniel W. *Construction Management*. Hoboken, N.J.: Wiley, 2006.

Harris, Cyril M. *Dictionary of Architecture and Construction*. 4th ed. New York: McGraw-Hill, 2005.

Harris, Frank, Ronald McCaffer, and Francis Edum-Fotwe. *Modern Construction Management*. Oxford: Blackwell, 2006.

Hornbostel, Caleb. *Building Design/Materials and Methods*. New York: Kaplan AEC Education, 2007.

Jackson, Barbara J. *Construction Management JumpStart: Construction Management Basics*. Berkeley, Calif.: Sybex, 2004.

Kerzner, Harold. *Project Management: A Systems Approach to Planning, Scheduling, and Controlling*. 9th ed. New York: Wiley, 2005.

Levy, Sidney M. *Project Management in Construction*. 5th ed. New York: McGraw-Hill, 2006.

Marshall & Swift/Boeckh. *Valuation Service*. New Berlin, Wis.: Marshall & Swift/ Boeckh, 2007 (published annually with updates).

O'Brien, James J., and Frederic L. Plotnick. *CPM in Construction Management*. 6th ed. New York: McGraw-Hill, 2005.

Peurifoy, R. L., William Burt Ledbetter, and Cliff J. Schexnayder. *Construction Planning, Equipment, and Methods*. 7th ed. New York: McGraw-Hill, 2005.

Pierce, David R. *Project Scheduling and Management for Construction*. Kingston, Mass.: R. S. Means, 2004.

Poage, Waller S. *The Building Professional's Guide to Contract Documents*. Kingston, Mass.: R. S. Means Company—Read Construction Data, 2003.

Rosen, Harold J. *Construction Specifications Writing: Principles and Procedures*. 5th ed. New York: Wiley, 2004.

R. S. Means Co. *Means Construction Cost Data*. Kingston, Mass.: Read Construction Data , 2007 (published annually).

R. S. Means Co. *Means Illustrated Construction Dictionary*. Kingston, Mass.: Read Construction Data, 2003.

Saporita, Ronald. *Managing Risks in Design and Construction Projects*. New York: ASME Press, 2006.

Wallace, Eric P. *Construction Guide: Accounting and Auditing*. Chicago: CCH Inc, 2007.

PART VIII. MAKING IT WORK

Asset and Property Management

Dickson, Doug. *Commercial Tenant Retention: Strategies for Today's Market*. Chicago: Institute of Real Estate Management, 2003.

Institute of Real Estate Management. *Glossary of Real Estate Management Terms*. Chicago: Institute of Real Estate Management, 2003.

Kyle, Robert C., Marie S. Spodek, and Floyd M. Baird. *Property Management*. Chicago: Dearborn Real Estate Education, 2005.

MacLaran, Andrew, ed. *Making Space: Property Development and Urban Planning*. London: Arnold, 2003.

Muhlebach, Richard F. *Insider's Tips to Operating a Successful Property Management Company*. Chicago: Institute of Real Estate Management, 2007.

Muhlebach, Richard F., and Alan A. Alexander. *Business Strategies for Real Estate Management Companies*. Chicago: Institute of Real Estate Management, 2004.

Pagliari, Joseph L., Jr. *Handbook of Real Estate Portfolio Management*. New York: McGraw-Hill, 1995.

ULI–the Urban Land Institute. *Asset Management*. Selected references. Washington, D.C.: ULI–the Urban Land Institute (updated annually).

ULI–the Urban Land Institute. *Property Management*. Selected References. Washington, D.C.: ULI–the Urban Land Institute, 2007 (updated annually).

Sales and Marketing Management

Christofferson-Cunningham, Ashley, and David Cathey. *Marketing and Selling to Generation X: A Unique Generation of Homebuyers*. Washington, D.C.: National Association of Home Builders, 2002.

Crosby, John V. *Cycles, Trends, and Turning Points: Practical Marketing and Sales Forecasting Techniques*. Lincolnwood, Ill.: NTC Business Books, 2000.

Kotler, Philip, and Gary Armstrong. *Principles of Marketing*. 11th ed. Englewood Cliffs, N.J.: Prentice Hall, 2005.

Kotler, Philip, and Kevin Lane Keller. *Marketing Management*. 12th ed. Englewood Cliffs, N.J.: Prentice Hall, 2005.

Lee, Nora. *The Mom Factor: What Really Drives Where We Shop, Eat, and Play*. Washington, D.C.: ULI–the Urban Land Institute, 2005.

Stroud, Dick. *The 50-Plus Market: Why the Future Is Age-Neutral When It Comes to Marketing and Branding Strategies*. London: Kogan Page, 2007.

Wilson, R.M.S., and Colin Gilligan. *Strategic Marketing Management: Planning, Implementation and Control*. Boston: Elsevier/Butterworth-Heinemann, 2005.

Young, Antony, and Lucy Aitken. *Profitable Marketing Communications: A Guide to Marketing Return on Investment*. Philadelphia: Kogan Page, 2007.

The Future

Baumohl, Bernard. *The Secrets of Economic Indicators: Hidden Clues to Future Economic Trends and Investment Opportunities*. Upper Saddle River, N.J.: Wharton School Publishing, 2005.

Bogart, William T. *Don't Call It Sprawl: Metropolitan Structure in the 21st Century*. Cambridge, England.: Cambridge University Press, 2006.

Bowles, Jonathan, and Tara Colton. *A World of Opportunity*. New York: Center for an Urban Future, 2007.

Flint, Anthony. *This Land: The Battle over Sprawl and the Future of America*. Baltimore: Johns Hopkins University Press, 2006.

Florida, Richard. *The Rise of the Creative Class and How It's Transforming Work, Leisure, Community and Everyday Life*. Jacksonville, Tenn.: Perseus Books Group, 2002.

Friedman, Thomas. *The World Is Flat: A Brief History of the Twenty-First Century*. New York: Farrar, Straus & Giroux, 2005.

Haas, Tigran, ed. *New Urbanism and Beyond: Contemporary and Future Trends in Urban Design*. New York: Rizzoli International Publications, 2008.

Hutter, Mark. *Experiencing Cities: A Global Approach*. Boston: Allyn & Bacon, 2007.

Hutton, Tom. *The New Economy of the Inner City: Regeneration and Dislocation in the 21st Century Metropolis*. London: Routledge, 2007.

Keiner, Marco, Martina Koll-Schretzenmayr, and Willy A. Schmid. *Managing Urban Futures: Sustainability and Urban Growth in Developing Countries*. Burlington, Vt.: Ashgate, 2005.

Kotkin, Joel. *Opportunity Urbanism: An Emerging Paradigm for the 21st Century*. Houston: Greater Houston Partnership, 2007.

Kresl, Peter Karl. *Planning Cities for the Future: The Successes and Failures of Urban Economic Strategies in Europe*. Cheltenham, U.K.: Edward Elgar, 2007.

Marshall, Stephen. *Cities: Design and Evolution*. New York: Routledge, 2007.

ORGANIZATIONS

General Real Estate and Planning

American Society of Landscape Architects (ASLA)
www.asla.org

Building Owners and Managers Association (BOMA)
www.boma.org

Commercial Investment Real Estate Institute (CIREI)
www.ccim.com

Commercial Real Estate Women (CREW)
www.crewnetwork.org/

Congress for the New Urbanism (CNU)
www.cnu.org

CoreNet Global
www.corenetglobal.com

Counselors of Real Estate (CRE)
www.cre.org

Design-Build Institute of America (DBIA)
www.dbia.org

Institute of Real Estate Management (IREM)
www.irem.org

International Downtown Association (IDA)
www.ida-downtown.org

International Real Estate Federation (FIABCI-USA)
www.fiabci-usa.com

Institute of Real Estate Management (IREM)
www.irem.org

Lincoln Institute of Land Policy (LILP)
www.lincolninst.edu

National Association of Realtors (NAR)
www.nar.org

National Council for Public-Private Partnerships
www.ncppp.org

National League of Cities
www.nlc.org

Real Estate Board of New York (REBNY)
www.rebny.com

Real Estate Educators Association (REEA)
www.reea.org

Real Estate Research Institute (RERI)
www.reri.org

Real Estate Roundtable
www.rer.org

Royal Institution of Chartered Surveyors (RICS)
www.rics.org

Women in Real Estate (WIRE)
www.womeninrealestate.org

Affordable Housing

American Institute of Architects
www.aia.org

American Planning Association
www.planning.org

Center on Budget and Policy Priorities
www.cbpp.org

Center for Community Change
www.communitychange.org

Council of Large Public Housing Agencies
www.clpha.org

Council of State Community Development Agencies
www.coscda.org

The Enterprise Foundation
www.enterprisefoundation.org

Fannie Mae
www.fanniemae.com

Ford Foundation
www.fordfound.org

Freddie Mac
www.freddiemac.com

Habitat for Humanity
www.habitat.org

Housing Assistance Council
www.ruralhome.org

Housing Partnership Network
www.housingpartnership.net

Joint Center for Housing Studies of Harvard University
www.gsd.harvard.edu/jcenter

Local Initiatives Support Corporation
www.lisc.org

Mortgage Bankers Association of America
www.mbaa.org

National Association of Counties
www.naco.org

National Association of Home Builders
www.nahb.org

National Association of Housing and Redevelopment
Officials
www.nahro.org

National Association of Local Housing Finance Agencies
www.nalhfa.org

National Association of Realtors®
www.realtor.org

National Coalition for the Homeless
www.nationalhomeless.org

National Community Development Association
www.ncdaonline.org

National Congress for Community Economic Development
www.ncced.org

National Council for State Housing Agencies
www.ncsha.org

National Housing Conference, Inc.
www.nhc.org

National Housing Law Project
www.nhlp.org

National Housing Trust
www.nhtinc.org

National League of Cities
www.nlc.org

National Low-Income Housing Coalition
www.nlihc.org

National Multi Housing Council
www.nmhc.org

National Trust for Historic Preservation
www.nthp.org

Neighborhood Housing Services of America
www.nhsofamerica.org

NeighborWorks America
www.nw.org

U.S. Census Bureau
Housing and Household Economic Statistics Division
www.census.gov

U.S. Conference of Mayors
www.usmayors.org

U.S. Department of Agriculture
Rural Development Agency
www.rurdev.usda.gov

U.S. Department of Housing and Urban Development
Office of the Secretary
www.hud.gov

U.S. General Accounting Office Resources, Community, and
Economic Development Division
www.gao.gov

United Way of America
www.unitedway.org

Urban Institute
www.urbaninstitute.org

ULI–the Urban Land Institute
www.uli.org

Specialized

American Bankers Association (ABA)
www.aba.com

American Hotel and Lodging Association (AH&MA)
www.ahma.com

American Industrial Real Estate Association (AIREA)
www.airea.com

American Resort Development Association (ARDA)
www.arda.org

American Seniors Housing Association (ASHA)
www.seniorshousing.org

Appraisal Institute (AI)
www.appraisalinstitute.org

Association of Foreign Investors in Real Estate (AFIRE)
www.afire.org

Construction Financial Management Association (CFMA)
www.cfma.org

Fannie Mae
www.fanniemae.com

Freddie Mac
www.freddiemac.com

International Council of Shopping Centers (ICSC)
www.icsc.org

Manufactured Housing Institute (MHI)
www.mfghome.org

Mortgage Bankers Association of America (MBA)
www.mbaa.org

National Apartment Association (NAA)
www.naahq.org

National Association of Home Builders (NAHB)
www.nahb.com

National Association of Industrial and Office Parks (NAIOP)
www.naiop.org

National Association of Real Estate Investment Managers (NAREIM)
www.nareim.org

National Association of Real Estate Investment Trusts (NAREIT)
www.nareit.com

National Council of Real Estate Investment Fiduciaries (NCREIF)
www.ncreif.com

National Multi Housing Council (NMHC)/American Seniors Housing Association (ASHA)
www.nmhc.org

Pension Real Estate Association (PREA)
www.prea.org

Society of Industrial and Office Realtors (SIOR)
www.sior.com

PERIODICALS

Journals and Magazines: General Real Estate and Planning

American City and County
www.americancityandcounty.com

Architectural Record
www.archrecord.com

Architecture Magazine
www.architecturemag.com

Banker & Tradesman
www.bankerandtradesman.com

Builder Magazine
www.builderonline.com

Building Design & Construction
www.bdcmag.com

Buildings Magazine
www.buildingsmag.com

Commercial Investment Real Estate Journal
www.ccim.com/magazine

Commercial Property News (CPN)
www.cpnonline.com

Design Cost & Data Magazine
www.dcd.com

Downtown Economics
www.uwex.edu/ces/CCED

Economic Development Quarterly
edq.sagepub.com

Engineering News-Record (ENR)
www.enr.com

Estates Gazette
www.egi.co.uk

Expansion Management Magazine
www.expansionmanagement.com

Global Real Estate Now
www.pwcglobal.com

Globe St.com
www.globest.com

Governing Magazine
www.governing.com

Institutional Real Estate, Inc.
www.irei.com

Journal of the American Planning Association (JAPA)
www.planning.org

Journal of Property Investment & Finance
www.emeraldinsight.com/jpif.htm

Journal of Property Management
irem.org

Journal of Real Estate Finance and Economics
www.jrefe.org

Journal of Real Estate Literature
cbeweb-1.fullerton.edu/finance/jrel

Journal of Real Estate Portfolio Management
cbeweb-1.fullerton.edu/finance/jrepm

Journal of Real Estate Research
business.fullerton.edu/finance/journal

Land Development Magazine
www.nahb.org

National Real Estate Investor (NREI)
www.nreionline.com

New Urban News
www.newurbannews.com

Planning
www.planning.org

Practical Real Estate Lawyer
www.ali-aba.org/aliaba/prel.htm

Professional Builder
www.housingzone.com

Property Week
www.property-week.co.uk

Real Estate Finance
www.aspenpublishers.com

Real Estate Finance Journal
west.thomson.com

Real Estate Forum
www.reforum.com

Real Estate Journal (Wall Street Journal)
www.realestatejournal.com

Real Estate Review
west.thomson.com

Real Estate Weekly
www.rew-online.com

Tierra Grande
recenter.tamu.edu/tgrande

Urban Affairs Review
uar.sagepub.com

Urban Land
www.uli.org

Journals and Magazines: Specialized

Assisted Living Success Magazine
www.alsuccess.com

Chain Store Age Magazine
www.chainstoreage.com

Development Magazine
naiop.org

Developments Magazine
www.arda.org

Eco-Structure
www.eco-structure.com

EDC Enviromental Design & Construction Magazine
www.edcmag.com

Golf Course Industry
www.golfcourseindustry.com

Green Builder Magazine
www.greenbuildermag.com

GreenSource Magazine
greensource.construction.com

Hotel Business
www.hotelbusiness.com

Hotel & Motel Management Magazine
www.hotelmotel.com

Hotels
www.hotelsmag.com

Hospitality Design Magazine
www.hdmag.com

Inside Self Storage
www.insideselfstorage.com

International Gaming & Wagering Business Magazine
www.igwb.com

Lodging Hospitality
www.lhonline.com

Midwest Real Estate News
www.mwrenonline.com

Multi Housing News
www.multi-housingnews.com

Multifamily Executive Magazine
www.multifamilyexecutive.com

Multifamily Trends
www.uli.org

Nursing Homes Long Term Care Management
www.nursinghomesmagazine.com

Parking
www.npapark.org

Parking Professional
www.parking.org

Resort & Recreation
www.resort-recreation.com

Resort Trades
www.thetrades.com

Retail Construction Magazine
retailconstructionmag.com

Retail Traffic
www.retailtrafficmag.com

Shopping Center Business
www.shoppingcenterbusiness.com

Shopping Centers Today
www.icsc.org

Sustainable Land Development Today
www.landdevelopmenttoday.com

Value Retail News
www.valueretailnews.com

Units
www.naahq.org

Index